2004

Fifth Edition

# POLICE ADMINISTRATION

*Structures, Processes, and Behavior*

**CHARLES R. SWANSON**

*University of Georgia*

**LEONARD TERRITO**

*University of South Florida*

**ROBERT W. TAYLOR**

*University of North Texas*

Prentice
Hall

Upper Saddle River, New Jersey 07458

**Library of Congress Cataloging-in-Publication Data**

Swanson, Charles R., 1942-
    Police administration : structures, processes, and behavior / Charles R. Swanson,
Leonard Territo, Robert W. Taylor.—5th ed.
        p. cm.
    Includes bibliographical references and index.
    ISBN 0-13-028573-0
        1. Police administration.    I. Territo, Leonard.    II. Taylor, Robert W.    III. Title.

HV7935 .S95 2001
363.2'068—dc21                                                                00-034680

Publisher: *Dave Garza*
Senior Acquisitions Editor: *Kim Davies*
Production Editor: *Lori Dalberg, Carlisle Publishers Services*
Production Liaison: *Barbara Marttine Cappuccio*
Director of Manufacturing and Production: *Bruce Johnson*
Managing Editor: *Mary Carnis*
Manufacturing Buyer: *Ed O'Dougherty*
Art Director: *Marianne Frasco*
Cover Design: *Joe Sengotta*
Cover Illustration: © *Tracey L. Williams/Courtesy of the Bernards Township Police
                Department, Basking Ridge, New Jersey*
Marketing Manager: *Chris Ruel*
Editorial Assistant: *Lisa Schwartz*
Composition: *Carlisle Communications, Ltd.*
Printing and Binding: *Courier Westford*

Prentice-Hall International (UK) Limited, *London*
Prentice-Hall of Australia Pty. Limited, *Sydney*
Prentice-Hall Canada, Inc., *Toronto*
Prentice-Hall Hispanoamericana, S.A., *Mexico*
Prentice-Hall of India Private Limited, *New Delhi*
Prentice-Hall of Japan, Inc., *Tokyo*
Prentice-Hall Singapore Pte. Ltd.
Editora Prentice-Hall do Brasil, Ltda., *Rio de Janeiro*

10 9 8 7 6 5 4 3 2 1
ISBN 0-13-028573-0

*For Paige, Traci, Kellie, Colin, and Maggie.*
> C. R. "Mike" Swanson

*To my daughter, Loraine, and my grandchildren, Matthew and Branden.*
> Leonard Territo

*To my wife, Mary, and to all the children of our family: Matt, Scott, Laura, and Shawna.*
> Bob Taylor

# CONTENTS

## 5 Concepts of Police Organizational Design    177

## 6 Leadership    209

## 9  Stress and Police Personnel        342

## 11   Legal Aspects of Police Administration    437

## 14 Productivity, Quality, and Program Evaluation: Measuring Organizational Performance    601

## 15 Organizational Change and the Future    627

# PREFACE

The field of police administration is dynamic and ever changing. Laws are modified, new problems occur, and administrative practices that were once accepted as gospel are challenged, modified, and in some cases, discarded. In this edition, as with the previous four editions, we have tried to provide the most current and useful information to the reader in an effort to help them deal with these dynamic forces and the ever-changing environment of police work.

Collectively the three authors have been police officers, detectives, administrators, and educators for over eighty years. We have studied, practiced, researched, taught, and consulted on police administration and an inevitable by-product of these experiences is the development of certain perspectives. It is these perspectives that form the rationale for this book.

There is much new information in this book the reader will find informative and useful. For example, Chapter Two, Community Policing is a new chapter which focuses on the impact of community policing on police administration. We also discuss the expanded coverage of the Chicago Alternative Policing Strategy (CAPS). In Chapter 3, Politics and Police Administration there is an expanded discussion on the issues of police brutality and scandal as well as discussions of militias, right-wing groups in the United States and school violence. In Chapter 8, Human Resource Management we discuss the arguments presented in favor of requiring a college education for police applicants as well as arguments presented by some groups opposing college education for police applicants. Also in this chapter we have added new material on the Administration of Discipline, Internal Affairs Units, and Retirement Counseling. In Chapter 9, Stress and Police Personnel we have expanded our discussion on police suicide and address in considerable detail the phenomenon known as Suicide by Cop (SbC), Stress and the Female Police Officer and Police Domestic Violence. In Chapter 11, Legal Aspects of Police Administration there is a feature on the now infamous New York City Abner Louima case and its impact along with a discussion of several other high profile cases that have occurred in recent years in New York City. There is also a discussion of a recent Supreme Court decision which limits liability for injuries and deaths associated with high speed police pursuit as well as an update and expanded discussion of sexual harassment in the workplace. In Chapter 12, Planning and Decision Making, we have provided updated material on the investigation of the Branch Davidian Seige in Waco, Texas, focusing on the potential coverup and misuse of military personnel during the engagement.

As with all previous editions, we have attempted to provide newspaper clippings, case studies and vignettes from our own experience. These are scattered throughout to illustrate points discussed in the narrative in order to make them more informative and interesting.

Finally, the mention of any product or firm in this book is intended for illustrative purposes only and does not necessarily constitute an endorsement or recommendation by the authors or the publisher.

# ACKNOWLEDGMENTS

Although it is insufficient compensation for their gracious assistance, we wish to recognize here the individuals and organizations who helped to make this book a reality. Unless asked to do otherwise, we have indicated their organizational affiliation at the time they made their contribution.

We would like to thank the following reviewers for their comments and suggestions for the fifth edition: Michael D. Paquette, Rutgers University; Clydell Duncan, Mott Community College; and Clyde L. Cronkhite, Western Illinois University. We would like to thank Kimberly Davies of Prentice Hall for her persistence and encouragement and Lori Dalberg, our project director who did a great job in keeping us on schedule and taking care of the many large and small details so necessary in order to have an accurate and well organized book.

Maryellin Territo, Marianne Bell, Carole Rennick, Shirley Latt, Jeannie Griffin, Linda Pittman, Dwayne Shumate, Charles Keeton, Leigh Prichard, and Donna Dickert provided typing and research assistance and made innumerable contributions.

Those who supplied photographs and written material and made suggestions about how to strengthen the book include Dr. Deanette L. Palmer for material on police retirement; Charlie Rinkevich and Peggy Hayward, Federal Law Enforcement Training Center, Glynco, Georgia; Chief David Couper, Madison, Wisconsin Police Department; Scott Wofford, Radio Shack, Fort Worth, Texas; the Drug Enforcement Administration; our colleague of 20 years, Jim Campbell, East Carolina University; Chief John Kerns, Sacramento, California Police Department; the U.S. Secret Service; Willie Ellison, Bureau of Alcohol, Tobacco, and Firearms; Deputy Superintendent Jim Finley, Illinois State Police; Larry Gaines, Eastern Kentucky University; Drs. Walter Booth and Chris Hornickj, Multidimensional Research Association, Aurora, Colorado; Lieutenant Rick Frey, Broward County, Florida Sheriff's Office; Chief Jim Everett, Austin, Texas Police Department; Captain Lawrence Akley, St. Louis, Missouri Metro Police Department; Chief Lee McGehee and Captain Glenn Whiteacre, Ocala, Florida Police Department; the Maricopa, Arizona Sheriff's Office; Inspector Vivian Edmond, Michelle Andonian, and Commander Dorothy Knox, Detroit, Michigan Police Department; Major Herman Ingram, Baltimore, Maryland Police Department; Commissioner Morgan Elkins and Captain Dennis Goss, Kentucky State Police; St. Paul, Minnesota Police Department; Thomas J. Deakin, John E. Ott, editor of the FBI Law Enforcement Bulletin, and William Tafoya, a futures expert, all three with the Federal Bureau of Investigation; our longtime friend Ron Lynch, University of North Carolina; the Tigard, Oregon Police Department; the California Highway Patrol; Dr. Zug Standing Bear, Colorado State University; Norma Kane, the Kansas City, Missouri Police Department; the San Diego, California Police Department; Janice Lowenberg, U.S. Probation and Parole; the Texas Department of Public Safety; the Philadelphia Police Department; Sergeant Maurice McGough, St. Petersburg, Florida Police Department; National Tactical Officers Association; Lieutenant James B. Bolger, Michigan State Police; the Denver Police Department; Colonel Carroll D. Buracker and Scott Boatright, Fairfax County, Virginia Police Department; Charles Tracy, Portland (Oregon)

State University; Major Dave Sturtz, Ohio State Patrol; the National Consortium for Justice Information and Statistics, Sacramento, California; Sheriff Sherman Block and Undersheriff T. H. Von Minden, Los Angeles County, California Sheriff's Office; Phoenix, Arizona Police and Fire Departments; Deputy Chief Troy McClain, Captain Terry Haucke, Dr. S. A. Somodevilla, and Sergeants Jody Thomas and Mark Stallo, Dallas, Texas Police Department; Mary Ann Wycoff, Police Foundation; Don Fish, Florida Police Benevolent Association; Captain Keith Bushey, Los Angeles, California Police Department; Deputy Chief Kevin Stoeher, Mt. Lebanon, Pennsylvania Police Department; Karen Anderson and Lisa Bird, LAN Publications Group; Lieutenant Rex Splitt, Craig, Colorado Police Department; Joseph Scuro, attorney, Dallas, Texas; Chief R. E. Hansen and Cynthia Shaw, Fayetteville, North Carolina Police Department; Dr. Mathew Prosser, Tyler, Texas; Officer David Hoffman, Anchorage, Alaska Police Department; LaNell Thornton, ElectroCom Automation, Arlington, Texas; Chief Paul Annee and Lieutenant Michael Spears, Indianapolis, Indiana Police Department; Lexington-Fayette, Kentucky Urban County Police Department; Dr. Gary Sykes, Dan Carlson, and Tracy Harris, Southwestern Law Enforcement Institute, Dallas, Texas; Environmental Systems Research Institute, Redlands, California; Nancy Brandon, Metro Software, Park City, Utah; Dr. Peter Nelligen, University of Texas at Tyler; Sheriff Jim Roache and Sarah Brooks, San Diego, California Sheriff's Department; Larry Yium, Director of Budget and Finance, Houston, Texas; Lois Roethel and Leslie Doak, Las Vegas, Nevada Police Department; the Knox County, Maine Sheriff's Department; Chief Jim Wetherington, a mentor, and Assistant Chief Sam Woodall, Semper Fi, Columbus, Georgia Police Department; Martha Bacile-Findley, University of Texas at Arlington; Sgt. Mike Parker, Los Angeles County Sheriff's Office; Chief Bennie Click, Assistant Chief Marlin Price, Assistant Chief Greg Holiday, Sgt. Mark Stallo, Dallas, TX Police Department; Chief Michael Jez, Denton, TX Police Department; Major John F. Meeks, Baltimore, MD Police Department; Mary Foss and Chief Randall Gaston, Anaheim, CA Police Department; Captain Tom Brennan, Newark, NJ Police Department; Lt. Robert O'Toole, Boston, MA Police Department; Commander Tim McBride, Los Angeles, CA Police Department; Superintendent Richard Pennington, New Orleans, LA Police Department; Sgt. Patrick Melvin, Phoenix, AZ Police Department; Officer Matthew Rastovski, Birmingham, AL Police Department; Lt. Doug Cain, Baton Rouge, LA Police Department; and Jeffrey Higgenbotham, a Special Agent in the Legal Division, FBI Academy, Quantico, Virginia, who contributed to the discussion on sexual harassment.

We would also like to thank Lou Reiter, formerly with the Los Angeles Police Department for his contribution of the material used in conjunction with the discussion of the Internal Affairs Unit. We also wish to thank Deanette L. Palmer, Ph.D., a psychologist with the Spokane, Washington Police Department for her contribution of material on Police Retirement. Lastly, we wish to thank Meredith A. Bowman of the Southeastern Public Safety Institute, St. Petersburg Jr. College, St. Petersburg, Florida, who contributed material on Stress and the Female Police Officer.

Charles R. "Mike" Swanson
Leonard Territo
Robert W. Taylor

## INTRODUCTION

If the many different purposes of the American police service were narrowed to a single focus, what would emerge is the obligation to preserve the peace in a manner consistent with the freedoms secured by the Constitution.[1] It does not follow from this assertion that our police alone bear the responsibility for maintaining a peaceful society; this responsibility is shared by other elements of society, beginning with each individual and spreading to each institution and each level of government—local, state, and federal. However, because crime is an immediate threat to our respective communities, the police have a highly visible and perhaps even primary role in overcoming the threat and fear of crime.

The preservation of peace is more complex than simply preventing crimes, making arrests for violations of the law, recovering stolen property, and providing assistance in the prosecution of persons charged with acts of criminality. In all likelihood, the police only spend something on the order of 15 percent of their time enforcing the law. The most substantial portion of their time goes toward providing less glamorous services that are utterly essential to maintaining the public order and well-being. Illustrative of these services are providing directions to motorists, mediating conflicts, evacuating neighborhoods threatened or struck by natural disasters, and serving as a bridge between other social service agencies and persons who come to the attention of the police, such as the mentally disturbed.

The degree to which any society achieves some amount of public order through police action depends in part upon the price that society is willing to pay to obtain it. This price can be measured in the resources dedicated to the public function and in the extent to which citizens are willing to tolerate a reduction in the number, kinds, and extent of liberties they enjoy. In this regard, totalitarian and democratic governments reflect very different choices. This point underscores the fact that the American police service cannot be understood properly if it is examined alone, as an island in a lake. A more appropriate and persuasive analogy is that policing is like a sandbar in a river, subject to being changed continuously by the currents in which it is immersed. As a profoundly significant social institution, policing is subject to, and continuously shaped by, a multitude of forces at work in our larger society.

The year 1890 is the date normally associated with the closing of the frontier and a milestone in our transition from a rural, agrarian society to one that is highly urbanized and industrialized. This period of time is a long one to have lived by current expectancies, but as a period of history, it is brief. Still, in this historically short time span, the changes that have taken place in this country are staggering.

Inevitably any attempt to highlight this period will have some deficits. However, the balance of this chapter does so to achieve two objectives: (1) to demonstrate the impact of social forces on policing and (2) to identify and

# —1—
# THE EVOLUTION OF AMERICAN POLICING

*The police at all times should maintain a relationship with the public that gives reality to the historic tradition that the police are the public and that the public are the police.*

SIR ROBERT PEEL

1

set the stage for some of the content treated in subsequent chapters. These two objectives will be met by presenting material organized under the headings of (1) politics and administration, (2) police professionalization, (3) the role of the police, (4) the impact of education, and (5) research on traditional policing.

## POLITICS AND ADMINISTRATION

Politics, stated simply, is the exercise of power. As such, it is value free, its "goodness" or "badness" stemming from its application rather than from some inherent character. Although police executives can occasionally be heard avowing to "keep politics out of the department," this unqualified posture is unrealistic. Personal politics exist in every organization, and democratic control of the policing mechanism is fundamental to our society. However, policing and partisan party politics have had a long and not entirely healthy relationship in this country.

In New York City, at the middle of the nineteenth century, the approval of the ward's alderman was required before appointment to the police force, and the Tammany Hall corruption of the same period depended in part on the use of the police to coerce and collect graft and to control elections.[2] During this same time, the election of a new mayor—particularly if from a party different from the incumbent's—signaled the coming dismissal of the entire police force and the appointment of one controlled by the new mayor.

Later, at the turn of the century, our cities were staggering under the burden of machine politics, corruption, crime, poverty, and the exploitation of women and children by industry.[3] The federal government, too, was not without its woes, as illustrated by the somewhat later Teapot Dome scandal that stained Warren G. Harding's administration.

Central to the Reformation period of 1900 to 1926 was the need to arouse the public and establish a conceptual cornerstone. Steffens exposed the plight of such cities as St. Louis, Minneapolis, Pittsburgh, and Chicago in *The Shame of the Cities* (1906); novels such as Sinclair's *The Jungle* (1906) called attention to abuses in the meat-packing industry; and Churchill addressed political corruption in *Coniston* (1911). The conceptual cornerstone was supplied by Woodrow Wilson's 1887 essay calling for a separation of politics and administration.[4] However impractical that might now seem, it is important to understand that to the reformers "politics" meant "machine politics" and all the ills associated with it.[5]

With an aroused public and a conceptual touchstone, rapid strides were made. In 1906, the New York Bureau of Municipal Research was formed, and by 1910, the city manager movement was under way. In 1911, the Training School for Public Service was established in New York, and by 1914, the University of Michigan was offering a degree in municipal administration. Further serving to strengthen the reform movement—whose center was the desire to separate politics (in the worst sense) and administration—was the issuance in 1916 of a model city charter by the National Municipal League, which called for a strict separation of these two elements. Further crystallization of the politics–administration dichotomy is found in White's *Public Administration* (1926), in which he praised the 1924 city manager's code of neutrality that stipulated that "no city manager should take an active part in politics," and in Willoughby's *Principles of Public Administration* (1927).

**FIGURE 1-1.** The entire Denver Police Department poses for an annual picture at the turn of the century, 1900. (Courtesy Denver, Colorado, Police Department.)

These events combined to produce movement toward reducing corruption, waste, fraud, and abuse in government; the desire to create a professionally qualified cadre of people committed to careers in public service; the rise of the civil service; emphasis upon proper recruitment, selection, and training of public employees; the freeing of government from the influence of machine politics; and the development of new theories, techniques, and models related to organizations. In short, these events were not only historical milestones; they unleashed a process of improvement that is still in progress today.

## POLICE PROFESSIONALIZATION

The terms *profession* and *professional* are tossed around with great abandon and a conspicuous lack of definition. The general absence of attention to definition has produced endless and futile debates as to whether policing is in fact a profession. The term *profession* is derived from the Latin *pro* (forth) and *fateri* (confess), meaning to "announce a belief"; at its early use, the word referred to public or open avowals of faith.[6] Cogan[7] notes that the earliest recorded use of the word *profession* as a learned vocation was in 1541 and that by 1576 the meaning had been generalized to mean any calling or occupation by which a person habitually earned his or her living. By 1675, a refinement of the secular use of the term occurred when it was associated with the act of professing to be duly qualified.[8]

Roughly since 1920, much of the serious work on professions has centered on specifying what criteria must be met to constitute a profession. The result is not a single definition but rather a collection of similar definitions that usually approximate the following: (1) an organized body of theoretically grounded knowledge, (2) advanced study, (3) a code of ethics, (4) prestige, (5) standards of admission, (6) a professional association, and (7) a service ideal, which may also be stated alternatively as altruism.[9] In 1960 Merton[10] reduced the values that make up a profession to (1) knowing (systematic knowledge), (2) doing (technical skill and trained capacity), and (3) helping (the joining of knowing and doing). Becker[11] has reduced the argument further to the pithy observation that in a debate as to whether a particular type of work can be called a profession, if the work group is successful in getting itself called a profession, it is one.

The rise of "professional" policing is associated initially with the paid, full-time body of police that stemmed from England's Peelian Reform of 1829. Despite the existence of similar bodies in this country from 1845 onward, the genesis of American professional policing is associated with the initiatives of August Vollmer, who was chief of police in Berkeley, California, from 1902 to 1932.

Without detracting one bit from Vollmer's genius, note that his tenure as chief parallels closely the reformation movement of 1900 to 1926, which, in addition to its politics–administration dichotomy concern, also had a heavy orientation toward good, progressive government. Carte summarizes the work of this giant by noting

> The image of professional policing as we know it today is largely the creation of one man, August Vollmer. Vollmer was a tireless crusader for the reform of policing through technology and higher personnel standards. Under his direction the Berkeley department became a model of professional policing—efficient, honest, scientific. He introduced into Berkeley a patrolwide police signal system, the first completely mobile patrol—first on bicycles, then in squad cars—modern records

**FIGURE 1-2.** August Vollmer, seated third from the left, at work in the Berkeley, California, Police Department about 1914. (Courtesy of the Berkeley Police Department.)

systems, beat analysis and modus operandi. The first scientific crime laboratory in the United States was set up in Berkeley in 1916, under the direction of a full-time forensic scientist. The first lie detector machine to be used in criminal investigation was built in the Berkeley department in 1921.

However, Vollmer's department was better known for the caliber of its personnel. He introduced formal police training in 1908, later encouraging his men to attend classes in police administration that were taught each summer at the University of California. Eventually he introduced psychological and intelligence testing into the recruitment process and actively recruited college students from the University, starting around 1919. This was the beginning of Berkeley's "college cops," who set the tone for the department throughout the 1920s and 30s and came to be accepted by police leaders as the ultimate model of efficient, modern policemen.[12]

The Pendleton Act of 1883 sought to eliminate the ills of the political spoils system in the federal government. Many states and local governments passed parallel legislation over the next 30 years, establishing civil service systems designed to protect government employees from political interference. Although these measures were intuitively attractive, their application was questioned early by one observer of the police, Fosdick, who wrote in 1920:

> In its application to a police department civil service has serious limitations. In the endeavor to guard against abuse of authority, it frequently is carried to such extremes that rigidity takes the place of flexibility in administration, and initiative in effecting essential changes in personnel is crippled and destroyed. Too often . . . civil service is a bulwark for neglect and incompetence, and one of the prime causes of departmental disorganization. Too often does the attempt to protect the force against the capricious play of politics compromise the principle of responsible leadership, so that in trying to nullify the effects of incompetence and favoritism, we nullify capacity and intelligence too.
>
> As a result of this divided responsibility between police executives and civil service commissions, there are in most large departments many men whose continuance in office is a menace to the force and to the community, but who cannot be dismissed because the proof of incompetence or dishonesty does not satisfy the requirements of the civil service law.[13]

It is a matter of some irony that there is a basic tension between Vollmer's trained and educated "professional" police officer and the early administration of civil service acts. The reason was that Vollmer was highly concerned with competence and performance—his notion of merit— whereas the measure of merit for many of the initial years of civil service was simply the degree to which political influence was kept out of appointments and promotion.[14]

Of significant consequence to the very structure of police organizations were the continuing efforts during the reformation period to separate politics and administration. One mechanism for doing so was to change the political structure; thus, in Los Angeles a council elected at large was substituted for the ward system.[15] Other reformers, persuaded that America was besieged by crime and that the police were our first line of defense, saw the police as analogous to the military. A second mechanism, therefore, was giving chiefs expanded powers, large and competent staffs, and the capability to actually control their departments.[16] In many cities, the precincts had previously operated largely or totally autonomously, and this second mechanism required centralization, which meant consolidating or eliminating precincts, as in New York City and elsewhere,[17] a further blow to ward boss control. The military analogy was so potent that its logical extension—recruiting military officers as police commissioners or chiefs—became a common practice for some years. Illustrative of this practice was the appointment in 1923 in Philadelphia of Marine Corps General Smedley Butler as director of public safety.

The highly centralized military analogy model (refer to Chapter 4) that became widely adopted and remains today as the dominant force of police organization is technically a bureaucratic structure that has been subjected to a number of criticisms. At the time of its adoption in American policing, it may have been an essential part of promoting police professionalism. For whatever its weaknesses, it brought with it an emphasis on discipline, inspections, improved record keeping, supervision, close-order drill, improved accountability, and other bits and pieces that contributed to the transformation of the police from semiorganized ruffians operating under the mantle of law into something entirely different.

The 1930s became a pivotal period as American police gained increasing legitimacy and authority in society.[18] Starting in 1931, the National Commission on Law Observance and Law Enforcement, popularly named after its chairman as the Wickersham Commission, presented a number of reforms for the police. Central to the commission's recommendations were provisions for civil service classification for police and enhanced support for education and training. Radelet[19] reports that "Take the police out of politics," a common slogan of the era, represented an important first step in gaining respectability. This step was a continuation of the separation of politics and administration, which first arose during the reformation period discussed earlier in this chapter.

The emphasis on law enforcement in American society was timely, as crime was perceived to be dramatically increasing. Stimulated by celebrated cases, such as the kidnapping of Charles Lindbergh's baby, the Federal Bureau of Investigation (FBI), under the direction of J. Edgar Hoover, began to emerge as a dominant entity in American policing. In 1935 the FBI created the National Police Academy, where local police leaders and officials were educated in the "professional" and "scientific" aspects of law enforcement.[20] This move was concurrent with the first major university programs (at the University of California at Berkeley, Michigan State University, and Northwestern University) devoted to the academic study of police practices. According to Kelling and Stewart, the decade that followed concretized the "reform" period from political "patsies" to professional agencies:

> Police departments nationwide had come to embrace an integrated and coherent organizational strategy that sought authority in criminal law; narrowed police function to crime control; emphasized classical organizational forms; relied on preventive patrol, rapid response to calls for service, and criminal investigation as its primary tactics; and measured its success by crime, arrest, and clearance data. . . . Indeed, with rare exception police defined themselves as professional organizations that should be kept out of the purview of citizens, academics and researchers, and other persons with an interest in police. Police business was just that: police business.[21]

Following World War II, interest in the police seemed to wane as economic development and social mobility gave rise to new issues—urban congestion, decaying values, and ethnic/racial unrest. It was not until the 1960s that significant attention was once again brought to bear on the functions and duties of the police.

The emerging racial tensions and social unrest of the early 1960s erupted into violent confrontation between minorities and police in most major cities. Fueled in part by the U.S. involvement in Southeast Asia, the police found themselves amid a nation divided both racially and socially. Occupying a very precarious position, police agencies reacted with a "get-tough" policy. The resulting riots were often characterized by widespread violence between predominantly white police departments and black communities. The nation began to focus on the police, specifically on the role of the police in society.

For the first time, major questions were being asked concerning what the police do. The National Advisory Commission on Civil Disorders, often referred to as the Kerner Commission, as it was headed by Governor Otto Kerner of Ohio, clearly outlined the problem:

> The policeman in the ghetto is a symbol of increasingly bitter social debate over law enforcement. One side, disturbed and perplexed by sharp rises in crime and urban violence, exerts extreme pressure on police for tougher law enforcement. Another group, inflamed against police as agents of repression, tends toward defiance of what it regards as order maintained at the expense of justice.[22]

This role conflict also called into question the legitimacy of policing as a profession. Were the police viable agents capable of controlling crime and disorder, or simply bullies who attempted to control a culturally divided American society? Such questions led to the identification of several conflicting and ambiguous roles for the police.

As a result of the previous "crime-fighting" era, police officers were considered law enforcers, charged with fighting crime, arresting criminals, and maintaining order. This image remains today and is reinforced by the popular media and continued community perception. Yet, at the same time, the police were touted as conflict managers, keepers of the peace, crime prevention specialists, and, to some degree, social service agents. In other words, the police were also supposed to *assist* citizens rather than *arrest* law violators.[23] To a large extent, this role ambiguity still exists as law enforcement agencies and their communities strive to define more accurately the evolving nature of policing.

# THE IMPACT OF EDUCATION

Major interest in police professionalization was renewed once again in the 1960s. During this time, the requirement of a high school diploma or a general equivalency degree became the minimum educational requirement for appointment. Character and background investigations became standard practice and increasingly more thorough. The use of the polygraph and psychological instruments to screen applicants became more widespread. Altogether, such factors signaled a shift from screening out the undesirable and hiring the rest to identifying and hiring those believed to be most able. At the state level, Police Officer Standards and Training Commissions (POSTs) were created, often with the incentive of Law Enforcement Assistance Administration (LEAA) grants to initiate operations and to ensure that uniform minimum standards—including training—were met.

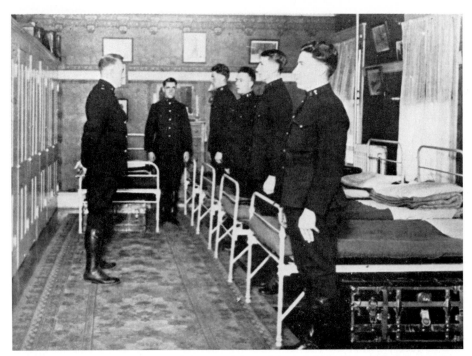

**FIGURE 1-3.** The military model at work in policing. A 1906 Pennsylvania State Police barracks inspection. (Courtesy of the Pennsylvania State Police.)

Training academies proliferated, and a few departments began to require a college degree as an entry-level educational requirement. More numerous, however, were the departments that required a few college credits, such as six or twelve, and the departments that required as a condition of employment that officers agree to obtain a certain number of college hours within a specified time after appointment. Written promotional tests gained in prominence, although many rank-and-file members objected to them, favoring seniority instead. Even some chiefs complained that written tests interfered with their ability to promote the most able persons. The length of recruit academy curricula increased steadily, and social science subjects were introduced. From 1965 on, the number of junior colleges, colleges, and universities offering police administration or criminal justice degrees grew steadily, if not exponentially, due initially to the availability of seed money to start such programs from the Office of Law Enforcement Assistance (OLEA), LEAA's predecessor. Law Enforcement Education Program (LEEP) funds from LEAA were offered to induce and support the studies of students with career interests in criminal justice.

Further impetus to the movement to educate in-service officers and infuse college graduates into police departments was gained by providing incentive pay for college credits, which is a supplement above the regular salary based on the number of college credits earned. "Professionalization" of the police and "education" became virtually synonymous in the eyes of many observers. Illustratively, while conspicuously failing to define professionalization, the 1967 President's Commission on Law Enforcement and Administration of Justice nonetheless clearly equated professionalism with education.

Thus, despite a variety of practices designed to foster a higher caliber of personnel, the hallmark from 1950 to 1970—particularly after 1965—was the at-

**FIGURE 1-4.** San Francisco police recruits learning to type in a 1937 class. Note the traffic lights that were used as a training aid. The use of such training programs was a central strategy in early attempts to professionalize the police. (Courtesy of the San Francisco Archives.)

tempt to promote police professionalism through education. Education was seen as a means by which to improve community relations, which had suffered and contributed to the urban riots of 1965–1968, to reduce police use of violence, to promote more judicious use of police discretionary powers, to counter the problem of corruption, and to accurately define the role of police in society.[24]

## RESEARCH ON TRADITIONAL POLICING

During the late 1970s, the issues of professionalism and the role of the police seemed to take a backseat to an ever-increasing public demand for efficiency and effectiveness. Unlike earlier years, law enforcement agencies were unable to expand their level of service delivery because of the reluctance of local officials to continually increase the police budget. This reluctance could be attributed to several factors. For example, some of the police expansion during the late 1960s and early 1970s could be traced to the creation of LEAA, which provided substantial financial resources to improve police operations. The decline of the agency during the 1970s severely cut what was once a relatively large fund for local police service improvement.

To make financial matters even worse, an inflationary economy had produced further constraints and burdens on urban police budgets. Major increases in gasoline prices and labor/personnel costs had forced many local governments to consider themselves in a state of crisis. New York City and Philadelphia laid off thousands of police officers in an attempt to recover from near economic collapse. Moreover, the social and political climate of the era focused on the scrutiny of government spending. Based in part on the public's cry for the efficient use of tax dollars, most city officials felt the need to conserve expenditures.

Still faced with rising crime and increased calls for service, police administrators looked for ways to improve the efficiency and effectiveness of existing resources. Fortunately, the ongoing research efforts of a few key institutions yielded some interesting, if not highly controversial, answers. Three important experiments once again set the stage for questioning what the police do:

**The Kansas City Patrol Experiment**

From October 1, 1972, to September 30, 1973, the Kansas City Police Department, along with the support of the Police Foundation, conducted a study to determine if routine patrol using conspicuously marked vehicles had any measurable impact on crime or the public's sense of security.[25] As noted in a report on the study, "police patrol strategies have always been based on two unproven but widely accepted hypotheses: first, that visible police presence prevents potential offenders; second, that the public's fear of crime is diminished by such police presence.[26]

The Kansas City experiment was conducted within fifteen beats in a 32-square-mile area with a resident population of 148,395 (see Figure 1-5). The beats were designated as reactive, proactive, and control areas. Reactive beats did not have preventive patrols; officers entered these areas only when a citizen called and requested service. When the officers were not responding to calls, they patrolled adjacent proactive beats on the boundaries of their own beats. With proactive beats, the routine preventive patrol was intensified to two to three times its usual level, whereas in control beats, the normal (usual) amount of patrolling was conducted. The following were noted in the evaluation of this experiment:

1. The amount of reported crime in the reactive, control, and proactive beats revealed only one significant statistical variation: The number of incidents under the category of "other sex crimes," including such offenses as exhibitionism and molestation (excluding rape), was higher in reactive areas than in control areas, but project evaluators felt this significance was most likely random.
2. There were no statistically significant differences found in regard to fluctuations in crimes that were not officially reported to the police.
3. No statistically significant differences in arrests among the three types of beats were found.
4. Security measures taken by citizens and businesses were not significantly altered with the variations in the level of patrolling.

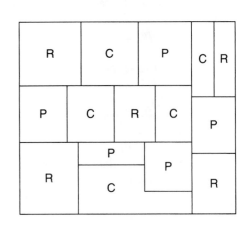

**FIGURE 1-5.** Schematic representation of the fifteen-beat experimental area of the Kansas City Patrol Experiment. [From George L. Kelling et al., *The Kansas City Patrol Experiment* (Washington, D.C.: Police Foundation, 1974), p. 9.]

5. There was little correlation found between the level of patrol and the citizens' and business persons' attitude toward the policing.

6. The citizens' fear of crime was not significantly changed by the alternations in the level of routine preventive patrol.

7. The time taken for police to answer calls was not significantly changed by variations in the level of routine preventive patrol.

8. The level of patrol had no significant effect on the incidence of traffic accidents.

The interpretations and findings of the Kansas City Patrol Experiment were highly controversial. Upon learning of the study, some local leaders felt that further increases in police manpower were not warranted and that decreases might even be justified. However, these persons failed to realize that a random moving patrol is not the only strategy of prevention available to police.

In 1973, the RAND Corporation was awarded a grant by the National Institute of Law Enforcement and Criminal Justice to undertake a nationwide study of criminal investigations in major metropolitan police agencies.[27] The purposes of the study were to describe how police investigations were organized and managed and to assess the contribution of various activities to overall police effectiveness. Before the RAND study, police investigators had not been subject to the type of scrutiny that was being focused on other types of police activity. Most police administrators knew little about the effectiveness of the day-to-day activities of their investigative units, and even less about the practice of other departments.

**The RAND Criminal Investigation Study**

**FIGURE 1-6.** Based in part on the RAND Criminal Investigation Study, some departments have used a team approach to solve crimes. Here members of a crisis team help children cope with the traumatic aspects of a family crime while maintaining their roles as detectives. (Courtesy Austin, Texas, Police Department.)

The RAND study focused on the investigation of serious crimes against unwilling victims (index offenses), as opposed to vice, gambling, and narcotics. The information on current practice was obtained by a national survey of municipal and county police agencies who employed more than 150 officers or jurisdictions with a population over 100,000. In order to obtain a representative sample, interviews and observations were conducted in over twenty-five departments. Data on the outcome of investigations were obtained from the FBI Uniform Crime Report tapes, from internal evaluations, and from samples of completed cases. In addition, data on the allocation of investigative efforts were obtained from a computerized work-load file maintained by the Kansas City Police Department.

The data from the national survey and the Uniform Crime Reports were then combined to analyze the relationship between departmental characteristics and apprehension effectiveness. In turn, case samples were analyzed to determine how specific cases were solved.

### Policy Recommendations

1. The RAND study strongly suggested that post-arrest investigation activities be coordinated more directly with the prosecutors, either by allowing prosecutors to exert more guidance over the practices and policies of investigators or by assigning investigators to the prosecutor's office. The purpose of this recommendation was to attempt to increase the percentage of cases that could be prosecuted.
2. Patrol officers were to be given a larger role in conducting preliminary investigations—to provide an adequate basis for case screening and to reduce or attempt to eliminate redundant efforts by an investigator.
3. Additional and improved resources were to be devoted to the processing of latent prints, and improved systems were to be developed for the organizing and searching of print files.
4. The study recommended that with regard to follow-up investigations for the cases a department selected to pursue, a distinction should be drawn between cases that merely required routine clerical processing and those that required legal skills or those of a special investigative nature.

The RAND study is still a subject of controversy within the police profession. Many police officials, especially those without detective experience, were sympathetic to the study in that it supported their own impressions of how investigators functioned. Others criticized the study for "telling us what we already knew." Some police chiefs became resentful because the study was used by city officials as an excuse to cut police budgets, and others refused to accept the findings because of the limited number of departments that were studied.[28]

There have not been any major attempts to extend or replicate the findings in the RAND study; a number of reports have been published with consistent findings. Bloch and Weidman's[29] analysis of the investigative practices of the Rochester, New York, Police Department and Greenberg's[30] efforts to develop a felony investigation decision model both resulted in findings that support the idea that preliminary investigations, which are carried out in a majority of arrests, can provide adequate information for screening cases. A report by the Vera Institute on felony arrests in New York City indicated that a substantial portion of felony arrests for street crimes involve offenders who are known to their victims,[31] and a report by Forst[32] on the disposition of felony arrests in Washington, D.C., demonstrates the importance of physical evidence and multiple witnesses in securing convictions for felony street crimes. In general these studies suggest that often much of the information needed to solve a case is supplied by the uniformed officer who does the original investigation as opposed to cases solved by a detective's follow-up investigation.

Team policing was one of the most dynamic experiments that altered traditional methods of policing in both the United States and Great Britain.[33] Table 1-1 contrasts the key features of traditional and team policing. Team policing was an innovation that enabled police personnel from various divisions to participate as full partners in the development of a superior police service delivery system.

**Team Policing**

**TABLE 1-1.  Comparison of Traditional and Neighborhood Team Policing**

| Traditional | Neighborhood Team Policing |
|---|---|
| 1. Smallest patrol unit (precinct or division) has 100 to 250 officers. | 1. Team has 20 to 30 officers. |
| 2. Supervision is quasi-military. | 2. Supervision is professional, with consultation, setting of objectives, an inservice training program, encouraging suggestions, permitting the exercise of responsibility within necessary limits. |
| 3. Shift responsibility includes eight-hour tours, with only unit commanders—captains or inspectors—responsible for around-the-clock operations. | 3. Team commander is responsible for all aspects of police service on an around-the-clock basis. |
| 4. Assignment is on the basis of the first available car to a call for police service—with priority for emergency calls. | 4. Team provides all police service for its neighborhood. Team members are sent out of the neighborhood only in emergencies. Nonteam members take calls in the neighborhood only in emergencies. |
| 5. Officers are rotated to new divisions or assignments. | 5. Officers are given extended assignments to a neighborhood. |
| 6. Special police units (tactical, detective, etc.) operate in local neighborhoods without informing local patrol officials. | 6. Special police units inform themselves of team goals and, whenever possible, consult in advance with the local team commander. |
| 7. Community relations is seen as "image building" (special units for community relations plus speaking engagements for officials). | 7. Community relations is seen as an essential patrol function, planned by team commander and the team, and consists of good police service, friendliness on street contacts, and attendance at meetings of various community groups. |
| 8. Reactive policing (responding to calls) or aggressive policing (stop and frisk and street interrogations) are prevalent. | 8. Decentralized planning (crime analysis, use of plainclothes or special tactics investigations, preventive programs, referral programs, service activities). |
| 9. Planning is centralized (innovation through orders from the chief or other important officials). | 9. Planning is decentralized (innovation by team commanders, subject to review by their superiors). |

From Peter Block and David Specht, *Neighborhood Team Policing* (Washington, D.C.: U.S. Government Printing Office, 1973), p. 2.

Generally, team policing involved combining the officers responsible for line operations into a team with a leader. Each officer involved in the team had an opportunity to perform the patrol, traffic, and detective functions and, where appropriate, the specialized functions of narcotics and vice and juvenile control. Community relations was not considered a specialization, because the function was the responsibility of every police officer. Each team was assigned a permanent sector or geographic area for which they were totally responsible. Authority for internal team assignments, scheduling, and complete police service was given to the team leaders. The team was held strictly accountable for police service in its assigned area.[34]

A number of police departments experimented with team policing, and the results were mixed. In New York City; Dayton, Ohio; and Holyoke, Massachusetts the programs were failures.[35] In New York City, officers continued to police in conventional ways, and low officer morale undermined the programs, as did similar problems in Dayton.[36] On the other hand, San Diego reported success in redefining the role of officers and in improving work-load management, and data from Rochester, New York, revealed improvement in crime control and investigative effectiveness. Furthermore, police from Albany, New York, and Los Angeles indicated that team policing was a qualified success in those cities in improving community attitudes about the police.[37]

A repeated theme in analyses of the failure of some attempts at team policing was the opposition of middle managers, whose importance was diminished because team policing reduces specialization and the number of levels in an organization. Wycoff and Kelling[38] report that the failures of team policing might have resulted more from implementation of change rather than from philosophy or ideas. They indicate several issues during the implementation process that deserve attention:

- Lack of planning and understanding of the change process existed throughout all levels of the organization.
- Ideas were imposed from the top or from outside the organization, often without support from the lower ranks.
- Mid-level managers and supervisors who were critical to success quickly became disaffected. They were not included in the planning, nor were they prepared for the role changes the new efforts would require.
- Changes in organizational processes or structures needed to support the new programs were not made and did not evolve on their own.
- An overall organizational philosophy supportive of the new programs did not exist. In each case, the new programs were add-ons, forced to sink or swim in an unprotected organizational environment.
- The overall effort was too much too fast.[39]

Hence, although team policing lost much of its luster during the mid-1970s, some of its failure might have been the consequence of poorly conducted organizational change rather than of the concept itself. There is also some limited research evidence that suggests that the implementation of team policing in large cities, but not necessarily smaller ones, may produce short-run benefits that "wash out" over time as the latent power of bureaucracy asserts itself;[40] Michels's[41] "iron law of oligarchy" states that modern large-scale organizations tend toward centralization, even if it runs contrary to the ideals and intentions of both the leaders and the led. Large police departments require a certain amount of specialization to handle diverse tasks efficiently, such as examining various physical evidence, and the amount of hierarchy required to coordinate the various specialized parts produces a tendency toward centralization. (Refer to Chapter 5 for a more thorough discussion of organizational design.) Interestingly, similar issues concerning team policing are currently being raised regarding the implementation of community policing programs of the 1990s.

## SUMMARY

The role of the police is to maintain the peace within a carefully established framework of individual liberties. By devoting more resources to policing and reducing rights, we could be more effective in crime control, but our system of government is incompatible with such a choice. Policing is an institution that does not stand alone; it is part of the larger society it serves and is influenced by the issues and forces that shape that society. For present purposes, we have discussed American policing as evolving within this arena. Our exploration can be characterized by the identification of significant developments.

1. *Politics and administration,* particularly the struggle to free policing from machine politics and the improvements resulting from the reformation period from 1900 to 1926

2. *Police professionalism,* including the early work of August Vollmer through the first university programs devoted to the study of policing

3. *Role of the police,* focusing on role ambiguity resulting from the violent confrontations between police and minorities during the 1960s

4. *Impact of education,* emphasizing education as the methodology to accomplish professionalism

5. *Research on traditional policing,* highlighting three important experiments during the 1970s (the Kansas City Preventive Patrol Experiment, the RAND Criminal Investigation Study, and team policing) and the failure of traditional methods to curb crime rates and integrate the police with the community

Within the context of these headings, we have touched on some of the issues confronting police administrators. The stage is now set to explore the new and innovative police philosophies that emerged during the 1990s. These community policing strategies will most certainly influence the administration of police agencies well into the new century.

## DISCUSSION QUESTIONS

1. Whose responsibility is it for maintaining an orderly society?

2. What is the conceptual cornerstone of the separation of politics and administration?

3. Of what consequence to policing was the reformation period from 1900 to 1926?

4. What were August Vollmer's contributions to American police professionalization?

5. Why were the 1930s considered a pivotal period in American policing?

6. Discuss the conflicting roles of the police.

7. What can be gained from the research of the 1970s regarding the effectiveness of traditional policing?

## NOTES

1. This section draws on and extends material found in the National Advisory Commission on Criminal Justice Standards and Goals, *Police,* Russell W. Peterson, chairman (Washington, D.C.: U.S. Government Printing Office, 1973), p. 13.

2. Thomas A. Reppetto, *The Blue Parade* (New York: Free Press, 1978), pp. 41–42.

3. Alice B. Stone and Donald C. Stone, "Early Development of Education in Public Administration," in *American Public Administration: Past, Present, and Future,* ed. Frederick C. Mosher (Tuscaloosa, Ala.: University of Alabama Press, 1975), pp. 17–18. The themes in this and the subsequent paragraph are reflected in Stone and

Stone's "Early Development" and sounded repeatedly in the literature. See Howard E. McCurdy, *Public Administration: A Synthesis* (Menlo Park, Calif.: Cummings, 1977), pp. 19–21; William L. Morrow, *Public Administration: Politics and the Political System* (New York: Random House, 1975), p. 25; Lynton K. Caldwell, "Public Administration and the Universities: A Half-Century of Development," *Public Administration Review,* 25 (March 1965), 52–60.

4. Woodrow Wilson, "The Study of Administration," *Political Science Quarterly,* 2 (June 1887), 197–222.

5. Edwin O. Stene, "The Politics–Administration Dichotomy," *Midwest Review of Public Administration,* 9 (April–July 1975), 84.

6. E. W. Roddenbury, "Achieving Professionalism," *Journal of Criminal Law, Criminology, and Police Science,* 44 (May 1953–1954), 109.

7. Morris L. Cogan, "Toward a Definition of Profession," *Harvard Educational Review,* 23 (Winter 1953), 34.

8. Everette Hughes, "Professions," in *The Professions in America,* ed. K. S. Lynn (Cambridge, Mass.: Riverside Press, 1965), pp. 1–14.

9. See, for example, Ernest Greenwood, "Attributes of a Profession," *Social Work,* 2:3 (1957), 45.

10. Robert K. Merton, "Some Thoughts on the Professions in American Society" (Address before the Brown University graduate convocation, Providence, R.I., June 6, 1960).

11. Howard Becker, "The Nature of a Profession," in the *Sixty-First Yearbook of the National Society for the Study of Education,* 1962. Also Harold L. Wilensky, "The Professionalization of Everyone?" *The American Journal of Sociology,* 70:2 (1964), 137–58.

12. Gene Edward Carte, "August Vollmer and the Origins of Police Professionalism," *Journal of Police Science and Administration,* 1:3 (1973), 274.

13. Raymond B. Fosdick, *American Police Systems* (Montclair, N.J.: A 1969 Patterson Smith Reprint of a Century Company Work), pp. 284–285.

14. Ibid., p. 271.

15. Robert M. Fogelson, *Big-City Police* (Cambridge, Mass.: Harvard University Press, 1975), p. 76.

16. Extended treatment of this line of thinking is found in Fogelson, "The Military Analogy," in *Big-City Police,* pp. 40–66.

17. Ibid., p. 77.

18. George L. Kelling and James K. Stewart, "The Evolution of Contemporary Policing," in *Local Government Police Management,* ed. William A.

Gellar (Washington, D.C.: International City Management Association, 1991), p. 7.

19. Louis A. Radelet, *The Police and the Community,* 3rd ed. (Encino, Calif.: Glencoe, 1980), p. 8.

20. See Kelling and Stewart, "Evolution of Contemporary Policing," for an excellent historical brief on the police.

21. Ibid., p. 9.

22. U.S. National Advisory Commission on Civil Disorders. *Reports of the National Advisory Commission on Civil Disorders* (Washington, D.C.: U.S. Government Printing Office, 1968), p. 157.

23. Conflicting role expectations for police have been a historical issue. See Radelet, *Police and the Community;* James Q. Wilson, *Varieties of Police Behavior: The Management of Law and Order in Eight Communities* (Cambridge, Mass.: Harvard University Press, 1968); Michael Banton, *Policeman in the Community* (New York: Basic Books, 1964); Jerome H. Skolnick, *Justice Without Trial: Law Enforcement in Democratic Society* (New York: John Wiley & Sons, 1966); and Peter K. Manning and John Van Maanen, eds., *Policing: A View from the Street* (Santa Monica, Calif.: Goodyear Publishing, 1978).

24. James Q. Wilson, "The Police and Their Problems," *Public Policy,* 12 (1963), 189–216.

25. See George K. Kelling et al., *The Kansas City Preventive Patrol Experiment* (Washington, D.C.: Police Foundation, 1974); Richard C. Larson, "What Happened to Patrol Operations in Kansas City: A Review of the Kansas City Preventive Patrol Experiment," *Journal of Criminal Justice,* 3 (Winter 1975), 267–97: Stephen E. Finberg, Kinley Larntz, and Albert J. Reiss, Jr., "Redesigning the Kansas City Preventive Patrol Experiment," *Evaluation,* 3:1–2 (1976), 124, 131. This section is a synopsis of the Kansas City Patrol Experiment as reported by Kelling et al., *Kansas City Preventive Patrol Experiment,* and H. J. Vetter and L. Territo, *Crime and Justice in America* (St. Paul, Minn.: West, 1984), pp. 161–63.

26. Kelling et al., *Kansas City Preventive Patrol Experiment,* p. 42.

27. This section is a synopsis of the RAND Criminal Investigator Study as reported by Peter W. Greenwood, *The RAND Criminal Investigation Study: Its Findings and Impacts to Date* (Santa Monica, Calif.: The RAND Corporation, July 1979), pp. 3–7, and Vetter and Territo, *Crime and Justice in America,* pp. 176–78.

28. Daryl F. Gates and Lyle Knowles, "An Evaluation of the RAND Corporation Analyses," *Police Chief,* 43 (July 1976), 20–24, 74, 77.

29. P. Bloch and D. Weidman, *Managing Criminal Investigations: Prescriptive Package* (Washington, D.C.: U.S. Government Printing Office, 1975).

30. B. Greenberg et al., *Felony Investigation Decision Model: An Analysis of Investigative Elements of Information* (Washington, D.C.: U.S. Government Printing Office, 1977).

31. The Vera researchers noted that in 56 percent of all felony arrests for crimes against the person, the victim had a prior relationship with the offender. In turn, 87 percent of these cases—as compared with only 29 percent of cases involving strangers—resulted in dismissals because the complainant refused to cooperate with the prosecutor. Once complainants "cool off," they are not interested in seeing the defendants prosecuted. Consequently, the Vera report recommends the use of neighborhood justice centers, rather than the courts, as the appropriate place to deal with most cases that involve prior relationships between victims and perpetrators.

32. B. Forst, *What Happens After Arrest* (Washington, D.C.: U.S. Government Printing Office, 1978).

33. Lawrence Sherman, Catherine Milton, and Thomas Kelly, *Team Policing: Seven Case Studies* (Washington, D.C.: The Police Foundation, 1973).

34. D. T. Shanahan, *Patrol Administration: Management by Objectives,* 2nd ed. (Boston, Mass.: Allyn and Bacon, 1985), p. 303.

35. William G. Gay, H. Talmadge Day, and Jane P. Woodward, *Neighborhood Team Policing: Phase I Report* (Washington, D.C.: U.S. Government Printing Office, 1977), p. 40.

36. Ibid., p. 40.

37. Ibid., p. 39, from Table 15.

38. See Mary Ann Wycoff and George L. Kelling, *The Dallas Experience: Organizational Reform* (Washington, D.C.: The Police Foundation, 1978).

39. Ibid.

40. Susette M. Talarico and Charles R. Swanson, "The Limits of Team Policing," *Police Studies,* 3:2 (Summer 1980), 21–29.

41. See Robert Michels, *Political Parties* (New York: Dover, 1959).

## INTRODUCTION

The failure of traditional law enforcement methods to curb rising crime rates during the 1970s and 1980s and to reintegrate the police with society gave rise to a new movement, generally referred to as "community policing." One of the first major critics of the traditional policing model was Herman Goldstein.[1] In his classic work, *Policing a Free Society,* Goldstein questioned the effectiveness of traditional police methods in safeguarding the constitutional rights and privileges celebrated in American society (e.g., freedom of speech and expression, due process, the right to privacy) versus the control of crime and the decay of social order. Goldstein pointed out that these two goals may be incompatible under the traditional police model and called for a closer link between the police and the community.

During this same time period, Wilson and Kelling's "broken windows" thesis emerged as a dominant theme in American policing debate.[2] Arguing that crime seemed to increase dramatically in neighborhoods where visible signs of social decay were present (e.g., graffiti on bridge structures, unkept lots with overgrown weeds, warehouses with broken windows), Wilson and Kelling suggested that the police needed to do more than just "crime control." Indeed, they argued that other functions of the police were as important, and maybe more important, than strictly enforcing the law and maintaining order. Police should focus more on a service orientation, building key partnerships with churches, youth centers, and other neighborhood groups in an effort to forge new alliances with the community. Crime was seen not as the sole purview of the police, but rather an entire community responsibility. Police administrators began to look for new techniques and operational strategies that emphasized more service than arrest. Decentralization of services, characterized by storefront operations and neighborhood centers, began to be commonplace in police organizations. Old programs such as the horse patrol and the "walking beat" officer were reintroduced to American policing as ways to bring the police and the community closer together.

Although Braiden[3] argues that community policing is "nothing new under the sun" because it only echoes the ideas expressed by Sir Robert Peel in the early 1800s, community policing does represent a refreshing approach to earlier problems. Community policing embraces the Peelian principle of police as members of the public giving full-time attention to community welfare and existence. Therefore, policing is linked to a myriad of social issues other than simply crime, including poverty, illiteracy, racism, teen-age pregnancy, and the like.[4]

Although precise definitions of community policing are hard to find, it generally refers to an operational and management philosophy that is uniquely identifiable. Primarily, community policing is characterized by ongoing attempts to promote greater community involvement in the police function. For the most part, the movement has focused on programs that foster five elements: (1) a commitment to crime prevention, (2) public scrutiny of the police, (3) accountability of police actions to the public, (4) customized police service, and (5) community organization.[5]

# —2—
# COMMUNITY POLICING

*Community policing changes the fundamental nature of the relationship between people and their police to one of mutual respect and trust.*

ROBERT C. TROJANOWICZ

**FIGURE 2-1.** Officers interact with community functions in order to provide customized police services appropriate to the city area. In this case, officers on horseback patrol the extensive park areas in Portland, Oregon. (Courtesy Portland, Oregon, Police Bureau.)

Community policing advocates argue that traditional policing is a system of response; that is, the police respond to calls for services *after* the activity occurs. Police response is then reactive and incident driven rather than proactive and preventive in nature. Further, a randomized motor patrol neither lowers crime nor increases the chances of catching suspects. Increasing the number of police, then, has limited impact on the crime rate because improving response time on calls for service has little relevance to preventing the original incident.[6] In addition, the role of the individual police officer is largely limited within the confines of patrol and response. Refer to Box 2-1 for a review of the research on traditional policing.

## BOX 2-1

### Review of Research on Traditional Policing

1. Increasing numbers of police does not lower the crime rate or increase the proportion of solved crimes.

2. Randomized motor patrol neither lowers crime nor increases the chances of catching suspects.

3. Two-person patrol cars are not more effective than one-person cars in lowering crime rates or catching criminals; they are also no safer.

4. Saturation patrol does not reduce crime; instead, it displaces crime.

5. The kind of crime that terrifies Americans most (mugging, rape, robbery, burglary, and homicide) is rarely encountered by police on patrol.

6. Improving response time on calls has no effect on the likelihood of arresting criminals or even in satisfying involved citizens.

7. Crimes are not solved through criminal investigations conducted by police—they are solved because suspects are immediately apprehended or someone identifies them (name or license number).

*Source:* Jerome H. Skolnick and David H. Bayley, *The New Blue Line* (New York: The Free Press, 1986).

| Questions | Traditional | Community Policing |
|---|---|---|
| Who are the police? | a government agency principally responsible for law enforcement | Police are the public and the public are the police; the police officers are those who are paid to give full-time attention to the duties of every citizen. |
| What is the relationship of the police force to other public service departments? | priorities often conflict | The police are one department among many responsible for improving the quality of life. |
| What is the role of the police? | focusing on solving crimes | a broader problem-solving approach |
| How is police efficiency measured? | by detection and arrest rates | by the absence of crime and disorder |
| What are the highest priorities? | crimes that are high value (e.g., bank robberies) and those involving violence | whatever problems disturb the community most |
| What, specifically, do police deal with? | incidents | citizens' problems and concerns |
| What determines the effectiveness of police? | response times | public cooperation |
| What view do police take of service calls? | deal with them only if there is no real police work to do | vital function and great opportunity |
| What is police professionalism? | swift, effective response to serious crime | keeping close to the community |
| What kind of intelligence is most important? | crime intelligence (study of particular crimes or series of crimes) | criminal intelligence (information about the activities of individuals or groups) |
| What is the essential nature of police accountability? | highly centralized; governed by rules, regulations, and policy directives; accountable to the law | emphasis on local accountability to community needs |
| What is the role of headquarters? | to provide the necessary rules and policy directives | to preach organizational values |
| What is the role of the press liaison department? | to keep the "heat" off operational officers so they can get on with their jobs | to coordinate an essential channel of communication with the community |
| How do the police regard prosecutions? | as an important goal | as one tool among many |

**FIGURE 2-2.** Traditional vs. community policing: Questions and answers [*Source:* Malcolm K. Sparrow, "Implementing Community Policing," *Perspectives on Policing* (Washington, D.C.: National Institute of Justice, November 1988), pp. 8–9.]

Community policing represents the emergence of a new perspective that is proactive and information based.[7] Oettmeier[8] explains that the proactive function requires accurate and timely information on which to develop directed strategies in response to identified crime and/or other disorder problems. The emphasis is placed on designing cooperative strategies within the community that interdict criminal activity before it occurs rather than on responding to the incident after it is reported. In this manner, the role of the police officer is greatly expanded with responsibility and authority to address wider social concerns and neighborhood problems. The individual officer emerges as a coordinator of municipal services and neighborhood security, actively seeking ways to prevent crime and better the quality of neighborhood life rather than simply responding to calls for service and reported crimes.[9] That crime is integrally linked to other urban problems dictates that the most effective responses require the coordination of activities from private citizens, the business sector, and government agencies *outside* the traditional criminal justice system.[10] These responses must address crime as one symptom of a much broader set of social problems. Figure 2-2 compares traditional and community policing via a series of questions and answers designed to clarify their fundamental differences.

Several cities have implemented community policing strategies in the past decade. Three of these experiments are presented as case examples that highlight various aspects of the community policing philosophy.

**Newport News, Virginia**

In 1983, under the direction of a new chief, Darrel Stephens, the Newport News Police Department developed a "problem-oriented" approach to policing. This new and innovative style of community policy focused on the department's traditional response to major, recurring problems. Its goal was to reassess the traditional, incident-driven aspects of police work and fundamentally change the way the Newport News Police Department viewed its mission. The resulting self-analysis yielded an important four-step, problem-solving methodology (commonly referred to as SARA) that has become an integral part of daily operations (see Figure 2-3).

<u>S</u>canning:    Instead of relying on broad, law-related concepts such as robbery, burglary, auto theft, and the like, officers are encouraged to group individual related incidents that come to their attention as "problems" and define these problems in more precise and useful terms. For example, an incident that typically would be classified simply as a "robbery" might be seen as part of a pattern of prostitution-related robberies committed by transvestites in center-city hotels. In essence, officers are expected to look for possible problems and accurately define them as part of their daily routine.

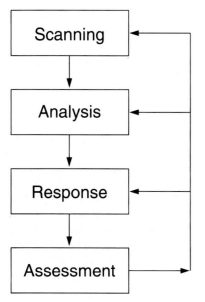

**FIGURE 2-3.** The problem-solving system used in Newport News, Virginia, Police Department. [*Source:* William Spelman and John E. Eck, "Problem Oriented Policing," *Research in Brief* (Washington, D.C.: National Institute of Justice, October 1986), p. 4.]

**Analysis:** Officers working on a well-defined problem then collect information from a variety of public and private sources, not just traditional police data such as criminal records and past offense reports. Officers rely on problem analysis guides that direct officers to examine offenders, victims, the social and physical environment, and previous responses to the problem. The goal is to understand the scope, nature, and causes of the problem and formulate a variety of options for its resolution.

**Response:** The knowledge gained in the analysis stage is then used to develop and implement solutions. Officers seek the assistance of citizens, businesses, other police units, other public and private organizations, and anyone else who can help to develop a program of action. Solutions may go well beyond traditional police responses to include other community agencies and/or municipal organizations.

**Assessment:** Finally, officers evaluate the impact and the effectiveness of their responses. Were the original problems actually solved or alleviated? They may use the results to revise a response, to collect more data, or even to redefine the problem.[11]

Goldstein[12] further explains this systematic process in his book, *Problem-Oriented Policing.* Destined to become a classic in the field, Goldstein's work attempts to give meaning to each of the four steps. For instance, a *problem* is expanded to mean a cluster of similar, related, or recurring incidents rather than a single incident. The assumption is that few incidents are isolated, as all are part of a wider set of urban social phenomena. Examples of such community problems are:

- Disorderly youth who regularly congregate in the parking lot of a specific convenience store
- Street prostitutes and associated "jack roll" robberies of patrons that continually occur in the same area
- Drunk and drinking drivers around the skid row area of the city
- Panhandlers, vagrants, and other displaced people living on the sidewalk in a business district
- Juvenile runaways, prostitutes, and drug dealers congregating at the downtown bus depot
- Robberies of commercial establishments at major intersections of a main thoroughfare of a suburban area that is a corridor leading out of a large central city[13]

Note that each of these problems incorporates not only a potential or real crime, but also a wider community/social issue. Further, each problem has been identified with a specific location. Goldstein[14] emphasizes that the traditional functions of crime analysis under the problem-solving methodology take on much wider and deeper importance. The pooling of data and subsequent analysis provide the basis for problem identification and response strategies. Therefore, the accuracy and timeliness of such information become a necessity for the department. However, the ultimate challenge in problem-oriented policing is not the identification of problems, but rather the integration of the community with the police in developing effective ways of dealing with them (see Box 2-2).

BOX 2-2

## Transitioning Your Community

**by Keith Carr, former sheriff**

**Blountville, Tenn.**

In rural law enforcement, moving from reactive to proactive responses to meet community needs is neither an automatic nor minor endeavor. To smoothly facilitate such a transition, the law enforcement chief executive officer must fully understand the community policing philosophy and be completely committed to its implementation.

To do it right, the CEO must be accessible to all levels of the changing agency as well as to outside agencies and citizens. Furthermore, the CEO should set the example for change internally. The agency's mission statement, goals, and objectives should reflect a commitment to excellence through community service.

An agency's managers and supervisors must be prepared to address the complaints that are sure to arise from the rank and file reflecting the opinion that community policing is mollycoddling troublemakers. It is difficult to convince many deputies who are accustomed to a traditional policing philosophy that it is more effective to attack the root causes of a problem rather than continue to strike at a problem's results. An effective leader can communicate that community policing techniques enhance rather than diminish conventional enforcement techniques.

Once this groundwork is laid, the next step is the appointment of an officer, committee, or group that coordinates the gradual move into community policing. The person or persons charged with this task must have a clear focus both of the concept of community policing and crime prevention. Not all crime prevention measures lead to, or support, the true concept of community policing. Through skilled coordination, you can avoid duplication of services, runarounds, and "passing the buck," and establish a full-service operation. This coordinating force will monitor the effort, design programs suited to the concept and guide into the practice of community policing those who have been specially trained and educated about the goals.

It is extremely necessary that the agency transitioning to community policing build strong partnerships with community members and with agencies and organizations representing the community. This can be accomplished through such measures as neighborhood watch programs, citizen law enforcement academy classes, citizen patrol groups, community service officers, and meetings with civic groups. Support for innovative school projects can be mined from community service agencies such as youth clubs, civic groups, church congregations, social service

agencies, and other organizations. Private businesses may also be enticed to participate both developmentally and financially in programs that can be shown to benefit youths. To be effective, program coordinators must be skilled in this area of partnership building.

Selling the community on the concept of trust and involvement that is essential to community policing is no easier than persuading officers established in their ways of enforcement to do an about-face. Citizen trust and involvement come one step at a time and become apparent when the calls for service increase in the area community policing is in effect. This is the alert to actively seek citizen participation in programs designed to involve citizens in the policing of their own communities.

A first step is to make officers as much a part of the affected community as possible. When that occurs, recommendations for services police could provide will begin to originate from officers in the field and flow up the chain of command to the CEO. The next step is to develop corrective measures, include the community as much as possible in the process and implement the new strategies. This concept, for all practical purposes, inverts the traditional power structure of most agencies.

Currently, the majority of law enforcement agencies react to crime by allowing criminals to dictate the placement of officers in the field. The response is for the agency to dispatch officers to react to the call for service. But the activity prompting the call for service will be repeated again and again—without the root cause ever being properly identified, much less attacked. Close community ties can make it possible for the patrol officer to anticipate a developing need for services and address it rather than make a rushed response after the fact to treat the symptoms of the problem. Patterns that lead to crime problems can be seen developing and then dealt with before they are allowed to coalesce into an insurmountable problem.

There is no single best approach to community policing. There are as many different good approaches as there are communities to serve. Each law enforcement executive officer entering into the effort must use cost-effective and valid methods applicable to each segment of the community and program. Programs that work in Cleveland, Ohio, or Fargo, N.D., will not necessarily work or function properly in the Tri-Cities area of Tennessee. But the basic concept of community members policing themselves in partnership with law enforcement is the undisputed wave of the future when it comes to keeping communities safe from crime.

*Source: The Community Policing Consortium*, issue 22, September/October 1998.

**Madison, Wisconsin** Community policing is not only a renewed emphasis on community and neighborhood involvement, but also a call for dynamic change in police organization and leadership. Community policing focuses on the quality of individual police service rather than the quantity (number) of arrests made, calls for service answered, cases cleared, and tickets written. As an example, the Madison, Wisconsin, Police Department has dramatically revised its mission statement and leadership principles (see Figure 2-4). During the last several years, the police department has slowly integrated community policing into its services.[15]

The Department's mission statement establishes several important goals: provide high quality, community-oriented police service with sensitivity; use problem-solving techniques and teamwork; and be open to the community. Accordingly, the department has adopted new management principles and created a decentralized facility called the Experimental Police District (EPD). The EPD serves as the department's testing ground for new ideas and methods, focusing on the implementation of new management strategies, teamwork, problem solving, and other community policing techniques.[16]

The emphasis on the quality of services and the vision of a community that is an active partner in promoting safety and security is in contrast with the

### VISION OF THE MADISON POLICE DEPARTMENT

We are a dynamic organization devoted to improvement, excellence, maintaining customer satisfaction, and operating on the Principles of Quality Leadership.

### MISSION STATEMENT

We believe in the DIGNITY and WORTH of ALL PEOPLE.

We are committed to:
- PROVIDING HIGH-QUALITY, COMMUNITY-ORIENTED POLICE SERVICES WITH SENSITIVITY;
- PROTECTING CONSTITUTIONAL RIGHTS;
- PROBLEM SOLVING;
- TEAMWORK;
- OPENNESS;
- CONTINUOUS IMPROVEMENT;
- PLANNING FOR THE FUTURE;
- PROVIDING LEADERSHIP TO THE POLICE PROFESSION.

We are proud of the DIVERSITY of our work force which permits us to GROW and which RESPECTS each of us as individuals, and we strive for a HEALTHFUL workplace.

### PRINCIPLES OF QUALITY LEADERSHIP

1. IMPROVE SYSTEMS and examine processes before blaming people.
2. Have a CUSTOMER orientation and focus toward employees and citizens.
3. Believe that the best way to improve the quality of work or service is to ASK and LISTEN to employees who are doing the work.
4. Be committed to the PROBLEM-SOLVING process; use it and let DATA, not emotions, drive decisions.
5. Be a FACILITATOR and COACH. Develop an OPEN atmosphere that encourages providing and accepting FEEDBACK.
6. Encourage CREATIVITY through RISK-TAKING and be tolerant of honest MISTAKES.
7. Avoid "top-down," POWER-ORIENTED decision-making whenever possible.
8. Manage on the BEHAVIOR of 95% of employees and not on the 5% who cause problems. Deal with the 5% PROMPTLY and FAIRLY.
9. Believe in, foster and support TEAMWORK.
10. With teamwork, develop with employees agreed-upon GOALS and a PLAN to achieve them.
11. Seek employees INPUT before you make key decisions.
12. Strive to develop mutual RESPECT and TRUST among employees.

**FIGURE 2-4.** Mission statement and leadership principles. (Courtesy of the Madison, Wisconsin, Police Department, 1995.)

traditional concept of policing. (Again, refer to Figure 2-4). In the Madison Police Department, considerable emphasis has been given to improving the quality of management and leadership within the agency so as to highlight organizational values and the importance of individual officers (see Chapter 6 on leadership).

These principles are consistent with modern "open-systems" thinkers (see Chapter 4, Organizational Theory) who argue that improving the quality of work life for employees within large, bureaucratic agencies will subsequently improve overall organizational effectiveness.[17] To achieve this end, the department established itself as a quality-driven, community-oriented service and developed the centralized position of quality coordinator to monitor a quality improvement process. This arrangement required continued input from members within the EPD as well as the development of an extensive internal survey. Customer surveys became an integral part of the quality improvement process, asking citizens to rate the individual officer responding to a call for service in seven areas: (1) concern, (2) helpfulness, (3) knowledge, (4) quality of service, (5) solving the problem, (6) putting the caller at ease, and (7) professional conduct. The questionnaire also asked citizens for recommendations on ways to improve.[18] These surveys have continued since late 1988, providing a substantial data bank on which to evaluate the aggregate performance of officers in the EPD. In addition, the Police Foundation and the

**FIGURE 2-5.** Within the EPD, officers focus on problem solving in traditionally high crime areas such as this public housing facility. Providing quality policing and an improved image are important parts of the community policing movement. (Courtesy Madison, Wisconsin, Police Department, 1995.)

Madison Comptroller's Office have completed outside evaluations of the EPD project. Several positive findings were revealed from these evaluation studies:

- Over 60 percent of all employees in the EPD believed that they had been more effective in solving crimes than they were in their previous assignments.
- Over 80 percent of all employees in the EPD reported a higher level of job satisfaction compared with previous assignments.
- Individual officers used considerably less sick time and earned substantially less overtime as compared to patrol officers working outside the EPD.
- The top five reasons that employees chose to work in the EPD were
    1. A more supportive management style
    2. Less rigid structure
    3. Greater input in decision making
    4. More autonomy
    5. A team atmosphere
- Overall crime dropped 1.1 percent and violent crime decreased 9.2 percent within the EPD while increasing 4.2 percent in other areas of the city.
- Residential burglaries decreased 24 percent in the EPD since 1986, while the rest of Madison suffered a 4.2 percent increase.
- EPD patrol speeding enforcement dropped 16.6 percent in one year, possibly indicating more community adherence to traffic laws.
- Finally and most importantly, citizen surveys indicated a vastly improved police image (noting improved satisfaction and concern with the police) within the EPD community as compared to the rest of the city.[19]

Community policing efforts in Madison are still evolving as successful organizational and community change takes place. The department is planning to establish four additional experimental police districts within the city in an attempt to bring the entire department gradually into the community policing philosophy. Successful implementation requires a strong vision of the quality of police service and the development of excellence in individual police leadership.[20] For the Madison Police Department, the resulting move to community policing has provided a vastly improved workplace, where employee growth, empowerment, and feelings of self-worth are encouraged and community support is subsequently fostered.

**Chicago, Illinois**   In January 1993, Mayor Richard Daley and then-Police Superintendent Matt L. Rodriguez announced the first major operational changes to set in place community policing in the City of Chicago. The new program, the Chicago Alternative Policing Strategy (CAPS), was designed to move the department from a traditional, reactive, incident-driven agency to a more proactive and community-oriented department. At first, CAPS was hailed as a method to combat crime, drugs, and gang activity in the inner city. However, as the implementation plan unfolded, a much broader mission statement evolved which focused on a combined effort with the community to "identify and solve problems of crime and disorder and to improve the quality of life in all of Chicago's neighborhoods."[21]

As in many large cities implementing community policing in the last five years, Chicago developed five prototype districts to serve as "laboratories" for testing new police ideas, innovations, and strategies. See Figure 2-6.

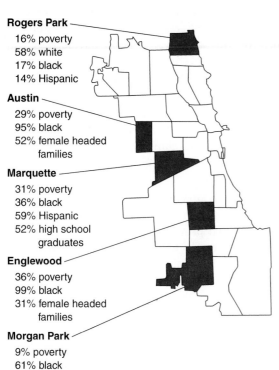

**Rogers Park**
16% poverty
58% white
17% black
14% Hispanic

**Austin**
29% poverty
95% black
52% female headed
    families

**Marquette**
31% poverty
36% black
59% Hispanic
52% high school
    graduates

**Englewood**
36% poverty
99% black
31% female headed
    families

**Morgan Park**
9% poverty
61% black
80% homeowners
62% long-term residents

**FIGURE 2-6.** Chicago's Five Experimental Districts (*Source:* Susan M. Harnett and Wesley G. Skogan, "Community Policing: Chicago's Experience," *NIJ Journal,* April 1999, p. 3.)

These districts could then refine the successful new programs and hence improve the CAPS model. Essentially, the new CAPS program echoed the methodology for implementing community policing in several other large metropolitan cities. For instance, in Houston, Texas, and New York City, under the direction of then-Commissioner Lee P. Brown, the transition to community policing occurred only in select neighborhoods or districts. Similar programs evolved in Phoenix, Arizona; Miami, Florida; Philadelphia, Pennsylvania; and Newark, New Jersey. Only a few cities have attempted to implement community policing strategies on a department-wide basis (Portland, Oregon, and Baltimore, Maryland). Most cities, and particularly large metropolitan communities, have realized that the implementation of community policing demands dramatic modification in the existing philosophy, structure, operation, and deployment of police.[22] The gradual evolution toward full-scale adoption essentially continues to redefine both the means and ends of community policing.[23]

CAPS has a number of key features aimed at improving and expanding the overall quality of police services in the City of Chicago as well as reducing crime.[24] These key features are:

**Crime control and prevention:** CAPS emphasizes both crime control and crime prevention. Vigorous and impartial enforcement of the law, rapid response to serious crimes and life-threatening emergencies, and proactive problem solving with the community are the foundations of the city's policing strategy.

**Neighborhood orientation:** CAPS gives special attention to the residents and problems of specific neighborhoods, which demands that officers know their beats (i.e., crime trends, hot spots, and community organizations and resources) and develop partnerships with the community to solve problems. Beat officers work the same beat on the same watch every day so they can more intimately know the beat's residents, its chronic crime problems, and the best strategies for solving those problems.

**Increased geographic responsibility:** CAPS involves organizing police services so that officers are responsible for crime control in a specific area or beat. A new district organizational structure using rapid-response cars to handle emergency calls allows newly created beat teams to engage in community policing activities. The beat teams share responsibility for specific areas under the leadership of a supervisory beat sergeant.

**Structured response to calls for police service:** A system of differential responses to citizen calls frees beat team officers from the continuous demands of 911 calls. Emergency calls are handled primarily by rapid-response sector cars, whereas nonemergency and routine calls are handled by beat officers or by telephone callback contacts. Sector officers also attend to community matters, and sector and beat teams rotate so that all officers participate in community policing.

**Proactive, problem-solving approach:** CAPS focuses on the causes of neighborhood problems rather than on discrete incidents of crime or disturbances. Attention is given to the long-term prevention of these problems and to the signs of community disorder and decay that are associated with crime (e.g., drug houses, loitering youths, and graffiti).

**Combined community and city resources for crime prevention and control:** CAPS assumes that police alone cannot solve the crime problem and that they depend on the community and other city agencies to achieve success. Hence, part of the beat officer's new role is to broker community resources and to draw on other city agencies to identify and respond to local problems. Mayor Daley has made CAPS a priority of all city agencies. Hence, the mayor's office ensures that municipal agencies are responsive to requests for assistance from beat officers.

**Emphasis on crime and problem analysis:** CAPS requires more efficient data collection and analysis to identify crime patterns and to target areas that demand police attention. Emphasis is placed on crime analysis at the district level, and beat information is recorded and shared among officers and across watches or shifts. To accomplish such a task, each district has implemented a local area network of advanced computer workstations employing a crime analysis system called ICAM (Information Collection for Automated Mapping). This new technology allows beat officers and other police personnel to analyze and map crime hot spots, to track other neighborhood problems, and to share this information with the community.

**Training:** The Chicago Police Department has made a significant commitment to training police personnel and the community in the CAPS philosophy and program. Intensive training on problem solving and community partnerships is being provided to district patrol officers and their supervisors. Innovative classroom instruction for the community and a program of joint police-community training have also been developed.

**Communication and marketing:** The Chicago Police Department is dedicated to communicating the CAPS philosophy to all members of the department and the community. This is a fundamental strategy of the CAPS program.

To ensure such communication, an intensive marketing program has been adopted, which includes a newsletter, roll call training, a regular cable TV program, information exchanges via computer technology (Internet and fax machines), and various brochures and videos. Feedback is collected through personal interviews, focus groups, community surveys, a CAPS hotline, and several suggestion boxes. The information collected through this marketing program assists in the refinement and development of the CAPS program.

**Evaluation, strategic planning, and organizational change:** The CAPS program is undergoing one of the most thorough evaluations of any community policing initiative in the United States. A consortium of four major Chicago-area universities (Northwestern, DePaul, Loyola, and the University of Illinois at Chicago) is conducting a three-year evaluation of the process and results in the prototype districts. In addition, the Chicago Police Department is conducting a variety of internal evaluations focusing on officer attitudes, morale, community perception, and the like. The information collected through systematic evaluation will be used to develop a broad strategic planning effort that includes representation from the community. The organizational changes that will be needed to fully implement the CAPS program will hopefully be identified, and specific action plans to carry out the implementation of community policing on a citywide basis will be developed.

CAPS represents one of the largest and most comprehensive community policing initiatives in the country. Refer to Figure 2-7. During its first year of operation, preliminary evaluation findings indicated that major crime and neighborhood problems were reduced, drug and gang problems were reduced, and public perception of the quality of police services were improved. Under this orientation, the community is viewed as a valuable resource from which powerful information and ties can be gathered. It aims "to increase the interaction and cooperation between local police and the people and neighborhoods they serve" to combat crime.[25] Hence, the major goals of community policing are not only to reduce crime but, more significantly, to increase feeling of safety among residents.[26] These two goals appear to be separate and distinct, but are actually very closely linked in the community policing process. This approach attempts to increase the visibility and accessibility of police to the community. Through this process, police officers are no longer patrol officers enforcing the laws of the state, but rather neighborhood officers. These officers infiltrate into local neighborhoods targeting specific areas in need of improvement. By involving themselves within the community the officers are more available to meet and discuss specific problems and concerns of each individual neighborhood and work to develop long-term solutions.[27] These solutions are the root of the proactive approach to policing. By listening to the public, the police will be better informed of the specific problems in each area. As cooperation between police and citizens in solving neighborhood problems increases, residents feel more secure.[28]

The major case studies presented (Newport News, Virginia; Madison, Wisconsin; and Chicago, Illinois) represent only three attempts to develop community policing initiatives in the United States. Peak and Glensor have identified a number of innovative approaches in selected American cities in their book devoted to community policing and problem solving.[29] These cities represent virtually every part of the United States and almost every type of local police agency: Austin, Texas; Hillsborough County, Florida; St. Louis, Missouri; Sacramento and San Diego, California; Reno, Nevada; Lumberton,

Chicago's community policing effort is more extensive and more organized than programs in most other jurisdictions, and it permeates the city to a greater extent than in most others. Below is an "at a glance" description of a typical, more limited program compared to Chicago's program.

### Chicago's Community Policing Model

*Police*

- The entire patrol division is involved.
- The program is fully staffed with permanent officers on regular shifts.
- Extensive training is given to both officers and supervisors.
- All districts and all shifts are involved.
- Program activities are supervised through the regular chain of command and through standard patrol operations.

*Residents*

- Residents are expected to take an active role in solving problems.
- Residents are encouraged to meet with police regularly to exchange information and report on actions taken.
- Public priorities play an important role in setting beat team priorities.
- Residents receive training in Chicago's problem-solving model.

*Municipal Services*

- Management systems are in place to trigger a rapid response to service requests.
- Agencies are held accountable by the mayor for the effectiveness of their response.
- Community policing is the entire city's program, not the police department's program.

### More Limited Community Policing Model

*Police*

- Small units are staffed by officers who have volunteered for a community policing assignment.
- Officers work overtime and are usually paid with temporary federal funding.
- Officers work on evening shift only.
- Little training is provided; officers' personal motivation propels the program.
- Officers are assigned only to selected areas.
- Program activities are supervised by the chief's office or from outside the routine command structure.

*Residents*

- Residents are asked to be the police department's "eyes and ears."
- Surveys or postcards are distributed to residents as a way of gathering information.
- Residents are called to meet occasionally, to publicize the program.
- Residents have no role in setting police priorities or operations.

*Municipal Services*

- Service agencies have no special responsibility to police or citizen groups.
- Service agencies believe community policing is the police department's program and should be funded by the police department's budget.

**FIGURE 2-7.** Chicago Community Policing At a Glance (*Source:* Susan M. Harnett and Wesley G. Skogan, "Community Policing: Chicago's Experience," *NIJ Journal,* April 1999, p. 8.)

**FIGURE 2-8.** Chicago police officer explains the "Officer Friendly" program to schoolchildren and their parents. (Courtesy Chicago, Illinois, Police Department, 1999.)

**FIGURE 2-9.** A major part of community policing emphasizes strengthening the relationship between the police and the community. Here, the Lumberton, North Carolina, Police Department's Great Dare Band performs a concert for a neighborhood youth rally. (Courtesy Chief Harry P. Dolan, Lumberton Police Department, 1999; photo by E. H. "Chip" Davis, Jr.)

North Carolina; Spokane, Washington; Abington, Virginia; Gresham, Oregon; and Brooklyn, New York. Certainly, these cities are not an exhaustive list of the communities implementing new police strategies.

**Community Policing and the Crime Bill of 1994**

In September 1994, Congress passed the Violent Crime Control and Law Enforcement Act of 1994, more commonly referred to as the crime bill. The act represented one of the most sweeping crime legislation bills in history, providing over $29 billion in additional funds to assist criminal justice agencies. While the bill earmarked $3 billion for new regional prisons and another $3 billion for boot camps for young adults, the key provision of the bill was the funding of additional police officers under the COPS (Community-Oriented Policing Services) program. Specifically, the bill provided a total of $8.9 billion for the allocation of 100,000 new local police officers over a five-year period (1995–2000).[30] As the name suggests, the COPS program requires local police agencies to clearly increase and support community policing efforts. In a direct manner, the crime bill reinforces the principles of community policing as a strategy to combat crime and improve the quality of life in the nation's cities.[31] In addition to adding new officers to the streets, the bill provides new avenues for agencies to purchase equipment, technology, and/or support systems. Again, these procurements must be aimed at increasing the level of community policing in an agency.

## COMMUNITY POLICING AND NEW INFORMATION TECHNOLOGIES

The evolution of community policing as a new methodology or strategy has included the development of sophisticated information technologies. Previous to the community policing movement, information technologies were best left to highly skilled technicians, separated from the day-to-day operations of the police. For the most part, information technologies were relegated to the collection and maintenance of vast amount of data. However, this role has changed as the tenets of community policing emerged and the need to analyze crime data became a priority. As Sparrow writes:

> Now, information systems are the essential circuitry of modern [police] organizations, often determining how problems are defined and how progress is evaluated. They frequently help determine how work gets done, often who does it, and sometimes what the work is.[32]

Information technologies have assumed a new and more vital role, due not only to the development of community policing, but also to the passage of the 1994 Crime Bill, which often provided the financial assistance and support for such technologies at the local level. These new technologies—crime analysis, geographic information systems, artificial intelligence and expert systems, and Internet communication—are now central to the support of community policing.

**Crime Analysis**

The statistical analysis of data and the organization of information into manageable summaries provide law enforcement with meaningful tools with which to combat crime. The crime problem has continued to grow in terms of quantity, sophistication, and complexity, thereby forcing police officers and investigators to seek additional help in enforcement techniques. The purpose of crime analysis is to organize massive quantities of raw information from databases used in automated records systems, and to forecast specific future events from the statistical manipulation of these data. In theory, crime analysis provides a thorough and systematic analysis of data on which to make rational decisions regarding past, present, and future actions(see Box 2-3).[33]

## BOX 2-3

### Analyzing This

### A police department in Kansas is mixing crime-analysis skills with common sense

*This story was developed as part of the U.S. Department of Justice's Technology Acquisition Project. The Institute for Law and Justice is leading the project in partnership with* **Government Technology.**

**by Raymond Dussault**
*Justice & Technology Editor*

Of all the new technologies being applied in the justice arena, perhaps only crime analysis and mapping draws from and reaches into so many areas of municipal government. Surprisingly, such a system, which provides many rewards to all parts of municipal government, is relatively easy and inexpensive to build.

When a police department decides to set up a crime-analysis unit, their base maps are drawn from planning and utilities departments. Inevitably, the data gathered cycles back to city council chambers and the mayor's office.

One example is Overland Park, Kan., a rapidly growing suburb of Kansas City, Mo. The city's crime-analysis unit, only about 6 years old, has been key to cracking jewelry-theft cases several hundred miles away and explaining the impact of new business projects within the city.

The foundation was laid in 1993, when Chief John Douglas, then the department's deputy police chief, became convinced that a major overhaul was needed in the way the department approached crime and community issues.

The city was under pressure, with a large influx of new residents fleeing Kansas City and a burgeoning workday population drawn by new job opportunities in the upscale community. The city now boasts a resident population of 138,000—with a daytime population of over 200,000—and is home to many large businesses, including Sprint's new international headquarters.

To meet the challenges of growth with a department consisting of 200 sworn officers and a civilian staff of 75, Douglas set out to build a crime-analysis and mapping unit that would help guide department decisions.

What he didn't realize was that he was taking the first step toward building a unit that would draw law enforcement from all over the country, hoping to pattern their success after Overland's.

**Humble Beginnings**
As a first step, Gerald Tallman was hired to build the unit. He started off with a lot of moral support and little more.

"When it started out, it was just Gerry and a 286. Now this team just keeps making me look better and better," said Captain Glenn Ladd, crime-analysis supervisor. "Either they're putting out great data or there's just so much of it no one can tell."

The team now consists of Tallman, assistant crime analysts Susan Wernicke and Jamie May, and five committed civilian volunteers. Tallman's old 286 is nowhere to be seen.

The team now runs maps, bulletins and statistical reports using seven 450 MHz Pentium III PCs. Those reports are accessible in-house, and crime bulletins are faxed regularly to federal, state and local law enforcement agencies in Kansas and Missouri.

Much of the team's work is produced with off-the-shelf software like Microsoft Excel, Word, Outlook, Power Point and FoxPro—helping to keep costs down—while their raw data is drawn from the department's server. But it's not hard for Tallman to look back.

"I was given a broad mission statement and a free reign; not much else," he said. "For the first six months, I don't even remember having a computer. I just researched and networked. I called cities all over the country to talk about what they were doing.

"Then I went to Colorado Springs, and spent three days with their unit. Next, it was a vendor fair—I had them flying in from all over to pitch their wares, but nothing I saw did everything we wanted. Finally, after looking at FoxPro, Lotus and Access, I settled on FoxPro as our software base."

*(continued)*

BOX 2-3  (continued)

Helping to cement the decision was the fact that the crime-analysis program that Tallman found—from the Institute for Police Technology and Management (IPTM)—was written in FoxPro. Still, even IPTM's program was not as user-friendly or versatile as needed.

Tallman negotiated to purchase the source code from IPTM, a $2,000 investment, and then hired a local consultant to revamp the program. That cost about another $5,000. But, in the end, the department's crime-analysis unit had a user-friendly program they named Target Crime Analysis.

## Busy Department

The Crime-Analysis Unit of the Overland Park Police Department is usually very busy. Some of its regular products include:

- Target Crime Analysis: This FoxPro-based program is used to maintain target crime databases and perform computer-aided analysis. It is networked via a LAN to the investigations division to track assigned caseloads.
- Daily Patrol Maps: Available on all department computers for patrol officers to view and perform simple queries. Data limited to most recent 48 hours.
- Weekly Persons and Property-Crime Maps: Provide crime type and location data for up to the last 90 days. The Persons map, which contains sex-crimes data, is for in-house use only, while the property crime map is posted in public areas.
- Persons and Property-Crime Bulletins: Word documents produced weekly which detail the last seven days' worth of persons and property crimes. Distributed in-house via e-mail and by fax to other law enforcement agencies in two states.
- Weekly Arrest Report: A Word document that contains pertinent information on arrested individuals and recently issued warrants. Distributed in-house via e-mail and by fax to other law enforcement agencies in two states.
- Crime Prevention Reports: Produced for neighborhood groups, homeowners' associations and individuals.
- Monthly Mall Report: Produced by the 10th of each month for investigations and patrol divisions.

### Reversal of Fortunes
In the five-and-a-half years since Tallman was searching the country for technology and application ideas, the tables have turned. In addition to local publicity, the department's use of crime mapping was included in a recently published book and highlighted at a national crime-mapping conference.

From this and word of mouth, the unit now receives calls and visits from departments as far away as Jamaica. The information and opportunities the crime-analysis unit provides are now being accessed by detectives, who went through a one-hour training class to learn how to utilize the software to create their own maps and reports.

Patrol officers can access, on a view-only basis, all crimes committed in their area during the 48 hours prior to their shift. In addition, the crime-analysis unit has provided information to the chief, City Council and community members to support informed decision making.

Officers and civilians at all levels of the department enthusiastically endorse the crime-analysis unit and the information it produces. Regular crime bulletins help information sharing across the department's two police districts, and at least one sergeant said he likes to turn to the unit when he thinks he sees a crime pattern developing. In several situations, the ability to spot a pattern has paid dividends.

When the unit noticed a string of construction-site burglaries involving another problem associated with the city's high growth rate—the unit's information led to erecting roadblocks on major thoroughfares. In addition to apprehending the thieves and recovering the stolen property, the roadblocks also led to tickets issued for safety and motor-vehicle violations.

In another situation, the unit picked up on a scam an elderly, well-dressed gentleman was running on shopping-mall jewelry stores. He would come in, ask to see several high-dollar items and then, when the clerk was distracted, take off with everything he could grab.

The unit issued a bulletin through its network, a copy of which ended up in Columbia, Mo., a two-and-a-half hour drive away. Columbia police officers saw the bulletin and caught the elderly suspect, who had decided to run his scam a little farther from home.

### Civil Benefits
Perhaps as telling as the numerous criminal trends the unit has helped stop is the role the unit has played in delivering information to the community. When an entertainment complex—including a bowling alley, night club and family restaurant—was proposed, neighborhood activists protested, believing the establishment would inevitably lead to crime.

The City Council turned to the unit for data. After some research, the unit presented information showing that the planned use of the land, based on other examples in the community, created fewer crime problems than almost any other use possible. In another instance, the unit's analysis led to increased support from the police chief.

"We had a group of people going to City Council meetings complaining that the department was not writing enough tickets to slow down speeders and stop-sign runners in their neighborhood. They felt that outsiders were using their community as a race track," explained Tallman. "The department stepped up patrols in the area and plotted the tickets for several weeks—locations, speed, who the speeders were—and at the next council meeting the chief was able to throw up this flip chart and say, 'Talk to your neighbors. They're the one's that we catch speeding there.' "

As with technology in police departments nationwide, the system is not always used to its full potential. Some officers still complain that the system is too complex. A few keep a tight grip on their pencil and paper, eschewing all things technological. Most, though, either utilize the system themselves or at least lean on the unit to provide needed data.

"This is about officer safety and serving the community, and we are doing that," said assistant analyst Wernicke. "Other agencies, we've noticed, won't even have their own data handy, but they use ours—and Kansas City patterned their unit after what we are doing. It's a good feeling."

*Source:* Raymond Dussault, "Analyzing This," *Government Technology,* October 1999, pp. 42–44.

Crime analysis is not limited solely to reported crime information. Attention has also been given to the statistical analysis of intelligence information. Kinney[34] reports that criminal intelligence analysis can support investigators, decision makers, and policy makers in their attempts to prevent and control crime.

Some of the more common crime analysis techniques are

- *Crime-specific analysis*—A tabular or graphic display of reported crimes within a given pattern of time and/or location. It is often used to detect robberies or burglaries that cluster in specific locations during various time periods.

- *Link analysis*—A graphic portrayal of associations and relationships among people, organizations, events, activities, and locations from a given point in time. This technique is a powerful analytic tool used to reveal the hidden connections among criminals and the structure of clandestine, organized criminal entities often found in street gangs, La Cosa Nostra families, white collar crime syndicates, large drug trafficking cartels, and terrorist organizations. Link analysis is invaluable in complex investigations, particularly those that have a "conspiracy" aspect, as is often found in racketeering and continuing criminal enterprise cases. Box 2-4 displays an automated, PC-based, link analysis system.

- *Telephone toll analysis*—Computerized reports derived from court-ordered long-distance telephone billings of suspects in illegal narcotics trafficking. Reports indicate number and frequency of calls that are displayed in numerical, chronological, and geographical order. Link analysis can be used to show the relationship between billing numbers and the numbers called.[35]

- *Visual investigative analysis (VIA)*—Charting that depicts key events of criminal activity in chronological order. VIA is used to show the degree of involvement of subjects. This method is especially convincing in conspiracy cases and can also be used as a planning tool to focus the resources of an investigative effort.[36] At a conference focusing on terrorism, a graphical VIA was presented on the Oklahoma City bombing incident.[37] Interestingly, the VIA effort displayed a horizontal graph, over 60 feet long, with over 1,200 entries.

- *Case analysis and management system (CAMS)*—Computerized case management in which large amounts of data are compiled and indexed for each retrieval of specific items. This system is used to clarify relationships and to calculate the probability of associations.[38]

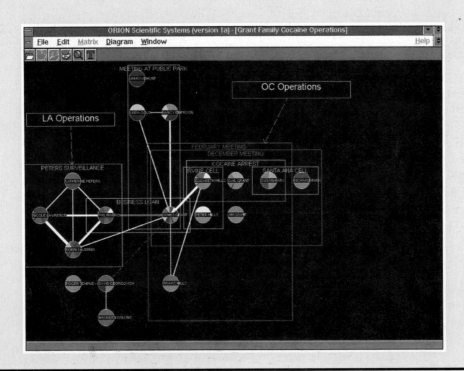

BOX 2-4

## Powerful Computer System Should Help Track Drug Flow

### The $7.5 million computer network will allow drug enforcement officers to share vital information with officers in other states

by Greg Jaffe

A new system of computers linking drug enforcement operations in Alabama, Mississippi and Louisiana opened Thursday on Gunter Park Drive in Montgomery.

The $7.5 million computer network will allow officers, who once depended on telephones and word of mouth when tracking the flow of drugs, to exchange and analyze reams of information instantly.

Previously, city, state and federal agencies had no place to pool information.

The programmers and analysts who staff the new Drug Operations Center will make information on drug trafficking immediately available.

Speakers from the state and federal governments invoked the "war on drugs" when discussing the center and praised the facility as a "state-of-the-art weapon."

"With the help of a sophisticated computer system, officers from these agencies will have a firm grip on the illicit drug operations throughout this area," Gov. Guy Hunt said at a ribbon-cutting ceremony for the facility. "This center combines law enforcement into one highly effective weapon."

Local law enforcement officers also promised that the network will make their collective fight to stem the flow of drugs more effective.

"The system isn't in full operation, but once it is, the results should be immediate," said Capt. Mike Jemison of the Alabama Department of Public Safety, who heads the facility.

The center, which is the core of the new Gulf States Initiative, was built with funds made available by Congress in 1990. The U.S. Department of Defense allocated $7.5 million for Mississippi, Louisiana and Alabama to build the computer network.

Next year, the three states will receive $3 million to keep the facility running. Gulf States Initiative offices in Louisiana and Mississippi will use hardware and software similar to the Alabama computer systems. The programmers will be trained at the Naval Air Station in Meridian, Miss.

*Source:* This Link analysis system used to track drug flow is courtesy of *The Montgomery Advertiser,* Montgomery, Alabama (November 6, 1992), p. 1B; and Orion Scientific Systems, McLean, Virginia.

Although not all of these techniques are fully automated, the basic procedures follow a flowchart configuration that provides a sound basis for software design. Combining these techniques with a statistical package (such as Excel, SPSS/X, ABSTAT, SAS, or STATPRO) produces a strong capability for forecasting and prediction.

**Geographic Information Systems (GIS)**

The last decade has given rise to the integration of automated database operations, crime analysis, and high-level mapping. The merger of these powerful programs is commonly referred to as *geographic information systems* (GIS).[39] Traditionally, map data and tabular data describing pieces of land such as police beats have been stored separately, but computer technology now provides the opportunity to merge the two yet preserve their independent natures. Unfortunately, only a few police departments have implemented GIS technologies on a mainframe, mainly due to expense and the developmental newness of the product. However, several PC-based mapping programs are making significant advances in the crime analysis field (see Box 2-5).

The new technology of desktop mapping allows the display of geographic information (spatial data) on computer monitors—topography, natural resources,

**BOX 2-5**

## GIS: A Successful Strategy for Reducing Crime

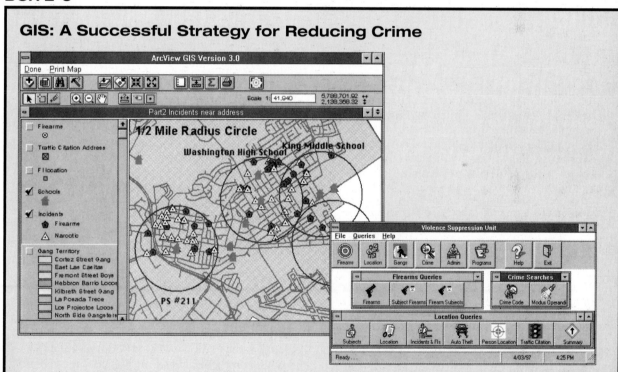

**Law Enforcement Agencies Have a New Partner in Their Fight Against Crime**

For the past several years a rapidly growing number of law enforcement agencies have been teaming up with geographic information system (GIS) professionals from ESRI® to develop better crime analysis techniques. These agencies are receiving a tremen-

dous benefit from GIS technology because it is helping them leverage their investments in personnel, equipment, and other resources.

With GIS, the traditional statistical information used in crime analysis is made available in map

*(continued)*

## BOX 2-5 (continued)

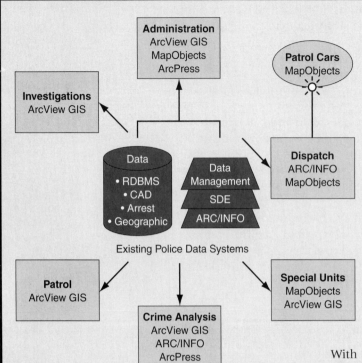

Administration
ArcView GIS
MapObjects
ArcPress

Patrol Cars
MapObjects

Investigations
ArcView GIS

Data
• RDBMS
• CAD
• Arrest
• Geographic

Data
Management
SDE
ARC/INFO

Dispatch
ARC/INFO
MapObjects

Existing Police Data Systems

Patrol
ArcView GIS

Crime Analysis
ArcView GIS
ARC/INFO
ArcPress

Special Units
MapObjects
ArcView GIS

format that shows specific crime patterns and geographical relationships among multiple factors associated with crime events. Drawing upon this integrated perspective, law enforcement agencies can be more effective in their efforts toward crime prevention, intervention, and community-oriented policing.

### Computer Mapping Making a Difference

GIS software from ESRI enables law enforcement and public safety personnel to capture, combine, and create an integrated picture of information in the form of interactive maps and reports on the desktop, laptop, or in the patrol car to

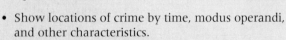
Crime

• Show locations of crime by time, modus operandi, and other characteristics.
• Determine crime "hot spots."
• Relate patterns of crime location with addresses of known offenders.
• Reveal patterns or trends in criminal activity.
• Show gang boundaries.
• Show census data.

Modus Operandi

The information used to create crime analysis GIS is gathered from existing computer systems, such as computer-

aided dispatch (CAD) and records management system (RMS), that store and maintain call-for-service, field interrogation, incident, arrest, and other geographic-related information. By relating these data to a simple street map, the crime-related data can be displayed by location and analyzed using proven crime analysis and geographic analysis tools and techniques.

### Deploy Personnel Where They Are Needed Most

Because GIS software from ESRI helps enhance the speed and quality of crime analysis, time and manpower can be redirected toward developing special enforcement efforts such as youth handgun violence. Additionally, beats can be redefined and improved according to changing demographics, fluctuations in criminal activity, and other dynamic conditions.

Location

With the growing emphasis on a proactive approach to controlling and preventing crime through community-oriented policing, law enforcement agencies are using ESRI GIS solutions to strengthen their efforts. Not only can crime analysts access and analyze information, but officers and commanders as well can easily use the GIS software mapping and reporting tools. Field officers can use the GIS to see calls for service, incidents, and arrests from prior shifts, and commanders can use the results of the GIS analysis to more strategically deploy staff and resources, as well as prepare specific maps and reports for presentations to community groups, elected officials, and others.

### Make Your Community Safer

Communities all over the United States are using GIS to integrate their current crime analysis programs with other information systems. By drawing upon demographic, housing, business, and other data resources, communities are better able to profile their neighborhoods and coordinate social, development, and other programs with crime prevention and police activities to make safer communities.

Incidents

In the City of Redlands, California, ESRI GIS software is being used to assist police officers in their efforts toward community-oriented policing. This technology is helping to enable the police department to establish flexible policies in areas such as determining beat boundaries and assigning officers to communities where they can be most effective.

President Clinton recognized the City of Salinas, California, for its efforts to reduce crime, specifically youth handgun violence, through federally funded programs. The crime analysis applications used by the City were developed from ESRI GIS software. The applications form the basis of a more comprehensive GIS that includes connectivity to additional data sources internal and external to the police department. Most importantly, with the implementation of its GIS, the City of Salinas has seen a reduction in crime committed by youths, and homicides have dropped; there were fewer than ten homicides in the City of Salinas in 1996, compared with twenty-one in 1995.

*Source:* Courtesy of Environmental Systems Research Institute, Inc. (ESRI), developer of ARC/INFO GIS Software, 1997.

transportation hubs, highways, utilities, political boundaries, and police beats. Geographic information systems combine these spatial representations with almost any other type of data an analyst wishes to enter. Textual and tabular data (attribute data) such as population density, crime locations, traffic patterns, demographic profiles, and voting patterns can be displayed and manipulated against map backgrounds. From this type of analysis, it is possible to overlay multiple map sets so that police researchers and executives can pictorially view the interrelationships among several variables. Thus, GIS technologies differ from previous types of crime analysis techniques and/or information systems in that their primary purpose is *not* purely cartographic, with emphasis on display and graphics, but rather the analysis, manipulation, and management of spatial data.

Geographic information system technologies have far-reaching implications not only in police operations as defined by crime analysis, but also as management and communications tools. For instance, by integrating the mapping of GIS with the navigational properties of global positioning systems (GPS), a powerful vehicle tracking system can be developed. Using a PC-based software package, real-time tracking can be accomplished for under $1,000 (see Box 2-6).

## BOX 2-6

### GIS/GPS Applications for Law Enforcement

**by Delrene Hills, Analyst,
Calgary Police Service**

*Source:* From the 1995 convention of the International Association of Crime Analysts in San Pedro, Calif.

#### Geographical Information Systems

GIS (geographical information systems) are computerized database systems which combine map images with other spatially referenced information. They are composed of two (2) types of data files (the maps and some descriptive data) and also some type of CAD software to display this information in a graphical format. For years in law enforcement, the analysis of spatial information has provided valuable clues to assist with the location and apprehension of perpetrators of various types of crime. Pin maps have traditionally been used and have been around almost as long as police departments. With the advent of computers, these maps have become much easier to create and manipulate, thus providing more valuable information. Additionally, the ability to generate maps quickly and easily by computer has increased the number of potential applications within law enforcement. Combining GIS systems with GPS (Global Positioning Systems) technology opens up even more possibilities.

There are two basic methods of storage and representation of this geographical information; these are vector and raster images. The raster image is a scanned graphic format file, which means an actual picture of the map is stored, while a vector-based system stores the information as a database of coordinate points along with some attribute information. Some software allows for a combination of these two methods. In order to be useful, the raster imaging must have some database attached to it as well or it would be very difficult to access that portion of the

*(continued)*

BOX 2-6 (continued)

file or files which you chose to view. This would be somewhat analogous to searching through the map book(s) for the street, city, state or country if the books had no associated indices, or grids.

GIS software should allow you to attach additional database information related to the application, such as crime occurrence information, demographic information and likely some boundary information related to manpower deployment. Typically, this additional information is referred to as layers. For some applications, engineering, planning and survey information can also be useful.

Numerous software packages are available on the market to display this information in a format which is both readable and useful, ranging in price from a few hundred dollars to a few hundred thousand, depending on the level of complexity and platforms. The choice of software is related to a number of factors such as requirements of the user, the hardware available and the application that it is intended for. Bear in mind that ease of use and cost of the system are often inversely related. A number of packages operate from DOS or Windows environments, and there are a larger number on the market every day as organizations move away from mainframes to CP networks. The software is also becoming more intuitive and user friendly as more general commercial applications are developed.

It does not matter how powerful your system is, however, nor how sophisticated your software is, if you do not have quality data files, then you will get 'garbage out'. Digital map files are increasingly available from a number of sources, both private and through government agencies. We are very fortunate in that the city of Calgary has devoted considerable time and resources to the creation of very detailed and accurate digital map files, which have been made available for our use. Additional data, such as occurrence information is usually obtainable from within the organization. In our case, a download of information from a mainframe database is required. The available format of the existing database files is another consideration when choosing software as there is generally a significant cost associated with converting these files.

### GIS Applications

There are a number of applications for geographical information systems in law enforcement:

1. Certain crimes have tendencies to show geographical patterns of occurrence. Identification of the patterns can aide with the apprehension of the perpetrators of these crimes. Additionally, spatial analysis is important for manpower deployment.

2. The integration of this occurrence information with demographic information can aide policy makers, as well as assist with Community Policing.

3. Crime prevention programs, such as CPTED (Crime Prevention through Environmental Design), can be targeted more effectively with this geographical information.

4. Court presentation of major crime scenes, such as homicides, can be enhanced through the use of maps.

5. The mapping of pursuit routes can be a useful investigative aide. Just as flow charts link temporal events, maps graphically show a spatial linking of events.

6. Deployment of manpower for major events or incidents can be done much more effectively through the utilization of maps.

7. Searches for suspects/evidence/victims require maps. The ability to see what areas have been physically searched greatly enhances the effectiveness and efficiency of the search. The use of digital maps allows for the plotting of these areas with ease, as well as the ability to transmit this data to other sites through the use of a modem.

8. There are tactical applications for maps with respect to positioning of swat/tactical unit members for the execution of search warrants, as well as various code situations such as snipers. A three-dimensional display of buildings allows for a visual representation of what the armed suspect has on view. Additionally, if the weapon type is known, perimeters can be calculated with a simple arithmetic calculation.

9. Emergency situations which require evacuations can be conducted more efficiently with a detailed map. If the map files have building outlines, and tax role information attached to the street addresses, it becomes possible to have immediate contacts and an idea of how many civilians may be in the area. Again, a visual display of the area enhances the commander's ability to make quality and timely decisions related to this evacuation thus minimizing the risk for injuries as well as legal liability.

### Global Positioning System

Essentially the GPS (Global Positioning System) consists of a constellation of 24 Navstar satellites orbiting the earth, with a maximum of 8 on 'view' at any one point in time. Originally intended for the precise guidance of U.S. military weapons, they are now the foundation of a growing assortment of commercial applications. From these satellites receivers on the

Personal computer-based vehicle tracking integrates the mapping of GIS with the navigational properties of global positioning systems (GPS). (Courtesy Trimble Navigation, Sunnyvale, California, 1997.)

ground can pick up positional data such as latitude, longitude and altitude. At least 4 satellites need to be visible to calculate a three-dimensional position. As well, through the Doppler Shift, velocity can be calculated. When it is tied in with a GIS system, this position can be displayed over more conventional urban navigational information, such as street addresses. A number of PC-based GIS systems, including MapInfo, now allow for this link.

From a static location positions from GPS receivers are quite precise. In the event that the receiver is not static, it is still possible to obtain centimeter accuracy with the use of a differential correction signal. This requires utilizing a base station and although the set up of a base station is likely beyond the scope of most law enforcement agencies, commercial firms are starting to supply this service for relatively modest annual fees. It can often be accessed utilizing a page frequency and hence, not even tie up any radio frequencies.

### GPS Applications

This inclusion of a GPS system with a GIS system allows for a number of other applications in law enforcement, as real-time positioning can now be added to the map.

1. Covert surveillance is possible with the placement of a GPS receiver and modem in the target vehicle. This reduces the amount of manpower required for the surveillance. Additionally, the ability exists to continue to track the suspect even if they leave the jurisdiction as the signals can be transmitted back with the use of a cellular phone and/or radio modem.

2. Systems which include a GPS component are increasingly being used for dispatch purposes in law enforcement, as well as other emergency services. When a call for service is received, the dispatcher knows instantly where it came from as well as the location of the nearest unit(s) available for response. The responding unit can also have a map and route to the call displayed in the vehicle. This means that response times are reduced, and officer safety is enhanced. These systems are also referred to as AVLN (Automatic Vehicle Location and Navigation) Systems.

3. GPS units, because they can give very precise positional data, are increasingly being used as survey instruments for engineering applications. For law enforcement, the survey of traffic fatality and major crime scenes are other applications.

4. GPS receivers linked with a GIS system provide precise positioning and locational tools for airborne

*(continued)*

## BOX 2-6 (continued)

units. These units have some unique problems with identifying their positions and/or a suspect's position due to the fact that they are unable to read any street signs or building identification numbers or names. The view of a map, with their own position indicated on it, allows the flight officer/observer to determine the exact location of the suspect(s) and communicate this to responding ground units.

Although each application for law enforcement is somewhat unique, many have a number of requirements consistent with other applications and often even other industry applications. Therefore, an 'off-the-shelf' GIS package may suffice, and in fact, has some distinct advantages over custom software. There are a number of these available, some with the ability to handle the real-time positioning provided by a GPS receiver. An important criterion when choosing a package is the source and format of the data files which pro-

vide the underlying map base. In addition to this, the ability to handle other database information such as occurrence date, site data, topographical or demographic information may be critical to a particular application, hence, the format of these may influence the software choice. Reformatting files can be difficult, expensive and may adversely affect the results. The accuracy, as well as how current these files are, is also critical to the application's effectiveness. In all cases, the platform chosen is dependent upon the hardware in place (or to be purchased) and this then may limit the software choices. Costs vary, as does functionality, however, buying the most expensive system does not necessarily give you the 'best' system. Systems which are onerous to obtain information from will *not* be effective, or in some cases, even utilized.

*Source:* International Association of Crime Analysts (IACA) *Bulletin,* (March 1996).

Police agencies can use GIS in dispatching police units by providing directions to locations; address histories; and locations of nearby fire and waste hazards, fire hydrants, alarm boxes, high power lines, water lines, and the like. Police managers can use GISs to provide graphic analysis of specific crime patterns, evaluate new policing strategies, and even track individual officer performance by area. Not surprisingly, GISs have emerged as powerful tools helping police executives make better-informed decisions (see Figure 2-10).

**Artificial Intelligence and Expert Systems**

Another type of information system having direct applications in law enforcement is *artificial intelligence* (AI). Most definitions of AI vary to emphasize the interdisciplinary nature of the subject. Artificial intelligence is a science and a technology based on disciplines such as computer science, biology, psychology, linguistics, mathematics, and engineering. The goal of AI is to develop computers that can think, as well as see, hear, walk, talk, and feel.[40] Basically, artificial intelligence can be defined as a shift from mere data processing to an intelligent processing of knowledge. The model for such development is the human body and brain. Artificial intelligence focuses on four major areas of research:

- *Natural language applications*—systems that translate ordinary human commands into language that computer programs can understand and execute; computer programs that read, speak, and understand human languages
- *Robotic applications*—machines that move and relate to objects as humans do; programs that focus on developing visual, tactile, and movement capabilities in machines
- *Computer science applications*—development of more advanced, fifth-generation computers and the replication of physical brain functioning such as that found in the human cell-computer interfacing and neural networks
- *Cognitive science applications*—programs that mimic the decision-making logic of the human brain, such as that found in expert systems, knowledge-based systems, and logic systems.

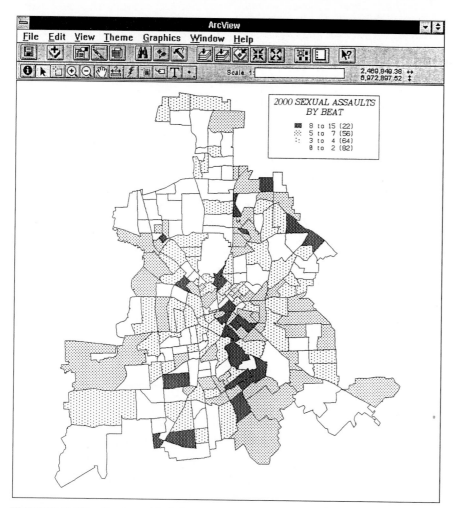

**FIGURE 2-10.** Geographic information systems (GIS) provide a wide array of maps and diagrams useful for crime analysis and decision making. (Courtesy Dallas Police Department, Sgt. Mark Stallo, 2000.)

Figure 2-11 provides a schematic view of the major application domains of AI.

It is this last area of cognitive science applications involving expert systems that police managers find most promising. Basically, expert systems attempt to supplant rather than supplement human efforts in arriving at solutions to complex problems. For instance, the state of Washington used a case analysis expert system to provide suspect profiles in the Green River homicide investigation.[41] The Baltimore, Maryland, Police Department uses an expert system (known as ReBES—Residential Burglary Expert System) to assist in solving burglary cases (see Box 2-7). The system correlates past suspect methods of operation with current burglary events to determine potential trends. About twenty-five specific items of information relating to a burglary are entered into the AI system, which provides a list of possible suspects, ranked in order of probability.[42] The Los Angeles Sheriff's Department uses a comprehensive database called CHIEFS to aid in homicide investigations. Other expert systems are being developed within the FBI's Behavioral Science Unit in Quantico, Virginia, to support investigations of organized crime, narcotics, arson, and terrorism.[43]

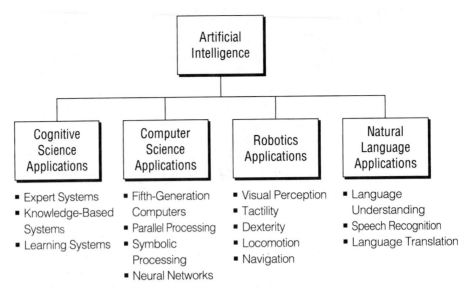

**FIGURE 2-11.** The major application domains of artificial intelligence [*Source:* J. A. O'Brien, *Management Information Systems: A Managerial End User Perspective.* (Homewood, IL: Irwin, 1990), p. 357.]

## BOX 2-7

### Sharing Expertise Through Knowledge-Based Systems

**by Joseph A. Esposito, Jr.***

#### A New Science Is Born

Artificial Intelligence, or AI as it is popularly known, is a relatively young science. In just 35 years, it has captured the interest of psychologists, linguists, and philosophers to form models of the human mind and to develop languages capable of expressing man's thought processes to solve problems by machines.

Ever since the invention of computers, programmers have sought ways to make machines "think" like a human. Therefore, it isn't too surprising that some of the earliest experiments with AI have been in robotics control, language recognition and translation, and complex problem solving through the application of expert knowledge. Of these, expert systems drawing upon expert knowledge have emerged as the most promising applications of AI in the near term.

Expert systems are the product of a special discipline of AI known as "knowledge engineering." The user of the system interacts with the system in a "consultation dialogue" much the same as he would

with a human expert. He explains the problem, performs suggested tests, and then asks questions about proposed solutions. The expert system can be viewed as an intermediary between the human expert whose knowledge is provided to the system during the "knowledge acquisition" phase and the human user who seeks the solution of problems during the "consultation" phase (Barr and Feigenbaum, 1981).

At the heart of expert systems are several new programming languages also called "fifth generation" languages. Three commonly used languages are LISP, PROLOG, and VT-Expert. Unlike earlier "procedural" languages which tell the computer how to solve a problem, the new "rule based languages" allow the computer to solve problems based upon internal rules and relationships. These are compared by the computer to outside data which describes the specific facts of the problem to be solved (Cameron, 1988).

Current research has been focused on the problems in expert system design. The systems are built through the interaction of a domain expert who possesses the expert knowledge to be applied to problems and the system designer (knowledge engineer) who stores the expert's knowledge in a database that is accessed during the consultation phase. Often the human expert has considerable difficulty in articulating his knowledge. Current systems are limited in scope. They lack the sense that humans have in determining when they are wrong. Nonetheless, expert

*Joseph A. Esposito, Jr. is a Criminal Justice Specialist with SCT, 962 Delaware Avenue, Lexington, KY 40505

systems have made inroads into many industries in recent years.

## Expert System Applications

The medical industry has been the forerunner in the race to utilize expert systems. Veratex, a medical and dental supplies company uses a knowledge-based system to assist telemarketers in understanding the technology they sell. The system will point out other products to offer when a customer calls in an order. For example, if a dentist buys X-ray film, then he or she also has to buy film holders (Haber, 1992).

Several rule-based systems have been built which assist physicians in the diagnosis and treatment of diseases. MYCIN, which uses 450 rules and 1000 facts, assigns a confidence factor to the diagnosis of meningitis and then suggests proper treatment according to what organism is suspected as the cause. Similar systems, PUFF and ONCONIN, perform similar analyses in pulmonary and cancer cases, respectively.

Other expert systems are used in private industry to diagnose diesel engine problems (CATS-1), to determine complex chemical structures (DENDRAL), and to predict the presence of ore in a given geographical area (PROSPECTOR). Southwest Ohio Steel in Cincinnati uses a system to help optimize the utilization of the company's inventory.

As with computers in general, expert systems have been slowly finding their way into law enforcement. Most of the work done thus far has been within projects conducted at the state and federal level. The FBI has created the DRUGFIRE system which serves as an intelligent front end to a relational database which contains forensic data and suspect descriptions and modus operandi for drug-related shootings. Their PROFILER system is used to produce lists of offender characteristics in homicides and rapes (Gramckow, 1992).

The Bureau of Justice Assistance funded the Jefferson Institute in development of the Residential Burglary Expert System (ReBES) which applies the experience of veteran burglary detectives to unsolved burglary cases. The Institute also created ROPES, a system which assists state and local agencies in the creation and maintenance of a repeat offender program.

The Alliance, NE Police Department has received national acclaim for its development of an expert system for its 20 officer agency ("When it Comes to Expert Systems," 1991). Their system focuses on their most persistent problem areas—burglary, theft, and vandalism—in a most unique way. Since their officers have access to laptop computers in their patrol cars, they can down-load the expert system into the computer for use at the investigation scene. Use of their system ensures that even a rookie has the benefit of an experienced investigator at his disposal. By virtue of its design, the system enforces a certain degree of consistency in the investigation of similar cases (Clede, 1992).

Except for providing fifth generation languages, the commercial sector has been relatively slow in introducing expert system products. Two notable exceptions—VIAC (Police*Ware, n.d.) and The Analyst's Notebooks (i2 Limited, n.d.)—are visual investigative tools which use link technology to produce a graphic description of a case. By deducing the importance of relationships between persons, places, and events, these products generate a visual time line (resembling a PERT chart) that aids in the comprehension of all the known facts in a case.

The information contained in these systems is extremely sensitive. For obvious reasons, expert knowledge of this nature would be devastating in the wrong hands. Thus the extension of these tools to all law enforcement agencies presents a real paradox (Cameron, 1988).

## How Can I Get Involved in AI?

Even after 35 years, AI—or more specifically, expert systems—are still in their infancy, not unlike crystal radios in the age of broadcasting. For the technically-minded, the Handbook of Artificial Intelligence provides a comprehensive bibliography of research in the field. PC AI Magazine, available at the local computer store, is also a source of information. For formal classes, contact IPTM about their Artificial Intelligence/Expert System training sessions.

Once you have decided to implement an expert system in your agency, you may find the need to network with others who have gone before you. CompuServe conducts an AI users forum which is a ready source of timely and current information. The International Criminal Justice/Law Enforcement Expert Systems Association (IC/LEESA) represents expert system users and innovators worldwide. Founded two years ago at the 1st International Symposium on Expert Systems promoted by the FBI National Academy (FBINA), this organization provides an opportunity for practitioners in the field to communicate and exchange experience and ideas.

We live in an Age of Information. Dr. Roger Depue, head of the Behavioral Sciences Unit at the FBINA, believes that expert systems will become common place in the 1990s in the more progressive agencies. Will yours be one of them?

*(continued)*

## BOX 2-7 (continued)

**References**

Barr, Avron, and Edward A. Feigenbaum (1981) *The Handbook of Artificial Intelligence.* Stanford, CA: HeurisTech Press.

Cameron, Jerry (1988) "Artificial Intelligence: Expert Systems, Microcomputers and Law Enforcement." *Law & Order* 36,3 (March): 61.

Clede, Bill (1992) "Alliance Solvability Factors Program." *Law & Order* 40,3 (March): 11.

Gramckow, Heike (1992) "1991 Meeting of the International Criminal Justice/Law Enforcement Expert Systems Association." *Police Computer Review* 1, 1: 18–19.

Haber, Lynn (1992) "A Little Knowledge." *Midrange Systems* 5,7 (April 7): 38.

i2 Limited (n.d.) "The Analyst's Notebook." Cambridge, England: author.

Police*Ware (n.d.) "Visual Investigative Aid on Computers." Anacortes, WA: author.

Stites, Clyde M. (1989) "Officers Trained in Use of Computerized Artificial Intelligence/Expert Systems." *Law & Order* 37,9 (September): 121.

"When it Comes to Expert Systems, No Agency is Too Small to Lead the Pack" (1991) *Law Enforcement News* 17, 335 (April 30): 1.

*Source: Police Computer Review,* 2:2 (1993), pp. 17–18.

**FIGURE 2-12.** One of the application domains of artificial intelligence (AI) (robotics) produces robots often used in law enforcement for special operations such as bomb disposal. (Photo courtesy of the Denver, Colorado, Police Department.)

AI development is not limited to traditional criminal investigations. For instance, in Chicago, an artificial intelligence program is used to identify traits or behavior patterns shared by officers who have been fired for disciplinary reasons. The program, called Brainmaker, is being used by the department as an automated "early warning system" intended to flag at-risk officers before they commit acts that could get them fired or arrested.[44]

On a more mundane level, expert systems are also being used to assist local police managers with complex planning and task scheduling. However, their greatest benefit may be in changing the way organizations behave by promoting a different perspective on problem solving. In law enforcement, this approach requires creative and innovative police executives who challenge traditional assumptions concerning the police function and mission. Indeed, with the development of expert systems that attempt to combine textbook guesses about a specific problem, executives need no longer rely on their own intuition or inspiration. What may have worked well in the past may appear foolish when contrasted to solutions based on expert systems.[45]

The future of expert systems and other AI applications holds great promise for law enforcement as the price and power of computer hardware improve and the sophistication of software development increases. The trend is clear. Police administrators will be using more AI-based technology as decision support systems in both operations and management.

## Fax Machines, Bulletin Board Systems (BBSs), and the Internet

Clearly, one of the most important technological advantages of the information age is the improvement of communication through the use of varied electronic media such as fax machines and computers. This improvement can be directly linked to the vast improvements in the speed, processing, and access capabilities of the personal computer and various network technologies.

The simplest digital device capable of transmitting electronic information from point to point is the fax machine. When the fax machine was first introduced into policing, it was relegated to special transmissions involving the communication of suspect photographs and fingerprints between and within agencies. Now, the fax machine is used in almost every aspect of police communication, from the standard transmission of police reports between precincts to the wide dispersal of suspect information. The FBI commonly uses fax transmissions of fingerprints for analysis in their lab. Local police agencies fax latent prints found at crime scenes to be compared to the vast inventory of prints held by the FBI in Washington, D.C.

In a recent survey exploring police computer bulletin board systems (BBSs) and other on-line electronic services, several agencies reported extensive use of such systems.[46] For instance, three agencies (Alaska Department of Public Safety; Marin County, California, Sheriff's Office; and the Newport News, Virginia, Police Department) reported frequent use of several different national services. The on-line, computerized bulletin board systems most often used by police agencies are the National Criminal Justice Reference Service (NCJRS) sponsored by the National Institute of Justice, the International Association of Chiefs of Police (IACP) Net, the Search BBS, Partnership Against Violence Network (PAVNET—refer to Box 2-8), the FBI BBS, and the Metapol BBS operated by the Police Executive Research Forum (PERF). Figure 2-13 displays the NCJRS home page, which acts as a gateway to various criminal justice agencies, shared information exchanges, other BBSs, and a host of research articles focusing on various aspects of the criminal justice system. In addition to these specialized BBSs, a number of "generic" on-line services (e.g., Compuserve, Prodigy, and America Online) are also used by police agencies. These services are most commonly used for research on policies, trends, and other issues related to policing. Other applications include information exchange, electronic mail, database access, downloading of software, on-line software support, legal research, file exchange, posting of information, and collaboration/networking with other agencies.

BOX 2-8

## PAVNET: A Model of Internet Use

The Internet can help convey information about how to respond to violence. At the federal, state, and local levels there is no lack of programs that deal with violence, addressing it from several perspectives, among them criminal justice, health, and education. Until recently, however, there was no easy way to find out what these programs are and where they operate. The NIJ-initiated Partnerships Against Violence Network (PAVNET) changed all that by centralizing this information and making it available online.

PAVNET Online, as the resource is called, is a compendium of information about hundreds of programs under way all over the country and includes information about technical assistance and funding. The information has also been published in traditional print format (and on computer diskettes), but Internet availability makes it possible for users to search, view, download, and copy the information whenever they want so that they need not buy and store hard copies or diskettes.

PAVNET represents the combined efforts of several federal agencies, each of which has contributed information from its own clearinghouse. A distributed data base structure is being constructed to enable each agency to upload and manage its own information and to link the agencies' systems. Although data will be entered from many sources, there is a single point of entry for the user, who will continue to perceive PAVNET as a centralized and seamless information resource.

### PAVNET Online "Structures"

Building the PAVNET structures was in large part the work of the U.S. Department of Agriculture's Extension Service, which was equipped with the necessary hardware and software. Information exchange among PAVNET users is being promoted by a listserv (or mail group), "pavnet-mg," and candidate programs for inclusion in the PAVNET data base are being solicited via the Internet.

### PAVNET II

Sound programs to reduce violence need to be linked to sound research. The success of PAVNET—it received a Vice Presidential award for helping to reinvent government—raised the possibility of creating a companion data base of research projects on violence now under way under federal sponsorship. NIJ is working with its partners in PAVNET to develop this resource.

*Source: NIJ Research in Action Bulletin* (March 1996), p. 5.

However, the electronic system used most widely by police to communicate more effectively on a global scale is the Internet.[47] The Internet is a worldwide network of computer systems and other computer networks that offers the opportunity for sending information to and receiving information from a vast audience from around the world. The unique benefits of the Internet are speed and efficiency combined with global reach. There are essentially no barriers to sending information and receiving information from as close as next door to around the world. Of particular importance to police agencies is the ease and speed with which information can be kept current. With the introduction of the World Wide Web, finding information on the Internet is very easy and user friendly. Several features of the Internet make it an ideal network technology for police and other criminal justice system practitioners:

1. The Internet acts as a gateway to a vast and varied array of information resources that may be physically located in distant repositories. Police agencies can access this information as well as establish worldwide communication links with other agencies.
2. The Internet facilitates dialogue among users and groups of users. Police agencies, for example, can "talk" to each other over the Internet, either directly or in dialogue structured and mediated by a third party. The Internet offers the capability of worldwide e-mail exchange.

**FIGURE 2-13.** The National Criminal Justice Reference Service (NCJRS) home page. (*Source:* The Internet, http://www.ncjrs.org., December 10, 1999.)

3. Information can be downloaded (or transferred) directly to a user's personal computer, eliminating printing and distribution costs often associated with hard paper copies.

4. Relatively easy searches of vast amounts of data can be accomplished on a worldwide basis, providing immediate access to important information. For instance, electronic publications and research bulletins focusing on the police and the criminal justice system are now commonplace on the Internet. New research and findings are available on-line from the National Institute of Justice and from prestigious research facilities such as RAND, Harvard University, and the Ford Foundation.[48]

5. The Internet promotes communication and information exchange between criminal justice agencies and practitioners, a problem that has traditionally plagued criminal justice coordination. Users can engage in electronic discussions with one another, one on one or in groups.

Local police agencies have capitalized on the use of the Internet, with many departments establishing their own home pages. Several departments have encouraged their communities to keep abreast of police activities through the Internet. A list of emergency services and phone numbers, names and descriptions of the most "wanted" fugitives in the community, periodic updates on a specific (usually high-profile) case, employment announcements and opportunities within the department, residential and commercial crime alerts, and even on-line crime reporting are now available through various departments on the Internet. Figure 2-14 reflects the home page of the Kansas City, Missouri, Police Department, which offers many of these services.

As worldwide communication and global reach via the Internet expand, policing will likely experience dramatic changes. As more agencies and individuals gain access, wider communication opportunities will exist. The United

**FIGURE 2-14.** Kcpd.org was created by members of the Kansas City, Missouri, Police Department to serve as the home of the K.C.P.D. Web Memorial, which pays tribute to those Kansas City, Missouri, police officers who died in the line of duty. It has since grown to include additional information regarding the police department. (*Source:* http://www.kcpd.org)

Nations recently linked various criminal justice research institutes from different countries, allowing for the first time a free exchange of information among countries on issues impacting the world community (e.g., international terrorism, environmental crime, gangs, and computer fraud). New and combined training sessions, various telecommunication partnerships, and interactive information exchanges will soon become commonplace on the Internet. The Internet could be viewed merely as a "tool of the information age"; however, in the past, some tools have been the catalysts for major changes in society. The greater access to information provided by the Internet is certain to make a major difference in the future, not only for police agencies and researchers, but also for individual communities addressing wider criminal justice issues.

## The Impact of New Technologies

Clearly, information technologies in policing have assumed a new and more vital role. They have taken on a new dimension, one that is central to the support of a new police strategy embraced in the tenets of community policing.

Herman Goldstein, in *Problem-Oriented Policing*, described the wide range of "problems" that should receive police attention.[49] He made it clear that problems may or may not be crime related. He also pointed out that varied dimensions of a problem must be identified by the police—geographic location, time, offender class, victim profile, behavior type, weapon, and other modus operandi elements. The new task for information technologies is analysis, in addition to the storage and maintenance of information. The analytic support for community policing, however, must permeate the entire organizational structure and not be just a function of the crime analysis division. Information technologies functionality must be much more flexible—ranging from support for quick, officer-level field inquiries, to longitudinal mapping of a specific neighborhood, to specific managerial performance measurements. Information technologies can no longer be separated from the integral parts of police management. They can no longer be relegated solely to the storage and maintenance of vast amounts of police data. Community policing is information based and information intensive and requires the ability to identify problems, suggest specific police responses, and

**FIGURE 2-15.** Houston officers patrol neighborhoods focusing on crime control and high-order maintenance activities. (Courtesy of the Houston, Texas, Police Department, 1996.)

evaluate their effectiveness. This function cannot follow the same information processing path as before.

Today's police officers must be equipped with information and training. The job still requires the ability to relate to various people under strained conditions in often hostile environments. Community policing involves new strategies that call for individual judgment and skill in relating to problems that are both criminal and noncriminal in nature. The police officer of the future must be able to relate to diverse groups of people in ways that stretch the imagination. To meet this challenge, police executives must ensure that three conditions exist. First, information technology development and design must support the emerging strategies in policing, particularly meeting the analytic demands embraced in community policing. Second, police officers and executives must manage technology rather than allow themselves to be managed by it. And finally, individual police officers must understand their role in the community as aided by, but not controlled by, the technological marvels of automation.

## PROBLEMS WITH COMMUNITY POLICING

Community policing is a dynamic new movement expressing a bold philosophy. Its goal is to allow police to concentrate on the root causes of crime and to combine efforts with other community resources in addressing crime. Police are viewed as proactive community agents who prevent crime, rather than reactive government forces that only respond to incidents and calls for service. Even considering the early successes, community policing has not been without criticism and conflict. Several academicians and practitioners have attempted to clarify some of the problems associated with community policing efforts.[50] As mentioned earlier, many of these same issues arose during the analysis of team policing efforts during the 1970s. Some fear that the concept of community policing may be expanding too rapidly and that the agencies and officers rushing to "jump on the bandwagon" may not understand or be fully prepared for the significant changes proposed. This, in turn, will lead to partial implementation, notable failures, and permanent damage to an otherwise valuable philosophy.

This discussion explores some of the problems associated with community policing in an effort to encourage caution and avoid the setbacks experienced by earlier innovators in police management. Community policing is a valuable concept, but it is not a panacea for eliminating crime in most communities. The following issues have been identified:

> **Lack of definition**—Despite the popularity (or perhaps because of it), the concept of community policing remains only loosely defined, referring to an array of programs as diverse as Neighborhood Watch, conflict mediation panels, buy-and-bust projects, and liaison programs to gay and other community groups. At best, community policing is a muddled term without exact meaning and precise definition. It appears that any strategy that is new is lumped within the community policing definition, regardless of how much community involvement or partnership it requires. As Strecher points out, community policing simply may be a turn away from one process toward another:

> The substance of community policing is difficult to pin down. When officers assigned in the COP mode are asked what they do, they paw the ground, shrug, and give answers such as "walk and talk," "grin and chin," "chat and charm," "schmooze," and most often, "maybe the brass will let us know." Peter Manning described community-oriented policing as more of an *ethos* than a method or concept, an ethos driven by the academic establishment rather than by developments in policing. Others refer to it as a philosophy of policing. Either term leaves unanswered the question of what community-oriented officers do, how their activities differ from those of traditional patrol officers, and how these activities might be evaluated.[51]

> Indeed, community policing in some departments may be more rhetoric than reality.[52]

> **Lack of "community"**—Ironically, some scholars argue that most cities do not have well-defined communities in which to organize partnerships with the police.[53] Indeed, the word *community* is one of those concepts which in itself is difficult to define. Who is the community? Can we have a single community with a single methodology for policing? Some might argue that if a true sense of community existed within a specific location, then police might not be needed at all.[54] The concept of the "American community" is warm and comforting, but in reality, there is little evidence that such an ideal exists.[55] Most demographic indicators show that the United States is becoming much more, not less, of a mass society. There is increasing cultural pluralism and moral fragmentation.[56] The middle class is diminishing and the underclass is growing, particularly in depressed inner city areas. The police are simply unable to organize communities that have disintegrated. Extremely poor neighborhoods, ghetto areas, and core inner cities are often characterized by

transient populations with few stable institutional ties and little or no identity, other than by vague reputation.[57] In such areas, the police have traditionally conducted high-level, order-maintenance duties. Trying to revive these locales and vastly improve the quality of life inside these areas may be an impossibility, and certainly one outside the scope of the police.

**Role confusion and low morale**—Poor definition and a nontraditional approach require officers and agencies to rethink their basic philosophies of work. To the extent that officers are to become all things to all people (and communities), some degree of role conflict, confusion, and stress (refer to Chapter 9) is inevitable.[58] For example, are police agencies to merge the traditional models of law enforcement, order maintenance, and social work, or are they to focus on entirely different roles such as those found in public housing, transportation, education, and/or refuse collection? This role conflict will become heightened as officers who entered policing with one set of perceptions come face to face with an entirely new array of tasks, duties, and philosophies. Clearly, the resulting ambiguity is almost certain to impact employee morale. In many departments advancing community policing strategies, documented cases of low morale persist.[59]

**Community policing is expensive**—As the trend toward community policing has grown, few cities have looked at the costs of the programs. In Houston, for example, only 20 neighborhoods were selected for the implementation of NOP, and still the cost exceeded $250 million per year![60] Patrol beats were redefined on the basis of neighborhoods rather than on traditional crime-related factors such as calls for services, type and seriousness of calls, geographic boundaries, and the like. The police union, in turn, argued that this redistricting jeopardized officer safety, pointing to an increase in officer assaults.[61] In other cities, the high cost of community policing is also noted. In 1993, the city of Phoenix, Arizona, approved a 0.1 percent tax increase to implement community policing programs, and in Oakland, California, a five-year, $54 million community policing program was initiated in 1995.[62]

Then too, what will happen when federal grants that support community policing cease? Will community policing fade as a new and innovative strategy? Since the passage of the Crime Bill in 1994, over $5.5 billion have been awarded directly to police departments to hire an additional 72,000 officers in about 9,000 agencies dedicated to community policing. An additional $1 billion has been spent on new, specific community policing programs and evaluation projects (e.g., neighborhood restoration, anti-gang initiatives, school programs, police ethics training). High costs in terms of money and people appears to be an indicative feature of community policing, especially if officers are to have a small enough beat to make a difference or if a department is to maintain a high level of response while developing a new strategy for each neighborhood. See Box 2-9.

**Lack of credible evaluation**—Community policing can best be described as a "reform" model for urban policing having vague conceptualization and limited empirical testing.[63] Murphy writes that a combination of methodologically limited research and reform ideals has allowed community policing advocates to effectively discredit the ideology, organization, and strategies of conventional policing.[64] In reality, the empirical evidence that traditional policing methods have failed is at best mixed. Further, what are the measurable advantages of community policing? Kelling[65] argues that traditional quantitative measures such as crime statistics and police response times are

BOX 2-9

## COPS Program Goal Won't Be Met by 2000

### Only 72,000 officers to be hired in time, audit predicts

by Kevin Johnson
USA TODAY

WASHINGTON—Taking aim at the Clinton administration's signature anti-crime program, the Justice Department's inspector general said the promise to put 100,000 additional police officers on the nation's streets by 2000 will be impossible to keep.

Inspector General Michael Bromwich also questioned Monday whether "several thousand" officers already funded under the Community Oriented Policing Services (COPS) program "will ever materialize."

Based on government projections, about 72,000 additional officers—not 100,000—will be deployed by 2000, a COPS program audit estimated.

"COPS officials informed us that their goal is to fund 100,000 new officers by the end of 2000," Bromwich said in the audit of the $8 billion program. "This is significantly different from having 100,000 new officers hired and actually deployed to the streets by the end of 2000, a goal that has been stated publicly by COPS and administration officials."

COPS authorities acknowledged Monday that there has been some "confusion" with the program's goal over the years. But spokesman Dan Pfeiffer said legislation passed in 1994 dictated only that the program would be funded by 2000.

Pfeiffer said the full complement of officers would be on the streets by 2002.

"This report does not portray an accurate picture of the tremendous impact the COPS program is having in communities across the nation," said Mary Lou Leary, the program's acting director.

"The COPS program works. Crime is down; more agencies than ever before are doing community policing; and we are well on our way to meeting the president's goal of adding 100,000 officers to the beat."

Leary said the inspector general had drawn broad conclusions based on previous audits of 149 communities that received grants, virtually all of which had been identified by COPS as problem cases.

"The 149 audits, some of which were conducted two years ago, represent less than 1.2% of the total universe of COPS grantees," Leary said.

COPS officials are challenging many of the findings in the previous audits, which were published in April.

Bromwich said the new audit is not "a verdict" on the concept of community policing or its contribution to reducing crime.

"Rather, this report assesses the management and administration of the COPS program, and the stewardship of billions of taxpayer dollars by the Department of Justice," Bromwich said.

By Khue Bui/AP/
Wide World Photos

**Bromwich:** Goal of 100,000 impossible

inappropriate for evaluating the success or failure of community policing. Others note that the usual means of measuring more subjective goals such as reducing fear and preventing crime may be far too costly and beyond the capabilities of most police organizations. If so, then by what criteria (refer to Chapter 14) will community policing programs be accurately evaluated?

According to Elizabeth Watson, former chief of police in Austin, Texas, virtually no evaluation of the NOP experience in Houston ever occurred.[66] Apparently no baseline data were ever developed previous to the implementation of NOP; no preconditional response patterns were explored; and no continuing data on changing community attitudes concerning fear, perception of crime, or feeling of security were ever collected. Unfortunately, responses from other cities implementing facets of community policing are even less encouraging. See Box 2-10.

**Conflict with accreditation standards**—Two of the most significant programmatic developments in American policing within the last decade have

BOX 2-10

# Does Community Policing Add Up?

## Need seen for ways of gauging effectiveness

by Jacob R. Clark

The term "community policing" has become a catch-phrase for a wide range of philosophies and strategies aimed at bringing the police and the community together in a closer working relationship to reduce crime and make neighborhoods safer.

As with many an evolving discipline, however, there is always the question of how to gauge the success of theoretical outcomes, and that principle appears increasingly to apply to community policing. Despite its rapid and widespread acceptance in recent years, there is still simmering uncertainty as to just how effective community policing strategies are in reducing crime and increasing public safety, and, more important, just how to gauge that effectiveness.

"Nobody is really measuring this in a formal way," said Chief of Personnel Michael Julian of the New York City Police Department, who, prior to his recent promotion, spent one year coordinating the NYPD's nascent community-policing program. "The academic studies talk about what you should measure, but they don't tell you how to measure."

Some work has occurred or is currently under way in several police departments, but police researchers readily admit that further study of community-policing evaluation methods is needed.

"There's not enough research being done," said Wesley G. Skogan, a professor of political science and urban affairs at Northwestern University who is currently involved in a three-year project to evaluate the Chicago Police Department's community policing efforts, which are now under way in five "prototype" neighborhoods. "President Clinton is talking about putting 100,000 more cops out there to do this, and they are doing this without a clue to its effectiveness."

### Old Dilemma, New Paradigm

To Boulder, Colo., Police Chief Thomas Koby, a key player in the development of Houston's pioneering Neighborhood-Oriented Policing program of the early 1980s, the evaluation of community policing programs presents the same dilemmas as any effort to gauge the effectiveness of police work.

"We've never had a way to measure police effectiveness, and community policing is not different policing. Policing is policing. We're talking about trying to approach something differently so we can have more effect than we've had in the past—which assumes that what we've been doing in the past wasn't effective. I'm not sure we know that. I assume it hasn't been, but it's difficult to prove because we've never evaluated policing before," he said.

Mark Moore, a professor of criminal justice policy and management at Harvard University's Kennedy School of Government, said the shift in the "paradigm of policing"—from the professional law enforcement or crime-fighting model to one that incorporates efforts to reduce fear—requires a rethinking of traditional evaluation methods, such as response times and statistics such as crime, arrest and clearance rates.

New measurements will need to consider fear, as well as crime-reduction, Moore contends. "Those things are now unmeasured by the traditional measures that we use," he told LEN. "Until we can find ways of measuring them, the new theory of policing in some sense will remain untested and probably unproduced, because the measurement of these things will produce this new form of policing as well as test it."

It's not a task that is going to occur overnight, Moore added. Police planners and administrators will need to "experiment with the different properties of these different measurements, just as we had to do for a long time on reported crime, response times and clearance rates. We went through a long period of development for those measures, and we'll probably go through a long period of development for these alternative measures as well."

### The Attraction of Numbers

Problem-solving efforts—like turning around criminogenic conditions in neighborhoods—are a big part of community policing, and evaluations need to be devised that can focus on how well these hard-to-quantify efforts are being carried out, said Bonnie Bucqueroux, the associate director of the National Center for Community Policing at Michigan State University's School of Criminal Justice.

Bucqueroux, who with her late colleague, Robert Trojanowicz, co-authored the recent book, "Community Policing: How to Get Started," says that traditional measures such as crime and arrest rates may not give a clear picture of the effectiveness of community-policing efforts.

"All too often, people—particularly politicians—are drawn to countable items because they are easier to run on," she said. "What [police] really need to do are

*(continued)*

# BOX 2-10 (continued)

more qualitative outcomes to find out whether people actually feel safer. The police have always been very good at quantifying activity. A much tougher challenge is to look at outcomes achieved at the street level."

## Talk to the Customers

Bucqueroux and others interviewed by LEN say that citizen surveys can provide a useful means of assessing the outcome of problem-solving and community-policing efforts. Bucqueroux argues that such surveys need to be department-specific and must be developed with community input.

While conferring with other agencies to develop evaluation methods may be useful, Bucqueroux pointed out, there is no "cookie-cutter evaluation process" that can be applied to every agency. "I really resist the idea that there is some sort of universal form out there that you can say, 'Here, just follow this,' " she said. "Police agencies like to do that. But the reality of community policing is that there are differences in the character of different police agencies. It has to be an organic process of development within each agency."

"It won't fly without the community," added John Clark, a professor of sociology at the University of Oregon who is helping the Portland Police Bureau to develop performance measures for community policing in a project funded by the National Institute of Justice. "Wise officers have known this forever, even during the era of strong-arm professionalism."

## Surprise Answers

Citizen surveys offer a variety of outcome measurements for police departments, as outlined by Moore. "We get a better measurement of criminal victimization than we do with reported crime—and potentially, a lot more information about circumstances. We get a very good measure of whether people are afraid or not, and that's the only way we can get that. We can find out whether citizens are satisfied with the quality of service and whether they have a trusting relationship with the police department. We could find out something about the self-defense mechanisms citizens are relying on in their own lives—whether they are relying mostly on the police or whether they're doing something on their own [such as] buying guns or locks or banding into groups."

Officials in community-policing agencies indicate that citizen surveys do indeed provide valuable information about what the public wants from police and how well the police respond to those needs. Some have learned that the perceptions of the two groups can be surprisingly different, as Assistant Chief David

Sinclair of the Lansing, Mich., Police Department confirmed.

"What we found in the beginning was that the things that we thought were very important, which primarily centered around Part I crimes, wasn't necessarily true," Sinclair told LEN. Lansing police officials found from the survey that people were more interested in the quality-of-life issues, such as uncollected trash, barking dogs, broken streetlights and hot-rodding teen-agers, he said. "It turned out that a lot more of those kinds of quality-of-life issues affected the vast majority of the population."

The San Jose, Calif., Police Department, whose community-policing effort turned one year old last month, is another agency that is still wrestling with ways to measure success. An initial survey of 1,600 citizens sought to determine the level of satisfaction felt toward the Police Department and the city in general, said Deputy Chief Tim Skalland, commander of the agency's Bureau of Field Operations.

The Lansing Police Department's experience repeated itself in San Jose, where residents seemed more concerned about quality-of-life issues, such as prostitution and homelessness. "The kinds of things we sort of always low-keyed were the things that were really important to them," said Skalland.

## What Officers Think

Equally important to some researchers is measuring the perceptions of individual officers as to their effectiveness in carrying out assignments and solving problems on their beats. Some agencies use the "management by objective" method, whereby officers and supervisors jointly plot goals to be met over a specific period of time. Afterward, they review accomplishments and shortfalls, and the supervisor gives advice on ways to achieve agreed-upon goals. "That method has proven the most successful for us," said Sinclair.

Sinclair added that the Lansing department's job description for its community police officers also serves as a basis for evaluating performance. Officers are expected to accomplish certain tasks, but are given the flexibility and the latitude they need to get the job done because supervisors know that some can accomplish more in less time than others.

That attitude is reflected in the trend away from the traditional "rigid, controlled" performance evaluations that tend to place officers and supervisors at odds, noted Bucqueroux.

"A lot of performance evaluation is really a hedge against lawsuits for unfair dismissals or disciplinary action," she noted. "Shifting the focus from trying to develop a system that's focused on the small number of bad actors to a system that really tries to encourage people to be as creative as they can requires a lot of rethinking."

## Team Players, Not Subordinates

In this arrangement, sergeants become "facilitators," and officers are treated as professionals and team players, not as subordinates. Citizens evaluate officers, and officers evaluate their supervisors. This was the kind of performance evaluation system that was implemented as part of Houston's Neighborhood-Oriented Policing program. The new system was the subject of a study released last month by the National Institute of Justice, which found that officers evaluated under the new procedures had more positive attitudes toward their NOP assignments and forged closer relationships with the citizens with whom they had contact.

In Houston, officers and sergeants were given a packet containing six forms used to measure performance. They included: the patrol officer's bi-annual assessment report, designed so that sergeants could evaluate officer performance across 22 different criteria reflecting the agency's expectations under NOP; the patrol officer's monthly worksheet, a tool used to guide the officers' on-duty actions; a community information form that was completed by citizens who worked closely with officers on projects; a calls for service/feedback form, which allowed the sergeant to obtain information on that most frequent form of citizen-officer contact; an investigator questionnaire designed to obtain information about the officer's knowledge and performance of preliminary or follow-up investigations; and the immediate supervisor assessment form, which gave the officer a chance to provide information about his sergeant's performance so that trends in their relationship could be identified.

Researchers Mary Ann Wycoff, a project director for the Police Foundation, and Timothy N. Oettmeier, acting director of Houston's Police Training Academy, found that the officers evaluated under the new process "reported having initiated problem-solving activities and having discussed area problems with other department personnel more frequently than did officers in a comparison group who were evaluated with the department's established evaluation process."

## Speaking Out

Surveys, while useful for gauging the strengths and weaknesses of community policing, can also be expensive. Police officials interviewed by LEN pointed to a number of less costly ways to get an idea of community policing's effectiveness, but again, the involvement of citizens in the process plays a crucial role.

In Fort Worth, Texas, the Police Department's Citizen on Patrol program of 1,800 volunteers was credited with contributing to a 24-percent reduction in crime last year. The volunteers, who serve as the "eyes and ears" of the police, are divided into groups who submit monthly reports on what they observe while on patrol, said Lieut. Pat Kneblick, a police spokeswoman.

Although the agency would like to conduct more citizen surveys, regular "community forums" give residents a chance to be heard and afford police brass an opportunity to learn whether programs are working. "Forums give citizens direct access to the upper ranks," Kneblick noted.

Such forums are also used by the Portland Police Bureau, and provide an impetus for citizens to give police input on dealing with community problems. "It's not easy to encourage cooperative problem-solving," noted Clark, the University of Oregon sociologist. "The public is not well-informed and most have more compelling things to do. We must put more effort into the sensible involvement of the public."

Some departments prepare "before-and-after" videotapes of neighborhoods to show the physical changes that occur after a community-policing effort is implemented. The Madison, Wis., Police Department routinely sends postcard surveys to citizens who have had contact with police in an effort to measure client satisfaction and get ideas on how to improve service.

## Less Obvious Indicators

Some agencies look at other, perhaps less obvious, indicators of effectiveness. "I know of one community that was going to look at whether library usage has gone up to find out if people feel safe enough to go out on the streets and take books out of the library," said Bucqueroux. "They wanted to look at some of the convenience stores and see whether they had more customers—particularly females—in the evening than before to get a handle on whether women felt safer on the street at night."

One of the first neighborhoods targeted by the San Jose PD's community policing effort was the Poco-McCreary section, which Skalland called "the worst neighborhood in the city." The deputy chief said an important indicator of the effort's effectiveness came last Halloween, when local children were able to trick-or-treat in the neighborhood for the first time in 25 years.

*(continued)*

## BOX 2-10 (continued)

"We didn't have to lock them in a school building and provide armed guards around the school so the kids could have some kind of Halloween function," he said. "They were actually able to go door-to-door. I'm not very scientific at this, but when kids can go out and trick-or-treat, I think that's a success."

Stephen Mastrofski, an associate professor of justice administration at Penn State University and a visiting fellow of the National Institute of Justice, suggests that an alternative evaluation measure lies in the level of citizen complaints filed against police officers for rudeness. Mastrofski, who conducted an NIJ-funded research project in Richmond, Va., to find out "what community policing looks like at the street level," said that complaints for rudeness make up the bulk of citizen complaints against officers.

"There's some considerable hope that community policing programs could increase the civility of the police toward the public, and, reciprocally, the public toward the police," he said. "That's not an easy thing to measure—that's one of the things we're working on—but when you have that, officers begin to pay attention to it."

### Getting Ambitious

Police agencies that have the money may want to turn to an outside consultant to gauge their programs, Skogan suggested, because they are generally more objective and are unfettered by the political agendas of community organizations and municipal officials.

"Program evaluation is harder and more expensive," he said. "There, you're talking about whether outcomes are different than if the agency decided not to proceed [with community policing] or whether the outcomes are different if they had tried something else—the expensive, high-tech end of evaluation. There, you really need consultants. They're expensive and probably not everybody should use them. But everybody should consume it, study it and learn from it when it's done."

In New York, police planners are developing an ambitious, high-tech system for evaluating community policing, partly in response to critics who say it is ineffective and lacks means to ensure accountability. Chief Julian said the change will include setting "objective criteria" and standard definitions for gauging police response to citizen-identified problems, and will shift the responsibility for assessment from the precinct commander to residents.

Previously, precinct commanders submitted quarterly, narrative reports on "priority conditions" in precincts—accounts that lacked objectivity, he said. "It was a creative writing experiment more than anything else. In every case, things always got 'better,' but nobody ever defined what doing better meant. In fact, they all used different terms to define success."

Under the proposed system, residents will tell police what they feel the neighborhood priorities should be, and strategies will be developed to solve problems based on community input. Forms will be used to measure and compare the success of police efforts to address like problems in all of the city's 75 precincts.

The information from the forms will eventually be entered into a department-wide data base. Computer files will document efforts made by police to address a particular problem and will provide contacts that encourage more information-sharing between precincts and ultimately, Julian envisions, between police departments.

"What we'd like to come out of this is not only a measurement tool, but an encyclopedia of successful, non-conventional strategies for each type of problem. This way, when [an officer] comes up with a problem in his district, he doesn't have to reinvent the wheel. He'll be able to go to files that will show what was done in a very user-friendly system. If he needs further information, he can go directly to the source."

*Source: Law Enforcement News,* April 15, 1994, pp. 1, 8 (John Jay College of Criminal Justice).

been community policing and police agency accreditation. The standards used by the Commission on Accreditation for Law Enforcement Agencies (CALEA) have come under scrutiny as being in conflict with the principles of community policing.[67] CALEA standards emphasize the formalization of organizational practices. To a vast extent, the standards tend to reinforce the efficiency orientation of the traditional and professional police model rather than the effectiveness orientation of community policing and problem solving. In terms of organizational structure and operation, the standards emphasize specialization, encourage centralization, implicitly produce taller hierarchies, and, most important, narrow police discretion. These principles inherently conflict with the basic philosophy of community policing.

**Increased potential for police favoritism**—According to O. W. Wilson, the central hierarchy of police structure provides a means with which to monitor and control subordinate (officer) behavior. Under traditional policing, the primary mission of the police is to maintain order and to enforce the law. There is little confusion whether to arrest. However, in most models of community policing, arrest is inherently secondary in importance.[68] Officers are encouraged to find other sanctions, short of arrest. Mastrofski, Worden, and Snipes write:

There is no consensus on what community policing is, but one has emerged regarding what it is not. It rejects law enforcement as the single, core function of police. Arrest is only a means to other ends. . . . Encouraging such discretion in law enforcement raises questions about whether and which extralegal influences might assume a larger role in shaping arrest decisions.[69]

These "extralegal influences" include the suspect's social status, race, gender, wealth, age, appearance, and behavior toward police. These are the foundations on which prejudice, discrimination, and harassment are usually based. Indeed, lady justice wears a blindfold so that she is not influenced by such issues. Why then should police use these characteristics in forming an arrest decision? Further, with unchecked authority and greatly increased discretion (characterized by flatter structures and encouraged "problem-solving" strategies), police officers patrol the same district or beat on the same shift in an attempt to build positive community relationships. But, what if officers become too friendly with some citizens, too attached to neighborhood interest groups, or too politically motivated? Will they be able to enforce laws from a neutral perspective, free from bias, and be able to identify white collar criminals as well as the more apparent and routine drug dealers, burglars, and thieves? Community policing requires officers to make broader decisions with much more community impact. Some scholars argue that such a condition is ripe for increased corruption and violates the principles of police neutrality.[70]

**Failure to understand the change process**—The basic concept of community policing as an instrument of change is a valuable and noble effort. However, in the long run, community policing may prove more frustrating for the police and the community as calls for service continue to escalate. Even in cities having well-developed community policing efforts, the citizenry still expect the police to react to calls for service and reduce crime. Basically, the community perception of the police as the "thin blue line" between order and chaos still exists. Police are still expected to quell neighborhood problems, stop abusive spouses, arrest criminals, give traffic tickets, and patrol in visible, marked police units. Failing to understand the change process (see Chapter 15) as long term, ongoing, and somewhat chaotic will doom community policing (as it did team policing) if considerable effort is not given to maintaining traditional perceptions of the police. Further, community policing requires extensive changes in police recruitment, selection, training, and organizational design (refer to Chapters 5 and 8). Many of these changes simply cannot be accomplished without the involvement of police labor unions, civil service boards, and other external entities. The change process will be long and fraught with difficulty, especially if crime rates continue to escalate in areas experimenting with community policing (see Box 2-11).

BOX 2-11

# How to Change

## Examining an organization in transition

**by Kelsey Gray, Ph.D.**

When a law enforcement agency embraces community policing, all department members become oriented to provide customer service and work toward a community-wide effort to prevent crime.

These same officers are often hampered by the existing hierarchical structure and regulations that keep decisions at the top, limit the amount and type of information dispersed, and require all actions to go through the "chain of command." These disparate organizational systems cause internal conflict that often limits the adoption of community policing.

Implementation throughout the entire department is difficult at best. Distrust of change, lack of confidence in management, and cynicism with respect to changing reward systems restrict implementation.

### Organizational Structure and Change

This inconsistency of purpose and values is the basis for conflict. Community policing requires structural and organizational change. Departments must examine their "organizational universe." This universe describes the total system in which the officer is working and includes values, goals, structure, internal climate and external stakeholders.

**Values.** At the core of an agency is a set of values—an underlying philosophy that defines its reason for existence. The values of community policing (including problem solving, partnerships and customer service) must drive the organization. The department's culture reflects these values in its structure and management, and through these values, members learn what actions are important.

It is critical that the agency's values are explicitly shared and modeled. Top managers are responsible for this step. Managers are often good at championing change of others, but poor at changing their own behavior. Culture is established by employees observing how things are and then drawing conclusions about their organization's priorities. They then set their priorities accordingly. For this reason, senior managers must incorporate the community policing philosophy into their own work.

**Goals.** Organizational goals are articulated values. They describe what the agency is striving for and delineate how results will be attained. For example, a goal to "enhance the involvement of community members in the identification and solution of community problems" implies a value based on citizen empowerment. Goals are not just budget items masked as action plans. They explain how the values will be implemented within the organization and must be outcome-based.

It is easy to opt into a community policing process, agree to the goals, but then exempt key employees from participating, or deny a particular unit's access to resources. Command staff must be held accountable for the goals, and agree on how they will share personnel commitment to community policing, allocate resources to ensure success, and evaluate processes that guarantee certain units are not excluded from change. Implementing community policing exposes many of the personal conflicts of interest that often lie undetected (or at least not discussed) within the department.

**Structure.** Structure involves more than just the organizational chart. The chart depicts the formal mechanisms and relationships that enable implementation of values and goals. There are five major structural areas: commander-officer relationships, communication patterns, decision-making procedures, accountability and commitment, and reward systems. Each of these areas must be congruent with the values, goals and structure. Only when the structural elements enhance, rather than inhibit these goals can members find job satisfaction.

As a department moves toward community policing, disorganization, inefficiency and ineffectiveness are often signs that roles and communication systems lack clarity.

**Climate.** A department's climate, or atmosphere, results from the structure. The climate is made up of all those unwritten rules and assumptions that drive behavior. Trust, risk-taking, support, competition, freedom, clarity of action, stress, conflict and morale are all elements of the climate. An agency's overall climate is built through a structure that supports its stated goals and values. The climate will indicate if there is incongruency among these elements. If the climate is poor, then morale plummets, trust in the system becomes nonexistent, jobs become competitive, and there is little opportunity or energy for innovation.

**Environment.** The outside environment influences the department's ability to accomplish its goals. Environmental influences may affect goal success or change priorities. Agencies without a well-developed value system are at the mercy of a changing environment. Goals may be altered based on partial information. Employees search for stability within the workplace and learn not to trust the new "initiatives" or "directives," knowing that within a short time all priorities will again change.

### Triangle of Responsibility

Because most law enforcement agencies have a traditional structure, many managers are unfamiliar with the opportunities presented by alternate structures, participative management and empowering leadership styles.

The key to community policing success is developing congruency among the three major components of management—responsibility, authority and accountability—or the "Triangle of Accountability." When an officer is given responsibility for particular outcomes, it is essential that the authority to make decisions and to take action accompanies this responsibility. Just as important is the requirement that he or she also be held accountable for his or her participation. When this triangle gets out of balance, department members become unsure of their jobs, their value, and how they will be held accountable.

### Organizational Development

Because the most difficult part of community policing is the implementation of its principles, managers often need assistance with implementing organizational change. Managers and officers need skills such as conflict management, interest-based problem solving and community (citizen) development. Direct consultation with citizens and/or volunteer networks are critical.

Effective organizations learn to involve environmental influences in appropriate and useful ways. Citizens, interest groups and politicians can be involved in enhancing community policing and providing the support necessary to build workable partnerships. Conducting community needs assessments and community policing evaluations are crucial for involving outside interests in appropriate ways. The data is clear that law enforcement agencies are powerless to reduce crime without the involvement and support of the community. These partnerships become critical to a department's success.

Rules that were developed because of past mistakes now stifle what we need in community policing—creativity and innovation. It is difficult for a manager to embrace risk taking, innovation and creativity without the guarantee of success. Community policing means allowing line officers to make decisions, take risks and then stand behind the decisions that they make. This balance of power allows innovation and creativity.

*Source: Community Policing Exchange, July/August, 1996, pp. 1–2.*

Community policing advocates a necessary and important reform. Its recognition of the close relationship of crime to other social problems is a big step in the evolution of American policing. However, the implementation of community policing is a concept in vogue. As Skolnick and Bayley[71] write, "community policing represents what is progressive and forward-looking" in American policing. Unfortunately, every new technique and strategy is being lumped under the rubric of community policing. As a result, within some professional circles, those agencies not involved in the community policing movement are labeled stagnant and backward. Such generalizations are without merit, especially considering the mixed evaluations on both traditional and community policing efforts.

## SUMMARY

Community policing presents the emergence of a new philosophy in policing characterized by ongoing attempts to promote greater community involvement in the police function. This perspective links social issues to crime, advocating the police as general problem solvers in cooperation with the community and calling for the reorganization of existing police agencies to foster improved leadership and a team atmosphere. Most cities across America have adopted community policing as a viable strategy to reduce crime and improve police-community relations. Police now use powerful, new information technologies to pinpoint and analyze crime and other social problems in their communities. Crime analysis, geographic information systems, artificial intelligence, and the Internet have greatly improved the police response to these problems.

The move to community policing has not been without significant problems. The lack of definition and role confusion among officers have caused poor morale and resistance within some departments. High expenses and a general failure to understand the change process within complex organizations have also resulted in negative implementation issues; and the failure to measure or evaluate community policing adequately as an effective strategy continues to plague many communities experimenting with this new strategy. However, despite some of these shortcomings, community policing continues to be an important evolutionary step in reform. Police will forever be changed from this dramatic movement of the 1990s. As we enter the new millennium, police will continue to explore the important linkages between community and crime, and will hopefully "muddle through" many of the implementation issues currently noted. The stage is now set to explore the fundamental principles of administration more fully and identify the current challenges awaiting future police managers.

## DISCUSSION QUESTIONS

1. Define *community policing.*
2. Describe the four-step, problem-solving system commonly referred to as SARA.
3. What were the positive findings associated with the EPD in Madison, Wisconsin?
4. What are the key features of the CAPS program in Chicago, and how does the Chicago effort differ from other community policing models observed around the country?
5. What was the impact of the 1994 Crime Bill on community policing?
6. Describe some of the more common crime analysis techniques used in community policing.
7. What is GIS? How does such a system enhance police services?
8. What are the four major application domains of AI? Which application holds the most promise for law enforcement, and why?
9. What is an on-line bulletin board system? What features make the Internet an ideal network technology for police and other criminal justice practitioners?
10. What are some of the problems associated with community policing?

## NOTES

1. Refer to Herman Goldstein, *Policing in a Free Society* (Cambridge, Mass.: Ballinger Press, 1977).
2. Refer to James Q. Wilson and George Kelling, "The Police and Neighborhood Safety: Broken Windows," *Atlantic Monthly,* 249 (1982), 29–38.
3. Chris Braiden, "Community Policing: Nothing New Under the Sun" (Edmonton, Canada: Edmonton Police Department, 1987).
4. Ibid., refer to Peel's Principle 7, as expressed on page 2.
5. Jerome H. Skolnick and David H. Bayley, *Community Policing: Issues and Practices Around the World* (Washington, D.C.: U.S. Department of Justice, 1988), pp. 67–70.
6. A number of researchers have documented the failures of traditional policing methods. Most notably, refer to A. J. Reiss, *The Police and the Public* (New Haven, Conn.: Yale University Press, 1971); Kelling et al., *Kansas City Preventive Parol Experiment;* M. T. Farmer, ed., *Differential Police Response Strategies* (Washington, D.C.: Police Executive Research Forum, 1981); L. W. Sherman, P. R. Gartin, and M. E. Buerger, "Hot Spot of Predatory Crime: Routine Activities and the Criminology of Place," *Criminology,* 27 (1989), 27–55; and W. H. Bieck, W. Spelman, and T. J. Sweeney, "The Patrol Function," in *Local Government Police Management,* ed. William A. Geller (Washington, D.C.: International City Management Association), pp. 59–95.
7. Timothy N. Oettmeier, "Endemic Issues in Policing: Matching Structure to Objectives" (Houston, Texas: Houston Police Academy), p. 11.
8. Ibid., p. 16.
9. William Spelman and John E. Eck, "The Police and Delivery of Local Government Services: A Problem-Oriented Approach," in *Police Practice in the '90s: Key Management Issues,* ed. James J. Fyfe (Washington, D.C.: International City Managers Association, 1989), p. 56.

10. Ibid.

11. The SARA methodology was adapted from William Spelman and John E. Eck, *Newport News Tests Problem-Oriented Policing* (Washington, D.C.: National Institute of Justice, SNI 201, January/February 1987), pp. 2–3; and Spelman and Eck, "Police and Delivery," 61.

12. Herman Goldstein, *Problem-Oriented Policing* (New York: McGraw-Hill, 1990).

13. This list was adapted, in part, from Goldstein, *Problem-Oriented Policing*, pp. 66–67.

14. Ibid., pp. 36–37.

15. Michael A. Freeman, "Community-Oriented Policing," *Management Information Services*, 21 (September 1989), 5–6.

16. "Creating a New Policing Environment in Madison: A Progress Report on the Experimental Police District" (Madison, Wis.: Madison Police Department, August 1989), p. 1.

17. Research focusing on the improvement of quality of life for individual workers is abundant in the open system literature, as described in Chapter 4. However, for a more recent articulation on the subject matter, see Warren Bennis and B. Nanus, *Leaders* (New York: Harper & Row, 1985); W. Edward Deming, *Out of the Crisis* (Cambridge, Mass.: MIT Center for Advanced Engineering Study, 1986); Thomas J. Peters, *Thriving on Chaos* (New York: Alfred Knopf, 1987); Thomas J. Peters and Nancy Austin, *A Passion for Excellence* (New York: Random House, 1985); Thomas J. Peters and Robert H. Wasserman, *In Search of Excellence* (New York: Harper & Row, 1982); John Naisbitt, *Megatrends* (New York: Warner Books, 1982); John Naisbitt and P. Auburdene, *Reinventing the Corporation* (New York: Warner Books, 1985); and John Gordon, *Leader Effectiveness Training* (New York: Bantam, 1975).

18. David C. Couper and Sabine H. Lobitz, *Quality Policing: The Madison Experience* (Washington, D.C.: Police Executive Research Forum, 1991), pp. 73–75.

19. Adapted from Couper and Lobitz, *Quality Policing*, pp. 83–88; and "Creating a New Policing Environment in Madison," (Washington, D.C.: Police Executive Research Forum, 1991), pp. 10–21.

20. Quality management and active leadership are critical elements for the implementation of community policing. See Mary Ann Wycoff and Wesley G. Skogan, "The Effect of a Community Policing Management Style on Officers' Attitudes," *Crime and Delinquency*, 40:3 (July 1994), 371–383.

21. City of Chicago, Department of Police, "Fact Sheet—The Chicago Alternative Policing Strategy (CAPS)," July 1995.

22. Arthur J. Lurigio and Wesley G. Skogan, "Winning the Hearts and Minds of Police Officers: An Assessment of Staff Perceptions of Community Policing in Chicago," *Crime and Delinquency*, 40:3 (July 1994), p. 319.

23. Mark Moore, "Problem-Solving and Community Policing," in *Modern Policing*, eds. M. Tonry and N. Morris (Chicago: University of Chicago Press, 1992), pp. 99–158.

24. The key features of the CAPS program presented in this text are adapted from Lurigio and Skogan, "Winning the Hearts and Minds of the Police Officers: An Assessment of Staff Perceptions of Community Policing in Chicago," p. 318, and Chicago Police Department, "Fact Sheet—The Chicago Alternative Policing Strategy (CAPS)," p. 1–2.

25. Stephen Mastrofski, Roger Parks, and Robert E. Worden, "Community Policing in Action: Lessons from an Observational Study," *Research Preview*, June 1998 (Washington, D.C.: National Institute of Justice).

26. Ibid.

27. Quint C. Thurman and Jihong Zhao, "Community Policing: Where Are We Now?" *Crime and Delinquency*, 43:3 (July 1997).

28. Mastrofski et al., p. 7.

29. Kenneth J. Peak and Ronald W. Glensor, *Community Policing and Problem Solving: Strategies and Practices* (Upper Saddle River, N.J.: Prentice-Hall, 1996), pp. 318–349.

30. U.S. Department of Justice, *The Violent Crime Control and Law Enforcement Act of 1994* (Washington, D.C.: U.S. Government Printing Office, 1994).

31. Gary Cordner, "Crime Bill Update: COPS-MORE," *Police Computer Review*, 4:1 (1995), 1–3.

32. Malcolm K. Sparrow, "Information Systems and the Development of Policing," *Perspectives on Policing* (Washington, D.C.: National Institute of Justice, March 1993), p. 1.

33. J. B. Howlett, "Analytical Investigative Techniques," *Police Chief*, 47 (December 1980), 42.

34. J. A. Kinney, "Criminal Intelligence Analysis: A Powerful Weapon," *International Cargo Crime Prevention* (April 1984), 4.

35. D. M. Ross, "Criminal Intelligence Analysis," *Police Product News* (June 1983), 45.

36. Ibid.

37. Conference on Domestic Terrorism, Southwestern Law Enforcement Institute, Richardson, Texas (April 16–18, 1996).

38. Ross, "Criminal Intelligence," 49.

39. For background material on the development of GISs, refer to Roger F. Tomlinson and A. Raymond Boyle, "The State of Development of Systems for Handling Natural Resources Inventory Data," *Cartographica,* 18 (1988), pp. 65–95; Donna Peuguet and John O'Callaghan, eds., *Design and Implementation of Computer-Based Geographic Information Systems* (Amherst, N.Y.: IGU Commission on Geographical Data Sensing and Processing, 1983); Robert C. Maggio and Douglas F. Wunneburger, "A Microcomputer-Based Geographic Information System for Natural Resource Managers," unpublished manuscript, Texas A&M University, Department of Forest Science, College Station, Texas, 1988; and Robert Rogers, "Geographic Information Systems in Policing," *Police Computer Review,* 4:2 (1995), 8–13.

40. James A. O'Brien, *Management Information Systems: A Managerial End User Perspective* (Homewood, Ill.: Irwin, 1990), p. 356.

41. W. Coady, "Automated Link Analysis: Artificial Intelligence–Based Tools for Investigator," *Police Chief,* 52 (1985), 22–23.

42. Edward C. Ratledge and Joan E. Jacoby, *Handbook on Artificial Intelligence and Expert Systems in Law Enforcement* (Westport, Conn.: Greenwood, 1989), chap. 8.

43. R. Krause, "The Best and the Brightest," *Law Enforcement Technology,* 3 (1986), 25–27.

44. See "Artificial Intelligence Tackles a Very Real Problem—Police Misconduct Control," *Law Enforcement News* (September 30, 1994), 1.

45. For more detailed information on this subject, refer to Robert W. Taylor, "Managing Police Information," in *Police and Policing: Contemporary Issues,* ed. Dennis J. Kenney (New York: Praeger, 1989), pp. 257–70.

46. The findings of this survey were reported by Gary Cordner, "Bulletin Boards," *Police Computer Review,* 4:3 (1995), 19–20.

47. Much of the section focusing on the Internet was adapted from G. Martin Lively and Judy A. Reardon, "Justice on the Net: The National Institute of Justice Promotes Internet Services," *NIJ Research in Action Bulletin* (Washington, D.C.: GPO, March 1996), 1–7.

48. A number of recent articles have extolled the virtues of accessing information on the Internet. For specific sources available, see Seth F. Jacobs, "On-Line Criminal Justice Resources," *Journal of Criminal Justice Education,* 6 (Fall 1995).

49. Herman Goldstein, *Problem-Oriented Policing* (New York: McGraw-Hill, 1990).

50. In the last three years, significant work has appeared in the literature questioning the effectiveness of community policing. See Jihong Zhao, Nicholas P. Lovrich, and Quint Thurman, "The Status of Community Policing in American Cities: Facilitators and Impediments Revisited," *Policing: An International Journal,* 22:1 (1999); Roger B. Parks, Stephen D. Mastrofski, Christina Dejong, and M. Kevin Gray, "How Officers Spend Their Time with the Community," *Justice Quarterly,* 16:3 (September 1999); Robert W. Taylor, Eric J. Fritsch, and Tory J. Caeti, "Core Challenges Facing Community Policing: The Emperor *Still* Has No Clothes," *ACJS Today,* 27:1 (May/June 1998); Lawrence F. Travis III and Craig N. Winston, "Dissension in the Ranks: Officer Resistance to Community Policing, Cynicism, and Support for the Organization," *Journal of Crime and Justice,* 21:2 (1998); Allan Y. Jiao, "Community-Oriented Policing and Policing-Oriented Community," *Journal of Crime and Justice,* 21:1 (1998); Albert P. Cardarelli, Jack McDevitt, and Katrina Baum, "The Rhetoric and Reality of Community Policing in Small and Medium-Sized Cities and Towns," *Policing: An International Journal,* 21:3 (1998); James Frank, Steven G. Brandl, and R. Cory Watkins, "The Content of Community Policing: A Comparison of the Daily Activities of Community and 'Beat' Officers," *Policing: An International Journal,* 20:4 (1997); Jihong Zhao and Quint C. Thurman, "Community Policing: Where Are We Now?" *Crime and Delinquency,* 43:3 (July 1997).

51. Victor G. Strecher, "Histories and Futures of Policing: Readings and Misreadings of a Pivotal Present," *Police Forum,* 1:1 (January 1991), 5–6.

52. Jack R. Greene and Stephen D. Mastrofski, eds., *Community Policing: Rhetoric or Reality* (New York: Praeger, 1991).

53. Samuel Walker, *The Police in America: An Introduction,* 2nd ed. (New York: McGraw-Hill, 1992), pp. 188–190; and Strecher, pp. 1–9.

54. The classic scholars such as Aristotle, Plato, Sir Thomas More, St. Thomas Aquinas, Jean-Jacques Rouseau, and Emile Durkheim argued that ideal community was self-governing and autonomous, void of the vices and tribulations expressed by man. Therefore, the need for police was nonexistent, as strife, discord, and contention were not part of the environment.

55. Strecher, p. 6.

56. Ibid., p. 6.

57. Peak and Glensor, *Community Policing and Problem Solving: Strategies and Practices,* p. 260.

58. Strecher, p. 6.

59. See J. F. Persinos, "The Return of Officer Friendly," *Governing,* 21 (1989), 56–61; and Dennis P. Rosenbaum, Sandy Veh, and Deanna I. Wilkinson, "Impact of Community Policing on Police Personnel: A Quasi-Experimental Test," *Crime and Delinquency,* 43:3 (July 1994), 331–353.

60. Cresap Management Audit (Washington, D.C.: Cresap, Inc., 1991), p. 10.

61. Ibid., p. 59.

62. Refer to Rick Del Vecchio, "Community Policing Plan for Oakland," *San Francisco Chronicle,* February 10, 1995, p. 5; and Dennis A. Garrett, "City Council Report to the City Manager," *San Francisco Chronicle,* February 7, 1995, p. 1.

63. C. Murphy, "Community Problems, Problem Communities, and Community Policing in Toronto," *Journal of Research in Crime and Delinquency,* 25 (November 1988), 392–410.

64. Ibid., 392–393.

65. George Kelling, "Police and Communities: The Quiet Revolution," *Perspectives on Policing* (Washington, D.C.: National Institute of Justice, 1988), p. 6.

66. Interview with then Deputy Chief Elizabeth Watson, Houston Police Department, at the Southwestern Law Enforcement Institute, Richardson, Texas, November 15, 1989.

67. For a detailed discussion of the potential conflict between community policing and CALEA standards, refer to Gary W. Cordner and Gerald L. Williams, "Community Policing and Accreditation: A Content Analysis of CALEA Standards," *Police Forum,* 5:1 (January 1995). Much of this section is adapted from this article and their awarded grant #92-IJ-CX-K038 from the National Institute of Justice, Office of Justice Programs, U.S. Department of Justice.

68. A number of scholars have noted the de-emphasis of law enforcement activities in the community policing philosophy. See David H. Bayley, "Community Policing: A Report from the Devil's Advocate," in *Community Policing: Rhetoric or Reality?,* eds. Jack R. Greene and Stephen D. Mastrofski (New York: Praeger Press, 1988); John P. Crank, "State Theory, Myths of Policing, and Responses to Crime," *Law and Society Review,* 28 (December 1994), 325–351; and Adam Clymer, "Crime Bill Clears Hurdle, but Senate Is Going Home Without Acting on Health," *The New York Times,* August 16, 1994, A1, A19.

69. Stephen D. Mastrofski, Robert E. Worden, and Jeffrey B. Snipes, "Law Enforcement in a Time of Community Policing," *Criminology,* 33:4 (January 1995), 541.

70. Refer to William F. McDonald, "Police and Community: In Search of a New Relationship," *The World and I,* (March 1992), 457; and Peter Nelligan and Robert W. Taylor, "Ethical Challenges in Community Policing," *Journal of Contemporary Criminal Justice,* 10:1 (March 1994), 59–66.

71. Skolnick and Bayley, *Community Policing,* p. 2.

## INTRODUCTION

In discussing the relationship between politics and police administration, it is important to distinguish between "Politics" and "politics." "Politics" refers to the attempts to impose external, partisan political influence on the operation of the department. For example, people are promoted because they know precinct committeepersons and ward chairpersons who have influence with the party in power. The department is manipulated for partisan, political advantage and forced to make financial contributions. Justice is not dispensed evenhandedly. This use of the word is negative. However, "politics" means governance of the city. Aristotle's original understanding of the word *politics* was "science of the polis," seeking the good of both citizen and city-state. The present-day police are its practitioners, as are politicians at their best. Politics with a small *p* avoids political leveraging and supports merit and job performance—all positive connotations. The art of governing a local community requires a commitment to take bad politics out of the police department and put the right kind back in.[1]

## —3— POLITICS AND POLICE ADMINISTRATION: EXTERNAL INFLUENCES AND CONTROLS

*Terrifying are the weaknesses of power.*
GREEK PROVERB

This chapter addresses a number of subjects involving the police that are often the focus of political debate and compromise. As such, these issues are often controversial in nature and tend to become more or less influential depending on the amount of attention expressed by specific individuals or parties in office. For instance, one of the most dynamic debates in Congress from 1993 to 1996 was over the development and refinement of the Violent Crime Control and Law Enforcement Act of 1994, commonly referred to as the crime bill (refer to Chapter 2). While the bill had almost unanimous support in providing federal money for an additional 100,000 local police officers under the COPS (Community-Oriented Policing Services) program, the bill also included stringent gun control measures—an issue that markedly divided Congress.

In November 1993, Congress passed the Brady Bill, which mandated a five-day waiting period for gun purchases, after overcoming a fierce lobbying effort mounted primarily by the National Rifle Association (NRA). The following year, in May 1994, the House of Representatives voted to ban 19 types of assault weapons and their look-alikes. And again, in 1994, Congress passed the entire crime bill inclusive of various gun control initiatives strongly supported by the Democratic Congress, President Clinton, and Attorney General Janet Reno. However, in 1995, touting a Republican majority, Congress initiated H.R. 2076, a $27.3 billion FY 96 Commerce, Justice, and State Appropriations Bill that dramatically cut over $4 billion in funding from the original deployment of 100,000 new police officers. Separate funding streams for community policing efforts were eliminated in the proposed bill. While President Clinton vowed to veto such a bill, one might believe that such a dramatic congressional change may be due to retaliation for the passage of rigorous gun control laws, which were part and parcel of the overall Crime Bill of 1994.[2]

Thus, we see how political issues have impacted the police. This type of activity is certainly not a new phenomenon to police executives who have had to manage agencies under such turbulent and dynamic environments. This chapter provides a thumbnail sketch of the political issues often confronting police administrators, including police accountability, state and local political forces, the state prosecutor, the judiciary, citizen involvement, and the media.

## POLICE ACCOUNTABILITY

Accountability of the police to other institutions conforms to the American notion of a system of checks and balances. There are, however, some questions about the actual means by which this accountability occurs and the degree to which it exists. It has been suggested that the degree of control over the police by political authority varies with the level of government at which the police functions take place. In this country, although cities and counties are legally creatures of the states under state constitutions, the states have traditionally divested themselves of much of their control over these jurisdictions and have allowed them to operate with considerable independence.[3] The existence of local autonomy has also been facilitated by the belief in home rule, which maintains that local government has the capability to manage its own affairs and that strong controls from the state capitol or the federal government are neither desirable nor consistent with American political philosophy. Nevertheless, the influences and controls being exerted upon local law enforcement from both the federal and state level have increased since the turbulent period of the 1960s.

Some argue that this encroachment of local hegemony will eventually result in a significant shift of control and political power away from the local level. In reply, the proponents of this development argue that the traditionally strong local control of policing has resulted in a degree of parochialism that has retarded the growth of professionalism. They also maintain that the increased involvement in local law enforcement by the state and federal government has produced important qualitative improvements in such areas as personnel selection standards, training, crime laboratory capabilities, and labor–management relations.

As we discussed in Chapter 2, the movement toward community policing places a renewed emphasis on police accountability. Under community policing, outside review and citizen involvement in the day-to-day operations of the police department are highlighted. The police are accountable to the community they serve. To this end, several types of review or oversight vehicles have been implemented in cities across the nation. These include citizen complaint desks, neighborhood substations staffed by volunteers, police–community relations committees, and outside review commissions. The transition to more citizen and community involvement has not been an easy one, often fraught with conflicting political agendas and open confrontation (see Box 3-1).

**Federal Influence in Law Enforcement**

Some authorities believe that trends occurring from the 1960s through the present have resulted in the partial nationalization of criminal justice. Up to the 1960s, it was safely said that criminal justice was almost completely the responsibility of state and local governments. Federal criminal statutes were

BOX 3-1

## Cop Review Panel Takes a Beating

by Christopher Lopez

The three-year effort by Denver's Public Safety Review Commission to hold cops accountable took an ominous twist yesterday when the board's chairwoman was told that the civilian oversight panel is too negative and confrontational. Several city council members said they probably won't vote to reappoint commission chairwoman Adrienne Benavidez.

The council is seeking a kinder, gentler commission to review complaints against Denver police. With three vacancies on the seven-member panel, and Benavidez on the ropes seeking reappointment, the timing is right if the council wants new blood. "If what they're looking for is a rah-rah session with the police department," Benavidez said, "then maybe they do need different commissioners on there."

The buzzsaw of criticism that Benavidez encountered yesterday at the council's personnel and public safety committee meeting was merely the latest head-butting involving the police-review commission, cops and the city council.

The review commission won a crucial victory two months ago when Chief Denver County Judge Andrew Armatas ruled that the commission can subpoena police officers and documents to assist in its investigations.

The Denver Police Protective Association is appealing that decision, and the city has spent $10,800 so far in outside attorney fees to represent the union in that battle, Benavidez said.

Before that issue arose, Police Chief Dave Michaud told his troops that they no longer had to appear in person to respond to inquiries by the police-review commission but, instead, could respond in writing.

That decision came last summer, when the police department felt under attack by the civilian board. "The issues were going too far afield," Deputy Chief Tom Sanchez said yesterday. "It was almost like a witch-hunt atmosphere." Sanchez said the police department isn't opposed to civilian review and is held accountable by various means, including public pressure. "We're replete with civilian oversight," Sanchez said, "including you all in the media. You're not afraid to go after anybody."

Derailing Benavidez's reappointment appears to be the council's first step to ensure that the review commission is more sensitive to police. It's up to Mayor Wellington Webb to recommend members to the board, but the city council must ratify the nominees. Webb is supporting Benavidez' reappointment, and one member of his staff predicted that most council members will come around and vote to reappoint her as well.

Councilman Dennis Gallagher, who told Benavidez that he probably won't back her, suggested that family members of police officers could sit on the commission to ensure that the board isn't so confrontational.

Councilwoman Joyce Foster suggested that former police officers could sit on the board. "It's balance I'm talking about," Foster said. "A balance toward impartiality." Foster said she perceives that the review commission isn't objective in investigating police complaints, a perception that comes from watching the commission's monthly meetings on the city's public access channel. "The tenor of the commission has been confrontational," Foster said, "and we don't solve problems and we don't develop trust in that type of forum."

Because the business of the commission is to investigate complaints against police, Benavidez said, the meetings usually are heated and confrontational. "We take what they say to heart," Benavidez said of the council's concerns. "But the nature of what we discuss is complaints against the police department, and we attempt to bring in another perspective."

*Source: Denver Post, January 17, 1996, p. A1.*

---

limited in their coverage, federal assistance to local law enforcement was generally in the areas of training and the processing of evidence, and the Supreme Court concerned itself with only the most notorious violations of constitutional rights by state and local authorities.[4] This trend was reversed in no small measure by a series of opinions rendered by the U.S. Supreme Court under the strong leadership of Chief Justice Earl Warren, which greatly strengthened the rights of accused persons in criminal cases. However, as the Supreme Court has become more conservative in the last two decades, an "erosion" of many of the landmark cases of the Warren era can be observed.

Significant judicial review of local police actions has been a somewhat recent practice.[5] However, during the period from 1961 to 1966—a period frequently referred to as the "due process revolution"—the U.S. Supreme Court took an activist role, becoming quite literally givers of the law rather than interpreters of it. The Warren court's activist role in the piecemeal extension of the provisions of the Bill of Rights, via the due process clause of the Fourteenth Amendment, to criminal proceedings in the respective states might have been a policy decision.[6] Normally the Supreme Court writes opinions in about 115 cases during any particular term. During the 1938–1939 term, only five cases appear under the heading of criminal law; a scant three decades later, during the height of the due process revolution, about one-quarter of each term's decisions related to criminal law.[7] The Supreme Court could scarcely have picked a worse period in which to undertake the unpopular role of policing the police; a burgeoning crime rate far outstripped population increases, and many politicians were campaigning on "law and order" platforms that all too often dissolved into rhetoric upon their election. The problem of crime increasingly came to the public's eye through the media. In sum, the high court acted to extend procedural safeguards to defendants in criminal cases precisely at a point in time when the public's fear of crime was high and there was great social pressure to do something about crime.

Fundamentally, the Supreme Court's role in the due process revolution was a response to a vacuum in which the police themselves had failed to provide the necessary leadership. The era of strong social activism by various special-interest groups was not yet at hand, and neither the state courts nor the legislatures had displayed any broad interest in reforming the criminal law. What institution was better positioned to undertake this responsibility? The Court may even have felt obligated by the inaction of others to do so. Therefore, it became the Warren court's lot to provide the reforms so genuinely needed but so unpopularly received. The high court did not move into this arena until after it had issued warnings that, to responsive and responsible leaders, would have been a mandate for reform.

Several key decisions were made by a split vote of the court and drew heavy criticism from law enforcement officers and others as handcuffing police in their struggle with lawlessness. These decisions included *Mapp* v. *Ohio* (1961), which banned the use of illegally seized evidence in criminal cases in the states by applying the Fourth Amendment guarantee against unreasonable searches and seizures; *Gideon* v. *Wainwright* (1963), which affirmed that equal protection under the Fourteenth Amendment requires that legal counsel be appointed for all indigent defendants in all criminal cases; *Escobedo* v. *Illinois* (1964), which affirmed that a suspect is entitled to confer with an attorney as soon as the focus of a police investigation of the suspect shifts from investigatory to accusatory; and *Miranda* v. *Arizona* (1966), which required police officers, before questioning suspects, to inform them of their constitutional right to remain silent, their right to an attorney, and their right to have an attorney appointed if they cannot afford to hire one. Although the suspect may knowingly waive these rights, the police cannot question anyone who, at any point, asks for a lawyer or indicates "in any manner" that he or she does not wish to be questioned.[8]

The impact of these decisions on police work was staggering. In an effort to curb questionable and improper tactics, the Supreme Court essentially barred the use of illegally obtained evidence in a criminal prosecution to prove guilt. This action, known as the *exclusionary rule*, rested primarily on the

## Supreme Court Decisions Affecting Law Enforcement: 1961 to 1966

judgment that deterring police conduct that violates the constitutional rights of an individual outweighs the importance of securing a conviction of the specific defendant on trial. A need for new procedures in such areas as interrogations, lineups, and seizures of physical evidence was created.

Although the decisions of the due process revolution initially were criticized by many law enforcement officers, over the years that view has changed as new generations of law enforcement officers come along for whom those decisions are simply the correct way to do things. Also, time has seen the exodus of some officers from the police profession who simply could not or would not adapt to a new way of "doing business." Finally, there was a growing willingness among law enforcement leaders to acknowledge not only that some of their tactics needed changing, but also that *Miranda* and other decisions had accomplished it.

**More Recent Supreme Court Decisions**

In more recent years, appointments to the Supreme Court by Presidents Ronald Reagan and George Bush have provided a conservative majority who have generated decisions more favorable to law enforcement. Beginning in the early 1970s and continuing through today, the Supreme Court has systematically eroded the basic principles set forth in the *Mapp* and *Miranda* decisions.[9]

Exceptions to the exclusionary rule developed in *Mapp* v. *Ohio* started in 1984. In *Massachusetts* v. *Sheppard* and *United States* v. *Leon,* the court held that evidence obtained by the police acting in "good faith," even if it is ultimately found to be illegally seized due to an error committed by the judge or magistrate, is still admissible in court.[10] In *Leon,* the court reasoned that the exclusionary rule was designed to deter police misconduct rather than punish the police for the errors of judges. Therefore, the Fourth Amendment's exclusionary rule should not be applied to bar the prosecution from using evidence that had been obtained by police officers acting in reasonable reliance on a search warrant issued by a neutral magistrate, even if that warrant is found to be invalid substantively for lack of probable cause. Critics of the decision suggest that the "good faith" exception will encourage police to provide only the minimum of information in warrant applications and hence undermine the integrity of the warrant process.[11]

The original decision on automobile stops and searches was developed in 1925 in *Carroll* v. *United States* (Figure 3-1).[12] As long as the vehicle was stopped due to reasonable and individualized suspicion (usually a traffic violation), the areas in plain view and the area around the driver were subject to search without a warrant. The mobility of the motor vehicle produced an exigent circumstance to the search warrant requirement. As long as the officer could develop probable cause that the vehicle was transporting contraband or other illegal substances, then a warrant was not required. In 1990, the court expanded the right to stop and search a vehicle without violation or individualized suspicion by allowing sobriety checkpoints and roadblocks. The court rejected the concept that sobriety checkpoints violated the Fourth Amendment, and allowed police agencies to stop vehicles without individualized suspicion.[13]

Nowhere is the erosion of a Warren court decision more obvious than in the cases impacting the *Miranda* v. *Arizona* doctrine. During the past 25 years, the court has systematically loosened the application of the Miranda warning, allowing evidence to be admitted under a variety of exceptions (refer to

**FIGURE 3-1.** The landmark case involving automobile stops and searches was developed in 1925 in *Carroll* v. *United States.* Here, a New York motorcycle officer shows the correct technique in stopping vehicles in 1921. (Courtesy AP/Wide World Photos, New York, 1996.)

Table 3-1). The most controversial and complex of these cases occurred in 1991. In *Arizona* v. *Fulminante,* the Court ruled that an error made by the trial court in admitting illegally obtained evidence (in determining that a confession was coerced) does not require an automatic reversal of the conviction if the error is determined to be harmless, that is, if there was no reasonable possibility that a different result would have been reached without the illegally seized evidence.[14] Even though Fulminante's confession was ruled to be "harmful," and subsequently reversed, the importance of the ruling was the establishment of a more conservative procedure for reversing cases, even when confessions were coerced and, hence, illegally obtained.

In the foreseeable future, the Supreme Court under the leadership of Chief Justice William Rehnquist will likely continue to expand police powers in such areas as search and seizure and interrogation. It is equally likely that the court will produce rulings that will reverse some of the gains made since the due process revolution of the Warren court regarding misconduct by the police.[15]

In an era of police reform characterized by significant Supreme Court decisions and sweeping programmatic changes (imbued in the new philosophy of community policing as described in Chapter 2), law enforcement continues to be plagued by the old problems of brutality and scandal. Recent celebrated cases (e.g., the Rodney King incident, the O. J. Simpson trial, and the Abner Louima case) have only revealed the tip of the iceberg. Police officers across the country have been accused of lying in court, falsifying or withholding evidence, grossly mishandling case investigations, corruption, racism, physical abuse

**Age-Old Problems in Policing: Brutality and Scandal**

**TABLE 3-1.  The Evolution of the *Miranda* v. *Arizona* Decision in 1966**

| | |
|---|---|
| **1791:** | The Bill of Rights takes effect, including the Fifth Amendment, which guarantees that no person "shall be compelled in any criminal case to be a witness against himself." |
| **1868:** | The Fourteenth Amendment is ratified, requiring that all rights guaranteed by the federal government also be honored by the states. This made the future Miranda ruling in 1966 apply to state and local law enforcement officers. |
| **1940s–1950s:** | Federal agents begin routinely reading suspects their rights without a Supreme Court demand that they do so. |
| **1963:** | Ernesto Miranda is arrested and charged with kidnapping and raping a woman in Phoenix, Arizona. After two hours of arduous interrogation, he signs a confession and is convicted of the crimes. He subsequently appeals his conviction on the basis that the confession was coerced by local law enforcement officers. |
| **1966:** | The Supreme Court rules 5-4 in *Miranda* v. *Arizona* that suspects must be read their rights in order to be questioned, but warns that the requirements are not a "constitutional straitjacket" and invites states and the federal government to adopt their own "procedural safeguards" to protect suspects' rights. |
| **1967:** | Miranda is retired without the confession and convicted again. He is sentenced to eleven years in prison in Arizona. |
| **1968:** | Congress passes the Omnibus Crime Control and Safe Streets Act, which suggests that the rights should be read in most cases but that they should not be absolutely required. Some would later argue that this law, codified as Section 3501, satisfied the Supreme Court's invitation to develop other safeguards. |
| **1972:** | Mr. Miranda is paroled. |
| **1976:** | Mr. Miranda is stabbed to death in a bar fight, and a suspect is questioned in the case. Advised of his rights, the suspect chooses to remain silent and is released. No one is every charged with the crime. |
| **1971–1994:** | Several key cases allow the admissibility of evidence based on their factual situation, hence eroding the *Miranda* v. *Arizona* decision: |

| | |
|---|---|
| *Harris* v. *New York* (1971) | Impeachment of credibility |
| *Michigan* v. *Tucker* (1974) | Collateral derivative evidence |
| *Michigan* v. *Mosley* (1975) | Questioning on an unrelated offense |
| *New York* v. *Quarles* (1984) | Threat to public safety |
| *Berkemer* v. *McCarty* (1984) | Roadside questioning of a motorist pursuant to routine traffic stop |
| *Oregon* v. *Elstad* (1985) | Confession obtained after warnings given following earlier voluntary but unwarned admission |
| *Moran* v. *Burbine* (1986) | Failure of police to inform suspect of attorney retained for him |
| *Colorado* v. *Connelly* (1986) | Confession following advice of God |
| *Connecticut* v. *Barrett* (1987) | Oral confession |
| *Colorado* v. *Spring* (1987) | Shift to another crime |
| *Arizona* v. *Mauro* (1987) | Officer-recorded conversation with defendant's wife |
| *Pennsylvania* v. *Bruder* (1988) | Curbside stop for traffic violation |
| *Duckworth* v. *Eagan* (1989) | Variation in warning |
| *Michigan* v. *Harvey* (1990) | Impeach testimony |
| *Illinois* v. *Perkins* (1990) | Officer posing as a inmate |
| *Pennsylvania* v. *Muniz* (1990) | Routine questions and videotaping DWI |
| *McNeil* v. *Wisconsin* (1991) | Questioning for other offenses after request for counsel at bail hearing |
| *Arizona* v. *Fulminante* (1991) | Harmless involuntary confessions |
| *Withrow* v. *Williams* (1993) | Habeas corpus review of Miranda errors must continue to be entertained in federal proceedings |

| 1994: | In a concurring opinion in *Davis* v. *United States,* Supreme Court Justice Antonin Scalia chastises the Justice Department for failing to invoke Section 3501 saying it "may have produced . . . the acquittal and the non-prosecution of many dangerous felons." As a result, the court ruled that the police can continue to question suspects in the face of an "ambiguous request for counsel." |
|---|---|
| 1994: | In *Beckwith* v. *United States,* the court rules that a formal custody interrogation, requiring Miranda warnings, requires that the police communicate to the suspect that he or she is under arrest and in custody. |
| 1997: | Attorney General Janet Reno issues a letter ordering federal prosecutors not to invoke Section 3501. |
| 1999: | A three-judge panel of the Fourth U.S. Circuit Court of Appeals in Richmond, Virginia, accepts Utah law professor Paul Cassell's argument that challenges the original 1966 ruling that required Miranda warnings for in-custody interrogations. Stating that " . . . Miranda is the most damaging thing that was done to law enforcement in the last half-century," Casell argued that any statement uttered by suspects could be used in a court as long as they were given voluntarily, even if the Miranda warning had not been given (*Dickerson* v. *United States*). |
| 2000: | Most legal scholars suggest that the Supreme Court will leave the Fourth U.S. Circuit Court ruling intact without explicitly endorsing it, perhaps revisiting the issue later if it should come up in a different jurisdiction and under different circumstances. |

*Source:* From *Criminal Procedure, 2nd edition,* by R. del Carmen. © 1991. Reprinted with permission of Wadsworth, a division of Thomson Learning. Fax 800 730-2215.

and violence, and even murder. The phenomenon has not been isolated, with several major cases highlighting police misconduct in rapid succession.[16]

Setting the stage in 1991, the now-infamous Rodney King beating by Los Angeles police exposed to the world the ugliness of police racism and brutality. However, Los Angeles is hardly the only place where police administer such "street justice" with disturbing regularity. Again in 1991, in New York City, five officers were indicted on murder charges in the death by suffocation of a 21-year-old Hispanic man suspected of car theft. The officers were accused of having hit, kicked, and choked Federico Pereira while he lay face down and "hog-tied"—his wrists cuffed behind his back while another set of cuffs bound his hands to one ankle. The case led to a sweeping investigation into New York City police brutality and corruption. In a 1993 scandal, a New York state trooper was convicted of falsifying fingerprint evidence to get convictions. In 1995, the O. J. Simpson case highlighted the actions of Detective Mark Fuhrman. Fuhrman testified that he found a bloody glove at O. J. Simpson's estate that matched one found two miles away near the bodies of Nicole Brown Simpson and Ronald L. Goldman (Figure 3-2). Such evidence, along with DNA matching of the blood on the glove, directly linked O. J. Simpson to the murder. Simpson's lawyers, however, were able to discredit Fuhrman as a liar and a racist who planted evidence, producing a tape-recorded conversation in which Fuhrman spoke of beating African American suspects (commonly referred to by Fuhrman as the "N-word") and repeatedly used other racial slurs and epithets.

On Saturday, August 8, 1997, police in New York City arrested Abner Louima in one of the most infamous police abuse cases of the decade. At the time of his arrest, Louima had no bruises or injuries. Three hours after his arrest, Louima was rushed by ambulance to the hospital in critical condition. Internal Affairs investigators confirmed that Louima had been severely beaten by officers during his arrest and subsequent transport to the jail. While in police custody, Louima was taken to a restroom and endured what

**FIGURE 3-2.** Mark Fuhrman testifying at the O. J. Simpson trial. His testimony lost credibility after his taped conversations revealed racial slurs and epithets, casting spurious doubts on the testimony of all police officers. (Courtesy of AP/Wide World Photos)

one investigator described as "torture." Police officers removed Louima's pants and began to sodomize him with a toilet plunger. Medical doctors confirmed that Louima's internal injuries were the result of blunt force trauma. Two of the five officers indicted for the beating and torture were found guilty and sentenced to prison.[17]

In 1999, again in New York City, four officers fired forty-one shots, killing an unarmed Amadou Diallo in the stairway of his apartment. Officers contend that they opened fire on Diallo because he "acted suspiciously" and they "thought he was armed with a gun." The Internal Affairs investigation revealed that four officers completely emptied their weapons (sixteen shots each) and one officer fired five times. It appeared one officer panicked and the others followed suit in the shooting. Three of the officers had been involved in other shooting incidents, an anomaly for the New York City Police Department where 90 percent of officers have never fired their weapon. The discrepancies in the officers' statements prompted a criminal investigation; all four officers were found not guilty of charges of second-degree murder.[18]

The problems of police deviance and misconduct have not been limited to local police. Federal agents and agencies have also come under attack, with the most embarrassing moments stemming from botched raids against the Branch Davidians in Texas and white separatists in Idaho. Even the much maligned Central Intelligence Agency was again attacked in 1995. CIA agents intentionally misled, exaggerated, and out-and-out lied to top government policy makers (including the president) regarding the level of threat posed by the Soviet Union throughout the 1970s and 1980s. The result was a waste of tens of billions of dollars on unnecessary weapons systems and defense projects aimed at bolstering the military strength of the United States.

These cases have not only marred the reputation of specific police agencies, but also have raised serious questions as to police accountability, autonomy, and ethics. Certainly, these are not new issues in American law enforcement. Historically, corruption has been a documented problem throughout the development of many East Coast departments. Police brutality, commonly accompanied by charges of racism, has been a constant complaint of many inner-city and ghetto residents. The riots of the early 1960s, as well as the more recent riots in Miami and Los Angeles, were all ignited by episodes of perceived police brutality. More seriously, the rash of celebrated cases of police deviance have produced a wide-sweeping public apathy toward the police. As one Los Angeles resident recently indicated, "I don't even put quarters in parking meters anymore. After Fuhrman, police in this town couldn't get a conviction for a parking ticket."[19] Tensions between minority groups, especially in inner-city, low-income areas, are exceptionally high. Continued reports of police brutality and harassment focus on racism (Figure 3-3). Some experts argue that these types of cases clearly undermine the public's confidence in the entire criminal justice system.[20]

As a result of these and similar incidents, serious questions concerning the ability of police internal affairs units to control effectively police misconduct and deviance has been questioned. Critics of the police argue that civil damage suits are a much more useful deterrent to police brutality than any type of internal disciplinary sanction.[21] Title 42 of the United States Code, Section 1983, titled *Civil Action for Deprivation of Rights,* specifically provides a mechanism for filing a civil tort action against individual police officers for violation of a suspect's constitutional rights. Infliction of mental and emotional distress, assault, battery, and excessive use of force, including use of deadly force, are routinely the grounds for a 1983 action against police officers (refer to Chapter 11 for more detail on Title 42 U.S.C., Section 1983). The damages under this section can be punitive and general and cannot be limited by recent state "tort reform" movements. Rodney King brought a $56 million civil suit under this section against all of the officers that were involved in the incident and the Los Angeles Police Department, reportedly $1 million for each blow against him. He was eventually awarded $3.5 million for sustained damages. In 1990 alone, the city of Los Angeles paid about $10.5 million in successful police misconduct suits. While the courts have ruled that police officers cannot be held individually liable for most actions undertaken on the job, taxpayer concern about the rising cost of lawsuits has revived the popularity of civilian review boards.[22] Such panels are at work in 26 of the nation's 50 largest cities (e.g., Philadelphia, New York, Kansas City, Chicago).[23] Despite the increase in civil litigation and public scrutiny, brutality and scandal still persist as a major problem in policing (see Box 3-2)

## Training and Police Ethics

In response to such criticisms or as a coincidence to the most sweeping changes in American policing, law enforcement has responded with reform through community policing. A few cities have revamped their training and supervision to make abuses less likely. Since 1988, all 2,400 police officers on the Metro-Dade county force have undergone violence-reduction training. Several new movements have entered the police training arena in an effort to raise the awareness of police ethics. One such program, partially funded by the Meadows Foundation, is located at the Southwestern Law Enforcement Institute (SWLEI) in Dallas, Texas. Intensive training seminars that apply classic ethical theories to more contemporary police problems are offered. Police officer trainers who teach courses on police ethics in law enforcement academies are particularly encouraged to attend seminars led by members of well-respected ethics centers, such as the Aspen Institute and Josephson Institute.

BOX 3-2

## A Bruised Thin Blue Line

### Cases of minority abuse undermine confidence in police

**by Angie Cannon and James Morrow**

An unarmed African street vendor is killed in the entrance of his apartment building in a barrage of 41 bullets fired by four white New York cops. Five white officers go on trial this month in the brutal beating of Haitian immigrant Abner Louima in Brooklyn. A 19-year-old black woman dies in a spray of police gunfire as she lies in a car in Riverside, Calif. In Pittsburgh, a black motorist is fatally shot by a white officer after a chase. New Jersey's top cop gets sacked for remarks that seem to point to race as an unspoken factor in traffic stops.

Is there a pattern here? Ask civil rights groups or minority residents in many of the nation's cities, and they'll say the cops are out of control; that police routinely use excessive force against blacks and Hispanics. "What you get is Jim Crow justice," says Ira Glasser, head of the American Civil Liberties Union. Not so, say police officials. "I'm not suggesting that there is no such thing as abusive cops, but to suggest that they are pervasive in the NYPD, the facts just don't support it," says Howard Safir, New York's police commissioner.

Charges of police misconduct toward minorities are nothing new. Accusations of abuse sparked the riots of the '60s and the grand juries of the '70s. Those who study policing say things are probably better now. But today's troubles come at a time when expectations of police are higher.

Many departments are more effective now because of new get-tough strategies that have cut crime, especially in minority neighborhoods. So what's up? Police watchdogs say it's two sides of the same coin: Aggressive policing works only if it's accompanied by aggressive vigilance to stamp out abuses.

The anecdotal evidence of abuse is powerful, but there are no hard statistics proving that police arbitrarily target minorities. Under a 1994 anticrime law, the Justice Department was supposed to track citizen complaints and police shootings. But Congress didn't provide the funds for the task. The department is investigating charges of misconduct by several police agencies, including those of New York City; New Orleans; Columbus, Ohio; and the state of New Jersey. President Clinton recently proposed $40 million more for police training and education and an additional $2 million to beef up minority police recruitment. "I have been deeply disturbed by recent allegations of serious police misconduct and continued reports of racial profiling that have shaken some communities' faith in the police," he said.

**Picking on minorities.** Aggressive new policing tactics have reduced crime. But many minorities say they're more worried about the cops than the crooks. Take New York City, where there were 629 murders last year compared with 2,262 homicides in 1990. New York's successful crackdown has been hailed as a model for the nation. Now, though, minority and civil liberties groups as well as some criminal justice experts say the Big Apple could become a model for what not to do. The killing of vendor Amadou Diallo, 22, last month unleashed a parade of protests and charges that Mayor Rudolph Giuliani's once heralded elite street-crimes unit picks on minorities.

New York City's and other police departments are trying to remedy the problem. New Orleans police set up an early-warning system to spot cops with repeat offenses. In the Newark, N.J., suburb of East Orange, Sgt. De Lacy Davis started Black Cops Against Police Brutality to teach kids how to handle police stops. "The goal is to leave that encounter with your life and limbs intact," says the 13-year veteran. After the Diallo shooting, New York officials launched a major drive to recruit more minorities. The NYPD is now more than two-thirds white, even though the city is only 43 percent white. Police Commissioner Safir says complaints of excessive force dipped 23 percent in the past two years since he raised the age (to 22) and education requirements (candidates need at least 60 hours of college and a C average).

Law enforcement experts say the key is holding officers accountable. "In good departments, there is strong leadership and an attitude that misconduct won't be tolerated," says Samuel Walker, a University of Nebraska criminal-justice professor. A new study shows that while complaints against New York cops are up since 1993, they're down by more than half in the 42nd and 44th precincts in the South Bronx. The reason: Those commanders require their officers to treat residents with respect, says the Vera Institute of Justice, a New York research group. They hold regular training sessions and routinely meet with officers with complaints against them.

**Apology accepted.** Observers say the Los Angeles department, notorious for its poor race relations after the 1991 Rodney King beating, is making strides, too.

To date, an estimated 250 police trainers have attended the seminars, resulting in over 10,000 officers from local and county jurisdictions being instructed on police ethics. A bulletin entitled *The Ethics Role Call* and an on-line bulletin board system (BBS), which provide officer reports and vignettes focusing on ethical constraints and problems confronted "on the job,"[24] are available through the SWLEI. (Refer to Box 3-3.)

As observed by Radelet and Carter,[25] the importance of applied ethics is that they help officers develop a reasoned approach to decision making instead of making decisions by habit. As such, a solid ethical background provides a guide for officers making complex moral judgments about depriving people of

**FIGURE 3-3.** Even in routine arrests, some force is often required. However, the recent highlighted cases involving African Americans and the police have again raised issues of brutality and racism. (Courtesy Michelle Andonian, Detroit, Michigan, 1996.)

BOX 3-3

## Ethics Conference Attracts Over 120 Participants

### "Walking the Talk" is theme of keynote address

The "Ethics Net" continues to be cast further each year, as evidenced by the geographical distribution of faculty and attendees at the 4th Annual Ethics Conference held October 26–27, 1995, at the Southwestern Law Enforcement Institute. Participants came from as far as Honolulu, Hawaii, and Washington, D.C., with faculty members being drawn from such widely separated spots as Los Angeles, California, and Toronto, Canada. In addition to the keynote, general session and luncheon addresses, the conference, for the first time, utilized a "breakout session" format. Attendees reported very favorably on that structure, pointing out that they were able to participate in a range of different ethics discussions including "Ethics and S.W.A.T.," "Leadership Ethics," "Demanding Disobedience," "Teaching Ethics," "Testifying" and "Street Ethics."

In his keynote address, "Walking the Talk of Ethics," Chief Charles Moose of Portland, Oregon, provided a vivid example of the process one might follow in role modeling behavior for others to emulate. While the act of moving his family into an inner city neighborhood has not been without difficulty, few can express doubts about the sincerity of his belief that there are things each individual can do to begin "taking back the city." This theme was carried forward in both the Thursday luncheon address by Chief Ben Click, of the Dallas Police Department, and the Friday general session address by Dr. Sam Souryal of Sam Houston State University. At the Friday luncheon, Mr. Chuck Doleac, Attorney at Law and Aspen Moderator, concluded the conference by painting a verbal portrait of policing as a truly noble profession.

Another "first" this year involved scheduling the conference so that it would be held concurrently with the end of the 60th School of Police Supervision. This format allowed the thirty-six graduates to interact with other individuals from around the country who shared strong interests in the area of law enforcement ethics. Feedback from those in attendance showed that the conference provided a fitting end to the four week school, challenging the graduates to recognize the importance of "walking the talk" of ethics in both their professional and personal lives. In his succinct closing remarks, Chuck Doleac summed up the theme of the conference by proposing that successful leaders will not be content to simply "administrate" organizations, but will find ways to "nobilitate" them as well.

*Source: The Ethics Roll Call,* Volume 2, No. 4.

their liberty and sometimes their lives. Given the largely unchecked discretion police officers exercise, it is incumbent that they be given an ethical foundation to ensure their decisions are just and legal. Many police agencies, especially those actively implementing a community policing philosophy, have emphasized the importance of maintaining police integrity and ethical decision-making. For instance, many departments have written value statements that attempt to integrate ethics, departmental mission, professional responsibility, fairness, due process, and empathy.[26] (Refer to Figure 3-4.) These statements clearly articulate managerial philosophy and behavioral expectations for officers. Again, as Radelet and Carter indicate:

> These statements should leave no question in the minds of officers about the department's position and expectation concerning any form of improper behavior. Because of the "moral" implications of the values, proper behavior is urged, not out of the threat of discipline, but because this type of behavior is "right."[27]

Additionally, community policing advocates have focused on changing the philosophy of police activity from order maintenance and arrest, which often encourages "street justice" scenarios, to a more dispute-resolution, mediation, and service orientation. Some agencies have responded by sending officers into depressed neighborhoods in an attempt to protect, serve, and often befriend

## Newport News, Virginia Police Department Statement of Values

**Value #1**
The Newport News Police Department is committed to protecting and preserving the rights of individuals as guaranteed by the Constitution.

**Value #2**
While the Newport News Police Department believes the prevention of crime is its primary responsibility, it aggressively pursues those who commit serious offenses.

**Value #3**
The Newport News Police Department believes that integrity and professionalism are the foundations for trust in the community.

**Value #4**
The Newport News Police Department is committed to an open and honest relationship with the community.

**Value #5**
The Newport News Police Department is committed to effectively managing its resources for optimal service delivery.

**Value #6**
The Newport News Police Department is committed to participating in programs which incorporate the concept of shared responsibility with the community in the delivery of police services.

**Value #7**
The Newport News Police Department actively solicits citizen participation in the development of police activities and programs which impact their neighborhood.

**Value #8**
The Newport News Police Department believes it achieves its greatest potential through the active participation of its employees in the development and implementation of programs.

**Value #9**
The Newport News Police Department recognizes and supports academic achievement of employees and promotes their pursuit of higher education.

**FIGURE 3-4.** Statement on values and integrity for the Newport News, Virginia, Police Department. [Courtesy Newport News, Virginia, Police Department and Louis Radelet and David Carter, *The Police and the Community,* 5th ed. (New York: Macmillan Publishing, 1994), p. 101.]

local residents. In many cases, the results have been positive, especially among minority youth groups (refer to Chapter 2). As one report indicates, "Episodes of police brutality are likely never to vanish entirely. But they could be significantly curtailed if more officers concluded that as long as their fellow police take the law into their own hands, *there is no law at all.*"[28]

The Commission on Accreditation for Law Enforcement Agencies (CALEA) is a private, nonprofit organization. It was formed in 1979 by the four major national law enforcement associations (International Association of Chiefs of Police [IACP], National Organization of Black Law Enforcement Executives

**Commission on Accreditation for Law Enforcement Agencies**

[NOBLE], National Sheriffs' Association [NSA], and Police Executive Research Forum [PERF]). The commission has developed a national set of 900 law enforcement standards for all types and sizes of state and local agencies. In some ways, CALEA can be viewed as a direct product of the reform era to professionalize the police. Nowhere is this more apparent than in the stated goals of the commission. Its standards are designed to

- Increase agency capabilities to prevent and control crime
- Enhance agency effectiveness and efficiency in the delivery of law enforcement services
- Improve cooperation and coordination with other law enforcement agencies and with other components of the criminal justice system
- Increase citizen and staff confidence in the goals, objectives, policies, and practices of the agency.[29]

The accreditation process is a voluntary undertaking. In the last decade, significant movement toward accreditation has been spurred by two developments. First, because most of the standards identify topics and issues that must be covered by written policies and procedures, successful accreditation offers a viable defense or "liability shield" against civil litigation.[30] Second, CALEA provides a nationwide system for change.[31] One of the most important parts of the accreditation process is self-assessment. During this stage, agencies undergo a critical self-evaluation that addresses the complete gamut of services provided by law enforcement. The agency is also later assessed by an on-site team of law enforcement professionals to determine whether it has complied with the applicable standards for a department of its type and size.

CALEA enjoys wide support among police executives and community leaders. In particular, when a city manager is seeking to hire a new police chief from outside of a troubled department, experience of candidates with the accreditation process is a substantial plus. In one city, officers received information on Christmas Eve that a rapist who had beaten and cut his victims was in a house in a county outside of their jurisdiction. Without any significant evaluation of the information, without a raid plan, using personnel who were untrained or had not previously trained together for conducting raids, and without a search warrant, the officers conducted a raid, killed a 74-year-old man in his own home who had no connection with the crime, and found out the rapist had never been there. In the aftermath, the community lost confidence in its police department. A member of the grand jury asked the police chief, "How do I know that your officers won't kill me or members of my family in my home tonight?" Departmental morale plunged to an all-time low. A management study of the department revealed that written policies and procedures were virtually nonexistent and identified other deficiencies as well. The chief of police retired, and a new chief was brought in from the outside with orders from the city manager to get the department accredited. In the process of accomplishing accreditation, the department regained its esprit de corps and the support of the community. The city manager said he believed that "no other mechanism besides accreditation could have done so much good so quickly in turning the department around."

Despite similar accounts and the reduction of liability risks that typically accompanies accreditation, the process is not without its critics. Some see it as "window dressing . . . long on show and short on substance"—a reference to the fact that some departments allegedly develop the necessary policies to meet the standards and then fail to follow them. Some city managers are reluctant to authorize their police departments to enter a process that takes an average of twenty-one months to complete at an average cost of $73,708.[32] This cost includes the modest CALEA accreditation fee, which ranges from $3,800 for a department with up to nine full-time employees to $14,700 for agencies with 3,000 or more full-time employees.[33] Other components of the average cost of accreditation include direct costs, such as purchases necessary to meet standards (e.g., first aid kits for all cars, body armor for special weapons, and tactics teams), modifications to facilities or capabilities (e.g., upgrading the evidence storage area and radio communication), and indirect costs, such as the cost of personnel actually doing the work necessary to meet standards (e.g., writing policies and procedures).[34] Others have maintained that the process is control oriented and at odds with important values set forth in community policing, such as individual initiative, participatory management, and organizational democracy. (Refer to Chapter 2 for a more thorough discussion of the perceived conflict between CALEA standards and community policing.)

In balance, however, it is clear that accreditation is an important national influence because it requires both self-scrutiny and external evaluation in determining the extent to which a law enforcement agency has met the 900 standards promulgated by experts in the field. It serves as a liability shield, promotes pride among employees, and stimulates confidence among the community. Moreover, it can play an important role in the economic development of a community. Business people seeking to relocate evaluate the communities they are considering on the basis of transportation, taxation, recreational opportunities, and the ability of local government to conduct its affairs professionally. In one instance a well-managed city of 300,000 lost a major prospective employer to another city due to one salient factor: the police department in the other city was accredited. As soon as this fact became known, the mayor directed the police chief to pursue accreditation by CALEA as a "top priority."

## THE ROLES OF STATE AND LOCAL GOVERNMENT IN LAW ENFORCEMENT

From the outset most Americans had a firm belief that the police should be controlled by local officials organized along municipal lines. For them, a national police, such as the Italian *carabinieri,* was inconceivable, and a state police, such as the German *polizei,* was undesirable.[35] However, the history of state and local relations in the area of law enforcement has often been a rocky and tumultuous one. Fogelson, for example, has noted that:

> By the mid-nineteenth century, it was plain that for most police departments local control meant Democratic control. Hence the Republican leaders, who generally spoke for the upper middle and upper classes, demanded state control, arguing that it would remove the police from partisan politics and improve the quality of law enforcement. Their Democratic opponents countered that state control would merely shift the focus of political interference and plainly violate the principle of self-government. The issue erupted in one city after another, with the Republicans usually getting their way. They imposed state control of the police in New York City in 1857, Detroit in 1865, Cleveland in 1866, New Orleans in 1868, Cincinnati in 1877, Boston in 1885, and Omaha in 1887. They also established metropolitan police departments, with jurisdiction over the central city and adjacent territory, in New York City in 1857, Albany in 1865, and a few other places thereafter.

Under these arrangements the state authorities appointed a board to manage, or at any rate to oversee, the big-city police. But the states did not contribute anything toward the upkeep of the police departments; nor, except in a few cases, did they authorize them to operate in the metropolitan area, much less throughout the entire state. Not until the early twentieth century did Pennsylvania, New York, and a few other states form statewide constabularies; and these forces, which patrolled mainly in small towns and rural districts, supplemented rather than supplanted the municipal police. Thus despite these changes, the American police remained decentralized to a degree unheard of anywhere in Western Europe. By the late nineteenth century, moreover, state control was well on the wane. The Democrats attacked it at every opportunity; and in the face of mounting evidence that the state boards had neither removed the police from partisan politics nor improved the quality of law enforcement, the Republicans were hard pressed to defend it. The issue was soon resolved, usually when the Democrats took office. The state authorities not only abolished metropolitan policing in New York and Albany in 1870 but also reestablished local control in Cleveland in 1868, New York in 1870, New Orleans in 1877, Cincinnati in 1880, Detroit in 1891, and Omaha in 1897. By 1900 the big-city police were controlled by local officials and organized along municipal lines everywhere in urban America except for Boston, Baltimore, St. Louis, Kansas City, and a few other places.[36]

The type of direct takeover of local law enforcement by the states described by Fogelson will very likely not occur again or at least not on the grand scale of the 1800s. However, we may see some isolated cases. For example, a decade ago some public officials in Georgia were urging the state to take over the administration of the Atlanta Police Department because of dramatic political upheavals that were affecting the morale and effectiveness of that department. A takeover by the state did not occur, but the political atmosphere was conducive to such a move.

Even if a state does not exercise its official political power to intervene in local police administration, it may be called on to exercise its influence in less apparent ways, in which case the influence may not always be proper or appropriate:

> Our department was going through a major reorganization and in the process was going to have to make about 50 promotions. One of the newly created positions was deputy chief. The only requirement for the position was that you had to have been a Major for one year. "Ed Hawks" had been a Major for about 8 months and he really wanted that deputy chief's position. Nobody believed that he even had a chance. He went to his cousin, who was close to the Governor, and talked to him. The Governor called the Mayor and expressed his "confidence" in what a great deputy chief Hawks would make. The mayor's son sat as a political appointee of the Governor on one of the most important state boards. So, the Mayor sat on the reorganization plan until the day after Ed Hawks had a year in grade as a Major—which meant that 50 promotions were held up for about four months—and then approved the implementation of the plan. . . . Hawks got promoted . . . crap like that is really demoralizing.[37]

In a positive vein, the impact of the state on the affairs of local law enforcement is continuing via the imposition of preemployment and training standards as well as through various funding formulas tied to these standards. The first state to impose minimum standards of training for police officers was California, in 1959. This move was soon followed by the states of New York,

Oklahoma, and Oregon. In 1970, the LEAA did make available discretionary grants to those states that wanted to implement minimum standards programs. Today all 50 states have mandated training for law enforcement officers. It must be noted, however, that much of the impetus for the implementation of minimum standards on a statewide basis comes from the local law enforcement community. Requirements related to the minimum standards for employment as police officers are administered through state organizations, often termed Police Officers Standards and Training Commissions (POST), which generally operate under three broad mandates: (1) to establish minimum standards for employment in a state, county, or local law enforcement agency; (2) to articulate curricula of training for police officers; and (3) to conduct and encourage research designed to improve all aspects of law enforcement.[38]

In its assessment of the role of the states in criminal justice planning, in general the National Advisory Commission on Criminal Justice Standards and Goals suggested that the State Planning Agencies (SPAs), which were created by the Omnibus Crime Control and Safe Streets Act of 1968 as the state-level organizations through which federal funds were funneled from the LEAA, bear a special responsibility for the formation of minimum statewide standards.[39] However, with the demise of LEAA in 1982 there has been a reduction or total dismantling of large state planning agencies.

## LOCAL POLITICAL FORCES

The special dimension of police politics varies from community to community, but law enforcement activities are governed for the most part by the dominant values of the local political culture.

James Q. Wilson, in his now-classic study of the police in eight communities, identified three distinctly different styles of law enforcement, all of which were reflective of the political culture of the communities they serve: (1) the "watchman" style of law enforcement emphasizes order maintenance and is found in economically declining cities with traditional political machines; (2) the "legalistic" style of law enforcement is found in cities with heterogeneous populations and reform-oriented, professional governments; law enforcement of both a reactive and proactive nature characterizes this style; and (3) in the homogeneous suburban communities, the "service" style of law enforcement is oriented toward the needs of citizens.[40]

In Wilson's studies, these variations in the community political culture manifested themselves in a number of ways that subsequently affected both the qualitative and the quantitative enforcement action taken by the police. Significant enforcement variations emerged in the areas of vice, juvenile offenses, order maintenance, and traffic enforcement. Numerous variations, linked to the community's political culture, also emerged in the police department's personnel entry standards, promotional policies, extent of specialization, and level of managerial skills. These, in turn, affected the overall operations of the department, which in turn impacted on the citizens' perception and confidence in its police department.

As indicated earlier, there is an unfailing, consistent, and close relationship between the type of law enforcement a community has and its dominant political culture. This is not to suggest, however, that any community's political culture is unalterably fixed. In fact, the reform movements that have been a part of the American political scene throughout much of its history have corresponded with the emergence of new political cultures. Each new dominant political culture in time leaves its own unique mark on the unit of government within its sphere of control.

## Strong Mayor

To some extent, the type of local government that a community has will have impact on the way police chiefs are selected, the freedom they will enjoy in the performance of their status, and their tenure. For example, with a strong mayor form of government, the mayor is elected to office and serves as the chief executive of the city. The city council constitutes the chief legislative and policy-making body. The mayor nominates a candidate to serve as police chief, with majority approval needed from the city council. Once approved, the candidate assumes the position of police chief and serves at the discretion of the mayor.

Ideally, the person selected by the mayor as police chief should possess the full range of managerial and administrative skills necessary to operate the police department. However, to a great extent, the kind of persons selected to serve as police chief will be determined by the mayor's professional qualifications, philosophy about the role of law enforcement, and political commitments. If the mayor is endowed with sound business or public administration skills and also has a "good government" philosophy, then the chief of police will very likely be selected on the basis of professional abilities rather than extraneous political factors. Unfortunately, on too many occasions in the past, this appointment has been a method of repaying political favors. A classical case of the misuse of this appointing authority was illustrated by the Wickersham Commission in 1931:

> . . . a few years ago the mayor of Indianapolis was called upon to introduce the police chief of that city to an assemblage of police chiefs during one of their conferences. In the course of his introductory remarks, the mayor said, "I know that my man is going to be a good chief because he has been my tailor for 20 years. He knows how to make good clothes; he ought to be a good chief."[41]

No big-city mayor would make this same choice today, but the choice will nevertheless still be a reflection of the mayor's personal value system and abilities, and of the political environment of the community.

In the strong mayor form of local government, the tenure of the chief of police is often linked directly to the mayor, and the nature of the relationship is such that the chief is quite dependent on the mayor for support and guidance on budgetary matters, enforcement practices, and a multitude of other areas essential to the overall success of the police department. If there is mutual respect between the police chief and the mayor, a strong professional and political bond will be formed. If the reverse holds true, however, significant antagonisms may begin to emerge. There are too many situations to enumerate positively or negatively that can affect the working relationship between a mayor and a police chief. One finds that the important differences that do emerge are frequently those that evolve out of philosophical and ethical differences rather than questions of legality. These are differences that can occur in any form of government.

## City Manager

There is no lack of supporters or detractors for every form of local government found in the United States. The proponents of the city manager form claim that it provides the most conducive atmosphere in which professional law enforcement can operate and minimizes external interference from outside controls. One of the reasons for this assessment is the balancing mechanisms developed over the years that are typically inherent in the city manager form of government: (1) the city manager is accountable to the elected members of the city council as a body rather than to any individual council member; (2) individual council members are prevented (by law of council rules) from giving administrative, operational, or policy direction to the city manager; (3) the council as a body may not give specific administrative direction to the city manager, who generally has exclusive executive authority over the city employees; (4) the city manager, consistent with civil service statutes and subject to employee appeals, has full authority to hire, promote, and discipline city personnel; (5) the city manager has broad authority within state municipal financial statutes to manage the budget and to depart from line item appropriations to meet unanticipated needs; and (6) the council as a body hires the city manager and may dismiss the city manager in its discretion without stating its cause. The city manager model is significant because it has been clearly successful in the American local political milieu and because its separation of the political policymaking body and the independent chief executive is realistically defined.[42]

The city manager more often than not is a professional administrator who is recruited for certain skills and training and appointed by the city council. A person with this background tends to make sincere efforts to select a competent individual to serve as police chief, because the manager's professional reputation is tied inextricably to the effective management of the city departments.

It is significant that city managers have sought qualified police chiefs and that they have in most instances based their selection on the professional qualifications of the candidate rather than on political or other extraneous considerations that too often have governed appointments to this position in the past.[43] This does not mean that the city manager form of government removes the chief from local politics, but it does create more distance and insulation than the one-to-one political relationship commonly found in the strong mayor form of government.

**City Councils**

The legally defined roles of city councils are fairly consistent throughout the United States; namely, they act as the chief legislative and policymaking body. Through its ordinance power, subject to constitutional and statutory provisions, including the city charter, the council carries out its legislative function; when within its authority, its enactments have the force of law and are binding on both administration and electorate. In addition to legislative and policymaking functions, the council, in common with most legislative bodies, holds the purse strings and exercises control over appropriations.[44] Thus, the immediate impact of a council's actions on the operation of a law enforcement agency is considerable.

The record of involvement by council members and other elected officials in police operations to the detriment of both the efficiency and effectiveness of the police establishment is a well-established fact. One observer of this problem has noted that:

> Local political leaders frequently promote more abuses of police power than they deter. In seeking favored treatment for a violator of the law or in exerting pressure

for police assistance in the sale of tickets to a fund-raising dinner, the politician only encourages the type of behavior he is supposed to prevent. Although such political interference into police work is not as extensive as it once was, it still exists.[45]

James F. Ahern, former chief of the New Haven, Connecticut, Police Department, discusses this issue at length in his book *Police in Trouble*. He describes as follows the extent to which political forces negatively affected the New Haven Police Department and the course of action he took to nullify them:

> There is nothing more degrading or demoralizing to a police department than the knowledge that every favor or promotion within it is controlled by hack politicians and outright criminals. And there is nothing more nearly universal. Five years ago, anyone with the most superficial knowledge of the workings of the New Haven Police Department could point to the political power behind every captain on the force. Every cop who wanted to get ahead had his "hook"—or, as they say in New York, his "rabbi." Everyone owed his success to a politician—from the Town Chairman on down—or to an influential underworld figure. Needless to say, in a situation like this there was no chance whatever of the department functioning in the public interest.
>
> A day after I had taken office, I closed the second-story back door to the Mayor's office and issued a renewal of a long-standing and long-ignored departmental order prohibiting any police officer from seeing the Mayor without the authorization of the chief.
>
> Given the incredible tangle of grimy politics that still existed in the lower levels of government and in the structures of the city's political parties, this action was largely symbolic. But as a gesture it was necessary. It would be immediately evident to everyone in the police department that if I would not permit the Mayor who had appointed me to influence departmental promotions or assignments, I certainly would allow no other politicians to influence them.
>
> Mayor Lee was aware of the connections between politics and police and was himself capable of intervening in the affairs of the police department to advance cops whom he considered honest and effective who otherwise would have been buried. Riding home with the Mayor in a car one day, I showed him a draft of my order. He frowned slightly, nodded, and then approved.
>
> But this order was only the opening shot in the war to end political interference in the police department. The far more substantive challenge was to make clear in every way possible, to every man in the department, that political influence of any kind was out. There was only one way to handle the problem, and it was somewhat heavy-handed. The men were made responsible for stopping interference themselves. They were warned that if politicians or underworld figures approached me with requests for promotions, transfers, or easy assignments for cops, the officers in question would be barred permanently from those positions.
>
> The immediate reaction among the cops was total incredulity. Political maneuvering had been the basis for advancement in the department for so long that it was doubtful whether they believed there was another way to be promoted. I would not be surprised if they thought that promotions in the department would freeze until I resigned or retired. But they did believe me. And they did convey the message to their hooks. For the time being, political interference in the department all but stopped.[46]

To suggest that the experience of New Haven is typical of most communities would be an inaccurate generalization, but there is little doubt that the council's fiscal control over the police department's budget and its legislative powers make it a political force that is never taken lightly by chiefs of police.

As a matter of fact, most police chiefs will go to great lengths to maintain the goodwill and support of their council members.

A study conducted in California showed that the average tenure of a police chief in that state was less than three years before the chief was fired or resigned.[47] Even though the tenure of police chiefs across the nation has somewhat improved since that time, the national average is still only about five years.[48] Of course, the reasons for change are numerous, including movement to another (oftentimes larger) police department, resignation, retirement, and, of course, dismissal. Much has been written about the need for some type of protection for police chiefs against the arbitrary and unjustified removal from office by an elected or political officeholder.[49] In some states, such as Illinois, statutory protections have been implemented to protect police chiefs against such actions. Special boards or commissions have been created for the sole purpose of establishing recruitment, selection, and retention policies for chiefs of police. In Illinois, the law prohibits the removal or discharge of a member of the fire or police department (including the chief) without cause; the individual must also be given written charges and an opportunity to be heard in his or her defense. While this is a state mandate, these protections are available only when there is no local ordinance prescribing a different procedure. If such an ordinance exists, the statute requires the municipal appointing authority to file the reasons for the chief's removal but does not require a showing of cause or a hearing.

New Hampshire affords significant protection to police chiefs. It requires written notice of the basis for the proposed termination, a hearing on the charges, and a finding of cause before the dismissal can be effected. Minnesota, on the other hand, provides no mandatory protections for police chiefs but does require that they be included in any civil service system adopted by a municipality.

A few other states have attempted to provide police chiefs with at least some job security whenever they have been promoted from within the ranks of the police department. Both Illinois and Ohio allow chiefs who resign or who are removed from their positions to return to the ranks they held within their departments before being appointed chiefs. Most states, however, offer very little protection.

Chiefs across the country are therefore forced to look for job protections in local civil service codes, local municipal ordinances, and such individual employment contracts as they are able to negotiate.[50]

However, for the most part, the ability to endure the realities of the position of chief of police requires a unique blend of talent, skill, and knowledge which are often not "guaranteed" in statute or law. The reality is that few protections exist for persons occupying the highest position of a police agency except for those developed in the person themselves. That is to say, the characteristics and qualities of excellent management and leadership imbued in the person are generally the reasons that a chief remains in office.

## THE POLICE CHIEF AND EXTERNAL INCIDENTS

Being a chief of police is difficult enough in a normal situation in which both internal and external factors often make it hard for the police chief to discern the public interest.[51] However, it is tolerable only if time and effort are available to solve a problem. Some situations and conflicts, however, are outside the chief's control, yet their occurrence may cost the police chief his or her job. Mintzberg[52] refers to these conflicts as "political arenas" and divides them into three types based on their duration, intensity, and pervasiveness.

The first type of political arena is "confrontation." In this most common type, the situational conflict is intense but brief and confined. An obvious example is the Rodney King incident, which occurred several years ago and put an end to the contract of Daryl Gates as the Los Angeles Chief of Police. The second political arena is a "shaky alliance," in which conflict is less intense but still pervasive. A shaky alliance may be a sequel to a confrontational situation. Chief Willie Williams, Daryl Gates's successor and the first outsider appointed as chief in over forty years, had to deal with both external (i.e., the impact of the King incident on the public) and internal pressures (i.e., resentful feelings from his own police officers). This was a shaky alliance, and at the end of his term in 1997, Williams's contract was not renewed. The third type of political arena, a "politicized organization," features pervasive but muted conflict that is tolerable for a time. This kind of conflict is commonplace in American policing, and survival of the agency's police chief depends on external support. Examples include riots resulting from allegations of police brutality such as those in 1996 in St. Petersburg, Florida, or the protracted JonBenet Ramsey homicide investigation in Boulder, Colorado. The "complete" political arena is the final situation in which the conflict is pervasive, intense, brief, and out of control. Fortunately, police chiefs seldom face this type of conflict. However, when it does occur, termination becomes a real possibility. Because of the common occurrence of the third type, the politicized organization arena, several expanded cases are offered.

In the St. Petersburg example, riots began on Thursday night, October 25, 1996, after a white police officer shot and killed a black man driving a stolen car. Police Chief Darrel Stephens was considered by many both within the community and law enforcement as an enlightened visionary leader. The front-page story on October 30, in the *St. Petersburg Times* reflected Stephens' philosophy:

> I've always believed that we would be able to keep something like this from happening. Personally, you look at what's happening and you have lots of questions about what more we could have done in this situation to keep it from developing. . . . In many respects, his [Stephens] actions at the scene reflect a policing philosophy and management style that have brought national attention to the St. Petersburg force, but have frustrated officers who prefer a tougher approach to crime or see the department as understaffed and overworked. Stephens now finds himself facing new scrutiny. Last Thursday's violence has been his administration's biggest crisis since he was hired in December 1992 to restore morale in a department troubled by racial friction and political factions.[53]

An editorial entitled "Help Stephens Succeed" in the *St. Petersburg Times,* on October 31, 1996, reported that,

> One casualty of the riot in south St. Petersburg could be the city's common sense approach to law enforcement community policing. That would be a shame and a setback for citizens, both black and white. In the aftermath of the fatal shooting . . . by a police officer and the ensuing chaos, some people are criticizing Police Chief Darrel Stephens' approach to law enforcement and his tempered reaction to rioters. Emotion rules such arguments and ignores history. Stephens was hired

four years ago to return stability and respect to the police department after the firing of combative Chief Ernest "Curt" Curtsinger. An expert on community policing, Stephens took some officers out of their patrol cars and put them in neighborhoods to help residents solve their problems. . . . Community policing cannot be expected to resolve the broader problems in St. Petersburg's poor black neighborhoods unemployment, broken families and the hopelessness of poverty. Those who hold the police responsible for such breaches in the nation's social fabric are misguided. Instead, St. Petersburg residents—both black and white—should be asking how they can help Stephens succeed. Black residents can invite police officers into their communities and offer their help. White residents can support measures that strengthen Stephens' work. We should not let the emotion of the moment stop progress toward a police force that serves all citizens.[54]

It is interesting that in the third arena of politicized support, not only did Stephens have the support of the *St. Petersburg Times* editorial staff, he also had the mayor's continued political support. On reelection to a second term, the mayor asked Stephens to become the city administrator for St. Petersburg in June 1997. The mayor and newly promoted city administrator quickly named a new police chief, an African American with a Ph.D., from within the ranks of the department. This all occurred within the span of several days during June.

In the JonBenet Ramsey murder investigation in Boulder, Colorado, Police Chief Tom Koby, the Boulder Police Department and the entire city of Boulder have been under intense national media scrutiny since the murder of the six-year-old JonBenet Ramsey on December 26, 1996. Both of Denver's major newspapers, the *Denver Post* and the *Rocky Mountain News* have been openly critical of the investigation and of Chief Koby. On June 8, 1997, an article in the *Rocky Mountain News* was titled "Ramsey Case a Tragedy of Errors." Similarly, the *Denver Post* printed the following headlines: "Cops Grumpy with Koby," "DA Brushes Off Koby Problems," "Is the Trail Too Cold?" "Mute Leaders," "Cops' Vote on Koby Negative," and "It's Ludicrous." As a yet unproductive (as this debate was finalized) investigation in a city in which murder cases are rare—and an unsolved murder case unheard of—it would appear that this case has polarized the department and city politicians. As a May 30, 1997, column in the *Denver Post* noted:

> Here is a glimpse into the inner workings of the city of Boulder: The troops, by a vote of 2 to 1 say they have lost confidence in Police Chief Tom Koby. Spense Havlik, deputy mayor of Boulder was "quite surprised" by the vote. Havlik must have spent most of April and May on Comet Hale-Bopp. Havlik's incredulous statement underscores a mystery as mystifying as JonBenet Ramsey's murder itself—where is the political and moral leadership in Boulder? Just like Chief Koby and District Attorney Alex Hunter—the two men supervising the investigation of the murder—Havlik doesn't have a clue. While the rank-and-file cops have no confidence in Koby, Councilman Havlik and most other political officers in the city are heartily endorsing the city's beleaguered police chief. Leading the parade for Koby are Mayor Leslie Durgin and City Manager Tim Honey, two people who also were surprised by the rank-and-file vote on Koby.[55]

On May 29, members of Boulder's police union voted 78 to 31 that they had no confidence in Chief Tom Koby's leadership. The vote came amidst rumblings that Boulder's elected officials were displeased with Koby's boss, City Manager Tim Honey (*Denver Post*, May 30, 1997). On June 8, 1997, the Rocky Mountain News reported "the night that Boulder City Manager Tim Honey tendered his forced resignation to the city council, he said, 'this investigation is going to lead to an arrest.' "

Chief Koby announced he would retire at the end of 1998, but his tenure as chief of police ended on June 28, 1998, when he was forced to step down by an acting city manager. He was terminated because of a combination of factors, including little or no support from the media, crumbling or divided political support within the city council, and support from less than 40 percent of the department's rank and file.

Without support from the mayor and the media, it is quite unlikely that Stephens would have been promoted to city administrator and may indeed have been in a situation similar to the one Koby experienced. Conversely, had Koby received positive editorials and strong political and rank and file support, it is likely his situation would have turned out differently.

In several cases, police chiefs either were terminated or their contracts were not renewed despite the lack of valid grounds. For example, the mayor of Cleveland, Ohio, ousted three police chiefs in a four-year period for political reasons. In 1992, Police Chief Elizabeth Watson was terminated by the newly elected mayor in Houston, Texas, because of her advocacy of community-oriented policing. She was criticized for reducing the effectiveness of the police as crime fighters. In 1996, Police Chief Philip Arreola of Milwaukee, Wisconsin, was forced to resign because of his failure to satisfy all of the constituencies. Police Commissioner William Bratton of New York was forced to resign after only twenty-seven months in the position, despite the fact that during his administration the city experienced the largest two-year decline of crime in its history.

Being a police chief today is very difficult. Chiefs can be terminated or forced to resign either because they do things too progressively or quickly (as in the case of Chiefs Watson and Arreola) or because they are perceived as doing things too slowly (as in the case of Chief Williams). Chiefs can even be forced to resign when their tenure is considered successful, as in the case of Commissioner Bratton.[56]

Should police chiefs be allowed to keep their positions if there is no evidence that they are incompetent, unethical, or involved in illegal activities? Should chiefs be terminated only for cause and not for personal or political reasons? Unfortunately, terminating police chiefs has become the norm. A recent Los Angeles city charter change guaranteed that no one will ever again hold the position as long as Gates did. In other cities where chiefs serve at the mayor's pleasure, they are virtually assured of a brief stay. All of the examples cited here are occurring at a time when big-city police chiefs as a group are more educated, more skilled at public relations, and better trained in management than ever before. Even the most adroit police chief tends to run into political conflicts. Whether by his or her own choice or by the mayor's or city manager's command, the chief is frequently terminated within a few years of a much-publicized arrival.[57]

Organizationally, replacing chiefs every few years can leave a department in a seemingly never-ending spiral of change, as each new chief strives to remedy the problems he or she was hired to solve and to create a loyal and cohesive command staff. Worse is the possibility that meaningful progress is not attempted because the rank and file believe that it is futile to begin a project that will never be finished: Just as progress is begun, there very likely will be another change.

Police chiefs who lack protection from arbitrary and unjustified termination cannot objectively and independently fulfill their responsibilities. The average tenure of most police chiefs is three to six years. For their contracts (an extremely limited number of actually formal contractual cases exist) to be renewed at the end of the term, or their status as an at-will appointee to be continued, compromises of the chief's sense of responsibility may be necessary, especially if his or her decisions run counter to those of city officials. A discussion of the lack of a reappointment agreement for Milwaukee's former Chief Philip Arreola states,

> He wasn't exactly fired, but months before his scheduled reappointment for a second term, word simply filtered out of City Hall that Mayor John O. Norquist no longer saw eye to eye with the chief. It was not a matter of scandal or of incompetence, it was a case of political failure—too many constituencies, all with clear-cut agendas, and no way to satisfy all of them at once. . . . It may seem curious for a city to can a respected police chief without any whiff of impropriety or misconduct, but in fact it is the norm these days, not the exception. The sacking of the police chief is part of the routine in urban America.[58]

The advent of community policing as the evolving contemporary policing strategy emphasizes enhanced relations between the police and the public and demands that police chiefs possess new skills and attitudes and become effective visionary leaders. In other words, chiefs must not be reluctant to pioneer innovative programs geared toward community problem-solving policing goals. The inherent risks, however, are obvious, and failure of these high-profile public projects may jeopardize the chief's position.

For a moment, let's consider where police chiefs come from. Most top police executives today, as in the past, reach their position as police chief in the twilight of their policing careers. Charles Gain, former chief of the Oakland, California, Police Department, argued that police chiefs in this twilight period tend to resist organizational change because they fear the loss of the position for which they have so long waited, and as they are in the final stages of their career, they engage in a "holding action"[59] Gain further comments that when chiefs make it to the top, they are not going to jeopardize their position by setting new goals and moving ahead.[60]

One researcher cites another example as demonstration of this bankrupt leadership style. Researchers of the Police Executive Development Project at Pennsylvania State University found that top police executives showed greater devotion for their personal moral standards than for the citizens they serve. Findings also indicated that top police executives showed greater submission to authority than does the general public. This subservient attitude has been formed as a result of working in a rigid organizational structure that demands and rewards obedience to authority.[61] The results of the project indicated that the average police executive failed to possess initiative, self-reliance, and confidence, because of a lifelong habit of submission and social conformity. The study concluded that these findings correlate to some extent with the suggestion that police chiefs tend to treat their job as a sinecure and are incapable of innovation at this late stage in their police careers.[62] Without some form of contract protection, it is difficult to expect any police chief to jeopardize his or her job by implementing a vision or a program that has any chance of failure.

**Future Trends**    In spite of the previous lack of job security for big-city police chiefs there is some evidence in some cases that this may be changing, in part because of the recent dramatic decrease in crime, a strong economy, and the desire of local government to improve services to its citizens (see Box 3-4).

## BOX 3-4

### Flush and Crime-Wary Cities Bid Up Pay for Police Chiefs

by Michael Janofsky

WASHINGTON, April 9—When the District of Columbia considered hiring the New Orleans Police Superintendent, Richard Pennington, as the capital's police chief, city officials in New Orleans did everything they could to keep him happy where he was.

That included the offer of a four-year contract with a raise of 50 percent, to $150,000, making Superintendent Pennington New Orleans's highest-paid city employee. Washington, meanwhile, turned to Charles H. Ramsey, second-in-command of the Chicago Police Department, offering him $150,000, which is $60,000 more than Mayor Marion S. Barry Jr. is paid and $40,000 more than Mr. Ramsey made in Chicago.

"I was really flattered," Mr. Pennington said of the competition for him. "I didn't want to start a bidding war. But when my Mayor said he would match whatever Washington was offering, that made me feel very comfortable."

With crime rates falling dramatically in many places around the country and a strong economy bolstering efforts by local governments to improve services, candidates for police chief with a proven record of success have become municipal superstars. Like free agents in baseball and highly skilled corporate executives, they are intensely recruited and highly paid—whether by the cities that lure them away or the cities that keep them in place.

Police chiefs are benefiting from the plummeting crime rates, though the reasons for the decline are the subject of debate. Some experts have cited other factors—including an aging criminal population and the weakening of the crack cocaine epidemic—as having had more impact on crime statistics than police work has had.

Nonetheless, a recent survey by the Police Executive Research Forum in Washington, which helps local governments find candidates for police chief, found that 25 percent of chiefs in cities with at least 50,000 people earned annual salaries of more than $100,000. One of the highest-paid chiefs,

Paul Meredith for The New York Times.    Alex Brandon for The New York Times.

Charles H. Ramsey, left, was named Washington's police chief after Richard Pennington, right, a candidate for the post, received a 50 percent raise to stay at the helm of the New Orleans Police Department.

Bernard C. Parks, who replaced Willie L. Williams last year in Los Angeles, is paid more than $200,000.

Mr. Pennington said he was the first New Orleans police superintendent to be given a contract.

The competition for talented municipal executives is not limited to police chiefs. With the Federal Government shifting more responsibility—and money—to the states to run programs, and states giving local governments more leeway in administering them, skilled executives recruited to lead welfare, public works and other municipal agencies are hot properties.

Officials in San Jose, Calif., searched two years for a director of information technology, offering an annual salary of $105,000, but they could not find a suitable candidate for that salary. They finally filled the position in February, hiring Ken Phillips, a computer company executive from Oregon, for about $140,000 a year.

"I've never seen anything like this," Normal Roberts, president of a Los Angeles company that helps local governments identify qualified candidates for senior positions, said of the salaries that leading candidates are winning. "In the last six months, at least 15 to 20 percent of all our recommended candidates have gotten offers, then counter offers to stay." In general, recruiters said, the demand for highly qualified department heads stemmed from the recession of the early 1990s, when many local governments were forced to pare their employment roles to avoid budget deficits. That often meant saving money by eliminating middle management positions.

But those cuts had a longer range impact, depleting future candidate pools in police departments and other government agencies for higher positions. Now, with the economy flush again and local governments eager to restore cannibalized departments, superior candidates for senior positions are widely sought.

Perhaps no candidates find themselves more coveted than a police chief or a second-in-command who can claim that his strategies of community policing helped drive down crime rates. In the early 1990s, when homicide and crack cocaine seemed unbeatable, many big cities fought their way through with strategies devised by their police chiefs.

Now, with murder rates dropping by as much as a third in some cities like New York and Minneapolis—although for reasons that remain the subject of heated debate—police chiefs like Mr. Pennington have become heroes in their cities with popularity ratings as high as any in the local government. In New Orleans, the murder rate has fallen by 40 percent over the last three years.

One of the biggest stars, William J. Bratton, the former New York City Police Commissioner and a former Boston police commander, has written a book, "Turnaround: How America's Top Cop Reversed the Crime Epidemic." Some of his senior disciples have been heavily recruited elsewhere, including John F. Timoney, who was recently named police commissioner in Philadelphia for $113,000 a year.

In most places, safe streets and neighborhoods contribute to a strong local tax base and civic pride, but only recently are police chiefs being recognized for the crucial role their programs play in the economic stability of a city or county.

"They have a huge impact on property values, the commercial viability of the community and the eagerness of people to enjoy themselves in public places," said Thomas C. Frazier, the Police Commissioner in Baltimore, where crime has fallen during his four years in charge. "They bring a lot of value added."

Police officials generally agree that police departments that are running smoothly promote from within when the job of chief becomes vacant. Outside candidates like Mr. Ramsey in Washington, are usually sought when past policies have failed, or corruption in the department demands that city leaders look elsewhere. The District's previous chief, Larry D. Soulsby, resigned last November amid ethical questions.

The Police Executive Research Forum survey, which polled 358 chiefs in cities with populations of 50,000 or more last September, found that 56.7 per-

cent of them had been promoted from within and 42.2 percent came from outside, a breakdown that has remained relatively constant over the years, said Chuck Wexler, the forum's executive director.

In either case, police chief is no longer the job it once was, simply marshaling forces to respond to one 911 call after another. Policing has changed dramatically in recent years, from reacting to crime to preventing it through a decentralized approach called community policing.

For the chief, that means developing programs that involve the department with citizens and community groups to help identify problems, devise solutions tailored to the neighborhood and evaluate results.

Even smaller communities now demand that their chief be well-schooled in community policing. "That was a big thing to us," said Kurt Kimball, city manager of Grand Rapids, Mich., who led a search that ended last month with the hiring of Harry Dolan, the police chief of Lumberton, N.C.

"The more he talked the talk, the more we realized he had walked the walk, albeit in a town one-tenth the size of ours," Mr. Kimball said of Mr. Dolan. "He even operated the police substations he set up."

Grand Rapids agreed to pay Mr. Dolan an annual salary of $80,000, a 53 percent increase over the $52,000 he was paid in Lumberton.

The higher salaries chiefs now receive also reflect a wider range of responsibilities. In addition to implementing new policing ideas, many chiefs, particularly those hired to lead departments in mid-sized and large cities, are involved more than ever with managerial issues, like budgets, union contracts, grievances, arbitration hearings and computer technology.

"It's a much different emphasis from years ago," said Dan Rosenblatt, executive director of the International Association of Police Chiefs in Washington, noting the shift from the image of chief as crime fighter. "These people are now like C.E.O.'s of major corporations."

With the expanding demands on a chief's time, many highly recruited candidates are far more educated than their predecessors of decades ago. Lee Brown, the Mayor of Houston who was New York City's police commissioner from 1990 to 1992 and Houston's police chief before that, said the first chief he worked under, in San Jose, had only a high school education. Houston's current chief, Clarence O. Bradford, has a law degree from the University of Houston.

The survey conducted by the Police Executive Research Forum found that more than half the

(continued)

## BOX 3-4 (continued)

chiefs who responded had a master's, doctoral or law degree.

"We always hear the same thing," said Mr. Wexler, the forum's executive director. "Cities want a strong leader, who is a visionary, a good manager, one with impeccable integrity and character and someone willing to move the department ahead. The competition to find them is fierce, and cities that have one want to hold on to him."

But just as the occasional free agent bats only .200 for his new team, some heavily recruited chiefs fail at their mission or do not survive the politics of the city. In New York, Mr. Bratton resigned in 1996 after crime had dropped significantly on his watch but amid tense relations with Mayor Rudolph W. Giuliani over who was responsible for it.

Some of Mr. Bratton's supporters have said the reason for the tension was the former commissioner's popularity, which rivaled that of his boss.

Mr. Williams, who built a strong reputation as Philadelphia's police chief before he was hired in Los Angeles to soothe the civic wounds of the Rodney King beating, was dismissed last year after his five-year contract expired.

The city's police commissioner acknowledged Mr. Williams's "ability to communicate with and reassure the community" but said that he had been "unable or unwilling to consistently translate his words into action."

Mr. Frazier, the Baltimore police commissioner, said: "For the city that needs a new chief, there's a huge risk. A police chief is probably the most important appointment a mayor or city manager could make. When there's an opening, 100 people come in and say they can do it, but only five really can. It's like turning around a big ship. You want to turn it as fast as you can but you can't tip it over. That's an art, not a science."

## POLITICS AND THE COUNTY SHERIFF

There are approximately 3,100 county sheriff's departments in the United States.[63] The county sheriff's office is unique among American law enforcement agencies in terms of both its role and its legal status.[64]

**The Sheriff's Role**   Sheriffs have a unique role in that they typically serve all three components of the criminal justice system, acting in: (1) law enforcement (e.g., in patrol, traffic, and criminal investigation); (2) the courts (e.g., as civil process servers and bailiffs); and (3) corrections (e.g., in county jails and probation). In many urban areas, civil process responsibilities consume more time and resources than criminal law enforcement. About 97 percent of all sheriff's departments are responsible for civil processing such as serving warrants and subpoenas. Over 98 percent of sheriffs perform work related directly to the county or state court system, and finally, about 87 percent of the sheriff's departments operate a county jail system.[65] The task can be very large and complex, as exhibited by the Los Angeles County Sheriff's Office (refer to Box 3-5).

In a few states, the county jails are operated by state departments of corrections. In most big cities, responsibility for the jail system is in the hands of a separate agency, but not always. Not all sheriff's departments play this three-part role. Some offer no police services, while others are not responsible for jails. One author has described four different models of sheriff's departments according to their responsibilities.[66] The full-service model carries out law enforcement and other police services, judicial processing, and correctional duties. The law enforcement model carries out only law enforcement duties while other duties are assumed by separate civil process and correctional

## BOX 3-5

### Big and Complicated

### The L.A. County Sheriff's Department operates the largest jail system in the free world

**by Mike Parker**

The L.A. County Sheriff's Dept. is among the nation's largest and most diverse law enforcement agencies. Here's just a few interesting facts about the L.A.S.D.

- The largest Sheriff's Department and third largest police agency in the nation.
- More than 13,000 employees, including more than 8,300 full-time sworn.
- Staffs and operates the largest jail system in the free world, with more than 18,000 inmates.
- Provides Municipal and Superior Court deputies for the largest County Court system in the nation.
- Sole police agency for more than 2.5 million of the county's 9.5 million people. This includes nearly half of the county's 88 cities and all of the unincorporated areas, totaling over 75 percent of the county's 4,083 square miles.
- Mutual aid coordinator for the region. Coordinating the response of federal, state and local public safety resources during earthquakes, civil unrest and other catastrophes.
- Patrol areas ranging from densely populated urban communities in South Central, East Los Angeles and West Hollywood to the beach city of Malibu, to the mountains of the Angeles National Forests, desert communities of the Antelope Valley and many suburban communities.
- Specialized units such as Aero Bureau, Substance Abuse & Narcotics Education (S.A.N.E.), Special Enforcement Bureau (SWAT, K-9, Motors, etc.), Emergency Services Detail (Search & Rescue), Mounted Enforcement Detail, Organized Crime Unit, and Arson/Explosives.

*Source: American Police Beat,* May 1996, p. 2.

agencies. The civil–judicial model involves only court-related duties. Finally, the correction–judicial model involves all functions except law enforcement.

In terms of size, most sheriff's departments are small. Nearly two-thirds of them employ fewer than twenty-five sworn officers, and a third employ fewer than ten. About half serve a population of less than 25,000.[67]

The county sheriff's legal status is unique in two ways. First, in thirty-seven states it is specified by the state constitution. As a result, major changes in the office of sheriff would require a constitutional amendment—a lengthy and difficult process.

Second, unlike most law enforcement executives, sheriffs are elected in all but two states. (In Rhode Island they are appointed by the governor; in Hawaii they are appointed by the chief justice of the state supreme court.) As elected officials, sheriffs are important political figures. In many rural areas the sheriff is the most powerful political force in the county. As a result sheriffs are far more independent than appointed law enforcement executives, because as discussed earlier, police chiefs can be removed by the mayors or city managers who appoint them. However, this is not to suggest that, because sheriffs enjoy greater independence than police chiefs, they are not subject to powerful political forces within their communities. Indeed, because the office is usually an elected position (in 48 of the 50 states), there is considerable media scrutiny and state accountability. Individuals seeking the position of sheriff must run for public office the same as any other public official. In fact, the office of sheriff is the only local law enforcement position recognized and decreed by many state constitutions, a holdover from the days when local sheriffs were the only law of the land. Refer to Box 3-6.

BOX 3-6

## Sheriff Overhauls Oklahoma Office, Arrests Stereotypes

TAHLEQUAH, Okla.—A no-smoking policy took effect when nurse Delena Goss became sheriff of Cherokee County.

No more "honorary deputy cards" handed out to citizens. No more sloppy grooming or trash talk by deputies on the radio.

Mrs. Goss, who in November became the second woman elected sheriff in Oklahoma history, spent her first month on the job overhauling the morale and procedures of an office besmirched by accusations of sexual battery and unprofessionalism.

She says women can handle the sheriff's job as well as men.

"The stereotype is cowboy hat, guns on both hips, out getting into fights," she said. "The reality is, the sheriff is administration. You put together a staff [and] delegate to make sure duties are done. It's mainly the business end of it."

But female sheriffs are still rare enough to raise interest.

The most recent estimate by the National Sheriff's Association counted 19 women as sheriffs in 1995.

Oklahoma had two female sheriffs decades ago who inherited the office when their husbands died. Rita Duncan of Pushmataha County beat two other Democrats in August to become the state's first elected woman sheriff.

Knowledge and managerial skill matter more than gender, said Mrs. Duncan, who has 13 years of experience in law enforcement.

She advised Mrs. Goss to "hang in there and be tough and support your people."

Keeping the peace in Cherokee County was never simple.

Larry McMurtry and Diana Ossana's new novel *Zeke and Ned*, set after the Civil War in and around Tahlequah, describes "a place so wild that the law had no chance of prevailing."

Mrs. Goss said drugs are the biggest crime problem in her county, home to Tenkiller Lake, Northeastern State University, the Cherokee Nation headquarters and tourism on the Illinois River.

The 35-year-old Cherokee County native left her job in the Tahlequah City Hospital emergency room to run an office with a $500,000 budget, a 32-bed jail and 20 employees, 17 of them men.

"She's doing an outstanding job," said County Commissioner G. V. Gulager. "There's a new spirit among employees, more accountability. There's a new kind of leadership that's refreshing to me as an employee of Cherokee County."

Mr. Gulager described Mrs. Goss as headstrong and practiced in making decisions during a crisis. Her gender makes no difference in law enforcement, he said.

And she agrees.

"My campaign theme was 'Time for a Change' because I was fed up with what was going on here," she said. "Nobody was doing anything about it."

Her predecessor, Andy Sellers, was charged last year with sexually battering a dispatcher. A grand jury recommended Mr. Sellers' ouster. He was accused of failing to control evidence and employees; misusing time by playing games with prisoners and staff; prejudicial treatment; allowing use of county equipment for personal gain; and allowing improper use of firearms.

His investigator, Terry Combs, was charged with grand larceny and two counts of sexual battery. Preliminary hearings are pending for both men.

It took a primary runoff for Mrs. Goss, who had worked as a sheriff's dispatcher in 1980, to win the Democratic nomination. She beat her Republican opponent 9,221 votes to 4,249 votes.

Unannounced visitors want time, and Mrs. Goss' door is open, her smile warm. Home life is also busy for the Civil War buff who is a stepmother and wife of an investigator for District Attorney Dianne Barker-Harrold.

Mrs. Goss doodled a pattern of diagonal lines while sitting through a recent 35-minute meeting of the County Commission. A resident who came to the meeting to complain about a car wash's water usage introduced herself to the new sheriff.

"Take care. Keep them straight," the woman said, winking.

Mrs. Goss has started to organize the Cherokee County Sheriff's Association for residents who want to help fight drugs and crime. She said the group will raise money to buy extra equipment for law enforcement.

She wants to beef up her reserves and to lobby for higher salaries in the department.

"The sheriff's office needs to be for everybody in the county, not just certain people," she said. Before, "there was a good ol' boy system here, big time."

*Source: Dallas Morning News*, December 21, 1996. Reprinted with permission of the Dallas Morning News.

The extent to which politics, in the negative sense, enters into the sheriff's race and subsequently into the operations of the sheriff's department will vary radically from community to community and even among sheriff's races. For example, in states in which sheriffs—because they are constitutional officers—are not bound by normal purchasing restrictions, some potential for abuse exists. If a candidate running for the office of sheriff has accepted a large donation from a certain business, there would be an expectation of reciprocity in return for such "support." This could result in purchases of cars from "loyal" car dealers, food for jail inmates from certain distributors, uniforms from a specific uniform company, and so forth. However, a sheriff who becomes too partisan in his or her purchasing risks disappointing other vendors. As such, a marshaling of support for the next candidate in the next election usually occurs. The "real politics" of such a situation is that while more purchases will be made from key supporting organizations, the incumbent must "spread around" enough purchasing to appease other vendors.

Then, too, there are potentials in any political environment for dirty campaigns, and sheriff's races are no exception.

Several years ago, an incumbent sheriff who realized he might not be reelected because of strong opposition from a highly qualified opponent, contacted one of his vice squad officers to see if he could create a situation that would be embarrassing to the opponent. The vice squad officer made contact with a young and exceptionally attractive prostitute, who also served as his informant. He asked her to approach the man running against the incumbent sheriff at his place of business and try to entice him into joining her in a nearby hotel to have sex. The preselected hotel room had been set up with audiovisual equipment so the entire event could be recorded. Once the planned act was recorded, the videotape would be sent to the candidate's wife along with copies to his minister and other key people in his life. It was felt that such a tape in the hands of these people would be sufficiently disruptive to the candidate's personal life to make him ineffectual as a campaigner. The prostitute, as instructed, did go to the business of the candidate and attempted to entice the individual to join her. The candidate, who was a politically astute individual, saw through this transparent farce and told the woman to leave his business. However, as soon as she left, he very discreetly followed her for a couple of blocks and saw her getting into an unmarked sheriff's department vehicle, which was being driven by the vice squad officer whom he recognized. When the election was held, the incumbent sheriff lost. Since this was only one of many "dirty tricks" attempted by a number of employees of the sheriff's department, the newly elected sheriff immediately "cleaned house" and fired everybody who he could prove, or suspected, was involved in the efforts to embarrass him.

Inside the sheriff's department, politics can also be a decisive factor in the operational effectiveness of the organization. It is no accident that increased enforcement activity by the local sheriff's office usually precedes an election. The activity usually focuses on highly visible suspects or signs of disorder. Characteristic events include the roundup of local prostitutes, the crackdown on street corner vagrants, the closing of "X-rated" video stores, which just happen to ensure considerable positive media attention. The interpretation is obvious, that the incumbent sheriff is "tough" on crime.

One of the most important political processes that impacts the internal organization is the absence of local or state civil service boards. In many states, employees of the county sheriff's office "serve at the pleasure" of the current sheriff. Therefore, if the incumbent sheriff decides either not to run for office or is defeated in the next election, the newly elected sheriff may decide to fire a high percentage of the employees currently working at the sheriff's department. Although a number of conflicting court cases have attempted to provide some sense of balance and order, this capability still exists in most states. As a result, most deputy sheriffs attempt to work in a politically neutral environment, trying not to favor one candidate over another. Such a condition results in a lack of continuity in the skill level of employees and affects the quality of service being delivered to the public. It also creates enormous job insecurity and provides a mechanism whereby unqualified persons may be elected to one of the highest positions of law enforcement in the community. Thus, the very nature of the electoral process and the enormous power inherent in the office can foster an environment in which politics prevails.

## STATE PROSECUTOR

The prosecutor, state's attorney, or district attorney is the chief law enforcement officer under the statutes of some states. However, despite this designation, the state prosecutor does not have overall responsibility for the supervision of the police.[68] Even so, the prosecutor's enforcement policies, procedures for review of all arrests before their presentation in court, and overall supervision of the cases prepared by the police do have an observable effect on police practices and enforcement policies. The initial contact of police officers with prosecutors occurs when the former brings a complaint to be charged. This encounter may be critical because it is an important point for making decisions about the disposition of the case and whether the complaint will be dismissed or reduced to a lesser offense. This discretionary power given the prosecuting attorney has tremendous influence on the ways and extent to which certain laws are enforced or ignored. Police chiefs who perceive that the prosecutor consistently reduces or fails to vigorously enforce certain types of violations may very likely divert their enforcement efforts and resources elsewhere. Then again, some chiefs may decide to "go public" and try to mobilize community support for enforcing the ignored violations. However, few police chiefs take this course of action, because it could result in a serious deterioration in the working relationship with the local prosecutor, a situation most would prefer to avoid.

From the prosecutor's perspective, a cordial relationship with the police is also a desired condition. This is not, however, always possible. For example, suspicions of corruption or other illegal activity by officers from a local police department cannot be ignored by the prosecutor. When prosecutor-led investigations become public knowledge or lead to indictments, a prosecutor's rapport with the police can be severely strained, requiring years to recultivate. The resulting tension may become high if officers believe that the prosecutor is "sticking it to the police department by dragging the thing out" or by not allowing affected officers to plea bargain to lesser charges, or if the prosecutor is suspected of furthering his or her career at the officers' expense (see Box 3-7).

## BOX 3-7

### S.F. Grand Jury Tells DA and Police: Get Your Acts Together

### Hallinan, Lau say they're already trying to improve their agencies' relationship

by Eric Brazil of the *Examiner* staff

District Attorney Terence Hallinan and Police Chief Fred Lau, acknowledging a kernel of truth in the grand jury's accusation that their departments' antagonistic relationship hurts San Francisco's criminal justice system, say they have begun working to repair it. The grand jury report released Wednesday said that the lack of cooperation between cops and district attorneys seems unique to San Francisco, far worse than in any other California county, said foreman Paul O'Leary.

But both Hallinan and Lau, while admitting flaws in the justice system, said that they are willing to start practicing the kind of cooperation the report recommended. "In a sense, we're already in the process, although not in a formalistic way," Hallinan said. "What's good about this (report) is that since I'm a new police chief, and we have a new DA, we can build for the future," Lau said. Both men and others familiar with the criminal justice system noted that some conflict between the two departments was virtually unavoidable.

**"Natural Tension" Exists**

"There's sort of a natural tension between them," said Katherine Feinstein, who headed the city's Office of Criminal Justice under former Mayor Frank Jordan. There were problems during her tenure, Feinstein said, but "they were intermittent and anecdotal."

Vincent Schiraldi, director of the Center on Criminal and Juvenile Justice in Washington, D.C., who held the same position for several years in San Francisco and served on Hallinan's transition team, said the report made a good point. But grand juries, as amateurs without a staff, can be influenced by "whoever wins the race to put their slant" on an investigation, he said, and sometimes they miss the mark or overstate their case. "They're good volunteers, but sometimes they get hoodwinked." On the other hand, Schiraldi said, San Francisco's criminal justice system has been afflicted with a perennial problem of lack of coordination. "Because there's no forum in which the whole community has input and

differences can be hashed out, ideas float out on their own," he said, and the result is "confusing, inadequate communication and an inefficient system."

Jurors called on Mayor Brown to lead an effort to streamline and rationalize the system—possibly by appointing a special commission—no later than September. Brown's press secretary, P. J. Johnston, said that while the mayor had only been briefed on the report,"he feels that the new administration, the new DA and the new chief are all working on the same page. He feels that coordination and streamlining are good ideas, but he's not sure that the city needs another study or a new commission."

The jury's report covers the administrations of Mayors Brown and Frank Jordan, District Attorneys Hallinan and Arlo Smith and Police Chiefs Lau and Tony Ribera. It found "a lack of common goals and incentives" by the two agencies and an adversarial attitude "manifested in such negative practices as risk aversion, game playing" and under-utilization of technology.

O'Leary said jurors were chagrined to learn that two detailed critiques of the city's criminal justice system—by the CSC/Index consulting firm and the Coro Foundation, a post-graduate public service fellowship program—which reached many of the conclusions included in the report, had been "regulated to the dustbin" by both agencies.

The jury said police report writing was so poor that "effective criminal prosecution . . . is at risk," noting that the approximately 55,000 felony arrests each year result in just 2,000 prosecutions.

**At Odds Over Prosecutions**

"I wouldn't be concerned about that," Schiraldi said. "I don't think that's particularly unusual in the state."

However, while the district attorney blames inadequate police reporting for its inability to prosecute many felons, the Police Department says the district attorney's office only takes sure-winner cases, the report said. "This blame game is a 'black eye' on the face of the criminal justice system," the jurors concluded.

Hallinan said his office and the Police Department already were working hard with each other on improving the quality of police reports. "It's key to the relationship between the cops and the DA," he said. "We don't meet until we get to court, and we have to go on the basis of their report. If they're not properly done, we're kind of flying blind." The report also criticized communications between the two departments, which it characterized as "inefficient, ineffective and even, at times, disdainful. The personnel in

*(continued)*

BOX 3-7 (continued)

each of these departments (do) not seem to have a clear understanding of each other's role and purpose and have no mechanisms in place to reverse this."

Hallinan said a certain amount of conflict between police and prosecutors was inevitable because "they are operating on the basis of probable cause, and we're operating on the basis of beyond a reasonable doubt."

Lau said he had turned the report over to Deputy Chief John Willet, his department's liaison with Hallinan's office. "It's too soon to say if it (the report) is really fair, but I consider the grand jury a good objective source of information," he said.

Hallinan said that he or his representative would soon be meeting with Willet to lay out a work program to achieve the ends that the grand jury was seeking.

*Source: San Francisco Examiner, June 27, 1996, p. A3.*

## THE JUDICIARY

Once the police have made an arrest and brought the arrestee before a judge, from pretrial release onward the case is within the domain of the judiciary. In its assessment of the relationships of the judiciary and the police, one governmental report noted that trial judges have acted as chief administrative officers of the criminal justice system, using their power to dismiss cases as a method of controlling the use of the criminal process. But, except in those rulings involving the admissibility of evidence, this has been done largely on an informal basis and has tended to be haphazard, often reflecting primarily the personal values of the individual trial judge.[69]

In contrast, the function of trial judges in excluding evidence that they determine to have been obtained illegally places them very explicitly in the role of controlling police practices. Trial judges have not viewed this role as making them responsible for developing appropriate police practices. However, many trial judges, when asked to explain their decisions, indicate that they have no more responsibility for explaining decisions to police than they have to private litigants.[70]

Occasionally, judges will grant motions to suppress evidence to dismiss cases that they feel should not be prosecuted because the violation is too minor or for some other reason. Use of a motion to suppress evidence in this manner serves to confuse the standards that are supposed to guide the police and has a disturbing, if not demoralizing, effect on them.[71]

If judges consistently interject their personal biases into the judicial process and make it very clear to police that they will dismiss certain categories of violations, the police may discontinue enforcing that particular law. This, in turn, may put the police on a collision course with certain segments of the community that favor the rigorous enforcement of those laws (see Box 3-8).

Skolnick, commenting on police–judiciary relationships, has noted that:

When an appellate court rules that police may not in the future engage in certain enforcement activities, since these constitute a violation of the rule of law, the inclination of the police is typically not to feel *shame* but *indignation*. This response may be especially characteristic of "professional" police, who feel a special competence to decide, on their own, how to reduce criminality in the community. The police, for example, recognize the court's power to bar admission of illegally seized evidence if the police are discovered to have violated the constitutional rights of the defendant. They do not, however, feel morally blameworthy in having done so; nor

BOX 3-8

## Police and Judges at Odds Over Releases

by John Harris
*American-Statesman Staff*

After police arrested Steven Clark on the afternoon of October 18 on suspicion of cashing bad checks, an investigator planned to seek a warrant to search his car in hopes of recovering an estimated $51,000.

But when Sgt. Joel Thompson arrived at work the next morning, he found he had missed his chance by 35 minutes.

Clark, 29, of Austin, had been released on personal bond at 7:25 A.M after Municipal Court Judge Nigel Gusdorf agreed the night before to release him to his attorney's custody, on the promise that he show up for arraignment later that morning.

He never showed up and has not been found. The money is missing, too.

Frustrated police say the release is the latest example of how municipal judges are too lenient in releasing suspects.

Gusdorf says there is nothing illegal or wrong with the practice, that jail officials tried to reach Thompson before personal bond was granted, and that some members of the Police Department are spreading incorrect information about court practices.

While some police officers occasionally "throw temper tantrums and act like little Saddam Husseins" over judges' actions, most officers recognize that the judges act within the law, Gusdorf said.

But similar disagreements between the judges and some police officers seem to arise every few months, signs of a lingering squabble that shows no signs of dissipating.

Part of the confusion stems from the Hobby rule, a local custom that allows people arrested for driving-while-intoxicated and misdemeanor cases to be released to their attorneys' custody overnight, if the person agrees to return to court the next morning to face charges.

Another agreement—between the Travis County Bar Association, the sheriff and the police chief—allows the jail to release inmates if no charges are filed within 24 hours of an arrest.

"The third situation is where a judge, obeying the law, has the right to (set) bail under the federal and state constitutions," Gusdorf said. That "is what happened in this case. That was me granting personal bond."

Thompson said he had planned to obtain a search warrant of Clark's car but was unable to do so after Clark was released. He had been arrested on suspicion of theft, forgery and evading detention after trying to escape from arresting officers.

"I don't know that I could have recovered the money, but I could at least have had the chance to," Thompson said. But the Travis County Central Booking Facility, where inmates usually are booked, "stays real full all the time, and they want us to process them as soon as possible."

### Origins of Hobby Rules

The Hobby rule got its name after the 1974 driving-while-intoxicated arrest of Lt. Gov. Bill Hobby. After Hobby was released to his attorney during the night, defense attorneys demanded their clients get the same treatment. The system was later broadened to include other non-violent misdemeanors.

But in another practice, sometimes called a "judge's Hobby," attorneys for persons accused of felonies seek personal bond from a judge, allowing their clients to be released with the understanding that they are to return the next morning for arraignment.

Gusdorf agreed that the term "Hobby" is often misunderstood and used loosely. Others say differences between the policies have grown too fuzzy.

"How do you grant personal bond when someone hasn't even been charged?" asked Senior Sgt. Sam Cox, president of the Austin Police Association. He said Clark's release shows the need for more consistency in court policies.

"We seem to be consistent in a lot of cases, but every month or two we seem to have cases that, wow, it defies common logic," Cox said. "If we have rules, we ought to stick with them."

The judges have cited a section of the Texas Code of Criminal Procedure that says a judge can assess a bail amount when a person is arrested, before a charge is filed.

But Assistant District Attorney Terry Keel said that particular statute "is just a rule of law that in determining the proper amount of bail to be set, the prisoner can ask the magistrate to look at all the available information."

"There is no interpretation of that article in the law anywhere that allows one to use that for the authority of what these municipal judges are doing, not in any way, shape or form," Keel said.

### Good Record for Lawyer and Client

Gusdorf said one reason he agreed to Clark's release on personal bond was that Clark's lawyer, Lowell Clayton, had a "perfect record" because his clients

*(continued)*

## BOX 3-8 (continued)

had always shown up for court the next day. Clark also had no prior criminal record, he said.

"We have to make about 4,000 bond decisions a month," Gusdorf said. "Of the municipal judges, I have the lowest bond forfeiture rate. If one of them fails to show, I'm not happy about it either.

"I did what I had to do under the law and made a judgment call," he said. "If something goes wrong, it's easy to play Monday-morning quarterback."

Betty Blackwell, vice chairwoman of the criminal law and procedures section of the county bar association, said she does not think people arrested in felony cases should be released to their attorneys as Clark was, but neither should they be placed in jail without charges being filed.

"My understanding was they were not to do that anymore," she said of Gusdorf's decision. But she said there was no formal agreement on the matter.

"I understand completely this officer's concern of people getting away and not getting to justice, but we also see regularly innocent people put in that horrible facility for 24 hours and not get released," she said.

Blackwell said part of the problem is that Austin patrol officers do not write affidavits showing probable cause for a person to be charged with a crime. That paperwork is written by sergeant-investigators.

Patrol officers could write the paperwork for approval by a judge, who then could set bail, Blackwell said. That would eliminate problems created when sergeant-investigators wait until the morning after a person is arrested to prepare charges, she said.

Gusdorf called the bail-setting procedure a "heavy responsibility" for a judge. "But you cannot have police officers leaning over judges and telling them what to do. That would be a police state."

*Source: Austin American-Statesman* (Texas), Nov. 11, 1990. © Austin American-Statesman. Reprinted with permission.

---

do they even accept such injunctions with good grace and go about their business. On the contrary, the police typically view the court with hostility for having interfered with their capacities to practice their craft. Police tend to rest their *moral* position on the argument that the "independence" and social distance of the appellate judiciary constitutes a type of government—by the courts—without the consent of the governed—the police. Thus, the police see the court's affirmation of principles of due process as, in effect, the creation of harsh "working conditions." From their point of view, the courts are failing to affirm democratic notions of the autonomy and freedom of the "worker." Their political superiors insist on "production" while their judicial superiors impede their capacity to "produce." Under such frustrating conditions, the appellate judiciary inevitably comes to be seen as "traitor" to its responsibility to keep the community free from criminality.

Antagonism between the police and the judiciary is perhaps an inevitable outcome, therefore, of the different interests residing in the police as a specialized agency and the judiciary as a representative of wider community interests. Constitutional guarantees of due process of law do make the working life and conditions of the police more difficult. But if such guarantees did not exist, the police would of course engage in activities promoting self-serving ends, as does any agency when offered such freedom in a situation of conflicting goals. Every administrative agency tends to support policies permitting it to present itself favorably. Regulative bodies restricting such policies are inevitably viewed with hostility by the regulated. Indeed, when some hostility does not exist, the regulators may be assumed to have been "captured" by the regulated. If the police could, in this sense, "capture" the judiciary, the resulting system would truly be suggestive of a "police state."[72]

## CITIZEN INVOLVEMENT

Citizen involvement in the policymaking process of law enforcement agencies is frequently met with considerable resistance from members of the law enforcement community. Many police administrators feel that their effectiveness rests on a high degree of autonomy. They view attempts to alter the way in which the law is enforced as efforts to negate the effectiveness of and to politicize the police. They argue further that during the last quarter-century law enforcement agencies have slowly but surely been successful in freeing themselves of partisan political interference and that public involvement by citizens will result in the police becoming instruments of pressure group politics and avowedly partisan to the most vocal and disruptive segments of society.[73]

One national commission took strong exception to this traditional posture of opposition to citizen involvement in policymaking. The commission's argument was that:

> In some areas of government activity, there is increasing utilization of citizen advisory committees as a way of involving members of the community in the policy making process. In some cases, the group may be advisory only, the governmental agency being free to accept or reject its advice. In other instances, the group is official and policies are cleared through the committee as a regular part of the policy making process. The advantages of both methods are that they serve as an inducement for the police administrator to articulate important policies, to formulate them, and to subject them to discussion in the advisory group. How effective this is depends upon the willingness of the group and the police administrator to confront the basic law enforcement policy issues rather than being preoccupied with the much easier questions of the mechanics of running the department. Where there is a commitment to exploring basic enforcement policy questions, the citizens' advisory group or policy making board has the advantage of involving the community in the decision making process, thus giving a broader base than would otherwise exist for the acceptance and support of enforcement policies.[74]

Hurricanes, floods, tornadoes, and other large-scale disasters have a tendency to bring the police and citizenry closer together. Nowhere was this more evident than in the aftermath of the bombing of the Alfred P. Murrah Building in Oklahoma City (1995). Individual members of the community worked hand-in-hand with police and other rescue personnel to assist the injured. The ruthless bombing left police exhausted and frustrated, except for the genuine support and care shown to them by the citizens of Oklahoma City (refer to Figure 3-5).

Citizen groups are varied, and they have different interests in police service. Chambers of commerce and service clubs generally promote police professionalism out of civic pride. Churches and church groups have historically campaigned against vice and corruption and for civil liberties and police–community relations (see Box 3-9).[75]

## Chambers of Commerce and Service Clubs

Local chambers of commerce and service clubs typically are supportive of efforts that lead toward efficient and clean government. Although such groups are characterized as being apolitical, they can exercise considerable influence. Their support for improving the quality of law enforcement in the community is frequently heard in the chambers of city hall and is demonstrated through various community projects intended to assist local law enforcement. Attuned police chiefs realize the benefit to be gained from the support of such groups, encourage personnel to become active members in these clubs, and frequently join one or two themselves. Support from these groups is not surprising when one considers that they are frequently comprised of men and women from the middle class who are well educated and deeply involved in many aspects of community leadership. Such groups often have mobilized behind a police

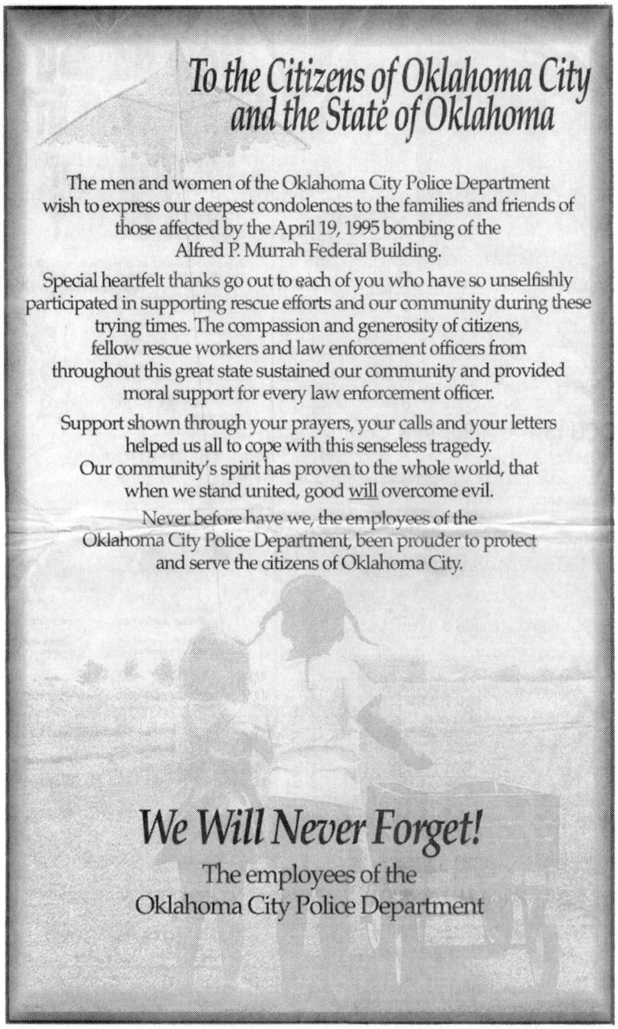

**FIGURE 3-5.** Citizens and the police can work together with mutual respect and understanding. (Ad appeared in *The Oklahoman*, July 2, 1995, p. A–17. Courtesy of the Oklahoma City Police Department.)

## To the Citizens of Oklahoma City and the State of Oklahoma

The men and women of the Oklahoma City Police Department wish to express our deepest condolences to the families and friends of those affected by the April 19, 1995 bombing of the Alfred P. Murrah Federal Building.

Special heartfelt thanks go out to each of you who have so unselfishly participated in supporting rescue efforts and our community during these trying times. The compassion and generosity of citizens, fellow rescue workers and law enforcement officers from throughout this great state sustained our community and provided moral support for every law enforcement officer.

Support shown through your prayers, your calls and your letters helped us all to cope with this senseless tragedy. Our community's spirit has proven to the whole world, that when we stand united, good will overcome evil.

Never before have we, the employees of the Oklahoma City Police Department, been prouder to protect and serve the citizens of Oklahoma City.

## We Will Never Forget!

The employees of the
Oklahoma City Police Department

chief to get much-needed budget increases for salaries, additional personnel, and equipment.

**Churches** The religious leaders and congregation members of a community's church groups represent one of the most potentially powerful pressure groups in the community. Their influence can, and frequently does, extend into the voting booth, which assures a high degree of responsiveness from local elected officials. Church leaders and their congregations almost always find an open door and a receptive ear at the office of their local police chief when they present their concerns. The problems that are frequently of greatest concern to such groups are vice related, such as prostitution, massage parlors, X-rated theaters, and adult bookstores. It is true that individual communities impose different standards and have varying levels of tolerance, but, if the church leaders of a community mobilize and call on their police chief to eradicate or reduce what they perceive to be a serious problem, there is a high probability that they will receive some positive response. And, if the police chief suggests that the police department cannot cope realistically with the problem because of limited

BOX 3-9

## Blacks Tell Council of Police Fear

by Richard Green

About 300 black citizens—many representing civic, church and community organizations—crowded into City Hall on Wednesday, to demand that council act to defuse tension between police and city residents.

"We want a peaceful city," said Frank Allison, president of the local chapter of the National Association for the Advancement of Colored People. "But police must be accountable."

If they are not, "young people will be fighting the police," Allison said. "Racism is alive in Cincinnati as much as it is in Tupelo, Miss."

The Rev. Donald Tye Jr., an associate pastor of the Tabernacle Baptist Church in Lincoln Heights, said: "Taxpayers are sick and tired of the arrogance of officers. If these bad feelings persist, there will be violence and blood on city streets."

The community leaders came to council chambers in response to last week's appearance of nearly 300 officers before council.

The police were protesting City Manager Gerald Newfarmer's ruling that Officer Bruce Hoffbauer used excessive force when he fatally shot a charging, unarmed man, Walter Brown of Corryville, in a hallway outside Brown's apartment Dec. 28. Hoffbauer is white; Brown was black.

In the emotional and often heated 90-minute session Wednesday, black leaders vented their concerns and recommendations. They seek:

- The firing of Hoffbauer.
- More staff and support going for the city's Office of Municipal Investigation, a civilian investigative unit that probes alleged wrongdoing of all city departments, including the police force.
- A crackdown on police brutality.

The request that drew a standing ovation from the audience was made by Theodore M. Berry, Cincinnati's mayor from 1972–1975 and its first black mayor.

He urged council to pass a charter amendment—which must be placed before voters—giving the city manager greater authority to hire and fire the police chief, whose job is now protected by the city's civil service rules.

"The buck stops with you," Berry told council members.

Resolving the questions about the Cincinnati Police Division should be council's direct responsibility, he said.

"The president of the United States is the commander in chief of the armed forces, and he removes officers in the field when they do not perform," Berry said. "The chief operating officer of this city should be able to do the same."

After his speech, Berry said he thought council would be "reluctant" to pass such a motion in an election year.

"I haven't approached any of them individually about it," Berry said. "I just put it out there today in the arena where it needs to be done. Council is where this problem is going to have to be done. Council is where this problem is going to have to be resolved."

Councilman Tyrone Yates—like Berry, a Charterite—said he would introduce such a motion within the next week. It would need the votes of six council members to be placed on the ballot.

While the citizens who came to the council meeting criticized Police Chief Lawrence Whalen directly, several blasted the police division.

"We do not advocate disrespect," said the Rev. Fred Shuttlesworth. "But we must demand the respect of those who are in control. And people are about ready to get back in the streets" to get that respect.

Mayor David Mann said council's Law and Safety Committee next week will begin looking into the issues raised at Wednesday's meeting.

"What we're talking about is dealing with a few bad apples," Mann said.

*Source: Cincinnati Enquirer* (Ohio), March 21, 1991. Used with permission of the Cincinnati Enquirer—Richard Green.

personnel and resources, these very same church groups will likely begin applying pressure on the city officials to give the police chief the needed resources. Thus, the religious leaders of the community can be powerful allies of the police chief in certain types of enforcement efforts. On the other hand, this same pressure group may force the chief to redirect resources away from areas that may have a higher priority.

# NEWS MEDIA

It is the responsibility of the police department and especially its top leadership to establish and maintain a cordial association with all media representatives.[76] Both the electronic and the print news media can be powerful friends or devastating antagonists of a local police department, and to a great extent this will be determined by the attitudes, policies, and working relationships among editors, news directors, and the police chief. When friction does occur between the police and the news media, as it invariably does in every community, it frequently emanates from the events surrounding a major crime or an unusual occurrence.

Often in the case of major crimes or incidents, police departments do not want to release information that will jeopardize the safety of the public or its officers, impair the right of a suspect to a fair and impartial trial, or impede the progress of an investigation. On the other hand, the news media have a different orientation and duty: to inform the public. Although their goals are often compatible, the police and the news media frequently disagree irreconcilably:

> In 1990, Mehrdad Dashti took 33 people hostage in a hotel bar in Berkeley, California. Dashti shot eight of his hostages, killing one of them. Police and television crews responded to the scene. Even though it was known that there was a television set in the bar on which Dashti could watch, one television station reported what the police were doing outside, including telling that an assault team had moved into position. At another time, a male hostage was shown shouting from the bar that he was about to be executed; he disappeared from the scene and a shot was heard. At the time no one knew that the bullet had missed or that the father was tuned to the station and left in turmoil. Police finally killed Dashti and freed the captives. And, the debate about real-time journalistics disclosures about sensitive police operations was on. Could not some information be held back by the news media without damage to journalistic ethics? In exercising their First Amendment rights should reporters make disclosures that could have cost the hostages their lives or needlessly endangered police officers committed to their rescue? A panel of police officials, journalists, and others discussed these and related issues at Columbia University without reaching any meeting of the minds, although television executives made a promise to "review their procedures."[77]

Another situation in which the police and other officials may be in conflict with the news media occurs when journalists uncover information that is of actual investigative or legal significance and, if police investigators, prosecuting attorneys, or defense attorneys want to confirm the information, decline to divulge from whom or how they got the information on the basis of protecting their sources. The argument of the news media is that failing to protect their sources could result in reduced information flowing to them, thus jeopardizing the public's right to know. However, a reporter's First Amendment right to protect sources is not absolute. Recognizing this, some states have enacted so-called shield laws. For both First Amendment rights and shield laws, the courts apply a "balancing test" to determine whether reporters can be required to release the identities of their sources: is there a compelling need for the information, that is, is the defendant's need for the information to make an effective defense greater than the need of a reporter to protect the identity of a source?

Other circumstances for potential tension or conflict in police–news media relationships include "off-the-record" police information appearing in the news media; the occasional claim by a police administrator that he or

**FIGURE 3-6.** The media hover while members of the Los Angeles Police Department Swat Team prepare for action as a suspected gunman emerges from cover. (Courtesy of *Police*, April 1988. Photograph by Mike Mullin.)

she was misquoted; and the involvement of press at the scenes of bank robberies, gangland killings, and hostage situations, or in the sensitive investigations of kidnappings and drug rings. From a legal standpoint, the police may release relevant information about a defendant if it is not prejudicial to the defendant's right to a fair trial. Many police departments have policies that protect the defendant's rights, but those policies may obstruct the needs of reporters to gather images and information for the public. For example, with respect to pretrial suspects, Kentucky State Police policy prohibits personnel from

1. Requiring the suspect to pose for photographers
2. Reenacting the crime
3. Disclosing that the suspect told where weapons, the proceeds of a crime, or other materials were located
4. Referring to the suspect as a "depraved character," "a real no-good," "a sexual monster," or by similar terms
5. Revealing that the suspect declined to take certain types of tests or that the suspect did take certain tests, for example, a blood alcohol test to determine the degree, if any, to which the suspect was under the influence of drugs or alcohol
6. Telling the press the results of any tests to which the suspect submitted
7. Making statements as to the guilt or innocence of a suspect
8. Releasing the identities of prospective witnesses or commenting on the nature of their anticipated testimony or credibility
9. Making statements of a purely speculative nature about any aspect of the case[78]

On the other hand, with the move toward community policing, many officers conduct crime prevention classes, crime block meetings, and media interviews. Some departments (such as that in Portland, Oregon) have taken a very positive approach to this issue, viewing these interactions as opportunities to communicate with the general public on police affairs. Box 3-10 reflects an informal guide for police officers in conducting public meetings and media interviews.

## BOX 3-10

### How to Work Well with the Media

by Jane Braaten

#### Bureau in More Public Role

Community policing—with its emphasis on teaching people about crime and crime prevention techniques—brings many Bureau employees into the forefront of public meetings and media interviews.

Many officers are participating on police-community efforts in which community members want media attention on successes so other neighborhoods can learn by example.

News stations, too, are trying to emphasize crime prevention information and neighborhood heroes in addition to crime scene summaries.

With all this going on, officers may find themselves as the right person to talk to about a partnership agreement or response team effort.

Here's a brief guide to making the best of media interviews.

#### What Will Reporters Ask?

If a reporter calls you to set up an interview, it pays to ask them what the topic is to see if you are the right person to handle those questions.

If you have agreed to be listed as the contact person for a project, however, there are basic questions you can anticipate being asked.

#### How Much Does It Cost?

Reporters, as watchdogs for the public, will ask about costs and funding sources. If your project calls for additional services or the installation of a traffic barrier, be prepared to talk cost or refer them to someone who can.

#### How Was the Decision Made?

What alternatives were looked at, how were they evaluated, etc. are all good questions if you are talking about drug free zones or street closures for cruising.

#### Who Disagrees with This Idea?

It is no secret to police personnel that the media likes reporting on controversies. So be prepared. Sgt. Roger Hediger in Forfeitures would refer reporters, if asked, to the appropriate person rather than waiting for the media to find someone who opposes forfeitures.

#### What Does This Mean?

As government communicators, this is often the question that we leave unanswered and wonder why the media chose not to cover our event. Take the time to include in the news release a brief sentence or two about why this particular event or project is significant.

#### What Does This Mean to People?

Reporters must take reams of data and hours of tape and turn it into brief stories that relate to their readers, listeners and viewers. Help them do this, and they will be better apt to understand your story and report on it. What would be of more interest—the number of foot patrollers or the testimony of neighbors who say that they see more families enjoying the park now.

#### How Should I Respond?

- **Make Sure You Are the Right Person.** Refer them to the right person if it's not you. This establishes you as a good contact and helps keep the peace internally.
- **Concentrate on the Audience.** The readers, listeners and viewers will never see or hear the questions or the reporter's tone of voice or demeanor. The public will see and hear only you.
- **Keep Your Cool.** Reporters sometimes ask essentially the same question several times to see if they can get more information. Stick to what you know you can answer.
- **Use Your Own Words.** Sometimes a question will come to you with wording intended to provoke a response, such as "Isn't this just window dressing?" or "Aren't these people lazy?" Again, remember that people at home can't hear the question so don't repeat it in your answer. Using the negative wording, even if you are discounting it, will make you sound defensive.
- **Realize Everything Is on the Record.** Off-color remarks, profanity, jokes—if they are spoken in front of a reporter, they are on the record. Off the record is a journalist's term, and its definition often varies greatly from what people think it is. The best advice is to say only what you would want to see in print.

- **Look at the Reporter.** Reporters make notes, check tapes and talk to the camera person. Avoid the temptation to look at the camera, or much of the interview will end up in the editing room.
- **Keep Sentences Short; Ideas in Brief.** Radio and TV reporters may be doing five stories a day. Handing them your 65-page report will not be effective. Prepare summaries.

## What to Do . . .

- **Be accurate and honest.** Many government agencies are under fire because somewhere along the way what they said to the public was not seen as credible.
- **Comply with all open meetings and public records law.** If you have questions about these, contact the Public Information Officer for assistance.
- **Avoid trying too hard to be clever or humorous.** What is viewed as funny varies from person to person. The risks are great if you use humor that is offensive to others.
- **Explain police terminology or acronyms.** It is OK to use terminology such as mission or SERT, but avoid jargon such as "do an after action" when "we will review the situation" would be better understood.
- **Figure out how to say "I don't know."** No one knows it all, but some people don't like to use the phrase "I don't know." Better to use it, or "I'll find out for you" or "I'll have someone call you with that" than blurt out incomplete information on the spot.
- **Volunteer important information.** Remember, you know more about your event than the reporter, that's why you are being interviewed.
- **Do follow up.** If reporters say they are interested in when the next foot patrol goes out or when the next meeting will be held, follow up with them.

## What Not to Do . . .

- **Quit worrying about the angle,** or the spin on a particular piece of information. There is a big difference between wanting to present the Bureau in a good light, which is fine, and orchestrating news or information to be misleading, which isn't.
- **Don't try to be philosophical.** Like humor, belief systems vary from person to person. What you may believe is universal philosophy probably isn't, and carries the risk of offending people.
- **Avoid hypotheticals.** Listen carefully to questions that start with "what if." Laws and regulations also require that people use common sense.
- **Don't use locker room talk or gallows humor.** Using phrases such as "nut case" or "jumper" are startling when seen in print or on the news, and certainly don't convey much compassion for the people and families involved. Avoid them.

## Press Conference How To

- **Make it an event.** If it's a partnership agreement signing, invite everyone who has played a part. If the event does not get a lot of coverage, it can still be a celebration.
- **Keep it brief.** The history of the project from start to finish can't be put in a 45-second story anyway. Keep the number of speakers (2–5) and the total amount of time they speak (15–20 minutes combined) brief.
- **Keep it focused.** Concentrate on three to five main points. Don't let it become a circus.
- **Get organized.** It doesn't have to be a formal, but it should be organized. Divide up tasks: facility, refreshments, invite speakers, greet people, hand out flyers, etc.
- **Give some thought to visuals.** If there are good visuals that help tell the story, include them. But don't contrive some gimmicky visual just to have one there.
- **Make sure the time and place are convenient.** Mornings are better, and buildings that are frequently used for public meetings are better for press conferences that are primarily announcements. If you do choose an unusual location, include a map in the press release if you want people to find their way there.
- **Keep people notified.** At a minimum, notify the PIO, Chief's Office, RU manager and your immediate supervisor of press conferences or events the media have been invited to.

## Press Release How To

- **Be accurate and be complete.** Reporters are working against the clock every day. Be sure your release contains everything they need to understand and get to your event.
- **Explain your event.** Be sure that names and titles are spelled correctly; give directions or a map if necessary; explain why the event is significant.
- **Provide extra copies.** Bring extra copies of the release, along with fact sheets or brochures if applicable, to the event or press conference.

## Where to Go for Help

- For assistance in working out a dispute with a reporter or assignment editor, talk to the Public Information Officer Lt. C. W. Jensen at 823-0010.
- For assistance in event planning, invitations, statistics or graphic displays, contact Planning and Support at 823-0283.

*Source: The Portland Police Bulletin,* March 30, 1997.

**FIGURE 3-7.** Public information officer being interviewed by a member of the media. (Courtesy of Scott Boatright, Fairfax County, Virginia, Police Department.)

Despite all potential and actual conflicting interests, the fact is that both the police and the news media have profoundly important duties in a free society. In the course of day-to-day activities, people of considerable conscience in both professions go about their jobs peacefully; police–news media clashes are atypical situations. Certainly, if the local news media believe that the police are being arbitrary, high handed, uncooperative, or worst of all, untruthful, then their news stories will reflect that dissatisfaction. Moreover, their coverage may even accentuate negative stories. For example, the dismissal of a felony charge because of insufficient evidence may lead to headlines such as "Shoddy Police Work Lets Burglar Go Free" as opposed to "Attorney Successfully Defends Local Man." Another consequence of a strained relationship with the news media could be minor or no coverage of favorable stories about the police, such as an awards ceremony. Thus, police administrators should exert a great deal of effort in seeing that all personnel understand the role of the press, that the applicable police department policies are current, that those policies are followed, and that open lines of communication with the news media are maintained.

## POLITICAL VIOLENCE AND TERRORISM

The last decade has seen the rise of international and domestic terrorism. The impact on local law enforcement agencies has been profound, as police administrators are confronted with yet another external issue. Police departments around the country have had to address new threats of violence, which are sometimes the result of federal actions or international foreign policy actions. For instance, in 1991, with the advent of Operation Desert Storm in the Persian Gulf, virtually every large metropolitan police department was placed on alert. Operational demands required police agencies to perform relatively new activities, included increasing airport and courthouse security, building antiterrorism barriers, beefing up intelligence-gathering sources, and monitoring activity in Middle Eastern communities. Even though an extensive federal structure has been developed to counter the terrorist threat, headed by the President's Interdepartmental Group on Terrorism, the first level of prevention (and defense) remains with uniform police officers on the street. The federal structure has come under considerable criticism for failing to coordinate antiterrorism activity, assess and analyze accurate intelligence information, and act quickly to prevent terrorist activities.[79]

The Federal Bureau of Investigation has been the focus of many of these allegations, primarily because it is the lead federal law enforcement agency responsible for investigating crimes involving terrorism. Recent events and poorly handled hostage situations (refer to Chapter 12, Planning and Decision Making) have forced the FBI and other government agencies to bolster their mission in the fight against terrorism. (See Box 3-11.)

**Defining Terrorism**

In the popular mind, terrorism is viewed as the illegitimate and violent actions of specific groups that violate the authority of rightfully established governments. Terrorism encompasses the threat of and/or use of violence for the purpose of achieving a specific set of political objectives or goals.[80] Historically, defining terrorism has been a very difficult venture, shaped and altered by a number of factors including our own national interests, government interpretations, the news media, hidden political agendas, and emotional human rights rhetoric.[81] By exploiting any one of these influences, it is possible to distort the facts of various actions and, hence, pass moral judgment on those who

## BOX 3-11

### Feds Fight Terrorism

Since the 1995 truck bombing in Oklahoma City, the federal government has spent billions of dollars creating or expanding a variety of counterterrorism programs. They include:

- **FBI Counterterrorism Center:** Develops overall strategies to combat foreign and domestic terrorism, working with other federal agencies.
- **Joint Terrorism Task Forces:** Groups of FBI officials and local law enforcement agencies who share information about possible terrorist threats. The number of groups is expected to be 22 by the end of the year, double the number in 1995.
- **The National Domestic Preparedness Office:** Designed to coordinate counterterrorism efforts among federal, state and local law enforcement agencies.
- **Rapid Deployment Teams:** Five sets of FBI agents who respond immediately to a terrorist attack.
- **Strategic Information and Operations Center:** Based in the main FBI building in

Washington, it is used as a headquarters for terrorism investigations.

- **National Infrastructure Protection Center:** Designed to protect the nation's roads, bridges, communications and financial systems. Also responsible for cyberterrorism investigations.
- **Hazardous Materials Response Unit:** Handles mostly chemical and biological threats.
- **LEGAT:** FBI Legal Attache offices posted in 36 countries. Credited with helping the 1998 investigation of bombings at two American embassies in East Africa.
- **The Office for State and Local Domestic Preparedness Support:** Run by the Justice Department, it hands out grants to state and local governments for counterterrorism equipment and training.
- **The Center for Domestic Preparedness:** Run by the Justice Department at Fort McClellan, Ala., the center trains local police officers, firefighters and emergency medical workers on what to do in the wake of a terrorist attack.

*Source: The Dallas Morning News*, April 19, 1999, p. 6A.
Reprinted with permission of *The Dallas Morning News*.

are labeled terrorists, for we in America assume that terrorism is what the bad guys do.[82] Such phrases as "guerrilla warfare," "revolutionary movement," "communist-supported terrorism," and "radical fundamentalist" only heighten ideological sentiment and play to emotion rather than intellect. Hence, we find the cliché that one man's terrorist is another man's freedom fighter to be truly an observation based on perspective and perception.[83] This is certainly the case in the United States, as some actions, such as the bombing of the World Trade Center in New York (1993), the Alfred P. Murrah Federal Building in Oklahoma City (1995), and TWA flight 800 (1996), are "terrorist," —while the sporadic bombings at abortion centers across the country are not.

Large, high-profile terrorist events greatly impact how members of society interact. Random acts of terrorism upset the framework of society, leaving only futile questions without rational answers. Essentially, terrorism tests the basic social structure of dependence and trust. If random bombings and acts of violence occur on a frequent basis at the most secure institutions of a society (e.g., federal buildings, police departments, churches, synagogues, hospitals), then people tend to lose faith in the existing social and governmental structure. Safety and security are severely compromised and questioned. Terrorism destroys the solidarity, cooperation, and interdependence on which social functioning is based and substitutes insecurity and distrust.

In the middle of this phenomenon are the police who are charged with maintaining law, order, safety, and security—an extremely difficult task, considering that the police are often targets of terrorism themselves.

**Middle East Conflict**
The list of potential international terrorist threats against the United States is almost unlimited considering the numerous political conflicts continuing in the international arena. Many of these threats are fueled by political, religious, and/or ideologically motivated causes. Certainly, terrorism from various Middle East groups has posed significant problems to American law enforcement. Historically, the root of conflict in the Middle East has been the establishment of Israel in 1948 and the subsequent U.S. support provided to that country. While peace between the two major groups (Israelis and Palestinians) was formally established in 1995, both sides still have major radical movements opposing the process. These groups often act out in the international arena, with the United States being a potential target. Confirmed activities by members of the JDL (Jewish Defense League), the PFLP (Popular Front for the Liberation of Palestine), Fatah Revolutionary Council, and a host of other splinter groups have caused concern to law enforcement. As if these groups were not enough, mercenary terrorists such as Carlos and Abu Nidal still foment activity in support of the highest bidder. These mercenary terrorists often work in concert with state-sponsored groups in the Middle East such as Al Sauqa (Syria), Amal (Lebanon), and the Third Hand (Libya).

Within the last decade, significant activities by Islamic fundamentalists have also sparked concern in the United States. Led by a variety of groups in Iran and Iraq, the movement is violently opposed to Western ideology and particularly the United States, characterized as the "great Satan" by Ayatollah Khomeini.[84] Such groups active in the international arena are Hezbollah (Party of God, responsible for the 1983 bombing of the Marine barracks in Beirut, Lebanon), Jihad (Holy War), and the Revolutionary Council of Iran. On February 26, 1993, the bombing of the World Trade Center killed five people. FBI experts contend that if the bomb had been just slightly larger and

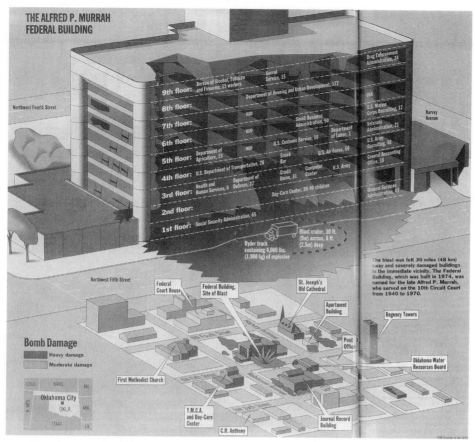

The Alfred P. Murrah Federal Building diagram with the following labels:

THE ALFRED P. MURRAH FEDERAL BUILDING

Drug Enforcement Administration, 24

9th floor: Bureau of Alcohol, Tobacco and Firearms, 15 workers — Secret Service, 15 — Department of Housing and Urban Development, 177

DEA

8th floor: HUD — U.S. Marine Corps Recruiting, 17 — Veterans Administration, 21

Harvey Avenue

7th floor: HUD — Small Business Administration, 50 — Department of Labor, 1 — U.S. Army Recruiting, 48

6th floor: HUD — U.S. Customs Service, 10 — U.S. Air Force, 50 — General Accounting Office, 18

5th floor: Department of Agriculture, 15 — Snack Bar — U.S. Army

4th floor: U.S. Department of Transportation, 28 — Credit Union, 31 — Computer Center — U.S. Army — General Services Administration, 43

3rd floor: Health and Human Services, 8 — Department of Defense, 22 — Day-Care Center, 20-40 children

2nd floor:

1st floor: Social Security Administration, 65

Northwest Fourth Street

Northwest Fifth Street

Blast crater, 30 ft. (9m) across, 8 ft. (2.5m) deep

Ryder truck containing 4,000 lbs. (1,800 kg) of explosive

The blast was felt 30 miles (48 km) away and severely damaged buildings in the immediate vicinity. The Federal Building, which was built in 1974, was named for the late Alfred P. Murrah, who served on the 10th Circuit Court from 1940 to 1970.

Bomb Damage
- Heavy damage
- Moderate damage

Federal Court House — Federal Building, Site of Blast — St. Joseph's Old Cathedral — Apartment Building — Regency Towers — Post Office — Oklahoma Water Resources Board — Journal Record Building — Journal Record Building

First Methodist Church — Y.M.C.A. and Day-Care Center — C.R. Anthony

Oklahoma City OKLA.
COLO. KANS. MO. N. MEX. OKLA. ARK. TEXAS LA.

**FIGURE 3-8.** Diagram of the Alfred P. Murrah Building in Oklahoma City showing the impact of the blast. (*Source: Time*, May 1, 1995. Diagram by Joe Lertola, pp. 58–59. © 1995 Time Inc. Reprinted by permission.)

more skillfully placed, the entire building may have collapsed causing untold devastation and death. Linkages to Islamic fundamentalist groups in Egypt were developed resulting in several indictments of Arab nationals living in the United States. One of those under suspicion was the blind cleric, Sheik Abdel Omar Rahman. Warrants for his arrest stirred additional turmoil in the movement aimed at the United States. Islamic fundamentalism has also been blamed for unrest and civil disorder in a number of other countries, including Egypt, Algeria, Zaire, India, Malaysia, and Japan. However, it is important to note that Islam is the world's second largest religion with over one billion followers, living primarily on the continents of Asia, Africa, and Europe.[85] In the coming decade, Islamic politics will continue to be combustible, with relations with the West more severely strained. As Islamic populations continue to grow in the former Soviet Union, China, India, Europe, and the United States, it will become more imperative to deal with political realities dispassionately and to transcend stereotypes.[86] Islam is not synonymous with violence,[87] and, thus, not every Muslim is a terrorist.

Certainly, the Middle East is not the only area ripe with terrorist activity aimed at the United States. Historical conflict in Northern Ireland has spawned the Provisional Irish Republican Army (PIRA), reportedly having

**Other International Threats**

significant financial contacts with groups in large East Coast cities (e.g., Boston, Philadelphia, New York).[88] Recent incidents in Germany, Italy, and France have indicated a "reawakening" of the Red Brigades, the Greens, and other cell groups expressing a left-wing, Marxist orientation.[89]

Then, too, a relatively new phenomenon called "narco-terrorism" continues to plague American police agencies as well as the international community. The most illustrative cases are seen in South America surrounding the highly lucrative cocaine business. Drug lords in the Medellin and Cali Cartels, have allied with the M-19 group in Colombia and Sendero Luminoso (Shining Path) in Peru for protection in cultivating and trafficking cocaine to the United States. Similar arrangements between drug dealers and anti-Western political groups (or states) have been observed in Cuba, Nicaragua, Panama, Bulgaria, and Burma.[90] More problematic to local police agencies is the connection between ethnic drug dealers (Haitians, Jamaicans, and Cubans) and foreign governments, which results in significant financing and armament supplying in support of drug trafficking to the United States.[91]

**Right-Wing Extremism**

The resurgence of right-wing, white-supremacist groups across the country was highlighted in the bombing of the Alfred P. Murrah Federal Building in Oklahoma City on April 19, 1995 (Figure 3-8). The blast killed 169 people, including 19 children, and injured more than 500 others. Convicted and sentenced to death, Timothy James McVeigh, held "extreme right-wing views and hated the federal government."[92] According to the FBI, the former army sergeant often wore military fatigues, sold weapons at gun shows, and attended militia meetings.[93] The incident focused attention on a number of right-wing groups and state militias which have traditionally expressed strong antigovernment and white-supremacist propaganda. These groups have also supported violence against minorities (African Americans, Asians, and Jews), homosexuals, and members of the U.S. Treasury Department (Bureau of Alcohol, Tobacco and Firearms and the Internal Revenue Service). While the number of members of each of these groups is relatively small, they pose a significant threat because of their ability to communicate and coordinate activities. The groups have multiple names and members, publish regular newsletters, maintain Internet web sites, and operate automated bulletin board systems. In some cases, documented collusion between these groups and local law enforcement officials has posed a significant threat. Many people are attracted to these groups because they identify themselves with fundamentalist Christianity. Much of their rhetoric focuses on patriotism as interpreted by their leaders, usually using a perversion of the Constitution or the Bible. These groups consist of well-armed ideologues who possess the potential for increased terrorism, at least in geographic pockets throughout the United States.[95] Figure 3-9 provides a list of the major right-wing groups active today.

The face of terrorism in the United States has changed in the past five years. More and more of the activities are characterized by random bombings aimed not at political agendizing or ransom delivery, but rather for "effect." That is, they are random acts of violence aimed at causing significant death, destruction, and widespread pandemonium through a society, leaving the larger community asking "Why?"

**Aryan Nations**—White-supremacist organization with strong separatist ideology. Led by Richard Butler of Hayden Lake, Idaho, a major figure in the Christian Identity Church, a pseudoreligious justification for white supremacy. The Nations recruits members from white prison gangs. Their goal is to develop an all-white homeland, to be called the "Northwest Mountain Republic," in Washington, Oregon, Idaho, Montana, and Wyoming.

**Covenant, Sword and Arm of the Lord**—This paramilitary group operated primarily in Texas, Arkansas, and Missouri. Eight members were arrested with illegal weapons, explosives, land mines, and an antitank rocket launcher in 1985. High Christian fundamentalism with survivalist mentality.

**Ku Klux Klan**—Primarily a southern states organization, with the largest memberships in Alabama, Georgia, North Carolina, and Mississippi. Several of the chapters have foregone the traditional cross-burning and hooded robes in favor of automatic weapons, paramilitary training camps and camouflage uniforms. In 1997, members of the KKK were indicted in a plot to blow up a natural gas plant in Texas, covering the planned armed robbery of an armored car. The group still maintains the white-supremacist and anti-Semitic beliefs prominently characterizing the KKK historically.

**Minutemen**—Paramilitary organization that was strongest during the 1960s. Small enclaves still exist which express strong anticommunist rhetoric and violence against liberals. Their insignia of the crosshairs of a rifle scope usually earmarks this group from other right-wing extremists.

**National Alliance**—Neo-Nazi group led by William L. Pierce, who started a new white enclave in rural West Virginia. Pierce is the author of *The Turner Diaries,* the saga of a family that survives the impending race war against African Americans and retreats to the mountains for safety.

**Posse Comitatus**—Loose-knit group attracting rural farmers. Strong antigovernment sentiment that claims that the Federal Reserve System and income tax are unconstitutional. Posse leaders have fused tax-protest doctrine with virulent anti-Semitism. Leader Gordon Kahl murdered two U.S. marshals in North Dakota and was subsequently killed in a shootout in 1983.

**Skinheads**—Violence-prone, neo-Nazi youth gang whose members are noted for their shaved heads. They express a strong white-supremacist, racist, and anti-Semitic ideology with close linkages to the Ku Klux Klan.

**The Order**—The most violent of the neo-Nazi groups, with several ties to the Aryan Nations. Responsible for the murder of a Jewish radio personality in Denver in 1984; at least two armored car robberies totaling $4 million in Seattle, Washington, and Ukiah, California, and a large bombing attempt in Coeur d'Alene, Idaho.

**White Aryan Resistance (WAR)**—The main white-supremacist group in California, headed by Tom Metzger, former Grand Dragon of the California Ku Klux Klan. Currently produces *Race and Reason,* a white-supremacist program shown on public-access cable TV.

**State Militias**—Active paramilitary organizations in almost every state (e.g., the Michigan Militia, the Republic of Texas Militia, the Arizona Vipers) expressing a strong white, Protestant, local constitutionalist perspective of government. They conduct a variety of paramilitary camps and are preparing for the "impending race war" of the future. Many groups have legitimate firearms licenses allowing automatic weapons and explosives. One group in Arizona is known to have purchased a WWII tank. Strong linkages to local police agencies have been documented. Members are strong gun owner advocates with a super patriotism and anti-federal government sentiment.

**FIGURE 3-9.** Major right-wing militant groups in the United States.[94]

# SCHOOL VIOLENCE

Similar to acts of terrorism, the recent tragedies stemming from school shootings seem to have no logical explanations. In the last three years, almost every state has suffered a tragic incident involving a school shooting or an episode of school violence in which students have lost their lives. Most of these incidents have not captured the nation's attention as did the shootings in Littleton, Colorado, (April 20, 1999) or Jonesboro, Arkansas, (March 24, 1998) in which several students were killed. Indeed, in these cases the nation stood shocked as innocent children and teachers were killed by random acts of irrational violence carried out by fellow students. In Littleton, the tragedy ended only when the young perpetrators committed suicide.

No other single incident has had such a profound impact on American feelings of safety and security than the shooting at Columbine High School in Littleton. Two heavily armed students dressed in black trench coats attacked fellow students with homemade bombs and automatic weapons. It remains the worst attack in an American school, with fifteen students and teachers dead (including the two gunmen) and another twenty-five wounded. The two students were among a handful of students called the "Trench Coat Mafia." They wore long, black coats, kept to themselves, generally followed the "goth" culture, and professed strong white-supremacist ideals. The term *goth* is short for "gothic," which refers to vampire novels and similar dark themes from centuries past. The goth culture is characterized by the absence of color—*black*. Therefore, members are often identified by their dyed black hair, black fingernails and lipstick, black boots, black clothing, and myriad of body tattoos and piercings. Followers of the movement are often associated with self-destructive and radically counterculture pop figures, such as shock-rocker Marilyn Manson and a variety of underground "death-rock" or "black-metal" bands such as King Diamond, Venom, Christian Death, KMFDM, and Cannibal Corpse.

Following a rash of other school shootings (refer to Box 3-12), the Columbine episode brought immediate attention to school safety. The newly researched statistics proved shocking! More than 3,930 students were expelled from school during the 1997-98 school year for bringing a firearm to school.[96] This figure was down roughly 30 percent from the previous year.

**FIGURE 3-10.** Students flee the deadly rampage at Columbine High School in Littleton, Colorado, which shocked the nation and renewed emphasis on school safety and security. (Courtesy of Kevin Higley/AP/Wide World Photos.)

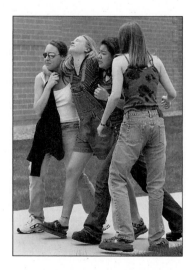

Closer analysis of student homicides also revealed that most student-related deaths at schools still occurred by known assailants rather than by random shootings such as at Columbine. In most cases, a rival gang fight or a sour boyfriend-girlfriend or student-teacher relationship was the underlying cause of the violence. From 1992 to 1998, more school children died at the hands of known acquaintances than during high-profile episodes of random violence.[97] These figures dramatically show that schools are anything but safe. Indeed, the Columbine incident drew significant attention not only because of its magnitude, but also because of its location. A normally serene, upper class, predominately white high school became the scene of a tragic shooting all too commonly associated with inner-city, ghetto neighborhoods.

The Columbine High School shooting sent shockwaves through the American public. The result has been an intense debate on several highly controversial subjects such as gun control, entertainment and media violence, and pop culture. School violence and random acts of terrorism leave us all with a sense of helplessness and desperation. These are phenomena that will be facing American police agencies throughout the foreseeable future. No place seems to be safe, and more intense demands are being made on the police to prevent and deter such acts of violence. Clearly, these external influences will continue to impact the role of the police in a highly political and dynamic manner.

## BOX 3-12

### Recent School Shooting Incidents

**October 1, 1997:** A 16-year-old boy in Pearl, Mississippi, kills his mother and then goes to his high school and shoots nine students, two fatally. He has been sentenced to life in prison while two others await trial on accessory charges.

**December 1, 1997:** Three students are killed and five others wounded while attending high school in West Paducah, Kentucky. A 14-year-old students pleads guilty and is serving life sentence for murder.

**March 24, 1998:** Two boys, 11 and 13, open fire from the woods on students conducting a fire drill at a middle school in Jonesboro, Arkansas. Four girls and a teacher are shot to death and ten others wounded; both boys are convicted in juvenile court of murder and can be held up to age 21.

**April 24, 1998:** A science teacher is shot to death by a 14-year-old in front of students at an eighth grade graduation dance in Edinboro, Pennsylvania.

**May 19, 1998:** Three days before his graduation, an 18-year-old honor student opens fire in the parking lot of his high school in Fayetteville, Tennessee, killing a classmate who was dating his ex-girlfriend.

**May 21, 1998:** A 15-year-old boy kills his parents and then opens fire on students at his high school in Springfield, Oregon. Two teenagers are killed and twenty others wounded.

**April 20, 1999:** Two heavily armed students attack students at Columbine High School in Littleton, Colorado, with homemade bombs and automatic weapons. In the worst attack ever in an American school, fifteen students and teachers (including the gunmen) are killed and another twenty are wounded.

**May 20, 1999:** A student opens fire at Heritage High School near Conyers, Georgia, just east of Atlanta. While there are no life-threatening injuries, six school mates are hospitalized with gunshot injuries.

**February 29, 2000:** A 6-year-old, first grade student shoots and kills his classmate, Kayla Rolland at Buell Elementary School in Flint, Michigan. No charges against the shooter are filed, since he is incapable of understanding right from wrong and the complexities of his actions. He meant only to scare his classmate. The student's 19-year old uncle, Jamelle James is indicted for felony manslaughter since he provided the shooter with easy access to a loaded firearm.

# SUMMARY

Police departments, like all administrative agencies, do not operate independently of external controls. Federal, state, and local governmental controls and influences are, in most instances, both legal and proper. The extent to which they impact on a law enforcement agency depends in part on national events and the unique political characteristics of each community.

This chapter has not identified all the possible external sources of influence and control that could affect law enforcement agencies. Instead, it has identified the most common and most influential to law enforcement agencies, categorizing them according to federal, state, or local origin. For example, the impact of decisions by the U.S. Supreme Court and local law enforcement is indisputable. Four of the most important decisions, *Mapp* v. *Ohio* (1961), *Gideon* v. *Wainright* (1963), *Escobedo* v. *Illinois* (1964), and *Miranda* v. *Arizona* (1966), have profoundly altered police practices regarding search and seizure and interrogation. In more recent years, appointments to the Supreme Court by Presidents Ronald Reagan and George Bush have provided a conservative majority whose decisions have been favorable to law enforcement. Thus, although there may be some dispute as to whether such decisions are "good" or "bad," there is little argument that such decisions deeply affect operations of police departments at all levels of government.

Even agencies without specific governmental connection can exert tremendous influence over the operations and professional image of local police departments. For example, the Commission on Accreditation for Law Enforcement Agencies (CALEA), a private nonprofit organization formed in 1979, has improved both the operations and the images of local police departments by providing the opportunity for them to become accredited and, thereby, to enjoy considerable professional status both in their local communities and at the national level with other law enforcement agencies.

The impact exerted on law enforcement by the state has increased dramatically since the 1970s, primarily via legislation that imposes preemployment and training standards on local police agencies. Further state intervention is not expected, except in those extraordinary cases involving rampant malfeasance, misfeasance, or nonfeasance.

The greatest control of the day-to-day operations of a police department emanates from the local level but is strongly affected by the local dominant values and political culture.

Two of the principle government actors exerting influence and control over law enforcement agencies will be the mayor in a strong mayor form of government and the city manager. Because the strong mayor and city manager have hiring and firing authority over the police chief, they can, if they choose, exert considerable control and influence over that office. There is little evidence that any particular form of government necessarily provides greater job security to the police chief than another; however, considerable evidence suggests that police executives who lack protection from arbitrary and unjustified removal have difficulty in fulfilling their responsibilities objectively and independently. Some states have systems offering statutory protection to police chiefs, but most do not. In states that do not provide protection, police chiefs across the country are forced to look for job protection in local civil service codes, local municipal ordinances, and any individual employment contracts they are able to negotiate. Thus, although occupying highly sensitive positions that require insulation from the political process, most police chiefs have limited job protection.

The influence of city council members is somewhat less direct than that of a strong mayor and city manager, but they can be equally formidable as they control the appropriations for the law enforcement agencies. The local prosecutor can also exert considerable influence and control on the law enforcement agency because of the ultimate authority to review all arrests before their presentation in court and overall supervision of cases prepared by the police. Police chiefs who perceive that the prosecutor consistently reduces or fails to enforce certain types of violations may direct their enforcement efforts and resources elsewhere.

Similarly, police operations and enforcement efforts may be influenced by the decisions of local judges. For example, if judges consistently interject their personal biases into the judicial process and make it clear to police that they will dismiss certain categories of violations the police may discontinue enforcing that particular law.

Police administrators have to contend with a number of political issues and problems outside their immediate control and jurisdiction. Terrorism represents one issue that historically has targeted police as victims. With the rise of right-wing paramilitary groups, and the dramatic increase in school violence, the future portends an even greater threat to the safety and security not only of police, but also of the entire population.

# DISCUSSION QUESTIONS

1. How do the authors differentiate between "Politics" and "politics"?

2. What is the significance of the U.S. Supreme Court decisions in each of the following cases: *Mapp* v. *Ohio* (1966), *Gideon* v. *Wainright* (1963), *Escobedo* v. *Illinois* (1964), and *Miranda* v. *Arizona* (1966)?

3. What is meant by the "erosion" of many of the landmark cases of the Warren court?

4. What has been the impact of highlighted media cases, such as the Rodney King, O. J. Simpson, and Abner Louima cases, which focus on police brutality and unethical conduct? What have police departments done to remedy some of these issues?

5. What four national law enforcement associations are credited with developing the Commission on Accreditation for Law Enforcement Agencies (CALEA)?

6. What three styles of law enforcement were described by James Q. Wilson, and what are their major features?

7. Briefly describe the three major forms of local government found in the United States. How does each form impact the selection and retention of the police chief?

8. Conflicts are divided into three political arenas. What are they?

9. In what two ways is the legal status of a county sheriff different from that of a police chief?

10. Discuss the conflict areas between the police and the news media.

11. Define terrorism and explain its impact on local law enforcement.

12. What are some of the characteristics of right-wing extremist organizations?

# NOTES

1. W. H. Hudnut III, "The Police and the Polis: A Mayor's Perspective," in *Police Leadership in America: Crisis and Opportunity,* ed. William A. Geller (Westport, Conn.: Praeger, 1985), p. 20.

2. "Congress Clears Bill to Eliminate COPS Program," *Crime Prevention News,* 95:23 (December 13, 1995), 1.

3. A. E. Bent, *The Politics of Law Enforcement* (Lexington, Mass.: D. C. Heath, 1974), p. 63.

4. N. G. Holten and M. E. Jones, *The Systems of Criminal Justice* (Boston: Little, Brown, 1978), p. 416.

5. Treatment of the Supreme Court's influence has been drawn from Thomas Phelps, Charles Swanson, and Kenneth Evans, *Introduction to Criminal Justice* (Santa Monica, Calif.: Goodyear Publishing, 1979), pp. 128–131.

6. In a legal sense, the Supreme Court opted for a piecemeal application when it rejected the "shorthand doctrine" (i.e., making a blanket application of the Federal Bill of Rights provisions binding on the states) in its consideration of *Hurtado* v. *California,* 110 U.S. 516 (1884); therefore, the statement should be read in the context that the activist role was a policy decision.

7. Fred P. Graham, *The Self-Inflicted Wound* (New York: Macmillan, 1970), p. 37. For a look at the police and due process see A. T. Quick, "Attitudinal Aspects of Police Compliance with Procedural Due Process," *American Journal of Criminal Law,* 6 (1978), 25–56.

8. T. R. Dye, *Politics in States and Communities* (Englewood Cliffs, N.J.: Prentice Hall, 1973), p. 214.

9. The concept of the "erosion" of the Mapp and Miranda decisions is commonly referred to in studies by Thomas Davies as cited in *The Oxford Companion to the Supreme Court of the United States,* ed. Kermit L. Hall (New York: Oxford University Press, 1992), p. 266; G. M. Caplan, *Modern Procedures for Police Interrogation* (Washington, D.C.: Police Executive Research Forum, 1992); and Rolando V. del Carmen, *Criminal Procedure: Law and Practice,* 3rd ed. (Belmont, Calif.: Wadsworth Publishing, 1995) pp. 317–336.

10. See *Massachusetts* v. *Shepard,* 468 U.S. 981 (1984) and *United States* v. *Leon,* 468 U.S. 897 (1984).

11. Justice William Brennan's dissent in *United States* v. *Leon.*

12. *Carroll* v. *United States,* 267 U.S. 132 (1925).

13. *Michigan Department of State Police* v. *Sitz,* 496 U.S. 444 (1990).

14. *Arizona* v. *Fulminante,* 111 S.Ct. 1246 (1991).

15. "Supreme Court on Police Powers," *Law Enforcement News,* 17:338, 339 (June 15/30, 1991), pp. 1, 9, 10.

16. Edward Timms, "Scandal Leaving Some Leary of Nation's Law Enforcement," *The Dallas Morning News* (September 25, 1995), p. 1.

17. Adapted from David Kocieniewski, "Injured Man Says Brooklyn Officers Tortured Him in Custody," *New York Times,* August 13, 1997, B1, B3; and "New York Officer to Plead Guilty in Beating," *Dallas Morning News,* May 25, 1999, p. A3.

18. Michael Cooper, "Officers in Bronx Fire 41 Shots, and an Unarmed Man is Killed," *New York Times,* February 4, 1999, A1, B5.

19. Anonymous Los Angeles resident, *USA Today* (September 22, 1995), 1.

20. Cathy Booth, Sylvester Monroe, and Edwin M. Reingold, "Law and Disorder," *Time,* 137:13 (April 1, 1991), 18–21.

21. Ibid., 21.

22. Ibid.

23. Louis A. Radelet and David Carter, *Police and the Community,* 5th ed. (New York: Macmillan Press, 1994), p. 46.

24. Interview with Dr. Gary Sykes, Director, Southwestern Law Enforcement Institute, Richardson, Texas (January 3, 1996).

25. Radelet and Carter, pp. 91–92.

26. Ibid., p. 99.

27. Ibid., p. 100.

28. Booth, Monroe, and Reingold, p. 21 [italics added].

29. Commission on Accreditation for Law Enforcement Agencies (CALEA), *Accreditation Program Overview* (Fairfax, Va.: CALEA, 1990), p. 4.

30. Gary W. Cordner, "Written Rules and Regulations: Are They Necessary?" *FBI Law Enforcement Bulletin* 58:7, p. 18.

31. Russell Maas, "Written Rules and Regulations: Is the Fear Real?" *Law and Order* (May 1990), p. 36.

32. Gerald Williams, *Making the Grade: The Benefits of Law Enforcement Accreditation* (Washington, D.C.: Police Executive Research Forum, 1989), pp. xv, xvii.

33. Ibid., pp. xv, xvii.

34. Ibid., pp. xvii, xviii.

35. Robert M. Fogelson, *Big-City Police,* (Cambridge, Mass: Harvard University Press, 1975), pp. 14–15.

36. Ibid., p. 14.

37. This vignette is based on one of the author's experiences while serving in law enforcement.

38. Information provided by the National Association of State Directors of Law Enforcement Training.

39. The National Advisory Commission on Criminal Justice Standards and Goals, *A National Strategy to Reduce Crime* (Washington, D.C.: U.S. Government Printing Office, 1972), p. 149.

40. James Q. Wilson, *Varieties of Police Behavior* (New York: Atheneum, 1973).

41. The President's Commission on Law Enforcement and Administration of Justice, *Task Force Report: The Police* (Washington, D.C.: U.S. Government Printing Office, 1967), p. 127.

42. A. H. Andrews, Jr., "Structuring the Political Independence of the Police Chief," in *Police Leadership in America,* ed. Geller, pp. 9, 10.

43. V. A. Leonard and H. W. Moore, *Police Organization and Management* (Mineola, N.Y.: Foundation Press, 1971), p. 21.

44. G. E. Berkeley et al., *Introduction to Criminal Justice* (Boston: Holbrook Press, 1976), p. 216.

45. Leonard and Moore, p. 15.

46. J. F. Ahern, *Police in Trouble* (New York: Hawthorn Books, 1972), pp. 96–98.

47. J. J. Norton and G. G. Cowart, "Assaulting the Politics/Administration Dichotomy," *Police Chief,* 45:11 (1978), p. 26.

48. Interview with staff assistants at the International Association of Chiefs of Police, Washington, D.C., December 8, 1995.

49. One of the most comprehensive collections of articles and essays focusing on the role of the chief of police is found in *Police Leadership in America: Crisis and Opportunity,* ed. William Geller (New York: Prager, 1985).

50. Janet Ferris et al., "Present and Potential Legal Job Protections Available to Heads of Agencies," *Florida Police Chief,* 14:5 (1994), 43–45.

51. G. L. Williams and S. Cheurprakobkit, "Police Executive Contracts: Are They a Foundation for Successful Tenure?" In *Controversial Issues in Policing,* ed. J. D. Sewell (Boston: Allyn and Bacon, 1999), pp. 105–112. (This discussion was adapted with permission from this source.)

52. H. Mintzberg, *Power in and Around Organizations.* (Engelwood Cliffs, N.J.: Prentice Hall, 1983).

53. T. Roche, "Chief's Policy Thrust Into Debate," *St. Petersburg Times,* October 30, 1996, 1A.

54. "Help Stephens Succeed," *St. Petersburg Times,* October 31, 1996, editorial page.

55. C. Green, "Boulder Leadership Missing In Action," *Denver Post,* May 30, 1997.

56. C. Mahtesian, "Mission Impossible," *Governing* (January 1997), 19–23.

57. Ibid.

58. Ibid.

59. J. Ruiz. *The Return of the Ultimate Outsider: A Civilian Administrator as the Top Cop.* Unpublished paper (1997).

60. Ibid.

61. Ibid.

62. Ibid.

63. See S. Walker, *The Police in America* (New York: McGraw Hill, 1992), p. 44; and B. A. Reaves, *Sheriff's Departments 1990,* U.S. Dept. of Justice, Bureau of Justice Statistics, p. 1.

64. National Sheriff's Association, *County Law Enforcement: Assessment of Capabilities and Needs* (Washington, D.C.: National Sheriff's Association, 1995), p. 1.

65. Reaves, p. 1.

66. L. P. Brown, "The Role of the Sheriff," in *The Future of Policing* ed. Alvin W. Cohn, (Beverly Hills, Calif.: Sage Publications, 1978), pp. 227–228.

67. Reaves, p. 1.

68. The President's Commission, *Task Force Report: The Police,* p. 30.

69. Ibid., p. 31.

70. Ibid.

71. Ibid.

72. J. H. Skolnick, *Justice Without Trial: Law Enforcement in a Democratic Society* (New York: John Wiley & Sons, 1966), pp. 228–229.

73. H. W. More, Jr., ed., *Critical Issues in Law Enforcement* (Cincinnati, Ohio: Anderson, 1972), p. 261.

74. The President's Commission, *Task Force Report: The Police,* p. 34.

75. Bent, p. 72.

76. E. M. Davis, "Press Relations Guide for Peace Officers," *Police Chief,* 39:3 (1972), p. 67.

77. Walter Goodman, "How Much Should TV Tell, and When?" *New York Times,* Oct. 29, 1990.

78. See General Order OM-F-4, "Release of Information to the News Media" issued by the Kentucky State Police, January 1, 1990.

79. Robert W. Taylor, "Managing Terrorist Incidents," *The Bureaucrat: A Journal for Public Managers,* 12:4 (Winter, 1984), 53–58; and "What's Wrong Inside: A Special Report on the FBI," *Time,* 149:17 (April 28, 1997).

80. Richard Schultz, "Conceptualizing Political Terrorism: A Typology," *Journal of International Affairs,* 4:8 (Spring/Summer, 1978).

81. Robert W. Taylor, "Defining Terrorism in El Salvador: La Matanza," *The ANNALS of the American Academy of Political and Social Science* (September, 1982), 107–110.

82. Brian Jenkins, *The Study of Terrorism: Definitional Problems* (Santa Monica, Calif.: The Rand Corporation, 1980), p. 1.

83. Taylor, "Defining Terrorism in El Salvador," p. 109.

84. John Hughes, "The Killing Fields of Iran," *Christian Science Monitor* (January 25, 1989), 18.

85. Shaw J. Dallal, "Islam and the U.S. National Interest," *The Link* (February–March 1993), 5.

86. John L. Esposito, *The Islamic Threat: Myth or Reality* (Oxford, England: Oxford University Press, 1992), p. IX.

87. See A. M. Rosenthal, "As You Sow," *The New York Times* (December 22, 1992), p. A21; E. McQuaid, "By Peace or the Sword," *The Jerusalem Post* (December 16, 1992); D. Pipes, "Fundamental Questions about Muslims," *The Wall Street Journal* (October 30, 1992), A11; and A. Permutter, "Wishful Thinking About Islamic Fundamentalism," *The Washington Post* (January 19, 1991), 16.

88. Scott S. Smith, "The Anglo-Irish Accord: Diverting Attention from the Real Issues," *Christian Science Monitor* (December 14, 1988), 15.

89. See Robert Kupperman and Jeff Kamen, "A New Outbreak of Terror is Likely," *The New York Times* (April 19, 1988), 6; and Alan Riding, "Rifts Threaten Plan to Remove Borders," *CJ International,* 6:5 (September/October 1990), 3.

90. David W. Balsiger, "Narco-Terrorism 'Shooting Up' America," *Annual Edition: Violence and Terrorism 990/91* (Guilford, Conn.: Dushkin Publishing, 1990), pp. 164–66.

91. Ibid.

92. "Families Scoff at Suspect's New Images," *The Sunday Oklahoman* (July 2, 1995), 24.

93. Ibid.

94. Adapted from several law enforcement intelligence reports. See also Cheryl Sullivan, "New Extremists exceed 'Jim Crowism' of KKK," *Christian Science Monitor* (January 12, 1992).

95. Radelet and Carter, *Police and Community,* p. 248.

96. Refer to Claudia Kalb, "Schools on the Alert," *Newsweek* (August 23, 1999), 42–44.

97. R. Taylor, E. Fritsch, and T. Caeti, *Juvenile Justice: Policy, Programs, and Practice* (Westerville, Ohio: Glencoe/McGraw-Hill, forthcoming 2001).

## INTRODUCTION

Formal organizations are not a recent innovation.[1] Alexander the Great and Caesar used them to conquer; the pharaohs employed them to build pyramids; the emperors of China constructed great irrigation systems with them; and the first popes created an organization to deliver religion on a worldwide basis.[2] The extent to which contemporary America is an organizational society is such that:

> We are born in organizations, educated by organizations, and spend most of our lives working for organizations. We spend much of our time . . . playing and praying in organizations. Most of us will die in an organization and when the time comes for burial, the largest organization of all—the state—must grant official permission.[3]

# —4—
# ORGANIZATIONAL THEORY

*Theory and practice are inseparable.*
DOUGLAS MCGREGOR

The basic rationale for the existence of organizations is that they do those things that people are unwilling or unable to do alone. Parsons notes that organizations are distinguished from other human groupings or social units in that to a much greater degree they are constructed and reconstructed to achieve specific goals; corporations, armies, hospitals, and police departments are included within this meaning, whereas families and friendship groups are not.[4] Schein defines an organization as:

> the rational coordination of the activities of a number of people for the achievement of some common explicit purpose or goal, through division of labor and function, and through a hierarchy of authority and responsibility.[5]

Blau and Scott identify four different types of formal organizations by asking the question of *cui bono,* or who benefits: (1) mutual benefit associations, such as police labor unions, where the primary beneficiary is the membership (see Box 4-1); (2) business concerns, such as Microsoft, where the owners are the prime beneficiary; (3) service organizations, such as community mental health centers, where a specific client group is the prime beneficiary; and (4) commonweal organizations, such as the Department of Defense and police departments, where the beneficiary is the public at large.[6]

These four types of formal organizations each has its own central issues.[7] Mutual benefit associations, such as police unions, face the crucial problem of maintaining the internal democratic processes—providing for participation and control by their membership. For businesses, the central issue is maximizing profits in a competitive environment. Service organizations are faced with the conflict between administrative regulations and providing the services judged by the professional to be most appropriate. In the case of a community mental health center, an illustration is that, following a reduction in funding, a regulation is placed into effect that requires all clients to be treated in group sessions when the psychiatric social worker believes the only effective treatment for a particular client is to be seen individually. The core reason that police managers must have a working knowledge of organizational theory stems from the fact that police departments are commonweal organizations.

## BOX 4-1

The key issue for a police department and other types of commonweal organizations is finding a way to accommodate pressures from two different sources, external and internal. The public, through its elected and appointed representatives, must have the means of controlling the ends served by its police department. This external democratic control feature also has the expectation that the internal workings of the police department will be bureaucratic, governed by the criterion of efficiency, and not also democratic. This is because democratic control by the members of a police department might be at the expense of lessening the police department's ability to affect the will of the community. Simultaneously, the large numbers of officers at the lower levels of the police department do not want to be treated like "cogs in a machine" and desire some voice in how the department operates (see Box 4-2). Thus, the

## BOX 4-2

challenge for police managers is how to maintain an organization that meets society's needs and the needs of the officers who work in it. This requires an understanding of such things as the different ways of organizing and the contrasting assumptions that various organizational forms make about the nature of people. Such knowledge is found within organizational theory.

This chapter consists of three major areas; each deals with different ways of thinking about how to organize work and work processes. Discussed more fully as they arise, the three major streams of thinking about work structures and processes to be treated are: (1) traditional organizational theory, upon which most police departments are based; (2) open systems theory, which represents a direct counterpoint to traditional theory; and (3) bridging theories, which to some greater or lesser degree show concern for the issues reflected both in traditional and open systems theories. Bridging theories do not fall neatly into either the traditional or the open systems category, yet reflect consideration of each, thus constituting a distinctly unique category. Within each of the three major streams of thinking about work structures and processes are illustrations of some of the specific techniques associated with various theorists and examples cast in a police context.

## TRADITIONAL ORGANIZATIONAL THEORY

Traditional theory is associated with organizations described as mechanistic, closed systems, bureaucratic, and stable. This body of knowledge evolved over centuries and crystallized between 1900 and 1940. The three stems of traditional organizational theory are (1) scientific management, (2) the bureaucratic model, and (3) administrative or management theory.

**Taylor: Scientific Management**

The father of scientific management was Frederick W. Taylor (1856–1915), and the thrust of his thinking was to find the "one best way" to do work. In addition to its status as a theory of work organization, Taylor's scientific management is a theory of motivation in its belief that employees will be guided in their actions by what is in their economic self-interest.

A Pennsylvanian born of Quaker-Puritan parents, Taylor was so discontented with the "evils" of waste and slothfulness that he applied the same careful analysis to finding the best way of playing croquet and of taking a cross-country walk with the least fatigue that was to be the hallmark of his later work in factories.[8] From 1878 to 1890, Taylor worked at the Midvale Steel Company in Philadelphia, rising from the ranks of the laborers to chief engineer in just six years.[9] Taylor's experience at Midvale gave him insight into the twin problems of productivity and worker motivation. He saw workers as deliberately restricting productivity by "natural soldiering" and "systematic soldiering."

*Natural soldiering* came from the natural inclination of employees not to push themselves; *systematic soldiering* came from workers not wanting to produce so much as to see their quotas raised or other workers thrown out of their jobs.[10] To correct these deficiencies, Taylor called for a "complete mental revolution"[11] on the part of both workers and managers, although it is certain that he faulted management more for its failure to design jobs properly and to give workers the proper economic incentives to overcome soldiering than he did workers for not producing.[12]

Taylor's scientific management is only loosely a theory of organization because its focus was largely upon work at the bottom part of the organization

Frederick W. Taylor
(Courtesy of the
Library of Congress.)

rather than being a general model. Scientific management's method was to find the most physically and time efficient way to sequence tasks and then to use rigorous and extensive controls to enforce the standards.

Taylor's conversation with "Schmidt" illustrates this:

"Schmidt, are you a high-priced man?"

"Vell, I don't know vat you mean."

"Oh yes, you do. What I want to know is whether you are a high-priced man or not."

"Vell, I don't know vat you mean."

"Oh, come now, you answer my questions. What I want to find out is whether you are a high-priced man or one of these cheap fellows here. What I want to find out is whether you want to earn $1.85 a day or whether you are satisfied with $1.15, just the same as all those cheap fellows are getting."

"Did I vant $1.85 a day? Vas dot a high-priced man? Vell, yes, I vas a high-priced man."

"Oh, you're aggravating me. Of course you want $1.85 a day—every one wants it! You know perfectly well that that has very little to do with your being a high-priced man. For goodness sake answer my questions, and don't waste any more of my time. Now come over here. You see that pile of pig iron?"

"Yes."

"You see that car?"

"Yes."

"Well, if you are a high-priced man, you will load that pig iron on that car tomorrow for $1.85. Now do wake up and answer my question. Tell me whether you are a high-priced man or not."

"Vell—did I got $1.85 for loading dot pig iron on dot car tomorrow?"

"Yes, of course you do, and you get $1.85 for loading a pile like that every day right through the year. That is what a high-priced man does, and you know it just as well as I do."

"Vell, dot's all right. I could load dot pig iron on the car tomorrow for $1.85, and I get it every day, don't I?"

"Certainly you do—certainly you do."

"Vell, den, I vas a high-priced man."

"Now, hold on, hold on. You know just as well as I do that a high-priced man has to do exactly as he's told from morning till night. You have seen this man here before, haven't you?"

"No, I never saw him."

"Well, if you are a high-priced man, you will do exactly as this man tells you tomorrow, from morning till night. When he tells you to pick up a pig and walk, you pick it up and you walk, and when he tells you to sit down and rest, you sit down. You do that right straight through the day. And what's more, no back talk. Now a high-priced man does just what he's told to do, and no back talk. Do you understand that? When this man tells you to walk, you walk; when he tells you to sit down, you sit down, and you don't talk back to him. Now you come on to work here tomorrow morning and I'll know before night whether you are really a high-priced man or not."[13]

Taylor also made other contributions, including the concept of functional supervision, the exception principle, and integrating cost accounting into the planning process.

For Taylor, authority was based not upon position in a hierarchy but rather upon knowledge; *functional supervision* meant that people were responsible for directing certain tasks despite the fact this meant that the authority of the supervisor might cut across organizational lines.[14] The *exception principle* meant that routine matters should be handled by lower-level managers or by supervisors and that higher-level managers should only receive reports of deviations above or below standard performances.[15] The integration of cost accounting into the planning process became part of some budgeting practices treated in Chapter 13.

Despite the success of scientific management in raising productivity and cutting costs, "Taylorism" was attacked from a variety of quarters. Union leaders saw it as a threat to their movement because it seemed to reduce, if not eliminate, the importance of unions. The management of Bethlehem Steel ultimately abandoned task management, as Taylor liked to refer to his system, because they were uncomfortable with such an accurate appraisal of their performance[16] and some liberals saw it as an exploitation of workers. Upton Sinclair charged that Taylor had given workers a 61 percent increase in wages while getting a 362 percent increase in work.[17] Taylor replied to this charge by saying that employees worked no harder, only more efficiently. In hearings before the U.S. House of Representatives in 1912, Taylor's methods were attacked thoroughly and he died three years later a discouraged man.

Scientific management did not disappear with Taylor, however. There remained a core of people devoted to its practice, including Henry L. Gantt (1861–1919); Watlington Emerson (1853–1931), also a promoter of the staff concept; Frank (1868–1924) and Lillian (1878–1972) Gilbreth; and Morris Cooke (1872–1960), who in *Our Cities Awake* (1918) called for the application of scientific management in municipal government. Gantt gained a measure of immortality by developing a basic planning chart, illustrated in Figure 4-1,

## State Police Testing Project

| Task Name | Duration | Start | End | 2001 | | | | |
|---|---|---|---|---|---|---|---|---|
| | | | | 12/Sep | 19/Sep | 26/Sep | 03/Oct | 1 |
| Order Project Equipment | 18.0 d | 13/Sep/01 | 06/Oct/02 | ████████ | | | | |
| Write Request for Computer, Printer, and Software | 2.0 d | 13/Sep/01 | 14/Sep/02 | ☐ | | | | |
| Obtain Administrative Approval for Equipment Request | 3.0 d | 15/Sep/01 | 17/Sep/02 | ☐ | | | | |
| Order Equipment & Software through Procurement | 3.0 d | 20/Sep/01 | 22/Sep/02 | | ☐ | | | |
| Equipment and Software on Order | 8.0 d | 23/Sep/01 | 04/Oct/02 | | ▭▭▭ | | | |
| Receive and Configure Equipment | 2.0 d | 05/Oct/01 | 06/Oct/02 | | | | ☐ | |
| Staff Project | 14.0 d | 13/Sep/01 | 30/Sep/02 | ██████ | | | | |
| Develop Job Descriptions | 2.0 d | 13/Sep/01 | 14/Sep/02 | ☐ | | | | |
| Announce Positions | 3.0 d | 15/Sep/01 | 17/Sep/02 | ☐ | | | | |
| Screen Applicants | 3.0 d | 20/Sep/01 | 22/Sep/02 | | ☐ | | | |
| Interview Finalists | 2.0 d | 23/Sep/01 | 24/Sep/02 | | ☐ | | | |
| Make Hiring Decisions | 1.0 d | 27/Sep/01 | 27/Sep/02 | | | ☐ | | |
| Train Staff | 3.0 d | 28/Sep/01 | 30/Sep/02 | | | ☐ | | |

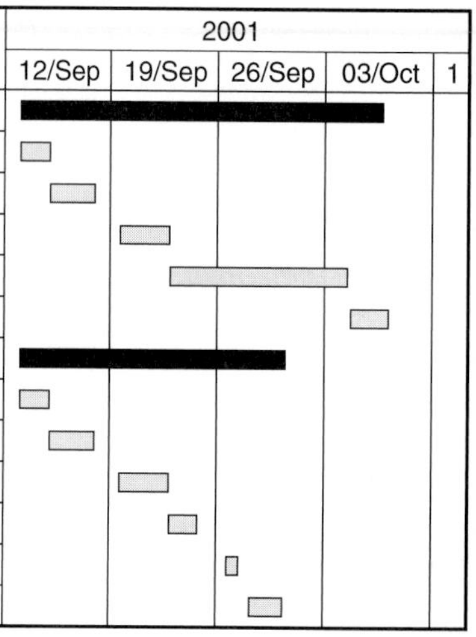

**FIGURE 4-1.** A portion of a Gantt Chart showing the start-up phase of a project.

that remains in wide use today and still bears his name. Developed during the summer of 1917, while Gantt worked at the Frankford Arsenal, the Gantt chart contained the then revolutionary idea that the key factor in planning production was not quantity, but time.[18] Some international interest in scientific management also remained after Taylor's death; in 1918 France's Ministry of War called for the application of scientific management as did Lenin in an article in *Pravda*.[19] It is, of course, ironic that a Marxist society should call for the use of a management system based on the principle that economic self-interest guides the behavior of workers.

The fact that the period when scientific management was a dominant force has "come and gone" does not mean that it is all history. Many of the techniques associated with scientific management such as time and motion studies and work flow analysis (depicted in Figure 4-2) remain in use in what is generally called industrial engineering. Other modern successors to scientific management were developed during World War II to support the war effort, and the refinement and more general application of these techniques is a post-1945 movement. The new techniques have alternatively been referred to as management science and operations research (OR), and their central orientation has been the application of quantitative and technical analysis to decision making.[20]

## Weber: The Bureaucratic Model

In popular usage, bureaucracy has come to mean:

> the slowness, the ponderous, the routine, the complication of procedures, and the maladapted responses of "bureaucratic" organizations to the needs which they should satisfy and the frustrations which their members, clients, or subjects consequently endure.[21]

Organizational "breakdown" (see example in Box 4-3) is far from the image of the ideal or pure bureaucracy developed by the towering German intellect Max Weber (1864–1920), the founder of modern sociology. For Weber,

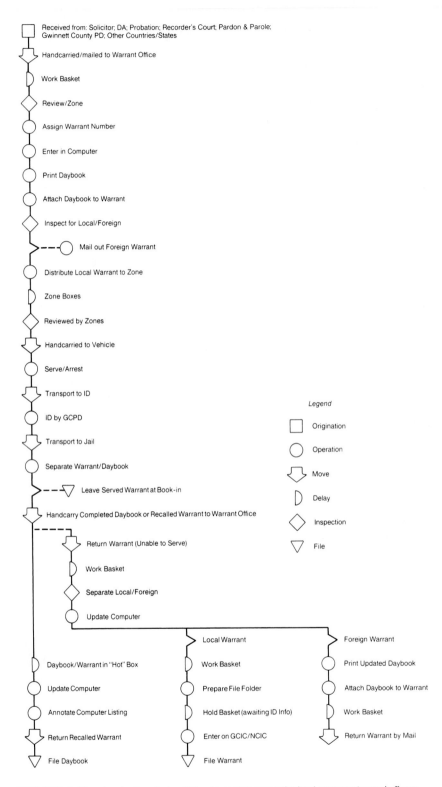

**FIGURE 4-2.** Analysis of sheriff's department criminal warrant work flow.

## BOX 4-3

### Woman Told Cops of Death Threat; She's Fatally Shot Four Days Later

by Alice McQuillan
**Daily News Staff Writer**
With Emily Gest and K.C. Baker

Four days before her spurned boyfriend shot her dead, Adela Buitrago told cops he had threatened to kill her with a knife, police said yesterday. As Buitrago's formal written complaint about her ex-lover was moving through the police bureaucracy, the murderous threat came true.

On Sunday, Pedro Game followed Buitrago, 35, to the Astoria, Queens, pool hall where she worked as a cashier and shot her several times in front of three witnesses, cops said. Hovering over her body, he then pressed a revolver to his chin and threatened to commit suicide. He fired but was only grazed and kept cops at bay for two hours until finally surrendering. Game, 41, was charged with murder, kidnapping and weapons possession.

Now the Police Department is looking into why Queens cops failed to investigate Buitrago's allegation immediately and arrest Game under tough new domestic violence policies. "Why did the police do nothing?" asked her brother, Gabriel Buitrago Escobar. "The police knew about the danger since last Wednesday."

In her complaint, filed Nov. 24, Buitrago said Game drove her to a desolate part of Astoria and threatened to knife her to death. She said this occurred Nov. 21—a week before Game allegedly made good on his threat and gunned her down at Alex's Club, a pool hall on 30th Ave.

"The department is investigating the handling of this complaint," said Sgt. Gerry Falcon, a police spokeswoman.

Buitrago tried to break off her relationship with Game after learning recently that he was married. For the 18 months they were together, Game had posed as a single man named William, Escobar said.

One reason the case might have slipped through the cracks is that Buitrago filed the menacing complaint in the 115th Precinct in Jackson Heights, where she lived, rather than with police in Astoria, where the threat occurred. A domestic-violence cop in the 115th Precinct recorded the complaint and faxed it to the 114th Precinct stationhouse in Astoria, a police source said.

It took several days for the complaint to be logged into that precinct's computer. It did not reach the squad's detectives until Sunday, the day cops say Game gunned down the woman he claimed to love.

Police are supposed to follow a tough must-arrest policy in domestic-violence cases in the wake of similar tragic incidents. If a complaint is made and the domestic relationship is confirmed, the offending party is supposed to be arrested, according to a police source.

"Cops treat these things pretty seriously, but this is just the opposite—it wasn't," said the source.

*Source:* © New York Daily News, L.P. reprinted with permission.

---

the choice was "only that between bureaucracy and dilettantism in the field of administration."[22] In this regard, Weber claimed that:

> Experience tends universally to show that the purely bureaucratic type of administrative organization—that is, the monocratic variety of the bureaucracy—is, from a purely technical point of view, capable of attaining the highest degree of efficiency and is in this sense formally the most rational known means of carrying out imperative control over human beings. It is superior to any other form in precision, in stability, in the stringency of its discipline, and in its reliability. It thus makes possible a particularly high degree of calculability of results for the heads of the organization and for those acting in relation to it. It is finally superior both in intensive efficiency and in the scope of operations, and is formally capable of application to all kinds of administrative tasks.[23]

Weber's bureaucratic model included the following characteristics:

1. The organization of offices follows the principle of hierarchy; that is, each lower office is under the control and supervision of a higher one. There is a right of appeal and of statement of grievances from the lower to the higher.

Max Weber (Courtesy of the Library of Congress.)

2. Specified areas of competence, meaning a division of labor, exist, in each of which the authority and responsibility of every organizational member is identified.
3. Official duties are bound by a system of rational rules.
4. Administrative acts, decisions, and rules are recorded in writing.
5. The "rights" associated with a position are the property of the office and not of the officeholders.
6. Employees are appointed on the basis of qualifications, and specialized training is necessary.
7. Organizational members do not own the means of production.[24]

Although not all of the characteristics of Weber's bureaucratic model can be revealed by an organizational chart, Figure 4-3 does depict two important features: (1) the principle of hierarchy and (2) a division of labor that results in specialization.

Weber's bureaucratic model rested on what he called rational-legal authority. This he contrasted to (1) traditional authority, which rested on an established belief in the sanctity of immemorial traditions and the legitimacy of the status of people exercising authority under those traditions, illustrated by kings or queens, and (2) charismatic authority, which stemmed from the exceptional sanctity, heroism, or exemplary character of an individual.[25]

# Organizational Chart
# Hawaii County Police Department

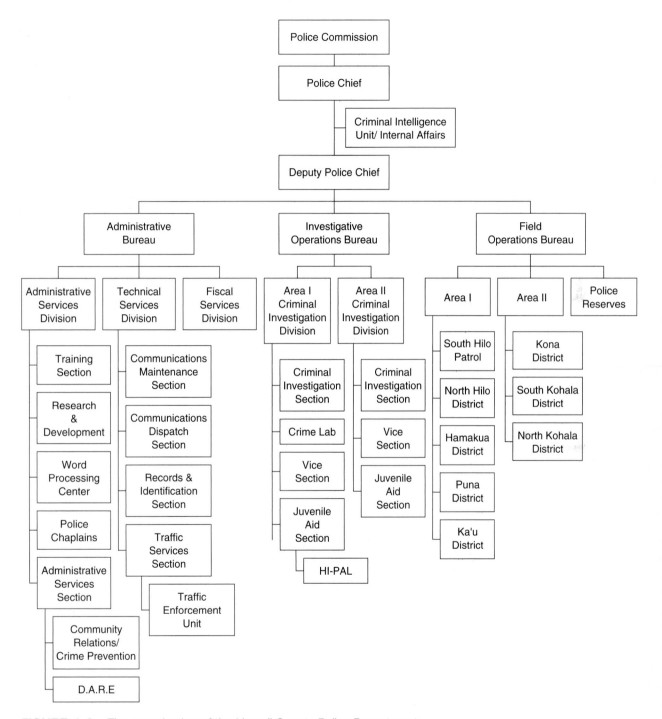

**FIGURE 4-3.** The organization of the Hawaii County Police Department.

Two dimensions to Weber's work are often not considered. First, on the one hand, he considered bureaucracy as the most efficient form of organization, and, on the other hand, he feared that this very efficiency constituted a threat to individual freedom by its impersonal nature and oppressive routine.[26] Second, Weber deplored the career professional of moderate ambitions who craved security; this type of person Weber saw as lacking spontaneity and inventiveness, the modern-day "petty bureaucrat."[27]

As a closing note, Weber did not invent the bureaucratic model; it had existed for centuries. Thus, whereas Weber spawned the formal study of organizations, it scarcely seems fair to lay at his feet any real or fancied inadequacies of the model or its operation. Moreover, although it would be difficult to overstate Weber's contributions, it must be borne in mind that whereas some people—such as Chester Barnard—read him in the original German,[28] his work was not translated into English and was not generally available until 1947, long after the bureaucratic model was well entrenched.

**Administrative Theory**

Administrative or management theory sought to identify generic or universal methods of administration. Its benchmark is the 1937 publication of Luther Gulick (1892–1993) and Lyndall Urwick's (1891–1983) edited *Papers on the Science of Administration*. In content, administrative theory is more compatible with the bureaucratic model than with scientific management because it concentrates upon broader principles. Administrative theory, also referred to as the principles approach, is distinguished from the bureaucratic model by its "how to" emphasis. At some risk of oversimplification, the principles both operationalize and reinforce features of the bureaucratic model. Consequently, because of the continuing pervasiveness of the bureaucratic model, the principles either explicitly or implicitly continue to play an important role in organizations, including police departments. The key contributors to this school are Henri Fayol (1841–1925), James Mooney (1884–1957) and Alan Reiley (1869–1947), and Gulick and Urwick.

Henri Fayol graduated as an engineer at the age of 19 from France's National School of Mines at St. Etienne and began a 40-year career with the Commentary-Fourchambault Company.[29] His contributions are based on writings that were an outgrowth of his experiences as a manager. Fayol's fame rests chiefly on his *General and Industrial Management* (1916). The first English edition of this appeared in Great Britain in 1923, and although his "Administrative Theory of the State" appeared in *Papers on the Science of Administration*, his main work, *General and Industrial Management*, was not widely available in this country until 1949. Fayol's principles included

1. A division of work, that is, specialization
2. Authority, namely, the right to give orders and the power to extract obedience—whoever exercises authority has responsibility
3. Discipline, in essence the obedience, application, energy and behavior, and outward marks of respect in accordance with the standing agreement between the firm and its employees
4. Unity of command, with an employee receiving orders from only one supervisor
5. Unity of direction, with one head and one plan for a group of activities having the same objective—unity of command cannot exist without unity of direction

6. Subordination of individual interest to the general interest—the interest of an individual or a group of employees does not prevail over the concerns of the firm

7. Remuneration of personnel—to be fair to the employee and employer

8. Centralization, a natural order of things—however, centralization or decentralization is a question of proportion, finding the optimum degree for the particular concern

9. Scalar chain, namely, the chain of superiors ranging from the ultimate authority to the lowest ranks, often referred to as the chain of command

10. Order, that is, a place for everyone and everyone in his or her place

11. Equity, namely, the combination of kindness and justice

12. Stability of tenure of personnel, which allows employees to become familiar with their jobs and productive—a mediocre manager who stays is infinitely preferable to outstanding managers who come and go

13. Initiative at all levels of the organization—this represents a great source of strength for business

14. Esprit de corps, harmony, and union of personnel—these constitute a great strength, and efforts should be made to establish them[30]

Fayol recognized that his scalar principle could produce disastrous consequences if it were followed strictly, since it would hamper swift action.[31] He therefore developed Fayol's gangplank, or horizontal bridge, discussed more fully in Chapter 7, as a means of combating this issue. Fayol's belief that a mediocre manager who stays is better than outstanding ones who come and go refound currency in the late 1970s, as many city managers retreated from hiring police chiefs from outside the organization. Although it can be argued with some validity that this movement was due to the increased qualifications of internal candidates, it is also true that the frequent recruitment, screening, and selection of "portable" police managers was an expensive, time-consuming, and, at least occasionally in terms of results, disappointing process.

Mooney and Reiley's *Onward Industry* (1931) was generally consistent with the work of Fayol, as were the subsequent revisions of this publication, which appeared in 1939 and 1947 under the title of *The Principles of Organization*.[32]

In "Notes on the Theory of Organization," which was included in *Papers on the Science of Administration*, Gulick coined the most familiar and enduring acronym of administration, POSDCORB:

> *P*lanning, that is, working out in broad outline the things that need to be done and the methods for doing them to accomplish the purpose set for the enterprise;
>
> *O*rganizing, that is, the establishment of the formal structure of authority through which work subdivisions are arranged, defined and co-ordinated for the defined objective;
>
> *S*taffing, that is, the whole personnel function of bringing in and training the staff and maintaining favorable conditions of work;
>
> *D*irecting, that is, the continuous task of making decisions and embodying them in specific and general orders and instructions and serving as the leader of the enterprise;
>
> *C*o-ordinating, that is, the all important duty of interrelating the various parts of the work;

_R_eporting, that is, keeping those to whom the executive is responsible informed as to what is going on, which thus includes keeping himself and his subordinates informed through records, research and inspection;

_B_udgeting, with all that goes with budgeting in the form of fiscal planning, accounting and control.[33]

Gulick acknowledged that his POSDCORB was adapted from the functional analysis elaborated by Fayol in _General and Industrial Management._ Urwick's "Organization as a Technical Problem," which appeared in _Papers on the Science of Administration,_ also drew upon the work of another Frenchman, A. V. Graicunas, for his treatment of the span of control. Urwick asserted that

> Students of administration have long recognized that, in practice, no human brain should attempt to supervise directly more than five, or at the most six individuals whose work is interrelated.[34]

Urwick, the Oxford-educated and military-career Englishman, also underscored management theory with his subsequent _Scientific Principles of Organization_ (1938).

**Critique of Traditional Theory**

Scientific management is decried because of its "man as machine" orientation, and ample life is given to that argument by even a casual reading of the conversation between Taylor and the legendary Schmidt. On balance, although Taylor's emphasis was on task, he was not totally indifferent to the human element, arguing that

> No system of management, however good, should be applied in a wooden way. The proper personal relations should always be maintained between the employers and men; and even the prejudices of the workmen should be considered in dealing with them.[35]

The bureaucratic model has no shortage of critics. The humanist Warren Bennis levels the following specific criticisms:

1. Bureaucracy does not adequately allow for the personal growth and development of mature personalities.
2. It develops conformity and "group think."
3. It does not take into account the "informal organization" and emerging and unanticipated problems.
4. Its systems of control and authority are hopelessly outdated.
5. It has no adequate judicial process.
6. It does not possess adequate means for resolving differences and conflicts between ranks and, most particularly, between functional groups.
7. Communication and innovative ideas are thwarted or distorted due to hierarchical divisions.
8. The full human resources of bureaucracy are not utilized due to mistrust, fear of reprisals, and so on.
9. It cannot assimilate the influx of new technology . . . entering the organization.
10. It modifies the personality structure such that each man becomes and reflects the full, gray, conditioned "organization man."[36]

Herbert Simon has mounted the most precise criticisms of the principles approach. He writes

> It is a fatal defect of the . . . principles of administration that, like proverbs, they occur in pairs. For almost every principle one can find an equally plausible and acceptable contradictory principle. Although the two principles of the pair will lead to exactly opposite organizational recommendations, there is nothing in the theory to indicate which is the proper one to apply.[37]

To illustrate his point, Simon notes that administrative efficiency is enhanced by keeping at a minimum the number of organizational levels through which a matter must pass before it is acted upon. Yet a narrow span of control, say, of five or six subordinates, produces a tall hierarchy. To some extent, Simon's criticism is blunted by invoking Fayol's exception principle and the gangplank, but in the main Simon's point that some of the principles contain logical contradictions is potent.

Less critical than both Bennis and Simon, Hage[38] describes bureaucracy in mixed terms and specifically as having

1. High centralization
2. High formalization
3. High stratification
4. Low adaptiveness
5. Low job satisfaction
6. Low complexity
7. High production
8. High efficiency

In *Complex Organizations* (1972), Charles Perrow mounted a major and articulate defense of the bureaucratic model, concluding that

> the extensive preoccupation with reforming, "humanizing," and decentralizing bureaucracies, while salutary, has served to obscure from organizational theorists the true nature of bureaucracy and has diverted us from assessing its impact on society. The impact on society in general is incalculably more important than the impact upon the members of a particular organization . . . bureaucracy is a form of organization superior to all others we know or can hope to afford in the near and middle future; the chances of doing away with it or changing it are probably non-existent in the rest in this century. Thus it is crucial to understand it and appreciate it.[39]

Relatedly, in *The Case for Bureaucracy* (1985), Charles Goodsell notes that denunciations of the "common hate object are fashionable, appealing, and make us feel good; they invite no retaliation or disagreement since almost everybody agrees that bureaucracy is bad . . ."but fashionable contentions are not necessarily solid ones.[40] Goodsell observes that:

> the attacks are almost always made in the tone of unremitting dogmatism. They are usually unqualified in portraying wicked behavior and inadequate outcomes. The pessimistic picture presented seems unbroken. The absolutism itself, it would seem, cannot help but strain our credulity. How can we believe that all public bureaucracies, all of the time, are inefficient, dysfunctional, rigid, obstructionist,

secretive, oligarchic, conservative, undemocratic, imperialist, oppressive, alienating, and discriminatory? How could any single human creation be so universally terrible in so many ways?[41]

Purely deductive models critical of bureaucracy abound, but they are—in the words of Alvin Gouldner—"a theoretical tapestry devoid of the plainest empirical trimmings."[42] Goodsell elaborates on this theme by observing that when empirical study is taken, single cases illustrating the conclusions desired are selected, and by concentrating on the problems, disorders, and dysfunctions of bureaucracy, rather than on what is working well, academics confirm both their own diagnoses and demonstrate the need for their own solutions.[43] Interestingly, Goodsell is able to muster a number of empirical studies that reveal positive evaluations of bureaucracies, including the police, by members of the public who have had direct contact with them; in general, these favorable evaluations are at least at the two-thirds level and many go beyond the 75 percent level.[44]

Despite philosophical criticisms and practical difficulties with the stems of traditional theory, in its entirety it must be appreciated for having formed the basic fund of knowledge on which the overwhelming majority of organizations in the world rest. Knowledge of traditional theory remains as an essential part of education and training for police leaders.

## OPEN SYSTEMS THEORY

Organizations described as flexible, adaptive, and organic are associated with open systems theory. This line of thought began its development in the late 1920s and is comprised of three major divisions: (1) human relations, (2) behavioral systems, and (3) open systems theory.

**Human Relations**

The human relations school developed in reaction to the mechanistic orientation of traditional organizational theory, which was viewed as neglecting or ignoring the human element.

**Mayo: The Hawthorne Studies**

In 1927, a series of experiments, which were to last five years, began near Chicago at the Western Electric Company's Hawthorne plant.[45] This work was guided by Elton Mayo (1880–1949), a professor in the Harvard School of Business, and his associate, Fritz Roethlisberger (1898–1974). Also involved in these studies was the plant manager, William Dickson.[46] From the perspective of organizational theory, the major contribution of the Hawthorne experiments is the view that organizations are social systems. Two research efforts, the telephone relay assembly study and the telephone switchboard wiring study,[47] were especially important to the development of the human relations school.

In the first study, five women assembling telephone relays were put into a special room and were subjected to varying physical work conditions.[48] Even when the conditions changed unfavorably, production increased. Mayo and his associates were puzzled by these results. Ultimately, they decided that (1) when the experimenters took over many of the supervisory functions, it became less strict and less formal; (2) the women behaved differently from what was expected because they were receiving attention, creating the famous "Hawthorne effect"; and (3) by placing the women together in the relay assembling test room, the researchers had provided the opportunity for them to become a closely knit group.[49] Based on these observations, the researchers concluded that an important influence on productivity was the interpersonal relations and spirit of cooperation that had developed among the women and between the women and their supervisors. The influence of these "human relations" was believed to be every bit as important as physical work conditions and financial incentives.[50]

In the telephone switchboard wiring study, fourteen men were put on a reasonable piece rate; that is, without physically straining themselves, they could earn more if they produced more. The assumption was that the workers would behave as rational economic actors and produce more since it was in their own best interest. To insulate these men from the "systematic soldiering" they knew to exist among the plant's employees, the researchers also placed these workers in a special room. The workers' output did not increase. The values of the informal group appeared to be more powerful than the allure of financial betterment:

1.  Don't be a "rate buster" and produce too much.
2.  If you turn out too little work, you are a "chisler."
3.  Don't be a "squealer" to supervisors.
4.  Don't be officious; if you are an inspector, don't act like one.[51]

Taken together, the relay assembly study and the switchboard wiring study raise an important question. Why did one group respond so favorably and the other not? The answer is that, in the relay assembly study, the values of the workers and the supervisors were mutually supportive, whereas in the switchboard wiring study, the objectives of the company and the informal group conflicted. The harder question is: Why was there mutuality in one situation and not the other? The basis of mutuality has already been discussed; the conflict is more difficult to account for, but it may have been the interplay of some things we know and some things we must speculate about:

1.  The researchers did not involve themselves in the supervision of the switchboard wiring room workers as they had with the relay assembly room employees.[52] The wiring room workers and their supervisor developed a spirit of cooperation, but it was one in which the supervisor was coopted by the informal group, which was suspicious of what would happen if output actually increased.[53]
2.  The way in which the subjects for both studies were selected is suspect and may have influenced the findings. The relay assembly women were experienced operators known to be friendly with each other and "willing and cooperative" participants, whereas the men were designated by the foreman.[54]
3.  The relay assembly-room workers were women and the switchboard wiring study employees were men. This difference in gender may have influenced the character of the responses. The studies were going on during the Depression; the women may have tried to hold onto their jobs by pleasing their supervisors, while the men restricted their output so there would be work to do and nobody would lose his job. In this context, both groups of employees can be seen as rational economic actors.

As a result of the Hawthorne studies, it was concluded that (1) the level of production is set by social norms, not by physiological capacities; (2) often workers do not react as individuals, but as members of a group; (3) the rewards and sanctions of the group significantly affect the behavior of workers and limit the impact of economic incentive plans; and (4) leadership has an important role in setting and enforcing group norms, and there is a difference between formal and informal leadership.[55]

When workers react as members of an informal group, they become susceptible to the values of that group. Thus, the informal group can be a powerful force in supporting or opposing police programs (see Box 4-4). Illustratively, a number of police unions started as an unorganized, informal group of dissatisfied officers. Although many factors contribute to the enduring problem of police corruption, such as disillusionment and temptation, an informal group that supports taking payoffs makes it more difficult

## BOX 4-4

### Chief Warns Police

Cleveland Police Chief Martin L. Flask has sent a stern warning to officers taking part in a recent slow-down on the writing of traffic tickets: You do so at the peril of future promotions and plum assignments.

In an order issued Wednesday, Flask said supervisors must immediately start counting the number of arrests and citations officers make for use in yearly performance evaluations. Flask and his advisers use these evaluations to help determine which officers should be promoted or given requested transfers.

Flask said yesterday that he still does not believe that officers have decided against enforcing the law. But in view of the recent drop in the issuance of tickets and misdemeanor citations—described by some officers as a protest against Mayor Michael R. White—the chief has decided to make officers more accountable for their actions.

But Flask denied that tracking citations amounts to a quota system.

"This is about fairness," he said. "We have officers making hundreds of arrests and getting letters of commendation, and in the same environment we have a few that don't work at the same level."

Robert Beck, president of the Cleveland Police Patrolman's Association, said the order's real purpose is to give White a way to single out and punish officers who have stopped or slowed their ticket-writing.

"I think it's improper," Beck said. "They certainly didn't negotiate this with us, and we plan to discuss it in the grievance committee."

Flask said the order should not be considered punitive, but is merely a form of accountability. Despite Flask's denials, Beck said the order is evidence that city officials have specific ticket quotas. He said supervisors regularly tell officers they need to issue more tickets, and Beck is fighting the recent transfer of two officers who were faulted for not writing enough citations.

Such pressure is one of the reasons for the decline in ticket-writing, Beck said. He said earlier in the week that frustrations with the mayor over pay, equipment and discipline are other reasons officers are writing fewer tickets. Court records show that in recent weeks, parking tickets, traffic tickets and arrest citations dropped by as much as 30 percent compared to the same period last year.

City officials initially said the drop was due to police preparations for the Aug. 21 Ku Klux Klan rally, but the figures continued to drop during the three weeks after the rally. Officers have told *The Plain Dealer* that the decline is due to an unorganized, informal slowdown to highlight their grievances with the mayor, including a department plan that would drastically cut some officers' overtime earnings.

The practice of evaluating officers is at least 21 years old. The evaluation, called the "Performance Rating Checklist," asks supervisors to rank officers from 1 to 10—with 10 being the best—for quality of work, quantity of work, dependability, and personal relationships. The supervisors are required to submit a separate report to justify a very high or very low ranking. The "quantity of work" section asks the supervisors to rank the officers' production, organization of time, industriousness, traffic enforcement and arrest record.

Flask's order said that effective immediately, "documentation shall be provided to support rating values regarding the 'Quantity of Work' section of the rating form. This documentation shall include Uniform Traffic Tickets written, Parking Infraction Notices issued, and arrests made."

The first batch of evaluations that will include the statistics is due Oct. 15 and includes officers whose last name begins with the letters S through Z.

*Source:* Reprinted with permission from *The Plain Dealer*©, September 24, 1999. All rights reserved.

to identify and prosecute "bad cops." In 1972, the Knapp Commission, investigating corruption in the New York City Police Department, distinguished between "meat-eaters" (those who overtly pursued opportunities to profit personally from their police power) and "grass-eaters" (those who simply accepted the payoffs that the happenstances of police work brought their way).[56] The behavior of the grass-eaters can be interpreted within the framework of the power that informal groups have. The Knapp Commission was told that one strong force that encouraged grass-eaters to accept relatively petty graft was their feeling of loyalty to their fellow officers. By accepting payoff money an officer could prove that he was "one of the boys" and could be trusted.

The foregoing discussion should not be interpreted to mean that informal groups always, or even frequently, engage in troublesome or unethical behavior, but rather as an illustration of the potency that such groups have. Astute police administrators are always alert for opportunities to tap the energy of informal groups to support departmental goals and programs.

As might be expected, the collision between the human relations school, fathered by Mayo's Hawthorne studies, and traditional organizational theory sent theorists and researchers in the various disciplines off into new and different directions. From among these at least three major themes are identifiable: (1) inquiries into what motivates workers, including the work of Maslow and Herzberg, which will be discussed shortly; (2) leadership, the subject of Chapter 6; and (3) work on organizations as behavioral systems, covered later in this chapter. As a concluding note, the term *human relations* has been used in law enforcement with two entirely different meanings. Particularly from the mid-1960s to the early 1970s, the term was used as a label for training that was basically race relations; when used in describing the major content areas of more recent police management seminars, its use denotes a block of instruction relating to individual and group relationships in the tradition of the Hawthorne studies.

Abraham Maslow (1908–1970) was a psychologist who developed the need hierarchy to explain individual motivation. The model appeared first in a 1943 article[57] and later received extended coverage in Maslow's *Motivation and Personality* (1954).

**Maslow: The Need Hierarchy**

Figure 4-4 depicts the need hierarchy. In Maslow's scheme, there are five categories of human needs.

1. Physiological or basic needs, such as food, shelter, and water
2. Safety needs, including the desires to be physically safe (see Box 4-5. If, as Maslow suggests, police officers have the need to be physically safe, why do some officers choose not to wear their protective vests?), to have a savings account for financial security, and to be safe in one's job, knowing that you will not be arbitrarily fired
3. Belongingness and love needs, such as the acceptance of one's work group in the police department and the affection of one's spouse, children, and parents
4. Esteem needs, including the desire for a stable, fairly based, and positive evaluation of one's self as evidenced by compliments, commendations, promotions, and other cues
5. Self-actualization needs, such as the want to test one's self-potential and gain a sense of fulfillment[58]

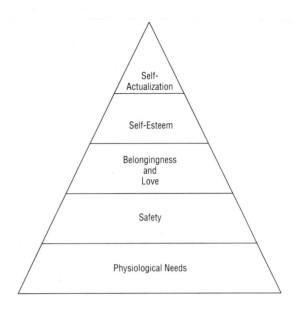

**FIGURE 4-4.** Maslow's need hierarchy.

The need hierarchy is arranged, like the rungs on a ladder, from the lower-order to the higher-order needs. A person does not move from one level to the next higher one until the majority of the needs at the level one is at are met. Once those needs are met, they cease to motivate a person, and the needs at the next level of the hierarchy predominate. To illustrate this, one does not attempt to self-actualize until one has feelings of self-confidence, worth, strength, capability, adequacy, and mastery;[59] these feelings are only generated with the meeting of the esteem needs. Conversely, if people's esteem needs are unmet, they feel inferior, helpless, discouraged, and unworthwhile and are unable to move to the self-actualization level and test themselves.

It is important to understanding the need hierarchy that the character of something does not necessarily determine what need is met but, rather, to what use it is put; money can be used to buy food and satisfy a basic need, or it can be put in a savings account to satisfy safety needs. Also, any process up the hierarchy can be reversed; the police officer who is fired or is given a lengthy suspension may be thrust into a financial situation in which the physiological needs will predominate. Police agencies that are managed professionally attempt to make appropriate use of theoretical constructs. For example, the fourth level of Maslow's need hierarchy is self-esteem, which includes the need for recognition as evidenced by compliments and commendations. Faced with a significant automobile theft problem in their state, Ohio state patrol officials wanted to develop a strategy that would have an impact upon the problem. One of the programs they developed was the Blue Max award.[60] In the Blue Max program each time a state trooper arrested a suspect in a stolen car he or she received a lightning bolt decal to place on the side of his or her patrol car. When troopers made their fifth apprehension in a year, they were given their own car for the rest of the year with a special license that read "ACE." At the end of the year the trooper who had made the most apprehensions received the coveted Blue Max award and was given a car reserved only for his or her use during the next year. In the first ten months in which the Blue Max program was operated, arrests of car thieves was up 49 percent as compared to the entire prior twelve months. The Blue Max program demonstrates the utility of Maslow's theory and how meeting organizational goals and individual goals can be compatible.

## BOX 4-5

### Officer Shot, Not Wearing Vest

**by Sheldon S. Shafer**

A 65-year-old man threatening to kill himself in his home instead shot and wounded a Louisville police officer yesterday, police said.

Later, while handcuffed, the man—Charles T. Hord—cut his own wrists in the back seat of a police car.

The wounded officer, Tommy Blair, 40, who is in his 11th year on the force, was in fair condition at University of Louisville Hospital after surgery. Blair had been shot once, in the side, with a handgun, police said.

Police charged Hord with first-degree assault, drug possession and two counts of wanton endangerment. He too was admitted to University, where he was in fair condition with multiple cuts on both arms, hospital spokesman Ken Marshall said.

The 3rd District commander, Maj. Wayne Kessinger, who is Blair's boss, called him an excellent officer who knows "just about everybody on his beat."

Hord's house is at 905 Brentwood Ave., four blocks south of Churchill Downs. Neighbors and relatives said he had been despondent since the death in February of his wife of 36 years, Vivian.

Diane Bonn-Allen, Hord's housekeeper, said she walked into his kitchen yesterday and saw him sitting at the table with a shotgun. Bonn-Allen said Hord told her he was going to kill himself and, because he could not read or write well, asked her to pen his last will and testament.

Bonn-Allen said she "tried to stall," and eventually went upstairs to get a cigarette and called police about 10:45 a.m. Officers Donna Lowhorn and Natalie Cunningham arrived within minutes, police said. Blair and Sgt. Rodney Estes arrived almost immediately as backups.

Police said Estes and Blair found Hord sitting in a chair with a shotgun pointed at his chin. The officers reported that Hord said he was "going to punch (his own) ticket." But he soon turned the shotgun toward the officers, police said.

Police said Estes lunged toward Hord and either grabbed the shotgun or pushed it aside. As Blair moved to take control of the shotgun, Hord reached under his buttocks and pulled out a .22-caliber revolver, police said.

As Estes and Blair struggled with Hord over the handgun, police said, it went off and the bullet hit Blair. He continued to help Estes until Hord was handcuffed.

Police said Blair was not wearing a protective vest, although it was not certain one would have deflected a bullet in the spot he was shot.

Officers then put the handcuffed Hord into a police car and started to take him downtown. Police said that somehow, even though his hands were restrained, Hord managed to remove a small surgical-like blade from his wallet and cut both of his arms. Police said Hord had been patted down by officers before he was put into the car.

Sharon McCoy, Hord's daughter-in-law, said he "has not been himself" since his wife died. Before her death, he was good-natured, but his behavior since then has become "erratic," McCoy said. She said Hord is a retired painter who was receiving disability payments because of a bad back.

Officer Lowhorn said police had made previous runs to Hord's home, but police would not elaborate on the nature of the calls.

Blair is the third Louisville police officer shot in the line of duty this year. All survived.

*Source: The Courier-Journal*, Louisville, Kentucky, August 24, 1999.

---

Because of their focus, neither the need hierarchy nor motivation–hygiene are organizational theories in the larger sense; they are included here because they are part of a stream of connected thinking. Motivation–hygiene theory developed from research conducted by Frederick Herzberg (1923– ), Bernard Mausner, and Barbara Snyderman on job attitudes at eleven work sites in the Pittsburgh area and reported on in *The Motivation to Work* (1959). The major statement of the theory, which evolved out of this earlier research, is found in Herzberg's *Work and the Nature of Man* (1966).

Herzberg saw two sets of variables operating in the work setting: (1) hygiene factors, which he later came to call maintenance factors, and (2) motivators. Table 4-1 identifies Herzberg's hygiene factors and motivators. The hygiene factors relate to the work environment; the motivators relate to the

**Herzberg: Motivation–Hygiene Theory**

The Blue Max medal and its presentation at an awards ceremony. (Courtesy of the Ohio State Patrol.)

work itself. Herzberg borrowed the term *hygiene* from the health care field and used it to refer to factors that if not treated properly could lead to a deterioration in performance, creating an "unhealthy" organization. Hygiene factors that are not treated properly are a source of dissatisfaction. However, even if all of them are provided, a police department does not have motivated officers, just ones who are not dissatisfied. Hygiene factors and motivators operate independently of each other; the police manager can motivate subordinates if they are somewhat dissatisfied with their salaries. However, the greater the level of dissatisfaction, the more difficult it becomes to employ the motivators successfully (see Box 4-6).

### TABLE 4-1. Herzberg's Motivation-Hygiene Theory

| Hygiene Factors | Motivators |
| --- | --- |
| Supervisory practices | Achievement |
| Policies and administration | Recognition for accomplishments |
| Working conditions | Challenging work |
| Interpersonal relationships with subordinates, peers, and superiors | Increased responsibility |
| Status | Advancement possibilities |
| Effect of the job on personal life | Opportunity for personal growth and development |
| Job security | |
| Money | |

From Frederick Herzberg, *Work and the Nature of Man* (Cleveland: World, 1966), pp. 95–96.

**BOX 4-6**

## Cop Morale Stuns Seattle Recruiters

Seattle police recruiters came to Atlanta this week looking for good cops who feel they're trapped in a bad situation.

Roughly 100 Atlanta officers have sent job applications to Seattle police in anticipation of the recruitment effort that started here Tuesday. At least 60 percent of those are officers with more than two years' experience, twice the percentage of seasoned cops who applied in nine other cities where Seattle police also searched for new hires.

Seattle recruiter Jim Ritter said his department picked Atlanta, and the other cities on their itinerary, because it has well-trained officers with "very low morale." While Ritter and others on the recruiting team talked to unhappy officers in the other cities they visited, the dissatisfaction displayed by Atlanta cops "was on a much larger scale," Ritter said. Atlanta, the final stop on a 10-city recruiting tour, left Ritter and his colleagues with an indelible impression.

"I have never seen morale this low in any of the other cities we've been to," Ritter said Tuesday as he and other recruiters prepared to test Atlanta police officers who gathered in a meeting room at Georgia Tech for testing and interview sessions. "We've been to at least nine other cities on this recruiting trip, and I found the morale problem here disturbing."

Other cities visited on Seattle's tour included Minneapolis-St. Paul, Austin, Texas, San Antonio, Raleigh, Denver, Charleston, S.C., and a handful of cities in Southern California. Ritter and Sgt. Mark Mount said they were particularly struck at the number of officers who expressed disappointment with APD. The most common complaints included low salaries, poor working conditions and the overall attitude of police administration toward rank-and-file officers and supervisors under the rank of major.

"Usually when we interview people in other cities, you'll get a handful who are dissatisfied," said Ritter, a 17-year veteran with Seattle. "Most of the officers feel they're just not important to the administration."

Neither Police Chief Beverly Harvard nor Mayor Bill Campbell answered questions, posed to them through their spokespersons, about the conclusions drawn by the Seattle recruiters.

Out-of-town recruiting is not unique to Seattle police. Atlanta police also recruit across the country. This year, Atlanta was particularly aggressive in its recruiting, trying to overcome a staffing shortage. The Atlanta department, with an authorized strength of 1,808 officers, counts about 400 vacancies, according to city records. Atlanta police have recruited in more than 10 cities since January, said Lt. C.J. Davis of APD's background and recruiting division. Atlanta police targeted cities where there are waiting lists for police candidates. According to departmental bulletins, Atlanta police lose from six to 10 officers a month. The reasons include resignations, retirements and firings.

Last year, officers expressed their anger after they received only half of the $4,000 salary increase they requested. The pay hike came only after police staged various protests that included a prayer vigil, a blue flu and two marches on City Hall. One of the main topics of contention among officers always has centered around the department's staffing levels. Police administration will not discuss the number of officers who work in the city, citing security issues. But according to pension records released by the city Wednesday, there are 1,423 active sworn police officers under the city's pension program. That number includes recruits in class at the Police Academy and recruits who are waiting to enter a new class next week, records showed.

Seattle is not the only jurisdiction fielding applications from Atlanta police. Cobb County police Chief Lee New says he personally receives two to three telephone calls a week from unhappy APD cops who want to work for him. DeKalb County police officials, meanwhile, said they've gotten 27 applications from APD officers so far this year.

But disenchantment on the job among police officers is not uncommon. John Violanti, a professor of criminal justice at Rochester Technical Institute in New York, said usually 20 percent of all officers in a police department will be unsatisfied with their job. While many officers stay on the force more than 10 years, many feel compelled to remain, trapped by retirement benefits and other perks that kick in only after a cop has worked in a department at least 20 years.

"The honeymoon period for a police officer is usually the first three years," Violanti said. "At about the eighth year of service, the officer begins to feel he's seen it all. They begin to get somewhat cynical. Unless they're working under good conditions, many of them are resigned to doing the minimum while on duty and going home at night."

*Source: The Atlanta Constitution, Oct 21, 1999.*

Note that police managers have more control over motivators than they do over basic hygiene factors; certain policies, such as automatically placing an officer involved in a shooting incident on suspension, may be mandated by the city administrator; the chief of police has little control over the status given the officer's job by society; and a chief cannot appropriate the money for higher salaries or improved fringe benefits.

In their leadership roles, police managers can try to influence, but they do not control such matters. It is over those hygiene factors that police managers do exercise control that they can do a considerable amount of good in reducing dissatisfaction and facilitating the use of the motivators or they can cause considerable unhappiness:

> The commander in charge of the uniformed division of a 100-officer department suddenly announced that officers were going to be placed on permanent shifts. Surprised and angered by this move, the officers and their wives mobilized to oppose the plan, and after a mass meeting with the commander, the plan was abandoned. The legacy of this incident was a period of barely subdued hostility, distrust, and low morale in the police department.

The nature of police work is in and of itself challenging, and some motivational effect is thus naturally occurring. Police managers can build on this by varying assignments appropriately. Measures that employ various of the other motivators include an established and active commendation system, the creation of field training officer and master patrol officer designations, an annual police awards banquet, an active staff development program, and a career system with various tracks, as discussed in Chapter 8.

Maslow's need hierarchy and Herzberg's motivation–hygiene theory can be interrelated; the physiological, safety, and belongingness and love needs of Maslow correspond to Herzberg's hygiene factors; the top two levels of the need hierarchy—esteem and self-actualization—correlate with Herzberg's motivators.

## Behavioral System Theory

By 1960, human relations in the tradition of the Hawthorne studies lacked vitality. Its successor, which traces its ancestry to that 1927–1932 period, was behavioral systems theory. The theorists associated with this school saw organizations as being composed of interrelated behaviors and were concerned with making organizations more democratic and participative. Behavioral systems theory is basically a post-1950 development; many of the people involved in this movement are also described in other ways. For example, Argyris, Likert, Bennis, Maslow, Herzberg, and McGregor are often referred to as organizational humanists and in one way or another are tied to organizational development, a concept treated later in this section.

## Lewin: Group Dynamics

Kurt Lewin (1890–1947) was a psychologist who fled from Germany in the early 1930s.[61] His interests were diverse and included leadership; force-field analysis, a technique sometimes used in decision making; change; and group dynamics. Lewin's force-field analysis is illustrated in Figure 4-5. In force-field analysis, driving forces push for some new condition or state, and restraining forces serve to resist the change or perpetuate things as they are. In using force-field analysis, if there are exactly opposing driving and restraining forces, the arrows of these opposing forces meet at the zero or balance line. In some instances, there might not be an exactly opposite force, in which case an arrow

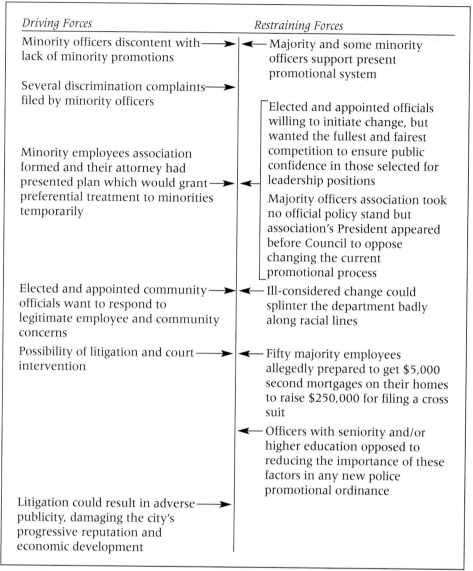

| Driving Forces | Restraining Forces |
|---|---|

Minority officers discontent with lack of minority promotions → | ← Majority and some minority officers support present promotional system

Several discrimination complaints filed by minority officers →

Minority employees association formed and their attorney had presented plan which would grant preferential treatment to minorities temporarily → | ← Elected and appointed officials willing to initiate change, but wanted the fullest and fairest competition to ensure public confidence in those selected for leadership positions

Majority officers association took no official policy stand but association's President appeared before Council to oppose changing the current promotional process

Elected and appointed community officials want to respond to legitimate employee and community concerns → | ← Ill-considered change could splinter the department badly along racial lines

Possibility of litigation and court intervention → | ← Fifty majority employees allegedly prepared to get $5,000 second mortgages on their homes to raise $250,000 for filing a cross suit

← Officers with seniority and/or higher education opposed to reducing the importance of these factors in any new police promotional ordinance

Litigation could result in adverse publicity, damaging the city's progressive reputation and economic development →

**FIGURE 4-5.** The use of force-field analysis regarding the decision to adopt a new police promotional ordinance.

is simply drawn, as in Figure 4-5, to the balance line. After all entries are made and the situation is summarized, the relative power of the driving and restraining forces must be subjectively evaluated. In this regard, the zero or balance line should be regarded as a spring that will be moved in one direction or another, suggesting the action that needs to be taken or the decision that needs to be made.

Lewin is also regarded as the father of the behavioral system school and founded the Research Center for Group Dynamics at the Massachusetts Institute of Technology.[62] In the same year as Lewin died, one of his followers, Leland Bradford, established a human relations effort at Bethel, Maine.[63] This undertaking was later to be called the National Training Laboratories for Group Development, which earlier focused on stranger T-group or sensitivity training, a method whereby behavior is changed by strangers in a group sharing their honest opinions of each other. The popularity of T-groups was greatest during the 1950s; its present use is diminished in large measure because some organizations that tried it were troubled by its occasional volatility and the fact that not all changes were positive:

> A division manager at one big company was described by a source familiar with his case as "a ferocious guy—brilliant but a thoroughgoing autocrat—whom everyone agreed was just what the division needed, because it was a tough, competitive business." Deciding to smooth over his rough edges, the company sent him to sensitivity training, where he found out exactly what people thought of him. "So he stopped being a beast," says the source, "and his effectiveness fell apart." The reason he'd been so good was that he didn't realize what a beast he was. Eventually, they put in a new manager.[64]

## Homans: External and Internal Systems

As a contemporary of Lewin's, George Homans (1910–1989) did work in the tradition of group dynamics. In *The Human Group* (1950), he advanced the idea that groups have both an internal and an external system.[65] The internal system is comprised of factors that arise within the group itself, such as the feelings that members of a group develop about each other during the life of the group. In contrast, the external system consists of variables in the larger environment in which the group exists, such as the administrative policies and supervisory practices to which the group is subject. Homans saw these two systems as being in a state of interaction and influencing each other.

For example, the decision of a chief of police to suspend an officer for three days without pay because of an accident while involved in a high-speed chase might result in a group of officers who saw the suspension as being unfair agreeing among themselves not to write any traffic citations during that time. This interaction brings the formal organization of the external system into conflict with the informal organization of the internal system. The formal sanction of the external system is countered with the informal sanction of reducing the city's revenue by the internal system.

Both Lewin and Homans have ties to the human relations school. Homans, for instance, drew upon the switchboard wiring room study to illustrate his concept of internal and external systems. Analytically, his work falls into the behavioral systems category and foreshadowed the dynamic interaction theme of open systems theory.

## Argyris: Immaturity–Maturity Theory and the Mix Model

Chris Argyris (1923– ) is a critic of the mechanistic model of organization and a leading proponent of more open and participative organizations. In *Personality and Organization: The Conflict Between System and the Individual* (1957), he states a theory of immaturity versus maturity. Argyris believes that, as one moves from infancy toward adulthood in years of age, the healthy individual also advances from immaturity to maturity. The elements of the personality that are changed during this process are summarized in Table 4-2. Simultaneously, Argyris views formal organizations as having certain properties that do not facilitate the growth into a mature state:

1. Specialization reduces the use of initiative by requiring individuals to use only a few of their skills doing unchallenging tasks.
2. The chain of command leaves people with little control over their work environment and makes them dependent upon and passive toward superiors.

**TABLE 4-2. Argyris's Immaturity-Maturity Changes**

| Infancy–Immaturity | → | Adulthood–Maturity |
|---|---|---|
| Passive | → | Self-initiative |
| Dependent | → | Relatively independent |
| Behaving in a few ways | → | Capable of behaving many ways |
| Erratic, shallow, quickly changed interests | → | Deeper interests |
| Short time perspective | → | Much longer time perspective |
| Subordinate position in the family | → | Aspirations of equality or superordinate position relative to peers |
| Lack of self-awareness | → | Self-awareness and self-control |

Data from p. 50 in *Personality and Organization: The Conflict Between System and the Individual* by Chris Argyris. Copyright © 1957 by Harper & Row Publishers, Inc., Reprinted by permission of the publisher.

3. The unity-of-direction principle means that the objectives of the work unit are controlled by the leader. If the goals do not consider the employees, then ideal conditions for psychological failure are set.

4. The narrow span of control principle will tend to increase the subordinate's feelings of dependence, submissiveness, and passivity.[66]

The needs of a healthy, mature individual and the properties of formal organizations therefore come into conflict; the ensuing response by the individual may take any of several forms:

1. The employee may leave the organization only to find that other organizations are similar to the one left.

2. To achieve the highest level of control over one's self permitted by the organization, the person may climb as far as possible up the organizational hierarchy.

3. The worker may defend his or her self-concept by the use of defensive mechanisms such as daydreaming, rationalizing lower accomplishments, developing psychosomatic illnesses, or becoming aggressive and hostile, attacking and blaming what is frustrating personally.

4. The individual may decide to stay in spite of the conflict and adapt by lowering his or her work standards and becoming apathetic and disinterested.

5. Informal groups may be created to oppose the former organization.

6. The employee may do nothing and remain frustrated, creating even more tension.[67]

In 1964 Argyris published *Integrating the Individual and the Organization*. The book's purpose was to present his thinking about how organizations could deal with the problem he had identified in *Personality and Organization: The Conflict Between System and the Individual*. Argyris doubted that it was possible to have a relationship between the individual and the organization that allowed the simultaneous maximizing of the values of both.[68] He did believe it was possible to reduce the unintended, nonproductive, side consequences of formal organizations and to free more of the energies of the individual for productive purposes; Argyris's mix model was the way in which this was to be done.[69] It is basically an attempt to "mix" or accommodate the interests of the individual and the organization. The mix model favors neither people nor the organization.

For example, Argyris saw the organization as having legitimate needs that were not people centered. He also believed that organizations cannot always provide challenging work. The fact, however, that some work was not challenging was viewed by Argyris as an asset to the individual and the organization; the unchallenging work provided some recovery time for the individual and allowed the organization's routine tasks to get done.[70]

**McGregor: Theory X and Theory Y**

Douglas McGregor (1904–1964) believed that

> Every managerial act rests on assumptions, generalizations, and hypotheses—that is to say, on theory. Our assumptions are frequently implicit, sometimes quite unconscious, often conflicting; nevertheless, they determine our predictions that if we do A, B will occur. Theory and practice are inseparable.[71]

In common practice, managerial acts, without explicit examination of theoretical assumptions, lead at times to remarkable inconsistencies in managerial behavior:

> A manager, for example, states that he delegates to his subordinates. When asked, he expresses assumptions such as, "People need to learn to take responsibility," or, "Those closer to the situation can make the best decision." However, he has arranged to obtain a constant flow of detailed information about the behavior of his subordinates, and he uses this information to police their behavior and to "second-guess" their decisions. He says, "I am held responsible, so I need to know what is going on." He sees no inconsistency in his behavior, nor does he recognize some other assumptions which are implicit: "People can't be trusted," or, "They can't really make as good decisions as I can."
>
> With one hand, and in accord with certain assumptions, he delegates; with the other, and in line with other assumptions, he takes actions which have the effect of nullifying his delegation. Not only does he fail to recognize the inconsistencies involved, but if faced with them he is likely to deny them.[72]

In *The Human Side of Enterprise* (1960), McGregor stated two different sets of assumptions that managers make about people:

*Theory X*

1. The average human has an inherent dislike of work and will avoid it if possible.
2. Most people must be coerced, controlled, directed, and threatened with punishment to get them to put forth adequate effort toward the achievement of organizational objectives.
3. The average human prefers to be directed, wishes to avoid responsibility, has relatively little ambition, and wants security above all.

*Theory Y*

1. The expenditure of physical and mental effort in work is as natural as play or rest.
2. External control and the threat of punishment are not the only means for bringing about effort toward organizational objectives. People will exercise self-direction and self-control in the service of objectives to which they are committed.

3. Commitment to objectives is a function of the rewards associated with their achievement.

4. The average human learns, under proper conditions, not only to accept but to seek responsibility.

5. The capacity to exercise a relatively high degree of imagination, ingenuity, and creativity in the solution of organizational problems is widely, not narrowly, distributed in the population.

6. Under the conditions of modern organizational life, the intellectual potentialities of the average human are only partially utilized.[73]

American police departments have historically been dominated by theory X assumptions. Even police departments with progressive national images may be experienced as tightly controlling environments by the people who actually work in them:

> The person leading a training session with about thirty-five managers of a West Coast police department observed that we often react to organizations as though they were living, breathing things. The managers agreed with this and noted the use of such phrases as "the department promoted me this year" and "the department hired me in 2000." They also understood that in fact someone, not the police department, had made those decisions. The managers were then divided into five groups and asked to make a list of what they thought the police department would say about them if it could talk. When the groups reported back, they identified a total of forty-two statements, some of which were duplicates of each other. These managers, all of whom were college graduates and many of whom held advanced degrees, indicated the police department would say such thing as "They are idiots"; "They don't have any sense"; "Watch them or they'll screw up royally." All of the statements reported had a theory X character to them.

Theory X assumptions are readily recognized as being those that underpin traditional organizational theory. For example, we can relate a narrow span of control to theory X's first two propositions. In contrast, theory Y is formed by a set of views that are supportive of Argyris's mix model; they postulate that the interests of the individual and the organization need not be conflictual but can be integrated for mutual benefit. The principal task of management in a theory X police department is control, whereas in a theory Y department it is supporting subordinates by giving them the resources to do their jobs and creating an environment where they can be self-controlling, mature, contributing, and self-actualizing.

The use of quality circles (QCs) or employee participation groups (EPGs) was one practice consistent with theory Y which was used in police departments. Widely used in Japanese industries and such American corporations as 3M, Union Carbide, Chrysler, and Lockheed, these procedures have been credited with achieving numerous productivity and product improvements while also enjoying the support of both management and labor.[74]

Quality circles are small groups of people, roughly between five to ten with seven being regarded as ideal, who perform the same type of work, such as uniformed patrol, training, or robbery investigation. This group or QC voluntarily agrees to meet at least once a week during regular duty hours for an hour to identify, discuss, analyze, and solve specified work-related problems that the group members have identified as being important. As practiced in the Dallas Police Department, QCs also

1. Were based on the premise that all members are of equal importance in making contributions
2. Used sergeants as leaders because they can "blend" in with the group, being more readily perceived as equals than are higher ranks
3. Provided formal training to the group leader and members in analytical techniques such as problem identification, data gathering, decision making, and making presentations
4. Had access to needed information and the use of experts in areas such as budgeting and systems analysis
5. Were assigned a facilitator—a top-level manager—to serve as a "go-between" and cut through "red tape" on behalf of the QC
6. Received the support of management to adopt all reasonable recommendations
7. Implemented the solution recommended to and approved by management

QCs were a valuable tool for police departments. Because circle members costed out their solutions, a greater awareness was created with respect to how a department's resources are used. The QCs' emphasis on improvement resulted in creative, cost-effective solutions. Each participating officer's knowledge of the department and its operating environment was enhanced and officers developed skills such as problem identification, planning, and decision making. Although certain topics were considered beyond the legitimate scope of a QC's inquiry—such as personalities and matters of law—the available range of topics was broad. QCs also reduced the potential for dissatisfaction and conflict by providing a forum to air concerns and devise solutions, which had the additional benefit of improving communication both horizontally, among peers, and vertically, up and down the chain of command. On the down side, if police administrators created QCs as a façade of participation, officers quickly became disillusioned and withdrew. Moreover, QC leaders and facilitators had to be properly trained in the interpersonal and group dynamics and had to be genuinely committed to the process or else meetings of the group devolved into classical, unproductive "gripe" sessions.

The fatal flaw in the use of QCs in policing and other organizations was that it made people at the bottom of the hierarchy assume too much responsibility for quality. As such, it was an isolated philosophy. Today, it is well understood that a successful quality movement requires that it be an organization-wide commitment and that it be a fundamental tenet of the organization, as opposed to an isolated practice. Additional information about the quality movement is found in Chapter 14, Productivity, Quality, and Evaluation of Police Services.

**Likert: Systems 1, 2, 3, and 4 and the Linkpin**

The work of Rensis Likert (1903–1981) is compatible with McGregor's theory X and theory Y in that fundamentally it contrasts traditional and democratic or participative management. In *New Patterns of Management* (1961), Likert identified four different management systems or climates: (1) exploitive authoritative, (2) benevolent authoritative, (3) consultative, and (4) participative group. In a subsequent publication, *The Human Organization* (1967), Likert extended and refined his notions of management systems, dropping the earlier designations and calling them system 1, system 2, system 3, and system 4, respectively. A partial description of these systems is given in Table 4-3.

**TABLE 4-3. Likert's Organizational and Performance Characteristics of Different Management Systems**

| Organizational Variable | System 1 | System 2 | System 3 | System 4 |
|---|---|---|---|---|
| Leadership processes used: | | | | |
| Extent to which superiors have confidence and trust in subordinates | Have no confidence and trust in subordinates | Have condescending confidence and trust, such as master has to servant | Substantial but not complete confidence and trust; still wishes to keep control of decisions | Complete confidence and trust in all matters |
| Extent to which superiors behave so that subordinates feel free to discuss important things about their jobs with their immediate superior | Subordinates do not feel at all free to discuss things about the job with their superior | Subordinates do not feel very free to discuss things about the job with their superior | Subordinates feel rather free to discuss things about the job with their superior | Subordinates feel completely free to discuss things about the job with their superior |
| Extent to which immediate superior in solving job problems generally tries to get subordinates' ideas and opinions and make constructive use of them | Seldom gets ideas and opinions of subordinates in solving job problems | Sometimes gets ideas and opinions of subordinates in solving job problems | Usually gets ideas and opinions and usually tries to make constructive use of them | Always gets ideas and opinions and always tries to make constructive use of them |

From *The Human Organization* by Rensis Likert. Copyright © 1967 McGraw-Hill Book Company. Used with permission of McGraw-Hill Book Company.

Basically, Likert's system 1 reflects the content of McGregor's theory X, whereas system 4 incorporates the assumption of theory Y; system 2 and system 3 form part of a continuum in contrast to the simple opposites of McGregor's theory X and theory Y. Likert argues that system 2 management concepts predominate in the literature and that these conceptual tools do not fit a system 4 management style, which he believes most people prefer.[75]

Assuming some linkage between what Likert saw as predominating in the literature and actual practice, one would expect to find most people reporting their organization to be a system 2 environment. In a study of 18 different-size local police departments in 15 different states throughout the country, Swanson and Talarico[76] asked 629 uniformed police officers actually assigned to field duties what type of management climate their department had. Some 16.6 percent of the officers reported a system 1; 42.9 percent a system 2; 35.9 percent a system 3; and only 4.6 percent a system 4. These data, then, provide some support for Likert's assertion.

Likert also contributes to the management literature by contrasting between the man-to-man and linkpin patterns or organization, depicted in Figure 4-6.[77] The man-to-man pattern is found in traditional organizations; the type of interaction characteristically is superior to subordinate, most often on an individual basis, and relies heavily on the use of positional authority. The linkpin pattern is found in the democratically and group-oriented system 4. In it, a police manager is simultaneously a member of one group, say, the chief's command staff, and the leader of another group, say, the operations bureau. The pattern of interaction is as a member of one group and as the leader

**FIGURE 4-6.**
Likert's man-to-man
and linkpin patterns.
[From *The Human
Organization* by
Rensis Likert.
Copyright © 1967
McGraw-Hill Book
Company. Used with
the permission of
McGraw-Hill Book
Company.]

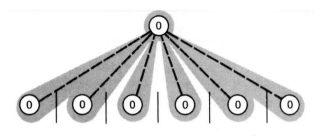

The Man-to-Man Pattern

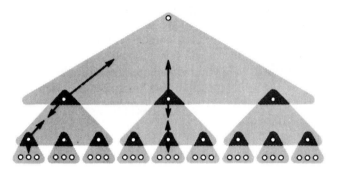

The Linkpin Pattern

of another, with the emphasis upon open, honest communications in an atmosphere of mutual confidence and trust. In a loose sense the traditional organization's managers perform a linkpin function, although it is man to man and is based on superior–subordinate interaction. However, in Likert's terms the linkpin function relies more on influence than on authority and connects groups rather than individuals.

**Bennis: Organizational Development**

An organizational humanist, Warren Bennis's (1925– ) criticisms of bureaucracy have been noted. Much of his work has been in the area of organizational development, which is:

> the name given to the emerging applied behavioral science discipline that seeks to improve organizations through planned, systematic, long-range efforts focused on the organization's culture and its human and social processes.[78]

Organizational development has two separate, but entwined, stems: the laboratory training stem and survey research feedback stem.[79] The laboratory approach involves unstructured experiences by a group from the same organization, the successor to stranger-to-stranger T-groups whose popularity had waned by the late 1950s. Laboratory training grew out of the work of Lewin and his Research Center for Group Dynamics.[80] The survey research feedback stem makes attitude surveys within an organization and feeds it back to organizational members in workshop sessions to create awareness and to promote positive change.[81] The survey research stem also grew out of Lewin's Research Center for Group Dynamics from which the senior staff—

which had included McGregor—moved to the University of Michigan following Lewin's death in 1947. There they joined with the university's Survey Research Center to form the Institute of Social Research, where some of Likert's work was done.

In a sense, organizational development began as a result of people rejecting stranger-to-stranger T-groups.[82] The laboratory stem began working with groups from the same organization, and the survey research feedback stem began using measurements. Fairly quickly, the focus spread from groups in the same organization to entire organizations. To illustrate the earlier point that many of the behavioral system theorists are tied to organizational development, note that McGregor employed such an approach with Union Carbide in 1957 and Argyris used it with the U.S. Department of State in 1967.

Organizational development as we know it today is an early 1960s movement. In his classic *Changing Organizations* (1966), Bennis describes it as having the following objectives:

1. Improvement in the interpersonal competence of managers
2. A change in value so that human factors and feelings come to be considered legitimate
3. Increased understanding between and within groups to reduce tensions
4. Development of more effective team management, meaning an increased capacity for groups to work together
5. Development of better methods of resolving conflict, meaning less use of authority and suppression of it and more open and rational methods
6. Development of open, organic management systems characterized by trust, mutual confidence, wide sharing of responsibility, and the resolution of conflict by bargaining or problem solving[83]

Chapter 15, Organizational Change and the Future, draws upon the literature of organizational development. To produce the types of climates Argyris, McGregor, Likert, and Bennis favor is hard work, and, despite good intentions by the organization at the outset, there is always the prospect of failure:

> The director of public safety in a major city wanted to implement a management by objectives (MBO) system. After discussions with the consultant who later directed the effort, it was agreed that this would take a long-term intervention. This effort focused on MBO as a rational management tool that had to be accompanied by behavioral shifts to be successful. The approach involved a survey research feedback component, training in MBO, and technical assistance in implementing it. After one year, the work had produced a good deal of paperwork, no small amount of confusion, and more than a little anger.
>
> The intervention failed because (1) the organization had not been prepared properly for change; (2) the project was seen as the director's "baby" and there was never widespread support for it; (3) many managers were threatened, denouncing it as "fad" or as an attempt by top management to find a way to evaluate them unfavorably; (4) not all managers were trained due to cost and scheduling difficulties; (5) success in part depended upon people in the organization taking responsibility for training lower-level managers and supervisors, a feat they did not accomplish; (6) the consultant's reservations about the likelihood of success given the specifics of the situation were never given sufficient weight by him or by others at the times they were voiced; (7) the time lines for the project were too ambitious; and (8) the resources dedicated to change were not sufficient.

**Organizations as Open Systems**

Systems theory concepts have been discussed since the 1920s, but they came into general use only as recently as 1960. A system is a grouping of separate but interrelated components working together toward the achievement of some common objective. General systems theory (GST), on which the biologist Ludwig von Bertalanffy and the sociologist Talcott Parsons have written, is a broad conceptual framework for explaining relationships in the "real world" without any consideration of the specifics of a given situation.

Organizations may be characterized as closed or open systems. In actuality, there are no entirely closed or open organizations; these are only terms used to describe the extent to which an organization approximates one or the other.

The closed system view of an organization assumes complete rationality, optimizing performances, predictability, internal efficiency, and certainty.[84] Because all behavior is believed to be functional and all outcomes predictable and certain, the closed organization can ignore changes in the larger environment, such as political, technological, and economic.[85] Thus, the closed system organization sees little need for interaction with its environment. The police chief who denies that he needs an automated management information system (MIS) prohibits subordinates from talking with politicians, prefers the "tried and true" over recent innovations, and refuses to justify budget requests carefully in a tight economic environment is reflecting a closed system view. Traditional organizational theory and the closed system fall into the same stream of thinking and are compatible.

The police department as an open system is depicted in Figure 4-7. Open systems are described by Katz and Kahn as having the following characteristics:

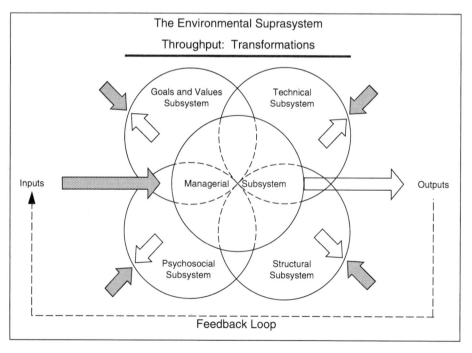

**FIGURE 4-7.** The police department as an open system. (From *Contingency Views of Organization and Management* by Fremont E. Kast and James E. Rosenzweig. © 1973, Science Research Associates, Inc. Reprinted by permission of the publisher with modifications.)

1. Open systems seek and continuously import sources of energy, including money, recruits, and information as inputs.

2. Once imported, the energy is transformed by the subsystems comprising the throughput function. For example, recruits are trained.

3. Although some energy is used by the subsystems in the throughput function, such as the efforts associated with training recruits, open systems export the bulk of the energy transformed into the environment as products, services, such as the trained recruits who are now assigned to patrol and respond to calls, and other forms.

4. There is a cyclical relationship between the inputs, the throughput, and the outputs as the services exported into the environment furnish the source of energy to repeat the cycle. Outputs both satisfy needs and create new demands for outputs.

5. All forms of organization move toward disorganization or death; this entropic process is a universal law of nature. To survive, open systems reverse the process by acquiring negative entropy. The cyclical character of open systems allows them to develop negative entropy by having energy flow continuously through them. Additionally, because open systems can import more energy than is expended, they have a storage capacity that allows them to survive brief interruptions of inputs. This may occur as one budget year ends and it is a short while until the city council enacts the new budget. Typically, the police department will have sufficient gasoline and other supplies to remain operational.

6. Open systems receive informational feedback as inputs from the larger environment in which they operate. As suggested by Figure 4-7, an open system has multiple points at which inputs occur. These inputs take place both through formal and informal exchanges. Police departments have a formally structured feedback loop to make them more responsive to control, and through it flows such things as technical evaluations of their programs and directions from the city council and the city manager. Open systems cannot absorb all informational and other inputs; excesses of inputs would overwhelm them. Therefore, open systems have a selective mechanism called "coding," which filters out some potential inputs and attunes them to important signals from the environment. A simple illustration of this principle is that, from among the dozens of daily telephone callers asking to talk to the chief of police, only a few actually get to do so. Switchboard operators, secretaries, and aides are taught to refer most callers to the appropriate department, handle the calls themselves, or connect them with someone empowered to deal with such matters. Yet the telephone calls of the city manager and certain other people will invariably find their way through these filters.

7. The continuous cycle of inputs, transformations, outputs, and feedback produces a steady state in an open system. A steady state is not a motionless or true equilibrium but a dynamic and continuous adjusting to external forces and of internal processes to ensure the survival of the system.

8. Over time open systems develop specialized subsystems, as shown in Figure 4-7, to facilitate the importation and processing of energy and to enhance their survival.

9. As specialization proceeds, its fragmenting effect is countered by processes that bring the system together for unified functioning, the purpose of the managerial subsystem depicted in Figure 4-7.

10. Open systems can reach the same final state even though they started from different sets of initial conditions and proceeded down different paths; this is the principle of equifinality.[86]

The subsystems identified in Figure 4-7 have been discussed in various ways; more specifically these overlapping subsystems have the following functions:

1. The managerial subsystem plays a central role in establishing goals, planning, organizing, coordinating, and controlling activities and in relating the police department to its environment (see Box 4-7).

## BOX 4-7

### The Distinctive Legacy of Chief Norm Stamper—As He Reached Out, Officers Felt Left Out

**by Linda Keene, Alex Fryer**
*Seattle Times* **Staff Reporters**

Retiring Seattle Police Chief Norm Stamper will be remembered reverently by many in the larger community and resentfully by some of those he led.

It is an unusual legacy—a flip-flop from that of many other police chiefs in major cities, who seem to alienate more citizens than officers.

Heralded in some quarters as an extraordinary ambassador who built bridges to disenfranchised groups under the mantra of community policing, Stamper is seen by others—including many under his command—as being just too soft, considerate of the wishes of outsiders but not tuned in to his own troops.

From the day he arrived in Seattle in early 1994, he stressed compassion over confrontation. He was a thinker, not a thumper, and some dubbed him the "philosopher" chief who made inroads to groups that had historically mistrusted police. If community policing had a poster child, it was Stamper.

"That's unquestionably his most distinctive legacy," said Hubert Locke, a professor in the Evans School of Public Affairs at the University of Washington. "I think he has taken that concept further in Seattle than perhaps in any other city. I think the city will be the better for it."

At its core, community policing is inclusive and tolerant, teaming cops and citizens to define local crime problems and together head them off, and Stamper often seemed like the perfect chief for Seattle. He recognized that this city was enamored with process, and he established an unprecedented number of advisory groups to appease that.

One of his early acts as chief was to march, in uniform, in a gay-pride parade on Capitol Hill. It was a bold move—his predecessor, Patrick Fitzsimons, wouldn't have dreamed of such a progressive display, and Seattle knew change was afoot.

So did his troops, many of whom noted with resentment that they were forbidden to march in uniform in parades with a Christian theme. In their estimation, Stamper's commitment to community policing bordered on pandering to special-interest groups.

Then there was the matter of his candor. He once told a newspaper columnist that for a brief time as a rookie, he had bought into a cop culture that condones gay bashing and racial slurs. The admission struck many readers as refreshingly honest. But it anguished his officers, who felt he had smeared them all.

#### 'His heart's in the right place'

Over time, the internal resentments grew so much that Stamper finally conceded earlier this year that he hadn't spent enough time with the rank and file. But by then, any effort to address that came too late. With the unrest at the World Trade Organization meetings, the internal discontent was blown wide open.

"It's hard not to like Norm Stamper, but many times we wished that he had offered us the same partnership that he offered the community," said Sgt. J. D. Miller, vice president of the Seattle Police Officers' Guild.

Officer Jim Kelly, who has been on the force eight years, agreed: "The general mood among officers was that he was overly invested in community policing—that it came at the expense of the nuts and bolts of law enforcement, like training."

Or like just plain minding the store. Though rumors circulated in the department for three years that a homicide detective had stolen money from a crime scene, nothing was done until a prosecutor got wind of it and charged the officer with theft.

Stamper later acknowledged he hadn't paid enough attention to internal investigations. But his admission came only after a panel of citizens looked into the case and recommended an unprecedented reform that also would become part of the Stamper legacy: that a civilian—not the police—watch over internal investigations.

Other law-enforcement officials noticed his weaknesses, too.

"His heart's in the right place, trying to do the right thing," said Donald Van Blaricom, former Bellevue police chief. "I just don't think he's tough enough. Sometimes you have to knock a few heads."

In February 1994, Seattle got its first feel for its next police chief when then-Mayor Norm Rice plucked him from a long list of applicants and put him in the final five.

From there, Stamper charmed his way into the job. It was a virtual schmooze-fest. Stamper was modest yet articulate; compassionate and tolerant; polite and restrained. This was no law-enforcement bully.

"I've often thought that he is the perfect chief for Seattle," said Brent Crook, a friend of Stamper's who works at the Department of Neighborhoods. "He has the same sensibilities of Seattle. He represents the breadth and depth of the city."

Stamper, 55, took on tough issues. He dramatically strengthened the domestic-violence unit, assigning 20 officers. Crime overall dropped during his tenure—as it did in most major U.S. cities—and allegations of unnecessary force by officers declined from 143 in 1994 to 64 last year.

Seattle City Attorney Mark Sidran characterized Stamper as the "Teflon chief."

"He was golden for a very long time," Sidran said, "and very popular with constituencies historically disaffected with police."

## He bridged the gap

Indeed, Stamper's outreach has been unprecedented. He created new advisory councils representing the Filipino, African-American, Southeast Asian, Korean, Hispanic, youth and gay communities. And then he spent countless nights in attendance.

"I have a high opinion of the chief," said state Rep. Ed Murray, a gay activist from the 43rd District.

"If the last week's events during WTO obscure what he's done to improve policing in Seattle, it would be unfortunate. He has made Seattle a safer and better place."

Before Stamper, Murray said, "there were complaints of police harassing gay and lesbian residents on Capitol Hill. That's dropped off dramatically."

Seattle City Councilwoman Margaret Pageler, who chaired the Public Safety Committee when Stamper became chief, said he made enormous strides in changing police culture.

"The first couple of years that I chaired the safety committee, there was anger and hostility from the minority communities, and substantial distrust within the gay community (toward police)," she said.

"Women felt embattled in the department, and there were only one or two officers who were out as gay or lesbian. I think he did a marvelous job of bridging the gap with those communities."

## Fears department will backslide

Sue Taoka agrees. As executive director of the Seattle Chinatown International District Preservation and Development Authority, she fears Stamper's resignation will be interpreted as an indictment of community policing.

"I'm very sad and scared that people will react and say, 'We tried that, and it didn't work,' and we'll end up in a reactionary mode. That could set us back years."

Pageler said she recognizes that concern but doesn't think the department will backslide.

"I'm saddened to see that he's retiring, but I'm not fearful about the department because one of his strengths has been to mentor subordinates," she said. "Rather than the previous, militaristic management style, where all the decisions were made by the chief, Norm has worked to make sure the assistant chiefs and captains are providing leadership. The result is a Police Department with a score of very fine men and women who will move up and provide leadership, and that's a wonderful legacy."

Asked if community policing might be de-emphasized under a new chief, Stamper said no: "The genie's out of the bottle. The city can't turn its back on community policing."

Sidran also thinks the city has grown to expect outreach. "I don't recall any police chief who had so assertively gone out and engaged the community on so many different levels as Norm Stamper," he said. "I have seen Norm at many, many community events, and his ability to engage with people is really quite impressive. In a positive sense, he's one of the best politicians I've seen in Seattle."

Yet officers say they feel neglected. That was exacerbated during the WTO, when Stamper publicly

*(continued)*

## BOX 4-7 (continued)

questioned the actions of a few officers and only later stressed his support for a majority.

"That left people feeling pretty empty," said Sgt. Miller. "Officers were dealing with the most violent protest since Vietnam and still returned safety to the streets. Show me the injuries. Yet, to pander to those few people (who complained about police conduct) as opposed to supporting the personnel, who gave so much, was unconscionable."

Amid all this lies a cautionary tale for the next chief: If you're too process-oriented and concerned with constituencies, it seems, the core mission might be forgotten. And without loyalty from the troops, no chief's vision can be carried out.

*Source:* Copyright 1999 Seattle Times Company. Used with permission.

2. Organizational goals and values represent an important subsystem; while the police department takes many of its values from the broader environment, such as the content of statutory law and appellate court decisions, it also influences society. An example illustrates the interplay between the police department's subsystems and the larger environment. Conditioned by the conservative nature of the organization in which they operate, which is reflected in the police department's goals and values subsystem, the top leadership of the managerial subsystem—in relating the police department to its environment—may take positions against abortions and the legalization of marijuana and for gun control and mandatory sentences.

3. The technical subsystem refers to the means required for the performance of tasks, including the knowledge, equipment, processes, and facilities used to transform inputs into outputs.

4. Individual behaviors, motivations, status and role hierarchies, group dynamics, and influence systems are all elements of the psychosocial subsystem.

5. The structural subsystem is concerned with the ways in which tasks are divided and how they are coordinated. In a formal sense, structure can be set forth by organizational charts, job descriptions, policies, and rules and regulations. Structure is therefore also concerned with patterns of authority, communication, and work flow. Also, the structural subsystem provides for a formalization of relationships between the technical and the psychosocial systems. However, many interactions that occur between technical and psychosocial subsystems bypass the formal, occurring informally.[87]

Knowledge of open systems theory is important to the manager because it provides a view of the police department that is more consistent with reality; the police department is not a closed system but, rather, an open one having many dynamic interactions with the larger society in which it is embedded. This interactive nature of policing is part of the core of the community police movement; thus, open systems theory and community policing are compatible orientations. Figure 4-8 demonstrates one aspect of the dynamic interactions a police department has with its larger environment, the relationship between the police department and external bodies in the fiscal management process.

Stressing the interrelatedness of the various subsystems and the interrelatedness of the police department with the larger world, open systems theory has the potential to foster increased cooperation. Also, the emphasis of open systems theory upon achieving objectives serves to reinforce the need for purposeful behavior and may lead to greater effectiveness in achieving goals.

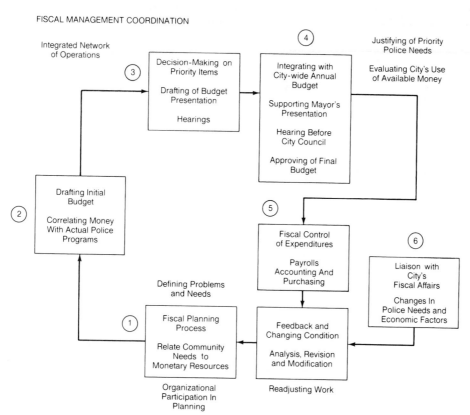

FISCAL MANAGEMENT COORDINATION

Integrated Network
of Operations

③ Decision-Making on
Priority Items

Drafting of Budget
Presentation

Hearings

④ Integrating with
City-wide Annual
Budget

Supporting Mayor's
Presentation

Hearing Before
City Council

Approving of Final
Budget

Justifying of Priority
Police Needs

Evaluating City's Use
of Available Money

② Drafting Initial
Budget

Correlating Money
With Actual Police
Programs

⑤ Fiscal Control
of Expenditures

Payrolls
Accounting And
Purchasing

⑥ Liaison with
City's
Fiscal Affairs

Changes In
Police Needs and
Economic Factors

Defining Problems
and Needs

① Fiscal Planning
Process

Relate Community
Needs to
Monetary Resources

Feedback and
Changing Condition

Analysis, Revision
and Modification

Organizational
Participation In
Planning

Readjusting Work

**FIGURE 4-8.** External relationships in the Houston Police Department's fiscal management process. [*Source:* Kent John Chabotar, *Measuring the Costs of Police Services* (Washington, D.C.: U.S. Department of Justice, National Institute of Justice, 1982), p. 114.]

**The New Paradigms of Administration**

Within the last few years, a new body of literature on administration, which draws on the physical and biological sciences, has begun to emerge. The two most important elements of this literature are chaos theory and quantum theory.[88] These are referred to as the new paradigms or models of administration and as the new sciences of administration. "Unfortunately, there is not one sentence, one paragraph, or even one book that can tell us what these new sciences are. They are a very loosely coupled set of ideas and findings"[89] that reflect some fundamental shifts in thinking about organizations. Due to the emerging nature of these theories, the purpose here is to provide a basic overview inasmuch as they are likely to be an increasingly prominent theme in the literature on administration. Both chaos theory and quantum theory have their roots in systems theory. Among early influential books applying these theories to organizations are Becker's *Quantum Politics,*[90] Wheatley's *Leadership and the New Science,*[91] Kiel's *Managing Chaos and Complexity in Government,*[92] and Zohar and Marshall's *The Quantum Society.*[93] Unlike other theorists and theories discussed in this chapter—such as Taylor and scientific management—chaos theory and quantum theory applied to administration do not have a single founder. Thus, the selection of theorists to associate with these theories, appearing in Table 4-4, is to a degree arbitrary.

The new paradigms may not necessarily be helpful to police managers concerned with the problem of efficient service delivery. The essence of these

## TABLE 4-4.  The Interrelationships of the Three Major Streams of Theories

| Theorists | Traditional Theories | Bridging Theories | Open Systems Theories |
|---|---|---|---|
| Taylor | Scientific management | | |
| Weber | Bureaucratic model | | |
| Fayol, Mooney and Reiley, Gulick, and Urwick | Administrative theory | | |
| Mayo | | | Hawthorne studies and human relations |
| Maslow | Bottom three levels of need hierarchy | | Top two levels of need hierarchy |
| Herzberg | Hygiene factors | | Motivators |
| Lewin | | | Group dynamics |
| Homans | | | Internal-external systems |
| Argyris | Immaturity | | Maturity |
| McGregor | Theory X | | Theory Y |
| Likert | System 1 | System 2     System 3 | System 4 |
| Bennis | | | Organizational development |
| Bertalanffy, Parsons, and Katz and Kahn | | | Systems theory |
| Kiel, Wheatley, Becker, and Zohar and Marshall | | | New paradigms |
| Barnard | | Cooperative system | |
| Simon and March | | Administrative man | |
| Burns and Stalker, Woodward, Sherman and Lawrence, and Lorsch | | Organizational contingency theory | |
| Vroom | | Expectancy theory | |
| Fiedler | | Situational leadership | |
| Katzell | | Theory Z | |

new paradigms is a broader look at administration in which chaos and complexity are not problems to be solved, so much as they are important aspects of organizational life by which the living system—e.g., a police department—adapts to its environment, renews and maintains itself, and ultimately changes itself through self-organization.[94]

Thus, the new paradigms do not simply offer innovative ways to manage police departments better; they question "the basic logic of most management philosophy,"[95] thereby asking different questions. For example, open systems theory holds that all organizations move toward disorganization or death, the entropic process discussed earlier in this chapter. The new paradigms raise several questions. What if the complexity of police departments and their ambiguity about their mission and methods are not sources of entropy, but instead important sources of the life-sustaining energy through which police departments organize themselves to adapt to these phenomena? Can police managers really separate themselves from the chaos they are trying to control when there is an event such as a natural disaster? Or do their very actions to control such events contribute to increased complexity by giving organizational systems new inputs to which they must react, for example, mobilizing all available on-duty personnel, recalling officers who are off duty, establishing a command post, evacuating citizens to safe areas, limiting access to devastated areas to prevent looting while granting entrance to insurance claims adjusters, operating a system for the collection and care of pets and other animals, providing a news media liaison officer, and coordinating with area hospitals and the Federal Emergency Management Agency.[96]

Chaos theory argues that when events such as natural disasters happen and gaining control of events is a slippery affair, new structures and processes emerge—such as task forces and ad hoc cooperation by individuals and groups—which are based on a recognition of their mutual interdependence. Helpful small actions taken everywhere—self-organization—produce the "butterfly effect." The butterfly effect ripples through the community, energizing people to use their talents and resources to help.

Chaos theory is illustrated by the following scenario. A city manager asked a consultant to do a management study of the police department. The "presenting symptoms" of the police department, as expressed by the city manager, were that the police department was in shambles, morale was low, and turnover was high. He therefore thought it was time to replace the chief of police. However, the consultant knew that the chief and the department had strong reputations and had just recently been reaccredited by the Commission on Accreditation of Law Enforcement Agencies (CALEA). Thus, the consultant suggested that before he commit to a study of the police department, he come and spend a few days assessing what—if any—intervention was needed.

During his investigation, the consultant learned that six months previously, the chief had instituted community-oriented policing, which had been strongly endorsed by departmental members. However, some opposition to COP now existed due in part to the fact that it required more reports—the archenemy of street officers. Shortly after the implementation of COP, the city manager ordered that 360-degree performance evaluations be used and that a continuous quality improvement program be implemented. This new method of written evaluation—from subordinates, co-equals, and superiors—frightened and angered members of the police department because it upset the established nature of things. Both COP and the continuous quality improvement program required many meetings, taking officers away from what they saw as "real police work." Roughly one year prior to this, the city's human resources director began recruiting only college graduates for the department. In the 36-officer police department, there was limited opportunity to advance, which frustrated the college graduates who began casting about for better opportunities. Furthermore, the city's salary administration plan—implemented a year before the drive to recruit only college graduates—offered very little in the way of financial advancement, which made veteran officers discontent and exacerbated the frustration of recent hires into the police department. At the same time, competing departments in the same area had increased their salaries and benefits, had much more attractive retirement plans, and offered greater potential for advancement into specialized units and supervisory assignments due to their greater size.

All police administrators know about organizational chaos. It is when too much happens too fast, things seem out of control, and collapse of the department seems not only possible, but even imminent.[97] Yet, somehow, out of this chaos, order does emerge as the department creates new structures and procedures to adjust to the new realities thrust upon it. Chaos theory, which has its roots in systems theory, is therefore described as the study of complex and

**Chaos Theory**

dynamic organizations which reveals patterns of order in what is seemingly chaotic behavior.[98] Chaos theorists argue that the language of systems theory—with its emphasis on maintaining the department's equilibrium—is "wildly incomplete."[99] What chaos theory teaches us is not to distrust chaos and stressfully uncertain times in an organization, but that it is in such times that real change is possible as new structures and procedures emerge from the very chaos administrators are trying to control.[100]

The consultant made his report to the city manager in the context of chaos theory and organizational change (the subject of Chapter 15). He told him that he found no basis for removing the chief, and that the department was simply suffering from "a normal case of chaos," which could be resolved by some new strategies and the passage of time. The department had been overwhelmed by large-scale changes being implemented so rapidly that none of them had yet taken root in the department, and each of the changes required more paperwork. Yet, out of the chaos of the ill-structured changes, progress was being made as new committees produced important reports resolving operational and administrative problems, and as individual officers made "butterfly-effect" contributions, such as developing new work schedules and reporting forms. Also pointed out at this meeting was the fact that some conditions which contributed to the low morale and turnover were projects mandated by the city manager.

The consultant asked the city manager to recall conditions in the department before the chief was selected from outside of the police department. The manager said there had been a burglary scandal in the police department and several officers had gone to jail, causing merchants to distrust the department. He went on to note that CALEA accreditation had restored confidence in the police department. Moreover, at the time, he didn't think the police department "could pull accreditation off due to the massive amount of work which had to be done."

The consultant made several recommendations to the city manager, including getting a police administrator with substantial experience in COP to be a "guru" to their chief; reducing the pace of change; reevaluating the city's pay, benefits, retirement plan, and recruiting policy; establishing a new career ladder as an alternative to movement up through the rank structure; increasing communications both ways between the chief and the city manager; using organizational awards and cash bonuses to reinforce the change process; and structuring the content of promotional examinations to reflect the new types of knowledge needed in the department. After considering the consultant's report, the city manager decided to retain the chief on the belief that some problems had been created for the chief and that "he is also the guy who made accreditation work when I thought it didn't have a prayer."

## Quantum Theory

Like chaos theory, quantum theory has its roots in different scientific disciplines, such as physics and biology.[101] Because quantum theory deviates sharply from the traditional scientific method, explaining it is difficult and can seem mystical and superstitious.[102]

Many management and policy problems involve significant proportions of "indeterministic elements," which means there are many things which we cannot know or understand in a given situation.[103] Police administrators cannot let such factors paralyze them; they live in a world in which they must resolve management and policy problems. In order to resolve them, they have to "fill in the blanks" by making assumptions and creating a "reality" which give them a context in which to respond. Gone is the expectation of objective reality, certainty, and simple cause-and-effect explanations; taking its place are subjectivity, uncertainty, and the recognition that "reality" is different things to different people because we construct our own realities.[104] Therefore, there are alternative explanations to the ones police administrators construct. Quantum theory also sees public institutions as energy fields, in which the focus is on not what is, but what could be.[105] Quantum theory's proposition that there are many things we do not know is consistent with Simon's concept of "bounded rationality"—the idea that because we cannot know everything our rationality is limited. Bounded rationality is discussed in Chapter 12, Planning and Decision Making.

Traditional police administrators argue that performance evaluations are meant to give officers objective feedback about their work behavior. Moreover, they assert that if we link these evaluations to pay increases and promotions, they become a powerful motivational tool for shaping the behavior of officers.[106] Quantum police administrators see these views of traditional administrators as "pure hogwash" for several reasons. For one, they believe that current performance evaluation systems are a hopelessly inadequate method of accurately portraying the complex behaviors of officers over a period of six months or a year. In addition, it is impossible for administrators to know all examples of success and failure by the officers they rate.

Quantum administrators also believe that the traditionalists' view that pay increases and promotions motivate the behavior of officers is too simplistic because the actual causes of behavior are more complex and are likely to include factors such as the officers' values and role concepts, their peer groups, their levels of ambition, the fact that any "reality" constructed about an officer's performance may or may not be consistent with the officer's own "reality," and that the same event can be considered both bad and good. Assume, for example, that a detective solved only three cases in the past six months out of an assigned load of 27 cases. Such a statistic is hardly impressive. But, what if all 27 cases were unsolved criminal homicides that had not been investigated any further in the past three years because all possible leads had been exhausted? What if an officer is drinking off duty in a bar and sees a burglary suspect who specializes in stealing fine jewelry from penthouses. This burglar has committed many recent "jobs" and the news media has been highly critical of the police department's inability to catch him. Assume that the burglar "makes" the off-duty officer and bolts for the door before the officer can call for help. The officer arrests the burglar, but only after a vicious fight. The suspect files suit against the department, claiming the officer used excessive force. The news media wonders why it is that "one intoxicated cop can arrest a burglar that an entire sober department couldn't even find," and criticizes the officer for not having his off-duty gun with him, which would have prevented the needless violence. Is this a good or bad job? On whose "reality" do you base your conclusions?

The quantum police administrator also says that in the very process of measuring things, such as an officer's performance, we change the officer's behavior, and it may or may not be for the better. To illustrate, Sergeant Abbruzzese has a hangover today, having gotten drunk yesterday after she came home and found her husband had left her for his accountant and had emptied their savings and checking accounts. Today, she completes Officer Dunagan's performance evaluation. Due to her immediate personal circumstances, she constructs a "reality" that is more critical than the "reality" that Officer Dunagan has of his own performance. Officer Dunagan subsequently leaves the department feeling that he has no future there.

**Critique of Open Systems Theory**

Mayo's human relations school has been challenged on a number of grounds:

1. It rests on questionable research methods, a point raised earlier.[107]
2. The viewpoint that conflict between management and the worker can be overcome by the "harmony" of human relations attributes too much potency to human relations and ignores the potential that properly handled conflict has for being a source of creativity and innovation.
3. The single-mindedness with which advocates insisted on the importance of human relations was evangelistic.
4. Entirely too much emphasis was placed upon the informal side of organization to the neglect of the formal.
5. The attention focused on the individual and the group was at the expense of consideration of the organization as a whole.[108]

Human relations is also criticized as having a pro-management bias from several different perspectives. First, it saw unions as promoting conflict between management and labor, a condition antithetical to the values of human relations. Second, by focusing on workers, the Hawthorne studies provided management with more sophisticated means of manipulating employees. Finally, the end of human relations is indistinguishable from that of scientific management in that both aim for a more efficient organization:

> Scientific management assumed the most efficient organization would also be the most satisfying one, since it would maximize both productivity and workers' pay. . . the Human Relations approach was that the most personally satisfying organization would be the most efficient.[109]

Although the Hawthorne studies never showed a clear-cut relationship between satisfaction and job performance,[110] the human relations position that satisfied people are more productive has become a widely held and cherished belief. It is a logically appealing and commonsense position whose endless repetition has accorded it the status of "fact." However popular this "fact," the unqualified assertion that satisfied people are more productive is at odds with the research findings; there is no consistent relationship between job satisfaction and productivity.[111]

This does not mean that police managers should be unconcerned about any possible consequences of job satisfaction and dissatisfaction. Quite to the contrary, there are profoundly important organizational and humane reasons that they should be very concerned. On the positive side, job satisfaction generally leads to lower turnover, less absenteeism, fewer cases of tardiness, and fewer grievances; it was the best overall predictor of the length of life in an impressive long-term study.[112] Conversely, job dissatisfaction has been found to be related to various mental and physical illnesses.[113] As a final note, some work on job satisfaction and productivity reverses the usual causal relationships, suggesting that satisfaction is an outgrowth of production.[114]

Maslow used a portion of his *Motivation and Personality* to attack the scientific method, claiming that its rigors limited the conclusions one could reach.[115] In turn, the scientific method has found it difficult to state the concepts of the need hierarchy in ways that they can be measured and the theory tested. Bennis[116] was baffled to discover that little had been done to test the need hierarchy. Despite the lack of research and the fact that the few existing studies do not support Maslow, there remains an almost metaphysical attraction to the need hierarchy,[117] a condition made even more perplexing by noting that Maslow's work on motivation came from a clinical study of neurotic people.[118]

In contrast to the lack of research on the need hierarchy, there has been considerable research on Herzberg's motivation-hygiene theory; after reviewing this evidence Gibson and Teasley conclude:

> It would be fair to summarize these efforts as mixed as regards the validation of the Herzberg concepts. The range of findings run from general support . . . to a vigorous condemnation of Herzberg's methodology.[119]

Behavioral systems theories have also been found wanting on a variety of grounds:

1. Insufficient attention has been paid to the organization as a whole, and too much emphasis has been placed upon the individual and groups.

2. Some theories, such as Argyris's immaturity–maturity theory, McGregor's theory X and theory Y, and Likert's systems 1, 2, 3, and 4, depend as much on setting the bureaucratic model up as a "straw man" to be knocked down as easily as they do their own virtues.

3. However attractive the arguments for organizational humanism, the data supporting them are not powerful and are sometimes suspect. For example, in commenting on McGregor's theory X and theory Y, Maslow notes that:

> a good deal of evidence upon which he bases his conclusions comes from my research and my papers on motivations, self-actualization, etc. But I of all people would know just how shaky this foundation is as a final foundation. My work on motivations came from the clinic, from a study of neurotic people. . . . I am quite willing to concede this . . . because I'm a little worried about this stuff which I consider tentative being swallowed whole by all sorts of enthusiastic people.[120]

Concerns have also been expressed regarding what actually is being measured. For example, Johannesson[121] claims that studies of job satisfaction and organizational climate are tapping the same dimension; critics of Johannesson term his conclusion "premature and judgmental,"[122] while others argue that job satisfaction is the direct result of organizational climate.[123] Moreover, some data suggest conclusions that differ from certain of the logical positions taken by behavioral systems theorists. Argyris's argument that the narrow span of control makes people passive and dependent is a case in point. From a study of 156 public personnel agencies, Blau[124] concluded that a narrow span of control provided opportunities for more mutuality in problem solving. Although not stated directly, this also suggests the possibility that wide spans of control may produce less collaboration, because the manager has less time to share with each subordinate, and a more directive relationship.[125]

4. In one way or another, humanistic theories depend upon open and honest communications among organizational members in an environment of trust and mutual respect. A compellingly attractive theme, it gives insufficient weight to the consequences that can and do flow when authenticity meets power. Along these lines, Samuel Goldwyn is reputed to have said to his staff

one day, "I want you all to tell me what's wrong with our operation even if it means losing your job."[126] The authenticity–power dilemma is not insurmountable; but it is a tall mountain whose scaling depends in large measure upon personally secure and nondefensive people dedicated to improving the organization and how it is experienced by its inhabitants.

5. In large measure the impetus to humanize organizations has been from the academic community; its belief that employees want more rewards than money from doing the work itself does not take into account the fact that some workers have a utilitarian involvement with the job. It simply provides the money necessary to live, and they save their energies and obtain their rewards from their families and other nonjob-related sources. Also, workers may not see attempts to broaden their jobs in the same light as theorists.[127]

Six American automobile workers spent four weeks in a Swedish Saab plant working to assemble engines as a team rather than on an assembly-line basis. Five of the six American workers reacted negatively to this experience. One of them expressed his dissatisfaction in the following way: "If I've got to bust my ass to be meaningful, forget it; I'd rather be monotonous."[128] Although neither controlling nor entirely persuasive, findings such as these at least provide another framework for thinking about theories of organization.

Despite the fact that open systems theory has enjoyed some popularity since 1960, its use has not penetrated into police departments to any discernible degree. Disarmingly straightforward as a concept, its application requires the investment of resources beyond the reach of most police departments, particularly when considered in relationship to needs perceived as more directly relevant to their mission.

Chaos theory and quantum theory do not offer a great deal of immediate assistance to police administrators looking for solutions to specific problems. Instead, they provide new lenses through which to look at administration. This allows police leaders to ask different questions. For example, a quantum belief is that a police department is an energy field and we should not focus only on what exists now, but also on what the possibilities are for the future. This could change the question from "How do we improve our Detective Division?" to "Assume there isn't a Detective Division and we are not going to create one. Under those conditions, what is the best use of the energy formerly vested in it?" Such questions have the potential to create exciting new possibilities for police departments in terms of organizational structure, the delivery of police services, and the roles of officers in departments. Because the application of the new paradigms to administration is in its formative stages, it will be some time before we know whether they will have a significant impact or simply become part of the landscape of thinking about organizations.

## BRIDGING THEORIES

As noted earlier in this chapter, bridging theories are those that display a certain degree of empathy for both the traditional and open systems perspectives. Trying to place a range of theories under the traditional or open systems streams of thinking is not unlike the experience of trying to fit a square peg in a round hole. This difficulty is created by the simple reality that the work of some theorists produces thinking that does not focus solely or even largely on a single dimension. Additionally vexing is the fact that over time the importance that theorists and others attach to their work may change. Perhaps equally perplexing to those newly introduced to organizational theory is the array of classification schemes for presenting work in this area—which also may change over time. For example, at one time organic models of organization were differentiated from general systems models, although in 1967 Buckley noted that the modern concepts of systems are now taking over the duty of the overworked and perhaps retiring concept of the organic organization.[129] All of this is by way of noting that ultimately classification becomes a matter of judgment. For present purposes, it is sufficient to understand that the designation "bridging theories" is intended to encompass a range of theories that can be conceived of as falling into the middle ground between traditional and open systems theory.

Under the broad heading of bridging theories, two subheadings of theories will be considered: general bridging theories and contingency theories. Note that, as the various theories are covered, mention is made of other ways in which these theories have been categorized.

Within this section, the work of Chester Barnard (1886–1961), James March (1928– ), and Herbert Simon (1916– ) is treated. Barnard's thinking has also been identified by others as part of the human relations, social systems, and open systems schools; March and Simon's efforts are sometimes categorized as being part of a decision theory school.

### General Bridging Theories

Chester Barnard's principal career was as an executive with American Telephone & Telegraph, although he had other work experiences as well. During World War II, he was president of United Service Organizations, and from 1952 to 1953 he was the Rockefeller Foundation's president. In 1938, he wrote *The Functions of the Executive,* which reflected his experiences and thinking. Among his major contributions are the following ideas:

1. Emphasis is on the importance of decision-making processes and a person's limited power of choice, as opposed to the traditionalist's rational man.

2. An organization is a "system of consciously coordinated activities or forces of two or more persons," and it is important to examine the external forces to which adjustments must be made.

3. Individuals can overcome the limits on individual performance through cooperative group action.

4. The existence of such a cooperative system depends on both its effectiveness in meeting the goal and its efficiency.

5. Efficiency, in turn, depends on organizational equilibrium, which is the balance between the inducements offered by the organization and the contributions offered by the individual.

6. The informal organization aids communication, creates cohesiveness, and enhances individual feelings of self-respect.

7. Authority rests upon a person's acceptance of the given orders; orders that are neither clearly acceptable nor clearly unacceptable lie within a person's zone of indifference.

8. Complex organizations are themselves composed of small units.

9. The traditional view of organizations is rejected as having boundaries and comprising a definite number of members. Included in this concept of organizations were investors, suppliers, customers, and others whose actions contributed to the productivity of the firm.

10. Executives operated as interconnecting centers in a communication system that sought to secure the coordination essential to cooperative effort. Executive work is the specialized work of maintaining the organization and its operation. The executive is analogous to the brain and the nervous system in relation to the rest of the body.[130]

These ideas of Barnard reveal an appreciation for both traditional and open systems theories. On the one hand, Barnard was concerned with formal structure, goals, effectiveness, and efficiency; on the other hand, he viewed organizations as cooperative systems, having an informal side and many relationships with the larger world. Effectively then, his thinking bridges the traditional and open systems streams of thinking.

Simon's *Administrative Behavior* has been mentioned with respect to its "proverbs" attack on the principles of organization, but it also made other noteworthy contributions. Simon believed that the "anatomy of an organization" was how the decision-making function was distributed; indeed, the central theme of *Administrative Behavior* is that organizations are decision-making entities.[131] Simon was, therefore, simultaneously interested in both structure and behavior. In *Organizations* (1958), March and Simon built on some of the ideas reflected in the earlier *Administrative Behavior. Organizations* presented March and Simon's "administrative man" who was a modification of the rational economic actor behaving in his own self-interest postulated by traditional organizational theory. Administrative man reflects the tension between the traditional theory's normative values of rationality, effectiveness, and efficiency and the open system's views of human behavior and the complexity of organizations. The administrative man

1. Lacks complete knowledge of the alternatives available to him in making decisions
2. Does not know the consequences of each possible alternative
3. Uses a simple decision-making model that reflects the main features of decision situations, but not the complexity of them
4. Make decisions characterized as "satisficing," which are short of optimizing but satisfy and suffice in that they are "good enough to get by"[132]

**Contingency Theory**

In the late 1950s and early 1960s, a series of studies was carried out in England and in this country that were to lead ultimately to the development of what is presently referred to as situational or contingency theory. This approach holds—with respect to organizing, managing, leading, motivating, and other variables—that there is no one best way to go about it. Contingency theory does not, however, also assume that all approaches to a situation are equally appropriate. It is a bridging theory in that it favors neither traditional nor open systems theory; rather, it is the specifics of a situation that suggest which approach should be used.

An early study important to the development of contingency theory was reported on by Burns and Stalker in 1961; as a result of their analysis of the operations of some English industries, they decided that

> we desire to avoid the suggestion that either system is superior under all circumstances to the other. In particular nothing in our experiences justifies the assumption that mechanistic systems should be superseded by the organic under condi-

tions of stability. The beginning of administrative wisdom is the awareness that there is no one optimum type of management system.[133]

In 1965, another English researcher, Joan Woodward, confirmed and extended the work of Burns and Stalker by her finding that a traditional management system was appropriate for a mass-production technology, whereas the organic, flexible, adaptive system was better suited for handling less highly repetitive tasks.[134]

In this country, the 1966 publication of Harvey Sherman's *It All Depends* was an early major statement with a contingency theme on organizations; Sherman, an executive with the Port of New York Authority, believed in a "pragmatic perspective":

> There can be no ideal design or arrangement that will fit all times, all situations, all objectives, and all values . . . these forces are in constant flux . . . it is well to reassess the organization periodically. The very design of the organization structure is a significant force in the total situation and changes in it can alter the total situation.[135]

Forces that Sherman felt were particularly important included

1. The enterprise's objectives and purposes, stated and implied
2. The nature of the work to be done
3. Technology, technological change, and the level of technological skills available to the organization
4. The technological and formal interrelationships within the enterprise
5. The psychology, values, and attitudes that prevail within the enterprise, particularly those of top management
6. The interpersonal and sociological relationship within the enterprise
7. Outside forces, such as changes in the economy, in technology, in laws, in labor relations, in the political situation and in broad sociological and cultural patterns[136]

In the recent past, there have been a number of examples of a contingency approach short of an entire theory of organization. In 1964, Vroom[137] developed a contingency model of motivation; Fiedler's[138] 1967 situational leadership approach is a contingency statement, as is Katzell's theory Z.[139] This last concept is basically a midpoint between McGregor's theory X and theory Y; that is, theory Z holds that, depending on the specifics of each case, it may be appropriate to employ either theory X or theory Y.

Altogether, the broad and more specific approaches to organizations and behavior, regardless of whether they were designated pragmatic, situational, or some other term, received so much attention that in 1970 Lorsch and Lawrence noted

> During the past few years there has been evident a new trend. . . . Rather than searching for the panacea of the one best way . . . under all conditions . . . investigators have more and more tended to examine the functioning of organizations in relation to the needs of their particular members and the external pressures facing them. . . . This approach seems to be leading to a "contingency" theory of organization.[140]

Before leaving contingency theory, it is appropriate to note that Burns and Stalker and Lorsch and Lawrence are also referred to in other literature as environmentalists, whereas Woodward is sometimes designated as a technologist. Environmentalists are theorists who state basically that various types of environments face and interact with organizations. These environments reflect various degrees of complexity and uncertainty that impact upon the organization and its operation. In contrast the theorists such as Woodward maintain that technology—in the sense of methods used to get the work done—has a significant impact on how an organization is structured.

**Critique of Bridging Theories**

Bridging theories, in a sense, simultaneously confirm and disconfirm both traditional and open systems theories. In so doing, they place traditional and open systems theories into a perspective of being useful given appropriate qualifications. Barnard's and March and Simon's statements provide helpful orientations that are, however, somewhat limited by the absence of understandable guidelines as to their applications. Contingency theories of organizations rest presently on relatively limited research, often involving small samples of specific types of organizations. This, added to the fact that some of the important research has been done abroad in a similar but different culture, does not provide powerful data from which to generalize. Nonetheless, contingency theories of organizations provide an alternative and promising way in which to think about organizations as monolithic types—either closed or open.

## SYNTHESIS AND PROGNOSIS

Table 4-4 summarizes the three major streams of thought: (1) traditional theories, (2) open systems, and (3) bridging theories. Note that Table 4-4 also illustrates the interrelationships among the theories. For example, McGregor's theory Y and Likert's system 4 are consistent with each other. There is not, however, an absolute correlation among all theories found under the same major heading; whereas Argyris's state of maturity is compatible with both theory Y and system 4, it only falls within the same stream of thought as the Hawthorne studies. Thus, the use of Table 4-4 depends in some measure on knowledge gained in the preceding pages. Too, throughout this chapter, reference has been made at various points to material covered that was not a theory of organization. To repeat, the purpose of including it was to connect systems of thought as they were developed. Therefore, Table 4-4 includes macro theories of organization, along with some micro level statements. Altogether, Table 4-4 does provide a comprehensive and easily understood overview of the theories covered and illustrates their interconnectedness.

For the vast majority of all organizations in the world, including the police, the bureaucratic model is going to remain overwhelmingly the dominant type of structure. This does not mean that police administrators should ignore or fail to try to reduce dysfunctional aspects of bureaucracy, but rather that reform efforts will generally take the form of improvements in how the bureaucratic model operates and is experienced by both employees and clients as opposed to abandoning it altogether. As discussed more fully in the next chapter, the police have experimented with structures that are alternatives to the bureaucratic model.

Attempts to modify bureaucracy may succeed temporarily in large police departments, if only because such efforts produce a Hawthorne effect. However, in large-scale organizations over time, the latent power of bureaucracy will assert itself—because it remains a superior form of organization for which there presently is no viable long-term alternative—and efforts such as team policing will largely fall away. We have a view, which may be incorrect and is based largely on impressionistic data, that the long-term implementation of true alternative models to the bureaucratic model may be possible only in smaller police departments of something in the order of less than 100 officers. This smaller scale facilitates interpersonal and group processes, such as communication, which can help maintain and institutionalize alternatives to the bureaucratic model. This is not a call to abandon efforts or experimentation with alternative organizational structures in policing; it is a call for realism and reason. The human systems approach is flawed by its small-group orientation in what is largely a large-scale organizational world. The data supporting the humanists, who make up a good part of the behavioral system theorists, are suspect on the basis of the often deductive posturing of this approach. What is left is that police managers must accept the bureaucratic form as a fact and embrace elements of the open system perspective largely on faith. Bridging theories, particularly contingency, represent a potentially rich source of satisfying the organizational imperatives of efficiency and effectiveness and of accommodating the needs of sworn officers and civilian employees.

## SUMMARY

External control of police departments requires that they be responsible to the societal demands placed upon them. This requirement carries with it the expectation that police departments will be efficiency oriented, but not internally democratic. This results in a basic tension between the existing bureaucratically structured department and some number of officers who want greater input into the organization and some increased control over work conditions and environment. Although it is relatively easy to grasp the fundamentals of this issue, obtaining a solution has proven difficult and requires knowledge of organizational theory.

Organizational theory can be summarized as consisting of three major streams of thought: traditional organizational theory, open systems theory, and bridging theories. Traditional theory is comprised of three stems: scientific management, the bureaucratic model, and administrative or management theory. Open systems theory also consists of three divisions: human relations, behavioral systems, and open systems theory. Bridging theories in some fashion represent the difficulty associated with putting a round peg in a square hole; bridging theories do not fall into either the traditional or the open systems streams of thought, but they

do show a certain affinity for both perspectives. In this sense bridging theories can be conceived of usefully as occupying the middle ground between traditional and open systems theories. The two components to bridging theories are general bridging theories and contingency theories.

Virtually all police departments rest on traditional organizational theory. Although lengthy critiques have been made of traditional theory, the data on which these critiques rest are not persuasive or powerful. Indeed, critiques have been made of all three major streams of organizational theory. For the foreseeable or near-term future—say, over at least the next three decades—significant movement away from the bureaucratic model by the police is unlikely. The police are hardly differentiated from most other organizations by this observation. The present reality is that bureaucratic organizations have achieved the very potency that Weber feared. The thorny but imminently necessary task facing police executives, perhaps their preeminent task, is to take the best features of the bureaucratic model and temper its debilitating effects with appropriate doses of other theoretical perspectives.

# DISCUSSION QUESTIONS

1. Why is knowledge of organizational theory important to police administrators and managers?

2. What is scientific management and what are three grounds on which it was attacked?

3. What are the seven characteristics of Weber's bureaucratic model?

4. Often overlooked in Weber's work on bureaucracy are two reservations that he expressed. What are they?

5. The most familiar and enduring acronym of administration was coined by Gulick. What is it and what does it mean?

6. Bennis makes certain criticisms of bureaucracy, whereas Perrow raises certain defenses. Respectively, what are they and how are they similar or dissimilar?

7. What are the major stems or divisions of traditional and open systems organization theories?

8. Elton Mayo is regarded as the father of the human relations school. With which other body of theory did human relations collide and what were the consequences?

9. How can Maslow's need hierarchy, Herzberg's motivation-hygiene theory, McGregor's theory X and theory Y, Argyris's immaturity-maturity statement, and Likert's systems perspective be interrelated conceptually?

10. What are the characteristics of an open system, and how can they be illustrated as being present in a police department?

11. Identify and discuss the new paradigms of administration.

12. What are bridging theories?

13. Under the heading of contingency theory, one finds both technological and environmental perspectives. What do these terms mean?

14. What is the future of the police organizational structure over the foreseeable, near-term future?

# NOTES

1. Amitai Etzioni, *Modern Organizations* (Englewood Cliffs, N.J.: Prentice Hall, 1964), p. 1.

2. Ibid., p. 1, with some additions.

3. Ibid., p. 1.

4. Talcott Parsons, *Structure and Process in Modern Societies* (Glencoe, Ill.: Free Press, 1960), p. 17.

5. Edgar H. Schein, *Organizational Psychology* (Englewood Cliffs, N.J.: Prentice Hall, 1965), p. 9.

6. Peter W. Blau and W. Richard Scott, *Formal Organizations* (Scranton, Pa.: Chandler, 1962), p. 43, with some changes.

7. The treatment of the central issues of the four types of formal organizations is taken from Blau and Scott, pp. 43 and 55, with some changes.

8. Daniel A. Wren, *The Evolution of Management Thought* (New York: Ronald Press, 1972), p. 112.

9. Ibid., p. 114.

10. Ibid., pp. 114–115.

11. See the testimony of F. W. Taylor before the Special Committee of the House of Representatives Hearings to Investigate Taylor and Other Systems of Shop Management, January 25, 1912, p. 1387.

12. Wren, *Evolution of Management Thought,* p. 115.

13. Frederick W. Taylor, *Principles of Scientific Management* (New York: Harper & Row, 1911), pp. 44–47.

14. See Frederick W. Taylor, *Shop Management* (New York: Harper and Brothers, 1911), for a discussion of this concept.

15. Ibid., p. 126.

16. Wren, *Evolution of Management Thought*, p. 132. Not only did Bethlehem Steel abandon the system, but it also fired Taylor.

17. Ibid., p. 131.

18. L. P. Alford, *Henry Lawrence Gantt* (Easton-Hive Management Series: No. 6, 1972; facsimile reprint of a 1934 edition by Harper and Brothers), pp. 207, 209.

19. Sudhir Kakar, *Frederick Taylor: A Study in Personality and Innovation* (Cambridge, Mass.: M.I.T. Press, 1973), p. 2.

20. Fremont E. Kast and James E. Rosenzweig, *Contingency Views of Organization and Management* (Chicago: Science Research Associates, 1973), p. 7.

21. Michael Crozier, *The Bureaucratic Phenomenon* (Chicago: University of Chicago Press, 1964), p. 3.

22. Max Weber, *The Theory of Social and Economic Organization*, trans. A. M. Henderson and Talcott Parsons (New York: Free Press, 1947), p. 337.

23. Ibid., p. 337.

24. Ibid., pp. 330–332, with limited restatement for clarity.

25. Ibid., p. 328.

26. On this point, see Nicos P. Mouzelis, *Organization and Bureaucracy* (Chicago: Aldine, 1967), pp. 20–21 and footnote 29 of that work.

27. H. H. Gerth and C. Wright Mills, *From Max Weber: Essays in Sociology* (New York: Oxford University Press, 1946), p. 50.

28. Wren, *Evolution of Management Thought*, p. 230.

29. Henri Fayol, *General and Industrial Management*, trans. Constance Storrs (London: Sir Isaac Pitman, 1949), p. vi.

30. Ibid., pp. 19–41.

31. Ibid., p. 34.

32. The 1939 edition was co-authored, but the 1947 edition appeared under Mooney's name.

33. Luther Gulick, "Notes on the Theory of Organization," in *Papers on the Science of Administration*, ed. Luther Gulick and L. Urwick (New York: August M. Kelley, a 1969 reprint of the 1937 edition), p. 13.

34. L. Urwick, "Organization as a Technical Problem," in *Papers on the Science of Administration*, p. 52.

35. Taylor, *Shop Management*, p. 184.

36. Warren Bennis, "Organizational Developments and the Fate of Bureaucracy," *Industrial Management Review*, 7:2 (Spring 1966), 41–55.

37. Herbert A. Simon, *Administrative Behavior* (New York: Free Press, 1945), p. 20. For additional criticism of the principles approach, see Dwight Waldo, *The Administrative State* (New York: Ronald Press, 1948).

38. J. Hage, "An Axiomatic Theory of Organizations," *Administrative Science Quarterly*, 10 (1965–1966), 305, Table 4.

39. Charles Perrow, *Complex Organizations* (Glenview, Ill.: Scott, Foresman, 1972), pp. 6–7.

40. Charles T. Goodsell, *The Case for Bureaucracy*, 2nd ed. (Chatham, N.J.: Chatham House Publishers, 1985), p. 11.

41. Ibid., pp. 11–12.

42. Alvin W. Gouldner, "Metaphysical Pathos and the Theory of Bureaucracy," *American Political Science Review*, 49 (June 1955), p. 501 as quoted by Goodsell at p. 12.

43. Goodsell, *Case for Bureaucracy*, pp. 12–13.

44. Ibid., p. 29.

45. As early as 1924, researchers from the National Academy of Sciences had experiments under way; for present purposes, the work at the Hawthorne plant is described following the arrival of Mayo.

46. The definitive report of this research is F. J. Roethlisberger and William J. Dickson's *Management and the Worker* (Cambridge, Mass.: Harvard University Press, 1939). Roethlisberger came from Harvard with Mayo while Dickson was a company administrator.

47. The designation of this study as the bank wiring study is also found in the literature; banks were telephone switchboards.

48. There were actually two relay assembly test room studies, one following the other. The second involved a change in the wage incentive and also confirmed the importance of the social group.

49. Roethlisberger and Dickson, *Management and the Worker*, pp. 58–59 and 180–183.

50. Bertram M. Gross, *The Managing of Organizations*, Vol. I (New York: Free Press, 1964), p. 163.

51. Roethlisberger and Dickson, *Management and the Worker*, p. 522.

52. On this point, see Roethlisberger and Dickson, pp. 179–186 and 448–458.

53. During the last two weeks of the switchboard wiring room study, there was a new supervisor, "Group Chief 2," who acted much more formally than did "Group Chief 1"; "GC-2" was regarded as a "company man." See Roethlisberger and Dickson, pp. 452–453.

54. Ibid., pp. 21 and 397.

55. Etzioni, *Modern Organizations*, pp. 34–37.

56. Whitman Knapp, chairman, Commission to Investigate Allegations of Police Corruption and the City's Anti-Corruption Procedures, *Commission Report* (New York, 1972), pp. 4, 65; also see Herman Goldstein, *Police Corruption* (Washington, D.C.: Police Foundation, 1975).

57. A. H. Maslow, "A Theory of Human Motivation," *Psychological Review*, 50 (July 1943), 370–396.

58. These five elements are identified in A. H. Maslow, *Motivation and Personality* (New York: Harper and Brothers, 1954), pp. 80–92. Maslow later added a sixth category, "metamotivation," but it has never received substantial interest. See "A Theory of Metamotivation," *Humanitas*, 4 (1969), 301–343.

59. Ibid., p. 91.

60. Robet M. Chiaramonte, "The Blue Max Award," *Police Chief*, 11:4 (1973), 24–25.

61. Wren, *Evolution of Management Thought*, p. 324; Lewin lived in this country for the fifteen years preceding his death in 1947.

62. Ibid., p. 325.

63. Ibid., p. 325.

64. This case is reported in Paul Hersey and Kenneth H. Blanchard, *Management of Organizational Behavior*, 3rd ed. (Englewood Cliffs, N.J.: Prentice Hall, 1977), p. 139, with credit to "The Truth Hurts" *Wall Street Journal*, no date. One of the key critics of T-groups has been George Odiorne.

65. George C. Homans, *The Human Group* (New York: Harcourt Brace, 1950), pp. 81–130.

66. Chris Argyris, *Personality and Organization: The Conflict Between System and the Individual* (New York: Harper and Brothers, 1957), pp. 58–66.

67. Ibid., pp. 76–122.

68. Chris Argyris, *Integrating the Individual and the Organization* (New York: John Wiley & Sons, 1964), p. 3.

69. For extended treatment of this subject, see Chris Argyris, pp. 146–191.

70. Ibid., p. 147.

71. Douglas McGregor, *The Human Side of Enterprise* (New York: McGraw-Hill, 1960), p. 6. Also see Louis A. Allen, "M for Management: Theory Y Updated," *Personnel Journal*, 52:12 (1973), 1061–1067.

72. Ibid., p. 7.

73. Ibid., pp. 33–57.

74. The information on QCs is drawn from W. Troy McClain "Focus on 'Quality Circles': In Quest of Improved Police Productivity," *Police Chief*, 52:9 (1985), 50–54; and Joyce L. Roll and David L. Roll, "The Potential for Application of Quality Circles in the American Public Sector," *Public Productivity Review*, 7 (June 1983), 122–142.

75. Rensis Likert, *The Human Organization* (New York: McGraw-Hill, 1967), p. 109.

76. Charles R. Swanson and Susette Talarico, "Politics and Law Enforcement: Implications of Police Perspectives" (Paper presented at the 1979 meeting of the Academy of Criminal Justice Sciences), Table VI of the appendix.

77. Likert, *Human Organization*, pp. 50–51.

78. Wendell L. French and Cecil H. Bell, Jr., *Organizational Development* (Englewood Cliffs, N.J.: Prentice Hall, 1973), p. xiv.

79. Ibid., p. 21.

80. Ibid., pp. 21–25.

81. Ibid., pp. 25–26.

82. Ibid., p. 24.

83. Warren G. Bennis, *Changing Organizations* (New York: McGraw-Hill, 1966), p. 118.

84. Stephen P. Robbins, *The Administrative Process* (Englewood Cliffs, N.J.: Prentice Hall, 1976), p. 259.

85. Ibid., p. 259.

86. Daniel Katz and Robert Kahn, *The Social Psychology of Organization*, 2nd ed. (New York: John Wiley, 1978), pp. 23–30, with some change.

87. Kast and Rosenzweig, *Contingency Views*, pp. 13–15, with changes and additions.

88. E. Sam Overman, "The New Science of Administration," *Public Administration Review*, 56:5 (September/October 1996), 487. Some of this author's ideas have been written into a police context by the authors.

89. Ibid., p. 487.

90. Theodore L. Becker, *Quantum Politics: Applying Quantum Theory to Political Phenomena* (New York: Praeger, 1991).

91. Margaret J. Wheatley, *Leadership and the New Science* (San Francisco: Berrett-Koehler, 1992).

92. L. Douglas Kiel, *Managing Chaos and Complexity in Government* (San Francisco: Jossey-Bass, 1994).

93. Danah Zohar and Ian Marshall, *The Quantum Society* (New York: William Morrow, 1994).

94. Linda F. Dennard, "The New Paradigm in Science and Administration," *Public Administration Review*, 56:5 (September/October 1996), 495.

95. Ibid., 495.

96. Ibid., 496. While Dennard writes generically about these questions, the authors have written her cogent ideas into a police context.

97. Overman, "The New Science of Administration," 487.

98. Ibid., 487.

99. Ibid., 487.

100. Ibid., 488.

101. Ibid., 487.

102. Ibid., 489.

103. Ibid., 489.

104. Ibid., 490.

105. Ibid., 489.

106. This example of a performance evaluation is drawn, with restatement, from Overman, 489–490.

107. The Hawthorne studies have continued to excite the imagination. See, for instance, H. W. Parsons, "What Caused the Hawthorne Effect?" *Administration and Society,* 10 (November 1978), 259–283; Henry Lansberger, *Hawthorne Revisited* (Ithaca, N.Y.: Cornell University Press, 1958).

108. These points are drawn, with change, from William H. Knowles. "Human Relations in Industry: Research and Concepts," *California Management Review,* 2:2 (Fall 1958), 87–105.

109. Etzioni, *Modern Organizations,* p. 39.

110. Edward E. Lawler, *Motivation in Work Organizations* (Monterey, Calif.: Brooks/Cole, 1973), p. 62.

111. Edwin A. Locke, "The Nature and Cause of Job Satisfaction," in *Handbook of Industrial and Organizational Psychology,* ed. Marvin D. Dunnette (Chicago: Rand McNally, 1976), p. 1332.

112. In this regard, see A. H. Brayfield and W. H. Crockett, "Employee Attitudes and Employee Performance," *Psychological Bulletin,* 52 (September 1955), 394–424; V. H. Vroom, *Motivation and Work* (New York: John Wiley & Sons, 1964); John P. Wanous, "A Causal-Correlation Analysis of the Job Satisfaction and Performance Relationship," *Journal of Applied Psychology,* 59 (April 1974), 139–144; Niger Nicholson, Toby Wall, and Joe Lischerson, "The Predictability of Absence and Propensity to Leave from Employees' Job Satisfaction and Attitudes Toward Influence in Decision Making," *Human Relations,* 30 (June 1977), 449–514; Philip H. Mirvis and Edward E. Lawler III, "Measuring the Financial Impact of Employee Attitudes," *Journal of Applied Psychology,* 62 (February 1977), 1–8; Charles L. Hulin, "Effects of Changes in Job Satisfaction Levels on Employee Turnover," *Journal of Applied Psychology,* 52 (April 1968), 122–126: A. H. Marrow, D. G. Bowers, and S. E. Seashore, *Management by Participation* (New York: Harper & Row, 1967); L. W. Porter and R. M. Steers, "Organizational Work and Personal Factors Related to Employee Turnover and Absenteeism," *Psychological Bulletin,* 80 (August 1973), 151–176; Frederick Herzberg et al., *Job Attitudes: Review of Research and Opinion* (Pittsburgh, Pa.; Psychological Service of Pittsburgh, 1957); E. Palmore, "Predicting Longevity: A Follow-up Controlling for Age," *Gerontologist,* 9 (1969), 247–250.

113. See A. W. Kornhauser, *Mental Health of the Industrial Worker: A Detroit Study* (New York: John Wiley & Sons, 1965); R. J. Burke, "Occupational and Life Strains, Satisfaction, and Mental Health," *Journal of Business Administration,* 1 (1969–1970), 35–41.

114. For example, Lyman Porter and Edward Lawler, *Managerial Attitude and Performance* (Homewood, Ill.: Dorsey Press, 1967); John E. Sheridan and John W. Slocum, Jr., "The Direction of the Causal Relationship Between Job Satisfaction and Work Performance," *Organizational Behavior and Human Performance,* 14 (October 1975), 159–172.

115. Frank K. Gibson and Clyde E. Teasely, "The Humanistic Model of Organizational Motivation: A Review of Research Support," *Public Administration Review,* 33:1 (1973), 91. Several of the points made in the treatment of Maslow are drawn from this excellent analysis.

116. Bennis, *Changing Organizations,* p. 196.

117. Walter Nord, "Beyond the Teaching Machine: The Neglected Area of Operant Conditioning in the Theory and Practice of Management," *Organizational Behavior and Human Performance,* 4 (November 1969), 375–401; also see Lyman Porter, "Job Attitudes in Management," *Journal of Applied Psychology,* 46 (December 1962), 375–384; Douglas Hall and Khalil Nougaim, "An Examination of Maslow's Need Hierarchy in an Organizational Setting," *Organizational Behavior and Human Performance,* 3 (February 1968), 12–35.

118. Maslow, *Motivation and Personality,* pp. 79–80.

119. Gibson and Teasley, "Humanistic Model," 92.

120. Abraham Maslow, *Eupsychian Management: A Journal* (Homewood, Ill.: Dorsey Press, 1965), 55–56.

121. R. E. Johannesson, "Some Problems in the Measurement of Organizational Climate," *Organizational Behavior and Human Performance,* 10 (August 1973), 118–144.

122. W. R. Lafollette and H. P. Sims, Jr., "Is Satisfaction Redundant with Organizational Climate?" *Organizational Behavior and Human Performance,* 13 (April 1975), 276.

123. J. M. Ivancevich and H. L. Lyon, *Organizational Climate, Job Satisfaction, Role Clarity and Selected Emotional Reaction Variables in a Hospital Milieu* (Lexington: University of Kentucky Press, 1972).

124. Peter Blau, "The Hierarchy of Authority in Organizations," *American Journal of Sociology,* 73 (January 1968), 457.

125. Perrow, *Complex Organizations,* p. 38.

126. Bennis, *Changing Organizations,* p. 77.

127. Jobs can be manipulated in three different ways: (1) jobs can be broadened by incorporating different tasks from the same skill level, referred to as "job enlargement"; (2) jobs can be made

larger by giving some of the supervisor's tasks to the subordinate, called "job enrichment"; and (3) job enlargement and job enrichment may be employed simultaneously, also called "job enrichment."

128. "Doubting Sweden's Way," *Time,* March 10, 1975, 44.

129. Walter Buckley, *Sociology and Modern Systems Theory* (Englewood Cliffs, N.J.: Prentice Hall, 1967), p. 43.

130. This concise summary of Barnard's contributions is drawn from Dessler, *Organization and Management,* pp. 44–45.

131. Simon, *Administrative Behavior,* p. 220.

132. James G. March and Herbert A. Simon, *Organizations* (New York: John Wiley & Sons, 1958), pp. 136–171.

133. Tom Burns and G. M. Stalker, *The Management of Innovation* (London: Tavistock, 1961), p. 125.

134. Joan Woodward, *Industrial Organization: Theory and Practice* (London: Oxford University Press, 1965).

135. Harvey Sherman, *It All Depends* (University: University of Alabama Press, 1966), p. 57.

136. Ibid., pp. 56–57.

137. Vroom, *Work and Motivation.*

138. Fred E. Fiedler, *A Theory of Leadership Effectiveness* (New York: McGraw-Hill, 1967).

139. Various names have been associated with theory Z. Writing in 1962, Harold J. Leavitt called for the use of "differentiating" approaches to structure and management, based on traditional and "newer" concepts, but did not use the term theory Z; see "Management According to Task: Organizational Differentiation," *Management International,* 1 (1962), 13–22. On September 4, 1961, Raymond A. Katzell gave the presidential address to the Division of Industrial Psychology, American Psychological Association and, after referring to McGregor's theory X and theory Y, called for the use of theory alpha and omega, which combined the best features of McGregor's opposites; see *American Psychologist,* 17 (February 1962), 102–108. Later, Lyndall F. Urwick specifically discussed what Leavitt generally, and Katzell more specifically, had addressed; see "Theory Z," *S.A.M. Advanced Management Journal,* 35:1 (1970), 14–21.

140. Jay W. Lorsch and Paul R. Lawrence, eds., *Studies in Organization Design* (Homewood, Ill.: Irwin and Dorsey Press, 1970), p. 1.

## INTRODUCTION

In the previous chapter, the major theoretical concepts associated with organizations and the ways in which they function were covered. In this chapter, further attention is given to how these theories actually work in police organizations, and additional related concepts are presented. Attention is also focused on line and staff relationships in police departments, why they evolved as they have, why dissension sometimes arises, and how this dissension can be minimized or eliminated.

## ORGANIZING: AN OVERVIEW

Police administrators modify or design the structure of their organization in order to fulfill the mission that has been assigned to the police. An organizational chart reflects the formal structure of task and authority relationships determined to be most suited to accomplishing the police mission. The process of determining this formal structure of task and authority relationships is termed *organizing*. The major concerns in organizing are: (1) identifying what jobs need to be done, such as conducting the initial investigation, performing the latent or follow-up investigation, and providing for the custody of physical evidence seized at the scene of a crime; (2) determining how to group the jobs, such as those responsible for patrol, investigation, and the operation of the property room; (3) forming grades of authority, such as officer, detective, corporal, sergeant, lieutenant, and captain; and (4) equalizing responsibility and authority, illustrated by the example that if a sergeant has the responsibility to supervise seven detectives, that sergeant must have sufficient authority to discharge that responsibility properly or he or she cannot be held accountable for any results.[1]

# —5—
# CONCEPTS OF POLICE ORGANIZATIONAL DESIGN

*We trained hard . . . but it seemed that every time we were beginning to form up into teams we would be reorganized. . . . I was to learn later in life that we tend to meet any new situation by reorganizing and a wonderful method it can be for creating the illusion of progress while providing confusion, inefficiency and demoralization.*

PETRONIUS, 210 b.c.

**Specialization in Police Agencies**

Central to this process of organizing is determining the nature and extent of specialization. Some 2,300 years ago, Plato observed that "each thing becomes . . . easier when one man, exempt from other tasks, does one thing."[2] Specialization or the division of labor is also one of the basic features of traditional organizational theory.[3] As discussed more fully later in this chapter, specialization produces different groups of functional responsibilities and the jobs allocated to meet those different responsibilities are staffed or filled with people who are believed to be especially qualified to perform those jobs. Thus, specialization is crucial to effectiveness and efficiency in large organizations. Yet, specialization makes the organizational environment more complex by complicating communication, by increasing the number of units from which cooperation must be obtained, and by creating conflict among differing interests and loyalties. Also specialization creates greater need for coordination and therefore additional hierarchy and can lead to the creation of narrow jobs that confine the incumbents and stifle their willingness or capacity to work energetically in support of the police department's goals. Police departments are not insensitive to the problems of specialization and attempt through various schemes to avoid the alienation of employees. Personnel can be rotated to different jobs, they can be given additional responsibilities that challenge them, they can be involved in organizational problem solving such as through the use of quality circles, and the police department can try different forms of organizational structures. Thus, although specialization is an essential feature of large-scale organizations, any benefits derived from it have their actual or potential costs.

One of the first police executives to explore systematically the relationship between specialization and the organizational structure was O. W. Wilson.[4] He noted that most small departments do not need to be concerned with widely developed specialization because their patrol officer is a jack of all trades. Conversely, in large departments particular tasks (such as traffic enforcement and criminal investigation) are assigned to special units and/or individuals within the organization. Specialization presents a number of advantages for large departments.

**Placement of responsibility**—The responsibility for the performance of a given task can be placed on specific units or individuals. For instance, a traffic division is responsible for the investigation of all traffic accidents and a patrol division is responsible for all requests for general police assistance.

**Development of expertise**—A narrow field of interest, attention, or skill can be the subject of a specialized unit. For instance, many police agencies have highly skilled special weapons and tactics (SWAT) teams that train regularly to respond to critical incidents, such as terrorist activities, hostage situations, or high-risk search warrants. Advanced training in this area yields increased officer safety and a high degree of expertise. Specialization is also helpful during the investigation of narrowly defined, technical crimes, such as bombings, computer fraud, and environmental dumping. (See Box 5-1.)

**Promotion of group esprit de corps**—Any group of specially trained individuals sharing similar job tasks, and to some degree dependent on each other for success, tends to form a highly cohesive unit with high morale.

**Increased efficiency and effectiveness**—Specialized units show a higher degree of proficiency in job task responsibility. For instance, a white-collar fraud unit will ordinarily be more successful in investigating a complex computer fraud than a general detective division.[5]

Specialization appears to be a sure path to operational effectiveness. It allows each employee to acquire expertise in one particular area so as to maximize his or her contribution to the overall department. However, as noted earlier, specialization has also been associated with increased friction and conflict within police departments. As units such as traffic, detective, and SWAT teams develop, an increase in job factionalism and competition also develops. The result may be a decrease in a department's overall job performance as individuals within each group show loyalty primarily or only to their unit. This traditional problem may be observed in the relationship between patrol officers and

**FIGURE 5-1.** Specialized patrol unit discusses geographical features of an area before saturation procedure in an effort to apprehend a rapist. (Courtesy of Maricopa County Sheriff's Office, Phoenix, Arizona.)

## BOX 5-1

### Midnight Dumpers Stalked by Eco-Cops

### S.F. agencies crack down on illegal garbage

by Jim Herron Zamora

It's midnight in a Hunters Point back alley. A pickup pulls up. The driver and a passenger jump into the bed of the truck and dump old tires, barrels of motor oil, wood scraps and other trash onto the pavement. As they start to leave, a dark van parked 100 feet away pulls into the truck's path. Undercover cops surround the dumpers. San Francisco's eco-cops make another bust.

Such scenes will become more frequent with the help of a new task force of San Francisco police, prosecutors, fire investigators and officials from the Health and Public Works departments.

Historically, criminal enforcement of environmental laws has been left to regulatory agencies that develop cases against egregious polluters and give the information to the district attorney or federal prosecutors. San Francisco police rarely became involved in toxic waste or dumping cases until December 1993, when a truck spilled bags of asbestos onto the Bay Bridge, closing the lower deck for eight hours. The police Environmental Crimes Unit was formed that month. But it consisted of only two people—Inspector Mike Mahoney and Officer Doug Frediani—who juggled dumping investigations with their caseloads in the hit-and-run detail.

The new task force allows four inspectors and one officer to investigate full-time. They also follow up on incidents of trash dumping or illicit hazardous-waste disposal reported to the departments of Health or Public Works. "We're going from a reactive to a proactive approach," Mahoney said. "We never really had the time to investigate every case. Pretty much what it used to be is that I would get a call or the Health Department. Our new game plan is to look at what's going on out there and track down the dumpers and the (waste) generators."

*(continued)*

# BOX 5-1 (continued)

### Boat, Copter Available

The expanded unit will be able to borrow San Francisco's police boat and new helicopter to look for polluters. "We'll use those to determine to if there are hot spots where they are discharging," Mahoney said. "That's something we've never done before."

Although the new unit will target big toxic polluters—such as the huge Triple A Machine Shop case in Hunters Point in the 1980s—investigators also hope to make a dent in a far more common problem: trash dumping. One example of the latter is the small-scale "midnight dumper" who tosses several 55-gallon drums of motor oil or other industrial solvents from a pickup at night, investigators said. Often property owners or the city are stuck with the work and expense of cleaning up the dumped toxics. Police said a small number of irresponsible businesses that hire people to dispose of their waste illegally make it harder for legitimate firms. "Either the taxpayers pay or honest business people get hit by people who cheat," Mahoney said.

### Car Wash Repeatedly Hit

Mahoney cited the problem of a still-unidentified midnight dumper who pulls a pickup into the back of a self-service car wash, dumps a load of 20 or so old tires, then drives off. "That business owner is then stuck with paying the cost of disposing of these tires," Mahoney said. The dumper has "gone to one car wash seven or eight times. This guy is responsible for a lot of stuff in the city because he has found a little niche."

Mahoney was luckier in the case of Lonnie Earl Adams, who had offered his services as a low-cost trash hauler in Bayview/Hunters Point. Police believe Adams frequently dumped loads on street corners and empty lots near the San Francisco Produce Market in the early morning. Based on a description by a night watchman, Mahoney set up a surveillance and caught Adams last month at the corner of Jerrold and Toland streets. "But because there was no hazardous waste in this truck full of garbage, we essentially only just gave him a ticket," Mahoney said. "If there were hazardous materials, we could have gotten him for a felony."

In the past decade, more and more local law enforcers, including the Los Angeles police and the sheriff's departments in Sonoma and Contra Costa counties, have formed environmental units. Frustrated by people dumping toxic waste in industrial neighborhoods, Oakland formed its police unit nine years ago.

### Not-So-Ingenious Solutions

Since then it has dealt with a wide variety of cases, including a dry-cleaning business that cut a hole in its floor and dumped solvents into the ground below. Not all dumpers resort to back alleys, said Sgt. Kenneth Parris, head of the Oakland unit. "We had a guy who dumped some construction rubbish, including asbestos pipe wrappings, at Mosswood Park in North Oakland," Parris said. "He offered to haul away someone's trash for a price cheaper than he could get rid of it at the dump." The hauler then backed his pickup onto the grass at Mosswood and dumped the material in a corner of the heavily used park.

But carelessness is a trait often found in illegal dumpers, Parris said. The trash included envelopes with addresses for the property owner who had hired the irresponsible hauler. "He lived less than three blocks away," Parris said. "The asbestos was dumped practically in his back yard."

*Source: San Francisco Examiner,* July 8, 1996, p. A-1.

---

detectives. Patrol officers are sometimes reluctant to give information to detectives because they feel detectives will take credit for their work. Specialization also increases the number of administrative and command relationships, complicating the overall organizational structure. Additionally, each unit requires a competent leader. In some instances this competent leader must also be a qualified specialist. A thorny problem here is when the specialist does not qualify for the rank usually needed to head a major unit. An example of such a problem is observed in the staffing of an air patrol unit in which the commanding officer may be a lieutenant or sergeant because that individual is the highest ranking officer with a pilot's license. In this case, the level of expertise (high) does not coincide with the level of rank (lower), which may cause difficulties when trying to deal with other commanding officers of units who hold the rank of captain or major.

Finally, specialization may hamper the development of a well-rounded police program. As specialization increases, the resources available for general uniformed patrol invariably decrease, often causing a lopsided structure wherein the need for general police services are second to the staffing of specialized programs and units (see Box 5-2).[6]

A police administrator's potential to direct the efforts of others personally and successfully is greater than one person and less than infinity. At the same time, the principle of hierarchy requires that each lower level of an organization be supervised by a higher level. The span of control recognizes both the limitations on potential and the importance of the principle of hierarchy. The span of control is the number of subordinates a police administrator can personally direct effectively. Depending on the nature of the activities performed by subordinates, the skills of the subordinates, their educational level, their experience, and other variables, some police administrators can effectively direct a relatively large number of officers, whereas others are fully employed supervising only a few. As a rule of thumb, seven is generally regarded as the upper limit one person can effectively supervise. Decisions regarding span of control directly influence the number of levels in the organization hierarchy and, hence, its complexity. Recently, the term *span of management* instead of *span of control* has been used to describe the number of personnel a supervisor can personally manage effectively. The term *span of management* is broader than *span of control* and also encompasses factors relating to an individual's capacity to oversee the activities of others directly, such as a police manager's ability, experience, and level of energy.[7]

The principle of hierarchy requirement that each lower level of organization be supervised by a higher level results not only in the use of multiple spans of control, but also in different grades of authority that increase at each successively higher level of the organization. This authority flows

## Hierarchy: Spans of Control and Grades of Authority

## BOX 5-2

### Chief Disbands Squad, Puts Officers in Uniform

by Bill Bryan

A special squad of detectives credited with combatting violent crime in St. Louis and lowering the city's murder rate has been disbanded.

Police Chief Ron Henderson says putting the 18 detectives of the Violent Crimes Task Force into uniform as members of the Mobile Reserve unit will bring much needed added police presence in high-crime areas.

Henderson also transferred 12 narcotics detectives —four from each of the three area stations—into Mobile Reserve. The moves, which become effective Monday, mean that Mobile Reserve will swell from 16 officers to 46.

"At every neighborhood meeting I go to, I keep hearing, 'We don't see the police,' " Henderson said.

"They want a stronger police presence, and I'm responding to their needs."

As for the loss of the narcotics units, Henderson said other units, plus Mobile Reserve, will take up the slack.

The Violent Crime Task Force was begun in August 1994 with a mission to target the city's most dangerous criminals while focusing on the most crime-ridden neighborhoods. The squad was highly successful with hundreds of arrests and hundreds of weapons seized.

When statistics disclosed that murder in St. Louis dropped 17 percent last year, the city's lowest level since 1990, many in the department credited the Violent Crimes Task Force with being partly responsible.

*Source: St. Louis Post Dispatch,* March 10, 1996, p. 5D. Reprinted with permission of the St. Louis Post-Dispatch, copyright 1996.

**TABLE 5-1.   Traditional Police Ranks Versus Alternative Titles**

| *Traditional Ranks* | *Alternative Titles* |
| --- | --- |
| Chief of police | Director |
| Deputy chief | Assistant director |
| Colonel | Division director |
| Major | Inspector |
| Captain | Commander |
| Lieutenant | Manager |
| Sergeant | Supervisor |
| Detective | Investigator |
| Corporal | Senior officer/master patrol officer |
| Officer | Public safety officer/agent |

downward in the organization as a formal grant of power from the chief of police to those selected for leadership positions. These different grades of authority produce the chain of command. Although there are many similarities from one department to another, the American police service does not have a uniform terminology for grades of authority and job titles.[8] In recent years some police departments have moved away from using traditional military-style ranks and have adopted, instead, alternative titles as summarized in Table 5-1. However, in many departments there remains a distinction between rank and title.[9] In these, rank denotes one's place in terms of grade of authority or the rank hierarchy, whereas title indicates an assignment. Where this distinction is made, a person holding the title of "division director," for example, may be a captain, major, or colonel in terms of the rank hierarchy.

## ORGANIZATIONAL STRUCTURE AND DESIGN

Tansik and Elliot suggest that when we consider the formal structure (or pattern of relationships) of an organization, we typically focus on two areas:

1. The formal relationship and duties of personnel in the organization, which include the organizational chart and job descriptions
2. The set of formal rules, policies, or procedures, and controls that serve to guide the behavior of organizational members within the framework of the formal relationships and duties.[10]

Organizational design focuses on two spatial levels of differentiation—vertical and horizontal, depicted in Figure 5-2. Vertical differentiation is based on levels of authority, or positions holding formal power within the organization; Table 5-2, later in this chapter, reflects one range of vertical differentiation found in police agencies. Persons with vertical authority have the power to assign work and to exercise control to ensure job performance.[11] In Figure 5-2 the deputy chief has a span of control of three, all of whom are captains, and all to whom he or she can give assignments and control.

Horizontal differentiation, on the other hand, is usually based on activity. However, in some cases, horizontal differentiation is based on specific projects

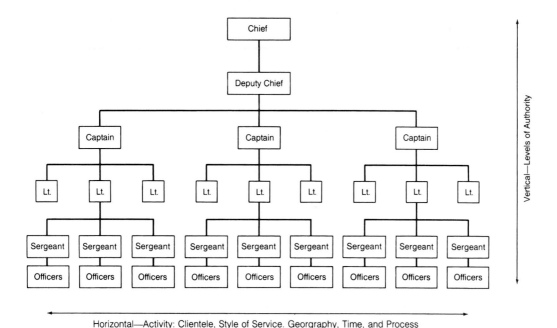

FIGURE 5-2. Organizational chart showing vertical and horizontal levels of differentiation. In some departments, especially large ones, a number of other ranks may be present within the chart.

or even geographical distribution. For instance, many state police departments are responsible for large geographical areas. Their organizational structure often reflects horizontal differentiation based on location rather than function. Some of the more common ways in which activities of personnel are grouped within an organization (on a horizontal dimension) are as follows:

**Grouping by clientele**—The simplest method of grouping within a police department is by clientele. Personnel are assigned by the type of client served, such as juvenile division, senior-citizen crime detail, mayor's security unit, and gang squad. Each group focuses on the needs of a special clientele, which may be either temporary or permanent. In this manner, officers become familiar with the specific enforcement problems and patterns associated with different client populations.

**Grouping by style of service**—A police department usually has a patrol bureau and a detective bureau. The grouping of uniformed patrol officers on the one hand and of plainclothes investigators on the other illustrates how the former are grouped by the nature of their services (conspicuous, preventive patrol, and preliminary investigations) and how the latter are grouped also by this same principle (follow-up investigations). This form of grouping also takes advantage of specialization of knowledge and skill and permits the pinpointing of responsibility for results.

**Grouping by geography**—Where activities are widespread over any given area, it may be beneficial to provide local command. Instances of this type of operation are large city precincts or district-type operations and state police posts that are located throughout a state. An example of this appears in Figure 5-4B, later in this chapter. Even in the headquarters building, activities that are related usually share the same floor. Instances of this arrangement are records, communications, and crime analysis in close proximity to each other. This permits supervisors to become familiar with operating problems of related units and to coordinate the various efforts by more direct and immediate control.

**Grouping by time**—This grouping occurs when the need to perform a certain function or service goes beyond the normal work period of a single eight-hour shift. Other shifts are needed to continue the effort. The division of the patrol force into three platoons, each of which is responsible for patrolling the city during an eight-hour period, is an example of this differentiation process. This form of grouping tends to create problems of coordination and unity of direction because top administrators work normal day hours whereas many of their officers perform their functions on the evening and midnight shifts. The need to delegate authority becomes critical under these circumstances.

**Grouping by process**—This involves the placing of all personnel who use a given type of equipment in one function. Examples include stenographic pools, crime laboratory personnel placed in a section to handle certain types of scientific equipment, and automotive maintenance units. This type of grouping lends itself to expertise involving a single process and makes the most efficient use of costly equipment.[12,13]

## Top-Down Versus Bottom-Up Approaches

The level of complexity within a police organization is largely determined by the amount of horizontal and vertical differentiation that exists.[14] Size is often, but not necessarily, related to complexity. Some organizations, even relatively small police departments, can be highly differentiated and quite complex in organizational design.

According to Hodge and Anthony,[15] the differentiation process can occur in two basic ways in police agencies. First, the "bottom-up" or synthesis approach focuses on combining tasks into larger and larger sets of tasks. For instance, a police officer's tasks may primarily involve routine patrol, but would dramatically increase in complexity when the officer was assigned preliminary investigative duties. Tasks become more complex and therefore require additional and varied levels of supervision and accountability. The bottom-up approach is shown in Figure 5-3A. Second, the "top-down" or analysis approach looks at the overall work of the organization at the top and splits this into increasingly more specialized tasks as one moves from the top to the bottom of the organization. The top-down approach considers the overall police mission —to protect and to serve the public. At the top level of a police agency, this can be defined into various administrative tasks such as budgeting, political maneuvering, and leadership, whereas at the street level, such a mission is carried out through activities such as patrol and arrest. This type of approach is shown in Figure 5-3B.

Both approaches are commonly found in police organizations. The top-down analysis is often used in growing organizations because it is easy to visualize the set of tasks to be accomplished and then to break these sets down into specific tasks and subtasks. The bottom-up approach is often used during periods of retrenchment where organizational growth has declined, because combining tasks such as those found in patrol and detective bureaus can consolidate jobs or even units.

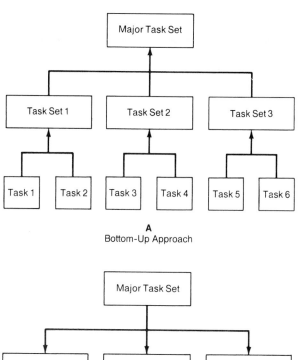

A
Bottom-Up Approach

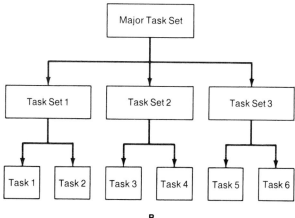

B
Top-Down Approach

**FIGURE 5-3.** The bottom-up and top-down approaches to building structure around differentiation. [*Source: Organizational Theory: An Environmental Approach* 1/E by Hodge, B. J./ Anthony, William P. Reprinted by permission of Prentice-Hall, Inc., Upper Saddle River, NJ.

**Flat Versus Tall Structure**

Some organizations have narrow spans of management with tall structures and many levels, whereas others reduce the number of levels by widening the span of management at each level. Many narrower spans of control make a police department "taller." Shown in Figure 5-4A, the California Highway Patrol (CHP) appears to have five levels. These levels are commissioner, deputy commissioner, assistant commissioner, field division chief, and area office commander. From a more functional perspective, each area office also has a chain of command consisting of four layers—captain, lieutenant, sergeant, and officer. Thus, when the rank layers in the area offices are considered, the CHP is a tall organization with a number of different levels of authority. Seven to nine levels of rank is fairly typical of large police organizations. Figure 5-4B displays each CHP area office by geographical grouping as described earlier in this chapter.

The complexity of a police department is increased by the proliferation of levels because they can negatively affect communication up and down the chain of command. For example, during urban riots police departments found that an initially small incident grew rapidly beyond the ability of a small group of officers to control it. The process of getting approval from

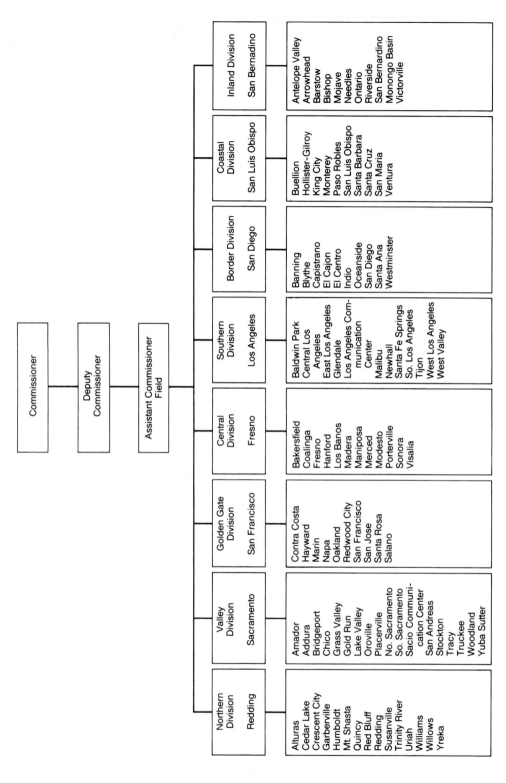

**FIGURE 5-4A.** Organizational chart for the California Highway Patrol (Field) with modification, showing five levels of control. (Courtesy California Highway Patrol, Sacramento, California, 1999.)

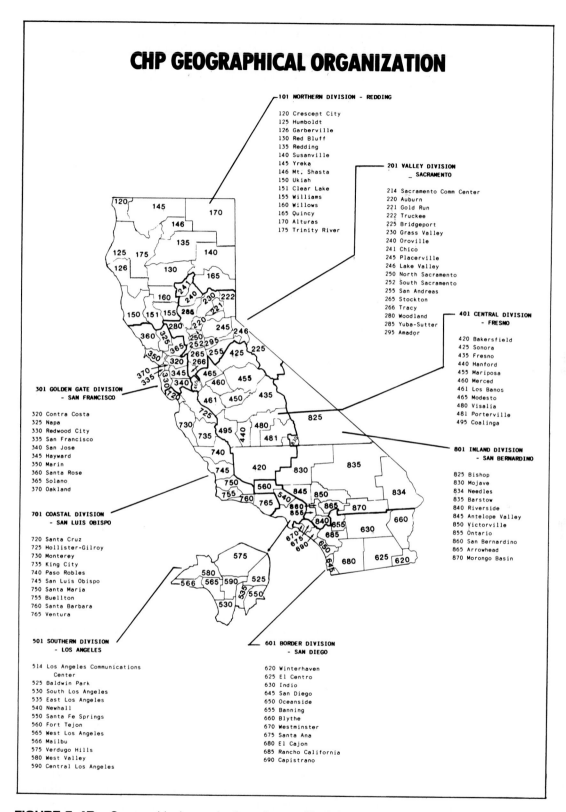

# CHP GEOGRAPHICAL ORGANIZATION

**101 NORTHERN DIVISION - REDDING**

120 Crescent City
125 Humboldt
126 Garberville
130 Red Bluff
135 Redding
140 Susanville
145 Yreka
146 Mt. Shasta
150 Ukiah
151 Clear Lake
155 Williams
160 Willows
165 Quincy
170 Alturas
175 Trinity River

**201 VALLEY DIVISION - SACRAMENTO**

214 Sacramento Comm Center
220 Auburn
221 Gold Run
222 Truckee
225 Bridgeport
230 Grass Valley
240 Oroville
241 Chico
245 Placerville
246 Lake Valley
250 North Sacramento
252 South Sacramento
255 San Andreas
265 Stockton
266 Tracy
280 Woodland
285 Yuba-Sutter
295 Amador

**401 CENTRAL DIVISION - FRESNO**

420 Bakersfield
425 Sonora
435 Fresno
440 Hanford
455 Mariposa
460 Merced
461 Los Banos
465 Modesto
480 Visalia
481 Porterville
495 Coalinga

**301 GOLDEN GATE DIVISION - SAN FRANCISCO**

320 Contra Costa
325 Napa
330 Redwood City
335 San Francisco
340 San Jose
345 Hayward
350 Marin
360 Santa Rose
365 Solano
370 Oakland

**701 COASTAL DIVISION - SAN LUIS OBISPO**

720 Santa Cruz
725 Hollister-Gilroy
730 Monterey
735 King City
740 Paso Robles
745 San Luis Obispo
750 Santa Maria
755 Buellton
760 Santa Barbara
765 Ventura

**801 INLAND DIVISION - SAN BERNARDINO**

825 Bishop
830 Mojave
834 Needles
835 Barstow
840 Riverside
845 Antelope Valley
850 Victorville
855 Ontario
860 San Bernardino
865 Arrowhead
870 Morongo Basin

**501 SOUTHERN DIVISION - LOS ANGELES**

514 Los Angeles Communications
    Center
525 Baldwin Park
530 South Los Angeles
535 East Los Angeles
540 Newhall
550 Santa Fe Springs
560 Fort Tejon
565 West Los Angeles
566 Malibu
575 Verdugo Hills
580 West Valley
590 Central Los Angeles

**601 BORDER DIVISION - SAN DIEGO**

620 Winterhaven
625 El Centro
630 Indio
645 San Diego
650 Oceanside
655 Banning
660 Blythe
670 Westminster
675 Santa Ana
680 El Cajon
685 Rancho California
690 Capistrano

**FIGURE 5-4B.** Geographical organization of area offices for the California Highway Patrol. (Courtesy California Highway Patrol, Sacramento, California, 1999.)

senior police officials to send additional officers took so long that by the time the officers arrived at the scene, the once small incident had grown into an uncontrollable riot. Thus, most departments shifted the authority to deploy large numbers of police officers downward, in some cases all the way to the individual police officer at the scene. This example illustrates several important principles:

1. Narrow spans of control make police departments taller.
2. Taller organizations are complex and may react slowly during crisis situations as effective communication is hampered by the number of different levels present within the chain of command.
3. Successful tall departments must develop policies and procedures that overcome problems created by increased complexity.

Many police agencies, such as the Phoenix Police Department, have redesigned their organizations to reflect larger spans of control or management and hence flatter organizational structures. Figure 5-5 represents only three major organizational levels—chief, division, and bureau. Although this structure is flatter than that of the CHP, traditional grades of authority, such as commander, lieutenant, sergeant, and officer ranks, continue to exist in the Phoenix Police Department. With higher educational standards for entry-level police officers and efforts toward professionalism, police organizational structures may reflect additional changes of this nature. Ultimately, however, the capacity to flatten out police organizational structures depends to no small degree on reducing the number of traditional ranks, a movement sure to be met with resistance because it means less opportunity for upward mobility.

McFarland[16] points out that flat structures associated with wider spans of control offer numerous advantages over the more traditional tall structures. First, they shorten lines of communication between the bottom and top levels. Communication in both directions is more likely to be faster and more timely. Second, the route of communication is more simple, direct, and clear than it is in tall organizations. Third, distortion in communication is minimized by a reduced number of people being involved. Fourth, and probably most important, flat structures are generally associated with employees with higher morale and job satisfaction as compared to employees in tall, structured organizations.

Flat structures do, however, place demanding pressures on supervisors, require high-caliber managers, and work best in organizations in which employees are held strictly accountable for measurable and objective results. Considering the role of the police and the continuing problems associated with evaluating police services, such a structure may cause inordinate stress on personnel. Top executives can attempt to direct the development of police agencies in such a way as to maintain structural balance. Some amount of hierarchy is needed for coordination, but the extremely tall police organization is neither needed nor particularly functional. In balance, no major city has successfully flattened out both the numbers of organizational layers or units and the traditional rank structure to any significant and continuing degree. Thus, any substantial flattening of a police organization is likely to be an experiment in organizational design rather than an institutionalized reform.

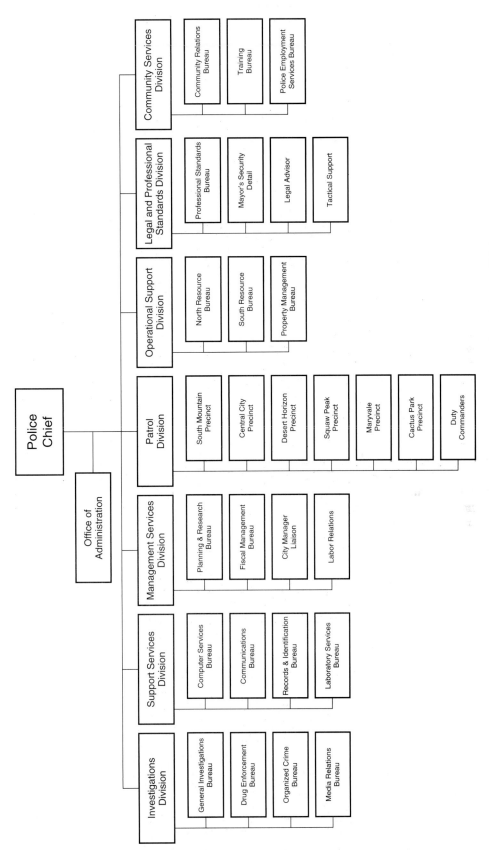

**FIGURE 5-5.** Flat organizational structure (Courtesy Phoenix Police Department, Phoenix, Arizona, 1999.)

# TYPES OF ORGANIZATIONAL DESIGN

Four basic structural types of design may be found within organizations such as police. They are line, line and staff, functional, and matrix. These types exist separately or in combination.

**Line Structure**    The line structure is the oldest, simplest, and clearest form of organizational design. As illustrated in Figure 5-6, authority flows from the top to the bottom of the organization in a clear and unbroken line, creating a set of superior–subordinate relations in a hierarchy commonly called the chain of command. A primary emphasis is placed upon accountability by close adherence to the chain of command.

The term *line* originated with the military and was used to refer to units that were to be used to engage the enemy in combat. *Line* also refers to those elements of a police organization that perform the work the agency was created to handle. Stated somewhat differently, line units contribute directly to the accomplishment of the police mission. Thus, the primary line elements of a police department are uniformed patrol, investigation, and traffic. Within police agencies the line function may also be referred to as "operations," "field services," or by some similar designation.

The pure line police organization does not have any supporting elements that are internal or part of it such as personnel, media relations, training, or fiscal management. Instead, the line police organization uses its total resources to provide services directly to the public. Typically found only in small towns, the line is the most common type of police organization due to the sheer frequency of small jurisdictions. However, most police officers work in larger departments that retain the basic line elements, but to which are added various

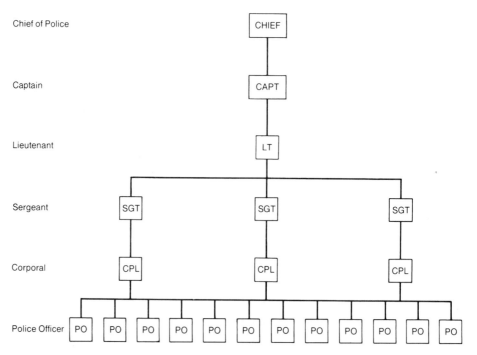

**FIGURE 5-6.**   Line organizational structure in a small police department. (Courtesy of the Tigard Police Department, Tigard, Oregon, 1999.)

types of support units. These larger police departments are often referred to as the line and staff form of organization.

As more demands for services are placed on police departments, there is a need to add internal support functions so that the line functions can continue to provide direct services to the public. The addition of support functions to the line elements produces a distinct organizational form: the line and staff structure. The addition of a staff component to the line structure offers a number of advantages because such units are helpful in

1. Providing expert advice to line units in special knowledge areas as demonstrated by the opinions of legal advisors
2. Relieving line managers from performing tasks they least prefer to do or are least qualified to do such as training and scientific analysis of physical evidence
3. Achieving department-wide conformity in activities that affect the entire organization such as disciplinary procedures
4. Reducing or eliminating special problems such as corruption because of the greater expertise they bring to bear on the issue and the greater amount of time they have to devote to the problem[17]

Staff functions will sometimes be further broken down into two types: auxiliary or support and administrative staff services. Under this arrangement, auxiliary or support units, such as communications and crime laboratory services, are charged with the responsibility of giving immediate assistance to the operations of line elements. In contrast, administrative staff units, such as personnel and training, provide services that are of less immediate assistance and are supportive of the entire police department. Table 5-2 identifies typical line, auxiliary/support, and administrative staff functions. Depending on factors such as the history of the police department and the chief's preferences, there is some variation as to how functions are categorized. Less frequently, legislative enactments may establish the organizational structure, which is another source of variation in how functions are categorized.

Figure 5-7 shows a line and staff structure. In it the field services bureau (composed of the patrol districts) is the primary line function of the organization and is highlighted intentionally (by the Boston Police Department) to show that purpose. The investigative services bureau is also a line function

**TABLE 5-2. Line, Auxiliary/Support, and Administrative Staff Functions**

| Line | Staff | |
| | Auxiliary/Support | Administrative |
| --- | --- | --- |
| —Uniformed Patrol | —Crime Laboratory | —Personnel |
| —Investigations | —Detention and Jail | —Training |
| —Vice and Narcotics | —Records | —Planning and Research |
| —Traffic Enforcement | —Identification | —Fiscal/Budgeting |
| —Juvenile Service | —Communications | —Legal Services |
| —Crime Prevention | —Property Maintenance | —Media Relations |
| | —Transportation and Vehicle Maintenance | |

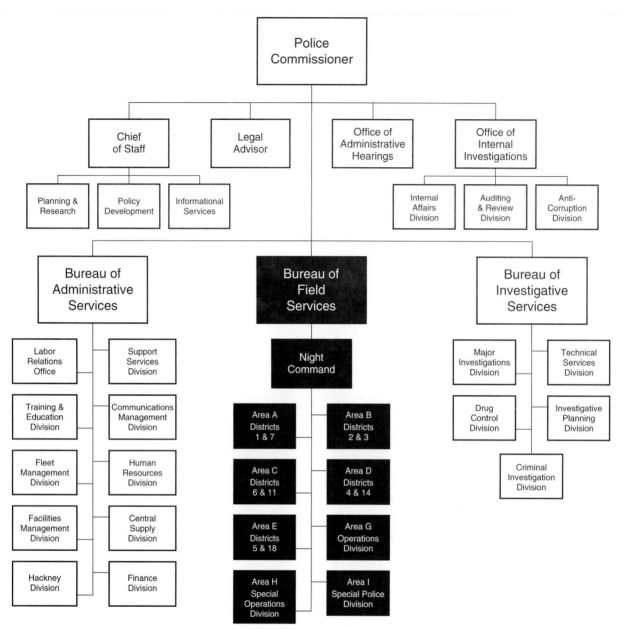

**FIGURE 5-7.** Line and staff structure in a police department. Note that line functions are grouped in the middle of the structure and highlighted as "Bureau of Field Services." (Courtesy Boston Police Department, 2000.)

but is not highlighted by the organization in contrast to the field services bureau. This may be attributed to the large number of personnel assigned to field services, or to the special attention the patrol function receives considering the community policing concepts described in Chapter 2. Interestingly, the Boston Police Department refers to the Bureau of Field Services as the "heart" of its organization. Illustratively, the bureau is positioned and emphasized in the center of the organizational structure. The administrative services bureau and upper echelon offices represent staff functions within the organization. Note in Figure 5-7 that two types of staff report directly to the chief of police: (1) the generalist, illustrated by the chief of staff, and (2) the specialist, illustrated by the legal advisor and internal investigations office.

## Functional Structure

The functional structure is one means by which the line authority structure of an organization can be modified. Hodge and Johnson[18] state that functional structure "is a line and staff structure that has been modified by the delegation of management authority to personnel outside their normal spans of control." Figure 5-9 shows a police department in which the intelligence unit is responsible to three different captains whose main responsibility is for other organizational units.

The obvious advantage of this type of structure is in the maximum use of specialized units. Successful police work requires the coordination of various subunits or specialized resources to attain a desired objective. All too often, a coordinated effort organization-wide is prevented by competing goals, energies, and loyalties to internal subunits. A classic example can be found between patrol and investigative bureaus:

> Examples of police subunits organized on the basis of purpose of function are investigative bureaus, homicide, robbery, burglary or vice control squads, traffic enforcement details, etc. Each of these units is responsible for some function or purpose of the police mission, e.g., detection, apprehension and prosecution of robbery suspects, prevention of traffic accidents and apprehension of violators, suppression

**FIGURE 5-8.** Units of the San Francisco's First Auxiliary Police Regiment pass in review in 1942. Although times have changed, many police agencies continue to support line officers with highly trained civilians acting in the capacity of auxiliary police officers. (Courtesy of the San Francisco Archives.)

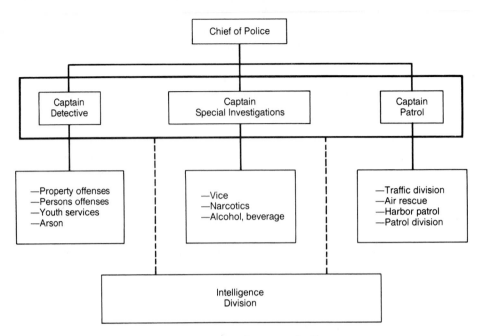

**FIGURE 5-9.** Functional structure in a police organization.

of vice activity, etc. Organization by purpose facilitates the accomplishment of certain assigned objectives by bringing trained specialists and specialized resources together under a single manager who can be held accountable for attainment of a desired state of affairs. The unit can be judged by what it accomplishes, not by its methodology. This type of organization is effective for gaining energies and loyalties of assigned officers because their purpose is clearly understood.

Difficulties arise when purposes overlap or conflict. A patrol unit and a specialized investigative unit may be jointly charged responsibility for the same task. For example, a local patrol precinct and a specialized robbery squad may share responsibility for reduction of the robbery rate in a certain high-crime area. Each of the units reports to a separate commander, both of whom are at least informally evaluated by how effectively robberies in that area are reduced. Each of the commanders may have his own ideas how this might be accomplished and each wishes to receive credit for improving the crime situation. This type of core-responsibility for the same results negates the advantage of specialization by purpose. It may result in the two units working at cross-purposes, refusing to share critical leads, and duplicating efforts. In this case, competition becomes dysfunctional and cooperation and communications between the patrol and investigative units are impaired.[19]

Some of these problems can be eliminated by police organizations using functional design. By forcing specific units to be responsible to a variety of other unit commanders, critical information is assured of reaching other line officers. Sharing is promoted while competing loyalties are diminished.

The major disadvantage of the functional design is that it increases organizational complexity. In Figure 5-9, members of the intelligence division receive instructions from several superiors. This can result in conflicting directions, and thus extensive functionalized structures are seldom found in police agencies. Law enforcement executives should explore the use of the functional design but be ever cautious of the potential confusion that could result if the process is not properly monitored and controlled.

One interesting form of organizational design is variously referred to as *matrix* or *grid* structure. In some cases, the style has been inclusively part of "project" or "product" management. The essence of matrix structure is in the assignment of members of functional areas (e.g., patrol, detective, and support services) to specific projects (e.g., task forces and crime-specific programs). The most typical situation in which the matrix approach is used is when a community has had a series of sensationalized crimes and the local police department announces it has formed a task force to apprehend the violator. One notable example of this occurred in 1981 in Atlanta, Georgia, where a task force comprised of over 300 federal, state, and local law enforcement officers searched for the murderer of young males in that city. As a result of that combined effort, Wayne Williams was arrested and convicted. The advantage of this type of organizational design is in the formation of specific groups of individuals, combining varied talents and levels of expertise in order to fulfill a designated mission or goal. Quite often, the matrix structure is used for relatively short periods of time when specific programs are conducted. After the assignment is completed, individuals return to their respective units.

Figure 5-10 displays the matrix design applied to a police organization. This chart reflects the basic line and staff elements found in most police agencies. However, four specific projects have been initiated that require use of personnel from five different units, which further requires each project to organize along the lines suggested by Figure 5-11.

Although the matrix structure greatly increases organizational complexity, it has been successful only in the short-term delivery of police services.

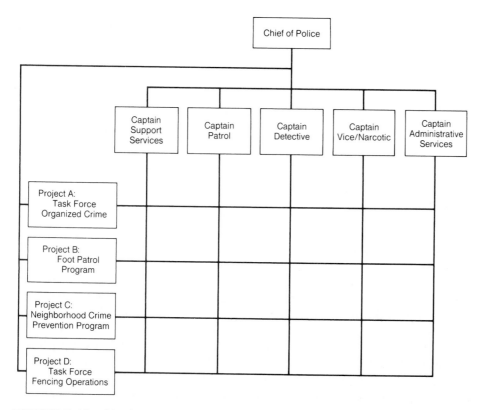

**FIGURE 5-10.** Matrix structure in a police organization.

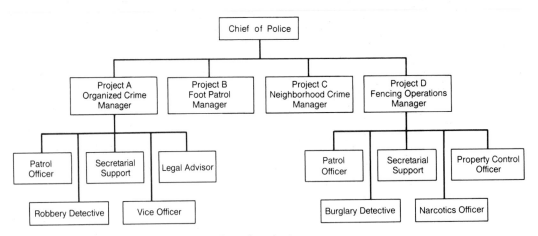

**FIGURE 5-11.** The detailed organization of projects.

# ORGANIZATIONAL STRUCTURE AND COMMUNITY POLICING

Within the last two decades, several studies have questioned the effectiveness of traditional police methods that focus on incident-driven, reactive approaches.[20] As a result, community policing methods have been offered that attempt to develop new, progressive strategies aimed at preventing crime and encouraging broad-based, problem-solving techniques. These approaches are being tried in several cities around the country with a mixed set of reviews (refer to Chapter 2).

These new styles of policing have called for radical changes in the police mission. As Trojanowicz points out:

> Community policing requires department-wide philosophical commitment to involve average citizens as partners in the process of reducing and controlling the contemporary problems of crime, drugs, fear of crime, and neighborhood decay, and in efforts to improve the overall quality of life in the community.[21]

This approach includes developing changes in executive philosophy and community perception of the police as well as organizational restructuring with an emphasis on decentralization of police services.[22]

**Decentralization Versus Centralization**

The impact of community policing on organizational structure is most apparent in agencies that have recently adopted decentralization strategies. The purpose behind such strategies is that police departments can more effectively serve their communities through an organizational design focusing on individual areas and neighborhoods rather than the entire city. Further, decentralization in organizational structure is seen as a much more flexible and fluid design in which to provide essential public and human services.[23]

Decentralization in police departments has primarily been conducted in the patrol division. A 1995 survey conducted by the Bill Blackwood Law Enforcement Management Institute of Texas found that a number of methodologies have been used in the decentralization process.[24] These include the use

## BOX 5-3

### Definitions of Key Terms Used in Decentralization

**Substations**—Generally operate 24 hours a day; have access, via computer links, to a majority of the department's files; have facilities for officers located in the building, including lockers, showers, exercise rooms, training capabilities through video link, and on-line briefing systems.

**Storefronts**—Approximately 1,000 to 1,500 square foot facilities located in strip centers or malls. They serve primarily as public information centers, with limited police resources.

**Mobile storefronts**—Function is similar to storefronts, but rather than using a structure to operate from, they are located in motor homes, vans, or buses that can be moved to different locations within a jurisdiction as needed.

*Source:* Courtesy of El Paso, Texas, Police Department, 1995.

of substations, storefronts, and mobile storefronts. Box 5-3 provides a working definition of these terms. Some police agencies use all three types of facilities in their approach to decentralization. For instance, the El Paso Police Department, El Paso, Texas (highlighted in Box 5-4), reports that decentralization through these types of facilities supports a much closer working relationship with their community.

Some departments have found limited advantages in decentralization. Whereas it may be advantageous to decentralize the patrol function, it may not prove feasible to decentralize other police activities, such as administrative services and investigation/detective bureaus.[25] High operational costs, personnel overlap, role confusion, and general inefficiency have been cited as reasons to avoid the decentralization process in some departments.[26]

**Community Policing Units Versus Departmental Philosophy**

Electing to compartmentalize the activities of the community policing concept, some departments have opted to provide such services solely through one unit or bureau. For instance, the Anaheim Police Department, Anaheim, California, has a single bureau devoted to community policing (see Figure 5-12). Through this unit, the Community Policing Team develops strategies that employ a total community effort involving the police department, city and county government, schools, churches, and businesses. These alliances form neighborhood partnerships. The mission of the Community Policing Bureau is to develop, promote, and implement community-based partnerships aimed at addressing various criminal and social problems confronting the city of Anaheim.[27] It is important to note that functions associated with community policing are relatively confined to the Community Policing Bureau.

In contrast, some departments (e.g., those in Portland, Oregon; Madison, Wisconsin; Dallas, Texas; and Minneapolis, Minnesota) have opted to implement the community policing concept holistically; that is, community policing is reflected in all aspects of the organization, and hence the organizational structure does not reflect a single unit devoted to community policing but rather an inferred assumption that the community policing philosophy is pervasive throughout the organization. In these cases, the organizational chart is reflective of the philosophical changes imbued in community policing. In the early 1990s, under the leadership of then Chief Lee Brown, the Houston Police Department acted as a model for community policing departments

BOX 5-4

## Decentralization in the El Paso Police Department

### The City of El Paso

El Paso, with a population exceeding 550,000, is the fourth largest city in the state. Across the border lies Ciudad Juarez, Mexico, with a population of over 1,216,000. The city's corporate limits encompass 247 square miles. Standing under the shadows of the Franklin Mountains, which divide the city in half, El Paso enjoys the unique status of being located at the crossroads of two nations, with a rich history spanning at least four centuries.

### The Police Department

**Demographics.** The 961-officer department (as of December 1994) consists of individuals from all nationalities and walks of life. When recruiting prospective officers, the department attempts to mirror the ethnicity of its citizens in an attempt to create a closer working relationship between the two. As such, the department is heavily represented by Hispanic officers.

**Crime Rates.** In 1993, major crime in El Paso was reduced by 3.5 percent. In 1994, crime was down by 13.7 percent. This reduction is record breaking. The department's modern record-keeping process dates back to 1972, and this is the largest, single decrease on record for at least 23 years.

**Community-Based Policing.** Continuing change was brought to the El Paso Police Department in 1993 and 1994 as it moved ahead in its transition to the concept of Community-Based Policing. The ultimate goal is to make El Paso a competitive city, with safe streets, strong neighborhoods, and a thriving economy. The department's approach is reflected in a published philosophy statement:

> Community-Based Policing is a philosophy and an organizational strategy that promotes a new partnership between people and their police. It is based on the premise that both the police and the community must work together to identity, prioritize, and solve contemporary problems such as crime, drugs, fear of crime, social and physical disorders, and overall neighborhood decay, with the goal of improving the overall quality of life in the area.

To accomplish this goal, the department implemented its four "Cornerstones of Community-Based Policing," which are the basic premises that drive Community-Based Policing in the El Paso Police Department. The four "cornerstones" are: (1) community involvement, (2) crime analysis, (3) problem-solving approach, and (4) call management. "The ultimate goal is for optimum cooperation and respect between the police and the public; and that officers be viewed as being part of rather than apart from the community."

**Regional Command Concept.** The department believes that community concerns differ from area to area, and from neighborhood to neighborhood. El Paso's geographical and cultural makeup is unique, with the city actually containing many communities in one. It is because of this unique composition that they have adopted the idea of developing a decentralized and personalized police approach.

In an effort to better accomplish this new mission, the department's organization structure has been reorganized and the Regional Command Facility Model has been developed. Under this Regional Command structure, the city will be divided into five regions—a central, east, west, northeast, and lower valley, each containing its own Regional Command Station. All the Regional Command Stations will be fully capable of providing a complete array of police services, to include a criminal investigation unit. At this time, three substations' CID units work out of Central Headquarters Command. All homicide and white-collar offenses are currently, and will remain, investigated by Central Command detectives. The Records, Identification, Communications, Tactical, Internal Affairs, Narcotics, and Intelligence units, which are located in the Central facility, remain centralized.

At present, the department has two, fully-operational Regional Command Centers located at the Central and Pebble Hills facilities, respectively. The current remaining three substations, which serve primarily as briefing rooms and temporary jail facilities, were replaced by Regional Command Centers by the end of 1996.

**Crime Analysis Unit.** The El Paso Police Department's Crime Analysis Unit began operation on January 3, 1995, after nearly a year of research and development. The unit is decentralized among five stations (two Regional Command Centers and three substations), with each command having a minimum of one crime analyst. However, a central crime analysis unit exists for the continued purpose of research and development of new software and work products, and to provide direction and training to the decentralized analysts. The Central Crime Analysis Unit consists of a supervisor, a systems analyst, and a crime analyst. The department does not utilize any civilian employees at this time; however, there are plans to hire one or more in the future.

The primary mission of the crime analysis unit is to assure that information is collected, analyzed, and distributed in a timely manner to accomplish the following: (1) patrol planning, (2) development of investigative leads, (3) support of SHOCAP Program, (4) support of crime prevention, and (5) administrative support. In short, the Crime Analysis Unit is one method by which the department more effectively utilizes its resources.

The method of data collection is direct entry by patrol officers and other Vax system users. The crime analysis module, master name file, etc., are used as long-term storage for the crime analysis unit. Data are then daily downloaded onto the hard disk in the file server and backed-up on a magnetic cartridge. Crime analysts at each station can then query the database which consists of the down-loaded data.

The Crime Analysis Unit is capable of producing 28 different types of reports, and other customized reports. The six reports that are generally produced on schedule are the: (1) crime analysis entry report, (2) repeat police calls by location, (3) weekly crime summary, (4) parole/probation bulletin, (5) juvenile investigation section/SHOCAP weekly crime summary, and (6) statistical bulletin. Distribution is normally through the RMS Electronic Mail System unless photographic images are necessary, in which case, hard-copy bulletins are prepared.

The department's Crime Analysis Unit is approximately 70 percent operational in terms of stated goals and expectations. For this reason, the department has not yet implemented a survey to evaluate the performance of the unit.

**Additional Departments/Services.** Although the following list is not exhaustive, it does contain the remainder of the primary departments and services which the El Paso Police Department utilizes. With the exception of those found in the Metro Section, most departments/services will be located in each Regional Command Center.

   **Metro Section**—Foot patrol, impact detail (undercover assignments), the bicycle unit, three-wheeler/parking enforcement controllers, and traffic enforcement detail.

   **Operations**—Community services, crime prevention unit, storefront operation, school resource officer, public information and headquarters building security (the information desk is manned

8:00 A.M.–4:00 P.M., Monday through Friday with civilian volunteers), safety education, D.A.R.E., gang diversion unit, civilian volunteer program, police chaplain, police explorer post, internal affairs, planning & research, asset forfeiture, inspections, court liaison, training, crisis management team, airport detail and support, bomb squad, canine section, R.O.P., pawnshop detail, crimes against persons, forgery/fugitive/theft, crime stoppers section, auto theft, auto theft task force, special investigations group, and juvenile investigation section.

## Functional Decentralization in El Paso

**Services provided by the headquarters (central command) only:** Foot patrol unit, three wheeler/parking enforcement controllers, public information and headquarters building security, planning & research, asset forfeiture, inspections, court liaison, records, communications, homicide investigation, auto theft/auto theft task force, and special investigations group (narcotics and vice/intelligence).

**Services provided by all regional commands:** Impact detail (plainclothes officers), traffic enforcement detail, crime prevention unit, storefront operation (regional commander supervisors), school resource officer, safety education, D.A.R.E., civilian volunteer program, all detectives with the exception of homicide, repeat offender program, pawnshop detail, and crime stoppers section.

**These sections are housed in separate facilities:** Tactical unit (special weapons and tactics, gang diversion unit and bomb squad), airport detail/airport support, canine section, and juvenile investigation section (child abuse unit, status offense unit, juvenile delinquency unit, and serious habitual offender comprehensive action program).

**Other services:** Bicycle unit (Central and East Valley regional commands), police chaplain (a volunteer position consisting of three chaplains who are on call for the entire department), police explorer post (police academy; however, they ride with all regional commands), in-service training (Central and Pebble Hills regional commands).

*Source:* Courtesy of El Paso, Texas, Police Department, 1995, and the Bill Blackwood Law Enforcement Management Institute of Texas, "Decentralization in Texas Police Departments," *TELEMASP Bulletin,* 2 (August 1995), pp. 1–11.

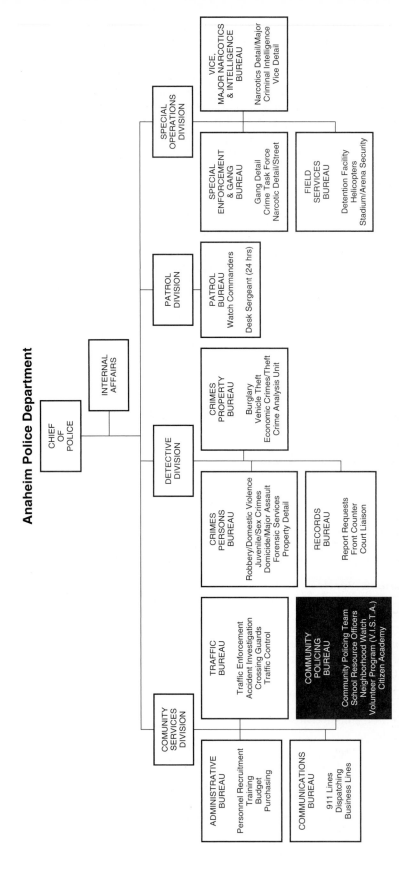

**FIGURE 5-12.** Organization chart showing one unit devoted to community policing (Courtesy Anaheim Police Department, Anaheim, California, 2000).

(refer to Figure 5-13). Reflective of these philosophical changes, the organizational chart of the department provides a new and dynamic look. Note that the focus of the department is on service delivery and support rather than the traditional modes of assignment. The police department is viewed more as a community organization than a control agency. As such, the organization is operated similarly to a service corporation that is fully responsible to an executive board comprised of police and community leaders. In this manner, community policing makes individual police officers accountable directly to the people of Houston. The chief of police acts more like a chairman of the board or as a chief executive officer for a major corporation than as a traditional police manager.

Although a number of community policing methods have been adopted across the country, several structural problems have been cited in the literature.[28] For instance, community policing revokes the paramilitary structure of the past 100 years. Traditional structures of police organizations have historically followed the principles of hierarchy that aim to control subordinates. These principles tend to stifle innovation and creativity, promote alienation and loss of individual self-worth, emphasize mediocrity, and diminish the ability of managers to lead (refer to Chapter 4). Community policing requires a shorter and flatter organizational design. Services are

**Traditional Design Versus Structural Change**

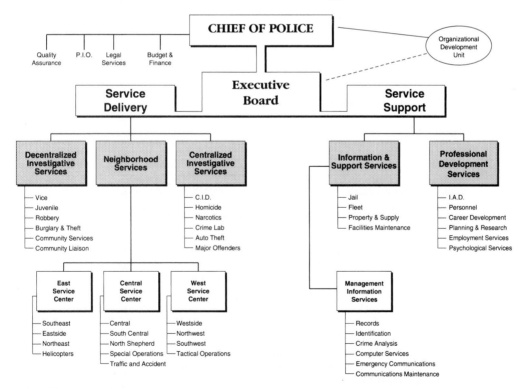

# Houston Police Department

**FIGURE 5-13.** Organizational chart of the Houston Police Department reflecting an emphasis on service delivery and support through a community-represented "executive board." (Courtesy of Houston, Texas, Police Department.)

decentralized and community based. Necessarily, such a design will be less formalized, less specialized, and less bureaucratic (rule oriented). Cordner[29] suggests that police agencies shift from written rules and regulations (which are primarily used to control officers) to a straightforward, situation-oriented approach. Community policing advocates empowering the individual officer with more discretion and more responsibility than traditional policing; hence, direction from the organization must emphasize shared values, participatory decision making, and a collegial atmosphere. Moreover, the organization of community policing is open and sensitive to the environment, with a built-in need to interact with members of the wider community and be "results oriented" rather than closed and internally defined. The differences in organizational structure between traditional policing and community policing are outlined in Table 5-3.

Some argue that community policing calls for too radical a change in organizational design, that such changes may be impossible under existing union and civil service constraints. Further, in Chapter 1, we discussed Michael's "iron law of oligarchy" which indicates that modern, large-scale organizations tend toward specialization and centralization.[30] However, these organizational traits appear to be in conflict with more progressive community policing structures. (See Table 5-3.) Large police departments require a certain amount of specialization to handle diverse tasks efficiently, such as examining various types of physical evidence or handling unique situations, and the amount of hierarchy required to coordinate the various specialized parts produces a tendency toward centralization. This structural conflict causes significant role confusion and ambiguity among officers who are assigned traditional law enforcement duties as well as more contemporary police tasks. As a result of such difficulties, the continued implementation of community policing should provide a dynamic arena for police organizational structure in the future.

### TABLE 5-3.  Organizational Structure

| Traditional Policing | Community Policing |
| --- | --- |
| 1. *Bureaucratic:* rigid, formalized—paper based, rule oriented—"by the book policing," standardized. | 1. *Nonbureaucratic:* corporate flexible—rules to fit situation—paper where necessary, collegial atmosphere |
| 2. *Centralized:* centralization of all management, support, operational, and authority functions | 2. *Decentralization:* of authority and management function to meet operational requirements—organization driven by front end—and community-based demand |
| 3. *Hierarchical:* pyramid with multiple rank levels | 3. *Flattened management (rank) structure:* additional rank at operational level |
| 4. *Specialization:* of varied police functions to increase efficiency (C.I.D. functions, crime prevention, etc.) | 4. *Generalization:* specialization limited—support generalist officer—patrol based |
| 5. *Closed organization orientation:* distinct from environment, resistant to environmental influence, internally defined agenda, means over ends | 5. *Open organization model:* interact with environment, open to change, sensitive to environment, results oriented |

Adapted from C. Murphy, *Contemporary Models of Urban Policing: Shaping the Future* (Ontario, Canada: Ministry of the Solicitor General, 1991), p. 2.

The rapid growth in size of many police agencies has been accompanied by a corresponding rapid growth in specialization and a need for the expansion of staff services to provide support for operating units. This expansion and division of responsibility, which occurs in all police departments except those that are a pure line form of organization, is sometimes fraught with difficulty and dissension. If left uncorrected, these conditions will have a serious negative effect on both the quality and the quantity of service a police agency is able to deliver to its citizens. The following represent some of the major causes of conflict between line and staff.

**The Line Point of View**

One of the basic causes of organizational difficulties, as line operations view them, is that staff personnel attempt to assume authority over line elements instead of supporting and advising them.[31] Line commanders feel that the chief looks to them for accountability of the operation; therefore, staff personnel should not try to control their operation because they are not ultimately responsible for handling line problems. Another commonly heard complaint is that staff personnel sometimes fail to give sound advice because their ideas are not fully thought out, not tested, or "too academic." This attitude is easy for line commanders to develop because of the belief that staff personnel are not responsible for the ultimate results of their product and therefore propose new ideas too quickly.

Communications problems sometimes emerge between the staff specialist and line commanders. Staff personnel on occasion fail to explain new plans or procedures and do not give line commanders sufficient time to propose changes. For example, a major staff project was installed in a patrol operation after only a very brief period of time had passed from its announcement until the starting date. Some attempts were made to prepare the personnel for the project by the use of general orders and memos, but this was left to line supervisors to do, and they did not have enough information to fully explain the new program. This resulted in confusion. Individual officers were unsure of what they were to do, so they did little. It took several weeks to recognize the problem and several more weeks to explain, train, and guide the personnel to operate under the new plan. After a three-month delay, the plan began to show results. However, the crime picture for this period was the worst in four years. The chief placed the blame at his precinct commanders' doors. They, in turn, blamed staff for poor preparation and lack of coordination.

Line commanders frequently claim that staff personnel take credit for successful operations and point the finger of blame at the line commander when programs fail. In one department a new report-writing program was installed under staff auspices. This program was designed to improve the statistical data that the staff group would use in preparing the various departmental reports and also to help the patrol commander to evaluate patrol personnel. During the first year of the program several flaws showed up that prompted staff to write a report that stated the patrol supervisors were not checking the reports carefully, and as a result erroneous information was appearing that made evaluation impossible. A retraining program was instituted and the defects were ironed out. The personnel assigned to do the training then wrote a report taking full credit for the improvement. The commander of the patrol division took a rather dim view of this self-congratulatory report because he along with some of his subordinates worked very closely with the training section in formulating the retraining program.

Operational commanders sometimes express the concern that staff personnel do not see the "big picture" because they have only limited objectives that reflect their own nonoperational specialties. For example, the personnel unit of one police department developed a test for the rank of lieutenant. Most of the sergeants who took the examination did poorly. Many became frustrated and angry because they had built up fine work records and believed that the examination procedure failed to measure their potential ability for the rank of lieutenant accurately. The members of the personnel unit who developed the examination procedure were not sympathetic and suggested that the department just did not have the caliber of personnel who could pass a valid examination. The line commanders claimed that the personnel unit did not know enough about the department's needs, and if they would put more effort into helping instead of "figuring out reasons why we're no good, then we'd be better off."

## The Staff Viewpoint

Staff personnel contend that line commanders do not know how to use staff. Instead of using their analytical skills, staff personnel feel that line commanders simply want to use them as writers. As an example, in one medium-sized department, the robbery case load was increasing at an alarming rate. When staff was approached to work on the problem, the detective chief told them how he saw the problem, asked them to prepare an order for his signature setting out the changes as he saw them, and refused any staff personnel the opportunity to contact the operating field units to determine what the problems were as they saw them.

Many staff personnel also feel that line officers are shortsighted and resist new ideas. As an example, a department had recently expanded and numerous personnel were promoted, but some of the personnel promoted to administrative and executive positions could not function effectively because they had not been properly trained to assume their new roles and responsibilities. The results were inefficiency and personal conflict. The planning and research officer had much earlier wanted to install a training program for career development for the ranks of lieutenant and above so there would be a trained group to choose from when needed. The planning and research officer blamed the line commanders for being shortsighted and not cooperating earlier to develop career development programs.

## Solutions

The problems of line and staff relationships can be corrected. What is needed is (1) a thorough indoctrination and training program and (2) clear definitions as to the tasks of each.

The line is principally responsible for successful operations of the department and therefore line employees must be responsible for operational decisions affecting them. Staff, on the other hand, exists to assist the line in reaching objectives by providing advice and information when requested to do so. This does not, however, prohibit staff from volunteering advice it believes is needed.

The use of staff assistance is usually at the option of line commanders but they must recognize that the chief can decide to use staff services to review any operation and that this decision is binding. As an example, the chief may order a planning and research officer to determine if patrol officers are being properly used. The patrol commander is responsible for making effective use of advice received under such circumstances. If the patrol commander disagrees with staff findings, then an opportunity for reply and review by a higher authority should be available.

Staff exists to help line elements accomplish the objectives of the department. To do this effectively, staff must know what line elements are doing. Illustratively, the personnel officer who does not know what tasks police officers must perform cannot effectively prepare selection standards for the hiring of personnel. Both staff and line must exert effort to ensure that staff stays in contact with what is going on in line units.

Line personnel are concerned primarily with day-to-day operating objectives within the framework of departmental goals. Staff can perform a valuable task for them by thinking ahead toward future problems and operations before they arise. The possibility of a plane crash is a subject that staff, in cooperation with line commanders, can anticipate. Thus, staff can accomplish time-consuming planning and the development of orders and procedures well before they are needed.

Line commanders should know what the various staff functions are and what they can contribute to the improvement of the line units. In some departments this can be done at meetings by allowing the staff heads to explain what they can do for the line commanders. At the same time line commanders can make known their expectations about staff support. Such discussions lead to closer coordination and to improved personal relationships that are essential for effectiveness. Staff's ideas will be more readily accepted if they demonstrate an understanding of line operations.

Staff activity deals primarily with change. However, people tend to resist change and ideas that threaten the status quo. Change by itself indicates the possibility that the old way is no longer acceptable. Staff should anticipate and dispel resistance to change by:

1. Determining to what extent the change proposed will affect the personal relationships of the people involved. Is the change a major one that will affect the social patterns established in the formal and informal organizations? Can the change be broken down into a series of small moves that will have less negative impact than a single large change?

2. Involving those most affected by the change in the early planning stages. When major changes are involved that will modify the relationships between line commanders and the people who work for them, opposition from commanders can be minimized if they participate from the early planning stages. Although it may not be possible for everyone to participate, the use of representative groups of employees is often effective in helping to facilitate change.

3. Communicating throughout the entire planning stage. The personnel who will be affected by the change will accept it better if: (a) they believe it will benefit them personally—that it will make their work easier, faster, or safer (the change should be tied in as closely as possible with the individual's personal goals and interests—job, family, future); (b) the personnel have an opportunity to offer suggestions, ideas, and comments concerning the change as it affects them—provided these suggestions are sincerely wanted and are given serious consideration; and (c) they are kept informed of the results of the change.

To achieve organizational objectives, a line commander should know how to use staff assistance. The specialized skills of staff people can be used to help achieve these goals more efficiently and economically. By involving staff in the problems of the line, staff personnel can become more effective by learning the line commanders' way of thinking. Line commanders must be able to identify their problems precisely before seeking assistance. They must not vaguely define a problem and then expect the staff unit to do all the work. It is also important for staff to keep other staff informed of decisions that will affect them. As an example, a department was given permission to hire and train 250 new officers, which was double the normal recruit class. The training unit was not advised of this until a week before the class was to start. Subsequently, many problems developed which could have been avoided.

## SUMMARY

This chapter elaborated on certain content from Chapter 4 and introduced related concepts. The major concerns in organizing are (1) dividing the jobs, (2) grouping the jobs, (3) forming grades of authority, and (4) equalizing authority and responsibility. Specialization has both advantages and disadvantages. The advantages include placement of responsibility, development of expertise, promotion of esprit de corps, and increased efficiency and effectiveness. Among the disadvantages of specialization are increased friction and conflict, decreased job performance, complication of the command structure, difficulty in finding sufficient qualified leaders, and hampering the development of a well-rounded police program. Organizational design focuses on two spatial levels of differentiation: vertical, based on levels of authority, and horizontal, based on activity. Some of the ways in which horizontal differentiation occurs is through grouping by: clientele, style of service, geography, time, and process. According to Hodge and Anthony, the differentiation process can occur in two basic ways: (1) the bottom-up or synthesis approach and (2) the top-down or analysis approach. Police departments can be considered tall or flat. Tall organizational structures have many different layers, which make them more complex and which can impair effective communication. Flat organizations have fewer layers, which is often the result of broadening the span of control, and tend not to suffer from as many communication problems as do the taller departments. Extremely tall organizations are neither needed nor particularly functional, although some amount of hierarchy is needed to coordinate the various parts of a large, complex organization. However desirable theoretically, no major city has made significant and continuing inroads into reducing both the layers of organization and the height of the traditional rank structure.

Four basic types of structural design may be found in police agencies: (1) line, (2) line and staff, (3) functional, and (4) matrix. These types can exist separately or in combination. Statistically the line form of organization appears most frequently, but most police officers work in a line and staff structure. Recent advances in community policing and problem-oriented policing are changing traditional perspectives on organizational structure. With a continued emphasis on citizen/community involvement in the police mission and the decentralization of police services, experimental methods offer new means in which to chart responsibility and accountability within an organization. Although there are controversial issues surrounding these innovative designs, their impact on future police organizational structure will be profound.

One of the continuing problems in all but the very smallest police departments is the tension between line commanders and staff specialists. Although the basic causes of these organizational difficulties are varied, several strategies can be employed as solutions.

## DISCUSSION QUESTIONS

1. What are some of the advantages and disadvantages of specialization?
2. Explain the concepts of vertical and horizontal differentiation as applied to organizational design.
3. What are the common ways of grouping activities?
4. What is meant by "tall" and "flat" organizational structures?
5. Identify and explain four basic types of structural design found in police agencies.
6. How have experimental police methods (such as community-oriented policing) influenced organizational structure and design?
7. What are the pros and cons of decentralizing the patrol division as a strategy for implementing community policing?
8. What are the essential differences between line and staff in police departments?
9. What are some of the major sources of tension in relationships between line and staff employees?

# NOTES

1. S. P. Robbins, *The Administration Process* (Englewood Cliffs, N.J.: Prentice Hall, 1976), pp. 17–18. This discussion of "Organizing an Overview" was adapted from this source.

2. *The Republic of Plato,* trans. A. Bloom (New York: Basic Books, 1968), p. 47.

3. For example, see Luther Gulick and L. Urwick, eds., *Papers on the Science of Administration* (New York: August M. Kelley, a 1969 reprint of the 1937 edition).

4. O. W. Wilson and R. C. McLaren, *Police Administration,* 3rd ed. (New York: McGraw-Hill, 1972), p. 79.

5. Ibid., p. 81.

6. Ibid., p. 83.

7. N. C. Kassoff, *Organizational Concepts* (Washington, D.C.: International Association of Chiefs of Police, 1967), p. 22.

8. Wilson and McLaren, *Police Administration,* p 56.

9. Ibid., p. 56.

10. D. A. Tansik and J. F. Elliot, *Managing Police Organizations* (Monterey, Calif.: Duxbury Press, 1981), p. 81.

11. Ibid., p. 81.

12. B. J. Hodge and W. P. Anthony, *Organizational Theory: An Environmental Approach* (Boston: Allyn & Bacon, 1979) p. 240.

13. Tansik and Elliot, *Managing Police Organizations,* p. 82.

14. Richard Hall, *Organizations: Structure and Process* (Englewood Cliffs, N.J.: Prentice Hall, 1972), p. 143.

15. This section is a synopsis of the "Nature and Process of Differentiation" found in Hodge and Anthony, *Organizational Theory,* p. 249.

16. Darlton E. McFarland, *Management: Foundations and Practices,* 5th ed. (New York: Macmillan, 1979), p. 316.

17. Ibid., p. 309.

18. B. J. Hodge and H. J. Johnson, *Management and Organizational Behavior* (New York: John Wiley & Sons, 1970), p. 163.

19. Joseph J. Staft, "The Effects of Organizational Design on Communications Between Patrol and Investigation Functions," in U.S. Department of Justice, National Institute of Justice, Research Utilization Program, *Improving Police Management* (Washington, D.C.: University Research Corporation, 1982), p. 243.

20. Several studies focusing on the failures of traditional police methods and advocating experimental styles have appeared in the last twenty years. Refer to G. Kelling et al., *The Kansas City Preventive Patrol Experiment: A Technical Report* (Washington, D.C.: Police Foundation, 1974); J. Dahman, *Examination of Police Patrol Effectiveness: High-Impact Anti-Crime Program* (McLean, Va.: Mitre Corporation, 1975); J. Schnelle et al., "Social Evaluation Research: The Evaluation of Two Police Patrol Strategies," *Journal of Applied Behavior Analysis,* 4 (August 1975), 232–40; W. Spelman and D. Brown, *Calling the Police: Citizen Reporting of Serious Crime* (Washington, D.C.: U.S. Government Printing Office, 1984); W. Spelman and J. Eck, *Problem Oriented Policing* (Washington, D.C.: National Institute of Justice, 1986); J. Eck and W. Spelman, *Problem Solving: Problem-Oriented Policing in Newport News* (Washington, D.C.: Police Executive Research Forum, 1987); L. Sherman, "Repeat Calls to Police in Minneapolis," *Crime Control Reports,* 4 (Washington, D.C.: Crime Control Institute, 1987); and H. Goldstein, *Problem-Oriented Policing* (New York: McGraw-Hill, 1990).

21. Robert C. Trojanowicz, "Community Policing Is Not Police Community Relations," *FBI Law Enforcement Bulletin,* 59 (October 1990), 8.

22. Ibid., 8–10.

23. Richard Kitaeff, "The Great Debate: Centralized vs. Decentralized Marketing Research Function," *Marketing Research: A Magazine of Management and Applications,* 6 (Winter 1993), 59.

24. This material and Box 5-3 are taken from the Bill Blackwood Law Enforcement Management Institute of Texas, "Decentralization in Texas Police Departments," *TELEMASP Bulletin,* 2 (August 1995), 1–11.

25. Las Vegas Metropolitan Police Department, Las Vegas, NV, "Staff Study Decentralization of the Burglary Function," 1989.

26. Ibid., p. 12.

27. Anaheim Police Department, Anaheim, Calif., "Community Policing Team Annual Report," 1994.

28. Several critiques of experimental police methods have been noted in the literature. See Robert W. Taylor and Dennis J. Kenney, "The Problems with Problem Oriented Policing" (paper presented at the Academy of Criminal Justice Sciences Annual Meeting, Nashville, Tennessee, March 1991); Kenneth W. Findley and Robert W. Taylor, "Re-Thinking Neighborhood Policing," *Journal of*

*Contemporary Criminal Justice*, 6 (May 1990), 70–78; Jerome Skolnick and D. Bayley, *Community Policing: Issues and Practices Around the World* (Washington, D.C.: National Institute of Justice, 1988); Jack Greene and Ralph Taylor, "Community Based Policing and Foot Patrol: Issues of Theory and Evaluation, in *Community Policing: Rhetoric or Reality?*, ed. Jack Greene and Stephen Mastrofski (New York: Praeger, 1988), pp. 216–19; and Stephen Mastrofski, "Police

Agency Accreditation: The Prospects of Reform," *American Journal of Police* (5 May 1986), 45–81.

29. Gary W. Cordner, "Written Rules and Regulations: Are They Necessary," *FBI Law Enforcement Bulletin*, 58 (July 1989), 17–21.

30. See Robert Michaels, *Political Parties* (New York: Dover, 1959).

31. Kassoff, *Organizational Concepts*, pp. 31–38.

## INTRODUCTION

During the 1970s and much of the 1980s, police departments placed considerable emphasis on rational management systems (such as sophisticated decision-making techniques) and the use of technology (e.g., computers). In an environment characterized by scarce resources for programs and a public demanding more and better services, chiefs of police tried to find new ways to improve productivity. This resulted in police chiefs thinking of themselves as managers as opposed to leaders. While rational management systems and technology remain important arrows in the quivers of police chiefs, the role of leadership in making police departments function at a high level reemerged as a vital concern by the very late 1980s as the community-oriented policing and quality movements began to take hold. Today, officials hiring police chiefs want to know what the candidates' visions are for the future of the agency, how they will stimulate employee participation, what efforts they will make to ensure that quality is driven by customer concerns, what methods they will use to ensure that agency improvement is continuous, how they will empower employees, and other related issues (see Box 6-1). These officials are less concerned about finding someone who can simply control a police department and more focused on identifying someone who can envision a better future and take the concrete steps to bring it about. These and other changes have placed such high demands on police leaders that they are retiring earlier in their careers.

# 6

# LEADERSHIP

*Leadership is not a spectator sport.*
KOUZES AND POSNER

Another factor that fostered concern with leadership in police organizations is that employees, who bring their own values, needs, and expectations into a police department, don't want to know just what to do, they want to know *why*. When these officers see better ways of doing things, they are not easily satisfied by answers such as "that's the way it has always been done." Today's employees do not want to be treated like mushrooms—kept in the dark and dumped on. They will work hard to achieve the police department's goals, but they also want the legitimacy of their own needs—such as being treated with dignity and respect—recognized. Finally, although some police chiefs still believe in "treating them rough and telling them nothing," they are rapidly following the path of dinosaurs because city managers are not willing to put up with high turnover rates, numerous grievances, and lawsuits.

## LEADERSHIP AND PERFORMANCE

The police leader is responsible for three equally important, but essentially different, broad responsibilities:

1. Fulfilling the mission of the police department
2. Making work productive and helping subordinates to achieve
3. Producing impacts. [1]

BOX 6-1

## Madison Police Department: Guiding Principles

### Systems

1. Improve Systems and Examine Processes.
   - Systems should support mission operations and relationships with other service providers and community groups.
   - Accountability for improving systems is personal at each level. Each member is responsible for their key role in the system.
   - Only through continuous evaluation of current systems can we provide the best ways to deliver our services.
   - It is everyone's responsibility to ensure the current processes and systems are both effective and efficient.

2. Have a Customer Orientation and Focus.
   - Customer is defined as the recipient of our work product or service each individual employee produces (DA, DA, citizens, etc.)
   - Provide high quality personalized service consistent with our organizational mission.
   - How could your job become more meaningful for yourself and the people you serve?
   - Toward each other and citizens.
   - District officers responding to the needs of district.

3. The Best Way to Improve the Quality of Work or Service Is to Ask and Listen to Employees at All Levels and Citizens Affected by the Problem and to Weigh That Input in Decision Making.
   - We encourage input recognizing input is advisory not binding.
   - Problem solving is a shared responsibility.

4. Be Committed to the Problem-Solving Process.
   - Concept to include both organizational and community problems.
   - Clarify types of data, emphasize use of best data available, use data in proper context.
   - Develop "bench marks" and baselines as an indicator of improvement.

### Leadership

5. Develop an Atmosphere of Trust, Honesty, and Openness That Fosters Constant Communication.
   - Providing and accepting feedback.
   - Willingness to share information

6. Support a Climate of Constant Improvement and Encourage Creativity Through Innovation.
   - Need to define innovation and the relationship between constant improvement.

7. Whenever Possible Seek Participation, Input and Concurrence Before Making Decisions.
   - We recognize that while performing our duties, we all need to take advantage of a wide variety of decision-making methods.
   - We have leadership at all levels of the organization.

8. The Majority of People Work Hard, Want to Succeed, and Are Trustworthy. It Is This Majority That Should Define the Approach to Our Work.
   - This is also the way that we should view the community.
   - This does not relieve us of the responsibility of dealing with problem behavior promptly and fairly.

### Teams

9. Believe In, Foster, and Support Partnerships and Teamwork.
   - Partnerships assign roles within the team.
   - Partnerships often include working with other agencies and community groups.
   - Team work assigns responsibilities for achievements.

10. Work Together to Develop Organizational, Team, and Individual Goals and Plans to Achieve Them.
    - All members of the team have responsibility for identifying the goals and developing the plans.

11. Consider Input Prior to Making Decisions Which Affect Others.
    - Recognize that most decisions affect others either directly or through issues of consistency, fairness, etc.

12. Treat Each Other with Respect and Trust.

*Source:* Madison, Wisconsin, Police Department, 1997. Note that these "guiding principles" are an elaboration of the points identified in Figure 1–10, under the "Principles of Quality Leadership."

A number of factors impinge on how well these responsibilities are met, such as the chief's leadership style, community preferences, available resources, and the selection process for a chief. Police leaders chosen by a competitive process or who are perceived by subordinates in the department as competent are viewed consistently as having greater expertise and, consequently, have more influence and power.[2] There are, additionally, "habits of minds" that police leaders who meet their three key responsibilities effectively must practice:

1. They know where their time goes and manage it actively. They identify and eliminate things that need not be done at all; they delegate to others things that can be done as well or better by someone else. And they avoid wasting their own time and that of others.[3]

2. They focus on outward contribution. They gear their efforts to results rather than to work. They start out with the question, "What results are expected of me?" rather than with the work to be done, let alone with its techniques and tools.

3. They build on strengths—their own strengths, the strengths of their superiors, colleagues, and subordinates, and the strengths in the situation—that is, on what they can do. They do not build on weakness. They do not start out with the things they cannot do.

4. They concentrate first on the few major areas where superior performance will produce outstanding results. They force themselves to set priorities and stay with their priority decision. They know they have no choice but to do first things first—and second things not at all. The alternative is to get nothing done.

5. They make effective decisions. They know that this is, above all, a matter of system—of the right steps in the right sequence. They know that an effective decision is always a judgment based on "dissenting opinions" rather than on "consensus on the facts." And they know that to make many decisions fast means to make the wrong decisions. What is needed are few, but fundamental, decisions. What is needed is the right strategy rather than razzle-dazzle tactics.

If, as has been suggested, leadership is an intangible, the effects generated by its presence or absence and its character are not. Consider the following examples:

- Police officers, operating a dirty patrol vehicle, approached a motorist they had stopped for a traffic violation. Unkempt in appearance, the officers had a conversation with the person which was correct on the surface, but which had an underlying tone of arrogance.

- A sergeant, already 35 minutes late getting off duty, was enroute to the station when a burglary in progress call was given to another unit; he volunteered to help and subsequently was shot to death by two burglars.

- The chief of police of a medium-sized city chronically complained to anyone who would listen that his commanders "aren't worth anything" and that he was "carrying the whole department on his back."

- A visitor to a city approached an officer walking a beat and asked where the nearest car rental agency could be found; the officer replied, "What the hell do I look like, an information booth?" and walked away. The next day she asked an officer standing on a street corner where the First National Bank Building was. The officer took the woman's arm, escorted her across the street and said, "Lady, you see that big building on the corner where we were just standing? Well, if it had fallen, we'd have both been killed by the First National Bank Building."

- Based on limited new information the commander of an investigations bureau reopened the case file on a convicted "no-good" who had already served 14 months for the offense in question. Subsequently, new evidence and a confession resulted in his release and the conviction of another person.

There are many different definitions of what leadership is, each reflecting certain perspectives. For example, leadership may be defined as the characteristics exhibited by an individual or as a function of a position within the police department's hierarchical structure, such as captain. However, a generally accepted definition is that *leadership* is the process of influencing organizational members to use their energies willingly and appropriately to facilitate the achievement of the police department's goals.

## THE NATURE OF LEADERSHIP, AUTHORITY, AND POWER

The given definition of leadership deserves some analysis. In Chapter 4, the basic rationale for the existence of organizations was given as being that they do those things that people are unwilling or unable to do alone. It therefore follows that police departments, as is true for other organizations, are goal directed. The behavior of its members should be purposeful and in consonance with the department's goals. By "using their energies appropriately," it is meant that morally and legally accepted means are employed in the discharge of duties. The terms *influencing* and *willingly* are related to the concepts of authority and power.

Although these are often treated synonymously, authority and power are allied, but separate, concepts. Authority is a grant made by the formal organization to a position, the incumbent of which wields it in fulfilling his or her responsibilities. The fact that a formal grant of authority has been made does not mean that the person receiving it also is automatically able to influence others to perform at all, let alone willingly:

> Officer James P. Murphy was among 50 officers to be promoted by the New York City Police Commissioner. Instead of accepting a handshake and his gold detective's shield, Officer Murphy removed the gold badge, placed it on the dais, and walked out of the ceremony. Officer Murphy took this action to protest the department's investigation of allegations that his unit—the Brooklyn Narcotics Tactical Team—had mistreated prisoners and lied about evidence to shore up shaky arrests. Officer Murphy was not believed to be a target of this investigation. A ranking police official with 40 years of service said he had never seen anything like Murphy's actions before.[4]

This incident illustrates that while the commissioner had the authority to promote Officer Murphy, he did not have the power to make him accept it. Some power to affect an officer's performance is inherent in positions of formal authority. But to a significant degree that power, as suggested by Barnard, is a grant made by the led to the leader. The leader whose subordinates refuse to follow is not totally without power, for subordinates may be given verbal or written reprimands or suspensions, or be forced or expelled from the organization, or be fined, imprisoned, or executed, depending upon the specifics involved.[5] The use of this type of power must be considered carefully; failure to invoke it may contribute to a breakdown in discipline and organizational performance; the employment of it may contribute to morale problems, may divert energy from achieving goals, and may have other negative side effects, including calling into question the abilities of the involved leader:

> A uniformed officer riding alone informed the radio dispatcher that he was stopping a possibly drunken motorist. His sergeant, who had only been promoted and assigned to the squad two weeks previously, heard the transmission and told the dispatcher that he would back up the officer. When the sergeant, a nine-year veteran of the force, but who had not served in any "street" assignment for the past six years, arrived, a Marine corporal was about to get into a taxi cab. When questioned by the sergeant, the officer who had stopped the Marine as a possible drunk driver related that the corporal had been drinking, but that it was a marginal case and after talking with him, the corporal agreed to park his car and had called the taxi cab from a nearby pay phone.
>
> The sergeant talked to the Marine and concluded that he had drunk sufficiently to be charged with driving under the influence and directed the officer to arrest him. The officer declined and the sergeant angrily said, "I think you don't want to arrest him because you're an ex-Marine. . . . Arrest him, that's a direct order." The officer refused again, the sergeant got into his car and left, and the Marine departed in the taxi cab.
>
> Later when the sergeant filed charges for refusal to obey the direct order of a superior, the officer was suspended without pay for two days. The other squad members felt the sergeant was not "streetwise" and had acted in a petty manner. Over time, it became apparent to the sergeant's superiors that he had lost the respect and confidence of the squad and could not regain it. The sergeant was then transferred to a minor staff position where he had responsibility for several functions but actually supervised no one.

Leadership also arises, as demonstrated by the Hawthorne studies, out of the informal side of an organization. Members of a work group give one or more of their members power by virtue of their willingness to follow them. This power may be given on the basis suggested by Weber's charismatic leader; thus, officers may look more to a seasoned and colorful officer in their squad or one who has been decorated several times for heroism than to their sergeant, who represents Weber's rational-legal type of authority. A variant of this situation is a problem more than occasionally in some departments as younger college-educated officers move up in rank rapidly, passing less educated veteran officers. Dismissing them as "test takers," the more experienced officers sometimes use the informal group to vie for leadership with the formally appointed leaders. If, however, the informal leaders support the police department's goals, they can be a significant additive and even help to compensate for mediocre formal leadership.

## THE POWER MOTIVATION OF POLICE MANAGERS

Power is an indispensable dimension of police departments. As we have seen, power is both a grant made from the led to the leader and an extension of the formal authority granted to a particular position such as sergeant. Power, however, is not always used for the same purpose; the term *power motivation* refers to the reasons, intentions, and objectives that underlie a police manager's use of power.[6]

Leadership requires that a person have an appreciation of the importance of influencing the outcome of events and the desire to play a key role in that process. This need for impact must be greater than either the need for personal achievement or the need to be liked by others. A police leader's desire for impact may take either of two forms; it may be oriented primarily toward (1) the achievement of personal gain and aggrandizement (a personalized power motivation), or (2) the need to influence others' behavior for the common good of the police department (a socialized power motivation). Additionally, police leaders have some desire to be accepted and liked, which is termed the *affiliation need.* Affiliation needs and aspirations are not power needs because they reflect a greater preoccupation with being accepted and liked than with having an impact on events.

Table 6-1 summarizes the differences between managers who use personalized power versus those who use social power. Hall and Hawker have developed an instrument for measuring personalized power, socialized power, and affiliative needs. In Figure 6-1, the shaded portions of the personalized, socialized, and affiliative columns represents what Hall and Hawker regard, based on research by McClelland and Burnham, as the theoretically ideal profile for managerial success; note that the ideal profile contains a mix of power motivations and affiliative needs. Affiliative needs serve as a check on power motivations, helping to keep them in proper proportions. In the application of Figure 6-1, differences of more than 25 percentile points are required to denote a genuine preference for one approach in comparison to another. The dotted horizontal lines across the personalized, socialized, and affiliative columns reflect the scores of 43 police

## TABLE 6-1. Personalized versus Social Power

| Police Managers with Personalized Power Tend to Be: | Police Managers with Socialized Power Tend to Be: |
|---|---|
| ▪ Impulsive and erratic in their use of power | ▪ Inhibited and self-controlled in their use of power |
| ▪ Rude and overbearing | ▪ Respectful of others' rights |
| ▪ Exploitative of others | ▪ Concerned with fairness |
| ▪ Oriented toward strength | ▪ Oriented toward justice |
| ▪ Committed to the value of efficiency | ▪ Committed to the value of working per se |
| ▪ Proud | ▪ Egalitarian |
| ▪ Self-reliant; individualists | ▪ Organization-minded; joiners |
| ▪ Excited by the certitudes of power | ▪ Ambivalent about power |
| ▪ Competitive | ▪ Collaborative |
| ▪ Concerned with exceptionally high goals | ▪ Concerned with realistic goals |
| ▪ Defensive—protective of own sense of importance | ▪ Nondefensive—willing to seek help |
| ▪ Inspirational leaders | ▪ Builders of systems and people |
| ▪ Difficult to replace—leave a group of loyal subordinates dependent on their manager | ▪ Replaceable by other managers—leave a system intact and self-sustaining |
| ▪ Sources of direction, expertise, and control | ▪ Sources of strength for others |

*Source:* From Jay Hall and James Hawker, "Interpreting Your Scores from the Power Management Inventory," © Teleometrics International, The Woodlands, Texas. Special permission for reproduction is granted by the authors and the publisher, all rights reserved. The Power Management Inventory can be used with a variety of occupations.

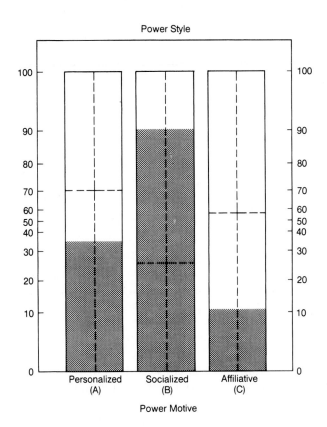

Power Style

**FIGURE 6-1.** The Mean Power Management Inventory scores for 43 police managers from one medium-sized depart-ment are indicated by the horizontal dotted lines and are contrasted from the ideal scores that are depicted by the shaded areas. (*Source:* Jay Hall and James Hawker, "Interpreting Your Scores from the Power Management Inventory," © Teleometrics International, The Woodlands, Texas: spe-cial permission for re-production of the figure is granted by the au-thors and the publisher, all rights reserved.)

Power Motive

managers from one medium-sized police agency and are intended as an illus-tration rather than as a generalization about police managers. Among the ob-servations that can be made about the profile of those 43 police managers as a group are (1) the preference for the use of personalized power as opposed to so-cialized power and (2) a desire to be liked (affiliative needs), which closely ap-proximates their preference for personalized power. This suggests that as a group these police managers are somewhat ambiguous about how to use power. They want to be seen as strong and self-reliant but also liked. Their scores also reflect the absence of a clearly unified approach to the use of power and the lack of a crystallized philosophy of management; as a result, they are probably seen as somewhat inconsistent by their subordinates.

## THE LEADERSHIP SKILL MIX

As depicted in Figure 6-2, a police department can be divided into three levels with various mixes of three broad categories of skills associated with them.[7] The ranks indicated at each of the three levels of the organization identified in the figure are illustrative only and will vary depending on departmental size and other factors. Additionally, in the discussion of these skills that follows, it should be noted that it is possible to include only a few of the many examples available.

Human relations skills involve the capacity to interrelate positively with other people and are used at all levels of a police department. Examples include motivation, conflict resolution, and interpersonal communication skills. The

**Human Relations Skills**

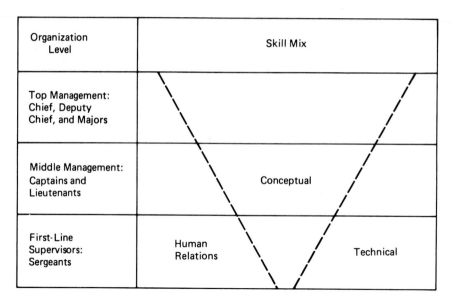

| Organization Level | Skill Mix | | |
|---|---|---|---|
| Top Management: Chief, Deputy Chief, and Majors | | | |
| Middle Management: Captains and Lieutenants | | Conceptual | |
| First-Line Supervisors: Sergeants | Human Relations | | Technical |

**FIGURE 6-2.** The leadership skill mix in a police department.

single most important human relations skill is communication; without it, nothing can be set in motion, and programs under way cannot be guided.

As one progresses up the rank hierarchy of a police department, typically one becomes responsible for more people but has fewer people reporting directly to him or her. The human relations skills of a police department's top managers remain important, however, as they are used to win political support for the agency's programs and to obtain the resources necessary to operate them. In particular, the chief's human relations skills are critical, as this person is the key representative of the department to the larger environment. The way in which he or she "comes across" is to a certain degree the way in which some significant others—such as the city manager and members of city council—are going to come to regard the police department. The question of the fairness of that fact aside, the practical implication is that the chief must be aware and fulfill the symbolic leadership role.

Within the department, top management must communicate their goals and policies downward and be willing to receive feedback about them. As mid-level managers, lieutenants and captains play an important linking function, passing downward in implementable forms the communications they receive from top management and passing upward certain communications received from first-line supervisors. Because sergeants ordinarily supervise directly the greatest number of people, they use human relations with great frequency, often focusing on such issues as resolving interpersonal problems, communicating the department's vision, stimulating employee participation in problem solving, and maintaining a customer focus.

**Conceptual Skills** Conceptual skills involve the ability to understand and also to interrelate various parcels of information, which often seem unrelated or the meaning or importance of which is uncertain. Although this skill is used at all levels of the police department, the standards for handling the information become less certain and the level of abstraction necessary to handle the parcels becomes greater as one moves upward. Illustrative is the difference between a sergeant helping a detective to evaluate the legal significance of certain evidence and the chief sorting out and interrelating facts, opinions, and rumors about a productive but controversial police program supported and opposed by some combination of political figures, public interest groups, and the news media.

## Technical Skills

Technical skills vary by level within a police department. Uniformed sergeants assigned to field duties must be able to help develop and maintain the skills of subordinates in such areas as the identification, collection, and preservation of physical evidence. As one progresses upward toward middle and top management, the range of technical skills narrows, and conceptual skills come to predominate. In that upward progression, the character of the technical skills also changes from being operations oriented to management oriented and gradually includes new elements, such as budgeting, planning, and the kind of decision making that increasingly requires the use of conceptual skills. To elaborate further, one may not be able to tell by the generic label whether a particular skill is, for example, technical or conceptual. A general understanding of the many aspects of financial management (see Chapter 14) is a conceptual skill, but the actual physical preparation of the budget is a technical skill required of middle-management or first-line supervisors, depending on the size and practices of a specific police department.

# THEORIES OF LEADERSHIP

Theories of leadership attempt to explain the factors associated with the emergence of leadership or the nature of leadership.[8] Included are (1) "great man" and genetic theories, (2) the traits approach, (3) behavioral explanations, and (4) situational theories.

"Great man" theories were advanced by Thomas Carlyle and Georg Wilhelm Friedrich Hegel.[9] Carlyle believed that leaders were unusually endowed individuals who made history. Reversing the direction of causality, Hegel argued that it was the events that produced the "great man." The "born leader" concept is associated with Francis Galton, who espoused that leaders were the product of genetics.[10]

It has also been maintained that leaders possess certain personality traits; for example, Field Marshal Montgomery[11] believed that, although leaders were made, not born, they had certain characteristics such as an infectious optimism, confidence, intellect, and the ability to be a good judge of character. Goode determined that the following traits were important for successful leadership:

1. The leader is somewhat more intelligent than the average of his followers. However, he is not so superior that he cannot be readily understood by those who work with him.

2. The leader is a well-rounded individual from the standpoint of interests and aptitudes. He tends toward interests, aptitudes, and knowledge with respect to a wide variety of fields.

3. The leader has an unusual facility with language. He speaks and writes simply, persuasively, and understandably.

4. The leader is mentally and emotionally mature. He has come of age mentally, emotionally, and physically.

5. The leader has a powerful inner drive or motivation that impels him to strive for accomplishment.

6. The leader is fully aware of the importance of cooperative effort in getting things done and therefore understands and practices very effectively the so-called social skills.

7. The leader relies on his administrative skills to a much greater extent than he does on any of the technical skills that may be associated directly with his work.[12]

Parenthetically, by administrative skills, Goode seems to mean what has been described previously as conceptual skills. Stogdill analyzed over two hundred studies and following the second review described a leader as being:

> characterized by a strong drive for responsibility and task completion, vigor and persistence in pursuit of goals, venturesomeness and originality in problem solving, drive to exercise initiative in social situations, self-confidence, and a sense of personal identity, willingness to accept consequences of decision and action, readiness to absorb interpersonal stress, willingness to tolerate frustration and delay, ability to influence other persons' behavior, and capacity to structure social interaction systems to the purpose at hand.[13]

From an organizational standpoint, the traits approach has great appeal: find out who has these characteristics and promote them, and successful leadership will follow. However, C. A. Gibb[14] has concluded that the numerous studies of traits do not reveal any consistent patterns, and Walter Palmer's[15] research does not provide support for the hypothesis that managerial effectiveness is a product of the personality characteristics of the individual.

Other theories of leadership focus on the behavior of managers as they operate. Whereas trait theories attempt to explain leadership on the basis of what the leader is, behavioral theories try to do the same thing by concentrating on what the leader does.[16] This is referred to as *style of leadership,* meaning the continuing patterns of behavior as perceived and experienced by others that they use to characterize the leader. Several of these approaches are discussed in the section that follows. Although not exclusively, many of the styles reflect elements of scientific management's task-centered and human relations' people-centered orientations.

Situational leadership theories postulate that effective leadership is a product of the fit between the traits or skills required in a leader as determined by the situation in which he or she is to exercise leadership.[17] Illustrative are Frederick Fiedler's contingency model,[18] Robert House's path-goal theory,[19] Robert Tannenbaum and Warren Schmidt's authoritarian-democratic leadership continuum, and Paul Hersey and Kenneth Blanchard's situational leadership theory. The last two are covered in detail in the next section because of their interrelatedness with leadership styles.

## STYLES OF LEADERSHIP

General interest in the topic of leadership and the various theories of it have generated both commentary and research on different schemes for classifying styles of leadership. The purpose of this section is to provide a sense of some ways in which this subject has been treated and to discuss certain of the contributions in this area.

Although these three styles of leadership had been identified in earlier works, the 1939 publication of Lewin, Lippitt, and White's[20] classical study of boys' clubs has closely identified these approaches with them.

The contrasting approaches to Lewin, Lippitt, and White's styles are detailed in Table 6-2. Briefly, they may be characterized as follows: (1) the authoritarian leader makes all decisions without consulting subordinates and closely controls work performance (see Box 6-2); (2) the democratic leader is group oriented and promotes the active participation of subordinates in planning and executing tasks; and (3) the laissez-faire leader takes a "hands-off" passive approach in dealing with subordinates.

White and Lippitt concluded that, although the quantity of work was somewhat greater under the autocratic leader, autocracy could generate hostility and aggression. The democratically controlled groups were about as efficient as the autocratically controlled ones, but the continuation of work in the former did not depend on the presence of the leader. Under the laissez-faire leader, less work was produced, the work quality was poorer, and the work was less organized and less satisfying to members of the group.[21]

**Lewin, Lippitt, and White: Authoritarian, Democratic, and Laissez-faire**

**TABLE 6-2. The Authoritarian, Democratic, and Laissez-faire Leadership Styles**

| *Authoritarian* | *Democratic* | *Laissez-faire* |
|---|---|---|
| 1. All determination of policy was by the leader. | 1. All policies were a matter of group discussion and decision, encouraged and assisted by the leader. | 1. Complete freedom for group or individual decision existed, with a minimum of leader participation. |
| 2. Techniques and activity steps were dictated by the authority, one at a time, so that future steps were always uncertain to a large degree. | 2. Activity perspective was gained during discussion period. General steps to group goal were sketched, and when technical advice was needed, the leader suggested two or more alternative procedures from which choice could be made. | 2. Various materials were supplied by the leader, who made it clear that he or she would supply information when asked. Leader took no other part in work discussion. |
| 3. The leader usually dictated the particular work task and work companion of each member. | 3. The members were free to work with whomever they chose, and the division of tasks was left up to the group. | 3. Nonparticipation of the leader was complete. |
| 4. The dominator tended to be "personal" in his or her praise and criticism of the work of each member, remained aloof from active group participation except when demonstrating. | 4. The leader was "objective" or "fact-minded" in his or her praise and criticism and tried to be a regular group member in spirit without doing too much of the work. | 4. Spontaneous comments on member activities were infrequent unless questioned and no attempt was made to appraise or regulate the course of events. |

*Source:* From Figure 1, p. 32 in *Autocracy and Democracy* by Ralph K. White and Ronald Lippitt. Copyright © 1960 by Ralph K. White and Ronald Lippitt. Reprinted by permission of Harper & Row, Publishers, Inc.; an earlier version of this appears in Kurt Lewin, Ronald Lippitt, and Ralph K. White, "Patterns of Aggressive Behavior in Experimentally Created Social Climates," *Journal of Social Psychology,* 10 (1939), p. 273.

## BOX 6-2

### Text of Evaluation of Police Chief Joe Pelkington by City Manager Chuck Coward

For the past two years we have worked together to address a number of situations and issues related to the leadership and operations of the Treasure Island **Police** Department. These issues were identified in 1997 through a series of employee meetings and during our briefing sessions, which were directed toward familiarizing me with the Treasure Island Police Department. I gave you direction on a number of programs which I believed would benefit the department. In addition, we spoke on several occasions about department leadership issues and the possibilities and difficulties of your continued service as police chief of the department, especially given a number of past situations and perceptions.

During the period of mid-1997 to mid-1999, several new programs were implemented and new employees were hired. Progress was made in many areas that have improved the department. However, in the past few months it appears that some of the initial problems that were identified in 1997 have reappeared. Two of our new hire officers have resigned and in recent employee meetings and exit interviews officers have cited issues such as employee favoritism, lack of professional development, and micro-management as key factors in their dissatisfaction and decision to leave.

In addition, I have now had two years to observe your management style and the performance of your department, its members and leaders. I believe that your management style is generally autocratic and not particularly well suited to the Treasure Island Police Department or community. I also believe that a number of past issues and incidents have damaged your credibility with some employees and foster a division among them.

I realize that this evaluation assessment may be difficult to accept. You have given this city 12 years of dedicated service. My conclusions are based on the following observations:

1. There exists in the department a climate of favoritism that is fostered by the same individuals being at the center of most activities to the exclusion of others who may not be encouraged to participate.

2. While you have implemented most of the programs I have suggested, you have not provided creativity in their application nor have you initiated other new programs that would benefit the department.

3. In general, my observation is that your leadership style is stale and rigid. It is representative of an autocratic style that neither recognizes nor encourages the full potential of the department employees, let alone a requirement of their full participation.

Given this situation, I believe that it is time to undertake some fundamental changes. As a start, it is my intent to hire a management consultant to review the management and operation practices of the department and make recommendations on programs and policies that can foster improvement. The focus of this review will be on participatory management practices and community policing programs. I expect your full participation in this review as well as the participation of all department employees.

Once this study is complete, a plan of action will be developed. Your willingness, ability and/or interest in implementing this action plan will then be for you and me to discuss. Hopefully, the best interests of all involved parties can be served; however, the needs of the city and its employees will receive top priority.

*Source: St. Petersburg* (Florida) *Times*, November 14, 1999.

---

**Tannenbaum and Schmidt: The Authoritarian–Democratic Leadership Continuum**

In 1958, Tannenbaum and Schmidt[22] published the leadership continuum depicted in Figure 6-3. They believed that the successful leader could choose to be more or less directive depending on certain factors:

1. Forces in the manager, such as his or her value system, confidence in subordinates, leadership inclinations, and need for security in uncertain situations

2. Forces in subordinates, including their needs for independence, readiness to assume greater responsibility, and interests, knowledge, and experience

3. Forces in the organization, illustrated by prevailing views and practices, the ability of the group to work together effectively, the nature of the problem, and the pressures of time.[23]

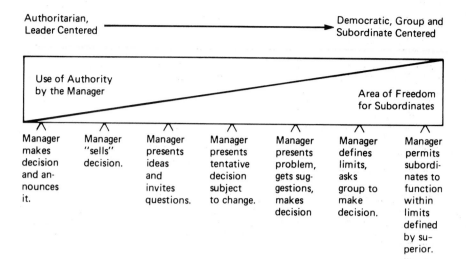

Authoritarian,
Leader Centered  ⟶  Democratic, Group and
Subordinate Centered

Use of Authority
by the Manager

Area of Freedom
for Subordinates

| Manager makes decision and announces it. | Manager "sells" decision. | Manager presents ideas and invites questions. | Manager presents tentative decision subject to change. | Manager presents problem, gets suggestions, makes decision | Manager defines limits, asks group to make decision. | Manager permits subordinates to function within limits defined by superior. |

**FIGURE 6–3.** The authoritarian-democratic continuum. [Reprinted by permission of the *Harvard Business Review*. Exhibit from "How to Choose a Leadership Pattern" by Robert Tannenbaum and Warren H. Schmidt (May–June 1973). Copyright © 1973 by the president and fellows of Harvard College; all rights reserved.]

Although their work is often simply presented as styles of leadership, by considering such variables and noting that these forces working together might suggest one leadership style instead of another, Tannenbaum and Schmidt's findings reflect a situational approach to leadership.

In 1967, Anthony Downs[24] described four types of leader behavior in bureaucratic structures: (1) climbers, (2) conservers, (3) zealots, and (4) advocates.

Climbers are strongly motivated by power and prestige needs to invent new functions to be performed by their unit, particularly functions not performed elsewhere. If climbers can expand their functions only by moving into areas already controlled by others, they are likely to choose ones in which they expect low resistance. To protect their "turf," climbers tend to economize only when the resultant savings can be used to finance an expansion of their functions.[25]

The bias of conservers is toward maintaining things as they are. The longer a person is in the same job and the older one becomes, the lower one assesses any chances for advancement, and the stronger one becomes attached to job security, all of which are associated with the tendency to become a conserver. Climbers may become conservers when they assess their probability for advancement and expansion to be low. Desiring to make their organizational lives comfortable, conservers dislike and resist change.[26]

The peculiarities of the behavior of zealots stem from two sources: (1) their narrow interest and (2) the missionary-like energy that they focus almost solely on their special interest. As a consequence, zealots do not attend to all their duties and often antagonize other administrators by their lack of impartiality and their willingness to trample over all obstacles to further their special interest. Zealots rarely succeed to high-level positions because of their narrowness and are consequently also poor administrators. An exception is when their interest comes into favor and they are catapulted into high office.[27]

Unlike zealots, advocates promote everything under their jurisdiction. To those outside their units, they appear highly partisan, but within their units they are impartial and fair, developing well-rounded programs. Loyal to their

**Downs: Leadership Styles in Bureaucratic Structures**

organizations, advocates favor innovation. They are also simultaneously more radical and more conservative than climbers. They are more radical in that they are willing to promote programs and views that may antagonize their superiors, if doing so will help their organization. They are more conservative because they are willing to oppose changes from which they might benefit but which would not be in the best overall interest of their organizations.[28]

**Van Maanen: Station House Sergeants and Street Sergeants**

In a study of a 1,000-officer police department, Van Maanen[29] identified two contrasting types of police sergeants: "station house" and "street." Station house sergeants had been out of the "bag" (uniform) before their promotions to sergeant and preferred to work inside in an office environment once they won their stripes; this preference is clearly indicated by the nickname of "Edwards, the Olympic torch who never goes out" given to one such sergeant. Station house sergeants immersed themselves in the management culture of the police department, keeping busy with paperwork, planning, record keeping, press relations, and fine points of law. Their strong orientation to conformity also gave rise to nicknames as suggested by the use of "by the book Brubaker" to refer to one station house sergeant.

In contrast, street sergeants were serving in the field when they received their promotions. Consequently, they had a distaste for office procedures and a strong action orientation as suggested by such nicknames as "Shooter McGee" and "Walker the Stalker." Moreover, their concern was not with conformity, but with "not letting the assholes take over the city."

In addition to the distinct differences already noted, station house and street sergeants were thought of differently by those whom they supervised: station house sergeants "stood behind their officers," while street sergeants "stood beside their officers." Each of these two different styles of working as a sergeant also has its drawbacks and strengths. Station house sergeants might not be readily available to officers working in the field, but could always be located when a signature was needed and were able to secure more favors for their subordinates than street sergeants were. Although immediately available in the field when needed, street sergeants occasionally interfered with the autonomy of their subordinates by responding to a call for service assigned to a subordinate and handling it or otherwise, at least in the eyes of the subordinate officer, "interfering."

A consideration of Van Maanen's work leads to some generalizations about the future careers of station house versus street sergeants. The station house sergeant is learning routines, procedures, and skills that will improve future promotional opportunities. Their promotional opportunities are further enhanced by contacts with senior police commanders who can give them important assignments and who can, if favorably impressed, influence future promotions. In contrast, street sergeants may gain some favorable publicity and awards for their exploits, but they are also more likely to have citizen complaints filed against them, more likely to be investigated by internal affairs, and more likely to be sued. Consequently, very aggressive street sergeants are regarded by their superiors as "good cops," but difficult people to supervise. In short, the action-oriented street sergeant who does not "mellow out" may not go beyond a middle manager's position in a line unit such as patrol or investigation.

**Blake and Mouton: The Managerial Grid**

Developed by Robert Blake and Jane Mouton,[30] the Managerial Grid© has received a great deal of attention since its appearance in 1962 in the *Journal of the American Society of Training Directors*. The grid is part of the survey research feedback stem of organizational development and draws upon earlier work done at Ohio State University and the University of Michigan.[31]

Depicted in Figure 6-4, the grid has two dimensions: (1) concern for production and (2) concern for people. Each axis or dimension is numbered from 1, meaning low concern, to 9, indicating high concern. The way in which a person combines these two dimensions establishes a leadership style in terms of one of the five principal styles identified on the Grid. The numbers associated with each of the styles reflect the level of concern for each of the two dimensions to the Grid. For example, 9,1 indicates maximum concern for production or the needs of the organization and a minimum orientation toward the needs of people in the organization.

Some of the leadership styles identified previously can be related readily to the grid. Authoritarian leaders are represented by the 9,1 style; laissez-faire leaders by the 1,1; and democratic leaders by the 5,5. Additionally, the 9,1 and 9,9 styles are consistent, respectively, with the streams of thought summarized in Chapter 4 under the headings of "Traditional Organizational Theory" and "Open Systems Theory."

The leadership style of an individual can be identified by using a questionnaire based on the work of Blake and Mouton. According to the grid, one moves from the "best" to the "worst" styles as one moves from a 9,9 through

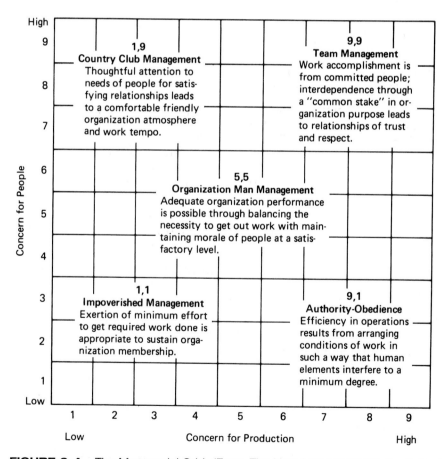

**FIGURE 6-4.** The Managerial Grid. (From *The New Managerial Grid* by Robert Blake and Jan Syrgley Mouton. Houston: Copyright © Gulf Publishing Company. Reproduced by permission.)

5,5; 9,1 and 1,9 to the 1,1. The most desirable combination of a primary and backup style is the 9,9 with a 5,5 backup.

A difficulty in using the grid questionnaire is that the data produced are no more accurate than the perceptions of self of the person completing the instrument. When working in an organizational development context, one way to overcome this is to have each manager complete the instrument and then to have each of his or her subordinates fill out on how they experience the manager.

**Hersey and Blanchard: Situational Leadership Theory**

Hersey and Blanchard's[32] situational leadership model was influenced greatly by William Reddin's 3-D management style theory. Although many situational variables are important to leadership—such as the demands of time, the leader, the led, the superiors, the organization, and job demands—Hersey and Blanchard emphasize what they regard as the key variables, the behavior of the leader in relationship to the followers.[33] Although the examples of situational leadership suggest a hierarchical relationship, situational leadership theory should have application when trying to influence the behavior of a subordinate, a boss, a friend, or a relative.[34]

Maturity is defined in situational leadership as the capacity to set high, but attainable, goals, the willingness to take the responsibility, and the education and/or experience of the individual or the group.[35] Age may be a factor, but it is not related directly to maturity as used in situational leadership theory.[36] An individual or group is not mature or immature in a total sense, but only in relationship to the specific task to be performed.[37] This task-relevant maturity involves two factors: (1) job maturity or the ability and technical knowledge to do the task, and (2) psychological maturity, or feelings of self-confidence and self-respect about oneself as an individual.[38]

Figure 6-5 depicts the situation leadership model; the various levels of follower maturity are defined as

- *M1:* The followers are neither willing nor able to take responsibility for task accomplishment.
- *M2:* The followers are willing but not able to take responsibility for task accomplishment.
- *M3:* The followers are able but not willing to take responsibility for task accomplishment.
- *M4:* The followers are willing and able to take responsibility for task accomplishment.[39]

Task behavior is essentially the extent to which a leader engages in one-way communication with subordinates; relationship behavior is the extent to which a leader engages in two-way communication by providing socioemotional support, "psychological strokes," and facilitating behaviors.[40] The definition of the four basic styles associated with these two variables operates like the Managerial Grid and is described in the following terms:

- *S1:* High-task—low-relationship leader behavior is referred to as "telling," because this style is characterized by one-way communication in which the leader defines the roles of followers and tells them what, how, when, and where to do various tasks.
- *S2:* High-task—high-relationship behavior is referred to as "selling," because with this style most of the direction is still provided by the leader. He or she also attempts through two-way communication and socioemotional support to get the follower(s) psychologically to buy into decisions that have to be made.

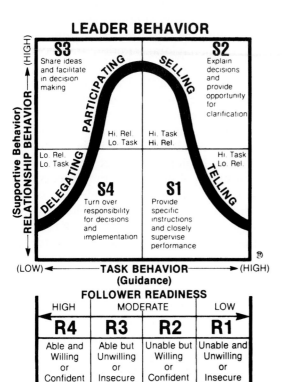

**FIGURE 6-5.** The situational leadership model. Situational Leadership® is a registered trademark of the Center for Leadership Studies, Escondido, CA. Used with permission. All rights reserved.

- *S3:* High-relationship—low-task behavior is called "participating," because with this style the leader and follower(s) now share in decision making through two-way communication and much facilitating behavior from the leader since the follower(s) have the ability and knowledge to do the task.
- *S4:* Low-relationship—low-task behavior is labeled "delegating," because the style involves letting follower(s) "run their own show" through delegation and general supervision since the follower(s) are high in both task and psychological maturity.

The bell-shaped curve in the style-of-leader portion of Figure 6-5 means that, as the maturity level of leader's followers develops from immaturity to maturity, the appropriate style of leadership moves in a corresponding way.[41]

To illustrate, the police leader who has a subordinate whose maturity is in the M2 range would be most effective employing an S2 style of leadership. The probability of success of each style for the four maturity levels depends on how far the style is from the high-probability style along the bell-shaped curve; Hersey and Blanchard describe these probabilities as for

- *M1:* S1 and S2 2nd, S3 third, S4 low probability
- *M2:* S2 High S1 and S3 secondary, S4 low probability
- *M3:* S3 High S2 and S4 secondary, S1 low probability
- *M4:* S4 High S3 2nd S2 3rd, S1 low probability[42]

Although it is easier said than done, the effective use of Hersey and Blanchard's model depends on police leaders developing or having a diagnostic ability and the flexibility to adapt their leadership styles to given situations.[43]

## Transactional and Transformational Leaders

In 1978, James Burns published a book that was simply titled *Leadership*. However modest the title, it was to become a very influential writing. In it, Burns identifies two types of leaders in the behavioral tradition: transactional and transforming.[44]

Most leader–follower relations are transactional: the leaders approach the followers with the idea that they will exchange one thing for another, such as raises and favorable assignments for good performance or personal loyalty. Each party to the transaction or "bargain" is aware of the resources of the other, and the purposes of both are entwined almost exclusively within the context of this relationship.[45] Transactional leaders emphasize values such as honesty, fairness, acceptance of responsibility, honoring commitments, and getting work done on time.[46] In contrast, transformational leadership occurs when leaders and followers interact in such a way that they are elevated and committed to—and sustained by—some great cause external to the relationship. Transformational leaders emphasize values such as justice, liberty, and equality. A classical example of transformational leadership is the preeminent role played by Martin Luther King, Jr., in the civil rights movement of the 1960s.

Burns's *Leadership* was written at a very broad level from a political science perspective; it was nearly another decade before his concepts began to be applied more narrowly to organizations. A 1984 article in the *Sloan Management Review* by Tichy and Ulrich[47] called for transforming leadership, as did two books the following year: *Leadership and Performance Beyond Expectations* by Bass[48] and *Leaders* by Bennis and Nanus.[49] Despite the importance of these writings, a later book emerged as most influential in galvanizing widespread interest in the transforming leader.

Published in 1987, *The Leadership Challenge: How to Get Extraordinary Things Done in Organizations* by James Kouzes and Barry Posner postulates that successful leaders have made ten behavioral commitments. These commitments are organized under five major headings:

### Challenge The Process

1. *Searching out challenging opportunities to change, grow, innovate, and improve*—Outstanding police leaders recognize that they must be change agents and innovators.[50] However, they also know that most innovations do not come from them.[51] Instead, these ideas often come from the officers who do the actual work and from the people who use the department's services.[52] "Leaders listen to the advice and counsel of others; they know that good ideas enter the mind through the ears, not the mouth."[53]

2. *Experimenting and taking risks, and learning from the accompanying mistakes*—"Leaders experiment and take risks (see Box 6-3). Since risk taking involves mistakes and failure, leaders learn to accept the inevitable disappointments. They treat them as learning opportunities."[54]

### Inspire a Shared Vision

3. *Envisioning an uplifting and ennobling future*—In the mold of Burns's transformational style, police leaders look forward to the future with visions and ideals of what can be.[55] "They have a sense of what is uniquely possible if all work together for a common purpose. They are positive about the future and they passionately believe that people can make a difference[56] (see Box 6-4).

BOX 6-3

## Seattle Police Chief Resigns in Aftermath of Protests

by Sam Howe Verhovek

Amid continuing criticism over the police department's handling of the protests last week in Seattle that eclipsed the World Trade Organization meeting here, the city's police chief announced today that he would resign

The chief, Norm Stamper, said he wished to "depoliticize" the investigations that are under way into police preparations for the global trade talks, which drew 35,000 protesters downtown. The demonstration quickly turned into a tumultuous affair, televised worldwide, in which the police sprayed tear gas and rubber pellets at many peaceful protesters along police lines near the meeting but failed to stop the window-smashing and looting by a relatively small group of vandals less than a block away. The national guard was called in to help restore order.

In his resignation letter to Mayor Paul Schell, Mr. Stamper praised his officers for the "restraint, discipline, perserverance and incredible courage" he said they showed in the face of the protests, and noted that there were no deaths or serious injuries reported in nearly a week of unrest.

But the police and Mr. Schell have been hit by complaints from all sides: from protesters and residents of neighborhoods in and around downtown who say the tear gas, pepper spray and rubber pellets they endured were wildly inappropriate; by merchants who say the vandalism caused at least $3 million in damages and much more than that in lost holiday sales, and even from some police officers, who have spoken up to assert that the department was completely unprepared.

In handing in his resignation, effective in March, Mr. Stamper may take a bit of political heat off Mr. Schell, although Mr. Schell made a point of dismissing suggestions that he had sought or forced the move.

"The decision was Norm's, and Norm's alone," Mr. Schell said at a news conference this morning, adding that he had tried to talk the chief out of resigning. But the mayor's critics, including some City Council members, quickly cast the resignation as an effort to make Mr. Stamper the scapegoat.

And the resignation may be only the beginning of the political fallout from an event that was intended to showcase Seattle as a world-class city and friend to both free speech and free trade. Mr. Schell, a Democrat up for re-election in 2001, turned back questions this morning about whether he himself might resign.

"I am not going to step down," he declared

Mr. Schell, a former director of community development and dean of the University of Washington's school of architecture and urban planning, had wanted to provide the protesters a broad forum to make their points, and he and Mr. Stamper had spent months working with protest leaders to ensure peace.

The mayor spoke of Seattle offering a model of "constructive debate" on trade issues, and as the protests got out of hand, he appeared stunned and saddened, saying: "This administration has people who marched in the 1960's. The last thing I wanted was to be mayor of a city that called in the National Guard."

For that approach, he has certainly drawn praise, and one snap poll last week by a local television station, KOMO-TV, the ABC affiliate here, found that 26 percent of Seattleites interviewed said they had a higher opinion of the mayor at the end of the week than at the beginning.

But in the main, he has been roundly criticized for the way the city prepared for and handled the protests. The City Council is opening hearings into the events, which will be open to protesters, residents, merchants, police officers and anyone else who wants to testify.

At least two civil-rights groups, the N.A.A.C.P. and the local chapter of the American Civil Liberties Union, are calling for investigations.

There was something of a subtext to the chain of events leading to the decision by Mr. Stamper, 55, to resign after nearly six years as head of the force. While widely praised in some quarters of this relatively liberal city for his outreach efforts, he was deeply unpopular with many conservative political leaders and with some police officers.

Half a year after taking over in 1994, he upset some officers when he wore his uniform in a gay-pride parade but forbade his officers from wearing theirs at a "March for Jesus" the same weekend.

In 1996, when one of his officers shot and killed an unarmed black man during a domestic-violence dispute, Mr. Stamper apologized at a community meeting organized by black leaders for what he termed a "wrongful death." Later, though, he told reporters he supported an inquest jury's conclusion that the shooting had been accidental.

In 1998, he told a columnist for *The Seattle Post-Intelligencer* that as a young police officer in San Diego, he had beaten up gays and used racial slurs to harass members of minority groups. "Gay bashing was not only acceptable, it was more or less required," he said,

*(continued)*

BOX 6-3 (continued)

and he added that he had "regularly jacked around young people and people of color."

While he expressed deep remorse for those actions and gained some praise for his candor, many police officers here and elsewhere were outraged, believing Mr. Stamper had branded them all racists and gay-bashers. After the column appeared, Mr. Stamper interrupted a vacation to apologize to veteran officers.

And most recently, Mr. Stamper's department was weathering a scandal over its failure to unearth details about a case in which a veteran homicide detective was suspected of stealing $10,000 from a crime scene and his sergeant was accused of covering up the crime. (A first trial of the detective ended in a hung jury.)

Mr. Stamper alluded to his roller-coaster history in his letter to Mr. Schell, saying, "Although my personal beliefs and political views have often been at odds with many of my colleagues, I've managed to love almost every moment of my career."

Still, Mr. Stamper's action today was clearly linked to the handling of last week's protests.

While merchants and many protesters were furious, so were police officers. Some have already talked of suing the city, and this morning the police union president, Mike Edwards, said that many officers had had deficient equipment and forced to spend as much as 20 hours straight on the police lines without food or other support.

Brett Smith, a 10-year veteran of the force, complained last week to the *Post-Intelligencer* that the department had been completely unprepared, despite warnings of a flood of protesters.

"It seemed like they closed their eyes and said, 'I hope nothing happens,' " he told the newspaper, which also reported news of Mr. Stamper's impending resignation in this morning's edition, hours before the mayor made it official.

Mr. Stamper said he had intended to resign next year anyway. "I think it's natural for people to say, 'Well of course the police chief is going to say this or say that, do this or do that because he wants to keep his job,' " he said at the news conference. "What I've said is, I'm not abandoning my job, I'm retiring from it."

Mr. Schell said that he had no intention of his leaving his job.

"The whole community's hurting, I'm hurting," the mayor said. "And I think that it's time to understand what happened, what can we learn from it as a community. And before we start assigning guilt, the first step is, let's get the facts. All of us, together. And then make our conclusions."

*Source:* Sam Howe Verhovek, *The New York Times,* December 8, 1999.

---

## BOX 6-4

### Evans Gives Top Brass a Shake-up

#### Move affects 19 hub officers, including 2 linked to scandal

**by Francie Latour**

In a sweeping shake-up of the commanding officers who serve at his discretion, Boston Police Commissioner Paul F. Evans yesterday elevated, reassigned, or demoted 19 command-level and lower-ranking officers, the broadest administrative changes in more than a decade.

The demotions included Night Superintendent John P. Boyle, one of Evans's closest associates, and Superintendent James M. Claiborne, one of the department's highest-ranking black officers. The transfers also included two other officers tainted by a racial scandal that brought disgrace to a nationally lauded department.

Evans promoted three sergeants to superintendent or deputy superintendent—a departure from his pledge to avoid elevating officers below the rank of lieutenant to command-level positions. Evans made the promise to counter widely held perceptions that such promotions were political and not merit-based.

The commissioner said the new lineup is part of his strategic Year 2000 plan, and insisted that the changes were neither punishment nor politically motivated. The changes came a day after President Clinton again touted the department' achievements in drastically lowering the rate of violent crime.

Problems in the department mounted over the years.

"I think the president being here says the department is doing a great job, and we can bask in the glow of that and become complacent," Evans said. "What today is about is I'm not going to become complacent. I'm going to make sure the community has what it deserves, which is to have the best possible police services."

But police and other sources yesterday said the changes reflect a department whose command staff has been mired in in-fighting and power struggles, choking innovative ideas from the rank and file and consuming the leadership in battles over who deserves the credit—or who gets the blame.

At the heart of those struggles, the sources said, was a deep-seated clash between Claiborne, who commanded the department's patrol officers, and Superintendent in Chief Robert P. Faherty, Evans's second in command.

"The bottom line is that the command structure of the Boston Police Department had become balkanized with endless infighting, so that the energy and leadership coming from the ground up was being blocked by a top-heavy bureaucratic command structure," a police source said yesterday.

Another source close to the shake-up said yesterday the Boyle and Deputy Superintendent Laurence J. Robicheau, an Evans confidant who was reassigned to the night shift, lost their positions because they were ineffective.

Sources yesterday said Claiborne was devastated by the news, and many of the rank-and-file officers he oversaw were stunned.

"He's hurt, he's angry," said a source close to Claiborne, whom many saw as a principal architect of Evans's strategic plan and one of Evans's proteges. "He had no idea this was coming before today."

While other command staff officers with close personal ties to Evans, such as Boyle, were given jobs within the Roxbury headquarters to cushion their fall, sources said, Claiborne was moved out of the building—returned to the rank of captain and transferred to a precinct in East Boston, across town from his home in Hyde Park.

"I think you're going to see turmoil, and I think you're going to see dissension," the source said of Claiborne's demotion.

While he acknowledged that the demotions were painful decisions, Evans denied that they were payback. In an interview yesterday, he praised Claiborne, in particular, for his accomplishments as a commander.

"People are going to speculate all they want, but the fact is I felt it was time to make a change," Evans said. "Is there any good time to give bad news to people? No. But I have absolute confidence in the integrity of all these people."

Among the most significant changes:

Claiborne is replaced by Sergeant Bobbie J. Johnson, the former deputy superintendent in charge of Area B, encompassing Roxbury and Mattapan. Robicheau, who led the prestigious Special Operations Unit during a racially tinged prank played on a black motorcycle lieutenant, now works in the patrol division.

Boyle is now a lieutenant detective assigned to the commissioner's office. It was unclear what his duties would be under his new assignment. His replacement is Sergeant Paul F. Joyce, who led the homicide division's cold-case squad.

Superintendent Donald Devine was reassigned from the investigative division to the police commissioner's office, but he is expected to retire soon.

Captain John S. Sullivan, who led the Mattapan precinct, is now in the department's Office of Labor Relations. Superintendent Pervis J. Ryans, the former night deputy commander, will become a captain and replace Sullivan.

Sergeant William H. Bradley was named deputy superintendent in charge of operations, the unit that includes the department's 911 phone system.

Though Claiborne loses his status as one of the highest-ranking black officers, Evans picked two more African-Americans to his command staff—Bradley and Sergeant Charles M. Horsley, a veteran homicide detective. Evans also selected Lt. Raphael Ruiz, the only Latino, for his staff.

The transfers will cost Claiborne, Ryans, and Boyle more than their positions: officials said they each will lose between $15,000 and $20,000 in pay.

Evans maintained that the reassignments have nothing to do with the recent scandals that have rocked the department, including allegations of fraud and extortion within the police unit that issues city taxi licenses, and a makeshift noose hung over the motorcycle of Lt. Val Williams, a black supervisor in the Special Operations Division.

In the aftermath of that incident, Evans concluded that the noose, made of crime scene tape and placed there by a subordinate, was a prank that involved no racial bigotry. But several observers, both within and outside of the 2,000-officer department, said the transfers of Robicheau and Bernard O'Rourke from that unit stemmed from the noose incident.

*(continued)*

## BOX 6-4 (continued)

Sources yesterday said that the transfer of Deputy Superintendent Thomas A. Dowd to Special Operations is a prelude to more changes within the unit.

"Dowd was brought in there to be the hatchet man, no question," sources said.

Reacting to the news yesterday, leading clergy applauded Evans for making the changes, which elevated many younger ranking officers.

"I think that Evans has to be commended for the courage and the audacity he has exhibited in making the changes needed to improve the quality of leadership performance in the department," said the Reverend Eugene Rivers, pastor of the Asuza Christian Community.

*Source: The Boston Globe,* January 20, 2000

4. *Enlisting others in a common vision by appealing to their values, interests, hopes, and dreams*—Visions seen only by the chief and his or her command staff are insufficient to create an organized movement such as community policing.[57] Police leaders must get others to see and be excited by future possibilities.[58] One study found that when senior executives were able to communicate their vision of the organization's future effectively, subordinate personnel reported significantly higher levels of
   a. Job satisfaction
   b. Commitment
   c. Loyalty
   d. Esprit de corps
   e. Clarity about the organization's values
   f. Pride in the organization
   g. Encouragement to be productive
   h. Organizational productivity[59]

   Thus, police leaders breathe life into dreams, communicating their visions so clearly that others in the department understand and accept them as their own.[60] They show others how their own values and interests will be served by this long-term vision of the future.[61]

### Enable Others to Act

5. *Fostering collaboration by promoting cooperative goals and building trust*—Police leaders develop collaborative and cooperative goals and cooperative relationships with others in the department, knowing that such relationships are the keys that unlock support for their programs.[62] Developing trust in organizations can be a difficult task if the people with whom you work have had their trust abused. One way to build trust is to delegate, for this process is fundamentally a system of trust.[63] Ultimately, you have to be a risk taker when it comes to trust, trusting others first and having faith that they will respond in kind.[64]

6. *Strengthening people by sharing information and power and increasing their discretion and visibility*—In some circles, power is thought to be like a pie; there is only so much and if I have more, then you have less. Kouzes and Posner[65] argue that this view is archaic and retards accomplishments in organizations. Their view is that when people hoard power, others feel less powerful or powerless, leading the less potent to zealously guard their prerogatives and thereby become arbitrary, petty, and dictatorial.[66] According to Kouzes and Posner, it is not centralized power, but mutual respect that sustains extraordinary group efforts; real leaders create an atmosphere of trust and human dignity and

nurture self-esteem in others.[67] They make others feel strong and capable,[68] and they empower other officers by such strategies as

a. Giving them important work to do on important issues
b. Giving them discretion and autonomy over their tasks and resources
c. Giving them visibility and recognition for their efforts
d. Building relationships for them by connecting them with powerful people and finding them sponsors and mentors.[69]

### Model the Way

7. *Setting the example for others by behaving in ways that are consistent with the leader's stated values*—Police officers are astute observers of behavior in organizations and are especially sensitive to differences between what their leaders say is important and how they behave. For instance, if patrol officers are told by their chief that the patrol division is the backbone of the department, but they are the last ones every year to get new cars, then the patrol officers will dismiss the chief's statement as "hype." "Leaders provide the standard by which other people in the organization calibrate their own choices and behaviors; in order to set an example, leaders must know their values and live by them.[70]

8. *Promoting small wins that reflect consistent progress and build commitment*—Some police chiefs fail because what they propose to do seems overwhelming and this frightens and paralyzes the very people whose support and enthusiasm are essential for success. A wiser strategy is to start with "small wins," doing things that are within the control of the department, that are doable, and that "get the ball rolling." These small wins form the basis for consistently winning, attract followers and deter opposition: it's hard to argue with success. Moreover, each gain preserves past progress and makes it harder to return to the previously prevailing conditions.[71]

### Encourage the Heart

9. *Recognize individual contributions to the success of every program*—Having high expectations for themselves and others is a must for police chiefs who wish to be successful; these expectations form the model to which others will adapt their behavior. But simply eliciting the behavior is insufficient. There must be a wide variety of ways police leaders can recognize and reward performance, such as praise, days off, cash awards, and formal award systems. For example, some departments grant officers an extra day off whenever they catch a burglar inside of a building. For a performance-reward system to be effective, three conditions must be met:

a. Personnel must know what is expected of them.
b. They must receive continuing feedback about their performance so errors can be corrected and solid practices reinforced.
c. Only people who meet or exceed standards of behavior should be rewarded, otherwise all rewards are cheapened and the system loses meaning.[72]

10. *Celebrate team accomplishments regularly*—The role of leaders in celebrations is often overlooked. Some police leaders conceive of their role in this area as limited to presiding over annual awards banquets and promotional ceremonies. However, this is a narrow view that is correct only when police department celebrations are limited to such occasions. As used here, *celebrate* simply means to gather people together to savor what they have accomplished and to

recognize it jointly. For example, a unit or team who put together a successful grant application could be invited to the chief's home with their spouses for a cookout. Or, investigators who have solved a particularly noteworthy case could, in addition to other recognitions, be the chief's guests at the monthly local chiefs meetings that are common throughout the country. There the chief could publicly introduce them and acknowledge their contributions. For Kouzes and Posner, such activities are both recognition tools and crucial ways of communicating important organizational values.

Transforming police leaders may act in a transactional style around particular issues without abandoning their transformational orientation. In fact, within the organizational setting it is essential that transformational leaders have transactional skills. Few transactional leaders, however, are able to convert to a transforming style because they lack that essential larger and ennobling vision of the future with which to excite potential followers.

The body of literature on transactional and transformational leadership is still evolving. Its most salient contribution is its emphasis on leadership as a primary force in elevating followers to higher levels of performance and purpose and carefully delineating the multiple roles of leaders as visionaries who articulate and teach organizational values.

**Total Quality Leadership**  Based on the pioneering work of Bell Laboratories' Walter Shewhart, Americans developed the concept of statistical quality control and applied it to production processes during the 1920s and 1930s.[73] After World War II, as the economy quickly expanded, the demand for products was so strong that quality control was less a priority for businesses, and they began issuing warranties to correct defective merchandise that consumers had purchased.[74] Also following World War II, the Japanese began applying statistical quality control methods and gradually expanded the notion of quality to be a broad philosophy of management involving everyone in the organization.[75]

Starting in the late 1970s and early 1980s, some American companies began using quality principles, largely due to strong competition from Japanese companies.[76] Roughly during this same period, public agencies began experimenting with some quality concepts, including a federal print shop that used a Total Quality Leadership (TQL) forerunner, Total Performance Management. In police departments, the earliest manifestation of the quality movement was the use of quality circles (see Chapter 15, Productivity, Quality, and Evaluation of Police Services, for further details on quality programs).

As community-oriented policing (COP, also referred to in some parts of the country as community-oriented policing and problem solving or COPPS) gathered steam, its natural relationship to the quality movement was quickly recognized. In fact, retired Madison, Wisconsin, Police Chief David Couper recalls that his department's COP program really did not get implemented until personnel bought into the notion that quality is important.[77] Many chiefs today take the position that to be successful, a COP program inherently must have a quality orientation. This is because COP entails delivering police services that are customized to the needs of the neighborhoods being served and because an essential component of quality is a customer focus.

TQL is customer driven. It focuses on meeting and exceeding customer needs and expectations by sustaining internal and external involvement in planning and implementing the continuous improvement of departmental processes.[78] "Quality" is recognized as the antithesis of waste and errors, which is the greatest drain on police resources; it is estimated that in the public agencies 30 to 45 percent of every budgeted dollar is virtually thrown away.[79] The major elements of a TQL system include customer focus, internal and external alignment, total involvement, and continuous improvement.[80]

## Customer Focus

TQL requires that the focal point of the police department is the customer or client.[81] Because TQL decisions are driven by data, the single most important source of data is feedback from the customer. This feedback is gathered by such methods as periodic surveys, input from neighborhood councils, citizens' letters, and police officers leaving evaluation questionnaires with those to whom they provide services. Chapter 4 noted that organizations exist to serve the needs of people who are unable or unwilling to do so for themselves. TQL understands that the agency's customers are the sole reason for the existence of the police department.

In traditional, incident-based policing (IBP), also referred to as respond-to-incidents (R2I), police officers respond to calls. Quality, if evaluated at all, is judged on whether the applicable policies and procedures were followed. Typically in IBP/R2I, no consideration is given to whether the customer is satisfied with the way the call was handled. The policies and procedures are met or "satisfied" as if they were the customer rather than the person receiving the service.[82] In contrast, TQL holds that the customer determines to what extent quality service has been delivered. No matter how technically proficient a police response is, if the customer isn't satisfied, the standard for total quality hasn't been met.

## Internal and External Alignment

The "total" in TQL refers to the fact that quality is everyone's responsibility rather than that of some special group or unit.[83] Internal alignment means that all of the police department's units and employees understand the organization's vision for the future (where it wants to be) and how the work they do fits into it.[84] External alignment is achieved when the police department is capable of meeting, and actually meets, the requirements of customers.[85] Who are these customers? They are both internal and external entities. Internally, when a records unit has not transcribed a report that was supposed to be ready for the detective bureau at 7:00 A.M. and the investigator assigned is upset, the records unit customer for that transaction is not satisfied. Externally, when a COP officer promises to meet with a group of citizens and "doesn't show," he or she has not met the customers' needs.

Police departments can achieve internal and external alignment by asking the customer three simple questions: What do you need from me? What do you do with what I give you? and Are there any gaps between what you need and what I give you?[86] But, as Harrison explained, "Alignment does not mean that the customer is always right."[87] A motorist who gets a ticket because she was doing 85 mph in a school zone in a dash to get to work on time has not had her needs met. In fact she has been thwarted by this untimely contact with the police. A person arrested for disorderly conduct who violently resists arrest and suffers some minor injury as he is taken into custody is not going to sing the praises of TQL while being booked. Yet, in many instances, effective communication about the customer's needs and the gap between them and the police response may lead to an adjustment of the customer's needs and/or a shift in the police response that reduce or eliminate the gap. The need for internal and external alignment is clearly in the tradition of open systems theory (see Chapter 4, Organizational Theory), which stresses the interdependence of units within a police department and recognizes the existence of multiple inputs from the larger environment in which the police department exists.

**Total Involvement**

Total involvement or participation holds that employees can make important contributions to the success of a police department and that one of the key tasks of leaders is to tap this vast pool of experience, knowledge, expertise, and creativity. To do this, TQL incorporates the following beliefs:

1. Our officers want to do good work.
2. Often, it is things in our departments—the policies and procedures, the lack of coordination, the systems that have been set up, and a failure to continuously reexamine such things—that keep us from doing the best possible work.
3. The people closest to the work, the people doing it, are often in the best position to identify problems and to develop solutions.
4. It is the responsibility of leaders to remove the barriers to doing the best possible job.
5. Leaders must create an environment in which those closest to the work have the opportunity and the willingness to identify problems and to forge lasting solutions.[88]

As depicted in Figure 6-6, there are a number of barriers when implementing TQL.[89] Foremost among these is the fact that 66 percent of employees don't really feel empowered. If employees do not believe they are really empowered and therefore do not participate, TQL cannot succeed. Only when employees have repeated experiences that demonstrate they are impacting on how the police department operates do they feel they are empowered. A key lesson from this is that when in the initial phases of implementing TQL, leaders must be patient. Officers will often believe "this is another management smoke-and-mirrors ploy" and that "none of this is real . . . the department isn't going to change just because we recommend a better way of doing things." This skepticism is based on what officers have personally implicitly or explicitly learned from some traditionally managed police departments: "what you think really isn't of a great deal of interest to us; just concentrate on doing your assigned job and leave the rest to us." In light of this, simply telling officers they are empowered is not enough. The embarrassingly simple truth is that only through the potency of personal learning can empowerment take on real meaning.

Total involvement is also enhanced when employees believe that they have quality leadership. Employees of the Madison, Wisconsin, Police Department identified these characteristics as those they associated with quality leaders:

1. Competent—They know their jobs
2. Champions—They "walk what they talk"
3. Fixers and improvers
4. Visible
5. Involved
6. Willing to take risks
7. Initiators
8. In touch with their employees
9. Providers of information about what's going on
10. Respectful of their employees.[90]

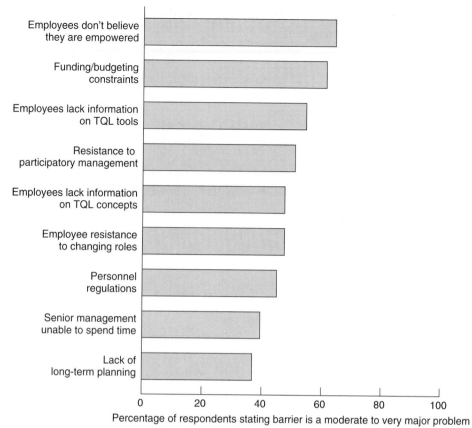

**FIGURE 6-6.** Barriers to Total Quality Leadership. (*Source:* General Accounting Office Report GAO/GGD-93-9BR, October 1992, p. 40.)

This list clearly communicates that TQL will require some supervisors to make significant shifts in how they lead. These shifts will be troubling and difficult to some, opposed by others, and impossible for a few. These shifts are discussed more fully in the subsequent section, "The Leadership Challenge."

There is a popular saying: "If it isn't broken, don't fix it."[91] This attitude reinforces the status quo. Things don't change because there is no imperative to change. The result is that while leaders from time to time react to the symptoms of problems, they often miss the underlying causes. They look for the "quick fix" and then go onto whatever problem pops up next. In such organizations, there is not much commitment because people do not believe they have much of a stake in things. "Eight (hours) and out" becomes the slogan. The police department limps along from one crisis to another in a reactive "hot stove" approach to management. Improvements are made only episodically, and they are usually triggered by some major crisis. The chief, planning and research, inspection, management control, or some other entity is responsible for improving the department.

TQL's view is that quality-driven police departments take a proactive approach to improvement. Everyone understands that improvement is his or her personal responsibility and that it must be continuous. Employees know what their jobs are and how they fit into the organization's commitment to satisfying internal and external customers. Although some problems are reacted to,

**Continuous Improvement**

more are prevented by employees trained in problem identification and solution techniques. Decisions are made on the basis of the best possible data, as opposed to opinions. The language and practice of quality permeates the department and becomes part of how it defines itself. The department uses its award and recognition systems to recognize contributions, further reinforcing the culture of continuous improvement. Over the long term, employee commitment and job satisfaction increase, while sick leave use, turnover, and customer complaints are reduced.[92] However, in the early phases of implementing a COP/TQL program, these indicators should not be expected to be as positive or even favorable, because the process of going from reactive policing to "this new system" is developmental and requires time. This means that police chiefs contemplating such a shift need to make sure that they get their political supporters on board before making any move.

**The Leadership Challenge**

Unless the leaders of a police department are willing to be evangelists about TQL, its prospects for succeeding are dim.[93] To do this, leaders must:

1. understand the shifts in leadership style that are required (these shifts are summarized in Table 6-3);
2. change themselves to any extent necessary;
3. set about improving the workplace. This is primarily accomplished by modeling the new required behaviors; and
4. ask employees to treat customers as they themselves are now being treated.[94]

Perhaps the most difficult "sell" for police leaders is to convince officers that the shift in orientation from the enforcement model to TQL's problem-solving model is in their own best interest.[95] The shift to TQL will mean fewer citizen complaints, more information coming into the department, and a reduction in officers simply being call-chasers, running from one call to another, because officers are solving the underlying problems. Not everyone will embrace the shift to a TQL approach because change is hard, the benefits of TQL are just promises

**TABLE 6-3.   The Leadership Shift Required by TQL**

| Former Leadership Style | TQL Leadership Style |
| --- | --- |
| Respond to incidents | Solve problems |
| Individual effort and competitiveness | Use of teamwork |
| Professional expertise | Asking customers and community orientation |
| "Go by the book," decisions by opinion | Use of data-based decision making |
| Tell subordinates | Ask and listen to employees, collaboration |
| Boss as patriarch and order giver | The leader's role is to coach and teach |
| Maintain the status quo | Create, innovate, experiment |
| Control and watch employees | Trust employees |
| Technology is more important than people | Employees are a better resource than machines |
| Blame employees when things go wrong | Errors mean flawed systems and processes |
| The police department is a closed system | The police department is an open system |

*Source:* David Couper and Sabine Lobitz, *The Quality Leadership Workbook* (Madison, Wis.: February 1993), p. 16, with modification.

in the beginning, the customer focus is foreign and somewhat scary, the image of crime fighter has more appeal than that of problem solver, and new roles must be mastered. Overcoming these factors takes strong, compassionate, and patient leadership, while never wavering on the commitment to TQL.[96]

The most important way for TQL leaders to find out how they are doing is to get feedback. Typically in police organizations the only formal feedback was through periodic performance evaluations done by "the boss." However, a small number of police departments are using 360-degree, or full-circle, evaluations in which superiors, subordinates, and peers have input. A variant of that is the so-called "reverse evaluation" in which subordinates rate their superiors on carefully chosen behaviors (see Figure 6-7). These forms are completed anonymously, tabulated in as aggregate data, and sent to the supervisor involved. This also becomes part of the supervisor's own evaluation when

**Use this form to rate your supervisor's behavior on the following scale:**
1 = Much more than satisfactory
2 = More than satisfactory
3 = Satisfactory
4 = Needs some improvement
5 = Needs much improvement

| Behavior | Circle the Rating |
|---|---|
| Is your supervisor available for questions/assistance as much as possible? | 1  2  3  4  5 |
| Is your supervisor in the field as much as possible during peak hours? | 1  2  3  4  5 |
| Does your supervisor listen to you? | 1  2  3  4  5 |
| Is your supervisor concerned about your personal safety? | 1  2  3  4  5 |
| Does your supervisor help you when you are backlogged with work? | 1  2  3  4  5 |
| Is your supervisor composed and reliable in emergency situations? | 1  2  3  4  5 |
| Does your supervisor use courtesy and tact when dealing with external customers? | 1  2  3  4  5 |
| Does your supervisor make the decisions to solve problems withing his/her authority? | 1  2  3  4  5 |
| Does your supervisor take corrective action with you when needed? | 1  2  3  4  5 |
| Do you see your supervisor as a coach and teacher? | 1  2  3  4  5 |
| Does your supervisor involve you in problem solving? | 1  2  3  4  5 |
| To what extent does your supervisor behave as though you are an internal customer? | 1  2  3  4  5 |
| Is your supervisor, within the limits of his/her authority, willing to experiment? | 1  2  3  4  5 |
| Does your supervisor value your input? | 1  2  3  4  5 |
| To what extent does your supervisor appropriately use teamwork to solve problems? | 1  2  3  4  5 |
| Does your supervisor use data to make decisions? | 1  2  3  4  5 |
| To what degree is your supervisor customer centered? | 1  2  3  4  5 |
| Does your supervisor trust you? | 1  2  3  4  5 |
| Are you treated as a valuable resource by your supervisor? | 1  2  3  4  5 |

Comments: _____

_____

_____

_____

_____

**FIGURE 6-7.** Sample supervisor feedback questions.

rated by his or her boss. There are some obvious risks in the use of full-circle and reverse evaluations, such as when a disgruntled employee "blasts" the supervisor being rated. However, such cases are usually easily identified and the value of such procedures, if the system is properly structured and administered, outweighs the risks.

## THE LEADER AND CONFLICT

Conflict is a condition in which at least two parties have a mutual difference of position, often involving scarce resources, where there is a behavior or threat of behavior through the exercise of power to control the situation or gain at the expense of the other party.[97] Competition differs from conflict in that, in the former, each party is bound to abide by the same rules.[98]

Conflict is a pervasive and perhaps inevitable part of human existence; *it is not inherently "bad" or "good,"* and its consequences depend mainly on how it is managed.[99] Viewed negatively, conflict is an energy-consuming and destructive phenomenon that divides individuals and groups within the police department, creates tension between representatives of the police department and other agencies, and results in acrimonious and combative exchanges. Viewed positively, conflict can

1. Stimulate interest
2. Prevent individual, group, and organizational stagnation
3. Be a source of creativity and change as alternative ways of viewing things are aired
4. Give individuals, groups, and organizations a distinctive identity by demarcating them from others
5. Create group and organizational solidarity
6. Be an enjoyable experience of testing and assessing the active use of one's full capabilities[100]

Although not unique to them, an unfortunate characteristic of many police departments is the view that conflict is destructive so that its positive aspects and potential benefits are overlooked and lost. To tap the useful dimensions of conflict, the police leader must be able to differentiate between pathologically and productively oriented situations. Pathological symptoms in conflict include

1. Unreliable and impoverished communication between the conflicting parties
2. The view that the solution of the conflict will result from the imposition of one view or position over the other
3. A downward spiral of suspicion and hostility that leads to oversensitivity to differences and the minimization of similarities[101]

Unresponded to, such symptoms are the prelude to hostile infighting, hardening of positions, and protracted opposition. In contrast, productively oriented conflict

1. Is characterized by open and honest communication, which reduces the likelihood of misperceptions and misunderstandings, allows each party to benefit

**TABLE 6-4. Leadership Style and Preference for Handling Conflict**

| Managerial Grid Leadership Style | Preference For Handling Conflict |
|---|---|
| 1/1 | Avoid it, withdraw when it occurs, ignore it, and do not take action. Conflict festers until it can no longer be ignored. |
| 1/9 | Gloss over differences, smooth things over, make appeals like "Why can't we all just get along? We're all cops here." The immediate conflict is resolved, but smoldering differences may remain. |
| 9/1 | Handle it quickly and decisively. Uses power of his/her position to announce unilaterally how it will be handled. Both sides may resent the solution. |
| 5/5 | Get the parties to negotiate with each and endorse solution or compromise. May sometimes develop and impose a compromise. In negotiation, both sides get some of what they want. |
| 9/9 | Parties to the conflict are brought together to collaborate on a true group decision. In collaboration the emphasis is on finding the best solution regardless of what the initial positions may have been. |

from the knowledge possessed by the other, and promotes a mutual and accurate definition of the issues

2. Encourages the recognition of the legitimacy of the other's interests and of the need to search for a solution that is responsive to the needs of each party
3. Fosters mutual respect and sensitivity to similarities and common interests, stimulating a comergence of positions[102]

The way in which police leaders will handle conflict is to some extent bound up in their leadership styles. Various methods for resolving conflict are summarized in Table 6-4. Each of the various methods identified may be appropriate or inappropriate at various times; to return to an earlier point, good diagnostic ability and flexibility are central attributes for leaders.

## LEADERSHIP AND ORGANIZATIONAL CONTROL

Because police leaders are responsible for the performance of their departments, they must be concerned with organizational control and organizational controls. *Organizational control* is synonymous with organizational direction and is normative, dealing with the future. In contrast, *organizational controls* consist of measurements of, information about, and analysis of what was and is.[103] Stated more simply, controls pertain to the means, control pertains to an end.[104]

Of necessity, the issues of organizational control and controls permeate police departments. Despite the definitions given, practical distinctions between them require some thought. For example, planning, budget preparation, and the written directive system of a police department—consisting of policies, procedures, and rules and regulations—are all control devices in that they all deal with preferred future states, positions, and behaviors. However, when an officer violates a rule and disciplinary measures are invoked, the system of controls is in operation. During the execution of a budget, a midyear review occurs in which performance over the first six months is summarized and analyzed and plans are made for the remaining six months. Thus, this midyear review incorporates features of the system of organizational controls and control. Similarly, quarterly evaluations of police programs incorporate features of the system of controls and control, whereas the final program evaluation report is in the main part of the system of controls. Despite such variations, it is apparent that informed control is a function of the system of controls.

To give the police leader control, controls must satisfy the following specifications:

1. They must be specific and economical.
2. They must be meaningful, relating to significant events.
3. They must use the appropriate indicators.
4. They must be timely.
5. Their limitations must be understood.
6. They must be as simple as possible.
7. They must be directed to those who can take the necessary action.[105]

Perhaps paradoxically, the tighter he or she attempts to control unilaterally, the less control a police leader actually has. A simple illustration of this point is taking a handful of sand and squeezing it forcefully; a great deal trickles out and is lost. Alternatively, the same amount of sand cupped loosely in the hand remains in place. By involving others, by sharing power, the police leader secures the greatest amount of control because individual commitment —the best and most effective type of control—is secured.

## SUMMARY

All police managers must be sensitive to their three main responsibilities: (1) contributing to the fulfillment of the department's mission, (2) ensuring that the effort of subordinates is productive and that they are achieving, and (3) producing impacts on their areas of responsibility. Meeting these key responsibilities effectively requires that the police managers practice certain "habits of mind," such as employing their time wisely, building on the strengths that they and their subordinates have, and concentrating on the results to be achieved rather than on the units of work to be accomplished.

Whereas leadership can be seen as the qualities displayed by an individual or as the function of a position, such as major, within a police department, a generally accepted definition is that leadership is the process of influencing the members of an organization to employ appropriately and willingly their energies in activities that are helpful to the achievement of the police department's goals. "Influencing" and "willingly" are related to the concepts of authority and power. In the main, authority is a grant made from above by the formal organization, whereas power is a grant made from below, being confirmed on the leader by the led. However, one

should not infer that those who have authority do not also have some power, for the bestowing of authority is accompanied inherently by at least some power.

Leaders at various levels of a police department have different blends of skills that they predominately employ. Human relations, conceptual, and technical are the three major types of skills that are employed in this skill mix. As one advances up the rank hierarchy of a police department, which can be organized under three groupings—first-line supervisors, middle managers, and top managers—the relative emphasis and importance of the three skills shift.

Leadership theories essentially try to establish what variables are related to the emergence of leadership or the nature of leadership itself. Illustrative are (1) great man and genetic theories associated variously with Carlyle, Hegel, and Galton; (2) the traits approach, which has historically enjoyed great appeal; (3) behavioral explanations, which center on what a leader does; and (4) situational statements, which maintain that effective leadership is the result of a good fit between the capabilities of a leader and the demands of a given condition.

The abundance of interest in the subject of leadership has produced alternative ways of classifying leadership styles. Schemes treated in this chapter include (1) authoritarian, democratic, and laissez-faire leaders; (2) the authoritarian-democratic continuum; (3) leader styles in bureaucratic structures; (4) traditional versus nontraditional police leaders; (5) station house versus street sergeants; (6) Managerial Grid styles; (7) situational leadership; (8) transactional and transformational leadership; and (9) total quality leadership.

A significant element of organizational life with which the police manager must deal is conflict, defined as a situation in which at least two parties have a mutual difference of position and in which one party employs or threatens behavior through the exercise of power to obtain control of the situation at the expense of the other party. Although the presence of conflict is often viewed as being undesirable, the absence of it is certainly unhealthy. Fundamental to any understanding of conflict is that the way in which it is handled is more a determinant of the "goodness" or "badness" of conflict rather than of any inherent characteristic of conflict itself. Leader styles may have certain pronounced preferences or tendencies for the way in which conflict is addressed; for example, the 9,1 style can be related to the use of power as a method of resolving conflict.

Organizational control and organizational controls are the devices by which the police manager shapes the course and events for the department. Organizational control and organizational direction can be equated usefully, and they are normative, futuristic statements. Measurements of, information about, and analysis of the past and present states are termed *organizational controls.* Organizational control and controls are differentiated further in that the former is a preferred state to be achieved, whereas the latter are the means of achieving that preferred state.

## DISCUSSION QUESTIONS

1. What is a generally accepted definition of *leadership?*

2. What are the definitions of *authority* and *power,* and how are they related?

3. What distinctions can be made between personalized and social power?

4. Within the skill mix, which skill is most essential to top management? Why?

5. The traits approach to leadership has enjoyed great popularity. What is it and what evidence is there to support it?

6. What differences are there among authoritarian, democratic, and laissez-faire leaders?

7. What are the two key dimensions and five principal styles of the Managerial Grid?

8. Compare Burns's transactional and transformational leaders.

9. There are five major components to TQL. Identify and briefly discuss the salient points of each component.

10. Why is TQL a natural adjunct to COP?

11. Can a police department implement TQL without implementing COP?

12. What is conflict, and is it good or bad for organizations?

13. Are there any differences between organizational control and controls? If so, what?

## NOTES

1. Peter F. Drucker, *People and Performance: The Best of Peter Drucker on Management* (New York: Harper's College Press, 1977), p. 28.

2. Patrick A. Knight and Howard M. Weiss, "Effects of Selection Agent and Leader Origin on Leader Influence and Group Member Perceptions," *Organizational Behavior and Human Performance,* 26 (August 1980), 17–21. Also, see Thomas Henderson, "The Relative Effects of Community Complexity and of Sheriffs Upon the Professionalism of Sheriff Departments," *American Journal of Political Science,* 19 (February 1975), 126.

3. Peter F. Drucker, *The Effective Executive* (New York: Harper & Row, 1966), p. 23 and pp. 36–39. Points 2 to 5 were taken from this source at page 24. Also see Eugene Raudsepp, "Why Managers Don't Delegate," *Journal of Applied Management,* 4:5 (1979), 25–27.

4. Jacques Steinberg, "Police Officer Rejects Promotion," *The New York Times,* June 2, 1991.

5. The flip side of the coin is the question, "Under what conditions do organizational members voluntarily elect to leave, stay and protest, or simply stay?" An important book addressing these issues

is Albert O. Hirschman, *Exit, Voice, and Loyalty* (Cambridge, Mass.: Harvard University Press, 1970).

6. The description of power motivation styles is drawn, with restatement into a police context, from Jay Hall and James Hawker, "Interpreting Your Scores from the Power Management Inventory" (The Woodlands, Texas: Teleometrics International, 1981).

7. Variants of this model appear in the literature; see, for example, Ronald G. Lynch, *The Police Manager,* 2nd ed. (Boston: Holbrook Press, 1978), Figure 1-2, p. 11; Calvin J. Swank, "Police Management in the United States: A Candid Assessment," *Journal of Police Science and Administration,* 4 (1976), 90–93; and Robert Katz, "Skills of an Effective Administrator," *Harvard Business Review,* 33:1 (1955), 33–42.

8. Ralph M. Stogdill, *Handbook of Leadership: A Survey of Theory and Research* (New York: Free Press, 1974), p. 17.

9. Thomas Carlyle, *Heroes, Hero-Worship and the Heroic in History* (New York: A. L. Burt, 1902) and G. W. F. Hegel, *The Philosophy of History* (Indianapolis: Bobbs-Merrill Company, Inc., 1952).

10. Francis Galton, *Hereditary Genius: An Inquiry into Its Laws and Consequences* (New York: D. Appleton, revised with an American preface, 1887).

11. Field Marshal Montgomery, *The Path to Leadership* (New York: Putnam, 1961), pp. 10–19. To some extent, Montgomery also holds with Carlyle in that the former asserted that the leader must be able to dominate and master the surrounding events.

12. Cecil E. Goode, "Significant Research on Leadership," *Personnel,* 25:5 (1951), 349.

13. Stogdill, *Handbook of Leadership,* p. 81, and "Personal Factors Associated with Leadership: A Survey of the Literature," *Journal of Psychology,* 25–26 (January 1948), 35–71.

14. C. A. Gibb, "Leadership," in *Handbook of Sound Psychology,* Vol. 2, ed. Gardner Lindzey (Reading, Mass.: Addison-Wesley, 1954).

15. Walter J. Palmer, "Managerial Effectiveness as a Function of Personality Traits of the Manager," *Personnel Psychology,* 27 (Summer 1974), 283–95.

16. Gary Dessler, *Organization and Management: A Contingency Approach* (Englewood Cliffs, N.J.: Prentice Hall, 1976), p. 158.

17. Stogdill, "Personal Factors," pp. 35–71; Dessler, *Organization and Management,* p. 169.

18. F. E. Fiedler, *A Theory of Leadership Effectiveness* (New York: McGraw-Hill, 1967). Fiedler has worked on a contingency approach to leadership since the early 1950s.

19. Robert J. House, "A Path–Goal Theory of Leader Effectiveness," *Administrative Science Quarterly,* 16 (September 1971), 321–38.

20. See K. Lewin, R. Lippitt, and R. White, "Patterns of Aggressive Behavior in Experimentally Created Social Climates," *Journal of Social Psychology,* 10 (May 1939), 271–99; R. Lippitt and R. K. White, "The Social Climate of Children's Groups," in *Child Behavior and Development,* ed. R. G. Baker, K. S. Kounin, and H. F. Wright (New York: McGraw-Hill, 1943), pp. 485–508; Ralph White and Ronald Lippitt, "Leader Behavior and Member Reaction in Three Social Climates," in *Group Dynamics: Research and Theory,* 2nd ed., ed. Dorwin Cartwright and Alvin Zander (New York: Harper & Row, 1960), pp. 552–553; Ronald Lippitt, "An Experimental Study of the Effect of Democratic and Authoritarian Group Atmospheres," *University of Iowa Studies in Childwelfare,* 16 (January 1940), 43–195.

21. White and Lippitt, "Leader Behavior," pp. 539–545 and 552–553.

22. Robert Tannenbaum and Warren H. Schmidt, "How to Choose a Leadership Pattern," *Harvard Business Review,* 36:2 (1958), 95–101.

23. Ibid., 98–101.

24. Anthony Downs, *Inside Bureaucracy* (Boston: Little, Brown, 1967).

25. Ibid., pp. 92–96.

26. Ibid., pp. 96–101.

27. Ibid., pp. 109–110.

28. Ibid., pp. 107–109.

29. John Van Maanen, "Making Rank: Becoming an American Police Sergeant," *Urban Life,* 13:2–3 (1984), 155–176. The distinction between station and street sergeants is drawn from Van Maanen's work with some restatement and extension of views. The speculation about future career patterns is the work of the present authors.

30. Robert R. Blake and Jane Srygley Mouton, "The Development Revolution in Management Practices," *Journal of the American Society of Training Directors,* 16:7 (1962), pp. 29–52.

31. The Ohio State studies date from the mid-1940s and identified the dimensions of consideration and structure; the University of Michigan studies date from the late 1940s and identified employee- and production-centered supervisors.

32. Paul Hersey and Kenneth H. Blanchard, *Management of Organizational Behavior: Utilizing Human Resources,* 3rd ed. (Englewood Cliffs, N.J.:

Prentice Hall, 1977), p. 105. Also, see William J. Reddin, *Managerial Effectiveness* (New York: McGraw-Hill, 1970).

33. Hersey and Blanchard, *Management of Organizational Behavior,* pp. 160–61.

34. Ibid., p. 161.

35. Ibid., p. 161.

36. Ibid., p. 163.

37. Ibid., p. 161.

38. Ibid., p. 163.

39. Ibid., p. 162.

40. Ibid., p. 168.

41. Ibid., p. 165.

42. Ibid., p. 168.

43. Ibid., p. 159.

44. James McGregor Burns, *Leadership* (New York: Harper & Row, 1978). For an excellent overview on leadership, see Edwin P. Hollander and Lynn R. Offermann, "Power and Leadership in Organizations: Relationship in Transition," *American Psychologist,* 45:2 (1990), 179–89.

45. Ibid., pp. 4, 19–20.

46. Ibid., p. 426.

47. Noel Tichy and David O. Ulrich, "The Leadership Challenge: A Call for The Transformational Leader," *Sloan Management Review,* 26:1 (Fall 1984), 59–68.

48. B. M. Bass, *Leadership and Performance Beyond Expectations* (New York: Free Press, 1985).

49. Warren Bennis and Bert Nanus, *Leaders* (New York: Harper & Row, 1985).

50. James M. Kouzes and Barry Z. Posner, *The Leadership Challenge: How to Get Extraordinary Things Done in Organizations* (San Francisco: Jossey-Bass, 1987), p. 38. This book does not focus on the police; hence, the authors have taken the liberty of writing its important lessons into the police context.

51. Ibid., p. 29.

52. Ibid.

53. Ibid.

54. Ibid.

55. Ibid., p. 79.

56. Ibid.

57. Ibid.

58. Ibid.

59. Ibid., p. 108.

60. Ibid., p. 79.

61. Ibid.

62. Ibid., p. 131.

63. Ibid., p. 155.

64. Ibid., pp. 159–160.

65. Ibid., p. 162.

66. Ibid., pp. 162–163.

67. Ibid., p. 131.

68. Ibid., p. 131.

69. Ibid., p. 175.

70. Ibid., p. 190.

71. Ibid., pp. 220–221.

72. Ibid., p. 245.

73. Stephen J. Harrison, "Quality Policing and the Challenges for Leadership," *The Police Chief,* 63:1 (January 1996), 26.

74. Ibid.

75. Ibid.

76. Ibid.

77. David Couper and Sabine Lobitz, "Leadership for Change: A National Agenda," *The Police Chief,* 60:12 (December 1993), 18.

78. Allen W. Cole, "Better Customer Focus: TQM and Law Enforcement," *The Police Chief,* 60:12 (December 1993), 23.

79. Robert Galloway and Laurie A. Fitzgerald, "Service Quality in Policing," *The FBI Law Enforcement Bulletin,* 61:11 (November 1992), 3, quoting A. C. Rosander, *The Quest for Quality in Services* (Milwaukee, Wis.: ASQC Quality Press, 1989).

80. Harrison, "Quality Policing and the Challenges for Leadership," is the general source for this discussion, although footnotes contained in the five-point discussion of TQL have been added by the present authors. Additionally, we have inserted our own views into Harrison's framework.

81. Ibid., pp. 26–27.

82. Ibid., p. 28.

83. Ibid.

84. Ibid.

85. Ibid.

86. Ibid., p. 31.

87. Ibid.

88. Ibid., pp. 31–32. Also see Sheila Berglund, "Employee Empowerment," *The FBI Law Enforcement Bulletin,* 62:12 (December 1993), 5–8.

89. Federal Government Accounting Office Report GAO/GGD-93-9BR, October 1992, p. 40.

90. David C. Couper and Sabine Lobitz, *The Quality Leadership Workbook* (February 1993), p. 55. No other publishing information is on this document.

91. Harrison, "Quality Policing and the Challenges for Leadership," p. 32.

92. Federal Government Accounting Office, "Management Practices: U. S. Companies Improve Performance Through Quality Efforts," NSIAD-91-190.

93. Galloway and Fitzgerald, "Service Quality in Policing," 3.

94. Couper and Lobitz, "Leadership for Change," 15, with the addition of the first point.

95. Galloway and Fitzgerald, "Service Quality in Policing," 4.

96. Ibid.

97. Albert E. Roark and Linda Wilkinson, "Approaches to Conflict Management," *Group and Organizational Studies,* 4 (December 1979), 441.

98. Ibid.

99. Ibid., p. 440; on this point, also see Kenneth Thomas, "Conflict and Conflict Management," in *Handbook of Industrial and Organizational Psychology,* ed. Marvin D. Dunnette (Chicago: Rand McNally, 1976), p. 889.

100. See Lewis A. Coser, *The Functions of Social Conflict* (Glenco, Ill.: Free Press, 1956); G. Simmel, *Conflict* (New York: Free Press, 1955); and M. Deutsch, "Toward an Understanding of Conflict," *International Journal of Group Tensions,* 1:1 (1971), p. 48.

101. Morton Deutsch, *The Resolution of Conflict* (New Haven, Conn.: Yale University Press, 1973), p. 353.

102. Ibid., p. 363.

103. Peter F. Drucker, *Management: Tasks, Responsibilities, Practices* (New York: Harper & Row, 1973), p. 494.

104. Ibid.

105. Ibid., pp. 496–505.

## INTRODUCTION

Effective communication is essential in all organizations in which people deal with one another. It is very difficult to imagine any kind of activity that does not depend on communication in one form or another. Today's police managers are aware that the efficiency of their personnel depends to a great extent on how well the efforts of individual members can be coordinated. Because coordination does not simply happen, managers must realize that communication is necessary if their subordinates are to obtain the understanding and cooperation required to achieve organizational and individual goals.

A major role of today's manager is that of communicator. Managers at all levels of the police organization spend an overwhelming amount of their time in the process and problems of communication.

Research in recent years has indicated that communication is the number one problem in management, and lack of communication is the employees' primary complaint about their immediate supervisors.[1] The information in this chapter is intended to provide police managers with an overview of both organization and interpersonal communications and provide specific information that will facilitate and enhance their communication skills.

# —7—

# ORGANIZATIONAL AND INTERPERSONAL COMMUNICATION

*The difference between the right word and the almost right word is the difference between lightning and lightning bug.*

MARK TWAIN

## THE COMMUNICATION PROCESS

An explanation of communication begins with a basic problem—it cannot be examined as an isolated event. Communication is a process, and so it must be understood as the totality of several interdependent and dynamic elements. In the aggregate, communications may be defined as the process by which senders and receivers interact in given social contexts. Another understanding of this definition is that the process of communication requires that we examine the several elements that make up the process; encoding, transmission, medium, reception, decoding, and feedback.[2] Figure 7-1 illustrates this process graphically.

**Encoding**—Experience cannot be transmitted as experience. In conveying an experience to another person, we do not relive that experience with that person. Even in the most scrupulous reproduction of an experience, every element cannot be duplicated. At the very least, the time period is altered, and intervening experiences have altered us as individuals.

To convey an experience or idea to someone, we translate, or encode, that experience into symbols. We use words or other verbal behaviors and gestures, or other nonverbal behaviors to convey the experience or idea. These symbols are our code; they stand for certain experiences; they are not experiences themselves.

**Transmission**—Encoding involves only the decision to use a symbol for some concept. The element of transmission involves the translation of the encoded symbols into some behavior that another person can observe. The actual

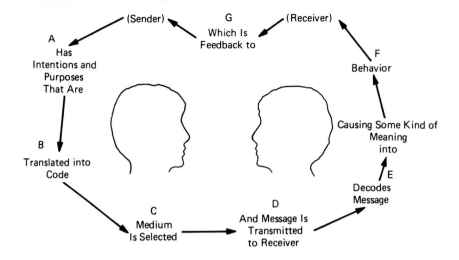

A. The sender has certain intentions, objectives, or purposes.

B. The sender translated these intentions into some code (language, nonverbal gesture, etc.), which becomes the message.

C. The sender then selects a medium (written or spoken words, music, art, etc.).

D. The sender uses the medium to transmit the message to the receiver.

E. The receiver "picks up" the message (listens, reads, watches, etc.) and decodes its meaning.

F. This meaning causes the receiver to behave in some manner.

G. This behavior gives the sender indications, or feedback, as to whether or not the receiver understood the meaning of the message.

**FIGURE 7-1.** The communication process. [From R. C. Huseman, "The Communication Process," in *Interpersonal Communication: A Guide for Staff Development* (Athens: Institute of Government, University of Georgia, August 1974), p. 22.]

articulation (moving our lips, tongue, etc.) of the symbol into verbal or non-verbal observable behavior is transmission.

**Medium**—Communication must be conveyed through some channel or medium. Media for communication may be our sight, hearing, taste, touch, or smell. Some other media are television, telephone, paper and pencil, computer, and radio. The importance of the choice of the medium should not be minimized. All of us are aware of the difference between a message that our superior delivers personally and the one that is sent through a secretary or by a memo. The medium, like the chosen symbol, has an effect on the meaning that the listener eventually attaches to the message in the process of decoding.

**Reception**—For the receiver, the reception of the message is analogous to the sender's transmission. The stimuli, the verbal and nonverbal symbols, reach the senses of the receiver and are conveyed to the brain for interpretation.

**Decoding**—The process of interpretation occurs when the individual who has received the stimuli develops some meaning for the verbal and nonverbal symbols and decodes the stimuli. For the receiver, then, decoding is analogous to the process of encoding for the sender. These symbols are translated into some concept or experience of the receiver. Whether the receiver is familiar with the symbols, or whether interference such as any physical noise or physiological problem occurs, determines how closely the message that the receiver has decoded approximates the message that the sender has encoded. The success of the communication process depends on the extent to which the receiver's decoded concept is similar to the concept of the sender. It is for this reason that we hear the phrase, "meaning is in people." Truly, the external verbal and nonverbal symbols that we usually call the message are in fact only stimuli. The actual message is the decoded or interpreted concept of the receiver. This decoded concept is the receiver's meaning for the external stimuli.

**Feedback**—When the receiver decodes the transmitted symbols, he or she usually provides some response or feedback to the sender. Feedback is a self-correcting mechanism. In our homes, thermostats, self-correcting mechanisms within the heating or cooling unit, will correct the temperature. In communication, responses to the symbols that we have sent act as regulators. If someone appears puzzled, we repeat the message or we encode the concept differently and transmit some different symbols to express the same concept. Feedback that we receive acts as a guide or steering device. Feedback promotes accuracy of communication. Feedback lets us know whether the receiver has interpreted our symbols as we intended. Feedback is, then, a crucial element in guaranteeing that the meaning that the sender intended to convey was in fact conveyed to the receiver.

- It is more effective to present both sides of an issue.
- Listeners tend to remember beginning and ends of presentations.
- Conclusions should be explicitly stated.
- Repetition in messages leads to increased acceptance.
- The most remembered messages arouse a need and then satisfy it.
- An emphasis on desirability of obtaining agreements helps facilitate agreement.

**General Observations Relative to the Content of the Message and its Appeal**

### The Communicator

The credibility of the communicator tends to be enhanced by:

- Past experience and reputation
- Professional and academic credentials acquired
- Recommendations by those who are respected regarding their reputation and accomplishments
- Public relations

### Selecting the Appropriate Media

- Sometimes when presenting a message, many different media can be employed.
- In some cases the media may have more of an impact on the audience than the verbal message content.
- The media can also distort the message.

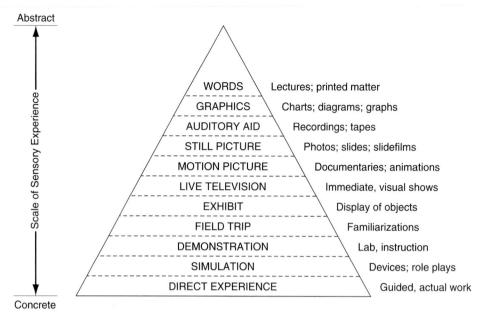

Abstract

Concrete

Scale of Sensory Experience

| | |
|---|---|
| WORDS | Lectures; printed matter |
| GRAPHICS | Charts; diagrams; graphs |
| AUDITORY AID | Recordings; tapes |
| STILL PICTURE | Photos; slides; slidefilms |
| MOTION PICTURE | Documentaries; animations |
| LIVE TELEVISION | Immediate, visual shows |
| EXHIBIT | Display of objects |
| FIELD TRIP | Familiarizations |
| DEMONSTRATION | Lab, instruction |
| SIMULATION | Devices; role plays |
| DIRECT EXPERIENCE | Guided, actual work |

**FIGURE 7-2.** Scale of sensory perception.

- Audiences tend to respond to messages that provide a reward and help retain a balance between their actual lives and their role perceptions.
- Remember that the audience to whom a message is being presented may not necessarily be homogeneous in terms of their attitudes, emotions, or values.

The more senses that are engaged in transmitting information, the more likely the message will be understood and remembered. Figure 7-2 displays a scale of sensory perception.

## COMMUNICATION BARRIERS

Barriers to communication, or communication breakdowns, can occur at any place in the system. They may be the result of improper techniques on the part of either the sender or the receiver.

### Sender-Caused Barriers

The sender hinders communications when

1. The sender is not clear about what is to be accomplished with the message.
2. The sender assumes incorrectly that the receiver has the knowledge necessary to understand the message and its intent and does not adapt the message to the intended receiver.
3. The sender uses a communication medium not suited for the message; for example, some messages are better transmitted face to face, others in writing or by illustrations.
4. The sender does not develop a mechanism for receiving feedback to determine if the message was understood correctly.

5. The sender does not interpret feedback correctly or fails to clarify the message on the basis of feedback from the receiver.
6. The sender uses language that causes the receiver to stop listening, reading, or receiving.
7. The sender analyzes the audience improperly.
8. The sender's background, experiences, and attitudes are different from those of the receiver, and the sender does not take this into account.

### Receiver-Caused Barriers

The receiver hinders communication when

1. The receiver is a poor listener, observer, or reader and therefore misinterprets the meaning of the message.
2. The receiver jumps to conclusions.
3. The receiver hears or sees only certain parts of the message.
4. The receiver tends to reject messages that contradict beliefs and assumptions.
5. The receiver has other concerns or emotional barriers, such as being mentally preoccupied.

### Other Barriers

Some other barriers to communication are

1. Noise, temperature, and other physical distractions
2. Distance or inability to see or hear the message being sent
3. Sender–receiver relationship, power structure, roles, and personality differences

## ORGANIZATIONAL COMMUNICATION

Organizational systems of communication are usually created by setting up formal systems of responsibility and explicit delegations of duties, such as implicit statements of the nature, content, and direction of communication that are necessary for the performance of the group. Consequently, formal communication is required by the organization and follows the accepted pattern of hierarchical structure. Delegated authority and responsibility determine the path that communication should take, whether upward or downward. Messages that travel through the formal channels of any organization may follow routine patterns; they may be expected at a given time, or presented in a standard form, and receive a regularized degree of consideration.[3]

Most police managers prefer a formal system, regardless of how cumbersome it may be, because they can control it and because it tends to create a record for future reference. However, motivational factors of the individual and organizations affect the flow of communication. Employees typically communicate with those who help them to achieve their aims and avoid communicating with those who do not assist, or may retard, their accomplishing those goals. They direct their communications toward those who make them feel more secure and gratify their needs and away from those who threaten or make them feel anxious or generally provide unrewarding experiences. In addition, employees communicate in a manner that allows them to increase their status, belong to a more prestigious group, attain more power to influence decisions, or expand their control. The moving transaction identified as organizational communication can occur at several levels and can result in understanding, agreement, good feeling, and appropriate behavior; the converse may also be true.[4]

**Downward Communication**

Classical management theories place primary emphasis on control, chain of command, and downward flow of information. Downward communication is used by management for sending orders, directives, goals, policies, procedures, memorandums, and so forth to employees at lower levels of the organization. Five types of such communication within an organization can be identified.[5]

1. Job instruction—communication relating to the performance of a certain task
2. Job rationale—communication relating a certain task to organizational tasks
3. Procedures and practices—communication about organization policies, procedures, rules, and regulations
4. Feedback—communication appraisal of how an individual performs the assigned task
5. Indoctrination—communication designed to motivate the employee[6]

Other reasons for communicating downward implicit in this listing are opportunities for management to spell out objectives, change attitudes and mold opinions, prevent misunderstandings from lack of information, and prepare employees for change.[7] A study conducted by Opinion Research Corporation some years ago revealed surprisingly that large amounts of information generated at the top of an organization did not filter down to the working levels. Studies of the flow of communications within complex organizations repeatedly demonstrate that each level of management can act as an obstacle or barrier to downward communication.[8] In perhaps the best controlled experimental research in downward communication, Dahle[9] proved the efficacy of using oral and written media together. His findings indicate the following order of effectiveness (from most effective to least effective):

1. Oral and written communication combined
2. Oral communication only
3. Written communication only
4. The bulletin board
5. The organizational grapevine

The research conducted thus far seems to indicate that most downward channels in organizations are only minimally effective. Findings indicate further that attempts at disseminating information downward in an organization should not depend exclusively on a single medium or channel.

**Upward Communication**

Even though police administrators may appreciate the need for effective upward communication, they may not translate this need into action.[10] It becomes apparent at once that to swim upstream is a much harder task than to float downstream. But currents of resistance, inherent in the temperament and habits of supervisors and employees in the complexity and structure of modern police agencies, are persistent and strong. Let us examine some of these deterrents to upward communication.

The physical distance between superior and subordinate impedes upward communication in several ways. Communication becomes difficult and infrequent when superiors are isolated so as to be seldom seen or spoken to. In large police organizations, executives may be located in headquarters or operating centers that are not easily reached by subordinates. In other police agencies, executive offices may be placed remotely or executives may hold themselves needlessly inaccessible.

The complexity of the organization may also cause prolonged delays of upward communication. For example, let us assume that a problem at the patrol officer level must be settled eventually by the chief executive or some other high-ranking officer. A patrol officer tells the sergeant about the problem, and they discuss it and try to settle it. It may take several hours or even a couple of days before all the available facts are compiled. The sergeant in turn brings the problem to the lieutenant, who feels compelled to reexamine all the facts of the problem and perhaps pursue it even further before forwarding it on to the next highest authority. Because each succeeding superior may be concerned that the problem could somehow reflect negatively on his or her ability, delays result that could mean that the problem is not brought to the attention of the chief executive for several weeks. In addition, as the information moves up the organizational ladder, there is a tendency for it to be diluted or distorted, as each supervisor consciously or unconsciously selects and edits information being passed up. The more levels of supervision the information passes through, the more it is filtered and the less accurate it becomes.

The attitude of superiors and their behavior in listening play a vital role in encouraging or discouraging communication upward. If, in listening to a subordinate, a supervisor seems anxious to end the interview, impatient with the subordinate, or annoyed or distressed by the subject being discussed, a major barrier to future communication may be created.

There is always the danger that a supervisor may assume the posture that "no news is good news," when in fact a lack of complaints or criticism may be a symptom that upward communication is operating at a dangerously low level.

Supervisors may also assume, often incorrectly, that they know what subordinates think or feel and also believe that listening to complaints from subordinates, especially complaints about departmental policies or even specific supervisors, is an indication of disloyalty. This attitude tends to discourage employees with justifiable complaints from approaching their superiors.

One of the strongest deterrents to upward communication is a failure of management to take action on undesirable conditions previously brought to their attention. The result is that subordinates lose faith both in the sincerity of management and in the value of communication.

Some executives feel that they are too involved in daily problems and responsibilities to provide adequate time for listening fully to their subordinates' ideas, reports, and criticism. Nevertheless, many time-consuming problems could be minimized or eliminated if superiors would take time to listen to their employees, for in listening they can discover solutions to present problems or anticipate causes for future ones. The subordinate who has free access to a superior can get answers to many budding problems and thus eliminate the heavier demands that will result when the problems have become much more complex, emotion laden, and possibly even out of control.

## Barriers Involving Subordinates

Communication may flow more freely downward than upward because a superior is free to call in a subordinate and talk about a problem at will. The subordinate does not have the same freedom to intrude on the superior's time and is also discouraged from circumventing the chain of command and going over a superior's head or from asking for an appeal from decisions made by superiors. Thus, neither the system available nor the rewards offered to the subordinate for upward communication equal those for downward messages.

Management, on the other hand, can speed the flow of information by the use of written policies, procedures, general orders, meetings, and so forth. There are rarely comparable organizational vehicles available for the upward flow of communications. Further, tradition, authority, and prestige are behind downward communications.

In communicating upward, a subordinate must provide explanations for the desired communication and, in the final analysis, must obtain acceptance from someone with greater status who is also likely to be more fluent and persuasive than the subordinate. The superior probably has worked in a similar position at one time and knows the attitudes, language, and problems at that level. On the other hand, the subordinate who is communicating with a superior rarely understands the responsibilities or difficulties the superior faces.

Finally, unless superiors are particularly receptive, subordinates generally prefer to withhold or temper bad news, unfavorable opinions, and reports of mistakes or failures. If a manager is defensive about listening to bad news, those who like and respect the manager will withhold information or minimize omissions and errors from friendly motives; others may withhold information from fear, dislike, or indifference.

## Horizontal Communication

When an organization's formal communication channels are not open, the informal horizontal channels are almost sure to thrive as a substitute.[11] If there is a disadvantage in horizontal communication, it is that it is much easier and more natural to achieve than vertical communication and, therefore, often replaces vertical channels rather than supplements them. Actually, the horizontal channels that replace weak or nonexistent vertical channels are usually of an informal nature. There are, of course, formal horizontal channels that are procedurally necessary and should be built into the system. Formal horizontal channels must be set up between various bureaus and divisions for the purposes of planning, interwork task coordination, and general system maintenance functions, such as problem solving, information sharing, and conflict resolution.

We can begin by acknowledging that horizontal communication is essential if the subsystems within a police organization are to function in an effective and coordinated manner. Horizontal communication among peers may also furnish the emotional and social bond that builds esprit de corps or a feeling of teamwork. Psychologically, people seem to need this type of communication, and police managers would do well to provide for this need and thus allow peers to solve some of their own work problems together.

Suppose, for example, that patrol sergeant A is having great difficulty communicating certain mutually beneficial information to detective sergeant B because the police department requires strict adherence to the chain of command in transmitting information. As indicated in Figure 7-3A, sergeant A would have to go up through the various hierarchical complexities of the patrol division and back down through the detective division to communicate with sergeant B. The time being wasted and the level-to-level message distortion occurring in the classically managed organization was recognized by Fayol[12] in 1916. Fayol pro-

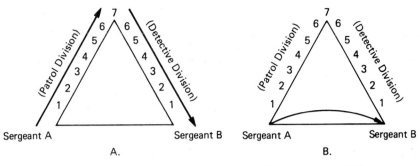

**FIGURE 7-3.** Horizontal lines of communication: A. Message path from sergeant A to sergeant B following the usual structured channels. B. Message path from segeant A to sergeant B following Fayol's bridge.

posed the creation of a horizontal bridge (see Figure 7-3B) that would allow more direct communications between individuals within an organization. The major limiting factor to the use of Fayol's bridge is a loss of network control and the subsequent weakening of authority and random scattering of messages throughout the system. Such random communication channels can lead to diagonal lines of communication, such as direct communication between sergeant A in the patrol division and sergeant B in the detective division. Diagonal lines of communication are not in and of themselves bad; however, they are very difficult to control from the management point of view.[13]

Despite the need for formal horizontal communication in an organization, there may be tendency among peers not to formally communicate task-related information horizontally. For instance, rivalry for recognition and promotion may cause competing subordinates to be reluctant to share information. Subordinates may also find it difficult to communicate with highly specialized people at the same level as themselves in other divisions.

In the main, then, formal horizontal communication channels are vital as a supplement to the vertical channels in an organization. Conversely, the informal horizontal channels, although socially necessary, can be detrimental to the vertical channels. Informal horizontal channels may not only carry false or distorted information but sometimes tend to replace the vertical channels.[14]

**The Grapevine**

The best-known system for transmitting informal communication is the grapevine, so called because it meanders back and forth like a grapevine across organizational lines. The grapevine's most effective characteristics are that it is fast, it can be highly selective and discriminating, it operates mostly at the place of work, and it supplements and relates to formal communication. These characteristics may be divided into desirable or undesirable attributes.

The grapevine can be considered desirable because it gives management insight into employees' attitudes, provides a safety valve for employees' emotions, and helps to spread useful information. Dysfunctional traits include its tendencies to spread rumors and untruths, its lack of responsibility to any group or person, and its uncontrollability. Attributes of the grapevine, its speed and influence, may work either to the good or to the detriment of the organization. The actual operation of the grapevine can be visualized in four ways (see Figure 7-4).[15]

1. The single-strand chain: A tells B, who tells C, who tells D, and so on.
2. The gossip chain: A seeks and tells everyone else, thus being the organizational "Paul Revere."

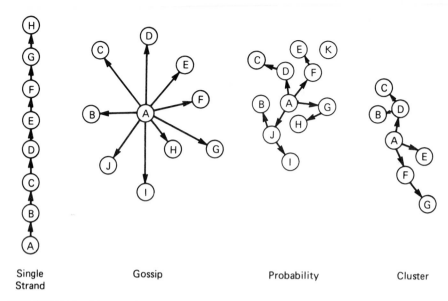

| Single Strand | Gossip | Probability | Cluster |

**FIGURE 7-4.** Types of communication grapevines. [From H. H. Albers, *Organized Executive Action: Decision Making and Leadership* (New York: John Wiley, 1961), p. 343.]

3. The probability chain: A communicates randomly to D, F, G, and J, in accord with the laws of probability; then D, F, G, and J tell others in the same manner.
4. The cluster chain: A tells three selected others; perhaps one of them tells two others; and one of these tells one other person.

The grapevine is a permanent factor to be reckoned with in the daily activities of management, and no competent manager would try to abolish it. Rather, the astute manager should analyze it and consciously try to influence it.[16]

**Communication Network Analysis**

One of the most effective methods of understanding organizational communication is through network analysis, a tool used to understand the pathways that communication takes in an organization. Networks are defined as individuals linked by patterned flows of information.[17] Network analysis provides a picture of human interaction in an organization. Information about who talks to whom can be obtained from each organizational member. When assembled from all members, a map emerges, taking the form of a total organizational sociogram. This map is the history of the communication process in an organization, and it is possible to locate each individual within that structure.

To show how network analysis might be used as a tool for communication assessment, we first describe communication network roles and then define "favorable communication climate," since it is assumed that a favorable climate is desired by all.

**Communication Network Roles**

Networks can be conceptualized as the regular, work-related, interpersonal patterns established between pairs of individuals in organizations.[18] More precisely, it is possible to separate groups of communicators and to classify all organizational members in various roles. Figure 7-5 shows various roles that exist in a communication network, such as *cosmopolites* (who relate the organization to its environment by providing openness); *isolates* (those who

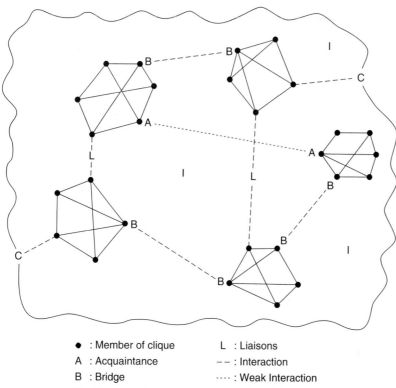

|  |  |
|---|---|
| ● : Member of clique | L : Liaisons |
| A : Acquaintance | – – : Interaction |
| B : Bridge | ···· : Weak Interaction |
| C : Cosmopolites | — : Strong Interaction |
| I : Isolates | |

**FIGURE 7-5.** This figure displays various organizational communication roles that result from communication network analysis. [*Source: OMEGA—Journal of Technical Writing and Communication,* Vol. 22(1)(1992), p. 97, "A Network Approach to Formulating Communications Strategy" by Patricia Karathanos and M. Diane Pettypool. Copyright Baywood Publishing Company, Inc.]

are not part of a network); *bridges* (who are members of a clique and link it with another); and *liaisons* (who link two or more cliques without being a member of a clique). An analysis of this communication network might provide understanding of an organization's communication climate.

Although organizational climate and communication climate are interdependent and inseparable, a distinction should be made between them. Much of the organization communication literature addresses the communication climate. The communication climate is generally seen as a composite of the following:[19]

## Communication Climate

- Supportive communication (responsiveness of higher levels to information from lower levels);
- Quality and accuracy of downward information;
- Superior–subordinate openness of communication;
- Upward communication (the extent to which messages are acknowledged and acted upon); and
- Information reliability.

The organizational climate must be considered a systemwide construct and must consider such things as technological readiness (the use of state-of-the-art work processes) and motivation climate (the extent to which policies and practices encourage personnel to perform). This differentiation is notable when one is considering ways to understand an organization's communication climate. Climate inventories, for example, measure perceptions of the *communication climate,* as described.[20] Network analysis can give us additional insight.

Casting climate with a focus on communication relationships can solve some of the conceptual problems with climate because communication linkages describe more concretely the vehicle by which perceptions are shared by many members.[21] By administering questionnaires and asking respondents to recall their communicative behavior during a specified time about relevant topics such as the handling of a crisis situation, and the types of communication employed, one can obtain a map (network) of communication interactions. Since networks tend to be stable over time, it becomes possible to compare different networks. Analysis of the data yields information about role behavior and the effectiveness of the communication process.

The importance of understanding communication networks cannot be underestimated. They provide a mechanism for understanding the *informal* means by which communication is processed throughout the organization. As discussed in Chapter 5, the size, structure, complexity, and design of an organization are interrelated. Large-scale, complex organizations have typically been associated with formal, centralized designs. In like manner, their communication processes have followed hierarchically based principles of top-down management, characterized by narrowly defined chains of command, which impede a free-flowing communication process. Conversely, organizations that follow a "matrix" model are more flexible and dynamic. They are less structured and more often display highly efficient, quality-oriented communication climates.

## INTERPERSONAL STYLES OF COMMUNICATION: THE JOHARI WINDOW

A cross-cultural study involving respondents from the United States, Japan, and Great Britain revealed that approximately 74 percent of the managers cited communication breakdown as the single greatest barrier to organizational excellence.[22] A fact of organizational life is that, when management is effective and relationships among organizational members are sound, problems of communication breakdown tend not to be heard.[23] It is only when relationships among organizational members are fraught with unarticulated tensions that complaints about communication breakdown begin to be heard.[24] Two important points are implicit in this discussion:

1. The quality of relationships in an organization may dictate to a large extent the level of communication effectiveness achieved.
2. The quality of relationships, in turn, is a direct product of the interpersonal practices of an organization's membership.[25]

The single most important aspect of interpersonal practices is the way in which parties to a relationship communicate with each other. In 1955, Joseph Luft and Harry Ingham developed a communication model for use in their group dynamics training programs; this model has come to be known as the

Johari Window, its designation as such arising from the use of portions of the first names of its developers.[26] Subsequently, Jay Hall and Martha Williams modified it to treat the Johari Window as an information flow and processing model. Through the use of a questionnaire developed by Hall and Williams, interpersonal styles of communication are identifiable.[27]

The Johari Window model is depicted in Figure 7-6 and has two key dimensions: exposure and feedback.[28] Exposure means the open and candid expression of the police manager's feelings, factual knowledge, guesses, and the like in a conscious attempt to share; together, these expressions are referred to as *information*. Untrue, frivolous, and kindred statements do not constitute exposure because they contribute nothing to promoting mutual understanding. Central to the use of exposure by the police manager is the desire to build trust and a willingness to accept a certain amount of risk. The feedback process entails the police leader's active solicitation of information that he or she feels others may have that he or she does not.

Figure 7-6 consists of four quadrants or regions, defined as follows:

1. Region I, termed the *arena,* is the area of the total space available in which information is shared equally and understood by the police manager and others. This facet of the interpersonal relationship is thought to be the part that controls interpersonal productivity. The underlying assumption is that productivity and interpersonal effectiveness are related directly to the amount of mutually held information in a relationship. Therefore, the larger region I

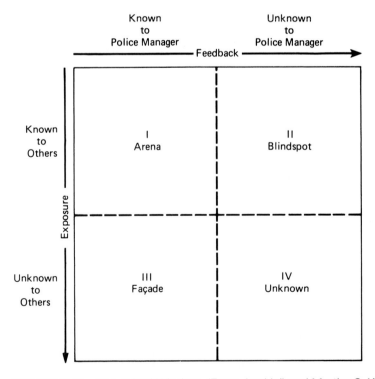

**FIGURE 7-6.** The Johari Window. (From Jay Hall and Martha S. Williams, "How to Interpret Your Scores on the Personal Relations Survey," © Teleometrics International, The Woodlands, Texas, 1967, with minor modification. Special permission for reproduction is granted by the authors Jay Hall, PhD, and Martha S. Williams, PhD, and publisher, Teleometrics International. All rights reserved.)

becomes, the more effective, rewarding, and productive becomes the relationship as well.

2. Region II, the *blindspot,* is that portion of the total space available that holds information known by others but unknown to the police manager. This area represents a handicap to the manager because one can scarcely understand the decisions, behavior, and feelings of others if one lacks the information on which they are based. However, others have a certain advantage to the extent that they have information unknown to the manager.

3. Region III, designated the *façade,* may also be considered an inhibitor of interpersonal effectiveness and productivity, due to an imbalance of information that favors the police manager. This is so because the police manager possesses information that is not known by others. The manager may withhold information that is perceived as potentially prejudicial to the relationship, out of fear, desire for power, or other related reasons. Essentially the façade serves as a protective front, but at the expense of keeping the arena from growing larger. Realistically, every relationship has a façade; the practical question is, how much is actually needed?

4. Region IV, the *unknown,* is the portion of the total space available that is unknown to both the police manager and others. This area is thought to contain psychodynamic data, unknown potentials, learned idiosyncrasies, and the database of creativity. However, as interpersonal effectiveness increases and the arena becomes larger, the unknown region shrinks.

As suggested, although the regions shown in Figure 7-6 are of equal size, when they are measured through the use of the Hall–Williams questionnaire, the Personnel Relations Survey, the regions vary in size. To illustrate, assume as shown in Figure 7-7 that there are two police managers. Manager B actively solicits information from manager A and as a result receives five "parcels" of information. Manager A is giving exposure, and manager B is receiving feedback, as depicted by the solid lines. Subsequently, the roles are reversed, and manager A receives seven parcels of information from manager B, as shown by the dashed lines. On the basis of this hypothetical exchange of feedback and exposure between managers A and B, the size of the quadrants or regions in their respective Johari Windows is established.

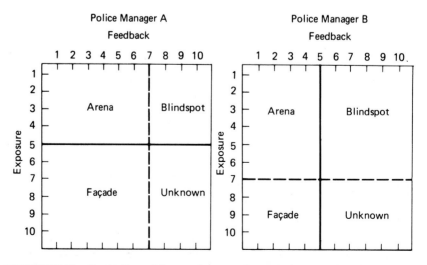

**FIGURE 7-7.**  Illustration of the exchange of exposure and feedback.

Figure 7-8 shows the four basic interpersonal communication styles, which may be described in the following terms:

**Type A**—This interpersonal style reflects a minimal use of both exposure and feedback processes; it is, in effect, a fairly impersonal approach to interpersonal relationships. The unknown region dominates under this style, and unrealized potential, untapped creativity, and personal psychodynamics prevail as the salient influences. Such a style would seem to indicate withdrawal and an aversion to risk taking on the part of its user; interpersonal anxiety and safety seeking are likely to be prime sources of personal motivation. Police managers who characteristically use this style appear to be rigid, aloof, and uncommunicative. This style may often be found in bureaucratic organizations of some type where it is possible, and perhaps profitable, to avoid personal disclosure or involvement. Persons using this style are likely to receive more than average hostility, because other parties to the relationship will tend to interpret the lack of exposure and feedback solicitation pretty much in terms of their own needs and how this interpersonal lack affects need fulfillment.

**Type B**—Under this approach, there is also an aversion to exposure, but it is coupled with a *desire* for relationships not found in type A. Thus, feedback is the only process left in promoting relationships, and it is much overused. An aversion to the use of exposure may typically be interpreted as a sign of basic

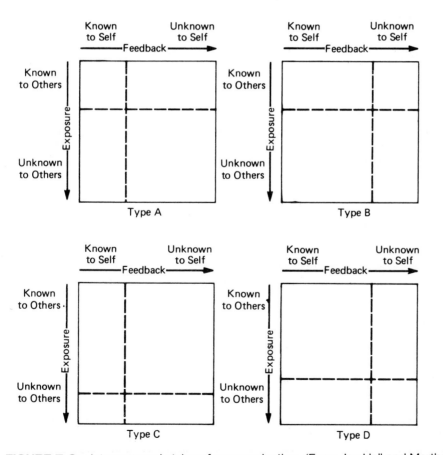

**FIGURE 7-8.** Interpersonal styles of communication. (From Jay Hall and Martha S. Williams, "How to Interpret Your Scores on the Personal Relations Survey," © Teleometrics International, The Woodlands, Texas.)

mistrust of others, and it is therefore not surprising that the façade is the dominant feature of relationships resulting from underused exposure coupled with overused feedback. The style appears to be a probing quasi-supportive, interpersonal ploy, and, once the façade becomes apparent, it is likely to result in a reciprocal withdrawal of trust by other parties. This may promote feelings of disgust, anxiety, and hostility on the part of others; such feelings may lead to the user's being treated as a rather superficial person without real substance.

**Type C**—This interpersonal style is based on an overuse of exposure to the neglect of feedback. It may well reflect ego striving and/or distrust of others' opinions. Individuals who use this style may feel quite confident of the validity of their own opinions and are likely to value authority. The fact is that they are often unaware of the impact they have on others. Others are likely to feel disenfranchised by individuals who use this style; they often feel that such people have little use for their contributions or concern for their feelings. As a result, this style often triggers feelings of hostility, insecurity, and resentment on the part of others. Frequently, others will learn to behave in such a way as to perpetuate the user's blindspot by withholding important information or by giving only selected feedback; as such, this is a reflection of the defensiveness that this style can cause others to experience.

**Type D**—Exposure and feedback processes are used to a great and balanced extent in this style; candor and openness coupled with a sensitivity to others' needs to participate are the salient features of the style. The arena becomes the dominant feature of the relationship, and productivity may be expected to increase as well. In initial stages, this style may promote some defensiveness on the part of others unused to honest and trusting relationships; but perseverance will tend to promote a norm of reciprocal candor over time such that trust and creative potential can be realized.[29]

Although it is not one of the basic styles, we designate a fifth commonly appearing style as type E. The type E style falls between types C and D, using both more exposure and feedback than type C but less than type D. In type E, there is slightly greater reliance on the use of exposure as opposed to feedback (see Table 7-1).

**TABLE 7-1.  Mean Johari Window Interpersonal Communication Styles for Various Groups of Police Managers**

| Group | Number in group | Communication with | | |
| --- | --- | --- | --- | --- |
| | | Subordinates | Colleagues | Superiors |
| 1 | 27 | E | E | E |
| 2 | 26 | E | C | B |
| 3 | 21 | A | C | C |
| 4 | 38 | B | C | E |
| 5 | 41 | E | C | E |
| 6 | 40 | E | E | E |
| 7 | 24 | E | C | E |
| 8 | 30 | D | D | D |
| 9 | 19 | C | D | C |

This is a sample of police managers from the southeastern United States, New Jersey, and Oregon. Managers from municipal and county police department and sheriffs' offices are represented.

The mean Johari Window scores for 325 police managers are plotted in Figure 7-9. Note that the Johari Window yields the style associated with communicating with three different groups—(1) subordinates, (2) colleagues, and (3) superiors—and that there is some variance among the scores. This variance is even more striking when examining the styles for eight different groups of police managers summarized in Table 7-1. Given such variance, it is difficult to make a unifying statement, but in general, type E is the most commonly occurring pattern among police managers.

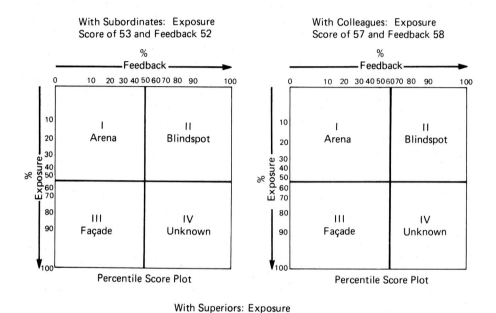

**FIGURE 7-9.** Mean Johari Window scores for 325 police managers. [The data depicted in these graphs are taken from Jay Hall, "Interpersonal Style and the Communication Dilemma: Utility of the Johari Window Awareness Model for Genotypic Diagnosis," *Human Relations,* 28 (1975), Table 3, p. 730. The graphs on which these data are displayed are taken from Jay Hall and Martha S. Williams, "How to Interpret Your Scores on the Personal Relations Survey," © Teleometrics International, The Woodlands, Texas, 1967. Special permission for reproduction is granted by the authors, Jay Hall, PhD, and Martha S. Williams, PhD, and publisher, Teleometrics International. All rights reserved.]

**TABLE 7-2. Relationship of Grid Management and Johari Window Styles**

| Grid Style | Johari Window Style |
|---|---|
| 9,9 Team management | Type D |
| 5,5 Organization management | Type E |
| 9,1 Authority-obedience | Type C |
| 1,9 Country club management | Type B |
| 1,1 Impoverished management | Type A |

As might be expected, there are correlations between Grid Management styles and Johari Window styles. These relationships are depicted in Table 7-2. To some extent these associations raise a "chicken and egg question" as to whether the choice of grid styles produces the Johari style or whether the reverse is true.

## CROSS-GENDER COMMUNICATIONS

Generally, an examination of the differences in the ways men and women communicate would be confined to scholarly books in the area of linguistics or perhaps to books in the popular market that examine male/female relationships. However, it is absolutely essential that police supervisors who must evaluate the actions of their subordinates understand that men and women in our society often communicate quite differently and may solve problems in dramatically different ways. A failure to understand these differences can result in erroneous evaluations of police officers' actions and even result in unfair criticism by fellow officers and superiors. The following scenario used to illustrate this point was witnessed by one of the authors.

A young woman pulled up to the pumps at a filling station to fill up her car. While at the pumps, a young man pulled up behind her in his vehicle. She did not see him pull up. He walked up to her from behind, turned her around, and slapped her across the face. An off-duty police officer in plainclothes and in his personal car was filling up his car at an adjoining pump and witnessed the assault. He immediately identified himself as a police officer and advised the man that he was under arrest. The officer requested the filling station attendant to call for a patrol unit. Prior to the arrival of the patrol unit, the assailant was placed in the front seat of the off-duty police officer's car unhandcuffed. Two uniformed officers arrived in separate police cars. One was a male and the other was a female. The off-duty officer explained to the uniformed officers what he had witnessed and requested their assistance in filling out the necessary paperwork and transporting the assailant to the county jail. However, as the officers were conversing, the assailant, who was still agitated, was loudly expressing his anger at his female companion who had apparently been out with another man the evening before. The female officer walked over to the assailant and in a very conciliatory way attempted to calm him down. The man was not threatening anyone, was not being aggressive, but was obviously still upset with the young woman he had assaulted. After a couple of minutes, the male officer became agitated with the prisoner "running his mouth." He walked over to the assailant and in very close physical proximity said very angrily, "If you don't shut your damn mouth, your ass is really going to be in trouble." At that point, the man proceeded to be quiet and was eventually handcuffed and transported to jail with no further difficulties.

Now let us assume that this scenario was being witnessed by a traditionally trained male supervisor. He might believe that the female officer should have been less conciliatory and more assertive and that her failure to be more assertive could have been interpreted as a sign of weakness by the arrested man, thereby encouraging him to become more belligerent. The supervisor might have assessed the male officer's approach as being more effective because he did, in fact, get the individual to quiet down and there were no further difficulties. However, let us assume, on the other hand, as sometimes happens, that the individual being arrested was sufficiently agitated that when the male officer spoke to him in this angry way, he in turn responded angrily and decided he would rather fight than go peaceably to jail. (Such scenarios are certainly not uncommon in police work.) If this had occurred, the outcome could have been quite different and someone could have been injured.

The fact of the matter is that the female officer was behaving in a way that women in our society are generally taught to behave when attempting to resolve a conflict, namely, in a nonconfrontal, conciliatory, nonphysical manner. In fact, this technique is recommended and employed in conflict resolution in many facets of police work.

Insights into the differences between the ways males and females communicate are important for police supervisors. If such insights are not present, the actions of female officers may be unfairly judged. Worse yet, if a female officer is criticized, she may believe that in order to be accepted by her peers and her supervisor she has to be overly aggressive, more confrontational, and more physical.

This is not to suggest that assertiveness is not a positive quality for police officers to possess. However, like anything else, too much can lead to unfortunate consequences.

Several years ago, Dr. Deborah Tannen, professor of linguistics at Georgetown University, wrote a book titled *You Just Don't Understand,* which examined differences in the ways men and women communicate.[30] The topic spawned a series of popular books focusing on communication differences between "the sexes," one even asserting that men and women were from different planets (*Men Are from Mars, Women Are from Venus*)![31] The issue of misunderstanding between men and women can lead to serious conflict not only in personal relationships, but also in the workplace. The following material from Tannen's book illustrates the differences in cross-gender communication.[32]

### Male-Female Conversation Is Cross-Culture Communication

If women speak and hear a language of connection and intimacy, while men speak and hear a language of status and independence, then communication between men and women can be like cross-culture communication, prey to a clash of conversational styles.

The claim that men and women grow up in different worlds may at first seem patently absurd. Brothers and sisters grow up in the same families, children to parents of both genders. Where, then, do women and men learn different ways of speaking and hearing?

Even if they grow up in the same neighborhood, on the same block, or in the same house, girls and boys grow up in different worlds of words. Others talk to them differently and expect and accept different ways of talking from them. Most important, children learn how to talk, how to have conversations, not only from their parents but from their peers. After all, if their parents have a foreign or regional accent, children do not emulate it; they learn to speak with the pronunciation of the region where they grow up. Anthropologists Daniel Maltz and Ruth Borker summarize research showing that boys and girls have very different ways of talking to their friends. Although they often play together, boys and girls spend most of their time playing in same-sex groups. And, although some of the activities they play at are similar, their favorite games are different, and their ways of using language in their games are separated by a world of difference.

Boys tend to play outside in large groups that are hierarchically structured. Their groups have a leader who tells others what to do and how to do it, and resist doing what other boys propose. It is by giving orders and making them stick that high status is negotiated. Another way boys achieve status is to take center stage by telling stories and jokes, and by sidetracking or challenging the stories and jokes of others. Boys' games have winners and losers and elaborate systems of rules that are frequently the subjects of arguments. Finally, boys are frequently heard to boast of their skill and argue about who is best at what.

Girls, on the other hand, play in small groups or in pairs; the center of a girl's social life is a best friend. Within the group, intimacy is key: differentiation is measured by relative closeness. In their most frequent games, such as jump rope and hopscotch, everyone gets a turn. Many of their activities (such as playing house) do not have winners or losers. Though some girls are certainly more skilled than others, girls are expected not to boast about it, or show that they think they are better than the others. Girls do not give orders; they express their preferences as suggestions, and suggestions are likely to be accepted. Whereas boys say, "Gimme that!" and "Get outta here!" girls say, "Let's do this," and "How about doing that?" Anything else is put down as "bossy." They do not grab center stage—they do not want it—so they do not challenge each other directly. And much of the time, they simply sit together and talk. Girls are not accustomed to jockeying for status in an obvious way; they are more concerned that they be liked.

### Styles in Conflict Resolution

Much of what has been written about women's and men's styles claims that males are competitive and prone to conflict whereas females are cooperative and given to affiliation. But being in conflict also means being involved with each other. Although it is true that many women are more comfortable using language to express rapport whereas many men are more comfortable using it for self-display, the situation is really more complicated than that, because self-display, when part of a mutual struggle, is also a kind of bonding. And conflict may be valued as a way of creating involvement with others.

To most women, conflict is a threat to connection, to be avoided at all costs. Disputes are preferably settled without direct confrontation. But to many men, conflict is the necessary means by which status is negotiated, so it is to be accepted and may even be sought, embraced, and enjoyed.

Walter Ong, a scholar of cultural linguistics, shows in his book *Fighting for Life* that "adversativeness"—pitting one's needs, wants, or skills against those of others—is an essential part of being human, but "conspicuous or expressed adversativeness is a larger element in the lives of males than of females." He demonstrates that male behavior typically entails contest, which includes combat, struggle, conflict, competition, and contention. Pervasive in male behavior is ritual combat, typified by rough play and sports. Females, on the other hand, are more likely to use intermediaries or to fight for real rather than ritualized purposes.

Friendship among men often has a large element of friendly aggression, dotted with sexual innuendoes and explicatives. Unfortunately, women often mistake these ritualized comments as the real thing. In the workplace, this type of "street language" can often result in serious charges of harassment and civil litigation, even though the offensive language was not directed at an individual (refer to Box 7-1). These are difficult situations from both male and female perspectives. In Chapter 11, we further discuss the issue of a "hostile environment" as a form of sexual harassment.

## BOX 7-1

### Metro Cops Policing Their "Street Language"

### Workplace complaints get officials' attention

**by Doug Payne**

Whatever it was that Cobb homicide detectives were saying that got Col. A. B. Allred demoted to captain, offended the wrong people.

Police Chief Culver Johnson won't even repeat it. "I was in the Navy six years and never heard anything like this," Johnson said.

But it wasn't just the words: "It was the manner in which it was said, the context, the timing, the place," he added. Taken altogether, Johnson said the detective's sexually explicit comments created a "hostile workplace environment."

Like many workplace managers, law enforcement officials around metro Atlanta and the country are trying to clean up the rough talk, usually from male officers.

"We [males] use it to maintain power, rather than having big clubs or sticks," said Scott W. Allen, a police psychologist with the Metro-Dade Police Department in Florida. "We use words as weapons."

If officers don't take the threat seriously, it can cost the city or county dearly, said Atlanta attorney Lee Parks, who was co-counsel in a case resulting in a $465,000 award in 1994 for five Clayton County Sheriff's Department female employees who said they were sexually harassed.

"Street language in a public safety environment is commonplace," Parks said. "That's the world they live in. That parlance sometimes carries over into the office or to their co-workers. And sometimes it just goes too far." Parks is representing six female employees of the Douglas County District Attorney's office who claim they were routinely demeaned and intimidated.

The nature of police work contributes to the problem, experts say.

"Any occupation that's stressful, that has life and death involved in it, that has a majority of males in it, has a higher usage of profanity," Allen said.

In the Cobb County case, the words were not directed at the female detective who objected to them; they were only heard by her. Her complaints about the language led to an internal investigation and ultimately Allred's demotion in January.

The Cobb Police Department's hierarchy was alerted to a problem early in 1995 when the female detective complained to her lieutenant about her co-worker's language. The complaint went up the chain of command to Allred, in charge of all of the department's detective units, who reportedly ordered his subordinates to "tone it down."

After her complaint, however, the woman was transferred out of the detective division back into the uniform division against her wishes, Johnson said. Then in October, she received a bad annual performance review. In a written objection to the review, the woman said that if her work was bad, it was because conditions in the homicide bureau bothered her so much that she couldn't do her job properly.

Johnson said that when he read the woman's performance review he ordered an internal investigation. It showed that homicide detectives were still using rough language.

Johnson ordered Allred, who has more than 25 years of service with the department, dropped two grades in rank. He was reassigned to command the Crimes Against Children unit based on Austell Road.

Legal experts say the line is fuzzy between what workplace behavior is OK and what is not OK, but they agree that courts perceive offensive language as a form of sexual harassment, whether or not it is directed at an individual.

In 1993 the U.S. Supreme Court ruled that no one has to suffer a nervous breakdown before a violation has occurred. The court held that "whether an environment is hostile or abusive can be determined only by looking at all the circumstances"—including the frequency of the offensive behavior, its severity and whether it interfered with anyone's job.

Metro area police departments have taken steps to combat the problem by forbidding offensive language on the job, police officials say. There are also training programs to help supervisors and rank-and-

*(continued)*

## BOX 7-1 (continued)

file employees recognize what a hostile workplace environment is and what to do about it.

The Gwinnett County Police Department has two policies concerning harassment, one that deals with conduct while dealing with the public and one concerning sexual harassment in the workplace, said Assistant Chief Mark Kissel.

The Fulton County Police Department's sexual harassment policy is read at roll calls and during training, "not because it's a problem but to keep it from becoming a problem," said Capt. Karen Harris, assistant commander of the department's communications division.

Cobb County has a departmental and a county policy that "puts employees and supervisors on notice that employees have a right to a harassment-free

workplace," Johnson said. The policies are stressed to supervisors and in a training course that all new employees must attend.

But the message apparently didn't sink in to detectives in one of the highest-profile offices in the department. "I have reiterated the requirement throughout the chain of command for all supervisors to review the no-harassment policy again with employees," Johnson said.

Allen, the Metro-Dade psychologist, said the word is out in his department: "Everyone in my police department, everyone, has to watch what they say, or you can be subject to immediate transfer—that day. It's that fast."

*Source: Atlanta Constitution (Georgia), February 16, 1996.*

Ong demonstrates the inextricable relationship between oral performance and "agonistic" relations. Oral disputation—from formal debate to the study of formal logic—is inherently adversative. With this in mind, we can see that the inclination of many men to expect discussions and arguments in daily conversation to adhere to rules of logic is a remnant of this tradition. Furthermore, oral performance is self-display and is part of a larger framework in which many men approach life as a contest.

Because their imaginations are not captured by ritualized combat, women are inclined to misinterpret and be puzzled by the adversativeness of many men's ways of speaking and miss the ritual nature of friendly aggression. At the same time, the enactment of community can be ritualized just as easily as the enactment of combat. The appearance of community among women may mask power struggles, and the appearance of sameness may mask profound differences in points of view. Men can be as confused by women's verbal rituals as women are by men's.

## CROSS-CULTURAL DIVERSITY IN COMMUNICATION

At least 90 percent of the messages that people send are not communicated verbally, but by posture, facial expressions, gestures, tone of voice, and so on.[33] These nonverbal messages express and shape attitudes toward others. No one teaches their meanings in school. Rather, people subconsciously learn the meaning of nonverbal messages by growing up in a particular culture. At the same time, they assume that everyone shares these meanings. In reality, just the opposite is true.[34]

Consider this scenario: A Nigerian cab driver runs a red light. An officer pulls him over in the next block, stopping the patrol car at least three car lengths behind the cab. Before the police officer can exit the patrol car, the cabbie gets out of his vehicle and approaches the officer. Talking rapidly in a high-pitched voice and making wild gestures, the cab driver appears to be out of control, or so the officer believes.

As the officer steps from his car, he yells for the cab driver to stop, but the cabbie continues to walk toward the officer. When he is about two feet away, the officer orders the cabbie to step back and keep his hands to his sides. But the cab driver continues to babble and advance toward the officer. He does not make eye contact and appears to be talking to the ground.

Finally, the officer commands the cab driver to place his hands on the patrol vehicle and spread his feet. What began as a routine stop for a traffic violation culminates in charges of disorderly conduct and resisting arrest.

This scene typifies many of the encounters that take place daily in the United States between law enforcement personnel and people of other cultures. A simple traffic violation escalates out of control and becomes more than a matter of communication and common sense. It represents two icebergs—different cultures—colliding with devastating results.

To understand the final outcome, we need to examine the breakdown in nonverbal communication. First, most Americans know to remain seated in their vehicles when stopped by the police. But the Nigerian exited his cab because he wanted to show respect and humility by not troubling the officer to leave his patrol car. The suspect used his own cultural rule of thumb (common sense), which conveyed a completely different message to the officer, who viewed it as a challenge to his authority.

The Nigerian then ignored the command to "step back." Most likely, this didn't make any sense to him because, in his eyes, he was not even close to the officer. The social distance for conversation in Nigeria is much closer than in the United States. For Nigerians, it may be less than 15 inches, whereas 2 feet represents a comfortable conversation zone for Americans.

Another nonverbal communication behavior is eye contact. Anglo-Americans expect eye contact during conversation; the lack of it usually signifies deception, rudeness, defiance, or an attempt to end the conversation. In Nigeria, however, people often show respect and humility by averting their eyes. While the officer saw the cabbie defiantly "babbling to the ground," the Nigerian believed he was sending a message of respect and humility.

Most likely, the cab driver was not even aware of his exaggerated gestures, high-pitched tone of voice, or rapid speech. But the officer believed him to be "out of control," "unstable," and probably "dangerous." Had the cab driver been an Anglo-American, then the officer's reading of the cabbie's nonverbal behavior would have been correct.

One of the primary results of a breakdown in communications is a sense of being out of control; yet, in law enforcement, control and action are tantamount. Unfortunately, the need for control combined with the need to act often makes a situation worse. "Don't just stand there. Do something!" is a very Anglo-American admonition.

With the Nigerian cab driver, the officer took control using his cultural common sense when it might have been more useful to look at what was actually taking place. Of course, in ambiguous and stressful situations, people seldom take time to truly examine the motivating behaviors in terms of culture. Rather, they view what is happening in terms of their own experiences, which is ethnocentric—and usually wrong.

Law enforcement professionals need to develop *cultural empathy*. They need to put themselves in other people's cultural shoes to understand what motivates their behavior. By understanding internal cultures, they usually can explain why situations develop the way they do. And if they know their own internal cultures, they also know the reasons behind their reactions and realize why they may feel out of control.

Here's another scenario. During face-to-face negotiations with police at a local youth center, the leader of a gang of Mexican American adolescents suddenly begins to make long, impassioned speeches, punctuated with gestures and threats. Other members of the group then join in by shouting words of encouragement and agreement.

A police negotiator tries to settle the group and get the negotiations back on track. This only leads to more shouting from the Chicano gang members. They then accuse the police of bad faith, deception, and an unwillingness to "really negotiate."

Believing that the negotiations are breaking down, the police negotiator begins to leave, but not before telling the leader, "We can't negotiate until you get your act together where we can deal with one spokesperson in a rational discussion about the issues and relevant facts."

At this point, a Spanish-speaking officer interrupts. He tells the police negotiator, "Negotiations aren't breaking down. They've just begun."

Among members of certain ethnic groups, inflammatory words or accelerated speech are often used for effect, not intent. Such words and gestures serve as a means to get attention and communicate feelings.

For example, during an argument, it would not be uncommon for a Mexican American to shout to his friend, "I'm going to kill you if you do that again." In the Anglo culture, this clearly demonstrates a threat to do harm. But, in the context of the Hispanic culture, this simply conveys anger. Therefore, the Spanish word "matar" (to kill) is often used to show feelings, not intent.

In the gang scenario, the angry words merely indicated sincere emotional involvement by the gang members, not threats. But to the police negotiator, it appeared as if the gang was angry, irrational, and out of control. In reality, the emotional outburst showed that the gang members wanted to begin the negotiation process. To them, until an exchange of sincere emotional words occurred, no negotiations could take place.

Each culture presents arguments differently. For example, Anglo-Americans tend to assume that there is a short distance between an emotional, verbal expression of disagreement and a full-blown conflict. African Americans think otherwise.[35] For African Americans, stating a position with feeling shows sincerity. However, white Americans might interpret this as an indication of uncontrollable anger or instability and, even worse, an impending confrontation. For most blacks, threatening movements, not angry words, indicate the start of a fight. In fact, some would argue that fights don't begin when people are talking or arguing, but rather, when they stop talking.

Anglo Americans expect an argument to be stated in a factual-inductive manner. For them, facts presented initially in a fairly unemotional way lead to a conclusion. The greater number of relevant facts at the onset, the more persuasive the argument.[36]

African Americans, on the other hand, tend to be more affective-intuitive. They begin with the emotional position, followed by a variety of facts somewhat poetically connected to support their conclusions. Black Americans often view the mainstream presentation as insincere and impersonal, while white Americans see the black presentation as irrational and too personal. Many times, arguments are lost because of differences in style, not substance. Deciding who's right and who's wrong depends on the cultural style of communication and thinking used.

Differences in argumentative styles add tension to any disagreement. As the Chicano gang leader presented his affective-intuitive argument, other gang members joined in with comments of encouragement, agreement, and support. To the police negotiator, the gang members appeared to be united in a clique and on the verge of a confrontation.

Sometimes, Anglo-Americans react by withdrawing into a superfactual-inductive mode in an effort to calm things down. Unfortunately, the emphasis on facts, logical presentation, and lack of emotion often comes off as cold, condescending, and patronizing, which further shows a disinterest in the views of others.

Law enforcement officers should remember that racial and cultural perceptions affect attitudes and motivate behavior. In close-knit ethnic communities, avoiding loss of face or shame is very important. Then too, loss of individual dignity and respect often comes with loss of economic means and wealth. In the community policing model described in Chapter 2, police officers are being asked to confront a myriad of social and criminal problems (e.g., juvenile runaways, neighborhood disputes, vagrants, gangs, homeless people). They often find themselves acting the role of mediator or facilitator between conflicting or competing groups. Their goal is to bring about compromise and share other potential resources in the community. As described in Box 7-2, police officers often act as coordinating agents, using their skills in negotiation and mediation to solve community and order-maintenance problems.

## BOX 7-2

### Operation Outreach: Homeless, Helpless or Hopeless?

**by Sergeant Mike Parker**

#### The Search

West Hollywood, Calif. It's after midnight. Deputy Bernie Patrick patrols slowly down the Sunset Strip, past the wealthy, the trendy, the tourists. Then he sees him, a shrouded figure shuffling along the sidewalk carrying a mangled knapsack. As Patrick moves closer to the man, a pungent smell rolls toward him. In spite of the warm summer air, the man wears multiple layers of clothing that reeks with odor.

Patrick approaches the man although he has violated no law. Casually, the deputy asks the man how he's doing and engages him in a "consensual encounter." After several minutes, Patrick mentions that a social worker from the West Hollywood Homeless Organization (WHHO) is nearby and asks the man if he is willing to speak with her. The man mumbles a half-hearted "okay." Hearing his reply, Gina Drummond, the social worker, gets out of Patrick's radio patrol car, greets the man and begins to talk to him about how he can get off the street.

#### Peace Work or Social Work?

Have peace officers become social workers after all? To the contrary, in the scenario above, the social worker was there to help the man find food and shelter, and the Los Angeles County sheriff's deputy was there to keep the peace.

Los Angeles County Sheriff Sherman Block strongly encourages his deputies to be involved in community partnerships. In fact, the department's community policing philosophy includes a directive for deputies to serve as facilitation agents. According to Block, deputies are to "act as a coordinating agent [and] use public and private resources to solve community crime and order-maintenance problems."

#### Operation Outreach

The West Hollywood Sheriff's Station received more than 300 documented patrol requests in one year. The reports centered on transient or homeless people loitering, camping, urinating, drinking, panhandling and so on. City hall also received scores of calls. Most were from residents upset at being awakened nightly by strangers rummaging through their trash to steal recyclables and food scraps. Operation Outreach was in essence, born as a result of "compassion fatigue."

Although many citizens complained about these disruptions, others were more concerned about the welfare of those homeless people not engaging in criminal activity. Public Safety Administrator Nancy Greenstein responded to citizen concern. Greenstein assured community members that both the public safety commission and the city council agreed that all

*(continued)*

# BOX 7-2 (continued)

West Hollywood Sheriff's Station Deputy Chris Hicks tells a local area transient about available shelter services. (Photo by Kelly Holland)

transient people would be treated as individuals and that homeless "sweeps" would not be conducted. The city's leaders were determined that West Hollywood not be perceived as antihomeless, a position with which the sheriff's department agreed.

In previous years, West Hollywood deputies referred homeless individuals to shelters and arrested criminal and fugitive transients for "letter of the law" violations such as outstanding warrants, public drunkenness, etc. Although this method had some success, it wasn't enough. In 1995, the department changed the way it handled transient people and expanded its program to include city environmental services staff and WHHO social workers. Under the new program, city employees rode with deputies to help identify the areas that generate the most complaints to city hall. This partnership worked so well that deputy sheriffs subsequently approached WHHO

shelter workers and suggested that they also join in, an idea that WHHO employees enthusiastically endorsed. Later, the department asked staff from a local shopping cart retrieval service to accompany them and collect abandoned and stolen carts.

For nearly a year, West Hollywood deputies have been teaming up with their partners, and together, the organizations address issues related to homelessness. At least once a month, the group approaches every visible transient person in the city. Those who are criminal or fugitive are arrested or cited; those who are homeless are referred to WHHO social workers.

Deputies differentiate between criminal or fugitive transient people and homeless people. In a recent operation, 14 transient people were arrested for public nuisance offenses or for having outstanding warrants; 32 additional people were referred on the spot to social workers. While more than 20 individuals declined services, a number accepted the help offered.

This teamwork approach has worked well. City officials also have accompanied deputies on night rides and register strong support for Operation Outreach. Citizen complaints to both the sheriff's department and city hall have dropped dramatically. Although significant progress has been made, West Hollywood is an international city that attracts new transient people daily.

Transient and homeless problems are not the sole responsibility of a law enforcement officer, a social worker, a neighborhood or even a city. These problems belong to everyone. Operation Outreach works, and the reason it works is because it allows a community to come together, build a positive rapport, and work collectively to resolve a long-term societal and criminal issue.

*Source: Sheriff Times* (Washington, D.C.: Community Policing Consortium, Summer 1996).

In complex urban societies, there is no assumption of indirect responsibility. If a matter must be resolved by intervention, then the police must appear neutral and service oriented, for the betterment of the greater good. Resolution is determined by a decision of right or wrong based on the facts or merits of the case. Compromise and respect for individual dignity, racial pride, and cultural heritage must characterize the communication process of the police.

**Cross-Cultural Training**
Because of naive assumptions, the criminal justice community seldom views cross-cultural awareness and training as vital. Yet, as society and the law enforcement workforce become more diverse, the ability to manage cultural diversity becomes essential. Those agencies that do not proactively develop cul-

tural knowledge and skills fail to serve the needs of their communities. More important, however, they lose the opportunity to increase the effectiveness of their officers.

Unfortunately, cross-cultural training in law enforcement often occurs after an incident involving cross-cultural conflict takes place. If provided, this training can be characterized as a quick fix, a once-in-a-lifetime happening, when in reality it should be an ongoing process of developing awareness, knowledge, and skills.

At the very least, officers should know what terms are the least offensive when referring to ethnic or racial groups in their communities. For example, most Asians prefer not to be called Orientals. It is more appropriate to refer to their nationality of origin, such as Korean American.

Likewise, very few Spanish speakers would refer to themselves as Hispanics. Instead, the term "Chicano" is usually used by Mexican Americans, while the term "Latino" is preferred by those from Central America. Some would rather be identified by their nationality of origin, such as Guatemalan or Salvadoran.

Many American Indians resent the term "Native American" because it was invented by the U.S. government. They would prefer being called American Indian or known by their tribal ancestry, such as Crow, Menominee, or Winnegago.

The terms "black American" and "African American" can usually be used interchangeably. However, African American is more commonly used among younger people.

Law enforcement executives need to weave cross-cultural awareness into all aspects of law enforcement training and realize it is not enough to bring in a "gender expert" after someone files sexual harassment charges or a "race expert" after a racial incident occurs. Three-hour workshops on a specific topic do not solve problems. Cross-cultural issues are interrelated; they cannot be disconnected.

## Overcoming Barriers to Cross-Cultural Communication

What can the law enforcement community do to ensure a more culturally aware workforce? To begin, law enforcement professionals must *know their own culture.* All personnel need to appreciate the impact of their individual cultures on their values and behaviors. Sometimes, the best way to gain this knowledge is by intensively interacting with those who are culturally different. However, law enforcement professionals must always bear in mind that culture, by definition, is a generalization. Cultural rules or patterns never apply to everyone in every situation.

The next step is to *learn about the different cultures found within the agency and in the community.* However, no one should rely on cultural-specific "guidebooks" or simplistic do's and don'ts lists. While such approaches to cultural awareness are tempting, they do not provide sufficient insight and are often counterproductive.

First, no guidebook can be absolutely accurate, and many cover important issues in abstract or generic terms. For example, several different nations comprise Southeast Asia. Therefore, when promoting cultural awareness, law enforcement agencies should concentrate on the nationality that is predominant within their respective communities, that is, Vietnamese, Laotian, Cambodian, and so on. At the same time, these agencies should keep in mind that cultures are complex and changing. Managing cultural diversity also means being able to adjust to the transformations that may be occurring within the ethnic community.

Second, relying on a guidebook approach can be disastrous if it does not provide the answers needed to questions arising during a crisis situation. It is much more useful to have a broad framework from which to operate when analyzing and interpreting any situation. Such a framework should focus on internal, not just external, culture. Knowing values, beliefs, behaviors, and thought patterns can only assist law enforcement professionals when dealing with members of ethnic communities.

Law enforcement professionals should also *understand the dynamics of cross-cultural communication, adjustment, and conflict.* When communication breaks down, frustration sets in. When this happens, law enforcement reacts. This presents a very serious, and potentially dangerous, situation for officers because of the emphasis placed on always being in control. Understanding the process of cross-cultural interaction gives a sense of control and allows for the development of coping strategies.

Finally, law enforcement professionals should *develop cross-cultural communicative, analytical, and interpretive skills.* Awareness and knowledge are not enough. Knowing about the history and religion of a particular ethnic group does not necessarily allow a person to communicate effectively with someone from that group. The ability to communicate effectively can only be learned through experience, not by reading books or listening to lectures. At the same time, being able to analyze and interpret a conflict between people of different cultures can also only be mastered through experience. (See Box 7-3.)

## BOX 7-3

### NYPD's "Streetwise" Cultural Sensitivity Training Gets Renewed Impetus

Cultural sensitivity training for rookie police officers in New York City had been in place well before the fatal shooting of Amadou Diallo in February, but in the wake of that incident a five-part curriculum developed by a public/private partnership has been raised to perhaps an even higher level of importance.

The training program, called "Streetwise: Language, Culture and Police Work in New York City," is now in its second year of funding by the Justice Department. The curriculum was created under the auspices of the New York State Regional Community Policing Institute (RCPI), one of 27 such institutes around the nation that enhance and provide training in community oriented policing and cultural diversity.

More than 2,500 NYPD rookies and in-service personnel—including some officers with the Street Crime Unit, which has been harshly criticized in the aftermath of the Diallo case—underwent the one-day training between April and May. In addition to providing a card that can be inserted into the officers' books containing basic expressions in Spanish, Haitian Creole, Russian and Mandarin Chinese, the curriculum includes a series of handouts that explore the cultural dimensions of each group and various city neighborhoods, along with an audio tape.

A fifth component, the African-Caribbean/American Experience, was developed by John Jay College of Criminal Justice, one of four partners that make up the RCPI, along with the New York City Police Department, the state Bureau for Municipal Police and the Citizens Committee for New York City, a nonprofit group.

The curriculum also discusses responses common to an individual group which could help defuse a potentially violent confrontation. Herbert Johnson, who led John Jay College's participation, said that in developing the Chinese component, a Chinese officer noted that those speaking in Mandarin often sound like they are arguing.

"Officers need to know that just because people are getting excited doesn't mean something is going to happen," Johnson told Law Enforcement News. "This is the way they express themselves. It's important when you know that, so you can react appropriately and not overreact."

In developing the program, the RCPI used focus groups in the community and within the NYPD, and participated in ride-alongs with officers, said project director Lancelott Smith. The program also includes a videotape portion that begins with a presentation by

Police Commissioner Howard Safir, and follows with a section in which training supervisors and a mentor officer discuss their experiences on the street and how important it proved under some circumstances to know basic expressions in the four languages.

Last year, some 1,041 rookie officers received the training—albeit without the newly developed African-Caribbean/American Experience component. But the death of Diallo, an unarmed African immigrant who was shot and killed by members of the department's Street Crime Unit in front of his Bronx apartment building, prompted a reevaluation of the program, said Johnson.

"I can certainly say it got everybody's attention," he said. "It may have even elevated the priority of the whole concept. Initially, I don't know how many people were on board with the importance of this as a training for law enforcement. With the Diallo case, it hit home the value it has and how important it can be in terms of strategies for law enforcement officers on the street."

As a result of the Diallo shooting, Johnson said, the emphasis within the African-Caribbean/American Experience segment may be broadened to include discussions of cultures from continental Africa.

Smith and Johnson said they are hopeful that the training will have an impact, although they acknowledged that bigotry and prejudice are difficult to change. Leadership, they said, is a crucial factor in augmenting the training. Bias is a societal problem and not exclusive to the police community, noted Johnson, but law enforcement stands a better chance of overcoming discrimination that other professions because of its paramilitary structure.

"I was in the military," said Johnson, "and the watchword was, 'We can't make you do anything, but we can make you wish you had done it.'" Law enforcement can have real success in making these changes, he said, if top leadership gets the word out that such behavior will not be tolerated.

*Source: Law Enforcement News, May 15/31, 1999*

## ORAL OR WRITTEN COMMUNICATION

**Suiting the Medium to the Recipient**

Although a potentially great variety of media is available for issuing orders, the individual issuing the orders is generally forced to choose from among a few existing ones that have nothing more than tradition in their favor. When certain media have become established, all subsequent material is made to fit them. If, for example, an organization has a personnel policy manual, it may become the pattern to announce through a routine revision of the manual even those changes that are of immediate and crucial interest to the employees. A change in the design of an application form would not elicit widespread interest, but a new system for computing vacation allowances is bound to interest everyone. Such differences in interest value are important factors in the proper selection of media, but the desired medium must be available in the first place.

**Written Communication**

There tends to be considerable confidence in the written word within complex organizations. It establishes a permanent record, but a transmittal of information in this way does not necessarily assure that the message will be unambiguous to the receiver. Sometimes, in spite of the writer's effort, information is not conveyed clearly to the recipient. This may result, in part, because the writer lacks the writing skills necessary to convey the message clearly and unambiguously. For example, the following information was taken from letters received by a county department and illustrates the difficulty some people have in communicating via the written form.

I am forwarding my marriage certificate and six children. I have seven but one died which was baptized on a half sheet of paper.

Mrs. Jones had not had any clothes for a year and has been visited regularly by the clergy.

Please find for certain if my husband is dead. The man I am living with can't eat or do anything until he knows.

I am very much annoyed to find you have branded my son illiterate. This is a dirty lie as I was married a week before he was born.

In answer to your letter, I have given birth to a boy weighing ten pounds. I hope this is satisfactory.

I am forwarding my marriage certificate and three children, one of which is a mistake as you can see.

Unless I get my husband's money pretty soon, I will be forced to lead an immortal life.

You have changed my little boy to a little girl. Will this make any difference?

I have no children as yet as my husband is a truck driver and works day and night.

I want money as quick as I can get it. I have been in bed with the doctor for two weeks and he doesn't do me any good. If things don't improve, I will have to send for another doctor.

Police administrators increasingly rely on written communication as their dominant medium for communication. The variety of duties that police officers perform, in addition to the officers' wide discretion in handling them, help to account for the proliferation of written directives. The breadth of police duties and functions generates a tremendous number of tasks and situations that are potential topics of written guidelines. When compounded by the need for discretion, simple, straightforward directives are rarely possible. Instead, lengthy directives specifying numerous factors and offering preferred responses for different combinations of those factors are much more common.[37]

The tendency to promulgate rules, policies, and procedures to enhance direction and control has been exacerbated by three contemporary developments. One is the requirement for administrative due process in police discipline, encouraged by court rulings, police officer bill of rights legislation, and labor contracts. More and more, disciplinary action against police employees necessarily follows an orderly process and must demonstrate violations of specific written rules. Thus police departments feel the increasing need to have written rules prohibiting all kinds of inappropriate behavior they want to punish, along with written procedures outlining the disciplinary grievance processes.

Another development motivating police departments to establish written directives is civil liability. Lawsuits against local governments, police departments, and police managers for the wrongful acts of police officers have become more common in recent years. Written guidelines prohibiting certain acts provide a principal avenue against civil litigation. In essence, police managers try to show that it was not their fault that officers erred. However, written policies and procedures are needed to make this avenue of defense available.

A third stimulus is the law enforcement agency accreditation movement. Although less than 10 percent of all police departments are presently accredited, many are either working toward accreditation or using the accreditation standards as a model for improvement. Agencies pursuing accreditation or simply looking to the program for guidance are clearly and strongly influenced by the possibility of enhancing their own policies and procedures.[38] For a more detailed discussion of the Commission on Accreditation for Law Enforcement Agencies, see Chapter 3, Politics and Police Administration.

The trend to rely on written communication as the principal medium for the transmittal of information also occurs quite frequently when dealing with individuals or groups outside the police department. Even in those cases for which the initial contact is made orally, a follow-up letter or memo is frequently filed in order to create a record of the communication. Such records are becoming routine partly as a result of the realization that they provide the greatest protection against the growing numbers of legal actions taken against police departments by citizens, activists, and interest groups.

## Oral Communication

Oral communication offers some distinct advantages to both the sender and the receiver.

The recipient of an oral order can probe for exactness wherever the meaning is not entirely clear, provided that the individual is not too unfamiliar with the subject matter. The recipient of the information may ask for a clarifying or confirming statement in writing, or a sketch or chart, or a demonstration of a manual operation. In this situation, both individuals can state their case so long as the elements of give and take are preserved.

The person issuing an order, on the other hand, has an opportunity for immediate feedback and can see whether the order has produced understanding or confusion. The person issuing the order can probably discern the recipient's attitude and determine whether it is one of acceptance or rejection, but the attitude of the person issuing the order will also be apparent to the recipient. It appears that an oral medium is highly suitable when it is believed that an instruction will be temporary. For example, a police sergeant instructing an officer to direct traffic at an intersection because of street construction will likely not put that instruction in writing if the problem is one of short duration. However, if the construction will be of long duration, a written order may be forthcoming, specifying that an officer will be assigned to direct traffic at this particular location until further notice. Further, the written order may also specify additional details such as the times the officer is expected to be at the location. Therefore, the method to be employed will sometimes be dictated by the duration of the problem.

## Electronic Media

Certain advantages are inherent in both oral and written orders and can be exploited according to each individual's situation. There are promising opportunities for using both oral and written form, where one or the other may have been used alone on previous occasions. For example, many police administrators have started using closed-circuit television combined with written communication to transmit to their officers information that may be especially sensitive or controversial. One police chief, upon creating an internal affairs unit, used his closed-circuit television to discuss the reasons that the unit was created and used that opportunity to answer a series of prepared questions that had been forwarded to him by officers who were concerned about the role and scope of this new unit. This televised presentation was given simultaneously with the newly developed procedure that detailed the organizational structure, the scope, and the responsibilities of this new unit.[39]

In the last ten years, electronic mail (e-mail) has become one of the most powerful communication media inside an organization. Capable of providing almost instantaneous communication with any member seated at a personal computer, e-mail provides an effective managerial tool for communication in all directions—horizontal, downward, and upward—within the organization. Transmitting over a computer network, e-mail provides a conduit for communication both internal and external to the organization. It is especially well suited for decentralized communication between units, such as between command headquarters and precinct offices.

At first glance, e-mail appears to be the perfect communication medium. It is reliable, security sensitive, and easy to use. It eliminates communication lag and provides managers with an ability to notify personnel of time-sensitive information accurately and consistently. However, as Box 7-4 indicates, ambiguity can exist even in the technologically advanced medium of e-mail. When the basic elements of the communication process between sender and receiver are muddied, communication is severely hampered or halted. Future communication techniques involving on-line video with e-mail, and teleconferencing, should further enhance the communication process[40] (refer to Chapter 13, Information Systems and Applications). In the meantime, there appears to be no substitute for a clear medium that provides immediate feedback and confirmation in the communication process.

## BOX 7-4

### Managers Aren't Always Able to Get the Right Message Across with E-Mail

**by Alex Markels**

Billions of electronic-mail messages pulse through corporate networks daily, and many of them are vitally important. Just as many, though, may be misleading, superfluous and even disruptive.

"E-mail is by far the most powerful tool a manager has," says Larry Crume, a vice president at software maker AutoDesk Inc. "But it's also the most abused."

In the U.S., more than 23 million workers are now plugged into e-mail networks, and three times that number will be connected by the year 2000, according to the Electronic Messaging Association in Washington. But experts say supervisors regularly—and mistakenly—employ e-mail to avoid face-to-face confrontations with workers.

Jaclyn Kostner, president of Bridge the Distance Inc., a company that holds seminars in "virtual leadership" for managers who work apart from their staffs, says one manager at a major telecommunications company that she advises subjects employees to "Friday afternoon dumps"—assignments via e-mail that arrive minutes before workers go home for the weekend.

Even worse, she says, some managers use e-mail to send performance reviews and other sensitive documents. "I know two people who received termination notices electronically," says Ms. Kostner.

Another problem of the medium is a lack of consensus among users as to what it represents. Is an e-mail message, in fact, mail, with all the weight of a letter or written interoffice memo? Or should it be regarded as an offhand remark?

The ambiguity creates misunderstandings. After Massachusetts Institute of Technology Professor Chris Schmandt rejected a portion of a graduate student's thesis, the student returned with an e-mail message written by the professor more than a year before. "He pulled out a piece of my old e-mail and said, 'Look, you told me to do this and I've done it. Therefore [the project] must be finished,' " says Mr. Schmandt, who teaches at MIT's Media Lab. Mr. Schmandt stuck to his rejection but concedes he should have been more careful. "I treated e-mail informally, like a phone call," he says.

Although some users treat e-mail as if it were written with disappearing ink, electronic messages can come back to haunt the indiscreet. [In 1995] Chevron Corp. paid $2.2 million to settle a sexual-harassment lawsuit filed against it by four female employees. Evidence presented by the women's lawyers included e-mail records listing 25 reasons why beer is supposedly better than women. (In settling, Chevron denied the women's allegations.)

E-mail users should also avoid heated electronic arguments, says Jeffrey Christian, president of executive recruiter Christian & Timbers in Cleveland. He learned this lesson when a subordinate recently sent him an e-mail proposal regarding management bonuses and how to motivate workers: "I disagreed completely, and my response was brash," Mr. Christian recalls. "I reacted from an emotional perspective, and it created a lot of unnecessary problems."

"Criticism and sarcasm just don't come across well on e-mail," says Brad Silverberg, a senior vice president of Microsoft Corp. "E-mail doesn't have the nuances of real-time human conversation." He says, for example, that subordinates often mistake his opinions for orders. Senior-level managers "lose track of the impact your mail may have on people," Mr. Silverberg says.

E-mail, however, is considered an indispensable tool at Microsoft during the hiring process, Mr. Silverberg says. As job candidates move through various levels of interviews during the company's rigorous one-day process, interviewers pass to one another e-mail highlighting the day's progress. "If the feedback is 'This is a person we really like,' then the nature of my interview changes," Mr. Silverberg says. "Instead of probing and questioning, I can turn to selling." He says this often helps the company make hiring decisions by the end of the interview day.

In fact, managers who shun e-mail "are somewhat out of the loop," says Robert Kraut, a professor at Carnegie Mellon University's Human Computer Interaction Institute. In a recent study of a major international bank, Mr. Kraut notes, "people who used e-mail were substantially more aware of what was going on in corporate headquarters."

Still, e-mail can be too much of a good thing. "I get 80 e-mails a day, and 60 of them are because I'm copied from multiple levels," says AutoDesk's Mr. Lynch. "I can put filters on my mailbox. But I tell my people the best filter is to show self-restraint."

In sending e-mail to the boss, some subordinates use the "George Factor," named for the "Seinfeld" television character who, after leaving his car in the company parking lot, was offered a promotion from bosses impressed that his car was there when they arrived at work and still there when they went home.

Ms. Kostner of Bridge the Distance says: "People have confessed to me that they do the e-mail after dinner but delay sending it until late at night."

*Source: The Wall Street Journal,* August 6, 1996. Reprinted by permission of The Wall Street Journal, © 1996 Dow Jones & Company, Inc. All Rights Reserved Worldwide.

# SUMMARY

Considerable evidence supports the premise that for administrators to be truly effective they must understand the dynamics involved in both organizational and interpersonal communication. It is not surprising to learn that administrators who are successful are also effective communicators and have created communication mechanisms within their organizations that avoid many of the pitfalls discussed throughout this chapter. To understand the process of communication, we have examined several elements that make up the process, namely, encoding, transmitting the medium itself, receiving, decoding, and feedback. Further, we have learned that barriers to communication or communication breakdowns can occur at any place in the system and may result from either the sender or receiver.

In order to understand the pathways that communication takes in an organization, we have suggested ways to analyze the communication network. By providing information about who talks to whom, an analysis reveals a picture of human interaction in an organization. This can provide clues for devising a communication strategy to foster a favorable communication climate.

Information flow is multidirectional (downward, upward, and horizontal). The police administrator must take every possible precaution to ensure that barriers are not created that can disrupt the smooth flow of information throughout the organization.

The discussion of the Johari Window in this chapter provided readers with an opportunity to examine and evaluate their interpersonal styles of communication and to assess other styles as well. It is hoped that the insight provides readers with an opportunity to make those adjustments deemed necessary to enhance their interpersonal communication styles.

In our discussion of cross-gender communication, we emphasized the importance of police supervisors understanding that men and women in our society often communicate quite differently and may solve problems in dramatically different ways. If they fail to understand these differences, it can result in an erroneous evaluation of a female police officer's action and may lead to unfair criticism by both her peers and her supervisors.

Because of the enormous cultural diversity existing in many parts of the United States today, it is absolutely essential that police officers understand as much as possible about the people they are serving. In our discussion of cross-cultural diversity, we provided some examples of the types of miscommunications that can occur and what the end results can be. We suggested ways of implementing cross-cultural training of police officers, which may prevent some of the communication breakdowns that can occur.

The police administrator may choose from among a number of ways to communicate. However, there tends to be considerable confidence in the use of written words in complex organizations. This is so in part because it establishes a permanent record for ready reference. On the other hand, not all communications can or should be in writing. As we have seen, oral communications can have distinct advantages to both the sender and the receiver. Further, there will be some instances in which a police administrator may wish to combine written, oral, and electronic communications.

In the final analysis, there can be little argument with the conclusion that effective communication is essential in all organizations. A communication breakdown in the process of law enforcement not only results in a less efficient organization, but may also result in unnecessary injury or death.

## DISCUSSION QUESTIONS

1. Discuss the elements that make up the communication process.

2. Discuss sender-caused barriers, receiver-caused barriers, and other barriers in communications.

3. Much of the organization communication literature addresses the communication climate, which is generally seen as a composite. What are the elements of that composite?

4. Discuss the five types of organizational communication that have been identified.

5. Discuss, in rank order from most effective to least effective, the means of downward communication, according to Dahle.

6. The physical distance between superior and subordinate may impede upward communication. Why?

7. What are the major desirable and undesirable traits of the organizational grapevine?

8. Discuss the four basic interpersonal styles of communication.

9. What are some of the basic differences in the styles of conflict resolution between men and women?

10. At least 90 percent of the messages that people send are not communicated verbally. What are the other means by which people communicate to each other?

11. What are the advantages in oral communication to both the sender and the receiver?

12. What are the advantages in combining both oral and written orders?

## NOTES

1. *Interpersonal Communication: A Guide for Staff Development* (Athens: Institute of Government, University of Georgia, August 1974), p. 15.

2. Much of the discussion in this chapter on the communication process was developed by R. C. Huseman and incorporated into the publication *Interpersonal Communication*, pp. 21–27.

3. P. V. Lewis, *Organizational Communication: The Essence of Effective Management* (Columbus, Ohio: Grid, 1975), p. 36.

4. Ibid., pp. 36–37.

5. Ibid., pp. 37–38.

6. D. Katz and R. L. Kahn, *The Social Psychology of Organizations* (New York: John Wiley & Sons, 1966), p. 239. As cited in Lewis, *Organizational Communication*, p. 38.

7. Lewis, *Organizational Communication*, p. 38.

8. R. L. Smith, G. M. Richetto, and J. P. Zima, "Organizational Behavior: An Approach to Human Communication," in *Readings in Interpersonal and Organizational Communication*, 3rd ed., eds. R. C. Huseman, C. M. Logue, and D. L. Freshley (Boston: Holbrook Press, 1977), p. 11.

9. T. L. Dahle, "An Objective and Comparative Study of Five Methods of Transmitting Information to Business and Industrial Employees" (Ph.D. diss., Purdue University, 1954). As cited in Smith, Richetto, and Zima, "Organizational Behavior," p. 12.

10. Much of the discussion in this chapter on upward communication has been taken from E. Planty and W. Machaver, "Upward Communications: A Project

in Executive Development," *Personnel,* 28 (January 1952), 304–319.

11. Much of the discussion in this chapter on horizontal communication has been taken from R. K. Allen, *Organizational Management Through Communication* (New York: Harper & Row, 1977), pp. 77–79.

12. H. Fayol, *General and Industrial Administration* (New York: Pitman, 1949), p. 34. As cited in Allen, *Organizational Management,* p. 78.

13. Allen, *Organizational Management,* p. 78.

14. Ibid., pp. 78–79.

15. K. Davis, "Management Communication and the Grapevine," *Harvard Business Review,* (September–October 1953), 43–49. As cited by Lewis, *Organizational Communication,* p. 41.

16. Lewis, *Organizational Communication,* pp. 41–42.

17. P. Karathanos and M. D. Pettypool, "A Network Approach to Formulating Communication Strategy," *OMEGA—Journal of Technical Writing and Communication,* 22: 1, 95–103. (This discussion from this article was adapted with permission.)

18. E. M. Rogers and D. L. Kincaid, *Communication Networks: Toward a New Paradigm for Research* (New York: The Free Press, 1981), pp. 31–78.

19. G. M. Goldhaber, H. Dennis, G. Richetto, and O. Wiio, *Information Strategies: New Pathways to Corporate Power,* (Englewood Cliffs, N.J.: Prentice Hall, 1979), p. 144.

20. K. H. Roberts and C. O'Reilly, III, "Some Correlations of Communication Roles in Organizations," *Academy of Management Journal,* 22:1 (1979), 42–57.

21. E. Reynolds and J. Johnson, "Liaison Emergence: Relating Theoretical Perspectives," *Academy of Management Review,* 7:4 (1992), 551–559.

22. J. Hall, "Interpersonal Style and the Communication Dilemma: Managerial Implications of the Johari Awareness Model," *Human Relations,* 27:4 (1974), 381. For a critical review of communication literature, see Lyman W. Porter and Karlene H. Roberts, *Communication in Organizations* (Irvine: University of California Press, 1972).

23. Hall, "Interpersonal Style," p. 382.

24. Ibid., p. 382.

25. Ibid., p. 382.

26. As Joseph Luft describes this, "It is fairly well known now that Johari does not refer to the southern end of the Malay Peninsula. That's Johore. Johari is pronounced as if it were Joe and Harry, which is where the term comes from. . . . Dr. Ingham and I developed the model during a summer laboratory session in 1955 and the model was published in the

Proceedings of the Western Training Laboratory in Group Development for that year by the UCLA Extension Office." See Joseph Luft, *Of Human Interaction* (Palo Alto, Calif.: Mayfield, 1969) p. 6.

27. This questionnaire is called the "Personnel Relations Survey" and is available from Teleometrics International, P.O. Box 314, The Woodlands, Texas 77380.

28. The description of the Johari Window is drawn, largely, with permission and minor modifications, from "How to Interpret Your Scores on the Personnel Relations Survey," © Teleometrics International, The Woodlands, Texas 77380.

29. The descriptions are taken by permission from "How to Interpret Your Scores," pp. 4–5, with minor modification.

30. Deborah Tannen, *You Just Don't Understand* (New York: Ballantine Books, 1990).

31. John Gray, *Men Are from Mars, Women Are from Venus* (Westport, Conn.: Harper Publishing, 1993).

32. Deborah Tannen, Ph.D., *You Just Don't Understand* (New York: Ballantine Books, 1990), pp. 42–44, 149–151. Copyright © 1990 by Deborah Tannen, Ph.D. By permission of William Morrow & Company, Inc.

33. G. Weaver, "Law Enforcement in a Culturally Diverse Society," *FBI Law Enforcement Bulletin* (September 1992) (this discussion of cross-cultural diversity in communication was taken with modification from this source), pp. 3–7.

34. Albert Mehrabian, "Communication Without Words," in *Readings in Cross-Cultural Communication,* 2nd ed., ed. Gary Weaver (Lexington, Mass.: Ginn Press, 1987), pp. 84–87.

35. Thomas Kochman, *Black and White Styles in Conflict* (Chicago: University of Chicago Press, 1981).

36. Edmund Glenn, D. Witmeyer, and K. Stevenson, "Cultural Styles of Persuasion," *International Journal of Intercultural Communication,* 1 (1977), 52–66.

37. G. W. Cordner, "Written Rules and Regulations: Are They Necessary?" *FBI Law Enforcement Bulletin,* 58:5 (1989), 18.

38. S. W. Mastrofski, "Police Agency Accreditation: The Prospects of Reform," *American Journal of Police,* 5:3 (1986), 45–81.

39. L. Territo and R. L. Smith, "The Internal Affairs Unit: The Policeman's Friend or Foe," *Police Chief,* 43:7 (1976), 66–69.

40. H. Brinton Milward and Louise O. Snyder, "Electronic Government: Linking Citizens to Public Organizations through Technology," *Journal of Public Administration Research and Theory,* 6 (1996), 261–275.

## INTRODUCTION

Most authorities who examine the major issues involved in law enforcement come regularly to the same inescapable conclusion: namely, that the ability of a police department to provide high-quality service to its citizens and to solve its major operating problems is significantly affected by the quality of its personnel and the ways in which they are managed.

As police departments have attempted to address external problems, such as rising crime rates, and internal problems, such as effectiveness of their operating units, they have undertaken many studies, entertained numerous theories, launched various experiments, and invested heavily in new equipment. In most of these efforts, however, it has been apparent that eventual success depends on the critically important element of human resources. Sound personnel practices, therefore, are the single most vital consideration in the quest for effective law enforcement.[1]

# —8—
# HUMAN RESOURCE MANAGEMENT

*There's only one corner of the world you can be certain of improving and that's your own self.*
ALDOUS HUXLEY

The subject of human resource management has gained considerable prominence and visibility within the law enforcement community over the past 40 years. A number of social, political, and economic factors have given impetus to this development, including (1) the civil disorders and rapidly increasing crime rates during the 1960s, which resulted in the creation of prestigious national commissions and numerous recommendations for improving the police service;[2] (2) expansion of the labor movement within law enforcement, resulting in the revision of personnel policies relating to working conditions, training, discipline, and promotions; (3) the Equal Employment Opportunity Act of 1972, which required police departments to eliminate personnel policies that unlawfully discriminated against minorities and women in both employment and career development; (4) the Civil Rights Act of 1991, which strengthened the Equal Employment Opportunity Act of 1972; (5) the Americans with Disabilities Act (ADA) of 1990, which made it unlawful to discriminate against persons having or perceived to have disabilities with respect to all employment practices, including recruitment, hiring, promotion, training, layoffs, pay, assignments, transfers, firing, leave, and benefits; (6) the willingness of police employees to litigate against practices and actions they feel are unjust; (7) the increased conferring of rights on public employees by the courts; and (8) greater willingness on the part of courts and juries to award large cash settlements to citizens injured by police officers because of some act deemed negligent. Acts of negligence often involve the injury or death of innocent bystanders because of careless use of firearms or police vehicles and are frequently linked to inadequate selection procedures, training, or supervision.[3,4] These factors require that considerable effort and time be directed to all areas of human resource management.

In larger departments, a sound human resource management unit needs to be adequately staffed and financed and report through the chain of command to the police chief. This unit must be specialized and have authority and responsibility to carry out its mission.[5] As a result of such factors as departmental philosophy, historical precedent, the chief executive's preference, intradepartmental power politics, and legislative requirements, broad statements about the functions of a human resource management unit are somewhat difficult to make.[6] However, the unit is generally responsible for the following:

1. Preparing policy statements and standard operating procedures relating to all areas of the administration of human resources, subject to the approval of the chief executive of the agency

2. Advising the chief executive of the department and other line officials on personnel matters

3. Maintaining a performance evaluation system

4. Creating an integrated management information system (MIS), which includes all necessary personnel data such as that pertaining to performance evaluation

5. Maintaining an energetic and results-producing program to recruit qualified applicants

6. Administering a carefully conceived process of selection; that is, administering a valid system for distinguishing those who are to be employed from those who may not be employed

7. Establishing criteria for promotion to the various ranks, along with a method for determining the relative qualifications of officers eligible for such appointments

8. Conducting a multifaceted staff development program for personnel of all ranks from entry through executive level

9. Developing and administering position classification and assignment studies to form the basis for staff assignment and evaluation

10. Developing a plan of adequate compensation, distributed fairly among rank assignments according to difficulty and responsibility of assignments and including provisions for differentials based on special assignments, shifts, or outstanding performance

11. Representing the agency during negotiations with police employee groups and at other meetings with representatives of organized employees, such as at meetings pertaining to grievances and related matters

12. Conducting exit interviews with resigning officers to identify, and subsequently correct, unsatisfactory working conditions

13. Providing advice to managers and supervisors at all levels concerning human resource problems, with special attention to leadership and disciplinary problems, and administering reviews of disciplinary actions and appeals

14. Conducting an ongoing personnel research program

15. Representing the police department to the central human resource management office or civil service commission[7]

Few police agencies have viable, adequately staffed, and sufficiently supported human resource management units that can maximize the agency's human resources. The most likely reasons for this problem are:

1. The failure of police management to determine its human resource objective. What does management really want its personnel arm—or, for that matter, its total personnel strength—to accomplish? Without clear-cut program objectives, it is difficult even for the best human resource administrator to adapt to the police function.

2. The inability or unwillingness of the police administrator to delegate clear-cut authority to accomplish the human resource goals. The absence of clear-cut lines of authority and responsibility is allowed to exist between field supervisors and the personnel staff. In some jurisdictions, civil service laws deny to the police chief and to other line managers sufficient authority over personnel matters. Without this authority, the human resource director is less than fully effective.

3. The inadequacy of total resources available to the police agency, leading to emphasis on field strength at the expense of personnel administration and frequently other management functions. Although it is politically attractive to the chief to get as many officers into the field as possible, these officers may be underutilized unless there is adequate management direction.

4. The intransigence of some police officials and unions against changes in personnel practices and policies.[8]

Moreover, it is not uncommon to find departmental policy implicitly stating that the human resource is less important than objects of capital expenditure. For example, in a number of cities, there are placards on the dashboards of police vehicles with a statement to the effect, "This car cost the taxpayers of _____$23,000—treat it with respect or you will be subject to disciplinary measures." Certainly no one would argue that a police officer having a vehicular accident is an unimportant event; accidents result in fewer cars being available for patrol service, thereby reducing coverage, and injuries may occur and liabilities may be created. But, in contrast, consider the sergeant with ten subordinates, each of whom earns $30,000 per year. Let us assume that the chief executive of that department sends the supervisor a memorandum at the beginning of each fiscal year stating, "You are responsible for the management of $300,000 of this organization's resources. Please ensure that the efforts of your subordinates are directed toward achievement of previously agreed-upon objectives." Would not this action, coupled with periodic monitoring, the implementation of any necessary corrective action, and comparison of year-end results with anticipated outputs, be more beneficial to the public?

## POLICE PERSONNEL SELECTION AND THE AMERICANS WITH DISABILITIES ACT

Although there are no hard-and-fast rules about the exact sequence of steps to be followed in the police hiring process, the steps themselves traditionally have been arranged in order from least to most expensive (see Figure 8-1). However, the 1990 federal Americans with Disabilities Act (ADA) has changed the traditional sequencing.

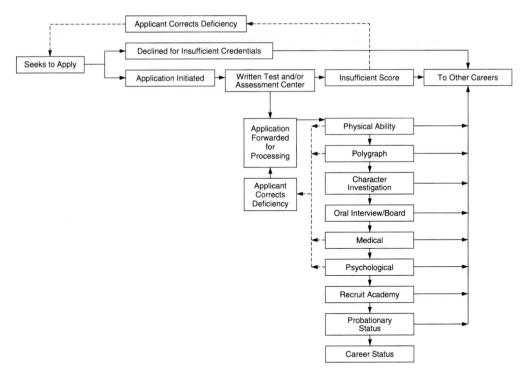

**FIGURE 8-1.** A model for processing police applicants. (From L. Territo, C. R. Swanson, and N. C. Chamelin, *The Police Personnel Selection Process,* © Bobbs-Merrill, Indianapolis, Indiana, 1977, p. 10). The original model has been modified to address changes brought about by the Americans with Disabilities Act (ADA).

The ADA was enacted by Congress to eliminate barriers to disabled persons in such areas as public transportation, telecommunications, public accommodations, access to government facilities and services, and employment. The ADA makes it unlawful to discriminate against people with disabilities in *all* employment practices, including recruitment, hiring, promotion, training, layoffs, pay, firing, job assignments, transfers, leave, and benefits. The ADA is applicable to both private- and public-sector employers. In 1994, all employers with fifteen or more employers were covered by its provisions. Although the federal Equal Employment Opportunity Commission (EEOC) has responsibility for the job discrimination provisions of the ADA, other federal agencies, such as the Department of Transportation and the Federal Communications Commission, oversee the parts of the ADA that fall within their areas of specialization.

The ADA covers both *actual* and *regarded* disabilities. Briefly, a disability is defined as a "physical or mental impairment that substantially limits a major life activity." A "regarded" disability case would be exemplified by a police administrator who, believing an employee had a disability, made an adverse employment decision on that basis; the administrator would then have violated that employee's rights under the ADA even if no disability existed. For instance, assume that Chief Joe Garcia transferred Officer Akisha Tyler from the patrol division to a job assignment involving clerical duties in the records division because he erroneously believed she was infected with the AIDS virus and he wanted to reduce her contact with the public. If Officer Tyler learned of Chief Garcia's reasons for making the transfer, she could file a complaint under the ADA. Moreover, even if she actually tested positive for the AIDS virus, such a transfer for that reason would be actionable unless she posed a significant health risk to others as determined by objective medical evidence and not through generalizations, fear, ignorance, or stereotyping. Also, if Officer Tyler had reached the point where she informed management of her disability or management reasonably determined that she could no longer perform field duties as a result of it, then reassignment to another less demanding position may be required. Among the significant provisions of the ADA and the guidelines issued by the EEOC for its implementation are:

1. Discrimination in *all* employment practices is prohibited, including job application procedures, hiring, firing, advancement, compensation, training, and other terms and conditions of employment such as recruitment, advertising, tenure, layoff, leave, and fringe benefits.[9] Job application sites must be accessible to those with disabilities. Although discrimination is prohibited, an employer is not required to give preference to a qualified applicant or worker with a disability over other applicants or workers.[10]

2. The ADA makes discrimination against individuals who have a relationship or association with a disabled person illegal.[11] For example, assume that Jane Johnson applies for a position in a police department for which she is qualified and that she has a disabled husband. It is illegal for the department to deny her employment solely on the basis of its unfounded assumption that she would take excessive leave to care for her spouse. Another illustration of a protected relationship or association is provided by a police officer who does volunteer work with dying acquired immunodeficiency syndrome (AIDS) patients. A chief of police who was uncomfortable with the officer's volunteer work and adversely affected any of the terms and conditions of the officer's employment would be in violation of the ADA. Similarly, police departments and other employers are prohibited from retaliating, for example, by transferring to undesirable precincts or hours of duty, against applicants or employees who assert their rights under the ADA.

3. The ADA expressly excludes certain conditions from protection,[12] including current illegal drug use, homosexuality, bisexuality, transvestitism, exhibitionism, voyeurism, gender identity disorder, sexual behavior disorder, compulsive gambling, kleptomania, pyromania, and psychoactive substance disorders resulting from current use of illegal drugs. However, former drug users who have successfully completed a rehabilitation program are covered by the ADA. Arguably, however, despite this provision, law enforcement employment could possibly be denied to former drug users because such applicants' prior conduct raised material questions about their judgment, criminal associates, willingness to abide by the law, and character.[13]

4. A person is defined by the ADA as disabled if that person has a physical or mental impairment that substantially limits one or more major life activities, has a record of such impairment, or is regarded or perceived as having such an impairment, even if they do not actually have it. Generally, a person is disabled if the person has any physiological disorder, condition, disfigurement, anatomical loss, or mental or psychological disorder that makes the individual unable to perform such functions as caring for him- or herself, performing manual tasks, walking, seeing, hearing, speaking, breathing, learning, or working to the same extent as the average person.[14] A person is not "substantially limited" just because he or she is unable to perform a particular job for one employer or is unable to perform highly specialized professions re-

quiring great skill or talent.[15] Protection against handicap discrimination does not include being able to work at the specific job of one's choice.[16]

5. A qualified individual with a disability is a person who meets legitimate skill, experience, education, or other requirements of an employment position that he or she is seeking and who can perform the "essential functions" of that position with or without reasonable accommodations.[17] Job descriptions will be considered highly indicative of what the essential functions of a job are, and they should be drafted with considerably greater care than that used by some personnel and police departments in the past. The "essential functions" provision states that an applicant will not be considered to be unqualified simply because of an inability to perform minor, marginal, or incidental job functions.[18] If an individual is able to perform essential job functions except for limitations caused by a disability, police departments and other employers must consider whether the individual could perform these functions with a reasonable accommodation. A reasonable accommodation is any change or adjustment to a job or work environment that permits a qualified person with a disability to enjoy benefits and privileges of employment equal to those of employees without disabilities.[19] Reasonable accommodations may include

   a. Acquiring or modifying equipment and devices
   b. Job restructuring
   c. Part-time or modified work schedules
   d. Reassignment to a vacant position
   e. Adjusting or modifying examinations—such as physical ability tests, training materials, or policies
   f. Providing readers and interpreters
   g. Modifying the physical work environment[20]

   Illustrations of this last point include installation of elevators, widening doorways, relocating work stations, and making break rooms accessible or relocating the break room so that the employee with the disability has opportunity to interact with other police employees. Failure to provide reasonable accommodation to a known physical or mental limitation of a qualified individual is a violation of the ADA unless it creates an undue hardship on the employer's operations.[21] Undue hardship means that the accommodation would be unduly costly, extensive, substantial, or disruptive, or would fundamentally alter the business of the employer.[22] Although some police departments may raise the "unduly costly" defense, the EEOC scrutinizes such claims carefully. Particularly when the accommodation needed for modified equipment, remodeled work space, or the development of new policies and examinations is a small fraction of the overall budget, claiming undue hardship may be viewed by the EEOC as a pretext for discrimination against applicants and employees with disabilities. Among the remedies federal courts have invoked in other types of civil rights cases in which the defendants claimed an inability to pay is requiring jurisdictions to borrow money to finance the ordered remedies. The requirement to make a reasonable accommodation is generally triggered by a request from an individual with a disability.[23] Without this request, police agencies are not obligated to provide one.[24]

6. The ADA does not encourage, prohibit, or authorize testing for illegal drugs in the workforce.[25] Drug testing is not a medical examination under the ADA. Solely from an ADA perspective, police and other employers can continue to

do preemployment drug screening of applicants and random tests of probationary and other employees.

7. Police applicants and employees often have medical conditions that can be controlled through medication or auxiliary means. Examples are persons whose diabetes or high cholesterol is mitigated through appropriate medication. Even though their medical conditions may have no significant impact on their daily lives, such individuals are covered by the ADA.[26] The ADA does not cover employees whose impairments are temporary (e.g., a broken arm), do not substantially limit a major life activity, are of limited duration, and have no long-term effects.[27]

8. No medical inquiries can be made of an applicant, nor can any medical tests be required or conducted, *before* a job offer is made, although the offer can be made contingent upon passing the medical test. Questioning applicants about their ability to perform job-related functions is permitted as long as the questions are not phrased in terms relating to a disability.[28] It is unlawful to ask applicants if they are disabled or the extent or severity of a disability.[29] It is permissible to ask an applicant to describe or demonstrate how, without reasonable accommodation, the applicant will perform job-related functions.[30]

## The Courts and the ADA

The federal Rehabilitation Act (RA) of 1973 (the forerunner to the ADA), state laws prohibiting employment discrimination on the basis of disabilities, and the ADA have formed the basis for a growing number of suits against police departments on behalf of people with disabilities. The cases that follow are intended to illustrate some of the issues addressed through litigation.

In *Kuntz* v. *City of New Haven*[31] (1993), plaintiff Walter Kuntz brought a suit under the RA. To establish a *prima facie* case of discrimination under the RA, Kuntz had to establish that (1) he was a handicapped person within the meaning of the act, (2) he was otherwise qualified for the position, (3) he was excluded or discharged from a position solely due to his handicap, and (4) the position was part of a program supported by federal funds. This last element did not require that Kuntz's individual position or the New Haven Police Department (NHPD) unit to which he was assigned be funded entirely with federal funds. This element of proof was satisfied by showing that both the City of New Haven and the NHPD received such funds. Sgt. Kuntz had suffered a heart attack four years previously and had undergone a triple bypass heart operation. Although he had passed the written and oral examinations for lieutenant, he was denied promotion twice solely due to his heart attack. The NHPD claimed that because lieutenants can be assigned as assistant shift commanders or as shift commanders, they must be able to apprehend suspects and to engage in high-speed pursuits. However, in fact, supervisors in the NHPD were rarely involved in high levels of physical stress. Kuntz exercised regularly and had a very strong record of performance in the various positions he had held before and after his heart attack. He worked side by side with "full-duty" lieutenants and successfully performed the same assignments given to such personnel. The medical opinion was that his health was normal for a person his age. Moreover, the NHPD's adoption of community policing also provided the opportunity to assign Kuntz to one of many lieutenant positions that did not entail physical exertion. These factors were sufficient for Sgt. Kuntz to overcome claims by the NHPD that his possible assignment to field duties would be dangerous to him, to other police officers, and to the public. The court held that the defendant had not shown that such risks were imminent and substantial, rising above the level of mere possibility. Kuntz was promoted to lieutenant and received back pay.

In Toledo, Ohio, police applicant Bombrys was disqualified from further employment consideration due to health and safety concerns because he was an insulin-dependent diabetic. Litigation was filed claiming protection under the ADA, the RA, the Ohio Civil Rights Act, and the due process clause of the Fourteenth Amendment. The city claimed that due to his medical condition, Bombrys could become confused on duty, combative, or even unconscious. Bombrys requested an accommodation: that he be allowed to carry the means to treat himself should it become necessary, pointing out that such an accommodation was not costly to the city nor did it change the basic functions of a police officer. The court issued a restraining order requiring the city to allow the plaintiff to enter and complete the police academy while the litigation went on. In *Bombrys* v. *City of Toledo*[32] (1993), the court held that the blanket exclusion of all insulin-dependent diabetics violated each of the protections cited in the plaintiff's suit. In so doing, the court noted that several cities do not categorically exclude diabetics from their police departments, and in these cities insulin-dependent diabetics were sent to a specialist who evaluated their ability to perform on a case-by-case basis. When the case was decided, Bombrys had completed the academy. The court noted that while Bombrys could not be summarily dismissed in a way that contravened the court's findings and the applicable law, the department was not prohibited from undertaking an investigation to determine if Bombrys was fit to perform the duties of a police officer. This was important in light of the fact that while on duty Bombrys suffered an insulin reaction and had to be taken to a hospital.

In *Champ* v. *Baltimore County*[33] (1995), a disabled police officer, James Champ, could not use one of his arms due to an on-duty motorcycle accident. Over the next 16 years, the police department used Champ in different light-duty assignments. Subsequent to his accident, Champ was recertified by the Maryland Police Training Commission in the driving of emergency vehicles and the use of firearms. Due to budgetary constraints that prevented the hiring of new officers, the police department began channeling long-term light-duty officers into non-law-enforcement positions. Then, the light-duty officers would be replaced by newly hired full-duty officers. Champ was placed on disability leave and subsequently filed suit under the ADA. The court found for the defendant in *Champ*. In so doing, it noted that the plaintiff could not perform the essential functions of a police officer (e.g., make a forcible arrest) and there was no reasonable accommodation that would allow him to do so. Champ was also deemed to be a direct threat to the welfare and safety of others due to his inability to perform the essential functions, since even if he were assigned to an "inside" position, he could still be subject to reassignment to field duties.

As this edition was being prepared, litigation was ongoing in *Phyllis Tower and Davey Sales* v. *City of Detroit Police Department*[34] (1996). *Tower* has the potential to become a landmark case with respect to the application of the ADA to police departments. The Detroit Police Department (DPD) had a lengthy history of finding long-term light-duty positions for officers who were injured on or off duty or who had various diseases, including multiple sclerosis. Over a period of years, the number of officers in such positions grew to about 350 of roughly 4,074 sworn positions. Around 1995, the DPD took the position that as a matter of safety for officers and the public, all officers had to be capable of performing the "24 essential functions of a police officer" and that the DPD was not required to make any "reasonable accommodation" to those who couldn't perform them. This position did not apply to officers temporarily assigned to a light-duty billet in anticipation of a full recovery from some injury or illness. However, the DPD's position did mean that all officers had to be able to perform the "24 essential functions" of a police officer regardless of whether they were assigned to inside or street duties, or they would be involuntarily separated from the service. This, the DPD asserted, was necessary in order to staff special events, to be able to respond to disasters and riots, and to perform police duties while off duty when necessary. Under city charter, the DPD can refer officers to the pension board without the officers' consent and thus they can be involuntarily retired if they cannot perform what the DPD claims are the 24 essential functions of a police officer. Officers injured on duty receive a pension of 66 percent of their current salaries, and officers injured off duty or who suffered a debilitating disease get a pension of 2 percent of their salaries per year if they are vested.

Plaintiffs Tower and Sales were involuntarily retired due to multiple sclerosis and filed an ADA suit on behalf of themselves and all similarly situated officers in the DPD. The plaintiffs noted that they had worked inside jobs for many years and that they performed the same duties as full-duty officers. Moreover, the plaintiffs had strong performance evaluations, including several perfect scores. During the discovery process, ample evidence was produced that showed that many full-duty officers working inside jobs were never called up to perform duties in the field or to staff special events such as parades. Additionally, because many of these special events were on holidays, many full-duty officers who were normally off bid to work so they could earn the premium rate holiday pay. The plaintiffs' expert pointed out that in the Chicago Police Department inside positions were simply found for officers who were going to be on restricted duty on a long-term basis without their having to request an ADA accommodation. In the San Francisco Police Department, restricted-duty officers were also placed in inside positions in which they could continue their careers. San Francisco was also in the early stages of identifying the number of positions into which long-term restricted-duty officers could be placed. Moreover, in the SFPD, the ability of restricted-duty officers to perform off-duty police action is not an issue due to the restrictions placed on all officers in such circumstances. The Detroit Police Officers Association (DPOA), a union, filed a grievance against the DPD claiming that management's very recent unilateral adoption of the 24 essential functions violated the collective bargaining agreement. If the DPOA prevails, a major component of the defendant's case is undermined. The plaintiffs' expert also argued that in a large line and staff organization (see Chapter 5, Concepts of Police Organizational Design), the DPD had inside jobs into which it could place long-term restricted-duty officers and that the blanket exclusion of all such officers from employment by the DPD was contrary to the *Bombrys* decision. Large police departments are watching the *Tower* case closely in light of the arguments raised and the fact that some police departments, such as Chicago and San Francisco, are both willing and able to find productive work for some number of long-term restricted-duty officers.

As the various components of the police selection process are described in subsequent sections of this chapter, some information about how the ADA and certain other legal provisions affect them are presented. In all cases, individuals and agencies should consult their own attorneys in order to be fully informed before deciding on a policy or course of action in such matters.

The recruitment of a well-qualified applicant pool is the starting place for the hiring process (see Box 8-1). This recruitment process often incorporates several different strategies, including police and personnel department representatives attending job fairs at churches, colleges, military bases, or other locations. On their own initiative, prospective applicants may also make a preliminary visit to the police department, civil service commission, or central personnel office to obtain employment information. The results of such a visit should be several. The individual should come away with sufficient knowledge to make an informed decision concerning a career in policing. This will be gained through literature prepared especially for that purpose and by access to someone who can respond to questions accurately and in detail. If an individual clearly does not meet the minimum standards for employment, he or she should be so advised and given some suggestions for possible remedial action, if any, that could be taken to qualify for consideration. Often overlooked by even seasoned personnel officers is the harm that can be done by treating an obviously unqualified prospective employee brusquely. Such action does little to mediate the person's disappointment and may cause the story of the treatment to be circulated among the individual's friends, reinforcing old stereotypes of the police and, in effect, dissuading other people from making application.

## BOX 8-1

### Recruiting Cops Is a Tough, Costly Process

**by Santiago Esparza**

Highland Park and Detroit police are in the midst of a recruiting drive that will shape the future of both departments.

Although more than 1,000 people showed up Monday at Cobo Convention Center to apply for the Detroit police academy, strict standards will doom most applicants, said Detroit Police Lt. Gary Brown, who oversees personnel and recruitment.

Brown said he needs to maintain a pace similar to Monday's to ensure there is a good pool of candidates from which to choose.

He said the Council of Baptist Pastors of Detroit and Vicinity Inc. has agreed to help him recruit. Brown has spoken to the congregations at Little Rock Baptist Church and Fellowship Chapel.

"If I attract 3,000, I'm only going to be able to hire 300 of them because of (strict standards)," Brown said. "We would like to have half that number (of) minorities."

Achieving those goals is tough because about 40 percent or 1,000 applicants of a class of 2,500—the amount of the last enrollment period—will be elimi-

nated due to criminal backgrounds or traffic violations that turned up during computer checks.

Another 400 will fail because of physical and written tests. About 50 percent of the remaining recruits will not make it past additional background checks. About 250 will be left after the remainder fail medical, oral board or psychological exams, Brown said.

"We do a complete computer check. We check with employer, do neighborhood surveys," he said. "They could have something in their background they haven't told us of."

Those checks are costly. The department routinely shells out $3,000 per applicant and as much as $10,000 per person.

Officials then pay about $15,000 per person once he or she makes it to the academy for 22 weeks of training. In addition, recruits earn base salary, which begins at $25,000.

Brown defends the expenses.

"Police work is demanding and the welfare and safety of the community is involved," he said. "This has to be one of the most thorough selections of any job."

Highland Park Police Chief David Simmons agrees.

"To find people suitable to be employed in the police department, you are looking at the cream of the

*(continued)*

BOX 8-1 (continued)

crop," he said. "In order for a person to be a cop, they have to have a basic love of people."

Another problem both departments face is that the brightest of candidates may not apply.

Both constantly compete with large employers such as the Chrysler Corp., which last week gave employees a bonus that averaged $7,800.

"Many of the people with the skills go to college and become doctors or lawyers," Brown said.

Detroit will have more than 400 positions open throughout the year. In addition, there are nearly 900 people who could possibly retire and those spots will need to be filled. Many of those officers are in command positions.

The situation is similar in Highland Park. Officials there recently hired 14 new officers to replace 27 retiring ones. And the city just received a $1.5 million federal grant to hire up to 14 more. They have not begun advertising the openings yet, but officials said they plan to do so soon.

The city's police department also pays thousands of dollars to conduct background checks. To cut costs, officials hire recruits who have already received training in criminal justice at a college. They also raid other police departments or hire laid-off officers, said Highland Park Mayor Linsey Porter at last week's City Council meeting.

"We need your sons and daughters," Porter said. "We want to make sure that our police department is representative of the community."

Raiding bigger departments is a practice mimicked by smaller departments across the state. They have hit the Detroit police hard in recent years. To fight this, Chief Isaiah McKinnon in August instituted new rules that mandate that recruits sign a contract with the department.

The recruits promise to work as Detroit police officers for at least three years or pay $5,400 to the department if they the take a post with a different force before that time. Brown said those who leave to work in other fields are not penalized.

Other departments have similar agreements. In Los Angeles, officers are required to pay back $60,000 to the police department if they leave for another force before serving at least five years. Highland Park has no such agreement.

"We can't stop them from leaving," Brown said. "But if they go to another department, they have to pay us. Two people have already done that: no questions asked."

Source: The Detroit News, January 30, 1997. Reprinted with permission.

Among local units of government, most individuals will be required to visit the central personnel office, which serves all departments of city government, and submit an application. Alternately, it is not uncommon to find a civil service commission, consisting of a board of three to five prominent citizens, existing independently of the central personnel office. In such situations, the board would typically direct a professional staff that would perform most of the actual work. Historically,[35]

The independent Civil Service Commission has often been limited to control over examinations for entry, promotions, and to the judicial function of hearing appeals from disciplinary actions.[36]

Where central personnel offices and civil service commissions exist concurrently in the same jurisdiction, the authority for matters not historically within the purview of the commission are retained by the central personnel office which constitutes no smaller number of functions or amounts of power. In some jurisdictions the central personnel office has virtually disappeared, supplanted by the civil service commission.

Regardless of which arrangement prevails, the person seeking to make an application will have to demonstrate the meeting of certain criteria before the application is accepted; among these are citizenship, attainment of minimum age, and related factors. The candidate's application form is one of the most important sources of information about a candidate for a law enforcement agency. The data included in this form will provide much of the focus for the personnel investigator's line of inquiry, as it includes specifics related to the following: personal data; marital status and former marital status, including divorces, annulments, or widowhood; educational background; military service; foreign travel; employment record; financial history; criminal and juvenile record; motor vehicle operator record; family background; references; and willingness to undergo a polygraph examination.[37] A conviction for a criminal arrest may or may not result in being disqualified for employment. Each conviction must be reviewed on the basis of its relevance to the job for which the applicant is applying. The application form should not request any information that is medical in nature, such as a history of illnesses and operations or medications currently being taken, as this would violate the ADA.

Where satisfactory proof of any of the basic criteria cannot be established, the application would be declined for insufficiency. An individual may later seek to reinstitute an application by correction of deficiencies or by obtaining and presenting additional documents.[38]

In 1972, Congress amended Title VII of the Civil Rights Act of 1964 and the EEOC was charged with the responsibility of administering its provisions. Title VII made it illegal to discriminate impermissibly against any person on the basis of race, sex, color, religion, or national origin in employment decisions. An example of a permissible discrimination is refusing to hire a man to model women's lingerie; in this situation hiring only women would constitute a bona fide occupational requirement (BFOQ). "Employment decisions" is defined broadly and includes hiring, demotion, transfer, layoff, promotion, and firing decisions. Any procedure or requirement used in making these decisions is a test and comes under the scrutiny of the EEOC. Thus, application forms, interviews, oral boards, written tests, probationary ratings, assessment centers, performance evaluations, education, background investigations, physical fitness or ability tests, and other logically related matters are all subject to EEOC review for a determination as to whether there has been an unlawful act of discrimination.

Initially the EEOC focused on entry-level requirements and testing because in many organizations there had been little progress in hiring minorities. In more recent years, the EEOC has directed greater attention to promotions and other personnel decisions as greater numbers of minorities have been hired and are affected by such decisions. A key concern of the EEOC is whether written tests and assessment center evaluations are job related and predictive of future job performance. A survey of employment practices in police agencies revealed that 91.9 percent of the departments responding to a survey used a written or cognitive test to determine eligibility for hiring.[39] Such written tests are relatively inexpensive, easy to administer, and can be quickly scored. Smaller jurisdictions may lease their examinations from firms specializing in such services, whereas larger cities and counties typically use one that has been developed by their own testing specialists, who often have been educated as industrial-organizational psychologists. Written entrance tests are usually given as an "assembled examination"—all of the candidates eligible to take it are brought together at the same time. In large cities such as New York and Chicago 25,000 or more applicants may take the written entrance examination simultaneously at public schools and other designated public properties designated as examination sites.[40]

**The Entrance Examination: The Written Test and/or Assessment Center**

In contrast, assessment centers are used by 22.6 percent of police agencies; local departments are somewhat more likely to use them than state police agencies.[41] Greater information on assessment centers is presented later in this chapter. Briefly, assessment centers are a series of behavioral tests or simulations in which candidates are given information and placed into mock situations where they are observed by teams of trained raters or assessors. The raters look for and evaluate the performance of candidates with respect to behaviors that are important to successful job performance as an entry-level police officer, such as oral communication skill. Assessment centers are expensive in comparison to written tests. The design of the simulations or mock situations—referred to as exercises—requires a great deal of thought, raters must be trained, the number of candidates each team of four to six assessors can reliably rate each day ideally should not be greater than six, scheduling is complex, the process is labor intensive due to the time devoted by the assessors, and the cost per candidate is higher as compared to the use of written tests. Despite some apparent disadvantages of assessment centers, some jurisdictions prefer them because they provide information about candidates' actual behavior, they yield more detailed information than written tests, and minorities tend to pass them at higher rates than those usually associated with written tests. A few jurisdictions use written tests on a pass-fail basis to screen candidates going to assessment centers, which ensures each prospect's minimum level of cognitive ability and thus makes the assessment center more cost effective.

The method by which a test can be shown to be associated with subsequent performance on the job is through a process of validation, the starting point for which is a job analysis. A job analysis reveals what the important tasks are for a position such as police officer as well as what specific knowledge and skills are needed to perform the job well.[42] Validation is a detailed undertaking whose thorough treatment is not possible here. However, some general statements are both proper and necessary. The question "Is this test valid?" seeks to determine whether it is appropriate (valid) to make a decision about a person's ability to perform a particular job based on that person's score on a particular test.

A test that discriminates against a group of prospective or current employees and cannot be shown to be valid is impermissible discrimination under EEOC guidelines. However, if a police department or other employer can show that different test scores are associated with different levels of performance on the job, then even if the test discriminates against some identifiable group, including minorities, the courts are likely to find that it is a permissible discrimination, unless some other test would adequately meet the employer's needs and produce less of a discriminatory impact.[43]

Under EEOC guidelines, discrimination in testing occurs when a substantially different rate of selection in hiring, promotion, or other employment decision works to the disadvantage of members of a race, gender, or ethnic group. This different rate of selection is termed "adverse impact" and is impermissible unless the test or other practice has been validated. As a rule of thumb, adverse impact occurs when the selection rate for any gender, race, or ethnic group is less than four-fifths (80 percent) of the selection rate for the group with the highest selection rate.[44] Table 8-1 illustrates how the so-called "four-fifths rule" is applied; in that hypothetical case adverse impact is demonstrated and will be judged to be impermissible if the test has not been properly validated.

**TABLE 8-1.  Hypothetical Group of Candidates for Employment as Police Officers**

|  | White | Black | Totals |
|---|---|---|---|
| Took test | 400 | 100 | 500 |
| Passed | 120 | 10 | 130 |
| Failed | 280 | 90 | 370 |
| Passing rate | 30%[a] | 10%[b] | 26% |

[a]120 (white passed) ÷ 400 (total white candidates) = 30% white selection rate
[b]10 (black passed) ÷ 100 (total black candidates) = 10% black selection rate
Adverse Impact Calculation:
10% (black selection rate) ÷ 30% (white selection rate) = 33.3% or less than 80% (four-fifths)

The four-fifths rule does not allow up to 20 percent discrimination; it is not a legal definition, but a means of keeping attention focused on the issue. Regardless of the amount of difference in selection rates, other unlawful discrimination may exist and may be demonstrated through appropriate means. To use an extreme example, assume that the president of the local minority employees' association is very militant and vocal about his opposition to the current chief of police's policies. Further assume that the president's daughter applies for a job with the police department. All other applicants taking the written test mark their answers in ink, but the daughter is required to use a pencil. Later, the daughter is told that she failed the test because she left half of the answer sheet blank. An examination of that sheet reveals that half of her answers were erased and that the majority of the erasures involved correct responses. In this situation, an impermissible discrimination would be shown even if there was no adverse impact on minorities overall.

**"Reverse Discrimination"**

Under EEOC guidelines all discrimination is prohibited and there is no recognized "reverse discrimination" theory. Yet, when the courts mandate preferential hiring and promotional opportunities for minorities to correct for past employment practices, problems arise. Majority individuals, who are typically white males, label the preferential treatment as "reverse discrimination" and at odds with the merit principle.

One of the regrettable side effects of trying to overcome years of blatant discrimination is the occasional tension between majority officers, who feel they have been passed over for promotion, and those who receive the preferential treatment. Despite the clear necessity to correct for long-standing discrimination in the workplace, the use of such practices is difficult for many officers to support. They feel that the "rules of the game" have been unfairly changed, that such preferential treatment needlessly endangers the public if the less able are hired or selected to lead. Even when a clearly superior minority officer, who would be promotable under any system, is selected ahead of them, their sense of anger may lead them to denigrate the minority officer's very real and substantial capabilities. Criticism of preferential consideration of minorities to correct long-standing abuses in hiring and promoting has come from different quarters, including the U.S. Commission on Civil Rights. Although such developments made civil rights leaders uneasy about the prospect of less support for their movement, two 1989 decisions by the Supreme Court both frightened and angered them, leading many to charge that the clock on civil rights was being turned backward. In *Wards Cove Packing*

v. *Antonio,* the court held that minorities could not be favored in hiring decisions and that the plaintiffs must disprove the claims of the employer—in this instance it was an Alaskan salmon cannery—that the adverse impact on minority hiring was based on factually neutral considerations.[45] In *Martin* v. *Wilks,* the court held that majority employees in the Birmingham, Alabama, Fire Department could challenge a consent decree because they had not been parties to the negotiations that had the effect of abrogating their rights.[46] Together these decisions made challenging employment decisions and practices more difficult for minorities, while facilitating challenges from majority employees of consent decrees favorable to minorities. Thus, to no small extent the Civil Rights Act of 1991 can be viewed as an attempt to strengthen the 1972 Title VII law administered by the EEOC as well as an effort to limit the impact of, or to negate, court decisions unfavorable to civil rights interests. Although the 1972 Title VII law did not allow for the award of punitive damages, the Civil Rights Act of 1991—also administered by the EEOC—does so on the following bases: (1) for employers who have more than 14 and fewer than 101 employees in each of 20 calendar weeks in the current or preceding year (referred to as the base period), up to $50,000; (2) for employers who have more than 100 and fewer than 201 employees for the base period, there is a cap or limit of $100,000 in punitive damages; (3) for employers who have more than 200 and fewer than 501 employees during the base period, $200,000; and (4) in the case of employers who have 500 or more employees during the base period, a maximum punitive damage award of $300,000.[47] Unquestionably this punitive damage provision is a significant development. Employers will abandon many questionable practices, employees will be more likely to litigate, and plaintiffs will be less likely to be satisfied with only the traditional EEOC remedies previously available to them, such as hiring or promotion, back pay, and orders to cease using the employment practices successfully challenged. However, under the Civil Rights Act of 1991 the punitive damage provision cannot be applied to a government, government agency, or political subdivision.

**Physical Ability Testing**

One study reported that 80.3 percent of responding police agencies presently use qualifying physical strength and/or ability tests.[48] However, before the enactment of Title VII in 1972, the principal physical requirement used in police officer selection was based on standards of height and weight. It is now recognized that these standards adversely affected the employment of women and some ethnic groups with small body size and are no longer rigidly used as hiring criteria because police departments consistently failed to, or were unable to, show the importance of these factors in job performance (see Box 8-2).[49] Interestingly, however, in *Robinson* v. *City of Lake Station* (1986), physical size was found to be a legitimate factor in hiring for the position of garbage packer.[50] It was noted the position required extensive lifting, changing oversized truck tires, and occasionally pushing trucks out of mud and snow.

As police departments moved away from rigid reliance on height and weight standards during the 1970s, many of them decided to use physical agility tests. Some departments adopted military-type obstacle courses or components of them. In general, police departments found it difficult to defend the use of this type of test when women—who typically failed the test at significantly higher rates than males—challenged it under EEOC provisions. For example, one department used a course that required applicants to scale a six-foot-high fence. Women who had been eliminated from further employment

**BOX 8-2**

### Minimum Height Rule for LAPD Officers Eliminated

**by Matt Lait**

The Los Angeles Police Commission on Tuesday abolished a requirement that officers stand at least 5 feet tall to join the LAPD. Department officials requested that the minimum height requirement be eliminated, saying they have found no evidence that shorter people were less capable of performing the duties of a police officer. Furthermore, they said such a requirement exposed the department to potential lawsuits from candidates who were rejected solely because of their height.

A couple of commissioners asked Los Angeles Police Chief Willie L. Williams if shorter officers had a greater tendency to rely on their weapons than taller officers, and the chief assured them there was no evidence to support such a theory. "There is no research within the department or nationally that shows that small stature individuals . . . [have] any negative impact on their ability to perform their jobs" because of their height, Williams said.

Department officials surveyed 16 police departments across the country, and none had minimum height requirements. Police officials and commissioners said the move is likely to attract more women and Asians to the department. The commissioners voted 4-0 to eliminate the requirement.

*Source: Los Angeles Times*, February 19, 1997. Copyright 1997, Los Angeles Times. Reprinted by permission.

consideration successfully challenged the practice and won when their attorney pointed out that a city ordinance forbade the construction of fences of greater than five feet in height, creating a *prima facie* case showing that the test was not job related. In *Harless* v. *Duck* (1980), a federal district court struck down a police department's use of a physical agility test that included the following components: (1) 15 pushups, (2) 25 situps, (3) a six-foot standing broad jump, and (4) a 25-second obstacle course.[51] The court ruled that although a job analysis showed the need for some physical activity on the job, it did not specifically define the amount of physical strength or extent of physical exertion required. Moreover, it was noted that the test was developed intuitively, there was no justification for the exercises chosen, and there were no benchmark scores. In contrast, in *Evans* v. *City of Evanston* (1989), women challenging a firefighters' physical agility test lost when the defendants were able to show that a job analysis had been done, the test faithfully imitated tasks firefighters are called on to perform in their work, and the test had been pretested on firefighters to determine scoring.[52]

By the 1990s, police departments were more inclined to describe their physical agility testing as physical fitness or ability tests. This shift represents more than a terminology change. It represents a content shift away from obstacle course–style testing toward measuring applicants' job-related anaerobic level (strength) and aerobic (cardiovascular) fitness.

Police departments wanting to create a defensible physical ability test should follow certain steps: (1) review the decisions in prior litigation carefully, (2) have a detailed job analysis done by a competent authority using sound methodology, (3) employ an exercise physiologist to link the physical tasks identified by the job analysis with specific physical abilities (e.g., upper-body strength) and then specify which physical test is best suited to assess an applicant's capability, (4) pretest the physical ability procedure to develop benchmark scores that are properly associated with acceptable job performance levels, (5) announce the components of the test in detail well before the test itself so that candidates know what to prepare for and have the time to do so, (6) administer the test in a consistent manner, (7) preserve all records of the test for the period of time dictated by applicable records retention laws or policies, and (8) be prepared for requests for reasonable accommodation under the ADA.

Because police departments, under the ADA, cannot ask any medical questions until a conditional job offer is made, some agencies are administering the physical ability test after the medical examination. The reason for this is to avoid the prospect that a candidate will die from some undisclosed medical condition during the physical ability test. Other departments are retaining it early in the selection process, but having candidates sign statements waiving any liability claims in the event of their own injury or death during the test. In addition, some agencies are also giving applicants a copy of the activities in the physical ability test and having them bring a written statement by a physician that they can participate. As a final note, when physical ability tests are administered on a pre-offer basis, police agencies should not gather any information about candidates' heart rates before and after the test or any other related measures because of their medical nature.

## The Polygraph Test in Preemployment Screening

The federal Employee Protection Act of 1988 prohibits the use of the polygraph in most private-sector preemployment screening, but all governmental bodies are exempt from this restriction.[53] However, a few state courts have prohibited even the police from using the polygraph in screening applicants.[54] Such state court decisions take precedent over the federal law. Nationally, 56.6 percent of police agencies reported using the polygraph in employment screening; municipal police departments are more likely (73.1 percent) than state police agencies (44.4 percent) to use it.[55] Typically most departments (83 percent) conducted their own examinations rather than contracting with a source outside of the department.[56]

The advantages to using the polygraph in screening police applicants include the fact that: (1) some potential candidates will decide not to apply because they feel that the polygraph examination will reveal prior acts that will disqualify them from further consideration, and (2) it sends a message to the community that the department is expending every effort to hire only the most fit people as officers.

Polygraph tests do not violate the ADA as long as no medical questions are asked when they are used *before* making a conditional offer of employment. At that point, questions about current medication or whether the employee is currently under medical care are impermissible.

## The Character Investigation

All police agencies conduct character or background investigations because, with the exception of observing the probationary officer's actual performance under varied field conditions, the single most important element of the process is the character investigation. The basic course of action in the character investigation is to review and verify all responses made by the applicant as to his or her education, military service, prior employment history, and related matters and to check the references listed and develop other references. The ADA mandates that any parts of the character investigation that are medical in nature cannot be pursued until a conditional offer of employment has been made.

An editor once stated that the three basic rules for great journalists were "check your facts, check your facts, and check your facts." These three basic rules also apply to conducting the character investigation; making assumptions or failing to verify "facts" independently will result in an increase in negligent hirings. This creates, as is discussed in Chapter 11, Legal Aspects of Police Administration, a liability problem because people who should not have been employed are hired.

A case history illustrates this point: On his initial employment form, an applicant to a large city department reported that he had served a tour of duty in the Coast Guard. Among the documents he showed the department's personnel investigators were the original copy of an honorable discharge as well as DD 214 (Armed Forces of the United States Report of Transfer or Discharge). The investigators believed the discharge and DD 214 to be authentic. Still, they obtained an authorization for release of military records and medical information from the candidate. This release was then sent to the appropriate military records center. Meanwhile, the candidate's character investigation went on with respect to other factors. The candidate reported on his application form that following his discharge from the Coast Guard, he and his wife had spent five months traveling the country on money they had saved, thus there was no employment history during that time. When the military record information arrived, it was learned that he had, in fact, been honorably discharged, but in less than 30 days had reenlisted and 2 months into that tour of duty, he got drunk, badly beat up his wife, and assaulted military authorities who were sent to his quarters on base to handle the domestic disturbance. Subsequently, he was dishonorably discharged from the service. When questioned about it, he readily admitted to these facts and added that he was betting that either the department wouldn't check or that the record of the second enlistment wouldn't yet be in his permanent personnel file if the department did check.

Such incidents have made many agencies realize that character investigations are very specialized and very demanding, and that a failure to properly conduct them will eventually produce results ranging from very serious to catastrophic.

## Oral Interviews and Oral Boards

*Oral interview* refers to a one-on-one interview between the applicant and some authority in the hiring process, such as the chief of police. In smaller jurisdictions the interview may actually take the place of a written test or assessment center. In other instances, although there may be a written test or an assessment center, the police chief may simply want a chance to see and talk with candidates before they are hired. In general, such interviews tend to be unstructured, free flowing, and either not scored or graded on a pass-fail basis. If legally challenged, unstructured interviews are difficult to defend because unskilled questioners may ask legally impermissible questions and because different candidates may be asked widely varying questions—a lack of standardization.

In contrast to interviews, *oral boards* usually involve a face-to-face contact between a three-member panel and the police applicant. Panel members may be police officials, representatives of the civil service or merit board, community members, or combinations of these people. A standard set of job-related questions is drawn up ahead of time, and panel members are trained in the use of the written evaluation form, which they incorporate into their consideration of each candidate. Such well-planned, systematic, structured systems are more reliable, have greater defensibility, and are better predictors of future job performance than unstructured interviews.[57]

## Medical and Psychological Testing of Police Applicants

In order to achieve maximum benefit, the police department must have a close relationship with the professionals who conduct medical and psychological examinations. The valid needs of the department must be communicated to the professionals, and professionals must be required to provide reliable information in the formats required by the department. Additionally, these professionals should also receive training on the ADA. Under the ADA, medical and psychological examinations may be administered only when a conditional offer to employ has been made.

Psychological tests deemed not to be medical tests by the ADA may be given prior to a conditional offer to employ. For example, a test designed to test an applicant's honesty may not be considered medical in nature. However, some tests, such as the Minnesota Multiphasic Personality Inventory (MMPI), include questions that may be considered disability related and therefore not allowable, for example:

1. I am bothered by an upset stomach several times per week.
2. I have a cough most of the time.
3. During the past year I have been well most of the time.
4. I have never had a fit or convulsion.
5. I have had attacks in which I could not control my movements or speech, but in which I knew what was going on around me.[58]

If an employer receives unsolicited medical information from a third party about the candidate's qualifications to perform the job, and the candidate is otherwise qualified, then the information cannot be used.[59] However, if an applicant volunteers information about a disability that makes her or him unqualified for the job, then no offer has to be made.[60]

# THE RECRUIT ACADEMY, PROBATIONARY PERIOD, AND CAREER STATUS

Widespread use of the police academy to train police rookies for their new responsibilities is a comparatively recent development. A survey of 383 cities by the Wickersham Commission in 1931 showed that only 20 percent of the municipalities provided police academy training.[61] At the time the use of the police academy was limited almost exclusively to the larger cities. In many jurisdictions new officers were simply equipped and told to go out and "handle things" or, at most, were assigned to work briefly with a veteran officer who "showed them the ropes."

Following World War II, there was increased recognition of the need to prepare newly hired personnel for police work, but, being a matter of local discretion, it remained largely undone. In 1959 California pioneered statewide legislation that statutorily established police minimum standards, including entry-level training or academy training. Today all states have legislation regulating entry-level police training.

It is important to note that although state statutes require a minimum number of hours, many jurisdictions choose to exceed that amount considerably, based on their own needs and philosophies. Police academy training is provided under a variety of arrangements. A state academy may offer the basic course, often referred to as mandate training; individual police agencies, usually the larger ones, operate their own academies; and regional academies provide training for police agencies in a multicounty area. Combinations of these arrangements exist in most states, and variations are possible. For example, for many years larger agencies that operated their own academies allowed smaller agencies to send recruits to their academies whenever they had unused seats. This practice initially was free under the "good neighbor" doctrine, but over time fiscal pressures have led to the use of fees.

Police academy training is frequently followed by placing new officers in the care of a field training officer (FTO). The FTO carefully monitors the development of the rookie under actual job conditions; often the rookie is rotated between shifts and FTOs to be further evaluated. FTO evaluations can be crucial in determining whether an officer stays with the department or is "washed out." Some agencies have adopted officer retention boards to review all evidence on each probationary officer and to recommend to the agency head whether an officer should be granted career (or permanent) employee status or released.

**FIGURE 8-2.** Officer instructing cadet on the proper way to complete a report form. (Photo courtesy of the Sacramento, California, Police Department.)

# COLLEGE EDUCATION FOR POLICE OFFICERS

Higher education for police officers can be traced to 1929, when the University of Southern California offered an advanced degree in public administration with a specialization in law enforcement. Michigan State University initiated its Bachelor of Science Degree in Police Administration in 1935. Higher education programs for the police grew slowly until the 1960s.[62]

During the 1960s, prominent groups, such as the International Association of Chiefs of Police and the International Association of Police Professors (now the Academy of Criminal Justice Sciences), began to issue public statements in support of higher education for law enforcement personnel.[63]

The President's Commission on Law Enforcement and Administration of Justice provided further impetus in its report, *The Challenge of Crime in a Free Society*. The commission recommended that all police officers be required to have two years of college education at a minimum and that all future police personnel be required to possess a bachelor's degree.[64] As the commission explained:

> Generally, law enforcement personnel have met their difficult responsibilities with commendable zeal, determination, and devotion to duty. However, the Commission surveys reflect that there is substantial variance in the quality of police personnel from top to bottom.
>
> . . . The Commission believes that substantially raising the quality of police personnel would inject into police work knowledge, expertise, initiative, and integrity that would contribute importantly to improved crime control.
>
> The word "quality" is used here in a comprehensive sense. One thing it means is a high standard of education for policemen. . . . A policeman today is poorly equipped for his job if he does not understand the legal issues involved in his everyday work, the nature of the social problems he constantly encounters the psychology of those people whose attitudes toward the law differ from his. Such understanding is not easy to acquire without the kind of broad general knowledge that higher education imparts, and without such understanding a policeman's response to many of the situations he meets is likely to be impulsive or doctrinaire. Police candidates must be sought in college. . .

The 1960s was a decade of social disruption and violence. Police confrontations with students at universities and with anti-Vietnam war protesters were common events. The inability of the police to cope with the ghetto riots and their apparent helplessness to curtail the spiraling crime rate led both liberal and conservative politicians to believe that higher education was desirable. The National Advisory Commission on Civil Disorders and similar commissions of this period reflect these views.[65]

The police were charged not only with being ineffective in controlling disorder, but also with aggravating and precipitating violence through harassment of minority ghetto dwellers, student dissidents, and other citizens. The National Advisory Commission on Civil Disorders discovered that, in America's cities, aggressive police patrolling and harassment resulted from society's fear of crime. This practice created hostility and conflict between the police and minorities. Finally, President Johnson's Commission on Campus Unrest also advocated the belief that education for police might assist in decreasing police/citizen confrontations. That commission found:

> Law enforcement agencies desperately need better educated and better trained policemen. There should be special monetary incentives for all who enter the police service with college degrees or who obtain degrees while in police service.[66]

The consensus was that to improve law enforcement, the quality of police personnel had to be upgraded through higher education. There is little doubt that law enforcement personnel had limited education. The median educational level of police officers in 1966 was 12.4 years. In December 1968, *Fortune* magazine estimated that fewer than 10 percent of American police officers had been to college; in October 1968, *Time* reported that Detroit police recruits were from the bottom 25 percent of their high school graduating classes.[67]

The 1960s focused on the need of criminal justice education. This need is determined by an analysis of the criminal justice system and by an assessment of the manpower requirements of the system's agencies.[68] Today, the need of the criminal justice field is for personnel with advanced degrees. New developments and techniques making criminal justice activities more sophisticated demand more sophisticated, well-prepared, well-schooled officers. Technology for policing has advanced by leaps and bounds to a point that a police officer in the 1960s would consider his role today to be science fiction!

Education is usually based on a solid foundation of liberal arts. A law enforcement practitioner—or a potential practitioner—must perceive policing as it relates to American society and the democratic process. Higher education exposes students to ideas, concepts, and problem-solving techniques. The educational process aims to develop individuals who know how to live within a group, individuals who understand conflicts in our society and who possess an understanding of motivation, stress, and tension of other people in our society. An individual with this knowledge and understanding has the ability to apply past information to new situations.[69]

A college education will not transform an intellectually wanting person into an accomplished one. However, all things being equal, the college-educated individual is more qualified and better prepared than the high school graduate. The college-educated person has more experience with people and new situations. His or her responsibility and adaptability to new surroundings have been tested. In addition, he or she has been exposed to various cultural characteristics and ethical and racial backgrounds. This exposure should eliminate or reduce prejudice and bias. More importantly, a formal education should teach individuals to check their judgments regarding prejudices in favor of a more tranquil analysis.[70]

A basic concern of higher education in law enforcement is the need to study and improve the system. Academic study of policing is needed to identify problems and to identify ways in which problems can be solved. Persons interested in research careers in criminal justice need higher education.[71]

As the importance of high-quality personnel was finally recognized in the 1960s, the drive to upgrade personnel began. However, in the 1970s, the National Advisory Commission on Criminal Justice Standards and Goals stated:

> Police agencies have lost ground in the race for qualified employees because they have not raised standards. College graduates look elsewhere for employment. Police work has often come to be regarded by the public as a second class occupation, open to anyone with no more than a minimum education, average intelligence, and good health.[72]

The Commission on Criminal Justice Standards and Goals found it ironic that educational levels were not increased for the police, because studies found that police officers with a college education generally performed significantly better than officers without a college education. According to the commission, upgrading the educational level of police officers should be a major challenge facing policing. Professions require a higher educational degree and, if police officers hope to be recognized as a profession, they need to take notice of the professional criteria. The Commission recommended that all police officers be required to possess a bachelor's degree by no later than 1982.[73] Even into the year 2000 the police, as a universal standard, did not yet require an under-graduate degree. At a time when we have more college graduates than ever in our society, still the police still do not require a college education. However, it should be noted that a study sponsored by the Police Executive Research Forum (PERF) found that approximately 62 percent of policing agencies serving jurisdictions with populations of more than 50,000 people had some form of incentive program to encourage education. This same study found that only approximately 14 percent of these departments had a mandatory requirement of a college degree as a prerequisite for employment.[74]

In the last forty years, police education has increased but not to the point where all entry-level police officers are required to have an undergraduate degree as a requirement for employment. If police departments are to increase their professionalism and if they have any expectations of meeting the demands placed on them by their communities, they must improve the educational level of all police officers. The 14 percent of departments requiring a college degree must increase to 100 percent for all sworn police personnel. American society is becoming increasingly more complex, sophisticated, better educated, multicultural, and multilingual; its police should do no less.

It is critical that police be familiar with the socioeconomic and cultural makeup of the community they serve. They must identify the cultural diversity among the people they protect. America's communities are heterogeneous, and a police officer with an adequate educational background should function better in the community than an officer unaware of various cultural differences among the numerous ethnic and racial groups. The police need to continue their pledge toward professionalism, and professionalism implies standards and proficiency. A Police Executive Research Forum study[75] hypothesized several advantages of college education for police officers:

- It develops a broader base of information for decision making.
- Course requirements and achievements inculcate responsibility in the individual and a greater appreciation for constitutional rights, values, and the democratic form of government.
- College education engenders the ability to flexibly handle difficult or ambiguous situations with greater creativity or innovation.
- Higher education develops a greater empathy for diverse populations and their unique life experiences.
- The college-educated officer is assumed to be less rigid in decision making and more readily accepts and adapts to organizational change.
- The college experience will help officers better communicate and respond to crime and service needs of a diverse public in a competent manner with civility and humanity.
- College-educated officers exhibit more "professional" demeanor and performance.
- The college experience tends to make the officer less authoritarian and less cynical with respect to the milieu of policing.

In spite of the arguments just presented in favor of a college education for police officers there are powerful political and social forces that are not fully supportive of this movement. The news story in Box 8-3 outlines some of these objections.

**Opposition to Higher Education**

## BOX 8-3

### College Degrees and Race Bias

The question of college education for police, an oft-debated ideal that has loomed over the profession for decades, is under scrutiny once again, and for all-too-familiar reason: the assertion that requiring police to have a college degree discriminates against minority groups.

The latest challenge has arisen in New Jersey, where the state chapter of the NAACP claims that a four-year college degree requirement for all State Police candidates is not job-related and disproportionately excludes black and Hispanic applicants.

The requirement was implemented in 1993 after the U.S. Justice Department lifted a consent decree mandating increased minority hiring.

According to a lawsuit filed in 1996 and now making its way through Mercer County Superior Court, African American and Latino representation in the State Police Academy classes has plummeted as a result of both the college requirement and a new written examination, which NAACP attorneys claim cuts a pool of applicants that is 20 percent minority to less than 8 percent.

In the two academy classes prior to 1993, according to the suit, 22.5 percent of those qualified to take the agency's written examination were African American and 9.4 percent were Latino. In the first three classes after the consent decree was lifted, however, blacks made up just 14.8 percent of those qualified to take the test, and Hispanics 6.7 percent.

Minorities made up 14.1 percent of the State Police ranks in March 1998, it said, but the next year that figure had fallen to 13.8 percent, and that percentage is seen likely to continue to decrease if more minorities fail to graduate from the academy.

"The overall effect of the State Police recruiting and selection process has been to reduce African American representation among members of the 114th, 115th and 116th classes from more than 22 percent of the qualified candidate pool to 6 percent of those hired," said the suit. "Hispanic representation was reduced from over 9 percent of those in the qualified candidate pool to 3 percent of those hired."

David Rose, who imposed and enforced the 1975 decree before his retirement from the Justice Department's Civil Rights Division in 1987, and who is now representing the NAACP, noted that in order to make something a prerequisite, an organization must first show that most of those who do not qualify under the new standard are unable to do the job. That is not true in this case, he told The Philadelphia Inquirer, noting that some of the highest-ranking members of the New Jersey State Police did not have a college education when hired. In fact, he claimed, no other state police agency has such a requirement.

However, the U.S. Supreme Court did let stand a lower court's ruling in a similar case more than a decade ago, which found while there may have been statistical discrimination in a 45-semester-hour college requirement implemented by the Dallas Police Department, it was not appropriate to abolish it in order to achieve racial equity within the agency.

An expert witness in that case, Dr. Gerald Lynch, president of John Jay College of Criminal Justice in New York, added that a study by the New York Police Department done a number of years ago had shown that 26 percent of blacks had attended college as compared with 22 percent of whites. "It was then that [then-Police Commissioner] Ben Ward was willing to consider higher education requirements for promotion," he told Law Enforcement News.

Two major black law enforcement organizations, the Guardians and the National Organization of Black Law Enforcement Executives, support those higher education requirements in New York, Lynch said, because they do not believe it will discriminate against African Americans. "It's a stalking horse that is actually erroneous," he said. "It sounds like it makes sense, but if you look at the facts, it doesn't really pan out."

A college-based police cadet program, which ultimately brings in more minorities and women than any other recruitment source, is the best way to go, said Lynch. "I believe the answer to all of this dilemma is to connect recruiting with college and university attendance and not just go out into the general public with these ads that are basically fluff and won't work."

Lou Mayo, executive director of the American Police Association, said that those departments that have instituted four-year degree requirements have

*(continued)*

**BOX 8-3 (continued)**

not found it difficult to recruit an adequate number of minority candidates. Two cases in point, he said, are the police departments of Portland, Ore., and Tulsa, Okla. "[Portland] Chief Charles Moose said they put the requirement in two years ago and have had no problem with that," said Mayo.

In Tulsa, a cadet program with an emphasis on minorities was established under an out-of-court settlement with the NAACP, he said. It allows candidates to work part-time at the department while completing a degree program with tuition reimbursement.

"At the end of the four years, they have a college degree so they win, and the Police Department has had four years to look them over and decide whether they want them as an officer, so they win," said Mayo. "The NAACP withdrew its suit based on this cadet recruitment plan for minorities."

Even within NOBLE's leadership, there is no "clear-cut" agreement on college requirements, said Bob Stewart, that group's executive director. What has seemed to occur in many jurisdictions, he said, is that the negotiated settlements arising from these challenges turn out to be the most comprehensive approach of all—as in the case of Tulsa, Stewart noted.

"It could be investing in a cadet program, putting some money into incentives for on the job schooling, and then setting a target for a college requirement for some point in the future," he told LEN. "That tends to cover all the bases."

New Jersey state officials, while acknowledging that the number of minority academy graduates dropped sharply in the years following the lifting of the decree, dismiss charges of racial discrimination. They point to other factors as primary contributors to the problem, including the inability to set minority hiring quotas, academy classes that do not coincide with college graduations, the heavy reliance on top scorers in the written exam, and poor recruitment efforts.

Robert J. Caccese, the director of operations and audits for the state Attorney General's office, said the college requirement is not the culprit. A college degree is necessary, he said, because unlike troopers in other states whose duties are mainly to patrol highways, New Jersey troopers in their first or second year on the job are expected to participate in a wide variety of duties, such as lab work, flying helicopters and working in the state's high-tech unit.

One of the problems has been that academy classes are predicated on having money in the budget, he said. With no academy classes between the years 1989 and 1993, many candidates opted for other jobs. In the future, classes will be scheduled in accordance with spring and winter commencements, said Caccese.

To correct other shortcomings uncovered in a report submitted last year by the Police Executive Research Forum, which was hired as a consultant to study the situation, the State Police has doubled the size of its recruitment staff to 12. The unit has increased the number of trips it now makes to colleges, said Caccese.

Also, in keeping with a PERF recommendation, the State Police is now taking recruits with scores that fall below the top 100 to achieve more ethnically diverse and balanced classes, Caccese said. The practice is legal, he told The Inquirer, as long as all those who are chosen have passed the test. A mentor program for female and minority candidates is also being implemented to ensure those candidates succeed at the academy, he added.

The NAACP's suit, however, disputes several of the assertions upon which the recent changes have been based. There are no studies that show minority candidates to be more likely to give up waiting for an academy class than white applicants, said Rose. And under State Police practices, he noted, the first five years of a trooper's career are spent patrolling the highways, not working in other areas of the agency.

*Source:* Reprinted with permission from *Law Enforcement News,* John Jay College of Criminal Justice (CUNY), 555 West 57th St., New York, NY 10019. May 15/31, 1999.

**Questions to be Answered**

It is apparent that the trend is toward a requirement that all entry police applicants have a college degree. The question now is, at what pace will this occur? Before making any dramatic changes in their standards, police administrators should try to answer the following questions in relation to the needs of their agencies and communities.

- Will the increased educational level of police officers result in both a quantifiable and qualitative improvement in the delivery of social and crime control services? Will the college-educated officer have difficulty in identifying easily with or understanding the problems of people of lower socioeconomic status with whom much of police contact exists?

- Does education have a relatively uniform impact upon individuals, or is there some variance by discipline, that generally makes certain college majors more or less suitable for police work? No general agreement exists, even among the proponents of higher education for police officers, about which academic skills are best suited to prepare individuals for a career in law enforcement.

- Are many values attributed to education merely correlates of it, being provided instead by other functions of the psychological makeup and drives of individuals who pursue a college education: that is, are college graduates more highly motivated to achieve professional success because they went to college, or did they go to college because they were highly motivated to achieve professional success and simply viewed the college degree as a vehicle through which this end could be achieved?

- Are there differences in the attitude and job performance of those who bring a college degree to the organization when compared with in-service officers who obtained a degree over an extended period of time?

- If education reduces authoritarianism, does it do so to the extent that the amount remaining decreases effective performance of field duties?

- Should a law enforcement agency that is highly traditional, bureaucratized, and authoritarian in its leadership philosophy try to recruit college-educated personnel?

- What types of problems may occur if college-educated personnel are recruited into police departments where the majority of the personnel from the supervisory ranks upward do not have a college degree?

- Since supervisory, managerial, and planning roles tend to be more complex than those undertaken at the line level, would a mandatory higher education requirement be more realistic if it were directed toward individuals filling these positions rather than those at the entry and line levels?

## WOMEN IN POLICING

Women are not new to policing. They have been in the ranks for decades, but their representation has traditionally been small. Since the early 1970s, however, more women have been applying for police positions. A recent study by the National Center for Women in Policing (NCWP) of 100 of the largest law enforcement agencies in the country revealed that in 1972, women represented 2 percent of all police officers in the agencies surveyed. By 1997, they represented almost 12 percent.[76]

However, this increase has occurred in the face of obstacles. While an increasing number of agencies have welcomed female officers, many simply have not; in fact, female applicants have often had to bring litigation against departments to overcome resistance. Women who entered major city departments in the '70s recount both passive and aggressive actions by male officers to make life uncomfortable for new female officers (see Box 8-4).

In view of both agency and individual resistance, the growth to 12 percent could be seen as a success. Still, critics are concerned that this growth is not as positive as it seems. They point out that recent growth (1990 to 1997) has been relatively slow, from 9.4 to 11.6 percent of the sworn workforce. Organizations that represent female police officers are concerned by this rate

## BOX 8-4

## Survey: Women Muscled Out by Bias, Harassment

by Kevin Johnson

ALBUQUERQUE—For years, Deputy Chief Sal Baragiola couldn't explain why this city's police department was having so much trouble adding women to its ranks.

The city went to its share of job fairs. It offered a competitive salary. But with the percentage of female officers in single digits, it was clear that they weren't doing enough to open doors to women. So during the last three years Albuquerque hired physical trainers to help women pass physical conditioning tests; the department switched to weapons that were better suited to a woman's smaller hand; and it even found a body armor manufacturer willing to tailor bulletproof vests to conform to women's breast sizes.

Today, women make up 13% of the force and that number is climbing. But Albuquerque is the exception rather than the rule among the nation's police departments, which in many cases offer women an inhospitable and at times hostile work environment.

"For a long time, they tried their best to squeeze us into men," Albuquerque patrolwoman Deedy Smith says. "The uniforms, the vests, the whole thing. This has always been a man's job."

In what is described as the most comprehensive analysis of women in policing, authorities say women remain grossly under-represented in the ranks; they are routine targets of gender bias and sexual harassment; and they have largely been unable to punch through a virtually bulletproof glass ceiling.

The survey of 800 police departments by the International Association of Chiefs of Police is to be published next week. Among its findings:

- Nearly 20% of the departments surveyed had no female officers at all. Overall, 12% of the nation's nearly 600,000 police officers are women, a number that has not moved appreciably in nearly a decade. This despite an unprecedented wave of police hiring since 1994 under a federal grant program designed to put 100,000 new officers on the nation's streets by 2000.
- Ninety-one percent of departments reported having no women in policy-making positions. Of the nation's 17,000 police departments, only 123 have women chiefs.
- Nearly 10% of the departments surveyed listed gender bias among the reasons that women were not promoted. That number has added significance since all of the survey's respondents were police chiefs or top department executives.

Women have won more than one-third of the lawsuits in which they charged police departments with gender bias or sexual harassment.

"You can imagine that there is some level of frustration here," says Susan Riseling, president of the National Association of Women Law Enforcement Executives. "Until we figure out what drives women away from this business, we're not going to see any progress."

The survey's findings have prompted the International Association of Chiefs of Police—the nation's largest association of law enforcement executives—to search for ways to increase the number of female police and to retain them.

"I accept this report as a clear mandate," IACP President Ronald Neubauer says. "They want our help to improve and expand the roles of women in policing, and they'll get it."

### Community policing

The push for more female officers reflects the shift by many departments to community policing, a philosophy in which law enforcement tries to be more responsive to community needs. The recent downturn in violent crime is attributed in part to community policing. And department executives believe they can be more successful by deploying officers who better reflect the makeup of their communities.

That means hiring more women.

"We just have to do a better job to get the word out," says Gaithersburg, Md., police Chief Mary Ann Viverette. "We have to reach girls at an early age when they are just forming opinions about what careers to pursue."

Among the report's recommendations: fairer screening procedures, tougher sexual harassment policies and sustained recruiting drives designed to attract women and keep them on the job.

More than 25% of the police departments that responded to the survey still express concerns about the ability of female officers to handle physical conflicts. But the survey also indicates that top law enforcement officials want more female officers and believe they possess superior skills in some other important categories.

For example, police executives said women often have exceptional interpersonal skills that enable them to defuse potentially volatile situations, especially domestic abuse cases.

### Keeping female officers

Getting women to consider a law enforcement career is hard enough. Keeping them on the job can be even more difficult. About 60% of women who leave police work do so between their second and fifth year on the job, according to the IACP survey. The reasons vary, but family pressures are the most frequently cited cause.

"I just lost one very good officer because she had to stay home with the kids," Viverette says. "Another moved from the area because she had to take care of aging parents."

And some aspects of police work place difficult demands on female officers—conditions that their male colleagues rarely face.

Officer Smith in Albuquerque says part of the reason her first marriage broke up was because her husband became uncomfortable with one of her undercover assignments.

"It was a super-secret operation," she says. "I was spending a lot of my time in bars because of it. I couldn't tell him anything. He couldn't handle it."

"I had to make a choice," Smith says. "I loved the job too much."

Viverette says making women aware of the kinds of pressures they will face in police work must become part of the recruiting and hiring process. And she says departments must become much more aggressive in recruiting.

Portland, Ore., has already begun a stepped-up recruiting drive.

As part of its push to hire more female and minority officers, Portland broke with tradition and hired a professional recruiter from outside the department. With 160 positions to fill during the next few years, recruiter Jennifer Lawrence has set a goal of seating a police academy class next year that is at least 25% female.

With women making up 16% of its force, Portland is already above the national average. Improving those numbers, however, will be difficult.

Portland is one of the few departments nationwide that requires candidates to have a four-year college degree, a requirement that limits the number of eligible candidates. The department also is competing with a robust economy and low unemployment rate that has cut the pool of job seekers.

As a result, Lawrence has expanded her recruiting efforts beyond the Portland metropolitan area to include five Western states.

"I think we can get the talent," she says. "But to do it, we have to go out of state. Because this is still a male-dominated profession, we have to be more focused in our search."

Portland police have stepped up recruiting efforts on college campuses and Lawrence is also tapping the military, a male-dominated environment that has had success in recruiting, promoting, and retaining women.

"They're out there," Lawrence says. "We just have to find them."

Pittsburgh is already one of the nation's most diverse police departments, with women making up 25% of its force. But it too is worried about recruiting and retaining women.

The department's makeup is largely the result of a federal court order that required Pittsburgh police to hire one white female, one black male and one black female for every white man hired between 1976 and 1992.

Pittsburgh police Commander Gwen Elliott says the number of women has begun to slip since the court order was lifted. "We're looking to hire some people in 2000," she says, "but we're worried about the lack of women candidates."

## A model department

Police executives point to Albuquerque as a potential model for other departments.

In the last three years, female recruits have increased from 8% of academy classes to 25% and women now represent nearly 13% of the force. When the next class enters the police academy in January, officials say one-third of the candidates will be women.

The improvements began after an intense review of department hiring practices revealed serious problems. Among the findings: department psychologists were eliminating a disproportionate number of female candidates.

Lt. Vicky Peltzer, who assisted the outside consultants doing the review, said the psychologists were disqualifying female candidates whose employment histories did not include law enforcement experience or other work traditionally listed by male candidates.

"We really don't know how many candidates we lost in that," Peltzer says.

But Peltzer, a 19-year veteran, points to officers like Deedy Smith as evidence that things are changing.

Smith, 46, patrols one of the city's toughest beats on Albuquerque's south side. She's there, Peltzer says, because she has proven she can do the job. And there isn't any job Smith would rather do.

"I've been in my share of scrapes," Smith says, a pair of silver hand-cuff earrings dangling from each lobe. "I got punched out by a plastic surgeon once because he didn't like getting arrested. It wasn't that bad."

And when it comes to women on the police force: "All I want to know is that when I'm in trouble out here, they'll be there when I need them. It doesn't matter whether it's a man or a woman."

*Source: USA Today,* Nov. 24, 1998. Copyright 1998, USA TODAY. Reprinted with permission.

of growth, particularly when compared to the ratio of women to men in the U.S. population.

The status of female officers is also a concern. Data from the NCWP study indicates that women hold 7.4 percent of top command positions nationwide and 8.8 percent of supervisory positions.

Several years ago in order to promote progress of women in policing, the International Association of Chiefs of Police (IACP) created an Ad Hoc Committee on Women in Policing. The committee concluded that a survey of IACP membership on women in policing issues would be an important first step. The survey was designed to query IACP members about their perspectives and opinions on:

- Status and roles of women in policing
- Recruitment and selection of female officers
- Support and mentoring of female officers
- Training and supervision as correlates of tenure, success, and promotion of female officers
- Attrition and resignation of female officers
- Gender discrimination and sexual harassment
- The degree to which a "glass ceiling" exists as a barrier to promotions
- Future directions for women in policing

Using the resources of the Gallup Organization, 800 IACP members were interviewed by telephone, using a survey instrument designed jointly by the IACP and Gallup. Survey respondents were male (97 percent), female (3 percent), chiefs of police (94 percent), and other positions (6 percent). Respondents represented agencies of all sizes: 277 agencies with fewer than 21 officers, 311 agencies with between 21 and 50 officers, and 210 agencies with more than 51 officers.

The survey revealed or confirmed critical information regarding the status and future of women in policing. While confirming that the number of women in law enforcement is growing and progressing through the ranks, it also revealed that:

- There are few women in policing, compared to their male counterparts.
- Female officers still face bias from male officers.
- Many departments lack strategies for recruiting women.
- Female officers may face gender discrimination and a "glass ceiling" that inhibits promotion.
- Sexual harassment still occurs in many departments.
- While the need is great, there are very few mentoring programs for female officers.

These and other issues uncovered in the survey make clear the need to support existing and future female officers. This may be accomplished in part by taking the following action.

- **Educate local agencies on the value of gender diversity in law enforcement.** Police departments must understand the value and impact of women in policing. Education must address the obstacles facing women as they enter and progress through the ranks.

- **Design a comprehensive approach to turn intentions into success.** While many agencies report an interest in hiring and promoting women, few have developed a long-term strategy to do so. Agencies need action plans to make gender diversity a reality. Recruitment is only a first step. It must be accompanied by an improved and welcoming culture, and it must occur in the absence of gender discrimination and sexual harassment.

- **Advertise and recruit to attract qualified women.** Local agencies must design and carry out effective marketing strategies that reach the intended audience of women and carry a compelling message. Many well-qualified women may not perceive law enforcement as a viable career. Only through sustained outreach can these misperceptions be dispelled.

- **Screen and hire to bring in the best candidates.** As women begin to apply in larger numbers, the screening, testing, and acceptance process must be scrutinized to ensure that it is in no way discriminatory.

- **Train on sexual harassment to foster a zero-tolerance approach.** Training curricula should respond to this issue. Zero tolerance must be the centerpiece of all such training. The curricula must address recognition of, response to, and effective resolution of all such incidents. The wealth of existing training curricula, in the private and government sectors, can provide the foundation for this task.

- **Train on recognition and reduction of gender discrimination.** While often subtle in form, gender discrimination is particularly heinous—limiting women unfairly from earned promotions or other leadership opportunities. Courses addressing this issue must address recognition and resolution of each incident.

- **Avoid actionable behavior and understand litigation issues.** Many agencies report pending or resolved litigation for both gender discrimination and sexual harassment. (See Chapter 11, Legal Aspects of Police Administration, for a more detailed discussion of this topic.)

- **Establish policies to improve the role of women in policing.** Local agencies should develop policies to recruit, retain, promote, and protect female officers from gender discrimination and sexual harassment. Agencies must have this battery of policies in place to respond fully to issues for women in policing.

- **Mentor women officers to strengthen the potential for longevity.** Agencies should establish effective mentoring programs in collaboration with national women in policing organizations, and efforts should be made to seek out examples of promising practices for mentoring programs to support female officers. Once identified, replication of these model programs can be promoted through a variety of educational/information avenues.

- **Improve promotional strategies to move women into leadership roles.** Local agencies must examine both the process of promotion and the trends in women being promoted within their agencies. Where progress of women toward leadership positions is weak, agencies must develop strategies to enhance the potential for women to seek and obtain higher rank.

- **Evaluate agency actions and underscore progress toward diversity.** As the previously cited actions are put into place, agencies must undertake a broad review of their approach to women in policing. Evaluations must address all aspects of women in policing, including recruitment, hiring, training, mentoring, and promotion, to assess an agency's relative success in bridging the gender gap.[77]

# THE FAIR LABOR STANDARDS ACT

The Fair Labor Standards Act (FLSA) is known as the "minimum wage law" and was passed following the stock market crash of 1929.[78] When initially passed, the FLSA applied only to the private sector, and federal, state, and local government employees were not covered by it. In 1985, the extension of FLSA coverage to government employees was held constitutional by the Supreme Court in *Garcia* v. *San Antonio Metropolitan Transit Authority.* The U.S. Department of Labor administers the FLSA.

As far as police officers are concerned, the most important aspect of FLSA is the requirement that under specific circumstances officers must be paid at an overtime rate or given compensatory time, which they can use like vacation days. Police officers commonly work a 28-day cycle, which means that if they exceed 171 hours during any such period, they must be paid overtime at the rate of 1.5 times their regular rate of pay or given compensatory time at the rate of 1.5 hours off for each hour of overtime worked.[79]

Officers can accrue up to 240 hours of compensatory time. If they leave the agency, any unused "comp time" is paid at their current rate of pay and not the rate they were being paid at the time they earned it.[80] Regardless of when officers are paid for their overtime hours, the pay must include any special supplements, such as shift differential, hazardous duty, and educational incentive pay.[81] Unless there is a collective bargaining agreement or some agreement with a group representing the officers to the contrary, employers cannot require officers to accept comp time in place of overtime pay nor do officers have a right to comp time instead of overtime pay.[82]

An important part of FLSA is determining what the "hours worked" by the employee were.[83] In general, "hours worked" means time spent in mental or physical exertion performing tasks the employer wants done or permits the employee to do. Prior to *Garcia,* officers were required to attend a preshift briefing or roll call of 15 to 30 minutes for which they were not paid.[84] Under FLSA, that time now counts as hours worked. In general, meal breaks, which are free of duties and last at least 30 minutes, do not count as hours worked. However, if an officer is not free to leave her or his workstation while eating, then the meal time counts as hours worked regardless of how long it lasts.[85] Time commuting to and from work is not part of the hours worked except in the case of an emergency call-out to some location substantially farther away than the workplace. Even then, only the time that exceeds the normal commute counts as hours worked.[86] The time spent by canine officers feeding and training dogs—including trips to the veterinarian—have consistently been held to be part of the hours worked by canine officers.[87] In most instances, officers who are "on call" in the evening or on weekends cannot count such time as part of their hours worked.[88] But, if on-call officers are frequently recalled to duty, then their on-call time may be counted as part of their hours worked, even if they spent part of that time sleeping.[89]

Salaried employees—those whose pay is fixed regardless of how long they work—are exempt or not covered by the FLSA.[90] However, if police supervisors and administrators are subject to short disciplinary suspensions without pay for violating the department's rules, then they are no longer exempt and are covered by the FLSA unless those suspensions are limited to major safety violations.[91] This synopsis of the FLSA reveals that it is yet another specialized aspect of personnel administration that requires constant attention as it continues to evolve (see Box 8-5).

**BOX 8-5**

## THE FAMILY MEDICAL LEAVE ACT

The Family Medical Leave Act (FMLA) of 1993 gave eligible employees the right to family or medical leave and subsequently to be able to return to their jobs.[92] At his or her discretion an employer can make the leave paid or unpaid. Almost all government employees are covered, including police officers. To be eligible for coverage, officers must have been employed by their department for twelve months and must have worked at least 1,250 hours during the twelve months before the FMLA leave request is made.

An eligible officer can take up to twelve weeks of leave during any twelve-month period for one or more of the following causes:

1. **Birth of a child:** This cause includes a biological child, adopted child, foster child, legal ward, step-child, or a child for whom the officer is acting in the role of a parent. If both spouses work for the same police department, then they are only entitled to a *combined* leave total of twelve weeks. At the police department's discretion, the leave may be taken intermittently as opposed to being in a continuous block of time.

2. **Care for family members:** Within the meaning of "family members" are the officer's spouse, child, or parent with a "serious health problem." However, brothers, sisters, and in-laws are not specifically covered by the FMLA. In most instances, child care leave is limited to children under eighteen years of age. However, leave may be granted when a child older than eighteen is incapable of self-care due to a physical or mental disability.

   The FMLA does not require that officers be granted leave to care for family members with routine illnesses such as the flu or other short-term ailments that are normally covered by the department's sick leave policy. A "serious health problem" is one that requires inpatient care in a hospital, hospice, or residential medical care facility, or that requires "continuing treatment" by a health care provider. "Continuing treatment" means that the family member has missed his or her normal activities—e.g., school or work—for more than three days and has been treated by or been under the supervision of a health care provider at least twice. Examples of medical conditions in a family member which would qualify an officer for leave are heart attacks, strokes, cancer, substance abuse treatment, pneumonia, severe arthritis, prenatal care, and stress. Conversely, FMLA coverage is not extended to situations in which the family member has had outpatient cosmetic surgery, orthodontic care, acne treatment, or other similar conditions.

3. **Self-care:** Officers are allowed to take care leave for themselves under the same conditions as those for family members. If the need for medical leave is intermittent, then the officer must try to schedule the leave when it is least disruptive to departmental functioning. In response to self-care leave requests, the department may require certification by the health care provider that the officer cannot perform the essential functions of her or his job and may transfer the officer to an equivalently paid position. Upon returning to duty, officers can be required to provide a medical fitness-for-duty report.

Police departments should have a carefully written policy on the FMLA. This policy should clearly identify what are the rights and responsibilities of officers and the department; how to apply for leave; whether FMLA leave is paid or unpaid; what benefits are continued or suspended during leave; how officers are restored to duty, including being reassigned to their former positions or an equivalent position; and how benefits that were discontinued during their leave are restored.

# PERFORMANCE EVALUATION

Performance evaluation is often disliked by both the supervisors doing the evaluation and the officers being evaluated. This occurs many times because the purposes of the performance evaluation are simply not understood.[93]

**Purpose of Evaluation**

**Employee Performance.** Appraisals serve as an aid in motivating employees to maintain an acceptable level of performance. In this sense, performance refers to more than just measurable units of work. Law enforcement is too complex an undertaking to base appraisals solely on how a person fulfills assigned tasks. In addition to an evaluation of how an officer performs physically, the appraisal must also address itself to aspects that are difficult to quantify, such as attitudes and traits, but are of utmost importance to the successful accomplishment of mission.

**Career Development.** Personnel evaluations, if administered properly, pinpoint strengths that can be developed and weaknesses that should be corrected, thereby furnishing administrators with a developmental and remedial device of considerable worth. Those employees who consistently maintain a level of performance above the standards set by the department can, based upon their evaluations, be assigned to more responsible duties. Conversely, officers who are unable to meet reasonable standards can be given the guidance, supervision, and training necessary to save a career before it flounders.

**Supervisory Interests.** Systematic evaluations encourage supervisors to take a personal interest in the officers under their command. Within this context, appraisals can have a humanizing effect on supervision by holding commanders responsible for the performance of subordinates. Ideally, the program will foster mutual understanding, esprit de corps, solidarity, and group cohesiveness.

**Selection Practices.**   When entry-level procedures are valid, most individuals selected for employment will make contributions to the department. If, however, many rookie officers in an agency are unable to perform adequately, something may be seriously wrong with the selection process. Personnel appraisal allows administrators to maintain a continuing check on entrance standards to determine if they are relevant or in need of modification.

**Salary Decisions.**   With the current managerial emphasis on rewards won on merit, personnel evaluations serve as a basis, often the only one, for pay increases. Officers with satisfactory appraisals will probably receive raises on time, whereas increases for those who fall below standards may be temporarily withheld.

## SALARY ADMINISTRATION

Salary administration is one of the most critical components in the personnel administration function. The ability of a police agency to compete with business and industry in attracting the most highly qualified personnel will be directly affected by the wages and other benefits offered. Thus, considerable administrative time and effort are expended in developing and updating pay plans and salary schedules to assure that the police agency is in a sound competitive position in the labor market.[94]

When a pay plan is being developed, it must accomplish several objectives, namely (1) to pay salaries that are equitable in relation to the complexity and responsibility of the work performed and to maintain internal equity in the relation of pay and employees; (2) to maintain a competitive position in the employment market and thereby attract and retain competent employees; (3) to provide data needed in budgeting, payroll administration, and other phases of financial and personnel management; (4) to stimulate personnel management and reward high-level performance; and (5) to provide an orderly program of salary policy and control.

Closely related to the development of the pay plan is the need for accurate information on existing employee benefits and trends regarding new benefits. Employee benefits can be classified into four basic categories: (1) income supplement (tax break) benefits, including issuance of uniforms, clothing allowance, paid medical and life insurance; (2) income supplement benefits, including overtime pay, stand-by pay, and shift pay differentials; (3) good life benefits, including paid vacations, holidays, and recreational facilities; and (4) protection benefits, including sick leave and other paid leave, retirement pensions, and workers' compensation.

There is considerable interest among police officers in a shorter workweek, early retirements, more paid holidays, longer vacations, payment for unused sick leave, and broader paid medical coverage for dental and eye care. Collective bargaining and rising expectations of employees are likely to increase the demands for new and improved fringe benefits. Every effort should be made to use employee benefits as a tool for attracting and retaining the best employees. Cost information on employee benefits is needed, not only to plan and implement a total compensation program, but also to permit thorough explanations to employees and the public.

## Salary Schedule

No standard salary structure can be applied universally in police departments, simply because of the structural diversity and variations in classifications that exist among them. There are, however, some standards that experience suggests should be applied in designing the policy salary schedule. For example, there must be enough ranges to permit salary differentiation among all the job classes in the classification plan and room enough in the total span of salaries to provide for significant differences in salary between successive ranks. The generally accepted rule of thumb is that pay grades should be at least 5 percent apart. Thus, if a law enforcement agency chooses to have var-

TABLE 8-2.  Sample Salary Schedule

| Rank | Step Grade | A | B | C | D | E | F | G | H |
|---|---|---|---|---|---|---|---|---|---|
| | 10 | 12.64 | 13.27 | 13.93 | 14.63 | 15.36 | 16.13 | 16.94 | 17.78 |
| | | 2,190.48 | 2,300.00 | 2,415.00 | 2,535.75 | 2,662.54 | 2,795.66 | 2,935.45 | 3,082.22 |
| | | 26,285.71 | 27,600.00 | 28,980.00 | 30,429.00 | 31,950.45 | 33,547.97 | 35,225.37 | 36,986.64 |
| Police Officer | 11 | 13.27 | 13.93 | 14.63 | 15.36 | 16.13 | 16.94 | 17.78 | 18.67 |
| | | 2,300.00 | 2,415.00 | 2,535.75 | 2,662.54 | 2,795.66 | 2,935.45 | 3,082.22 | 3,236.33 |
| | | 27,600.00 | 28,980.00 | 30,429.00 | 31,950.45 | 33,547.97 | 35,225.37 | 36,986.64 | 38,835.97 |
| Corporal | 12 | 13.93 | 14.63 | 15.36 | 16.13 | 16.94 | 17.78 | 18.67 | 19.60 |
| | | 2,415.00 | 2,535.75 | 2,662.54 | 2,795.66 | 2,935.45 | 3,082.22 | 3,236.33 | 3,398.15 |
| | | 28,980.00 | 30,429.00 | 31,950.45 | 33,547.97 | 35,225.37 | 36,986.64 | 38,835.97 | 40,777.77 |
| Detective | 13 | 14.63 | 15.36 | 16.13 | 16.94 | 17.78 | 18.67 | 19.60 | 20.58 |
| | | 2,535.75 | 2,662.54 | 2,795.66 | 2,935.45 | 3,082.22 | 3,236.33 | 3,398.15 | 3,568.05 |
| | | 30,429.00 | 31,950.45 | 33,547.97 | 35,225.37 | 36,986.64 | 38,835.97 | 40,777.77 | 42,816.66 |
| | 14 | 15.36 | 16.13 | 16.94 | 17.78 | 18.67 | 19.60 | 20.58 | 21.61 |
| | | 2,662.54 | 2,795.66 | 2,935.45 | 3,082.22 | 3,236.33 | 3,398.15 | 3,568.05 | 3,746.46 |
| | | 31,950.45 | 33,547.97 | 35,225.37 | 36,986.64 | 38,835.97 | 40,777.77 | 42,816.66 | 44,957.49 |
| Sergeant | 15 | 16.13 | 16.94 | 17.78 | 18.67 | 19.60 | 20.58 | 21.61 | 22.69 |
| | | 2,795.66 | 2,935.45 | 3,082.22 | 3,236.33 | 3,398.15 | 3,568.05 | 3,746.46 | 3,933.78 |
| | | 33,547.97 | 35,225.37 | 36,986.64 | 38,835.97 | 40,777.77 | 42,816.66 | 44,957.49 | 47,205.37 |
| | 16 | 16.94 | 17.78 | 18.67 | 19.60 | 20.58 | 21.61 | 22.69 | 23.83 |
| | | 2,935.45 | 3,082.22 | 3,236.33 | 3,398.15 | 3,568.05 | 3,746.46 | 3,933.78 | 4,130.47 |
| | | 35,225.37 | 36,986.64 | 38,835.97 | 40,777.77 | 42,816.66 | 44,957.49 | 47,205.37 | 49,565.63 |
| Lieutenant | 17 | 17.78 | 18.67 | 19.60 | 20.58 | 21.61 | 22.69 | 23.83 | 25.02 |
| | | 3,082.22 | 3,236.33 | 3,398.15 | 3,568.05 | 3,746.46 | 3,933.78 | 4,130.47 | 4,336.99 |
| | | 36,986.64 | 38,835.97 | 40,777.77 | 42,816.66 | 44,957.49 | 47,205.37 | 49,565.63 | 52,043.92 |
| | 18 | 18.67 | 19.60 | 20.58 | 21.61 | 22.69 | 23.83 | 25.02 | 26.27 |
| | | 3,236.33 | 3,398.15 | 3,568.05 | 3,746.46 | 3,933.78 | 4,130.47 | 4,336.99 | 4,553.84 |
| | | 38,835.97 | 40,777.77 | 42,816.66 | 44,957.49 | 47,205.37 | 49,565.63 | 52,043.92 | 54,646.11 |

*Source:* Courtesy of Stephen E. Condrey, Carl Vinson Institute of Government, University of Georgia, Athens, 1998.

ious grades of patrol officers, a 5 percent differentiation should exist in addition to longevity considerations. Differentials between major ranks (i.e., sergeant, lieutenant, captain, etc.) should be at least 10 percent and preferably 15 percent.

A sample salary schedule is presented in Table 8-2. Notice that the range from minimum to maximum is broad enough to allow not only salary growth within a given pay range but also recognition through merit increases or pay-for-knowledge compensation systems (e.g., successful completion of a series of courses and designation as a Master Patrol Officer).

| I | J | K | L | M | N | O | P | Q | R |
|---|---|---|---|---|---|---|---|---|---|
| 18.67 | 19.60 | 20.58 | 21.61 | 22.69 | 23.83 | 25.02 | 26.27 | 27.59 | 28.97 |
| 3,236.33 | 3,398.15 | 3,568.05 | 3,746.46 | 3,933.78 | 4,130.47 | 4,336.99 | 4,553.84 | 4,781.53 | 5,020.61 |
| 38,835.97 | 40,777.77 | 42,816.66 | 44,957.49 | 47,205.37 | 49,565.63 | 52,043.92 | 54,646.11 | 57,378.42 | 60,247.34 |
| 19.60 | 20.58 | 21.61 | 22.69 | 23.83 | 25.02 | 26.27 | 27.59 | 28.97 | 30.41 |
| 3,398.15 | 3,568.05 | 3,746.46 | 3,933.78 | 4,130.47 | 4,336.99 | 4,553.84 | 4,781.53 | 5,020.61 | 5,271.64 |
| 40,777.77 | 42,816.66 | 44,957.49 | 47,205.37 | 49,565.63 | 52,043.92 | 54,646.11 | 57,378.42 | 60,247.34 | 63,259.71 |
| 20.58 | 21.61 | 22.69 | 23.83 | 25.02 | 26.27 | 27.59 | 28.97 | 30.41 | 31.93 |
| 3,568.05 | 3,746.46 | 3,933.78 | 4,130.47 | 4,336.99 | 4,553.84 | 4,781.53 | 5,020.61 | 5,271.64 | 5,535.22 |
| 42,816.66 | 44,957.49 | 47,205.37 | 49,565.63 | 52,043.92 | 54,646.11 | 57,378.42 | 60,247.34 | 63,259.71 | 66,422.69 |
| 21.61 | 22.69 | 23.83 | 25.02 | 26.27 | 27.59 | 28.97 | 30.41 | 31.93 | 33.53 |
| 3,746.46 | 3,933.78 | 4,130.47 | 4,336.99 | 4,553.84 | 4,781.53 | 5,020.61 | 5,271.64 | 5,535.22 | 5,811.99 |
| 44,957.49 | 47,205.37 | 49,565.63 | 52,043.92 | 54,646.11 | 57,378.42 | 60,247.34 | 63,259.71 | 66,422.69 | 69,743.83 |
| 22.69 | 23.83 | 25.02 | 26.27 | 27.59 | 28.97 | 30.41 | 31.93 | 33.53 | 35.21 |
| 3,933.78 | 4,130.47 | 4,336.99 | 4,553.84 | 4,781.53 | 5,020.61 | 5,271.64 | 5,535.22 | 5,811.99 | 6,102.58 |
| 47,205.37 | 49,565.63 | 52,043.92 | 54,646.11 | 57,378.42 | 60,247.34 | 63,259.71 | 66,422.69 | 69,743.83 | 73,231.02 |
| 23.83 | 25.02 | 26.27 | 27.59 | 28.97 | 30.41 | 31.93 | 33.53 | 35.21 | 36.97 |
| 4,130.47 | 4,336.99 | 4,553.84 | 4,781.53 | 5,020.61 | 5,271.64 | 5,535.22 | 5,811.99 | 6,102.58 | 6,407.71 |
| 49,565.63 | 52,043.92 | 54,646.11 | 57,378.42 | 60,247.34 | 63,259.71 | 66,422.69 | 69,743.83 | 73,231.02 | 76,892.57 |
| 25.02 | 26.27 | 27.59 | 28.97 | 30.41 | 31.93 | 33.53 | 35.21 | 36.97 | 38.82 |
| 4,336.99 | 4,553.84 | 4,781.53 | 5,020.61 | 5,271.64 | 5,535.22 | 5,811.99 | 6,102.58 | 6,407.71 | 6,728.10 |
| 52,043.92 | 54,646.11 | 57,378.42 | 60,247.34 | 63,259.71 | 66,422.69 | 69,743.83 | 73,231.02 | 76,892.57 | 80,737.20 |
| 26.27 | 27.59 | 28.97 | 30.41 | 31.93 | 33.53 | 35.21 | 36.97 | 38.82 | 40.76 |
| 4,553.84 | 4,781.53 | 5,020.01 | 5,271.64 | 5,535.22 | 5,811.99 | 6,102.58 | 6,407.71 | 6,728.10 | 7,064.50 |
| 54,646.11 | 57,378.42 | 60,247.34 | 63,259.71 | 66,422.69 | 69,743.83 | 73,231.02 | 76,892.57 | 80,737.20 | 84,774.06 |
| 27.59 | 28.97 | 30.41 | 31.93 | 33.53 | 35.21 | 36.97 | 38.82 | 40.76 | 42.79 |
| 4,781.53 | 5,020.61 | 5,271.64 | 5,535.22 | 5,811.99 | 6,102.58 | 6,407.71 | 6,728.10 | 7,064.50 | 7,417.73 |
| 57,378.42 | 60,247.34 | 63,259.71 | 66,422.69 | 69,743.83 | 73,231.02 | 76,892.57 | 80,737.20 | 84,774.06 | 89,012.76 |

# ASSESSMENT CENTERS

An assessment center is both a process and a place. As a process, it is most often used as a means of evaluating the behavior of candidates for the purpose of determining whether they can perform a particular job, such as that of sergeant. As a place, the physical site might be continuously dedicated to conducting assessment centers, or it might be used for this purpose on an ad hoc basis, such as rooms in a hotel.

Candidates in an assessment center are put through a series of situations, which are also called simulations or exercises. Box 8-6 is from handout materials given to candidates for the rank of sergeant at an orientation and illustrates three different types of exercises. In the case of the role-play described in Box 8-6, the candidate—who takes the role of Sgt. Fletcher—has 30 minutes to prepare for the exercise. During this time, she or he is placed alone in a room set up like an office. The candidate studies the role-play materials, which include memos, newspaper articles, attendance rosters, letters from citizens, and other documents, until the preparation period is over. The candidate, along with all of her or his materials and notes, is then taken to another room where she or he meets "Lt. Goldstein," who has been trained in how to relate to "Sgt. Fletcher." Also in the room are two to three trained assessors who take no part in the conversation between Lt. Goldstein and Sgt. Fletcher. As the conversation goes on, the assessors take notes about Sgt. Fletcher's behavior. These notes then are compared against checklists to establish to what extent the candidate "got" the things he or she should have during their meeting with Lt. Goldstein. This completed checklist then forms the basis for the numerical score the candidate later receives. Other exercises are variants on this basic procedure.

## BOX 8-6

### Descriptions of Three Different Assessment Center Exercises

You will participate in three different exercises:

#### 1. The Role Play Exercise

In this exercise you take the identity of Sergeant T. Fletcher in the Uniform Patrol Division. For the purpose of this exercise, "today" is always December 5, 1997. It is also always "10:00 A.M." Effective "today," you are promoted to sergeant. You are assigned to "A" shift. The shift commander is Lt. Goldstein. For the three months, you have been assigned to Ireland's National Police to study its methods of community policing. While you were gone, Lt. Goldstein was hired from outside of the GPD to command "A" shift. Thus, you have never met Lt. Goldstein.

Lt. Goldstein had some concerns about "A" shift. So, she gathered up some materials (the pages you will review during the 30-minute preparation period for this exercise) which relate to these concerns. Your job is to study the materials with a "fresh eye" and then meet with Lt. Goldstein to discuss your understanding of the situation and to provide your recommendations. This meeting with Lt. Goldstein cannot last longer than 20 minutes.

#### 2. The Written Exercise

Following the meeting with Lt. Goldstein, you will have one hour to write a memo to Lt. Goldstein to document the meeting for the record. This will be done in a separate room. Make sure that you follow Lt. Goldstein's directions for writing this memo.

#### 3. The Oral Presentation Exercise

Lt. Goldstein was supposed to speak before a community group at lunch today. However, Lt. Goldstein has just been taken to the hospital with chest pains. You are assigned to speak in Lt. Goldstein's place. You have access to a packet of correspondence between your lieutenant and the community group. You have 30 minutes to study these materials and then you are to make the presentation to the group (the assessors), which cannot last longer than 20 minutes.

*Source:* Gainesville, Georgia, Police Department, Sergeants Assessment Center Orientation Handout, 1997.

**FIGURE 8-3.** A candidate is filmed during an Assessment Center simulated press conference. (Photo courtesy of the Fairfax County, Virginia Police Department.)

The first modern-day experiments with assessment centers were conducted by the Germans in World War I. Their objective was to select persons suited for intelligence assignments that required certain unique characteristics.[95] Simulation exercises were reactivated in World War II by German and British military psychologists to aid in the selection of military officers. In the United States, the Office of Strategic Services (OSS) used similar procedures for selecting intelligence agents. Candidates taking part in the OSS testing program participated in a wide range of paper-and-pencil tests, interviews, and simulations over a period of several days. The simulations were intended to reflect aspects of field intelligence work under wartime conditions, and some were, therefore, designed to be highly stressful.[96]

In the private sector, the use of assessment centers was pioneered by AT&T in 1956. For the most part, it was another 20 years before even a modest number of public agencies were using the concept.

The first step in developing the simulation exercises used in an assessment center is to identify the behaviors that are important to successful job performance. For example, if the assessment center is being conducted to identify those who are qualified to advance from the rank of lieutenant to captain, then it is necessary to determine which behaviors (skills) are required to perform a captain's duties properly. Ideally, these skills would be identified as the result of a carefully conducted job analysis. Because of the technical skill, cost, and time required to perform a job analysis, many departments substitute a less rigorous job analysis consisting of a few interviews with job incumbents or a senior police commander's list of requisite skills. Care should be taken, however, with such substitutes, because an improperly

**Historical Development of Assessment Centers**

**Development of Simulation Exercises**

conducted or inadequate job analysis leaves a testing process open to legal challenge on the basis that it lacks validity.

Continuing with the example of a captain's assessment center, the skills identified as essential for effectiveness are termed *dimensions*. Illustrations of dimensions include

1. Decisiveness
2. Judgment
3. Oral communication
4. Stress tolerance
5. Written communication
6. Planning
7. Flexibility

Once the dimensions are identified, simulation exercises that provide a context in which to evaluate the candidates' skill degrees must be developed. The common denominator in all exercises is that candidates competing for promotion assume the role that they would actually have to perform if selected for advancement. In addition to the three exercises described in Box 8-6, common types of exercises include

1. The in-basket, in which candidates assume the role of a newly promoted captain who comes to the office and finds an accumulation of paperwork that must be dealt with. Included in the accumulated material may be such things as new regulations, requests for transfers, complaints against officers, letters from citizens, reports on shooting incidents, requests from officers to attend special training schools or to have special days off, notification from the training bureau that certain officers must be at the pistol range on particular days for their annual qualification firing, and other similar types of information. The length of time for in-basket exercises varies from 90 minutes to as much as four hours.

2. A leaderless group discussion (LGD), in which captain candidates are told that as recent promotees to the rank of captain, they have been appointed by the chief to a committee to study a particular problem in their department and they should come up with specific recommendations to solve it. Among the problems often given in this exercise are how to improve community relations, how to defend the department's budget against proposed reductions, and how to cut down on the number of on-duty traffic accidents by officers. Ideally, there are four to five candidates in an LGD exercise, which may last from 45 to 90 minutes. Over the past 10 years, a number of large corporations have stopped using LGDs because they do not resemble actual work situations: someone is always in charge. Some consultants have followed this practice. Despite these developments, many police departments continue to use LGDs, a matter they would probably be wise to reevaluate.

3. The written problem analysis, in which candidates are asked to analyze a problem in their department and to send a memo to the chief containing their rationale, alternatives considered, and recommended course of action. The problem may be an actual one in their agency or one that is specially written for the exercise. Depending on how complex the problem is, this exercise may last from 45 minutes to two hours.

Even when candidates have been given a detailed orientation to the assessment center process, they often become confused, thinking that they are being evaluated on the basis of a particular exercise. Moreover, they may become very upset if they think they "blew" an exercise. However, as depicted in Table 8-3, candidates are being assessed on the basis of their cumulative performances on each dimension. Thus, candidates' final standings are not based solely on how they did on the in-basket or any other single exercise, but rather on how well they performed on each dimension as it was repeatedly assessed over a number of exercises. Some candidates, thinking that they have failed an exercise, lose their confidence and fail to do well in those remaining. Their failure to manage themselves is regrettable from two perspectives: (1) whatever troubled them about their performance on an exercise might not have been a dimension that was assessed on that exercise, and (2) even if it had been assessed, they might have done so well in other exercises on that dimension that they were still competitive. It is part of the assessment center process for candidates to experience and manage their own feelings. However, candidates occasionally get very angry with assessment center directors who do not comfort or encourage them.

The assessment center technique offers a number of advantages over written tests and other management identification techniques. A number of important managerial abilities, such as planning and organizing, establishing priorities, leadership, relevant analytical skill, sensitivity to the needs of subordinates, management control, stress tolerance, and communications effectiveness, are very difficult to measure adequately with the use of written tests alone. Also, because of the job relevance and the involved procedures, assessment center results are generally readily accepted by individuals who object to traditional testing procedures. Some of the more significant advantages to the assessment center method are:[97]

## Advantages of the Assessment Center

1. The exercises are simulations of on-the-job behaviors.
2. A large amount of information is generated by each participant in a relatively short time.
3. A variety of methods is used.
4. The exercises are constant for all participants.

## TABLE 8-3. Illustration of a Dimension-Exercise Matrix

| | | Exercises | | | |
|---|---|---|---|---|---|
| Dimension | In-basket | Leaderless Group Discussion | Oral Presentation | Written Problem Analysis | Individual Role Play |
|---|---|---|---|---|---|
| 1. Decisiveness | X | X | X | X | X |
| 2. Judgment | X | X | X | X | X |
| 3. Written communication | X | 0 | 0 | X | 0 |
| 4. Oral communication | 0 | X | X | 0 | X |
| 5. Planning | X | 0 | X | X | X |

X = assessed
0 = not assessed

5. There is a consensus of judgment among the assessors for each participant.

6. The observers typically have no personal involvement with the participants.

7. The observers are well trained in evaluation procedures.

8. The observers are able to devote full attention to the task of assessing.

9. Information obtained can be used effectively to develop personnel. Individuals are provided with specific behaviorally referenced indicators of strengths and weaknesses, and developmental programs can be planned to strengthen weaknesses so that an individual may be promotable in the future.

10. Assessors receive valuable training in behavioral observation techniques, and this training carries over to their regular job performance.

**Assessors** The role of the assessor is not to make promotion decisions. The assessors are to analyze behavior, make judgments about behavior, organize the information in a report, and make the report available to the individual making the promotion decision.[98]

As typically found in business organizations, assessors are managers who are one and sometimes preferably two levels higher than the position for which people are applying. This is based on the assumption that prior experience in the job facilitates judgment of the candidate's aptitude for the position and is far enough away from the candidate to be assessed to ensure greater objectivity than their immediate supervisors might exercise. Also not to be overlooked is the credibility of the assessment center concept when upper-level officers are involved.[99] Depending on the number of candidates to be assessed and the time allotted for assessment, anywhere from three to six assessors may be needed.

Because the assessors may not be thoroughly familiar with the mechanics of operating the center and the instruments, a prime concern is training each assessor in the skills of being a keen observer of human behavior. A natural starting point in training is for prospective assessors to participate in the exercise themselves so they may experience the behavior they will be observing. Training in interviewing, observation of specific behavior, and precise analysis are also very important. Such training will very likely have to be provided by a professional who has extensive experience in this area of management. However, a large number of assessors may be trained at one time and the expense spread over considerable time as the assessors are used over the years whenever assessment centers are convened.[100]

# RECOVERING THE COST OF TRAINING POLICE OFFICERS

Cities and counties often encounter the problem of providing new officers with recruit training only to watch them later depart for other opportunities, often with larger police or sheriff's departments. The original police employer suffers the loss of a trained employee in addition to the cost of training someone to take his or her place. These repetitive costs add up to substantial losses.

One response by local agencies has been to hire only officers who are already trained. Although in many instances this practice works well, it contains a substantial risk in that some of these officers have questionable incidents in their backgrounds, incidents that may be overlooked in the interest of economy. Also overlooked by some jurisdictions is the increased liability risk: one police department of eight "recycled officers" had committed so many acts for which the city had been successfully sued that the insurer told the city it was withdrawing all insurance coverage.

A growing number of jurisdictions have reduced repetitive costs through the use of training contracts, which may be used for both entry-level and specialized or advanced courses. The total cost of providing the training, including an officer's compensation and the course tuition, is calculated. These costs are identified in a contract between the jurisdiction and the officer, in which as a condition of attending the course, the officer agrees that if he or she voluntarily leaves before a specified term, he or she will repay a corresponding amount. In the case of entry-level training, the police or sheriff's department contract may require the officer to repay one twenty-fourth of the training cost for each month absent from a 24-month base period. For example, an officer under this arrangement who left after 12 months would have to repay 50 percent of the cost of the initial training. If the base period for repayment was 36 months and the officer left after 12 months, then 12/36ths of the agreed-upon period of service would have been completed and the officer would owe 66 percent of the training cost to the initial employer.

## EMPLOYING CIVILIANS IN POLICE WORK

Police departments initially restricted civilians to clerical type positions. Later, in order to reduce costs, free officers for field duty, and bring greater efficiency to such work, departments began expanding the roles of civilians. As suggested by Table 8-4, the selective use of civilians in certain command assignments has also proven its value. Often, civilian commanders of selected units within a police department have both a substantive expertise—such as crime analysis—and a depth of experience that make them particularly effective.

### TABLE 8-4. Potential Civilian Command Assignments

Depending on the size and needs of the agency, the following assignments exemplify some suitable posts for civilian commanders.

- Accounts payable/receivable
- Affirmative action administrator
- Audit and inspection program
- Budget administration
- Code enforcement
- Computer systems management
- Contract administration
- Cost recovery program
- Crime analysis
- Cultural awareness director
- Custodian of records/personnel files
- Environmental design review
- Graffiti abatement program
- Internal ombudsman
- Jail management
- Neighborhood watch/business watch
- Outreach program development
- Payroll supervisor
- Personnel recruiting and selection
- Records and communications
- Risk management program
- Television programs
- Training program development and administration
- Workers compensation administrator

*Source:* Joseph L. Colletti, "Why Not Hire Civilian Commanders?" *FBI Law Enforcement Bulletin* 65, no. 10 (October 1996), p.10.

The Santa Ana, California, Police Department has taken the civilianization process even further by creating the position of police service officer (PSO). For years, the Santa Ana Police Department had used nonsworn personnel to supplement enforcement officers. The scope of their duties, however, was limited and traditionally restricted to parking control and desk assignments. A management decision was made to create the PSO position, which greatly expanded the duties of nonsworn personnel to encompass virtually every aspect of police service except those specifically restricted to sworn officers due to job hazards and required job skills. The rationale for this decision was that a large percentage of police calls were service oriented rather than enforcement related and that many of the services being provided by sworn police officers could be handled by nonsworn PSOs. Box 8-7 details the tasks performed by the PSOs of the Santa Ana Police Department.

## BOX 8-7

### Police Service Officer Assignments

**Front Desk**
- Answer incoming calls regarding information and police matters.
- Assist citizens who come to the front desk.
- Take reports over the phone or in person on petty thefts, grand thefts, vehicle burglaries, habitual runaways, annoying or obscene calls; information reports on malicious mischief, lost property, patrol checks, supplemental reports.
- Female PSOs assist police officers in pat-down searches of female prisoners.
- Sign off traffic citations.

**Community Oriented Policing (C.O.P.) Program**
- Scheduling and handling C.O.P. meetings.
- Organize and distribute C.O.P. bulletins, Crime Warning Bulletins, Crime Alert Bulletins and Area Crime Resume.
- Maintain area crime statistics.
- Coordinate residential burglary seminars and home security inspections with the Community Service Officers.
- Assist other police agencies in setting up a community watch program in their city.
- Recruit and train block captains.
- Maintain an updated block captains' information list.
- Maintain an on-going relationship with block captains and community watch members.
- Serve as an advisor to the area executive board and city-wide executive board.
- Assist in organizing special citywide C.O.P. events such as C.O.P. Track Meet, Golf Tournament, Block Captains' Picnic, etc.

**Patrol**
- Mark abandoned vehicles and store them.
- Handle all types of crime reports which are not in progress.
- Handle minor non-emergency calls to assist citizens.
- Handle recontacts on crime reports to obtain further information.
- Accident reports—injury and non-injury.
- Crime Scene Investigation.

**Civilian Accident Investigator**
- Traffic accidents—injury and non-injury; if the C.A.I. is the closest to an injury accident or a no-detail accident, they respond Code 3.
- Render first aid, give mouth to mouth resuscitation and/or CPR when necessary.
- If it is a hit and run accident, perform CSI (Crime Scene Investigation) and follow up on leads in an attempt to locate the suspect.
- Lay flare patterns and do traffic control when needed.

**Community Police Offices**
- Answer telephones and handle citizen inquiries.
- Take reports over the phone or in person on petty thefts, grand thefts, vehicle burglaries, habitual runaways, annoying or obscene phone calls; information reports on malicious mischief, lost property patrol checks and supplementals.
- Sign off citations for non-moving violations.
- Maintain list of referral numbers for citizens who come in or call for such assistance.
- Keep a monthly pin map showing problem areas, specifying burglaries of residential, commercial or vehicles; also armed robberies are pinned.

**Career Criminal Apprehension Program (C-CAP)**
- Analyst/Trainee (Crime Analysis)
- Processing and submitting criminal information and data for computer entry.

- Daily compilation and dissemination of "Daily Investigative Supplemental," consisting of outstanding warrants, stolen vehicles, wanted persons, field interviews and photo requests to patrol and areas of the department.
- Monitoring outstanding warrant/stolen vehicle log.
- Daily pin-mapping of residential burglary cases, by area and team grids.

### Juvenile Investigation
- Log all bike thefts and all impounds (recoveries and founds) in logs and compare both logs for possible matching.
- This PSO is assigned all bicycle theft reports.
- Processes Child Abuse Registry reports as a resource to the investigators and assigns case numbers to them.

### General Investigation—Theft/Pawn Detail
- Handles petty theft reports of gasoline and some shoplift cases from department stores.
- Assists outside agencies and citizens making pawn inquiries.
- Files and reviews all reported pawn slips for completeness and for known sellers of stolen property.
- Checks on traceable (serialized) pawns and office equipment repair records.
- Notifies other agencies when stolen property has been located.
- At least once a week, walks through in uniform all pawn shops and secondhand businesses.
- Investigates all applications filed for Second-hand Business Licenses and Security Guard Licenses.

### General Investigation—Crimes Against the Elderly Detail
- The PSO assigned to this detail is responsible for crime prevention programs for seniors; which includes scheduling and presenting meetings and seminars on a variety of crime prevention subjects.
- Assists in follow-up of certain cases, including victim assistance and referral.
- Prepares and distributes Crime Warning Bulletins for seniors.
- Maintains crime statistics.

### General Investigation—Crimes Against Persons Detail
- Responsible for investigation of lewd and annoying phone calls, indecent exposures, and misdemeanor assaults.
- Maintains mug files.
- Responsible for the placement and maintenance of VARDA (robbery and burglary) alarms.

### Special Investigation—Vice Detail
- Handles and/or coordinates investigations regarding the issuance of permits and licenses by the Chief of Police and the City Manager. (These include dance permits, bingo, massage, escort services, modeling, and ABC licenses.)
- Performs premise inspections with regard to these licenses and permits.
- Maintains liaison with other city departments to insure proper and timely reports and inspections as needed.
- Responsible for all record keeping and correspondence related to these licenses and permits, as well as liaison with the City Council.
- Under direction of supervisor, performs background investigations as related to municipal code and vice enforcement.
- Assists as needed with vice investigations.

### Court Liaison
- Prepares and packages DUI cases involving injury or accident for review by the D.A.
- Files these cases with the Central Court.
- Types complaints for DUIs with no accident or injury involved, approves the complaints and files them.
- Prepares and packages warrant cases for D.A. review and files them in Central Court.
- Walks through warrants on misdemeanor cases.
- In absence of sworn court liaison officer, the PSO assigned to this position prepares and packages all in-custody cases.

### Media Relations
- With department's sworn public information officer (lieutenant), this PSO serves as liaison between news media and the police department.
- Responsible for publicity of departmental programs and events.
- Assists in organizing special events.
- Maintains records of media coverage.
- Responsible for preparation of some departmental brochures and other publications.

### Community Crime Resistance
- Provides training workshops to block captains.
- Responsible for preparation and layout of a bimonthly departmental publication and assisting with a publication of the C.O.P. Block Captains' Association.
- Serves as liaison between the police department and the C.O.P. Block Captains' Association.

*(continued)*

## BOX 8-7 (continued)

**Reserves' Office**

- Recruitment of Reserve applicants.
- Assists with all phases of screening/selection process.
- Conducts and/or coordinates all background investigations on potential Reserve Officers.
- Maintains statistical data and confidential personnel files for Reserves.
- Arranges for monthly training and updates on laws and pertinent information for Reserves.
- Ensures P.O.S.T. requirements are continually met as changes occur.
- Once a Reserve is appointed, assigns to an area in keeping with the Team Policing concept. Assists with "call-ups" in emergency/disaster situations and coordinates assignments of Reserves where and as needed on a special basis.
- Serves as liaison between Reserve Officers and other departmental sections/personnel.
- Responsible for monthly communication with all Orange County Reserve Coordinators for updates, etc.
- Coordinates recruitment, screening and placement of Civilian Volunteers, who perform a wide variety of services for the department, based on their expertise, experience and technical skills.

**Traffic Safety Officer**

- The PSO assigned to this position is responsible for the total administration of the adult crossing guard program, which includes the hiring of adult crossing guards, training, supervision, liaison between schools, children and the guards, and scheduling. This PSO is also responsible for ordering and maintaining supplies and working out specific traffic problems which affect locations manned by adult crossing guards.
- This PSO is also responsible for the School Safety Patrol, which includes liaison with schools, ordering and maintaining supplies and coordinating field trips.
- Bicycle safety programs are a responsibility of this position. This includes presenting films and lectures, ordering and distributing literature, providing obstacle courses for coordination of bicycle rider, bicycle licensing, and inspection of bicycles for defects.
- Presents films, lectures and literature on pedestrian safety.
- Responsible for mechanical inspection of each tow truck, catering truck, ice cream truck, taxi and produce truck, then attaches city sticker.
- Performs background research for tow truck and taxi company permits.
- Writes citations for Santa Ana Municipal Code vehicle violations and California Vehicle Code parking violations.

*Source:* Santa Ana, California, Police Dept.

## THE ADMINISTRATION OF DISCIPLINE

In almost all encounters with the public, police officers and nonsworn employees exercise this authority appropriately. At times, however, citizens raise legitimate questions about how this authority had been used. Unfortunately, there are also times when police personnel abuse this authority. Therefore, departments must establish a system of discipline that minimizes abuse of authority and promotes the department's reputation for professionalism.[101]

**System of Discipline**    The most effective disciplinary system combines the reinforcement of the right set of values in all employees with behavioral standards that are consistently and fairly applied. Each employee must understand and be guided by these standards that have been established in the department's (and city's) general orders, rules, regulations, and procedures.

Employees should be expected to conduct themselves, both in interactions with one another and with the public, in a manner that conveys respect, honesty, integrity, and dedication to public service. In turn, employees should be treated fairly, honestly, and respectfully by everyone in the department, regardless of authority, rank, or position within the organization.

All employees make judgment errors from time to time when carrying out their responsibilities. Each error in judgment offers a learning opportunity for the employee and the department, although some errors come with greater consequences than others for the public, the department, and the employee.

Even so, the department has an obligation to make its expectations as unambiguous as possible to employees. At the same time, it has an equal obligation to make clear the consequences for failing to meet those expectations. While meeting both obligations can be difficult, the latter is obviously more complex. Circumstances often contribute to errors in judgment and poor decisions that administrators must consider when determining the appropriate consequences for behavior found to be improper.

Employees often admit they would like the department to provide a list of prohibited behaviors, along with the penalties for engaging in those behaviors. Yet, experience has shown that employees directly involved in the disciplinary process, either as the subject of the process or in a review capacity, want to consider the results on one's actions in light of the circumstances that might have contributed to the violation. This consideration is critical to apply discipline fairly and consistently.

A number of factors should be considered when applying discipline. Granted, not all factors may be considered in every case, and some may not apply at all in particular situations. There may also be a tendency to isolate one factor and give it greater importance than another. Yet, these factors should be thought of as being interactive and having equal weight, unless circumstances dictate otherwise. These factors include employee motivation, degree of harm, employee experience, employee's past record, and intentional/unintentional errors.

## Determining Factors

**Employee Motivation.** A police department exists to serve the public. Therefore, one factor to consider when examining an employee's conduct should be whether the employee was acting in good faith. An employee who violates policy in an effort to accomplish a legitimate police action should be given more positive consideration than one who was motivated by personal interest.

**Degree of Harm.** The degree of harm resulting from employee error is another factor when deciding the consequences for errant behavior. Harm can be measured in terms of monetary costs to the department and community, such as repairs to a damaged vehicle, or in terms of personal injury claims for excessive force.

Another way to measure harm is by the impact of employee error on public confidence. An employee who engages in criminal behavior, such as selling drugs, corrodes public trust in the police if discipline does not send a clear, unmistakable message that this behavior will not be tolerated.

**Employee Experience.** Employee experience also has a bearing on the type and the extent of discipline. A relatively new employee, or a more experienced officer in a new assignment, should be given greater consideration for judgmental errors. Accordingly, errors by veteran employees may warrant more serious sanctions.

**Employee's Past Record.** To the extent allowed by law, policy, and contractual obligations, an employee's past record should be taken into consideration when determining disciplinary actions. An employee who continually makes errors should expect the penalties for this behavior to become progressively more punitive. Less stringent consequences should be administered to employees with records that show few or no errors. When determining disciplinary action, every consideration should be given to employees whose past records reflect hard work and dedication to the department and the community.

**Intentional/Unintentional Errors.** Supervisory personnel need to consider the circumstances surrounding the incident to determine whether the employee's error was intentional or unintentional. Obviously, the type of error will govern the extent and severity of the discipline.

The unintentional error occurs when an employee's action or decision turns out to be wrong, even though at the time, the employee believed it to be in compliance with policy and the most appropriate course to take based on information available.

Unintentional errors also include those momentary lapses of judgment or acts of carelessness that result in minimal harm (backing a police cruiser into a pole or failing to turn in a report in a timely fashion). Employees should be held accountable for these errors, but the consequences should be more corrective than punitive, unless the same or similar errors persist.

Employees make intentional errors when they take action or make a decision that they know, or should know, to be in conflict with law, policy, procedures, or rules at the time. Generally, intentional errors should carry greater consequences and be treated more seriously.

Within the framework of intentional errors, certain behaviors are entirely unacceptable, such as lying, theft, physical abuse of citizens, and equally serious breaches of trust placed in the police.[102] However, the type of police officer who generally causes the most grief and embarrassment to a police department is the one who is prone to violence.

## Profile of Violence-Prone Police Officers

Several years ago the National Institute of Justice conducted a survey of numerous police psychologists in an effort to develop a profile of officers who had been referred to them for the use of excessive force. Their answers did not support the conventional view that a few "bad apples" are responsible for most excessive force complaints. Rather, their answers were used to construct five distinct profiles of different types of officers, only one of which resembled the "bad apple" characterization.

The data used to create the five profiles constitutes human resource information that can be used to shape policy. Not only do the profiles offer an etiology of excessive force and provide insight into its complexity, but they also support the notion that excessive force is not just a problem of individuals but may also reflect organizational deficiencies. These profiles are presented in the ascending order of frequency, along with possible interventions.

**Officers with personality disorders that place them at chronic risk.** These officers have pervasive and enduring personality traits (in contrast to characteristics acquired on the job) that are manifested in antisocial, narcissistic, paranoid, or abusive tendencies. These conditions interfere with judgment and interactions with others, particularly when officers perceive challenges or threats to their authority. Such officers generally lack empathy for others. The number who fit this profile is the smallest of all the high-risk groups.

These characteristics, which tend to persist through life but may be intensified by police work, and may not be apparent at preemployment screening. Individuals who exhibit these personality patterns generally do not learn from experience, nor do they accept responsibility for their behavior. Thus, they are at greater risk for repeated citizen complaints.

**Officers whose previous job-related experience places them at risk.** Traumatic situations such as justifiable police shootings put some officers at risk for abuse of force, but for reasons totally different from those of the first group. These officers are not unsocialized, egocentric, or violent. In fact, personality factors appear to have less to do with their vulnerability to excessive force than the emotional "baggage" they have accumulated from involvement in previous incidents. Typically, these officers verge on burnout and have become isolated from their squads. Because of their perceived need to conceal symptoms, some time lapses may occur before their problems come to the attention of others. When this happens, the triggering event is often a situation in which excessive force was used and the officer has lost control.

In contrast to the chronic at-risk group, officers in this group are amenable to critical-incident debriefing, but to be fully effective, the interventions must be applied soon after involvement in the incident. Studies recommend training and psychological debriefings, with follow-up, to minimize the development of symptoms.

**Officers who have problems at early stages in their police careers.** The third group profiled consists of young and inexperienced officers, frequently characterized as "hotdogs," "badge happy," "macho," or generally immature. In contrast to other inexperienced officers, individuals in this group are characterized as highly impressionable and impulsive, with low tolerance for frustration. They nonetheless bring positive attributes to their work and could outgrow these tendencies and learn with experience. Unfortunately, the positive qualities can deteriorate early in their careers if field training officers and first-line supervisors do not work to provide them with a full range of responses to patrol encounters.

These inexperienced officers were described as needing strong supervision and highly structured field training, preferably under a field training officer with considerable street experience. Because they are strongly influenced by the police culture, such new recruits are more apt to change their behavior if their mentors show them how to maintain a professional demeanor in their dealings with citizens.

**Officers who develop inappropriate patrol styles.**  Individuals who fit this profile combine a dominant command presence with a heavy-handed policing style; they are particularly sensitive to challenge and provocation. They use force to show they are in charge, as their beliefs about how police work is conducted become more rigid and this behavior becomes the norm.

In contrast to the chronic risk group, the behavior of officers in this group is acquired on the job and can be changed. The longer the patterns continue, however, the more difficult they are to change. As the officers become invested in police power and control, they see little reason to change. Officers in this group are often labeled "dinosaurs" in a changing police profession marked by greater accountability to citizens and by adoption of the community policing style of law enforcement.

If these officers do not receive strong supervision and training early in their careers, or if they are detailed to a special unit with minimal supervision, their style may be reinforced. They may perceive that the organization sanctions their behavior. This group would be more responsive to peer program or situation-based interventions in contrast to traditional individual counseling. Making them part of the solution, rather than part of the problem, may be central to changing their behavior.

**Officers with personal problems.** The final risk profile was made up of officers who have experienced serious personal problems, such as separation, divorce, or even perceived loss of status, that have destabilized their ability to function effectively on the job. In general, officers with personal problems do not use excessive force, but those who do may have elected police work for all the wrong reasons. In contrast to their peers, they seem to have a more tenuous sense of self-worth and higher levels of anxiety that are well masked. Some may have functioned reasonably well until changes occurred in their personal situation. These changes undermine confidence and make it more difficult to deal with the fear, animosity, and emotionally charged patrol situations.

Before they resort to excess force, these officers usually exhibit behavior while on patrol that is erratic and signals the possibility they may indeed lose control in a confrontation. This group, which is the most frequently seen by psychologists because of excessive-force problems, can be identified by supervisors who have been properly trained to observe and respond to the precursors of problem behavior. Their greater numbers should encourage departments to develop early warning systems to help supervisors detect "marker behaviors" signifying that problems are brewing. These officers benefit from individual counseling, but earlier referrals to psychologists can enhance the benefit and prevent their personal situations from spilling over into their jobs.[103]

# THE INTERNAL AFFAIRS UNIT

Every police agency needs a functional Internal Affairs Unit (IAU) or person charged with the responsibility to oversee the acceptance, investigation, and adjudication of complaints about police performance. The size of this unit depends on the workload.[104]

In most smaller agencies (25 or fewer employees) the internal affairs function will normally be undertaken by the chief of police or assigned to the second in command. In smaller sheriff's departments this duty is often handled by the chief deputy, usually on an as needed basis. In all other police agencies the internal affairs function should be designated as an IAU or some other terminology, such as the current favorite Professional Standards Unit. This unit or person can be assigned other ancillary duties depending on the workload. Regardless of the designation or position in the agency, this function should be directly responsible to the chief of police or sheriff. Only in larger agencies should this function be assigned to a secondary layer within the organization such as an assistant or deputy chief of police or chief deputy/undersheriff.

Two primary philosophies guide the assignment of persons to investigate personnel complaints. Much of this is based on whether the agency views this function as principally one of investigation or one of supervision. Investigations can be conducted very well by a first-level officer or detective just as they do in purely criminal matters. Internal affairs and personnel complaint investigations, however, are an essential element of agency control, discipline, and the supervisory function; thus, they should be conducted by a supervisor. This can be invaluable experience in the development of supervisors and future managers of the agency.

The agency that elects to assign these investigations to first-level officers should restrict the task strictly to the investigative function. Conclusions and recommendations should be a function for supervisory or command level personnel. The investigation of allegations of misconduct against fellow officers can be a difficult task for the assigned officer. It is even more difficult to require first-level officers to do it. Usually they are in the same bargaining unit with the accused and may have to work directly with them in the future. Thus, investigating officers should not be held accountable for making conclusions, findings, or recommendations; their responsibility should be limited to fact finding.

Assignments to internal affairs should be limited in tenure. Two years would not be an unreasonable period of time. It should be considered as a career development opportunity to enhance the employee's understanding of discipline and supervisory techniques. Longer tours of duty can adversely affect an employee's outlook and inhibit his/her eventual return to other assignments in the agency. The regular rotation of personnel may assist in eliminating the "headhunter" reputation given to some IAU operations. Some agencies have been successful in encouraging members to undertake this assignment by offering them a reasonable guarantee of a selected assignment following their tour in internal affairs.

## Time Limits

An emerging issue is the imposition of rigid and inflexible time limits for filing a complaint, completing the investigation, and/or imposing discipline in a sustained case. Currently there is no clear or common trend in law enforcement on this issue. One incentive for this movement is that such a policy would be beneficial for accused officers and employees in minimizing unnecessary delays in reaching closure on the allegation(s). On the other side, however, is the basic principle of administrative investigations that requires the agency to do everything reasonable to reach the truth of the matter. The ultimate issue appears to be whether a delay is unreasonable and unexplainable.

Some current examples of this practice follows. One large agency has a charter provision requiring that misconduct be discovered within one year of occurrence or no discipline beyond a written reprimand may be given. One state mandates by statute that the complaint of misconduct be filed within 60 days of occurrence. Another large agency by administrative ruling must conclude the investigation and assess discipline within 120 days of the complaint or no discipline can be imposed. Another agency, by mayoral decision, has forestalled any imposition of discipline unless the investigation is concluded and discipline administered within 45 days of the agency's notice of misconduct or the date when it should have been aware of possible employee misconduct.

## Investigations by Line Supervisors

If field supervisors are to be used for some administrative investigations, the agency should ensure they are adequately prepared for the task. This can be done through specific training and by use of a thorough exemplar for guidance.

Immediate supervisors of the accused officer can normally conduct a reasonable administrative investigation. Their closeness to the accused member or the probability of continued daily contact between the two should not be considered hindrances to an effective investigation. Discipline is a function of supervision. Immediate supervisors should not be allowed to avoid direct involvement in this essential supervisory task.

## Proactive Enforcement Operations

A Police Foundation study conducted several years ago reported that 11 percent of the police agencies surveyed indicated they conducted some form of proactive enforcement involving police misconduct. Some areas of misconduct that might be conducive to this type of administrative policing are:

- Involvement with narcotics
- Theft
- Unauthorized information release
- Perjury or false affidavits
- Sexual misconduct
  — Traffic stops of females
  — Voyeuristic activities
  — Repeated contacts with vulnerable persons (prostitutes, addicts, and runaways)
  — Citizen initiated contacts for sex
- Excessive, unnecessary use of force

Agencies which are engaging in these forms of proactive enforcement may also refer to them as "integrity checks." Some are staged calls for officers response to burglaries or vehicle impound that contain some form of valuable property. The officer's conduct is checked to determine whether the property was properly inventoried and booked into evidence. Some agencies have used decoys when specific employee misconduct is suspected.

Some important considerations that should be evaluated before deciding to engage in any proactive administrative enforcement are:

- Resources and equipment
- Mutual aid provisions
- Ethical issues
- Agency environment

## Investigations by Another Agency

Most police agencies, except very large ones, are not equipped nor staffed for large scale intense, critical operations. Frequently in such cases operative personnel are recruited from adjacent agencies, state and federal units, and/or community outreach sources.

However, an agency's reliance on an outside entity to conduct an investigation does not relieve it of its responsibility for ultimate accountability. Outside agencies are sometimes reluctant to become involved in these administrative investigations. Some look at the task within the narrow framework of the possible criminal wrongdoing. This can seriously reduce the ability of an agency to use the investigation for the more intensive administrative analysis and subsequent determination whether discipline may be warranted. It must be noted that the outside entity's investigation does not bring the administrative aspect to final closure. That investigation focuses primarily on criminal wrongdoing and will not normally make a satisfactory administrative finding in determining if any departmental policies or procedures have been violated.

In smaller agencies, investigations of the chief of police or other top administrators are often conducted by an outside unit. Some jurisdictions will designate the city manager or personnel director to conduct these investigations. Most, however, will look to some other outside agency (usually state or federal) for this service.

The use of polygraphs and voice stress detection equipment in administrative investigations is controversial. Agency employees normally cannot be compelled to submit to such an examination. The results of this form of examination rarely can be used in disciplinary hearings or appeals even if given voluntarily by an agency employee.

**Use of the Polygraph or Voice Stress Detection Equipment**

The polygraph and voice stress examination, however, can be useful when dealing with complainants and other civilian witnesses. This form of examination should be done only after the person has given a complete and formal statement. The final approval for requesting a person to submit to such an examination should be by the chief of police or his/her designee. The polygraph or voice stress should not be used as a means of intimidating or coercing a person. The investigator should explain that the results are simply a method of verifying the statement. This, of course, may be necessary when there is little physical evidence or disinterested witnesses.

*Refusal to submit to a requested polygraph or voice stress examination does not negate the validity of the person's statement or allegation.* This refusal should be noted in the investigative report. Should a person submit to the examination and, in the examiner's opinion, show deception, the person must be reinterviewed and confronted with this inconsistency. It is becoming more difficult to admit the examiner's opinion in any formal hearing, whether criminal or administrative. However, this process can give the examiner and/or the investigator with valuable information upon which s/he can further develop the case. Skillful interviewing techniques both before and after the examination often can provide the investigation with more valuable information than the test itself.

The greatest value of these types of detection devices is to rule out issues, provide new direction for the investigation, and serve as one factor in the final adjudication of the complaint allegation.

**Chemical Tests**

Investigators conducting administrative investigations should attempt to maximize the use of chemical testing for the presence or absence of alcohol or drugs.

Complainants and civilians should be requested to consent to such chemical tests should there be objective symptoms or a reasonable suspicion that substance abuse might be involved and have some relevance to the complaint. When a civilian dies from police actions, traffic accident involving a police vehicle or pursuit, or an in-custody death, the medical examiner usually conducts a complete toxicological examination. The investigator should ensure that this will be done and the results should be included in the investigative report along with the autopsy report. Other times when a civilian refuses to consent voluntarily to a chemical test, the investigator is required to follow the legal standards for obtaining a forced sample. This could be under the authority of the Vehicle Code or by warrant. If neither is successful, any observations should be fully noted in the investigative report.

Chemical testing of agency personnel is a vital element in an administrative investigation and maintenance of a professional police organization. A police agency cannot tolerate substance abuse by employees. Case law has continuously upheld the right of police agencies to require an employee to submit to a chemical test when done in a reasonable manner and under specific criteria. These should be delineated in the agency written policy. The following are the four times when such a test is warranted:

1. The employee exhibits objective symptoms of alcohol or other drug use, or there is a reasonable suspicion that the employee is using drugs illegally.
2. The employee's actions have caused death or serious injury of another person.
3. The test is consistent with the agency's policy on random drug screening.
4. The test is necessary to rule out an allegation that an employee is under the influence of alcohol or other drugs or engaging in the use of illegal drugs.

The investigator should normally request the employee to consent to such a test, particularly when it is being used to rule out an allegation. If the employee refuses, the investigator and/or the employee's immediate supervisor should order the employee to submit to the test in cases involving categories 1, 2, or 3. The employee cannot be ordered to submit to a chemical test simply to rule out an allegation (category 4) without some evidence of substance abuse or a reasonable suspicion.

The best chemical test is the urine specimen. It is less intrusive and does not require involvement of medical personnel, and it can detect drugs in the system for a longer period of time after use. A breath test is still applicable in cases involving symptoms of alcohol influence. A urine sample might be warranted should the breath results be lower than what the objective symptoms would lead a reasonable investigator to suspect. Investigators should be alert to the possible use and influence of anabolic steroids, particularly among police agency employees. (See Chapter 9 Stress and Police Personnel for a more detailed description.) It should be noted that the employee does not have a right to the type of test to be used in an administrative investigation. Employees do have the right to have a test of their choice at their own expense. This cannot be allowed to interfere unnecessarily with the progress of the investigation.

Investigators should tape record as much of the contact with employees as possible when they are suspected of involvement with or use of illegal drugs. Normally the employee should be ordered to the police facility if she or he isn't there already. This is the most reasonable approach for several reasons. First, it is the most discreet. Second, it allows for closer supervisory control and validates the job relationship of the investigation. The investigator and any involved supervisor should view this activity as simply a contact to collect a piece of evidence, rather than any form of interview or interrogation that would then necessitate additional formal procedures.

It is not unreasonable to allow the employee to have some form of representation present during this investigatory contact, if the employee requests. However, should the delay be extended for more than an hour, the test or sample should be taken to avoid the drug being flushed through the system.

## Photo and Physical Lineups

Both the use of a photo lineup and physical lineup are reasonable investigatory tools. This is particularly important when multiple officers are involved in an incident that leads to an allegation of misconduct. The agency should maintain a file of photographs of all employees both in uniform, with and without hat, and in civilian clothing. It should be the policy of the agency to update these photos every five years.

Both of these forms of lineups for identification must follow the criminal standards of care for objectivity. Whether using a photo display or physical lineup, the persons involved must be similar in appearance. Photo lineups are less intrusive and easier to conduct, but facial hair changes can cause problems.

It should be noted that agency employees do not have a right to refuse to participate in a physical lineup. Likewise they do not have a right to prohibit the use of their photograph in a photo lineup. As with any professional investigation, the photo lineup used should be preserved and become part of the investigative documents.

**Financial Records**

In some cases such as corruption, bribery, or theft, the financial records of the employee may become an integral part of the investigation. This information normally should be obtained through warrant unless voluntarily provided by the employee.

**Use of Covert Collection Techniques**

Some allegations of misconduct may warrant the use of covert collection techniques. Investigators should adhere to the agency's policies and procedures when using any of these investigative techniques. Examples of these covert techniques are visual surveillance, decoy operations, controlled buys and electronic/aural surveillance. If informants are to be used, the agency's guidelines on identification, control, and use of informants must be followed.

## RETIREMENT COUNSELING

Inherent in the law enforcement officers' life stage of retirement are issues of finance, lifestyle, leisure time, identification, psychological needs, and marriage and family adaptation.[105] For some police officers it also often involves retirement issues that are significantly different from those of the general population. Most police officers have spent their careers living decidedly separate from the community in which they serve. They live with a level of stress far surpassing that of most persons and experience the acute physiological and psychological ramifications of that stress. The realities of their work often necessitate the development of a small, closed system of support, if any exists at all. Typically, their support system includes those with whom they work on a daily basis. Separation from the work environment includes the possibility of isolation and further withdrawal and most certainly brings new challenges to the officer's immediate family system as this unit becomes the predominant support system.

**Psychological Impact**

Retirement from law enforcement does, in fact symbolize loss of identity, of authority, and of family. According to Rehm[106] a key psychological factor in deciding to stay on the job past the time of retirement eligibility involves unfulfilled needs as described by Maslow's Theory of Self-Actualization (previously discussed in Chapter 4, Organizational Theory). When reflecting on their careers, police officers may not be able to see any signs of lasting impact on the department or on the community to which they have dedicated their service. The legal system creates a revolving door that oftentimes places the same individuals (criminals) in prison time after time for brief periods. The result may be an officer's sense of powerlessness to impact that system. Staying long past the point of effectiveness may be an attempt to remedy that situation and to fulfill that psychological need. Sticking with the job without consideration of physical and psychological fitness for duty can result in shame, humiliation, poor morale, and heightened liability for the officer, for fellow officers, and for the department.

Officers who have relied primarily on police support networks struggle with loss of consortium when their everyday lives no longer include active police work. The absence of being at the center of what is happening in the community, privy to specific confidential information, often results in a sense of isolation, which may lead to the tendency to withdraw further.

Loss of structure provided by the profession for so many years is oftentimes a difficult phenomenon with which to cope. For many, this structure played a significant role in an internal sense of peace and control. It provided the officer with a sense of purpose and specific direction. Without it, the retired officer may experience an intense transition for a period of time, which can include a sense of hopelessness and chaos. As a result the retired officer may resort to ineffective coping mechanisms to deal with the subsequent anxiety, fear, and loneliness.

For most police officers, their identity has been punctuated (and, for some, summarized) by their uniforms, their service weapons, and their badges. They may feel stripped naked upon relinquishing these symbols. This may also be followed by feelings of fear, perceived decrease in status, and a generalized sense of loss.

In post-retirement counseling sessions, officers frequently report that "all I know how to do is to be a cop." Some believe they are unqualified for other employment opportunities after retirement. They frequently fail to recognize the repertoire of skills developed as a result of their careers. Police work requires the refinement of fluid skills rather than simply the development of more crystallized abilities. They have become master problem solvers as a vital part of their role. Conflict resolution has become second nature. Their communication skills far surpass those of the general community. They are self-starters requiring little supervision; they tend to be dependable, reliable, and ethical; they are uncharacteristically brave; and they generally consider the needs of others above themselves. These skills and qualities represent critical foundational pieces to a myriad of other jobs. Specific counseling regarding the transfer and marketability of skills and abilities can be invaluable in assisting officers with this transition.

**Family Impact**

Most families of police officers have learned to function under unique circumstances. Shift work, rotating days off, working off-duty jobs to augment income, overtime, court responsibilities, on-call status, community contact—all of these sacrifices force police spouses, to learn to function within a multiplicity of roles. The spouse of one retiring police officer recently reported, "I have spent the last 30 years running the household, raising the children, managing our finances, playing both father and mother, and now that he is home full-time, he insists on criticizing me and telling me what to do! I spent years waiting for him, learning how to live without him. Now, all of a sudden, he is my constant companion. He is driving me crazy! He doesn't know what to do with himself without his job to go to everyday, and I don't know what to do with him here. I still love him very much, but I am afraid we can't adjust." For many, this marks the beginning of a new marriage with different agreements about roles and responsibilities, and with the need for the development or discovery of common interests, goals, and ways of being together. For some, it unfortunately marks the end of the marriage.

The average age of retirement for police officers often coincides with the time at which their children are leaving home. For those officers whose focus has been more job than family related or whose shiftwork has not been conducive to family life, there may be unfinished business with those children. This may need to be resolved for the maintenance or establishment of a healthy future relationship.

Additionally, families must deal with other significant losses. Net income decreases by as much as 50 percent, and medical and dental coverage previously available may no longer be offered at the same level of coverage or cost. Vacation pay and sick time are no longer a part of everyday life. Annual raises to offset the cost of living have become things of the past.

As reported by Rehm,[107] the Bureau of Labor estimates that individuals require an income equal to approximately 70 to 80 percent of their working income to maintain the same standard of living after retirement. For many, this means working at least part-time in addition to retirement investments. Unfortunately, many officers do not begin thinking about retirement early enough. Family demands render heavy investment in outside individual pension plans difficult, if not impossible. Optimally, retirement planning should begin at the outset of one's career, with regular review and adjustment as one's career progresses. If the officer can anticipate the date of retirement within three to five years, planning is significantly enhanced. In addition to financial options, such as deferred retirement option plans,[108] officers can also begin to consider post-retirement employment options.

**Planning**

Career management should, ideally, be a consistent ongoing part of officers' entire work life. Annual or biannual meetings with supervisors as part of the evaluation process could include planning of goals and directives for officers to maintain peak interest in their careers. Identification of strengths and exploration of placement options keep officers sharp and invested in their careers.

Some research suggests that job dissatisfaction can affect attitude.[109] There is some evidence that at least some officers work extra (non-police) jobs because they are not receiving adequate satisfaction from their police jobs.[110] Satisfaction with a career choice and the factors that determine that satisfaction or lack of it are valuable information during the initial screening and selection process. That information could also be useful in diagnosing behavioral problems and, more importantly, in prevention of problems altogether throughout the course of an officer's career.[111]

The results of a study conducted by Primm, Palmer, and Hastings[112] demonstrate a difference in the reported job satisfaction between those officers who involve themselves in extracurricular activities and those who do not. These activities represent additional time and energy devoted to the career in an area of special expertise. Older officers with many years on the job may be successfully motivated and experience greater satisfaction if they become involved in these activities. While these interventions may well serve to increase the effective life span of the career, it is ironic that the more satisfying the career, the more difficult it is to shape a satisfactory retirement.[113] Therefore, it seems imperative that there be a balance between ensuring a satisfying career and systematically preparing for retirement by encouraging officers to pursue outside interests as their time to retire approaches.

As officers age, planning meetings could include discussion of impending retirement. Ideally, this should begin three to five years prior to retirement.

Planning is significantly impacted by the retirement system under which officers were hired. Since most officers are not likely to be ending their work years at the point of leaving the department (generally around age 50), officers could be counseled about possibilities such as returning to school for new training, continuing education in their field, exploring and planning self-employment options, and looking at new work sites as post-retirement possibilities. Since most will have been outside the market for quite some time, seeking assistance with one's job-seeking skills, including resume writing and interviewing techniques, would be helpful.

Financially, officers should receive counseling regarding their specific status and needs. Planning for post-retirement needs assists officers in determining the best time for retirement to ensure their financial stability.

Ideally, psychological intervention with police officers should begin at the beginning. In the post-academy, specific attention could be paid to discussion about the potential psychological impact of the job, both on officers and on their families. During the work life of officers, annual visits to the department psychologist would assist in identifying problems with job satisfaction and performance, psychological health and wellness, and potential family difficulties. Intervention at this stage often results in successful alleviation of the problems and adds significantly to the productive work and family life of officers. Ongoing psychological services made available to officers and dependents afford opportunities for stress reduction, addressing of duty-related difficulties, family conflict intervention, and alleviation of symptomology associated with depression or anxiety. The early establishment of seeking and accepting psychological service as needed may likely result in an easier decision to seek assistance at the end of their careers.

In collaboration with field supervisors conducting annual job performance reviews and identifying those officers considering retirement, referral could be made for counseling with the police psychologist to explore reasons for retirement and potential post-retirement issues. Additionally, spouses and family members need to be included in the counseling process to ensure a smooth transition and family stability. They, too need to explore and address their feelings regarding this major life transition and to develop a working understanding of what to expect of their loved ones.

One method of beginning to address all of these retirement issues would be to have a series of seminars for all officers approaching retirement. These in-services could cover issues such as community resources, retirement benefits, insurance, job-seeking techniques, psychology of retirement, and financial management.[114] Additionally, a special seminar for family members would serve to begin to prepare them for the transition and provide them an outlet for their concerns.

Lastly, the department plays a huge role in the post-retirement psychological adjustment of its officers. Retirement should be a time of celebration of a job well done. Far too often, officers simply slip away without acknowledgment or even notice until time has passed without their presence. A formal, public send-off with overt acknowledgment of the contributions made by retiring officers helps to bring to a close their years of commitment and service. Presenting the officers' gun and badge as a gift symbolizes their contribution and sacrifice. A formal letter from the chief of police summarizing the officers' accomplishments and articulating the appreciation of the department and of the city provides tangible validation of a job well done.

# SUMMARY

Because the quality of the service that a police department delivers to its citizens can never exceed the quality of its personnel, human resource management is one of the most important areas in police administration today. In this chapter we examined some of the major components of police human resource management, drawn upon the latest state-of-the-art information from a wide variety of disciplines, and suggested ways in which police administrators can improve the overall effectiveness of their agencies within the confines of the resources available to them.

We began by discussing the functions of the human resource unit. We outlined the basic responsibilities of the unit and the process employed in selecting police officers—clearly one of the most important components of human resource management. In conjunction with this process, we discussed the impact of the Americans with Disabilities Act. We also discussed some of the major components of the selection process, including the entrance examination, reverse discrimination, physical ability testing, the polygraph, the character investigation, all interviews in all boards, and medical and psychological testing of police applicants.

The effort for providing higher education for police officers can be traced to 1929 but the real impetus for the movement started in the 1960s, a decade of social disruption and violence. Police confrontations with students in universities and with anti-Vietnam War protesters were common events. The inability of the police to cope with the ghetto riots and their apparent helplessness to curtail the spiraling crime rate led both liberal and conservative politicians to believe that higher education was desirable. It is generally agreed that college education would not transform an intellectually wanting person into an accomplished one, but all things being equal, the college educated individual is more qualified and better prepared than the high school graduate. However, in spite of arguments presented in favor of a college education for police officers, there are still powerful political and social forces that do not fully support this movement.

In this chapter we also discussed the need to support female officers, current and future. We recommend that the following actions be taken to educate local agencies on the value of gender diversity in law enforcement, design a comprehensive approach that turns intentions into success; advertise and recruit to attract qualified women; screen and hire with the intention of bringing on the best candidate; train on sexual harassment to emphasize a zero tolerance approach; train on gender discrimination, recognition, and reduction; avoid actionable behavior and understand litigation issues; establish policies to improve the role of women in policing; mentor women officers to strengthen the potential for longevity; recruit promotional strategies and move women into leadership roles; and evaluate agency actions and understand progress toward diversity.

Two federal laws that have impacted on law enforcement were also discussed in detail, the Fair Labor Standards Act and the Family Medical Leave Act.

One of the more controversial components of human resource management, performance evaluation, is often disliked and misunderstood both by the individuals doing the evaluation and by those being evaluated. This occurs because the purposes of such evaluations are simply not understood by many of the people involved. The major purposes of performance evaluation are to aid employees in maintaining acceptable levels of behavior, to assist in career development, to encourage supervision to take a personal interest in officers under their command, to make salary decisions, and to evaluate the selection procedure.

Salary administration is one of the most critical components in the personnel administration process. The ability of a police agency to compete with business and industry in attracting the most highly qualified personnel will be directly affected by the wages and other benefits offered.

The task of selecting people for entry-level or promotional positions in law enforcement has produced various techniques over the years, none of which is strong in its predictive aspect. One attempt at finding a more reliable way to predict future performance is through an assessment center. An assessment center is both a process and a place. This multiple-assessment strategy involves multiple techniques, including various forms of job-related simulations, and may include interviews and psychological tests.

On the topic of civilians in police work, the literature indicates that civilians are being employed by police departments in rapidly growing numbers and in an increasing variety of activities. It seems that this trend is likely to continue.

The most effective disciplinary system combines the reinforcement of the right set of values and all employees' behavioral standards that are consistent and fairly applied. Each employee must understand and be guided by these standards that have been established in the departments' general orders, rules, regulations, and procedures.

Every police agency needs a functional Internal Affairs Unit (IAU) or Professional Standards Unit or a person charged with the responsibility to oversee the acceptance, investigation, and adjudication or complaints of police performance. The size of this unit depends upon the workload. Those individuals performing functions within this unit should be directly responsible to the chief of police or sheriff. Only in large agencies should this function be assigned to a secondary layer within the organization such as an assistant or deputy chief of police or chief deputy/undersheriff.

Finally, we discussed retirement counseling for police officers. Inherent in law enforcement officers' last stage of retirement are the issues of finance, lifestyle, leisure time, identification, psychological needs, and marriage and family adaptation. For some police officers retirement also involves issues that are significantly different from those of the general population. Most police officers have spent their lives living decidedly separate from the community in which they serve. They live with a level of stress far surpassing that

of most persons and experience the acute physiological and psychological ramifications of the stress. It is important for administrators to understand these factors and do everything possible to assist police officers in making a smooth transition from career law enforcement to civilian life. One of the methods to begin addressing factors involved in the retirement process is a series of seminars for all officers approaching retirement. These in-service courses covers issues such as community resources, retirement benefits, insurance, job-seeking techniques, psychology of retirement, and financial management. In addition, a special seminar for family members would serve to begin to prepare them for the transition and would provide an outlet for their concerns.

## DISCUSSION QUESTIONS

1. Since 1960, the subject of human resource management has gained considerable prominence and visibility within the law enforcement community. What are some of the major social, political, and economic factors that have given impetus to the movement?

2. Why did Congress enact the Americans with Disabilities Act (ADA) of 1990?

3. What are the significant provisions of the Americans with Disabilities Act?

4. What two decisions were made by the U.S. Supreme Court in 1989 that caused civil rights leaders to become uneasy? What was the essence of those two decisions?

5. What was the significance of *Robinson* v. *City of Lake Station* (1986) and *Evans* v. *City of Evanston* (1989), as they relate to physical ability testing?

6. Law enforcement agencies using the polygraph in preemployment screening have indicated there are very specific benefits derived from its use. What are these benefits?

7. What are the advantages of a college education for police officers cited by the Police Executive Research Forum?

8. What question should police administrators answer before making dramatic changes in their educational requirements for police officers?

9. What courses of action were recommended by the International Association of Chiefs of Police to support female officers, current and future?

10. What function does the field training officer (FTO) serve in relation to new officers?

11. What provisions of the Fair Labor Standards Act impact most directly on police officers?

12. What conditions must be met before a police officer is eligible to take advantage of the provisions of the Family Medical Leave Act?

13. Under the Family Medical Leave Act, a police officer may be eligible to take up to twelve weeks of leave during any twelve-month period of time for one or more of which causes?

14. What are the major purposes of performance evaluations?

15. Pay plans must accomplish several objectives. What are they?

16. What is an assessment center?

17. What are the advantages of the assessment center?

18. Name several options municipalities might seek to recover the financial investment made in training new police officers.

19. A number of factors should be considered when applying discipline. What factors were discussed in this text?

20. Five profiles of violence-prone officers were discussed in this chapter. Identify each.

21. Why should assignments in internal affairs units be limited in tenure?

22. When is chemical testing of agency personnel warranted?

23. What types of issues are inherent in a law enforcement officer's life stage of retirement?

# NOTES

1. O. G. Stahl and R. A. Staufenberger, eds., *Police Personnel Administration* (Washington, D.C.: Police Foundation, 1974), p. 111.

2. For a detailed analysis of these findings and recommendations, see The President's Commission on Law Enforcement and the Administration of Justice, *Task Force Report on the Police* (Washington, D.C.: U.S. Government Printing Office, 1967); *Report of The National Advisory Commission on Civil Disorder* (New York: *New York Times,* 1968).

3. W. W. Schmidt, "Recent Developments in Police Civil Liability," *Journal of Police Science and Administration,* 4:3 (1976), 197–202.

4. D. M. Walters, "Civil Liability for Improper Police Training," *Police Chief,* 38:11 (1971), 28–36.

5. W. D. Heisel and P. V. Murphy, "Organization for Police Personnel Management," in *Police Personnel Administration,* ed. O. G. Stahl and R. A. Staufenberger (Washington, D.C.: Police Foundation, 1974), p. 1.

6. L. Tenito, C. R. Swanson, Jr., and N. C. Chamelin, *The Police Personnel Selection Process* (Indianapolis, Ind.: Bobbs-Merrill, 1977), p. 3.

7. Heisel and Murphy, "Organization for Police Personnel Management," pp. 8–11.

8. Ibid., pp. 1–2.

9. U.S. Equal Employment Opportunity Commission, *The Americans with Disabilities Act: Your Responsibilities as an Employer* (Washington, D.C.: U.S. Government Printing Office, 1991), p. 2.

10. Ibid., p. 3.

11. U.S. Equal Employment Opportunity Commission and U.S. Department of Justice, *The Americans with Disabilities Act: Questions and Answers* (Washington, D.C.: U.S. Government Printing Office, July 1991), p. 7.

12. Jeffrey Higginbotham, "The Americans with Disabilities Act," *FBI Law Enforcement Bulletin,* 60:8 (1991), 26.

13. Ibid., 26–27.

14. Ibid., 26.

15. Ibid., 26.

16. Ibid., 26.

17. Ibid., 26.

18. Ibid., 26.

19. Ibid., 26.

20. U.S. Equal Employment Opportunity Commission, *Americans with Disabilities Act: Your Responsibilities as an Employer,* p. 4.

21. Ibid., p. 5.

22. Ibid., p. 5.

23. U.S. Equal Employment Opportunity Commission, *Americans with Disabilities Act: Questions and Answers,* p. 4.

24. Ibid., p. 4.

25. Ibid., p. 6.

26. Jody M. Litchford, "The Americans with Disabilities Act," *Police Chief,* 58:1 (1991), 11.

27. U.S. Equal Employment Opportunity Commission, *Americans with Disabilities Act: Your Responsibilities as an Employer,* p. 10.

28. Ibid., p. 10.

29. Ibid., p. 6.

30. Ibid., p. 6.

31. *Kuntz* v. *City of New Haven* et al., No. N-90-480(JGM), March 3, 1993.

32. *Bombrys* v. *City of Toledo,* No. 3:92CV7592, June 4, 1993.

33. *Champ* v. *Baltimore County* et al., No. HAR 93-4031, April 19, 1995.

34. United States District Court, Eastern District of Michigan, Southern Division, Case No. 96-73369.

35. Territo, Swanson, and Chamelin, *Police Personnel Selection Process,* p. 10.

36. Heisel and Murphy, "Organization for Police Personnel Management," p. 5.

37. Territo, Swanson, and Chamelin, *Police Personnel Selection Process,* pp. 12, 13.

38. Ibid., p. 12.

39. Philip Ash, Karen Slora, and Cynthia F. Britton, "Police Agency Selection Practices," *Journal of Police Science and Administration,* 17:4 (1990), 262.

40. Ibid., 263.

41. Ibid., Table 4, 265.

42. U.S. Equal Employment Opportunity Commission, "Adoption of Questions and Answers to Clarify and Provide a Common Interpretation of the Uniform Guidelines on Employee Selection Procedures," *Federal Register,* Mar. 2, 1979, p. 12007.

43. Ibid., p. 12003.

44. Ibid., p. 11998.

45. 43 *FEP Cases* 130 (1989).

46. 57 *Law Week* 4616 (1989).

47. Civil Rights Act of 1991, Title 1, Section 1977A.

48. Ash, Slora, and Britton, "Police Agency Selection Practices," p. 264.

49. Walter S. Booth and Chris W. Horwick, "Physical Ability Testing for Police Officers in the 80s," *Police Chief*, 1:1 (1984), 39–41.

50. 630 F.Supp. 1052 (1986).

51. 619 F.2nd 611, U.S. *cert den*, 449 U.S. 872 (1980).

52. 881 F.2nd 382 (1989).

53. Ash, Slora, and Britton, "Police Agency Selection Practices," p. 265.

54. Ibid.

55. Ibid.

56. Ibid.

57. Robert M. Guion, "Personnel Assessment, Selection, and Placement," in *Handbook of Industrial and Organizational Psychology*, vol. 2, eds. Marvin D. Dunnette and Leaetta M. Hough (Palo Alto, Calif.: Consulting Psychologists Press, 1991), p. 347.

58. "Minnesota Multiphasic Personality Inventory-2," The University of Minnesota Press, 1989, #28, #36, #141, #143, and #182 as quoted in Paula N. Rubin, *Americans with Disabilities Act and Criminal Justice: New Employees*, U.S. Department of Justice, National Institute of Justice–Research in Action, October 1994.

59. Ibid.

60. Ibid.

61. The President's Commission on Law Enforcement and Administration of Justice, *Task Force Report: The Police* (Washington, D.C.: U.S. Government Printing Office, 1967), p. 137.

62. M. J. Palmiotto, "Should a College Degree Be Required for Today's Law Enforcement Officer?" in *Constitutional Issues in Policing*, ed. James D. Sewell, (Boston: Allyn and Bacon, 1999), pp. 70–75. (This discussion was adapted with permission from this source.)

63. R. W. Kobetz, *Law Enforcement and Criminal Justice Education Directory, 1975–76*. (Gaithersburg, MD: IACP, 1997).

64. The President's Commission on Law Enforcement and Administration of Justice, *The Challenge of Crime in a Free Society*. (Washington, D.C. Government Printing Office.)

65. J. B. Jacobs and S. B. Magdovitz, "At LEEP's End? A Review of the Law Enforcement Education Program." *Journal of Police Science and Administration*, 5:1 (1977), 7.

66. National Advisory Commission on Criminal Justice Standards and Goals, *The Police* (Washington, D.C.: U.S. Government Printing Office, 1973).

67. Jacobs and Magdovitz, "At LEEP's End?"

68. J. J. Sienna, "Criminal Justice Higher Education—Its Growth and Directions," *Crime and Delinquency*, 20:4 (1974), 389–397.

69. W. R. Anderson, "The Law Enforcement Education Act of 1967," *The Congressional Record*, H.R. 188, (1967) January.

70. W. H. Hewitt, "The Objectives of Formal Police Education," *Police*, 9:2 (1964), 25–27.

71. Sienna, "Criminal Justice Higher Education."

72. National Advisory Commission on Criminal Justice Standard and Goals, *The Police*, p. 367.

73. Ibid. p. 367.

74. D. L. Carter, A. D. Sapp, and D. W. Stephens, *The State of Police Education: Police Direction for the 21st Century* (Washington, D.C.: Police Executive Research Forum, 1986b).

75. D. L. Carter, A. D. Sapp, and D. W. Stephens, "Higher Education as a Bonafide Occupational Qualification (BFQ) for Police: A Blueprint," *American Journal of Police*, 7:2 (1988a), 16–18.

76. "The Future of Women in Policing," *The Police Chief*, LXVI:3 (March 1999), 53 and 54.

77. Ibid., pp. 55 and 56.

78. Will Aitchison, *The Rights of Police Officers*, 3rd ed. (Portland, Ore.: Labor Relations Information System, 1996), p. 361. This source has been paraphrased in preparing this section.

79. Ibid., p. 362.

80. Ibid., p. 375.

81. Ibid., p. 371.

82. Ibid., p. 374.

83. Ibid., p. 362.

84. Ibid., p. 363.

85. Ibid.

86. Ibid., p. 366.

87. Ibid., p. 365.

88. Ibid.

89. Ibid.

90. Ibid., p. 378.

91. Ibid.

92. Part of the information in this section is drawn from J. Higginbotham, "The Family and Medical

Leave Act of 1993," *FBI Law Enforcement Bulletin* (December 1993), 15–21.

93. W. Dopp and P. M. Whisenand, *Police Personnel Administration,* 2nd ed. (Boston: Allyn & Bacon, 1980). Much of the discussion on performance evaluation was taken from this source.

94. J. N. Matzer, Jr., *Personnel Administration: A Guide for Small Local Governments* (Washington, D.C.: Civil Service Commission). Much of the information in this chapter dealing with salary administration was taken from this source.

95. D. P. Slevin, "The Assessment Center: Breakthrough in Management Appraisal and Development," *Personnel Journal,* 57 (April 1972), p. 256.

96. M. D. Dunnette and S. J. Motowidlo, *Police Selection and Career Assessment* (Washington, D.C.: U.S. Government Printing Office, 1976), p. 56.

97. R. J. Filer, "Assessment Centers in Police Selection," in *Proceedings of the National Working Conference on the Selection of Law Enforcement Officers,* ed. C. D. Spielberger and H. C. Spaulding (Tampa, Fla.: University of South Florida, March 1977), pp. 105, 106.

98. W. J. Kearney and D. D. Martin, "The Assessment Center: A Tool for Promotion Decisions," *Police Chief,* 42:1 (1975), p. 32.

99. Ibid.

100. Ibid.

101. Darrel W. Stephens, "Discipline Philosophy," *The FBI Law Enforcement Bulletin,* 63:3 (March 1994), 21.

102. Ibid., p. 22.

103. Ellen N. Scrivner, "Controlling Police Use of Excessive Force: The Role of the Police Psychologist," U.S. Department of Justice, Office of Justice Programs, *National Institute of Justice,* October 1994, 2–4.

104. L. Reiter, *Law Enforcement Administrative Investigations* (Tallahassee, Fla.: Lou Reiter and Associates, 1998) (This discussion of internal affairs units was adapted with permission from this source, pp. 3–6 through 3–11 and pp. 6–9 through 6–12).

105. Jeanette L. Palmer, Ph.D. "Police Retirement: Life After the Force," *American Criminal Justice Association Journal,* Vols. 60–61, Nos. 1–4 (Spring/Summer 1998, Fall/Winter 1999), 18–20. (This discussion was adapted with permission from this source.)

106. B. Rehm, "Retirement: A New Chapter Not the End of the Story," *FBI Law Enforcement Bulletin,* 65:9 (1996), 6–12.

107. Ibid.

108. T. Carlton, "Police Pension and Retirement System," *FBI Law Enforcement Bulletin,* 63:4 (1994), 23.

109. V. H. Vroom, "Ego-Involvement, Job Satisfaction, and Job Performance," *Personnel Psychology,* 15 (1962), 159–177.

110. M. G. Grant, "The Relationship of Moonlighting to Job Dissatisfaction in Police Officers," *Journal of Police Science and Administration,* 5 (1977), 193–196.

111. M. Primm, D. Palmer, and P. Hastings, "An Examination of Career Satisfaction in Professional Police Officers: A Field Study," *American Criminal Justice Association L.A.E. Journal,* Vols. 58–59 (1997–1998), 42–45.

112. Ibid.

113. L. Harrison, "The More Satisfying the Career, the More Difficult It Is to Shape a Satisfactory Retirement," *Police Chief* (October, 1981).

114. J. Violanti, "Police Retirement: The Impact of Change," *FBI Law Enforcement Bulletin,* 59(3) (1992), 12–15.

## INTRODUCTION

Historically, U.S. business and industry have been slow to identify and provide for the needs of workers. Largely because of the labor union movement, the U.S. worker has achieved a variety of benefits, ranging from increased wages to comprehensive medical care and retirement programs. The inclusion of mental health compensation as a significant management issue has evolved through a combination of union pressures and simple economics. A healthy, well-adjusted worker means increased efficiency and higher production for the corporation. As a consequence, job related stress "has moved from the nether world of 'emotional problems' and 'personality conflicts' to the corporate balance sheet. . . . Stress is now seen as not only troublesome but expensive.[1]

# 9

# STRESS AND POLICE PERSONNEL

*If, under stress, a man goes all to pieces, he will probably be told to pull himself together. It would be more effective to help him identify the pieces and to understand why they have come apart.*
R. RUDDOCK

Government and public service sectors generally lag behind industry and business in employee benefit innovations, and the mental health issue is no exception. However, the private sector's concern with the wide-ranging effects of job-related stress on workers is also shared by those in law enforcement. More and more literature on stress factors in policing is becoming available to the law enforcement executive for use in developing programs designed to reduce stress among police personnel.[2]

## WHAT IS STRESS?

Despite the volumes of research published on stress, the phenomenon remains poorly defined. Hans Selye, the researcher and theorist who pioneered the physiological investigation of stress, defines *stress* in the broadest possible terms as anything that places an adjustive demand on the organism. Identified as "the body's nonspecific response to any demand placed on it," stress may be either positive (*eustress*) or negative (*distress*) (see Table 9-1).[3] According to this distinction, many stressful events do not threaten people but provide them with pleasurable challenges. The excitement of the gambler, the thrill of the athlete engaged in a highly competitive sport, the deliberate risk taking of the daredevil stunt man—these are examples of stress without *distress*. For many people, this kind of stress provides the spice of life.

Basowitz and his associates define stress as those stimuli that are likely to produce disturbances in most people. The authors postulate a continuum of stimuli that differ in meaning and in their anxiety-producing consequences:

At one end are such stimuli or cues, often highly symbolic, which have meaning only to single or limited numbers of persons and which to the observer may appear as innocuous or trivial. At the other end are such stimuli, here called stress,

## TABLE 9-1.  Changes to the Body at the Alarm Stage

| | |
|---|---|
| Heart rate increase | Blood flow increases to heart, lungs, and large muscles |
| Blood pressure increase | Perspiration, especially to palms |
| Large muscle groups tense | Digestive secretions slow |
| Adrenaline rush | Dry mouth due to saliva decrease |
| Increase blood sugar | Bowel activity decreases |
| Hypervigilance | Extremities become cool |
| Pupils dilate | Sphincters tighten |
| Increased hearing acuity | More white blood cells enter the bloodstream |
| Increased blood clotting | Cholesterol remains in the blood longer |
| Increased metabolism | Dilation of the lung passages and increased respiration |

*Source: Stress Management for Law Enforcement Officers* by Anderson/Swenson/Clay, © 1995, Reprinted by permission of Prentice Hall, Inc., Upper Saddle River, NJ.

which by their explicit threat to vital functioning and their intensity are likely to overload the capacity of most organisms' coping mechanisms.[4]

The authors also distinguish between pathological, neurotic, or harmful anxiety and the normal, adaptive, or healthy form of anxiety. In the first instance, anxiety is defined as a conscious and painful state of apprehension unrelated to an external threat. This kind of anxiety may render an individual incapable of distinguishing danger from safety or relevant information and cues from irrelevant ones. Ultimately one's psychological and physiological functioning can become so reduced that death occurs. As the authors state, anxiety in this severe form is generally derived from "internal psychological problems and therefore is chronically present, leading to more serious, long-lasting somatic and psychological changes."[5] In the second instance, anxiety is defined as a state of increased alertness that permits maximum psychological and physiological performance. A state of fear, according to this formulation, is a simple form of anxiety characterized by the life-threatening or harmful nature of the stimuli. Unlike the more severe, harmful forms, simple forms of anxiety are temporal and beneficial to the individual. Of course, distinctions among the various levels of anxiety are difficult to make. For example, a person may react to a minimally threatening stimulus as though his or her life were in imminent danger. The fear response may have been appropriate and the overreaction inappropriate (perhaps indicative of psychological disturbance). Anxiety, then, can be defined as the individual's ability to cope with, or respond to, threatening situations.

## Biological Stress and the General Adaptation Syndrome

Selye has formulated what he calls the general adaptation syndrome (GAS) to describe on the biological level how stress can incapacitate an individual. The GAS encompasses three stages of physiological reaction to a wide variety of *stressors*—environmental agents or activities powerful enough in their impact to elicit a reaction from the body. These three stages are (1) alarm, (2) resistance, and (3) exhaustion.

The alarm stage, sometimes referred to as an *emergency reaction*, is exemplified on the animal level by the so-called "fight or flight" syndrome. When an animal encounters a threatening situation, its body signals a defense alert. The animal's cerebral cortex flashes an alarm to the hypothalamus, a small structure in the midbrain that connects the brain with body functions. A powerful hormone called ACTH is released into the bloodstream by the hypothalamus and is carried by the bloodstream to the adrenal gland, a part of the endocrine, or ductless gland, system. There ACTH triggers the release of adrenin, which produces a galvanizing or energizing effect on the body functions. The heart pounds, the pulse races, breathing quickens, the muscles tense, and digestion is retarded or inhibited (see Table 9-1). The adjustive function of this reaction pattern is readily apparent, namely, preparing the organism biologically to fight or to run away. When the threat is removed or diminished, the physiological functions involved in this alarm, or emergency reaction, subside, and the organism regains its internal equilibrium.

If the stress continues, however, the organism reaches the resistance stage of the GAS. During this stage, bodily resources are mobilized to deal with the specific stressors, and adaptation is optimal. Although the stressful stimulus may persist, the symptoms that characterized the alarm stage disappear. In short, the individual seems to have handled the stress successfully.

Under conditions of prolonged stress, the body reaches a point where it is no longer capable of maintaining resistance. This condition characterizes the exhaustion stage. Hormonal defenses break down, and many emotional reactions that appeared during the alarm stage may reappear, often in intensified form. Further exposure to stress leads to exhaustion and eventually to death. Even before this extreme stage has been reached, however, excessive hormonal secretions may result in severe physiological pathology of the type that Selye calls "diseases of adaptation," for example, ulcers, high blood pressure, and coronary susceptibility.[6]

## Psychological Stress

While life-threatening situations have understandably received considerable attention from researchers and theorists, there are many other circumstances in which the stress involved threatens something that the individual deems valuable: self-esteem, authority, and security, for example. The human being's highly developed brain, accumulated knowledge, and ability to perceive and communicate through the medium of symbols lead him or her to find unpleasant or pleasant connotations in an incredible number of situations and events. Human beings react not only to tangible, physical stresses but also to symbolic or imagined threats or pleasures.[7] The effects of the stimulus can vary widely, depending on a person's culture, personal and family background, experiences, and mood and circumstances at the time. The objective nature of an event is not nearly as significant as what the event means to a particular individual at any given time. People can influence the nature of stress through their ability to control and anticipate events in the environment. As anticipation can simplify stress, the lack of it does so even more. The unanticipated event often has the greatest impact on an individual and leaves the most persistent aftereffects.[8]

## Reactions to Stress

Most people adjust their behavior to daily stress according to their adaptive range. At the high end of the range, when a person encounters an extremely demanding situation, his or her first reaction is usually anxiety, a varying mixture of alertness, anticipation, curiosity, and fear. At the low end of the range, when confronted with a stressful situation, an individual experiences a condition of overload. The ability to improvise deteriorates, and behavior is likely to regress to simpler, more primitive responses. Regardless of personality type, people under high stress show less ability to tolerate ambiguity and to sort out the trivial from the important. Some authorities report that people become apathetic and inactive when stress is either minimal or absent.

As stress increases slightly, the person becomes attentive and more active. When stress increases further, the individual becomes either interested and curious or wary and cautious. Greater stress then results in emotional states of unpleasant anxiety or pleasant expectation. When stress becomes extreme, anxiety may increase until it threatens to overwhelm the individual. At this point, panic, accompanied by paralysis, flight, or attack, may occur. Under high levels of emotion, an individual becomes less discriminating and tends to make either disorganized or stereotyped responses, to lose perceptual judgment, and to idealize and overgeneralize.[9] As one police psychologist puts it, "People under stress make mistakes." In policing where job-related stress is involved, the kind of mistakes that are likely to occur can result in potentially irreparable, even fatal, consequences.[10]

## STRESS IN LAW ENFORCEMENT

Police work is highly stressful—it is one of the few occupations in which an employee is asked continually to face physical dangers and to put his or her life on the line at any time. The police officer is exposed to violence, cruelty, and aggression and is often required to make extremely critical decisions in high-pressure situations.

Stress has many ramifications and can produce many varied psychophysiological disturbances that, if sufficiently intense and chronic, can lead to demonstrable organic diseases of varying severity. It may also lead to physiological disorders and emotional instability, which can manifest themselves in alcoholism, a broken marriage, and, in the extreme, suicide. Three-fourths of the heart attacks suffered by police officers are from job-related stress, studies have shown. As a result, courts have ruled that a police officer who suffers a heart attack while off duty is entitled to worker's compensation.[11] In California, a court held that the suicide of a probationary sergeant was directly related to his job stress. This ruling established the eligibility for certain benefits to the surviving family members. Thus, even a superficial review of the human, organizational, and legal impacts of stress-related health problems should sensitize every administrator toward the prevention, treatment, and solution of these problems.

## JOB STRESS IN POLICE OFFICERS

In law enforcement, stressors have been identified in various ways.[12] Researchers such as Kroes,[13,14] Eisenberg,[15] Reiser,[16,17,18,19] and Roberts[20] have all conducted extensive studies into law enforcement occupational stress, and although they do not group these stressors in identical categories, they tend to follow similar patterns. Most of the law enforcement stressors can be grouped into four broad categories: (1) organizational practices and characteristics, (2) criminal justice system practices and characteristics, (3) public practices and characteristics, and (4) police work itself.

One group of researchers interviewed 100 Cincinnati patrol officers about the elements of their job that they felt were stressful. Foremost on their list of items were the courts (scheduling, appearances, and leniency), the administration (undesirable assignments and lack of backing in ambiguous situations), faulty equipment, and community apathy. Other items listed but not with so great a frequency were changing shifts, relations with supervisors, nonpolice work, other police officers, boredom, and pay.[21]

A survey of twenty police chiefs in the southeastern United States confirmed these findings. These chiefs, when asked about situations they felt were stressful for line personnel, listed lack of administrative support, role conflicts, public pressure and scrutiny, peer group pressures, courts, and imposed role changes.[22]

While working with the San Jose Police department, one researcher was able to identify numerous sources of psychological stress that were basically reflections of his personal observations and feelings while performing the functions of a patrol officer for approximately two years. Some of these sources of psychological stress were poor supervision; absence or lack of career development opportunities; inadequate reward reinforcement; offensive administrative policies; excessive paperwork; poor equipment; law enforcement agency jurisdiction; isolationism; unfavorable court decisions; ineffectiveness of corrections to rehabilitate or warehouse criminals; misunderstood judicial procedures; inefficient courtroom management; distorted press accounts of police incidents; unfavorable attitude by the public; derogatory remarks by neighbors and others; adverse local government decisions; ineffectiveness of referral agencies; role conflict; adverse work scheduling; fear of serious injury, disability, and death; exposure to people suffering and in agony, both physically and mentally; and consequences of actions, their appropriateness, and possible adverse conditions.[23]

## POLICE STRESSORS

Violanti and Aron distributed the 60-item Police Stress Survey (PSS) to a random sample of 110 officers in a large New York state police department.[24] Ninety-three percent of those sampled (N=103) completed the PSS and returned it. Table 9-2 displays the results of this survey. The single most potent stressor was killing someone in the line of duty. The empathy police officers have for victims is revealed by the fact that the fourth most potent stressor was handling child abuse cases, which ranked ahead of other well-known stressors such as high-speed chases, using force, responding to felony-in-progress calls, and making death notices.

The stressors in Table 9-2 can be factored into two components: (1) those that are organizational/administrative and (2) those that are inherent in the nature of police work. Within these stressors there were some variations. Sergeants in charge of substations reported the most organizational/administrative stress, while detectives reported the least. For officers in the 31- to 35-year-old range, the single most powerful stressor was shift work. However, for officers over 46 years of age, the mean values of all stressors dropped. This is

## TABLE 9-2. Police Stressors Ranked by Mean Scores

| Stressor | Mean Score | Stressor | Mean Score |
|---|---|---|---|
| Killing someone in line of duty | 79.38 | Excessive paperwork | 43.15 |
| Fellow officer killed | 76.67 | Court leniency | 42.65 |
| Physical attack | 70.97 | Disagreeable regulations | 42.27 |
| Battered child | 69.24 | Ineffective judicial system | 42.00 |
| High speed chases | 63.73 | Family demands | 41.84 |
| Shift work | 61.21 | Politics in department | 40.64 |
| Use of force | 60.96 | Inadequate supervision | 40.11 |
| Inadequate dept. support | 60.93 | Public criticism | 39.52 |
| Incompatible partner | 60.36 | Assigned new duties | 39.22 |
| Accident in patrol car | 59.89 | Ineffective corrections | 39.08 |
| Insufficient personnel | 58.53 | Inadequate salary | 38.45 |
| Aggressive crowds | 56.70 | Change from boredom to high stress | 38.06 |
| Felony in progress | 55.27 | Making arrests alone | 37.23 |
| Excessive discipline | 53.27 | Personal insult from citizen | 36.67 |
| Plea bargaining | 52.84 | Negative public image | 36.17 |
| Death notifications | 52.59 | Increased responsibility | 33.03 |
| Inadequate support (super.) | 52.43 | Exposure to pain and suffering | 33.01 |
| Inadequate equipment | 52.36 | Exposure to death | 32.06 |
| Family disputes | 51.97 | Second job | 31.51 |
| Negative press coverage | 51.80 | Lack of participation in decisions | 31.10 |
| Court on day off | 51.06 | Public apathy | 29.50 |
| Job conflict w/rules | 50.64 | Promotion competition | 29.46 |
| Fellow officer not doing job | 49.02 | Promotion or commendation | 28.79 |
| Lack of recognition | 48.10 | Non-police tasks | 27.94 |
| Physical injury on job | 47.10 | Demands for high morality | 26.14 |
| Making quick decisions | 45.82 | Politics outside dept. | 25.48 |
| Restrictive court decisions | 44.82 | Strained non-police relations | 23.60 |
| Getting along w/supervisors | 44.48 | Boredom | 23.25 |
| Disagreeable duties | 43.90 | Minor physical injuries | 23.23 |
| Mistreatment in court | 43.50 | Racial conflicts | 22.53 |

*Note:* Overall mean score = 44.78.

*Source:* Reprinted from *Journal of Criminal Justice*, Volume 23, John M. Violanti and Fred Aron, "Police Stressors: Variations in Perception Among Police Personnel," pages 287–294, Copyright 1995, with kind permission from Elsevier Science Ltd., The Boulevard, Langford Lane, Kidlington OX5 1GB, UK.

probably due in part to the accommodations that such officers have learned to make as well as the nature of the jobs that people more senior in their careers hold. For African Americans, the highest-ranking stressor was inadequate support by the police department. Table 9-3 provides a checklist of stress symptoms.

## TABLE 9-3.  Stress Symptoms Checklist

| | |
|---|---|
| Trouble getting to sleep or staying asleep | Constipation |
| Nightmares | Nausea, upset stomach |
| Feeling anxious and tense | Vomiting |
| Pulling or twisting hair | Appetite increase or decrease |
| Sweating (when not exercising) | Weight loss/ or gain |
| Blurred vision | Increase in use of alcohol or medications |
| Skin rash | Upper respiratory colds |
| Irregular menstruation | Shortness of breath |
| Restlessness | Difficulty breathing |
| Itching | Memory blanks |
| Biting nails | Rush of ideas |
| Shaking or trembling | Daydreaming |
| Chest pains | Confusion |
| Impatience | Poor concentration |
| Irritability | Indecision |
| Thoughts of hurting others | Worrying |
| Feeling inferior to others | Persistent intrusive thoughts |
| Feeling unattractive | Feeling impending danger |
| Feeling lonely | Desire to escape or hide |
| Decreased interest in social activities | Feel tight bands around head or body |
| Blaming self | Sense of choking or tightness in throat |
| Oversleeping | Numbness in parts of the body |
| Awakening too early in morning | Muscular weakness in part of the body |
| Grinding teeth | Decreased sex interest |
| Tightness in jaw | Feeling guilt, shame, or embarrassment |
| Tension headaches | Thoughts of death or suicide |
| Muscular stiffness and aches | Fatigue, lack of energy |
| Nervous tics and mannerisms | Apathy |
| Cold hands or feet | Lack of pleasure in things |
| High blood pressure | Feeling depressed |
| Racing heart or palpitations | Crying spells |
| Dizziness or lightheadedness | Feeling trapped |
| Diarrhea | Future looks hopeless |

*Source: Stress Management for Law Enforcement Officers* by Anderson/Swenson/Clay, © 1995. Reprinted by permission of Prentice Hall, Inc., Upper Saddle River, NJ.

# ALCOHOLISM AND POLICE OFFICERS

Alcoholism in government and industry is not only widespread but also extremely costly—a fact established most convincingly by many independent researchers. Some 6.5 million employed workers in the United States today are alcoholics. Loss of productivity because of the disease of alcoholism has been computed at $10 billion.[25]

Although precise figures are not available to substantiate a high incidence of alcoholism among police, department officials have reported informally that as many as 25 percent of the officers in their respective departments have serious alcohol abuse problems.[26]

Alcohol problems among police officers manifest themselves in a number of ways. Some of these are a higher than normal absentee rate before and immediately following the officer's regular day off, complaints of insubordination by supervisors, complaints by citizens of misconduct in the form of verbal and physical abuse, intoxication during regular working hours, involvement in traffic accidents while under the influence of alcohol on and off duty, and reduced overall performance (see Table 9-4).

**TABLE 9-4. Signs of Alcohol Abuse as Reported by Alcoholic Police Officers and Their Supervisors**

| Supervisors' Observations | Alcohol-Abusing Officers' Signs |
|---|---|
| Leaving post temporarily | Hangover on job |
| Drinking at lunchtime | Morning drinking before work |
| Red and bleary eyes | Absenteeism; day or half-day |
| Mood changes after lunch | Increased nervousness, jitteriness |
| Lower quality of work | Drinking at lunchtime |
| Absenteeism; day or half-day | Hand tremors |
| Unusual excuses for absences | Drinking during working hours |
| Loud talking | Late to work |

*Note:* From "Signs of Developing Alcoholism" by Seafield 911, in *Supervisor's Training Manual,* 1991, Davie, FL, Seafield 911.

**FIGURE 9-1.** An Oklahoma County Sheriff's deputy cradles a tiny victim of the devastating Oklahoma City bombing incident. (Courtesy *The Daily Oklahomian,* Oklahoma City, Oklahoma.)

It has been suggested further that policing is especially conducive to alcoholism. Because police officers frequently work in an environment in which social drinking is commonplace, it is relatively easy for them to become social drinkers. The nature of police work and the environment in which it is performed provides the stress stimulus.[27]

Traditionally, police departments adhered to the "character flaw" theory of alcoholism. This outdated philosophy called for the denunciation and dismissal of the officer with an alcohol problem.[28] Today, police departments attempt to rehabilitate officers and typically they are separated from the service only after such attempts have failed. Police departments now have a broad mix of employee assistance programs (EAPs) to assist officers with their drinking problems, including self-assessment checklists (see Table 9-5), peer counseling, in-house psychologists and those on retainers, and support groups.

**Departmental Programs**

There is no single "best way" for a department to assist its officers with a drinking problem, but some agencies have enjoyed a fair degree of success for their efforts. For example, the Denver Police Department has used its closed-circuit television system to teach officers who are problem drinkers and encourage them to join the in-house program. A major portion of the in-house program was designed to persuade the problem drinker, after he or she has digested a sufficient amount of the educational aspect, to enter the Mercy Hospital CareUnit® and achieve the status of a recovering alcoholic.[29]

It is the responsibility of the individual police agency and its administrators to act on the fact that alcoholism is a disease and to create a relaxed atmosphere and an in-house program for the dissemination of information relative to this problem. As indicated earlier, the objective of such a program is

---

**TABLE 9-5.  Alcohol Self-Assessment Checklist**

Each of the following conditions or behaviors has been found to be associated with alcohol abuse or problem drinking. Check the ones that apply to you. This exercise will sensitize you to what to look for when evaluating a person for alcohol abuse potential.

_____  1. Drinking alone regularly.

_____  2. Needing a drink to get over a hangover.

_____  3. Needing a drink at a certain time each day.

_____  4. Finding it harder and harder to get along with others.

_____  5. Memory loss while or after drinking.

_____  6. Driving skill deteriorating.

_____  7. Drinking to relieve stress, fear, shyness, insecurity.

_____  8. More and more family and friends worrying about drinking habits.

_____  9. Becoming moody, jealous, or irritable after drinking.

_____ 10. "Binges" of heavy drinking.

_____ 11. Heavy weekend drinking.

_____ 12. Able to drink more and more with less and less effect.

None of these represents a certain indicator of alcohol abuse or problem drinking. They are all signs that problems may be developing, or already exist.

---

*Source:* Theodore H. Blau, *Psychological Services for Law Enforcement* (New York: John Wiley & Sons, 1994), p. 198. Copyright © 1994 by Theodore H. Blau. Reprinted by permission of John Wiley & Sons, Inc.

ultimately to persuade individual officers to enter a care unit for treatment. The combination of unsatisfactory performance, excessive costs, and the almost certain progressive deterioration of the individual officer to the point of unemployability, if the illness goes unchecked, creates a situation that conscientious chiefs of police should neither tolerate nor ignore.[30]

An essential point to remember is that, if drinking affects an officer's health, job, or family, immediate action is essential—the officer is probably an alcoholic.

Reports by the Denver Police Department indicate that the organization benefited in specific ways since the implementation of its alcohol abuse program. Some of these specific benefits have been

1. Retention of the majority of the officers who had suffered from alcoholism
2. Solution of a set of complex and difficult personnel problems
3. Realistic and practical extension of the police agency's program into the entire city government structure
4. Improved public and community attitudes by this degree of concern for the officer and the officer's family and by eliminating the dangerous and antisocial behavior of the officer in the community
5. Full cooperation with rehabilitation efforts from the police associations and unions that may represent officers
6. The preventive influence on moderate drinkers against the development of dangerous drinking habits that may lead to alcoholism. In addition, an existing in-house program will motivate some officers to undertake remedial action on their own, outside the scope of the police agency program.[31]

## DRUG USE BY POLICE OFFICERS

Drug abuse by police officers has garnered a great deal of attention.[32] A national study of 2,200 police officers found that 10 percent had serious drug problems.[33] As a result of this condition, police administrators have had to grapple with such issues as:

- What positions will the employee unions or other employee organizations take if drug testing is proposed?
- Who should be tested for drugs? Entry level officers? Regular officers on a random basis? All officers before they are promoted? Personnel assigned to high-profile units such as bomb disposal and special tactics and response?
- When does a supervisor have "reasonable suspicion" of a subordinate's drug use?
- Who should collect urine or other specimens and under what conditions?
- What criteria or standards should be used when selecting a laboratory to conduct the police department's drug testing program?
- What disciplinary action is appropriate when officers are found to have abused drugs?
- What duty does an employer have to rehabilitate employees who become disabled as a result of drug abuse?[34]

In recent years, issues around testing sworn officers for drugs have been debated and litigated. In the early days of such litigation, court rulings were sometimes wildly contradictory, with most courts striking down such requirements, typically on the basis that it was an unwarranted intrusion into officers' constitutional right to privacy.[35] Nevertheless, three major principles have emerged from the many random drug cases decided by the courts. The first was that drug testing—both on the basis of reasonable suspicion and when conducted on a random basis—does not violate the federal constitution. The second was that although drug testing may not violate federal constitutional rights, it may not be permissible under the constitutions of some states. The third principle was that in states that have granted collective bargaining rights to police officers (see Chapter 10, Labor Relations), drug testing cannot be unilaterally implemented by the employer. Instead, it must be submitted to the collective bargaining process.

The selection of officers for drug testing must be truly random and part of a clearly articulated drug testing policy (see Box 9-1). The courts will not support the police department's operation of a nonrandom drug testing program, except when there is reasonable suspicion to test for the presence of drugs. Although no clear guidelines exist as to how often random drug testing can occur, a state court in New York held in 1994 that testing 10 percent of all sworn officers each month was reasonable.[36]

**Anabolic Steroids**   When police administrators consider the use of illegal drugs by their personnel, they typically think of the traditional illegal drugs such as marijuana,

## BOX 9-1

### Drug Testing General Order

**Policy**

It is the policy of this department that the critical mission of law enforcement justifies maintenance of a drug free work environment through the use of a reasonable employee drug-testing program.

The law enforcement profession has several uniquely compelling interests that justify the use of employee drug-testing. The public has a right to expect that those who are employed to protect them—either directly or in support functions—are at all times both physically and mentally prepared to assume these duties. There is sufficient evidence to conclude that the use of controlled substances and other forms of drug abuse will seriously impair an employee's physical and mental health, and thus, job performance.

Where law enforcement agency employees participate in illegal drug use and drug activity, the integrity of the law enforcement profession, as well as public confidence in it, are destroyed. This confidence is further eroded by the potential for corruption created by drug use.

Therefore, in order to ensure the integrity of the department, and to preserve public trust and confidence in a fit and drug-free law enforcement profession, this department shall implement a drug-testing program to detect prohibited drug use by sworn employees.

**Definitions**

1. *Sworn Employee*—Those employees subject to the provisions of Kentucky Revised Statutes, Chapter 16.

2. *Supervisor*—Those employees assigned to a position having day-to-day responsibility for supervising subordinates, or who are responsible for commanding a work element.

3. *Drug Test*—The production and submission of urine by an employee, in accordance with departmental procedures, for chemical analysis to detect prohibited drug usage.

4. *Reasonable Suspicion*—That quantity of proof or evidence, based on specific, objective facts and any rationally derived inferences from those facts about the conduct of an individual that would lead a reasonable officer based upon his training and experience, to suspect that the individual is or has been using drugs while on or off duty. Reasonable suspicion is less than probable cause, but substantially more than a mere hunch. Reasonable suspicion does not exist unless the reasons for suspicion are articulable.

5. *Probationary Employee*—For the purposes of this policy only, a probationary employee shall be considered to be any person who is conditionally employed with the department as a law enforcement officer.

## Procedures/Rules

1. *Prohibited Activity.* The following rules shall apply to all applicants, probationary and formally vested sworn employees, while on and off duty:

   No employee shall use or possess any controlled substance, as defined in Chapter 218A of the Kentucky Revised Statutes, in any manner violative or any state or federal law.

   No employee shall ingest any controlled substance, as defined in Chapter 218A of the Kentucky Revised Statutes, unless as prescribed by a licensed medical practitioner and shall be in compliance with the use of medication on duty rule of conduct.

   Any employee who unintentionally ingests, or is made to ingest, a controlled substance shall immediately report the incident to his/her supervisor so that appropriate medical steps may be taken to ensure the officer's health and safety.

2. *Applicant Drug-Testing.* Applicants for the position of Kentucky State Police officer shall be required to take a drug test as a condition of employment. Applicants shall be disqualified from further consideration for employment under the following circumstances:

   a. Refusal to submit to a required drug-test intended to determine the presence of any illegal drug or controlled substance; or

   b. A confirmed positive drug-test indicating drug use prohibited by this policy.

3. *Employee Drug Testing/Mandatory and Random Basis.* Sworn officers shall be required to take drug tests as a condition of continued employment in order to ascertain prohibited drug use, as provided below:

   Sworn officers graduating from the Kentucky State Police Academy in Cadet Class 162 and all subsequent Classes, and all Aircraft Support Section personnel, shall submit to random drug-testing on a mandatory basis. All other sworn officers *may* submit to random drug-testing on a voluntary basis. Also, any sworn officer *may* submit to post-accident or other post-incident drug-testing on a voluntary basis when the use of drugs could become an issue.

   No sworn officer shall be caused to submit to random drug-testing more than twice in a two-year period.

4. *Employee Drug-Testing/Promotion or Transfer Basis.* To be eligible for any promotions within the department, or a transfer to the Aircraft Support Section, the Drug Enforcement/Special Investigation Branch, the Special Response Team or Drug Interdiction work, all sworn officers shall submit to random drug-testing on a mandatory basis.

5. *Employee Drug-Testing/"Reasonable Suspicion" Basis.* Sworn officers shall be required to take drug tests as a condition of continued employment in order to ascertain prohibited drug use, as provided below:

   Any officer having a reasonable suspicion to believe that another employee is illegally using, or in possession of, any controlled substance shall immediately report the facts and circumstances to his supervisor or, if the supervisor is unavailable, any superior officer.

   Any supervisor or superior officer who receives such a report from a subordinate shall immediately contact the suspect officer to observe his behavior and demeanor, or take any other necessary and appropriate steps to determine whether reasonable suspicion exists to suspect that the officer has violated this policy. If it is determined that "reasonable suspicion" exists, the following steps shall be taken immediately:

   a. The suspect officer's vehicle and all issued weapons shall be secured and the suspect officer shall not be allowed to engage in any law enforcement activity.

   b. The suspect officer's post or section commander, or acting post or section commander, shall be immediately apprised of all details.

   It shall be the responsibility of the post or section commander, or the acting post or section commander, to determine whether sufficient grounds exist under the "reasonable suspicion" standard to order the suspect officer to submit to a search and/or a drug test. An administrative search may be conducted at any time.

   No officer while on duty shall refuse to submit to a search of his person or of any state property under his custody or control, including any personally owned containers found therein, upon reasonable grounds to suspect that the officer is in possession of any contraband controlled substance. If a search is ordered, the post or section commander, or acting post or section commander, who issued the order shall conduct the search.

   If a drug test is ordered, the post or section commander, or acting post or section commander, shall be responsible for adhering to the drug-testing procedures set forth in this policy.

   If the suspect officer complies with the mandated search and/or drug test order, the officer shall be placed on non-disciplinary administrative leave with pay until such time is a final determination of policy compliance has been made.

*(continued)*

# BOX 9-1 (continued)

6. *Selection and Notification.* On two Mondays each month the Personnel Branch shall arrange the random selection, by computer, of the employees to be drug-tested within the next thirty (30) days. The Personnel Branch notifies the appropriate post or section commanders, by telephone, of the random selections. Any employee randomly selected is to be drug-tested as soon as practicable, but no later than thirty (30) days from the time of selection.

   The post or section commander schedules the employee's drug test to occur in a timely and efficient manner. No employee is to be called in from off-duty. The post or section commander notifies the employee, by telephone (not by radio), of the time and place for drug-testing on the day testing is to occur. The employee shall have no prior warning.

7. *Drug-Testing Procedures.* The employee to be drug-tested arrives at the time and place set by the post or section commander.

   Forensic Laboratories personnel, post or section commanders, or acting post or section commanders are the only agency personnel authorized to administer drug-tests. Sworn personnel administering the test shall be of the rank of Lieutenant or higher. The only exception will be Driver's Testing Section. Sergeants assigned to this section are authorized to administer drug tests due to the dispersed nature of the section's personnel, and the unavailability of higher ranking supervisory personnel.

   Personnel authorized to administer drug-tests shall require positive identification from the employee to be tested before the testing area is entered.

   The testing personnel shall escort the employee to a private office. Here, a pre-test interview shall be conducted by testing personnel in order to ascertain and document any recent use of prescription or non-prescription drugs, or any indirect exposure to drugs that may result in a false positive test result. Additionally, the DT-1 authorization form shall be explained.

   The employee completes the medical questionnaire and signs the DT-1 form.

   The testing personnel shall affix peel-and-stick labels denoting the employee's identification number to two (2) specimen containers and hand the containers to the employee. (Note: The medical questionnaires, DT-1 forms, labels and specimen containers are to have been stored under lock-and-key by the post commander to preclude tampering.)

   The testing personnel shall escort the employee to the testing area—either a bathroom or an office. The testing area must be *private, secure* and *previously-screened* by the testing personnel to document that it is free of foreign substances.

   The employee shall provide the urine specimen in privacy; no one will witness and no disrobing will be involved.

   Where the employee appears unable or unwilling to give a specimen at the time of the test, testing personnel shall document the circumstances on the drug-test report form.

   The employee shall be permitted no more than eight hours to give a sample, during which time he or she shall remain in the testing area, under observation. Reasonable amounts of water may be given to the employee to encourage urination. Failure to submit a sample shall be considered as refusal to submit to a drug-test.

   When the employee hands the filled containers to the drug testing personnel, they shall be immediately checked for temperature. The drug testing personnel shall ensure that the containers are properly-lidded and then seal the lids with tamper-proof tape. (Note: If requested by the employee, special arrangements shall be made by the testing personnel for the employee to hand the specimen containers to testing personnel of the same sex.)

   The employee then ensures that his or her identification number on the containers' labels matches his or her identification number on the list held by the post or section commander and signs off on the list.

   The testing personnel shall then place the containers into a plastic bag, and store the bag in a secured repository until forwarded to the laboratory for testing.

   The testing personnel shall provide the employee a copy of the signed DT-1 form and forward the list matching employee identification numbers and employee names, the employee's completed medical questionnaire and the employee's signed DT-1 form to the Employee Assistance Program.

   Whenever there is reason to believe that an employee may have altered or substituted the specimen, a second specimen shall be obtained the same day under direct observation of the drug testing personnel.

8. *Drug-Testing Methodology.* The testing or processing phase shall consist of a three-step procedure:
   - Initial screening test at the Kentucky State Police Forensic Laboratories.
   - Confirmation test at an independent laboratory recognized and approved by the College of American Pathologists or the National Institute of Drug Abuse.
   - A second confirmation test at the Kentucky State Police Forensic Laboratories.

   The urine sample is first tested using the initial drug screening procedure. An initial positive test result will not be considered conclusive; rather, it will be classified as "confirmation pending." Notification of test results shall be held until the confirmation test results are obtained.

   A specimen testing positive will undergo one confirmation test and, if still testing positive, a second confirmation test. The confirmation procedure shall be technologically different and more sensitive than the initial screening test.

   The drug screening tests selected shall be capable of identifying marijuana, cocaine, and every major drug of abuse including heroin, amphetamines and barbiturates. Personnel utilized for testing will be certified as qualified to collect urine samples or adequately trained in collection procedures.

   Drug screening shall be by immunoassay techniques. A detectable concentration of amphetamines, barbiturates, benzodiazepines, cocaine, marijuana, opiates, propoxyphene or such other drugs determined to be subject to abuse shall be considered a positive test result.

   Drug confirmation shall be by technologically different and more sensitive technique than the drug screening, such as gas chromatography or mass spectrometry.

   The laboratories selected to conduct the analysis shall be experienced and capable of quality control, documentation, chain-of-custody, technical expertise, and demonstrated proficiency in urinalysis.

   Laboratory results shall be forwarded to the Employee Assistance Program Coordinator.

   The Employee Assistance Program Coordinator shall report negative drug test results to the employee. Employees having negative results shall receive a memorandum from the Employee Assistance Program Coordinator stating that no illegal drugs were found. If the employee requests such, a copy of the letter shall be placed in the employer's personnel file.

   The Employee Assistance Program Coordinator shall report "presumptive" positive drug test results to the Medical Review Officer and the Commissioner. "Presumptive" positive drug test results are those results showing positive for the presence of drugs in laboratory analysis, but which have not yet been verified by the Medical Review Officer.

   The Commissioner may authorize an immediate non-disciplinary administrative leave for an employee upon report of a "presumptive" positive result.

   Employees having a "presumptive" positive result shall receive a memorandum from the Medical Review Officer instructing them to contact his office within three days of receipt of the letter. A confidential meeting shall be arranged to discuss the test result. If not legal cause of the "presumptive" positive result is found, the test result shall be recorded as a positive. The Medical Review Officer shall notify the Employee Assistance Program Coordinator of the positive result, the Employee Assistance Program Coordinator shall notify the Internal Affairs Section, and the Internal Affairs Section shall notify the employee.

   Any employee who breaches the confidentiality of testing information shall be subject to discipline.

9. *Chain of Evidence—Storage.* Each step in the collecting and processing of the urine specimens shall be documented to establish procedural integrity and the chain of custody. Where a positive result is confirmed, urine specimens shall be maintained in secured, refrigerated storage for an indefinite period.

10. *Drug-Test Results.* All records pertaining to department-required drug tests shall remain confidential, and shall not be provided to other employers or agencies without the written permission of the person whose records are sought. Drug test results and records shall be stored and retained by the Employee Assistance Program Coordinator for a period of two years.

11. *Drug Testing Violations.* As prescribed in the drug testing policy, failure to submit to a mandated drug test or having a confirmed positive result from an illegal drug or breaching the confidentiality of drug testing information is a Class A violation.

*Source:* Courtesy of the Kentucky State Police.

cocaine, heroin, amphetamines, barbiturates, and so forth. However, drugs that are abused more than many people realize are anabolic steroids.

**Background**

The use of anabolic steroids by athletes began in the late 1940s.[37,38] It is estimated that 80 to 99 percent of male body builders[39] and perhaps as many as 96 percent of professional football players have used these drugs, as have many other athletes.[40] Sixty-eight percent of interviewed track and field athletes had used steroids in preparation for the 1972 Olympics in Munich.[41] Since then, the International Olympic Committee has banned all anabolic drugs, and the top six performers in each Olympic event are now tested for nontherapeutic drugs of all types. Despite such developments, steroid use is widespread. The Mayo Clinic has estimated that more than one million Americans are regular steroid users.[42]

The law enforcement community is not exempt from this form of drug abuse. For example, the U.S. Bureau of Customs was investigating the smuggling of anabolic steroids into this country. Their investigation led them to certain health clubs in North Carolina, where it was determined that state patrol officers were illegally using anabolic steroids. The North Carolina State Patrol joined the investigation, and subsequently three troopers were terminated. In Miami Beach, a physical training sergeant noticed that one of his female charges was "bulking up" too fast. This female also displayed street behavior that led a department supervisor to recommend that she be assigned to non-street duties. It was subsequently established that she had been using anabolic steroids. In addition to using steroids themselves, officers in New York have been convicted of selling anabolic steroids.

**Adverse Health Impact**

There are recognized medical uses of anabolic steroids. Among the conditions for which anabolic steroids may be therapeutically appropriate are deficient endocrine functioning of the testes, osteoporosis, carcinoma of the breast, growth retardation, and severe anemia.[43]

The use of anabolic steroids, as summarized in Table 9-6, is associated with a number of potential outcomes that are adverse to an individual's health.

**TABLE 9-6.  Adverse Effects of Anabolic Steroids**

| *Men* | *Women* | *Both Sexes* |
|---|---|---|
| ■ Breast enlargement<br>■ Testicular atrophy with consequent sterility or decreased sperm count<br>■ Impotence<br>■ Enlarged prostate | ■ Breast diminution<br>■ Clitoral enlargement<br>■ Facial hair growth<br>■ Deepened voice<br>■ Menstrual irregularities<br>■ Excessive body hair<br>■ Baldness | ■ Increased aggression known as "'roid rage"<br>■ Increased risk of heart disease, stroke, or obstructed blood vessels<br>■ Acne<br>■ Liver tumors, jaundice, and peliosis hepatitis (blood-filled cysts)<br>■ Pre-teens and teenagers accelerated bone maturation leading to permanent short stature |

*Source:* Charles Swanson, Larry Gaines, and Barbara Gore, "Police Use of Steroids," *FBI Law Enforcement Bulletin,* 60:6 (1991), pp. 19–23.

These risks are even greater when anabolic steroids are taken under the direction of a self-appointed "roid guru" or when self-dosing, because the typical usage under these and related circumstances is ten to one hundred times greater than typical medical dosages.[44] Further complicating the nontherapeutic use of steroids is self-treatment with preparations not legally available in the United States and veterinary preparations such as Boldenone (Equipose®), for which it is difficult to estimate dosage equivalency,[45] virtually assuring dosages well beyond those recognized as medically appropriate.

Unknown, or less well known, to anabolic steroid abusers than the previously noted risks are certain affective and psychotic symptoms. Charlier[46] maintains "aggressive behavior is almost universal among anabolic steroid users." There are documented case histories of severe depression, visual and auditory hallucinations, sleep disorders, thoughts of suicide, outbursts of anger, anorexia, psychomotor retardation, and irritability.[47] In a survey of health club athletes who used steroids, 90 percent reported steroid-induced aggressive or violent behavior.[48] Pope and Katz conducted a study of 39 male and two female anabolic steroid abusers whose psychiatric histories were generally unremarkable. Yet five subjects had psychotic symptoms and others had manic episodes or periods of major depressions:

> One 23-year-old man bought a $17,000 automobile. . . . When he stopped taking anabolic steroids he realized he could not afford the payments and sold the car. A year later, while taking steroids again, he impulsively bought a $20,000 sports car. . . . Another subject bought an old car and drove it into a tree at 40 miles per hour while a friend videotaped him. . . . A third subject believed his mind was influencing the pictures on television and promised a friend he would show God to him.[49]

Although not physically addicting, steroids can cause a psychological dependence. Goldstein[50] discusses three stages of drug abuse: initial stage of exploration, continuing stage of regular usage, and cessation from use. People are attracted to steroid use for a variety of reasons, all of which center on developing a more domineering physique. Initial users are generally "turned on" to the drugs by other abusers or seek them out at health clubs or gyms, where such drugs are commonly abused. The continuation stage occurs after initial use, when subjects have experienced some success with the drug. Thereafter, subjects become obsessed with their larger physiques, increased strength, or sexual appeal. Exercise becomes easier whenever steroids are used, and pain and a lack of strength appear when the drugs are discontinued. This process may continue until subjects are confronted with difficulties that result from their drug dependency. Cessation of usage will come only when the subjects become disinterested or are confronted with their problems.

## Anabolic Steroids: The Legal Environment

The Drug Enforcement Administration has the major responsibility for enforcing the federal Controlled Substances Act (CSA), which is intended to minimize the quantity of drugs available for illegal use. The CSA places a substance into one of five schedules based on such factors as potential for abuse and whether there is a recognized medical use of the substance. Most over-the-counter (OTC) and prescription drugs do not fall within one of the CSA schedules and responsibility for enforcement efforts relating to them rests with the Food and Drug Administration (FDA) and state agencies. The FDA determines whether a substance falls within the OTC or prescription category; each state then has the legal power to determine who can legally prescribe and dispense OTC and prescription substances. The federal Anti-Drug Act of 1988—also referred to as the Omnibus Drug Abuse Initiative—created a special category of anabolic steroids within the prescription class, and all violations involving the sale or possession with intent to distribute anabolic steroids are now felonies.

Even before the passage of the Anti-Drug Act, it was illegal to possess anabolic steroids without a prescription in all 50 states. Thus, all officers in this country using anabolic steroids without a prescription have committed an illegal act.

Awareness of the nature and impact of illegal anabolic steroid use is seen in litigation. "Anabolic steroid–induced rage" has been used as a defense in sexual assault cases; in one instance the judge accepted this argument as a mitigating factor when sentencing a defendant in a sexual assault. Liability is one of the most critical issues regarding steroid usage. It is only a matter of time before it will be alleged in a state tort or federal civil rights lawsuit that "but for the failure of the police department to conduct a proper background and drug screening, the anabolic steroid–induced violent assault on my client would never have occurred" (negligent selection) or that "but for the failure of the police department to properly train its supervisors on how to identify the manifestations of anabolic steroid abuse, then the physical trauma to Mrs. Johnson would not be an issue before this court today" (failure to train and failure to supervise). Although there are almost limitless liability scenarios, there is only one inescapable conclusion: if administrators do not confront this issue quickly, harm will be done to citizens, officers, families, and public treasuries.

## Administrative Concerns and Anabolic Steroids

Regarding administrative attitudes toward steroid use, people in the internal affairs, public information, and command positions, as well as staff psychologists, of 30 police departments across the country were interviewed. With few exceptions, the response was "that's not a problem in this department and we've never had a problem with it." Yet replies of that nature are deceiving. For example, a departmental representative who had stated in the morning that steroid abuse was not a problem called back in the afternoon, saying "I've been thinking . . . one of our retired officers runs a gym frequented by our officers and some of them have gotten very muscular awfully quick." Police officials readily recognize cocaine or marijuana abuse as a police personnel problem, but for the most part they still are not aware of the seriousness of steroid abuse. If this situation is not soon corrected, departments will be confronted with increasing numbers of steroid-related problems.

As a practical matter, however, the agendas of most police departments are already crowded with pressing issues. Drug-testing programs are costly to develop and implement and may be opposed by police unions or elected officials who want their support. Even where in place, however, general drug tests will not detect the presence of anabolic steroids; a separate test is required, representing an additional cost for which to budget. Moreover, present information about police officer use of anabolic steroids is fragmented and impressionistic. Thus, full agendas, other priorities, difficulties in implementing drug-testing programs, politics, cost, and the lack of available information combine to limit the amounts of organizational attention that will be given to police officer use of steroids in the near future.

Considerable difficulty exists in studying police suicide.[51] Researchers often find that information on officer suicide either is not collected or departments are reluctant to allow access to such data.[52]

In addition, police suicides may be misclassified routinely as either accidents or undetermined deaths. Because police officers traditionally subscribe to a myth of indestructibility, they view suicide as particularly disgraceful to the victim officer and to the profession.[53]

The police represent a highly cohesive subculture whose members tend to "take care of their own."[54] The desire to shield victim officers, their families, and their departments from the stigma of suicide may lead investigators to overlook certain evidence intentionally during the classification process. One study of the Chicago Police Department estimated that as many as 67 percent of police suicides in that city had been misclassified as accidental or natural deaths.[55]

Failure to correct for such biases could lead to false conclusions regarding the causes and frequency of police suicides. Therefore, accurate research must go beyond official rates; the preliminary results of an ongoing study of police suicides over a 40-year period indicate that nearly 30 percent of police suicides may have been misclassified.[56] (See Box 9-2)

## BOX 9-2

### Code of Silence Doesn't Help

**by Gary Fields and Charisse Jones USA TODAY.**

SAN DIEGO—More than 300 federal, state and local law enforcement officers were added to the National Law Enforcement Officers Memorial in Washington, D.C., last month. San Diego police Capt. Lesli Lord and Detective Anthony Castellini were not among them.

The two officers—she was among the highest ranking women in the department, and he a winner of the department's medal of valor—killed themselves within 48 hours of each other last year, becoming the fourth and fifth San Diego officers to commit suicide since 1992. During that same period, not a single San Diego officer was killed in the line of duty.

It is the pomp and ceremony of an official law enforcement funeral that the public remembers—the 21-gun salute, the officers lining the streets in dress blues mourning a colleague killed while protecting the public.

Yet research by USA TODAY and the findings of several studies show that most departments lose more officers to suicide than they do to violence in the course of their jobs.

"We're losing about 300 officers a year to suicides," says Robert Douglas, executive director of the National P.O.L.I.C.E. Suicide Foundation and a retired Baltimore police officer.

"If a jumbo jet with 300 people went down every year, do you think the FAA would ground the jumbo jets and find out what was going on? You bet they would."

There are no national reports on police suicide and no memorials for those officers who take their own lives. The code of silence and shame that prevents many officers from seeking professional help when they are angry or depressed also prevents them from discussing the specter of suicide. But the statistics that do exist are troubling.

**Disturbing statistics**

The nation's largest police organization, the Fraternal Order of Police, studied suicides among 38,800 of its 270,000 members in 1995 by looking at insurance records in 92 local chapters in 24 states. They found a suicide rate of 22 deaths per 100,000 officers. The national rate is 12 per 100,000 people, according to the Centers for Disease Control and Prevention.

That study focused on small- and medium-size departments ranging from 16 to 3,000 officers.

*(continued)*

# BOX 9-2 (continued)

Although no such study has been done for the nation's largest departments, a USA TODAY survey of the nation's largest law enforcement agencies found equally disturbing statistics.

- In New York, 36 officers have been killed in violent confrontations with suspects while on the job since 1985. During the same period, 87 officers have taken their own lives, a suicide rate of 15.5 per 100,000.
- In Los Angeles, 11 officers have been slain on duty since 1989. Twenty have killed themselves. The suicide rate is 20.7 per 100,000.
- In Chicago, 12 officers have been slain while on duty since 1990. Twenty-two officers have killed themselves, a rate of 18.1 suicides per 100,000 officers.

And it is not just a local law enforcement problem. The FBI, which would be the third largest police agency in the country if it were a department, has lost four special agents in the line of duty since 1993. Eighteen special agents have killed themselves during that period, a rate of 26.1 per 100,000. The U.S. Customs Service lost seven agents to suicide in 1998, alone. That translates to a rate of 45.1 per 100,000. None were slain that year in the line of duty.

Indeed, suicide has been a chronic problem among law enforcement officers for years, a silent killer largely hidden from public view by a police culture that jealously guards its image of strength. Its causes are wide-ranging, from the stresses of a job that requires split-second decisions with life and death consequences, to the normal human struggles with family, career, alcoholism and depression that can be exasperated by the isolation many law enforcement officers feel from society.

"The majority of police officers do not kill themselves," says Andre Ivanoff, professor of social work at Columbia University, who specializes in suicidal behaviors.

For example, San Antonio, Houston, Dallas and Phoenix have reported no police suicides in the last five years. But the fact that police are public servants whose suicide rates rank fourth behind dentists, doctors and entrepreneurs, Ivanoff says, "should make everyone uncomfortable."

A review of the nation's 10 largest police departments, various studies and dozens of interviews indicate that suicide is among the most serious problems facing law enforcement today. The issue is of such concern that the FBI is planning a seminar on suicide for officers at its academy in Quantico, Va., this September.

Departments from Miami to Los Angeles have launched programs to address the problem, sending police psychologists from precinct to precinct and requiring everyone from cadets to commanders to take classes about suicide.

**Never prepared**

The sheriff's department in Orange County, Calif., had warned Sylvia Banuelos about a different kind of death when her husband, Ernesto first entered the sheriff's academy. She was required to take a class from a captain who tried to prepare deputies' families for an uncertain future.

"He said, 'If I tell you your officer will not be killed, I'd be lying,' " she remembered. " 'Every officer has a bullet with his name on it.' Line-of-duty death, it's something I think wives accept. But suicide is never an option. You never think it's going to be suicide."

But Ernesto Banuelos did not die on the street. He shot himself to death one morning in 1997. Despite a growing acknowledgement of the problem, the topic of suicide remains taboo among much of law enforcement's rank and file. To some extent, psychologists say, that is merely a reflection of society as a whole—uncomfortable with the idea of people taking their own lives. But experts say that those who make their living projecting strength and control are especially reluctant to admit that they need psychological help. They fear they will be perceived as weak.

"Cops don't talk about that kind of stuff," says Jerry Sanders, former San Diego police chief. "They either do it. Or they don't."

In many departments, "if it's known you've thought about suicide, or you're depressed, it's next to impossible for you to progress through the ranks," says Ivanoff, who worked on a 1994 project that evaluated New York City police officers' attitudes about suicide. "Because of the negative effect it can have on your career, officers are extremely reluctant to identify each other as needing help and will go to great lengths to 'protect' somebody who needs help rather than helping them get it."

The stress that often leads an officer to commit suicide is at least partially the result of unrealistically high expectations of being a successful cop. "If you're a carpenter and you drop your hammer, you bend over and pick it up," says Don Sheehan, director of the stress management program at the FBI's Behavioral Sciences Unit. "What happens to a police officer who drops his gun during a bank robbery or misspeaks during a trial? They have to always be in control. Officers learn very early on that they have to always be right."

Many departments are reticent about the subject of suicide, afraid of being held liable if the death is linked to stress on the job, and fearful that all cops will be tarnished if the public learns an officer took his or her own life. As a result, those who have studied the issue say it is very difficult to get an accurate tally of suicides because many departments do not keep official statistics. And some say questionable incidents, such as reports of officers accidentally killing themselves while cleaning their guns, may actually be efforts to mask suicides.

Douglas recalls a Boston officer whose death was listed as accidental by the department but ruled a suicide by the medical examiner.

"How do you accidentally discharge your firearm into your mouth?" he asks. "She was sitting on her bed and shot herself in the mouth and they said she was cleaning her gun?"

### 'It could be me'

Because those who commit suicide are not killed in the line of duty, they are seldom given an official department funeral. Their families also are not entitled to various benefits, such as the $143,943 that each family of an officer slain in the line of duty receives from the Justice Department.

Many relatives also lament that they are suddenly ignored by their loved one's colleagues, unceremoniously banished from the law enforcement fraternity.

"I have lost friends in law enforcement and that's really hurt me," says Banuelos, whose husband, Ernesto, shot himself to death in March 1997. "They won't come around. They don't want to be seen with me."

She believes that some of the deputies who worked alongside her husband simply do not know what to say. And, she says, that sometimes they are silenced by their own fear.

"Maybe they've contemplated suicide before," says Banuelos, a mother of four who now counsels despondent officers. "Maybe they've been where Ernie was and it scares them to get that close. Maybe they know it's happened more often and they worry that 'it could be me.'"

### A department's pain

The pain of police suicide often reaches beyond the family to tear at the department as a whole.

In San Diego last year, when two of the department's most promising officers killed themselves in unrelated suicides in as many days. The sadness was palpable in the silence, visible in the morning roll calls. In a press conference with the media, the chief broke down and cried. "Police departments aren't normally quiet and this was a quiet place," says Sanders, the current president and CEO of United

Way in San Diego who was the city's police chief at the time. "And we were going to lineups for about a week talking to people and you could see the signs of this in the quietness, and the questions, and in people kind of staying close to each other for support."

Both officers were undergoing counseling for emotional problems at the time of their deaths, Sanders says. Captain Lesli Lord, 45, a married mother of three children, was one of the five highest-ranking women in the department, officials say. She had been on the police force just shy of 20 years when she shot herself to death at her home.

The next evening, the body of Detective Anthony Castellini was discovered by his girlfriend, dead from a self-inflicted gunshot wound to the head. He was a 12-year department veteran who had been separated from his wife and children for 18 months. In 1989, he had been awarded the department's medal of valor for pulling a suspect from a vehicle moments before it burst into flames.

After the suicides, the department sent counselors to the city's police stations. Sanders says the department's psychological services were "booked solid for weeks." And he spoke to the media about the deaths, as he had been willing to do with each of the five suicides that occurred during his six-year tenure.

Sanders says that he wanted to "let people know that we respected them as members of the department and weren't going to hide the fact they had been in our department."

### Tough to diagnose

There is no particular profile of the officer who will attempt suicide. He or she may be a few years out of the academy or at the end of their career, and their personal crises run the gamut. Divorce and the break-up of relationships are common problems. But those who kill themselves may also be suffering from stagnated careers, under investigation for alleged misconduct or drinking heavily. Throw the ever-present firearm into the cauldron and the mix is deadly.

"Having the means is extremely important," says Ivanoff, who notes that the suicide rate among British police officers who don't carry guns is much lower than in the United States. "And it's not just having the means. It's intimate familiarity and comfort with it . . . This is not something that happens by mistake."

Experts say an officer who may be contemplating suicide often lacks energy or motivation, becomes withdrawn and may actually talk about suicide. Troubled officers also sometimes become accident-prone or targets of numerous citizen complaints.

*(continued)*

## BOX 9-2 (continued)

Communication can break the cycle. But officers are often isolated, distrustful of anyone outside law enforcement. And the hostility they sometimes bring home after a day of dealing with antagonistic situations can erode the one solid safety net the officers have—their family.

"It's difficult to go from an almost combat situation to home life," says John Violanti, author of *Police Suicide: Epidemic in Blue.* "It tears on one's psychological ability to adjust."

Many officers doubt they can receive confidential help. Michael Markman, chief of personnel for the New York City Police Department, says that despite a wide array of services available for everything from marriage counseling to alcohol abuse and depression,

only about 1% of the officers who need help seek counseling. Still, many departments are trying to shed light on the problem.

In Los Angeles, police psychologist Debbie Glasser says her department plans to hire 12 psychologists in the next six months to join the 10 already on staff. They will work alongside officers in stations around the city.

"We're hoping that by having all the psychologists out and about it's demystify psychology and just make it seem like it's part of everyday police work," she says. "I tell people it takes more courage to go get help . . . It's just like calling for back-up."

*Source:* Copyright 1999, *USA TODAY,* Reprinted with permission.

---

**Why Officers Commit Suicide**

Studies have revealed several factors related to police suicide. Suicides have been found to be more common among older officers and are related to alcoholism, physical illness, or impending retirement.[57] Other clues have been cited to help explain the high rate of self-inflicted death among police officers: the regular availability of firearms, continuous duty exposure to death and injury, social strain resulting from shift work, inconsistencies within the criminal justice system, and the perception among police officers that they labor under a negative public image. In addition, research confirms a higher propensity for suicide among males, who dominate the police profession.[58] Table 9-7 lists suicide rates for several major U.S. law enforcement agencies.

A study of the Detroit Police Department found that the vast majority of Detroit police officers who took their lives were white young men, high school

---

### TABLE 9-7. Law Enforcement Agencies' Suicide Rates

The suicide rate in the United States is about 12 per 100,000 residents, according to the Centers for Disease Control. Suicide rates in some of the nation's largest law enforcement agencies:

| | New York P.D. 1985–98 | Chicago P.D. 1990–98 | FBI 1993–98 | Los Angeles P.D. 1990–98 | San Diego P.D. 1992–98 | U.S. Customs 1998–99[1] |
|---|---|---|---|---|---|---|
| Department size | 40,000 | 13,500 | 11,500[2] | 9,668 | 2,000 | 10,826[3] |
| Killed in the line of duty | 36 | 12 | 4 | 11 | 0 | 0 |
| Committed suicide | 87 | 22 | 18 | 20 | 5 | 7 |
| Suicide rate per 100,000 | 15.5 | 18.1 | 26.1 | 20.7 | 35.7 | 45.6 |
| Compared to national suicide rate | +29.1% | +50.9% | +116.6% | +72.5% | +197.5% | +280% |

1 - Through May 28, 1999     2 - Special agents     3 - Inspectors, special agents and officers

*Source:* Copyright June 1, 1999, *USA TODAY.* Reprinted with permission.

educated, and married. Alcohol abuse was fairly common among the sample (42 percent), as was a formal diagnosis of psychosis (33 percent). However, marital difficulties appeared to be the most prevalent problem among the Detroit sample.[59]

Examination of twenty-seven cases of police suicide in Quebec found that one-half of the officers had a history of psychiatric and/or medical problems, and many had severe alcohol problems. Most officers in the sample experienced difficulties at work, and *in every case,* a notable drop in work performance had been observed in the six months prior to the suicide.[60]

Among the occupational factors surrounding police suicide, frustration is often cited as particularly important. Almost unfailingly, officers enter policing with high ideals and a noble desire to help others. Over time, this sense of idealism may transform into hardcore cynicism.

## Frustration and Helplessness

The roots of frustration emanate from the central irony of American policing: Society charges police officers with the task of regulating a public that does not want to be regulated. For individual officers, the resulting frustration is exacerbated by a largely unsympathetic press, a lack of community support, and a criminal justice system that values equity over expediency. A sense of social isolation often ensues, compelling officers to group together in a defensive stance. When an officer feels that the frustration is no longer tolerable or that no coping alternative is available, suicide may become an attractive option.[61]

It also is possible that feelings of helplessness are brought about by the nature of the job.[62] A sense of helplessness is a disturbing realization for anyone, but especially for police officers who are conditioned to view themselves as super-heroes capable of anything. Suicide is one way of dealing with helplessness and emotional pain. The finality of the ultimate solution may be an attempt to restore feelings of strength, courage, and mastery over the environment.[63]

**FIGURE 9-2.** Sylvia Banuelos, whose husband, Ernesto, killed himself in 1997, holds his service badge at the gravesite. Ernesto Banuelos was an Orange County, Calif., sheriff's deputy. Behind her are her children, Matthew, left, Adam, Andrew and Justin. Photo by Bob Riha, Jr. *USA Today* June 1, 1999, Copyright. Reprinted with permission. (See story in Box 9-2)

## Access to Firearms

Another factor that distinguishes police officers from the general population has been implicated in the high number of police suicides. That is, most law enforcement officers carry or have access to firearms. An ongoing study of police suicides in the United States reveals that 95 percent involved the use of the officer's service weapon.[64]

Another study compared suicides in New York City and London. While the police suicide rate in New York City was twice that of the general population, the police suicide rate in London, where officers do not carry firearms, was similar to that of the city's civilian population.[65]

The police firearm holds special significance for officers. It is a very potent symbol of the power of life and death. Society entrusts law enforcement officers with the authority to use their weapons and to take the life of another person in certain situations. In police suicides, officers, in effect, are claiming the right to take their own lives. After all, the weapon has been issued as a means to stop misery and to protect others from harm. Despondent officers may view suicide in such a way.

## Alcohol Abuse

Alcohol abuse, discussed earlier in this chapter, has also been implicated as a significant contributing factor in police suicides. One study documented alcohol abuse in 60 percent of the suicides in the Chicago Police Department.[66] Administrators should be aware that alcoholism may lead to other work problems, such as high absenteeism, traffic collisions, or intoxication on duty. Given the established correlation between alcoholism and suicide, these symptoms should not be ignored. They should be considered indications of a larger problem.

## Fear of Separation From the Police Subculture

As officers near the end of their law enforcement careers, another potential threat appears—separation. To individual officers, retirement may mean separation from the camaraderie and protection of police peers. During their years of service, officers may have clustered with other officers due to a general isolation from society and its prejudices toward the police. Upon retirement, these officers must enter the very society that they perceive as alien and hostile.

While the benefits of retirement may be viewed positively by the majority of officers, separation from the police subculture can be a frightful and devastating prospect for others. Fear coupled with increasing age (a definite suicide risk factor), loss of friends, loss of status as a police officer, and a loss of self-definition leave some retiring officers vulnerable to suicide. A recent study found a ten-fold increase in risk of suicide among police retirees.[67]

## Recognizing the Warning Signs

Identifying at-risk officers is the first step toward helping them.[68] Is there any common pattern to be found in police suicidal behavior? In truth, any member of the department could become depressed and commit suicide under certain circumstances. However, a long trail of evidence typically leads to the final act. Many suicidal people have mixed feelings about dying and actually hope to be rescued. About 75 percent give some kind of notice of their intentions.[69] If recognized and taken seriously, these early warning signs make prevention and intervention possible.

Typically, multiple problems plague suicidal police officers, so supervisors should look for a cluster of warning signs. These might include a recent loss, sadness, frustration, disappointment, grief, alienation, depression, loneliness, physical pain, mental anguish, and mental illness.

The strongest behavioral warning is a suicide attempt. Generally, the more recent the attempt, the higher the risk factor for the officer. Police training officers need to incorporate education about suicide warning signs as a regular part of the department's mental health program.

When officers who have consistently been good performers begin to fail to perform at the optimal level for an extended period of time, the problem could be related to a major depressive episode. Clinicians agree that depression can be so serious that it results in a homicide followed by suicide.

Supervisors should refer officers to a certified mental health professional, even setting appointments and making arrangements for the officers to be there. The department's responsibility does not end there, however. Supervisors should monitor the situation to ensure that officers are evaluated and receive continued support and counseling.[70]

## SUICIDE BY COP

Upon hearing the term "suicide by cop," (SbC) the average person would probably think of police officers who take their own lives. However, to law enforcement officers, this phrase refers to an individual who wishes to die and uses the police to effect that goal. The following cases serve as an example of this phenomenon.[71]

A nineteen-year-old was spotted driving erratically by a Nassau County, N.Y., police officer who pulled over the college student's car. As the officer exited his patrol vehicle, the student got out of his car and approached the police officer with what appeared to be a firearm. Despite the officer's repeated pleas for him to drop the weapon, the student continued to advance. Faced with the prospect of his own impending death, the officer fired three times, killing the student. Only later did the officer learn that the weapon wielded by the suspect was nothing more than a toy gun.

A thirty-six-year-old man walked into a central Tucson, Arizona, convenience store, slammed a gun on the counter, and demanded the clerk call police to come kill him. An hour later, he lay dying in an empty lot with two bullets in his body: one in the chest from a police officer's gun; the other, a self-inflicted gunshot wound to the head.[72]

In another case, Philadelphia police responded to a burglary-in-progress call at a local school. Upon arrival, the suspect fired twice at the police. A subsequent chase through the school corridors followed. A police dog eventually cornered the subject. As the officers approached, they found the subject crouched and pointing a gun at them. The officer fired, killing the subject. The police later found the subject's gun was a starter pistol, incapable of firing live rounds. Furthermore, family members later identified the subject's voice on police tapes as the person who placed the initial burglary call to the police.[73] Finally, police learned the subject had been previously hospitalized as a result of a suicide attempt.[74]

Other occasions exist in which the suicidal intent of a subject is clearly evident, but due to particularly patient and attentive police work, a shooting does not occur and a death is avoided. Such an example occurred in this case: An officer patrolling a hotel parking lot observed a man pushing a woman onto the floor of a vehicle. The woman was nude and bloody from the waist down. The officer approached the vehicle and noticed that the man's blue jeans were covered with blood. The man began walking toward him, yelling profanities and shouting, "Go ahead, kill me." As the officer drew his weapon and pointed it at the subject, he ordered the man to the ground. The subject kept walking toward him, saying, "Kill me, you chicken. Shoot me in the head, kill me." The officer backed up, trying to keep a safe distance, as the subject kept putting his hands in his pockets and behind his back. Backup officers surprised the subject from behind and subsequently subdued him.[75] All of the above cases reasonably imply that suspects acted in such a manner to ensure police officers would shoot them.

**Profile of a Suicide by Cop**

The following represents a behavioral profile of a potential SbC victim; however, it should not be used alone to classify an individual as suicidal:

- He is often a member of a lower socioeconomic class, who has integrated aggressive behavior as a problem-solving model. He may seek to destroy himself because of depression, desperation, and/or a need to punish society—by his death—for the "wrongs" it has committed against him.

- Because of his aggressive lifestyle, poor self-concept, and individual social standards, he may not view death at his own hands (true suicide) as a socially acceptable method of death. Therefore, he may confront law enforcement officers in a way that he knows will require them to use deadly force. He may use any means necessary—including killing an officer or an innocent bystander— to bring about his own death in a way that he believes will allow society to perceive him as a victim of others, not of himself.

- If, prior to his confrontation with the authorities, the individual has killed another, especially a significant other, the guilt hypothesis would suggest that he believes society's hatred of his offense— and, therefore, himself—will be satisfied only by his own violent death at the hands of the authorities. The SbC may subconsciously agree with the norms of society—norms that he has internalized within his own social consciousness, but against which he has consistently fought when presented as the standard by other social groups. The individual and his sense of self-worth thus become a legitimate target for aggression.

**Indicators of a Potential SbC**

- As the subject of a self-initiated hostage or a barricade situation, he refuses to negotiate with authorities.
- He has just killed a significant other in his life, especially if the victim was a child or the subject's mother.
- He demands that he be killed by the police.
- He sets a deadline for the authorities to kill him.
- He has recently learned he has a life-threatening illness or disease.
- He indicates an elaborate plan for his own death, one that has taken both prior thought and preparation.
- He says he will only "surrender" (in person) to the officer in charge, such as the chief or the sheriff.
- He indicates he wants to "go out in a big way."
- He presents no demands that include his escape or freedom.
- He comes from a low socioeconomic background.
- He provides the authorities with a "verbal will."
- He appears to be looking for a manly or macho way to die.
- He has recently given away money or personal possessions.

- He has a criminal record indicating past assaultive behavior.
- He has recently experienced one or more traumatic events in his life that affect him, his family, or his career.
- He expresses feelings of hopelessness and helplessness.

Although this list is not all-inclusive, the presence of one or more of these indicators will help to identify a person who is possibly depressed and/or suicidal. A combination of these indicators should be considered evidence of a possible SbC, especially if this individual confronts the authorities in a way that could bring about his own death.[76]

## Police Officers as Victims

Retired NYPD Director of Psychological Services Harvey Schlossberg indicates that an SbC shooting is often tantamount to a "psychological assault" on the officer involved in the shooting. When an officer determines that the suspect's weapon was inoperative, or that the suspect was otherwise responsible for a confrontation to bring about his death at the hands of the authorities, the officer may question his reaction to this confrontation.

Society may be quick to identify the dead SbC suspect as the victim in this incident, when the real victim was the officer forced into the situation by a suicidal person. We must be equally quick to provide the individual and departmental support needed by the victim officer in such circumstances. The officer must be made to understand that his/her actions were ethically correct and professionally justified.[77]

## CRITICAL INCIDENT STRESS

A critical incident is defined as a psychologically distressing experience that is outside of the range of usual human experience.[78] Thus, by definition, the single most potent stressor—killing someone in the line of duty—is a critical incident. A veteran officer over the course of a career generally deals with abusive language, sudden assaults, traffic fatalities produced by drunken drivers, abused children, and other similar incidents.[79] Over time, although these are stressful occurrences, they become part of the "normal" job experiences of police officers. Thus, it is the other traumatizing events that most officers seldom or never experience—such as killing someone in the line of duty, handling the remains of victims in plane crashes, being present at the scene of mass suicides, and assisting victims of natural disasters such as earthquakes—that rise to the level of critical incidents for police officers. Naturally, these stressors are uniquely inherent in the job, but officers also have critical incidents in their personal lives, such as the death of a child or spouse or divorce.[80]

A critical incident threatens the officer's very survival or ability to continue to function. It is of such intensity that it is likely to produce post-traumatic stress disorder (PTSD) in the average officer[81] (see Table 9-8). Critical incidents have the following common characteristics:

1. The event is sudden and unexpected.
2. The event is a threat to the officer's existence or well-being.
3. The event may include some element of loss, such as of a partner or some physical ability.
4. The event may cause a sudden shift in the officer's values, confidence, or ideals.[82]

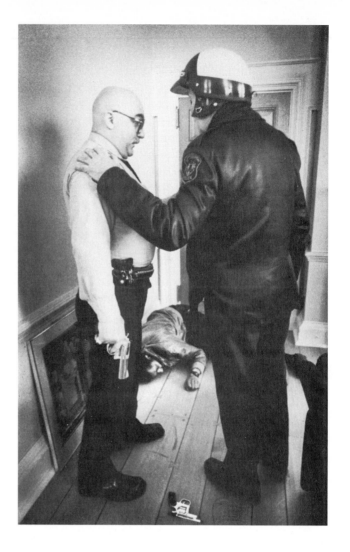

**FIGURE 9-3.**
Pittsburgh police officer, left, is comforted by a fellow police officer after shooting a suspect after the man shot and wounded his wife. (Photo courtesy John Kaplan, Pittsburgh, Pa. Press.)

The responses of police officers who kill someone in the line of duty vary. In some cases, officers experience incredible guilt, feel immobilized, and perhaps even believe they have compromised their religious beliefs.[83] The other extreme is comprised of individuals who experience no guilt, as in the case of one officer who said to a police psychologist, "Doc, isn't it alright if I don't feel guilty? If I had another gun, I would have shot him six more times."

Police departments place an officer who has wounded or killed someone on administrative leave while a "shooting team" decides whether it was "righteous." Additionally, many of them require an officer involved in a shooting to get counseling from a designated provider within 24 hours of the incident. This is important because officers are experiencing all of the effects of the shooting incident, plus being concerned about the shooting team's finding. Moreover, the earlier there is skilled intervention, the less traumatic the incident is for the officer in the short and long term.

About 58 percent of police departments have a psychological unit.[84] However, only 31 percent of all departments give officers access to an in-house psychologist. The prevailing pattern is for officers to be referred to a mental health professional outside of the agency. This is due to the fact that concerns about confidentiality are most easily satisfied; there is less danger of records

## TABLE 9-8. Symptoms of Post-Traumatic Stress Disorder

| Physical Reactions | Emotional Reactions | Cognitive Reactions |
|---|---|---|
| • Headaches | • Anxiety | • Debilitating flashbacks |
| • Muscle aches | • Fear | • Repeated visions of the incident |
| • Sleep disorders | • Guilt | • Nightmares |
| • Changed appetite | • Sadness | • Slowed thinking |
| • Decreased interest in sexual activity | • Anger | • Difficulty making decisions and solving problems |
| • Impotence | • Irritability | • Disorientation |
| | • Feeling lost and unappreciated | • Lack of concentration |
| | • Withdrawal | • Memory lapses |

*Source:* Arthur W. Kureczka, "Critical Incident Stress," *FBI Law Enforcement Bulletin* 65, no. 2/3 (February–March 1996), p. 15.

## BOX 9-3

### Officers Face Stress Fallout from Gunfight

**by Jeff Leeds**

Flush from their televised takedown of the North Hollywood bank bandits, Los Angeles police officers involved in Friday's shootout now face another test: a crucial six-week period in which they will probably suffer flashbacks, anxiety, depression and, perhaps for the first time, cope with their own vulnerability. "The crash is going to come," said LAPD psychologist Kris Mohandie, coordinator of the department's Behavior Science unit.

For the moment, the officers who exchanged gunfire with two robbers outside the Bank of America branch seem exuberant in public, exchanging jokes and munching lasagna donated by grateful residents. But their emotional high is quickly fading.

Mohandie's unit is warning officers at police station roll calls to watch for early signs of post-traumatic stress disorder, and psychologists will hold a series of debriefings this week to encourage officers to release feelings of anger, frustration or fear that they may experience as a result of being outgunned.

Police officials also have taken steps to mute potential echoes of the shootout, asking a crew from the television show "High Incident" to call off plans to film a scene involving machine gun fire on Oxnard Street, not far from the bank, on Wednesday.

But there is already evidence that officers face a difficult road to recovery.

For Officer Eddie Guzman, who ducked for cover behind his patrol car as one of the bandits sprayed it with gunfire moments after emerging from the bank, it wasn't until he returned to his vehicle Friday night and found it punctured with eight armor-piercing rounds that the incident began to wear on him. "I realized how close I really was," he said softly as his eyes welled up. That night, he couldn't fall asleep until 3 A.M. The next night, he was at home trying to relax with his wife and children, who were watching an action film on television. The rattle of machine gun fire and calls of "Officer down" suddenly screamed from the TV. "That type of thing just takes you back," Guzman said, choking up.

Officer John Goodman rushed to the bank as calls of a robbery in progress came over the radio. He ran up to a car parked about 60 feet from the bank entrance to warn the driver to take cover. Something told him to look up. His eyes locked with a man in body armor carrying a machine gun, and he dove for cover as the van next to him exploded into glass and metal shards. While pinned down, he saw four officers fall in a hail of gunfire. The image still haunts him. "It plays every time I open my eyes," Goodman said.

Within a week of the incident, the rush of adrenaline that swept over most officers at the battle scene will ebb, psychologists say, forcing them to confront the fact that they were in a potentially deadly conflict. The next four to six weeks are a cooling-off period in which it is normal for officers to replay the incident in their minds and even have trouble sleeping.

Officers involved in shootouts and other so-called "critical incidents" often second-guess themselves in

*(continued)*

## BOX 9-3 (continued)

the weeks afterward, Mohandie said. Others may doubt themselves the next time they drive by the spot where the shootout unfolded, confront a suspect or have to draw their gun. Some officers remain skeptical of even their own department's psychologists, Mohandie said. And in trying to comfort officers involved in the shootout, psychologists must overcome a paradox: Police officers trained to conceal fear now must openly display it to recover.

For Officer Loren Farell, who was in his patrol car across the street from the bank Friday morning when he saw a husky man toting a machine gun walk inside, one emotion has risen above all others in the wake of the event. "Anger. You know why? None of us got to fire a round. We were pinned down. We were in no way, shape or form in control," Farell said. "It just reminds us of our vulnerability. I feel there's nothing I can do about it. The bad guy always chooses where and when." Farell said he plans to run "a couple miles" to begin relieving stress, but said he does not expect any long-term effects. "I'm not one to get a syndrome," he said.

To work out their frustrations, officers must find ways to accept and vent their emotions, through talking, exercise and even maintaining a healthy diet, without turning to alcohol or abusive behavior, said Officer Kevin Kirsch, who oversees the LAPD's peer counseling program. Dozens of the department's 220 peer counselors, many of them officers who have lived through shootings, have met one-on-one with officers who participated in Friday's bank shootout.

Other law enforcement agencies have developed a wide array of strategies to help officers deal with on-the-job trauma. At the Laguna Beach Police Department, officials replace the uniform of every officer involved in a shooting to remove any reminders of traumatic events. At the Los Angeles County Sheriff's Department, officers who fire their weapons at suspects are removed from fieldwork for five days, and psychologists interview them within 24 hours of the incident, following up two weeks later and then six months later. They also meet with peer counselors. In training, deputies watch a department-produced video about how the partners and friends of Deputy Nelson Yamamoto, a deputy killed in 1992, dealt with his loss.

"There's a whole romanticized notion of what a cop should be, that they should be invulnerable," said Michael S. Broder, stress manager for the Philadelphia Police Department. "We try to teach them in the academy that this is a very self-defeating attitude. The reality is, no one finds a situation like that [North Hollywood robbery] easy."

Audrey Honig, director of employee support services for the Los Angeles County Sheriff's Department, said that about 33% of officers involved in critical incidents suffer memory loss of some portion of the event. Between 14% and 33% suffer some kind of acute reaction, such as repeated flashbacks. For many officers, the most arduous part of the recovery comes after they have finished their initial debriefings or counseling sessions and they must return to the streets.

"That is the hardest part of the job—to get back in a radio car and go back to the same area," said Sgt. Rock Pattullo, a sheriff's deputy peer counselor who has been involved in five shootings. "I tell [fellow deputies], 'Hey, when I had to put back on my Sam Brown, my chest was just thumping out.' They realize it's OK to have that anxiety."

Part of that anxiety comes from the forced realization by law enforcement officers that a badge and a gun mean little to better-equipped criminals, experts say. "You come on the job, you're given the power of life and death, citizens have to follow your orders," said Georgette Bennett, a sociologist who helped the New York Police Department develop its psychological services unit. "Now here you are in this situation, absolutely humiliated, where your authority doesn't mean a damn thing. To be trained to be in authority and then finding out on the street it means nothing—out of that comes a lot of the extreme behavior."

On-the-job stress is a major reason why police have disproportionately high rates of suicide, alcohol abuse and divorce, studies show. Still, LAPD officials say only a fraction of retiring officers, about 15 a year, retire on stress-related disability pensions.

Police Protective League Director Dennis Zine, who did not witness the shootout firsthand, said he went to church Sunday and found himself envisioning police officers in coffins. "Without God's mercy, we would've lost some cops," Zine said. "I wouldn't be surprised if some officers quit."

But most stay to face the streets again.

*Source: Los Angeles Times,* March 6, 1997. Copyright 1997, Los Angeles Times. Reprinted by permission.

**FIGURE 9-4.** Capt. Terry Hyndman, south region commander of the Indiana Department of Natural Resources, can't hold back the emotion as he remembers his friend and fellow officer, First Sgt. Karl Kelley, during memorial services at the U.S. Capitol during National Police Week. (© 1999, Terri Cavoli.com)

falling into unauthorized hands, and the officer is likely to feel more comfortable when the station house is not also the counseling location.[85]

## STRESS AND THE FEMALE POLICE OFFICER

Most of the early research on police officer stress focused on male officers. This is not surprising when one considers that law enforcement positions were filled almost exclusively with men up until the 1970s. The literature that does exist on female officers' stress tends to compare the performance between male and female officers or measure male attitudes toward females.[86] Starting in the mid to late 1970s the gender gap in police positions started to close. For example, there are now almost 72,000 female police officers employed in the American police agencies with one in ten in policy-making positions and 123 serving as police chiefs.[87] However, in spite of this modest progress it has been suggested that female officers still face not only the same stressors as their male counterparts but some others that are unique to them. We know that in the past this has been true. For example, not too many years ago, it was common for police administrators to dismiss the notion that women could adequately perform functions normally falling within the exclusive domain of male officers—such as patrol work, nonfamily-related crime investigations, swat teams, riding a motorcycle, and so forth. Legislative, administrative, and judicial action have long since resolved the question of whether or not women should be permitted to perform these functions, and women have put to rest the questions about their ability to handle these tasks. There is ample empirical evidence to support the proposition that carefully selected and carefully trained females can be as effective as police officers as carefully selected and carefully trained males. This, however, is not meant to suggest that women have been universally and enthusiastically accepted by their male counterparts.[88] For example, we know that in the past the first assignment for police women, like their male counterparts, was in the operating units, which traditionally had been comprised exclusively of men. These women faced certain psychological pressures that would not be encountered by men or for that matter by women who would follow in their footsteps months or even years later. The first female officers performed their duties in an atmosphere of disbelief on the part of their supervisors and peers in their ability to deal physically and emotionally with the rigors of street work, particularly patrol functions. It must be remembered that peer acceptance is one of the greatest pressures operating within the police organization.[89] The desire to be identified as a "good officer" is a strong motivating force, and a failure to achieve that goal in one's eyes and in the eyes of one's peers can have a devastating and demoralizing effect.

For the rookie female officer, attaining the approval of her peers can be an even more frustrating task than it is for her male counterparts. As is true for her male counterparts, she must overcome her doubts about her own ability to perform her duties effectively, but unlike her male counterpart, she must also overcome the prejudice stemming from societal influences depicting the female as the "weaker sex" in every respect.[90] Also, unlike her male counterpart, she will very likely receive little support from her family, friends, and perhaps even her husband or other close male companions. Thus, she experiences additional stresses when she chooses a career in law enforcement that would not be imposed upon men.

## Studies of Male and Female Officers

As previously suggested, the majority of early studies on police stress used only male subjects, because women filled a very small number of law enforcement positions. The early research involving women in law enforcement that does exist consists generally of comparative studies of performance between males and females or measures of males' attitudes toward females.

A 1973 study by Bloch and Anderson[91] in Washington, D.C., found that men and women performed in generally the same manner when on patrol. The women handled the same types of calls and had similar results in handling violent citizens. Citizens showed the same level of respect for both male and female officers. The women were found to have a less aggressive style of policing and were better able to defuse potentially violent situations. The male patrol officers and superior officers, however, expressed negative attitudes toward women. The male officers believed they were better able to handle violent situations and rated the women as less competent, stating that they preferred not to work with the women.

Another study done in St. Louis County in 1975 by Sherman arrived at a similar conclusion.[92] The women were found to be equally effective in handling calls with violent citizens as their male counterparts. The study, along with the department's performance evaluations, showed that the performance of the women was no different from that of the men. The men, however, had some of the same negative attitudes toward the women as in the Washington, D.C., study. Neither of these studies addressed the question of stress in the female officer. One could infer that the attitudes of the male officers would be reflected in their interaction with female officers, and those experiences in turn would cause additional stress for female officers. However, the studies did not address this question.

A study done by Schwartz and Schwartz in 1981 found the major stress in female officers was lack of support within the organization.[93] They found that women were subjected to harsher treatment than men and received little support from management and supervisors. There were also no assistance programs made available specifically for women.

In 1982, Glaser and Saxe found six psychological stressors that affect women officers. These included: (1) doubts about competence and self-worth in doing a traditionally male job; (2) lack of support from men both on and off the job; (3) necessity to develop greater assertiveness and authority in voice and stature; (4) inappropriate expectations regarding physical training, odd hours, and quasi-military environment; (5) an inability to work fifteen-hour days and still maintain a household; and (6) a necessity to develop new defense mechanisms for stress, which were more appropriate to law enforcement.[94]

In a 1983 study, Wexler and Logan found that women officers experienced the same stressors as their male counterparts along with stressors unique to them. Wexler and Logan developed a category of female-related stressors consisting of four stressors: negative attitudes of male officers, group blame, responses of other men, and lack of role models.[95]

In this study 80 percent of the women surveyed reported experiencing stress from negative attitudes of male officers. These negative attitudes included both official and individual harassment. The official harassment included having no separate locker rooms and being physically locked out of the police station. Types of individual harassment included questions about the women's sexual orientation, refusal to talk to the women, and blatant anti-women comments.[96]

A study done by Norvell, Hill, and Murrin found that higher stress levels in women officers resulted from dissatisfaction with their coworkers.[97] Overall, however, the women did not have higher stress levels or lower job satisfaction than male officers. Males seemed to have more stress, more daily hassles, and greater emotional exhaustion than females, and they had greater job dissatisfaction than females.

Daum and Johns conducted a study specifically targeted at women officers. Their study showed women did not feel they received enough acceptance and credit for the job they were doing. The women surveyed felt ostracized from the males and felt they were being evaluated according to "male" criteria. Most did not, however, regret the decision to enter law enforcement.[98]

## Female Law Enforcement Officer Stress Today

To assess more accurately whether or not the stresses facing women entering law enforcement today are still greater and somewhat different than those exerted upon their male counterparts, two Florida law enforcement agencies were studied. The agencies were the Largo Police Department, which is a medium-sized municipal agency in Pinellas County, Florida, and the Pinellas County Sheriff's Office, which is a large, urban county agency serving the Clearwater/St. Petersburg area.

All the female patrol officers and patrol sergeants in each agency were surveyed along with a proportionate, matched sample of male officers. The males were matched to the females by age, years of service, and rank. Fifty-six subjects participated.

## Findings

Researchers suspected prior to conducting the study that the findings would show that females continue to experience stresses unique to them. However, the results showed this not to be the case. As a matter of fact, the findings of this survey indicated that male and female patrol personnel in these two agencies experienced similar levels of stress. In addition, the female officers of these two agencies no longer experienced unique gender-related stressors. It seems that over the years, as both law enforcement and the community at large have become accustomed to the idea of women in law enforcement, that female officers, at least with these two agencies, experienced less stress than their earlier counterparts. As law enforcement has become accepted as an appropriate career for females, they no longer have the personal stressors associated with negative attitudes from family or from men they are dating. In addition young female officers now have significant role models within their agencies. Women officers now feel the same stress associated with the job as their male counterparts. It would also seem that as both males and females take more equal roles in family raising, the stress that female officers once experienced when handling dual roles has lessened.

The highest levels of stress experienced by male and female officers seemed to be involved with critical incidents, such as the violent death of an officer in the line of duty (94.4 percent), the suicide of an officer who was a close friend (94.4 percent), taking a life (87.2 percent) or shooting someone (83.6 percent) in the line of duty, and dismissal (83.8 percent). Going through a divorce or separation (74.1 percent), also ranked high, along with responding to a scene involving the death of a child (73.8 percent). Interestingly, these findings following the same pattern found by Sewell. In Sewell's study, officers rated the following as the five most stressful events they could experience: violent death of a partner in the line of duty, dismissal, taking a life in the line of duty, shooting someone in the line of duty, and suicide of an officer who is a close friend.

These findings underscore the need for department heads to be sure that all personnel involved in any critical incident be given immediate mandatory critical incident stress debriefing, and be allowed to continue in counseling for as long as it takes the officer to recover from the incident. Officers who are dealing with a divorce or separation or who are recovering from the death of a close friend should also have counseling available to them, to help with the recovery process.

## POLICE DOMESTIC VIOLENCE

Given the stressful nature of police work, it is not surprising that officers sometimes have difficulty keeping what happened to them at work separate from their home lives. "Leave it at the office" is a common admonition to officers. While the intent of this message is clear, it is often hard to do so consistently.[99]

It is not known how many acts of domestic violence police officers commit in their own homes. The reasons for the nonreporting of such incidents include victims with low esteem who think they "got what they deserved," threats from their attackers of more severe physical harm if the victims do call the police, and the belief that fellow officers will not take action against "one of their own." Box 9-4 examines the crime of domestic violence by police officers.

## BOX 9-4

### New York Police Lag in Fighting Domestic Violence by Officers

**by David Kocieniewski and Kevin Flynn**

In the fall of 1995, Officer Anthony Nieves was accused of two offenses that could hardly have been more different.

Already a suspect in the murder of one girlfriend, he was arrested for harassing another. Then he was caught, while off duty, sprinting onto the field at Yankee Stadium to high-five a player.

Yet when the police officials considered the incidents, they imposed punishments that could hardly have been more similar.

His antics at the stadium earned him a 30-day suspension.

Harassing his girlfriend earned him a 29-day suspension.

The way the Nieves case was handled is not unusual for the New York City Police Department, which critics say has long been complacent in its approach to domestic abuse complaints against its officers—complaints that are rising sharply.

A review of department records shows that officers found guilty of domestic abuse in administrative proceedings are rarely fired, and that some are punished with suspensions of just 15 days—the same penalty given to officers caught sleeping on the job or taking an unjustified sick day.

Law enforcement and domestic violence experts say the department, despite its size and a climbing number of abuse complaints, is far less aggressive in detecting and punishing domestic abusers on the force than are departments in other large cities.

Already this year, the Police Department said it had received 821 complaints of domestic abuse by officers, from threats to actual assaults, a 40 percent increase over the total for last year. In the last three years, more than 120 officers have been arrested on charges relating to domestic violence.

In one high-profile case, Officer Patrick J. Fitzgerald, a patrolman in the 34th Precinct, shot and killed himself, his wife and their two children in September at the family's home in Orange County, N.Y. Relatives of Officer Fitzgerald's wife, Leeanne, said afterward that she had called the 34th Precinct station house several times to complain that he was abusing her, but that the calls were not taken seriously. Police officials have said they cannot find any record of such calls.

"There is a culture in the Police Department that just doesn't want to admit how serious this problem is," said Eleanor Pamm, a domestic violence expert at John Jay College of Criminal Justice and a member of the Mayor's Task Force on Domestic Violence. "And until they get serious about it, the situation isn't going to get any better. People are going to continue to suffer."

Domestic violence experts say that when police officers, with their ready access to guns, are involved in household disputes, arguments that would otherwise end in bruises or wounded feelings can quickly escalate into bloodshed. Over the last three years in New York, domestic incidents involving officers have claimed 10 lives by murder or suicide. Three more spouses died under suspicious circumstances, according to investigators.

New York police officials say they are vigilant in rooting out abusive officers and punishing colleagues who try to protect them. But abuse by officers, both on and off duty, is difficult to combat, experts said. A feeling of futility often prevents victims from reporting abuse, and a code of silence among officers frequently makes them reluctant to turn in their peers.

Except in the most serious crimes, prosecutors generally leave the punishment of officers up to the department's internal disciplinary system. But records show that the department rarely punishes officers severely for any offenses, even when the accusations involve domestic violence.

Police departments in other large cities have made greater strides in addressing domestic abuse among officers, according to domestic violence experts. In Baltimore, officials set up an elaborate network in 1997 to monitor complaints against officers who lived in outlying suburbs. In Los Angeles, officials created a five-member investigative team last year devoted solely to accusations of battering by officers. In Chicago, the department hired full-time counselors in 1994 to help victims of police domestic abuse follow through on their complaints.

New York City has adopted none of these strategies.

Patrick Kelleher, the First Deputy Police Commissioner in New York, said that, given the size of the 40,000-member force, he would describe the abuse problem as "relatively small, but very serious."

In the last three years, according to police statistics, the department has suspended 162 officers without pay for domestic violence, and fired 13. Since a 1995 domestic dispute in which an officer was killed, the department has required that a captain respond to the scene to every abuse complaint against an officer. Mr. Kelleher said the department is installing new policies, including a pilot program tried once earlier this year in which officers with a history of domestic violence attend an eight-week course in stress reduction and conflict resolution.

"I'm really not familiar with what's happening in other cities, like Chicago," Mr. Kelleher said, "But I do know we are light years ahead of where we were a few years ago."

But Donald C. Sheehan of the Federal Bureau of Investigation, a special agent coordinating the bureau's effort to reduce family violence by officers, said: "New York hasn't been able to get a grip on the problem. What it takes is a commitment from the highest level of the department, and we just haven't seen that yet."

*(continued)*

BOX 9-4 (continued)

## The Police Response

### A Plea for Help Is Heeded Too Late

Bliss Verdon thought the Police Department could help her when her former boyfriend, a transit police officer, began harassing her in May 1997.

When Ms. Verdon, a 25-year-old social worker, reported that Officer Rodney Dilbert had left an angry and abusive diatribe on her answering machine, a sergeant went to her home in Queens to investigate. While he was there, Officer Dilbert called and the sergeant took the telephone, saying he would handle the matter "cop to cop," according to a police report. He scolded Officer Dilbert, but filed no official report with the Internal Affairs Bureau.

Three weeks later Officer Dilbert was back. He trailed Ms. Verdon on the subway, shoved her into a parked car and tried to force his way into the office building where she worked, according to police records. Frightened, she went to the 115th Precinct station house near her home to file a complaint. But police commanders who would speak only on the condition of anonymity said precinct supervisors were delayed in investigating the complaint because they were busy handling another matter—the political fallout from having given a state senator a traffic summons.

Two days later, officials decided Officer Dilbert was not an imminent threat and took no action.

Although Ms. Verdon called the station again, it was not until June 10 that her complaint was assigned to transit investigators. By then it was too late. That evening, Officer Dilbert killed Ms. Verdon, shooting her eight times with his service pistol while she used a phone booth near her home, then killed himself.

Police Commissioner Howard Safir fired one of the six supervisors involved in the Verdon case and forced another to retire, but he said the tragedy was caused by a failure of "individuals, not the system." Ms. Verdon's mother, Jo-Ann Cote, still blames the department.

"My daughter didn't have to die," Ms. Cote said. "She did everything she could do to make them aware of this man threatening her, this man who had their gun. The Police Department just didn't want to deal with it."

Ms. Verdon's case is an example of why domestic violence experts say the spouses of abusive police officers are especially vulnerable. Officers are often reluctant to turn in their colleagues. And some abusive officers use their connections inside the criminal justice system to block their victims' appeals for help. Some women are so sure the law enforcement system is stacked against them that they will not report the crime, the experts said.

"These women are really all alone out there," said Maria Guarracino, of the Archdiocese of New York, who counsels victims of police spousal abuse. "There are just so few places for them to turn."

It took two complaints of domestic abuse against Michael Ferrante, a Bronx narcotics detective, to get the department to take serious action.

Officer Ferrante was accused of hitting his estranged wife, Lisa, during an encounter in Yonkers in 1994, according to the police. But his wife declined to press charges, and he was not arrested. The Police Department did open an administrative case against him, but found the allegations of abuse "unsubstantiated," even though Mrs. Ferrante had been treated

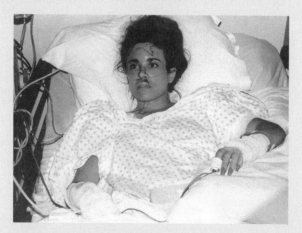

**FIGURE 9-4.** Accused in stabbing Michale Ferrante, a Bronx narcotics detective, above, is charged with attempted murder in the stabbing of his girlfriend, Carol Nanna, left. The police say he punctured her lung and nearly severed her left arm. (The New York Times)

at a hospital for facial injuries. Within three months, Officer Ferrante was back on full duty.

After that incident, the detective began threatening his girlfriend, Carol Nanna, 30, according to her family. But Ms. Nanna said she never called the police to report the threats. "I was always afraid to because he was a cop, and I always felt they stuck together," she said.

In May of this year, Ms. Nanna finally moved out of their home in Yonkers after Officer Ferrante threatened her with his gun, she said. She reported the threat to the police, and Officer Ferrante was stripped of his gun the next day.

Six days later, as Ms. Nanna sat in her car at an intersection, Officer Ferrante attacked her with a knife, according to the police, slashing her face, puncturing her lung and nearly severing her left arm, injuries from which she has yet to fully recover.

Officer Ferrante is awaiting trial on a charge of attempted murder. His lawyer, Paul Goldberger, declined to comment.

Ms. Nanna's family said the Police Department had taken too long to act against Officer Ferrante.

"If you threaten anybody, you should not be a police officer," said Susan Milo, Ms. Nanna's mother. "As far as I am concerned, they are not doing enough, because they are not monitoring these situations."

## A Comparison: Other Cities Use Stiffer Penalties

Some experts contend that police work, with its emphasis on giving orders and establishing control, attracts many men with a propensity for domestic violence. Although police officials generally reject that view, almost all large police departments have taken steps to address the problem—some more aggressively than others.

In 1996, a new Federal law required police departments to take guns away from officers who had been convicted of domestic abuse. When New York reviewed the personnel history of its police force that year, it found that 88 officers had criminal records for domestic abuse. But the department could not move against them because their cases had been dismissed under probation programs and erased from the court records.

Some police departments decided to place officers with histories of abuse in special monitoring programs. Others studied psychiatric tests the officers took as candidates to devise new screening questions to weed out other abusive candidates. New York did not follow up on the 88 officers with a history of family violence, said Mr. Kelleher, the First Deputy Commissioner in New York.

In several cities, officials said they viewed abusive officers as threats to more than just their spouses.

"This officer is carrying our weapon and he is supposed to be serving the citizens," said Col. Margaret Patten of the Baltimore police. "That may sound lofty, but do we want a criminal being responsible for upholding the law?"

Under Baltimore's "zero tolerance" policy, the department fires any officer found to have been involved in domestic abuse. "We don't care if the victim doesn't want to prosecute," Colonel Patten said. "We have a responsibility to go forward."

This year, Baltimore has received 49 complaints of domestic abuse by its officers, and has fired nine, the police department said. Meanwhile in New York, where the force and the number of complaints are more than 10 times larger, officials have fired two.

In Chicago, the focus of the domestic violence program is less punitive. Officials recognize that battered spouses are often financially dependent on their abusers and unlikely to report violence if they feel doing so will cost an officer his job. Jan Russell, one of the department's domestic violence counselors, said abrupt firings can also make officers so desperate they only grow more abusive.

Chicago police commanders try to recognize and curb potentially abusive behavior long before it becomes criminal. Nonetheless, officials of the 13,500-member department, which received 319 domestic abuse complaints against its officers last year, fired eight for domestic offenses. That same year, New York, a department nearly three times as large, dismissed seven.

The New York police have tried to balance counseling efforts with punishments calibrated to the offense.

Mr. Kelleher, the New York police official, called the zero-tolerance approach "the easy way out" because it relieves officials weighing the merits of each case. Although there are no guidelines for punishing officers, many defense lawyers say Commissioner Safir has handed out stricter punishments than his predecessors.

"We try to do what is the best thing for everyone concerned," Mr. Kelleher said. "For the officer, for the victim and for the department—with the emphasis on the victim."

But a review of police administrative hearings shows that officers found guilty of domestic violence, or of failing to report their colleagues' abuse, have not been severely punished.

In the Nieves case, the officer was punished no more severely for the abuse complaint than for the

*(continued)*

## BOX 9-4 (continued)

ball park prank, even though his girlfriend said she had been terrified when he scaled her fire escape and broke the window to her apartment after a fight. When he was finally disciplined, police administrators who made the decision were holding personnel records showing that he had been placed on modified duty because he was a suspect in the murder of a previous girlfriend.

Officer Nieves, who was never charged in the murder, has since been returned to full duty. Investigators said their inquiry has stalled, but that Officer Nieves remains a suspect. Both Officer nieves and his lawyer, Joseph Librie, would not comment.

In a second case, two Brooklyn officers pleaded guilty last year to administrative charges of helping a fellow officer cover up the shooting of his wife. The officer whose wife was shot, Milton Calderon of the 72d Precinct, was fired by an administrative judge who said she suspected he had been involved in the shooting, which he had blamed on his 3-year-old daughter. But the two officers who responded to the Calderon house were suspended for 30 days and placed on probation for a year, even though the judge found they never reported the shooting, enabling Officer Calderon to destroy evidence.

Police records also show that since 1995, five officers who violated court orders of protection were punished by suspensions of 20 or fewer days, the same penalty imposed on officers who lose their identification cards. In other cases, officers found guilty in departmental trials of beating their spouses received 15-day suspensions.

Beyond disciplining officers, the Police Department offers free counseling that Mr. Kelleher credits with improving, even saving, the lives of officers and their family members. One of the largest programs is the Membership Assistance Program that was setup by the department and the patrolmen's Benevolent Association in 1994 after a series of police suicides. It deploys 120 peer counselors in the city's 76 precincts, and they evaluate troubled officers and make about 400 referrals a year to outside therapists.

But many police officers spurn such counseling, fearing they will be stigmatized or disciplined if they acknowledge having a personal problem. One former officer, Ronald Marchetta, has sued the department,

asserting that when he came to the department for help in his troubled marriage, a police psychiatrist breached the confidentiality of his therapy and provided the department with information that was used to force him into retirement.

The department said that it plans to expand its recent program offering stress management training to abusers, and that it may work with suburban police departments to insure that the city's department is informed of domestic complaints against officers who live outside the city.

### Open Secrets: Signs of Trouble Go Unnoticed

As more details have emerged about the case of Officer Fitzgerald, who killed his family and himself, it has become a lesson in how oblivious officers can be to signs that a colleague's marriage is in desperate trouble—signs that experts say officers should be trained to notice.

Friends of Officer Fitzgerald maintain that neither they, nor the department, had any way of knowing that he might snap one day and kill his wife and children.

"No one could have foreseen this, never in a million years," said Officer Peter Ciaccio, one of Officer Fitzgerald's closest friends. "They were never that type. I could never see that he would do this, because he loved those kids. And he loved her, even with everything that was going on."

But the Fitzgeralds' stormy marriage was an open secret among officers in the 34th Precinct, according to police investigators.

Both the officer and his wife had received court orders of protection. Her relatives say she called the precinct station to complain. State police were called at least once to the family's house in Greenville.

Despite those outward signs, department supervisors said they were unaware of the strains in the family until Sept. 25, when the couple's daughter, Ashley Fitzgerald, 7, called 911 in a futile effort to protect her family and herself from her father's rage.

"You kind of wonder, what will it take to finally make them deal with this?" said Dr. Pamm, of the Mayor's Task Force on Domestic Violence. "I mean, how many bodies do they need before they realize it is a major problem?"

*Source: The New York Times,* November 1, 1998.

Of critical concern to departments is how to screen and select new officers to minimize the risk of hiring officers who may engage in domestic violence.[100] To understand the connection between the various forms of family violence, it is essential to investigate whether a recruit has a history or likelihood of engaging in child abuse, domestic violence, or elder abuse. The process of investigating recruits must be handled in two stages: preemployment screening and investigation, and post-conditional offer of employment.

**Early Warning and Intervention**

All candidates should be asked about any history of perpetrating child abuse, domestic violence, or elder abuse, and past arrests or convictions for such crimes. They should be asked whether they have ever been the subject of a civil protective order. If the candidate answers positively to any of these questions or the department uncovers any information in the background check that indicates a history of violence, the candidate should be screened out of the hiring process.

During the background investigation, a check should be made for restraining orders issued in any jurisdiction where the candidate has lived.

**Preemployment Screening and Investigation**

If the candidate's background investigation does not indicate a history of child abuse, domestic violence, or elder abuse, the department should proceed with a psychological examination, which should include indicators of violent or abusive tendencies. This portion of the screening process should be conducted by an experienced clinical psychologist or psychiatrist.

**Post-Conditional Offer of Employment**

Departments must make it clear to all officers the department has a zero tolerance policy on domestic violence and the department should share this information with family members of the officer. Departments should look to develop a line of communication directly with the partners of recruits and officers. For example, a department can hold a family orientation day prior to graduation. Family members should be provided with instructions on whom to contact within the department if any problems arise. The dual purpose of establishing such contact is to underscore the department's zero tolerance policy and to provide victims with an avenue for direct communication with a department employee who is trained in handling such calls.

**Zero Tolerance Policy**

An individual or family member of an officer may recognize early indicators of a police officer's potential violence such as issues of power and control. The power and control may take the forms of restricting contact with family and friends, requiring the partner to turn over his/her paycheck, or limiting activities outside the home. Victims may communicate their concerns "informally" at first, such as calls to an officer's supervisor. These informal contacts must be treated with care, since this is a critical opportunity for a department to provide intervention using early intervention/prevention strategies. The model policy calls for a formal system of documenting, sharing, and responding to information from concerned partners and family members.

Departments need to provide officers and their families with nonpunitive avenues of support and assistance before an incident of domestic violence occurs. Departments must establish procedures for making confidential referrals to internal or external counseling services with expertise in domestic violence. These referrals can be made upon the request of an officer or family members or in response to observed warning signs.

**Department Responsibilities**

Officers will not be entitled to confidentiality anytime they or family members disclose to any member of the department that the officer has engaged in domestic violence. Confidentiality should be extended to partners or family members who report an officer as a matter of safety. A report of such criminal conduct must be treated as an admission/report of a crime and investigated both criminally and administratively.

Departments must understand that other officers may become involved in an officer's domestic violence situation by engaging in inappropriate activities that serve to interfere with cases against fellow officers who are engaged in such acts as stalking, intimidation, harassment, or surveillance of victims, witnesses, and/or family members of victims or witnesses. If this occurs, these officers must be investigated and sanctioned and/or charged criminally where appropriate.

## Supervisor Responsibilities

Typically, an abusive person engages in certain patterns of behavior. These may include repeated actions of increasing control directed at his/her partner preceding an incident of physical/criminal violence.

The early indicators of potential violence are not limited to home life; the department may detect warning signs in an officer's behavior prior to a domestic violence incident. Supervisors must receive specific training on warning signs and potential indicators of violent or controlling tendencies. Warning signs that may indicate a likelihood of violent behavior include increased use of force in arrest situations, drug/alcohol problems, frequent tardiness or absences, verbal disputes, physical altercations, and other aggressive behavior.

When supervisors become aware of a pattern of controlling or abusive behavior exhibited by officers, the supervisors have a responsibility to document the information and notify their immediate ranking supervisor, who will then inform the chief in accordance with the department's chain of command. After making proper notification supervisors should inform officers that the behaviors have been documented. A recommendation can be made to officers that they participate voluntarily in a counseling/support program to address the identified issue or behavior.

In cases where behavior violates departmental policy, a department can seize the opportunity to mandate participation in a batterer intervention program in addition to any appropriate sanctions.

Early prevention/intervention strategies employed by a department at this phase of the continuum have tremendous potential not only to reduce future violence, but also to save victims' lives and officers' careers. The range of services that can be made available includes the following:

- Employee assistance program referral (Discussed in greater detail later in this chapter.)
- Internal professional counseling (police psychologist)
- External professional counseling (contract/referral)
- Advocacy support from local agencies
- Peer support program (with clear reporting and confidentiality guidelines)

The department will need to ensure that the quality and expertise of these resources are sound. Collaboration with local domestic violence victim advocacy organizations is recommended.

As part of the department's zero tolerance policy, all officers need to understand their responsibility to report definitive knowledge they have concerning domestic violence on the part of an officer. Departments must be prepared to investigate and possibly sanction and/or charge criminally any officer who fails to report such knowledge or cooperate with an investigation.

In addition, all officers need to know they will be investigated and sanctioned and/or charged criminally if they engage in activities such as stalking, surveillance, intimidation, or harassment of victims or witnesses in an attempt to interfere with investigations of other officers accused of domestic violence.

In the event that an officer is the subject of a criminal investigation and/or a protective or restraining order, the officer is responsible for informing his or her supervisor and providing copies of the order and timely notice of court dates, regardless of the jurisdiction.

## Police Officer Responsibilities

A department's response to 911 calls involving police officer domestic violence immediately sets the tone for how a situation will be handled throughout the remainder of the continuum. Further, the unique dynamics between the offending and responding officers (for example, collegiality and rank differential) often make on-scene decisions extremely difficult.

A department must take the following actions, all of which are critical steps in responding to allegations of domestic abuse by police officers.

## Incident Response Protocols

**Communications Officer/Dispatcher Documentation.**   When a call or report of domestic violence involves a police officer, the dispatcher should have a standing directive to document the call and immediately notify both the on-duty patrol supervisor and the chief of police. This directive ensures that key command personnel receive the information and prevents the call from being handled informally.

**Patrol Response.**   Any officer arriving at the scene of a domestic violence call/incident involving a police officer must immediately request the presence of a supervisor at the scene regardless of the involved officer's jurisdiction.

**On-Scene Supervisor Response.**   The on-scene supervisor has responsibilities for the following:

- Securing the scene and collecting evidence
- Ensuring an arrest is made where probable cause exists
- Removing weapons in the event of an arrest
- Considering victim safety
- Notifying the police chief or sheriff if the incident occurs outside the officer's jurisdiction

The on-duty supervisor must respond to the call and assume all on-scene decision making. Leaving the decision making to officers of lesser or equal rank to the suspect officer puts the responding officer in a difficult situation. The presence of a ranking officer on the scene resolves this problem. The policy recommends that in police officer domestic violence cases no fewer than two officers, with at least one of senior rank to the accused officer, be present. This is also the case when serving arrest warrants and civil protective orders.

**Crime Scene Documentation.**   Recanting or reluctant witnesses and victims are not uncommon when domestic violence occurs. Police on the scene of a 911 call must take specific actions to document all evidence, including color photographs/videotape of injuries, overturned/damaged furniture, interviews of neighbors and family members, and documentation of threats from the officer. Documentation of this evidence will be essential to the successful prosecution of the case with or without the victim's presence in court.

**Arrest Decisions.**   Policies on arrest for domestic violence incidents vary among state, county, and local jurisdictions. In all cases, responding officers should base arrest decisions on probable cause. When a crime has been committed, an arrest shall be made, as in all other cases. The on-scene supervisor is responsible for ensuring an arrest is made if probable cause exists or submitting written documentation to explain why an arrest was not made. All officers need sufficient training to enable them to determine which party is the primary (i.e., dominant) aggressor in domestic violence situations. Every effort should be made to determine who is the primary aggressor to avoid the unwarranted arrest of victims.

**Weapon Removal.**   If an arrest is made, the on-scene supervisor shall relieve the accused officer of his or her service weapon. Some police officers may have several weapons at their home. Where multiple weapons are present, removing only the service weapon of the officer leaves the victim entirely vulnerable to further violence. While federal, state, and local laws vary on how and when such weapons can be removed, police have broad powers to remove weapons in certain circumstances, particularly if an arrest is being made. Where application of the law is questionable, the on-scene supervisor should suggest that the officer in question voluntarily relinquish all firearms. The supervisor can also simply ask victims if they want to remove any weapons from the home for safekeeping by the department.

In situations where no arrest has been made, the on-scene supervisor should consider removing the accused officer's weapon as a safety consideration.

After weapons are removed, decisions need to be made about how long they will or can be held. Where court orders of protection are in place, these orders may also affect decisions on gun removal/seizure.

When the accused officer is the chief/director/superintendent of the department, a specific protocol must be in place to document and report the incident to the individual who has direct oversight for the chief, director, or superintendent.

When police respond to a domestic violence incident involving an officer from another jurisdiction, all responding officers, investigators, and supervisors shall follow the same procedures to be followed if responding to a domestic violence complaint involving an officer from their own department. The on-scene supervisor shall notify the chief of police from the accused officer's department verbally as soon as possible and in writing within 24 hours of the call.

Departments may be faced with domestic violence situations where the victim is a police officer. If this occurs, standard domestic violence response and investigation procedures should be followed. The department should take steps to protect the privacy of the officer and make referrals to confidential counseling services. The department should not allow the reported incident to impact negatively upon the assignments and evaluation of the victimized officer.

If both the victim and offender in a domestic violence situation are police officers, the protocols established by the department should remain substantially the same. Safety of the victim should be the paramount concern. In the event that an order of protection has been issued, a department will need to make careful decisions concerning work assignments for accused officers pending administrative and criminal investigations. Gun removal in this situation becomes extremely complex. In the development of the policy, individual departments should seek legal guidance to ensure the rights of all concerned are protected.

**Department Follow-Up.**   The department or supervisor should require a debriefing of all officers involved in a response to the scene of a police officer domestic violence case and may include communications officers. At the debriefing, the department's confidentiality guidelines should be reviewed. In addition, a command-level critical incident management review of every domestic violence case involving an officer should be conducted.

The department must take responsibility for conducting an assessment to determine the potential for further violence on the part of the accused officer. A specifically trained member of the command staff should review a checklist of risk factors with the accused officer. In addition the evaluation should be supplemented by interviews with the victim, witnesses, and family members. Information gained from the assessment should be used to determine appropriate sanctions, safeguards, and referrals. The command officer assigned as the victim's principal contact should discuss the risk factors with the victim as part of safety planning.

## RESPONDING TO STRESS

### The Officer's Responsibility

Some police officers think that stress is just "a fairy tale . . . something that those who can't hack it can blame for their problems." Thus, the first step toward taking responsibility is for officers to recognize that unchecked stress can cause them to be sick more frequently, to engage in self-destructive behaviors (such as substance abuse), to live life less fully, to lose their families, and simply to be more uncomfortable every day than they need to be. The second step for officers is to monitor their own bodies and actions for stress, even though this capacity for self-awareness and introspection is difficult for some people to develop. Simply put, officers need to be in touch with what they are feeling, to think about what they have said and done, and to ask: Why? The final step is to take steps to help eliminate or reduce stress, the so-called stress inoculations activities. Among these activities are:

1. Rigorous physical exercise that lasts 20 to 30 minutes, at least three times per week.[101]
2. Maintaining a proper diet, e.g., minimizing the intake of foods high in salt and cholesterol.
3. Getting adequate rest—not drinking caffeine within five hours of going to bed and trying to get eight hours of sleep.
4. Developing leisure interests and hobbies such as hiking, tying flies, rock climbing, gardening, collecting stamps, writing poetry and fiction, learning a foreign language, and photography—in other words, learning new things that excite and refresh the mind.[102]

5. Meditating and praying.

6. Avoiding maladaptive responses to stress, such as smoking and drinking.

7. Establishing support groups.

8. Developing a network of friends, including people outside of the department.

9. Monitoring yourself. Refer yourself for help before you have to be referred. You will avoid some problems, reduce others before they become entrenched, and get more out of the helping process.

10. Using relaxation techniques such as biofeedback, yoga, progressive muscle relaxation, Tai chi, imagery, and breathing exercises.[103]

11. Making sure your career and other expectations are consistent with your actual situation.[104]

## Employee Assistance Programs

Although the evolution has been slow in development, a variety of employee assistance services are currently available within police departments.[105] The growth of assistance programs in the law enforcement field can be traced back to the early 1950s.[106] Many programs, such as those initiated in Boston, New York, and Chicago, were created to deal primarily with alcohol abuse programs.

In the 1970s, agencies such as the Los Angeles Sheriff's Office, the Chicago Police Department, and the San Francisco Police Department expanded their programs to include problems not related to alcohol. In 1980, mental health professionals began providing personal and job-related counseling services to FBI personnel. Mental health professionals were also used to assist FBI managers with a variety of employee-related matters.[107] By 1986, many of the largest police departments in the United States had formed "stress units" or other sections to provide help for officers having personal or occupational difficulties. In the early 1990s, the United States Customs Service provided stress management training for both its supervisory and nonsupervisory personnel throughout the country.[108] The majority of law enforcement agencies with 100 or more officers now have written policies regarding providing counseling assistance services for their officers.[109]

## Benefits of the Employee Assistance Program

As the leaders and developers of an employee assistance program (EAP) plan, implement, evaluate, and refine their program, it is critical not only to involve labor and management but also to facilitate cooperative and trusting relationships among all those involved. Identifiable, mutual, and cooperative tasks and activities are not only beneficial to labor and management but to the EAP itself. The following are some benefits noteworthy and deserving of special attention.

**Increased Probability of Success.** The active, mutual, and cooperative involvement of both labor and management with an employee assistance program increases the program's probability for success. This without a doubt is important to the program.

**Increased Referrals.** A well-run and effective employee assistance program will serve approximately 8 to 10 percent of the total number of individuals who have access to it (e.g., employees and their immediate family members). Achieving a rate such as this without full labor and management cooperation and involvement is very unlikely. An EAP must be postured to respond to the needs of its constituency group.

**Joint Training Sessions.**   The training sessions typically conducted by EAP staff members are attended by representatives from both labor and management. Not only does this provide serendipitous opportunities for cooperative interaction on behalf of labor and management representatives, but on behalf of the EAP staff as well. For example, the EAP professional enjoys the opportunity to work with both supervisors from management and employee representatives in a noncrisis, nonproblem-oriented situation, to train mixed intervention teams focusing on employee concerns, to educate and market the program, and above all to assist critical supervisory personnel on knowing how to assist troubled workers in recognizing they have a problem and recommending where to go for assistance. This is absolutely essential if seriously troubled employees are to be identified and helped.

In the ultimate sense, the vast majority of the previously discussed benefits of mutual cooperation and trust on behalf of labor and management will directly and indirectly result in benefits to employees. Of the numerous identifiable benefits to employees, the following five appear to be worthy of special attention.

**Benefits to the Employee**

**A Meaningful Employee Benefit.**   First of all, it is important to remember that the mere existence of a good EAP is a meaningful employee benefit. Moreover, those that are supported jointly by labor and management tend to be more efficient, more effective, and helpful to a larger proportion of the employees and their families who have access to them. EAPs with joint labor-management support also tend to facilitate the existence of other positive qualities within the agency (e.g., high morale), and with the existence of joint labor-management support the longevity and continuance of the EAP assuredly is on more solid ground.

**Real Help in Response to One's "Cry for Help."**   In most instances, it takes caring, trained, and cooperating individuals to recognize and helpfully respond to a hurting employee's cry for help. For example, many authorities in the field of alcoholism believe that people troubled with alcohol or other drugs suffer from a "catch 22" situation. Part of them wants to hide their problem and not be found out, but another part wants to be identified and helped. When labor and management cooperatively and in trusting ways work together with an effective EAP, the latter alternative is more likely to be the affected outcome.

**Stigma Reduction.**   When both labor and management jointly communicate and demonstrate that to be troubled is to be human, a much more trusting environment exists and employees tend to feel more comfortable asking for and accepting help and assistance. It is not easy for employees and/or families to admit they need help. The cultural stigma that suggests people should be able to solve their own problems without help from others, especially among law enforcement personnel, can be a very powerful influence and may make people reluctant to seek assistance. However, when supervisors or peers recommend that employees seek assistance from the EAP, an altogether different atmosphere exists—and assistance is then more likely to be sought.

**Feeling Cared For as a Person.**   No one advocates coddling, especially in the workplace. At the same time, however, employees do not like to feel as if they are "a dispensable tool" or "just a badge number." When employees have feelings like these, morale tends to go down, job satisfaction dwindles, and quite often productivity suffers. Nonetheless, in environments where labor, management, and the EAP cooperatively, trustingly, and mutually work together, employees are more apt to feel that others care about them as people. This attitude, in turn, tends to enhance morale, job satisfaction, and productivity.

**Affordable Access to Help.**   One of the primary reasons why employees seek help and assistance early from an EAP is that they can afford to. Effective EAPs are well financed, at least to the extent that feared economic hardship is not an up-front deterrent to seeking help. Affordability, in terms of the perceptions of troubled employees, also means they can seek assistance and help without immediate fears that it could cost them their jobs (or benefits, opportunities for promotion, etc.). In an ideal EAP environment, troubled employees do not consider whether or not they can afford to seek help; they consider why they cannot afford *not* to seek help. Hopefully, their considerations produce the conclusion that seeking help is the best course.[110]

Here is an example of a case handled by an EAP in one agency. A self-referred couple arrived to see the employee assistance program counselor. They requested to come into the session together. The husband was thirty years old and the wife was twenty-seven. They had dated for four years before getting married, and at the time had been married for seven and one-half years and had one child, an eighteen-month-old son. The husband was a college graduate and his wife, who had a two-year junior college degree, was working as a medical secretary. When they sat down to talk with the counselor, they were both very nervous and uncomfortable. Nonetheless, after an atmosphere of trust and acceptance was established and the purpose of the assessment sessions was explained, toward the end of the first session the husband volunteered that he had had an affair. He stated he felt relieved after he was "found out" (after about three months), but still felt guilty and responsible—not only for his wife's pain and hurt but for the feelings of the other woman as well. The wife explained she indeed did feel hurt and betrayed, and she also felt very indignant in view of the fact that the other woman was a friend and coworker in the same medical complex where she was working.

Two days later, each of them came in for individual, one-hour sessions. She revealed that before her husband's affair, she had been feeling down, caught in the trap of work and child care, and possibly not as attentive to herself as she had been previously. He expressed feelings of inadequacy as a provider. He believed he should have been further along in his career and generally felt quite frustrated. He also indicated he had not shared these feelings with his wife (seeing them as his problem).

At that juncture, it appeared quite clear to the counselor that in the absence of other possible coexisting and/or confounding problems, they needed to see a marriage counselor to help them learn to communicate with each other more meaningfully and share with each other their feelings of inadequacy and being trapped. It is important to note that in view of their having had pulled apart from each other and his three-month affair, the counselor might have drawn a premature and inaccurate assessment that they were having "sexual-boredom problems." Had this been the case, inappropriate treatment could have been recommended, and this would have been very unfortunate. Nonetheless, an accurate assessment was gleaned, an appropriate referral was made, and the couple's readiness for help had been established by the counselor.

Through follow-up (with appropriate signed releases for follow-up information), the EAP counselor learned that the couple had seen a marriage therapist, had improved their interpersonal communications, and had regained the meaningfulness from their relationship that they both desired. Moreover, the husband was allowing himself to feel more adequate, and he was becoming more assertive as to his own needs. The wife became aware that she had not been taking care of herself and was not assertive to her own needs. She joined an inexpensive spa and began feeling "less down and more attractive." She started communicating her needs and feelings to her husband; in the process she received more attention from him and, importantly, was feeling more adequate.

This is somewhat of a typical marital situation that an EAP counselor may encounter. When clients come to an EAP with severe psychiatric problems, mental health concerns, and serious physical problems, the importance of thorough and accurate diagnosis, the use of appropriate medical and para-medical professionals, facilities, and centers in the community, and the facilitation of readiness for help can be even more demanding of the professional assessment and counseling skills of the case manager.[111]

## SUMMARY

Our objective throughout this chapter has been to present clear and straightforward discussions of major subjects in the area of stress that can be read with profit and interest by a person who does not necessarily possess a scientific background and training. We have tried to provide the reader with an orientation and introduction to the general topic of stress and some of its principal effects in terms of psychological, physiological, and social consequences and to acquaint the reader with some of the basic concepts and terminology relating to stress that are beginning to attain wider currency among law enforcement personnel. It is quite apparent that some stress factors are unique to policing; others are comparable to the sorts of stress encountered in other occupations and professions. However, the latter's meaning and significance for the present account lie in how they interact with the unique stress factors in policing to create special problems in coping effectively with the total stress situation.

There is little doubt that some unmistakable trends are developing in the study and prevention of stress-related problems in police work. It appears that in the future we will witness a greater number of law enforcement administrators directing their professional efforts and organizational resources toward the creation of services that can deal effectively with job-related health and personal problems. The organizational changes that result will manifest themselves in a number of ways. We can expect to see an increasing number of law enforcement agencies implementing psychological and psychiatric assessment of police applicants. This will be done in part to screen out the emotionally unstable applicant. Further, we will witness a dramatic increase in the number of law enforcement agencies that will make available to their personnel and their families in-house professional mental health specialists as well as referral services to community-based mental health specialists. We will also see a greater number of in-service training courses on this subject for both patrol officers and supervisors to assist them in recognizing and coping with job stress and the physical and psychological conditions associated with it.

This trend toward greater organizational sensitivity is indeed a welcome change and certainly long overdue. It is hoped that it will result in the reduction of alcohol- and drug-related problems, suicide, marital and other family problems, and premature retirements. In the final analysis, the police officers, family, and the organization will be the beneficiaries.

## DISCUSSION QUESTIONS

1. What is the general adaptation syndrome?

2. How do most people react to stress?

3. What types of changes take place in the body at the alarm stage?

4. Most law enforcement stressors can be grouped into four broad categories. What are these categories?

5. Alcohol-related problems among police officers manifest themselves in a number of ways. What are they?

6. What are some of the specific benefits reported by the Denver Police Department since it implemented its alcohol abuse program?

7. What three major principles have emerged from the many random drug cases decided by the courts?

8. What are the recognized medical uses of anabolic steroids?

9. What are the most common factors related to police suicide?

10. What are some of the typical warning signs that an officer may be contemplating suicide?

11. What are indicators of a potential Suicide by Cop (SbC)?

12. What is critical incident stress?

13. What are some of the most common characteristics of a critical incident?

14. What types of problems did the first women in law enforcement face that were not experienced by their male counterparts?

15. What steps can be taken to screen and select new officers to minimize the risk of hiring officers who may engage in domestic violence?

16. Ayres has concluded that eleven management and organizational issues cause considerable stress in police officers. What are these issues?

17. What are some of the benefits to employees of an employee assistance program?

# NOTES

1. K. Slogobin, "Stress," *New York Times Magazine,* November 20, 1977, 48–55.

2. For a comprehensive treatment of literature on police stress, see L. Territo and James D. Sewell, eds., *Stress Management in Law Enforcement* (Durham, N.C. Carolina Academic Press, 1999).

3. H. Selye, *Stress Without Distress* (Philadelphia: Lippincott, 1974), p. 60.

4. H. Basowitz, *Anxiety and Stress* (New York: McGraw-Hill, 1955), p. 7.

5. Ibid., p. 4.

6. Selye, *Stress Without Distress,* pp. 35–39.

7. J. C. Coleman, "Life Stress and Maladaptive Behavior," *The American Journal of Occupational Therapy,* 27:3 (1973), 170.

8. O. Tanner, *Stress* (New York: Time-Life Books, 1978).

9. For a comprehensive treatment of defensive behavior patterns, see J. M. Sawrey and C. A. Tilford, *Dynamics of Mental Health: The Psychology of Adjustment* (Boston: Allyn & Bacon, 1963), pp. 40–67.

10. J. G. Stratton, "Police Stress: An Overview," *Police Chief,* 45:4 (April 1978), 58.

11. "Compensation for Police Heart Attacks Allowed," *Crime Control Digest,* 9:10 (1975), 3.

12. Stratton: "Police Stress," 58.

13. W. H. Kroes, B. L. Margolis, and J. Hurrell, "Job Stress in Policemen," *Journal of Police Science and Administration,* 2:2 (1974), 145–55.

14. W. H. Kroes, *Society's Victim—The Policeman* (Springfield, Ill.: Charles C. Thomas, 1976).

15. T. Eisenberg, "Labor–Management Relations and Psychological Stress," *Police Chief,* 42:14 (1975), 54–58.

16. M. Reiser, "Stress, Distress, and Adaptation in Police Work," *Police Chief,* 43:1 (1976), 24–27.

17. M. Reiser, R. J. Sokol, and S. J. Saxe, "An Early Warning Mental Health Program for Police Sergeants," *Police Chief,* 39:6 (1972), 38–39.

18. M. Reiser, "A Psychologist's View of the Badge," *Police Chief,* 37:9 (1970), 24–27.

19. M. Reiser, "Some Organizational Stress on Policemen," *Journal of Police Science and Administration,* 2:2 (1974), 156–65.

20. M. D. Roberts, "Job Stress in Law Enforcement: A Treatment and Prevention Program," in *Job Stress and the Police Officer: Identifying Stress Reduction Techniques,* ed. W. H. Kroes and J. Hurrell (Washington, D.C.: U.S. Department of Health, Education, and Welfare, 1975), pp. 226–33.

21. Kroes et al., "Job Stress in Policemen," 145–155.

22. S. A. Somodevilla, et al., *Stress Management in the Dallas Police Department* (Dallas: Psychological Services Unit, Dallas, Texas, Police Department, 1978), p. 6.

23. Eisenberg, "Labor–Management Relations," 54–58.

24. John M. Violanti and Fred Aron, "Police Stressors: Variations in Perceptions Among Police Personnel," *Journal of Criminal Justice,* 23. 3 (1995), 287–294.

25. L. Dishlacoff, "The Drinking Cop," *Police Chief,* 43:1 (1976), 32.

26. Kroes and Hurrell, "Stress Awareness," in *Job Stress and the Police Officer,* p. 241.

27. Ibid., p. 241.

28. Ibid.

29. Dishlacoff, "The Drinking Cop," 39.

30. Ibid.

31. Ibid.

32. On this point, see Mary Niederberger, "Random Drug Test for Police Opposed," *Pittsburgh Press,* April 6, 1989; Rob Zeiger, "14 Fired Officers Returned to Duty," *Detroit News,* July 22, 1988; Shelly Murphy, "Court Upholds Drug Tests for Hub Cops," *Boston Herald,* May 13, 1989; Marilyn Robinson, "Drug Use Cuts Police Recruits by Nearly 50%," *Denver Post,* July 15, 1983; and David Schwab, "Supreme Court Backs Drug Tests for South Jersey Police Officers," *Newark Star-Ledger,* April 4, 1989.

33. J. J. Hurrell and R. Kliesmet, *Stress Among Police Officers* (Cincinnati, Ohio: National Institute of Occupational Safety and Health, 1984), p. 12.

34. *Newlun* v. *State Department of Retirement Systems,* 770 P.2d 1071 (Wash. App. 1989). Relatedly, *McElrath* v. *Kemp,* 27 Govt. Emp. Rel. Rep. (BNA) 605 (D.D.C. 1989), deals with an alcoholic employee who had relapses after being treated and was terminated, but was reinstated later.

35. Will Aitchison, *The Rights of Police Officers,* 3rd ed. (Portland, Ore.: Labor Relations Information System, 1996); pp. 228–233 is the source of the information in this paragraph, with restatement by the authors.

36. *Delaraba* v. *Nassau County Police,* 632 N. E.2d 1251 (N.Y. 1994).

37. C. Swanson, L. Gaines, and B. Gore, "Use of Anabolic Steroids," *FBI Law Enforcement Bulletin,* 60:8 (1991), 19–23. This discussion of anabolic steroids was adapted from this source.

38. R. F. Doerge, ed., *Wilson and Grisvold's Textbook of Organic Medicinal and Pharmaceutical Chemistry* (Philadelphia: Lippincott, 1982), pp. 679–684.

39. Schuckitt, "Weight Lifter's Folly: The Abuse of Anabolic Steroids," *Drug Abuse and Alc Newsletter,* 17:8 (1988); and Hecht, "Anabolic Steroids: Pumping Trouble," *FDA Consumer* (September 1981), pp. 12–15.

40. Couzens, "A Serious Drug Problem," *Newsday,* Nov. 26, 1988.

41. Doerge, *Wilson and Grisvold's.*

42. Couzens, "A Serious Drug Problem."

43. A. G. Gilman et al., *Goodman and Gilman's The Pharmacological Basis of Therapeutics* (New York: Macmillan, 1985), pp. 1440–1458.

44. Harrison G. Pope and David L. Katz, "Affective and Psychotic Symptoms Associated with Anabolic Steroid Use," *American Journal of Psychiatry,* 145:4 (1988), p. 488.

45. Ibid.

46. Charlier, "For Teens, Steroids May Be Bigger Issues than Cocaine Use," *Wall Street Journal,* Oct. 4, 1988.

47. Pope and Katz, "Affective and Psychotic Symptoms," 187–190.

48. Cowart, "Physician-Competitor's Advice to Colleagues: Steroid Users Respond to Education, Rehabilitation." *JAMA,* 257:4 (1987), 427–428.

49. Pope and Katz, "Affective and Psychotic Symptoms," pp. 489, 487.

50. Goldstein, p. 14.

51. J. M. Violanti, "The Mystery Within: Understanding Police Suicide," *FBI Bulletin* (February 1995), 19–23.

52. J. H. Burge, "Suicide and Occupation: A Review," *Journal of Vocational Behavior,* 21 (1982), 206–222.

53. J. Skolnick, *Police in America* (Boston: Educational Associates, 1975), p. 21.

54. J. M. Violanti, "Police Suicide on the Rise." *New York Trooper* (January 1984), pp. 18–19.

55. M. Wagner and R. Brzeczek, "Alcohol and Suicide: A Fatal Connection," *FBI Law Enforcement Bulletin,* March 1983, 7–15.

56. Slogobin, "Stress."

57. J. Schwartz and C. Schwartz, "The Personal Problems of the Police Officer: A Plea for Action," in *Job Stress and the Police Officer,* eds. W. Kroes and J. Hurrell (Washington, D.C.: U.S. Government Printing Office, 1976), pp. 130–141.

58. S. Labovitz and R. Hagehorn, "An Analysis of Suicide Rates Among Occupational Categories," *Sociological Inquiry,* 41 (1971), 67–72; also Z. Nelson and W. E. Smith, "The Law Enforcement Profession: An Incidence of High Suicide," *Omega,* 1 (1970), 293–299.

59. B. I. Danto, "Police Suicide," *Police Stress,* 1 (1978), 32–35.

60. G. Aussant, "Police Suicide," *Rural Canadian Mounted Police Gazette,* 46 (1984), 14–21.

61. Basowitz, *Anxiety and Stress.*

62. M. Heiman. "Suicide Among Police," *American Journal of Psychiatry,* 134 (1977), pp. 1286–1290.

63. P. Bonafacio, *The Psychological Effects of Police Work* (New York: Plenum Press, 1991); also S. Allen, "Suicide and Indirect Self-Destructive Behavior Among Police," in *Psychological Services for Law*

*Enforcement,* eds. J. Reese and H. Goldstein (Washington, D.C.: U.S. Government Printing Office, 1986).

64. Slogobin, "Stress."

65. P. Friedman, "Suicide Among Police: A Study of 93 Suicides Among New York City Policemen 1934–40," in *Essays of Self Destruction,* ed. E. S. Schneidman. (New York: Science House, 1968).

66. Basowitz, *Anxiety and Stress.*

67. C. W. Gaska, "The Rate of Suicide, Potential for Suicide, and Recommendations for Prevention Among Retired Police Officers," doctoral dissertation, Wayne State University, 1980.

68. T. E. Baker and J. P. Baker "Preventing Police Suicide," *FBI Law Enforcement Bulletin* (October 1996), 24–26.

69. See for example, J. M. Violanti, J. E. Vena, and J. R. Marshall, "Disease Risk and Mortality Among Police Officers: New Evidence and Contributing Factors," *Journal of Police Science and Administration,* 14 (1986), 17–23; and K. O. Hill and M. Clawson, "The Health Hazards of Street Level Bureaucracy Mortality Among the Police," *Journal of Police Science,* 16 (1988), 243–248.

70. Violanti, "Mystery Within," 22.

71. Daniel B. Kennedy, Robert Homant, and R. Thomas Hupp, "Suicide by Cop," *FBI Law Enforcement Bulletin,* 67:8 (1998), 21.

72. D. Scoville, "Getting to Pull the Trigger," *Police,* 22:11 (1998), 36.

73. Kennedy, Homant, and Hupp, "Suicide by Cop," 22.

74. Richard N. Jenet and Robert J. Segal, "Provoked Shooting by Police as a Mechanism for Suicide," *The American Journal of Forensic Medicine and Pathology,* 6 (March, 1985), 274–275.

75. Although the hotel parking lot incident involved an armed, uniformed security officer rather than a sworn police officer, it was believed that the expressive career felon would have exhibited the same behavior. Ironically the subject was eventually sentenced to death for the murder of the woman's husband, which had occurred only minutes before the security had arrived at the scene.

76. Clinton R. Vanzandt, "Suicide by Cop," *The Police Chief* (July 1993), 29.

77. Ibid., p. 30.

78. Theodore Blau, *Psychological Services for Law Enforcement* (New York: John Wiley & Sons, 1994), p. 164. With some restatement, this section is drawn from this work, pp. 164–170.

79. Ibid., p. 165.

80. Ibid., pp. 167–168.

81. Ibid., p. 165.

82. Ibid., pp. 165–166.

83. Walter Lippert and Eugene R. Ferrara, "The Cost of Coming Out on Top: Emotional Responses to Surviving the Deadly Battle," *FBI Law Enforcement Bulletin* (December 1981), 6–10. This discussion of post-shooting trauma was adapted from the source.

84. Frances A. Stillman, *Line of Duty Deaths: Survivor and Departmental Responses,* National Institute of Justice, Research Brief, January 1987. This discussion of line of duty deaths was adapted from this source.

85. Blau, *Psychological Services for Law Enforcement,* p. 213.

86. Meredith A. Bowman, *Female Specific Police Stress: A Study of the Stressors Experienced by Female Police Officers.* Unpublished master's thesis, Department of Criminology, University of South Florida, Tampa, Florida, 1999. Much of the information discussed regarding female stress resulted from research completed for this master's thesis.

87. K. Johnson, "Survey: Women Muscled Out by Bias, Harassment," *USA Today* (November 24, 1998), 1–2.

88. C. R. Swanson, L. Territo, and R. W. Taylor, *Police Administration* (New York: Macmillan, 1988), pp. 215–216.

89. Brenda Washington. "Stress Reduction Techniques for the Female Officer." in *Job Stress and the Police Officer,* eds., W. H. Kroes and J. J. Hurrel Jr. (Washington, D.C.: U.S. Government Printing Office, December 1975), p. 36.

90. Ibid., p. 36.

91. Bloch and Anderson as cited in J. Balkin. "Why Policemen Don't Like Policewomen," *Journal of Police Science and Administration,* 16 (1988), 29–38.

92. Sherman as cited in Balkin, "Why Policemen Don't Like."

93. J. A. Schwartz and C. B. Schwartz as cited in P. W. Lunneborg, *Women Police Officers: Current Career Profile.* (Springfield, Ill.: Charles C. Thomas, 1989).

94. Glaser and Saxe as cited in Lunneborg, *Women Police Officers.*

95. J. G. Wexler and D. D. Logan, "Sources of Stress Among Women Police Officers," *Journal of Police Science and Administration,* 11 (1983), 46–53.

96. Ibid.

97. N. K. Norvell, H. A. Hills, and M. R. Murrin, "Understanding Female and Male Law Enforcement Officers," *Psychology of Women Quarterly,* 17 (1993), 289–301.

98. J. M. Daum and C. M. Johns, "Police Work from a Woman's Perspective," *The Police Chief,* 19 (1994), 339–348.

99. L. D. Lott, "Deadly Secrets: Violence in the Police Family," *FBI Law Enforcement Bulletin* (November 1995), 12–15. This discussion was adapted from this article.

100. "Police Officer Domestic Violence," *Concepts In Issue* Papers Washington, D.C.: (Violence Against Women Officers, Office Justice Programs and Office of Community-Oriented Policing. U.S. Department of Justice), pp. 3–5.

101. Wayne Anderson, David Swenson, and Daniel Clay, *Stress Management for Law Enforcement Officers* (Englewood Cliffs, N.J.: Prentice Hall, 1995), p. 221.

102. Ibid., p. 222.

103. Ibid., p. 220.

104. Many of these factors are identified in Robert W. Shearer, "Police Officer Stress: New Approaches for Effective Coping," *The Journal of California Law Enforcement,* 25:4 (1991), pp. 97–104.

105. Max Bromley and William Blount, "Criminal Justice Practitioners," in *Employee Assistance Programs,* eds. in William R. Hutchison, Jr., and William G. Emener (Springfield, Ill: Charles C. Thomas Publisher, 1997), p. 400.

106. J. T. Reese, *The History of Police Psychological Service* (Washington, D.C.: U.S. Department of Justice, 1987).

107. C. Milofsky, E. Astrov, and M. Martin, "Stress Management Strategy for U.S. Customs Workers," *EAP Digest,* 14:6 (1994), 46–48.

108. Reese, *History of Police Psychological Service.*

109. Bromley and Blount, "Criminal Justice Practitioners," p. 401.

110. Fred Dickman and William G. Emener, "Union Involvement: A Key Ingredient to Successful Employee Assistance Programs," in *Employee Assistance Programs,* eds. William S. Hutchison and William G. Emener (Springfield, Ill: Charles C. Thomas Publishing, 1997), pp. 100–104.

111. William G. Emener and Fred Dickman, "Case Management, Caseload Management, and Case Recording and Documentation: Professional EAP Service," in *Employee Assistance Programs,* eds. William R. Hutchison and William G. Emener, (Springfield, Ill: Charles C. Thomas Publisher, 1997), pp. 121–122.

## INTRODUCTION

No single force in the past 50 years has had as much impact on the administration of police agencies as collective bargaining by officers. Police unions represent a major force that must be reckoned with by police managers. This chapter deals with the powerful phenomenon of collective bargaining under the following headings: (1) the unionization of the police, (2) the impact of unions, (3) the basis for collective bargaining, (4) police employee organizations, (5) establishing the bargaining relationship, (6) conducting negotiations, (7) grievances, (8) job actions, (9) use of surveillance, and (10) administrative reaction to job actions. This coverage provides a broad overview with supporting details, sufficient to understand the topic and also to create an appreciation for both its complexities and subtleties.

# —10—

# LABOR RELATIONS

*"You, a lowly policeman is going to tell me
how to run my department! . . . Get out!"
and you had to go; he hated me. . . .*

RANK-AND-FILE ORGANIZATION LEADER JOHN CASSESE
ON AN EARLY MEETING WITH NEW YORK CITY
POLICE COMMISSIONER KENNEDY.

## THE UNIONIZATION OF THE POLICE

From 1959 through the 1970s, a number of events combined to foster public-sector collective bargaining. These significant forces were (1) the needs of labor organizations, (2) the reduction of legal barriers, (3) police frustration with the perceived lack of support for their "war on crime," (4) personnel practices in police agencies, (5) salaries and benefits, (6) an increase in violence directed at police, and (7) the success of the groups in making an impact through collective action.[1]

**The Needs of Labor Organizations**

The attention of labor organizations was devoted almost entirely to the private sector until the 1960s. However, as the opportunity to gain new members became increasingly constrained because of the extensive organization of industrial workers, unions cast about for new markets, and statistics such as these impressed them:

> Public service is the most rapidly growing major sector of employment in the United States. In the last 30 years public employment has tripled, growing from 4.2 million to 13.1 million employees. Today nearly one out of five workers in the United States is on a government payroll.[2]

Thus, as with any organization that achieves its primary objective, labor groups redefined their sphere of interest to include public employees. Concurrently, there were stirrings among public employees to use collective action to improve their lot.

**The Reduction of Legal Barriers**

Although workers in the private sector had been given the right to bargain collectively under the federal National Labor Relations Act of 1935, it was another quarter of a century before the first state enacted even modest bargaining rights for public employees. Beginning with the granting of public sector collective bargaining rights in Wisconsin in 1959, many of the legal barriers that had been erected in the wake of the Boston police strike of 1919 began to tumble. Other states that also extended such rights to at least some classes of employees at an early date included California (1961) and Connecticut, Delaware, Massachusetts, Michigan, Oregon, Washington, and Wyoming, all in 1965. Many other states followed this lead, particularly from 1967 to 1974.[3] President John F. Kennedy granted limited collective bargaining rights to federal workers in 1962 by Executive Order 10988. The courts, too, were active in removing barriers; for example, in *Atkins* v. *City of Charlotte* (1969), the U.S. district court struck down a portion of a North Carolina statute prohibiting being or becoming a union member as an infringement on the First Amendment right to free association.[4] While *Atkins* involved firefighters, the federal courts reached similar conclusions involving Atlanta police officers in *Melton* v. *City of Atlanta* (1971)[5] and a Colorado deputy sheriff in *Lontine* v. *VanCleave* (1973).[6]

Historically, the police have felt isolated in their effort to control crime. This stems from two factors: perceived pubic hostility and the impact of the due process revolution.

**Police Frustration with Support for the War on Crime**

The police perceive a great deal more public hostility than actually exists. Illustrative of this is a survey of one big-city department, which found that over 70 percent of the officers had an acute sense of citizen hostility or contempt.[7] In contrast, a survey conducted by the National Opinion Research Center revealed that 77 percent of the respondents felt that the police were doing a "very good" or "pretty good" job of protecting people in their neighborhoods, and a 1965 Gallup poll showed that 70 percent of the public had a great deal of respect for the police.[8] These data notwithstanding, the police saw the public as hostile, and the most persuasive "evidence" of this emerged in the attempts to create civilian review boards, which carried several latent messages to police officers. First, it created anger with its implied allegation that the police could not, or would not, keep their own house in order. Second, it fostered the notion that politicians were ready to "throw the police to wolves" and thus were part of "them."

Particularly among street-level officers, the reaction of the police to the whirlwind of Supreme Court decisions, discussed in Chapter 3, was one of dismay at being "handcuffed" in attempts to control crime. It tended to alienate the police from the Supreme Court and to contribute toward a general feeling that social institutions that should support the police effort in combatting crime were, instead, at odds with it.

Past practices become precedent, precedent becomes tradition, and tradition, in turn, becomes the mighty anchor of many organizations. By the late 1960s, the tendency to question the appropriateness of certain traditions was pervasive. Police rank-and-file members were no exception. This tendency was heightened by the increased educational achievement of police officers. Although management's general performance was often judged to be suspect, traditional personnel practices were the greatest concern, as these directly affected the individual officer.

**Personnel Practices**

Among the practices that were most distasteful to rank-and-file members were the requirement to attend, unpaid, a thirty-minute roll call immediately before the eight-hour tour of duty; uncompensated court attendance during off-duty time; short-notice changes in shift assignments; having to return to the station from home for minor matters, such as signing reports, without pay or compensatory time for such periods; favoritism in work assignments and se-lection for attendance at prestigious police training schools; and arbitrary dis-ciplinary procedures. Gradually, the gap between officers and management widened. Officers began turning to employee organizations to rectify collec-tively the shortcomings of their circumstances. Subsequently, the solidarity of police officers was to prove of great benefit to employee organizations.

In addition to providing material for ferment through illegal, ill-conceived, abrasive, or insensitive general personnel practices, police managers often un-wittingly contributed to the resolve and success of police unions by their treat-ment of leaders of police employee associations. In Atlanta, the chief of police transferred the president of the Fraternal Order of Police fifty-one times in forty-five days for his outspokenness,[9] and in Boston, Dick MacEachern, founder and president of the then fledgling Police Patrolmen's Association, was transferred repeatedly from precinct to precinct and Mayor White subsequently refused to sign MacEachern's disability pension for the same reason.[10] Such ac-tions provide free publicity, create a martyr (an essential for many social move-ments), put the leaders in contact with people they ordinarily would not meet, increase group cohesiveness, and provide compelling confirmation in the minds of rank-and-file members why they need and should join a union.

## Salaries and Benefits

As did other government workers in the 1960s, police officers felt that their salaries, fringe benefits, and working conditions were not adequate. In 1961, mining production workers were averaging $111 a week in earnings, lithogra-phers $114, tire and inner-tube producers $127, and telephone line construc-tion workers $133,[11] whereas the pay of police officers averaged far less. Even by 1965, the salary range for patrol officer in the larger cities, those with more than 100,000 in population, was only between $5,763, and $6,919.[12] The rank-and-file members believed increasingly that, if what was fairly theirs would not be given willingly, they would fight for it. In New York City, the Patrolmen's Benevolent Association (PBA) was believed to have been instrumental, from 1958 to 1969, in increasing entry-level salaries from $5,800 to $11,000 per year; obtaining longevity pay, shift differential pay, and improved retirement benefits; and increasing the death benefit from $400 to $16,500.[13] In 1968, the Boston PBA, in negotiating its first contract—which required mediation—obtained in-creased benefits for its members, such as an annual increase of $1,010, time and a half for all overtime including court appearances, and twelve paid holidays.[14]

## Violence Directed at the Police

In 1964, there were 9.9 assaults per 100 officers; in 1969, this figure rose to 16.9. Before 1968, the killing of police officers by preplanned ambushes was unheard of; in that year, there were seven such incidents.[15] The escalating violence had considerable psychological impact on the police, who saw themselves as sym-bolic targets of activists attacking institutional authority. Rank-and-file members began pressing for body armor, special training, the placement of special weapons in police cars, and sharply increased death benefits.

## The Success of Other Groups

During the 1960s the police witnessed mass demonstrations on college cam-puses, which used many of the tactics associated with the civil rights move-ment. Among the campus demonstrations that were highly publicized were the University of California at Berkeley (1964–1965), the University of Chicago (1965), Columbia University (1968), and San Francisco State College (1969). By 1970, campus demonstrations reached the point that, within ten days of President Richard Nixon's announcement to invade enemy sanctuaries in

Cambodia, a total of 448 campuses were either shut down or otherwise affected by campus unrest.[16]

The analogy was not lost on the police: if concerted action could impact foreign policy, it could also be a potent force in winning benefits for the police. Moreover, the police began supplying their own success models. In 1966, Mayor Lindsay of New York City appointed an independent Civilian Review Board. In resistance, the PBA filed a petition to have the issue put to a citywide referendum and in the ensuing publicity campaign spent an estimated $250,000 to $1,000,000 to defeat the measure, not a small feat as both Senators Robert Kennedy and Jacob Javits had allied themselves with the mayor.[17]

## THE IMPACT OF UNIONS

Despite the fact that police unionism as a viable force has had a history of less than 30 years, its impact has been considerable. Traditionally, public officials in general and law enforcement executives in particular have opposed the idea of police unions. A 1944 publication of the International Association of Chiefs of Police (IACP) concluded that police unions could accomplish nothing.[18] In a 1967 address to the State House at Annapolis, Maryland, Baltimore Police Commissioner Donald Pomerleau concluded that "a police union is not compatible with police responsibility."[19]

When such objections are distilled and analyzed, what often remains is the fear that police unions will result ultimately in reduced executive prerogatives (see Box 10-1). There can be little serious question that such fears have a reasonable and factual basis. As co-equal to management at the bargaining table, police unions represent a new power center that has in many instances effectively diminished management's unilateral and sometimes ill-considered exercise of control. In some matters administrators have simply made bad bargains, giving away prerogatives vital to the ability to manage properly. Far more difficult to assess are the consequences to the times that police executives have failed to act, or have acted differently, in anticipation of the union's stand.

## BOX 10-1

### Iowa Ticket Probe Gets New Venue

### Judge keeps chief from questioning officers until the Council Bluffs police union can file a grievance with the state

by Patrick Strawbridge
World-Herald Staff Writer

The Council Bluffs police chief's attempt to question his department's officers about the voiding of traffic tickets is headed for arbitration before the State Public Employee Relations Board.

Pottawattamie County District Judge James Heckerman ruled Wednesday that a temporary restraining order against the chief will be dissolved Jan. 31. He allowed the order to remain in place for five days so that the department's police union, which objects to the scope of the investigation, can file a grievance.

The dispute over the chief's actions stems from an ongoing investigation into the voiding of traffic tickets by Council Bluffs police officers. One officer has been placed on administrative leave, and Police Chief James Wilkinson said the department is still trying to determine whether other officers wrongly voided traffic tickets or knew that others were.

*(continued)*

## BOX 10-1 (continued)

As part of his effort to determine the extent of the practice, Wilkinson prepared a written survey to be given to each officer in December. When the department's police union found out about the survey, it sought and obtained a judge's order preventing Wilkinson from distributing the survey.

Police Detective Keith Jones, the union's president, said he feared that innocent officers were being unfairly involved in the investigation, and objected to Wilkinson's demands that everybody answer the questions or face discipline.

"We just don't want all 116 officers dragged into this," Jones said. "This puts a black mark on the whole department."

The restraining order remained in place for six weeks, until Wednesday's hearing. After listening to testimony from Wilkinson and Jones, Heckerman decided that the union had not exhausted its administra-

tive remedies to stop the survey. So he told the union to file a grievance to the policy and take it up with the Public Employee Relations Board, and told the city not to discipline any officers for refusing to answer the questions while that grievance is being pursued.

The end result: the survey remains unanswered and the union will keep fighting for the right of officers to not answer the questions.

"I don't believe they have that right," Wilkinson said during Wednesday's hearing.

Any information that came from the survey could be used in internal investigations and prompt disciplinary action but could not be used in a court of law. Therefore, Wilkinson said, the city isn't asking anybody to give up a right against self-incrimination.

*Source: Omaha World-Herald,* January 27, 2000.

---

Police unions have impacted on public policy decisions in many ways. For example, in various cities they have thwarted the use of civilian review boards; advocated the election of "law and order" candidates; resisted the replacement of two-officer cars with one-officer cars; litigated to avoid layoffs; lobbied for increased budgets, especially for raises; caused the removal of chiefs and other high-ranking commanders; advocated the elimination of radar guns from patrol vehicles because of potential adverse health risks associated with their use; and opposed annexation and the firing of union members (see Box 10-2).

Police labor organizers often maintain that there is only one color that counts, the color of the uniform. Despite this low-pitched plea for solidarity among rank-and-file members, police employee associations and unions are believed by some observers to have contributed to racial tensions. The president-elect of the Boston Police Patrolmen's Association told a forum on crime and violence that "if black men want to go out and fornicate and don't want to take care of their nests . . . then we have a problem." The comment set off a firestorm of reaction from both African Americans and whites.[20] Other instances that have served to heighten racial tensions include the opposition of police unions to civilian review boards and the use of their support to help elect white candidates running against African Americans. Such incidents have created the feeling among African Americans that white-dominated employee organizations are insensitive to issues affecting minorities. Consequently, African Americans have tended to form their own organizations to address issues of importance to them.

It is incautious to make categorical statements about the impact of unionism on police professionalization, as it has had both positive and negative effects. Until the mid-1960s, police professionalization was conceived of as including all sworn officers. To the extent to which unionism drives a wedge between those at the lower reaches of the department and management, it negates police professionalization as it has been conceived of for many years. In addition, professionals traditionally do not participate in labor movements. However, as many professional groups, such as the American Association for

BOX 10-2

## Reno Panel Reaffirms Officers

**Associated Press**

RENO—The city Civil Service Commission is standing by its decision not to fire two police officers who have been convicted of misdemeanor domestic violence.

City officials said the commission's action on Thursday sets the stage for a court battle to force the firings of officers Lynn Drake and Mark Markiewicz.

"We're going to court," said Rick Gonzales, the city's labor relations manager. "We will proceed with the layoffs."

Police union president Ron Dreher said any move against the officers would be fought.

"The city has no authority to lay them off," Dreher said. "They would be violating their own policies, which say the civil service commission has the sole authority to do a layoff.

"The city can't just ignore it's own rules."

Drake and Markiewicz have been on restricted duty for more than two years, when passage of an amendment to the federal Brady Bill made it illegal for anyone convicted of domestic violence charges to carry a firearm.

Four years ago, Drake admitted to disturbing the peace after his ex-wife filed a claim that his discipline of their daughter was abusive. Markiewicz, found guilty in the battery of his ex-wife, contended he used a special tactic to get a knife away from her when she threatened suicide.

Police Chief Jerry Hoover has said the two men are good officers but need to be replaced with officers who are legally able to carry guns.

Commission Chairman Bill Moon cast the tie-breaking vote on Thursday to keep the officers employed.

"Our position says we don't feel the city properly handled the situation," Moon said. "We couldn't in a clear conscious agree to lay them off."

City Attorney Patricia Lynch, who appealed for a rehearing after commissioners earlier rejected the layoffs, said commissioners overstepped their authority.

*Source: Las Vegas Review-Journal, May 8, 1999.*

the Advancement of Science, the American Society of Civil Engineers, the American Nurses Association, and the American Association of University Professors (whose members have traditionally been considered professionals), come to act like unions, there may be some redefinition of the relationship between a profession and unionism. The differences between labor and management have also served to foster a high degree of professionalization in the administration of police departments to deal with the existence and demands of unions.

Where the objectives of the union and the police administrator are the same, the union can be a powerful ally. Even when they are not the same, the union may line up behind a chief and provide support if the cost to the union is not too great. In such instances it may be simply a case of a display of police solidarity, the fact that the union likes a city manager or mayor even less than it likes the chief, the desire to improve the union's image by supporting something from which there is no apparent gain, or for some other reason. Also, when the union exercises its considerable political muscle, it can defeat important policy and program initiatives by the police chief, such as halting the use of one-officer cars as an alternative to two-officer units. It is here that the union confronts the police executive at a basic point: the control of the police department. One chief left a unionized department to take a similar position in another state that did not allow public-sector collective bargaining. Over a period of time the city formerly employing him had given up control over many administrative matters as a substitute for demands made by the union for economic gains. As the chief himself put it: "I realized I had to get out because the union could do two things I couldn't; it could stop the department and it could start it." Although an extreme example, it does bring clearly into

**FIGURE 10-1.** Instructor from the Management Science Unit, Federal Bureau of Investigation Academy, addressing police executives at a labor relations seminar sponsored by the Massachusetts Criminal Justice Training Council. (Photo courtesy of the Federal Bureau of Investigation.)

focus the issue of who controls the department for what purpose. Moreover, it squarely raises the issue of accountability: if police chiefs control increasingly less of their departments, to what extent can they be properly held accountable? Finally, presuming that a chief wants to administer for the common good, for the safety of the general public, but cannot do so, then for whose benefit is the department being operated?

## THE BASIS FOR COLLECTIVE BARGAINING

Because each state is free to decide whether and which public-sector employees will have collective bargaining rights under what terms, there is considerable variety in such arrangements. In states with comprehensive public-sector collective bargaining laws, the administration of the statute is the responsibility of a state agency that carries a designation such as the Public Employees Relation Commission (PERC) or the Public Employees Relations Board (PERB). Despite the variety in state laws, they can be summarized by three basic models: (1) binding arbitration, 2) meet and confer, and 3) "bargaining not required."[21] Table 10-1 reflects the use of these models in the various states.

**The Binding Arbitration Model**   The binding arbitration model is used in 25 states. There, public employees are given the right to bargain with their employers. If the bargaining reaches an impasse, the matter is submitted to a neutral arbitrator who decides what the terms and conditions of the new collective bargaining agreement will be, usually applying standards mandated by state statute.[22] In all states in which binding arbitration is used, there is an accompanying ban on the right to strike.[23]

| State | Binding Arbitration Model | Meet-and-Confer Model | Bargaining-Not-Required Model | State | Binding Arbitration Model | Meet-and-Confer Model | Bargaining-Not-Required Model |
|---|---|---|---|---|---|---|---|
| Alabama | | | X | Montana | X | | |
| Alaska | X | | | Nebraska | | | X |
| Arizona | | | X | Nevada | X | | |
| Arkansas | | | X | New Hampshire | X | | |
| California | | X | | New Jersey | X | | |
| Colorado | | | X | New Mexico | | X | |
| Connecticut | X | | | New York | X | | |
| Delaware | X | | | North Carolina | | | X |
| District of Columbia | X | | | North Dakota | | | X |
| Florida | | X | | Ohio | X | | |
| Georgia | | | X | Oklahoma | X | | |
| Hawaii | X | | | Oregon | X | | |
| Idaho | | | X | Pennsylvania | X | | |
| Illinois | X | | | Rhode Island | X | | |
| Indiana | | | X | South Carolina | | | X |
| Iowa | X | | | South Dakota | | | X |
| Kansas | X | | | Tennessee | | | X |
| Kentucky | | | X | Texas | | | X |
| Louisiana | | | X | Utah | | | X |
| Maine | X | | | Vermont | X | | |
| Maryland | | | X | Virginia | | | X |
| Massachusetts | X | | | Washington | X | | |
| Michigan | X | | | West Virginia | | | X |
| Minnesota | X | | | Wisconsin | X | | |
| Mississippi | | | X | Wyoming | | | X |
| Missouri | | | X | | | | |

*Source:* Will Aitchison, *The Rights of Police Officers,* 3rd ed. (Portland, Oregon: Labor Relations Information System, 1996), p. 10.

Public employers have challenged such laws as an unconstitutional delegation of legislative authority and as interfering with the home rules status of local governments; however, almost uniformly the courts have not upheld these challenges.[24]

Only three states use the meet-and-confer model, which grants so few rights to public employees that it is also referred to as the "collective begging" model. Like the binding arbitration model, officers in meet-and-confer states have the right to organize and to select their own bargaining representatives.[25] Public employers are required to meet promptly and in person for a reasonable period of time with the officers' labor organization, to try to agree on matters that are permissible topics of discussions, and to bargain in good faith.[26] When an impasse is reached in meet-and-confer states, police officers are at a considerable disadvantage. Their only legal choices are to accept the employer's best offer; try to influence the offer through political tactics, (see Box 10-3), such

**The Meet-and-Confer Model**

as appeals for public support; or take a permissible job action.[27] States that give public employees weak or no collective bargaining rights experience more labor strife,[28] such as work slowdowns during which officers write very few traffic tickets (which deprives the employer of revenue) and epidemics of the "blue flu" (sick-outs).

**The "Bargaining Not Required" Model**

The twenty-two states that follow this mode either do not statutorily require or do not allow collective bargaining by public employees (see Box 10-3).[29] In the majority of these states, laws permitting officers to engage in collective bargaining simply have not been passed.[30] In a few states, such as Indiana, the courts have struck down collective bargaining laws passed by the legislature.[31] The attorney generals in several of these states have issued opinions, in the absence of state statutes on the subject, that prohibit public-sector collective bargaining. Yet, in other of these states, local units of government have elected to voluntarily bargain with their police officers.[32] This bargaining may be conducted on a verbal or "handshake" basis or as a written agreement, an executive order, a resolution by the local legislative body, or a local ordinance.

**Closed, Open, and Agency Shops**

States with collective bargaining laws must also address the issue of whether an individual employee must be a member of a union that represents his or her class of employees in a particular organization. In a closed shop, employees must be dues-paying members or they will be terminated by the employer. Open shops have exactly the opposite arrangement; employees have a choice whether or not to join, even though the union has an obligation to represent them. Agency shops take the middle ground: if employees are not dues-paying members, they must pay their fair share of applicable union costs.

## BOX 10-3

### Police, Firemen Share KC Picket Line March

by Melissa Moy
The Kansas City Star

About 100 protesters representing police officers and firefighters picketed Monday in favor of collective bargaining.

The protesters from the Missouri State Fraternal Order of Police and the International Association of Fire Fighters Local No. 42 demonstrated outside the Hyatt Regency Crown Center hotel, where the Missouri Municipal League was holding its annual convention.

The league, an association of Missouri cities and towns seeking to improve relations with state government, is offering training sessions and seminars for city officials and employees at the convention.

Protesters organized by the Fraternal Order of Police seek collective bargaining rights and want the league to stop using tax dollars to lobby against them in the state legislature, said Thomas Mayer, state president of the order.

The municipal league disagreed.

Gary Markenson, executive director of the league, said the Fraternal Order of Police wanted outside arbitration for benefits and conditions. He said the use of a third party was in opposition to the league's beliefs.

"Cities are great supporters of public employees," Markenson said. "They give them everything they can."

Mayer said: "This (the picket line) is just the very first action unless we get some kind of commitment from them to stop lobbying against us with tax dollars."

*Source:* Reprinted by permission of *The Kansas City Star,* September 14, 1999.

Knowledge of the various police employee organizations is essential to an administrator because these organizations tend to have their own philosophies and orientations. It is somewhat difficult to identify police employee organizations and those for whom they bargain accurately because one organization will succeed another and groups of police officers may choose to drop their affiliation with one union in favor of another.[33] Consequently, any such description is not unlike a photograph in that it depicts situations at a given time. In general, examples of organizations that seek to organize police officers may be divided into two broad categories: unions whose parent is an industrial union, and independent, police-only unions. The "police-only" designation, as discussed later in this chapter, is not always as exclusive of other types of employees as it might first appear.

The AFL-CIO has a number of unions through which police officers can be represented in the collective bargaining process, including the American Federation of State, County, and Municipal Employees (AFSCME), the International Union of Police Associations (IUPA), the Service Employees International (SEIU), the Communications Workers of America (CWA), the American Federation of Government Employees (AFGE), and the International Brotherhood of Teamsters (IBT).

## Industrial Unions as the Parent Organization

## AFSCME

AFSCME, founded in 1936, is the largest all-public employee organization with an industrial union as a parent. In 2000, it represented 35,000 police officers nationally with major strength in Connecticut, Illinois, and Wisconsin, and growing strength in Western states such as Utah and North Dakota.[34] One of its earliest members was the Portland (Oregon) Police Association, which was chartered in 1942.

When fewer than 10 police officers are to be represented, AFSCME places them in locals with a mix of different types of public employees, such as a city-wide local. AFSCME has had good success in creating state-level, police-only councils such as AFSCME's Council 15, Connecticut Council of Police Unions, which represents some 52 municipal departments. A similar situation exists with respect to the State of Hawaii Organization of Police Officers (SHOPO), AFSCME Local 3900.

## IUPA

IUPA grew out of the National Conference of Police Associations (NCPA), which was founded in 1954 to foster the exchange of information among police employee organizations. Twelve years later, NCPA evolved into the International Conference of Police Associations (ICPA) when some Canadian police associations linked up with it. By 1973, ICPA had decided to become a union and charter police locals. By 1978, it claimed to represent 182,000 officers in 400 locals. At ICPA's Toronto, Canada, convention in the spring of 1978, the membership fought about whether to affiliate with the AFL-CIO. At ICPA's winter meeting in 1978 in Phoenix, their president Ed Kiernan and 28 regional vice-presidents resigned to form a new organization, the International Union of Police Associations (IUPA). This defection, along with large numbers of dues-paying members (which resulted in $300,000 in debts), doomed ICPA. The AFL-CIO originally rejected IUPA's request for a charter, but finally granted one to the organization in 1979. Although IUPA got off to a fast start, by 1983 its numbers had dwindled to about 10,000. An effort to revitalize

IUPA was successful, and by early 1997 it represented 80,000 officers nationally. By 2000, IUPA had 480 locals, including the Virginia Coalition of Police and Sheriffs, the Salt Lake Police Association, the Yonkers Police Department, the Minot Police Employees' Union, and the Los Angeles County Professional Peace Officers Association (see Box 10-4).

**SEIU**    Historically, SEIU attempted to organize officers in two ways. The first was through a subordinate organization, the National Union of Police Officers (NUPO), which bolted from SEIU. NUPO subsequently became a very marginal player in unionizing the police and is out of existence, according to SEIU officials. The second way SEIU organized the police was to charter police locals.

In 1970, the then-independent International Brotherhood of Police Officers (IBPO), which had been founded in Rhode Island in 1964, affiliated with the National Assembly of Government Employees (NAGE). NAGE then affiliated with SEIU in 1982. Presently, SEIU largely relates to police officers through IBPO. Traditionally, IBPO's strength has been in New England and in Western states. SEIU also has some police officers in its State Employee Associations (SEAs). For example, New Hampshire's SEA, SEIU Local 1984, includes the Bedford and Keene Police Departments. However, IBPO is the predominate SEIU means of organizing the police for collective bargaining.

**CWA**    The Communications Workers of America organizes police officers for the purpose of collective bargaining through a subordinate organization, the National Coalition of Public Safety Officers (NCPSO). Florida, Texas, Maryland, West Virginia, New York, New Jersey, Iowa, Georgia, New Mexico, and Arizona were areas of NCPSO strength in early 2000 with some 35,000 members.

One of NCPSO's largest statewide groups is the Florida Police Benevolent Association (FPBA). In 1963, the Dade County (Miami area) Police Benevolent Association (DCPBA) was formed. As a result of expertise gained there, former DCPBA leaders established FPBA in 1972. In 1996, the FPBA partnered with

## BOX 10-4

### Houston Police Officers' Union Affiliates with the I.U.P.A.

The International Union of Police Associations, AFL-CIO, would like to welcome the newest affiliate, the Houston Police Officers' Union. On October 4, 1999, the Houston Police Officers' Union (HPOU) voted in a constitutional election to affiliate with the I.U.P.A. As Local 2, the HPOU brings more than 4,700 new members to the International. This is the result of a year long negotiation process designed to unify all of Houston's Police Officers into one powerful union under the AFL-CIO umbrella.

The I.U.P.A. is elated by the affiliation of the Houston Police Officers' Union. This affiliation will truly empower the police officers of Houston and strengthen the I.U.P.A.'s presence in Texas. HPOU President Hans Marticiuc called the passage of the

package, "the final step in our journey to unify our department. The issue was to build minority caucuses within the HPOU structure to give Hispanic, African American, and Asian officers a meaningful voice in the union." The HPOU is a progressive and powerful union and will control the upcoming negotiations with the city in 2000.

Over the past several years the I.U.P.A. has affiliated several large law enforcement associations under the AFL-CIO umbrella including the Boston Police Patrolmen's Association, the Santa Ana Police Officers Associations, and the Ohio State Troopers. Currently, the I.U.P.A. is seeking a certification election to represent the Florida State Law Enforcement Officers. This is truly an exciting time of growth and prominence for the I.U.P.A.'s membership.

*Source:* http://www.sDDi/IUPA/leadstry0.html.

NCPSO to offer its members benefits provided by the AFL-CIO. This arrangement meant the end of FPBA's status as an independent, "police-only" union. Additionally, FPBA picked up the protection of the AFL-CIO's "no-raiding" policy, which forbids one AFL-CIO union from trying to take existing members from another AFL-CIO union. The no-raiding policy was important to FPBA because it had just expended $250,000 in fighting off an AFL-CIO union trying to take its members away and FPBA saw this as opening shot in a long line of expensive battles that it wished to avoid. FPBA has charters, which provide almost all of their own expertise in labor relations, and chapters, which are more dependent on FPBA's staff for assistance in contract negotiations, grievance hearing representation, and other related matters. Another large NCPSO state organization is the Combined Law Enforcement Associations of Texas (CLEAT), with a membership of some 16,000. Peoria, Arizona, is home to one of the smaller unions, Local 7077, AZ-COPS (see Box 10-5). It came into being as a result of many of the forces that have historically led to police unionization: comparatively lower pay, intermittent salary increases, "good old boy" promotions, and inconsistent discipline.[35]

**AFGE** Among federal workers, AFGE, which was founded in 1932, is AFSCME's counterpart. In 1997, it represented personnel from a number of federal agencies, including the Border Patrol (Council 83) and the U.S. Marshal's Office (Council 210). Among other groups it represents are U.S. Department of Agriculture food inspectors, personnel at the Kennedy Space Center, and workers in the Social Security Administration. Like AFSCME, AFGE's members are public employees.

**IBT** The International Brotherhood of Teamsters (IBT) has had some interest in organizing officers for about 30 years. More recently, it has been more aggressive in such efforts. Historically, the IBT placed officers in mixed public–private

## BOX 10-5

### Peoria (Arizona) Police Officer Association Promotes Awareness Of Line-Of-Duty Deaths

In 1998, COPS received a letter from Mrs. Dolly Craig of Philadelphia, PA, stating she'd be putting blue lights in her window that holiday season. The lights would remember her son-in-law, Danny Gleason, a Philadelphia (PA) Police Officer who was killed in the line of duty in 1986, and her daughter, Pam, Danny's widow, who was killed in an auto accident earlier in 1988. She thought others might like to share her idea. Dolly's idea is now her legacy.

COPS shared the idea with others. Now thousands of blue lights shine nationwide during the holiday season to honor and remember those law enforcement officers who have given their lives in service to the profession. The blue lights also thank those officers who continue to work America's dangerous streets each and every day of the year.

Law enforcement agencies sponsor holiday parties for the disadvantaged, the elderly, the infirm. What will we do "for our own" this holiday season? Will your agency decorate in blue lights this holiday season? Will your agency remember the surviving families of your fallen officers this holiday season? Will your agency send a special greeting card? Or have a special holiday floral arrangement with one blue candle delivered to their home? Will you invite them to your agency party and then insure they feel welcomed? Will your agency send Santa Claus to visit younger children?

Concerns of Police Survivors
www.nationalcops.org
cops@nationalcops.org

*Source: Behind the Badge,* official publication of the Peoria (Arizona) Police Officers Association, December 1999.

membership locals or in all-public employee locals, such as Teamsters Local 633, which represents 20 law enforcement agencies in New Hampshire and some school principals.

**Independent Police Associations**

Independent police associations, which may be national, state, or local in nature, have two important characteristics: first, they are not affiliated with any other union, and second, they represent, with a few exceptions (such as civilians working in police departments and correctional officers), only police officers. Two forces foster the existence of independent police associations that represent officers for the purpose of collective bargaining. The first is that police officers believe their responsibilities are so unique that they must stand alone. The second force springs from the fact that some jurisdictions, such as New York City, have laws that grant collective bargaining rights to police officers only if they are not affiliated with a national labor union or a labor organization that advocates the right to strike.[36] Thus, New York City police officers are represented by the independent Patrolmen's Benevolent Association.

The largest independent police association is the Fraternal Order of Police (FOP), which in 2000 had approximately 280,000 members. However, the FOP does not bargain for all of its members. Founded in 1915, the FOP's strength is in the northeastern, southern, and midwestern states. Because engaging in collective bargaining was something in which the FOP did not want to engage, they moved into that area somewhat reluctantly. In many localities, the FOP remains a fraternal organization, which was its original purpose, while in others it is a union. For example, Capitol City FOP Lodge 141 bargains for sworn members—with the exception of some higher ranks—of Michigan State University's Department of Police.

The New Jersey Policemen's Benevolent Association (NJPBA) was formed in 1896, when officers from several cities met in Patterson to discuss how salaries, working conditions, job security, and pensions could be improved. By 2000, roughly 100 years later, the NJPBA had grown to 30,000 members in municipal, county, state, and federal agencies with over 350 locals in New Jersey. In addition to other services, the NJPBA provides members with a dental fund, dental insurance, and assistance to the families of officers injured or killed in the line of duty.

Lake County, California, is located about 120 miles northwest of Sacramento. In 1970, the Lake County Deputy Sheriffs Association (LCDSA) was formed to represent its members in bargaining. Over a period of time, the LCDSA—an independent union—began accepting jailers as members. Although the jailers were not sworn, the fact they all worked together initially made it a good fit. The jail staff grew dramatically, while the number of deputies grew slowly. Eventually, the needs of the jailers dominated the agenda and deputies began to feel disenfranchised. Just in the last several years there has been a split in the organization and the deputies left to form the Lake County Sheriff's Deputies Association (LCSDA). The LCSDA contributes to the community with a number of civic programs, including sponsoring a little league team and providing scholarships.[37] In its new iteration the LCSDA remains an independent police union.

Because police unions affiliated with an industrial union will continue to work to gain new members and can sometimes offer a better benefits package, many currently independent police associations like the LCSDA are vulnerable to raids by them. The future for many independent police associations that bargain for their members is written in the recent shift of the Florida PBA from independence to partnering with the National Coalition of Public Safety Officers, a Communications Workers of America organization. While this shift is dramatic in terms of the long-standing autonomy of the Florida PBA, it merely represents another milestone in such shifts which have been happening for about the past twenty-five years.

In addition to those already noted, a number of police organizations do not engage in collective bargaining, but nonetheless provide fraternal contacts and advocate for their members. Examples of these include the Coalition of Hispanic American Police Officers (CHAPA, see Box 10-6); the Police Emerald Isle Association, the most venerated of which is New York City's; the Italian American Police Association; the Rhode Island Minority Police Officers Association (RIMPA, see Box 10-7); the International Association for Women Police; the Portuguese American Police Association; the National Organization of Black Law Enforcement Executives (NOBLE); and the Latino Peace Officer Association.

**Other Police Organizations**

## BOX 10-6

### CHAPA—Coalition of Hispanic American Police Associations

The Coalition of Hispanic American Police Associations (CHAPA) is a not-for-profit corporation dedicated to providing a national perspective and definitive voice on issues facing Hispanics in Law Enforcement, and enhancing the role of Hispanic law enforcement officers in dealing with problems in Hispanic communities. CHAPA will realize these goals by publicly advocating policies and programs at the Local, State and Federal levels that result in equitable representation and treatment of Hispanics throughout the civil rights enforcement and judicial systems, especially in police departments and law enforcement agencies.

CHAPA is committed to developing strategies and training programs that promote the hiring, appointment and advancement of Hispanics at all levels of the criminal justice system, and make law enforcement a viable, fruitful and respected career for Hispanics. CHAPA actively seeks to eliminate substandard, and inferior police and government service to Hispanic communities and actively promotes the utilization of competent bilingual and culturally sensitive personnel to serve Spanish speaking clients and implement outreach services and programs, such as Community Oriented Policing to the Hispanic community.

*Source:* http://claraweb.co.santa-clara.ca.us/sheriff/chapa.htm, February 6, 2000.

## BOX 10-7

### Rhode Island Minority Police Officers Association: Mission and Goals Statement

**Mission Statement**

The Rhode Island Minority Police Association was founded in 1980 by seven minority law enforcement officers from various agencies around the State who joined in an effort to promote fraternalism and soli-

darity among the members of the minority law enforcement community. Their goal was to provide a focal point for members of the minority communities throughout the State of Rhode Island to bring their questions, concerns and complaints regarding issues of police activity, the justice system in general, and minority law enforcement officers, specifically.

*(continued)*

## BOX 10-7 (continued)

The Mission of the Rhode Island Minority Police Association is three-fold. First, as an organization representing the needs and concerns of law enforcement personnel, we are ever watchful of issues which have a directed impact, both adverse and positive, on the employment, promotion and retention of minority law enforcement officers in every facet of the Criminal Justice System. Whether they be employed in traditional or non-traditional agencies, it behooves us to provide guidance, support, and assistance in their efforts for equality of employment in their chosen field.

We are dedicated to the task of improving the individual proficiency of our members in the performance of their activities among law enforcement officers; encouraging legislative, social, charitable and educational activities and change for and amongst minority law enforcement; and to increase the efficiency of the law enforcement profession and thus more firmly establish the confidence of the public in the service.

Secondly, as a community oriented organization, we have both a responsibility and an obligation to the members of the minority community state-wide, whom we serve. We are responsible to them for being both the conscience and guardians of the Criminal Justice System, and ensuring that all members of the community are treated Justly, Fairly, and EQUALLY. We are further obligated to them to increase the awareness of the community, and to enhance the quality of life in the African American community.

Finally, we are committed to the education of our youth, as it is they who must, and shall, reap the benefits of our labors. Only through education can the children of our community be provided with the resources to overcome cultural ineptitude and racial ignorance. It is only through education that they, and we, may embrace those methods which will make us stronger in both mind and spirit, and to bring about the changes which must come.

*Source:* http://www.RIMPA.com, February 6, 2000.

## ESTABLISHING THE BARGAINING RELATIONSHIP

**The Process**   Assuming the existence of some legal provision for collective negotiations, the process of establishing a bargaining relationship is straightforward, although fraught with the opportunity for disputes. The mere fact that most members of a police department belong to a single organization does not mean that it automatically has the right to represent its members for the purposes of collective bargaining.[38] Those eligible to be represented may in fact select an organization to which they already belong for this purpose, or they may select another one. This choice must be made, however, in ways that conform to the legislation providing for collective bargaining if the employee organization hopes to gain certification by the PERC.

The union begins an organizing drive (see Box 10-8), seeking to get 30 percent of the class or classes of employees it seeks to represent to sign authorization cards, of which Figure 10-2 is typical. Once this goal is reached, the union notifies the police department. An election is held and to prevail, the union must get 50 percent plus one officer to prevail (see Box 10-9). If management believes that the union has obtained a majority legitimately and that it is appropriate for the class or classes of officers to be grouped together as proposed by the union, it will recognize the union as the bargaining agent of the officers it has sought to represent. Once recognized by the employer, the union will petition the PERC or other body responsible for administering the legislation for certification. In such cases, the PERC does not check the authorization cards, but only the appropriateness of the grouping of the officers. If the grouping is deemed appropriate by the PERC or similar administrative body, then the employee organization is certified as the bargaining representative.

BOX 10-8

## Unions Court Sheriffs' Deputies

by Kathryn Wexler

A court ruling encourages efforts to organize deputies in Hillsborough and elsewhere.

A vigorous and unusual appeal went out to Hillsborough County sheriff's deputies Friday.

"The choice is clear. It is your time," read a mass mailing sent by the West Central Police Benevolent Association to 978 patrol deputies. "Don't let fear and intimidation keep you from being in better control of your livelihood."

A recent Florida Supreme Court ruling—which some attorneys say is ambiguous at best—is fueling efforts by unions statewide to organize sheriff's deputies. Not since the court forbade deputy sheriffs to collectively bargain in 1978 have unions tried so hard to galvanize mass support, officials said Monday.

"We're definitely thrilled," said Ernie George, president of the Florida Police Benevolent Association. "We've started organizing here in Palm Beach County and we're looking to organize Central Florida, the Orange County Sheriff's Office and all those."

In Pinellas County, "the blue cards have just come in," reported Jack Soule, an officer with the St. Petersburg Police Department and president of the Pinellas PBA chapter, referring to the cards 30 percent of deputies at any given department must sign for a union to hold an election.

But confidence about the ruling is mostly limited to union officials and their supporters. State regulators said Monday they weren't sure what to make of it.

"The decision is not quite clear" on the rights of sheriff's deputies, said Steve Meck, general counsel for the state Public Employees Relations Commission, which oversees efforts to unionize public workers.

Flagler County, with about 70 deputies, is the first agency since the Jan. 13 ruling to submit petitions with the commission in order to hold a union election.

PBA officials said Brevard County, with 330 deputies, now has the number of signatures it needs to file as well.

And in Hillsborough County, about 200 of the necessary 294 cards have been signed since the mailings several days ago, said West Coast PBA president Jim Thompson.

Meck said the commission will hold a hearing on whether deputies' duties differ enough from those of other public employees to continue to prohibit them from choosing a union. He said the court did not overrule the 1978 case, which shielded sheriffs' departments from unions, but that it did question its validity.

The recent lawsuit was brought on behalf of an Orange County deputy clerk of court who claimed she was fired for trying to organize a union. The court ruled that clerks do have the right to organize, and also discussed the status of deputy sheriffs.

Pinellas County Sheriff Everett Rice said he won't resist orders to allow a union, if that's what his employees want, but added, "I think the best bargaining agent for deputy sheriffs is the sheriff himself."

Hillsborough County Sheriff Cal Henderson was out of town Monday and could not be reached for comment.

Col. David Gee said things like raises are determined more by budgetary constraints than unions.

"The county only has so much money, and whether there's a union or not, you're only going to get certain benefits that they can afford," Gee said.

The Broward County Sheriff's Office unionized five years ago when local legislation gave employees that right. Four other counties—Miami-Dade, Duval, Escambia and Alachua—have similar laws.

Pat Hanrahan, a Broward sheriff's deputy who has negotiated union contracts, said he understands sheriffs' resistance to unions.

"A sheriff normally doesn't support (a union) because he feels it's taking his power away; and two, they can't get rid of bad cops," Hanrahan said. But if collective bargaining is so bad, Hanrahan said, "why does every municipality have that right?"

Pat Sullivan, sheriff of Arapahoe County, Colo., and an official with the National Sheriff's Association, said courts disallowed unions in sheriffs' departments because, unlike appointed police chiefs, elected sheriffs can be held liable for their employees' actions. And he challenged the contention that sheriffs run agencies according to whim.

"There's still due process," Sullivan said.

But reversing that viewpoint appears likely, say even some skeptics of a new policy.

"Times have changed," said Rice, the Pinellas sheriff. "To say (the right to collective bargaining) doesn't include sheriff's deputies is old thinking."

*Source: St. Petersburg (Florida) Times, February 1, 2000.*

# AFSCME COUNCIL 15
## AFL-CIO
### 290 Pratt Street ■ Meriden, CT 06450

PLEASE PRINT

Local Union No._____     Date_____

Applicant's Name_____

Home Address_____

_____

Home Phone No._____     Social Security No._____

Employer_____

Dept._____     Classification_____

Worksite_____     Work Phone No._____

I, the undersigned, hereby designate the American Federation of State, County, and Municipal Employee, AFL-CIO, as my duly chosen and authorized representative on matters relating to my employment in order to promote and protect my economic welfare.

Signature of Applicant_____

Received by_____

APPLICATION FOR MEMBERSHIP/AUTHORIZATION FOR REPRESENTATION

**FIGURE 10-2.** A typical authorization card.

If the employee organization is not recognized by management, it can petition PERC for an election; the petition must be accompanied by signed and dated representation cards from 30 percent of the group of employees the union seeks to represent. A secret vote is then held at the direction of the PERC, with the ballot including the union or unions that are contesting the right to represent the officers along with the choice of no union. The union that receives a majority of the votes from among the officers who both are eligible to be represented by the employee organization and who actually cast ballots is then certified. Alternately, a majority of those casting ballots may vote for no union. In the event that no majority is achieved, a runoff election is necessary.

**The Opportunity for Conflict**

In establishing the bargaining relationship, there is ample opportunity for disputes to develop. Management may undertake a campaign to convince officers that they are better off without the union at the same time that the union is mounting its organizing drive. The employee organization may wish access to bulletin boards, meeting space, and mailing lists to publicize the advantages of unionizing to the officers, all of which management may not wish to provide. The decision as to what is an appropriate grouping of officers for the purposes of collective bargaining, technically referred to as *unit determination,* is profoundly significant and one about which management and the union may have sharp differences.

Questions such as the following may arise: Are lieutenants part of management and therefore not eligible for representation by the union for purposes of collective bargaining? Should civilian radio dispatchers be part of the same bargaining unit as uniformed officers? Should detectives be in a bargaining unit by themselves? These decisions are important because they may

BOX 10-9

## Lakeland Police Vote to Reject PBA

**by Jill Farrell King**
**The Tampa Tribune**

LAKELAND—Department and city officials applaud the voting results which rejected union representation.

Lakeland Police officers and sergeants rejected union representation by the Police Benevolent Association in a vote this week.

Of the 215 officers and sergeants eligible, 111 opposed the union while 87 were in favor. Seventeen didn't vote.

"I'd like to thank the officers for keeping the team within the department," said Police Chief Sam V. Baca. "The only solution to concerns and issues will come from within the department and not through a third party."

The West Central Florida Police Benevolent Association lobbied to represent the officers after many officers and sergeants filed requests for representation with the Public Employees Relations Commission, said PBA President Jim Thompson.

The West Central Florida PBA represents many police departments, including Tampa.

The voting was Wednesday at Lakeland Police headquarters on Massachusetts Street. PBA representatives came out for the vote wearing "Vote Yes" T-shirts and waving "PBA" signs.

Prior to the vote, the city and police brass had mandatory meetings with police officers where they talked about the benefits of remaining nonunion, Baca said.

However, Thompson said the union would have provided better benefits and working conditions for the department.

"That's the message we tried to get across," Thompson said. "We wanted them to become unionized and have a collective bargaining voice."

City Manager Gene Strickland said he isn't against unions but doesn't think they belong within the Lakeland Police Department.

"We're not saying unions are bad; we're saying that we have a department that works well without union representation and we can continue to progress without making our employees pay dues and be represented by an outside party," Strickland said.

Baca said department supervisors will continue to address employees' concerns and problems.

He said he heard rumors that those who voted in favor of the union would be retaliated against.

"There is no such thing in my management concept," Baca said. "We're all a team and all members of the Lakeland Police Department will be treated fairly and with dignity and respect."

*Source: The Tampa Tribune, September 4, 1999.*

affect the operation of the police department; determine, to some degree, the dynamics of the employee organization; impact upon the scope of bargaining; affect the stability of the bargaining relationship; or even be decisive in the outcome of a representation election.[39]

Both the union and management are pragmatic when it comes to defining the appropriate bargaining unit. In general, both may prefer a broad unit, the union, because the numbers will give it strength, while management resists the proliferation of bargaining units because each one that is recognized officially must be bargained with separately. Here, too, despite a similar orientation, disputes may arise. The union may know that it has the support of only one category of employees, for the purposes of illustration, detectives, and seeks to represent them as a single bargaining unit. Management may feel that particular union is too militant and, consequently, favors, as a part of a hidden agenda, the inclusion of detectives in a wider unit as a means of promoting the election of a more moderate union that is also seeking to represent employees. What constitutes an appropriate unit may be defined by state law. The most common method of unit determination, however, is for the PERC or similar administrative body to make decisions on a case-by-case basis, applying certain criteria stipulated in the legislation.[40] Among the criteria often identified are the desires of the employees, the "community of interests" shared by employees, the need to avoid creating too many bargaining units, the effects on efficiency of operations, and the history of labor relations in the police department.

Legislation establishing the right to bargain collectively enumerates certain unfair labor practices for management and employee organizations. Certain of these may come into play during the union's organizing period, particularly if management mounts a countering campaign.

It is an unfair labor practice sometimes referred to as an "improper practice" or "prohibited practice," for a public employer to:

(1) interfere with, restrain, or coerce public employees in the exercise of their enumerated rights;
(2) dominate or interfere with the formation or administration of an employee organization;
(3) discriminate in regard to hire or tenure of employment or any term or condition of employment to encourage or discourage membership in any employee organization;
(4) discharge or otherwise discriminate against an employee because he had filed charges or given testimony under the act; and
(5) refuse to bargain in good faith with the duly designated bargaining agent.

Similarly . . . It is an unfair labor practice for an employee organization to:

(1) restrain or coerce employees in the exercise of their enumerated rights;
(2) cause or attempt to cause an employer to interfere with, restrain, or coerce employees in the exercise of their enumerated rights;
(3) restrain or coerce employers in the selection of their representatives for the purposes of collective bargaining or the adjustment of grievances; and
(4) refuse to bargain in good faith.[41]

The interpretation of these provisions is a function of the PERC; for example, a police union may claim that the employer is engaging in an unfair labor practice by having its managers conduct a surveillance of the union's meeting place during organizing rallies. After conducting a preliminary investigation, the PERC, if substantiating evidence were found to support the claim, would order a hearing. In this example, assuming the necessary presentation of evidence, the PERC would issue a cease-and-desist order requiring the police department not to engage in such activities, which clearly is an unfair labor practice by the employer.

## NEGOTIATIONS

### Selection of the Management and Union Teams

Figure 10-3 depicts a typical configuration of the management and union bargaining teams. The union's chief negotiator will usually not be a member of the bargaining unit; rather he or she will be a specialist brought in to represent it. This ensures a certain level of expertise, wider experience, an appropriate degree of objectivity, and an autonomy that comes from knowing that, once the bargaining is over, he or she will not be working daily for the people sitting across the table. It is not automatic that the union president will be a member of the bargaining team, although customarily some union officer is, and often it is the president. Accompanying the union's chief negotiator and president will be two or three team members who have conducted in-depth research on matters relating to the bargaining issues and who will have vari-

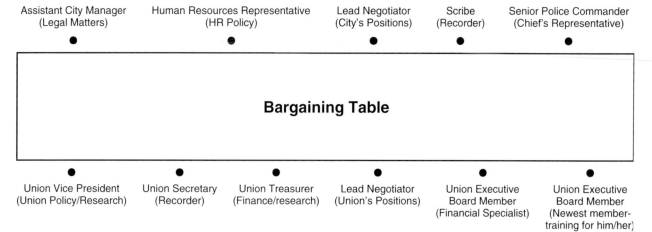

| Assistant City Manager (Legal Matters) | Human Resources Representative (HR Policy) | Lead Negotiator (City's Positions) | Scribe (Recorder) | Senior Police Commander (Chief's Representative) |

**Bargaining Table**

| Union Vice President (Union Policy/Research) | Union Secretary (Recorder) | Union Treasurer (Finance/research) | Lead Negotiator (Union's Positions) | Union Executive Board Member (Financial Specialist) | Union Executive Board Member (Newest member-training for him/her) |

**FIGURE 10-3.** The Management and Union Bargaining Teams. Although the composition of management's and the union's bargaining teams varies somewhat from one jurisdiction to another and even within jurisdictions over time, the configuration shown above approximates the "typical" municipal situation. Occasionally a member of City Council also sits in as an observer. (Courtesy of Chuck Foy, Past President, Peoria (Arizona) Police Officers Association.)

ous types of data, facts, and documents—such as wage and benefit surveys, trends in the consumer price index, and copies of recent contracts for similarly sized jurisdictions—with them. Although there will only be several union research team members at the table, they will have had assistance in gathering their information from others in the union. Unless the union's chief negotiator is an attorney, there will seldom be an attorney sitting at the table with the union's team.

The composition of management's negotiating team is also depicted in Figure 10-3; the chief negotiator may be the director of labor relations or human resource director for the unit of government involved or a professional labor relations specialist. Some jurisdictions prefer the latter because, if there are acrimonious occurrences, once the bargaining is over the director of labor relations can step back into the picture and assume a relationship with the union that is unscarred by any incidents. The chief of police should not appear at the table personally, but a key member of the command staff who has his or her confidence should. The appearance of the chief at the table makes the task of leadership more difficult; to appear there on equal footing with the union's bargaining team on one day and then to step back atop the organizational hierarchy on the next requires greater adjustments by both the chief and the union members than the creation of any benefits associated with her or his presence are worth.

The issues, the way in which they are presented, and the flexibility that both sides have will impact strongly on how the bargaining sessions will go. Perhaps equally important are the decisions made as to who will represent each side in what role at the table. It is not uncommon in evolving or newly established bargaining relationships to find that both parties put great effort into preparing for negotiations but make the selection of their representatives without the same thought. Zealots, those with "axes to grind," and firebrands are poor choices, as are those with sarcastic, acrid, or abrasive personalities. The purpose of bargaining is to produce a bilateral written agreement to which both parties will bind themselves during its lifetime. This is not only a profoundly important task, but one that is sufficiently difficult without including people on either side who have an agenda other than negotiating in good faith or whose personalities create yet another obstacle. For these reasons, management must exercise careful consideration in deciding who will represent the police department at the table and, if necessary, influence the selection of the city's other representatives.

## The Scope of Bargaining

The scope of bargaining refers to the decision as to what aspects of the employment relationship should, or should not, be subject to joint determination at the bargaining table.[42] Management prefers a narrow scope of negotiations because it means less shared power; the union's preference is for the widest possible scope. The topics about which bargaining may occur are often divided into three categories by state or local enactments: (1) mandatory topics, which represent subjects about which both parties must bargain in good faith if the issue is raised by the other party; (2) permissive topics, which the parties may negotiate about, although it is not mandatory; and (3) prohibited topics, about which the parties cannot bargain.[43]

As a general matter, police departments are not required to negotiate policy decisions with unions, but when such decisions affect the terms and conditions of employment, the effect of the policy decision becomes negotiable. For example, when the Cedar Rapids, Iowa, Police Department unilaterally implemented a policy requiring physical performance tests and also promulgated a new sick leave policy that required employees to get a physician's certificate at their own expense, the union challenged the effect of both policies. Subsequently, the Iowa PERB held that both policies were mandatory subjects of bargaining.[44] In Spokane, Washington, the same determination was made when the union objected to the city's creation of a police review board with the ability to review departmental disciplinary files.[45]

An employer cannot wait until a contract lapses and then unilaterally make changes in mandatory topics while there is no contract. To do so is an unfair labor practice by management. In addition to state or local enactments identifying the topics that are mandatory subjects for bargaining, the scope of mandatory topics may be extended by language in the collective bargaining agreement itself. For example, many agreements have broadly worded "maintenance of benefits" or "continuance of existing conditions" clauses similar to that enjoyed by police officers in Buffalo, New York:

> All conditions or provisions beneficial to employees now in effect which are not specifically provided for in this agreement or which have not been replaced by provisions of this agreement shall remain in effect for the duration of this agreement, unless mutually agreed otherwise between the Employer and the Association.[46]

The effect of these clauses is to give the union a right through the grievance procedure to challenge an employer's decision in such matters. This right must be exercised promptly by the union or the right to bargain over it is deemed waived. Thus, when the employer gives notice that it is changing some past practice, unions should carefully determine whether some conditions beneficial to its members are being lost.

## Preparing for Negotiations

Management can ill afford to simply wait until the employee organization prepares its demands and presents them; effective action requires considerable effort on management's part before it receives the union's proposal. Management's negotiating team must be selected; agreement with the union obtained on the site where the actual negotiations will take place; the bargaining schedule established in conjunction with the union; and various types of data and information gathered, tabulated, and analyzed. Although final preparations for negotiating will begin several months before the first bargaining sessions, the preparation process is a continuous one; management should begin preparing for the next negotiations as soon as these are completed. The demands not obtained by the union in the past year may be brought up again in this year's bargaining sessions, and management should be prepared for this.

Various types of records should be kept and summaries made of such factors as the union membership; types and outcomes of grievances; the costs of settling grievances; the numbers, kinds, and consequences of any contract violations by the employee organization; the subject matters brought before the union–management committee during the life of the expiring contract and the disposition of them; and the themes reflected in the union's newsletter. Additionally, just as the employee organization's bargaining team is doing, the management team must be familiarizing itself with changes in the consumer price index and provisions of recent contracts in similarly situated jurisdictions and conducting its own wage and benefit survey or cooperating with the union on one.

From all these and other sources, it is essential that management do three things. First, it must develop fairly specific anticipations as to what the union will be seeking and the relative importance of each demand to the union. Second, it must develop its position with respect to the anticipated preliminary demands that it believes the union will present. Third, it must develop the objectives that it seeks to achieve during the forthcoming process of bilateral determination. If it is not already an institutionalized practice, arrangements should be made to have the union submit its demands in writing prior to the first scheduled round of negotiations. These demands may be submitted either in the form of a proposed contract or as a "shopping list," which simply lists the demands being made. The presentation of the demands in writing before the first bargaining session allows for a more productive use of the time allotted for the first negotiating session.

If management has done a good job, there will be relatively few surprises when the proposed contract is submitted. Surprises do not indicate that management's preparation was wasted; the knowledge gained through the process of anticipating the union's demands adds to the negotiating team's depth of understanding and overall confidence, key ingredients of bargaining table success. It is difficult to know precisely when management's bargaining team is prepared, but the employee organization will easily detect and capitalize on a lack of preparation.

## The Negotiating Sessions

The publicity and attending atmosphere preceding the negotiating sessions focus considerable attention on them and may be barometers of, or influence, the way in which they unfold. However, prebargaining publicity is also part of attempts to influence public opinion, to impress the public or rank-and-file members with the city's or union's resolve, and to create a façade behind which both sides may maneuver for advantage. Thus, one should not be too encouraged or discouraged about the content of such publicity; it should be considered and evaluated, but not relied on solely as an informational source.

The number of bargaining sessions may run from one to several dozen, lasting from thirty minutes to ten or more hours, although half-day sessions are more common, depending on how close or far apart the union and management are when they begin to meet face to face (see Figure 10-4). Traditionally, any means of making verbatim transcripts, such as the use of a stenographer or tape recorder, have generally been excluded from the bargaining sessions, as it was believed that they tended to impede the progress of negotiations because people would begin speaking for the record.

In a related vein, the enactment of Florida's "sunshine law" opened up many previously closed governmental meetings to the general public, including bargaining sessions, and stirred up some controversy. Advocates of the legislation argued that it opened government up to the people and would make it both more responsive and responsible. With respect to its application to collective negotiations, critics of the law maintained that the real bargaining would be done secretly, that the scheduled public bargaining sessions would be merely a ritualistic acting out of what had been agreed on privately, and that real negotiating would be difficult because both sides would tend to "play to the audience." This last point is underscored by one negotiator's wry observation that bargaining under the sunshine law was like "a Roman circus with kibitzers."[47]

At the first meeting, friendly conversation may be passed across the table or there may be merely strained greetings before the formal session begins. Much like the prenegotiations publicity, this may, or may not, be reflective of how the session will go. Friendly conversation may suggest that rapid and amicable bargaining will follow, but, instead, no mutually acceptable positions are reached because the friendly conversation has veiled only thinly the hostility or aggressiveness of one or both sides, which quickly comes to the fore. On the

**FIGURE 10-4.** Representatives of the Florida Police Benevolent Association at the bargaining table with State of Florida officials during the negotiations for members of the State Law Enforcement Supervisors Unit. (Photo courtesy of the Florida Police Benevolent Association.)

other hand, strained greetings may reflect the heavy responsibility that each party to the negotiations feels, and quick progress may follow.

In the initial session, the chief negotiator for each party will make an opening statement; management's representative will often go first, touching on general themes such as the need for patience and the obligation to bargain in good faith. The union's negotiator generally will follow this up by voicing support for such sentiments and will outline what the union seeks to achieve under the terms of the new contract. Ground rules for the bargaining may then be reviewed, modified as mutually agreed on, or developed. The attention then shifts to the terms of the contract that the union is proposing and the contract is examined thoroughly in a "walkthrough" during which time management seeks to learn what the union means by particular wording. This is a time-consuming process but of great importance because both parties need to share a common understanding of what it is they are attempting to commit each other to, or there will be frequent unresolved conflicts and many complex and expensive grievances filed during the lifetime of the contract. For purposes of illustration, the union may have proposed that "vehicles will be properly maintained to protect the health and safety of officers." Discussion of this proposal may reveal that their expectations are much more specific:

1. This is to apply to all vehicles, including marked, semimarked, and unmarked.
2. Each patrol vehicle, whether marked, semimarked, or unmarked, will be replaced at 60,000 miles.
3. All vehicles will be equipped with radial tires.
4. Plexiglas® protectors will be installed between the front and rear seats.
5. Shotguns in locking mounts accessible from the front seat will be provided for in all marked and semimarked cars.
6. First-aid kits of a particular type will be placed in all vehicles.

Another illustration is reflected in Table 10-2; assuming that the union is seeking a two-year contract and wants a 20 percent raise during the lifetime,

**TABLE 10-2. Alternative Ways to Costing Out a 20% Raise Over a Two-Year Contract**

| | | |
|---|---|---|
| 1. 10% increase each year of contract | | |
| Year 1 cost: 10% of 980,000 | = | $98,000 |
| Year 2 cost: 10% of year 1 wages, $1,078,000 | = | 107,800 |
| plus continuation of year 1 | = | 98,000 |
| | | $303,800 |
| 2. 15% increase in year 1; 5% in year 2 | | |
| Year 1 cost: 15% of $980,000 | = | $147,000 |
| Year 2 cost: 5% of year 1 payroll of $1,127,000 | = | 56,350 |
| plus continuation of year 1 | = | 147,000 |
| | | $350,350 |
| 3. 20% in year 1; nothing in year 2 | | |
| Year 1 cost: 20% of $980,000 | = | $196,000 |
| Year 2: no new increase but continuation | | |
| of year 1 raise | = | $196,000 |
| | | $392,000 |

of the contract, there are several ways that the cost of that raise might be spread. Management must find out what the union is bargaining for in very specific terms and then cost it out so that the administration knows the budgetary implications of its commitments and counterproposals beforehand.[48] The walkthrough may take several sessions to complete; during this time, little bargaining is being done, as management is basically attempting to obtain clarity about what the union's expectations are.

For bargaining purposes, the union will have categorized each clause in the proposed contract as being (1) "expendable," meaning that under certain circumstances it will be withdrawn as a symbol of good faith; (2) a "trade-off," indicating that it will be dropped as total or partial payment for obtaining some other benefit; (3) "negotiable," meaning that the benefit needs to be obtained in one form or another; and (4) "nonnegotiable," meaning that the benefit is wanted exactly as proposed.[49] Management will study the information gained from the walkthrough for several days, and then both parties will return to the table. Management then responds to the union's proposal by indicating which clauses it (1) "accepted," (2) "accepted with minor modification," (3) "rejected," and (4) wishes to make its own proposals and counterproposals to. Management cannot simply reject a clause out of hand; to do so would not constitute bargaining in good faith. Instead, it must give a reason for the rejection that is reasonable, such as an actual inability to pay.

Having been told formally of management's position on the contract proposed, the bargaining begins, concentrating on the items on which agreement can be reached immediately or fairly rapidly. Such an approach helps to foster a spirit of mutualism that can be useful in dealing with the issues about which there are substantial differences. As bargaining enters the final stages, the issues that must be dealt with usually become fewer but also more difficult in terms of securing agreement about them (see Box 10-10).

At such points, "side trips" may threaten to make the sessions unproductive. These side trips may involve wild accusations, old recriminations, character assassinations, or discussion of a specific clause in philosophical or intellectual terms as a means of not dealing with the concrete realities that may be threatening and anxiety provoking for one or both parties. At these times a caucus or even a slightly longer space of time than ordinary until the next session may give enough time for tempers to calm or for more perspective to be gained.

Ultimately, unless a total impasse is reached, agreement will be obtained on the terms of a new contract. The union's membership will vote on the contract as a whole. If approved by the membership, the contract then goes before the necessary governmental officials and bodies, such as the legislative unit that appropriates the funds, for its approval.

**Bargaining Impasse Resolution**

Even parties bargaining in good faith may not be able to resolve their differences by themselves and require the invocation of some type of impasse resolution technique. The essence of all impasse resolution techniques is the insertion of a neutral third party who facilitates, suggests, or compels an agreement. Of present concern are three major forms of impasse resolution: mediation, fact-finding, and arbitration. All, several, or only one of these techniques may be provided for in a particular jurisdiction.

## BOX 10-10

### Cops Target Merit System; City Counters with List of Concessions

by Fran Spielman

Chicago Police officers are demanding a 19 percent pay raise over 2 1/2 years, another paid holiday and an end to merit promotions, but the city wants major concessions in return, sources said Tuesday.

Instead of basing 80 percent of district and shift assignments on seniority, the Daley administration wants a 60-40 split to prevent a proliferation of rookie officers in high-crime districts. Forty percent of all vacancies would be filled by management prerogative under the city's proposal.

The mayor also wants to double—from one year to two—the probationary period for new police officers, bring back the mandatory retirement age of 63 and overhaul disciplinary procedures to make it easier for the city to punish police wrongdoing and harder for the union to defend wayward members.

Fraternal Order of Police President Bill Nolan refused to comment on the union's demands or the city's counterproposal.

The *Chicago Sun-Times* reported July 26 that four of the city's most dangerous police districts are saddled with the largest number of rookies because of a police contract that awards district assignments and shifts on the basis of seniority.

Daley responded by saying the Police Department needs more flexibility to make certain there are seasoned officers in every district on every shift. He refused to reveal specific percentages.

At a union meeting Tuesday, Nolan spelled out the specifics and told his members what the union wants in return.

In addition to the 19 percent pay raise over 2.5 years, the FOP's demands include one more personal day and one additional holiday; 30 minutes of overtime per day for rank-and-file officers and a requirement that overtime be doled out on the basis of seniority; no employee contributions to medical, dental or optical insurance; a 36 percent increase in the $550-per-quarter duty availability pay, and a $200 increase in the annual uniform allowance.

The FOP also wants to end all merit promotions and drop the requirement that candidates for promotion complete two years of college.

The average salary for a 15-year veteran police officer now stands at $53,610. A 19 percent pay raise would raise that to $63,795.

*Source: Chicago Sun-Times, September 22, 1999.*

---

## Mediation

"Mediation arises when a third party, called the mediator, comes in to help the adversaries with the negotiations."[50] This person may be a professional mediator, a local clergyman whom both parties respect and have confidence in, or some other party. The mediating will most often be done by one person, although three- and even five-member panels may be used.

In most states mediation may be requested by either labor or management, although in some states both parties must request it, and in others the PERC can intervene on its own initiative. The mediator may be appointed by the parties to the negotiations or by a governmental body. Meeting with labor and management either jointly and/or separately,[51] the task of the mediator is to build agreement about the issue or issues involved by reopening communications between the two groups.

The mediator will remove himself or herself from a case when (1) an agreement is reached, (2) one of the parties to the negotiations requests his or her departure, (3) the agreed-on time comes to use the next step in the impasse resolution procedure, or (4) the mediator feels that his or her acceptability or effectiveness is exhausted.[52] Because the mediator is without any means to compel an agreement, a chief advantage to the process is that it preserves the nature of collective bargaining by maintaining the decision-making power in the hands of the involved parties. Balancing this advantage, however, is the belief that the effectiveness of mediation depends on a certain level of sophistication by those conducting the negotiations, and where this condition does not exist, the mediator may spend more time simply educating the two parties than in helping them resolve their differences.[53]

**Fact-Finding**

The designation of this technique as fact-finding is something of a misnomer; the parties to an impasse are often in agreement as to what the facts are. Much of the work in fact-finding is the interpretation of facts and the determination of what weight to attach to them.

Appointed in the same ways as are mediators, fact-finders also do not have the means to impose a settlement of the dispute. Fact-finders may sit alone or as part of a panel, which often consists of three people. If a panel is used, a common procedure is for management and labor each to appoint a representative, and those two pick the third person, who is designated as the neutral. If the two appointed members cannot agree on the third, then the PERC, the American Arbitration Association (AAA), or another body or official as provided for in the applicable state law will do so. In some states the representatives that management and labor placed on the panel have no part in the selection of the neutral, which is left to the PERC. Rarely does a panel consist of three neutrals, due to the cost. If a single fact-finder is used, the parties may agree on one: he or she may be appointed by a body such as the PERC; or a group such as the AAA supplies a list of names and labor, and then management and the union take turns striking off names from a list of seven until only one remains, that person being then appointed as the fact-finder.

The fact-finding hearing is quasi-judicial, although less strict rules of evidence are applied. Both labor and management may be represented by legal counsel, verbatim transcripts are commonly made, and each side generally presents its position through the use of a single spokesperson along with some exhibits. Following the closing arguments, the fact-finder will prepare the report containing his or her recommendations that must be submitted in a specified number of days, such as within thirty days of appointment or ten days following the close of the hearings.

In the majority of instances, the fact-finder's recommendations will be made public at some point. However, the report should first be given to the two parties for their use for some specified period of time so that they might carry out further negotiations free of distractions. Although there is some minor debate as to whether fact-finders should even make recommendations, the majority position is described aptly by the view that fact-finding without recommendations is "as useful as a martini without gin."[54]

**Arbitration**

In most respects—including the selection and appointment of arbitrators and as a process—arbitration parallels fact-finding; it differs chiefly in that the "end product of arbitration is a final and binding decision that sets the terms of the settlement and with which the parties are legally required to comply."[55] Although the term "advisory arbitration" is occasionally encountered, it is a contradiction of terms because arbitration is compulsory and binding, "advisory arbitration" is, instead, another term that is used occasionally to describe the process of fact-finding.[56] Arbitration may be compulsory or voluntary:

> It is compulsory when mandated by law, regulation and/or Executive Order and is binding upon the parties even if one of them is unwilling to comply. On the other hand it is voluntary when the parties undertake of their own volition to use

the procedure. Voluntarism could be the result of a statute which permits, rather than requires, the parties to submit disputed issues to binding arbitration on their own initiative. It could also arise from the parties' own initiative with respect to future contract impasses pursuant to a permanent negotiation procedure.[57]

Even when entered into voluntarily, however, arbitration is compulsory and binding upon the parties who have agreed to it.

Although some states now permit strikes under certain conditions, the more prevalent public policy choice has been no strikes, particularly with respect to providers of services viewed as critical, most notably correctional, police, fire, and hospital workers. Simultaneously the final step provided for in resolving most bargaining disputes has been some provision short of arbitration. The net result was that labor was denied the use of its ultimate tactic, the strike, and also had no neutral "final court of appeal" in which to resolve a bargaining impasse. The inherent unfairness of this situation became easier to deal with as public sector collective bargaining began gaining acceptance, and the number of states providing arbitration grew. Although compulsory arbitration tended initially to be provided for only those occupational groups viewed as providers of critical services, there has been some movement to broaden the coverage to include other or all types of employees.

One form of bargaining impasse arbitration that emerged in 1973 is final offer selection (FOS). In FOS, each party submits its last offer, and the arbitrator or arbitrators select, without modification one of them as being final and binding. Although FOS may be done on an item-by-item basis, it is usually done on a package or whole-contract basis.[58]

Although court cases have challenged the use of arbitration on the basis of its being an unlawful delegation of power, the courts have generally upheld its use.[59] Moreover, even in considering the ability to pay, several courts have held that the employer must make available the funds necessary to implement an agreement that has been reached by the parties.[60]

## GRIEVANCES

### Why Grievances Are Inevitable

There is a notion that, once the bargaining is completed and an agreement signed, the most difficult part of labor relations has been passed through and easy times are ahead. Such a notion is natural. Bargaining is high drama, with a great deal of attention focused on it by the news media and the community. The production of an agreement acceptable to both the union and management is in fact a significant achievement. Beyond it, however, is the day-to-day administration of the contract during its lifetime. Because the contract outlines the duties and rights of each party in its dealings with the other, it is ironically not only the basis for accord, but also for conflict:

> It would, of course, be ideal for all concerned, including the public, if in the negotiation of the agreement both parties were able to draft a comprehensive document capable of foreseeing and forestalling all potential disputes which might arise during its life. Unfortunately, such crystal-ball vision is usually lacking, particularly when the parties are pressured to obtain agreement in a period of negotiation tensions and time deadlines. It is not humanly possible in a new collective bargaining relationship to draft such a perfect document.
>
> Therefore it is inevitable that questions will arise concerning the interpretation and application of the document drafted in the haste and pressure of contract

negotiations. What is the meaning of a particular clause of the agreement? How does it apply, if at all, to a set of facts which occurred after the agreement was signed? These questions are not at all uncommon in any contractual relationship.[61]

**The Definition of a Grievance**

Whereas in common usage a *grievance* is a complaint or expression of dissatisfaction by an employee with respect to some aspect of employment, what can be grieved formally is usually defined within the contract itself. Grievances may be limited to matters discussed specifically in the contract, primarily contract related, or anything pertaining to the job, as is seen in these clauses from three different agreements:

1. A grievance is defined as a complaint arising out of the interpretation, application or compliances with the provisions of this agreement (see Box 10-11).

## BOX 10-11

### City Reverses Lobbying Policy, Police Union Protests Change

**By Susan Greene**
**Denver Post Staff Writer**

The city of Denver has reversed a long-standing policy allowing political lobbying by on-duty police officers.

But the police union is protesting—and says the change is part of a vendetta by City Councilman Ed Thomas and a feud with the mayor's office over photo radar.

For at least 30 years, the city has paid a full-time police officer to lobby city and state lawmakers on behalf of the union.

"It's how it's always been handled," said union President Mike Stack, a police sergeant. "We need to protect the interest of law enforcement."

That quiet arrangement came into question during this year's legislative session when officer and Police Protective Association official Kirk Miller lobbied, while on duty, against the city's photo radar-enforcement program. The union was miffed that radar vans weren't staffed by police, arguing the program was about money, not safety.

Denver Mayor Wellington Webb, Manager of Safety Butch Montoya and Police Chief Tom Sanchez lobbied in support of continuing photo radar in Denver.

Councilman Ed Thomas, a former longtime Denver cop, complained it's inappropriate for police officers to oppose city policy on city time.

"Officers shouldn't be lobbying on the public dime, especially on issues conflicting with public-safety interests," he said.

The councilman also complained that PPA members were working on duty to oppose him during his spring re-election campaign—a charge the union denies.

The PPA was angered by Thomas' opposition to last year's ballot measure allowing city employees to live outside Denver, and by his plan to force cops who moonlight to buy insurance to cover them in excessive-force cases. Last spring, the union supported Kevin Shancady in his unsuccessful quest for Thomas' seat.

City attorneys agreed with Thomas that on-duty officers shouldn't push political or union causes. Based on their legal opinion, Sanchez in June advised the union and other police-employee groups "that it's improper to engage in political activities," including lobbying and political campaigning.

"We have 1,450 police officers and we need every one of them working out in the field as much as possible," he said, noting cops are free to lobby or campaign while not at work.

The PPA, in response, last week filed a grievance with the city under its collective-bargaining agreement.

Stack said the union "feels that lobbying is protected under our contract." He defended the old practice of taxpayers funding a police officer to push the union's agenda.

"It's been our experience that when policy makers want to talk to someone about law enforcement, they want to talk to a police officer, not a professional lobbyist," he said.

Stack blamed Thomas for triggering the controversy.

"He's just upset because we didn't endorse him in the last election," he said.

Thomas responded: "It's about cleaning up a 30-year-old, ill-conceived plan."

The union's grievance is expected to go to arbitration in the coming months.

*Source: The Denver Post,* July 23, 1999.

2. For the purpose of this agreement the term "grievance" shall mean the difference of dispute between any policeman and the Borough, or a superior officer in the chain of command, with respect to the interpretation, application, claim or breach, of violation of any of the provisions of this agreement, or with respect to any equipment furnished by the Borough.

3. A grievance, for the purposes of this article, shall be defined as any controversy, complaint, misunderstanding or dispute arising between an employee or employees and the City, or between the Brotherhood and the City.

## The Grievance Procedure

The grievance procedure is a formal process that has been the subject of bilateral negotiations and that is detailed in the contract. It involves seeking redress of the grievances through progressively higher levels of authority and most often culminates in binding arbitration by a tripartite panel or a single neutral. A typical sequence of steps would include the following:

> Grievances shall be presented in the following manner and every effort shall be made by the parties to secure prompt disposition of grievances:
>
> *Step 1.* The member shall first present his grievance to his immediate supervisor within five (5) days of the occurrence which gave rise to the grievance. Such contact shall be on an informal and oral basis, and the supervisor shall respond orally to the grievance within five (5) working days.
>
> *Step 2.* Any grievance which cannot be satisfactorily settled in Step 1 shall be reduced to writing by the member and shall next be taken up by his division commander. Said grievance shall be presented to the division commander within five (5) working days from receipt of the answer in Step 1. The division commander shall, within five (5) working days, render his decision on the grievance in writing.
>
> *Step 3.* Any grievance not satisfactorily settled in Step 2 shall be forwarded, in writing, within five (5) working days, to the Chief of Police, who shall render his written decision on the grievance within five (5) working days.
>
> *Step 4.* If the grievant is not satisfied with the response of the Chief of Police, he will forward his written grievance within five (5) working days to the City Manager, who will have ten (10) working days to reply, in writing.
>
> *Step 5.* If the grievance has not been settled to the satisfaction of the grievant in Step 4, the matter will be subject to arbitration. An arbiter will be selected, without undue delay, according to the rules of the American Arbitration Association. The arbiter will hold an arbitration hearing. When the hearing has ended, the arbiter will be asked to submit his award, in writing, within fifteen (15) days. His decision shall be final and binding on both parties.[62]

Because the union must share equally the cost of arbitration with management, the decision to take a grievance to the last step is customarily the prerogative of the union rather than the individual officer who is grieved.

Not only are the steps of the grievance procedure enumerated in the agreement, but also such matters as the manner of selecting the tripartite panel or the single neutral, along with their duties and powers. If the panel is used, management and the union each appoints one member and those two appoint the third; where the two cannot agree on the neutral, the contract may provide for the referral of the choice of a chairperson to a designated agency,[63] such as the AAA, the Federal Mediation and Conciliation Service, or a state agency. Where a single arbitrator is used, a variety of techniques are employed in selection, ranging from agreement on the person by the union and management on a case-by-case basis, to the appointment of a permanent arbitrator during the lifetime of the contract, to having an outside agency submit a list of qualified arbitrators from which management and the union take turns eliminating names until only one remains or they agree to accept any of some number remaining, such as three.

The arbitration hearing is quasi-judicial with more relaxed rules of evidence than are found in either criminal or civil proceedings. The burden of proof is on the grieving party, except in discipline cases where it is always on the employer. The parties may be represented by legal counsel at the hearing, and the format will generally be obtaining agreement of what the issue is, the opening statements by each side (with the grieving party going first), examination and cross-examination of witnesses, and closing arguments in the reverse of the order in which the opening statements were made.

## Arbitration Issues and Decision Making

Despite the many different types of matters that can be and are grieved, the largest single category of cases, about 90 percent of the total, brought to an arbitration hearing are those involving discipline against the officer. Although some arbitration decision making is not difficult because one side chooses to take a losing case to arbitration, because of its symbolic importance, the need to appear supportive of union members, or to be seen as strongly supporting one's managers, other decisions are complex as they seek to obtain equity in a maze of conflicting testimony, ambiguous contract language, changes from past practices, credibility of evidence, and valid and persuasive cases by both parties that emphasize the relative importance of different factors. Arbitrators often employ checklists in conducting the hearings to ensure that all relevant points are covered.

If an employee is found to have done what he or she was accused of, the arbitrator may then consider certain factors that might mitigate the severity of the penalty, including the officer's years of service to the department; the provocation, if any, that led to the alleged offense; the officer's previous disciplinary history, including the numbers, types, and recency of other violations; the consistency with which the applicable rule is enforced; and the penalties applied for similar offenses by other officers.[64]

One study of police grievances that were arbitrated reveals that the officer involved in the grievance was assigned to uniformed patrol 84 percent of the time, another police officer was involved in the incident slightly more than half the time (56 percent of the cases), the grieving officer's supervisor supported him or her 14 percent of the time, and in exactly three-quarters of the cases the involved officer had a clear disciplinary record.[65] Given that police unions must be selective in terms of the cases they take to arbitration, the results are not too surprising: the union won 77 percent of the grievances.

A key advantage to arbitration is the speed with which issues are heard and a decision made as compared with seeking resolution of the dispute in court. The deadline for issuance of the award may be established by statute; the parties; some governmental authority, such as PERC; the arbitrator, if he or she is acting as an independent and his without other guidance; or the body appointing the arbitrator.[66] The AAA requires arbitrators to render their decisions in writing within thirty days of (1) the conclusion of the hearing; (2) the receipt of the hearing transcript, if one has been made; or (3) the receipt of posthearing briefs.[67] In general, except in such instances as fraud or bias by the arbitrator, the hearing officer's decision, where binding arbitration is provided for, will not be reviewed by the courts.

*Job action* is a label used to describe several different types of activities in which employees may engage to express their dissatisfaction with a particular person, event, or condition or to attempt to influence the outcome of some matter pending before decision makers, such as a contract bargaining impasse. Job actions carry the signal "we are here, organized, and significant, and the legitimacy of our position must be recognized."

Through job actions, employees seek to create pressure that may cause the course of events to be shifted to a position more favorable or acceptable to them. Such pressure may come from a variety of quarters, including the city manager, elected officials, influential citizens, merchant associations, political party leaders, and neighborhood groups. Under such pressure, administrators may agree to something that they might not under more relaxed circumstances. When ill-advised agreements are made, they may be attributable at a general level to pressure but on a more specific plane to such factors as stress, miscalculations, the desire to appear responsive to some superior or constituency, or the mistaken belief that the implications of a hastily conceived and coerced agreement can be dealt with effectively later. Four types of job actions are recognizable: the vote of confidence, work slowdowns, work speedups, and work stoppages.

**The Vote of Confidence**

The vote of confidence, which typically produces a finding of no confidence (see Box 10-12), has been used somewhat sparingly in law enforcement. An extreme example of that infrequent use is the Massachusetts State Police, whose members for the first time in their 129-year history, gave their commander a vote of no confidence in 1994.[68] Such a vote is how rank-and-file members signal their collective displeasure with the chief administrator of their agency. Although such votes have no legal standing, they may have a high impact because of the resulting publicity.

In mid-1996, the Houston Police Officers Association's board issued a vote of no confidence against then-Chief Sam Nuchia. Within six months, Nuchia was gone from the department. A year before, in Prince George's County, Maryland, 300 members of the Fraternal Order of Police voted no confidence in the department's command hierarchy.[69] Five officers had been ordered to a warehouse to meet FBI agents investigating the alleged beating of a citizen. Upon arriving, the five officers had been ordered to strip, which produced a fiery protest and the no-confidence vote.

Although the vote of no confidence may produce a change in leadership and policies, on rare occasions it creates the opposite effect. Years ago in Houston, the chief received a no-confidence vote. Members of the city council and the chamber of commerce quickly supported the chief, labeling the vote a sign that he was "clamping down" on police officers and making much-needed changes in the department.[70]

## BOX 10-12

### Police Vote Criticizes Mayor, City Manager

COMPTON—The Police Officers Assn. overwhelmingly voted "no confidence" in the mayor and city manager as a result of last summer's removal of the city's police chief and a top captain, officers announced Monday.

"The mayor and city manager have allowed the Police Department to become extremely politicized," said Det. Ed Aguirre, president of the association. "Morale within the ranks has deteriorated and the efficiency of the department has been reduced."

A city spokesman could not be reached for comment.

The results of the "no confidence" vote, taken at a Saturday association membership meeting, will be presented tonight to the Compton City Council, Aguirre said.

In August, Compton city officials abruptly placed Police Chief Hourie Taylor and Capt. Percy Perrodin, the department's second in command, on administrative leave. At the time, city officials would not comment on the action. The city still has not issued a public statement explaining why Taylor and Perrodin were placed on leave.

"Our association has pledged to support Chief Taylor and Capt. Perrodin, who were removed from their positions without any cause," Aguirre said. "Police officers are tired of being embarrassed by the mayor."

Mayor Omar Bradley is the target of a recall petition prompted by city staff problems, including the controversy over the removals. The petition has raised other questions about Bradley, including his vote to give $50,000 to a Meals on Wheels program run by his aunt, who is on the council. It also challenged recent council votes to increase car allowances and provide credit cards to council members.

*Source:* Copyright, 2000, *Los Angeles Times,* February 1, 2000. Reprinted by permission.

**Work Slowdowns**  Although officers continue to work during a slowdown, they do so at a leisurely pace, causing productivity to fall. As productivity drops, the unit of government employing the officers comes under pressure to restore normal work production. This pressure may be from within the unit of government itself; for example, a department may urge officers to write more tickets so more revenue is not lost. Or citizens may complain to politicians and appointed leaders to "get this thing settled" so the police will answer calls more rapidly and complete the reports citizens need for insurance purposes. In 1997, New York City police officers protesting stalled contract negotiations staged a ticket-issuing slowdown which resulted in a loss of $2.3 million dollars in just two months. This action also produced strong conflict within the rank and file among officers who did and didn't support the slowdown. In order to counter New York City Police Department pressure to stop the ticket slowdown, the Patrolmen's Benevolent Association—which represents the city's 29,000 officers—picketed outside traffic courts, denouncing what it called the administration's traffic ticket quota policy.[71]

The adoption of new technologies in a police department, intended to speed up police responses, also offers the opportunity to create a work slowdown. In 1997, 150 Alexandria, Virginia, police officers turned in their department-issued pagers to protest a pay scale that lagged behind neighboring jurisdictions. The pagers were used to call in off-duty officers in specialized units, such as homicide and hostage negotiations, when needed. Detective Eric Ratliff, president of Local 5, International Union of Police Associations, said "I won't sugar-coat it. The response time of specialized units . . . will be slower. What this does is take us back to the early '80s, before we had pagers, which is basically where our pay is."[72] In East Hartford, Connecticut, the police union contract approved by the city council in March

1997 included a provision to pay officers required to carry beepers an extra $1,500 annually, avoiding the wholesale return of pagers that Alexandria experienced.[73]

As the term suggests, work speedups are an acceleration of activity resulting in the overproduction of one or more types of police services. The purpose is to create public pressure on elected and appointed government leaders to achieve some union-desired goal. The purpose of a work speedup may be to protest a low pay increase proposed by the employer, to force the employer to make more or particular concessions at the bargaining table, or to pressure the employer to abandon some policy change that adversely affects union members. Examples of speedups include "ticket blizzards" and sudden strict enforcements of usually ignored minor violations such as jaywalking, littering, or smoking in prohibited areas. **Work Speedups**

Work stoppages are the biggest hammer in any union's toolbox. The ultimate work stoppage is the strike, which is the withholding of *all* of labor's services (see Figure 10-5). This tactic is most often used by labor in an attempt to force management back to the bargaining table when negotiations have reached an impasse. However, strikes by public employees are now rare. In 1969, public employee strikes peaked at 412.[74] Today, there are fewer than 50 a year. The reasons for the sharp decline in strikes include the extension of collective bargaining rights to many public employees, state laws prohibiting strikes, the fines that may be levied against striking unions and employees, and the fact that striking employees may be fired. President Ronald Reagan's wholesale dismissal of the air traffic controllers remains a potent lesson for unionists. Additionally, the climate of the 1990s was not favorable to unionism. The growing conservatism in this country and the view that the unions are adept at getting what they want at "our expense" are also factors that make both private and public unions less likely to **Work Stoppages**

**FIGURE 10-5.** Policemen on strike, Albuquerque, New Mexico. (Photo copyright © Michael Douglas, The Image Works.)

## BOX 10-13

### Pawtucket Police Hit by the 'Blue Flu' Bug

**Associated Press**

PROVIDENCE—Pawtucket police came down with a case of the "blue flue" Friday, with all but a few officers scheduled to work the day and evening shifts calling in sick.

Mayor James E. Doyle denounced the job action, which was an apparent protest of his administration's refusal to pay police officers their annual $1,000 clothing allowance, The Providence Journal reported.

Twenty-eight officers, most of whom have seniority and can take time off with pay, called in sick.

The sickout was the first anybody could remember in the history of the department.

Police officials had to order some officers to come in from vacations and days off to fill the shifts.

The police department would not comment yesterday on the sickout and whether it was continuing, referring calls to a spokesman who couldn't be reached.

Police Chief George L. Kelley III said Friday the department was functioning at full staff but the sickout was costing the city more than $2,000 in overtime per shift.

"I understand one [officer] had to go on sick leave because his son had chicken pox," he said. "It was probably the only legitimate excuse all day."

The mayor said the sickout would hurt morale and damage the department's reputation.

"To have officers jeopardize the life and public safety of people in this city is unconscionable and unforgivable," he said.

The mayor's administration has said the unpaid clothing allowance is an issue that should be resolved over the bargaining table.

A police union spokesman denied that the sickout was organized or sanctioned by the union. State law does not allow police officers to engage in a work stoppage, slowdown, or strike.

*Source: The Boston Globe,* August 1, 1999.

---

strike.[75] In states in which public-sector bargaining is not allowed, tough laws affecting strikers have served to make public employees think long and hard before striking. Even in those states, many public employers know what they have to do in order to reap the benefits of a well-trained and seasoned workforce, and they do so to prevent the labor unrest that would impede economic development. Companies are not likely to relocate to cities that cannot govern effectively. Without these relocations, a city's budget becomes increasingly tight because tax revenue is flat or falling, residents and business are hit with increased and new taxes, and they begin to leave to find more hospitable locations in which to live and work.

Short of a strike by all officers are briefer work stoppages, which may affect only specialized assignments or involve a large number of police officers, but not all of them, in epidemics of the "blue flu" (see Box 10-13) that last only a few days. Work stoppages of this type are an important police labor tactic. While, like strikes, these briefer collective actions may be intended to force management back to the table, they are also used occasionally to punctuate the extreme displeasure of officers with a policy, for example, one unreasonably restricting moonlighting by officers, or with particular actions by officials inside and outside of the department, for example, the decision of a district attorney to prosecute a police officer on what is seen as a public-image-enhancing, but "thin" case. These briefer job actions sometimes follow a vote of no confidence.

In Boston, three members of the department's sexual assault unit—a specialized unit—refused to be on call overnight for emergencies, protesting the fact that the officers were not well paid for such assignments.[76] Los Angeles officers staged their third blue flu or "copout" when 45 percent of the daily workforce called in sick for two days in a row, just as the tourist season was beginning. This protest was made because officers had been working twenty-one months without a contract or pay raise and wanted to move the bargaining process forward.[77] In East St. Louis, police officers angry that firefighters made more money called in sick for one day—during which county and state police officers stepped in to patrol the streets. As a result, the city agreed to grant salary increases.[78] Ninety-five of 130 disgruntled Cook County, Illinois, deputies assigned to court security duties called in sick. Officials estimate that in the juvenile court alone, some 700 cases had to be postponed. Other public employers who have experienced blue flu epidemics recently include New Orleans, Louisiana; Pontiac, Michigan; and Sacramento County, California.

Although union job actions frequently center on economic factors, unions also take stances on other factors. In Washington, D.C., during 1997, Ron Robertson, president of the local Fraternal Order of Police, asked the federal government to take over the police department because the public and officers were in a "killing field."[79] Two days prior to Robertson's request, an officer working alone was shot four times and killed as he sat in his patrol car at a traffic light outside of a night club. The city's inability to staff two officers to a car had been a continuing union concern.

**Police Unions: The Political Context**

While contract negotiations were ongoing between the state and State Police Association of Massachusetts (SPAM), the association opted at the last minute not to air an ad that blamed Governor Weld for the death of a state trooper who was gunned down by a convicted murderer who had been released early by the parole board. In the midst of the state–SPAM negotiations, Governor Weld reappointed one of the members of the parole board. This member had voted for the murderer's early release, prompting the preparation of the ad. Despite the fact that the ad was not aired, a controversy ensued. Weld aides asserted that the union's tactics were designed to make the governor capitulate to the union's demands, and one of the governor's political allies, a state senator, called the ad "the lowest." The union responded by stating that the state senator was "intruding into the collective bargaining process and acting beyond his realm."[80]

When Riverside County, California, deputies beat two suspected undocumented Mexican immigrants after a well-documented high-speed chase, which was seen in homes everywhere on the evening news, the AFL-CIO took strong exception. AFL-CIO Executive President Linda Chavez-Thompson said, "our movement will not tolerate this kind of brutality, nor will we excuse officers because the situation [was] volatile . . . this is not a question of immigration rights, but of basic civil and human rights."[81]

The Lautenberg Amendment to the federal "Brady Bill" gun control legislation retroactively denies anyone convicted of a domestic violence misdemeanor from having a gun. When applied to police officers and federal agents, this controversial law ends their careers. Women's rights groups have supported the law because it denies a firearm to "cops who batter." Police unions have been angered by the retroactive application of the law, claiming it is unfair to take away an officer's livelihood with no advance notice. The Grand Lodge of the Fraternal Order of Police filed a lawsuit challenging the constitutionality of the law, a move supported by a number of unions, including the Detroit Police Officers Association.

Police unions also use high-visibility, high-impact tactics to further their objectives. Fraternal Order of Police Lodge 89 in Prince George County,

Maryland, spent $7,000 to erect billboards assailing what they saw as County Executive Wayne Curry's inaction on rising crime and an understaffed police department. Other police unions have used radio stations to broadcast thirty- to sixty-second messages designed to "bring heat" on politicians by mobilizing the public to their side. The Florida PBA has a "Van Plan" which delivers 100 uniformed police officers every day to the state legislature while legislators are in session to lobby for bills the FPBA supports. Some police unions also have in-state toll-free numbers that can be automatically connected to the offices of key legislators so members can lobby for their bills. When a sheriff spoke against the FPBA before a legislative committee, the FPBA campaigned against him in the next election; the incumbent was defeated, a strong showing of po- litical muscle by the union.

In 1996, when Aurora, Illinois, Mayor David Pierce had a political fund- raiser, 100 members of the police union picketed the affair to protest a lack of progress in stalled contract negotiations.[82] Conversely, in St. Louis, mayoral can- didate Clarence Harmon was backed in 1997 by three police groups, including the 1,250-member St. Louis Police Association. Not coincidentally, Harmon is the city's former police chief and had promised expanded community policing, a gun buy-back program—which when previously implemented took 7,600 guns off the streets in a month—and other efforts, including the reduction of domestic vi- olence. However, the city's Ethical Society of Police—a minority organization— was trying to decide which candidate to endorse. The Society and Harmon had been at odds over affirmative action and promotions while he was chief.[83]

Unions have also found parades and other community events to be vehi- cles for highlighting their concerns. In New York City, 150 police officers protested the city's contract offer by picketing the parade and shouting, "Crime is down and so is our pay." In Methuen, Massachusetts, a police union pay dis- pute threatened the cancellation of the city's annual Christmas Parade.[84]

# THE USE OF SURVEILLANCE IN THE LABOR–MANAGEMENT RELATIONSHIP

One of the most controversial tactics in the labor–management relationship is the use of surveillance to obtain information to influence the decision-making process. It may be used by police unions, police associations in states without collective bargaining rights, small informal groups of police employees, and employers.

Police officers have well-developed skills that make this tactic particularly effective when those being observed have relationships or habits that would bring discredit on them if publicly disclosed. In a state that did not have a public-sector collective bargaining law, a new chief was brought into the "Whiteville" Police Department from another state. Having previously run a unionized department, this chief thought he could have total control of the "Whiteville" officers due to the absence of a union in their department with which to contend. Initially the department was very cool to the chief because he was the first outsider brought in to run it. Within six months, however, everyone had warmed to him because he purchased new equipment the offi- cers had long wanted.

Unfortunately, this "honeymoon" was short-lived, coming to a swift and bitter end when the chief moved to reorganize the department. During the prior chief's administration, "Whiteville" had wanted to give officers a raise, but under the existing pay plan many officers were "topped out" and would have had nowhere to go for promotion. At this point the city's classification and compensation plan should have been updated, but the city went for the quick fix: raises were given to everyone, including the topped-out officers, who were promoted "in place" without changes in their assignments or responsibilities. Corporals were made sergeants without any supervisory responsibilities, sergeants became lieutenants, and so on. Approximately 80 percent of the department ended up with some type of rank.

To implement his new organizational structure, the new chief wanted to "roll back" people to their former ranks. Although the chief did not attempt to reduce the pay of these people, the response from the department was fairly immediate, widespread, and vocal. The "outsider" issue was resurrected as personnel protested that because the community had become accustomed to seeing them with their new ranks it would appear that they were being demoted and would thus be viewed as less reliable police officers. The roll back took place and departmental personnel litigated. When a chief from a nearby jurisdiction committed suicide, a copy of the newspaper article covering it was edited to read as if it had happened to "Whiteville's" chief and was placed on department bulletin boards. T-shirts showing the chief's face, circled and crossed out, which were referred to as the "chief buster" shirts, were defiantly worn around the department by some of the officers.

A small group of officers resorted to the use of surveillance to get information with which to drive the chief out of the department. While his wife was out of town, the chief reportedly "hosted" the visit of a woman from another state. Several days later, a copy of material appeared in the city manager's office, allegedly containing photographs of the chief picking the woman up in his departmental car in another jurisdiction, copies of the chief's credit card imprint at a hotel, logs of when the chief and the woman entered and left the hotel, the times lights went on and off in the woman's room, and other details. Ultimately, the chief left the department, but not before he unwisely called a departmental meeting in which he explained that he had sought marital counseling, exposing himself to even further disregard.

In light of these events, the very real threat of surveillance tactics within police departments, however sparingly they may be used, becomes clear. Police administrators must keep their personal lives on an exemplary plane or risk public exposure of professionally crippling information.

## ADMINISTRATIVE REACTION TO JOB ACTIONS

### Anticipatory Strategies

There are no simple answers for what police administrators should do in the face of a job action. A short period of ignoring a work slowdown may see its natural dissipation, or it may become more widespread and escalate. Disciplinary action may effectively end a job action, or it may simply serve to aggravate the situation further, causing the job action to intensify and become more protracted. In choosing a course of action, one must read the environment, assess the situation, review alternatives, decide on a course of action, implement it, monitor the impact, and make adjustments as necessary. In short, it is a decision-making process, albeit a delicate one.

The best way in which to handle job actions is for both management and the union to take the position that they have mutual responsibilities to avoid them. This may, however, not be uniformly possible; a union leadership that is seen to be too cooperative with management may, for example, be discredited by rank-and-file members and a sickout may occur. Negotiations that do not meet expectations, however unrealistic, of militant union members may produce a walkout. In general the following can be expected to reduce the possibility of a job action:[85]

1. The appropriate city officials, both appointed and elected, union leaders, and management must be trained in the tenets and practices of collective bargaining, particularly as they relate to mutual trust and the obligation to bargain in good faith.

2. Formal and informal communications networks should be used freely within city government, the police agency, and the union for the transmission of messages between them. The timely sharing of accurate information is essential to good labor relations in that it reduces the opportunity for misinformation or noninformation to create distance and build barriers.

3. On a periodic basis, key managers from the police department, along with the staff and its labor relations unit, should meet with union leaders and the representatives, including elected officials, of the city who are responsible for the implementation of its labor relations program. This serves to strengthen existing communications networks, it establishes the possibility to open new networks, and it is a continuing affirmation of the mutualism that is central to the process of collective bargaining.

4. Well before any job actions occur, management must develop and publicize the existence of a contingency plan that contemplates as many of the problems as reasonably can be foreseen with respect to each type of job action. For example, in planning for a strike, one must consider such things as how the rights and property of nonstrikers will be protected.[86] What security measures are to be invoked for government buildings and property? What are the minimum levels of personnel and supplies required? What special communications arrangements are necessary? Does the city's insurance extend to coverage of potential liabilities to employees and property? What legal options exist and who has authority to invoke them under what circumstances? What coordination arrangements are needed with other police departments and governmental agencies? What effect will various strike policies have on labor relations after the strike? How will nonstriking officers and the public react to various strike policies? May a striking employee injured on the picket line be placed on sick leave? Do striking employees accrue leave and retirement credit for the time they were out?

5. In attempting to determine the possibility of various job actions, the philosophy, capabilities, strengths, weaknesses, and propensities of the union, its officers, negotiators, legal counsel, and its members must be assessed. That, along with an estimate of the financial resources of the union, will be useful in anticipating the actions in which it is likely to engage and toward which planning can be directed. Although the hallmark of good planning is that it provides for future states of affairs, management is most likely to underestimate the union's capabilities, and the planning bias should, therefore, be toward an overstatement of what is possible.

**During the Job Action** Using a strike as an illustration, police managers must appreciate its long-range implications. The striking officers are engaging, as is the employer, in a power struggle that has an economic impact on both parties. The union is not attempting to divest itself of its employer, and for both legal and practical reasons, the employer cannot unilaterally rid itself of its relationship with the union; at some point in the very near future, it is most likely that they will resume their former relationship.[87] Considering this, managers must be temperate in their private and public remarks regarding striking officers; emotionally laden statements and cynical characterizations regarding strikers may provide a degree of fleeting satisfaction, but at some cost to the rapidity with which antagonisms may be set aside and the organization restored to its normal functioning. The union leadership and the rank-and-file membership have the same obligation; in the face of either management or the union not fulfilling their obligation, it becomes even more important that the other side be restrained in their remarks, or the ensuing trail of recriminations and biting comments will lead only to a degeneration of goodwill and the production of hostility, both of which will have negative effects on future relations.

Managers should strive to maintain a fair and balanced posture on the subject of the strike, and their dominant focus should be on ending it. Additionally,

1. No reaction to a strike or other job action should be taken without first anticipating the consequences of a reaction from the union and the officers involved. For example, the decision to seek an injunction ordering the officers to terminate the action and return to work could result in the officers disobeying the order and forcing a confrontation with the court issuing the order. A public statement that all officers involved in the action will be fired places the chief in the difficult position after the conflict is terminated of either firing participating officers or, in the alternative, losing face with his employees.

2. All management responses to a strike should be directed toward terminating it only, and not toward an ulterior purpose, such as trying to "bust" the union. There have been job actions in which the employer's sole objective was to destroy the union, an objective that frequently results in aggravated hostility between the employer and the union, the chief and officers participating in the action and among the officers themselves. The long-range effect of this approach is to injure the morale of the police department, affecting the quality of police services and ultimately the level of service to the public.[88]

The degree of support that nonstriking employees, the media, the public, and elected and appointed officials will give management in the event of a strike is a product not only of the soundness of management's position but also of how effective management is in communicating. For a department whose workforce is depleted by a walkout, personnel are a scarce resource and not to invest it in communications efforts is a natural temptation tinged heavily by the reality of other needs that must also be considered. To be borne in mind, however, is the perspective that the effective use of some personnel in communications efforts may shorten the strike.

It is essential during a strike that communications be rapid, accurate, consistent, and broadly based. Nonstriking employees may be kept informed by the use of the daily bulletin, briefings, or other devices. Letters may be sent to the homes of striking officers informing them of the applicable penalties for their actions, the status of negotiations, and management's present position with respect to these issues. Facsimile letters for this and other actions should already have been prepared as part of the development of the contingency plan.

Personal appearances by police managers before neighborhood groups, professional associations, civic clubs, and other similar bodies can be useful in maintaining calmness in the community, in providing one means of informing the public of special precautionary measures that they can take to protect themselves, and in galvanizing public opinion for management's position. Care must be taken to ensure that in this effort the needs of lower socioeconomic groups are not overlooked; they are not likely to be members of the Kiwanis or the local bar association, and special attention must be given as to how they too will be informed and their needs listened to.

**In the Aftermath**   At some point either the strike will collapse or an agreement will be reached, or both sides will agree to return to the bargaining table upon the return of personnel to the job. Often, a tense atmosphere will prevail for some time. Nonstrikers will resent any threats made and any damage to their personal property. Those who walked out will view those who continued to work as not having helped to have maintained the solidarity necessary for effective job actions. Union members dissatisfied with what the strike did or didn't produce may engage in petty harassments of nonstrikers, display thinly veiled contempt for management, or surreptitiously cause damage to city property. Management's posture during the strike can in part reduce the tensions inherent in the poststrike adjustment period, but it cannot eliminate the need for responsible action by the union or overcome the intransigence of a subversely militant union.

As soon as an agreement ending the strike is reached, a joint statement with the union should be released announcing the settlement and highlighting its key features, and letters should be sent to the homes of all officers urging them to put aside the matter and to return to the business of public service with renewed commitment. All personnel in the department should take particular care not to discriminate between those who struck and those who did not.

Among the other items of business that must be handled after a strike relate to whether strikers are to be disciplined, although the union will typically insist on amnesty for all striking officers as a precondition to returning to the job; what disciplinary measures are to be taken against those who destroyed private or public property during the course of the strike; what measures are to be taken against those who undertook various actions against officers who did not walk out; and the securing of a union commitment not to act in any way against nonstrikers and to actively discourage such actions by union members.

As a final note, there has been some experimentation with reconciliation meetings of parties to promote goodwill. Experience has demonstrated that, in most cases, the wounds are so fresh and the feelings so intense that it simply creates the opportunity for an incident; in one notable instance, a reconciliation party resulted in two hours of strictly staying in groups of strikers and nonstrikers and ultimately in a mass fight at the buffet table.[89]

## SUMMARY

From 1959 through the 1970s seven forces were at work contributing to the evolution of collective bargaining by public sector employees, including (1) the needs of labor organizations, (2) the reduction of legal barriers, (3) police frustration with a perceived lack of support in the war on crime, (4) insensitive personnel practices, (5) inadequate salaries and fringe benefits, (6) a sharp upswing in violence directed at the police, and (7) the success of other groups in using collective action to attain their objectives.

Because each state is free to extend or deny collective bargaining rights to police officers, state laws and local enactments regulating bargaining vary. In states with legislation allowing bargaining, the law is typically administered by a state agency referred to as a Public Employee Relations Commission (PERC) or by some similar title. Three models account for collective bargaining practices: (1) binding arbitration, (2) meet and confer, and (3) bargaining not required.

States with collective bargaining laws must also address the issue of whether an individual employee must be a member of a union that represents his or her class of employees in a particular organization. In a closed shop, employees must be dues-paying members or they will be terminated by the employer. Open shops are exactly the opposite arrangement: employees have a choice whether or not to join even though the union has an obligation to represent them. Agency shops take the middle ground: if employees are not dues-paying members, they must pay their fair share of applicable union costs.

Employee organizations that bargain for their members are unions. There are two categories of police unions: those whose parent is an industrial union, and independent, "police-only" unions. Merely because a majority of officers belong to a police employee organization does not mean that the association bargains for the officers. An appropriate number of signed authorization cards must be obtained from the group of officers that the union seeks to represent, and the grouping of the officers—the unit—must be determined to be appropriate by the PERC. Under certain conditions, an election by secret ballot may be required and any of three outcomes may arise: (1) the union or a particular union from among several competing unions may gain a majority vote, (2) there may be a runoff election, or (3) the officers eligible for union membership may vote for no union.

During the time that a bargaining relationship is being established, there are frequent chances for conflict to occur. These may represent conflicts over access to bulletin boards, meeting space, or more substantial matters. Of particular concern to both management and the union is that each party observe the other's rights and not engage in unfair labor practices.

Considerable effort is expended before management and the union arrive at the bargaining table; the members of the respective bargaining teams must be selected with care; the issues to be presented must be identified and researched; a site must be selected; and common procedures must be agreed on by both parties, among other matters.

Bargaining can be tough work, with progress difficult to come by. Even when there has been a general spirit of mutualism among the negotiating parties, a single hotly contested item can grind progress to a halt. In these situations, a cooling-off period may be sufficient to get negotiations back on track, or it may be necessary to resort to one of the major forms of resolving bargaining impasses.

The achievement of a written contract obtained through bilateral negotiations is a noteworthy accomplishment, one often heralded in the media. However, the hard work is not over. For a year or whatever period the contract covers, the parties to the agreement must daily live under the terms that they have mutually agreed will regulate their relationship. Despite the best of intentions and efforts and the existence of well-intended and reasonable people, it is inevitable that differences are going to occur as to what a particular clause means, allows, requires, or prohibits. When presented formally, these differences are called grievances and ultimately may be settled by arbitration.

When unionized officers are displeased with such things as the progress of negotiations or when they want to influence or protest a decision, they may engage in job actions such as (1) votes of confidence, (2) work slowdowns, (3) work speedups, and (4) work stoppages. Although strikes by police are almost always illegal, numerous examples of them exist. The administrative handling of job actions is an issue requiring sensitivity and good judgment. The best posture regarding job actions is one in which management and the union agree that they have a joint obligation to avoid them; however, management as a practical matter must plan for the worst scenario, and its bias should be to overestimate the negatives in the situation to be faced. In contrast, management's public pronouncements must be statesmanlike.

## DISCUSSION QUESTIONS

1. Identify and briefly discuss the seven factors that led to police unionism.
2. What are the three models of collective bargaining that summarize practices in the various states?
3. Identify the two broad categories of police unions and give three examples of each.
4. What makes the survival of independent police unions a challenge?
5. Define open, closed, and agency shops.
6. What do CHAPA, RIMPA, and similar associations have in common?
7. With respect to the scope of bargaining, how do the views of management and the union contrast?
8. To what do the terms *mandatory, permissive,* and *prohibited* refer?

9. Identify and briefly discuss three major types of bargaining-impasse resolution.

10. Are grievances inevitable during the contract administration period? Why or why not?

11. State and briefly describe four major forms of job action.

12. What can police leaders do to limit the possibility of job actions by unionized officers?

# NOTES

1. These themes are identified and treated in detail in Hervey A. Juris and Peter Feuille, *Police Unionism* (Lexington, Mass.: Lexington Books, 1973).

2. C. M. Rehmus, "Labor Relations in the Public Sector," Third World Congress, International Industrial Relations Association, in *Labor Relations Law in the Public Sector*, ed. Russell A. Smith, Harry T. Edwards, and R. Theodore Clark, Jr. (Indianapolis, Ind.: Bobbs-Merrill, 1974), p. 7.

3. The Public Service Research Council, *Public Sector Bargaining and Strikes* (Vienna, Va.: Public Service Research Council, 1976), pp. 6–9.

4. 296 F.Supp. 1068, 1969.

5. 324 F.Supp. 315, N.D. Ga., 1971.

6. 483 F.2d 966, 10th Circuit, 1973.

7. President's Commission on Law Enforcement and Administration of Justice, *Task Force Report: The Police* (Washington, D.C.: U.S. Government Printing Office, 1967), p. 144.

8. Ibid., p. 145.

9. Charles A. Salerno, "Overview of Police Labor Relations," in *Collective Bargaining in the Public Sector*, ed. Richard M. Ayres and Thomas L. Wheeler (Gaithersburg, Md.: International Association of Chiefs of Police, 1977), p. 14.

10. Rory Judd Albert, *A Time for Reform: A Case Study of the Interaction Between the Commissioner of the Boston Police Department and the Boston Police Patrolmen's Association* (Cambridge, Mass.: M.I.T. Press, 1975), p. 47.

11. From various tables, U.S. Department of Labor, *Employment and Earnings*, 8:4 (October 1961).

12. Bureau of the Census, *Statistical Abstract of the United States*, 1975 (Washington, D.C.: U.S. Government Printing Office, 1975), p. 162.

13. John H. Burpo, *The Police Labor Movement* (Springfield, Ill.: Charles C. Thomas, 1971), p. 34.

14. Albert, *A Time for Reform*, p. 29. Several recent studies have reported that market forces other than unions explain better the rise in public employees' salaries than does union activity.

15. These data were extracted from the Federal Bureau of Investigation's *Uniform Crime Reports* (Washington, D.C.: U.S. Government Printing Office, 1965 and 1970).

16. William W. Scranton, chairman, *Report of the President's Commission on Campus Unrest* (Washington, D.C.: U.S. Government Printing Office, 1970), p. 18.

17. Sterling D. Spero and John M. Capozzola, *The Urban Community and Its Unionized Bureaucracies* (New York: Dunellen, 1973), p. 183.

18. International Association of Chiefs of Police, *Police Unions and Other Police Organizations* (Washington, D.C.: International Association of Chiefs of Police, 1944), pp. 28–30.

19. From the March 16, 1967 statement of Commissioner Donald Pomerleau on the unionization of the Baltimore Police Department at the State House, Annapolis, Maryland.

20. Joe Sciacca, "Cop Union Chief's Comment Draws Fire," *Boston Herald*, Dec. 12, 1990.

21. Will Aitchison, *The Rights of Police Officers*, 3rd ed. (Portland, Ore.: Labor Relations Information System, 1996), p. 7.

22. Ibid.

23. Ibid.

24. Ibid, p. 8.

25. Ibid.

26. Ibid., pp. 8–9.

27. Ibid., p. 8.

28. Dane M. Partridge, "Teacher Strikes and Public Policy," citing Ichniowski, *Journal of Collective Negotiations in the Public Sector*, 25:1 (1996), 8.

29. Aitchison, *The Rights of Police Officers*, p. 9.

30. Ibid.

31. Ibid.

32. Ibid.

33. Portions of this section, revised and with additional information through 1997, are drawn from Charles R. Swanson, "A Topology of Police Collective Bargaining Employee Organizations," *Journal of Collective Negotiations in the Public Sector*, 6:4 (1977), 341–346.

34. Interview with Garry Waterhouse, AFSCME Council 15, Connecticut Council of Police Unions, April 4, 1997.

35. We are indebted to Chuck Foy, President, Local 7077, for his assistance on April 7, 1997, with the

information on the CWA, the NCPSO, and AZCOPS.

36. Aitchison, *The Rights of Police Officers,* p. 12.

37. Thanks to Roger Hakeman, President, LCDSA, for his help with this material on April 9, 1997.

38. William J. Bopp, *Police Personnel Administration* (Boston: Holbrook Press, 1974), p. 345.

39. See Richard S. Rubin et al., "Public Sector Unit Determination Administrative Procedures and Case Law," Midwest Center for Public Sector Labor Relations, Indiana University Department of Labor Contract J-9-P-6-0215, May 31, 1978.

40. In this regard, see Stephen L. Hayford, William A. Durkee, and Charles W. Hickman, "Bargaining Unit Determination Procedures in the Public Sector: A Comparative Evaluation," *Employee Relations Law Journal,* 5:1 (Summer 1979), 86.

41. These points are drawn from the private-sector National Labor Relations Act, Section 7 amended, which has served as a model for the portion of many public-sector laws pertaining to unfair labor practices.

42. Paul Prasow et al., *Scope of Bargaining in the Public Sector—Concepts and Problems* (Washington, D.C.: U.S. Department of Labor, 1972), p. 5. For a more extended treatment of the subject, see Walter Gershenfeld, J. Joseph Loewenberg, and Bernard Ingster, *Scope of Public-Sector Bargaining* (Lexington, Mass.: Lexington Books, 1977).

43. Aitchison, *The Rights of Police Officers,* p. 18.

44. Ibid., pp. 41 and 32.

45. Ibid., p. 25.

46. Ibid., pp. 19–20.

47. Donald Slesnick, "What Is the Effect of a Sunshine Law on Collective Bargaining: A Union View," *Journal of Law and Education,* 5 (October 1976), 489.

48. On costing out contracts, see Marvin Friedman, *The Use of Economic Data in Collective Bargaining* (Washington, D.C.: Government Printing Office, 1978).

49. Charles W. Maddox, *Collective Bargaining in Law Enforcement* (Springfield, Ill.: Charles C. Thomas, 1975), p. 54.

50. Arnold Zack, *Understanding Fact-Finding and Arbitration in the Public Sector* (Washington, D.C.: Government Printing Office, 1974), p. 1.

51. Ibid., p. 1; most characteristically the mediator meets with labor and management separately.

52. Zack, *Understanding Fact-Finding,* p. 1.

53. Thomas P. Gilroy and Anthony V. Sinicropi, "Impasse Resolution in Public Employment," *Industrial and Labor Relations Review,* 25 (July 1971–1972). 499.

54. Robert G. Howlett, "Fact Finding: Its Values and Limitations—Comment," Arbitration and the Expanded Role of Neutrals, Proceedings of the Twenty-Third Annual Meeting of the National Academy of Arbitrators (Washington, D.C.: Bureau of National Affairs, 1970), p. 156.

55. Zack, *Understanding Fact-Finding,* p. 1.

56. Ibid.

57. Ibid.

58. Council of State Governments and the International Personnel Management Association, *Public Sector Labor Relations* (Lexington, Ky.: Council of State Governments, 1975), p. 38.

59. One exception is *City of Sioux Falls* v. *Sioux Falls Firefighters Local 813, 535,* GERR B-4 (1973), a Fourth Judicial Circuit Court of South Dakota decision.

60. Council of State Governments, *Public Sector Labor Relations,* p. 31.

61. Arnold Zack, *Understanding Grievance Arbitration in the Public Sector* (Washington, D.C.: U.S. Government Printing Office, 1974), p. 1.

62. Maddox, *Collective Bargaining,* p. 109.

63. Zack, *Understanding Grievance Arbitration,* p. 4.

64. Maurice S. Trotta, *Arbitration of Labor-Management Disputes* (New York: Amacon, 1974), p. 237, with changes.

65. See Helen Lavan and Cameron Carley, "Analysis of Arbitrated Employee Grievance Cases in Police Departments," *Journal of Collective Negotiations in Public Sector,* 14:3 (1985), 250–251.

66. Zack, *Understanding Grievance Arbitration,* p. 32.

67. Ibid.

68. Indira A. R. Lakshmanan, "State Police Fault Colonel," *Boston Globe,* February 1, 1994, 24.

69. Terry M. Neal, "300 PG Officers Vote No-Confidence in Commanders," *Washington Post,* August 16, 1995, Section D, p. 3.

70. David Marc Kleinman, "Zinging it to the Chief," *Police Magazine,* 2:3 (1979), 39.

71. Michael Cooper, "Police Picket Traffic Courts, As Pact Protests Go On," *The New York Times,* January 27, 1997, Section B, p. 3.

72. Peter Finn, "Police Officers Send Pointed Message: More Than 150 Pagers Turned In To Protest Alexandria Pay Scale," *Washington Post,* January 24, 1997, Section B, p. 6.

73. Stephanie Reitz, "Council Approves Police Contract in East Hartford," *The Hartford Courant,* March 19, 1997, B-1.

74. Jack Rabin, Thomas Vocino, W. Bartley Hildreth, and Gerald J. Miller, eds., *Handbook of Public Sector Labor Relations* (New York: Marcel Dekker, 1994), p. 6.

75. On these and related points see Robert P. Engvall, "Public Sector Unionization in 1995 or It Appears the Lion King Has Eaten Robin Hood," *Journal of Collective Negotiations in the Public Sector,* 24:3 (1995), 255–269.

76. Indira A. R. Lakshmanan, "3 Allegedly Protest On-Call Police Duty," *Boston Globe,* July 10, 1995.

77. Daniel B. Wood, "Police Strike Hits L.A. as Tourist Season Opens," *Christian Science Monitor,* June 3, 1994, 2.

78. Kim Bell, " 'Blue Flu' Strikes in St. Louis," *St. Louis Post-Dispatch,* May 30, 1993, Section D, p. 1.

79. *Detroit Free Press,* February 8, 1997.

80. Don Aucoin, *The Boston Globe,* September 27, 1997.

81. http://204.127.237.106/newsonline/96apr22/beatings.html.

82. Hal Dardick, "Cop Union at Odds with Mayor," *Chicago Tribune,* May 21, 1996.

83. Lorraine Lee, "3 Police Groups Back Harmon," *The St. Louis Post-Dispatch,* January 29, 1997.

84. Caroline Louise Cole, "Pay Dispute Could Stop City's Parade," *Boston Globe,* December 1, 1996.

85. On September 29, 1976, Richard M. Ayres presented a paper, "Police Strikes: Are We Treating the Symptom Rather than the Problem," at the 83rd International Association of Chiefs of Police Meeting, Miami Beach, Fla. Although it is not quoted here, some of his themes may be identifiable and his contribution in that regard is acknowledged.

86. This list of questions with modifications and additions is drawn from Charles C. Mulcahy, "Meeting the County Employees Strike," in *Collective Bargaining in the Public Sector,* eds. Ayres and Wheelen, pp. 426–430. Also see Carmen D. Saso, *Coping with Public Employee Strikes* (Chicago: Public Personnel Association, 1970).

87. Harold W. Davey, *Contemporary Collective Bargaining* (Englewood Cliffs, N.J.: Prentice Hall, 1972), p. 195.

88. John H. Burpo, *Labor Relations Guidelines for the Police Executive* (Chicago: Traffic Institute, Northwestern University, 1976), p. 14, with modifications and additions.

89. Lee T. Paterson and John Liebert, *Management Strike Handbook* (Chicago: International Personnel Management Association, 1974), p. 42.

## INTRODUCTION*

One of the primary characteristics of our nation's law is its dynamic nature. Rules of law are promulgated in three basic ways: by legislation, by regulation, and by court decision. Statutes and ordinances are laws passed by legislative bodies, such as the U.S. Congress, state legislatures, county commissions, and city councils. These lawmaking bodies often produce legislation that establishes only a general outline of the intended solution to a particular problem. The legislation authorizes a particular governmental agency to fill in the details through rules and regulations. Such rules and regulations have the full force of the law.

When the solution to a legal dispute does not appear to be specifically provided by an existing statute, rule, or regulation, a judge may rely on prior decisions of that or other courts which have previously resolved disputes involving similar issues, referred under the common law as precedent. Case decisions can be reversed or modified by a higher level court or by passage of new legislation. Sometimes judges must develop their own tests or rules to resolve an issue fairly through creative interpretation of a statute or constitutional provision.

Clearly, the fluid nature of our lawmaking system renders it impossible to offer a definitive statement of the law that will remain true forever or perhaps even for very long. The task of stating rules of law is complicated further by the vast number of legislative bodies and courts in this country. Statutes and judge-made law may vary considerably from state to state and from one court to another. However, interpretations of the U.S. Constitution and federal law by the U.S. Supreme Court are binding on all other courts, be they state or federal, and, therefore, are given special attention in this chapter.

The reader should view the material that follows as instructive background rather than as an authoritative basis for action. Police administrators should always seek qualified legal counsel whenever they face a problem or a situation that appears to possess legal ramifications. A primary objective of this chapter is to make police administrators more capable of quickly determining when they face such a problem or situation.

# —11—

# LEGAL ASPECTS OF POLICE ADMINISTRATION

*Law is order, and good law is good order.*
ARISTOTLE

## LIABILITY FOR POLICE CONDUCT

One of the most troubling legal problems facing police officers and police departments in recent years has been the expanded impact of civil and criminal liability for alleged police misconduct. It is commonplace to hear police spokespersons

---

*Jack Call and Donald D. Slesnick were the co-authors of this chapter in the first edition; Slesnick and Janet E. Ferris were the co-authors in the second edition; and the authors of *Police Administration* have assumed responsibility for it in this edition with Robert W. Taylor and Gregory P. Orvis having revised and updated much of the material.

complain that law enforcement officers are widely hampered by the specter of being undeservedly sued for alleged improper performance of duty. Although one may argue that the magnitude of police misconduct litigation may be overstated, the amount of litigation appears to be increasing, and is apparently accompanied by a movement toward larger monetary damage awards.

## BASIC TYPES OF POLICE TORT ACTIONS[1]

Law can be divided into two parts: criminal law and civil law. Police officers and other criminal justice practitioners are generally more familiar with criminal law because they deal with it on a daily basis. Each "piece" of the law addresses a specific type of action. For instance, criminal law focuses on crimes, whereas civil law applies to torts.

Barrineau defines *crime* as a public injury, an offense against the state, punishable by fine and/or imprisonment. It is the violation of a duty one owes the entire community; the remedy for a breach of such duty is punishment (fine or imprisonment) imposed by the state. Crimes are exemplified in the FBI Crime Index (murder, assault, robbery, rape, burglary, larceny, auto theft, and arson), wherein each crime is composed of specific elements and has an affixed penalty.

On the other hand, a *tort* is a private injury inflicted on one person by another person for which the injured party may sue in a civil action. Such action may bring about liability that leads to an award of money damages. Tort actions encompass most personal injury litigation. The injured party initiates the lawsuit and is called the *plaintiff*. The sued person is called the *defendant* and is often referred to as the *tort feasor*.[2] Examples of tort actions that are brought against police officers are allegations of criminal violations such as assault and battery (police brutality). However, most commonly they are civil actions brought about by false arrest, false imprisonment, invasion of privacy (through illegal search and seizure), negligence, defamation, and malicious prosecution.[3]

There are three general categories of torts that cover most of the suits against police officers: negligence torts, intentional torts, and constitutional torts.[4]

### Negligence Torts

Our society imposes a duty on individuals to conduct their affairs in a manner that does not subject others to an unreasonable risk of harm. This responsibility also applies to criminal justice practitioners. If a police officer's conduct creates a danger recognizable as such by a reasonable person in like circumstances, the officer will be held accountable to others injured as a result of his or her conduct. In negligence suits, defendants will not be liable unless they foresaw, or should have anticipated, that their acts or omissions would result in injury to another. The key in negligence suits is *reasonableness*. Was the conduct or action reasonable in the eyes of the court? Examples of negligence involving police officers often arise from pursuit driving incidents in which the officers violate common traffic laws, such as speeding, running a stop sign, or failing to control their vehicles, which results in the injury or death of another person.

### Intentional Torts

An intentional tort is the voluntary commission of an act that to a substantial certainty will injure another person. It does not have to be negligently done to be actionable. Therefore, an intentional tort is really a *voluntary* act such as assault, false arrest, false imprisonment, and/or malicious prosecution.

The duty to recognize and uphold the constitutional rights, privileges, and immunities of others is imposed on police officers and other criminal justice practitioners by statute, and violation of these guarantees may result in a specific type of civil suit. Most of these suits are brought under Title 42, U.S. Code, Section 1983, in federal court.[5]

In our system of government, there are court systems at both federal and state levels of government. However, federal courts are intended to be courts of somewhat limited jurisdiction and generally do not hear cases involving private, as opposed to public, controversies unless a question of federal law is involved or the individuals involved in the lawsuit are residents of different states. Even then, the suit may usually be decided in a state court if both parties to the controversy agree to have the dispute settled there. As a result, historically most tort suits have been brought in state courts.

A major trend in the area of police misconduct litigation is the increase in the number and proportion of these suits that are being brought in federal court. The most common legal vehicle by which federal courts can acquire jurisdiction of these suits is commonly referred to as a "1983 action." This name derives from the fact that these suits are brought under the provisions of Section 1983 of Title 42 of the U.S. Code. This law, passed by Congress in the aftermath of the Civil War and commonly referred to as the Civil Rights Act of

## Constitutional Torts

## Title 42, U.S. Code, Section 1983

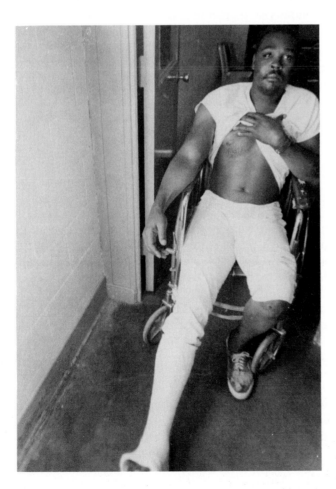

**FIGURE 11-1.** Rodney King in the Los Angeles County jail 48 hours after his arrest on March 3, 1991. (Photo courtesy Roger Sandler, Los Angeles, Calif.)

1871, was designed to secure the civil rights of the recently emancipated slaves. It prohibits depriving any person of life, liberty, or property without due process of law. Specifically, Section 1983 states

> Every person who, under color of any statute, ordinance, regulation, custom, or usage of any State or Territory, subjects, or causes to be subjected, any citizen of the United States or any other person within the jurisdiction thereof to the deprivation of any rights, privileges, or immunities secured by the Constitution and laws, shall be liable to the party injured in an action at law, suit in equity, or other proper proceeding for redress.[6]

After 90 years of relative inactivity, Section 1983 was resuscitated by the U.S. Supreme Court in the landmark case, *Monroe* v. *Pape* (1961).[7] In this case, the Court concluded that when a police officer is alleged to have acted improperly, for example, in conducting an illegal search, that officer can be sued in federal court by alleging that he or she deprived the searched person of his or her constitutional right under the Fourth Amendment to be free from unreasonable searches and seizures. A critically important element of Section 1983 is that the violation must have occurred while the officer was acting "under color of State law," that is, while the officer was on duty and acting within the scope of employment as a sworn police officer. Unless there is direct personal participation by police supervisory personnel, they are not generally liable for Section 1983 damages even if there are broad allegations of failure to properly train and supervise policemen who are liable in the Section 1983 lawsuit.[8]

**Bivens Action**    Section 1983 is the primary civil rights statute involved in litigation against municipal and state police officers. However, the statute rarely applies to federal agents (such as officials of the FBI, Secret Service, and Drug Enforcement Administration) because its terms require that the plaintiff be acting under "color of State law." Federal officials can be sued under one of two complaints—a *Bivens* action against individuals, but not the United States for violations of constitutional rights, and a tort action against the United States under the Federal Tort Claim Act (FTCA).[9] The actions can be combined in one lawsuit.

Essentially, a *Bivens* action is a judicially created counterpart to a Section 1983 tort action. The Supreme Court has permitted suits against federal officials (not, however, against the United States) for violations of constitutional rights that would otherwise be the subject of a Section 1983 action against a state or local officer. Its name is derived from the landmark case, *Bivens* v. *Six Unknown Federal Narcotics Agents* (1971), wherein the U.S. Supreme Court held that a cause of action for violation of the Fourth Amendment (search and seizure clause) can be inferred from the Constitution itself.[10] Hence, federal courts have jurisdiction to hear federal question cases involving suits against federal employees in their individual capacities.[11]

The preceding discussion demonstrates that three basic types of tort actions may be brought against police for misconduct: traditional state law torts, Section 1983 torts, and *Bivens* torts. This classification is important in that the type of tort action brought will determine who can be sued, what kind of behavior will result in liability, and which immunities might be available to the defendants.

At common law, police officers were held personally liable for damage caused by their own actions that exceeded the boundaries of permissible behavior. This rule applied even though the officer might have been ignorant of the boundary established by the law. Unjust as many of such results may often seem, the rule establishes one of the traditional risks of policing.

A more difficult question concerns whether the supervisors of the officer and/or the governmental unit by which he or she is employed can be sued for that individual's misbehavior. Generally, an effort to impose liability on supervisors for the tortious conduct of their employees is based on the common law doctrine of respondent superior. That doctrine, also called vicarious liability, developed along with the growth of industrial society, and reflected a conscious effort to allocate risk to those who could afford to pay for the complained of damages.[12]

Although American courts have expanded the extent to which employers can be sued for the torts of their employees, they have traditionally been reluctant to extend the doctrine of vicarious liability to police supervisors and administrators.[13] There appear to be two primary reasons for this reluctance.

The first is that police department supervisors and administrators have limited discretion in hiring decisions.[14] The second reason is that police officers are public officials whose duties are established by the governmental authority that created their jobs rather than by their supervisors or police administrators.[15] Therefore, police supervisors do not possess as much ability to control the behavior of their employees as their counterparts in private industry.

The court decisions that have refused to extend vicarious liability to police supervisors or administrators do not go so far as to insulate them from liability for acts of their subordinates in all cases. If the supervisor authorized the misbehavior, was present at the time of the misbehavior and did nothing to stop it, or otherwise cooperated in the misconduct, he or she can be held partially liable for the officer's tortious behavior.[16] However, these situations are not classic examples of vicarious liability; rather, they are instances in which it can be said that the supervisor's own conduct is, in part, a cause of the injury giving rise to the lawsuit.[17]

Nevertheless, the growing area of negligence as a Section 1983 cause of action has caused concern within police supervisory ranks. The courts have supported several negligence theories applicable to police supervision and management. The following is a discussion of important negligence cases and subsequent legal development in this area.[18]

**Negligent Hiring.** The law enforcement administrator and the local government entity have a duty to "weed out" those obviously unfit for police duty. Further, the courts have held that an employer must exercise a reasonable standard of care in selecting persons who, because of the nature of their employment (such as policing), could present a threat of injury to members of the public.[19]

**Negligent Assignment, Retention, and Entrustment.** Police administrators who know, or should have known, of individual acts or patterns of physical abuse, malicious or threatening conduct, or similar threats against the public by officers under their supervision must take immediate action. If an internal investigation sustains an allegation of such serious conduct by an officer, appropriate action by a police chief could be suspension—followed by assignment to a position with little or no public contact—or termination. A police chief failing to take decisive action when required could be held liable for future injuries caused by the officer. In addition, entrustment of the "emblements of office" (e.g., a badge, a gun, a nightstick) subjects a municipality and appropriate administrators of a municipal agency to liability whenever injury results from the known misuse of such emblements. In other words, administrators and supervisors have a duty to supervise errant officers properly.[20]

**Negligent Direction and Supervision.** The administrator and/or supervisor have the duty to develop and implement appropriate policies and procedures. Therefore, a written manual of policies and procedures is an absolute must. This manual must provide clear instruction and direction regarding the position of police officer, be widely disseminated, and be accompanied with training so that all officers understand the significance of the manual.[21] Further, the courts have held that supervisors must "take corrective steps" where evidence indicates that official policy is being abridged and/or the public is being placed at an "unreasonable risk" due to the actions of a police officer. Inaction on the part of the police supervisors and/or administrators is enough to establish negligence if there is a pattern or custom of police abuse and accession to that custom by police supervisors and/or administrators.[22] For example, the failure of a police sergeant to order the termination of a high-speed pursuit of a minor traffic violator through a congested downtown business area that results in serious personal injuries or deaths to members of the public is sure to bring litigation based on an allegation of failure to supervise.

**FIGURE 11-2.** As described in Chapter 2, community policing places additional responsibility on the supervisor to instruct and direct officers during routine incidents. Neighborhood disturbances are often characterized by high emotion and potentially violent confrontations, which may require the presence of a supervisor at the scene. The failure to provide such direction and/or supervision can result in a negligence tort action. (Photo courtesy of the Lexington–Fayette Urban County, Kentucky, Police Department.)

**Negligent Training.** The local unit of government and the administrator or supervisor of a police department have an affirmative duty to train their employees correctly and adequately. In a recent landmark case (*City of Canton* v. *Harris*), the Supreme Court limited the use of inadequate police training as a basis for Section 1983 actions. The Court held that inadequate police training may form the basis for a civil rights claim "where the failure to train amounts to deliberate indifference to the rights of persons with whom the police come in contact" and such official indifference amounts to "policy or custom." Therefore, it is incumbent on the plaintiff to prove that the training program is inadequate as to the expected duties of an officer and that the deficiency of training is closely related to the ultimate injury[23] (see Box 11-1).

## BOX 11-1

### Written Policies Best Defense Against Police Liability Exposures

**by Michael Schachner**

ATLANTA—Police departments can best manage potential liability by implementing written policies and procedures and then training officers to adhere to them, according to a liability management consultant.

Police chiefs and municipal risk managers also must make a greater effort to supervise and guide subordinates to control police liability exposures, he said.

In light of recent highly publicized cases of police brutality, like the Rodney King case in Los Angeles (*BI*, March 25), law enforcement officers now are under a tremendous amount of scrutiny regarding the use of force, observed G. Patrick Gallagher, director of the Institute for Liability Management in Leesburg, Va.

"Jury sensitivity toward police violence is way up, while police credibility is down. Supervisors must do more to look over their subordinates—not overlook their actions," Mr. Gallagher said during a session at the 12th annual Public Risk Management Assn. conference in Atlanta earlier this month.

"The police chief and risk manager can't manage liability if they can't manage their people. The greatest exposure to liability exists when the police chief knows what's going on but doesn't do anything," he explained.

Mr. Gallagher said that while police work is a "tough line of business where the adrenaline gets pumping," supervisors of line officers must implement a systematic approach to instructing officers about the proper use of force, one which addresses liability and increases effectiveness. Any approach also must detail disciplinary measures the department will take against officers who violate policy.

"As a leader, you need to guide with a plan and vision," Mr. Gallagher said.

That plan should include:

- A complete program of policies and procedures. "You have to have these. There are no short cuts," Mr. Gallagher asserted.

  Policies are usually formal written rules. They are formal when issued by the police chief, but they become informal when modified by supervisors, he noted.

  "You need policies for every little thing you do," agreed Richard Shaffer, police chief for the city of Harrisburg, Pa., in another session during the PRIMA conference. "Whether it be in the use of firearms, foot pursuit or vehicle operation, you must have written policies governing the procedures."

- Training. "You have to train your people in departmental policies. Officers do go through the academy, but they don't come out with an understanding of your department's policies," Mr. Gallagher said.

  "For example, a shooting case can become a problem—not because the officers lacked the skills to fire their weapons properly, but because they weren't trained as to when to shoot," he explained.

  "You can't have police on the street with a gun or performing a high-speed chase when they haven't completed proper training courses. We wouldn't have pilots flying airplanes under the promise that they'll soon be attending flight school," Mr. Gallagher said.

- Supervision and discipline. Officers who commit egregious acts do not feel that they will be held personally responsible, Mr. Gallagher said. "Often, the police department doesn't feel pain or loss in a lawsuit. Change your policy so that the officers know that they'll be held directly responsible for what they do on the street," he advised. Supervision and discipline, "combined with policy and training, is your defense in court," Mr. Gallagher said.

*(continued)*

BOX 11-1 (continued)

"If you have clearly written policies, training and supervision, you can control a case. You can't control a robbery or a high-speed car chase at 2 a.m., but if you have done everything else, it forces the plaintiff to fight you based on the incident only, rather than on five fronts."

"If you have policies and training, the chief, the department and the city are much better protected," Mr. Shaffer agreed.

- Review and revision. Risk managers and police department heads must pay close attention to police liability lawsuits filed locally or nationally, court decisions and any new state or local statutes that affect law enforcement and adjust their policies and procedures accordingly, Mr. Gallagher urged.
- A legal adviser, who does not necessarily have to be the city attorney.

Mr. Gallagher recommended that the public entity responsible for a law enforcement body employ a full-time specialist knowledgeable about police work who would advise the chief and city attorney after an incident, handle post-incident press relations and be a liaison between the department and a plaintiff.

"This specialist should be able to offer advice, but not necessarily legal counsel. Many city attorneys just don't understand police work," Mr. Gallagher said.

A problem in implementing the program often develops, though, because many risk managers cannot establish a partnership with the police chief and the department's other ranking officers, according to Mr. Gallagher.

"Hopefully, the relationship between the police department and the risk manager is good," Mr. Shaffer said. "But if the chief is not open to communication, then the risk manager should go straight to the mayor, who is likely the only one who'll be able to change the police chief's mind," he said.

"But don't start out by trying to stuff your risk management program down the throat of the police chief," Mr. Shaffer warned. "You have to remember that cops aren't risk managers—they're police officers, and they don't know your lingo and speech."

In developing a liability management program, departments should study the programs in place at similar police departments around the country and use them as models, Mr. Gallagher advised.

"Try to identify five departments that you would call leaders. Examine their leadership, training courses and values and employ them for yourself. There are plenty of very good police departments out there—they just have to be identified," Mr. Gallagher said.

*Source: Business Insurance, May 27, 1991, p. 3.*

---

The two areas of negligence that have been the greatest sources of litigation under Section 1983 in recent years have been negligent supervision and negligent training. Incidents arising out of the use of deadly force have certainly raised significant questions regarding training and will be covered later in this chapter.

A second difficult question with respect to who may be sued for damages caused by police misconduct concerns the liability of the police department and the governmental unit of which the department is a part.[24] To answer this question, it is necessary to briefly consider the concept of sovereign immunity.

Under common law in England, the government could not be sued because the government was the king, and in effect, the king could do no wrong. Although this doctrine of sovereign immunity was initially adopted by the American judicial system, it has undergone extensive modification by court decisions and acts of legislative bodies.

The courts were the first to chip away at the doctrine as it related to tort action in state courts. Most of the courts taking this action did so on the basis that the doctrine had been created initially because the times seemed to demand it, and thus the courts should abrogate the doctrine because modern times no longer justified it. Kenneth Culp Davis,[25] a commentator on administrative law, reported that 18 courts "had abolished chunks of sovereign immunity" by 1970, 29 had done so by 1975, and 33 by 1978.

Davis noted that the trend toward abrogation of sovereign immunity by judicial action was on the wane by 1976 and that the state legislatures had become the primary movers toward limiting or eliminating the doctrine. As a result of combined judicial and legislative action, by 1978 only two states still adhered fully to the traditional common law approach that government was totally immune from liability for torts occurring in the exercise of governmental functions.[26]

Lawsuits brought in federal courts against state and local officials are analyzed somewhat differently. The courts first examine the claim asserted by the plaintiff in the case and then determine whether the relief requested can be imposed against the defendants named in the action. For governmental officials and governmental entities named as defendants, the plaintiff's ability to succeed will depend on which immunities are available to those defendants. These immunities will be applied to determine whether governmental defendants remain in the lawsuit and whether damages can be assessed against them.

In federal lawsuits against a state, or state officials sued in their official capacities, the courts have concluded that the Eleventh Amendment to the United States Constitution precludes awards of monetary relief.[27] The courts have arrived at this result by deciding that the essence of the Eleventh Amendment is its protection of state treasuries against damage awards in federal court. The U.S. Supreme Court recently extended this principle to bar the recovery of attorneys' fees against state officials sued in their official capacity under 42 U.S.C. 1983.

The Eleventh Amendment does not, however, preclude courts from ordering state officials to do certain things in the future,[28] even if such orders will require the expenditure of substantial sums from the state treasury.[29] The rationale behind such orders is that federal courts can require that the actions of state officials comport with the federal constitution. The U.S. Supreme Court decided in 1984 that the federal constitution does not allow those courts to consider allegations that a state official violated state law; such claims must be addressed in state courts.

Individuals pursuing damage claims under Section 1983 against local government officials, and state officials who are sued in their individual rather than official capacities will have to overcome the defense available to such parties of "qualified, good-faith immunity." Such official immunities are not creatures of Section 1983; they arose from traditional, common law protections that were historically accorded to government officials. Basically, the good faith immunity doctrine recognizes that public officials who exercise discretion in the performance of their duties should not be punished for actions undertaken in good faith. Imposing liability on public officials in such situations would inevitably deter their willingness to "execute . . . [their] office with the decisiveness and the judgment required by the public good."[30]

Over the years, the courts have struggled to develop a test for "good faith." In 1975, the U.S. Supreme Court articulated such a test that considered both the official's state of mind when he committed the act in question (the subjective element) and whether the act violated clearly established legal rights (the objective element).[31]

However, seven years later the Supreme Court decided that the subjective element of the text should be dropped, leaving only the standard of "objective reasonableness."[32] Now, a court must determine only whether the law at issue was "clearly established" at the time the challenged action occurred.

Furthermore, if the plaintiff's allegations do not show a violation of clearly established law, a public official asserting good faith immunity will be entitled to dismissal of the lawsuit before it proceeds further.[33]

The immunities available to state and local officials are generally designed to protect individuals from liability arising out of the performance of official acts. With the Eleventh Amendment providing similar protection to the states, the question of the immunity of a local government was raised. Initially, the U.S. Supreme Court concluded that Congress had not intended to apply 42 U.S.C. 1983 to municipalities, thereby giving municipalities what is called "absolute," or unqualified immunity from suit.[34] Upon reexamination of this issue in the 1978 case *Monell* v. *Department of Social Services*,[35] the court decided that Congress had intended for Section 1983 to apply to municipalities and other local government units. The court further concluded that although certain other immunities were not available to a municipality in a Section 1983 lawsuit, the municipality could not be held liable solely because it employed an individual who was responsible for Section 1983 violations. The court made it clear that local government entities will be liable under Section 1983 only when that government's policies or official procedures could be shown to be responsible for the violation of federally protected rights.

Unfortunately, the *Monell* decision did not fully articulate the limits of municipal liability under Section 1983. The result has been considerable litigation to establish when a deprivation of federally protected rights actually results from enforcement of a municipal policy or procedure, and at what point an official's actions can be fairly treated as establishing the offending policy.[36]

More recently, the Supreme Court has held that "single acts of police misconduct" do not, by themselves, show that a city policy was involved in the alleged tortious act.[37] A lower federal court has since acknowledged that it may be questionable whether an alleged policy of inadequate training or negligent hiring will suffice to impose liability on a municipality for the unconstitutional actions of its police officers.[38]

## SCOPE OF LIABILITY

In general, state tort actions against police officers provide a greater scope of liability than do the Section 1983 and *Biven* suits. That is, in tort actions under state law, a greater range of behavior is actionable.

The types of torts under state law that commonly are brought against police officers may be categorized as intentional or negligence torts. An intentional tort is one in which the defendant knowingly commits a voluntary act designed to bring about certain physical consequences. For example, the tort of assault is the purposeful infliction on another person of a fear of a harmful or offensive contact. If X points an unloaded pistol at Y, who does not know the pistol is unloaded, X has created in Y an apprehension that Y is about to experience a harmful contact from a bullet. X voluntarily lifts the pistol and points it at Y, fully expecting that it will cause Y to be apprehensive about being hit by a bullet. Thus, X is liable to Y for the intentional tort of assault.

The tort of negligence involves conduct that presents an unreasonable risk of harm to others which, in turn, is the proximate cause of an actual injury. Whereas in an intentional tort the consequences following an act must be substantially certain to follow, in the tort of negligence the consequences need only be foreseeable. When X drives through a stop sign, even though unintentional, and hits the side of Y's car, X's behavior presents an unreasonable risk of harm to others and is the proximate cause of the damage to Y's car. Although X would have been negligent for "running the stop sign" even without hitting the other car, he or she would not have committed the tort of negligence in that no injury was caused (see Box 11-2).

Recently, the Supreme Court limited the scope of liability in reference to negligence as an element of deprivation of constitutional rights in Section 1983 and *Bivens* actions. In *Daniels* v. *Williams* (1986), the petitioner sought to recover damages as a result of injuries sustained in a fall caused by a pillow negligently left on the stairs of the city jail in Richmond, Virginia. The court held that the petitioner's constitutional rights were "simply not implicated by a negligent act of an official causing *unintentional* loss or injury to life, liberty, or property."[39] This case has had a profound impact on limiting Section 1983 and *Bivens* actions to intentional torts; hence, the sheer volume of such cases has significantly decreased in past years. It is important to note, however, that the Supreme Court "has not changed the rule that an intentional abuse of

---

**BOX 11-2**

## Agency and Officer Liability— A Case Example

In some instances juries may determine that both the law enforcement agency and the officer should be liable for the actions of the officer. The following case illustrates this point.

A police officer on routine patrol observed a motorcycle fail to stop for a stop sign. There were two men on the motorcycle. The officer pulled in behind the motorcyclist and activated his emergency equipment. The motorcyclist pulled over and stopped. The officer approached the driver and advised he stopped him for failing to stop at the stop sign. The driver took exception to the officer's observations and very sarcastically and profanely denied that he failed to stop. The officer became angry at the attitude of the driver and ordered both men to get off the motorcycle. They complied with his instructions. The verbal confrontation between the officer and the men escalated, and the officer proceeded to strike the driver across the head with a metal flashlight, knocking him to the ground. The passenger at that point became angry, very loud, and also profane, at which point the officer struck this individual several times across the head with the flashlight, knocking him to the ground. Both men eventually had to be taken to the hospital for their injuries. The driver had sustained permanent brain damage as a result of being struck in the head with the flashlight. The men were both charged with disorderly conduct, assault and battery on a police officer, and resisting arrest.

The officer completed his report and provided statements to the internal affairs unit that the men had physically threatened him and he was merely defending himself. There were no eyewitnesses to this incident other than the officer and the two arrested men.

As a result of their investigation, the internal affairs unit determined that the charges made by the two men could not be substantiated, and the police chief ruled in favor of the officer. Prior to this incident, neither of the men on the motorcycle had any police record.

At the criminal trial, both men were found not guilty. A civil action was initiated against the officer and his department by the two men. At the civil trial it was learned that this same officer had been investigated on numerous occasions for excessive force, and his actions had resulted in at least ten people being hospitalized in the past seven years because of the force he used in making arrests. In every case his department cleared him of any wrongdoing.

Upon hearing the evidence, the jury concluded, based in great part upon the officer's previous record, that he used excessive force in this case and his department, by their previous inaction, had condoned his actions and were guilty of negligent retention.

The jury returned a defense verdict which imposed $100,000 in punitive damages against the officer for his excessive and unnecessary use of force, and $250,000 against his agency for failing to take proper action against this officer, by either counseling, disciplining, reassigning, or dismissing him.

**FIGURE 11-3.** When police officers use wholesale "round-up" procedures on gang members without probable cause to arrest or search, they may run the risk of being sued under the Section 1983 tort claims of harassment, false imprisonment, and malicious prosecution. (Photo courtesy of the *FBI Law Enforcement Bulletin*, 1990.)

power, which shocks the conscience or which infringes a specific constitutional guarantee such as those embodied in the Bill of Rights," still implicates serious liability.[40]

As noted earlier in this chapter, many lawsuits against police officers are based on the intentional torts of assault, battery, false imprisonment, and malicious prosecution.[41] Suits against police officers for intentional torts can be brought as state tort actions, Section 1983 suits, or *Bivens* suits. Although suits against police officers for negligence torts can be brought as state tort actions, the issue is not so clear-cut with regard to Section 1983 and *Bivens* suits.

Generally damages assessed in civil litigation for negligence are ordinary (compensatory) damages that are paid by the employing governmental entity (or its liability insurance carrier) on behalf of the defendant officer. Therefore, as a general rule, the individual employee is not required to pay ordinary damages that result from a civil negligence suit. This is so because normally when governmental employees are performing their duties within the scope of employment, they are deemed to be the agents or representatives of the employing agency, and therefore not personally liable for their acts. However, where punitive damages are assessed for conduct that is grossly negligent, wanton, or reckless, individuals who have been responsible for such acts are personally liable, and, generally speaking, these assessments are not absorbed by the employing governmental entity nor by liability insurance. Thus, law enforcement employees who act in reckless, wanton, or grossly negligent manners will be subject to, and personally liable for, punitive damage awards.

In this constantly changing area of the law, the U.S. Supreme Court has established a rule that police are entitled to "qualified" immunity for acts made in good faith that can be characterized as "objectively reasonable." In *United States v. Leon*[42] the court focused on the objectively ascertainable question of whether a reasonably well-trained officer would have known that the act committed was illegal. Subsequently, the court following that logic held that if police personnel are not "objectively reasonable" in seeking an arrest warrant, they can be sued personally for many damages despite the fact that a judge has approved the warrant. In fact, the court stated that a judge's issuance of a warrant will not shield the officer from liability if a "well-trained officer in [his] position would have known that his affidavit failed to establish probable cause and that he should not have applied for the warrant."[43] However, the Supreme Court modified its position in a later case when an FBI agent conducted a warrantless search of a resident's home for a fugitive, by holding that an alleged unlawful warrantless search of an innocent third party's home does not create an exception per se to the general rule of qualified immunity. The Court held that the relevant question is whether a reasonable officer would have believed the search lawful once the clearly established law and the information possessed by the agent were taken into consideration and, if the answer is yes, whether the agent is protected by qualified immunity from civil liability.[44] Still, whereas public officials exercising discretion (for example, judges and prosecutors) have absolute immunity for their unreasonable acts, the only person in the system left to sue for damages for a wrongdoing will be the police officer, unless his or her acts can be attributed to the policy or procedural custom established by the employing governmental agency.

## TRENDS IN TORT LIABILITY FOR POLICE SUPERVISORS AND ADMINISTRATORS

Although there has been a traditional reluctance to hold police supervisors or administrators liable for the misbehavior of their subordinate officers, some courts have been increasingly willing to extend liability to these officials where the plaintiff has alleged negligent employment, improper training, or improper supervision.[45]

Under the first of these, negligent employment, a police official may be held liable for his failure to conduct a thorough investigation of a prospective employee's suitability for police work if he or she hires an applicant with a demonstrated propensity "toward violence, untruthfulness, discrimination or other adverse characteristics."[46] Of course, under this theory, the injuries suffered by the plaintiff would have to have been the result of the negative trait that had been demonstrated by the individual before employment as an officer. If the negative trait is not demonstrated until after employment, a party injured by the officer may be able to sue a police official successfully for negligently retaining the officer or otherwise failing to take appropriate remedial action. In some circumstances, the official may not be able to dismiss an officer who has demonstrated unfitness, but he or she still might be found liable if he or she negligently assigns the unfit officer to duties where the public is not protected adequately from the officer's particular unfitness. Finally, the official is potentially liable for negligently entrusting a revolver to an officer who has a history of alcohol or drug abuse or misuse of a weapon.

Suits alleging that police officials improperly trained a police officer have been particularly successful where firearms were involved in inflicting the injury. Courts have stressed that the "law imposes a duty of extraordinary care in the handling and use of firearms,"[47] and that "public policy requires that police officers be trained in the use of firearms on moving and silhouette targets and instructed when and how to use them."[48] Suits alleging lack of necessary training are also becoming increasingly successful in cases involving the use of physical force to overcome resistance, the administration of first aid, pursuit driving (see Box 11-3), and false arrest.[49]

## BOX 11-3

### When a High-Speed Chase Goes Wrong, Should the Police Be Liable?

by Laurie Asseo
The Associated Press

WASHINGTON, Dec. 9—The Supreme Court was asked today to sharply limit police officers' legal liability for injuries or deaths in high-speed chases like one that killed a California teenager.

"There is a simple remedy in this case, and that is to pull over and stop and yield to lawful authority," said Terence J. Cassidy, the lawyer for Sacramento County Sheriff's Deputy James E. Smith.

Smith wants the justices to throw out a federal lawsuit brought by the parents of Philip Lewis, 16, who was killed in 1990 when Smith's car accidentally struck him in a chase at speeds approaching 100 mph.

Lewis' parents say Smith violated their son's constitutional rights by engaging in a dangerous pursuit.

"This is a phenomenal problem" that kills hundreds of people every year, said the Lewises' lawyer, Paul J. Hedlund. Smith's chase of Lewis, who was a passenger on a motorcycle, was an "incredibly reckless act," Hedlund added.

#### The Court's Debate

But some justices appeared skeptical.

"It was at most an irresponsibly speedy chase," said Justice Antonin Scalia. "Is there any evidence that there was an intent to kill anybody?"

Chief Justice William H. Rehnquist said, "Do you think that high-speed auto chases are the sort of things the (Constitution's) 14th Amendment was designed to prevent? In 1868?"

Hedlund responded, "Although the framers didn't know about cars, they certainly knew about arbitrary, abusive, oppressive government . . . depriving

innocent people of their lives every day without any justification."

Cassidy, the deputy's lawyer, said he should be granted immunity from the lawsuit. Also, he said Smith should be held legally liable only if his actions were taken with malicious intent.

"There is a rational purpose more often than not in a substantial number of police pursuits," Cassidy said. Claims involving such chases should be handled under state law, not federal law, he added.

But Justice David H. Souter said other federal claims that a police officer used unreasonable force also involve the same purpose of apprehending a suspect.

"Why don't we, in effect, dismiss all of those cases on the same analysis?" Souter asked.

The Supreme Court will issue by July what could be an important ruling on police immunity.

#### A Police Chase

Lewis was struck by Smith's police car on the night of May 22, 1990. A deputy in another car had tried to stop the motorcycle, and when it took off Smith followed in pursuit.

The chase forced two other cars and a bicyclist off the road.

The pursuit ended when the motorcycle skidded to a halt. Smith's car hit Lewis while trying to stop, knocking him nearly 70 feet down the road. Lewis was pronounced dead at the scene.

The youth's parents, Teri and Thomas Lewis, sued. But a federal judge threw out their claim that Smith violated their son's rights.

The 9th U.S. Circuit Court of Appeals reinstated their lawsuit, saying the Lewises could force the deputy to pay damages if they could show he acted with "deliberate indifference . . . or reckless disregard."

Smith appealed to the Supreme Court, arguing that he should not have to go to trial because his conduct did not "shock the conscience," and that he

Another emerging theory of recovery against police officials is an allegation of failure to properly supervise or direct subordinate officers. This type of suit is typically brought where officials have failed to take action to rectify a recurring problem exhibited in the conduct of police operations by subordinates.[50] An interesting recent development in this area concerns the situation in which the police department issues a written directive that establishes a policy more stringent than the law requires. In several cases involving such a situation, the courts have held that the written directive establishes a standard of conduct to which police officers must conform or face the possibility of civil liability for their actions.[51]

**FIGURE 11-4.** Police officers responding to hostage and/or barricaded suspect situations often require specialized training in crisis negotiations and use of firearms. In this case, a man was taken hostage at a local television station while the suspect shouted demands from the control room. After hours of skilled negotiations on the part of local detectives, the hostage was released without harm, avoiding potential liability stemming from the incident. (Photo courtesy of the Phoenix, Arizona, Police Department, 1991.)

The last area to which courts have given recent increased attention concerns cases in which it is alleged that the police officer failed to provide needed medical care to people with whom the officer came in contact.[52] Although the incidents giving rise to such allegations can occur in a variety of situations, they seem to occur with greatest frequency when the plaintiffs have been in custody or have been mistakenly thought to be intoxicated when they actually were suffering from a serious illness. These cases are based on four theories of recovery: (1) failure to recognize and provide treatment for injury, (2) failure to provide treatment upon request, (3) failure to provide treatment upon recognition of an injury, and (4) negligent medical treatment. Suits in the first three categories may allege either negligent conduct or intentional behavior. Some courts have held that police officers do not have a duty to care for injured persons with whom they come in contact,[53] although such a holding is not likely to occur when the injured person is in their custody.

# ADMINISTRATIVE DISCIPLINE: DUE PROCESS FOR POLICE OFFICERS

The Fifth and Fourteenth amendments to the U.S. Constitution state that "no person shall be . . . deprived of life, liberty, or property, without due process of law."

**Liberty and Property Rights of Police Officers**

There are two general types of situations in the disciplinary process in which an employee of a law enforcement agency can claim the right to be protected by the guarantees of due process.[54] The first type involves those situations in which the disciplinary action taken by the government employer threatens liberty rights of the officer. The second type involves a threat to property rights.

Liberty rights have been defined loosely as those involving the protection and defense of one's good name, reputation, and position in the community. It has, at times, been extended further to include the right to preserve one's future career opportunities as well. Thus, when an officer's reputation, honor, or integrity are at stake because of government-imposed discipline, due process must be extended to the officer.[55]

It should be noted that the use of the "liberty rights" approach as a basis for requiring procedural due process has proven extremely difficult. The Supreme Court further restricted the use of this legal theory by holding that it can be utilized only when the employer is shown to have created and publicly disseminated a false and defamatory impression about the employee.[56]

The more substantial and meaningful type of due process guarantee is that pertaining to the protection of one's property. Although the general concept of property extends only to real estate and tangible possessions, the courts have developed the concept that a person's property also includes the many valuable intangible belongings acquired in the normal course of life such as the expectation of continued employment. However, not all employees are entitled to its protection.

The courts have consistently held that an employee acquires a protected interest in a job only when it can be established that there exists a justifiable expectation that employment will continue without interruption except for dismissal or other discipline based on just or proper cause. This expectation of continued employment is sometimes called "tenure" or "permanent status."

In 1972, the Supreme Court issued two landmark decisions on tenure.[57] In one of these cases, the plaintiff was a state university professor who had been hired under a one-year contract, and had been dismissed at the end of that year without notice or a hearing. The court held that the professor was not entitled to notice or a hearing because under the circumstances the professor had no tenure because he had no justifiable expectation of continued employment after his contract expired. Therefore, he had no vested property interest protected by the Fourteenth Amendment. The other case also involved a state university professor employed on a one-year contract, but this professor had taught previously in the state college system for ten years. Under these circumstances, the Court held that the professor had acquired de facto tenure (a justifiable expectation of continued employment) and, therefore, possessed a vested property interest protected by the Fourteenth Amendment.

Because property rights attach to a job when tenure has been established, the question of how and when tenure is established becomes crucial. Public employment has generally used certain generic terms, such as "annual contract," "continuing contract," and "tenure" in the field of education or "probationary" and "permanent" in civil service systems to designate the job status of employees. However, court decisions indicate that it is the definition of these terms as established by the employer rather than the terms themselves that determines an employee's legal status. Thus, the key to the establishment of the rights of an employee is the specific wording of the ordinance, statute, rule, or regulation under which that person has been employed.[58]

Merely classifying job holders as probationary or permanent does not resolve the property rights question. Whether or not a property right to the job exists is not a question of constitutional dimension; rather, the answer lies in a careful analysis of the applicable state and local laws that might create legitimate mutual expectations of continued employment.[59]

Federal courts have been inclined to read employment laws liberally so as to grant property rights whenever possible. For example, the Fifth Circuit Court of Appeal found that a city employment regulation that allows termination "only for cause" created a constitutionally protected property interest.[60] A federal district court held that a Florida statute (Section 112.532) known as the "Law Enforcement Officers' and Correctional Officers' Bill of Rights," created a property interest in employment because of its disciplinary notice provisions.[61] That approach is consistent with those of other jurisdictions in which state statutes have been interpreted to give property interests in a job to local government employees.[62]

Once a liberty or property right has been established, certain due process guarantees attach to protect the employee. The question becomes "What process is due?"

The question of due process for police officers falls into two categories: procedural and substantive. The former, as its name implies, refers to the legality of the procedures used to deprive police officers of status or wages, such as dismissal or suspension from their job. Substantive due process is a more difficult and elusive concept. We will simply define substantive due process as the requirement that the basis for government disciplinary action is reasonable, relevant, and justifiable.

Kenneth Culp Davis has identified twelve main elements of a due process hearing:

## Procedural Due Process

(1) timely and adequate notice, (2) a chance to make an oral statement or argument, (3) a chance to present witnesses and evidence, (4) confrontation of adverse

witnesses, (5) cross-examination of adverse witnesses, (6) disclosure of all evidence relied upon, (7) a decision based on the record of evidence, (8) a right to retain an attorney, (9) a publicly-compensated attorney for an indigent, (10) a statement of findings of fact, (11) a statement of reasons or a reasoned opinion, (12) an impartial deciding officer.[63]

The courts have not examined all the trial elements in the context of the police disciplinary process. However, there are cases that have held that police officers must be informed of the charges on which the action is based,[64] given the right to call witnesses,[65] confronted by the witnesses against them,[66] permitted to cross-examine the witnesses against them,[67] permitted to have counsel represent them,[68] have a decision rendered on the basis of the record developed at the hearing,[69] and have the decision made by an impartial hearing officer.[70]

A question that has proven particularly troublesome for the courts is whether or not due process requires that an evidentiary hearing be held before the disciplinary action being taken. In *Arnett* v. *Kennedy,* a badly divided Supreme Court held that a "hearing afforded by administrative appeal after the actual dismissal is a sufficient compliance with the requirements of the Due Process Clause."[71] In a concurring opinion, Justice Powell observed that the question of whether a hearing must be accorded before an employee's removal "depends on a balancing process in which the government's interest in expeditious removal of an unsatisfactory employee is weighed against the interest of the affected employee in continued public employment."[72] In *Mathews* v. *Eldridge,* the U.S. Supreme Court set forth the competing interests that must be weighed to determine what process is due: (1) the private interest that will be affected by the official action; (2) the risk of an erroneous deprivation of such interest through the procedures used, and the probable value, if any, of additional or substitute procedural safeguards; and (3) the government's interest, including the function involved and the fiscal and administrative burdens that the additional or substitute procedural requirement would entail.[73]

In 1985, the court further clarified the issue of pretermination due process in *Cleveland Board of Education* v. *Loudermill.*[74] The court found that public employees possessing property interests in their employment have a right to "notice and an opportunity to respond" before termination. The court cautioned that its decision was based on the employee's also having an opportunity for a full posttermination hearing. Therefore, assuming that a public employee will be able to challenge the termination in a full-blown, evidentiary hearing after the fact, pretermination due process should include an initial check against mistaken decisions: essentially, a determination of whether there are reasonable grounds to believe that the charges against the employee are true and support the proposed action. The court went on to describe an acceptable pretermination procedure as one that provides the employee with oral or written notice of the charges against him or her, an explanation of the employer's evidence, and an opportunity to present his or her side of the story. The court reasoned that the governmental interest in the immediate termination of an unsatisfactory employee is outweighed by an employee's interest in retaining employment and the interest in avoiding the risk of an erroneous termination.[75]

Thus, it is clear that those public employees who can legitimately claim liberty or property right protections of due process for their jobs are guaranteed an evidentiary hearing. Such a hearing should be conducted before disciplinary action is taken unless the prediscipline protections just mentioned are provided, in which case the full-blown hearing could be postponed until afterward.

For those administrators with a collective bargaining relationship with their employees, where minimal procedural safeguards are provided in contractual grievance-arbitration provisions, that avenue of relief may very well provide an acceptable substitute for constitutionally mandated procedural rights.[76]

As mentioned earlier, due process requirements embrace substantive as well as procedural aspects. In the context of disciplinary action, substantive due process requires that the rules and regulations on which disciplinary action is predicated be clear, specific, and reasonably related to a valid public need.[77] In the police environment, these requirements present the greatest challenge to the commonly found departmental regulations against conduct unbecoming an officer or conduct that brings discredit upon the department.

**Substantive Due Process**

The requirement that a rule or regulation be reasonably related to a valid public need means that a police department may not intrude into the private matters of its officers in which it has no legitimate interest. Therefore, there must be a connection "between the prohibited conduct and the officer's fitness to perform the duties required by his position."[78] In addition, the conduct must be of such a nature as to adversely affect the morale and efficiency of the department or have a tendency to destroy public respect for and confidence in the department.[79] Thus, it has been held that a rule prohibiting unbecoming conduct or discrediting behavior cannot be applied to the remarks of a police officer that were highly critical of several prominent local figures but were made to a private citizen in a private conversation in a patrol car, and were broadcast accidentally over the officer's patrol car radio.[80]

The requirements for clarity and specificity are necessary to ensure (1) that the innocent are not trapped without fair warning, (2) that those who enforce the regulations have their discretion limited by explicit standards, and (3) that where basic First Amendment rights are affected by a regulation, the regulation does not operate unreasonably to inhibit the exercise of those rights.[81]

The courts' applications of these requirements to unbecoming conduct and discrediting behavior rules have taken two courses. The first course, exemplified by *Bence* v. *Breier,* has been to declare such regulations unconstitutional because of their vagueness. In its consideration of a Milwaukee Police Department rule that prohibited "conduct unbecoming a member and detrimental to the service," the court found that the rule lacked

> inherent, objective content from which ascertainable standards defining the proscribed conduct could be fashioned. Like beauty, their content exists only in the eye of the beholder. The subjectivity implicit in the language of the rule permits police officials to enforce the rule with unfettered discretion, and it is precisely this potential for arbitrary enforcement which is abhorrent to the Due Process Clause.[82]

The second course taken by the courts has been to uphold the constitutionality of the regulation because, as applied to the officer in the case at hand, it should have been clear to him that his behavior was meant to be proscribed by the regulation. Under this approach, the court is saying that there may or may not be some circumstances in which the rule is too vague or overbroad, but the rule is constitutional in the present case. Thus, it should be clear to any police officer that fleeing from the scene of an accident[83] or making improper advances toward a young woman during the course of an official investigation[84] constitutes conduct unbecoming an officer or conduct that discredits the police department.

Many police departments also have a regulation prohibiting neglect or dereliction of duty. Although on its face such a rule would seem to possess some of the same potential vagueness and overbreadth shortcomings characteristic of the unbecoming conduct rules, it has fared better in the courts because the usual disciplinary action taken under neglect-of-duty rules nearly always seems to be for conduct for which police officers could reasonably expect disciplinary action. The courts have upheld administrative sanctions against officers under neglect-of-duty rules for sleeping on the job,[85] failing to prepare for planned demonstrations,[86] falsification of police records,[87] failure to make scheduled court appearances,[88] failure to investigate a reported auto accident,[89] and directing a subordinate to discontinue enforcement of a city ordinance.[90] The courts have refused to uphold disciplinary action against a police chief who did not keep eight-to-four office hours,[91] and against an officer who missed a training session on riot control because of marital problems.[92]

**Damages and Remedies**

In determining an employee's entitlement to damages and relief, the issue of whether the employer's disciplinary action was justified is important. For example, when an employee's termination was justified, but procedural due process violations occurred, the employee can recover only nominal damages in the absence of proof of actual compensable injuries deriving from the due process violation. Upon proof of actual injury, an employee may recover compensatory damages, which would include damages for mental and emotional distress and damage to career or reputation.[93] However, injury caused by the lack of due process when the termination was justified will not be compensable in the form of back pay.[94]

## CONSTITUTIONAL RIGHTS OF POLICE OFFICERS

**Free Speech**

The First Amendment of the U.S. Constitution prohibits Congress from passing any law "abridging the freedom of speech." It has been held that the due process clause of the Fourteenth Amendment makes this prohibition applicable to the states, counties, and cities as well.[95]

Although freedom of speech is one of the most fundamental of all constitutional rights, the Supreme Court has indicated that "the State has interests as an employer in regulating the speech of its employees that differ significantly from those it possesses in connection with regulation of the speech of the citizenry in general."[96] Therefore, the state may place restrictions on the speech of its employees that it could not impose on the general citizenry. However, these restrictions must be reasonable.[97] Generally, disputes involving infringement of public employee speech will be resolved by balancing the interests of the state as an employer against the employee's constitutional rights.[98]

There are two basic situations in which a police regulation or other action may be found to be an unreasonable infringement on the free speech interests of an officer. The first is when the action is overly broad. A Chicago Police Department rule prohibiting "any activity, conversation, deliberation, or discussion which is derogatory to the Department" was ruled overly broad because it prohibited all criticism of the department by police officers, even if the criticism occurred in private conversation.[99] The same fate befell a New

Orleans Police Department regulation that prohibited statements by a police officer that "unjustly criticize or ridicule, or express hatred or contempt toward, or. . . which may be detrimental to, or cast suspicion on the reputation of, or otherwise defame, any person."[100]

A second situation in which a free speech limitation may be found unreasonable is in the way in which the governmental action is applied. The most common shortcoming of police departmental action in this area is a failure to demonstrate that the statements by the officer being disciplined adversely affected the operation of the department.[101] Thus, a Baltimore police regulation prohibiting public criticism of departmental action was held to have been applied unconstitutionally to a police officer who was president of the police union and who had stated in a television interview that the police commissioner was not leading the department effectively and that "the bottom is going to fall out of this city."[102] In this case, no significant disruption of the department was noted. However, when two officers of the Kinloch, Missouri, Police Department publicly complained of corruption within city government, the Court held that the "officers conducted a campaign . . . with complete disregard of chain of command motivated by personal desires that created disharmony among the 12-member police force."[103] Because the allegations were totally unfounded and were not asserted correctly through channels instituted by state "whistle-blower" procedures, the dismissals were upheld.

A more recent basis for enforcing employees' First Amendment freedom of speech is that of public policy. The Eighth Circuit held that discharging an employee who violated the police department's chain of command by reporting misconduct to an official outside of the city violated the employee's First Amendment rights. The court reasoned that the city's interest in maintaining discipline through the chain-of-command policy was outweighed by the public's vital interest in the integrity of its law enforcers, and by the employee's right to speak out on such matters.[104] However, the same court upheld a department's refusal to promote a fire captain who, as union president, had issued a letter to the public in which he accused the chief of destroying the department.[105]

It appears that one's right to speak openly about the policies of a police department may well depend on four important factors: (1) the impact of the statements on the routine operations of the department, (2) the truth of the statements, (3) the manner in which the statements were made regarding existing policy orders involving chain-of-command and state whistle-blower regulations, and (4) the position occupied by the officer. For instance, statements made by dispatchers, clerks, and first-line officers in a large department that have relatively little impact may be given much more tolerance than supervisory or command personnel complaining of departmental policy, because the degree of influence, validity, and credibility significantly increases with rank.

**Other First Amendment Rights**

A basic right of Americans in our democratic system of government is the right to engage in political activity. As with free speech, the government may impose reasonable restrictions on the political behavior of its employees that it could not impose on the citizenry at large. It is argued that if the state could not impose some such restrictions, there would be a substantial danger that employees could be pressured by their superiors to support political candidates or causes that were contrary to their own beliefs under threat of loss of employment or other adverse action against them for failure to do so.[106]

At the federal level, various types of partisan political activity by federal employees are controlled by the Hatch Act. The constitutionality of that act has been upheld by the U.S. Supreme Court.[107] Many states have similar statutes, which are usually referred to as "little Hatch" acts, controlling political activity by state employees. The Oklahoma version of the Hatch Act, which was upheld by the Supreme Court,[108] prohibited state employees from soliciting political contributions, joining a partisan political club, serving on the committee of a political party, being a candidate for any paid political office, or taking part in the management of a political party or campaign. However, some states, such as Florida, specifically prohibit local governments from limiting the off-duty political activity of their employees.

Whereas the Supreme Court decisions might appear to have put to rest all controversy over the extent to which the government can limit political activity by its employees, that has not been the case. In two more recent cases, lower courts have placed limits on the authority of the state in limiting the political activity of state employees.

In Pawtucket, Rhode Island, two firefighters ran for mayor and city councilmember, respectively, in a nonpartisan election, despite a city charter provision prohibiting all city employees from engaging in any political activity except voting and privately expressing their opinions. In granting the firefighters' requests for an injunction against the enforcement of this provision, the court ruled that the Supreme Court precedents did not apply to the Pawtucket charter provision because the statutes upheld in the prior decisions had prohibited only partisan political activity. However, the Court of Appeals vacated the injunction after applying a balancing test that weighed the government's interests against the employees' First Amendment rights, finding that the government has a substantial interest in regulating the conduct and speech of its employees that is significantly different than if it were regulating those of the general public.[109] In a very similar case in Boston, the court upheld the police departmental rule at issue there on the basis that whether the partisan–nonpartisan distinction was crucial was a matter for legislative or administrative determination.[110]

In a Michigan case, the court declared unconstitutional two city charter provisions that prohibited contributions to or solicitations for any political purpose by city employees because they were overly broad.[111] That court specifically rejected the partisan–nonpartisan distinction as crucial, focusing instead on the office involved and the relationship to that office of the employees whose political activity was at issue. For example, the court saw no danger to an important municipal interest in the activities of a city employee "who is raising funds to organize a petition drive seeking a rate change from the Public Service Commission."[112]

Thus, whereas the Supreme Court has tended to be supportive of governmental efforts to limit the political activities of government employees, it is clear that some lower courts intend to limit the Supreme Court decisions to the facts of those cases. Therefore, careful consideration should be given to the scope of political activity to be restricted by a police regulation, and trends in the local jurisdiction should be examined closely.

The cases just discussed dealt with political activity, as opposed to mere political affiliation. May police officers be relieved of their duties because of their political affiliations on the basis that those affiliations impede their ability to carry out the policies of superiors with different political affiliations? The Supreme Court addressed this question in a case arising out of the sheriff's department in Cook County, Illinois.[113] The newly elected sheriff, a Democrat, had discharged the chief deputy of the process division and a bailiff of the juvenile court, both of whom were nonmerit system employees, because they were Republicans. The Court ruled that it was a violation of these employees' First Amendment rights to discharge them from non-policy-making positions because of their political party memberships.[114]

Nonpolitical associations are also protected by the First Amendment. However, it is common for police departments to prohibit officers from associating with known felons or other persons of bad reputation on the basis that "such associations may expose an officer to irresistible temptations to yield in his obligation to impartially enforce the law, and . . . may give the appearance that the community's police officers are not themselves honest and impartial enforcers of the law." Sometimes the prohibition is imposed by means of a specific ordinance or regulation, whereas in other instances the prohibition is enforced by considering it conduct unbecoming an officer. Of course, if the latter approach is used, the ordinance or regulation will have to overcome the legal obstacles discussed earlier, relating to unbecoming conduct or discrediting behavior rules.

As with rules touching on the other First Amendment rights, rules prohibiting associations with criminals and other undesirables must not be overly broad in their reach. Thus, a Detroit Police Department regulation that prohibited knowing and intentional associations with convicted criminals or persons charged with crimes except in the course of an officer's official duties was declared unconstitutional because it proscribed some associations that could have no bearing on an officer's integrity or the public's confidence in an officer. The Court cited as examples an association with a fellow church member who had been arrested on one occasion years ago, and the befriending of a recently convicted person who wanted to become a productive citizen.[115]

The other common difficulty with this kind of rule is that it is sometimes applied to situations in which the association has not been demonstrated to have had a detrimental effect on the performance of the officer's duties or on the discipline and efficiency of the department. Thus, one court has held that a police officer who was a nudist but was fully qualified in all other respects to be a police officer could not be fired simply because he was a practicing nudist.[116] On the other hand, another court upheld the firing of a police officer who had had sexual intercourse at a party with a woman he knew to be a nude model at a local "adult theater of known disrepute."[117] The court viewed this behavior as being of such a disreputable nature that it had a detrimental effect on the discipline and efficiency of the department.

The First Amendment's protection of free speech has been viewed as protecting means of expression other than verbal utterances.[118] That issue as it relates to an on-duty police officer's personal appearance has been addressed by the Supreme Court decision in *Kelley* v. *Johnson*,[119] which upheld the constitutionality of a regulation of the Suffolk County, New York, Police Department that established several grooming standards for its male officers. The Court in *Kelley* held that either a desire to make police officers readily recognizable to the public or a desire to maintain an esprit de corps was a sufficiently rational justification for the regulation. The issue of personal grooming and style continues to be a subject of hot debate in departments across the nation, particularly as officers move closer to their constituencies through community policing endeavors. Refer to Box 11-4.

BOX 11-4

## Officer Says Department's Mustache Policy Is Splitting Hairs

SAN FRANCISCO—He shows it off in Hollywood movies, uses it as a public relations tool and says even the mayor likes it.

But that's not good enough for the Police Department, which says Officer Kenneth Cantamout has to prune the long, curly handlebar mustache he's cultivated for 12 years.

On Friday, a judge ruled in favor of the department and upheld its order to trim.

Officer Cantamout said he'll appeal—and he may even ask fashion-conscious Mayor Willie Brown for help.

The mayor has "seen it and has always liked it," he said.

Maybe, but the mayor isn't going to intervene, a spokesman said Saturday.

Departmental regulations prohibit mustaches that extend more than a quarter of an inch beyond the end of the lips.

Officer Cantamout's mustache is long enough that he can twirl it into curls, which he then anchors neatly with mustache wax when he's on duty.

The department maintains that because he does not conform to regulations, his appearance undermines departmental morale and damages the force's public image.

"The department needs to have a standardized appearance," a spokesman said. "These policies are clear and in effect."

The trouble started after Officer Cantamout was transferred to the transit patrol division last December. For the previous six years, he had worked in administration with little public contact. But after his transfer, other officers began complaining.

Officer Cantamout says the mustache has become his trademark and helps break the ice with the public when he's on the beat.

"One of my most valuable tools is my mustache," he said.

It's also won the aspiring actor bit parts in commercials and movies, including *The Rock* and the upcoming *George of the Jungle.*

"If it's such a violation and such a problem, why was I allowed to have it for 12 years?" he asked.

Officer Cantamout filed a lawsuit to block the directive, claiming it was partly in retaliation for a department complaint he filed in 1993. But on Friday, Superior Court Judge William Cahill ruled that Officer Cantamout failed to prove that the order was retaliatory.

Officer Cantamout acknowledges that he's become tired of the battle, but he's determined to see it through for the sake of his hard-to-maintain image.

"It's high maintenance and takes a lot of work with all the wax and stuff," he said. "The easy thing to do would be to cut it off, but I'm going to go down fighting."

*Source: Dallas Morning News* (Texas), April 20, 1997, p. 7A. Reprinted with permission of the Dallas Morning News.

## SEARCHES AND SEIZURES

The Fourth Amendment to the U.S. Constitution protects "the right of the people to be secure in their persons, houses, papers, and effects, against unreasonable searches and seizures. . . ." This guarantee protects against actions by states and the federal government.[120] Generally, the cases interpreting the Fourth Amendment require that before a search or seizure can be effectuated, the police must have probable cause to believe that a crime has been committed and that evidence relevant to the crime will be found at the place to be searched. Because of the language in the Fourth Amendment about "persons, houses, papers, and effects," for years the case law analyzed what property was subject to the amendment's protection. However, in an extremely important case in 1967, the Supreme Court ruled that the amendment protected individuals' reasonable expectations of privacy and not just property interests.[121] Interestingly, twentieth-century technology has brought forth a number of key Fourth Amendment issues regarding privacy, especially involving private communications and wire taps. In a case involving a police officer suspected of gambling, the Supreme Court held that the use of a pen register did not require the same constitutional safeguards as those surrounding a wire tap. The pen register uses a "trap and trace" device that records phone numbers and the duration of each call but does not capture any type of communication between parties. The Court reasoned that no warrant or probable cause was needed as the Fourth Amendment was applicable to captured communication only, and that there was no reasonable expectation to privacy regarding the actual phone number.[122]

The Fourth Amendment usually applies to police officers when at home or off duty as it would to any other citizen. However, because of the nature of the employment, a police officer can be subjected to investigative procedures that would not be permitted when an ordinary citizen was involved. One such situation arises with respect to equipment and lockers provided by the department to its officers. In this situation the officer has no expectation of privacy that merits protection.[123] The rights of prison authorities to search their employees was at issue in a 1985 Iowa case. There the court refused to find a consent form signed as a condition of hire to constitute a blanket waiver of all Fourth Amendment rights.[124]

Another situation involves the ordering of officers to appear at a lineup. Requiring someone to appear in a lineup is a seizure of his or her person and, therefore, would ordinarily require probable cause. However, a federal appeals court upheld a police commissioner's order to sixty-two officers to appear in a lineup for the purpose of identifying officers who had allegedly beaten several civilians. The court held that in this situation "the governmental interest in the particular intrusion (should be weighed) against the offense to personal dignity and integrity." Because of the nature of the police officer's employment relationship, "he does not have the full privacy and liberty from police officials that he would otherwise enjoy."[125]

To enforce the protections guaranteed by the Fourth Amendment's search and seizure requirements, the courts have fashioned the so-called "exclusionary rule," which prohibits the use of evidence obtained in violation of the Fourth Amendment in criminal proceedings. However, in a series of recent cases, the Supreme Court has redefined the concept of "reasonableness" as it applies to the Fourth Amendment and the exclusionary rule. In *United States* v. *Leon* and the companion case of *Massachusetts* v. *Sheppard,* the court held that the Fourth Amendment "requires officers to have reasonable knowledge of what the law prohibits" in a search.[126] In essence, *Leon* and *Sheppard* began to develop the concept of "totality of circumstances" confirmed in *Illinois* v. *Gates,* that is, that evidence cannot be suppressed when an officer is acting "under good faith" whether or not a warrant issued is good on the surface.[127] These cases have far-reaching implications in civil actions against police officers, in that officers enjoy the benefits of qualified immunity when they are acting in good faith and under the belief that probable cause does exist.[128] Indeed, the Court has held that only a clear absence of probable cause will defeat a claim of qualified immunity.[129]

Finally, the exclusionary rule and the above mentioned cases have an important bearing on disciplinary hearings involving the police. In *Sheetz* v. *Mayor and City Council of Baltimore,* the Court held that illegally seized drugs in the possession of an officer could be used in an administrative discharge proceeding against that officer.[130] The Court reasoned that only a bad faith seizure would render the evidence inadmissible because the police are not motivated to seize illegally for the purpose of use in an administrative discharge proceeding; hence, the exclusionary rule was not applicable and the officer's firing was upheld.

# RIGHT AGAINST SELF-INCRIMINATION

On two occasions the Supreme Court has addressed questions concerning the Fifth Amendment rights of police officers who are the subjects of investigations. In *Garrity* v. *New Jersey*,[131] a police officer had been ordered by the attorney general to answer certain questions or be discharged. He testified and the information gained as a result of his answers was later used to convict him of criminal charges.

The Fifth Amendment protects an individual from being compelled "in any criminal case to be a witness against himself."[132] The Supreme Court held that the information obtained from the police officer could not be used at his criminal trial because the Fifth Amendment forbids the use of coercion of this sort to extract an incriminating statement from a suspect.

In *Gardner* v. *Broderick*,[133] a police officer had declined to answer questions put to him by a grand jury investigating police misconduct on the grounds that his answers might tend to incriminate him. As a result, the officer was dismissed from his job. The Supreme Court ruled that the officer could not be fired for his refusal to waive his constitutional right to remain silent. However, the court made it clear that it would have been proper for the grand jury to require the officer to answer or face discharge for his refusal so long as the officer had been informed that his answers could not be used against him in a criminal case and the questions were related specifically, directly, and narrowly to the performance of his official duties. The court felt that this approach was necessary to protect the important state interest in ensuring the police officers were performing their duties faithfully.

In their ruling, the Supreme Court set forth a basic standard for disciplinary investigations of police officers. Referring to *Garrity,* the Court ruled that although a police agency can conduct an administrative investigation of an officer, it cannot in the course of that investigation compel the officer to waive his or her privilege against self-incrimination. As it has been interpreted, *Garrity* requires that before a police agency can question an officer regarding an issue that may involve disciplinary action against the officer for refusal to answer questions, the agency must

1. Order the officer to answer the questions
2. Ask questions that are specifically, directly, and narrowly related to the officer's duties
3. Advise the officer that the answers to the questions will not be used against the officer in criminal proceedings[134] (see Box 11-5).

If the officer refuses to answer appropriate questions after being given these warnings and advisement, then he or she may be disciplined for insubordination.

As a result of these cases, it is proper to discharge police officers who refuse to answer questions that are related specifically and directly to the performance of their duties and who have been informed that any answers they do give cannot be used against them in a criminal proceeding.[135]

Historically, it was not uncommon for police departments to make use of polygraph examinations in the course of internal investigations. The legal question that has arisen most frequently is whether an officer may be required to submit to such a procedure under threat of discharge for refusal to do so. There is some diversity of legal authority on this question, but the majority of

## BOX 11-5

### Disciplinary Interview Advice of Rights

The following is a sample warning given to police officers during a disciplinary setting. Note that the "advice of rights" statement is *not* the warning mandated in criminal cases under the *Miranda* decision. In a disciplinary interview, *Miranda* has no application.

I wish to advise you that you are being questioned as part of an official investigation of the Police Department. You will be asked questions specifically directed and narrowly related to the performance of your official duties or fitness for office. You are entitled to all the rights and privileges guaranteed by the laws and the constitution of this state and the Constitution of the United States, including the right not to be compelled to incriminate yourself (and to have an attorney of your choice present during questioning). I further wish to advise you that if you refuse to testify or to answer questions relating to the performance of your official duties or fitness for duty, you will be subject to departmental charges which would result in your dismissal from the Police Department. If you do answer, neither your statements nor any information or evidence which is gained by reason of such statements can be used against you in any subsequent criminal proceeding. However, these statements may be used against you in relation to subsequent departmental charges.

*Source: Police Discipline and Labor Problems Workbook* (Chicago: Americans for Effective Law Enforcement, Inc., 1989), pp. 2–8.

---

courts that have considered it have held that an officer can be required to take the examination.[136]

An Arizona court overturned a county merit system commission's finding that a polygraph examination could be ordered only as a last resort after all other investigative efforts had been exhausted, and held that

> a polygraph is always proper to verify statements made by law enforcement officers during the course of a departmental investigation as long as the officers are advised that the answers cannot be used against them in any criminal prosecution, that the questions will relate solely to the performance of official duties, and that refusal will result in dismissal.[137]

On the other hand, a more recent decision of the Florida Supreme Court held that the dismissal of a police officer for refusing to submit to a polygraph test constituted "an unjust and unlawful job deprivation." Further, the court recognized that granting to public employers a carte blanche authority to force employees to submit to unlimited questioning during a polygraph test would conflict with the employees constitutional right of privacy, and would abrogate his or her protection against self-incrimination.[138]

Further, the use of the polygraph test to screen job applicants for police jobs has fallen under severe criticism. In 1987, a federal judge declared the test to be both unconstitutional and unreliable and ordered the city of Philadelphia to reconsider the applications of individuals denied positions due to their failure to pass a polygraph test. Conversely, the Court of Appeals reversed the District Court holding and stated that the use of polygraph tests for preemployment screening did not violate either equal protection or substantive due process.[139]

As a result of these cases and the resulting ambiguity concerning polygraph testing and the Fifth Amendment, most jurisdictions have limited the use of the polygraph by statute and/or administrative regulation. Also, most agencies have developed extensive internal policies to limit the use of the polygraph and to expressly detail circumstances in which the test may be used to corroborate officer statements.

# OTHER GROUNDS FOR DISCIPLINARY ACTION

**Conduct Unbecoming an Officer**

By far the largest number of police disciplinary cases arise under rules prohibiting conduct unbecoming an officer. These rules have traditionally been vague and overbroad in order to control officers both on and off duty.[140] Most "conduct unbecoming" regulations have been challenged for being unconstitutionally vague.[141] The basis of this claim rests in the concept of reasonableness as applied to the misconduct.[142] In a leading case, the California Supreme Court held that the permissible application of a "conduct unbecoming" regulation turns on whether the officer could reasonably anticipate that his or her conduct would be the subject of discipline:

> We construe "conduct unbecoming" a city police officer to refer only to conduct which indicates a *lack of fitness* to perform the functions of a police officer. Thus construed, [the rule] provides a sufficiently specific standard against which the conduct of a police officer in a particular case can be judged. Police officers . . . will normally be able to determine what kind of conduct indicates unfitness to perform the functions of police officer.[143]

A wide variety of conduct has been held to fall appropriately within the scope of a "conduct unbecoming" regulation. It is important to note that the regulation must reasonably warn the officer of what type of conduct would be considered unbecoming and that said conduct would tend to affect the officer's

**FIGURE 11-5.** The routine traffic stop has been the setting for activities that commonly fall within the scope of "conduct unbecoming an officer." Complaints often include verbal abuse, swearing, unprofessional conduct, and/or sexual harassment by police officers. Some agencies have placed hidden cameras and microphones in police vehicles, in part to defend themselves against such allegations. (Photo courtesy of the *FBI Law Enforcement Bulletin*, 1990.)

performance of his or her duties adversely or cause the department to fall into public disrepute.[144] Some of the activities that commonly fall within the scope of a "conduct unbecoming" regulation and that have been upheld by the courts include associating with crime figures or persons with a criminal record,[145] verbal abuse and swearing,[146] off-duty drinking and intoxication,[147] criminal conduct,[148] dishonesty,[149] fighting with coworkers,[150] insubordination,[151] and a number of improprieties involving sexual activity.

The cases in this area tend to fall into two general categories: cases involving adultery and cases involving homosexuality.

## Sexual Conduct

Most cases are in general agreement that adultery, even though committed while the policeman was off duty and in private, created a proper basis for disciplinary action.[152] The courts held that such behavior brings adverse criticism on the agency and tends to undermine public confidence in the department. However, one case involving an Internal Revenue Service agent suggests that to uphold disciplinary action for adultery, the government would have to prove that the employing agency was actually discredited; the court further stated that the discreditation would not be presumed from the proof of adulterous conduct.[153]

More recently, the Supreme Court justices appeared to be divided on the issue of extramarital sexual activity in public employment. In 1984, the Sixth Circuit held that a Michigan police officer could not be fired solely because he was living with a woman to whom he was not married (a felony under state law). In 1985, the Supreme Court denied review of that decision over the strong objection of three justices who felt the case "presented an important issue of constitutional law regarding the contours of the right of privacy afforded individuals for sexual matters."[154]

In those cases involving sexual improprieties that clearly affect an officer's on-the-job performance, the courts have had far less controversy. In a series of cases, the court has consistently supported the disciplinary action attached to the department's "conduct unbecoming" regulation, including cases in which officers were cohabiting or in which the sexual activities were themselves illegal (e.g., public lewdness, child molestation, sexual activity with prostitutes, and homosexuality).[155] In fact, the courts have upheld internal regulations barring the employment of spouses, due in part to the concern for an officer's work performance (see Box 11-6).

The issue of homosexual activity as a basis for discharge was recently presented to the Supreme Court. Oklahoma had a law permitting discharge of schoolteachers for engaging in "public homosexual activity." The lower court held the law to be facially overly broad and therefore unconstitutionally restrictive. The Supreme Court affirmed the decision.[156] Another federal court held that the discharge of a bisexual guidance counselor did not deprive the plaintiff of her First or Fourteenth Amendment rights. The counselor's discussion of her sexual preferences with teachers and other personnel was not protected by the First Amendment. Her equal protection claim failed because she did not show that the heterosexual employees would have been treated differently for communicating their sexual preferences.[157]

In an equally important federal case involving thirteen lesbian deputies terminated from the Broward County, Florida, Sheriff's Department, the Court held that homosexuals are not a suspect class accorded strict scrutiny under the equal protection clause, and, therefore, the dismissal did not deprive the plaintiffs of any constitutional or equal protection right.[158]

BOX 11-6

## Officer Who Wed Colleague Denied Reinstatement

PASADENA—A former Pasadena police officer who lost her job for marrying a fellow officer was denied reinstatement Wednesday by the Pasadena Civil Service Commission.

"I'm disappointed, but I wasn't really surprised," Kerri Burch Fry said. "I don't understand why it's OK to have other people in the department (who are) related but not married officers."

Mrs. Fry, 27, was forced to resign after she married a fellow officer with whom she already had a child. She had asked the service commission to reinstate her to the police department where she had worked for six years.

Unemployed now, she said she plans to appeal the commission's ruling.

She was dismissed earlier this month under a department nepotism policy. Under that policy, if two officers marry, the one having the least seniority automatically must resign.

Mrs. Fry is married to Lt. Jack Fry, 35, who has been with the department for 12 years.

During the hearing Wednesday, Mrs. Fry contended the police administration punished her for taking wedding vows although officials had known of the couple's past live-in relationship and the baby she had months before their marriage.

"It condones officers living together. They knew we lived together and had a child, but we did the right thing and got punished for it. Our child has a right to bear her father's name," she said.

Mrs. Fry said city nepotism laws are discriminatory because they are selectively enforced by department leaders.

Mrs. Fry's husband voluntarily took the stand under an arrangement that prohibited questioning from attorneys.

Pointing to his wife, Officer Fry said: "I've put my life on the line for this department. I can't understand why this lady here can't do the same thing and still be married—why we can't have a personal life.

"It's telling me, 'We trust you to lay your life on the line but we don't trust you to marry somebody who has that same dedication.'"

Police Chief Lee Gilbert testified that the no-spouses law prevents potential favoritism between spouses and other management problems.

"It would be a management nightmare for me to manage 10 to 15 married couples, worrying about deploying them and keeping them separate," he said.

"The conflict of interest is obvious. We're a relatively small department."

*Source: Dallas Morning News,* Aug. 18, 1989, p. 26A. Reprinted with permission of the Dallas Morning News.

---

Finally, the courts have upheld the right of the states to make laws prohibiting sodomy and thus developing the argument that homosexuality is a criminal violation that may be a viable basis for discharging a police officer. In a 1987 case, a federal court of appeals upheld the FBI's policy of not hiring homosexuals on the grounds that agents must be able to work in any state in the country, half of which have criminal laws prohibiting homosexuality or sodomy.[159]

## RESIDENCY REQUIREMENTS

A number of local governments have established requirements that all or certain classes of their employees live within the geographical limits of the jurisdiction. These residency requirements have been justified by the governments imposing them as desirable because they increase employees' rapport with, and understanding of, the community. When police officers were concerned, it has been asserted that the presence of off-duty police has a deterrent effect on crime and results in chance encounters that might lead to additional sources of information.

Before 1976, challenges to the legality of residency requirements for public employees dotted the legal landscape. In 1976, the Supreme Court in

*McCarthy* v. *Philadelphia Civil Service Commission* ruled that Philadelphia's residency requirement for firefighters did not violate the Constitution.[160]

Since the *McCarthy* decision, the legal attacks on the residency requirements have subsided. The cases now seem to be concerned with determining what constitutes residency. The most obvious means of attempting to avoid the residency requirement (by establishing a second residence within the city) appears doomed to failure unless the police officer can demonstrate that he or she spends at least a substantial part of his or her time at the in-city residence.[161] A strong argument has been made that, in areas where housing is unavailable or prohibitively expensive, a residency requirement is unreasonable.[162] In upholding the application of such requirements, courts have focused on the issues of equal enforcement and the specificity of the local residency standard.[163]

## RELIGIOUS BELIEF OR PRACTICE

In part, Title VII of the Civil Rights Act of 1964 prohibits religious discrimination in employment. The act defines religion as including "all aspects of religious. . . practice, as well as belief, unless an employer . . . is unable to reasonably accommodate to an employee's . . . religious . . . practice without undue hardship on the conduct of the employer's business."[164] Title VII requires reasonable accommodation of religious beliefs, not accommodation in exactly the way the employee would like. Title VII also does not require accommodation that spares the employee any cost whatsoever.[165] For example, an Albuquerque firefighter who was a Seventh-Day Adventist refused to work the Friday night or Saturday day shifts because they fell on what he believed to be the Sabbath day. Although department policy would have permitted the firefighter to avoid working these shifts by taking leave with pay, taking leave without pay, or trading shifts with other firefighters, he refused to use these means and insisted that the department find other firefighters to trade shifts with him or simply excuse him from the shifts affected by his religious beliefs. The department refused to do either. Under these circumstances, the court ruled that the department's accommodations to the firefighter had been reasonable and that no further accommodations could be made without undue hardship to the department. Therefore, the firefighter's discharge was upheld. However, as the court itself emphasized, decisions in cases in this area depend on the particular facts and circumstances of each case.[166] Recently, the courts have held that the termination of a fundamental Mormon police officer for practicing plural marriage (polygamy), in violation of state law, was not a violation of his right to freely exercise his religious beliefs.[167]

## MOONLIGHTING

Traditionally, the courts have supported the authority of police departments to place limits on the outside employment of their employees.[168] Police department restrictions on moonlighting range from a complete ban on outside employment to permission to engage in certain endeavors, such as investments, rental of property, teaching of law enforcement subjects, and employment designed to improve the police image. The rationale in support of moonlighting prohibitions is that "outside employment seriously interferes with keeping the [police and fire] departments fit and ready for action at all times"[169] (see Box 11-7).

BOX 11-7

## Off-Duty Job Can Create Problems for Police

**by Lisa Olsen,** *Staff Writer*

At Lynnhaven Mall in Virginia Beach, nearly half the security staff carries government-issued guns, badges and the clout of full arrest powers. They're off-duty cops.

In Smithfield, people who need their grass cut or snow shoveled can call 4 Seasons Lawn Care, a company owned and operated by the town's police chief.

In Chesapeake, city officials spent only $7,500 to gut and renovate a police precinct building in 1988. They saved money by hiring four off-duty officers for the five-month job.

Moonlighting has become an institution for Hampton Roads police officers, who often seek second or third jobs to supplement starting salaries that range from about $17,000 to $21,000 a year. More than half the officers in Hampton Roads work second jobs. But it can be dangerous for them and the public they serve, state and national experts say.

A second job does more than add to income, they say: It contributes to stress, burnout and the risk of accidents or injury. It also creates troubling conflict-of-interest questions that often aren't addressed by police policies.

"It's certainly dangerous for the officer who has to take a second job to make ends meet and is still expected to be alert and prepared," said Robert E. Colvin, a former police officer and the executive director of the Virginia State Crime Commission.

Police departments in Virginia Beach, Norfolk, Chesapeake and Hampton limit part-time work to 20 hours a week, but there are no such limits in Portsmouth, Smithfield, the Sheriff's Department in Isle of Wight County, and in Newport News and Hampton Roads.

"Probably everyone at one time or another has worked part time during their career," said Robert P. Haynes, police spokesman for Norfolk. "At one time in their career, it has been part of their routine. Almost 100 percent."

Security work provides the majority of part-time jobs held by police, but Hampton Roads officers do everything from practicing law to washing cars.

Most police departments restrict officers from working in bars or in liquor stores, but other rules are less common. In most cases, police chiefs or other supervisors routinely approve jobs, although many policies prevent officers from taking work that could interfere with police work or present a conflict of interest.

At least three Hampton Roads police officers use their training in accident investigations to work as expert witnesses, although they work only outside the cities where they are employed.

Top police officials often authorize moonlighting by officers, but they rarely have second jobs themselves. Smithfield Police Chief Claiborne A. Havens is an exception. Havens, who owns a lawn care business with his wife, employs several of his officers to cut lawns.

Part-time work has become such an institution that several Hampton Roads police departments, especially in fast-growing Chesapeake and tourist-driven Virginia Beach, regularly take calls from businessmen asking for off-duty officers to take security posts.

"I know at the Oceanfront, a lot of hotels use (off-duty police officers) in the summertime," said Master Police Officer Lewis B. Thurston, a Virginia Beach department spokesman. Thurston works off-duty at Lynnhaven Mall.

That practice has led to shootings, heated debates and lawsuits elsewhere in the country, said Dr. James J. Fyfe, a criminal justice professor at American University in Washington and a former New York City police officer.

"The big ethical dilemma," Fyfe said, "is whether police officers should be permitted to work as hired guns.

"I have a problem with that because I think if a police officer carries a gun and wields his power in the public interest and is expected to be fair and objective, it seems to me to be a bit twisted if he works in a hotel or a bar as a security guard. . . . It seems to me he's using his enforcement power and wearing his guns for private interest and he can't be objective."

Off-duty officers who work without radio contact or patrol cars are more vulnerable to attack than on-duty officers and can become aggressive more quickly under pressure, said Virginia Beach lawyer Kenneth W. Stolle, a former police officer.

Stolle worries about the consequences.

"If (the officer) gets hurt, is he eligible for compensation? If someone else gets hurt, who do they sue?" Stolle asked. "It's a no-win situation. The police departments don't want to force the officers not to work. At the same time, there is a lot of liability attached to what they do."

A Virginia Supreme Court decision said that a city or county can be held responsible for the actions of an off-duty officer when he or she is enforcing the law and using police powers.

Virginia Beach was sued for $300,000 in 1987 by a man who had been shot by an off-duty officer moonlighting as a store security guard. However, the officer was fired after an investigation, and the city did not have to pay.

Fyfe said moonlighting, especially as security guards, can lead to more police shootings. In a study of 2,900 police shootings in New York City from 1971 to 1975, he found that about 20 percent involved off-duty officers who were moonlighting or simply off-duty. Of those, half were found to be "bad shootings"—cases where officers did not follow policy. After that study, New York City prohibited its officers from taking second jobs, Fyfe said.

Shootings, though, are not nearly as common as sheer exhaustion among moonlighting officers.

Haynes, of Norfolk, once worked part time in radio and television news, a job that pushed his work week to 70 or 80 hours.

"I'm an example of one who burned out," he said. "As much as I love it, I'm not going to do that anymore."

*Source: Norfolk Pilot* (Virginia), Aug. 13, 1990.

However, in a Louisiana case, firefighters offered unrefuted evidence that moonlighting had been a common practice before the city banned it; during the previous sixteen years, no firefighters had ever needed sick leave as a result of injuries suffered while moonlighting; there had never been a problem locating off-duty firefighters to respond to an emergency; and moonlighting had never been shown to be a source of fatigue that was serious enough to impair a firefighter's alertness on the job. Under these circumstances, the court ruled that there was not a sufficient basis for the prohibition on moonlighting and invalidated the ordinance.[170]

It is important to note that in several cases involving off-duty officers moonlighting (as private security guards or store detectives), the same legal standards imposed on sworn officers acting in the capacity of their jobs apply. The court has held that off-duty officers act "under color of State law" and are subject to Section 1983 liability while working in a private security or "special patrolman" capacity.[171] Therefore, it follows that police agencies and departments may be liable under the same ramifications, opening up a new wave of future litigation involving police officer off-duty employment.

## MISUSE OF FIREARMS AND DEADLY FORCE

The last two decades have been witness to an enormous increase in the number of lawsuits filed against police departments for wrongful deaths. In the vast majority of these cases the issue is not that an officer injured an innocent third party while shooting at a "bad guy," but rather that the "bad guy" should not have been shot in the first place.

Unfortunately, in the past, police officer training has too often focused on the issue of how to shoot and not when to shoot. Many times when a problem does arise relating to the use of deadly force, it is not that the officer failed to qualify at the police pistol range or that the weapon malfunctioned, but that the officer made an error in judgment.

The police chief and his or her legal counsel must question whether this error in judgment was merely a human error resulting from the pressure of the moment, or whether the police department failed to provide proper guidelines to the officer. If proper guidelines were made available to the officer, did the police department incorporate these guidelines into its formal training program?

**FIGURE 11-6.** Officers enter a suspected drug house during a search warrant execution. Police firearms regulations should provide direction during those incidents in which the probability for the use of deadly force may be high. (Photo courtesy of the Derry, New Hampshire, Police Department and the *FBI Law Enforcement Bulletin,* 1990.)

Let us examine what areas a use-of-deadly-force policy should cover and the formalized mechanisms by which officers can be trained to understand this policy.

**Tennessee versus Garner, 1985**

Until 1985, the courts nationwide had not established a standard of law regarding the use of deadly force. Likewise, law enforcement agencies had not developed a standard, written directive that would establish national guidelines. While most larger police agencies had established use-of-deadly-force policies, those policies certainly were not consistent in form or content.[172]

On March 27, 1985, all of this started to change when the United States Supreme Court ruled unconstitutional a Tennessee law that permitted police officers to use deadly force to effect an arrest.[173] The Tennessee statute on the police use of deadly force provided that if, after a police officer has given notice of an intent to arrest a criminal suspect, the suspect flees or forcibly resists, "the officer may use all the necessary means to effect the arrest."[174] Acting under the authority of this statute, a Memphis police officer shot a juvenile, Garner, as he fled over a fence at night in the backyard of a house he was suspected of burglarizing. The officer ordered him to halt but he failed to stop. The officer then fired a single shot and killed him. The officer used deadly force despite being "reasonably sure" that the suspect was unarmed and believing him to be 17 or 18 years old and of slight build. The father subsequently brought an action in federal district court, seeking damages under 42 U.S.C.S. 1983 for asserted violations of his son's constitutional rights. The district court held that the statute and the officer's actions were unconstitutional. The Court of Appeals reversed and the U.S Supreme Court affirmed the Court of Appeals' decision.

The Court held that the Tennessee statute was unconstitutional insofar as it authorized the use of deadly force against, as in this case, an apparently unarmed, nondangerous fleeing suspect. Such force may not be used unless necessary to prevent the escape and the officer has probable cause to believe that the suspect poses a significant threat of death or serious physical injury to the officer or others. The Court's reasoning was as follows:

1. Apprehension by the use of deadly force is a seizure and subject to the Fourth Amendment's reasonableness requirement. To determine whether such a seizure is reasonable, the extent of the intrusion on the suspect's rights under that amendment must be balanced against the governmental interests in effective law enforcement. This balancing process demonstrates that, notwithstanding probable cause to seize a suspect, an officer may not always do so by killing him. The use of deadly force to prevent the escape of all felony suspects, whatever the circumstances, is constitutionally unreasonable.

2. The Fourth Amendment, for purposes of this case, should not be construed in light of the common-law rule allowing the use of whatever force is necessary to effect the arrest of a fleeing felon. Changes in the legal and technological context mean that the rule is distorted almost beyond recognition when literally applied to criminal situations today.

   Whereas felonies were formerly capital crimes, few felonies are now. Many crimes classified as misdemeanors, or nonexistent, at common law are now felonies. Also, the common-law rule developed at a time when weapons were rudimentary. The varied rules adopted in the states indicate a long-term movement away from the common-law rule, particularly in the police departments themselves; thus, that rule is a dubious indication of the constitutionality of the Tennessee statute. There is no indication that holding a police practice, such as that authorized by the Tennessee statute, will severely hamper effective law enforcement.

3. While burglary is a serious crime, the officer in this case could not reasonably have believed that the suspect—young, slight, and unarmed—posed any threat. Nor does the fact that an unarmed suspect has broken into a dwelling at night automatically mean he is dangerous.

**Evaluation of Written Directives**

As suggested earlier, when an alleged wrongful death case is being evaluated, the adequacy of the police department's policy must be considered. Generally speaking, an adequate policy will address the following topics: defense of life and fleeing felons, juveniles, shooting at or from vehicles, warning shots, shooting to destroy animals, secondary guns, off-duty weapons, and registration of weapons.

**Defense of Life and Fleeing Felon**

State laws and departmental policies still remain fairly diverse even after *Garner,* although with narrower bounds. No longer can these provisions leave officers virtually untethered as in the extreme case of one small American town whose only gun guidance to its officers was the homily "Never take me out in anger; Never put me away in disgrace."[175]

The range of firearms policies hereafter is likely to be from the "defense-of-life" regulations, which permit shooting only to defeat an imminent threat to an officer's or another person's life. At the other extreme, a minimal compliance with the *Garner* rule permits shooting at currently nonviolent fleeing suspects whom the officer reasonably believes committed a felony involving the threat but not the use of violence. Both approaches are currently employed by many large police departments.

The defense-of-life approach significantly reduces the possibility of wrongful death allegations.

**Juveniles**

For the most part, police departments do not instruct their officers to make a distinction between adults and juveniles in using deadly force. This is not based on a callous disregard for youthful offenders; rather, it is based on the pragmatic view that an armed juvenile can kill with the same finality as an armed adult. Further, it is often difficult, if not impossible, to tell if an offender is a juvenile or an adult.

**Shooting at or from Vehicles**

The trend in recent years has been to impose severe limitations on police officers shooting at or from vehicles except as the ultimate measure in self-defense or the defense of another when the suspect is using deadly force by means other than the vehicle.

Some of the reasons presented against shooting at or from vehicles are: difficulty in hitting the target, ricochets striking innocent bystanders, population densities, difficulty in penetrating the automobile body and steel-belted tires, an inability to put a stop to the vehicles momentum even when the target suspect is hit, damage that might result from causing the vehicle to go out of control, difficulty in hitting a moving target, and striking an innocent passenger in the fleeing vehicle.[176]

There is little question that if a motorist is trying to run a police officer down and the officer has no reasonable means of escape, then the officer has every right to defend his or her life. What often happens, however, is that the officer starts shooting at a vehicle when he or she is no longer in danger. For example, if a vehicle attempts to run a police officer down and the officer is able to take evasive action and get out of harm's way, under the provisions of many police departments' policies, the officer would no longer be permitted to shoot at the vehicle since the officer is no longer in danger. Naturally, if the driver turns the vehicle around and comes back toward the officer, the officer once again has the right to protect his or her life.

**Warning Shots**

There seems to be a general consensus among administrators that department policies should prohibit warning shots, as they may strike an innocent person. Privately, however, officials may fear something else: that officers shooting at and missing a suspect may claim that they were merely firing a warning shot and attempt to avoid answering for their actions. In addition, police officials point out that warning shots rarely accomplish their purpose, especially if suspects know that officers will not or cannot shoot them.[177]

**Shooting to Destroy Animals**

Police departments generally allow their officers to kill an animal either in self-defense, to prevent substantial harm to the officer or others, or when an animal is so badly injured that humanity requires its relief from further suffering. A seriously wounded or injured animal may be destroyed only after all attempts have been made to request assistance from the agencies (i.e., humane society, animal control, or game warden) responsible for disposal of animals. The destruction of vicious animals should be guided by the same rules set forth for self-defense or the defense and safety of others.[178]

Police officers in the United States are all conspicuously armed with a revolver or semiautomatic handgun. This fact is recognized, and for the most part approved, by most of our citizenry. A second fact not commonly known is that many police officers also carry a concealed secondary weapon. There are stated reasons for the practice: officers are concerned about being disarmed (with sound justification) during a confrontation; officers are less likely to be caught off guard when confrontation is not anticipated; and officers can less conspicuously be prepared to protect themselves during routine citizen stops. Regardless of the rationale, the practice is considered acceptable by knowledgeable police officials, but treated by many police administrators as something understood but not formally admitted.

A major criticism of backup weapons is that they may be intended as "throwaways" in the event an officer shoots an unarmed suspect. In order to protect the officer from such allegations, it is generally recommended that there be a strict policy of registering all backup guns with the department.[179]

**Secondary Weapons**

The rationale for officers to be armed while off duty is based on the assumption that police officers within their own jurisdictions are on duty 24 hours a day, and are therefore expected to act in their official capacity if the need to do so occurs. This, for the most part, was the policy of many police departments. Until recently, an officer who failed to comply with this regulation was subject to disciplinary action if a situation occurred that needed police action, such as responding to a robbery in progress, and the officer could not respond because he or she was unarmed.

Many police departments now make being armed while off duty optional but still compel their officers to register any weapons they choose to wear off duty with the department and to qualify regularly with the weapons. Most police departments also designate the type of ammunition the officers may carry in all weapons they use irrespective of whether they are used on duty or off duty.[180]

**Off-Duty Weapons**

Most police departments require their officers to use only department-approved weapons on and off duty and further require that the weapons be inspected, fired, and certified safe by the departments' armorers. Further, the firearms must be registered with the departments by make, model, serial number, and ballistics sample.[181]

**Registered Weapons**

It does a police department little good to have an adequate use-of-deadly-force policy if its officers are not familiar with all aspects of that policy. Following are some examples of formalized administrative means by which officers can become familiar with their agencies' policies:

**Familiarization with the Department's Policy**

1. **Recruit Training**—Instructions dealing with the deadly-force policy should be incorporated into the unit of instruction dealing with firearms training. As suggested earlier, the judgmental aspects of using deadly force are as important as the hands-on skill development of police officers in firearms training. Such a unit of instruction should involve a discussion of the numerous situations that officers will typically encounter and what course of action would keep these officers in strict compliance with their departments' policies and minimize wrongful deaths.

**FIGURE 11-7.** Police use of deadly force requires extensive training in firearms techniques that can be validated and documented by qualified personnel. (courtesy of the Lexington–Fayette Urban County, Kentucky, Police Department, 1990.)

2. **Field Training Officer**—The field training officer to whom the rookie officer is assigned immediately upon graduation from the police academy is responsible for continuing the training process started by the police academy and for evaluating the suitability of the rookie for police work. Such programs frequently incorporate training features designed to reinforce topics covered in the formal classroom setting of the academy. This component of the training program should be examined to be certain it deals with the topic of police use of deadly force.

3. **Roll-Call Training**—A part of this training, which typically occurs just prior to the officers going on patrol, can be spent in reviewing newly developed departmental policies, procedures, and regulations, including those dealing with the use of deadly force.

4. **In-Service Training**—In-service training classes typically range from one to five days. It is quite clear that the *Garner*[182] decision has resulted in many police departments rethinking and rewriting their use-of-deadly-force policies. The importance of the *Garner* decision will not be fully appreciated if a police department merely rewrites its policy and hands it out to its officers with no explanation. It is imperative that some explanation be provided, preferably by legal counsel, so that there is no misunderstanding about what this policy means. This familiarization and orientation can occur in conjunction with the firearms requalification training that officers have to go through regularly, or it can be treated within the context of an in-service training course.[183]

The legal theory underlying most pursuit-related lawsuits is that the police were negligent in conducting a pursuit.[184] A negligence action is based on proof of the following four elements: (1) the officer owed the injured party a duty not to engage in certain conduct, (2) the officer's actions violated that duty, (3) the officer's negligent conduct was the proximate cause of the accident, and (4) the suing party suffered actual and provable damages.[185] Negligence litigation focuses on the alleged failure of an officer to exercise reasonable care under the circumstances.

**Duty Owed**

Courts first determine the duty owed in a pursuit situation by examining the officer's conduct in light of relevant laws and department regulations. With the exception of some police departments that prohibit all pursuits, police officers have no duty to refrain from chasing a criminal suspect even when the risk of harm to the public arising from the chase is foreseeable and the suspect is being chased for a misdemeanor.[186] In *Smith* v. *City of West Point*,[187] the court stated that police ". . . are under no duty to allow motorized suspects a leisurely escape."[188] However, police do have a duty of care with respect to the manner in which they conduct a pursuit. This duty is derived from state statutes, court decisions defining reasonable care, and departmental pursuit policies.

Statutes in most jurisdictions confer a special status on police and other authorized emergency vehicles, exempting them from certain traffic regulations, such as speed limits, traffic signals, and a right of way.[189] Statutes exempting emergency vehicles from ordinary traffic regulations generally make the privilege conditional upon: (1) the existence of an actual emergency, (2) the use of adequate warning devices, and (3) the continued exercise of due care for the safety of others. Whether a governmental unit or its officers may be held liable depends in large part on the construction of such statutes. As a general rule, police drivers are not liable for negligence as a matter of law solely because they disregard a traffic regulation during an authorized emergency run. However, these statutes provide no protection against liability for an officer's reckless driving. Drivers of emergency police vehicles have a statutory duty to drive with due regard for the safety of others.

Court decisions defining the reasonable care standard constitute a second source from which to derive a duty owed by police pursuit drivers. Most courts have translated the reasonable care standard into a duty to drive with the care that a reasonable, prudent officer would exercise in the discharge of official duties of a like nature.[190] Reasonable care is a relative term depending on the exigencies of the situation and the degree of care and vigilance reasonably dictated by the circumstances of the chase.

A third source from which to derive a duty owed by police pursuit drivers is department policy. A law enforcement organization's policies, procedures, and training material concerning high-speed pursuits are generally admissible as evidence in lawsuits against the department or its officers for the negligent operation of a pursuit vehicle.[191] For example, in order to ascertain the standard of care applicable to a particular pursuit situation, a court could admit into evidence a police department regulation defining the proper speeds at which police cars responding to emergency calls were supposed to enter intersections when proceeding against red traffic signals. Depending on the jurisdiction involved, departmental pursuit policies may be merely a guideline to assist juries in determining the reasonableness of pursuit conduct, or they may actually constitute a duty owed, the violation of which would be considered negligent.

**Proximate Cause**    Liability must be based on proof that police conduct in breaching a duty owed was the proximate cause of a pursuit-related accident. Proximate cause is difficult to establish in cases involving the intervening negligence of other drivers, such as a case in which a fleeing motorist collides with an innocent person. In such cases, some courts impose liability on the officer and the department if the accident was a foreseeable consequence of police negligence.[192] For example, if police pursue without activating their lights and siren and an innocent citizen enters an intersection without being warned of the pursuit and collides with the pursued vehicle, the police may be liable because the accident was the proximate and foreseeable result of their failure to adequately warn other drivers of the pursuit. In *Nelson* v. *City of Chester, Ill.,*[193] the court held that the city's breach of its duty to properly train its police officers in high-speed pursuit might be found to be the proximate cause of the pursued driver's death, notwithstanding the contributing negligence of the pursued driver.

Legal barriers to civil actions, such as immunity, have been removed in many jurisdictions by a combination of legislation and judicial decisions, even though the extent of immunity continues to vary.[194] Statutes in most states have limited sovereign immunity to discretionary as opposed to ministerial decisions. Accordingly, the decision to pursue is viewed as discretionary, rendering the public entity immune, but the manner of pursuit is a ministerial decision for which there is no general grant of immunity. *Rhodes* v. *Lamar*[195] used this bifurcated approach to hold that the decision to institute a pursuit is a discretionary decision for which a sheriff enjoyed sovereign immunity, but liability was not precluded if the pursuit was conducted in a manner that violated a reasonable duty of care. In *Fagan* v. *City of Vineland,* the Court of Appeals allowed the municipality to be sued directly under Section 1983 when the pursuit causing a constitutional tort was pursuant to municipal policy or custom. Furthermore, the court allowed the municipality to be held liable for lack of training its officers in high-speed pursuit even if none of the officers involved in the pursuit at issue violated the Constitution.[196]

**Federal Civil Rights Act**    Pursuit-related liability under the federal Civil Rights Act, 42 U.S.C. 1983, requires proof that an officer's conduct violated a constitutionally protected right.[197] In *Cannon* v. *Taylor,*[198] the U.S. Court of Appeals for the 11th Circuit concluded that "a person injured in an automobile accident caused by the negligent, or even grossly negligent, operation of a motor vehicle by a police officer acting in the line of duty has no Section 1983 cause of action for violation of a federal right."[199] Automobile negligence actions are grist for the state law mill, but they do not rise to the level of a constitutional deprivation.[200] The common thread running through the cases is that negligent conduct during a pursuit does not suffice to trigger jurisdiction under 1983. However, a municipality may be held liable under Section 1983 if there was no or inadequate high-speed pursuit training for its officers, even when the officers involved with a pursuit were not individually negligent.[201]

Certain techniques employed by police during a pursuit may raise constitutional issues cognizable under 1983. For example, in *Jamieson By and Through Jamieson* v. *Shaw*[202] the court held that the constitutionally permissible use-of-force standard set forth by the Supreme Court in *Tennessee* v. *Garner*[203] was violated when a passenger in a fleeing vehicle was hurt when the vehicle hit a so-called deadman roadblock after officers allegedly shined a bright light into the driver's eyes as the vehicle approached the roadblock. In *Bower* v. *County of Inyo*,[204] a high-speed pursuit of over 20 miles ended when the fleeing suspect was killed when his vehicle hit a tractor-trailer which police had placed across the road as a roadblock. The Court of Appeals held that police use of a roadblock could constitute a constitutional violation of substantive due process if it was designed as an intentional deathtrap where the approaching driver does not have a clear option to stop because the roadblock is concealed around a curve or inadequately illuminated. The Supreme Court went further in stating that the deceased driver was unreasonably "seized" when the roadblock was placed completely across the highway in a manner likely to kill the driver, and that the police officers were liable under the Fourth Amendment and Section 1983 for the use of excessive force.[205]

Pursuit-related litigation usually involves an inquiry into whether the manner in which the pursuit was conducted was reasonable under the circumstances of that case. Each pursuit situation is different and requires a particularized assessment. Following is a brief discussion of certain factors that most frequently determine the extent of pursuit-related liability.

**Factors Determining Liability**

**Purpose of Pursuit.**   This factor relates to the need or reason for a pursuit. Does the purpose of the pursuit warrant the risks involved? What is the nature and seriousness of the suspected offense? Is the fleeing motorist suspected of committing a serious crime or only a misdemeanor? Was the motorist already operating the vehicle in a reckless and life-threatening manner before the pursuit started, or had the motorist committed a minor, nonhazardous traffic violation prior to the pursuit but then started driving in a reckless and life-threatening manner after the pursuit was initiated? Is there a need for immediate apprehension or has the suspect been identified so that apprehension at a later time is possible?

**Driving Conditions.**   This factor involves a general assessment of equipment, weather, roadway and traffic conditions, and the experience and personal ability of the drivers involved in the chase.

**Use of Warning Devices.**   The use of adequate visual and audible warning devices, such as flashing lights and a siren, is not only a statutory mandate for most pursuit situations, but also assures to the greatest extent possible that other vehicles and pedestrians are alerted to approaching emergency vehicles and to the need to yield the right of way.

**Excessive Speed.**   Whether a particular speed is excessive depends on the purpose of the pursuit, driving conditions, and the personal ability of a police driver to control and effectively maneuver the vehicle. Speed when crossing an intersection against a light or sign is an especially critical consideration, since statistics suggest that most pursuit-related collisions occur at intersections.[206] Liability may be based on the failure to sufficiently decrease speed when approaching an intersection so that a complete stop can be made to avoid a collision.

**Disobeying Traffic Laws.**   Pursuit vehicles are statutorily obligated to use due care for the safety of others when disobeying traffic laws, such as operating a vehicle on the wrong side of the road, passing on the right, going the wrong way on a one-way street, passing in a "no passing" zone, or proceeding against a traffic signal. These dangerous and high-risk driving situations should be avoided because police are generally held liable for any resulting accidents.[207]

**Roadblocks.**   Special care is required when using roadblocks to ensure that innocent persons are not placed in a position of danger and that the fleeing motorist is afforded a reasonable opportunity to stop safely.[208] To reduce the risk of liability, it is recommended that roadblocks only be used when authorized by a supervisor and only as a last resort to apprehend a fleeing motorist who is wanted for a violent felony and who constitutes an immediate and serious threat. Although the Supreme Court stated that a roadblock could be a Fourth Amendment unreasonable seizure granting Section 1983 liability,[209] the Court of Appeals for the First Circuit qualified the definition of "seizure" to apply to roadblock accidents constituting a "misuse of power" as opposed to the "accidental effects of otherwise lawful governmental conduct."[210]

**Continuation of the Pursuit.**   The decision to continue a pursuit in a reckless manner can create liability. A pursuit should be terminated when the hazards of continuing outweigh the benefits and purpose of the pursuit. The pursuit should be terminated when the level of danger created by the pursuit outweighs the necessity for immediate apprehension. If it is reasonable to conclude that the fleeing motorist will not voluntarily stop and that there is no realistic way of stopping the motorist without recklessly endangering others, the pursuit should be terminated because the risks are greater than the government's interest in the pursuit. Dangerous pursuits should be terminated when the fleeing suspect has been identified and there is no continuing need for immediate apprehension. Because some officers may be reluctant to terminate a pursuit out of fear that fellow officers will view the voluntary termination as an act of cowardice or timidity, it is advisable for departments to place the responsibility for supervising and terminating a pursuit on supervisory personnel not directly involved in the pursuit.[211]

## Departmental Responsibility for Liability Reduction

To reduce the risks and liability associated with vehicular pursuits, law enforcement organizations must carefully evaluate their pursuit policies, training, supervision, and post-incident evaluations. Liability reduction is accomplished through sound management controls and a reduction in the number of pursuit-related accidents.

## Policy Development

The function of a well-written pursuit policy is to state the department's objectives, establish some ground rules for the exercise of discretion, and educate officers as to specific factors they should consider when actually conducting a vehicular pursuit. Where feasible, a comprehensive policy statement should give content to terms such as *reasonable* and *reckless* and provide officers with more particularized guidance. A policy should be tailored to a department's operational needs, geographical peculiarities, and training capabilities. A written policy also provides a basis for holding officers accountable for their pursuit-related conduct.

Lack of adequate training may contribute to many pursuit-related accidents. **Training**
The natural tendency for many police drivers is to become emotionally involved and therefore lose some perspective during a pursuit. They are also required to drive different police vehicles with unique handling characteristics
under various road and weather conditions. It is easy to lose control of a vehicle that is driven beyond its or the driver's capabilities, and law enforcement
organizations can be held liable for failing to provide adequate driver training
to prepare officers to safely handle vehicles in pursuit situations.[212] The extent
and type of training required depend on a department's operational needs and
objectives. A minimal level of cost-effective training can be accomplished by
emphasizing defensive driving techniques and carefully instructing officers
about departmental pursuit policies and relevant state regulations concerning
the operation of emergency vehicles.

Police departments are responsible for providing adequate supervision of offi- **Supervision**
cers involved in a pursuit. Experts who have studied the emotionalism and psychology associated with pursuits recommend that, as soon as possible after a
pursuit has been initiated, a supervisor who is not in any of the pursuit vehicles should be tasked with the responsibility of supervising the pursuit.[213] The
supervisor who is not immediately involved is in a better position to oversee
objectively the pursuit and decide whether it should continue and under what
circumstances. The supervisor should track the location of the pursuit, designate the primary and secondary pursuit vehicles, and maintain tight controls
on the desire of other officers to get involved or parallel the action. Effective
communication between the pursuing vehicles and the supervisor is essential.
The failure to transmit information concerning the location of a pursuit or the
condition of the pursued driver may contribute to a subsequent accident.

Law enforcement organizations should provide for an ongoing process of eval- **Evaluation and**
uation and documentation of pursuit-related incidents. All pursuits, including **Documentation**
those successfully terminated without an accident, should be routinely cri-
tiqued to determine whether departmental policy was followed and the extent
to which any policy modification, training enhancement, or other remedial action is warranted.

## TESTING IN THE WORK ENVIRONMENT

It is common for police departments to require that their officers not be under **Alcohol and**
the influence of any intoxicating agent while on duty. Even in the absence of **Drug Testing**
such specific regulation, disciplinary action has been upheld when it was taken
against an officer who was suspected of being intoxicated while on duty by
charging him with neglect of duty or violation of a state law.[214]

Regulations that prohibit being under the influence of an intoxicating or
mind-altering substance have been upheld uniformly as reasonable because of
the hazardous nature of a police officer's work and the serious impact his or
her behavior or misbehavior is sure to have on the property and safety of others. The necessity to require a clear head and rational action, unbefuddled by
alcohol or drugs, is clear.[215] A Louisiana court upheld a regulation that prohibited an officer from consuming alcoholic beverages on or off duty to the extent that it caused the officer's behavior to become obnoxious, disruptive, or
disorderly.[216]

Effective enforcement of regulations against an officer's being under the influence of drugs or alcohol will occasion situations when a police supervisor or administrator will order an officer to submit to one or more tests to determine the presence of the prohibited substance in the subject's body. It has been held that a firefighter could be ordered to submit to blood sampling when reasonable grounds existed for believing that he was intoxicated and that it was permissible to discharge the firefighter for his refusal to comply with the order.[217] More recently the courts have also been asked to review police department policies that require officers to submit to urinalysis for the purpose of determining the presence of drugs or alcohol. In *United States* v. *Jacobsen,* the Supreme Court defined the concept of search and seizure:

> A "search" occurs when an expectation of privacy that society is prepared to consider reasonable is infringed. A "seizure" of property occurs when there is some meaningful interference with an individual's possessory interests in that property.[218]

According to the Supreme Court, removing urine from an individual's body is a search within the meaning of the Fourth Amendment. Consequently, when a government agency tests an employee's urine, due process must be applied, which involves providing probable evidence of illegal activity. In the case of public employer drug testing, the search is justified from the beginning, when "reasonable grounds exist for suspecting that the search will turn up evidence of work-related drug use."[219]

A reasonable search depends on a "balancing test" set forth by Justice Sandra Day O'Connor:

> A determination of the standard of reasonableness applicable to a particular class of searches requires balancing the nature and quality of the intrusion on the individual's Fourth Amendment interests against the importance of the governmental interest alleged to justify the intrusion. In the case of searches conducted by a public employer, we must balance the invasion of the employee's legitimate expectations of privacy against the government's need for supervision, control, and the efficient operation of the work place.[220]

The Supreme Court ruled on two cases in the late 1980s that would become landmark for drug testing in the public sector. In *Skinner* v. *Railway Labor Executives' Association,* the Supreme Court upheld a mandatory drug-testing program in cases in which the government had no reasonable suspicion about any particular public employee but had a substantial interest in maintaining public safety.[221] In a case even more important to police agencies, the Supreme Court considered in *National Treasury Employees Union* v. *Von Raub* whether the U.S. Customs drug-testing program was constitutional. The customs service drug-tested employees who sought promotion to positions that required seizing or safekeeping illegal drugs, carrying firearms, or handling classified documents. The Court held that such employees have a diminished expectation of privacy and that drug testing is a minimal intrusion that is far outweighed by the government's interests.[222]

The prevailing view appears to be that totally random, unscheduled drug testing is unacceptable, but that particular officers can be required to submit to urinalysis if there exists a "reasonable suspicion" that the officer has been using a prohibited substance.[223] The results of such compulsory tests are appropriate evidence for introduction in administrative discharge proceedings.[224] Decisions involving other governmental employees and similar kinds of personal intrusions (e.g., strip searches of prison guards) seem to support the view that random testing is unreasonable under the Fourth Amendment[225] (see Box 11-8). However, without a definitive decision from the Supreme Court on random drug testing, lower federal court decisions concerning public agency personnel appear to allow random drug testing without reasonable suspicion of individual drug abuse if: (1) an employer knows that drugs are used in their workplace; (2) the testing will not totally disrupt the employee's privacy expectation; and (3) the jobs are "safety-sensitive" in nature.[226]

In an attempt to skirt the issue of mandatory or random testing, some departments have incorporated drug testing as a "usual and customary" part of a required medical examination. For instance, the Philadelphia Police Department requires a medical examination for all individuals attempting to secure employment under the following conditions: (1) when an officer is first hired; (2) when an officer is transferred to a "sensitive" position (i.e., vice and narcotics division, SWAT, and hostage negotiation teams); (3) when an officer is promoted to a higher rank; and (4) when an officer returns to duty after an extended period of time (i.e., long illness, disability, or suspension). Drug abuse is viewed as a medical malady and subject to disclosure similar to the findings of other tests that show spinal problems, poor vision, hearing loss, and the like. Hence, drug testing can be viewed as a routine part of the medical examination for pre-employment to a new position.

## BOX 11-8

### Drug Abuse Has Huge Costs to Police Workplace

**by Dr. Gregory P. Orvis, University of Texas at Tyler**

With 10,000 tons of marijuana, 50 to 75 tons of cocaine, and almost 6 tons of heroin a year being consumed illegally by Americans and an estimated 10 to 23 percent of American workers using drugs in the private sector workplace, there have been increasing doubts concerning drug abuse in the criminal justice workplace. A recent survey of police agencies has increased the worries about drug abuse among police officers in particular.

Dr. D. L. Carter and Dr. M. Britz recently surveyed 520 police agencies. Over half reported that they knew of particular police officers abusing drugs. Almost 40 percent reported that marijuana was the most frequent drug being used illegally by police officers, whereas almost 36 percent reported that cocaine was the drug of choice among such officers. Drs. Carter and Britz also reported a mean of seven officers a year per agency being investigated by the police agency for drug abuse. They further inferred that recreational use of illegal drugs is prevalent among police officers because of socialization into the drug culture, job stress, and public apathy towards drug abuse in general.

Such drug abuse by police officers can be costly to both the police agency as well as the taxpayer. The U.S. Chamber of Commerce estimated that a drug-abusing employee is over three times more likely to be involved in a workplace accident, over two times more likely to request time off, and three times more likely to be late for work. Drug abuse by employees is also associated with rising medical costs for employers, with drug abuse directly attributed to half of the national cost of accidents.

Employees' drug abuse costs employers directly through a loss of worker productivity and workplace accidents and indirectly through increasing medical premiums. The costs are even greater, although less measurable, when the employees are police officers and the employer is the public. It is no wonder that many police agencies are turning to drug testing in order to keep the costs down.

*Source:* Gregory P. Orvis, "Drug Testing in the Criminal Justice Workplace," *American Journal of Criminal Justice*, 18:2 (Spring 1994), pp. 289–305.

In Arlington, Texas, all police officers are required to take an annual medical examination and perform acceptable physical agility tests that "qualify" them for continued employment. The department links these tests to "insurability" through policies and regulations. Officers with physical disabilities (including alcohol and drug addiction) cannot be insured through the city of Arlington. An important note regarding both the Arlington and Philadelphia police departments is the attitude expressed about officer drug abuse. Each department views the problem as a medical issue; therefore, extensive programs for counseling and rehabilitation have been established. Although these regulations have *not* been court tested, it appears reasonable that a comprehensive look at the issue of drugs in the workplace will support drug testing as a routine part of a medical examination.

# TERMS AND CONDITIONS OF EMPLOYMENT

**Wage and Hour Regulations**
The Fair Labor Standards Act (FLSA) was initially enacted by Congress in 1938 to establish minimum wages and to require overtime compensation in the private sector. In 1974, amendments to the act extended its coverage to state and local government employees and established special work period provisions for police and fire. However, in 1976 the U.S. Supreme Court ruled that the extension of the act into the realm of traditional local and state government functions was unconstitutional.[227] Almost a decade later, the Supreme Court surprisingly reversed itself, thus bringing all local police agencies under the coverage of the FLSA.[228] Shortly thereafter, Congress enacted the Fair Labor Standards Amendments of 1985 (effective April 15, 1986), which set forth special wage and hour provisions for government employees in an effort to reduce the monetary impact of the overtime requirements on state and local governments.

Generally, all rank-and-file law enforcement officers are covered under the FLSA. Exemptions include elected officials, their personal staffs, and those employees in policy-making positions. The law requires that overtime be paid to police personnel for all work in excess of 43 hours in a seven-day cycle or 171 hours in a 28-day period. Employers are allowed to establish or negotiate a work/pay period as they see fit within those boundaries. (The FLSA sets minimum standards that may be exceeded by offering greater benefits.) The appropriate wage for overtime hours is set at 1 1/2 times the employee's regular rate of pay. This may be given in money or compensatory time. Public safety officers may accrue a maximum of 480 hours of "comp" time, which, if not used as leave, must be paid off upon separation from employment at the employee's final regular rate or at the average pay over the last three years, whichever is higher.

Of special interest to police agencies is that off-duty work and special details for a separate independent employer voluntarily undertaken by the employee are not used for calculating overtime payment obligations. Thus, specific hourly rates may still be negotiated for such work.

Because the new provisions discussed previously were only recently placed into effect, it is exceedingly difficult to offer definitive guidance to police administrators as to the precise application and interpretation of the 1985 amendments. Therefore, readers should seek legal guidance to ensure that wage and hour regulations are appropriately implemented and enforced.

State and local governments have adopted a variety of personnel policies to ensure that police officers are in adequate mental and physical condition in order to perform the normal and the unexpected strenuous physical activities of the job satisfactorily and safely. Based on the assumption that increasing age slows responses, saps strength, and increases the likelihood of sudden incapacitation because of breakdowns of the nervous and/or cardiovascular systems, many police departments and state law enforcement agencies have established mandatory hiring and retirement ages.

During the 1970s the courts allowed employers much latitude in enforcing retirement age requirements, finding such standards to be rationally related to a legitimate state interest in seeing that officers were physically prepared to protect the public's welfare.[229] In more recent decisions, however, the Supreme Court has significantly restricted the employer's ability to require that an employee be terminated upon reaching a certain age.

The Age Discrimination in Employment Act (ADEA) is a federal law that prohibits discrimination on the basis of age against employees who are between the ages of 40 and 70, unless age is shown to be a "bona fide occupational qualification (BFOQ) reasonably necessary to the normal operation of the particular business."[230] The Supreme Court has held that the BFOQ exemption is meant to be an extremely narrow exception to the general prohibition of age discrimination contained in the ADEA.[231] For an employer to demonstrate successfully that its age-based mandatory retirement rule is valid, it must first prove the existence of a job qualification reasonably necessary to the essence of its operation. Second, the employer must show that it has reasonable cause, based on fact, for believing that substantially all persons in the prohibited age group would be unable to perform the job duties safely and efficiently, or that it is impractical or impossible to accurately test and predict the capabilities of individuals in the excluded group.[232]

In another 1985 decision, the Supreme Court stated that stereotypical assumptions about the effects of aging on employee performance were inadequate to demonstrate a BFOQ. Instead, the Court held that employers are required to make a "particularized, factual showing" with respect to each element of the BFOQ defense.[233]

The federal courts have considered an ADEA challenge to a New York state law setting a maximum age of 29 for those applying for jobs as police officers. The court concluded that age 29 was not a BFOQ and ruled that the requirement was a violation of the law. The court noted that the employer has the same burden of proof to justify an age-based hiring standard as it does to justify an age-based retirement requirement.[234]

# SEXUAL HARASSMENT

The increasing number of women joining law enforcement agencies poses a challenge to law enforcement managers and executives. As in many other professions, women joining the law enforcement ranks are sometimes stereotyped by those who believe that they are not capable of being good police officers. Moreover, the addition of women to a male-dominated profession, where notions of machismo may prevail, can create a situation in which

**FIGURE 11-8.** Employment discrimination on the basis of age and/or race is prohibited by federal law. (Photo courtesy of the Longview, Texas, Police Department.)

women are singled out and made to feel unwelcome solely because of their gender, regardless of their work performance.[235]

The challenge to law enforcement managers and executives is to break down the inaccurate stereotypes attached to women and eliminate any notion of disparate treatment of employees based on gender. Although common sense and good management practice dictate these must be done, the law requires it.[236] Under Title VII of the 1964 Civil Rights Act, commonly referred to simply as Title VII, when an employer causes, condones, or fails to eliminate unfair treatment of women in the workplace, liability may be found.[237]

**Sexual Harassment: A Definition**

It is somewhat difficult to provide a precise definition of conduct that constitutes sexual harassment; it is apparently more easily recognized than defined. Sexual harassment falls within the broader, prohibited practice of sex discrimination and may occur when an employee is subjected to unequal and unwelcome treatment based solely on the employee's sex.

Specific guidance on the types of conduct that would constitute sexual harassment is provided in the Equal Employment Opportunity Commission's (EEOC's) *Guidelines on Discrimination Because of Sex.*[238] These guidelines, although not carrying the force of law, "constitute a body of experience and informed judgment to which courts and litigants may properly resort for guidance."[239] The guidelines describe sexual harassment as follows:

> Unwelcome sexual advances, requests for sexual favors, and other verbal or physical conduct of a sexual nature constitute sexual harassment when (1) submission to such conduct is made either explicitly or implicitly a term or condition of an individual's employment; (2) submission to or rejection of such conduct by an individual is used as the basis for employment decisions affecting such individuals; or (3) such conduct has the purpose or effect of unreasonably interfering with an in-

dividual's work performance or creating an intimidating, hostile, or offensive working environment.[240]

In general, sexual harassment can take two forms. First, sexual harassment exists when an employee is requested or required to engage in or submit to a sexual act as a term or condition of a job benefit or assignment. Second, sexual harassment may arise when the comments, conduct, or actions of the employer, supervisors, or coworkers create an unwelcome and hostile work environment for an employee, based on gender. Both denigrate the workplace and must be prevented.

Because by general definition sexual harassment falls into two categories, it is not surprising that courts have imposed liability on employers and coworkers for participating in, condoning, or permitting sexual harassment at work under two parallel theories. These two theories upon which liability may be found have been referred to as *quid pro quo liability* and *hostile environment liability*.[241]

**Sexual Harassment: Theories of Liability**

Quid pro quo liability is established when a sexual act is the condition precedent before an individual is hired or promoted or becomes the recipient of any other job benefit. The converse is also true. Quid pro quo liability can be found where the refusal to engage in a sexual act is the reason for the refusal to hire, the firing, a denied promotion, or a withheld job benefit. Unlike the hostile working environment theory, the plaintiff in a quid pro quo case must show that the sexual demand was linked to a tangible, economic aspect of an employee's compensation, term, condition, or privilege of employment.[242]

The second legal theory on which sexual harassment can be predicated is the hostile working environment. Individuals who must work in an atmosphere made hostile or abusive by the unequal treatment of the sexes are denied the equal employment opportunities guaranteed to them by law and the Constitution.[243] As the Court of Appeals for the 11th Circuit said:

> Sexual harassment which creates a hostile or offensive environment for members of one sex is every bit the arbitrary barrier to sexual equality at the workplace that racial harassment is to racial equality. Surely, a requirement that a man or woman run a gauntlet of sexual abuse in return for the privilege of being allowed to work and make a living can be as demeaning and disconcerting as the harshest of racial epithets.[244]

The elements of a hostile environment case were most clearly spelled out in *Henson* v. *City of Dundee*.[245] To prevail in such a suit, the court noted that a plaintiff must establish four elements. First, as in all Title VII cases, the employee must belong to a protected group, which requires only "a simple stipulation that the employee is a man or a woman."[246] Second, the employee must show that he or she was subject to unwelcome harassment. Third, the harassment was based on sex, and but for the employee's gender, the employee would not have been subjected to the hostile or offensive environment. Fourth, the sexual harassment affected a term, condition, or privilege of employment.

It can easily be seen that the greatest attention is focused on the last three factors. If a plaintiff can establish each of those elements, with membership in a protected group being a given, then a claim of sexual harassment has been stated and liability may attach. Because these three factors form the core of the sexual harassment claim, each will be discussed in turn.

**Unwelcome Sexual Harassment**

In 1986, the Supreme Court had the occasion to address the issue of what constituted unwelcome sexual harassment. In *Meritor Savings Bank* v. *Vinson*,[247] a bank employee alleged that following completion of her probationary period as a teller-trainee, her supervisor invited her to dinner and, during the course of the meal, suggested they go to a motel to have sexual relations. The employee first declined but eventually agreed because she feared she might lose her job by refusing. Thereafter, over the course of the next several years, the employee alleged that her superior made repeated demands of her for sexual favors. She alleged she had sexual intercourse forty to fifty times with her superior, was fondled repeatedly by him, was followed into the women's restroom by him, and was even forcibly raped on several occasions. In defending the suit, the defendant-bank averred that because the employee had voluntarily consented to sexual relations with her superior, the alleged harassment was not unwelcome and not actionable.

The Supreme Court disagreed. The Court stated that "the fact that sex-related conduct was 'voluntary,' in the sense that the complainant was not forced to participate against her will, is not a defense to a sexual harassment suit brought under Title VII."[248] Sexually harassing conduct is unwelcome if the "employee did not solicit it or invite it, and the employee regarded the conduct as undesirable or offensive."[249]

The determination of whether specific conduct, even if "voluntary," constitutes unwelcome sexual harassment is a fact-bound inquiry.[250] Each case brings different facts and parties, leading to potentially different results. However, the courts have provided some guidance as to the types of facts that are relevant in determining whether the conduct considered in a sexual harassment suit was unwelcome.

For example, in *Meritor Savings Bank* v. *Vinson*,[251] the Supreme Court noted

> While "voluntariness" in the sense of consent is not a defense to such a claim, it does not follow that a complainant's sexually provocative speech or dress is irrelevant as a matter of law in determining whether he or she found particular sexual advances unwelcome. To the contrary, such evidence is obviously relevant.[252]

Thus, the Supreme Court ruled that to some extent,[253] the employee's own conduct is at issue when he or she files suit alleging sexual harassment. The nature of relevant employee conduct extends to the employee's participation in office vulgarities and sexual references,[254] the employee's nonwork conduct where a moral and religious character particularly sensitive to sexual jokes is claimed,[255] and proving that the employee actually initiated the sexual advance or innuendo.[256] Also relevant to the issue of "unwelcome" conduct is whether and when the employee complained. At least one court has ruled that a failure to report instances of alleged sexual harassment, where the opportunity and mechanism to do so existed, was proof that the conduct later complained of was not genuinely offensive or unwelcome.[257]

Whether the conduct is unwelcome is a "totality of circumstances" analysis. Conduct alleged to be sexual harassment must be judged by a variety of factors, including the nature of the conduct; the background, experience, and actions of the employee; the background, experience, and actions of coworkers and supervisors; the physical environment of the workplace; the lexicon of obscenity used there; and an objective analysis of how a reasonable person would react to and respond in a similar work environment.[258] However, rather than risk making an incorrect ad hoc determination of whether conduct is or is not unwelcome in each instance of alleged sexual harassment, police managers should be prepared to take appropriate action when conduct directed against employees because of sex first appears to be offensive and unwelcome.

**Harassment Based on Sex**

As stated earlier, the second major element of a Title VII claim of hostile environment sexual harassment requires that the harassment be directed against an employee based on the employee's gender.[259] Conduct that is offensive to both sexes is not sexual harassment because it does not discriminate against any protected group.[260] The essence of a disparate treatment claim under Title VII is that "an employee . . . is intentionally singled out for adverse treatment" on the basis of a prohibited criterion.[261]

The prohibited criterion here is, of course, an employee's gender. In quid pro quo cases, this requirement is self-evident. The request or demand for sexual favors is made because of the employee's sex and would not otherwise have been made. However, discrimination based on gender is not always as clear in a hostile environment case. "In proving a claim for a hostile work environment due to sexual harassment, . . . the plaintiff must show that but for the fact of her [or his] sex, [the employee] would not have been the object of harassment."[262]

The term *sexual harassment* usually brings to mind sexual advances or acts, comments, and jokes relating to sexual activities. However, whereas sexual harassment includes all those types of conduct if they are unwelcome, the concept itself is broader. Any unwelcome conduct aimed at an employee that would not have occurred but for the employee's sex is sexual harassment. For example, in *Hall* v. *Gus Construction Co.*,[263] three female employees of a road construction firm filed suit alleging sexual harassment by fellow male employees. The conduct the women complained of included the use of sexual epithets and nicknames, repeated requests to engage in sexual activities, physical touching and fondling of the women, the exposure of the men's genitals, "mooning," the displaying of obscene pictures to the women, urinating in the women's water bottles and gas tank of their work truck, refusal to perform necessary repairs on the work truck until a male user complained, and refusal to allow the women restroom breaks in a town near the construction site. The defendant construction company argued that some of the conduct—such as the urinating in water bottles and gas tanks, the refusal to perform needed repairs on the truck, and the denial of restroom breaks—could not be considered as sexual harassment because the conduct, although perhaps inappropriate, was not sexually oriented.

The court disagreed. It concluded that the "incidents of harassment and unequal treatment . . . would not have occurred but for the fact that [the employees] were women."[264] Intimidation and hostility toward women because they are women can obviously result from conduct other than explicit sexual advances. Additionally, there is no requirement that the incidents, sexually oriented or not, be related to or part of a series of events. Sexual harassment can be based on repeated, though unrelated, events.[265]

Police managers and executives should be aware that any type of unwelcome conduct that is directed at an employee because of that person's gender may constitute sexual harassment. The lesson, as before, is to be alert and stifle any conduct that threatens disparate treatment because of the employee's sex.

**Harassment Affecting a Condition of Employment**

Title VII prohibits discrimination based on sex with respect to "compensation, terms, conditions, or privilege of employment."[266] Although it can readily be seen how the quid pro quo theory of a sexual harassment claim is sex discrimination with regard to compensation, terms, conditions, or privileges of employment, how can a sexually hostile environment affect a condition of employment, if no economic or tangible job detriment is suffered?[267]

The answer is simple. One of the conditions of any employment is the psychological well-being of the employees.[268] Where the psychological well-being of employees is adversely affected by an environment polluted with abusive and offensive harassment based solely on sex, Title VII provides a remedy. "The language of Title VII is not limited to 'economic' or 'tangible' discrimination. The phrase 'terms, conditions or privileges of employment' evinces a congressional intent 'to strike at the entire spectrum of disparate treatment of men and women' in employment."[269]

However, this is not to say that any conduct, no matter how slight, directed against an employee because of sex constitutes a hostile working environment. "For sexual harassment to be actionable, it must be sufficiently severe or pervasive to alter the conditions of the victim's employment and create an abusive working environment."[270] Isolated incidents[271] or genuinely trivial ones[272] will not give rise to sexual harassment liability. Not every sexual epithet or comment will affect the conditions of employment to a sufficient degree to create a hostile environment in violation of Title VII. Nonetheless, law enforcement management must realize that Title VII obligates it to provide a workplace where the psychological health of its employees is protected against sexual harassment.

## Grounds for Sexual Harassment Claims

Generalizations about the kinds of conduct that translate into a legal finding of sexual harassment are difficult because each case is a fact-oriented determination involving many factors. However, an analysis of the cases indicates that at least three broad categories of conduct can be identified that, if found, generally lead to a legal finding of sexual harassment.

First, invariably when allegations of quid pro quo sexual harassment are proved, liability follows.[273] That such is the case is not surprising. Demands for sex acts in exchange for job benefits are the most blatant of all forms of sexual harassment. In addition, whenever a job benefit is denied because of an employee's refusal to submit to the sexual demand, a tangible or economic loss is readily established. The primary difficulty in a quid pro quo case is in carrying the burden of proof and establishing that the alleged event(s) actually occurred. Because such incidents usually occur in private conversations, the cases often involve a one-on-one contest of testimony.[274] However, if the employee sufficiently proves the event(s) happened, courts readily conclude that sexual harassment existed.

Second, courts frequently conclude sexual harassment exists where the alleged conduct was intentionally directed at an employee because of the employee's gender, was excessively beyond the bounds of job requirements, and actually detracted from the accomplishment of the job. When the conduct becomes so pervasive that the offending employee's attention is no longer focused on job responsibilities and significant time and effort is diverted from work assignments to engage in the harassing conduct, courts will generally conclude that sexual harassment exists.

This principle can be illustrated by examining two law enforcement-related cases. In *Vermett* v. *Hough*,[275] a female law enforcement officer alleged sexual harassment by her coworkers. One specific act alleged to have been offensive to her was a male officer placing a flashlight between her legs from behind. The court ruled that the conduct was nothing more than "horseplay"[276] and a stress-relief mechanism in a high-pressure job. The "horseplay" was viewed by the court to be more indicative of the female's acceptance as a coworker than sexual harassment. Moreover, horseplay was an occasional part of the police station behavior but not on an inordinate basis.

The second case, *Arnold* v. *City of Seminole*,[277] illustrates the other side of the coin—out-of-control office joking leading to sexual harassment. In *Arnold,* a female officer chronicled a series of events and conduct to which she was subjected because she was female. Among the offensive conduct that created a hostile working environment were the following: (1) a lieutenant told her he did not believe in female police officers; (2) superior officers occasionally refused to acknowledge or speak to her; (3) obscene pictures were posted in public places within the police station with the female officer's name written on them; (4) epithets and derogatory comments were written next to the officer's name on posted work and leave schedules; (5) false misconduct claims were lodged against her; (6) work schedules were manipulated to prevent the female officer from being senior officer on duty, thus denying her command status; (7) she was singled out for public reprimands and not provided the required notice; (8) members of the female officer's family were arrested, threatened, and harassed; (9) other officers interfered with her office mail and squad car; (10) attempts to implicate the female officer in an illegal drug transaction were contemplated; and (11) the female officer was not provided equal access to station house locker facilities. Based on this amalgam of proof, which far exceeded any colorable claim of office camaraderie, the court ruled that the female officer had indeed been subjected to an openly hostile environment based solely on her gender.

A note of caution is in order. The line between innocent joking that contributes to esprit de corps and offensive sexual harassment can be a fine one. Police managers should be cognizant of such conduct and be prepared to take immediate and corrective action at the first moment it appears to be in danger of exceeding acceptable bounds.

The third category of sexual harassment generally arises from conduct or statements reflecting a belief that women employees are inferior by reason of their sex or that women have no rightful place in the workforce. For example, where a supervisory employee stated, among other things, that he had no respect for the opinions of another employee because she was a woman, sexual harassment was found.[278] Similarly, a supervisor who treated his male employees with respect but treated his women employees with obvious disdain, used the terms *babe* and *woman* in a derogatory fashion, and indicated his belief that women should not be working at all was found to have sexually harassed his female employees.[279]

Although the law alone cannot realistically dispossess people of their personal prejudices, it can require that they not exhibit them in the workplace. Police managers have the responsibility to see that they do not.

One of the primary goals of Title VII is to eliminate sexual harassment from the workplace.[280] However, to the extent it does not, civil liability remedies are available against both employers and offending coworkers. Both are matters of concern for law enforcement managers.

The Supreme Court in *Meritor Savings Bank* v. *Vinson*[281] made it clear that an employer would not be held liable simply because sexual harassment occurred in the workplace. Rather, the Court ruled that employer liability would be guided by agency principles, although it declined "to issue a definitive rule on employer liability."[282]

## Liability for Sexual Harassment

The lower courts have consistently applied agency principles to effect a remedy for sexual harassment. Three such principles can be identified. First, where a supervisory employee engages in quid pro quo sexual harassment, that is, the demand for sex in exchange for a job benefit, the employer is liable. As one court explained:

> In such a case, the supervisor relies upon his apparent or actual authority to extort sexual consideration from an employee. . . . In that case the supervisor uses the means furnished to him to accomplish the prohibited purpose. . . . Because the supervisor is acting within at least the apparent scope of the authority entrusted to him by the employer when he makes employment decisions his conduct can fairly be imputed to the source of his authority.[283]

Second, in cases where a plaintiff has successfully proved that sexual harassment by supervisory employees created a hostile working environment, courts will hold employers liable. The Fourth Circuit Court of Appeals noted this to be the rule:

> Once the plaintiff in a sexual harassment case proves that harassment took place, the most difficult legal question typically will concern the responsibility of the employer for that harassment. Except in situations where a proprietor, partner or corporate officer participates personally in the harassing behavior, the plaintiff will have the additional responsibility of demonstrating the propriety of holding the employer liable under some theory of respondent superior.[284]

Third, if the sexually hostile working environment is created at the hands of coworkers, employers will be liable only if they knew or reasonably should have known of the harassment and took no remedial action. It is the burden of the offended employee to "demonstrate that the employer had actual or constructive knowledge of the existence of a sexually hostile working environment and took no prompt and adequate remedial action."[285] Actual knowledge includes situations in which the unwelcome, offensive conduct is observed or discovered by a supervisory or management-level employee and supervisory employees are personally notified of the alleged sexual harassment.[286] Constructive knowledge arises when the sexually harassing conduct is so widespread or pervasive that knowledge is imputed to the employer.[287] Absence of actual notice to an employer does not necessarily insulate that employer from liability[288] (see Box 11-9).

These three principles suggest the manner in which sexual harassment liability can be prevented. Law enforcement managers and executives must not engage or participate in any conduct that constitutes sexual harassment. In addition, when such conduct comes to their attention, corrective action must be taken. Further, management has an affirmative obligation to monitor the workplace to ensure sexual harassment does not become a widespread practice.

Although the remedies available under Title VII are directly against the employer only and are limited by statute to primarily equitable relief,[289] not including compensatory damages,[290] other remedies may also be available to impose liability against employers or coworkers for sexual harassment claims. In addition to the relief available under Title VII, a plaintiff may seek monetary damages for a violation of federal civil and constitutional rights[291] as well as for state tort violations.[292] The important point to be noted is that

**BOX 11-9**

## Sexual Harassment: What Is It?

### CEOs' standards higher than judge's in Jones case

**by Matthew Robinson**
**Investor's Business Daily**

While the nation's chief executive grapples with numerous sex charges, more than six in 10 top corporate officers don't think similar conduct would be tolerated in their offices.

In fact, 67% say they doubt they'd be able to keep their jobs if several of their employees charged them with sexual misconduct, according to an exclusive poll of leaders of the country's fastest-growing companies.

Fully 87% of them don't think politicians should be governed by different moral and ethical standards than business leaders. And 97% of business leaders put a high premium on honesty and integrity.

They also take a strong stand against sexual harassment. Nine in 10 have formal policies against it, and 56% put managers through preventive training.

Three-quarters don't even think dating their employees is appropriate. In fact, one in six has a written policy against dating subordinates.

Ethics aside, one CEO says, fooling around with workers is just stupid. It makes leaders and their companies vulnerable to blackmail.

What constitutes sexual harassment?

The majority of top executives think it involves one or more of the following:

- Requests for sex in exchange for a benefit like a job, promotion or raise.
- Demands for sex under threat of termination, demotion, pay cut or some other penalty.
- Indecent exposure.
- Sexually explicit language.
- Gender-related comments or physical descriptions.

How does that square with last week's ruling in the Paula Jones case?

In tossing out Jones' charge that Bill Clinton sexually harassed her, a federal judge concluded that there was not "tangible" proof that Jones suffered in her state job after she refused the then-governor's sexual advances.

But that still left the matter of Clinton allegedly exposing himself to Jones—"boorish and offensive" behavior, if true, opined the judge. Was that harassment? No, ruled the judge.

That's at odds with executives' thinking.

Ninety-eight percent of them say indecent exposure *is* sexual harassment—second only to sexual propositions tied to job perks or penalties.

The judge's decision "really flabbergasted me—as it did everybody," said Wilburn Smith, president of Ada, Okla.-based Pre-Paid Legal Services Inc. "This person can sexually harass, but it's not OK for everybody else."

"I can tell you if I did that in my company," he added, "I would be history in a week."

Last month, *IBD* and Technometrica Institute of Policy and Politics asked 210 CEOs and CFOs of leading companies to take part in a poll on leadership and conduct. Exactly 100 responded.

The panel of executives was picked in July '97 based on their companies' earnings and stock growth.

The IBD/TIPP poll found that the cream of American business leaders view moral behavior as critical to their success. But they say politicians seem to be ruled by a different set of mores.

President Clinton apparently is a textbook example. On moral leadership, 73% of executives give him an "F."

Strict workplace policies on sexual conduct grew out of the increased awareness generated by sex-harassment charges against then-Sen. Bob Packwood and against Clarence Thomas during '91 hearings on his nomination to be a Supreme Court justice.

Some executives think it ironic that a president who claims to champion feminist causes is being accused of sexually harassing women who worked for him. Former White House aide Kathleen Willey has claimed Clinton groped her.

"There are a lot of good Clinton jokes running around out there, but employees are afraid to tell them for fear of sexually harassing someone," said James Durrell, chief financial officer of Harris Savings Bank Financial in Harrisburg, Pa.

Some 55% of top officers think it is "unlikely" that a CEO could "retain his or her job" in the face of

### Risky Business

 **Q:** How would you define sexual harassment in the workplace?

| | |
|---|---|
| Requests for sex tied to incentives or penalties | 99% |
| Indecent exposure | 98% |
| Displays of sexually oriented photos or clippings | 85% |
| Sexually explicit language | 74% |
| Gender-related comments or physical descriptions | 61% |
| Incidental body contact | 28% |
| Greetings involving kissing and/or hugging | 25% |

*Source: IBD/TIPP Poll of CEOs, CFOs, March 24–31.*

*(continued)*

BOX 11-9 (continued)

"allegations of sexual misconduct by several of the company's employees." Another 12% think it is "somewhat unlikely."

"If Clinton had to work in this environment, where he is subjected to the same rules and regulations and doesn't have people running around him putting their spin on this stuff, I don't think Clinton would get away with it," Durrell said. "Most boards of directors would have gotten rid of him by now."

For many, it's puzzling that Clinton, despite so many scandals, is still popular—as shown by his high job-approval ratings.

Most top executives don't think he's doing a good job. Overall, they give him a "C−" grade. He scores lowest on moral leadership, statesmanship and upholding constitutional principles.

Only 3% of officers rate his private conduct as good. And 86% say it's poor. By comparison, only 20% think political leaders in general act badly. Of course, 72% of executives rate their own conduct good, while none thinks they behave badly.

Why are politicians able to live by different rules?

"A lot of these people are lawyers, or they are around lawyers," Smith said. "In Washington, D.C., in front of one of the buildings it says, 'Equal Justice for All.' But that simply isn't true. A lot of these politicians can afford a lot more 'justice' than most folks."

"In the real America," he added, "real people can't get away with what they can get away with."

Durrell says the booming economy is insulating Clinton from public disgrace.

"The only reason Clinton survives politically is because people look at what's actually going on economically in the country and tend to identify it with him," he said.

Some 87% of executives say their moral and ethical behavior has a "great" effect on worker morale. And half say customer loyalty is greatly affected by how honest they are.

## Pillars Of Success

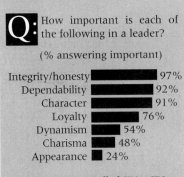

**Q:** How important is each of the following in a leader?

(% answering important)

| | |
|---|---|
| Integrity/honesty | 97% |
| Dependability | 92% |
| Character | 91% |
| Loyalty | 76% |
| Dynamism | 54% |
| Charisma | 48% |
| Appearance | 24% |

*Source: IBD/TIPP Poll of CEOs, CFOs, March 24–31.*

In fact, the vast majority of executives rate honesty, dependability and character as the most important traits of a leader. They rank charisma and looks last.

Ethics are key to success, they say.

"Price has become a little more sensitive with the changes in the economy, so maybe it's No. 1," said Dan Tuchter, CEO for Houston-based Midcoast Energy Resources. "But No. 2 right behind it is honesty and your reputation."

Durrell agrees.

"My experience has been over the years (that) most business people treat each other like they are basically honest," he said. "Once that integrity is destroyed, it's awfully hard to get back. You can spend the rest of your career trying to get it back."

Mega-investor Warren Buffett told a Harvard Business School audience that character is the most important of the three qualities he looks for when considering someone for a key job. He said the other two, intelligence and energy, can actually be liabilities if strong character is lacking.

And Buffett's advice for success was simple: "You should try to behave in an honorable manner all the time."

CEOs concur. Overwhelmingly, they think setting higher standards for themselves in both their public and private lives is critical.

Some 95% agree that business leaders "have an obligation to maintain certain standards of private conduct."

This can mean setting an example—even outside the office.

"One of my personal rules is that I don't visit bars or drink with my people," Smith said. "It just leaves the wrong impression."

*Source:* Reprinted by permission of *Investment Business Daily*, April 6, 1998, p. A–1.

liability may not be appropriate where no sexual harassment exists or where the employer takes swift remedial action.[293] The primary goal of law enforcement managers and executives should be to prevent the occurrence of any type of sexual harassment. If it does exist, sexual harassment must quickly be confronted and stopped. If this is done, no liability will attach.

**Policy Development**

One of the most important steps toward eradicating workplace harassment, and thus minimizing the chances of liability for harassment, is the development of an agency policy prohibiting harassment in the workplace. A written policy begins the process of establishing the agency's philosophy that workplace harassment is prohibited conduct that will not be condoned. It provides officers with notification of what acts are prohibited. In addition, it provides a shield for those officers who do not want to participate in harassing behavior but do so because of group pressure. Finally, a written policy informs all employees of their right not to be subjected to harassment and how to remedy the situation should harassment occur.[294]

Development of a policy prohibiting harassment is an issue of importance to all law enforcement executives, whether or not they currently have such a policy in place. The *Meritor* case suggests that employer liability for maintaining a hostile work environment will be determined by weighing all of the facts of the case, including whether or not the employer had a well-developed policy prohibiting workplace harassment.

It is crucial to note, however, that *Meritor* emphasizes that having a policy will not necessarily shield the employer from liability.[295] Law enforcement executives familiar with policy implementation and civil liability will appreciate that a bad policy is often as damning as no policy. Further, once a policy is established, it must be enforced. Even the best of policies provides no protection if it is not followed.

Several points should be considered when developing a quality policy that will meet the necessary legal standards. The policy must be clearly written so that it is easily understood. There should be a statement within the policy that discriminatory harassment is illegal, is prohibited by the agency, and will be dealt with through disciplinary action. This statement should have a prominent position within the policy.

It is crucial that the policy clearly delineate specific types of conduct that are prohibited. The scope of workplace harassment is defined legally and is not assumed to be common knowledge. Many agencies choose to include in their policies a set of examples and/or definitions of harassment. This is an excellent practice because it provides notice to employees of the types of activity prohibited while continually reinforcing that knowledge.

On the other hand, many agencies provide a brief legal definition of workplace harassment and then rely on special training programs to provide more specific examples of discriminatory harassment.

The rationale behind this approach is that by stating a set of examples in the policy, it may be misconstrued as an exclusive list of prohibited conduct. The benefit of the model policy approach is that it allows officers to focus on specialized training and examine for themselves whether certain conduct could be construed as unwelcome harassment. Where this approach is adopted, it is imperative that the agency provide special training on harassment for its officers, which is discussed in the next section.

Finally, the policy should state how an employee can register a complaint of harassment. Again, clarity in drafting is necessary so that employees do not bypass agency remedies because of frustration. A complex, multistep procedure, or one that is too vague, can lead to misunderstandings and thus frustrate both the employees' and agency's attempts to eliminate harassment.

A copy of the policy should be distributed to every employee, regardless of rank. The policy will have little impact if access is limited to those employees with the initiative to seek it out. A rather popular and effective way to make sure the policy is read and continuously reinforced is by the use of posters. Many agencies place posters discussing workplace harassment in conspicuous places within their administrative complexes. The use of both posters and a policy on harassment signals employees that the agency is serious about prohibiting workplace harassment.

## Training

The boundaries of what constitutes prohibited harassment can often be confusing. While a written policy provides a good framework for delineating prohibited acts, the law enforcement executive should also consider implementing training programs to combat harassment.

A good training program will help instill and reinforce the agency's philosophy against harassment. Special training programs that are carefully developed can be a valuable tool in fleshing out the policy description of what acts are prohibited. The training program should explain the agency's policy, philosophy, and applicable laws pertaining to workplace harassment. Such training should be used at the recruit level and on a regular basis with the entire agency.

A number of companies offer special training programs using speakers and/or videos that focus on workplace harassment. The Equal Employment Opportunities Commission regional office may be able to suggest such a program. In addition, the International Association of Chiefs of Police has developed a training course devoted to workplace harassment and can develop a custom program for any law enforcement agency that so requests. The cost of any of these programs is a small price when compared to the costs of discrimination litigation.

## Supervision

No law enforcement agency can fulfill its duty to maintain a workplace free of harassment without the assistance and support of its supervisors. Apathetic or hostile supervisors can quickly undermine an otherwise effective and meaningful policy against harassment through their actions or nonactions in implementing the policy. By contrast, through their daily supervision of employees, supervisors can assist the agency in spotting, stopping, and preventing harassment.

Supervisors' responsibilities include watching for signs that harassment may be occurring in their unit. As agency liability may turn on the effectiveness or negligence of supervisors in monitoring the workplace, it is important that supervisors receive thorough training in identifying harassment.

## Complaint Procedure

The development of an effective complaint procedure is the most important action that the agency can take to stop workplace harassment and minimize liability. The *Meritor* case emphasized the importance of maintaining an accessible and effective complaint procedure as a factor to be considered in determining employer liability for maintaining a hostile work environment.[296]

## Employee Responsibilities

Employees are encouraged to assist victims of harassment by reporting any observed incidents, or at least by encouraging the victim to complain. Victims of harassment often feel that everyone agrees with the harasser and that they are powerless. This feeling of isolation may keep victims from realizing that other employees may also be subject to the harassment and not reporting it. Support from coworkers can encourage the employees to file complaints.

Finally, law enforcement executives should encourage employees to document each incident of harassment, regardless of the severity. Harassment, especially sexual harassment, can often begin with acts so slight that the targeted employee may not know what is intended. As a result, the dates upon which the alleged harassment occurred may be inexact. The documentation should include information such as the time, date, and location of the incident; the actions taken by the harasser and employer; the names and actions of any bystanders; and any physical or stress problems resulting from the incident.

Employers should encourage victims of harassment to make clear that the harassing conduct is offensive and unwanted. Employees should be encouraged to report incidents of harassment as soon as possible.

## SUMMARY

In recent years there has been a significant increase in the amount of litigation involving police agencies and their officers. A substantial portion of this litigation has stemmed from efforts by citizens to receive compensation for injuries allegedly caused by department policy and the actions of police department employees. Such suits are brought as state tort actions, Section 1983 claims, or *Bivens* suits. In state tort actions, the plaintiff alleges that his or her injury was caused by conduct that constitutes a tort under state law, such as assault, battery, false imprisonment, or false arrest. A Section 1983 claim is brought under a federal statute that permits relief from infringements of rights created by the Constitution or by federal law by persons acting under color of state law. A *Bivens* action also provides relief from infringements of constitutional rights and serves primarily to fill some "holes" left by Section 1983.

All three types of suits have limitations on who can be sued. The police supervisor and administrator are generally not liable solely by virtue of their status as the employer of the officer whose conduct caused the injury, unless the supervisor or administrator specifically authorized or cooperated in the officer's conduct that led to the injury. However, in an increasing number of cases, supervisors and administrators have been found liable for the misbehavior of their subordinates when plaintiffs were able to demonstrate that the former were negligent in the employment, training, or retention of their subordinates.

The governmental body that employs the officer accused of culpable behavior was traditionally shielded from liability by the doctrine of sovereign immunity. In recent decades, the protection of sovereign immunity in state tort actions has been eroded substantially by legislative and judicial action, but it remains an important restriction on the amount of recovery that can be obtained against the government.

Plaintiffs seeking recovery for injuries caused by police conduct are also limited by the judicial extension of immunity to public employees. In suits based on federal law, an absolute immunity is extended to prosecutors, and to judicial and quasi-judicial officials. A qualified immunity is extended to other officials while they are acting in a discretionary capacity, in good faith, and in a reasonable manner. However, a defendant is not acting in good faith if his or her conduct violates settled law. In state tort actions, absolute immunity is still usually extended to public officials in their exercise of discretionary functions.

Disciplinary actions against police officers raise issues concerning procedures that are required by the due process guarantees of the U.S. Constitution. Due process protections apply when property interests or liberty interests of a public employee may be affected by disciplinary action. Supreme Court cases suggest that in determining when property and liberty interests evoke due process guarantees, the court will carefully examine whether the local government intended to create a protected interest in the public employee.

When due process is mandated, procedural protections are required by the Constitution in taking disciplinary action against a police officer. Court decisions have extended to the police officer rights to be given notice of the charges, to call witnesses, to be confronted by and cross-examine adverse witnesses, to have counsel, and to have a decision based on the record of a hearing conducted by an impartial party. The evidentiary hearing may be postponed until after the disciplinary action is taken when risk-reducing protections, such as written notice of and opportunity to rebut the reasons for the action, are afforded the employee.

Due process also requires that disciplinary rules be clear, specific, and reasonably related to a valid job requirement. Accordingly, a disciplinary rule must address conduct that has an impact on an officer's fitness to perform his or her duties, adversely affects departmental morale or efficiency, or undermines public confidence in the department. The rule must be clear enough to give fair warning, to control the discretion of administrators, and to avoid a "chilling effect" on the exercise of constitutional rights by officers. Many departments prohibit conduct "unbecoming an officer" or "tending to bring discredit upon the department." The application of due process protections to rules of this nature has resulted in some rules being declared unconstitutional for vagueness. Other courts have upheld the constitutionality of such rules because in various disciplinary situations, it should have been clear to the officer that the rule was intended to prohibit his or her conduct.

Sometimes disciplinary rules attempt to prohibit conduct of police officers that is protected by the Constitution. Rules infringing upon the free speech of officers may be upheld if the legitimate interest of the governmental employer is found to be more important than the officer's free speech interest. However, such rules frequently run afoul of the Constitution because they are too broad, or because the department failed to demonstrate that the officer's speech produced an unjustifiable adverse effect on the department's ability to perform.

Rights regarding political participation are also protected by the First Amendment to the Constitution. However, the federal Hatch Act and similar state laws that prohibit nearly all partisan political activity by public employees have been upheld by the Supreme Court. Nevertheless, courts have struck down prohibitions that extended to nonpartisan political activity or political activity, which seemed only remotely related to an important governmental interest. Dismissals of non-policy-making public employees for reasons of political party affiliation have been held illegal.

In other areas affected by the First Amendment, courts have generally upheld rules prohibiting police officers from associating with criminals or other undesirables so long as the rule is not too broad, and it can be demonstrated that the association has a detrimental effect on the department's operation. With regard to freedom of expression, the Supreme Court has upheld the establishment of grooming standards for police officers.

Courts have held that the Fourth Amendment protection against unreasonable searches and seizures does not prevent a department from searching lockers and equipment issued to officers, or from ordering officers to appear in a lineup when there is a strong governmental interest at stake.

The constitutional right against self-incrimination does not prohibit a police department from ordering an officer to answer questions directly related to the performance of his or her duties. Although there is some disagreement among courts considering the question, most courts have also held that officers may be required to take polygraph examinations under the circumstances just described.

Other issues apply to disciplinary action against police officers:

1. "Conduct unbecoming" has been defined as a lack of fitness to perform the functions of a police officer, including associating with crime figures, fighting, dishonesty, off-duty drinking, insubordination, and a wide array of other inappropriate activity.

2. Adultery has generally been upheld as a proper basis for disciplinary action.

3. Homosexuality comes to the forefront when an employee's sexual preference impairs the efficiency of the agency; only flagrant displays of homosexual conduct have generally been found to have such an effect.

4. A department can require its officers to live within the geographical limits of its jurisdiction.

5. A department must reasonably accommodate the religious practices of its officers without imposing an "undue hardship" on itself or other employees.

6. Moonlighting may be prohibited.

7. Regulations relating to the use of weapons issued to officers will be upheld so long as they are reasonable.

8. Regulations prohibiting intoxication or impairment of an officer's ability to perform while on duty as a result of the influence of drugs or alcohol carry a strong

presumption of validity. Police officers can probably be ordered to take blood, breathalyzer, or urinalysis tests when there is a reasonable suspicion of abuse or influence.

In administrative matters unrelated to the disciplinary process, the Supreme Court has held that police departments must comply with the minimum wage and overtime requirements of the Fair Labor Standards Act. Persons between the ages of 40 and 70 may not be discriminated against in employment decisions unless age is a bona fide occupational qualification reasonably necessary to the operation of the department's business.

The best way for law enforcement administrators to prepare to respond to potential incidents of sexual harassment allegations and lawsuits in the workplace is to establish a clear policy and procedure. First, the policy must identify that conduct that constitutes sexual harassment. Second, the policy and procedure must prohibit the offensive conduct and provide for appropriate remedial and punitive measures that should be taken if the policy is violated. Third, the policy and procedure should establish a mechanism for the thorough and timely investigation of all sexual harassment complaints. Finally, law enforcement management must effectively resolve each incident of sexual harassment.

## DISCUSSION QUESTIONS

1. What are the two vehicles by which federal courts can acquire jurisdiction of tort suits that have traditionally been brought in state courts?

2. What is the difference between a crime and a tort?

3. Explain the three general categories of torts. How do they differ?

4. What does "acting under color of State Law" mean? How does this statement relate to Section 1983 actions?

5. What is a *Bivens* action?

6. List and discuss the negligence theories applicable to police supervision and management.

7. What are procedural and substantive due process?

8. What are the twelve elements of a due process hearing?

9. In what three ways are the rules of law promulgated?

10. What are liberty rights and property rights?

11. Discuss some of the grounds for disciplinary action often brought against police officers.

12. Discuss the important elements in *Tennessee* v. *Garner.* Exactly how did this case impact police use of deadly force?

13. Under what circumstances can an officer use deadly force? List some of the important aspects of training in a deadly-force case that a department might offer to defend against a negligence suit.

14. What four elements must be proved in order to sue the police for negligence in a high-speed pursuit? List some of the important management controls that might be taken to reduce liability related to high-speed pursuits.

15. What is the "balancing test," as referred to in alcohol and drug testing in the workplace?

16. What policy recommendations have been made in order to reduce the potential for sexual harassment allegations and lawsuits against police departments?

## NOTES

1. Much of this section is taken, with some addition, from H. E. Barrineau III, *Civil Liability in Criminal Justice* (Cincinnati, Ohio: Anderson, 1987), pp. 3–5.

2. Ibid., p. 3.

3. False arrest is the arrest of a person without probable cause. Generally, this means making an arrest when an ordinarily prudent person would not have concluded that a crime had been committed or that the person arrested had committed the crime. False imprisonment is the intentional illegal detention of a person. The detention that can give rise to a false imprisonment claim is any confinement to a specified area and not simply incarceration in a jail. Most false arrests result in false imprisonment as well, but there can be a false imprisonment after a valid arrest also, as when the police fail to release an arrested person after a proper bond has been posted, the police

unreasonably delay the arraignment of an arrested person, or authorities fail to release a prisoner after they no longer have authority to hold him or her. "Brutality" is not a legal tort action as such. Rather, it must be alleged as a civil (as opposed to a criminal) assault and/or battery. Assault is some sort of menacing conduct that puts another person in reasonable fear that he or she is about to have a battery committed upon him or her. Battery is the infliction of harmful or offensive contact on another person. Harmful or offensive contact is contact that would be considered harmful or offensive by a reasonable person of ordinary sensibilities. See Clarence E. Hagglund, "Liability of Police Officers and Their Employers," *Federation of Insurance Counsel Quarterly,* 26 (Summer 1976), p. 257, for a good discussion of assault and battery, false arrest, false imprisonment, and malicious prosecution as applied to police officers.

4. Although a fourth category (strict liability tort action) does exist in the wider body of law, such a general category is rare in police officer litigation. Therefore, for the purposes of this book, strict liability actions are not discussed. Under strict liability, one is held liable for one's act irrespective of intent or negligence. The mere occurrence of certain events will necessarily create legal liability. A good example of such cases is often found in airplane disasters in which the air transportation company is strictly liable for the passengers' health and well-being regardless of other factors.

5. The definitions of *negligence, intentional torts,* and *constitution torts* are taken from Barrineau, *Civil Liability.*

6. Title 42, U.S. Code Section 1983.

7. See *Monroe* v. *Pape,* 365 U.S. 167, 81 S.Ct. 473 (1961). The plaintiff and his family sued 13 Chicago police officers and the city of Chicago, alleging that police officers broke into their home without a search warrant, forced them out of bed at gunpoint, made them stand naked while the officers ransacked the house, and subjected the family to verbal and physical abuse. The court held that the definition of "under color of State law" for Section 1983 purposes was the same as that already established in the criminal context, and also concluded that because Section 1983 provides for a civil action, the plaintiffs need not prove that the defendants acted with a "specific intent to deprive a person of a federal right" (365 U.S. at 187). The court also held that municipalities (such as the city of Chicago, in this case) were immune from liability under the statute, although the Supreme Court later overruled this part of *Monroe* v. *Pape,*

holding that municipalities and other local governments are included among "persons" open to a Section 1983 lawsuit. See *Monell* v. *Dept. of Social Services of the City of New York,* 436 U.S. 658, 98 S.Ct. 2018 (1978). [Citations to case opinions give the volume number in which the opinion is located followed by the name of the reporter system, the page number, the court if other than the Supreme Court, and the year in which the opinion was rendered.]

8. The resuscitation of Section 1983 hinges on the misuse and abuse of power imbued to individuals acting as police officers. All municipal and county law enforcement officers take an oath to uphold and enforce the laws of a specific state in which their municipality resides. Therefore, municipal police officers are squarely within the confines of Section 1983. "Misuse of power," possessed by virtue of state law and made possible only because the wrongdoer is clothed with the authority of state law, is action taken "under the color of law." *United States* v. *Clasic,* 313 U.S. 299, at p. 326, 61 S.Ct., 1031 at p. 1043 (1941) as quoted in *Monroe* v. *Pape.* Thus, private citizens cannot be sued under Section 1983 unless they conspire with state officers. (See *Slavin* v. *Curry,* 574 F.2nd. 1256 [5th Cir. 1978], as modified by 583 F.2nd. 779 [5th Cir. 1978].) Furthermore, if a state officer has immunity to a Section 1983 lawsuit, private citizens who conspired with him do not have "derivative immunity" to the lawsuit. (See *Sparks* v. *Duval County Ranch Co., Inc.,* 604 F.2d 976 [5th Cir. 1979] at p. 978.) In addition, see *Sanberg* v. *Daley,* 306 F. Supp. 227 (1969) at p. 279.

9. Most tort actions against the U.S. government must be brought under the FTCA. The FTCA is a partial waiver of sovereign immunity, with its own rule of liability and a substantial body of case law. Federal employees can be sued for violation of constitutional rights and for certain common-law torts. For more information, refer to Isidore Silver, *Police Civil Liability* (New York: Mathew Bender, 1987), Section 1.04, from which this material is taken.

10. See *Bivens* v. *Six Unknown Federal Narcotics Agents,* 403 U.S. 388, 91 S.Ct. 1999 (1971). Also, refer to Silver, *Police Civil Liability,* Section 8.02.

11. Silver, *Police Civil Liability,* Section 8.02.

12. See William L. Prosser, *Handbook of the Law of Torts,* 4th ed. (St. Paul, Minn.: West, 1971), p. 69, for a good discussion of the philosophical basis for and development of the doctrine of vicarious liability.

13. Wayne W. Schmidt "Recent Developments in Police Civil Liability," *Journal of Police Science and Administration,* 4 (1976), 197, and the cases cited therein.

14. "[T]he Courts have very generally drawn a distinction between a sheriff and a chief of police, holding that the deputies of the former are selected exclusively by the chief of police, and are themselves officers and do not act for the chief of police in the performance of their official duties," *Parish* v. *Meyers,* 226, at p. 633 (Wash. 1924).

15. *Jordan* v. *Kelly,* 223 F. Supp. 731 (1963) at p. 738, followed in *Mack* v. *Lewis,* 298 F. Supp. 1351 (1969).

16. Ibid., p. 739.

17. Schmidt, "Recent Developments," p. 197.

18. Although this list does not include all types of negligence theories regarding Section 1983 action against police supervisors and managers, it does provide a starting point in understanding this issue. This part has been adapted from Barrineau, *Civil Liability,* pp. 59–60.

19. See *Peter* v. *Bellinger,* 159 N.E.2nd. 528 (1959); *Thomas* v. *Johnson,* 295 F. Supp. 1025 (1968); *McKenna* v. *City of Memphis,* 544 F. Supp. 415 (1982), affirmed in 785 F.2d 560 (1986); *McGuire* v. *Arizona Protection Agency,* 609 P.2nd 1080 (1908); *Di Cosal* v. *Kay,* 19 N.J. 159, 450 A.2nd 508 (1982); *Pontiac* v. *KMS Investments,* 331 N.W. 2d 907 (1983); and *Welsh Manufacturing Div. of Textron, Inc.* v. *Pinkertons, Inc.,* 474 A/2md 426 (1984).

20. See *Moon* v. *Winfield,* 383 F.Supp. 31 (1974); *Murray* v. *Murphy,* 441 F.Supp. 120 (1977); *Allen* v. *City of Los Angeles,* (No. C-9837) LA Sup. Ct. (1975); *Stengel* v. *Belcher,* 522 F.2d 438 (6th Cir. 1975); *Dominguez* v. *Superior Court,* 101 Cal App.3d 6 (1980); *Stuessel* v. *City of Glendale,* 141 Cal. App.3d 1047 (1983); and *Blake* v. *Moore,* 162 Cal. App.3d 700 (1984).

21. See *Ford* v. *Breiser,* 383 F.Supp. 505 (1974); *Dewel* v. *Lawson,* 489 F.2d 877 (10th Cir. 1974); *Bonsignore* v. *City of New York,* 521 F.Supp. 394 (1981), affirmed in 683 F.2d 635 (1st Cir. 1982); *Webster* v. *City of Houston,* 689 F.2d 1220 (5th Cir. 1982), reversed and remanded on the issue of damages in 739 F.2d 993 (5th Cir. 1984); and *District of Columbia* v. *Parker,* 850 F.2d 708 (D.C. Cir. 1988), cert. den. in 489 U.S. 1065, 109 S.Ct. 1339 (1989).

22. See *Marusa* v. *District of Columbia,* 484 F. 428 (1973); *Webster* v. *City of Houston,* supra; and *Grandstagg* v. *City of Borger,* 767 F.2d (5th Cir. 1985), cert. den. in 480 U.S. 917, 107 S.Ct. 1369 (1987).

23. *City of Canton* v. *Harris,* 389 U.S. 378, 103 L.Ed. 412, 109 S.Ct. 1197 (1989) at pp. 1204–1205; *Merritt* v. *County of Los Angeles,* 875 F.2d 765 (9th Cir. (1989); *Owens* v. *Haas,* 601 F.2d 1242 (2nd Cir. 1979), cert. den. in 444 U.S. 980 (1980).

24. Prosser, *Handbook of the Law of Torts,* pp. 977–978.

25. Kenneth Culp Davis, *Administrative Law of the Seventies* (Rochester, N.Y.: Lawyers Cooperative, 1976), p. 551; p. 207, 1978 Supplement.

26. In most states in which abrogation of sovereign immunity has occurred, the abrogation has not been total. In some states, the abrogation is an unconditional waiver of the sovereign immunity, but the waiver extends only to certain activities, to cases in which the employee had a particular state of mind, to cases in which liability is not to exceed a designated monetary amount, or to cases that are limited to a particular level of government. In some states, the insured is responsible for the potential loss. Yet another approach taken by some states is not to allow government units to be sued but to require indemnification of public employees who have been sued successfully. (For an example, see *Florida Statutes,* Chapter 768.28.)

27. *Hans* v. *Louisiana,* 134 U.S. 1, 10 S.Ct. 504 (1890); *Edelman* v. *Jordan,* 415 U.S. 651, 94 S.Ct. 1347 (1974); *Scheuer* v. *Rhodes,* 416 U.S. 232, 94 S.Ct. 1683 (1974).

28. *Alabama* v. *Pugh,* 438 U.S. 781, 98 S.Ct. 3057 (1978).

29. *Davis* v. *Sheuer,* 46 U.S. 183, 104 S.Ct. 3012 (1984).

30. *Scheuer* v. *Rhodes,* at p. 240.

31. *Wood* v. *Strickland,* 420 U.S. 308, 95 S.Ct. 992 (1975).

32. *Harlow* v. *Fitzgerald,* 457 U.S. 800, 102 S.Ct. 2727 (1982).

33. *Mitchell* v. *Forsyth,* 472 U.S. 511, 105 S.Ct. 2806 (1985).

34. *Monroe* v. *Pape,* supra note 7.

35. 436 U.S. 658, 98 S.Ct. 2018 (1978).

36. See, for example, *Rookard* v. *Health and Hospitals Corp.,* 710 F.2d 41 (2nd. Cir. 1983).

37. *Oklahoma City* v. *Tuttle,* 471 U.S. 808, 105 S.Ct. 2427 (1985); but see *Pembauer* v. *Cincinnati,* 475 U.S. 469, 106 S.Ct. 1292 (1986).

38. *Fundiller* v. *City of Cooper City,* 777 F.2d 1436 (11th Cir. 1985).

39. *Daniels* v. *Williams,* 474 U.S. 327, 106 S.Ct. 662 (1986).

40. *New* v. *City of Minneapolis,* 792 F.2d 724, at pp. 725–726 (8th Cir. 1986). See also *McClary* v. *O'Hare,* 786 F.2d 83 (2nd Cir. 1986).

41. Hagglund, "Liability of Police Officers," p. 257.

42. *United States* v. *Leon,* 468 U.S. 897, 104 S.Ct. 3430 (1984).

43. *Malley* v. *Briggs*, 475 U.S. 335, 106 S.Ct. 1092 (1986).

44. *Anderson* v. *Creighton*, 483 U.S. 635, 107 S.Ct. 3034 (1987).

45. Schmidt, "Recent Developments."

46. Ibid., p. 198.

47. *Wimberly* v. *Patterson*, 183 A.2d 691 (1962) at p. 699.

48. *Piatkowski* v. *State*, 251 N.Y.S. 2d 354 (1964) at p. 359.

49. Schmidt, "Recent Developments," p. 199.

50. *Fords* v. *Breier*, 383 F.Supp. 505 (E.D. Wis. 1974).

51. *Lucas* v. *Riley*, Superior Court, Los Angeles County, Cal. (1975); *Delong* v. *City of Denver*, 530 F.2nd 1308 (Colo. 1974); *Grudt* v. *City of Los Angeles*, 468 P.2nd 825 (Cal. 1970); *Dillenbeck* v. *City of Los Angeles*, 446 P.2nd 129 (Cal. 1968).

52. AELE Law Enforcement Legal Defense Manual, "Failure to Provide Medical Treatment," Issue 77-6 (1977).

53. Ibid., and cases therein.

54. See, generally, Joan Bertin Lowy, "Constitutional Limitations on the Dismissal of Public Employees," *Brooklyn Law Review*, 43 (Summer 1976), p. 1; Victor G. Rosenblum, "Schoolchildren: Yes, Policemen: No—Some Thoughts About the Supreme Court's Priorities Concerning the Right to a Hearing in Suspension and Removal Cases," *Northwestern University Law Review*, 72 (1977), p. 146.

55. *Wisconsin* v. *Constantineau*, 400 U.S. 433, 91 S.Ct. 507 (1970); *Doe* v. *U.S. Department of Justice*, 753 F.2d 1092 (D.C. Cir. 1985).

56. *Codd* v. *Velger*, 429 U.S. 624, 97 S.Ct. 882 (1977). See also *Paul* v. *Davis*, 424 U.S. 693, 96 S.Ct. 1155 (1976), which held that injury to reputation alone does not constitute a deprivation of liberty. Also see *Swilley* v. *Alexander*, 629 F.2d 1018 (5th Cir. 1980), where the court held that a letter of reprimand containing untrue charges that was placed in an employee's personnel file infringed on his liberty interest.

57. *Board of Regents* v. *Roth*, 408 U.S. 564, 92 S.Ct. 2701 (1972); *Perry* v. *Sinderman*, 408 U.S. 593, 92 S.Ct. 2694 (1972).

58. *Arnett* v. *Kennedy*, 416 U.S. 134, 94 S.Ct. 1633 (1974); *Bishop* v. *Wood*, 426 U.S. 341, 96 S.Ct. 2074 (1976). See Robert L. Rabin, "Job Security and Due Process; Monitoring Administrative Discretion Through a Reasons Requirement," *University of Chicago Law Review*, 44 (1976), pp. 60, 67, for a good discussion of these cases; also *Bailey* v. *Kirk*, No. 82-1417 (10th Cir. 1985).

59. See Carl Goodman, "Public Employment and the Supreme Court's 1975–76 Term," *Public Personnel Management*, 5 (September–October 1976), pp. 287–289.

60. *Thurston* v. *Dekle*, 531 F.2d 1264 (5th Cir. 1976), vacated on other grounds, 438 U.S. 901, 98 S.Ct. 3118 (1978).

61. *Allison* v. *City of Live Oak*, 450 F.Supp. 200 (M.D. Fla. 1978).

62. See for example *Confederation of Police Chicago* v. *Chicago*, 547 F.2d 375 (7th Cir. 1977).

63. Davis, *Administrative Law*, p. 242.

64. *Memphis Light Gas & Water Division* v. *Craft*, 436 U.S. 1, 98 S.Ct. 1554 (1978).

65. *In re Dewar*, 548 P.2d 149 (Mont. 1976).

66. *Bush* v. *Beckman*, 131 N.Y.S. 2d 297 (1954); *Gibbs* v. *City of Manchester*, 61 A. 128 (N.H. 1905).

67. *Morrissey* v. *Brewer*, 408 U.S. 471, 92 S.Ct. 2593 (1972).

68. *Goldman* v. *Kelly*, 397 U.S. 254, 90 S.Ct. 1011 (1970). See also *Buck* v. *N.Y. City Bd. of Ed.*, 553 F.2d 315 (2d Cir. 1977), cert. den. 438 U.S., 98 S.Ct. 3122 (1978).

69. *Morrisey* v. *Brewer*, supra note 67.

70. *Marshall* v. *Jerrico, Inc.*, 446 U.S. 238, 100 S.Ct. 1610 (1980) and *Hortonville J.S.D. No. 1* v. *Hortonville Ed. Assn.*, 426 U.S. 482, 96 S.Ct. 2308 (1976); *Holley* v. *Seminole County School Dist.*, 755 F.2d 1492 (11th Cir. 1985).

71. 94 S.Ct. 1633, 416 U.S. 134 (1974), at p. 157.

72. Ibid. at pp. 167–168.

73. 96 S.Ct. 893, 424 U.S. 319 (1975), at p. 335.

74. 105 S.Ct. 1487, 470 U.S. 532 (1985).

75. Ibid. at p. 1494.

76. *Gorham* v. *City of Kansas City*, 590 P.2d 1051 (Kan. S.Ct. 1979) and *Winston* v. *U.S. Postal Service*, 585 F.2d 198 (7th Cir. 1978).

77. *Bence* v. *Breier*, 501 F.2d 1185 (7th Cir. 1974), cert. den. in 419 U.S. 1121, 95 S.Ct. 804 (1975).

78. *Perea* v. *Fales*, 114 Cal. Rptr. 808 (1974), p. 810.

79. *Kramer* v. *City of Bethlehem*, 289 A.2d 767 (1972).

80. *Rogenski* v. *Board of Fire and Police Commissioners of Moline*, 285 N.E.2d 230 (1972). See also *Major* v. *Hampton*, 413 F.Supp. 66 (1976), in which the court held that an IRS rule against activities tending to discredit the agency was overbroad as applied to a married employee who had maintained an apartment for illicit sexual liaisons during off-duty hours.

81. *Grayned* v. *City of Rockford*, 92 S.Ct. 2294, 408 U.S. 104 (1972), at pp. 108–109.

82. *Bence* v. *Breier,* supra note 77, at p. 1190.

83. *Rinaldi* v. *Civil Service Commission,* 244 N.W. 2d 609 (Mich. 1976).

84. *Allen* v. *City of Greensboro, North Carolina,* 452 F.2d 489 (4th Cir. 1971).

85. *Petraitis* v. *Board of Fire and Police Commissioners City of Palos Hills,* 335 N.E. 2d 126 (Ill. 1975); *Haywood* v. *Municipal Court,* 271 N.E. 2d 591 (Mass. 1971); *Lewis* v. *Board of Trustee,* 212 N.Y.S. 2d 677 (1961). Compare *Stanton* v. *Board of Fire and Police Commissioners of Village of Bridgeview,* 345 N.E. 2d 822 (Ill. 1976).

86. *DeSalvatore* v. *City of Oneonta,* 369 N.Y.S. 2d 820 (1975).

87. *Marino* v. *Los Angeles,* 110 Cal. Rptr. 45 (1973).

88. *Guido* v. *City of Marion,* 280 N.E. 2d 81 (Ind. 1972).

89. *Carroll* v. *Goldstein,* 217 A.2d 676 (R.I. 1976).

90. *Firemen's and Policemen's Civil Service Commission* v. *Shaw,* 306 S.W. 2d 160 (Tex. 1957).

91. *Martin* v. *City of St. Martinville,* 321 So. 2d 532 (La. 1975).

92. *Arnold* v. *City of Aurora,* 498 P.2d 970 (Colo. 1973).

93. *Carey* v. *Piphus,* 435 U.S. 247, 98 S.Ct. 1042 (1978).

94. *County of Monroe* v. *Dept. of Labor,* 690 F.2d 1359 (11th Cir. 1982).

95. *Gitlow* v. *New York,* 268 U.S. 652, 45 S.Ct. 625 (1925).

96. *Pickering* v. *Board of Education,* 88 S.Ct. 1731, 391 U.S. 563 (1968), at p. 568.

97. *Keyishian* v. *Board of Regents,* 385 U.S. 589, 87 S.Ct. 675 (1967).

98. *Pickering* v. *Board of Education,* supra note 96.

99. *Muller* v. *Conlisk,* 429 F.2d 901 (7th Cir. 1970).

100. *Flynn* v. *Giarusso,* 321 F.Supp. 1295 (E.D. La. 1971), at p. 1299. The regulation was revised and later ruled constitutional in *Magri* v. *Giarusso,* 379 F.Supp. 353 (E.D. La. 1974). See also *Gasparinetti* v. *Kerr,* 568 F.2d 311 (3rd Cir. 1977), cert. den. in 436 U.S. 903, 98 S.Ct. 2232 (1978).

101. *In re Gioglio,* 248 A.2d 570 (N.J. 1968); *Brukiewa* v. *Police Commissioner of Baltimore,* 263 A.2d 210 (Md. 1970); *Kannisto* v. *City and County of San Francisco,* 541 F.2d 841 (9th Cir. 1976), cert. den. in 430 U.S. 931 S.Ct. 1552 (1977). Compare *Magri* v. *Giarusso; Hosford* v. *California State Personnel Board,* 141 Cal. Rptr. 354 (1977); *Simpson* v. *Weeks,* 570 F.2d 240 (8th Cir. 1978).

102. *Brukiewa* v. *Police Commissioner of Baltimore,* supra.

103. *Perry* v. *City of Kinloch,* 680 F.Supp. 1339 (1988).

104. *Brockell* v. *Norton,* 732 F.2d 664 (8th Cir. 1984).

105. *Germann* v. *City of Kansas City, Mo.,* 776 F.2d 761 (8th Cir. 1985).

106. *Broaderick* v. *Oklahoma,* 413 U.S. 601, 93 S.Ct. 2908 (1973), and *Reeder* v. *Kansas City Bd. of Police Comm.,* 733 F.2d 543 (8th Cir. 1984).

107. *United Public Workers* v. *Mitchell,* 330 U.S. 75, 67 S.Ct. (1947); *U.S. Civil Service Commission* v. *National Association of Letter Carriers,* 413 U.S. 548, 93 S.Ct. 2880 (1973).

108. *Broaderick* v. *Oklahoma,* supra note 106.

109. *Magill* v. *Lynch,* 400 F.Supp. 84 (R.I. 1975), vacated in 560 F.2d 22 (1st Cir. 1977), cert. den. in 434 U.S. 1063, 98 S.Ct. 1236 (1978).

110. *Boston Police Patrolmen's Association, Inc.* v. *City of Boston,* 326 N.E. 2d 314 (Mass. 1975).

111. *Phillips* v. *City of Flint,* 224 N.W. 2d 780 (Mich. 1975). But compare *Paulos* v. *Breier,* 507 F.2d 1383 (7th Cir. 1974).

112. Ibid. at p. 784.

113. *Elrod* v. *Bruns,* 427 U.S. 347, 96 S.Ct. 2673 (1976). See also *Ramey* v. *Harber,* 431 F.Supp. 657 (1977), cert. den. in 442 U.S. 910, 99 S.Ct. 823 (1979), and *Branti* v. *Finkel,* 445 U.S. 507, 100 S.Ct. 1287 (1980).

114. *Connick* v. *Myers,* 461 U.S. 138 (1983); *Jones* v. *Dodson,* 727 F.2d 1329 (4th Cir. 1984).

115. *Sponick* v. *City of Detroit Police Department,* 211 N.W. 2d 674 (Mich. 1973), at p. 681, but see *Wilson* v. *Taylor,* 733 F.2d 1539 (11th Cir. 1984).

116. *Bruns* v. *Pomerleau,* 319 F.Supp. 58 (D. Md. 1970). See also *McMullen* v. *Carson,* 754 F.2d 936 (11th Cir. 1985), where it was held that a Ku Klux Klansman could not be fired from his position as a records clerk in the sheriff's department simply because he was a Klansman. The Court did uphold the dismissal because his active KKK participation threatened to cripple the agency's ability to perform its public duties effectively.

117. *Civil Service Commission of Tucson* v. *Livingston,* 525 P.2d 949 (Ariz. 1974).

118. See, for example, *Tinker* v. *Des Moines School District,* 393 U.S. 503, 89 S.Ct. 733 (1969).

119. 425 U.S. 238, 96 S.Ct. 1440 (1976).

120. *Mapp* v. *Ohio,* 367 U.S. 643, 81 S.Ct. 1684 (1961).

121. *Katz* v. *United States,* 389 U.S. 347, 88 S.Ct. 507 (1967).

122. *Smith* v. *Maryland,* 442 U.S. 735, 99 S.Ct. 2577 (1979) and *Chan* v. *State,* 78 Md. App. 287, 552 (1989). The "expectation to privacy" clause was developed in *Katz* v. *United States,* supra note 121, a case that involved warrantless electronic surveillance of a public telephone booth. The Court

said that "the Fourth Amendment protects people, not places. What a person knowingly exposes to the public, even in his own home or office, is not subject of Fourth Amendment protection. But what he seeks to preserve as private, even in an area accessible to the public, may be constitutionally protected. . . . There is a two-fold requirement, first that a person have exhibited an actual expectation of privacy, and second that the expectation by one's society is prepared to recognize it as reasonable/legitimate."

123. See *People* v. *Tidwell,* 266 N.E.2d 787 (Ill. 1971).

124. *McDonnell* v. *Hunter,* 809 F.2d 1302 (8th Cir. 1987).

125. *Biehunik* v. *Felicetta,* 441 F.2d 228 (2nd Cir. 1971), cert. den. 403 U.S. 932, 91 S.Ct. 2256 (1971).

126. *United States* v. *Leon,* 468 U.S. 897, 104 S.Ct. 3430 (1984) and *Massachusetts* v. *Sheppard,* 468 U.S. 981, 104 S.Ct. 3424 (1984).

127. *Illinois* v. *Gates,* 462 U.S. 213, 103 S.Ct. 2317 (1984).

128. The concept of the "good faith-reasonable belief" defense as either a qualified or an absolute immunity has significant case history. See Isadore Silver, *Police Civil Liability,* chapters 4 and 7.

129. See *Floyd* v. *Farrell,* 765 F.2d 1 (1st Cir. 1985), *Malley* v. *Briggs,* 475 U.S. 335, 106 S.Ct. 1092 (1986), *Santiago* v. *Fenton,* 891 F.2d 373 (1st Cir. 1989), and *Hoffman* v. *Reali,* 973 F.2d 980 (1st Cir. 1992).

130. *Sheetz* v. *Mayor and City Council of Baltimore, Maryland,* 315 Md. 208 (1989).

131. 385 U.S. 493, 87 S.Ct. 6126 (1967).

132. The states are bound by this requirement as well. *Malloy* v. *Hogan,* 378 U.S. 1, 84 S.Ct. 489 (1964).

133. *Gardner* v. *Broderick,* 392 U.S. 273, 88 S.Ct. 1913 (1968).

134. These procedural rights in police disciplinary actions have often been referred to as the "Garrity Rights." They were developed through a series of cases, see *Lefkowitz* v. *Turley,* 414 U.S. 70, 94 S.Ct. 316 (1973), and *Confederation of Police* v. *Conlisk,* 489 F.2d 891 (1973), cert. den. in 416 U.S. 956, 94 S.Ct. 1971 (1974). Further, as the rights appear here, see Will Aitchison, *The Rights of Law Enforcement Officers* (Portland, Ore.: Labor Relations Information System, 1989), p. 118.

135. See *Gabrilowitz* v. *Newman,* 582 F.2d 100 (1st Cir. 1978). Cases upholding the department's authority to order an officer to take a polygraph examination include *Eshelman* v. *Blubaum,* 560 P.2d 1283 (Ariz. 1977); *Dolan* v. *Kelly,* N.Y.S. 2d 478 (1973); *Richardson* v. *City of Pasadena,* 500 S.W. 2d 175 (Tex. 1973); *Seattle Police Officer's Guild* v. *City of Seattle,* 494 P.2d 485 (Wash. 1972); *Roux* v. *New Orleans Police Department,* 223 So. 2d 905 (La. 1969); *Coursey* v. *Board of Fire and Police Commissioners,* 234 N.E. 2d 339 (Ill. 1967); *Frazee* v. *Civil Service Board of City of Oakland,* 338 P.2d 943 (Cal. 1959); and *Hester* v. *Milledgeville,* 777 F.2d 1492 (11th Cir. 1985). Cases denying the department's authority include *Molino* v. *Board of Public Safety of City of Torrington,* 225 A.2d 805 (Conn. 1966). *Stape* v. *Civil Service Commission of City of Philadelphia,* 172 A.2d 161 (Pa. 1961), and *Farmer* v. *Fort Lauderdale,* 427 So.2d 187 (Fla. 1983), cert. den. in 464 U.S. 816, 104 S.Ct. 74 (1983).

136. *Eshelman* v. *Blubaum,* supra note 135, at p. 1286.

137. *Farmer* v. *City of Fort Lauderdale,* supra note 135.

138. *Faust* v. *Police Civil Service Commission,* 347 A.2d 765 (Pa. 1975); *Steward* v. *Leary,* 293 N.Y.S. 2d 573 (1968); *Brewer* v. *City of Ashland,* 86 S.W. 2d 669 (Ky. 1935); *Fabio* v. *Civil Service Commission of Philadelphia,* 373 A.2d 751 (Pa. 1977).

139. *Anderson* v. *City of Philadelphia, Pennsylvania,* 668 F.Supp. 441 (1987), reversed by 845 F.2d 1216 (3rd. Cir. 1988).

140. See Aitchison, *The Rights of Law Enforcement Officers,* pp. 58–62.

141. See *Bigby* v. *City of Chicago,* 766 F.2d 1053 (7th Cir. 1985), cert. den. in 474 U.S. 1056, 106 S.Ct. 793 (1986); *McCoy* v. *Board of Fire and Police Commissioners* (Chicago), 398 N.E. 2d 1020 (1979); *Davis* v. *Williams,* 588 F.2d 69 (4th Cir. 1979); *Parker* v. *Levy,* 417 U.S. 733, 94 S.Ct. 2547 (1974); *Bence* v. *Brier,* 501 F.2d 1184 (7th Cir. 1974), cert. den. in 419 U.S. 1121, 95 S.Ct. 1552 (1977); and *Gee* v. *California State Personnel Board,* 85 Cal Rptr. 762 (1970).

142. Whether or not reasonable people would agree that the conduct was punishable so that an individual is free to steer a course between lawful and unlawful behaviors is the key to "reasonableness." Refer to *Cranston* v. *City of Richmond,* 710 P.2d 845 (1986), and *Said* v. *Lackey,* 731 S.W. 2d 7 (1987).

143. *Cranston* v. *City of Richmond,* supra.

144. See *City of St. Petersburg* v. *Police Benevolent Association,* 414 So. 2d 293 1982, and *Brown* v. *Sexner,* 405 N.E. 2d 1082 (1980).

145. *Richter* v. *Civil Service Commission of Philadelphia,* 387 A.2d 131 (1978).

146. *Miller* v. *City of York,* 415 A.2d 1280 (1980), and *Kannisto* v. *City and County of San Francisco,* 541 F.2d 841 (1976), cert. den. in 430 U.S. 931, 97 S.Ct. 1552 (1977).

147. *McIntosh* v. *Monroe Police Civil Board,* 389 So. 2d 410 (1980), *Barnett* v. *New Orleans Police Department,* 413 So. 2d 520 (1982), and *Allman* v. *Police Board of Chicago,* 489 N.E.2d 929 (1986).

148. *Philadelphia Civil Service Commission* v. *Wotjuski,* 525 A.2d 1255 (1987), *Gandolfo* v. *Department of Police,* 357 So. 568 (1978), and *McDonald* v. *Miller,* 596 F.2d 686 (1979).

149. *Monroe* v. *Board of Public Safety,* 423 N.Y.S. 2d 963 (1980).

150. *Redo* v. *West Goshen Township,* 401 A.2d 394 (1979).

151. *Brase* v. *Board of Police Commissioners,* 487 N.E. 2d 91 (1985).

152. *Major* v. *Hampton,* 413 F.Supp. 66 (1976).

153. *City of North Muskegon* v. *Briggs,* 473 U.S. 909 (1985).

154. *National Gay Task Force* v. *Bd. of Ed. of Oklahoma City,* 729 F.2d 1270 (10th Cir. 1984).

155. See *Whisenhund* v. *Spradlin,* 464 U.S. 964 (1983) and *Kukla* v. *Village of Antioch,* 647 F.Supp. 799 (1986), cohabitation of officers; *Coryle* v. *City of Oil City,* 405 A.2d 1104 (1979), public lewdness; *Childers* v. *Dallas Police Department,* 513 F.Supp. 134 (1981) and *Fout* v. *California State Personnel Board,* supra, child molesting; *Fugate* v. *Phoenix Civil Service Board,* 791 F.2d 736 (9h Cir. 1986), sex with prostitutes; *Doe* v. *Commonwealth Attorney,* 425 U.S. 901, 96 S.Ct. 1489 (1976), *Smith* v. *Price,* 616 F.2d 1371 (5th Cir. 1980), and *Bowers* v. *Hardwick,* 478 U.S. 186, 106 S.Ct. 2841 (1986), sodomy as a state law prohibiting homosexuality.

156. *Bd. of Ed.* v. *National Gay Task Force,* 729 F.2d 1270 (10th Cir. 1984), affirmed in 470 U.S. 903, 105 S.Ct. 1858 (1985).

157. *Rowland* v. *Mad River Sch. Dist.,* 730 F.2d (6th Cir. 1984), cert. den. in 470 U.S. 1009, 105 S.Ct. 1373 (1985).

158. *Todd* v. *Navarro,* 698 F.Supp. 871 (1988).

159. *Padula* v. *Webster,* 822 F.2d 97 (D.C. 1987).

160. *McCarthy* v. *Philadelphia Civil Service Comm.,* 424 U.S. 645, 96 S.Ct. 1154 (1976).

161. *Miller* v. *Police of City of Chicago,* 349 N.E. 2d 544 (Ill. 1976); *Williamson* v. *Village of Baskin,* 339 So. 2d 474 (La. 1976); *Nigro* v. *Board of Trustees of Alden,* 395 N.Y.S. 2d 544 (1977).

162. *State, County, and Municipal Employees Local 339* v. *City of Highland Park,* 108 N.W. 2d 544 (1977).

163. *Hameetman* v. *City of Chicago,* 776 F.2d 636 (7th Cir. 1985).

164. 42 U.S.C. S2003(j).

165. *Pinsker* v. *Joint Dist. No. 281,* 554 F.Supp. 1049 (1983), affirmed in 735 F.2d 388 (10th Cir. 1984).

166. *United States* v. *City of Albuquerque,* 12 EPD 11, 244 (10th Cir. 1976). See also *Trans World Airlines* v. *Hardison,* 432 U.S. 63, 97 S.Ct. 2264 (1977).

167. *Potter* v. *Murray City,* 760 F.2d 1065 (10th Cir. 1985), cert. den. in 474 U.S. 849, 106 S.Ct. 145 (1986).

168. *Cox* v. *McNamara,* 493 P.2d 54 (Ore. 1972); *Brenkle* v. *Township of Shaler,* 281 A.2d 920 (Pa. 1972); *Hopwood* v. *City of Paducab,* 424 S.W. 2d 134 (Ky. 1968); *Flood* v. *Kennedy,* 239 N.Y.S. 2d 665 (1963). See also *Trelfa* v. *Village of Centre Island,* 389 N.Y.S. 2d 22 (1976). Rules prohibiting law enforcement officers from holding interest in businesses that manufacture, sell, or distribute alcoholic beverages have also been upheld. *Bock* v. *Long,* 279 N.E.2d 464 (Ill. 1972); *Johnson* v. *Trader,* 52 So. 2d 333 (Fla. 1951).

169. Richard N. Williams, *"Legal Aspects of Discipline by Police Administrators,"* Traffic Institute Publication No. 2705 (Evanston, Ill.: Northwestern University, 1975), p. 4.

170. *City of Crowley Firemen* v. *City of Crowley,* 264 So. 2d 368 (La. 1972).

171. See *Rojas* v. *Alexander's Department Store, Inc.,* 654 F.Supp. 856 (1986), and *Reagan* v. *Hampton,* 700 F.Supp. 850 (1988).

172. Kenneth James Matulia, "The Use of Deadly Force: A Need for Directives in Training," *The Police Chief* (May 1983), p. 30.

173. Kenneth James Matulia, "A Balance of Forces: Model Deadly Force and Policy Procedure," *International Association of Chiefs of Police* (1985), pp. 23 and 24. See also *Tennessee* v. *Garner,* 471 U.S. 1, 105 S.Ct. 1694 (1985).

174. *Tennessee* v. *Garner,* 471 U.S. 1 (1985).

175. *Tennessee* v. *Garner,* supra.

176. *Matulia,* "A Balance of Forces," p. 72.

177. Catherin H. Milton, Jeanne Wahl Halleck, James Lardnew, and Gray L. Albrecht, *Police Use of Deadly Force* (Washington, D.C.: Police Foundation, 1977), p. 52.

178. Matulia, "A Balance of Forces," p. 52.

179. Ibid., p. 77.

180. Ibid., p. 77

181. Ibid., p. 78

182. 471 U.S. 1, 105 S.Ct. 1694 (1985).

183. Matulia, "A Balance of Forces," p. 78.

184. Daniel L. Schofield, "Legal Issues of Pursuit Driving," *FBI Law Enforcement Bulletin* (May 1988),

23–30. (This discussion was adapted from this source.)

185. Richard G. Zivitz, "Police Civil Liability and the Law of High Speed Pursuit." 70 *Marquette L. Rev.* 237 (1987), pp. 237–279.

186. *Jackson* v. *Olson,* 712 P.2d 128 (Or. App. 1985).

187. 457 Do. 2d 816 (Miss. 1985).

188. Ibid. at p. 818.

189. See generally Annotation, "Emergency Vehicle Accidents," 24 *Am. Jur. Proof of Facts,* p. 599.

190. See generally Annotation, "Liability of Governmental Unit or Its Officer for Injury to Innocent Occupants of Moving Vehicle as a Result of Police Chase." 4 *A.L.R.* 4th 865. See also, *Breck* v. *Cortez,* 490 N.E. 2d 88 (III. App. 1986).

191. See generally Annotation, "Municipal Corporation's Safety Rules or Regulations as Admissible in Evidence in Action by Private Party Against Municipal Corporation or its Officers or Employees for Negligent Operation of Vehicle." 82 *A.L.R. 1285.*

192. See *Fiser* v. *City of Ann Arbor,* 339 N.W.2d 413 (Mich. 1983).

193. 733 S.W.2d 28 (Mo. App. 1987).

194. For a general discussion of immunity, see David Charlin, "High-Speed Pursuits: Police Officer and Municipal Liability for Accidents Involving the Pursued and an Innocent Third Party," 16 *Seton Hall L. Rev.* 101 (1986).

195. 490 So. 2d 1061 (Fla. App. 1986).

196. *Fagan* v. *City of Vineland,* 22 F.3d 1283 (3rd Cir. 1994).

197. 42 U.S.C. 1983 provides in relevant part: "Every person who, under color of any statute, ordinance, regulation, custom, or usage, of any State of Territory, subjects or causes to be subjected, any citizen of the United States or other person within the jurisdiction thereof to the deprivation of any rights, privileges, or immunities secured by the Constitution and laws, shall be liable to the party injured in an action at law, suit in equity, or other proper proceedings for redress."

198. 782 F.2d 947 (11th Cir. 1986).

199. Ibid. at p. 950.

200. Ibid.

201. See *Allen* v. *Cook,* 668 F.Supp. 1460 (W.D. Okla. 1987). See also *Fagan* v. *City of Vineland,* supra note 196.

202. 772 F.2d 1205 (5th Cir. 1985).

203. 471 U.S. 1, 105 S.Ct. 1694 (1985). The Supreme Court held that the use of deadly force to apprehend an unarmed fleeing felon was an unreasonable seizure which violated the Fourth Amendment.

204. 817 F.2d 540 (9th Cir. 1987). In *City of Miami* v. *Harris,* 490 So. 2d 69 (Fla. App. 1985), the court held that a city can be liable under 1983 for a pursuit policy that is adopted with a reckless disregard of whether such policy would cause loss of life without due process.

205. *Brower* v. *County of Inyo,* 489 U.S. 593, 109 S.Ct. 1378 (1989).

206. A discussion of empirical studies regarding pursuits is set forth in Geoffrey P. Alpert, "Questioning Police Pursuits in Urban Areas," in *Critical Issues in Policing: Contemporary Readings,* ed. R. G. Dunham and G. P. Alpert (Prospect Heights, Ill.: Waveland Press, 1989), pp. 216–229.

207. *Jackson* v. *Olson,* supra note 186.

208. See Annotation, "Municipal or State Liability for Injuries Resulting from Police Roadblocks or Commandeering of Private Vehicles," 19 *A.L.R.* 4th 937.

209. *Brower* v. *County of Inyo,* supra note 205.

210. *Horta* v. *Sullivan,* 4 F.3d 2 (1st Cir. 1993), at p. 10.

211. See note, "*State* v. *Harding:* Municipal Police Authority and the Fresh Pursuit Statute," 39 *Main L. Rev.,* 509 (1987).

212. See, for example, *Nelson* v. *City of Chester, Ill.,* 733 S.W. 2d 28 (Mo. App. 1987); *Biscoe* v. *Arlington County,* 738 F.2d 1352 (D.C. Cir. 1984).

213. Alpert, "Questioning Police Pursuits in Urban Areas," pp. 227–228.

214. *Reich* v. *Board of Fire and Police Commissioners,* 301 N.E.2d 501 (Ill. 1973).

215. *Krolick* v. *Lowery,* 302 N.Y.S. 2d 109 (1969), at p. 115, and *Hester Milledgeville,* 598 F.Supp. 1456, at p. 457, n.2 (M.D. Ga. 1984), modified in 777 F.2d 1492 (11th Cir. 1985).

216. *McCracken* v. *Department of Police,* 337 So. 2d 595 (La. 1976).

217. *Krolick* v. *Lowery,* supra note 215.

218. 466 U.S. 109, 104 S.Ct. 1652 (1984), at p. 1656.

219. *National Federation of Federal Employees* v. *Weinberger,* 818 F.2d 935 (1987). See also related cases *National Treasury Employees Union* v. *Von Raab,* 816 F.2d 170 (1987), and *Lovvorn* v. *City of Chattanooga, Tennessee,* 846 F.2d 1539 (1988).

220. *O'Connor* v. *Ortega,* 480 U.S. 709, 107 S.Ct. 1492, (1987).

221. 489 U.S. 602, 109 S.Ct. 1402 (1989).

222. Supra note 189.

223. *City of Palm Bay* v. *Bauman,* 475 So. 2d 1322 (Fla. 5th DCA 1985).

224. *Walters* v. *Secretary of Defense,* 725 F.2d 107 (D.C. Cir. 1983).

225. *Security of Law Enforcement Employees, District Counsel 82* v. *Carly,* 737 F.2d 187 (2d Cir. 1984); *Division 241 Amalgamated Transit Union* v. *Suscy,* 538 F.2d 1264 (7th Cir. 1976) cert. den. in 429 U.S. 1029, 97 S.Ct. 653 (1976); *McDonnell* v. *Hunter,* 612 F.Supp. 1122 (S.D. Iowa 1984), aff'd 746 F.2d 785 (8th Cir. 1984).

226. For a comprehensive review of the cases in this area, see Gregory P. Orvis, "Drug Testing in the Criminal Justice Workplace," *American Journal of Criminal Justice,* 18:2 (Spring 1994), 290–305.

227. *National League of Cities* v. *Usery,* 426 U.S. 833, 96 S.Ct. 2465 (1976).

228. *Garcia* v. *San Antonio Transit,* 469 U.S. 528, 105 S.Ct. 1005 (1985), overruled *National League of Cities,* supra note 227.

229. *Massachusetts Board of Retirements* v. *Murgia,* 427 U.S. 307, 96 S.Ct. 2562 (1976).

230. 29 U.S.C. 623 (*f*).

231. *Western Airlines* v. *Criswell,* 472 U.S. 400, 105 S.Ct. 2743, at p. 2751 (1985), and *Dothard* v. *Rawlinson,* 433 U.S. 321, 329, 97 S.Ct. 2720 (1977).

232. *Usery* v. *Tamiami Trail Tours, Inc.,* 531 F.2d 224 (5th Cir. 1976).

233. *Johnson* v. *Mayor and City Council of Baltimore,* 472 U.S.5353, 105 S.Ct. 2717, at p. 2722 (1985).

234. *Hahn* v. *City of Buffalo,* 770 F.2d 12 (2nd Cir. 1985).

235. Jeffrey Higgenbotham, "Sexual Harassment in the Police Station," *FBI Law Enforcement Bulletin,* 57 (September 1988), pp. 22–28. This discussion of sexual harassment was adapted from this article.

236. 42 U.S.C. S2000e-2(a)(1) makes it "an unlawful employment practice for an employer . . . to discriminate against any individual with respect to his compensation, terms, conditions, or privileges of employments, because of such individual's . . . sex."

237. See, for example, 41 U.S.C. S2000e-5 and 2000e-6.

238. 29 C.F.R. S1604.11 (1987).

239. *General Electric Co.* v. *Gilbert,* 97 S.Ct. 401, 429 U.S. 125 A, at pp. 141–142 (1975).

240. 29 C.F.R. S1604.11(a).

241. *Katz* v. *Dole,* 709 F.2d 251 (4th Cir. 1983).

242. *Henson* v. *City of Dundee,* 681 F.2d 897 (11th Cir. 1982). See also *Vernett* v. *Hough,* 627 F.Supp. 587 (W.D. Mich. 1986).

243. See U.S. Constitution, Amendment 14.

244. *Henson* v. *City of Dundee,* supra note 242, at p. 902.

245. Supra note 242.

246. Ibid. at p. 903.

247. 106 S.Ct. 2399 (1986).

248. Ibid. at p. 2406.

249. Ibid.

250. *Moylan* v. *Maries County,* 792 F.2d 746 (8th Cir. 1986), reheard as *Staton* v. *Maries County,* 868 F.2d (8th Cir. 1989).

251. *Meritor Savings Bank* v. *Vinson,* 447 U.S. 57, 106 S.Ct. 2399, at p. 2406 (1986).

252. Ibid.

253. Ibid. at p. 2407.

254. The Supreme Court noted that a trial court must exercise its discretion to decide whether the relevance of the evidence is outweighed by the danger of unfair prejudice, but may not establish a per se rule excluding such evidence. Ibid.

255. See *Loftin-Boggs* v. *City of Meridian,* 633 F.Supp. 1323 (S.D. Miss. 1986) aff'd, 824 F.2d 921 (5th Cir. 1987), cert. den. in 484 U.S. 1063, 108 S.Ct. 1021 (1988).

256. *Laudenslager* v. *Covert,* 45 F.E.P. Cas. 907 (Mich. Ct.App. 1987).

257. *Highlander* v. *K.F.C. National Management Co.,* 805 F.2d 644 (6th Cir. 1986).

258. See *Silverstein* v. *Metroplex Communications,* 678 F.Supp. 863 (S.D Fla. 1988); *Neville* v. *Taft Broadcasting Co.,* 42 F.E.P Cas. 1314 (W.D. N.Y. 1987). However, in *Meritor Savings Bank* v. *Vinson,* supra note 251, the Supreme Court refused to hold that the failure of an employee to use an employer's grievance procedure automatically insulated the employer from liability. That issue was "plainly relevant" but not conclusive. 106 S.Ct. at 2409.

259. *Rabidue* v. *Osceola Refining Co.,* 805 F.2d 611 (6th Cir. 1986); see also 29 C.F.R. S1604.11(b) 260.

260. *Henson* v. *City of Dundee,* supra note 242. See also *Bohen* v. *City of East Chicago, Ind.,* 799 F.2d 1180 (7th Cir. 1986) (conduct equally offensive to men and women is not a violation of equal protection.)

261. *Henson* v. *City of Dundee,* supra note 244, at p. 903.

262. Ibid. at p. 904.

263. 842 F.2d 1010 (8th Cir. 1988).

264. Ibid. at p. 1014.

265. *Vermett* v. *Hough,* 627 F.Supp. 587 (W.D. Mich. 1986).

266. 42 U.S.C. S2000e-2(a)(1).

267. See *Meritor Savings Bank* v. *Vinson,* supra note 251, at p. 2404. The existence of a tangible effect on a condition of employment is inconsequential. No economic or tangible job detriment need be suffered.

268. *Rogers* v. *EEOC,* 454 F.2d 234 (5th Cir. 1971), cert. den. in 406 U.S. 957 (1972); *Meritor Savings Bank* v. *Vinson,* supra note 236, at p. 2405. See also *Broderick* v. *Ruder,* 685 F.Supp. 1269 (D.D.C. 5/13/88). (Sexual activities in the workplace between other employees can affect the psychological well-being of an employee and create a hostile environment.)

269. *Meritor Savings Bank* v. *Vinson,* supra note 251, at p. 2404 (citations omitted).

270. Ibid. at p. 2406.

271. See *Fontanez* v. *Aponte,* 660 F.Supp. 145 (D. Puerto Rico 1987); *Sapp* v. *City of Warner Robins,* 655 F.Supp. 1043 (M.D. Georgia 1987); *Strickland* v. *Sears, Roebuck & Co.,* 46 F.E.P. Cas. 1024 (E.D. Va. 1987); *Petrosky* v. *Washington-Greene County Branch,* 45 F.E.P. Cas. 673 (W.D. Pa. 1987).

272. See *Moylan* v. *Maries County,* supra note 250; and *Katz* v. *Dole,* supra note 241.

273. See, for example, *Arnold* v. *City of Seminole,* 614 F.Supp. 853 (E.D. Oklahoma 354-18 1985). See also discussion at note 48 and accompanying text, *infra.*

274. See *Lake* v. *Baker,* 662 F.Supp. 392 (D.D.C. 1987).

275. 627 F.Supp. 587 (W.D. Michigan).

276. Ibid. at p. 599.

277. Supra note 273.

278. *Porta* v. *Rollins Environmental Services,* 654 F.Supp. 1275 (D.N.J. 1987), aff'd, 845 F.2d 1014 (3rd Cir. 1988).

279. *DelGado* v. *Lehman,* 665 F.Supp. 460 (E.D. Va. 1987).

280. See *Arnold* v. *City of Seminole,* supra note 273 at p. 872. See also 29 C.F.R. S1604.11(*f*).

281. Supra note 12.

282. *Meritor Savings Bank* v. *Vinson,* supra note 251, at p. 2408.

283. *Henson* v. *City of Dundee,* supra note 242, at p. 910.

284. *Katz* v. *Dole,* supra note 241, at p. 255.

285. Ibid. at p. 255.

286. *Hall* v. *Gus Construction Co.,* 842 F.2d 1010, at p. 1061 (8th Cir. 1988).

287. *Sapp* v. *City of Warner Robins,* 655 F.Supp. 1043, at p. 1050 (M.D. Ga. 1987). See also *Hall* v. *Gus Construction Co.,* supra note 286, at p. 1016.

288. See, e.g., *Arnold* v. *City of Seminole,* supra note 280, *Hall* v. *Gus Construction Co.,* supra note 286, *Henson* v. *City of Dundee,* supra note 242, *Lipsett* v. *Puerto Rico,* 864 F.2d 884 (1st Cir. 1988). See also the five-post test established in *Chamberlim* v. *101 Reality, Inc.,* 915 F.2d 777 (1st Cir. 1990), at p. 783–785.

289. *Meritor Savings Bank* v. *Vinson,* supra note 251, at p. 2408.

290. See 42 U.S.C. S2000e-5(g).

291. See, for example, *Arnold* v. *City of Seminole,* supra note 273, at p. 871.

292. See, for example, *Johnson* v. *Ballard,* 644 F.Supp. 333 (N.D. Ga. 1986); *Bohen* v. *City of East Chicago, Ind.,* supra note 260; *Brown* v. *Town of Allentown,* 648 F.Supp. 831 (D.N.H. 1986); *Hunt* v. *Weatherbee,* 626 F.Supp. 1097 (D. Mass. 1986).

293. See, for example, *Brown* v. *Town of Allentown,* supra note 292; *Priest* v. *Rotary,* 634 F.Supp. 571 (N.D. Cal. 1986); *Owens* v. *Tumage,* 46 F.E.P. Cas. 528 (D.N.J. 1988).

294. International Association of Chiefs of Police, "Harassment in the Workplace" (Arlington, Va.: 1990), pp. 6–7, 9–10.

295. *Meritor Savings Bank* v. *Vinson,* supra note 251, at p. 72.

296. Ibid.

# INTRODUCTION

Decision making is a complex process that includes not only procedures for reaching a sound decision on the basis of pertinent knowledge, beliefs, and judgments but also procedures for obtaining the required knowledge, ideas, and preconditions. Moreover, in the case of important decisions, these procedures may involve many minor decisions taken at various stages in the decision-making process. For example, a chief's decision to automate the records division by purchasing a computer and software usually follows a series of decisions. First, the chief decides that the present manual system is not adequate. Second, a decision is made to evaluate the number of systems available on the open market. This decision probably accompanied the decision to address the city council to request additional funding with which to purchase the necessary equipment. And finally, the chief resolves that records division personnel must be retrained to operate in an automated system. These minor decisions are only part of the overall process in arriving at a major decision. Thus, the decision to take a certain action, if sound, should be based on the judgment that this action probably will have more desirable results than any other action, and this judgment may be based on conclusions as to the probable consequences of alternative decisions.[1]

————12—

# PLANNING AND DECISION MAKING

*The essence of ultimate decision remains impenetrable to the observer, often, indeed, to the decider himself. . . . There will always be the dark and tangled stretches in the decision-making process—mysterious even to those who may be most ultimately involved.*

JOHN F. KENNEDY

Decision making also involves the application of our knowledge, our experience, and our mental and moral skills and powers to determine what actions should be taken to deal with a variety of problem situations. Moreover, this decision-making process includes the application of logic for testing conclusions and the use of ethics for testing judgment.[2] For instance, an individual officer's decision to arrest a violent, drunk husband at a family disturbance will usually be based on the officer's past knowledge that if the current situation is left unattended, the probable result will be a criminal act involving assault, wife or child abuse, or even murder. Ethically, the officer is bound to deter crime and as such will take the necessary course of action to prevent the physical harm of any family member.

Decision making is a responsibility that all police officers come to accept routinely. These decisions may be as ordinary as deciding whether to write a motorist a traffic citation or as complex as a split-second decision whether to shoot at someone. The quality and types of decisions made by police managers in their policy formulation and by the street-level officer in invoking arrest action will be based, in part, on the personality characteristics of the individual making the decision, the recruiting and career development practices of the police department, and, equally important, the type of community being served. For example, one merely has to read the works of Wilson[3] and Skolnick[4] to conclude that enforcement decisions that appear to be quite adequate for one community may be totally unacceptable for another; that recruitment practices that would be acceptable to one community would draw objections from another. Thus, police administrators can follow no single model to make the best decisions all the time. However, certain principles, when understood and applied carefully, can result in good decisions much of the time. Although sometimes not understood as such, planning is basically part of the decision-making process, and as such will be treated accordingly.

# PLANNING

Police administrators sometimes do not appreciate the importance of planning because of their pattern of career development. It is ironic that the pattern of career development for typical police managers carries with it seeds that sometimes blossom into a negative view of planning. Having spent substantial portions of their careers in line divisions, such as patrol and investigative services, police managers may see planning as "clerical" or "not real police work." Further, because many agencies have a "planning and research" unit, there is a natural tendency to believe that planning should occur only in that area by individuals assigned to that task. However, planning is an integral element of good management and good decision making.[5] Management needs to anticipate and shape events; it is weak if it merely responds to them.[6] The police manager whose time is consumed by dealing with crises is symptomatic of a department with no real planning or decision-making process. Police departments are sometimes said to be practicing "management by crisis"; in fact, it is "crisis by management."[7] That is, the lack of attention given by police managers to planning creates an environment in which crises are going to occur with regularity. This is so because management by crisis produces a present-centered orientation in which considerations of the future are minimal. In contrast, planning can be expected to

1. Improve analysis of problems
2. Provide better information for decision making
3. Help to clarify goals, objectives, and priorities
4. Result in more effective allocation of resources
5. Improve inter- and intradepartmental cooperation and coordination
6. Improve the performance of programs
7. Give the police department a clear sense of direction
8. Provide the opportunity for greater public support
9. Increase the commitment of personnel

In short, competent planning is a sure sign of good police administration and the first step in accurate decision making.[8]

## Definitions of Planning

There are no simple definitions of planning. The word *planning* became common terminology in the vocabulary of criminal justice with the introduction of the Omnibus Crime Control and Safe Streets Act of 1968. However, what appeared to be missing in that now-famous document was an examination of what planning actually involved, or what it meant in the operation of criminal justice organizations. Hudzik and Cordner[9] have defined planning as "thinking about the future, thinking about what we want the future to be, and thinking about what we need to do now to achieve it." Stated more succinctly, planning involves linking present actions to future conditions. Mottley defines planning as

A management function concerned with visualizing future situations, making estimates concerning them, identifying the issues, needs and potential danger points, analyzing and evaluating the alternative ways and means for reaching desired goals according to a certain schedule, estimating the necessary funds and resources to do the work, and initiating action in time to prepare what may be needed to cope with changing conditions and contingent events.[10]

There is also the assumption that planning is oriented toward action, which means that thinking is only a part of planning; the real purpose is determining what an organization should do, and then doing it. And finally, planning is associated with empirical rationalism: planners gather and analyze data and then reach an objective conclusion.

## PLANNING APPROACHES

A variety of approaches are employed in the planning processes. Each is unique and can be understood as a *method* of operationalizing the word *planning*. There are basically five major approaches to planning: (1) synoptic, (2) incremental, (3) transactive, (4) advocacy, and (5) radical.

**Synoptic Planning**

Synoptic planning or the rational-comprehensive approach is the dominant tradition in planning. It is also the point of departure for most other planning approaches, which, in general, are either modifications of synoptic planning or reactions against it. Figure 12-1 represents the typical synoptic model. It is based on "pure" or "objective" rationality and attempts to assure optimal achievement of desired goals from a given situation.[11] This model is especially appropriate for police agencies as it is based on a problem-oriented approach to planning. It relies heavily on the problem identification and analysis phase

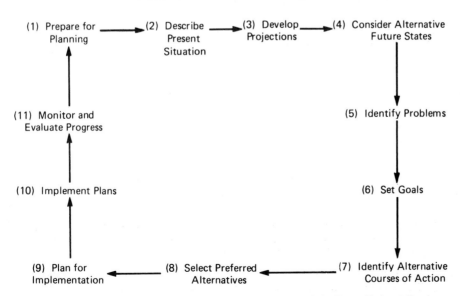

The Synoptic or Traditional Planning Model

FIGURE 12-1. The synoptic or traditional planning model. [From Robert Cushman, *Criminal Justice Planning for Local Governments* (Washington, D.C.: U.S. Government Printing Office, 1980), p. 26, with minor modification.]

of the planning process and can assist police administrators in formulating goals and priorities in terms that are focused on specific problems and solutions that often confront law enforcement. For instance, police administrators are more apt to appreciate a planning model centered around problem-oriented goals and priorities (such as the reduction of burglaries in a given residential area) than around more abstract notions (such as the reduction of crime and delinquency).[12] Then, too, police departments are designed for response, and it is easier to mobilize individual officers and gain cooperation between police units if concrete goals and objectives are set in reaction to a given problem.

Synoptic planning consists of eleven progressive steps. Each step is designed to provide the police manager with a logical course of action.[13]

## Prepare for Planning

Hudzik and Cordner[14] point out that the most important aspect of planning is that it takes place in advance of action. Therefore, the task of planning should be a detailed work chart that specifies (1) what events and actions are necessary, (2) when they must take place, (3) who is to be involved in each action and for how long, and (4) how the various actions will interlock with one another.[15]

Police managers need to understand that when a course of action and its consequence seem "patently clear," a grand planning event may be unnecessary and inefficient. However, when consequences are not clear, or when undiscovered courses of action may be better, the value of planning increases greatly.[16] This assumes that decision making is ongoing and that planning attempts to predict or at least partially control the future.[17] Police managers, then, must be prepared to address the vast array of possibilities that may arise from a given course of action. It is during this stage that the police chief organizes the planning effort with a central theme—what are we trying to accomplish and what type of information is required to understand the problem?

## Describe the Present Situation

This step is often forgotten or overlooked by police administrators because of the desire to eliminate the problem immediately. Planning must have a means for evaluation, and without an accurate beginning data base, there is no reference point on which to formulate success or failure. Weiss[18] states that a primary purpose of planning is in evaluation, or comparing "what is" with "what should be." To this end, police chiefs following this model must describe the current situation: describe crime and criminal justice system functions (What exactly do police, courts, and corrections do?), and analyze community characteristics associated with crime (Is the community conservative or liberal? Does any religious or political agenda affect the situation?).

## Develop Projections and Consider Alternative Future States

Projections should be written with an attempt to link the current situation with the future, keeping in mind the desirable outcomes. One projection should at least dwell on the status quo. What will happen if the police do nothing? In some instances, it may be best to eliminate police presence. For example, a police chief may decide that the best course of action is to reduce police visibility. This tactic has been successful where a high probability for violence between a group of people and the police exists—such as rock concerts, outlaw biker parades, and demonstrations. It is important for the police executive to project the current situation into the future to determine possible, probable, and desirable future states while considering the social, legislative, and political trends existing in the community. What may work in one city may not work in another. For instance, a parade of gay activists marching in San Francisco may be a somewhat common occurrence, whereas the same type of activity in another city may be received differently.

The discovery of problems assumes that a system to monitor and evaluate the current arena is already in place. The final step in the synoptic model addresses this concern. However, closely related to the detection and identification of issues is the ability of the police manager to define the nature of the problem; that is, to be able to describe the magnitude, cause, duration, and expense of the issues at hand. This provides a clear conceptual picture of the present conditions confronting the chief in which to develop means for dealing with the problem. It is here that the chief develops a detailed understanding of the problem and ensuing issues. At this point, the planning process allows for estimations of the gap between the probable future and desired outcomes—or how serious and complex the problem really is. A complete understanding of the problem leads to the development of means to deal with the issues.

**Identify and Analyze Problems**

A goal is an achievable end state that can be measured and observed. Making choices about goals is one of the most important aspects of planning.[19] However, without the previous steps, goal setting has little meaning. It makes no sense to establish a goal that does not address a specific problem. Remembering that police departments are "problem-oriented," choices about goals and objectives should adhere to the synoptic model.

**Set Goals**

Hudzik and Cordner point out that several kinds of choices must be made concerning goals:

> Several kinds of choices must be made. First, choices must be made about preferred states or goals. An important and sometimes ignored aspect of this choice involves the choice of the criteria for measuring goal attainment. This is often hard, much harder than setting the goal itself. For example, the goal of a juvenile treatment program may be to reduce recidivism among those treated. Yet, in measuring goal attainment several questions arise. First, what constitutes recidivism? Technical or status violation? Arrest for criminal violation? Conviction on a criminal violation, and only for those crimes against which the juvenile program may have been directed? Also, over how long a period will recidivism be monitored? A year? Two years? Five years? Ten years? It is not that those questions cannot be answered, but securing agreement on the appropriate criteria becomes a major difficulty.[20]

The following steps attempt to link set goals with desired outcomes through the establishment of specific means.

Alternatives are means by which goals and objectives can be attained. They may be policies, strategies, or specific actions aimed at eliminating a problem. Alternatives do not have to be substitutes for one another or perform the same function. For instance, improving officer-survival skills through training, modifying police vehicles, issuing bulletproof vests, using a computer-assisted dispatch program, and increasing first-line supervision may all be alternatives in promoting officer safety.

**Identify Alternative Courses of Action**

It is important that the activities (the means) that a police department engages in actually contribute to the achievement of goals (the ends). If the means are not connected to the ends, then a police agency could expend a great deal of resources in activities that keep personnel busy, but do not contribute to fulfilling key objectives or responsibilities.

**Means-Ends Analysis.**  Depicted in Figure 12-2 is a means-ends analysis chart. This is one method of trying to ensure that the police department's programmatic efforts and expenditures make an appropriate contribution toward arriving at the desired state. Means-ends analysis charting is also a very effective method in which alternatives can be identified in the planning process.

The following procedure is used to develop a means-ends analysis chart:

1. At the center of a page, state the objective you are trying to achieve. In the case of Figure 12-2, this is stated as "to reduce assaults on officers by 50 percent in fiscal year (FY) 2001 as compared to fiscal year 2000." Note that an objective differs from a goal in that an objective can be achieved within one year.

2. Identify the "whys" of trying to attain the objective. Place these statements above the objective on the work page. Figure 12-2 identifies four such "whys," namely reduce medical costs, reduce potential for civil suits, reduce officer stress, and improve officer retention.

3. Identify and select the "hows" to obtain the objective. Referring again to Figure 12-2, four major "hows" or means are specified: use technology, in-

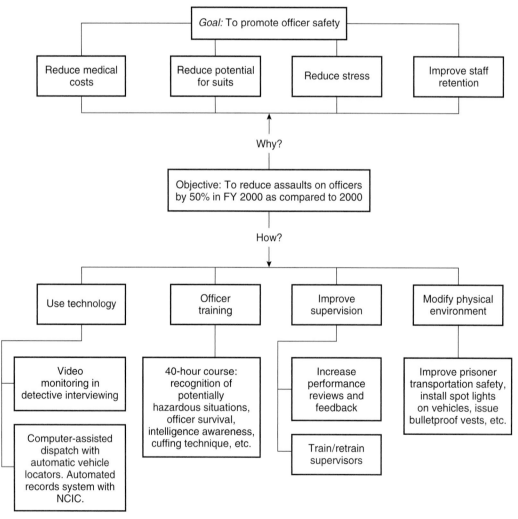

**FIGURE 12-2.**  Means-ends analysis chart.

crease officer training, improve supervision, and modify the physical environment.

The police manager should realize that the means-end analysis chart does not select alternatives; that is discussed in the following step of the synoptic planning model. However, means-ends analysis is an excellent method of brainstorming that assists the police chief in identifying alternative courses of action designed to achieve specific goals and objectives.[21]

**Select Preferred Alternatives**

The selection process for deriving a preferred course of action or alternative is often fraught with complexity. The issue has been researched for several decades by scholars in business management, public administration, systems science, and criminal justice in order to assist decision makers in this process. Three basic techniques to select alternatives are discussed here: (1) strategic analysis, (2) cost-effectiveness analysis, and (3) must-wants analysis.

**Strategic Analysis.** The first study addressing the selection of preferred courses of action originated at the U.S Naval War College in 1936 and has been popular in police management circles.[22] Since that time, the model has been refined into a more systematic and objective treatment.[23] The process is shown as a diagram in Figure 12-3. To visualize how the technique can be applied and selections made, it will be helpful to use an example currently confronting law

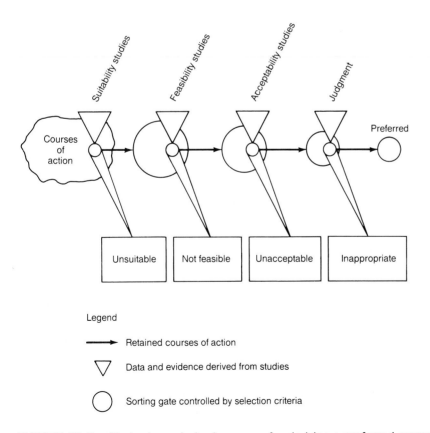

**FIGURE 12-3.** Strategic analysis: A process for deriving a preferred course of action.(*Source:* C. M. Mottley, "Strategic Planning," *Management Highlights,* 56, September 1967.)

enforcement managers, for example, the issue of automating a records division with particular reference to the improvement of officer-generated reports by use of laptop computers.

Given a set of possible alternatives or courses of action, the number of alternatives can be reduced in the following ways.

First, make suitability studies of all alternatives. That is, each course of action is evaluated in accordance with general policies, rules, and laws. For example, in all jurisdictions it is illegal to maintain an automated records system that contains arrest and conviction data of juveniles to safeguard the juvenile's reputation. A manual records system is deemed more secure because access can be totally controlled.

Second, subject the retained and suitable alternatives to feasibility studies. These include the appraisal of the effects of a number of factors weighed separately and together. Continuing with the example, the feasibility of an automated records system would be judged on the basis of meeting (1) the existing standards of operation (e.g., Will an automated records system do everything the manual system can do?); (2) the conditions of the operational environment (e.g., Is the police department facility large enough to accommodate a computer? Is it air-conditioned? Does it have proper electrical outlets?); (3) the restrictions imposed by the state of the art (e.g., Is the desired software compatible with the existing computer system?); and (4) limitations on the resources available (e.g., Is the cost for an automated records system beyond police funding approval? Can the records division personnel be retrained and how much will that cost?).

Third, analyze the retained courses of actions (those judged to be suitable and feasible) in acceptability studies. Four principal factors are combined and enter into this evaluation: (1) the cost of each alternative, (2) the performance, (3) the effect of the alternative on the entire system, and (4) the time involved in implementation and setup. These factors are applied to each alternative to reveal critical limits and trade-offs. Finally, a judgment is rendered that selects the preferred course of action.

**Cost-Effectiveness Analysis.** This technique is sometimes called cost-benefit or cost-performance analysis. The purpose of this form of selection is that the alternative chosen should maximize the ratio of benefit to cost. The concept is based on economic rationalism: calculations are made "scientifically" through the collection of data and the use of models in an attempt to maximize benefits and minimize costs. A model is a simplified representation of the real world that abstracts the cause-and-effect relationships essential to each course of action or alternative.[24] Using the example of automating a records division, each course of action would be analyzed in an attempt to compare the cost in dollars of each segment of the system (mainframe, software, laptop computers) with the benefits (increased officer safety, more efficient crime analysis, and subsequent apprehension that diminishes property loss and injury). In the analysis of choice, the role of the model (or models, for it may be inappropriate or absurd to attempt to incorporate all the aspects of a problem into a single formulation) is to estimate for each alternative (or course of action) the costs that would be incurred and the extent to which the objectives would be attained.[25] The model may be as complex as a set of mathematical equations or as simple as a purely verbal description of the situation, in which intuition alone is used to predict the outcomes of various alternatives. Figure 12-4 is the structure of cost-effectiveness analysis.

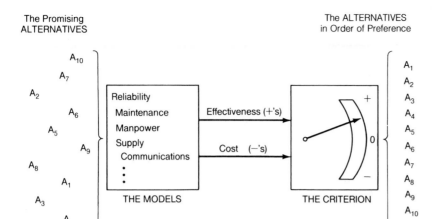

The Promising
ALTERNATIVES

The ALTERNATIVES
in Order of Preference

**FIGURE 12-4.** The structure of cost-effectiveness analysis.[*Source:* E. S. Quade, "Systems Analysis Techniques for Planning-Programming-Budgeting," in F. J. Lyden and E. G. Miller, *Planning, Programming, Budgeting: A Systems Approach to Management* (Chicago: Markham, 1972), p. 250.]

It is important to note that each alternative is weighed against a criterion: the rule or standard by which to rank the alternatives in order of desirability. This provides a means to analyze cost against effectiveness.[26] Unlike strategic analysis, alternatives are not dismissed from the process but ranked in order of preference.

**Must-Wants Analysis.**  This method of selecting a preferred course of action combines the strengths of both strategic and cost-effectiveness analyses. Must-wants analysis is concerned with both the subjective weights of suitability, feasibility, and acceptability and the objective weights of costs versus benefits.

In this method of selection a must-wants chart is developed to assist the police administrator. This methodology is particularly well-suited for comparing like brands or models of equipment (in the case of personal weapons, for example, the strengths and weaknesses of 9 mm semiautomatic pistols versus .38 caliber revolvers; or for personal computers, the pros and cons of selecting among an IBM, Compaq, or Packard-Bell personal computer). In this example, Figure 12-5 provides a chart for evaluating three popular police patrol vehicles, namely, the Chevrolet Caprice Classic, the Chevrolet Camaro, and the Ford Crown Victoria.

The must-wants chart is constructed in the following manner:

1. "Musts" are placed at the top of the page. These are conditions that are set by the police chief or selecting committee and that *absolutely* have to be met in order for an alternative (in this case, a specific police patrol vehicle) to continue to be a viable choice. Failure of any alternative to meet a must condition immediately eliminates it from further consideration. In Figure 12-5, note that Alternative B, the Chevrolet Camaro, did not conform to the must of being a full-size, four-door sedan. Because the 1999 Chevrolet Camaro was available only in two-door models, it was eliminated.

2. "Wants" are conditions, performances, characteristics, or features that are desirable but not absolutely necessary. They are listed below the musts, and corresponding data for each want are completed for each alternative that was not discarded at the previous step.

| Musts | Alternative A: Chevrolet Caprice | Alternative B: Chevrolet Camaro | Alternative C: Ford Crown Victoria |
|---|---|---|---|
| Total purchase price not to exceed $24,000 | $23,700 | $22,900 | $23,500 |
| Dual airbags (driver & passenger side) | yes | yes | yes |
| Power-assisted, four wheel disc, antilock brake system | yes | yes | yes |
| Heavy-duty, automatic transmission | yes | yes | yes |
| Full-size, four-door sedan | yes | NO, NO GO | yes |
| Front & rear heavy-duty suspension | yes | | yes |
| Goodyear police pursuit radial tires | yes | | yes |

| Wants | wt. | | sc. | wt. × sc. | | sc. | wt. × sc. |
|---|---|---|---|---|---|---|---|
| Minimum total price | 7 | $23,700 | 8 | 56 | $23,500 | 9 | 63 |
| High engine displacement | 4 | 350 cu. in. | 7 | 28 | 281 cu. in. | 5 | 20 |
| High horsepower | 7 | 260 @ 5000 rpm | 8 | 56 | 210 @ 4500 rpm | 7 | 49 |
| Excellent acceleration (0 to 60 mph) | 6 | 8.02 secs | 8 | 48 | 9.1 secs | 6 | 36 |
| Good acceleration (0 to 100 mph) | 3 | 21.47 secs | 9 | 27 | 25.18 secs | 6 | 18 |
| Good top speed | 4 | 139 mph | 7 | 28 | 135 mph | 6 | 24 |
| Good quarter mile run from stop to finish (seconds/top speed) | 5 | 16.14 sec/88 mph | 7 | 35 | 16.89 sec/83.83 mph | 7 | 35 |
| Excellent braking—Stopping distance from 60 mph | 7 | 133.1 feet | 7 | 49 | 133.4 feet | 7 | 49 |
| Excellent turning capability | 6 | 43 feet | 7 | 42 | 39 feet | 9 | 54 |
| Large fuel capacity | 4 | 23 gallons | 7 | 28 | 20 gallons | 5 | 20 |
| Heavy frame and body | 5 | 4,249 lbs. | 8 | 40 | 3,974 lbs. | 7 | 35 |
| Excellent ergonomics: | | | | | | | |
|   Front seating area | 9 | comfortable/roomy | 9 | 81 | slightly cramped | 7 | 63 |
|   Interior headroom | 8 | 39.2—very good | 8 | 64 | 38.4—good | 6 | 48 |
|   Rear seating area | 5 | easy entry & exit | 8 | 40 | tight and "bouncy" | 7 | 35 |
|   Clarity of instrumentation | 4 | good | 7 | 28 | fair | 6 | 24 |
|   Communications accessibility | 4 | good | 8 | 32 | good | 8 | 32 |
| High EPA mileage | | | | | | | |
|   City | 10 | 17 mpg-very good | 8 | 80 | 17 mpg-very good | 8 | 80 |
|   Highway | 8 | 26 mpg-excellent | 9 | 72 | 23 mpg-good | 7 | 56 |
|   Combined | 9 | 20 mpg-excellent | 9 | 81 | 19 mpg-very good | 8 | 72 |
| **Performance totals of wants objectives:** | | | | **915** | | | **813** |

**FIGURE 12-5.** Must-wants chart for selecting a police patrol vehicle. [*Source: 1996 and 1999 Model Year Patrol Vehicle Testing*, prepared by Michigan State Police (Washington, D.C.: National Institute of Justice, Office of Justice Programs, November 1995 and October 1998)] The "results" in the illustration of must-wants analysis are hypothetical and should not be used as a basis of action.

3. Weight (the column marked "wt." in Figure 12-5) reflects the subjective importance of the want as determined by the police chief or selection committee. Weight has a scale of 1 (lowest) to 10 (highest).

4. Score (the column marked "sc." in Figure 12-5) is the evaluation of the actual existence of wants by the chief or committee. A scale of 1 to 10 is also used in this column. The score is set by the evaluator to reflect an assessment of the

| Alternative A: Chevrolet Caprice | | | | Alternative C: Ford Crown Victoria | | | |
|---|---|---|---|---|---|---|---|
| | Probability | Seriousness | $P \times S$ | | Probability | Seriousness | $P \times S$ |
| Relatively large turning circle (difficult to perform u-turns) | 8 | 7 | 56 | Relatively small gas tank, will require more frequent refueling | 5 | 3 | 15 |
| 100,000-mile bumper-to-bumper warranty is extra, $1,800 | 9 | 8 | 72 | Smaller vehicle with smaller inside and trunk volume | 6 | 8 | 48 |
| Chevrolet does not have a CNG option for fuel | 6 | 5 | 30 | Department master mechanics are all GM trained, service & parts agreement with GM | 8 | 6 | 48 |
| Dealership is downtown, will be more difficult for precincts to access | 9 | 8 | 72 | Overall EPA mileage is lower in all categories, reducing cost savings | 9 | 7 | 63 |
| **TOTALS:** | | | **230** | | | | **174** |

**FIGURE 12-6.** Possible adverse consequences worksheet—police patrol vehicles.

subjective or actual existence of the want. In this example, the wants under "excellent ergonomics" are subjective evaluations, while "EPA mileage—city, highway, combined" are objectively determined by an outside source. In general, the scoring of wants should be based on a limited number of factors because too many could distort the choice of an option.

5. The weight and score for each want are multiplied (wt × sc. in Figure 12-5) and summed. The sum of each wt. × sc. column is called the performance total of wants objectives.

6. The second part of the must-wants chart, shown in Figure 12-6, is called the "possible adverse consequences worksheet." On this worksheet, statements concerning possible detriments or negative outcomes are listed for each alternative. The probability and seriousness of each comment are subjectively scored. The probability of an adverse consequence happening is scored on a scale from 1 (very unlikely) to 10 (certain to happen). Seriousness is scored on the same type of scale, with 1 representing "extremely unserious" and 10 denoting "very serious." The final scores are summed and used in the last choice, the selection step.

7. Some advocates of using the must-wants chart recommend that the totals of the possible adverse consequences worksheet be considered only advisory, whereas others recommend that the performance totals for each alternative be mathematically reduced by the value of the possible adverse consequences score. If this latter approach is used, the alternative with the highest total points should be chosen. Referring to Figure 12-7, Alternative A, the 1999 Chevrolet Caprice Classic, would be selected as the primary police patrol vehicle for the agency, with a total point score of 685.

Despite the "rational" and "objective" appearance of the must-wants analysis approach, there are a number of subjective scores, weights, and probabilities in the chart. The "bottom line" values in Figure 12-7 (685 and 639) were calculated on subjective measures. The real value in must-wants analysis is in

|                                    | *Alternative A*<br>*Chevrolet Caprice Classic* | *Alternative C*<br>*Ford Crown Victoria* |
|------------------------------------|:---------------------------------:|:------------------------------:|
| Must-have objectives:              | All met                           | All met                        |
| Wants performance total:           | 915                               | 813                            |
| Possible adverse consequences total: | (230)                           | (174)                          |
|                                    | **685**                           | **639**                        |

**FIGURE 12-7.** The final step in must-wants analysis—selecting an alternative. The alternative with the highest point value should be chosen. (Again, the facts and figures presented are for illustrative purposes only and should not be the basis for action.)

the methodology. The chief must not become a captive of the device and follow the results mechanically. He or she should use a must-wants chart to consider and weigh the intangibles that are not easily quantifiable between alternatives. The value of must-wants analysis is not in the end product, but rather in the sharpening of differences or similarities between alternatives or courses of action.

As with must-wants charts, the other two approaches (strategic and cost-effectiveness analyses) are methods of selecting a preferred alternative or choosing a desired course of action. In the final analysis, the judgment of the police chief plays a key and indisputable role, one that cannot be taken lightly; the chief cannot afford to be ill-informed about the alternative courses to be made.

**Plan and Carry Out Implementation**

Once a preferred course of action is selected, the next step in the synoptic planning model is to implement the chosen alternative. Implementation requires the chief to execute plans that fulfill the objectives or goals of the process. The classic work on implementation was conducted by Pressman and Wildavsky[27] in Oakland, California. In that study, the authors contend that the process of implementation alone can produce complexities in the future. An example of this phenomenon is observed in any organization undergoing change. The very process of change often causes anxieties within personnel, disputes over responsibilities, and restructuring of the organization. Organizational change is discussed in Chapter 15. But as an illustrative point, consider again the case of automating a police records division. Certainly, the automation process will cause most of the records clerks to reassess their value as workers. Some may think that the computer will eliminate their position, whereas others will resist being retrained because they have little or no previous familiarity with computers. Then too, who will manage the new computerized center? What will happen if the software has minor "bugs" or faults? Who will fix the hardware if it breaks? Thus, a whole series of new issues and questions arises from the implementation of a computer into a police department.

In any event, the police administrator must be aware that implementation requires a great deal of tact and skill. It may be more important "how" an alternative is introduced to a police department than "what" it actually is.

**Monitor and Evaluate Progress**

The final step of the synoptic planning model is evaluation: Were the objectives achieved? Were the problems resolved? The answer to these questions should be obtained through a system that monitors the implementation process.

**FIGURE 12-8.** Officers using a laptop computer via a cellular telephone hook-up in a marked police vehicle. (Courtesy of St. Petersburg, Florida, Police Department and GTE Mobilnet, Inc.)

Evaluation requires comparing what actually happened with what was planned for—and this may not be a simple undertaking.[28] Feedback must be obtained concerning the results of the planning cycle, the efficiency of the implementation process, and the effectiveness of new procedures, projects, or programs. This is an important step of synoptic planning—trying to figure out what, if anything, happened as a result of implementing a selected alternative. It is for this reason that baseline data are so critical (Step 2—Describe the present situation). Hudzik and Cordner[29] point out that evaluation completes the cycle of rational planning. The issue of identifying problems must be considered again. Does the original problem still exist or was it solved? Is there a new problem?

Considerable attention has been given to synoptic planning because it is the most widely used approach in police management. Most other approaches have been derived from the model just described. Synoptic planning basically comprises four activities: preparing to plan, making a choice between alternatives, implementation, and evaluation. The eleven-step approach is a refinement of this cyclical process.

The approaches to follow are other methods commonly used in business forecasting or social planning. Although these approaches are not used as extensively in police management as the synoptic approach, they too deserve some attention.

**Summation of the Synoptic Planning Approach**

Incremental planning levels a series of criticisms at synoptic planning, including its tendency toward centralization, its failure to appreciate the cognitive limits of police executives (decision makers), and unrealistic claims of rationality.

**Incremental Planning**

Incrementalism concludes that long-range and comprehensive planning are not only too difficult, but inherently bad. The problems are seen as too difficult when they are grouped together and easier to solve when they are taken one at a time and broken down into gradual adjustments over time. The incremental approach disfavors the exclusive use of planners who have no direct interest in the problems at hand and favors a sort of decentralized political bargaining that involves interested parties. The incrementalists feel that the real needs of people can best be met this way and the "tyranny of grand design" avoided.[30]

**Transactive Planning**

Transactive planning is not carried out with respect to an anonymous target community of "beneficiaries" but in face-to-face interaction with the people who are to be affected by the plan. Techniques include field surveys and interpersonal dialogue marked by a process of mutual learning. For example, in planning a crime-prevention program in a particular neighborhood, the police might go to certain randomly selected houses to talk to residents about unreported crime, their concerns and fears, and the rise in residential burglary rates. The residents receive crime prevention techniques and a more secure feeling knowing that the police are concerned about their neighborhood. The police department also receives benefits: intelligence information is gathered about strange persons or cars in the area, a more aware citizenry is likely to detect and report crimes, and a more supportive public attitude concerning the police is developed.

**Advocacy Planning**

Advocacy planning grew up in the 1960s in the adversary procedures modeled by the legal profession. This approach is usually associated with defending the interests of the weak—the poor and politically impotent, for example—against the strong. Beneficial aspects of this approach include a greater sensitivity to the unintended and negative side effects of plans.

**Radical Planning**

Radical planning has an ambiguous tradition with two mainstreams that sometimes flow together. The first mainstream involves collective action to achieve concrete results in the immediate future. The second mainstream is critical of large-scale social processes and how they permeate the character of social and economic life at all levels, which, in turn, determine the structure and evolution of social problems.

## TYPES OF PLANS

From an applications perspective, the planning process yields an end product— the plan. These can be categorized by use and are delineated into four groups:[31]

1. Administrative or management plans include formulation of the department's mission statement, goals, and policies; the structuring of functions, authority, and responsibilities; the allocation of resources; personnel management; and other concerns whose character is that they are prevalent throughout the agency. An administrative plan from the Anchorage, Alaska, Police Department appears as the appendix to this chapter. Note that this plan is expressed as a general order. General orders are issued to cover standing or long-term situations. In contrast, special orders are issued to cover unique nonrecurring events, such as a visit by the president of the United States, which last for only a limited and specific period of time. Parenthetically, the announcement of promotions, transfers, and other such actions are made known in personnel orders.

2. Procedural plans, in line with many but certainly not all management plans, are ordinarily included as part of a police department's written directive system, a copy of which is assigned to every officer and is updated periodically. Procedural plans are the guidelines for the action to be taken under specific circumstances and detail such matters as how evidence is to be sent or transported to the crime laboratory, the conditions under which male officers may search arrested females and the limits thereto, and how to stop and approach traffic violators.

3. Operational plans are often called *work plans* and describe specific actions to be taken by line units (patrol officers, precinct groups, and/or division teams). Work plans are usually short and terse, giving both direction and time constraints in accomplishing a given task. In community policing ventures, the work plan usually focuses on a defined community need in a specific neighborhood. In Portland, Oregon, the police bureau provides a guideline for officers and managers to follow in developing work plans for specific projects and/or programs. Box 12-1 displays this guideline, focusing on reducing crime in residential housing units. Note that the work plan is tied to the much larger, more comprehensive strategic plan that provides overall mission, value, and goal statements.

## BOX 12-1

### How to Develop Work Plans

**by Jane Braaten,**
**Planning and Support Division**

Managers are currently working to submit workplans on major projects and programs within their divisions. Since the task of completing workplans may fall to others within the division, *The Bulletin* offers this brief how-to guide:

The Portland City Council requires the Police Bureau to report back on progress made on the 1994–96 Strategic Plan and also to report on what services were provided with the funds allocated in the budget. To provide this report, information on major programs and projects needs to be captured.

Current workplan forms are one page and ask for the project title, timelines, strategy number(s) and outcomes. The strategy number is gleaned from the Strategic Plan.

#### Strategy Numbers

The plan contains four goals, 21 objectives and 108 strategies, and they are all numbered. Each goal has three to nine objectives and each objective has two to 13 strategies.

In the plan, Strategy 1.4.2 means Goal 1 Reduce crime and fear of crime, Objective 1.4 Increase early intervention and Strategy 1.4.2 Implement approaches to reach school age children.

Goals are expressions of what the Bureau as a whole is attempting to accomplish. Objectives are ex-

pressions of how all or some divisions will accomplish the goal. Strategies are expressions of how a division or unit will accomplish the objective. Programs and projects describe activities that will be conducted to accomplish the strategy.

Here's a way to look at the Strategic Plan:

For example, an individual division implements a training and coaching project to improve the skill level and job satisfaction of its employees.

The manager then reports on the project as supporting Strategy 3.7.1 (Goal 3 Empower personnel, Objective 3.7 Improve employee community policing training, Strategy 3.7.1 Expand specialized training for line, supervisory, management, investigative and nonsworn personnel).

*(continued)*

BOX 12-1 (continued)

Another example might be a problem-solving effort at a housing or apartment complex with chronic calls for theft from autos.

The manager would report the project as supporting Strategy 1.2.7 (Goal 1 Reduce crime and fear of crime, Objective 1.2 Increase problem solving, Strategy 1.2.7 Expand efforts to identify and target chronic call locations).

The manager might also report it under Strategy 1.1.1 (Goal 1 Reduce crime and fear of crime, Objective 1.1 Improve crime response, Strategy 1.1.1 Develop improved methods for identifying and addressing "minor" crimes that have a significant impact on neighborhood livability).

### Outcomes

The workplans also report on outcomes, i.e. what are the expected results that the Bureau will see as a result of doing this program or project.

Looking at the previous examples, a workplan might list:

- Provide eight hours of training
- Implement coaching program

or

- Establish neighborhood foot patrol
- Expand Block Watch participation by 50 percent
- Reduce reported crime for theft from auto by 50 percent

Notice how the outcomes can be either numerical (number of hours of training or number of reported crimes) or narrative (program implemented or foot patrol established).

### Bureau-Wide Reports

Reports combining all of the major programs and projects throughout the agency will be shared with all managers to post within each division. These reports will give all employees a quick reference for who's doing what in the Bureau.

*Source:* Portland Police Bureau, Portland, Oregon, *The Bulletin,* August 18, 1994, p. 2.

4. Tactical plans involve planning for emergencies of a specific nature at known locations. Some tactical plans are developed in anticipation of such emergencies as the taking of hostages at a prison or a jailbreak and are subject to modification or being discarded altogether in peculiar and totally unanticipated circumstances. Other tactical plans are developed for specific situations as they arise, such as how to relate to a demonstration in the park or a march on city hall. Although well-operated police agencies invest considerable effort in developing tactical plans that may seldom or never be used, their very existence stimulates confidence among field officers and lessens the likelihood of injury to officers, the public, and violators.

## EFFECTIVE PLANS

Regardless of how plans are classified, the bottom line is that organizations with a formal and continuous planning process outperform those without one. This discrepancy in performance increases as the larger environment becomes more turbulent and the pace and magnitude of change increase.[32] This is the type of environment that police administrators have faced in recent years and is illustrated by Proposition 12 in California, which severely limited police expansion; fuel shortages and the attending swift rise in fuel prices; the unionization of police officers and job actions, such as strikes and demonstrations; the escalation of litigation by the public and police department employees; and times of fiscal restraint producing cutbacks in the availability of resources.[33]

Considering these and other circumstances, police administrators must not only have a planning process and plans but also must be able to recognize characteristics of effective plans.

1. The plans must be sufficiently specific so that the behavior required is understood.
2. The benefits derived from the achievement of the goals associated with the plan must offset the efforts of developing and implementing the plan, and the level of achievement should not be so modest that it is easily reached.
3. Involvement in their formulation must be as widespread as is reasonably possible.
4. They should contain a degree of flexibility to allow for the unforeseen.
5. There must be coordination in the development and implementation of plans with other units of government whenever there appears even only a minimal need for such action.
6. They must be coordinated in their development and implementation within the police department to ensure consistency.
7. As may be appropriate, the means for comparing the results planned for versus the results actually produced must be specified before implementation. For tactical plans, this often takes the form of an analysis, referred to as the *after-action report.*

## PLANNING AND DECISION MAKING

As stated previously, planning is the first integral part of decision making. Planning is primarily concerned with coming to understand the present situation (problem) and widening the range of choices (alternatives or courses of action) available to the police chief (decision maker). Therefore, planning is aimed at providing information (a plan) whereas decision making is aimed at using this information to resolve problems or make choices.[34]

## DECISION MAKING

The literature dealing with decision making in the police management field is not very extensive, and most of it is devoted to methods of applying the decision-making process. Whereas in theory it should be easy to divide decision-making processes into discrete, conceptual paradigms, in reality, it is extremely difficult to separate one approach from another.

However, three models derived from decision-making theory appear to be basic in most of the literature. They are (1) the rational model, (2) the incremental model, and (3) the heuristic model.

**The Rational Model**

The traditional theory of management assumes that people are motivated predominantly by "economic incentives" and will, therefore, work harder given the opportunity to make more money. The "economic actor" concept also prevails in early decision-making theory. In Chapter 4, the scientific management approach developed by Taylor was presented. Within this concept, the economic person is presumed to act in a rational manner when faced with a decision-making situation. The assumptions for this rational behavior are (1) that a person has complete knowledge of all alternatives available to him or her, (2) that a person has the ability to order preferences according to his or her own hierarchy of values, and (3) that a person has the ability to choose the best alternative for him or her. Money is usually used as a measure of value for the decision maker. It is considered only natural that a person will want to work harder if that person can maximize the return of money by so doing. But these assumptions are difficult for a person to achieve in real life. Just by looking at the first assumption—that a person has knowledge of all available alternatives and their consequences in any given decision situation—we can see how impossible it would be to fulfill these requirements in most circumstances.

There is some evidence to suggest that administrative rationality differs from the "economic actor" concept of rationality because it takes into account an additional spectrum of facts relative to emotions, politics, power group dynamics, personality, and mental health. In other words, the data of social science are facts just as much as the carbon content of steel, but they are difficult and, in many cases, impossible to quantify with a high degree of accuracy.[35]

Police administrators bring to administrative decision making their own personal value system that they inject into the substance of decision making while clothing their decision with a formal logic of the "good of the organization." They clothe the decision with the official mantle of the department's logic and respectability while their eyes remain fixed on more personal goals. But this does not lead to chaos, because there is frequently a large element of commonality in personal value systems as related to organizational goals.[36] For example, the police executive who develops and directs a specialized unit to solve a series of murders will be accomplishing a law enforcement goal: to apprehend criminals. Although the executive's personal motives are to gain public success of his or her unit, the personal objectives are in line with the organizational goals. Thus, conflict does not arise, unless the personal values begin to compete with the department's mission.

In an earlier chapter the work of Gulick and Urwick was discussed as a description of administrative behavior focusing on the work of the chief executive. Part of their theory includes the act of making rational choices by following prescribed elements of work (PODSCORB). Their contribution set the stage for the rational model of decision making by suggesting that executives follow orderly and rational steps before making decisions. Subsequently, Simon[37] responded to these assumptions in his article "The Proverbs of Administration," in which he outlined several requirements for a scientifically based theory of administration. Simon's article was then included in his *Administrative Behavior* (1947).[38]

Simon explains that rational choices are made on a "principle of efficiency." His model of rationality contends that there are three essential steps in decision making; (1) list *all* of the alternative strategies, (2) determine and calculate *all* of the consequences to each strategy, and (3) evaluate *all* of these consequences in a comparative fashion.[39] Whereas Simon is given credit for the development of this approach, its comprehensive expansion can be observed in the literature of several other theorists. Drucker's concept of the "Effective Executive," Iannone's "style" in *Supervision of Police Personnel,* and Sharkansky's decision-making model in *Public Administration* all exhibit an expansion of Simon's original work.[40] The rational model, now often referred to as the rational-comprehensive model, sets forth a series of formalized steps toward "effective" decision making. These steps can be generally observed and listed as follows:

1. Identify and define the problem.
2. Ascertain *all* information regarding the problem.
3. List *all* possible alternatives and means to solving the problem.

4. Analyze the alternatives and assess the facts.
5. Select the appropriate alternatives; find the answer.

It is important to observe the elaboration on Simon's original method. The decision-making model assumes an ideal condition whereby the decision maker is aware of *all* available information related to the problem and has an unlimited amount of time in which to explore and narrow down proposed alternatives by a "rational" and comparative process. Unfortunately, actual practice rarely allows for the ideal.

Highly criticized for being too idealistic and irrelevant to the administrative functions of a police organization, the rational decision-making model has been subjected to harsh criticisms. Many of these criticisms were noted as limitations by proponents of the method. For instance, Sharkansky[41] provided a detailed discussion of "roadblocks" to the fulfillment of the rational-comprehensive model in practical administration. He documented constraints of all available data and emphasized contingencies in the human ability to make decisions. Additionally, Simon elaborated on the concept of a "rational man." Noting that man was "bounded" by a triangle of limitations, he stated

> On one side, the individual is limited by those skills, habits, and reflexes which are no longer in the realm of the conscious . . . on a second side, the individual is limited by his values and those conceptions of purpose which influence him in making decisions . . . and on a third side, the individual is limited by the extent of his knowledge that is relevant to his job.[42]

It is apparent that Simon understood not only the decision-making process but also the human factors associated in the term of *rationality*. A prerequisite to effective decision making is an acute awareness of the social, environmental, and organizational demands placed on the administrator. Simon[43] accurately stresses that one's ability to make rational decisions is bounded by the limitation of his or her knowledge of the total organization. From this critical observation, Simon formulates a modified rational-comprehensive idea entitled "bounded rationality."[44] The emphasis, of course, is on man's inherent limitations to make decisions. Refer to Figure 12-9.

**The Incremental Model**

Another important approach concerning the modification of rational decision making is the "incremental" and "muddling through" theories explored by Lindblom.[45] Based on his study of governmental institutions in the United States, Lindblom states that the decision-making process is so fragmented and so complex, incorporating the interaction of various institutions, political entities, pressure groups, and individual biases, that rationality can have only a marginal effect. That is, the police administrator faces a set of limiting political factors (such as the mayor's wish to be reelected) that prevent the decision-making process from being truly rational. For elected sheriffs, the political agendas may be so strong that purely rational decision making is inhibited.

Lindblom asserts that decision making is serial, that it is limited by time and resources as it gropes along a path where means and ends are not distinct, where goals and objectives are ambiguous, and where rationality serves no purpose. Contending that police managers and administrators "play things safe" and opt to move very slowly (incrementally) in decision making, Lindblom[46] proposes that managers "muddle through" problems rather than analytically choosing decisions. In Lindblom's view, decision

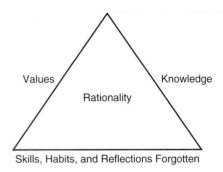

**FIGURE 12-9.** Simon's concept of bounded rationality.

Values      Knowledge

Rationality

Skills, Habits, and Reflections Forgotten

making that occurs through a series of incremental steps provides the police administrator (and hence the public) with a number of safeguards against error:

> In the first place, past sequences of policy (decision) steps have given him knowledge about the probable consequence of further similar steps. Second, he need not attempt big jumps toward his goals that would require predictions beyond his or anyone else's knowledge, because he never expects his policy (decision) to be a final resolution of a problem. His decision is only one step. . . . Third, he is in effect able to test his previous predictions as he moves on to each further step. Lastly, he often can remedy a past error fairly quickly—more quickly than if policy (decision) proceeded through more distinct steps widely spaced in time.[47]

Lindblom's ideas have support, if not in theory, at least in practice, as many police managers find them to be "a description of reality."[48]

**The Heuristic Model**

In another opposing concept to rationality and logic, Gore[49] identifies the crucial element of humanism in decision making. He presents a "heuristic model" appropriately referred to as "the gut level approach" when considering the police organization. The seasoned patrol officer frequently refers to an unknown quality or phenomenon known as "moxie" or the ability to be "street-wise." This unknown dimension is captured in Gore's decision-making method for police administrators. In an antithesis to the rational model, Gore identifies a process by which a decision is the product of the maker's personality. Gore views the heuristic process "as a groping toward agreements seldom arrived at through logic . . . the very essence of those factors validating a decision are internal to the personality of the individual instead of external to it."[50] Whereas the rational method is concrete, formalized by structure and calculations, the heuristic concept is nebulous, characterized by "gut feelings reaching backward into the memory and forward into the future."[51]

For Gore, decision making is basically an emotional, nonrational, highly personalized, and subjective process. Therefore, the facts validating a decision are internal to the personality of the individual instead of external to it. The key word in this statement is *validating;* it is intended to convey a sense of personal psychological approval or acceptance. The optimum situation is to select that decision alternative that creates the least anxiety or disruption to the individual's basic needs, wants, and desires. In effect, every "objective" decision should be modified or adjusted to meet the emotional needs of the various members of the police department who will be affected by the decision. The passage from which this statement was taken provides additional insight into Gore's heuristic decision-making scheme.[52]

Whereas the rational system of action evolves through the identification of causes and effects and the discovery of ways of implementing them, the heuristic process is a groping toward agreement seldom arrived at through logic. The very essence of the heuristic process is that factors validating a decision are internal to the personality of the individual instead of external to it. Whereas the rational system of action deals with the linkages between a collective and its objectives and between a collective and its environment, the heuristic process is orientated toward the relationship between that private core of values embedded in the center of the personality and its public counterpart, ideology. The dynamics of personality are not those of logic but rather those of emotion.[53]

In other words, although logic and reason may be the basic intellectual tools needed to analyze a given problem or to structure a series of solutions to a given situation, logic and reason may not prove to be completely effective in establishing intraorganizational agreement in connection with any given decision.[54]

Applauded for its contribution to the decision-making process, Gore's approach is also highly criticized as being too simplistic and nonscientific. Souryal[55] writes that "Gore's analysis is too unreliable . . . it could complicate an existing situation, promote spontaneity, discredit the role of training and delay the advent of professionalism" in police organizations. This is an unfair assessment of the method. Gore views heuristic applications as adjuncts or alternatives to rational models. Further, some type of credibility must be assessed to that vague, unknown, and nonmeasurable entity we call "experience," "talent," or the "sixth sense." It was these elements that Simon had so much trouble with in calculating his "bound and limited" argument regarding the rational model. In any event, Gore's contributions remain as an opposite to decision making based solely on figures, formulas, and mathematical designs.

## Alternative Decision-Making Models

A more recent attempt to outline various approaches to the decision-making process is Allison's[56] account of the 1962 Cuban Missile Crisis. He contends that the rational decision-making model, although most widely used, is seriously flawed. Allison presents two additional models (the organizational process model and the government politics model) to explain decision making during crisis events that police and other government agencies often face. The organizational process model is based on the premise that few government decisions are exclusively the province of a single organization. In other words, police agencies are dependent on information and advice from other governmental units (like the mayor's office, the FBI, and the district attorney's office) to make major decisions that affect public policy. The government politics model purports that major government policies are rarely made by a single rational actor, such as the chief of police. Rather, policy and general decision making is the outcome of a process of bargaining among individuals and groups to support those interests. Implicit in both of the models is that the decision maker requires direction from his or her internal staff as well as support from other governmental agencies in the making of important decisions. This is especially true during crisis situations.[57]

Other alternative models to decision making have evolved from the systems approach to management as described in Chapter 4. These techniques are vastly influenced by large, complex systems of variables. The application, collection, and analysis of data from decision making within the organization is called "operations research."[58] In response to a need for a management–science that addressed complex problems involving many variables, such as government planning, military spending, natural resource conservation, and national defense budgeting, operations research employs the use of mathematical inquiry, probability theory, and gaming theory to "calculate the probable consequences of alternative choices" in decision making.[59] As a result, techniques such as Program Evaluation and Review Technique (PERT) and Planning, Programming, and Budgeting Systems (PPBS) were developed for use in managerial planning, forecasting, and decision making.[60] By their very nature, these techniques must structure the system for analysis by quantifying system elements. This process of abstraction often simplifies the problem and takes it out of the real world. Hence, the solution of the problem may not be a good fit for the actual situation.

PERT is a managerial attempt to convert the disorganized resources of people, machines, and money into a useful and effective enterprise by which alternatives to problem solving can be assessed. This process is conducted by a cost-effective analysis or an estimation for each alternative of the costs that would be incurred and the extent to which the objectives would be attained, which is similar to those discussed in the synoptic model.

Another model, the decision tree, is illustrated in Figure 12-10. In this model, the probabilities for various outcomes are calculated for each branch of the tree. In the example used in Figure 12-10, the first branch of the trunk has three possible outcomes: (1) arrest at the scene by a patrol officer, (2) no arrest at the scene, and (3) arrest at the scene by a detective. Note in Figure 12-10 that the probabilities for those three events total 1.0, which is the mathematical

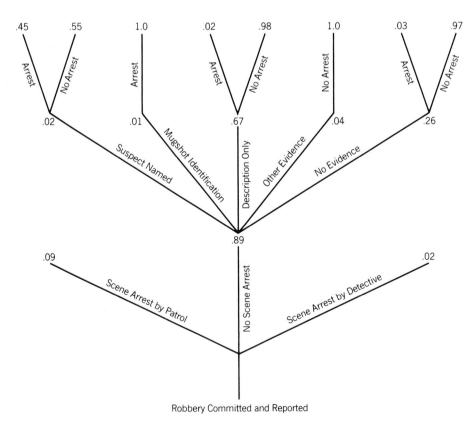

**FIGURE 12-10.** Decision tree of hypothetical probabilities of various outcomes in a robbery investigation.

value for certainty; all possible outcomes for that branch of the example are accounted for. The next higher branch of the example decision tree deals with the various types of evidence obtained from investigation and the final branches deal with the probability of arrest associated with the gathering of each type of evidence. Decision trees are very useful in analyzing situations and for reference when series of decisions that flow from one event are involved. For example, decision trees would be useful to the commander of a detective bureau in formulating policy and guidelines on when to continue or inactivate an investigation based on the types of evidence that were involved in order to make best use of investigative resources. In this regard, decision trees can be seen as a tool of operations research. If an administrator is facing a decision for which there are no actual data, a decision tree can still be useful in analyzing the situation and the "probabilities" can be the administrator's own subjective estimations based on past experience.

These approaches are highly sophisticated elaborations of the rational model using quantitative techniques. The weakness of the methods is in their practicality to real-world situations in which time and resources are not directly structured to gather intelligence about every problem and possible alternative. Further, these models assume that human biases will not enter the decision-making process. The most critical aspect of the approaches appears to be in their overriding insistence that decision making is not a human activity but the product of some scientific, computerized, and unimpressionable robot that digests quantitative information.

Wildavsky[61] has continually warned that the application of decision making to costs, benefits, resources, and budgets frequently results in the adoption of meaningless data and places unwarranted stimuli into the process.

## DECISION MAKING DURING CRISIS INCIDENTS

Police agencies, like all governmental organizations and private entities, are not immune to the necessity of effective decision making during crisis events. In this chapter, we have examined decision making in law enforcement from the traditional aspects of planning, organizational needs, theoretical models, and administrative roles. As such, we focused on the classic models of decision making presented by Simon, Lindblom, and Gore. However, recent highly publicized events, including the ATF (Bureau of Alcohol, Tobacco and Firearms) raid on Branch Davidians in Waco, Texas (1993), the FBI (Federal Bureau of Investigation) siege of the Weaver family at Ruby Ridge, Idaho (1992), and the police department bombing of MOVE headquarters in Philadelphia (1985) have highlighted the need for an examination of police executive decision making during crisis incidents. The purpose of this analysis is to bring applications of the various decision-making models to reality. It is not intended to be taken as a critical editorial, pointing out "where the strong man stumbled," but rather as an educational essay designed to identify the commonalities of the incidents and bring potential reason to action. It should not be taken lightly that each incident began with a sense of duty, good faith, honor, and courage yet ended in tragic losses of careers, agency reputations, and human life.

During the early years of the 1990s, a young charismatic religious leader began to develop a group of followers known as the Branch Davidians. The group settled slightly northeast of Waco, Texas, and began building a well-fortified

**The Branch Davidians, Waco, Texas (1993)**

compound in which to protect themselves from the outside world and the impending "Last Judgment Day." Their spiritual leader, David Koresh (commonly referred to by followers as the "Lamb of God"), was a high school dropout with a perceived mystical ability to teach from the apocalyptic Book of Revelation in the New Testament.

Police investigations of the Branch Davidians did not begin until late in 1992, when ATF agents were contacted by a postal driver who reported seeing hand grenades in a partially opened package delivered to the Waco compound. As a result of the investigation, an arrest warrant for Koresh was issued, along with a search warrant to seek out additional illegal weapons and explosives at the Waco compound.

In the early morning hours of February 28, 1993, tactical teams totaling approximately 75 men stormed the Waco compound. The agents were met with a fusillade of heavy gunfire. In the resulting exchange, four ATF agents and six Branch Davidians were killed. The incident prompted a 51-day standoff between federal agents and the Branch Davidians. Immediately following the initial confrontation between ATF and the compound occupants, the Federal Bureau of Investigation assumed control of the operation. While negotiations during the ordeal were targeted initially at a peaceful resolution, the FBI began preparations to reenter the compound by force, using armored vehicles to break through heavily fortified walls and distribute a debilitating dose of CS tear gas. The gas was supposed to be nonlethal, wouldn't permanently harm adults or children, and wouldn't cause fire during the delivery stage. As time lingered and negotiations lulled, Attorney General Janet Reno gave orders to commence with the assault. At 6:00 A.M. on April 19, 1993, several M-60 military tanks reconfigured with tear gas delivery booms began breaking through the compound walls (refer to Figure 12-11). Within hours of the operation, fire broke out. Fanned by 35 mile-per-hour winds, the fire raged and the compound was rapidly incinerated. Seventy-two bodies were found among the remains, including several children.

Unfortunately, the flames of Waco have not been extinguished. In 1999, the Texas Rangers and lawyers for the Waco survivors revealed a blatant cover-up by the Federal Bureau of Investigation. For six years, the FBI insisted that the Branch Davidians burned their own compound and denied to Congress that its agents fired any flammable tear gas canisters in the attack on April 19, 1993. Renewed investigations revealed that not only did the FBI mislead Congress, but top decision makers may have overtly lied, finally admitting that the FBI did indeed fire at least two pyrotechnic M651 grenades at the Branch Davidian bunker. Even more troubling was the revelation that the U.S. military provided federal law enforcement agents with more than $1 million worth of support (supplying tanks, helicopters, aerial reconnaissance, munitions, and support personnel) during the standoff at Waco. At least ten military advisors or observers attached to the U.S. Army's elite Delta Force were present at various times throughout the incident. The entire action came dangerously close to violating the Posse Comitatus Act, prohibiting the use of federal soldiers to act as police officers or in a law enforcement capacity within the borders of the United States. Further, Attorney General Janet Reno admitted that her decision to allow the FBI to rush the Davidian compound was heavily based on tales of Koresh abusing children. Later, a Justice Department "clarification" said that there was no evidence of child abuse. According to Reno, the FBI convinced her that

# THE LAST ASSAULT

At 5:55 A.M. on April 19, an FBI hostage negotiator called the Branch Davidians to tell them that agents were about to inject tear gas. A cult member threw out the phone. Six hours later almost everyone inside was dead.

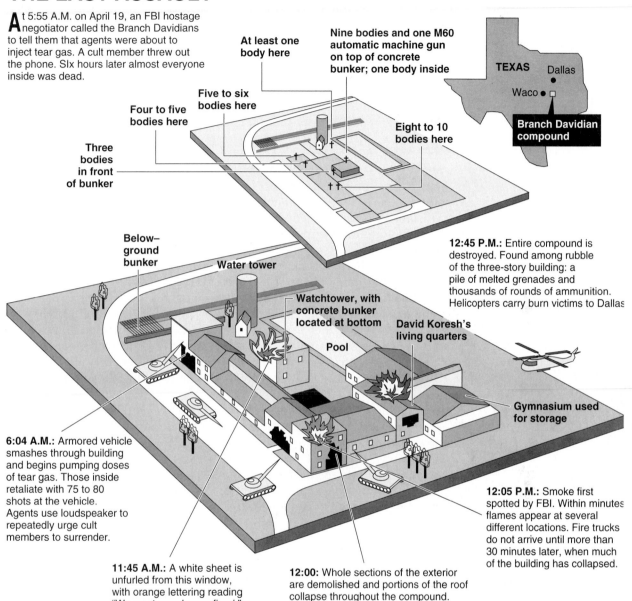

**At least one body here**

**Nine bodies and one M60 automatic machine gun on top of concrete bunker; one body inside**

**Five to six bodies here**

**Four to five bodies here**

**Three bodies in front of bunker**

**Eight to 10 bodies here**

**TEXAS** Dallas

Waco

**Branch Davidian compound**

**Below–ground bunker**

**Water tower**

**Watchtower, with concrete bunker located at bottom**

**David Koresh's living quarters**

**Pool**

**Gymnasium used for storage**

**12:45 P.M.:** Entire compound is destroyed. Found among rubble of the three-story building: a pile of melted grenades and thousands of rounds of ammunition. Helicopters carry burn victims to Dallas

**6:04 A.M.:** Armored vehicle smashes through building and begins pumping doses of tear gas. Those inside retaliate with 75 to 80 shots at the vehicle. Agents use loudspeaker to repeatedly urge cult members to surrender.

**11:45 A.M.:** A white sheet is unfurled from this window, with orange lettering reading "We want our phones fixed."

**12:00:** Whole sections of the exterior are demolished and portions of the roof collapse throughout the compound.

**12:05 P.M.:** Smoke first spotted by FBI. Within minutes flames appear at several different locations. Fire trucks do not arrive until more than 30 minutes later, when much of the building has collapsed.

**FIGURE 12-11.** The siege of the Branch Davidians near Waco, Texas, resulted in a serious questioning of police (FBI) tactics, operations, and decision making. (*Newsweek*, May 3, 1993, illustration by Dixon Rohr. © 1993, Newsweek, Inc. All rights reserved. Reprinted by permission.)

Koresh was a suicidal madman bent on destroying himself and others within the compound; however, she was never shown a letter by Koresh dated just days before the attack, which promised that he would come out peacefully after completing his writing. The resulting publicity and trials have caused serious questioning of the FBI's tactics, operations, and decision making.

In March 1992, federal prosecutors indicted Randy Weaver, a known white separatist, on a charge of selling two sawed-off shotguns to an undercover federal informant. The job of arresting Mr. Weaver, who had fled to his secluded and fortified retreat at Ruby Ridge, Idaho, was assigned to the U.S. Marshal Service. On August 12, 1992, marshals began their surveillance of the Weavers' cabin and surrounding terrain under the code name "Operation Northern Exposure."

Nine days later, on August 21, Randy Weaver, his 14-year-old son, Sam Weaver, and a family friend, Kevin Harris, followed their dog into the woods adjacent to the cabin. Deputy U.S. Marshals surveilling the cabin were discovered and an exchange of gunfire occurred between the two groups. Sam Weaver and one U.S. Marshal were fatally wounded. Confusion and speculation about who fired first and whose bullets killed the two victims continues to plague the investigation. In any event, information soon reached Washington, D.C., that federal agents were under attack at Ruby Ridge and that assistance was badly needed. The FBI deployed their HRT (Hostage Rescue Team) to the location, beginning an eleven-day standoff between the FBI and the Weaver family.

Under normal circumstances, the HRT snipers followed specific rules of engagement that dictated the use of deadly force only under the threat of "grievous bodily harm." Although the reasoning behind changing this operational policy at Ruby Ridge, and who was responsible for it, are unclear, FBI snipers were told that they "could and should fire at any armed adult male" in the cabin. Hence, on August 22, one day after the initial confrontation and the deaths of Sam Weaver and a U.S. Marshal, FBI snipers fired on cabin occupants to protect a surveillance helicopter. The resulting shots struck Kevin Harris and Vicki Weaver (Randy Weaver's wife), who was standing just inside the cabin holding her infant child. Although Mrs. Weaver died of her wounds, FBI personnel did not learn of her death until Randy Weaver surrendered nine days later.

The actions of the FBI were debated in Congress and a special Senate Judiciary Subcommittee was formed to investigate the incident (refer to Box 12-2). Both Randy Weaver and Kevin Harris were acquitted of murdering the U.S. Marshal in the initial confrontation.

## BOX 12-2

### FBI's Ruby Ridge Order "In Error"

WASHINGTON (AP)—The Justice Department's former No. 2 official testified Friday that the FBI was "clearly in error" when it issued a directive that snipers should fire at armed adults at the Idaho homestead of white separatist Randy Weaver.

At the same Senate hearing, the author of a Justice Department task force report on the August 1992 Ruby Ridge siege stood by the report's conclusion in June 1994 that the FBI shooting directive was unconstitutional. The Justice Department recently disputed that finding, saying it remains an open question that is part of a pending criminal investigation.

The report's author, Barbara Berman, then assistant counsel in the department's Office of Professional Responsibility, also said she hadn't seen notes described by suspended former FBI Deputy Director Larry Potts, which Potts said demonstrate he did not approve the improper shooting rules.

Former Deputy Attorney General George Terwilliger said, "I do not believe" the order that preceded the FBI's killing of Weaver's wife Vicki, "was meant to be an unlawful license to kill."

That shooting by an FBI sniper during the 11-day Ruby Ridge siege came as Mrs. Weaver stood behind the door of the family's mountainside cabin holding her infant daughter on Aug. 22, 1992. A day earlier, the Weavers' 14-year-old son, Sam, and Deputy U.S. Marshal William Degan died in a gunfight that occurred as federal agents checked out Weaver's property in anticipation of arresting him on a weapons charge.

Terwilliger told the Senate Judiciary subcommittee on terrorism, technology and government information that the language using the word "should," while not unconstitutional, was "clearly in error."

Terwilliger said he was on vacation during the siege and that his top deputy, Jeffrey Howard, handled the Justice Department's liaison with the FBI in the operation's first days.

Howard told The Associated Press on Thursday that he was told by Potts, who was the assistant FBI director in charge of its criminal investigative division in 1992, or Potts' top aide, Daniel Coulson, early in the siege that Sam Weaver had been shot. That conflicts with the Justice Department task force report, which found that the teenager's shooting wasn't known until the third day of the standoff, when his body was found.

The subcommittee planned to call Howard to testify Tuesday about his statements to the AP. Also expected to appear was Kevin Harris, a Weaver family friend who was wounded at Ruby Ridge and, along with Weaver, acquitted of Degan's murder in 1993.

Sen. Dianne Feinstein, D-Calif., saying she detected a "syndrome of plausible deniability" in the testimony by Terwilliger and other former officials, told him, "What Washington seems to be saying is, 'We had no part in it.'"

Terwilliger conceded that he bears some responsibility for what happened, but said, "This was an operational situation, and the FBI is in charge of operations."

Berman testified she had been unable to determine who approved the unique FBI rule saying snipers "could and should" shoot at armed adult males at Ruby Ridge. There was insufficient documentation to decide whether someone in Washington or FBI agents on the scene approved the order, Berman said.

"We could not explain why there were no records available for us to look at," said Berman, who is now first assistant U.S. attorney in Milwaukee.

Sen. Herbert Kohl of Wisconsin, the subcommittee's senior Democrat, asked Berman, "Is this a lawyerlike way of saying that documents were removed or updated?"

Berman said she was unable to reach such a conclusion. She said she did not believe there was a cover-up, only a "disagreement" within the Justice Department.

Appearing briefly, former FBI Director William Sessions told the panel he was vacationing at the time of Ruby Ridge and let top FBI aides handle the matter, while he stayed in touch by telephone.

Potts, who is among five top FBI officials now under suspension amid a federal criminal investigation of the destruction of some Ruby Ridge documents at FBI headquarters, testified Thursday that the Justice Department is withholding evidence that would exonerate him.

Potts said his contemporaneous notes, showing that he gave FBI snipers permission to shoot at armed adults but never told them that they "should" do so, "are in the possession of the Department of Justice, which has refused to make them available to me or my attorney."

"I am confident these notes will fully corroborate my testimony," Potts asserted.

On Friday, however, Berman said she hadn't even seen the notes Potts was describing. She told the AP that she knew such notes existed, but did not know their content. She said she never received them.

A Justice Department official said away from the hearing that release of the documents Potts wants "could endanger an ongoing investigation."

*Source: The Dallas Morning News,* September 23, 1995, p. 1C. Reprinted with permission of the Dallas Morning News.

---

In the early 1970s, a charismatic African American named Vincent Leaphart developed an organization entitled American Christian Movement for Life. The group's name was later shortened to MOVE, a name that apparently was not an acronym. As the organization grew, it developed an "anarchistic, back-to-nature philosophy, the main tenets of which were reverence for all animal life, rejection of the American Lifestyle, and absolute refusal to cooperate with the system."[62] Leaphart changed his name to John Africa and began recruiting members in Philadelphia.

**MOVE in Philadelphia, Pennsylvania (1985)**

Initial complaints against MOVE members concerned tension with land-lords and neighbors concerning sanitary problems, numbers of unleashed and uncontrolled pets, and a general harassment of surrounding popula-tions. The group became involved in numerous demonstrations in the neigh-borhood and used loudspeakers to "harangue" neighbors and area citizens all through the day and night. The Philadelphia Police Department, acting under then Mayor Frank Rizzo's "get tough and mean business" policy had numerous confrontations with the group. In 1975, the MOVE group began fortifying its apartment complex by constructing an eight-foot wall around the complex. In 1978, the city blockaded the MOVE headquarters and turned off all electricity and water. When police began demolition of the wall, gunfire erupted, ending with one officer being fatally shot and eight others wounded. Ten MOVE members were arrested and sentenced to prison for the murder of the Philadelphia police officer. Although John Africa was also arrested in 1981 by federal authorities in New York City, he was subse-quently acquitted and moved to Philadelphia to rejoin his group. This time, headquarters for MOVE was located in a quiet, medium-income residential community of Philadelphia rather than the ghetto neighborhood they had used in the past. The group once again began using harassment and intimi-dation tactics against the neighboring residents. Physical assaults and rob-beries were not uncommon and area residents appealed to local and state politicians for help.

On May 9, 1985, a plan was drafted and accepted by all Philadelphia and Pennsylvania agencies to "evacuate and evict" the MOVE members from their residential headquarters. On May 12, the Philadelphia Police Department approached the building with arrest and eviction warrants. MOVE members were requested to surrender. After a day-long siege, in-volving the use of high pressure water hoses to knock down barricaded walls and doors, tear gas and smoke distribution, and open gunfire exchanges, the incident appeared to be at a standstill. The next morning, on May 13, Police Commissioner Gregore Sambor bellowed one last plea over a bullhorn: "Attention, MOVE. This is America. You have to abide by the laws of the United States."[63] What followed was one of the most devastating police ac-tions to date. Commissioner Sambor made the decision to drop two, one-pound charges of DuPont Tovex—a TNT-related blasting agent used in mining—on MOVE's rooftop. The bomb sparked a fire, which was fueled by stored gasoline inside the house. The resulting conflagration reduced most of two tree-lined blocks to smoldering rubble. Sixty-one houses were destroyed, 250 people were left homeless, and 11 MOVE members, including 5 chil-dren, were killed during the episode, which resulted in over $7 million in damages (refer to Figure 12-12).

In all probability the decision to use a bomb during the May 13th MOVE in-cident will always cause a stir in the City of Philadelphia. Police Commissioner Gregore Sambor, himself a 35-year police veteran, retired soon after the event, and then Mayor Wilson Goode, a young and promising African American politi-cian, failed to be reelected. The decision was not without some rationality: the bomb was supposed to be nonincendiary and an air strike from above was cho-sen to avoid further endangering police officers on the ground. The decision to use explosive entry devices was not unreasonable after some 90 minutes of a full-fledged firefight (the day before), during which over 7,000 rounds of police ammunition were expended. As expressed by one officer, "We wanted action but we never expected this!"

## ANATOMY OF A DISASTER

The plan was to dislodge the rooftop bunker that gave MOVE members a deadly vantage point over the street. But from the start, the operation went awry—ending in blazing tragedy for the city and its mayor.

**1**

Police evacuate the immediate neighborhood and firefighters begin water barrage of MOVE house to dislodge bunker. Gunfight follows.

STAKEOUT UNITS IN
SECOND-FLOOR ROOMS

**3**

Helicopter sweeps low over MOVE house and police drop explosive charge on rooftop bunker. A fire erupts that destroys 60 surrounding houses.

WATER
CANNONS

BUNKER

LOUDSPEAKERS

SWAT TEAM

BOARDS

**2**

Police break through cellar wall two houses away from MOVE house, but are met with gunfire from sect members who have broken through their own basement wall and barricaded themselves. Police retreat.

MOVE-HOUSE
BASEMENT

B OHLSSON—Newsweek

**FIGURE 12-12.** The anatomy of a disaster. Incremental steps in Philadelphia's attempt to evict MOVE. (*Newsweek*, May 27, 1985. © 1985 Newsweek, Inc. All rights reserved. Reprinted with permission.)

## Analyses of Decisions During Crisis Events

At first glance, these three incidents represent a series of individual decisions that seriously depart from the major theoretical models presented by Simon, Lindblom, and Gore. However, on closer inspection, each decision maker may have started out with firm plans to adhere to the cool, step-by-step, purely rational model prescribed by Simon, but was swayed by the emotionality and national attention of the incident as it unfolded. Similar to the incremental model, each incident followed its own course, without direction or clear goal, disjointed and separated from a logical, straightforward path. Surely, decision makers relied on their "gut-level" feeling at the time. Who could not have been influenced by watching the news footage of fallen ATF agents being dragged in retreat from the Branch Davidian compound in the early morning hours of February 28, 1993?

The decision-making models developed by Simon, Gore, and Lindblom are not the only credible efforts to help students understand the decision-making process. Indeed, their models may be more appropriate for noncrisis, routine administrative ventures.

Irving Janis and Leon Mann have outlined a decision-making model based on *psychological conflict* that emphasizes the decision-making process under stress.[64] In contrast to the cool, intellectual (rational) process presented by Simon, Janis and Mann indicate that decision making involves "hot" emotional influences, similar to Gore's theory. The need to make a decision is inherently stressful. When a decision maker is faced with an emotionally consequential, no-win choice, how he or she copes with the problem depends on two major factors—hope and time. This process causes great stress as the factors of hope and time are rarely within the control and purview of the decision maker. This can be uniquely observed in protracted, high-stress incidents involving the police, such as those observed in Waco, Ruby Ridge, and the MOVE incident in Philadelphia.

When the decision maker has control of time and has hope that conciliation is possible, that person's efforts are more likely to follow the desired pattern of the "vigilant decision maker."[65] The vigilant model closely resembles the familiar rational-comprehensive model developed by Simon. The vigilant decision maker: (1) thoroughly canvasses a wide range of alternatives; (2) surveys a full range of objectives to be fulfilled and the values implicated by choice; (3) carefully weighs the costs and risks of negative consequences, as well as the positive consequences that could come from each alternative; (4) intensively searches for new information relevant to further evaluation of the alternatives; (5) correctly assimilates and takes account of new information or expert judgment to which he or she is exposed, even when the information or judgment does not support the course of action initially preferred; (6) reexamines the positive and negative consequences of all known alternatives, including those originally regarded as unacceptable, before making a final choice; and (7) makes detailed provisions for implementing or executing the chosen course of action, with special attention to contingency plans that might be required if various known risks were to materialize.[66]

While Janis is better known among students of politics, policy, and management for his earlier work on "groupthink,"[67] his development with Leon Mann of the concept of the vigilant decision maker has provided a practical model for measuring administrative responsibility. Most notable is the excellent essay by Jack H. Nagel in applying the decision-making theories of Janis and Mann to the 1985 MOVE incident in Philadelphia.[68] In his highly critical work, Nagel identifies several decision-making paradoxes which, unfortunately, are not uncommon in similar incidents (e.g., the SLA [Symbionese Liberation Army] shoot-out in Los Angeles in 1968, the AIM [American Indian Movement] siege of Wounded Knee in 1977, the FBI shootings at Ruby Ridge, and the ATF raid on Branch Davidians in Waco).

These paradoxes are identified and elaborated on by Taylor and Prichard.[69] All of the incidents have commonality. They were all police-precipitated—that is, each incident grew from the police advancing on the homes of well-armed, openly defiant, and hostile groups of individuals. Each incident grew from earlier encounters with the police, often highly charged, emotional encounters involving everything from civil and slander suits against the police for harassment to police–group shootings. In all of the incidents, the police intelligence concerning the actual location of the assault and/or the number and armament of the suspects was in gross error. To complicate the issue, the primary decision maker was not at the scene. In both the Waco and Ruby Ridge incidents, critical decisions were made in Washington, D.C., several thousand miles away. In the Philadelphia MOVE incident, Mayor Wilson Goode never visited the actual location of the incident. Then, too, the incidents were characterized by an overreliance on technology. Decision makers believed that tear gas, or in the MOVE incident, Tovex, would not ignite and burn, but rather force hostages and suspects from their barricaded positions. The illusion of invulnerability also impacted each incident—who would believe that suspects would not surrender to a large, powerful, tactically trained, well-armed group of federal agents? This certainly was the case in the ATF raid on Branch Davidians in Waco. The overreliance on intellectual rationality failed as police decision makers underestimated the power and control of a charismatic leader in a relatively small, religiously inspired group. Further, the belief that police SWAT (Special Weapons and Tactics) agents could act like an effective, highly specialized military unit performing a "surgical strike" on a bunker belonged more in the movies than in reality. Police officers and agents are simply not experienced, trained, or equipped to handle such encounters. Contrary to popular belief, highly trained police tactical units are rarely successful since they must rely on meticulous timing, superlative intelligence, surprise, and the ability to use deadly force effectively. None of these conditions existed in the protracted events of Waco, Ruby Ridge, or the like.

Finally, in each incident, the decision maker himself lost hope for a peaceful outcome. When such a condition occurs, the decision maker enters the downward spiral of "defensive avoidance."[70] The pattern is characterized by procrastination and delay, followed by passing the buck and other ways of denying personal responsibility, followed by bolstering and gaining superficial support from others. The distorted view produced by bolstering results in a spreading of responsibility and an exaggerated value of the chosen course of action. More often than not, the chosen course is a "do something" reaction. The Philadelphia police officer's statement that "we wanted action . . . " is indicative of the bolstering phenomenon. As Janis and Mann state, the process of defensive avoidance "satisfies a powerful emotional need—to avoid anticipatory fear, shame, and guilt."[71] Delay followed by haste can result in wishful thinking, oversimplification of the problem, and the selection of the force option. Confusion, catastrophe, and denial soon follow.

## Crisis Events in the Future

Several new directions for handling such crisis events in the future can be developed from the lessons of the past. These recommendations have been adopted as policy for the new FBI Critical Incident Response Group, created in 1994 as a response to the Waco and Ruby Ridge encounters. See Box 12-3, which discusses the 1996 standoff between the FBI and the Montana "freemen."

BOX 12-3

## Standoff Tests FBI Crisis Plan

### Agency takes measured response in Montana

**by David Jackson**

WASHINGTON—Three years after the Branch Davidian siege, which ended in flames on the Texas plains, the FBI faces a crucial test of its new crisis-management rules at a remote Montana sheep ranch.

Now entering its sixth day, a standoff with Montana "freemen" is being conducted by the FBI's Critical Incident Response Group, created the year after the Waco disaster, in which more than 80 people died.

"The FBI has gone to great pains to ensure that there is no armed confrontation, no siege, no armed perimeter and no use of military-assault type tactics or equipment," Attorney General Janet Reno said during a congressional budget hearing this week.

In other words, no more Wacos. No more Ruby Ridges, either, the name of the Idaho mountain where an FBI sniper in 1992 shot and killed the unarmed wife of white separatist Randy Weaver.

In addition to the loss of lives, the Waco and Ruby Ridge incidents proved politically embarrassing for the FBI, which took heavy criticism during a series of congressional hearings.

"They clearly misinterpreted the response of both the Weaver family and the Branch Davidians," said Chip Berlet, a senior analyst with Massachusetts-based Political Research Associates, which studies right-wing movements. "They obviously understand now that these people are not the equivalent of bank robbers with hostages, which is the style they used with the Weavers and the Davidians."

On Friday, a Montana freemen leader who was arrested this week said the standoff would end in violence "worse than Waco."

Federal law enforcement officials are playing down any similarity between those incidents and the latest siege in Montana. For one thing, they said, agents at Waco and Ruby Ridge were seeking to arrest leaders, David Koresh and Mr. Weaver.

The Montana standoff, on the other hand, began with the arrests Monday of LeRoy Schweitzer and Daniel Petersen Jr., freemen leaders charged with writing millions of dollars in forged checks and money orders. Officials also alleged that the freemen plotted the deaths of federal officials, including a judge involved in the foreclosure on their ranch near Jordan, Mont.

The Montana freemen are one of dozens of groups nationwide who have rejected the legitimacy of the federal government. The freemen have gone so far as to establish their own courts of law, which sometimes issue arrest warrants for representatives of the "illegitimate" government.

About a dozen freemen are holed up inside the ranch, surrounded by an estimated 100 armed federal agents scattered across the countryside. Federal officials said they are eager to make sure that Jordan does not join Waco and Ruby Ridge to form a trinity of armed confrontation between the government and citizens.

As he was being led from a court hearing Friday, Mr. Petersen said: "You watch folks, when it goes down, it's going to be worse than Waco," according to a witness.

Federal officials refuse to speculate how long the standoff could last, saying they are prepared to stay for months if necessary to bring about a peaceful resolution.

"This is an opportunity for them to do their thing," said one law enforcement official, who did not want to be identified. "They have a chance over the next few months to test their negotiating skills."

It is probably the biggest test the Critical Incident Response Group has faced, officials said. The new approach is designed to fix three major problems evident at either Waco or Ruby Ridge: a relative lack of federal agents to handle extended barricade situations, poor relations between tactical agents and hostage negotiators and confused lines of authority within the FBI.

In developing the response group, the FBI doubled the membership of its Hostage Rescue Team, which numbered 52 at the time of Waco, officials said. Many of the new members came from existing Special Weapons and Tactics (SWAT) teams.

In addition, at least nine SWAT teams, totaling about 355 agents, underwent intensive training with the Hostage Rescue Team in order to provide support in crisis situations. FBI Director Louis Freeh and Ms. Reno also underwent crisis training at the FBI Academy in Quantico, Va.

Edward S. G. Dennis Jr., a Philadelphia lawyer who evaluated the Justice Department's performance at Waco, said the increase in personnel alone should help improve the chances for a peaceful resolution in Montana.

"You can stay out there longer," Mr. Dennis said. "You can rotate people on and off."

And patience is a virtue, Mr. Berlet said, when dealing with groups with a paranoid view that the government is out to get them—a view reinforced by Waco and Ruby Ridge.

"The key is to not rush them and not put them into confrontational situations where they make snap judgments," Mr. Berlet said. "The test of any democracy is often the patience of its law enforcement officers."

The new rules also were designed to remove any doubt as to who is in charge during barricade incidents: the FBI director. Mr. Freeh announced the creation of the response group on April 18,1994, a day before the first anniversary of the fire that killed Davidian leader David Koresh and more than 80 followers, including young children.

"We must always employ prevention and persuasion," Mr. Freeh said then. "If they fail, we still must do everything possible to save lives. At the same time, we can never falter in our efforts to arrest those responsible for crimes."

Robin L. Montgomery, the special agent in charge of the response group, was dispatched to Montana this week. He answers directly to Mr. Freeh.

Members of other anti-government groups said the best way to defuse the situation in Montana would be to pull out all federal officials, and have local law enforcement officers negotiate a surrender.

"Those people will recognize the authority of the sheriff," said Ed Dosh of the Militia of Montana. "They do not recognize the authority of the federal government. They put the sheriff in office; he's an elected official."

Federal officials said they are obligated to be in Montana because they believe federal laws were broken. They are optimistic of a peaceful resolution, given the success of a much smaller operation last month in Louisiana.

A freeman in Coushatta, La., surrendered five days after refusing, at gun point, to accept a warrant for failure to pay child support. James DeSarno, the special agent in charge of the FBI's New Orleans office, said he decided to pull out a SWAT team from around the freeman's house after consulting with the Critical Incident Response Group.

"I wasn't going to give that guy a platform to spout that anti-government stuff," Agent DeSarno said. "I didn't feel we should get into a confrontation with this guy."

*Source: The Dallas Morning News,* March 30, 1996, pp. 1A and 10A.

## The Montana Freemen

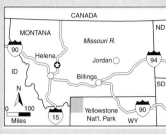

- **Description:** The Montana "freemen" are part of the Christian Identity Movement; others call themselves "Christian Patriots."

- **Beliefs:** The Christian Identity Movement holds that white North Americans are God's chosen people. Members reject the legitimacy of the federal government.

- **Freemen leaders:** LeRoy Schweitzer and Daniel Petersen Jr., who were arrested this week on federal charges.

- **Justus Township:** Established by Mr. Schweitzer, Mr. Petersen, and Rodney Skurdal last September at a Montana sheep ranch near Jordan. They consider the township an alternative government to the one in place.

- **Common-law courts:** Organizations that monitor the white supremacy movement have identified Justus Township as a focal point of "common-law courts," which are increasingly popular within the Christian Identity Movement and other anti-government groups. These courts issue "arrest warrants" and "tax liens" against their enemies in the "illegitimate government."

- **Numbers:** Justus Township is believed to include no more than 20 people, but researchers estimate that similar "freemen" groups and common-law courts operate in about 30 states, including Texas. They estimate there are 25,000 "hard-core activists" in the white supremacy movement, about 60 percent of whom consider themselves "freemen" of one sort or another.

*Sources: Dallas Morning News* research; Coalition for Human Dignity. Reprinted with permission of the Dallas Morning News.

Recommendations for protracted conflict can be summarized as follows:

1. Nagel strongly argues that policies to deal with such events must be institutionalized.[72] That is, they must be concrete, written directives that reflect the overall philosophy of the department or agency. These policies must not be changed arbitrarily during a crisis event or for a specific operational strategy. Further, policies must identify key players and decision makers during such

events. Who is the primary decision maker? Who is in charge of operational management? Who is in charge of coordination, communication, logistics, and so on? These are critical positions and must be identified in writing, well before an incident occurs.

2. Police agencies must adopt a philosophy that clearly articulates the importance of safety and security of human life during such incidents. The force option through the use of SWAT team assault, selective sniper fire, and tear gas distribution must be absolute, last resorts. The primary philosophy must emphasize a patient, no-force negotiation strategy rather than a tactical solution for outcome. This is not a new concept. Frank Bolz and others have pressed for this type of departmental philosophy for the last 20 years.[73]

3. Police agencies must consider withdrawal as a strategy. Certainly, in most of these cases, the police could have arrested the primary leaders of these groups outside the confinement of a barricaded compound. The use of more modern surveillance equipment using FLIR (Forward Looking Infra-Red) and wall-penetrating radar technology could do much to increase the accuracy of intelligence and the development of an arrest plan *before* a barricaded standoff occurs.

4. Police executives must reconsider the role and use of SWAT teams. Their role must be limited to containment and use during routine search warrant executions. They should not be used as a skilled military group capable of executing high-risk operations requiring precision and exceptional teamwork. Here, police executives must fight the "testosterone syndrome" of SWAT team commanders who argue that their training and expertise prepare SWAT teams for such missions. They simply do not. The comparison between police SWAT teams and military strike force teams (such as the Navy SEALS or Army Delta Force) must be broken. The rules of engagement for each unit are unique, as are the desired goals or outcomes.

5. Training for protracted conflicts must include the top-level decision makers as well as operational commanders and chiefs. Attorney generals, governors, city managers, mayors, councilpersons, and top police executives must be trained in coping with such conditions. Significant attention must be paid to the development of a policy that emphasizes the no-force, negotiation option. Further, decision makers should be trained to recognize the characteristics of "defensive avoidance" and "groupthink" before courses of action are taken.[74] Mock scenarios and role playing should accompany the training.

6. During crisis incidents, outside and neutral referees or observers should assist in the situation. These individuals should be well versed in the no-force, negotiation option and should act as "coaches" for the negotiation team. These individuals should have no ownership or responsibility in the situation and should be paid a small fee for their time only. These are not high-level consultants but, rather, well-trained neutral observers with whom operational managers and top-level decision makers can review potential tactics and strategies. Outside observers must be protected from any type of potential ensuing liability through the agency involved. Their main purpose is to act as a "reality check and review" for actions to be taken by the police.

We must recognize that decision making during these types of protracted events, when the suspects appear to be anything but rational, is always a very difficult task. It is also a very human endeavor and, as such, mistakes will inevitably occur. Remember that the purpose of studying these cases is not to criticize the agencies involved (hindsight is always 20-20) but rather to offer students and police executives alternatives to past experiences and tactics. No one decision-making model guarantees success. However, we owe it to the brave men and women who died in these past incidents to ensure that future decision makers always attempt to maximize the two most important factors in the negotiation strategy—hope and time. This can be accomplished by eliminating the force options of direct assault, selective sniper fire, and tear gas dispersal.

Up to this point, we have concentrated mainly on individual decision making. However, police administrators rarely act alone. They are surrounded by deputy chiefs, bureau commanders, and division captains who provide input into the working structure of a police department. Group actions in the decision-making process are critically important to the success or failure of a specific decision and therefore require exploration.

## GROUP DECISION MAKING

Research on group problem solving reveals that this approach has both advantages and disadvantages over individual problem solving. If the potential for group problem solving can be exploited, and if its deficiencies can be avoided, it follows that group problem solving can attain a level of proficiency that is not ordinarily achieved. The requirement for achieving this level of group performance seems to hinge on developing a style of leadership that maximizes the group's assets and minimizes its liabilities. Because members possess the essential ingredients for the solution, the deficiencies that appear in group solutions reside in the processes by which group solutions are developed. These processes can determine whether the group functions effectively or ineffectively. With training, a leader can supply these functions and serve as the group's central nervous system, thus permitting the group to emerge as a highly efficient entity.[75]

A number of advantages are found in group decision making. They are:

**Group Assets**

**Greater Total Knowledge and Information.**   There is more information in a group than in any of its members; thus, problems that require use of knowledge (both internal and external to the police agency) should give groups an advantage over individuals. If one member of the group (e.g., the police chief) knows much more than anyone else, the limited unique knowledge of lesser-informed individuals could serve to fill in some gaps in knowledge.

**Greater Number of Approaches to a Problem.**   Most police executives tend to get into ruts in their thinking, especially when similar obstacles stand in the way of achieving a goal, and a solution must be found. Some chiefs are handicapped in that they tend to persist in their approach and thus fail to consider another approach that might solve the problem in a more efficient manner. Individuals in a group have the same failing, but the approach in which they are persisting may be different. For example, one police administrator may insist that the best way to cope with the increasing number of robberies of local convenience stores in a community is to place the businesses under surveillance by specially trained police officers who are equipped with sufficient firepower to either arrest or shoot the robbers if necessary. Another police administrator might insist that the best way to reduce the number of robberies is through the implementation of crime-prevention programs designed to employ procedures that would make the businesses in question either less attractive or less vulnerable to robberies (e.g., keep the amount of cash available down to a minimum, remove large signs from the front of the store windows that block the view of passing patrol cars and other motorists). It is sometimes difficult to determine which approach or approaches would be most effective in achieving the desired goal. But undue persistence or allegiance to one method tends to reduce a decision group's willingness to be innovative.

**Participation in Problem Solving Increases Acceptance.**   Many problems require solutions that depend on the support of others to be effective. Insofar as group problem solving permits participation and influence, it follows that more individuals accept solutions when a group solves the problem than when one person solves it. When the chief solves a problem alone, then he or she still has the task of persuading others. It follows, therefore, that when groups solve such problems, a greater number of persons accept and feel responsible for making the solution work. A solution that is well accepted can be more effective than a better solution that lacks acceptance. For example, the decision to establish a crime-prevention program in a ghetto neighborhood must have support from the level of chief to individual beat officer. Although other measures to reduce crime (like increasing the number of patrol officers or stricter enforcement of juvenile gang activity) might have a more substantial impact, it is important to remember that most of the program participants must support the effort.

**Better Comprehension of the Decision.**   Decisions made by an individual but that are to be carried out by others must be communicated from the decision maker to the decision executors. Thus, individual problem solving often requires

**FIGURE 12-13.**   A common group decision-making technique: the decision table. (Photo courtesy Tyler, Texas, Police Department.)

an additional state—that of relaying the decision reached. Failures in this communication process detract from the merit of the decision and can even cause its failure or create a problem of greater magnitude than the initial problem that was solved. Many police organizational problems can be traced to inadequate communication of decisions made by superiors and transmitted to officers who have the task of implementing the decision. The chances for communication failures are reduced greatly when the individuals who must work together in executing a decision have participated in making it. They not only understand the solution because they saw it develop, but also are aware of the several other alternatives that were considered and the reasons they were discarded. The common assumption that decisions supplied by superiors are reached arbitrarily, therefore, disappears. A full knowledge of goals, obstacles, alternatives, and factual information tends to open new lines of communication, and this communication in turn is maximized when the total problem-solving process is shared.

This maxim is especially important concerning law enforcement because officers assigned to regular "beats" or "districts" often provide the administrator with additional information or new dimensions to the problem. Additionally, almost any new program aimed at reducing crime in a specific area (neighborhood crime prevention or neighborhood watches) must necessarily include the patrol officer for implementation and success.

Notwithstanding the benefits of group decision making, a number of liabilities are worth mentioning as a precautionary measure: **Group Liabilities**

**Social Pressure.**   Social pressure is a major force for increasing conformity. The desire to be a good member and to be accepted may become more important than whether or not the objective quality of a decision is the most sound. Problems requiring solutions based on facts, independent of personal feelings and wishes, can suffer in group problem-solving situations.

It has been shown that minority opinions in leaderless groups have little influence on the solution reached, even when these opinions are the correct ones. Reaching agreement in a group often is confused with finding the right answer, and it is for this reason that the dimensions of a decision's acceptance and its objective quality must be distinguished.

**Individual Domination.**   In most leaderless groups, a dominant individual emerges and captures a disproportionate amount of the influence in determining the final outcome. Such individuals can achieve this end through a greater degree of participation, persuasive ability, or stubborn persistence (wearing down the opposition). None of these factors is related to problem-solving ability, so that the best problem solver in the group may not have the influence to upgrade the quality of a solution (which the individual would have had if left to solve the problem alone). The mere fact of appointing a leader causes this person to dominate a discussion. Thus, regardless of the individual's problem-solving ability, a leader tends to exert a major influence on the outcome of a discussion. In police circles, the influence of the chief's opinion is undeniable. All too often, the chief dominates the group process so much that participation is squelched. The chief needs to be aware of his or her influence and make a cognitive effort to listen rather than dominate.

**Conflicting Secondary Goals: Winning the Argument.**   When groups are confronted with a problem, the initial goal is to obtain a solution. However, the appearance of several alternatives causes individuals to have preferences, and, once these emerge, the desire to support a particular position is created. Converting those with neutral viewpoints and refuting those with opposing viewpoints now enter the problem-solving process. More and more, the goal becomes having one's own solution chosen rather than finding the best solution. This new goal is unrelated to the quality of the solution and, therefore, can result in lowering the quality of the decision.

**Groupthink.** The theory of "groupthink" was first introduced by Irving Janis in 1972, and was briefly discussed earlier in this chapter.[76] Groupthink is an interesting psychological phenomenon which most often occurs in tight, cohesive groups that are isolated from other political and decision-making bodies. This condition often occurs within police leadership circles, especially during crisis events. The political pressure and stress to make a decision coupled with the presence of a strong leader escalates the condition. Groupthink is most often characterized by a serious lack of methodical procedure, which forces a misperception of the problem and a hurried search for answers. During groupthink, there is considerable focus on a shared rationalization that bolsters the least objectionable alternative as a solution, a suppression of unfavorable outcomes, and an illusion of unanimity and invulnerability. Indeed, Janis and Mann warn that the decision-making process may be so intense that more effort is expended on striving for concurrence than on finding an appropriate decision.[77] During such conditions, the leader should attempt to remain impartial, listening to ideas and alternatives. He or she must invite dissent and encourage individual advisors to express their reservations about suggested solutions. The leader should challenge the group's actions and play the devil's advocate, asking what might go wrong and what the possible adverse consequences might be to the proposed actions. Finally, outside experts or critical evaluators should be asked to review agreed-upon actions or plans. The leader must accept criticism of his or her own judgments as well as those proposed by the group. Janis and Mann are quick to point out that groupthink occurs not only during crisis times, but also during rather mundane policy-making meetings.[78] It is incumbent that the leader, as well as individual members of the group, be ever on guard for the signs and characteristics of groupthink. The best defense to such a condition is continual, open debate and discussion. This requires a highly democratic and participatory leadership style (refer to Chapter 6). In addition, this practice needs to be reinforced by the development of a methodological procedure that encourages dissent and, of course, the acceptance of criticism by all parties involved.

**Factors That Can Serve as Assets or Liabilities**

Depending on the skill of the discussion leader, some elements of group decision making can be assets or liabilities:

**Disagreement.** Discussion may lead to disagreement and hard feelings among members or it may lead to a resolution of conflict and hence to an innovative solution. The first of these outcomes of disagreement is a liability, especially with regard to the acceptance of solutions; the second is an asset, particularly where innovation is desired. A chief can treat disagreement as undesirable and thereby reduce both the probability of hard feelings and innovation. The skillful police administrator creates a climate for disagreement without risking hard feelings because properly managed disagreement can be a source of creativity and innovation. The chief's perception of disagreement is a critical factor in using disagreements. Other factors are the chief's permissiveness, willingness to delay reaching a solution, techniques for processing information and opinions, and techniques for separating idea elicitation from idea evaluation.

**Conflicting Versus Mutual Interests.**   Disagreement in discussions may take many forms. Often, participants disagree with one another with regard to the solution, but when the issues are explored, it is discovered the solutions are in conflict because they are designed to solve different problems. Before there can be agreement on a solution, there must be agreement as to the problem. Even before this, there should be agreement on the goal and on the various obstacles that prevent the goal from being reached. This is where the synoptic planning model can be an invaluable tool. Once distinctions are made among goals, obstacles, and solutions (which represent ways of overcoming obstacles), the opportunities for cooperative problem solving and reduced conflict are increased.

Often, there is also disagreement regarding whether the objective of a solution is to be of the highest quality or merely acceptable. Frequently a stated problem reveals a group of related but separate problems, each requiring a separate solution so that a search for a single overall solution is impossible. Communications are often inadequate because the discussion is not synchronized, and each person is engaged in discussing a different aspect of the problem. Organizing the discussion to explore systematically these different aspects of the problem increases the quality of solutions. The leadership function of guiding such discussions is quite distinct from the function of evaluating or contributing ideas.

When the discussion leader helps separate different aspects of the problem-solving process and delays the inclination of the group to come to a quick but not well-thought-out solution, both the quality of the solution and acceptance of it improve. When the leader hinders or fails to facilitate the isolation of these processes, there is a risk of deterioration in the group process. The leader's skill thus determines whether a discussion drifts toward conflicting interests or whether mutual interests are located. Cooperative problem solving can only occur after the mutual interests have been established, and it is interesting how often they can be found when a discussion leader makes this a primary task.

**Risk Taking.**   Groups are more willing than individuals to reach decisions that involve risk. Taking risks is a factor in the acceptance of change, but change may represent either a gain or a loss. The best protection against the latter outcome seems to be primarily a matter of the quality of a decision. In a group situation, this depends on the leader's skill in utilizing the factors that represent group assets and avoiding those that make for liabilities.

**Time Requirements.**   In general, more time is required for a group to reach a decision than for an individual to reach one. Insofar as some problems require quick decisions, individual decisions are favored. In other situations, acceptance and quality are requirements, but excessive time without sufficient returns also presents a loss. On the other hand, discussion can resolve conflicts, whereas reaching consensus has limited value. The practice of hastening a meeting can prevent full discussion, but failure to move a discussion forward can lead to boredom and fatigue, and group members may agree to anything merely to put an end to the meeting. The effective use of discussion time (a delicate balance between permissiveness and control on the part of the leader), therefore, is needed to make the time factor an asset rather than a liability. Unskilled leaders either tend to be too concerned with reaching a solution and, therefore, terminate a discussion before the group's agreement is obtained, or tend to be too concerned with getting input, allowing discussion to digress and become repetitive.

**Who Changes.**   In reaching consensus or agreement, some members of a group must change. In group situations, who changes can be an asset or a liability. If persons with the most constructive views are induced to change, the end product suffers, whereas if persons with the least constructive points of view change, the end product is upgraded. A leader can upgrade the quality of a decision because the leadership position permits the individual to protect the person with the minority view and increase the individual's opportunity to influence the majority position. This protection is a constructive factor because a minority viewpoint influences only when facts favor it.

In many problem-solving discussions, the untrained leader plays a dominant role in influencing the outcome, and when the person is more resistant to changing personal views than are the other participants, the quality of the outcome tends to be lowered. This negative influence of leaders was demonstrated by experiments in which untrained leaders were asked to obtain a second solution to a problem after they had obtained their first one. It was found that the second solution tended to be superior to the first. Because the dominant individual had influenced the first solution and had won the point, it was not necessary for this person to dominate the subsequent discussion that led to the second solution. Acceptance of a solution also increases as the leader sees disagreement as producing ideas rather than as a source of difficulty or trouble. Leaders who see some of their participants as troublemakers obtain fewer innovative solutions and gain less acceptance of decisions than do leaders who see disagreeing members as persons with ideas.

**Brainstorming**   Brainstorming is a special case or type of group decision making developed initially in advertising to help trigger creativity. The idea behind brainstorming is to bring a group together and to establish an environment in which individuals within the group can present any idea that seems to apply even remotely to the subject being considered with the understanding that criticism will be withheld unless it can somehow improve on the original idea.[79] The practitioners of brainstorming have been able to determine some specific procedures that improve the effectiveness of the brainstorming sessions. Whiting points out that

1. The sessions should last 40 minutes to an hour, although brief 10- to 15-minute sessions may be effective if time is limited.
2. Generally, the problem to be discussed should not be revealed before the session.
3. The problem should be stated clearly and not too broadly.
4. A small conference table that allows people to communicate easily should be used.[80]

This approach can be useful in dealing with many public policy or administrative problems. When the major problem is one of discovering new ways of dealing with a situation, brainstorming may prove useful. One of the most difficult aspects of brainstorming, however, is creating a situation in which it can occur. Most of the "rules of the game" are based on an implicit level of trust between individuals that sometimes does not exist in a politically volatile organization. This kind of trust must be developed for the procedure to be successful; thus, people tend to become freer and better able to use the process as they have repeated experiences with it.[81]

## PERSONALITY CHARACTERISTICS OF DECISION MAKING

Katz and Kahn have suggested that among the more important personality dimensions of policy makers that may affect their decisions are (1) their orientation to power versus their ideological orientation, (2) their emotionality versus their objectivity, (3) their creativity versus their conventional common sense, and (4) their action orientation versus their contemplative qualities.[82]

**Ideology versus Power Orientation**

A police department dominated by a power-driven chief will find its policy decisions moving in the direction of survival and aggrandizement of the chief rather than toward the healthy development of the total department. The following actual case illustrates how this may occur.

A newly appointed police chief selected from outside his department made a decision to implement team policing in one section of the city. The experiment enjoyed some success, and as a result the chief was beginning to gain national recognition via articles in police journals, guest speaker appearances at national conferences, and so forth. There was considerable speculation within the ranks of his police department that the chief was using the police department as an experimental laboratory to test the team policing concept and also as a staging area of self-aggrandizement in the hopes of eventually moving to some larger police department.

The team policing project had been in operation for approximately six months when the chief made a decision to implement it throughout the entire city. The decision was made, in fact, because this would have been the first time team policing had been tried on such a large scale in the United States and would most certainly thrust the police chief into the national spotlight.

The chief's entire command staff was opposed to the move because there were still some personnel and operational problems that had not been worked out in the experimental team policing area. In addition, there was considerable resistance to the concept among rank-and-file personnel. There was sufficient evidence to support all these concerns. A confrontation occurred between the police chief and his entire command staff. The command staff threatened to resign en masse if the chief tried to implement the plan. The city manager became embroiled in the confrontation and decided to support the command staff. The chief was fired, and with his dismissal the entire team policy project was abandoned.

In the final analysis, the chief's quest for self-aggrandizement and his own personal ambitions were perceived by his command staff and many rank-and-file officers as not being congruent with the organizational welfare or with their own personal welfare.

However, in some instances, the power interest of the police executive and organizational welfare coincide. The questions to be answered are: How pertinent are the contributions of the leader to the organization, and what is left for the department when the top leader has moved on?

A police department may have a remarkable chief executive whose brilliant rise in the agency has been accompanied by new organizational developments and substantial benefits to the organization, and when this does occur, such a person may be classified as having an ideological orientation. In reality, however, few organization leaders are ideological crusaders or power-driven survivalists or self-aggrandizers. Most decision makers represent combinations of these value orientations and often use practical compromises to achieve power.

## Emotionality versus Objectivity

All individuals are to some extent susceptible to interjecting emotional components into the decision-making process. To a great extent, the degree to which either one's emotions or one's objectivity intervene will depend on the characteristics of the decision makers and the variables involved in the situation calling for a decision. However, some decision makers seem to possess a higher degree of chronic emotional biases with accompanying momentary emotional impulses than do others. For example, time after time in World War II, Hitler made military decisions reflecting his need to project the image of Germans as supermen. His armies, though outflanked, were never to withdraw but were to fight to the death. The Germans suffered unnecessary losses on the Russian front, in Egypt, and finally on the Western front because decisions were made not only on the basis of objective military strategy and tactics but also on the basis of Hitler's unconscious need to avoid any display of weakness.

Some personality characteristics are capable of activating defense mechanisms in the decision-making process. These psychological characteristics can block or distort the analysis of the problem or the assessment of consequences. Experimentation has shown that defense mechanisms can change the perception of incoming information. Threatening and unpleasant facts are often denied, ignored, or distrusted. Police executives whose defensiveness results in their avoiding certain types of unpleasant information may be reinforced in their blindness by subordinates who keep such facts from them.

## Creativity versus Common Sense

Some individuals are gifted in originality; they are able to see new relationships and to impose new structure on old facts. Others may have a marked ability in making commonsense judgments requiring the evaluation of many relevant factors and the accurate prediction of likely outcomes. Although not logically antithetical, these two abilities do not often occur in the same person. Some individuals by virtue of their enthusiasm, originality, and creativity do not examine the flow of their ideas with searching criticism. Such an attitude would inhibit the creative process. On the other hand, the person seeking to make a balanced judgment and concerned with giving the appropriate weight to competing plausible notions is unlikely to produce a new solution. Occasionally, the two abilities are combined in a person who can move from a phase of creativity to a phase of criticism.

In general, the power to make policy is in the hands of people of good judgment rather than with creative police managers. The police chief with good judgment can single out subordinates to perform the innovative function. Creative police managers can supplement their talents by surrounding themselves with individuals of good sense, yet still have the problem of making the final judgment. It is understandable, then, that the most original minds in any organization are rarely found in top positions. The complexities of organizational life, with its many conflicting demands on the police chief, require critical and judgmental abilities at this level.

Another personality characteristic relevant to organizational functioning is the capacity for action, the ability to act on judgments. Many people have excellent ideas; not nearly as many translate their ideas or even make their decisions into the required implementing actions. Many individuals make that translation in what is called the "action paragraph," acting only when the situation compels it or when they are otherwise forced to perform. As a result, the opportunity for action is sometimes lost entirely.

**Action Orientation versus Contemplation**

In the final analysis, an understanding of personality characteristics is essential if one is to understand the decision-making process. An individual's intellect, reasoning powers, emotions, and biases enter into most decisions, and even when decisions appear to be based almost entirely on hard data, the data that are selected for inclusion in the decision-making process are influenced to some degree by emotion and feeling.[83]

**Impact of Personality Traits on Decision Making**

In fact, it is rarely possible to make decisions that are completely free from inherent discrimination of some kind. Biases may be introduced into the process in many ways, and, whether through ignorance or carelessness, many decision makers appear to overlook the bias of their methods. They tend to use the decision-making process with which they are most comfortable or familiar without any real concern for their fairness. This practice may produce conflict in circumstances when the chief is called on to defend a decision from attack by advocates of a rejected course of action who contend that their disadvantaged position resulted from biased or unfair decisions.[84]

Holland's study of decision making and personality concluded that

> Intelligent persons can think their own thoughts. Moreover, a measure of critical introspection is imperative in a well-lived life. They must recognize outward signs of anxiety, depressions, peculiar habits and mechanisms and view these as symptoms of causes which lie in repressed drives or counter drives. Most highly civilized people are shocked when they recognize powerful negative emotions in themselves. Yet we all have hostilities and fears and we can learn to discharge these without damage. Administrators can admit punitive, egotistical drives for power and omnipotence and deal with these wisely, with a sense of amusement at themselves or even recognize irrational, perfectionistic compulsions as signs of their own overdeveloped conscience. They can get their centers of gravity back in their own hands and away from the primitive impulses and counteracting inhibitions.[85]

## COMMON ERRORS IN DECISION MAKING

Analysis of the decision-making process indicates that certain types of errors occur at a higher frequency than others. Nigro and Nigro[86] have indicated that these are: (1) cognitive nearsightedness, (2) the assumption that the future will repeat the past, (3) oversimplification, (4) overreliance on one's own experience, (5) preconceived notions, (6) unwillingness to experiment, and (7) reluctance to decide.[87]

The human tendency is to make decisions that satisfy immediate needs and to brush aside doubts of their long-range wisdom. The hope is that the decision

**Cognitive Nearsightedness**

will prove a good one for the future also, but this actually is to count on being lucky. The odds for such good fortune to occur consistently across all decisions are poor.

Attempting to find a solution that is a "quick fix" may create infinitely greater difficulties in the future. An example of this phenomenon is observed in barricaded hostage situations, in which the chief wants to assault the location immediately with a SWAT team. In crisis situations such as this, time has always proven to be an ally of the police.[88] Unfortunately, the complicated environment in which police officials function sometimes creates pressure to act on relatively narrow considerations of the moment. Also related to cognitive nearsightedness is the "narrow view," or the consideration of only one aspect of a problem while neglecting all other aspects of that problem, as occurred in the Branch Davidian, Ruby Ridge, and MOVE incidents.

## Assumption That the Future Will Repeat Itself

In making decisions, police officials must try to forecast future conditions and events. Human behavior controls many events; in relatively stable periods of history, the assumption can safely be made that employees, client groups, and the public in general will behave much as they have in the past. The present period is, however, far from stable; many precedents have been shattered, and police officers along with other public employees can behave in sometimes surprising ways. Very rarely do dramatic changes occur without some warning signals. Early trends frequently can serve as valuable indicators of future behavior, but the police administrator must make the effort to be aware of these trends and develop strategies to cope with them.

## Oversimplification

Another tendency is to deal with the symptom of a problem rather than with its true cause because the actual cause may be too difficult to understand. It is also easier for those participating in a decision-making process to understand a simpler solution: it is more readily explained to others and therefore more likely to be adopted. Although a less-involved solution may actually be the better one, the point is that the decision maker looking for an acceptable answer may take the first simple one, no matter how inferior it may be to other, somewhat more complicated, alternatives.

## Overreliance on One's Own Experience

In general, law enforcement practitioners place great weight on their own previous experience and personal judgment. Although the experienced police executive should be able to make better decisions than the completely inexperienced one, a person's own experience may still not be the best guide. Frequently, another police executive with just as much experience has a completely different solution and is just as certain that his or her solution to a problem is the most satisfactory one. In fact, past success in certain kinds of situations may be attributable to chance rather than to the particular action taken. Thus, there is frequently much to be gained by counseling with others whose own experience can add an important and uniquely different dimension to the decision-making process.

## Preconceived Notions

In many cases, decisions allegedly based on facts actually reflect the preconceived ideas of the police executive. This appears to be dishonest, and it is dishonest if the facts are altered to justify the decision. However, in many cases, individuals are capable of seeing only those facts that support their biases. Administrative decisions might be better if they were based on social science findings, but such findings are often ignored if they contradict the ideas of the police chief.[89] In administrative policymaking, conclusions are often supported by a structure of logic that rests dangerously on a mixed foundation of facts and assumptions.[90] Decision makers may appear as if they are proceeding in an orderly way from consideration of the facts to conclusions derived logically from them, when, in fact, what sometimes occurs is that the conclusion comes first and then the facts are found to justify them.

**Unwillingness to Experiment**

The best way in which to determine the workability of a proposal is to test it first on a limited scale. However, pressure for immediate large-scale action often convinces the police chief that there is no time to proceed cautiously with pilot projects, no matter how sound the case for a slow approach. Sometimes police executives are reluctant to request funding and other needed support for the small-scale implementation of new programs for fear that such caution may raise doubts about the soundness of the programs. In all fairness to the cautious police administrator, sometimes this assessment has merit.

**Reluctance to Decide**

Even when in possession of adequate facts, some people will try to avoid making the decision. Barnard speaks of the natural reluctance of some people to decide:

> The making of a decision, as everyone knows from personal experience, is a burdensome task. Offsetting the exhilaration that may result from a correct and successful decision is the depression that comes from failure or error of decision and in the frustration which ensues from uncertainty.[91]

## SUMMARY

Decision making is an integral part of the responsibilities of all administrators, yet it is clear that some individuals are more effective at it than others. We have attempted to examine the decision-making process in a way that would assist readers in evaluating and enhancing their own decision-making skills

Planning was discussed as an integral first step in the decision-making process. Special attention was given to the synoptic planning model and three methods of selecting a preferred course of action: strategic analysis, cost-effectiveness analysis, and must-wants analysis. Other planning approaches mentioned were the incremental transactive, advocacy, and radical techniques. Various types of plans were identified as well as the characteristics of effective plans.

The major strengths and weaknesses of major decision-making models were discussed, including rational decision making, incremental decision making, and heuristic decision making. Significant attention was given to decision making during crisis events, focusing on three important incidents (the siege of the Branch Davidian compound in Waco, Texas; the FBI shooting involving the Weaver family in Ruby Ridge, Idaho; and the bombing of the MOVE headquarters in Philadelphia, Pennsylvania). Through analysis of each incident, we noted similar decision-making flaws and provided several recommendations for handling future encounters of this nature.

The discussion of group decision making noted that this approach has some very distinct advantages and disadvantages. The advantages of group decision making include a greater knowledge and information from the group than from any of its members; a greater number of approaches to a problem likely to be considered; an increase in the potential for acceptance by individual members; and a better understanding of the decision. The liabilities of group decision making include the desire to be a good group member and to be accepted, which tends to silence disagreement and favors groupthink; the potential of individual domination from a person who does not possess the greatest problem-solving ability; and conflicting secondary goals, such as the desire to win an argument rather than to obtain the best possible solution.

**FIGURE 12-14.** During future crisis situations, police executives will be forced to make decisions influencing a wide range of organizational, community, and political issues. (Photo courtesy of the San Diego Police Department.)

The ways in which one's own personality characteristics can affect the types of decisions one makes were examined. These characteristics include orientation to power versus ideology, emotion versus objectivity, creativity versus conventional common sense, and action versus contemplation. Certain decision-making errors occur with a higher frequency than others: cognitive nearsightedness, assumption that the future will repeat the past, oversimplification, overreliance on one's own experience, preconceived notions, unwillingness to experiment, and reluctance to decide.

## DISCUSSION QUESTIONS

1. Discuss the synoptic planning approach. Describe three methods of selecting a preferred course of action.

2. Compare and contrast five planning approaches.

3. What are the differences between administrative, procedural, operational, and tactical plans?

4. Discuss Simon's concept of "bounded rationality."

5. Explain Lindblom's theory of incremental decision making.

6. How does Gore view the decision-making process?

7. Explain the psychological phenomena of "defensive avoidance" and "groupthink." How do they impact decision-making during crisis events?

8. What are some of the important recommendations, developed in this chapter, for handling future crisis events?

9. According to Katz and Kahn, what are some of the more important personality dimensions of policy makers that will affect their decisions?

10. Analysis of the decision-making process indicates that certain types of errors occur at a higher frequency than others. What are they?

## NOTES

1. G. S. Fulcher, *Common Sense Decision-Making* (Evanston, Ill.: Northwestern University Press, 1965), p. 4.

2. Ibid., pp. 4–5.

3. J. Q. Wilson, *Varieties of Police Behavior* (Cambridge, Mass.: Harvard University Press, 1978). In this study, Wilson considers how the uniformed officers of eight communities deal with such offenses

as assault, theft, drunkenness, vice, traffic violations, and disorderly conduct. He also analyzes the problems facing the police administrator both in deciding what patrol officers ought to do and then in getting the officer to do it, how patrol officers in various cities differ in performing their functions, and under what circumstances such differences are based on explicit community decisions.

4. J. H. Skolnick, *Justice Without Trial* (New York: John Wiley & Sons, 1966). This book is based on the author's actual participation as a detective plus comparative community and case material. He discusses key issues such as the organization of the police in America; the effects of police bureaucracy on criminal justice, narcotics, and vice investigation; the informer payoff and its consequences; and the relation between the police and black citizens. His findings are analyzed in light of organizational and legal controls over the police and their effect on the decision-making processes with law enforcement.

5. Israel Stollman, "The Values of the City Planner," in *The Practice of Local Government Planning*, ed. Frank S. So et al. (Washington, D.C.: International City Management Association, 1979), p. 13.

6. Ibid., p. 13.

7. Robert C. Cushman, *Criminal Justice Planning for Local Governments* (Washington, D.C.: U.S. Government Printing Office, 1980), p. 8; five of the elements identified are provided by Cushman, and the others have been added.

8. Ibid., p. 8.

9. John Hudzik and Gary Cordner, *Planning in Criminal Justice Organizations and Systems* (New York: Macmillan, 1983), p. 1.

10. Charles M. Mottley, "Strategy in Planning," in *Planning, Programming, Budgeting: A System Approach to Management*, 2nd ed., ed. J. F. Lyden and E. S. Miller (Chicago, Ill.: Markham, 1972), p. 127.

11. The term *pure* or *objective rationality* is taken from the alternative planning models identified by Tony Eddison, *Local Government: Management and Corporate Planning* (New York: Harper & Row, 1973), pp. 19–23.

12. Cushman, *Criminal Justice Planning*, p. 4.

13. The synoptic model is thoroughly discussed in R. C. Cushman, *Criminal Justice Planning*. Some of the following information relating to the model is paraphrased from that work.

14. Hudzik and Cordner, *Planning in Criminal Justice*, p. 10.

15. Ibid., p. 24.

16. Ibid., p. 10.

17. Ibid.

18. Carol Weiss, *Evaluation Research: Methods of Assessing Program Effectiveness* (Englewood Cliffs, N.J.: Prentice Hall, 1972), p. 7.

19. P. Davidoff and T. A. Reiner, "A Choice Theory of Planning," *Journal of American Institute of Planners* (May 1982), 103–115.

20. Hudzik and Cordner, *Planning in Criminal Justice*, p. 14.

21. R. G. Lynch, *The Police Manager* (Boston: Holbrook, 1975), p. 144.

22. U.S. Naval War College, *Sound Military Decisions* (Newport, R.I.: U.S. Naval War College, 1942).

23. The following discussion of strategic analysis is taken from Charles M. Mottley's "Strategic Planning," *Management Highlights*, Release 56, Office of Management Research, U.S. Department of the Interior (September 1967), pp. 103–119.

24. E. S. Quade, "System Analysis Techniques for Planning-Programming-Budgeting," in *Planning, Programming, Budgeting*, ed. Lyden and Miller, p. 249.

25. Ibid.

26. Ibid.

27. J. L. Pressman and Aaron Wildavsky, *Implementation* (Berkeley, Calif.: University of California Press, 1973).

28. Hudzik and Cordner, *Planning in Criminal Justice*, p. 196.

29. Ibid.

30. The last portion of this paragraph is taken, with some restatement, from Stollman, "Values of the City Planner," pp. 14–15.

31. A number of sources identify plans according to their use: see O. W. Wilson, *Police Planning*, 2nd ed. (Springfield, Ill.: Charles C. Thomas, 1962), pp. 4–7; Vernon L. Hoy, "Research and Planning," in *Local Government Police Management*, ed. Bernard L. Garmire (Washington, D.C.: International City Management Association, 1977) pp. 374–375.

32. Stanley S. Thune and Robert J. House, "Where Long-Range Planning Pays Off," *Business Horizons*, 13 (August 1970), 81–90.

33. For information on managing organizational decline and cutback, see Elizabeth K. Kellar, ed., *Managing with Less* (Washington, D.C.: International City Management Association, 1979); Jerome Miron, *Managing the Pressures of Inflation in Criminal Justice* (Washington, D.C.: U.S. Government Printing Office, 1979).

34. Hudzik and Cordner, *Planning in Criminal Justice*, p. 195.

35. J. M. Pfiffner, "Administrative Rationality," *Public Administration Review,* 20:3 (Summer 1960), 126.

36. Ibid., 128.

37. Herbert A. Simon, "The Proverbs of Administration, *Public Administration Review,* (Winter 1946), 53–67.

38. Herbert A. Simon, *Administrative Behavior* (New York: Macmillan, 1961; a reprint of 1947 edition), p. 39.

39. Ibid., p. 40.

40. For a complete discussion of the rational-comprehensive model, see Peter F. Drucker, *The Effective Executive* (New York: Harper & Row, 1967); N. F. Iannone, *Supervision of Police Personnel* (Englewood Cliffs, N.J.: Prentice Hall, 1970); and Ira Sharkansky, *Public Administration* (Chicago: Markham, 1972).

41. See Sharkansky, *Public Administration,* p. 44, and Sam S. Souryal, *Police Administration and Management* (St. Paul, Minn.: West, 1977), p. 315.

42. Simon, *Administrative Behavior,* p. 40.

43. Ibid.

44. See Paul M. Whisenand and R. Fred Ferguson, *The Managing of Police Organizations,* 2nd ed. (Englewood Cliffs, N.J.: Prentice Hall, 1978), pp. 202–203, for a discussion of Simon's "bounded-rationality" concepts.

45. Charles F. Lindblom, *The Policy-Making Process* (Englewood Cliffs, N.J.: Prentice Hall, 1968).

46. Ibid., p. 209.

47. Charles F. Lindblom, "The Science of Muddling Through," *Public Administration Review,* 19 (Spring 1959), p. 86.

48. Jack Kuykendall and Peter Unsinger, *Community Police Administration* (Chicago: Nielson-Hall, 1975), p. 132.

49. William J. Gore, *Administration Decision-Making: A Heuristic Model* (New York: John Wiley & Sons, 1964).

50. Ibid., p. 12.

51. Souryal, *Police Administration,* p. 318.

52. L. G. Gawthrop, *Bureaucratic Behavior in the Executive Branch* (New York: Free Press, 1969), pp. 98–99.

53. Gore, *Administrative Decision-Making,* p. 12.

54. Gawthrop, *Bureaucratic Behavior,* p. 99.

55. Souryal, *Police Administration,* p. 319.

56. Graham T. Allison, *Essence of Decision: Exploring the Cuban Missile Crisis* (Boston: Little, Brown, 1971).

57. Some of this discussion was excerpted from an excellent review of Allison's book by Robert B. Denhardt, *Theories of Public Organization* (Monterey, Calif.: Brooks/Cole, 1984), pp. 81–85.

58. John Ott, "The Challenging Game of Operations Research," in *Emerging Concepts of Management,* ed. Max S. Wortmann and Fred Luthans (London: Macmillan, 1970), p. 287.

59. Ibid.

60. Peter P. Schoderbeck "PERT—Its Promises and Performances," in *Emerging Concepts,* ed. Wortmann and Luthans, p. 291; and E. S. Quade, "Systems Analysis Techniques for Planning-Programming-Budgeting," *RAND Report,* p. 332 (Santa Monica, Calif.: RAND Corporation, 1966), p. 7.

61. Aaron Wildavsky, *Speaking Truth to Power: The Art and Craft of Police Analysis* (Boston: Little, Brown, 1979), p. 84.

62. John H. Nagel, "Psychological Obstacles to Administrative Responsibility: Lessons of the MOVE Disaster," *Journal of Policy Analysis and Management,* 10:1 (1991), 3.

63. Marci McDonald, "Attention, MOVE. This is America," *McLeans* (May 27, 1985), 28–29.

64. Irving L. Janis and Leon Mann, *Decision Making: A Psychological Analysis of Conflict, Choice, and Commitment* (New York: The Free Press, 1977).

65. Ibid., Chapter 1.

66. Ibid., pp. 11–15.

67. Irving L. Janis, *Victims of Groupthink* (Boston: Houghton Mifflin, 1972).

68. Nagel, "Psychological Obstacles."

69. Robert W. Taylor and Leigh A. Prichard, "Decision-Making in Crisis: Police Responses to Protracted Critical Incidents." Paper delivered at the Academy of Criminal Justice Sciences Annual Meeting, Las Vegas, Nevada, March 13, 1996.

70. The concept of "defensive avoidance" was first developed by Janis and Mann in *Decision Making: A Psychological Analysis of Conflict, Choice, and Commitment.* However, Nagel uniquely applied the concept to reality in his article, "Psychological Obstacles to Administrative Responsibility: Lessons of the MOVE Disaster."

71. Janis and Mann, *Decision Making,* p. 85.

72. Nagel, "Psychological Obstacles," p. 21.

73. The concept of a negotiated solution to crisis events has been developed over the last twenty years. See Frank A. Bolz and Edward Hershey, *Hostage Cop* (New York: Rawson, Wade Publisher, 1979); Ronald C. Crelinsten and Denis Szabo, *Hostage-Taking* (Lexington, MA: Lexington Books, 1979); Murray S. Miron and Arnold P. Goldstein, *Handbook for Hostage Negotiations: Tactical Procedures,*

*Negotiating Techniques and Responses to Non-Negotiable Hostage Situations* (New York: Harper and Row, 1979); and Robert W. Taylor, "Hostage and Crisis Negotiation Procedures" in *Police Civil Liability*, ed. Leonard Territo (New York: Hanrow Press, 1984).

74. See Nagel, Janis and Mann, and Taylor and Prichard.

75. N. R. F. Maier, "Assets and Liabilities in Group Problem Solving: The Need for Integrated Function," *Psychology Review*, 74:4 (1967), 239–248. Much of the information in this chapter dealing with the discussion of group decision making was obtained from this source.

76. See Irving L. Janis, *Victims of Groupthink* (Boston: Houghton Mifflin, 1972).

77. Janis and Mann, *Decision Making*, pp. 398–400.

78. Ibid.

79. W. Gortner, *Administration in the Public Sector* (New York: John Wiley & Sons, 1977), p. 124.

80. C. S. Whiting, "Operational Techniques of Creative Thinking," *Advanced Management Journal*, 20:28 (1955), pp. 24–30.

81. W. Gortner, *Administration in the Public Sector*, p. 124.

82. Much of the discussion on the four personality dimensions of decision makers that follows has been drawn extensively from D. Katz and R. L. Kahn,

*The Social Psychology of Organizations* (New York: John Wiley & Sons, 1966), chapter 10, "Policy Formulation and Decision-Making," pp. 290–294.

83. A. J. DuBrin, *Fundamentals of Organizational Behavior* (New York: Pergamon Press, 1974), p. 76.

84. A. Easton, *Decision-Making: A Short Course for Professionals*, Lessons I (New York: John Wiley & Sons, 1976), p. 35.

85. H. K. Holland, "Decision-Making and Personality," *Personnel Administration*, 31:3 (1968), 28–29.

86. Much of the information in this chapter dealing with the discussion of common errors in decision making was obtained from F. A. Nigro and L. G. Nigro, *Modern Public Administration* (New York: Harper & Row, 1977), pp. 226–232.

87. Katz and Kahn, *Social Psychology*, p. 285.

88. Robert W. Taylor, "Hostage and Crisis Negotiation Procedures: Assessing Police Liability," *TRIAL Magazine*, 19:4 (1983), 64–71.

89. See, for example, A. Leighton, *Human Relations in a Changing World* (Princeton, N.J.: Princeton University Press, 1949), p. 152.

90. Ibid.

91. C. Barnard, *The Functions of the Executive* (Cambridge, Mass.: Harvard University Press, 1938), p. 189.

# APPENDIX: ANCHORAGE POLICE DEPARTMENT
# POLICY STATEMENT

Municipality of Anchorage
Anchorage Police Department
General Order No. 91-3

DATE:       October 25, 1999

TO:         All Personnel

FROM:       Duane S. Udland, Deputy Chief of Police

SUBJECT:    Victim's Rights Act of 1991, Confidentiality Requirements

The Victim's Rights Act of 1991 (A.S. 12.61.100–150) became effective September 15, 1991. This Act restricts public access to certain information contained in our files, our press releases, and in court documents.

**Protected Information That May Not be Released:**

1. The *residence address, business address, or telephone number of any victim or witness* to any crime. (This applies to crimes only, not to violations or infractions that carry no jail time.)
2. The *name of the victim* of the following crimes:
   Kidnapping involving physical or sexual assault
   Sexual Assault—First, Second and Third degree
   Sexual Abuse of a Minor—First through Fourth degrees
   Incest
   Unlawful Exploitation of a Minor
   Indecent Exposure
3. NOTE: This Act should not be construed to limit the release of the name of any kidnapping victim needed to facilitate the recovery of the missing victim or to conduct the necessary investigation of the crime.

Effective immediately, the following policies will be followed in regards to the release of information:

**Release of Records to the Public:**

1. Police reports will only be released by the Records Section and Crime Prevention Unit personnel in accordance with their unit procedures.
2. Police reports or other records, such as papers, photographs, court files, or notebooks may **only** be released to the public **after** they have been examined for the presence of protected information and that information has been deleted or made unreadable.
3. Other Law Enforcement agencies, Municipal Prosecutors, and District Attorneys may request and obtain complete copies of any police report. If the identity of the person requesting the report is not known to the employee, proper identification will be required.
4. According to the Alaska Department of Law, the release of police reports to insurance companies does not constitute a release of protected information and is not restricted under the Act.

**Media Releases:**

1. Press releases may **not** contain any protected information. Personnel providing authorized releases will insure that they do not contain the names of

Sexual Assault, Sexual Abuse of a Minor, Incest, Indecent Exposure or Kidnapping victims; and that **no** victim or witness addresses or phone numbers are given.

2. Although the Act does not apply to verbal communications, it is the policy of the Anchorage Police Department that protected information will not be released in any form.

## Required Court Certification

The Court System now requires that a Certification Form be attached to all paperwork being filed in any criminal case, including all criminal complaints, misdemeanor citations, and search warrants. Most often, the prosecutor's office will handle this requirement. Occasionally, officers will submit paperwork directly to the court system and will then secure this form through the Clerk of the Court's office. This applies to **crimes only,** not to violations or infractions that carry no jail time.

Law enforcement officers can sign the forms in good faith, and will be in compliance with the Victim's Rights Act of 1991, if the complaint or other court document does not contain:

1. the address or telephone number of any victim or witness (other than the defendant), unless the address is used to identify the place of the crime. **This applies in all cases.**

2. The name of the victim, but instead uses initials to identify the person. If the victim is a minor, you must also use initials to identify the minor's parent or guardian. **This applies in sex and kidnapping cases only.**

3. In some cases, it may be necessary to use some protected information in search warrant applications or criminal complaints. In those instances, the court clerk's office should be notified and they will have to take the necessary precautions to guard against the disclosure of the court files.

## INTRODUCTION

The historical importance of financial management to this country's very existence is unmistakable; the issue of taxation without representation was part of the conflict with England that led ultimately to the American Revolution. The present importance of financial management in government is readily established by examining the content of daily newspapers. (See Box 13-1).[1] Stories note the arrest and indictment of an official for embezzling public funds, the defeat or passage of a bond referendum to construct a jail, an auditor's report that describes the police department's accounting procedures for handling funds for informants and narcotics purchases as "woefully inadequate," the closing of a school or precinct station because funds were no longer available to operate it, or the efforts of local officials to obtain the state legislature's approval to levy new taxes or to increase the levels of existing ones.

# —13—
# FINANCIAL MANAGEMENT

*Not least among the qualifications of an administrator is his ability as a tactician and gladiator in the budget process.*

FREDERICK C. MOSHER

The fact that some police administrators think that budgeting and financial management is "only detailed clerical work" and therefore unattractive and unimportant deserves some attention here. First, financial management does involve some detailed effort. The product of that effort is attended by the possibility of uncomfortable or potentially severe consequences for misjudgment or oversight. For example, when gasoline prices exceed projections, some police agencies are forced to limit the numbers of miles patrolled daily, the purchasing of smaller cars, the cost of driver training programs to increase fuel economy, and the need to return to the legislative body for additional funds. In this last regard, the Maryland State Police had to request an additional $525,000 in one year, and Detroit's citywide annual budget for gasoline was found to have been inadequate by some $2,000,000.[2] The best budget preparation process in the world cannot anticipate unforeseeable emergencies, and thus little harm is done to the reputation of an agency when a budgetary shortfall occurs (see Box 13-2). However, when items are not included in a budget request through oversight, considerable embarrassment is created. Illustrative of such an oversight was the failure of a sheriff to request any ammunition in his annual budget, which required him to go before the county commissioners considerably red-faced to specially request it. Lest one think that such events happen only in small departments, one state police agency forgot to request the $4 million in funds it needed to provide recruit training for newly hired troopers, resulting in a one-year hiring freeze.

A second factor related to viewing financial management as unattractive work is that it offers little of the excitement, attention, or perhaps even glamour that directing a noteworthy major investigation does. However, success in obtaining and shepherding resources increasingly involves the need for creativity and is a potentially rich source of job satisfaction. As to financial management not being "real police work," the validity of that statement diminishes as one advances up the hierarchy, incurring at each successive level a set of new responsibilities that renders operational prowess less relevant.

BOX 13-1

## Wiscasset Police Department Feeling Budget-Cutting Pinch

### by Robert Conlin

Nearly 50 percent of the staff has left in less than a year, putting a strain on a department used to more.

The next time a neighbor turns up the music too loud or a garbage can goes missing from a Wiscasset resident's yard, it's likely that the familiar dark blue car of the Wiscasset Police Department won't be as quick to the scene as in the past.

Budget cuts, attrition and a promotion for one of the Wiscasset's top police officers have been the impetus for the departure of three of the department's eight officers in the past 10 months, with a fourth contemplating a move as well.

Since July, when Robert McFetridge left to go to the Boothbay Harbor Police Department, Police Chief Carl Fleck has seen his department trimmed nearly in half. With 87 percent of the department's budget devoted to salaries and a mandate to slash town budgets across-the-board, at least two of the departures were expected, but Fleck is unsure whether replacements are on the way.

"Obviously, with the budget cuts, everything is in transition," he said Tuesday. "We have a couple of reserves coming in, but we'll have to wait until after the Town Meeting to see about any other replacements."

The department's budget was $361,000 in 1997, while this year, the selectmen are proposing a $259,000 budget. With nearly a third of its resources on the chopping block, the department was obviously prepared to operate at less than full strength from years past.

Following on the heels of McFetridge's departure, Officer Wayne Appleby transferred to a job as aquatics director at the Wiscasset Community Center in December. The two were paid salaries of $18,400 and $31,000 respectively.

However, the imminent departure of Lt. David Tims, the second-in-command at the department, to a job as Chief of Police in Southwest Harbor was not anticipated. Tims was paid $36,200 this year.

Neither is the possible departure of Officer Eric Powell, who is currently undertaking the rigorous Maine State Police multi-level testing. Powell was paid $30,900 this year.

Should he be accepted, the department's patrol staff would have been reduced by half in less than a year.

There's little doubt that Fleck had more than adequate staffing in the past. Eight officers for a town of 3,500 is almost unheard of in Maine and a direct result of Maine Yankee's tax bill. However, that funding is drying up and the department is learning how to make do with less.

"We are asking people to have some patience. There will be some delays compared to what residents have been used to. I can say that any emergency calls will get dealt with as quickly as in the past. Both the Lincoln County Sheriff's Department and, if needed, the Maine State Police will help us if necessary," Fleck stressed. "However, there will be some delays for non-emergency calls."

Sheriff William Carter of the Lincoln County Sheriff's Department, which patrols 458 square miles of Lincoln County with nine officers, said he has talked to Chief Fleck and offered any necessary help.

"We've done back-up for the town in the past. It won't be all that different. We'll do for Wiscasset what we do for all the towns in the county, which is be there to help when needed," he said. "The cutbacks will change the way people perceive the department, though. They will have to make do like the rest of the towns in the county. This is rural Maine. You don't have a police officer on your doorstep right after you call 911."

The Sheriff's Department is adding two officers for the summer, which will ease the burden should the seasonal surge in tourist traffic drive up calls.

Wiscasset's police department has averaged some 2200 calls a year for the past three or four years, and Fleck doesn't expect any marked increase. Most of those calls are non-emergency in nature.

For example, the department responded to 17 assaults, 55 thefts, nine burglaries and six auto thefts last year. They made 114 arrests in total.

Both Fleck and Carter acknowledge that Wiscasset has had more than ample police protection in the past and that its current size is more in line with statewide police staffing.

Fleck, who has always been a chief who is out on patrol, has picked up Appleby's DARE program to the schools. He said Tuesday that the town will continue to be covered 24 hours a day, that the department will make the transition, that Wiscasset residents can count on them being there.

"I want people to call us. If calls come in, we'll take them. It doesn't matter if it's eight officers or five, we'll be there for residents of this town," he explained. "But people have to be aware that the department has been fortunate in the past—just like every agency in this town—and there will be an adjustment period for everyone."

*Source:* Robert Conlin, *Wiscasset* (Maine) *Newspaper*, March 26, 1998.

BOX 13-2

## Protecting KKK Rallies Busting Cities' Budgets; $800,000 Spent Across State this Year

### From Staff and Wire Reports

On June 26, about 200 police officers representing four separate departments converged around the Montgomery County courts building. Their mission: Keep the peace during a Ku Klux Klan rally and a counter-demonstration.

The officers—from Dayton, Kettering, Miamisburg and the county sheriff's office—outnumbered members of the American Knights of the Ku Klux Klan and the counter-protestors about 10 to 1.

Dayton police projected $24,000 in overtime costs for the event, which Detective Carol Johnson called "uneventful."

As Ohio approaches a record number of Ku Klux Klan rallies this year, the heavily guarded events have cost taxpayers about $800,000 in security and preparation expenses.

Some people argue that if anti-Klan protesters would just stay away, the security would be unnecessary. But officials say they have little choice but to be as prepared as possible.

While Dayton's money could certainly be used for other things, Johnson said that if the police presence kept things calm, "I guess we could say it was worth the money spent. It's better to have us and not need us."

As rallies increase and take their financial toll on communities, the state is poised to provide additional help. Attorney General Betty Montgomery said that for the first time her office will make free metal detectors and fences available for use during rallies.

*Source: The Dayton* (Ohio) *Daily News,* October 10, 1999.

## POLITICS AND FINANCIAL MANAGEMENT

In addition to other political forces, the budgets for state and local units of government are often shaped by politics at the national level. Roughly 30 years ago, there was a great deal of financial assistance which flowed from the federal to other levels of government. Over the ensuing years, many state and local units of government have been under fiscal pressure because of a cutback in federal assistance and occasional economic downturns. Under conditions of fiscal stress, jobs have been cut and/or services reduced or eliminated. Further exacerbating these fiscal pressures has been the "devolution" or shifting of some responsibility for programs, such as welfare, from the federal to the state level and then on to local units of government. Although some funding has accompanied the devolution, state and local resources are increasingly strained. Altogether, these pressures force state legislatures, county commissions, and city councils to make some very unpleasant decisions (see Box 13-3).

Budgeting is inherently a political process. Anything done through government entails the expenditure of public funds.[3] If politics is regarded in part as a conflict over whose preferences shall prevail in the determination of policy, the outcome of this struggle is recorded in the budget.[4] Thus, the single most important political statement that any unit of government makes in a given year is its budget. Essentially the budget process confronts decision makers with the gambler's adage, "put your money where your mouth is."[5] Because increasing demands often are made on resources that are declining, stable, or outstripped by the claims made on them, the competition for appropriated funds is keen and often fierce as the police and other departments seek to make the best case they can for their own budget. Beset by competing demands from each department of government, assailed by informal "arm twisting," influenced by media reports of public opinion on various subjects, confronted by special-interest groups with different priorities, and in consideration

BOX 13-3

## East Palo Alto Has Tough Vote in Budget Crisis

### Parks Dept. faces ax in move to save cops' jobs

**by Carolyne Zinko, Chronicle Staff Writer**

East Palo Alto officials say they have no way to keep paying the salaries of 15 police officers—about half of the force—unless they eliminate the city's Parks and Recreation Department.

The City Council was scheduled to vote last night on the drastic measure recommended by City Manager Monika Hudson. The money is needed to replace a federal law enforcement grant that is due to expire in June.

In emotionally charged testimony before the vote, some 35 residents and city employees lined up to blast the council for insensitivity in the proposed lay-off, and expressed concern for the programs and children who would be affected.

Facing cuts are two full-time employees and seven part-time employees in the Parks and Recreation Department, along with the phones and computers they use.

"These (Parks and Recreation) workers are some of the only male role models that these kids know," said Marcus Butler, 20, a special education teacher.

"Bell Street Gym isn't just a gym," he said of the Parks and Recreation facility. "It is a counseling center, a right of passage for males and females in our community."

William Webster, a local resident, agreed: "For you to take this out of the community is ludicrous."

Webster complained that the proposal would eliminate the community services director, Meda Okelo, who has worked for the city for 11 years.

Still, Councilman R. B. Jones indicated that because the city has limited funds, there would be little to discuss.

Jones said the council had earlier told Hudson that "we want to keep the same level of police protection that we have."

"It would not be an option to dissolve the East Palo Alto Police Department and go to the rent-a-cop sce-nario," he said, referring to the contracting of police services from another law enforcement agency.

"It will hurt," he said. "It's a small town and we all know each others' families . . . but I don't know of a better plan."

The move is intended to free some $905,000 during the next two years.

Hudson said she selected the Parks and Recreation Department because several other recreation facilities could fill the gap.

The city has several parks and runs an open gym and a pool. The local YMCA told city officials it could expand its programs in town. Meanwhile, a new Boys & Girls Club is due to open in several months, Hudson said.

The Police Department will also face the loss of one officer under the plan.

Hudson said the city accepted the $3 million federal grant, part of a police hiring program in 1997, on the condition that it make a "good faith effort" to re-tain the officers when the grant expired or face the prospect of having to pay the money back. The grant expires in June.

Coupled with redevelopment efforts that have sprung up in part because of a marked reduction in crime in recent years, the city is anxious to find a way to keep as many officers employed as possible.

The city logged dozens of murders a year at the beginning of the 1990s but had only one killing last year.

"When I looked at having to make a cut, (Parks and Recreation) seemed a wiser cut than police services," Hudson said.

The cutbacks are intended to last 18 months, but those positions could be brought back once the city's financial fortunes improve, Hudson said.

The city has a $10 million budget—$4 million in grants allocated for specific purposes and $6 million in general fund money, two-thirds of that already going to the Police Department.

*Source: © The San Francisco Chronicle, January 19, 2000, reprinted by permission.*

of their own values and judgments, those who appropriate the funds are making a highly visible and often controversial political decision when they enact a budget. Because legislatures allow public officials, such as city managers and police chiefs, some discretion in how they execute a budget, they too are making political decisions whose impact may evoke strong reactions.

Although its political orientation is inescapable, a budget is more than an indicator of who won and who lost, who was able to form effective coalitions and work out acceptable compromises and who was not able to perform this feat, and whose policies are in ascendancy and descendancy; it is also a key managerial tool.[6]

## STATE AND LOCAL FINANCIAL MANAGEMENT

**The States' Role in Local Finance**

There are numerous examples of private-sector organizations that have had severe financial problems, including Chrysler, Lockheed, and Penn Central. Historically, local governments have also not been without a certain degree of financial frailty. In the last 150 years, more than 6,000 units of local government have defaulted on their financial obligations, although about two-thirds of these came during the decade that followed the economic crash of 1929.[7] States simultaneously contribute to, and attempt to help, local government avoid financial difficulties. They contribute to the problem by mandating programs that require the expenditure of local funds. Examples of such mandated programs include the training of peace officers, proscribing levels of police service, and establishing special disability and retirement benefits for police.[8] Our national government also contributes in a similar fashion; for example, it is estimated that programs legislated by the federal and state government cost Iowa cities $50 million to $60 million annually.[9]

As the sovereign and superior governmental entity for the geographic areas they encompass, states have constitutional responsibilities over local government.[10] Under the legal doctrine known as Dillion's rule,[11] no local government may organize, perform any function, tax citizens, or receive or spend money without the consent of the state. With an eye toward helping local government avoid financial woes, state laws, which vary, may control (1) the revenue structure of local governments and methods of tax collection; (2) budgeting, accounting, and financial reporting practices; (3) cash collection, deposit, and disbursement procedures; and (4) procedures for incurring debt, the types of debts that may be issued, and the level of debt that is allowable.

**Local Administration**

In addition to whatever requirements are established by the federal and state governments, the practice of local financial management is also shaped by a number of other forces, including the city charter, ordinances, executive orders, regulations, and practices. Of considerable impact is the political structure of the unit of government. In city manager and strong mayor cities, these figures play dominant roles in their respective systems in the development of what is termed an executive budget. In weak mayor systems, the city council is the dominant force in the development of what is termed a legislative budget. Under this arrangement, a city council budget committee has responsibility for preparing the budget. A budget staff frequently serves this committee by providing administrative support. The heads of the various departments, including the police, and their budget staffs deal directly with the council budget committee and its staff in formulating the budget. Under the declining commissioner plan, three to seven elected officials serve as both members of the local legislative branch of government and as heads of one or more departments of city government. One of the commissioners receives the title of mayor, but it is largely ceremonial, akin to a weak mayor system. Under the commissioner plan, the budget preparation process may follow any of several patterns: (1) the commission as a whole may be the dominant force, (2) the commission may have a budget officer attached directly to it, or (3) the preparation of the budget may be guided by a budget officer assigned to the commissioner of finance, but who serves at the pleasure of the commissioners as a whole to ensure responsiveness to them.

## DEFINITIONS OF A BUDGET

The word *budget* is derived from the old French *bougette,* meaning a small leather bag or wallet.[12] Initially, it referred to the leather bag in which the chancellor of the exchequer carried the documents to English Parliament stating the government's needs and resources.[13] Later, it came to mean the documents themselves. Currently, *budget* has been defined in many ways, including a plan stated in financial terms, an estimate of future expenditures, an asking price, a policy statement, the translation of financial resources into human purposes, and a contract between those who appropriate the funds and those who spend them.[14] To some extent, all these are true and help us to understand something about budgets, but they lack the feature of being comprehensive.

Even more comprehensive definitions of a budget reflect different notions. The definitions that follow represent, successively, the budget as a management tool, the budget as a process, and the budget as politics:

> The budget is a comprehensive plan, expressed in financial terms, by which a program is operated for a given period of time. It includes: (a) the services, activities, and projects comprising the program; (b) the resultant expenditure requirements; and (c) the resources usable for their support.[15]
>
> The budget is a unified series of steps taken to implement a government's policy objectives. It involves the development of a documented work program . . . the careful linkage of the program with a formal, comprehensive financial plan, and the carrying out of the entire scheme through an administrative arrangement.[16]
>
> The budget is a device for consolidating the various interests, objectives, desires and needs of our citizens.[17]

Budgets may also be defined as operating and capital. An operating budget is usually for one year and is for items that have a short life expectancy, are consumed in the normal course of operations, or are reincurred each year. Included in operating budgets are batteries, paper, duplicating and telephone expenses, as well as salaries and fringe benefits. There is a great deal of diversity in how different jurisdictions treat their capital budgets. "Capital project" or "capital improvement plan" (CIP) is often used to denote expenditures to buy land or to construct or for a major renovation of public facilities. Normally three to five years are needed to complete the development of, and pay for, a CIP. Depending on the guidelines that a jurisdiction uses, vehicles, furniture, and other equipment may or may not be included in the CIP. If not included in the CIP, such objects as police vehicles, radios, desks and chairs, binoculars, and microcomputers may be included in the operating budget under the heading of "capital item," "capital outlay," or just simply "capital." Table 13-1 illustrates a capital budget for a police department. Operating and capital improvement budgets are normally acted on separately by the legislative body to which they are presented for consideration.

| Project Name | Capital Budget 1998 | Future Year Estimates | | | | |
| --- | --- | --- | --- | --- | --- | --- |
| | | 1999 | 2000 | 2001 | 2002 | 2003 |
| 1 West Station | $0 | $500,000 | $1,602,125 | $0 | $0 | $0 |
| 2 Card Access System | 12,800 | 0 | 0 | 0 | 0 | 0 |
| 3 Reconfiguration of Central Dist/Hdqtrs | 13,500 | 0 | 0 | 0 | 1,000,000 | 0 |
| 4 Executive Section Remodeling | 19,000 | 0 | 0 | 0 | 0 | 0 |
| 5 Evidence Storage/Processing Facilities | 48,800 | 0 | 0 | 0 | 0 | 0 |
| 6 East Station | 0 | 0 | 0 | 0 | 400,000 | 1,255,000 |
| 7 South Station | 0 | 0 | 0 | 0 | 0 | 0 |
| 8 Microwave Link Replacement | 0 | 258,000 | 0 | 0 | 0 | 0 |
| 9 Eastside Tower Link | 0 | 58,000 | 0 | 0 | 0 | 0 |
| 10 Add Equipment to Tower Locations | 0 | 0 | 0 | 900,000 | 0 | 0 |
| 11 Replace all MPD radios | 0 | 0 | 0 | 0 | 1,300,000 | 0 |
| 12 Optical Imaging System | 0 | 63,000 | 0 | 0 | 0 | 0 |
| **Total** | $94,100 | $879,000 | $1,602,125 | $900,000 | $2,700,000 | $1,255,000 |

*Source:* Madison, Wisconsin, Police Department.

## THE BUDGET CYCLE AND ROLES

Some governments require all their departments to budget for a two-year period called a biennium. The Kentucky State Police represents agencies that practices biennium budgeting. Most governments, however, budget for a shorter time, called a fiscal year (FY). A fiscal year is a twelve-month period that may coincide with a calendar year, although commonly its duration is from July 1 of one year until June 30 of the next; in the federal government, it is from October 1 of one year until September 30 of the following year. A budget that took effect on July 1, 2001, and terminated on June 30, 2002, would be described as the FY 02 budget. Both biennium and annual or fiscal year budgeting systems have fundamental strengths and weaknesses. The biennium approach fosters long-range planning and analysis, but it is more likely to be affected by unforeseen contingencies because of its longer time horizon. Fiscal year budgets provide for a more frequent scrutiny of programs, but they may be costly in that they emphasize thinking in small increments of time to the neglect of more sweeping considerations such as economic trends.

The budget cycle consists of four sequential steps that are repeated every year at about the same time in a well-organized government: (1) budget preparation (2) budget approval, (3) budget execution, and (4) the audit. Fiscal years and the budget cycle overlap. For example, while a police department is executing this year's budget, it will at various times be faced with an audit of last year's and the preparation of next year's. Within each of the steps, a number of things occur that affect the dynamics of budgeting and with which the police manager must be familiar to be effective.

Given that the executive budget predominates, whether in the form of the president's, a governor's, a strong mayor's, or a city manager's, this discussion of the elements of the budget cycle will assume for purposes of illustration a city manager form of government.

Long before the police department or any other unit of city government begins the preparation of its annual submission, a great deal of effort has been expended, principally within the department of finance or other similarly titled unit. Figure 13-1 depicts the general and detailed organization of such a body.

Included in this preliminary effort are revenue forecasts, determinations of how much money from existing departmental budgets will not be expended, analyses of how population shifts will affect demands for various types of public

---

**Finance Department**

**Administration Division:**
- Oversees the functions of the Finance Department
- Tracks and collects all accounts receivables
- Manages the city's debt portfolio
- Manages utility system revenue
- Provides financial management services to all city departments

**Account Division:**
- Manages annual audit, general ledger system, bank reconciliation process, debt payment, and tracking special district budgets
- Revenue collection
- Processes biweekly payroll
- Accounts for fixed assets
- Processes accounts payable checks

**Sales Tax Division:**
- Administers all provisions of the Westminster Municipal Code pertaining to sales and use taxes, admissions tax, accommodations tax and franchise fees
- Conducts field audits of businesses which are engaged in business within the city
- Processes tax receipts and handles taxpayer inquiries

**Treasury Division:**
- Administers central cashiering program for city revenues
- Administers the utility billing programs for water and sewer
- Manages the investment portfolio for the city
- Administers the banking contract for the city

**Risk Management Division:**
- Manages the workers' compensation self-insurance program
- Coordinates with the Colorado Intergovernmental Risk Sharing Agency (CIRSA)
- Oversees management of the city's property and liability insurance program
- Offers employee safety trainings, conducts facility inspections, and facilitates the meetings and activities of the City Safety Committee
- Administers contracts for employee medical and dental benefits, life insurance, survivors income benefit, and long-term disability
- Administers organization-wide wellness program, including the annual Health and Fitness Fair and various exercise challenges throughout the year

**FIGURE 13-1.** Organization of the Westminster, Colorado, Finance Department, January 30, 2000.

services, and the development of the city's budget preparation manual. Budget preparation manuals tend to focus on the technical aspects of budget, such as responsibilities, definitions, and instructions on completing forms.

Ordinarily accompanying the budget preparation manual is a memorandum from the city manager that discusses the general fiscal guidelines to be followed by the departments in preparing their budget requests. The content of this memorandum essentially reflects the data generated by the preliminary effort discussed previously, supplemented by whatever special information or priorities the city manager may have.

In some jurisdictions the city manager will formally or informally go before the city council to get members' views as to their priorities in terms of spending levels, pay raises, new hirings, and programs. This does not constitute a contract between the city manager and the council; rather, it is an exchange of information that is binding on neither but that can eliminate time-consuming and costly skirmishes later. In other jurisdictions, the council may unilaterally issue a statement of their expectations, or the city manager and department heads may have to try to establish the council's expectations through reading their statements to newspapers or informal contacts with individual council members.

An important element of the budget preparation manual is the budget preparation calendar, which is the time schedule a city follows from the time it begins to prepare a budget until the budget is approved. From the standpoint of a chief of police, there are actually two budget preparation calendars: the one established by the department of finance's budget officer and the one the police department develops that duplicates the timetable of the city's overall budget preparation but that also establishes a timetable and set of responsibilities within the police department. Table 13-2 shows an internal budget preparation calendar for a large police department.

Upon receipt of the city's budget preparation manual and the city administrator's fiscal policy memorandum, the chief of police will have the planning and research unit, assuming that this is where the department's fiscal responsibility is located as budgeting is most fundamentally a planning process, prepare the internal budget calendar and an internal fiscal policy memorandum. This material establishes the chief's priorities within the context of the directions he or she has been given, just as the city manager's fiscal policy memorandum does for the city. The budget preparation manual with the city manager's and chief's cover memorandums attached is then distributed to the police department's major units where the budget building actually takes place.

Just how far down the organizational hierarchy involvement in this process goes is related somewhat to the size of the police department. In small departments where there is little or no functional specialization, the chiefs may actually prepare the budgets alone or with minimal input from their watch commanders. In some instances, most often when the city manager has a high need for control, small department chiefs may have little or no input into preparing the budget request for their departments and may never actually see the budget under which their departments operate. In police departments sufficiently large for functional specialization, the lowest supervisory ranks in the smallest organizational entities should be involved in preparing the budget request for their own operation; when their request is completed, it is submitted to the next largest organizational entity in the police department's structure, where it is reviewed, returned for any adjustments, resubmitted, and becomes part of the request initiated by that next largest organi-

## TABLE 13-2. A Budget Preparation Calendar for a Large Police Department

| What Should Be Done | By Whom | On These Dates |
|---|---|---|
| Issue budget instructions and applicable forms | City administrator | November 1 |
| Prepare and issue budget message, with instructions and applicable forms, to unit commanders | Chief of police | November 15 |
| Develop unit budgets with appropriate justification and forward recommended budgets to planning and research unit | Unit commanders | February 1 |
| Review of unit budget | Planning and research staff with unit commanders | March 1 |
| Consolidation of unit budgets for presentation to chief of police | Planning and research unit | March 15 |
| Review of consolidated recommended budget | Chief of police, planning and research staff, and unit commanders | March 30 |
| Department approval of budget | Chief of police | April 15 |
| Recommended budget forwarded to city administrator | Chief of police | April 20 |
| Administrative review of recommended budget | City administrator and chief of police | April 30 |
| Revised budget approval | City administrator | May 5 |
| Budget document forwarded to city council | City administrator | May 10 |
| Review of budget | Budget officer of city council | May 20 |
| Presentation to council | City administrator and chief of police | June 1 |
| Reported back to city administrator | City council | June 5 |
| Review and resubmission to city council | City administrator and chief of police | June 10 |
| Final action on police budget | City council | June 20 |

zational entity. This process is repeated until each of the largest organizational entities, normally designated as bureaus, has a budget request that covers its entire operations for the forthcoming fiscal year.

The planning and research unit will then review the bureau budget requests for compliance with technical budgeting instructions and the priorities of the chief and the city manager. Here and elsewhere, there is often a great deal of communication between the police department's designated liaison with the city budget officer regarding waivers from certain requirements, clarification of guidelines, and other related matters. After any necessary adjustments are made by the bureaus, the planning and research unit will prepare a consolidated budget for the entire police department and submit it to the chief with its recommendations. Following this, the chief will have a series of meetings with the staff of the planning and research unit and the bureau commanders to discuss the department's budget.

In these meetings, the interplay of the stakes, issues, personalities, internal politics, value differences, personal agendas, and other variables create an atmosphere that is tense and sometimes heated. The chief both mediates and contributes to conflicts. One key way in which the chief contributes to mediating and promoting conflict is by using the budget as a means of rewarding "the faithful" and disciplining "the disloyal." In a very real sense, a chief can harm a subordinate's interests more than he or she can help them; programs can be cut back, assigned low priorities, and eliminated with a greater likelihood of success than can initiating requests for additional personnel, special equipment, and funds to support travel to conferences.

Also considered during these meetings between the chief and key staff members are questions of overall budget strategy. Such questions include what priorities to assign different programs, how to best justify requests, and how large a request to make. Police administrators must be able to justify the contents of their department's budget proposal. Any portion of a request for which a persuasive defense cannot be made fosters the belief in budget analysis that more, perhaps much more, of the request can be cut. This, in turn, invites even closer scrutiny and some cuts that go beyond "trimming the fat" and go to "cutting muscle and bone." However, if the city's central budget office operates in the role of "cutters" and "defenders of the public treasury," to some extent the practical question is not whether to "pad the budget," but rather where and how. This may take the form of requesting funding for one or a few programs that are justifiable, but can essentially serve as "sacrificial lambs" while at the same time not endangering the rest of the request. The alternative is to present a budget from which the chief can tolerate no cuts and hope that at some other point of consideration the essential cut funds will be restored. There is a fine point involved here; if the chief is seen as someone who simply routinely pads the budget, he or she will lose the respect and confidence of those involved in the budgetary process. If, however, the chief is skillful in these maneuvers, his or her reputation may be enhanced as being an effective advocate for the department, a programmatic innovator, and a realist who can be flexible in budget negotiations. Based on such considerations and input, the chief makes decisions and directs the planning and research unit to develop the police department's budget request that is going to be submitted to the city manager. This document is then forwarded to the city manager with a cover letter from the chief of police. This cover letter highlights the detailed budget request, calls attention to new initiatives and past successes, and may warn of consequences if funds are not forthcoming or appropriated.

The city manager will, in turn, treat the police department's budget in the same manner as the unit budgets were treated within the police department. The city manager's budget office will consolidate the requests from the various departments, the heads of which will meet with the city manager and the budget officer to discuss their requests. Subsequently, the city manager will direct the city's budget officer to make certain changes, often cuts, and prepare a draft of the citywide budget that the city manager will recommend to the council. This recommended budget will then be sent to the council with a cover letter not unlike the one the chief sent the city manager, except that it will be in the broader perspective of the city's needs and may call attention to such variables as the legal requirement for a balanced budget, that is, one in which expenditures do not exceed revenues.

**Budget Approval**   Having received the city manager's recommended budget, the city council will commence its consideration, which begins with an analysis of the budget by the council's budget officer, if it has one. Subsequently, the city manager will appear before the council to answer whatever questions the members have. At some point, the heads of each department and their key staff members may appear before the council as the budget request for their department is being considered. (See Box 13-4, an example of a State Police Superintendent appearing before the state's legislative body.) The appearance of representatives

## BOX 13-4

### Oregon State Police Superintendent Howland's Introductory Remarks at the FY 1999–2001 Legislative Budget Presentation

This budget will bring positive benefits to both Oregon citizens and public safety agencies. In addition to adding new patrol positions, this budget increases the Department's forensic and criminal identification services throughout the state. The enhancements to our statewide crime labs will allow the Department to more readily keep pace with the work load demands for forensic services in support of local law enforcement.

This budget represents the *beginning phase*, after 18 years of decline, of restoring a greater level of patrol services to local communities by the addition of 100 new uniform patrol troopers.

Although the full benefits of these positions will not be realized until after July 2001, the addition of these new patrol troopers will begin a process of bridging the public safety "service gaps" that local communities and our public safety partners have identified for State Police patrol service.

Once fully phased in, the new uniform patrol troopers will provide for an enhanced level of police response to local transportation safety and crime issues.

Today, we are not able to respond to all emergency calls for service that are received. Also, many local law enforcement agencies are having to leave their patrol areas to respond to calls for State Police service on state and interstate highways. This is because there are no patrol troopers available or close enough to take the calls.

For example, in 1997 alone, we received over 8,200 calls for service where we had no patrols available to respond. Of these, we received over 2,000 reported drunk drivers and over 5,000 driving complaints where we had no patrols available to respond.

We also had over 9,000 calls for service during 1997 that were referred to other agencies for disposition. We estimate that at least one half of these (4,500) were calls that we had no patrol available and other agencies had to respond for us. We had the same level of unanswered calls for service in 1998.

The addition of 100 new troopers positions will increase our ability to respond to calls for service and help local law enforcement agencies as well. In fact, we estimate that with these new positions over 20,000 service hours will be returned back to local law enforcement.

These new positions will also provide for a much needed increase in the availability of emergency backup for both local law enforcement agencies and our own patrol troopers that are often out there working alone in remote areas of the state.

Your Department of State Police is very grateful for the addition of 100 new uniform patrol trooper positions in this budget.

These 100 new positions represents less than one fourth of what Oregon communities have identified as State Police service gaps. Oregon communities have identified the need for an additional 316 patrol troopers that remain unfunded and unfilled.

Today, there are other funding bills being considered that would return to the legislature a future funding option from the State Highway Trust Fund. Funding a portion of the Patrol Division from the State Highway Trust Fund would represent a long term and stable funding option for filling the service gaps.

We agree that it makes sense to fund a portion of State Police uniform patrol activities from the Highway Fund as a component of highway safety.

The Department of State Police is committed to acquiring the troopers necessary to assume those state services that meet the priority needs of local communities.

In closing, I want to offer a special thanks to the representatives of Oregon TV, radio and newspaper media. Thank you for your interest in our Resource GAP Analysis budget process, for attending the many local community meetings held by our individual officers and for delivering the message of communities on the need for additional State Police troopers.

Thank you.

*Source:* Oregon State Police, June 7, 1999.

of the individual departments may be opposed by the city manager who sees such appearances as a threat to his or her power, fiscal policies, or other matters, because it presents the opportunity for department heads to get cuts made by the city manager restored to the police budget.

For example, a police department's budget requested no new personnel in accordance with the city administrator's restrictions.[18] However, when presenting the budget request to the council, police officials included a frank description of conditions, using simple and carefully selected graphics. Immediately subsequent to this presentation, the city council added 90 new positions to the police department's budget. This incident also gives rise to considering how a police administrator can be effective in obtaining funds from appropriators. In the case in which the police department got 90 new positions, the positions given to the police department required reducing the budgets of several other departments. The following represent some things believed to be important to being successful in getting appropriations:[19]

1. Have a budget that is carefully justified.
2. Anticipate the environment of the budget hearing; find out by examining news reports and through conversations the priorities of the council members. Talk to department heads who have already presented their budgets to learn what types of questions are being asked. Analyze local, regional, and national papers to identify criticisms being made of the police and current issues and innovations. For example, during 1997–2000, the New York City Police Department changed the color scheme on its 1,600 Chevrolet Caprice patrol cars, thereby saving $1,000,000 in painting costs.[20] The cars—which had been painted blue and white—are now white with green and blue stripes. Because the news media publicizes the potential for savings through such means throughout the country, alert police administrators will anticipate that their own city council members are aware of the savings created by the New York City Police Department's shift in color schemes and will be prepared to respond to their questions about the feasibility of making a similar shift.
3. Determine which "public" will be at the police department's budget hearing and prepare accordingly. As the issues change from year to year, so will the portion of the community that is sufficiently aroused to participate in these proceedings. A child killed by a vehicle while crossing an unguarded intersection, a series of violent robberies in the downtown area, the rapes of several elderly women, and incidents of "gay bashing" are likely to mobilize such groups as the parent–teacher association, the chamber of commerce and the merchants association, the Grey Panthers, or gay rights groups.
4. Help shape the environment by planting questions with sympathetic council members, the answers to which put the police department in a favorable light.
5. Make good use of graphics (Figure 13-2). In budget presentations the use of carefully selected colors adds to the impact of graphics. In using graphics it is

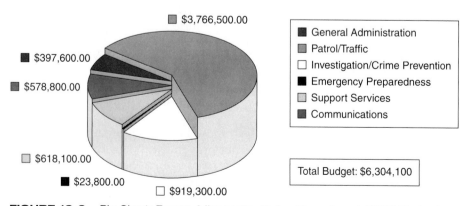

**FIGURE 13-2.** Pie Chart: Eagen, Minnesota, Police Department FY'99 Budget.

important to be selective and not "go overboard"; short case histories of police successes are natural and potent adjuncts to graphics.

6. Rehearse and critique the presentation several times using role playing; the use of videotaping is especially helpful in this regard.

7. Have the physical layout checked before the presentation so it is known where electrical outlets are, where the screen should be situated, and if an extension cord is needed for any audiovisual equipment.

8. Develop a reputation for being an able and economical administrator.

9. Take advantage of unusual situations to dramatize the need for special police equipment or additional personnel.

10. Be a political realist.

After the police and all other departments have appeared before it, the city council will give directions to the city manager. These directions may take any of several forms, such as cutting the overall city budget request by $1.5 million with or without any guidance as to where the cuts are to be made or directing that certain programs cut by the manager be reinstated, again with or without guidance in where to find the funds. When all adjustments are made to the satisfaction of the city council, the budget is adopted by the passage of an ordinance by a simple majority vote.

Table 13-3 shows the approval process for the Sausalito Police Department. Note that the columns show "FY '98 Actual Expenditures" (which include the original budget, plus or minus any amendments to it); a "First Nine Months of FY '99 Expenditures" column (the actual expenditures and encumbrances through September 30, 1999); a column for "Requested Change for FY '00"; and a final column labeled "City Council Approved Changes for FY '00" (the budget with which the police department starts its next fiscal year). Budget formats are discussed in detail later in this chapter. For present purposes, it is sufficient here to point out that Table 13-3 is the line-item budget format.

A city's comprehensive budget approval document would reflect: (1) the police department's original request; (2) the amount recommended by the mayor or city manager; (3) the amount of spending endorsed by the council; (4) the dollar amount of increase or decrease; and (5) the percentage change.

## Budget Execution

The budget execution function has four objectives:

1. To provide for an orderly manner in which the police department's approved objectives for the fiscal year are to be achieved.

2. To ensure that no commitments or expenditures by the police department are undertaken, except in pursuance of authorizations made by the city council.

3. To conserve the resources of the police department that are not legitimately required to achieve the approved objectives.

4. To provide for a suitable accounting, at appropriate intervals, of the manner in which the chief's stewardship over entrusted resources has been discharged.[21]

These objectives are supported by three different mechanisms: (1) a system of allotment, (2) accounting controls, and (3) management controls.[22]

## The Allotment System

Once an appropriations ordinance has been enacted by the city council, money can be expended legally by that unit of government. Once this has happened, it is theoretically the responsibility of the city's finance office to

**TABLE 13-3. The FY '00 Budget Approval Process**

| Account Number | Wages & Benefits | FY '98 Actual Expenditures | First 9 Months of FY '99 Expenditures | Revised FY '99 Budget | Requested Change for FY '00 | City Council Approved Change for FY '00 |
|---|---|---|---|---|---|---|
| 601 005 | Salaries | 1,350,994 | 1,040,724 | 1,417,456 | 72,460 | 1,489,916 |
| 601 008 | Deferred Comp | 114 | 421 | 576 | 18 | 594 |
| 601 010 | Wages | — | 89,358 | 123,000 | — | 123,000 |
| 601 014 | Training Overtime | 24,045 | 15,275 | 27,000 | — | 27,000 |
| 601 015 | Overtime | 57,381 | 65,777 | 78,000 | (18,000) | 60,000 |
| 601 020 | Holiday Pay | 37,688 | 21,210 | 41,931 | 2,489 | 44,420 |
| 601 045 | Retirement | 27,011 | 16,953 | 19,663 | (7,092) | 12,571 |
| 601 050 | Safety Retirement | 167,301 | 146,808 | 207,649 | (83,723) | 123,926 |
| 601 052 | Medicare Taxes | 13,111 | 16,768 | 23,685 | 481 | 24,166 |
| 601 060 | Health Insurance | 98,905 | 80,260 | 110,000 | 10,019 | 120,019 |
| 601 080 | Uniform Allowance | 16,820 | 15,747 | 17,230 | (955) | 16,275 |
| | **SUB TOTAL** | **1,793,370** | **1,509,301** | **2,066,190** | **(24,303)** | **2,041,888** |

| Account Number | Services & Supplies | FY '98 Actual Expenditures | First 9 Months of FY '99 Expenditures | Revised FY '99 Budget | Requested Change for FY '00 | City Council Approved Change for FY '00 |
|---|---|---|---|---|---|---|
| 601 120 | Books & Periodicals | 1,126 | 431 | 1,000 | — | 1,000 |
| 601 125 | Chemicals & Gases | 416 | — | 200 | — | 200 |
| 601 135 | Clothing & Uniforms | — | 107 | 820 | — | 820 |
| 601 150 | Equipment Parts | 8,091 | 7,279 | 9,400 | 600 | 10,000 |
| 601 160 | Firearms | 1,948 | 1,235 | 2,000 | 500 | 2,500 |
| 601 165 | Foods | 775 | 393 | 550 | 250 | 800 |
| 601 175 | Fuel | 19,734 | 15,512 | 20,000 | — | 20,000 |
| 601 190 | Hardware Supplies | 359 | 187 | 400 | — | 400 |
| 601 205 | Identification Markers | 1,573 | 1,852 | 2,000 | 600 | 2,600 |
| 601 210 | Janitorial Supplies | 232 | 529 | 500 | — | 500 |
| 601 230 | Miscellaneous | 2,595 | 7,961 | 9,000 | 1,600 | 10,600 |
| 601 235 | Office Supplies | 5,858 | 2,290 | 5,500 | — | 5,500 |
| 601 250 | Photography Supplies | 1,231 | 962 | 1,200 | — | 1,200 |
| 601 270 | Safety & Protection | 4,892 | 456 | 5,000 | — | 5,000 |
| 601 310 | Surety Bond | 500 | 500 | 500 | — | 500 |
| 601 355 | Building Maintenance | 799 | 335 | 750 | — | 750 |
| 601 370 | Equip. Maintenance | 17,162 | 8,218 | 14,000 | 7,500 | 21,500 |
| 601 375 | Auto. Maintenance | 9,200 | 8,787 | 10,000 | — | 10,000 |
| 601 410 | Conferences, Meetings | 2,788 | 2,120 | 3,000 | 600 | 3,600 |
| 601 440 | Memberships & Dues | 1,926 | 1,905 | 2,000 | 1,570 | 3,570 |
| 601 445 | Mileage & Bridge Tolls | 153 | 128 | 180 | — | 180 |
| 601 510 | Education & Training | 13,347 | 9,362 | 14,000 | — | 14,000 |
| 601 530 | Janitorial Services | 390 | — | 1,000 | — | 1,000 |
| 601 560 | Other Professional | 306,069 | 200,268 | 296,823 | — | 279,092 |
| 601 575 | Postage | 2,420 | 1,752 | 2,000 | — | 2,000 |
| 601 580 | Printing & Copying | 5,163 | 1,265 | 4,000 | 3,500 | 7,500 |
| 601 630 | Building Rent | 41,519 | 31,139 | 41,640 | — | 41,640 |
| 601 655 | Equipment Rental | 210 | 378 | 378 | (68) | 310 |
| 601 670 | Utilities | 31,303 | 18,615 | 25,000 | 3,000 | 28,000 |
| 601 760 | Depreciation | 24,766 | 18,575 | 24,766 | — | 24,766 |
| 601 810 | Auto Equipment | 23,334 | 23,028 | 23,028 | 972 | 24,000 |
| 601 840 | Office Equipment | 12,237 | 2,704 | 7,900 | (5,100) | 2,800 |
| 601 845 | Other Equipment | 11,063 | 3,900 | 4,550 | 18,050 | 28,600 |
| 601 855 | Radio Equipment | 6,401 | — | 0 | — | — |
| 601 922 | Encumbrances | 4,523 | 43,620 | 0 | — | — |
| | **SUB TOTAL** | **564,103** | **415,793** | **533,085** | **33,573** | **554,928** |
| | **GRAND TOTAL** | **2,357,473** | **1,925,094** | **2,599,275** | **9,271** | **2,596,816** |

*Source:* Sausalito, California, Police Department.

break each department's approved budget up into allocations for specific periods of time. When actually used, this procedure—referred to ordinarily as the allotment system—usually employs a three-month period known as a quarter. However, because the spending patterns of the various departments do not fall into neat "quarters" and vary widely, establishing the actual needs of each department is a time-consuming process. Therefore, despite the attention that allotment systems receive in the literature, many units of government have elected to rely on other mechanisms, such as budget status reports, as a means of monitoring spending and exercising control.

**Accounting Controls**

A police department's budget officer, acting on behalf of the chief, will have a system of accounts to ensure that expenditures do not exceed the available resources. Separate budget ledgers are established for the major cost centers involved. Figure 13-3 illustrates the use of cost centers. Expenditures must be authorized by means of appropriate forms and supporting documents. The police department's budget officer wields considerable power in this regard, and occasionally his or her decisions will be appealed to the chief.

Here a certain dilemma exists that must be dealt with on a case-by-case basis: if the chief supports too many appeals, the budget officer loses some effectiveness and the chief may find him- or herself deluged with appeals; if no appeals are supported, the police department may lose some effectiveness because of the lack of equipment or may lose the chance to capitalize on some unusual opportunity.

Periodic reports on accounts are an important element of control in that they serve to reduce the likelihood of overspending. Additionally, they identify areas in which deficits are likely to occur. Although police agencies budget

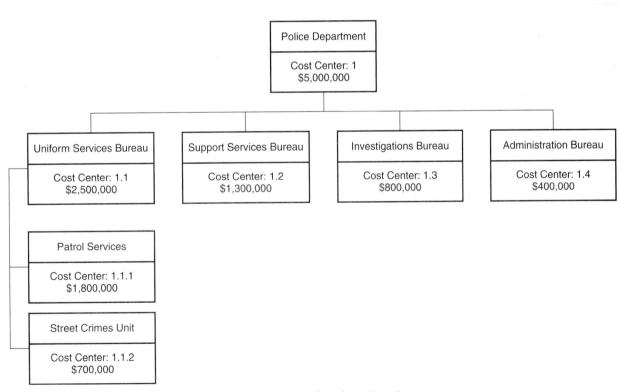

**FIGURE 13-3.** Illustration of major cost centers in a police department.

for unusual contingencies, deficits may occur because of increased gasoline prices, extensive overtime, natural disasters, or other causes. Table 13-4 is a budget status report; from the standpoint of managerial use, it incorporates several deficiencies:

1. The "% Used" column reflects only the total in the "Expenses to date" column without consideration of the amount obligated, but for which no disbursements have been made. This leads to a misimpression as to the amount of funds actually available for use.
2. There is no provision for comparing the percentage of the budget used with the percentage of the budget year that has lapsed to make some judgment about the coinciding of expenditures with the passage of time.

**Management Controls** The last element of budget execution is management controls, without which financial controls are incomplete. Management controls reach down and throughout a police department to regulate the use of resources. Often, the character of these controls is prospective in that they prevent financial obligations from being incurred. Examples include a chief's placing a freeze on hiring or requiring that, when a specific percentage of expenditures in budget cat-

**TABLE 13-4.   A Police Department's Budget Status Report, January 31, 2000**

| Line Item | Amount Budgeted | Expenses to Date | Amount Obligated | Balance to Date | % Used |
|---|---|---|---|---|---|
| Salaries | $1,710,788 | $848,161.05 | $ 0.00 | $862,626.95 | 49.58% |
| Training | 15,000 | 5,374.47 | 6,098.00 | 3,527.53 | 35.83 |
| Professional services | 1,000 | 828.40 | 115.00 | 56.60 | 82.84 |
| Travel | 4,500 | 2,077.55 | 834.06 | 1,588.39 | 46.17 |
| Dues and subscriptions | 1,021 | 383.83 | 164.11 | 473.06 | 37.59 |
| Communications | 19,557 | 8,669.28 | 1,273.01 | 9,614.71 | 44.33 |
| Utilities | 35,000 | 17,213.81 | 1,420.36 | 16,365.83 | 49.18 |
| Office supplies | 21,000 | 7,988.76 | 3,274.99 | 9,736.25 | 38.04 |
| Printing | 7,000 | 3,725.43 | 1,854.75 | 1,419.82 | 53.22 |
| Repairs to equipment | 55,129 | 25,979.00 | 3,363.11 | 25,786.89 | 47.12 |
| Real property maintenance | 4,500 | 2,946.50 | 374.28 | 1,179.22 | 65.48 |
| Equipment leasing | 2,600 | 1,438.71 | 352.39 | 808.90 | 55.34 |
| Riot agents | 1,000 | 0.00 | 0.00 | 1,000.00 | 0.00 |
| Ammunition | 2,500 | 524.07 | 745.00 | 1,230.93 | 20.96 |
| Investigation fee | 4,000 | 2,057.46 | 538.00 | 1,404.54 | 51.44 |
| Xerox | 7,000 | 2,370.36 | 625.60 | 4,204.04 | 33.86 |
| Fuel and lubricants | 108,000 | 42,103.88 | 10,000.00 | 55,896.12 | 38.99 |
| Janitorial supplies | 4,000 | 1,082.73 | 808.46 | 2,308.81 | 27.07 |
| Uniforms | 31,500 | 10,004.56 | 3,955.75 | 17,539.69 | 31.76 |
| Protective equipment | 6,530 | 1,007.18 | 1,118.31 | 4,404.51 | 15.42 |
| Intoximeter | 800 | 220.53 | 82.60 | 496.87 | 27.57 |
| Cash match | 812 | 0.00 | 0.00 | 0.00 | 0.00 |
| Pistol team | 1,500 | 803.96 | 681.10 | 14.94 | 53.60 |
| Swat team | 3,000 | 66.74 | 600.00 | 2,333.26 | 2.22 |
| Capital teams | 84,173 | 13,713.62 | 63,685.82 | 6,773.56 | 16.29 |

egories is reached, his or her approval is required for any additional expenditures or obligations. Management controls are also retrospective in that a chief may have to initiate corrective action.

Illustrative of this would be preparing a budget amendment request to take surplus funds from one account to cover an account in which a deficit exists. Transfer-of-funds requests go from the police department to the city's budget officer, through the city manager, and to the city council for their approval if they exceed any latitude given to the city manager by the council for budget administration.

Management controls may also be both retrospective and prospective; the midyear review affords the chief and his command staff the opportunity to examine financial performance and progress toward departmental objectives during the first half of the fiscal year and to plan and take any necessary corrective action for the remaining period. Monitoring actions will occur on a more frequent basis, such as monthly or quarterly, but the midyear review represents a major milestone.

The term *audit* refers to the act of verifying something independently.[23] (See Box 13–5). The basic rationale for an audit has been expressed in the following way:

**The Audit**

> A fundamental tenet of a democratic society holds that governments and agencies entrusted with public resources and the authority for applying them have a responsibility to render a full accounting of their activities. This accountability is inherent in the governmental process and is not always specifically identified by legislative provision. This governmental accountability should identify not only the object for which the public resources have been devoted but also the manner and effect of their application.[24]

Audits are concerned with three broad areas of accountability: (1) financial, which focuses on determining whether the financial operations of the police department are conducted properly, whether its reports are presented accurately, and whether it has complied with the applicable laws and regulations; (2) management, which concerns whether the police chief and his subordinate managers are using resources in an efficient and economical manner, along with the identification of any cases of inadequate, inefficient, or uneconomical practices; and (3) program, which determines whether the benefits and objectives that the city council intended to arise and achieve from the operation of the police department during the fiscal year were actually created and attained, along with the causes of any nonperformance.[25]

Figure 13-4 depicts the participants in the audit process; those in the role of auditors vary—for example, they may be part of a state's system of monitoring local finances or, if that provision does not exist, they may be representatives of private-sector firms that complement the city's internal audit function. Auditors look for

1. Unauthorized transfers of funds between accounts
2. Failure to compile and submit financial reports punctually
3. Year-end accounting manipulations that move liabilities from one fiscal year to the next
4. The use of commingled accounts to disguise the use of grant funds for unauthorized purposes

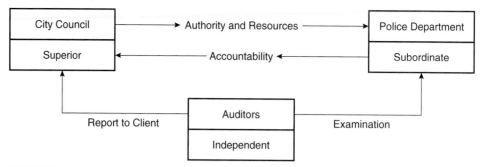

**FIGURE 13-4.** The audit process and roles.

5. Improper computations
6. The disbursements of funds without adequate documentation
7. The use of bond proceeds for projects other than those authorized
8. Expenditures in excess of appropriations
9. The lack of compliance with established bidding procedures[26]

Before the audit report is submitted, it will be discussed with the chief of police, and any errors of fact or representation in the report will be adjusted. Matters relating to differences of opinion or judgment between the auditors and the chief are usually the subject of a letter from the chief to the city council. After reviewing the auditor's report, the city council may request the formal appearance of the chief to discuss the report or direct the city manager to cause any corrective action required to be initiated.

Although audits may reveal weaknesses and thus are a source of potential professional embarrassment, police managers should welcome them because of the advantages they hold for improved information for decision making, the potential to increase the police department's effectiveness and efficiency, and the opportunity to correct deficiencies that might otherwise lead to the loss of grant funds or other negative consequences.

## BUDGET FORMATS

At the turn of this century, there was nothing that resembled the budget cycle just described. The situation in California was portrayed by Governor Young as follows:

> When I first entered the legislature in 1909 there was little short of chaos as far as any orderly provisions for state expenditures were concerned. There had been no audit of state finances for over twenty years. The finance committees of the two houses were scenes of a blind scramble on the part of the various institutions and departments of the state in an endeavor to secure as large a portion as possible of whatever money might happen to be in the treasury. Heads of institutions encamped night after night at the committee rooms, each alert for his own interest regardless of the interests of other institutions.[27]

Not only were other states similarly situated, but conditions were not any better in local governments at that time; cities had not yet recovered from the havoc wrought by political rings stealing and squandering enormous sums of public money in earlier years, and waste and extravagance flourished.[28] There were no systematic procedures for handling fiscal matters, there was no comprehensive or long-term financial planning, the total cost of operating a city's government was often unknown or suspect, and one could not tell in advance if the year would end with a surplus or deficit.[29] The practices of the federal government were not sharply differentiated from those of the state and local governments of that time. In 1885, eight committees of the House of Representatives had authority to recommend appropriations; later, this was increased to ten. The Senate was not far behind with appropriating authority given to eight of its standing committees.[30] The assertion of Senator Aldrich in 1909 that the Congress had enacted $50 million of wasteful appropriations gave dramatic publicity to the need for reform.[31]

The center of power in budgeting at the turn of the century was with the legislative body; the following factors characterized legislative budgeting at that time:

1. There was no central official who was empowered to review or revise departmental estimates or to make recommendations to the legislature.
2. Most frequently each department's requests were submitted separately, often at different times.
3. Each agency classified accounts in its own way.
4. Departmental requests were often presented as a lump sum without supporting detail.
5. Requests were not related in any way to revenues anticipated.
6. Each department bargained separately with the appropriations committees.
7. There was little or no supervision of department spending.[32]

Illustrative of several of these points is that when President Taft prepared a budget for the national government for the 1914 fiscal year and submitted it to Congress, it was coldly received and practically ignored.[33] However, strong forces were at work that led to budgeting reforms at all levels of government. The most significant development was the advent of the executive budget, in which every department submitted its estimates to the chief executive of the unit of government involved or a designated representative, creating centralized control. Centralized control hastened, if not made possible, standardized budget cycles, budget formats, and other tools.

The forces that contributed to budgeting reforms include the writings about municipal corruption by such "muckrakers" as Ida Tarbell, Ray Baker, and Lincoln Steffens;[34] the 1899 Model Municipal Corporation Act, which proposed a budget system under the direct supervision of the mayor; the influence of the scientific management movement; the formation of the New York Bureau of Municipal Research in 1906, which brought together such luminaries as Frederick Cleveland, William Allen, and Henry Bruère, who undertook an immediate study of New York City's budgeting and published in 1907 the influential *Making a Municipal Budget;*[35] the good government and city manager movements during the second decade of the century; and the 1916 issuance of a model city charter by the National Municipal League. It is interesting to note that the rise of the executive budget, with its centralized control and standardized budget cycles and formats developed in the cities, spread to the states between 1915 and 1925[36] and only appeared in the federal government in 1921 with the passage of the Budget and Accounting Act.

The flow of these events is important from two key perspectives; first, it accounts for the control orientation of the first budget format widely adopted; second, it underpins the notion that each prevailing budget format is understood and appreciated best as a product of the period in which it evolved.

Six different budget formats are covered in the sections that follow. Some have enjoyed a period of dominance, but these periods are difficult to identify precisely because the rhetoric of the budget literature and actual practices do not always coincide. The *line-item budget* remains the single most commonly employed budget format and is associated generally with the period 1915 to just after World War II. *Performance budgets* came into vogue following World War II until about 1960. The *planning-programming budget system* was a dominant theme in the literature from 1960 to 1971, but it was never practiced widely outside of the federal government. *Programmatic budgets* evolved during the early 1970s, and variants of it presently abound. *Zero-based budgets* gained attention in the literature in the early 1970s, but they have not been adopted widely by state and local governments. *Hybrid budgets* have always existed, and in actual practice most budgets incorporate features of several different formats.

When attempting to decide which type of a budget a police department uses, the test is not which label is applied—because labels are often used almost indiscriminately—but rather what the emphasis of the format is.

## The Line-Item or Object-of-Expenditure Budget

The line-item or object-of-expenditure budget[37] is the oldest and simplest of budget types. It is the basic system on which all other budget types rely because of its excellence as a control device. As suggested by Table 13-5, the line-item budget derives its identity from its character; every amount requested, recommended, appropriated, and expended is associated with a particular item or class of items; it is therefore described as an input-oriented budget. A budgetary format keyed to objects of expenditure fosters control in a number of ways:

1. Control is comprehensive because no item escapes scrutiny.
2. There are multiple points at which control can be exercised.
3. Control is exact in that expenditures for very specific items can be regulated.[38]

The structure of a line-item budget typically involves the use of about four major categories, each of which has a number of standardly defined categories that are used throughout city government. In police departments large enough for functional specialization, there will be an overall budget and the budget will be broken down into smaller line-item budgets for the various organizational entities such as patrol, investigation, and crime prevention. These smaller budgets serve further to facilitate control and serve as the basis of allocations within the police department. Workload indicators for past years and the forthcoming budget year may also be included as part of a line-item budget. Typically such things as numbers of (1) arrests by various categories, (2) calls for service, (3) traffic and parking citations, (4) accident investigations, and (5) criminal investigations, along with other indicators, such as miles patrolled, will be included.

The line-item budget has five rather straightforward advantages: (1) it is easy to construct; (2) because incremental changes in the appropriations are made annually on the basis of the history of expenditures, the likelihood of the police department having a budget that is grossly inadequate is reduced;

TABLE 13-5.   The Mishawaka, Indiana, 1999 Police Budget

1 PERSONAL SERVICES

*Salaries and Wages*

| | | | |
|---|---|---|---|
| 411-01 | Police Chief | 42,434.00 | |
| 411-02 | Assistant Chief | | |
| | 3 @ 38,935.00 | 116,805.00 | |
| 411-03 | Captains | | |
| | 5 @ 35,371.00 | 212,226.00 | |
| 411-04 | Lieutenants | | |
| | 10 @ 34,641.00 | 346,410.00 | |
| 411-05 | Sergeants | | |
| | 17 @ 33,933.00 | 576,861.00 | |
| 411-06 | Corporals | | |
| | 42 @ 33,451.00 | 1,404,942.00 | |
| 411-07 | Patrol Officer | | |
| | 20 @ 31,451.00 | 629,020.00 | |
| 411-08 | Executive Secretary | 21,007.00 | |
| 411-09 | Administrative Secretary | | |
| | 3 @ 20,815.00 | 62,445.00 | |
| 411-10 | Secretaries/Transcriptionist | | |
| | 5 @ 20,511.00 | 102,555.00 | |
| 411-11 | Desk Personnel | | |
| | 6 @ 23,183.00 | 139,098.00 | |
| 411-12 | Parking Personnel | 20,511.00 | |
| 411-13 | Janitor 2 @ 20,142.00 | 40,284.00 | |
| 411-14 | Radio Systems Coordinator | 27,040.00 | |
| 411-15 | Administrative Assistant/ | | |
| | Property Clerk | 23,300.00 | |
| 411-17 | Training Coordinator | 26,282.00 | |
| 411-30 | Crossing Guards 20 @ 4,957 | 99,140.00 | |
| 411-60 | Substitute Crossing Guard | 2,000.00 | |
| 411-18 | Dispatch Shift Supervisor | | |
| | 3 @ 23,683 | <u>70,149.00</u> | 3,962,509.00 |

*Employee Benefits*

| | | | |
|---|---|---|---|
| 413-05 | Group Life Ins | 7,500.00 | |
| 413-06 | Uniform Allowance | | |
| | 99 @ 1,175.00 | 107,000.00 | |
| 413-92 | Holiday Pay | | |
| | 99 @ 1,654.00 | 163,746.00 | |
| 413-94 | Uniform Allowance/Parking | 500.00 | |
| 413-95 | Uniform Allowance/Cross | | |
| | Guards 20 @ 170.00 | <u>3,400.00</u> | 282,146.00 |

*Other Personal Services*

| | | | |
|---|---|---|---|
| 415-91 | Overtime/Court-time | <u>300,000.00</u> | <u>300,000.00</u> |
| | | | 4,544,655.00 |

2 SUPPLIES

*Office Supplies*

| | | | |
|---|---|---|---|
| 421-02 | Printing Supplies | 8,000.00 | |
| 421-90 | Office Supplies | 13,000.00 | |

*(continued)*

**TABLE 13-5.   (continued)**

| | | | |
|---|---|---:|---:|
| *Operating Supplies* | | | |
| 422-35 | Photo Supplies | 6,800.00 | |
| 422-36 | Flares, Ammunition, Etc. | 12,000.00 | |
| 422-37 | Polygraph Supplies | 150.00 | |
| 422-38 | Batteries/Radio Supplies | 5,000.00 | |
| 422-39 | Miscellaneous Supplies | 2,500.00 | |
| *Repairs and Maintenance Supplies* | | | |
| 423-90 | Equipment Repair Supplies | 5,000.00 | |
| 423-91 | Building Maintenance Supplies | 7,500.00 | |
| *Other Supplies* | | | |
| 429-10 | Seminar Supplies/ Refreshments | 500.00 | |
| 429-92 | Community Relations Supplies | <u>4,500.00</u> | 64,950.00 |
| 3  OTHER SERVICES AND CHARGES | | | |
| *Professional Services* | | | |
| 431-05 | New Hire Testing | 7,000.00 | |
| 431-15 | Computer Upgrades/ Support | 6,000.00 | |
| *Repairs and Maintenance* | | | |
| 436-02 | Radio/Equipment Repair | 5,000.00 | |
| 436-91 | Service Contracts | 29,000.00 | |
| 436-92 | Building Repair/Maintenance | 9,000.00 | |
| 436-93 | Computer Maintenance | 5,000.00 | |
| *Other Services and Charges* | | | |
| 439-03 | Procedure Update Project | | |
| 439-04 | Civil Defense | 4,000.00 | |
| 439-05 | Special Expense | 9,000.00 | |
| 439-09 | Miscellaneous Charges | 950.00 | |
| 439-90 | Subscriptions, Dues, Etc. | 2,000.00 | |
| 439-91 | Travel and Training | 40,000.00 | |
| 439-94 | Canine Expenses | 3,000.00 | |
| 439-95 | Crime Stoppers Program | 5,000.00 | |
| 439-96 | Youth Services Bureau | <u>7,500.00</u> | 132,450.00 |
| 4  CAPITAL OUTLAYS | | | |
| *Machinery and Equipment* | | | |
| 444-01 | Equipment/Furnishings | 30,000.00 | |
| 444-03 | Maintenance Equipment | 4,000.00 | |
| 444-04 | Law Enforcement Equipment | 36,000.00 | |
| 444-05 | Training Equipment/ Supplies | 4,000.00 | |
| 444-06 | Computer Upgrades | 7,000.00 | |
| *Other Capital Outlays* | | | |
| 449-01 | Safety Vests | 16,875.00 | |
| 449-90 | Clothing/Equipment (New officers) | <u>20,000.00</u> | <u>117,875.00</u> |
| | | | 4,859,930.00 |

*Source:* Mishawaka, Indiana, Police Department.

(3) it is easy to understand; (4) it is easy to administer; and (5) control is comprehensive. On balance, there are also some clear disadvantages to this budget format: (1) the emphasis on control results in an orientation toward the input to the detriment of managing toward results; (2) long-range planning is neglected; (3) any correlations between the input and results occur at only a very gross level, such as numbers of arrests made; and (4) it has limited utility with respect to evaluating performance.

As a final note, the line-item budget format tends to favor continuation of the police department's status quo—a disadvantage to the reform chief but an advantage to one who has less energy and drive.

The key characteristic of a performance budget is that it relates the types and volume of work to be done to the amount of money spent.[39] As an efficiency-oriented tool, the performance budget can be described as input-output centered. The single most important consequence of performance budgeting is that it increases the responsibility and accountability of police managers for output as opposed to input.[40] As a management-oriented system, the performance budget incorporates the following features:

1. A cost structure consisting of the various programs under which related functions or activities are clustered
2. A detailed system of work-load and unit-cost measures
3. A line-item component for fiscal control

**The Performance Budget**

Although the origin of the performance budget is not universally agreed upon, public-sector milestones in the advocacy of its elements and its use and places of adoption are identifiable. This lack of agreement is perhaps best accounted for by the fact that performance budgeting did not spring into use fully developed but rather evolved over time.

In 1912 the Taft Commission on Economy and Efficiency, which opposed the line-item format, recommended one element associated with performance budgeting—the organization of expenditures around the types of work being done. From 1913 to 1915, the Borough of Richmond, New York City, experimented with a cost data budget,[41] and during the 1920s, periodic mention of this type of budget appeared in the literature.[42] As early as 1939, the Municipal Finance Officers Association advocated a model emphasizing activities grouped under functions. The U.S. Department of Agriculture worked with project and activity budgeting in 1934, and about the same time the Tennessee Valley Authority employed a budget classification of programs and accomplishments.[43] Shortly following the adoption of the city manager form of government in Richmond, Virginia, in 1948, a performance-type budget was implemented.[44]

These various developments received both attention and impetus with the report of the first Hoover Commission in 1949, which called for adoption of a format referred to specifically as a "performance budget." This recommendation was reinforced by the report of the second Hoover Commission in 1955, which applauded the progress made and called for even greater use. In 1950, the federal Budget and Accounting Procedures Act, although not specifically using the term *performance budgeting*, gave further encouragement to its use. Cincinnati began experiments with performance budgeting in about 1950,[45] Maryland adopted it in 1952,[46] and Boston followed in 1955.[47] During the 1950s and very early 1960s, a number of cities experimented with it, including San Diego, Cleveland, Phoenix, Rochester, and Los Angeles.[48]

The advantages of the performance budget include (1) a consideration of outputs; (2) the establishment of the costs of various police efforts; (3) an improvement in the evaluation of programs and key managers; (4) an emphasis on the responsibility of police managers for output; (5) an emphasis on efficiency; (6) the increased availability of information for managerial decision making; (7) the enhancement of budget justification and explanation; and (8) an increased responsibility of police managers, which leads to some decentralization and thus greater participation.

The disadvantages of the performance budget include (1) its expense to develop, implement, and operate given the extensive use of cost accounting techniques and the need for additional staff (Figure 13-5 shows the complexity of using cost accounting to determine total costs); (2) the difficulty and controversies surrounding choosing appropriate work-load and unit-cost measures; (3) the tendency to generate data more suitable for police managers than for policy makers; (4) its emphasis on efficiency rather than effectiveness; (5) its failure to lend itself to long-range planning; (6) the questionable need, according to police managers, for much of the data; and (7) its frequent inability to relate community needs systematically to police work-load and unit-cost measures.

**The Planning-Programming Budgeting System (PPBS)**

In principle, PPBS or PPB was born and died in the federal government, and its use in state and local government was always negligible. An understanding of it is, however, important in that it is a significant segment of the literature of budgeting and represents part of the stream of thinking and practice devoted to improving budgeting.

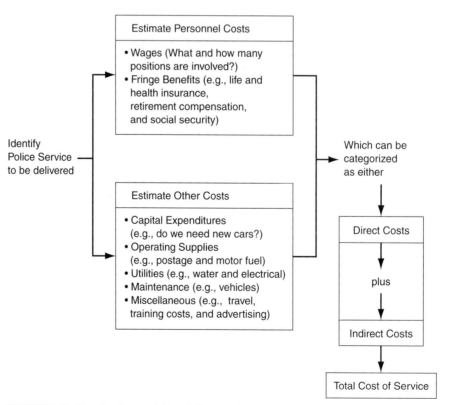

**FIGURE 13-5.** Costing out the delivery of police services.

To some extent every budget system incorporates planning, management, and control processes.[49] However, only one of these processes can predominate. Although PPBS treated the three basic budget processes as compatible and complementary, they were not regarded as equal; PPBS was predicated on the primacy of planning.[50] This future orientation of PPBS was to transform budgeting from an "annual ritual" into "formulation of future goals and policies"[51] on a long-range basis. Thus, the singularly unique function of PPBS was to implement policy choices by allocating the resources necessary for their accomplishment. The characteristics of a classical PPBS system include

1. A program structure
2. Zero-based budgeting, to be discussed in detail later in this chapter
3. The use of cost-budget analysis to distinguish between alternatives
4. The use of a budgetary time horizon, often five years
5. The systematic relating of the three basic budgetary processes by a crosswalk system to provide a diversified and comprehensive information base.

General Motors documents reveal that in 1924 it was using a basic PPBS method to identify major objectives, to define programs essential to these goals, and to allocate resources accordingly.[52] The RAND Corporation was a major contributor to the development of PPBS in a series of studies dating from 1949.[53] By the mid-1950s a few states such as California, Illinois, Kentucky, Washington, North Carolina, and Pennsylvania were using elements of a PPBS system. It remained, however, for Secretary Robert McNamara to introduce PPBS into the Department of Defense for the system to emerge fully in government. In 1965 President Johnson issued a directive calling for its use in the federal government. The "Five-Five-Five" project, fully operational in 1967, sought to test a "true" PPBS system in five states, counties, and cities.[54]

One survey revealed that only 28 percent of the cities and 21 percent of the contacted counties had implemented a PPBS system or significant elements of it.[55] Also in 1971, the death of PPBS was announced in the federal government by a memorandum from the Office of Management and Budget. The general interest in PPBS faded rapidly as did its practice in the few states and local governments that had adopted it.

Implied and partial explanations of the demise of PPBS are sprinkled throughout the literature and include "fantastic terminological tangles used with a false sophistication" and the absence of a precise definition of PPBS.[56] Because PPBS was born and died in the federal government, analysis of its demise there is most appropriate. The most lucid and complete dissection of PPBS becoming an "unthing" in federal agencies is provided by Schick,[57] who attributes the following factors as leading to its death:

1. PPBS failed because it did not penetrate the vital routes of putting together and justifying a budget. Always separate, but never equal, the analysts had little influence over the form or content of the budget.
2. Many analysts failed to comprehend the connection between their work and budgeting. Because they came to PPBS with little administrative or budgetary experience, they did not recognize that the fate of analysis hinges on its use in budgeting.
3. The government-wide application of the Department of Defense's PPBS gave little consideration to the preferences or problems of individual departments.

4. For all its talk about an integrated planning and budgetary system, the Bureau of the Budget kept the two apart, quarantining its tiny PPBS operation from the powerful budget review staffs and promulgating separate PPBS and budget instructions.

5. PPBS had become a threat to budgeters and an embarrassment to reformers, reminding the latter of their failure to deliver and the former of the inadequacies of their process.

6. PPBS was introduced without much preparation, inadequate support, and a leadership with too few resources to invest in its behalf.

7. There was neither an adequate number of analysts nor sufficient data, and PPBS did not have enough time to make up the deficit.

8. The implementors of PPBS were arrogantly insensitive to budgetary traditions, institutional loyalties, and personal relationships.

9. PPBS was conceived almost exclusively from an executive perspective, as if Congress did not exist.

10. PPBS failed to penetrate because budgeters did not let it in and PPBS'ers did not know how to break down the resistance.

The explanation that PPBS failed because of agency subversion is rejected by Schick, who feels that most departments gave it a try.[58] Another explanation rejected by Schick is that offered by Thompson, who contends that the emphasis on rationality and analysis is at odds with the American political process.[59] Among the police departments that employed a PPBS at one time are those in Phoenix, Arizona; Dayton, Ohio; Dade County, Florida; and San Diego, California.

## The Programmatic or Results Budget

*Programmatic* or *program budget* is a term that has been used to describe a variety of practices. In the 1950s and 1960s, it referred to, along with functional or activity budgets, simply using programs as cost centers with little additional data. During the 1960s and early 1970s, it was a popular shorthand used to refer to a PPBS system. In the contemporary sense, it refers to budgets that emphasize the results achieved or outcomes produced.

While the literature of budgeting and the practice of federal budgeting was being dominated by PPBS from 1960 to 1971, the practice of local governmental budgeting was quietly undergoing change. Performance budgeting, with its emphasis on work-load and cost measures, did not disappear entirely, and there was considerable interest in the achievement of policy aspects of PPBS. The result was the evolution of a budget type that incorporated features from the performance and PPBS formats and is referred to as a results, outcomes, objectives, or programmatic—in the contemporary sense—budget. In general, a programmatic budget typically includes:

1. A statement of need as established by legal mandates, executive orders, the population to be served, or other related indicators

2. A program structure

3. The identification of objectives to be achieved within each of the identified programs

4. A brief work plan

5. Limited and carefully selected work-load and cost measures for each of the identified programs

6. A line-item component for fiscal control.

Additionally, multiyear projections may be included, although the practice is probably more honored in its breach than in its observance.

Table 13-6 illustrates a portion of a programmatic budget for a sheriff's office. A review of the six elements identified previously as typically being included as part of the structure of the programmatic format and of Table 13-6 reveals that all six elements are present. Note, however, that, whereas some of the elements are clearly immediately identifiable (e.g., there are work-load and cost measures and a line-item component for fiscal control), other elements, although present, are less immediately identifiable. For example, no overall program structure is presented, but it can be properly inferred from the "Program: Law Enforcement Services" budget portion that there is a larger structure that encompasses other programs such as detention and investigations.

The advantages of the program budget include (1) an emphasis on the social utility of programs conducted by the police department; (2) a clear relationship between policy objectives and expenditures; (3) organizational behavior that is directed at the attainment of specific objectives; (4) its ability to provide a good basis for justifying and explaining the budget; (5) its facilitating citizen understanding of police programs and objectives; (6) its establishing a high degree of accountability; and (7) its format and the wide involvement in formulating objectives, which lead police officers at all levels of the department to understand more thoroughly the importance of their roles and actions.

The disadvantages of this budget type include (1) its cost in terms of time and dollars to develop, implement, and administer; (2) the fact that police managers may be resistant to increased accountability; (3) difficulties associated with developing appropriate objectives and performance measures; (4) the fact that the city council may rely on the line-item portion of the budget to make adjustments in appropriations, negating the policy value of this format and causing serious problems in the execution of programs; and (5) the fact that police managers responsible for the various programs may not have been or may not be interested in developing the skills necessary for directing large-scale and complex programs.

## Zero-Based Budgets

The concept of a zero base is not new. It is one of the elements associated with PPBS, and the FY 1964 budget submitted by the U.S. Department of Agriculture was a zero-based budget. An analysis of that experience revealed that it produced only $200,000 in changes in the department's budget while consuming at least 180,000 person-hours of effort.[60]

Based on Peter Phyrr's use of a zero-based budget (ZBB) at the Texas Instruments Company, Jimmy Carter, then Governor of Georgia, implemented it in that state during the early 1970s. After election to national office, Carter announced that ZBB would be implemented in the federal government for FY 1979. Other governmental adopters have included New Mexico; Montana; New Jersey; Texas; Arlington County, Virginia; Wilmington, Delaware; and Orange County, Florida. Some agencies, such as the Portland, Oregon, Police Bureau, at one time used variants that incorporate many of the features of a ZBB.

As popularly understood in the most literal sense, ZBB implies preparing a budget without any reference to what was done before.[61] This interpretation has been widely condemned as naive and impractical;[62] such an application would unproductively use enormous amounts of energy, and the product would be likely to confuse, if not overwhelm, decision makers. As actually practiced, ZBB involves the use of marginal analysis techniques to see how

**TABLE 13-6. A Portion of the San Diego County Sheriff's Department Programmatic Budget**

| PROGRAM: Law Enforcement Services | DEPARTMENT: SHERIFF |
|---|---|
| PROGRAM #: 12002 | ORGANIZATION #: 2400 |
| MANAGER: Myron Klippert, Assistant Sheriff | REFERENCE: 1996–97 Proposed Budget—Pg. 13–12 |

**Authority:** Government Code 26600-26602 requires the Sheriff to preserve the peace, to make arrests, to prevent unlawful disturbances, which come to his attention, to investigate public offenses which have been committed. The County Charter (Section 605) requires the Sheriff to provide the County efficient and effective police protection and to perform all the duties required of him by law. The Government Code (51301 and 51304) authorizes intergovernmental agreements for the provision of law enforcement services.

| | 1993–94 Actual | 1994–95 Actual | 1995–96 Actual | 1995–96 Budget | 1996–97 Budget | % Change |
|---|---|---|---|---|---|---|
| **Direct Cost** | | | | | | |
| Salaries & Benefits | $62,183,262 | $65,052,375 | $71,053,078 | 66,493,489 | $74,635,287 | 12.2 |
| Services & Supplies | 2,249,840 | 4,316,016 | 3,188,631 | 2,689,380 | 3,041,049 | 13.1 |
| Other Charges | 71,796 | 305,148 | 331,126 | 331,000 | 340,535 | 2.9 |
| Operating Transfers | 0 | 0 | 0 | 0 | 0 | 77 |
| Fixed Assets | 515,033 | 408,394 | 186,223 | 287,677 | 314,129 | 9.2 |
| Vehicle/Comm. Equip. | 146,034 | 180,000 | 346,825 | 346,825 | 448,888 | 29.4 |
| **Total Direct Cost** | **$65,165,965** | **$70,261,931** | **$75,105,883** | 70,148,371 | **$78,779,888** | 12.3 |
| **Program Revenue** | (31,896,554) | (33,042,420) | (36,456,464) | 35,276,590) | (39,202,283) | 11.1 |
| **Net General Fund Contribution** | $33,269,411 | $37,219,511 | $38,649,419 | 34,871,781 | $39,577,605 | 13.5 |
| **Staff Years** | 1,085.00 | 1,107.80 | 1149.09 | 1,131.67 | 1197.00 | 5.8 |
| **Positions** | 1,093 | 1,122 | 1,174 | 1,146 | 1,200 | 4.7 |

## Program Mission

To provide the County of San Diego with efficient and effective direct law enforcement services, which include protecting life and property, preserving the peace, making arrests, preventing unlawful disturbances, and investigating public offenses which have been committed. To provide specialized investigative support, which includes investigation of homicides, kidnapping, arson, bombings, fraud, forgery, juvenile intervention, child endangerment, gambling, prostitution, pornography, narcotics violations, and gang activities. A vital tool used by the specialized investigative units is the Crime Lab, which processes evidence used to support arrests and court proceedings. Regional Services also includes emergency services such as Special Weapons and Tactics (SWAT), Special Enforcement Detail (SED), Underwater Recovery, Aerial Support, and Emergency Planning.

## 1995–96 Actual to 1995–96 Budget Comparison

Salaries and Benefits are over budget due primarily to midyear additions approved by the Board of Supervisors and continued underfunding of overtime. Services and Supplies are over budget due to the continued underfunding of vital crime lab services. Fixed Assets are under budget due to a change in equipment needs.

## Achievement of 1995–96 Objectives

- Construction has begun on the 800 MHz project.
- Priority 1 and 2 response times were 8.4 minutes in the incorporated area, 12.2 minutes in the unincorporated areas and 23.9 minutes in the rural area.
- The Sheriff's Department investigated approximately 3,736 violent crimes and approximately 18,060 property crimes, and achieved clearance rates of 57% and 12% respectively.

## 1996–97 Program Outcome and Output Objectives

The following performance indicator represents only a portion of this program's activities and divisions.

1. Law Enforcement Operations—Patrol: Maintain current priority 1 and 2 response times of 12.4 minutes for the unincorporated areas, 22.5 minutes for the rural areas and 8.7 minutes for the contract cities.

    a. Provide the current minimum number of 214 patrol units operating in a 24-hour period.

## 1996–97 Adopted Subprogram Activities

The activities of this program are summarized as follows:

1. *Law Enforcement Operations—Northern Command* [388.00 SY; E = $24,370,869; R = $20,063,961] including support personnel is:
   - Mandated/Discretionary Service Level.
   - Responsible for all law enforcement in the northern unincorporated area of San Diego County and for five contract cities.
   - Increased by 12.00 staff years and 12 positions related to the midyear board actions on contract cities services adjustments. Three of these positions are unincorporated area detectives.
   - Increased by 8.00 staff years and 8 positions due to a department-wide position reconciliation.
   - Increased by 4.25 staff years and 1 position for full year funding of the Community Oriented Policing Program (C.O.P.S. Ahead grant).
   - Increased by 2.00 staff years and 2 positions due to a reorganization within the Sheriff's Department.
   - Increased by 2.00 staff years and 2 positions for the Community Oriented Policing Program (C.O.P.S. Universal grant).

2. *Law Enforcement Operations—Southeastern Command* [433.50 SY; E = $29,020,771; R = $15,568,086] including support personnel is:
   - Mandated/Discretionary Service Level.
   - Responsible for all law enforcement in the southeastern unincorporated area of San Diego County and for four contract cities.
   - Increased by 16.00 staff years and 16 positions related to the midyear board actions on contract cities services adjustments. Nine of these positions are unincorporated area detectives.
   - Increased by 8.50 staff years and 2 positions for full year funding of the Community Oriented Policing Program (C.O.P.S. Ahead grant).
   - Increased by 9.00 staff years and 9 positions for the Community Oriented Policing Program (C.O.P.S. Universal grant).
   - Increased by 8.00 staff years and 8 positions due to a reorganization within the Sheriff's Department.
   - Increased by 1.00 staff year to full year for the two positions which were added to the unincorporated area of Ramona based on increased False Alarm Revenue Fees.
   - Decreased by 5.00 staff years and 5 positions due to a department-wide position reconciliation.
   - Decreased by .42 staff years and one position due to the funding reduction from the Peace Officers' Research Association of California (PORAC).

3. *Law Enforcement Support Command* [375.50 SY; E = $25,388,248; R = $3,570,236] including support personnel is:
   - Mandated/Discretionary Service Level.
   - Responsible for regional specialized investigative support and highly technical emergency services response.
   - Increased by 2.00 staff years and 2 positions for the Crime Lab.
   - Increased by 1.00 staff year and 1 position for the North County Gang Task Force.
   - Increased by 4.00 staff years and 4 positions due to a department-wide positions reconciliation.
   - Decreased by 2.00 staff years and 2 positions due to the addition of three Sheriff's Supervising Emergency Service Dispatchers and the deletion of 5 Sheriff's Emergency Service Dispatchers.
   - Decreased by 1.00 staff year and 1 position due to the deletion of one Sergeant position from the High Intensity Drug Trafficking Area (HIDTA) program.
   - Decreased by 4.00 staff years and 4 positions due to a reorganization within the Sheriff's Department.

*(continued)*

**TABLE 13-6. (continued)**

**Performance Measures**

| | 1993–94 Actual | 1994–95 Actual | 1995–96 Actual | 1995–96 Budget | 1996–97 Budget |
|---|---|---|---|---|---|

The following performance indicators represent only a portion of this program's activities and divisions. The Sheriff's Department has been working to further refine viable measures for each activity.

**ACTIVITY A: LAW ENFORCEMENT OPERATIONS—PATROL**

**% of Resources 17%**

OUTCOME (Planned Result)

| | 1993–94 Actual | 1994–95 Actual | 1995–96 Actual | 1995–96 Budget | 1996–97 Budget |
|---|---|---|---|---|---|
| Priorities 1 & 2 | | | | | |
| Incorporated Response Times | 8.8 | 8.7 | 8.4 | 8.9 | 8.7 |
| Unincorporated Response Times | 12.7 | 12.4 | 12.2 | 12.8 | 12.4 |
| Rural Response Times | 22.5 | 22.3 | 23.9 | 21.6 | 22.5 |
| EFFECTIVENESS (Input/Outcome) | | | | | |
| Cost to achieve Priority 1 & 2 response times | N/A | $32,431,384 | $33,419,939 | $30,347,484 | 32,160,802 |
| OUTPUT (Service or Product) | | | | | |
| Number of Patrol Units Dispatched in a 24-Hour Period | N/A | 207 | 210.5 | 206 | 214 |
| EFFICIENCY (Input/Output) | | | | | |
| Cost to Staff a 24-Hour Patrol Unit | N/A | $156,673 | $158,764 | $147,318 | $150,284 |

Direct costs consist of the salaries and benefits for Patrol Sergeants and Patrol Deputies. The indirect cost for Captains, Lieutenants, office support staff and services and supplies were allocated to the Law Enforcement operational areas of Patrol, Detectives, Traffic, Community Service Officers, Special Purpose Officers and Crime Prevention. Only the Patrol portion of the indirect costs have been included. Cost for vehicles, fuel and maintenance are not included. This is a new performance measure as of FY95/96.

*Source:* Courtesy of the San Diego, California, Sheriff's Department.

various levels of funding affect the delivery of services. The heart of ZBB is a four-step analytical process:

1. *Establishment of budget decision units.* The decision unit (DU) represents the smallest entity for which a budget is prepared in the police department. Every DU has an identified manager empowered to make all decisions regarding the budget submission. As a practical matter, DUs tend to coincide with the police department's organizational structure.

2. *Budget unit analysis.* The police manager responsible for the DU must conduct a detailed appraisal of the purpose and operations of the unit before any consideration of costs. This critical examination includes asking the zero-base question of what consequences would there be if this DU were eliminated, clarifying objectives, describing current operations, analyzing for potential productivity improvements, and specifying the measures that can be used best to justify and monitor the DUs' work load and performance.[63]

3. *Service-level analysis.* The manager responsible for the DU must next define the service priorities and structure them into a series of incremental packages of activities, resources, and projected performances. Called "decision packages"

in some ZBB systems and "service levels" in others, these incremental packages are the building blocks for the budget request ultimately submitted by the police department. The first package is designated as the base, the minimum service level, and is the deepest possible programmatic and economic reduction short of the total elimination of the DU. The second package provides an additional level of service above the base; the third package provides an increment of service above the second package; and so forth.

4. *Ranking.* After the lower level DU managers in the police department have prepared the decision packages, they are placed in a priority ranking by the department's command staff in a group session. Table 13-7 reflects the priority ordering for 37 packages used by the Portland Police Bureau in developing its fiscal 1981 request. Note that the first five choices represent the base for certain key areas of the organization but that the sixth choice, an incremental increase in precinct operations services, was given a slightly higher priority than the base for special operations. The priority list, also referred to as a ranking table, is important because once a level of funding is selected, the "line is drawn," meaning that lower priority packages are not funded. In the case of the Portland Police Bureau's fiscal 1981 requests, packages 23 to 37 fell below the line.

The advantages of a ZBB include (1) a fresh approach to planning requires police managers to ask the question, "Why are we doing this?"; (2) the duplication of effort is identified and eliminated; (3) emphasis can be given to priority programs; (4) marginally effective and nonproductive programs can be rationally eliminated; (5) there is better information for managerial decision making;[64] (6) the evaluation of the police department's performance and that of its subordinate managers is strengthened; (7) it improves communications between different levels of the police department; (8) budget information and justification are improved; (9) it fosters better linkages between police operational planning and budgeting; and (10) police managers are involved in budgeting in a more substantive way.[65] The disadvantages include (1) the number of decision packages may become overwhelming—the use of ZBB in state government in Georgia, for example, contained an estimated 10,000 of them; (2) the process of developing the system and each annual budget request requires the use of considerable resources; (3) the process is weakened considerably by poorly prepared decision packages; (4) police managers may not be very motivated to undertake critical self-examinations; and (5) the system may implicitly foster a belief that increased funds are the only way in which to increase services, causing police managers to neglect other means of improving productivity.

The ZBB represents the last major innovation designed to improve budgeting. In 1980, some knowledgeable observers of the budgetary scene predicted that ZBB would experience the same sort of mercurial fall that PPBS did. Although ZBB has not been officially pronounced as deceased, by 1986 it was infrequently practiced as described herein. Moreover, the Portland, Oregon, Police Department no longer practices it as shown in Table 13-7. Portland adopted ZBB during a time of financial pressure; as these pressures declined there was more resistance from managers throughout the city who did not want to go through the ZBB process. As a consequence, Portland moved to a budget with a program structure and no performance indicators. Subsequently, police managers found that they did not have the data to resist budget cuts—one estimate is that as a result of budget cuts after abandoning

## TABLE 13-7. Portland, Oregon, Police Bureau Package Ranking and Summary*

| (1) Rank | (2) Package Name/Number/Description | | (3) Full-time Positions 1980–81 | (4) Approved Budget 1979–80 | (5) Discretionary Request 1980–81 | (6) Total Request 1980–81 |
|---|---|---|---|---|---|---|
| 1 | PO-1 | Precinct operations base | 372.38 | $10,735,358 | 12,112,450 | $12,150,118 |
| 2 | SER-1 | Services base | 17.38 | 819,008 | 757,399 | 807,116 |
| 3 | INV-1 | Investigations base | 204.76 | 5,862,717 | 6,307,822 | 6,356,935 |
| 4 | REC-1 | Records base | 76.06 | 1,459,476 | 1,461,595 | 1,595,200 |
| 5 | MGT-1 | Management base | 20.93 | 545,964 | 740,111 | 740,527 |
| 6 | PO-2 | Current service level | 28.84 | 663,261 | 713,371 | 713,371 |
| 7 | SO-1 | Special operations base | 11.27 | 445,500 | 427,424 | 447,676 |
| 8 | TRA-1 | Traffic base | 65.90 | 2,397,426 | 2,663,063 | 2,664,588 |
| 9 | CPD-2A | Locks project | 6.06 | 234,282 | 2,406 | 231,351 |
| 10 | SER-2 | Current service level | 13.08 | 324,770 | 359,831 | 371,645 |
| 11 | REC-2 | Current service level | 8.14 | 128,795 | 137,645 | 137,645 |
| 12 | REC-3 | CRISS conversion | 4.00 | — | 86,447 | 86,447 |
| 13 | INV-2 | Current service level | 7.50 | 218,586 | 217,212 | 220,467 |
| 14 | CPD-1 | Crime prevention base, target level | 11.32 | 804,371 | 392,396 | 571,179 |
| 15 | TRA-2 | Current service level | 10.22 | 318,810 | 317,638 | 317,638 |
| 16 | SER-3 | Affirmative action, court coordinator, word processor | 5.00 | — | 83,988 | 83,988 |
| 17 | MGT-2 | Current service level (word processor) | 1.16 | — | 32,144 | 32,144 |
| 18 | MGT-3 | Legal advisor | 1.00 | — | 16,508 | 16,508 |
| 19 | PO-4 | Horses, horse patrol (6) | 7.00 | — | 225,853 | 225,853 |
| 20 | REC-4 | Shelving | — | — | 127,000 | 127,000 |
| 21 | PO-6 | Reserves | — | — | 9,154 | 9,154 |
| 22 | INV-5 | Cameras, bureau request | — | — | 2,004 | 2,004 |
| | | Total request | 872.00 | | 27,079,161 | $27,794,384 |
| 23 | PO-3 | Annexation | 12.00 | | 270,240 | 270,240 |
| 24 | INV-3 | CJO | 2.00 | | 53,333 | 53,333 |
| 25 | CPD-2B | GF transition | — | | 175,844 | 175,844 |
| 26 | REC-5 | Property room | — | | 5,000 | 5,000 |
| 27 | INV-4 | Paraprofessional | 2.00 | | 34,551 | 34,551 |
| 28 | TRA-3 | Prior current service level | 10.00 | | 251,211 | 251,211 |
| 29 | REC-6 | Current years planned service level | 8.00 | | 105,903 | 105,903 |
| 30 | SER-4 | Evaluation system, background checks | 2.00 | | 76,159 | 76,159 |
| 31 | SER-5 | LET, instructors | 8.00 | | 151,889 | 151,889 |
| 32 | REC-7 | Purge record files | 6.00 | | 83,495 | 83,495 |
| 33 | INV-7 | Prior current service level | 7.00 | | 159,508 | 159,508 |
| 34 | INV-6 | New ID technicians | 4.00 | | 66,034 | 66,034 |
| 35 | MGT-4 | Command coordinator | 1.00 | | 32,921 | 32,921 |
| 36 | REC-8 | New files | — | | 24,000 | 24,000 |
| 37 | PO-5 | Horses, horse patrol(2) | 2.00 | | 49,187 | 49,187 |
| | | Total all packages | 936.00 | | $28,618,436 | $29,333,659 |

*The Portland Police Bureau no longer uses ZBB.

*Source:* Courtesy of Portland, Oregon, Police Bureau.

ZBB, the police department's response time to calls gradually increased by approximately two minutes. The legacy of ZBB is that many departments that use a line-item or some other format have incorporated the use of decision packages into the budget request process. For example, in Fort Worth, Texas, a decision package (DP) is a narrative and financial description of a service or a program that is part of the police department's budget request. In Fort Worth there are four types of DPs:

1. Reduction or elimination of an existing service or program
2. Continuation of an existing service or program
3. Expansion of an existing service or program
4. Addition of a new service or program

Thus, although on the wane, ZBB has contributed to the evolution of budgetary practices and the DP continues to be part of the language and practice of financial management.

## Hybrid Budgets

Although it is important to understand the orientations of different budgeting systems, their emphases, and their relative advantages and disadvantages, budget systems can be discussed with a great deal more purity than they exist in actual practice. Most police budget systems are a hybrid of several approaches that are blended together to meet the particular needs of a unit of government. Given the different approaches, the relative emphasis that can be placed on them, and the sheer frequency of hybrid budget systems, one should not be startled when examining a police department's budget to find that it is not clearly one type or another. Nor should judgments be made too quickly about the "rightness" of what has been done. To understand and appreciate it in context, one must understand the needs, resources, and priorities that led to its implementation, another manifestation of the political nature of financial management.

# STRATEGIES FOR SUPPLEMENTING THE POLICE BUDGET

Police departments can employ a variety of tactics to reduce the cost of delivering services, such as using volunteers and replacing officers with less costly civilian positions whenever possible. This section focuses on strategies for supplementing the department's budget by (1) obtaining grants from federal agencies and general foundations, (2) implementing donation programs, (3) taking advantage of forfeiture laws, (4) initiating user fees, (5) enacting police tax legislation, and (6) applying for Internal Revenue Service rewards and reimbursements.[66]

## Federal and General Foundation Grants

Over the past thirty years, grant-awarding organizations—such as the now defunct Law Enforcement Assistance Administration (LEAA) and to a lesser extent general foundations—have been important sources of funding external to the normal budgeting process of police departments. Some recipients of grants, despite provisions to prohibit such employment, have substituted the money for resources that otherwise would have been appropriated or expended by the involved unit of government.

Grants have been used for a variety of endeavors, including the purchase of vehicles, riot equipment, and communications centers; for training; to create regional crime laboratories, frequently emphasizing the examination of narcotics evidence; and to develop special efforts in such areas as crime prevention, alcohol safety–accident prevention, family crisis intervention, and programs for rape victims and the elderly. Many police agencies became adept at getting grants by locating potential grantors in the *Federal Directory of Domestic Aid Programs* and elsewhere and by preparing well-conceived, responsive proposals.

The reasons for pursuing grants have been varied. Occasionally, it was done simply to get the city manager "off the back" of the chief or to provide evidence that the chief was an innovative administrator. In other instances, law enforcement agencies accepted grants urged on them by the funding source for experimental or demonstration projects. In such cases, at least some police agencies had little commitment to the "pet project" of the grantor but accepted the grant in the belief that it would create goodwill at the time when the grantor was considering some future proposal from that police department or in the belief that enough equipment or other resources would remain as a useful residue from the project, regardless of its other merits. Often missing in the various machinations involved in getting the money was a strong management analysis of certain factors:

1. What problem or need, if any, will go unmet in the absence of the grant funds?
2. What would be the probable qualitative and quantitative impact of not meeting the problem or need?
3. What would be the qualitative and quantitative impact on police services of using the grant funds?
4. If a multiyear grant, what are the consequences and probabilities of midproject termination or reduced funding?
5. How many sworn and civilian employees will be added to the total personnel complement who may have to be continued on the payroll at the end of the project?
6. Will any equipment or facilities be acquired that nongrant funds ultimately will have to maintain?
7. What obligations are incurred with respect to continuing the effort initiated following the termination of the grant period?
8. Must the police department provide some matching contribution to the project? If so, how much? Can it be an in-kind match, such as providing space, or must the match be in equal funds? If actual funds are required, will they come from the police department's budget or from a special municipal fund established for just such purposes?
9. What operational or financial procedures have to be changed to meet grant requirements?
10. What ongoing programs will be brought under new state or federal regulations as a result of receiving the grant, in what way, and at what costs?
11. What will be the cost of the administrative overhead outside of the police agency necessary to support the administration of the grant?[67]

None of this is intended to ignore the existence of many exemplary projects that have improved the delivery of police services to the public. However, even in some number of excellent projects, there have been side costs, and the potential for these hidden costs increases inversely with the amount of management planning done when considering whether to take grant funds offered or whether to apply for grant funds. It is also important to note that some police chiefs have deliberately chosen not to raise certain of the identified issues—to the chagrin of their city managers and sometimes at risk of their own jobs—to initiate badly needed programs that could not be funded through the normal budget process.

Donation and fund-raising programs may be operated by the police or on behalf of individual officers or departments. They can also be characterized as those involving a single issue or those that are ongoing.

## Donation and Fund-Raising Programs

The San Francisco Police Department appealed directly to the public for contributions when a police dog was killed at a shootout at a homeless camp and there was no money budgeted to replace him.[68] Chicago restaurateur Andreas Angelopolous held a fund-raiser at his Athena restaurant for paralyzed Officer James Mullen, which helped bring the total donations to over $60,000.[69] In a number of major cities, such as New York and Baltimore, nonprofit police foundations raise money continuously in order to give training scholarships to officers, create specialized units, such as bomb disposal, or for other activities related to strengthening the police department. The New Orleans Police Foundation raised $200,000 from the Metropolitan Association of Realtors, which was used to help revamp the police department.[70] In Mandeville, Louisiana, a group of local businesses formed a private, nonprofit foundation whose first project was to donate $18,000 to the police department to help in narcotics arrests.[71] Bank South donated funds to the Atlanta Police Department to buy new bikes for the department's Bicycle Patrol Unit.[72] A Lakewood, Colorado, officer gathered 125 used bulletproof vests and arranged to ship them to English constables.[73] In Washington, D.C., the GoGo Alliance offered to hold a concert for the benefit of police officers and promised free attendance for a year to their performances to anyone turning in a gun at the concert.[74] This offer was spurred by criticisms of the group linking its performances to violence, including the fatal on-duty shooting of Officer Brian T. Gibson in Washington, D.C.

Not all donation programs are used to help the police. In Denver, the Sunshine Foundation—an offshoot of the Colorado State Patrol—raised money to help a 17-year-old cancer victim buy a $13,000 prosthesis to replace his amputated leg.[75] During one Christmas season, Detroit police officers gave away 104 new bicycles, helmets, and T-shirts to needy youngsters.[76] The funds for these gifts were raised through police and public contributions. Michigan police officers traveled to Oklahoma City to deliver cards, gifts, and financial assistance to children who survived the bombing.[77] Houston officers, with the help of the nurses and employees at Texas Children's Hospital, delivered toys and gifts to women and children at a shelter for battered women during the winter holidays.[78]

The essence of forfeiture laws is twofold: (1) criminals should not be allowed to profit financially from their illegal acts, and (2) the assets of criminals that are subject to seizure can be put to work against them by funding additional law enforcement initiatives (see Box 13-5). There is a wide variety of state statutes regarding forfeitures, but they generally cover cash and property from four categories of crime:

## Forfeiture Laws

1. Narcotics
2. Transportation of contraband goods

BOX 13-5

## State's Seizure Policies Faulted

### Auditor criticizes law on drug money

**Karen Dillon, The Kansas City Star**

Flaws and gray areas in the law allowed Missouri law enforcement agencies to circumvent state statutes when they seized drug money, according to a report to be released today.

The Missouri auditor's report was undertaken this year because of concerns that police had found a way to keep much of the drug money they seized instead of sending it to public education, as legislators intended.

Under state law, police must report all drug money they seize to county prosecutors. The money is to be handled by state courts, which normally would send that money to education.

*The Kansas City Star* reported in January that in many cases police simply gave seized money to federal agencies, which kept part and returned the rest, usually 80 percent, to police.

The auditor's report is expected to be addressed in a legislative hearing on the issue today in St. Louis. A copy of the report was obtained by *The Star.*

Auditor Claire McCaskill said she hoped the report would educate legislators about the complexity of the issue.

"There is not one quick fix to the problems associated with forfeitures in Missouri," McCaskill said. "It is going to take an effort in several different places to have forfeiture policies follow what the legislative policy intended."

Her report, which was based on a survey of law enforcement in Missouri, showed that $47 million was seized in the state in a three-year period, with Missouri police agencies receiving more than $19 million back from federal agencies.

Five agencies, including Kansas City police, received 71 percent of the $19 million.

The report finds several problems in the state law.

"Differences between state and federal law, the gray area of task forces and the problems with the way state laws are written create an environment where local law enforcement circumvents state law and uses the federal instead," McCaskill said.

According to the report:

State drug laws need to define when police have actually seized cash or property. Currently state law simply requires police to report money they seize to a county prosecutor. But some police agencies have said they did not technically seize money in a search of a person or property—they were only holding it until a federal agent arrived on the scene.

Some parts of the law are too restrictive. For example, people who are charged in drug cases must be convicted of a felony before the state can confiscate their property. The law should provide some exemptions to that requirement, the report said.

Under state law, local officers assigned to a federal task force must still follow state laws when seizing property. But the report says those officers could be subject to conflicting state and federal regulations.

The report also questions some actions of law enforcement:

Law enforcement agencies failed to always report to the county prosecutor when they seized money or property. "The prosecutors have not been given the opportunity to determine how to proceed with these potential forfeiture cases," according to the report.

Prosecuting attorneys and the attorney general have interpreted state law to prohibit them from confiscating cash when drugs are suspected but are not present in a search. For that reason, officials have said, law enforcement turns that money over to federal agencies.

In actuality, according to the report, cash can be forfeited under state law when no one claims it.

Even in the small number of cases that were filed in state court, judges often transferred money to a federal agency, even though they did not need to under state law.

The report also points out that the $47 million in seizures makes up less than 1 percent of the funding Missouri provides to local schools. The $3.5 million the Missouri Highway Patrol received back from the federal government also is less than 1 percent of its budget.

Some legislators, however, have said that sending the money to education is not the issue. They say they don't care where the money goes as long as it doesn't stay with law enforcement. They believe police agencies that generate revenue by seizures have a conflict of interest and an opportunity for abuse.

*Source: The Kansas City Star, October 12, 1999.*

3. Organized crime, racketeering, and unlawful gambling
4. Targeted crimes (e.g., in North Carolina vehicles used in serious drunk-driving cases may be forfeited)

Upon seizing airplanes, cash, cars, boats, guns, or other property subject to their state's forfeiture law, law enforcement officers may initiate forfeiture proceedings by making a request to the prosecutor or by retaining a lawyer for that purpose. Care is taken to protect the rights of others who were not involved in the crime and who have a financial interest in the forfeited property, such as a lender who has a lien on an airplane. Four patterns exist regarding the way forfeited property is handled:

1. All benefits from the forfeiture go to the unit of government's general fund.
2. The police may keep all property, typically using cars for undercover operations and aircraft for surveillance, but if the property is later sold, the proceeds of the sale go to the unit of government's general fund.
3. The police may keep or sell the property, but if it is sold, the police can keep up to only some ceiling amount, such as $50,000, and any excess goes into a trust fund to which the department can apply for specific uses.
4. All property and cash can be kept by the police department.

The public accepts certain types of user fees for special services that cost the police department something to produce, such as copies of traffic accident reports. Other examples of user fees that are readily accepted include permits for parades and other special events and charges for copies of photographs or videotapes. However, although it actually costs police departments to produce all services, the public often complains about being charged some user fees because the service received is seen as part of the basic responsibility of the department. For example, police departments that began charging people for opening car doors when they had accidentally locked their keys inside had to beat a retreat from this practice due to public reaction, as well as complaints from locksmiths. Residential burglar alarms can create a number of false alarms, often due to mistakes made by homeowners in setting or deactivating them. Repeated runs by patrol units to respond to these false alarms is a wasteful drain on police services. Cities have reacted to this in several ways. In Denver, the police will not respond to an alarm unless it has been registered with the city and a fee has been paid. Other jurisdictions charge homeowners a flat fee of $35 to $50 to respond to a false alarm after three such incidents at their homes.

A common type of police tax is the special district tax. Under this arrangement, specific groups request that in their area an additional tax be levied, the funds from which then go to enhance police services in that area. The groups are varied and include downtown business associations, malls, boat owners at marinas, and civic associations for particular neighborhoods. Taxes levied in this manner are seldom controversial, although there have been instances in which community leaders argue that the poor neighborhoods that need protection the most can't afford to provide for increased police presence. A group proposed a special taxing district for New Orleans' French Quarter, a measure that was quickly dropped due to a lack of interest.[79] Sometimes taxes to be used for the police are levied indirectly; in St. Charles Parish, Louisiana, authorities placed a tax on the Waterford 3 Nuclear Plant, which was used to give

**User Fees and Police Taxes**

sheriff's deputies a hefty 13 percent pay increase,[80] the cost of which will be passed on to electrical customers.

In California, the unilateral imposition of special taxes; increases in user fees for local government services; and special property assessments for police, fire, library, and other purposes sparked taxpayer revolt, resulting in the passage of Proposition 218. "Prop 218" requires local governments to win approval from the majority of voters before they can continue or increase existing levies and before they can place new ones into effect.[81]

## Internal Revenue Service Rewards and Reimbursements

Police Departments may be able to supplement their budgets with two types of funds available from the Internal Revenue Service (IRS): (1) rewards and (2) reimbursement for investigations, under certain conditions.

Realizing that it often arrested racketeers who had not properly reported their income, the Atlanta Police Department approached the IRS about collecting the 10 percent informers fee on unpaid taxes. Subsequently, the city council passed an ordinance allowing the Atlanta Department of Public Safety to apply for rewards on behalf of the city, to be deposited in a special account earmarked for law enforcement activities. The IRS does not divulge the identities of agencies who have received such awards, their amounts, or other related information.

The Internal Revenue Service reimburses state and local agencies for certain types of investigations. State and local law enforcement agencies which provide information that substantially contributes to the recovery of at least $50,000 in federal taxes on illegal drug dealing or related money laundering may receive reimbursement for their investigative efforts. The reimbursement cannot exceed 10 percent of the unpaid taxes recovered. If more than one agency is involved, the IRS must equitably allocate that 10 percent amount among the various agencies involved. An agency is not eligible for the reimbursement if it will receive or has received reimbursement under a federal or state forfeiture program or under state revenue laws. A key requirement for agencies seeking reimbursement is that they must indicate their intent to do so when they first provide the information to the IRS.

## SUMMARY

Some police executives view financial management as an unattractive responsibility. Successful police executives know that money is the fuel on which police programs operate. The unwillingness to invest a high level of energy in acquiring and managing financial resources pre-establishes the conditions for mediocre or worse performance by the police department.

Government activities inherently involve public funds; thus financial management is a political process. Illustrative of the entwining of politics and financial administration are state provisions for monitoring and controlling certain aspects of local government finance; the budget preparation instructions given to the various departments by the mayor, city manager, or finance director; the internal dialogue within a police department when deciding how much to request; the development of the city's consolidated budget; the ap-

propriations decision by the city council; and decisions made in the course of executing the budget.

Typically, local government budgets for a 12-month period are referred to as a fiscal year. In properly administered governments, there is a sequence of four steps that are termed the budget cycle and that are repeated at approximately the same time each year: (1) budget preparation, (2) budget approval, (3) budget execution, and (4) the audit.

Numbers are the basic language in which budgets are expressed; the way in which those numbers and any accompanying narrative are organized is termed the budget format. The oldest, simplest, and most universally employed budget is the line item, because of its ease of construction and the potential for control that it offers. In fact, because of its control feature, it is the base on which all other formats rest. Each budget format can be associated loosely with a time in which it was a dominant force; sometimes this domination was far greater in the literature than in actual practice. Nonetheless, from the line item forward, each format can be viewed as an attempt to improve and reform the practice of financial management.

In addition to the use of volunteers and the substitution of less costly civilian positions for sworn positions whenever feasible, police executives can strengthen their budgets by (1) federal and general foundation grants, (2) donation and fund-raising programs, (3) forfeitures, (4) user fees and police taxes, and (5) IRS rewards and reimbursements.

## DISCUSSION QUESTIONS

1. How can politics and financial management be related usefully?

2. What is the budget cycle and what are the major steps in it?

3. How do the federal and state governments shape the practice of local financial management?

4. What is a fiscal year? What are some examples of different fiscal years?

5. What can police managers do to enhance the likelihood of getting their departmental budgets enacted?

6. If you were a police manager undergoing an audit of the department's last fiscal year budget, what are some things you would expect to see examined?

7. What are the advantages and disadvantages of the following budget formats?

   a. Line item
   b. Performance
   c. PPBS
   d. Programmatic
   e. ZBB

8. What is the significance of hybrid budgets?

9. You are the recently appointed director of planning and research for the department, and the chief of police has just sent for you. The chief tells you that the department may apply for a grant from a federal agency. The chief is seeking your advice as to whether or not to apply. What kinds of perspectives would you encourage the chief to consider?

10. Identify and discuss strategies for supplementing the police budget.

## NOTES

1. This idea and several of the examples in the next sentence are taken from Felix A. Nigro and Lloyd G. Nigro, *Modern Public Administration*, 5th ed. (New York: Harper & Row, 1980), p. 337.

2. See National Highway Traffic Safety Administration, "The Impact of Fuel Costs on Law Enforcement" (Washington, D.C.: Mimeographed, February 1, 1980), 11 pp. For a view of some models on police financial stress, see Charles H. Levine, "Police Management in the 1980s: From Decrementalism to Strategic Thinking," *Public Administration Review*, 45 (November 1985), 691–700.

3. Roland N. McKean, *Public Spending* (New York: McGraw-Hill, 1968), p. 1.

4. Aaron Wildavsky, *The Politics of the Budgetary Process*, 2nd ed. (Boston: Little, Brown, 1974), p. 4.

5. S. Kenneth Howard, *Changing State Budgeting* (Lexington, Ky.: Council of State Governments, 1973), p. 13.

6. Harold F. Gortner, *Administration in the Public Sector* (New York: John Wiley & Sons, 1977), p. 315.

7. Advisory Commission on Intergovernmental Relations, *City Financial Emergencies* (Washington, D.C.: U.S. Government Printing Office, 1973), from Table 2-1, p. 10.

8. Advisory Commission on Intergovernmental Relations, *State Mandating of Local Expenditures* (Washington, D.C.: U.S. Government Printing Office, 1978), from Table IV-4, p. 55.

9. "Inflation, Limits, Mandates, Strain Budgets," *Iowa Municipalities*, 34:7 (1979), 3. Also see George E. Hale and Marian Lief Palley, "The Impact of Federal Funds on the State Budgetary Process," *National Civic Review*, 67:10 (1978), 461–64, 473.

10. The information in this paragraph is taken from John E. Peterson, C. Wayne Stallings, and Catherine Lavigne Spain, *State Roles in Local Government Financial Management: A Comparative Analysis* (Washington, D.C.: Government Finance Research Center, 1979), pp. 1, 5. The Government Finance Research Center is a nonprofit professional service organization that serves as the research arm of the Municipal Finance Officers Association.

11. The rule is described in Peterson, Stallings, and Spain, *State Roles,* p. 4, as follows: "Dillion's Rule, first espoused by John F. Dillion, a justice of the Supreme Court of Iowa, from 1862 to 1869, and later accepted by courts in many other states and the U.S. Supreme Court, establishes the full legal superiority of the state over local governments." Dillion himself stated the rule as follows: "It is a general and undisputed proposition of law that a municipal corporation possess and can exercise the following powers, and no others: First, those granted in express words; second, those necessarily or fairly implied in or incident to the powers expressly granted; third, those essential to the accomplishment of the declared objects and purposes of the corporation—not simply convenient, but indispensable. Any fair, reasonable, substantial doubt concerning the existence of power is resolved by the courts against the corporation, and the power is denied." In states that have a constitutional provision conferring home rule powers on cities, Dillion's Rule is used by the courts in interpreting the scope of home rule powers.

12. A. E. Buck, *The Budgets in Governments of Today* (New York: Macmillan, 1945), p. 5.

13. See James C. Snyder, "Financial Management and Planning in Local Government," *Atlanta Economic Review* (November–December, 1973), pp. 43–47.

14. Wildavsky, *Politics of the Budgetary Process,* pp. 1–4.

15. Orin K. Cope, "Operation Analysis—The Basis for Performance Budgeting," in *Performance Budgeting and Unit Cost Accounting for Governmental Units* (Chicago: Municipal Finance Officers Association, 1954), p. 8.

16. James W. Martin, "An Economic Criteria for State and City Budget Making," *Public Administration Review,* 24 (March 1964), p. 1.

17. Fritz Morstein Marx, "The Bureau of the Budget: Its Evolution and Present Role, II," *American Political Science Review,* 39 (August 1945), p. 871.

18. This case is taken from William P. Gloege, "Successful Police Department Budgeting," *Police Chief,* 44:5 (1977), 58–59.

19. These strategies, with some change, are essentially those identified by Wildavsky, *Politics of the Budgetary Process,* pp. 63–123.

20. Clifford Krauss, "New Color Scheme, Mostly White, to Reduce the Cost of Painting Police Cars," *New York Times,* June 25, 1996.

21. Lennox L. Moak and Kathryn W. Killian, *A Manual of Techniques for the Preparation, Consideration, Adoption, and Administration of Operating Budgets* (Chicago: Municipal Finance Officers Association, 1973), p. 5, with changes.

22. These three types of controls are identified in J. Richard Aronson and Eli Schwartz, eds., *Management Policies in Local Government Finance* (Washington, D.C.: International City Management Association, 1975), pp. 86–87, and are drawn on with changes here.

23. Lennis M. Knighton, "Four Keys to Audit Effectiveness," *Governmental Finance,* 8 (September 1979), p. 3. Also see Kenneth S. Caldwell, "Operational Auditing in State and Local Government," *Governmental Finance,* 3–4 (May 1974–1975), pp. 36–43.

24. The Comptroller General of the United States, *Standards for Audit of Governmental Organizations, Programs, Activities, and Functions* (Washington, D.C.: General Accounting Office, 1972), p. 1.

25. These three types of accountability are drawn, with modification, from U.S. Comptroller General, *Standards of Audit.*

26. Peter F. Rousmaniere, ed., *Local Government Auditing* (New York: Council on Municipal Performance, 1979), from Tables 1 and 2, pp. 10, 14.

27. A. E. Buck, *Public Budgeting* (New York: Harper and Brothers, 1929), p. 12.

28. Ibid.

29. Ibid.

30. Jesse Burkhead, *Government Budgeting* (New York: John Wiley & Sons, 1956), p.11.

31. Ibid., p. 17.

32. Allen Schick, *Budget Innovation in the States* (Washington, D.C.: Brookings Institution, 1971), pp. 14–15.

33. Buck, *Budgets in Governments,* p. 40.

34. Burkhead, *Government Budgeting,* p. 13.

35. Ibid.

36. In 1913, Ohio became the first state to adopt the executive budget.

37. Budget purists would argue that there are technical differences between line-item and object-of-expenditure budgets. In common usage and practice, however, they are synonymous.

38. Schick, *Budget Innovation,* p. 23; Schick lists a total of 10 ways in which the line-item budget fosters control, but these three sum them up adequately.

39. Malchus L. Watlington and Susan G. Dankel, "New Approaches to Budgeting: Are They Worth the Cost?" *Popular Government,* 43 (Spring 1978), 1.

40. Burkhead, *Government Budgeting*, p. 155, with change.

41. Herbert Emmerich, chairman, "Symposium on Budget Theory," *Public Administration Review*, 213 (Winter 1950), 26.

42. See, for example, A. E. Buck, "Measuring the Results of Government," *National Municipal Review* (March 1924), 152–157.

43. Burkhead, *Government Budgeting*, p. 134.

44. Robert B. Elmore, "Performance Budgeting in Richmond, Virginia," *Municipal Finance*, 28:2 (1955), p. 77.

45. Vernon E. Koch, "Cincinnati's Budget Developments," *Public Administration Review*, 20:20 (Spring 1960), 79.

46. John A. Donaho, "Performance Budgeting in Maryland," *Municipal Finance*, 28:12 (1955), 69.

47. Joseph P. Lally, "Performance Budgeting in Boston," *Municipal Finance*, 28:2 (1955), p. 80.

48. Burkhead, *Government Budgeting*, p. 137.

49. Allen Schick, "The Road to PPB: The Stages of Budget Reform," *Public Administration Review*, 26 (December 1966), 244.

50. Ibid., pp. 245–246.

51. Ibid., p. 244.

52. David Novick, ed., *Program Budgeting* (New York: Holt, Rinehart and Winston, 1969), p. xxvi xxvi.

53. Ibid., p. xxiv.

54. For information on this project, see Council of State Governments, *State Reports on Five-Five-Five* (Chicago: Council of State Governments, 1968). The involved states were California, Michigan, New York, Vermont, and Wisconsin; the counties were Dade (Florida), Davidson (Tennessee), Los Angeles (California), Nassau (New York), and Wayne (Michigan); and the cities were Dayton, Denver, Detroit, New Haven, and San Diego.

55. International City Management Association, *Local Government Budgeting, Program Planning and Evaluation* (Urban Data Service Report, May 1972), p. 7. Also see Selma J. Mushkin, "PPB in Cities," *Public Administration Review*, 29:2 (1969), pp. 167–177.

56. These two examples are drawn from Roger H. Jones's "Program Budgeting: Fiscal Facts and Federal Fancy," *Quarterly Review of Economics and Business* (Summer 1969), p. 45.

57. Allen Schick, "A Death in the Bureaucracy: The Demise of Federal PPB," *Public Administration Review*, 33 (March–April 1973), pp. 146–156.

58. Ibid., p. 148.

59. Ibid., p. 149.

60. Joseph S. Wholey, *Zero-Base Budgeting and Program Evaluation* (Lexington, Mass.: Lexington Books, 1978), p. 8.

61. Graeme M. Taylor, "Introduction to Zero-Base Budgeting," in *Experiences in Zero-Based Budgeting*, ed. Joseph L. Herbert (New York: Petrocelli, 1977), p. 3.

62. Ibid.

63. The descriptions of budget unit and service-level analysis are drawn with some changes from J. Robert Krebill and Ronald F. Mosher, "Delaware Budgets for Productivity," *State Government*, 53 (Winter 1980), pp. 20–21.

64. Robert F. Littlejohn, "Zero-Base Budgeting," *Police Chief*, 45 (December 1978), p. 35.

65. Points 6 through 9 are restatements of matter found in Taylor, "Introduction to Zero-Base Budgeting"; the article also appeared in *Bureaucrat*, 6 (Spring 1977), pp. 33–55.

66. The information on donation programs, forfeitures, user fees, police taxes, and IRS rewards is drawn from Lindsey D. Stellwagen and Kimberly A. Wylie, *Strategies for Supplementing the Police Budget* (Washington, D.C.: U.S. Department of Justice, National Institute of Justice, 1985), with some restatement.

67. Some of these 11 points are identified by Wayne Stallings in "Improving Budget Communications in Smaller Local Governments," *Governmental Finance* (August 1978), p. 24.

68. "S.F. to Replace Slain Fog, Needs $5,500," *San Francisco Chronicle*, August 25, 1995, Section A, p. 20.

69. Andrew Martin, "Restaurant Joins Effort for Paralyzed Officer," *Chicago Tribune*, November 6, 1996, Section 2C, p. 6.

70. "Police Group Gets $200,000 Pledge," *The Times-Picayune*, December 14, 1996, Section B, p. 4.

71. Glen Justice, "Group to Buy Cops Equipment," *The Times-Picayune*, May 19, 1996, Section OTMN, p. 1.

72. Charmagne Helton, "Bank South Says Police Deserve a Pedal," *The Atlanta Constitution*, February 2, 1995.

73. Marilyn Robinson, "Police Recycle Used Vests," *The Denver Post*, October 7, 1996.

74. Cindy Loose, "GoGo Alliance Offers to Give Concert to Aid Police," *The Washington Post*, February 11, 1997, Section B, p. 5.

75. "Cops Aid Cancer Victim," *The Denver Post*, March 6, 1994, Section C, p. 2.

76. Santiago Esparza, "Charities: 104 Ride Off on New Bikes, Thanks to Donations," *The Detroit News,* December 19, 1996.

77. Larry Perl, Mike Martindale, and John Larabee, "Michigan Cops Drive Message Home to Kids Hurt in Bomb Blast," *The Detroit News,* May 10, 1995, Section BW, p. 3.

78. Eric Hanson, "Blue and White Santas," *Houston Chronicle,* December 23, 1996, Section A, p. 21.

79. Bruce Eggler, "Tax District for Quarter Fizzles Out," *The Times Picayune,* September 12, 1996.

80. Rhonda Bell, "St. Charles Cops Get Raise, Thanks to N-Plant," *The Times Picayune,* January 4, 1997.

81. Editorial, "Storm of Concern on Prop 218," *Los Angeles Times,* January 27, 1997.

## INTRODUCTION

Returning to a theme from an earlier chapter, organizations do what we as individuals cannot or will not do. Organizations are intended to meet the needs of people. Police departments provide for our safety and protection. A logical extension of this aim is that as citizens and police leaders we should make sure that the agencies that protect us are well operated and that we have ways for knowing if they are doing a good job or a bad job. But the fact is that historically we have used very gross measures (e.g., is the crime rate rising or falling?). Overall, there has been a conspicuous absence of well-crafted performance measures for many decades.

Over the last fifteen years public, scholarly, and police interest in trying to develop measures of performance has accelerated. A number of factors have combined to form a potent impetus toward better measurement of the activities of police departments. Notable among these factors are the drive toward productivity improvement, the legacy of the management by objectives (MBO) movement; the tie between quality management and the community policing movement; and the federal Government Performance and Results Act (GPRA), variants of which have been adopted both by some states and some local units of government. Essentially, GPRA-type legislation requires leaders to be more responsible for the performance of their departments by requiring the use of performance measures (PMs).

# —14—

# PRODUCTIVITY, QUALITY, AND PROGRAM EVALUATION: MEASURING ORGANIZATIONAL PERFORMANCE

*We have no choice but to learn to manage the service institutions, such as the police, for performance and productivity.*
PETER F. DRUCKER

## PRODUCTIVITY

Classically, productivity is considered to be a ratio of output to input. Thus, productivity seeks to specify the relationship between inputs into a police department (such as the money allocated to the patrol division) to the outputs or results (e.g., how much does it cost to answer each call for service? See Box 14-1). If, for example, it costs $210 to answer each call for service in FY '01 and it costs $178 in FY '02, a substantial productivity gain is created. If you have 100 officers and their productivity is increased 25 percent, it's like having one-fourth more officers, but not having to pay for them.

Productivity gains may be achieved by a number of methods, including:

1. Redesigning jobs, such as having volunteers and lower earning civilians perform tasks formerly carried out by higher earning officers. (For example, in some communities trained civilians investigate "fender benders" that do not involve death or serious personal injury.)
2. Introducing new technology, such as Automated Fingerprint Identification Systems (AFIS), which makes it possible for computers to do high speed searches of massive fingerprint files.

BOX 14-1

## Citing Low Productivity, Little Ferry Cuts K-9 Unit

**by Monique El-Faizy,** *Staff Writer*

LITTLE FERRY—When dog handlers in several Bergen County police departments won costly legal battles last year over payment for the time they spent caring for their furry friends, council members decided to be proactive. They devised a payment plan they hoped could help them avoid similar litigation.

The arrangement—in which the borough agreed to take on more of the dogs' expenses and compensate their handlers for their time—saved the borough from litigation but resulted in the end of the K-9 unit.

Acting on the advice of Police Chief Donald Fleming, the council voted this week to discharge its doggies.

"It's not cost effective," said Councilwoman Roberta Henriquez.

The dogs have served well, but not well enough to earn their chow. Tango and Yambo assisted in about nine arrests over the past three years, Fleming said, but that arrest rate isn't high enough to justify the roughly $20,000 per year the dogs cost the department.

By cutting the unit, the department would also regain the two work days the handlers were given each month for training time.

The dogs were brought in on a trial basis three years ago, and Fleming decided they weren't really needed.

"I really thought it was going to be a lot better than it was," he said. "If they had made some good arrests, I think it would have been worthwhile."

What's more, when the department really needs a dog, it can rely on the county police to provide one of theirs.

"It's a service we get from the county for free, so why burden the taxpayers with that?" Henriquez asked.

The fate of the Little Ferry dogs is uncertain, but everyone is hoping they will stay with their handlers. Legally, the town is required to open bidding on them, but both Fleming and Henriquez said they doubted anyone would bid against the current masters.

*Source:* Reproduced with permission of *The Bergen* Record of Hackensack, New Jersey, February 12, 1999.

3. Redesigning work processes so unneeded steps can be eliminated, such as the requirement that the approval of a supervisor must be obtained before a vehicle can be impounded.

4. Redesigning forms so that unused information is not collected and eliminating forms that call for redundant information.

5. Delegating decisions and tasks to the lowest level where they can be made effectively, freeing up the more costly time of upper echelon leaders to deal with more complex problems.

6. Identifying wasted space that can be used to house time-saving equipment (see Box 14-2).

7. Training officers in new ways of doing their jobs more effectively (see Box 14-3).

Effectiveness (Did we get the right job done using acceptable methods? Did we achieve our goal?) and efficiency (What did it cost us to do this job or to achieve this goal?) are the twin pillars of productivity. Both must exist before you can measure productivity by comparing current against past performance for the same period. Historically, the quality of service has either been ignored or there has been some minimal attention to it as part of the effectiveness statement. However, with the rise of the quality movement in public sector organizations, quality has become a separate measure (e.g., how many requests for copies of traffic accident reports from motorists were responded to within 24 hours of the receipt of the request?). Table 14-1 provides examples of performance measures for these concepts.

## BOX 14-2

### Solving the Crime

### Police expect to know 'who done it' a lot faster with latest in lab technology

by Paul Bird, *Staff Writer*

GREENWOOD, Ind.—Dust wafted in corners. Boxes were stacked here and there. The dark, dingy room had a musty smell.

For years, the southeast corner of Greenwood Police headquarters' second floor had seen little use.

But with a renovation and the addition of thousands of dollars' worth of scientific equipment, the area has been transformed into a high-tech crime laboratory.

The improvements bring Greenwood another step closer to becoming the premier player in the high-tech age of forensics in central Indiana, said Chief Robert Dine.

The transition from wasted space to high-tech lab was guided by Deputy Police Chief Albert Hessman. He oversaw construction of the department's first lab in 1987 at the direction of then-Police Chief Charles Henderson, now the city's mayor.

That lab had about 1,000 square feet and allowed for basic testing.

The original plan—developed nearly a decade ago—called for developing a shooting range on the headquarters' second floor, but those plans were delayed because of lack of money. Then it was determined the noise and other environmental issues—lead and toxic gases—would poison the air throughout the building.

The Police Department received approval last fall from the Board of Works and the City Council to proceed with the lab project.

"We transferred $180,000 from the existing budget from 1999 to purchase equipment and remodel," Dine said. "It was all of us working to make the city better."

Last week, huge ventilation hoods were moved onto the second floor through square holes cut into the building's east second-floor walls.

The hoods carry away toxic gases from tests.

The additional space and equipment promote safety for the scientists and samples being examined. One common test for fingerprints generates cyanide gas.

Hessman is guiding the expansion with the help of scientists Eva Marie Lewis, who specializes in drug identification and toxicology, and Jennifer M. Wood, a specialist in serology and DNA analysis.

Lewis explained that the renovation, new equipment and other upcoming changes will allow full analysis of body fluids and sophisticated DNA testing.

"We are not there yet, but with some additional equipment we will be," she said.

Another redesigned area is the photo lab.

"We have moved to digital photography for routine evidence collection, and it is working well," Hessman said. "We have issued these cameras to the road officers."

The lab already serves all police agencies in Johnson County.

What Greenwood and other country residents gain is quicker justice. For example, lab work must be completed in drug cases before they can proceed in court.

"It eliminates delays caused by waiting for reports from other agencies," Dine said. "Our only shortcomings are in firearm ballistics and questioned documents. We will continue to send them to the State Police lab."

Hessman said the lab will move closer to meeting accreditation from the American Society of Crime Laboratory Directors, a national organization that sets standards for crime labs. Accreditation would make the lab eligible for federal grant money.

"We're becoming independent and will not have to rely on outside agencies," said Dine.

*Source: The Indianapolis Star, January 28, 2000.*

---

Gains in productivity rarely occur by themselves. They result when the leadership of a department is serious about managing for specific results. Police leaders know what they want to happen, they see that the necessary procedures are put in place to help them focus on the results they want, and they monitor progress toward those results. Whether a productivity improvement program is large or small, simple or complex, experience has demonstrated that there is a basic checklist of conditions that must be satisfied for it to be developed and implemented successfully. Police leaders must have

**Implementing a Productivity Program**

1. The courage and determination to initiate and sustain the program.
2. The analytical capacity to determine what needs to be done, what can be done, and how to do it.

BOX 14-3

## Police Recruits' Training Expanded Greatly at Academy

### 'Problem solvers,' not responders, sought

by Christine Clarridge, Seattle Times staff reporter

For the first time in more than two decades, Washington state's law-enforcement academy is expanding its training procedures.

The changes are, in part, sparked by the desire of law-enforcement agencies to provide new recruits with more and better training to handle the wider spectrum of responsibilities faced by police.

New recruits will now undergo a nearly six-month training program that almost doubles the hours spent in field-training, exercises and class studies.

During training, police recruits will be expected to learn a wide range of skills, from issuing tickets and calming violent drug users to getting cows out of the roadway.

Recruits will be expected to learn the ins and outs of the state's legal system, and how to write a report that will hold up in court.

They'll have to know how to make split-second decisions about when to shoot and when not to shoot. And they'll have to look calm doing it, said Commander Mark Mann of the Criminal Justice Training Center in Burien.

The Burien center and branches at Sand Point and in Spokane train every police officer in the state, except for the State Patrol, which has its own training program.

With $1.5 million in funding from the Legislature, the expansion reflects a change in society and its expectations, according to Mann.

"What we're coming from is an era in which cops ran from call to call, like pinballs," he said. "But now we find that the public does not want just problem responders. They want us to be problem solvers."

For example, he said, a series of 911 calls from a fearful elderly person might have police responding night after night. But new recruits will be taught to pick up on the pattern and then seek the services of people who can help, he said.

"We're training our new officers to be resource providers," said Mann.

3. The active support or, failing that, at least the neutrality of relevant others, such as the city or county manager, the legislative body, the interested public and the union.

4. The ability to overcome resistance from other departments of government, such as personnel or central purchasing, who may resist the writing of new job and equipment specifications because they impinge on established control practices.

5. Overall, the cooperation of the people within the police department. Even if large numbers of personnel are committed, lesser numbers of well-situated people opposing the program can mean failure.

6. The organizational control system and controls to facilitate and reinforce the changes to be made.

7. Competent persons responsible for the changes.[1]

A key and positive way of reinforcing the changes to be made is a widespread system of incentives that makes efforts to improve productivity have some "payoff" to those involved. Police administrators may be guaranteed that some portion of the savings generated by productivity improvements will be made available to them for new or expanded programs.[2] For example, in some jurisdictions police officers with perfect attendance for 90 days are given an extra day off, a measure that reduces the use of sick days considerably.

Basically, productivity improvements can be made in two ways: (1) increasing the level of output while holding the level of resources used constant,

## TABLE 14-1. Examples of Performance Measures for Effectiveness, Efficiency, and Quality

**Measure of Effectiveness:** Reduce the number of civil suits filed against the department by 25% in 2000 as compared to 1999.

### Calculation of Effectiveness:

The number of civil suits in 1999 (assume 12) −
The number of suits in 2000 (assume 8)

_____ × 100 = Percent Change

The number of civil suits in 1999

$12 - 8 = \quad\quad 4$

_____ = .33 × 100 = 33% decrease in civil suits

$\quad\quad 12$

**Measure of Efficiency:** Reduce the average cost of answering calls for police service by 15% in 2000 as compared to 1999.

### Calculation of Efficiency

The average cost of answering calls for service in 1999 (assume $210) −
The average cost of answering calls for service in 2000 (assume $178)

_____ × 100 = Percent Change

The average cost of answering calls for service in 1999

$\$210 - \$178 = \quad\quad \$32$

_____ = .1523 × 100 = 15.23% decrease in cost

$\quad\quad \$210$

**Measure of Quality:** Increase the percentage of requests for traffic accident reports sent within 24 hours of receipt of the request from 70% in 1999 to 90% in 2000.

### Calculation of Quality

The number of requests handled within 24 hours in 1999 (assume 1,473) −
The number of requests handled within 24 hours in 2000 (assume 2,032)

_____ × 100 = Percent Change

The number of requests handled within 24 hours in 2000

$1{,}473 - 2{,}032 = \quad\quad 559$

_____ = .2750 × 100 = 27.5% increase in timely response

$\quad\quad 2032$

or (2) maintaining or increasing the level of output with a decrease in the level of resources used. Productivity improvement does not mean working harder; it means working "smarter."

One way of working smarter is to have an effective volunteer program. Some cities have trained cab drivers to be alert for suspicious people and situations and to notify the police. Essentially this creates more eyes and ears for patrol officers. Disabled persons and other volunteers can be trained and authorized to issue citations when able-bodied people park in handicapped spaces. In communities with large bodies of water, civilian boaters can be trained to serve in the same role as the taxi cab drivers previously discussed. Other police agencies have used volunteers to keep mug books updated, to conduct crime analyses, to maintain equipment, and to take care of police horses. A special case of using volunteers occurs in retirement communities, where large numbers of skilled people with flexible schedules can be helpful in a myriad of ways, including analyzing the financial data in white collar crimes and determining the best use of various technologies.

Productivity improvement efforts are possible in both large and small police departments. In terms of sequential steps, the implementation of a productivity improvement effort involves:

1. Selecting a program, subprogram, or activity for concentrated study, such as a neighborhood crime watch program.
2. Determining the true objectives of the program (e.g., to increase crime prevention awareness within specific neighborhoods and thereby reduce reported street crime).
3. Choosing the appropriate analytical procedures for eliciting information, such as interviewing victims or surveying officers.
4. Designing several program improvement options; for example, new technology, improved procedures, increasing employee motivation, contracting out service, and so on.
5. Forecasting direct and indirect impacts of program options, such as decreased fear of crime and safer and more secure public feeling.
6. Implementing the program—putting the selected program option into effect. This includes developing strategies for overcoming individual, organizational, and institutional barriers.
7. Evaluating the program—determining how well the new or adjusted program works when compared with the original program.[3]

**Management Style and Productivity**

The overall strategy involved in implementing a productivity improvement program may take one of three forms: (1) centralized, (2) nondirective, and (3) decentralized.[4] In a highly centralized system, the productivity staff might have responsibility for:

1. Establishing and imposing performance targets and timetables on the operating agencies
2. Identifying the programs or activities for which productivity improvements will be developed
3. Analyzing programs and activities
4. Designing and scheduling productivity improvement projects
5. Managing the implementation of productivity improvement projects
6. Operating a central information and control system on all productivity improvements
7. Negotiating or controlling negotiations with employee unions on productivity improvements[5]

The case for a centralized system is that it unites trained analysts with elected officials and ties productivity improvements to the power of the budget. Against it is the inherent danger of resistance from the police or other departments when change is experienced or perceived as being imposed. In the nondirective approach the city manager "makes no bones" about his or her interest in productivity improvements, but it is left to the department heads to decide a course of action. For those who seek improvements, the city manager provides substantial assistance in eliminating bureaucratic obstacles and obtaining expert help and is otherwise actively supportive. No pressure is placed on the "laggards" save the example set by the city manager and the responsive department heads; over time, increasingly more departments join the effort. Decentralization places responsibility for improvements with the heads of operating agencies, and although there is a reduction in central control, there is also less tension from imposed change and a closer linkage between the analysts and operations—improving both—because they are housed within each department of government.

**Management by Objectives**

A management approach that is a natural adjunct to productivity programs and that enhances them is management by objectives (MBO) or some alternative designation of it, such as policing by objectives (PBO).[6] The concept of MBO is widely attributed to Peter Drucker, author of *The Practice of Management* (1954). In general, the use of MBO in government can be described as a late-1960s, early-1970s movement. Its adoption has not been universal.

MBO can be defined as having a result, as opposed to an activity, orientation to managing with an underlying philosophical bias in participative management. Drucker elaborates on this philosophical bias by describing MBO as a common and explicit understanding between managers and their subordinates regarding what their contributions to the organization will be over a definite period of time (See Box 14-4).[7] Where MBO has been tried by police departments and has failed, its lack of success most often has been caused by using it as a purely technical management system implemented without a shift from reliance on traditional organizational theory precepts to the use of bridging or open systems theories, which stress the importance and worth of officers at all levels of the department. Stated in terms of leadership orientations, the MBO system implemented under a 9,1 (authority obedience) orientation incurs a greater risk of failure than under the 5,5 (organization management) or 9,9 (team management) approaches.

## BOX 14-4

### Downplaying Patrols and Embracing Communities, the State Police is Setting its Sights on Being . . .

### A Force of Change

**by Kyle Niederpruem,** *Staff Writer*

Trooper John D. Bowling is spending his work time a little differently these days. He's no longer just a traffic cop in a cruiser.

On this day, he's reading a book—and on taxpayer time.

He's spending a few afternoon hours at Richmond's Townsend Community Center with a gaggle of children, many of whom live in nearby government-subsidized housing. And his bosses approve.

"People talk to me now," Bowling said. "They used to see me as the enemy."

The Indiana State Police no longer measure success by the number of tickets written or arrests made. Once the lifeblood of this 66-year-old department, the numbers went down dramatically in some of the state's most populated districts from 1996 to 1998.

In District 52, which covers Boone, Johnson, Marion and Shelby counties, the number of traffic violations cited dropped to 18,491 in 1998 from 31,514 in 1996.

Should motorists be alarmed as troopers spend less time on the roads?

"If you live here, you should be frightened to enter the interstate system," said Trooper Mark Smith, who is a board director of the Indiana State Police Alliance and patrols Marion County roads.

But the plummeting statistics do not worry the man in charge. Superintendent Melvin Carraway barely looks at them. He says they are meaningless markers of the old way of doing business.

*(continued)*

## BOX 14-4 (continued)

Under the new model, district commanders write business plans. Troopers are "empowered" to craft personal performance goals that include community details that pull them off the interstates. Those who can't conform to this new way of working—and thinking—are placed in "rescue" mode, a form of probation.

Maj. Kelvis T. Williams, chairman of the Association of Indiana State Troopers representing about 150 minority employees in the department, said it's a better way.

"It's power down to the trooper, an opportunity to do a lot more," he said. In the old days—Williams has worked under four different superintendents in 22 years—"a sergeant was breathing down your neck (asking), how many tickets have you written?"

Moving away from the old style of management, however, hasn't made everyone a happy camper.

One trooper who favors the freedom in his work detail still complains about his aging equipment, a 1971-issue radio in his car that cuts out when his strobe lights are on at the same time.

It also doesn't fix the longtime grumble of low pay, even with a recent salary boost approved by lawmakers. Trainees who had been paid $19,396 now make $27,563, a 42 percent increase. Officers serving in their first year on the force now make $28,804.

Lt. Joan E. Malayter-Brubaker, district commander at the Bremen post, remembers what the superintendent said to her troops.

"I can't give you new radios, cars or a pay raise. But this is reality. Empower your people, and tell me what you can do. Tell 'em public service is as important as criminal arrests. Do it the way you see fit," she recalled from Carraway's visit.

She believes the same. People fail only if they don't try.

Since this evaluation system has been in place, only two State Police employees out of 1,200 have been brought up on administrative charges for disciplinary action after being placed in "rescue" mode. No one has been fired.

In her district, traffic arrests and criminal arrests have increased in the past year, one of the few geographical areas where statistics—the old measuring tool—increased markedly from 1996 to 1998.

But can the public be convinced that a lower number of traffic tickets means safer highways? That depends largely on other numbers. Statistics don't bear out a rise in roadway fatalities that correlates to the drop of reported traffic violations.

District commanders say if a trooper is freed up to concentrate on a traffic trouble spot, a danger zone where accidents are routine can be fixed.

The old way meant sitting on an intersection during rush hour writing tickets. A trooper in the new regime calls state transportation officials. Together, they document hazards and make necessary fixes.

Bowling says it happened last year on I-70. In a 12-mile construction zone on the east side of the state, there were four fatalities in a few short months over the summer.

The trooper began working with highway workers to reconstruct the zone with message boards, longer transition lanes and passing restrictions. The measure of success came over the Thanksgiving weekend. There was a crush of traffic and some property damage accidents, but no fatalities.

"This is more what a state trooper should do," said Bowling.

The new way of thinking covers a variety of on-the-clock programs that do take troopers off the road: after-school reading programs, power-point presentations to motel owners about drug trafficking, helping small towns find qualified marshal candidates and writing "Ask a Trooper" columns for local high schools.

Those constitute the new way of doing business. But they are also initiatives that can't easily be evaluated or measured for success.

Herb Davis, director of the Townsend Community Center, looks at his evolving relationship with Bowling as an investment.

"I think over the long term it helps reduce crime. I have no statistics to bear that out. The troopers can reach some of these young kids who might potentially get in trouble."

At the center, Bowling spends quality time reading a morality tale tailored for tots. It starts with a group of kids who grab a woman's purse at the mall.

"What would you do?" he asks.

They perk up with a rush of hands.

"Run home!" one shouts.

"I'd tell my mom and dad about it," another suggests.

Their questions follow in a staccato rush.

"You been shot?"

"Ever arrest someone you know?"

"Have you killed anyone?"

Bowling says that for these children who often see police only in the worst light—when Mom or Dad is arrested—this is bonding at its best.

But the outreach aspect of a law enforcement department that was first started when noisy cars began to push horse-drawn carriages off the road still has its contrary traditionalists.

## nples of Mission
ements

### are State Police

ance the quality of life for all Delaware citizens
itors by providing professional, competent and
ssionate law enforcement services.

### o County (Nebraska) Sheriff's
tment

eriff's Department will involve the communi-
l the people of the county in all policing activ-
at directly affect the quality of life.
Sheriff's Department will maintain crime pre-
1 as its primary goal, while vigorously pursu-
se who commit crimes.
Sheriff's Department will ensure that its polic-
ategies will preserve and advance democratic

Sheriff's Department will structure service de-
1 a manner as to reinforce the strengths of the
communities and rural areas.
Sheriff's Department will encourage public in-
arding the development of policies that di-
ffect the quality of life in Buffalo County.
Sheriff's Department will manage its re-
carefully and effectively.

The Sheriff's Department will seek the input of
employees into matters that affect job satisfaction
and effectiveness.

The Sheriff's Department will maintain the highest levels of integrity and professionalism in all its
members and its activities.

The Sheriff's Department will seek to provide stability, continuity and consistency in all departmental
operations.

The Sheriff's Department will conduct themselves
both personally and professionally in a manner that
is above reproach by the people of the communities
and county it serves.

### Hobbs (New Mexico) Police Department

We, the members of the Hobbs Police Department,
are committed to being responsive to our community in the delivery of quality service. Recognizing
our responsibility to maintain order, while affording
dignity and respect to every individual, our objective is to improve the quality of life through a community partnership which promotes safe, secure
neighborhoods. The values of the Hobbs Police
Department evolve around People, Leadership,
Service and Performance.

*Objectives* are end states that can be achieved in one year or less. Well-
stated objectives have three characteristics:

- Target specific
- Quantified
- Identified time frame

The following statement of an objective illustrates the use of these three characteristics: Objective One—to have 100 percent of all sergeants complete 120 hours
of supervisory training during FY 2002. These characteristics are important because they provide a basis for determining whether or not the organization accomplished what it set out to do. These characteristics also help explain one underlying reason for resistance to planning in general and goal and objective
setting in particular; formal statements of expectations are generated, impacting
on *responsibility* and *accountability,* the very essence of program evaluation.

The achievement of the identified objectives is then reinforced by the development of work plans, as shown in Figure 14-2. The specificity of the action plan allows for (1) monitoring; (2) taking corrective action as needed, as
the basis of evaluating; and (3) improved planning and decision making.

**acles and
Benefits**

MBO systems can fail for a variety of reasons. Stein[11] conducted a study in
which the attitudes of lower-level and midlevel management personnel using
MBO were examined. The results of the study revealed a number of problems
associated with the MBO system. The three most critical problems were

Smith, for example, says the primary responsibility of any trooper isn't about community outreach, the "warm and fuzzy" image-building stuff.

"The rush away from numbers has gotten us away from law enforcement," Smith said. "We should own the interstate system."

Smith is often one of only two troopers assigned per shift to the highways crisscrossing Marion County. Yet he grudgingly admits that the new system does "give you a little bit of freedom."

Davis is a witness to the value of off-road activity, and he sees the value for taxpayers.

"If you look at dollars spent, ther kids have an understanding, an apt spect for law enforcement and a ser how much better off is the commu

"Could they still do their job cruiser? Sure. But there would b turns."

For sure, Davis believes, for the

*Source: The Indianapolis Star,* January

The underlying rationale of MBO can be summarized as such: the better a manager understands what he or she hopes to accomplish (the better he or she knows his or her objectives), the greater will be his or her chances for success.[8] In a sense, MBO provides the manager with a blueprint that guides him or her toward the objective he or she has set. Others suggest, "if one knows where he is going, he finds it easier to get there, he can get there faster, and he will know when he arrives.[9]

Figure 14-1 summarizes the major steps commonly involved in the MBO process. The formulation of long-range goals is preceded by the development of the police department's *mission statement,* which is the broadest, most comprehensive statement that can be made about the overall purpose of the police department.[10] The mission statement recognizes either explicitly or implicitly legislatively mandated roles, professional tenets, community preferences, and related sources (see Box 14-5).

*Goals* are end states or conditions that take one or more years to achieve. Complex goals (e.g., designing, obtaining approval for, procuring, and placing a new jail communications system into operation) may take three to five years. Goals may also be stated in such a fashion that the pursuit of them is continuous (e.g., "to promote officer safety and performance by providing a variety of basic and in-service training experiences"). Because of the time-horizon associated with goals, they are supported by more immediately achievable (and subsequently measurable) objectives.

1. Develop long-range goals.
2. State measurable objectives that will be accomplished during a specific period of time.
3. Review goals and objectives to make sure they are challenging but obtainable.
4. Develop work plans that contribute to the achievement of goals and objectives.
5. Develop effectiveness, quality, and efficiency measures.
6. Implement and monitor work plans.
7. Modify work plans as needed.
8. Evaluate performance of work plans as compared to the planned-for results.

**FIGURE 14-1.** Steps in developing an MBO process.

| GOAL | To provide a management environment that facilitates achieving department goals while providing for the career needs of its employees. | |
|---|---|---|
| OBJECTIVE | To develop and place into operation by August 4, 2000 a new telecommunications center. | TARGET DATE<br>August 4, 2000 |
| DIVISION<br>Administration | | PERSON RESPONSIBLE<br>Janice Saylors |

| ACTION PLAN | TARGET DATE |
|---|---|
| Development and Construction of a Police Department Communications Center to Be Operational by August 4, 2000. | |
| A.  Equipment selection to include equipment options | Jan. 31, 2000 |
| B.  Develop equipment specifications | Feb. 25, 2000 |
| C.  Site plan and specifications completed | Feb. 25, 2000 |
| D.  Bids released on communications equipment and construction | Mar. 3, 2000 |
| E.  Bids received by city of purchasing office | Mar. 28, 2000 |
| F.  Bids awarded for equipment and construction by city council | Apr. 1, 2000 |
| G.  Communications equipment ordered from successful bidder | Apr. 2, 2000 |
| H.  Construction begins on communication center | Apr. 14, 2000 |
| I.  Delivery and installation of communications equipment | Jul. 23, 2000 |
| J.  Construction work in center completed | Aug. 1, 2000 |
| K.  Communications center operational | Aug. 4, 2000 |

| PREPARED BY | Colin Cummings | DATE PREPARED<br>October 30, 1999 |
|---|---|---|
| APPROVED BY | Chief Doc Mercer | DATE APPROVED<br>November 5, 1999 |

**FIGURE 14-2.** A work plan.

1. Difficulty in defining objectives that were both meaningful and measurable
2. Insufficient follow-up, monitoring, and updating of the program
3. Lack of commitment by management to the purposes and concepts of MBO.[12]

Further, it should be remembered that the implementation of MBO requires large-scale organizational change. However, a fully developed and properly implemented MBO system may require two to five years of sustained effort in large organizations before it takes hold. A review of the research on MBO reveals that it has the potential to

1. Increase goal specificity
2. Increase awareness of goals
3. Contribute to improved planning
4. Result in greater specificity in identifying and defining problems
5. Produce better resource allocation
6. Have a favorable effect on productivity
7. Improve superior-subordinate relationships
8. Increase the receptivity of superiors to new ideas and suggestions

9. Make greater use of subordinates' ability and experiences
10. Improve interpersonal and organizational communications
11. Increase motivation and job satisfaction among employees
12. Increase objectivity in evaluating performances[13]

From these points, one could conclude, as one chief wryly did, that "MBO will do everything but take out the garbage." Given its potential utility, why aren't fully developed MBO systems being used in every police department? There may be no single answer, but from experience some observed reasons are that (1) it is easier to maintain the status quo than to enter into the change process; (2) some police leaders are unable or unwilling to part with highly centralized control; (3) MBO has been oversold in that, as compared with its benefits, not as much attention has been given to the reality that it takes sustained hard work to achieve changes; it cannot simply be dropped into the police department like a set of spark plugs into a car; (4) some managers do not really want to know the answer to the question, "How well am I (or are we) doing?"; (5) reports of failures in the use of MBO have discouraged some potential adopters; and (6) the costs involved in developing the system and training personnel in both MBO's technical and the behavioral aspects are high.

Additionally, research suggests that MBO may have certain dysfunctional consequences if not implemented properly: (1) over time, officers may become indifferent to it as "just another management procedure"; (2) when participation in objective setting does not reach the lower levels of the organization, it is likely to fail, making future innovations more difficult to implement; (3) it can create excessive paperwork with an emphasis more on building a paper record than on achieving results; and (4) easily quantifiable objectives may be substituted for more important, but more difficult to measure, ones.[14] Despite such barriers, MBO is an important management tool.

## The Thorns in Productivity Measurement

Whereas the concept of productivity is deceptively simple, trying to employ it meaningfully in policing presents challenges. The fact that such challenges exist does not, however, mean that productivity improvement efforts (PIEs) should not be undertaken. At present, productivity measurement in policing are still in a relatively early stage. However, the heightened concern for "getting the most for the buck," has resulted in the use of more formal PIEs and PMs. Relatedly, the most fundamental obligation that managers seeking public appropriations have is to demonstrate that they have exercised careful stewardship over the resources previously entrusted to them. Failing a demonstration of that, on what grounds can police managers reasonably expect effectively to advance a case for any additional funding?

A key issue in using PMs is developing a definition of output. If part of the role of the police is preventing crime, how, for example, do you measure how many crimes the police prevented? A related problem is establishing that there is some relationship between police effort and outcome. To illustrate, if reported crime decreases or increases, it may be the result of a reduction in, or an increase in, public confidence that the police cannot or can do something about crime. This shift in public confidence may occur quite independently of anything that the police may or may not do; such a shift may be caused by rumors, statements by political candidates, or the errors in news reports that occasionally happen under the pressure of deadlines. Additionally, if specific police programs aimed at particular crime problems do not yield results, the police may be tempted to discourage the filing of complaints or assign the complaints to another crime category. In a city with a rash of robberies, the uniformed officers may be told at roll call to "make sure you really have a robbery; some of those reports coming in as robberies are actually larcenies, and it's causing extra paperwork in getting them classified properly." The words spoken notwithstanding, the real message is "we're taking a lot of heat about these robberies and one way or another we've got to reduce them." In some jurisdictions, there are allegations that the police have "cooked" the crime statistics.

Other problems relating to measuring productivity include the following: (1) an increase in police productivity may be accompanied by a reduction in the quality of output; (2) the achievement of a given productivity level does not mean that the level of services being provided is consistent with community desires or needs; (3) there is difficulty in developing adequate and appropriate measures for staff functions such as personnel and training; (4) achieving the desired level of productivity in one area may make it difficult to achieve the desired level in another; and (5) performance measures must be clearly defined at the beginning of their use. If, for example, a police chief wants to reduce the cost of responding to calls for service, what elements make up that cost? Does it include only the officer's time at the scene or does it include travel time and vehicle costs? How are vehicle costs to be calculated? Is it just gas? Does it assume a flat 25 cents per mile from where the officer got the call to where the request for service is? What about depreciation on the vehicle?

In some cases, the crime control and community relations functions may come into conflict. For example, assume that a police department assigns officers in teams to various high-crime neighborhoods. All members of the team are dressed to blend into the street life where they are assigned and one or more serve as decoys. When offenders attempt to victimize the decoys, the other team members close in and make an arrest. After seven months, the arrest and conviction rates for serious offenses are five times higher among team officers as compared with the rates for conventionally deployed officers. However, in the course of these special operations, six minority citizens have been shot to death and two others wounded as they attempted to commit violent felonies involving the decoys as victims. As a result, the minority community is aroused, and their relations with the police are reaching new lows. Thus we have two desirable goals that are in conflict, namely, improved community relations and the reduction of violent street crime.

## MBO, Productivity, and Quality Improvement Efforts

Figure 14-3 depicts the integration of an MBO system and a productivity improvement effort (PIE). Although an MBO system and PIE have some overlapping features—which is why MBO is a natural adjunct to a productivity program—there are some differences. The starting place for an MBO system is the mission statement, which is a global orientation, whereas the starting place for a PIE is selecting a program, a subprogram, or an activity for concentrated study.

Three separate types of performance measures are identified in Figure 14-3: (1) efficiency, used to denote the efficiency of the service delivery system rather than the individual worker; (2) quality; and (3) effectiveness. Typically, when a productivity system is introduced, the measures of efficiency and effectiveness draw the early attention. Subsequently, concern for what will happen or what is happening to the quality of service delivery emerges and measures are adopted or developed to deal with this concern.

To illustrate, in 1950, W. Edwards Deming was invited by the Union of Japanese Scientists and Engineers to speak to leading industrialists who were

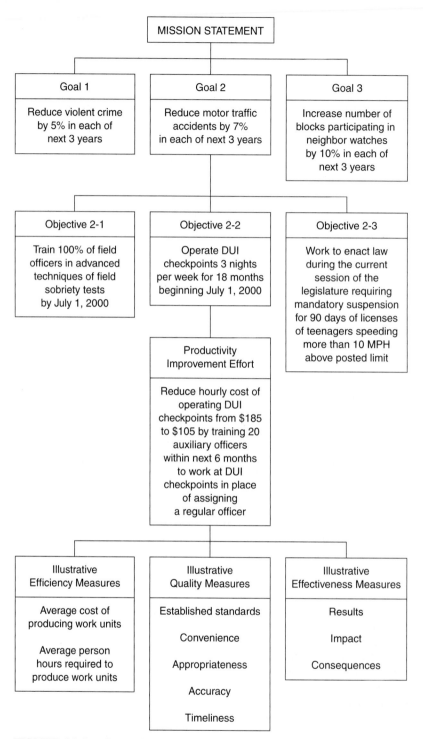

**FIGURE 14-3.** Examples of efficiency, quality, and effectiveness performance measures were provided in Table 14-1.

concerned about breaking into foreign markets.[15] At that time Japan used typical management and efficiency measures and had a deserved reputation for poor quality goods. Deming convinced them that Japanese quality could be the best in the world if they adopted his methods, which center on 14 points (see Box 14-6).[16] The industrialist took Deming's philosophy to heart and the rest is history.[17] Each year Japanese industry presents on television the coveted Deming prize to the company that has achieved the greatest gains in productivity. Its past winners have included Nissan, Hitachi, and Toyota.[18] In 1985, Texas Instruments became the first American recipient of a Deming award.[19] Events such as these sparked considerable private- and public-sector interest in this country. Quality circles (QCs)—discussed in Chapter 4, "Organizational Theory"—quickly sprang up everywhere. However, by the 1990s, QCs were seen as being nothing more than "quick fixes" that were based on the faulty assumption that by training workers at the lower levels of the organization, quality would take care of itself. In contrast, Deming's view of quality is that it permeates every aspect of the organization (total quality management, or TQM; also, refer back to Chapter 6, "Leadership" and the information on Total Quality Leadership—TQL). In 1987, President Reagan signed the Malcolm Baldrige National Quality Improvement Act. Named after a former secretary of commerce, the act mandated the creation of a quality award for manufacturing, service, and small businesses, with a limit of two awards per year in each of those categories.[23] The National Institute of Standards and Technology (NIST) was responsible for the development of standards that organizations could use to evaluate their quality improvement efforts. NIST developed a seven-category, 1,000-point scoring system and a three-level judging process to evaluate applicants for a Baldrige Award.[24] Past Baldrige winners included Xerox, Cadillac, Motorola, and the first awardee in the service category, Federal Express. Among the criticisms of the Baldrige

## BOX 14-6

### Deming's 14 Quality Points

1. Create constancy of purpose toward improvement of product and service, with a plan to improve competitive position and stay in business.

2. Adopt the new philosophy. We are in a new economic age. We can no longer live with commonly accepted levels of delays, mistakes, defective materials and defective workmanship.

3. Cease dependence on mass inspection. Require, instead, statistical evidence that quality is built in to eliminate the need for inspection on a mass basis.

4. End the practice of awarding business on the basis of price tag. Instead, depend on meaningful measures of quality, along with price.

5. Find problems. It is management's job to work continually on improving the system.

6. Institute modern methods of training on the job.

7. Institute modern methods of supervision.

8. Drive out fear so that everyone may work effectively for the company.

9. Break down barriers between departments.

10. Eliminate numerical goals, posters, and slogans that seek new levels of productivity without providing methods.

11. Eliminate work standards that prescribe numerical quotas.

12. Remove barriers that rob employees of their pride of workmanship.

13. Institute a vigorous program of education and retraining.

14. Create a structure which will push on the prior 13 points every day.

Source: Howard S. Gitlow and Shelly J. Gitlow, The Deming Guide to Quality and Competitive Position (Englewood Cliffs, N.J.: Prentice Hall, Inc., 1987), p. 20.

Award were that it didn't predict financial success for a company and that it really didn't recognize superior quality because Cadillac had yet to distinguish itself in stellar ratings of automobiles such as the J. D. Powers survey.[25] However, the General Accounting Office reported that there was a cause-and-effect relationship between the TQM practices embodied in the Baldrige Award and corporate performance as measured by employee relations, customer satisfaction, or profitability.[26] Unfortunately, the Baldrige Award was eliminated in the mid-1990s by a budget-slashing Congress. It is now administered by the American Society for Quality CASQ.

Law enforcement's equivalent of the Malcolm Baldrige Award is the Webber Seavey Award for Quality Policing, which is jointly sponsored by the International Association of Chiefs of Police (IACP) and Motorola (see Figure 14-4). Established in 1993, this award is named after the first president of the International Association of Chiefs of Police. The Seavey Award was created solely to recognize outstanding police performance worldwide. In order to compete for the award, a police agency must submit a description of a quality-driven project which it has initiated to instill continuous service improvement to the community being served.

The Reading (Pennsylvania) Police Department was one of three winners of the 1999 Seavey Award.[20] Like many other agencies, the RPD was inundated with 911 emergency and other priority calls for services. As a result of this high volume, patrol officers had little time to focus on underlying problems, resulting in a high crime rate and unsatisfied customers. The city's drug trade has also increased dramatically, spawning a rise in violence, weapons violations, disturbance calls, and gang activities. The city's police department had seen its calls for service climb 20 percent over the last seven years, from 60,514 calls in 1992 to 75,963 in 1998. Many of these calls were 911 emergency calls demanding immediate response. The department's patrol officers

**FIGURE 14-4.** The Webber Seavey Award for Quality Policing. (Courtesy of the International Association of Chiefs of Police.)

became hard pressed to respond to citizen calls for service, and many lower priority calls were never answered due to this increased workload and growing crime rate. It is safe to characterize police response as being "911" driven and almost completely reactive.

In addition, a series of neighborhood meetings hosted by city government throughout the city revealed the residents also had other concerns about their neighborhoods. They complained about burglaries and thefts, loud car stereos, unruly and disrespectful groups, traffic and parking problems, and trash-strewn streets and properties. Residents felt that their ability to enjoy their homes and neighborhoods was seriously impinged by these conditions.

The RPD created and implemented plans designed to raise the quality of life in the city by improving the methods in which officers are deployed, taking stricter enforcement action, and instituting innovative methods of police response. The solutions were identified to be the establishment of a series of new full-time and part-time special units, a renewed partnership between management and the police union, and an emphasis on creating a team focus on fighting crime in the city. Included in these actions were the establishment of Quality of Life units that provided more timely response to citizens' calls regarding disturbances, noise, and parking problems, and a High Crime Detail that tracked and apprehended offenders responsible for multiple crimes.

The results were impressive. Response time improved to quality of life type calls for service, and laws and ordinances were more rigorously enforced. Arrests of all types were up 14 percent since 1996 and arrests for disorderly conduct, a prime Quality of Life (QOL) offense, were up 30 percent. Prostitution arrests were also up by 51 percent since 1996, and there were numerous arrests for violations of the city's revised noise ordinance. Drug investigations by police increased 32 percent. Perhaps the most notable result was the effect this effort had on the city's crime rate, which decreased 23 percent over the first two years these plans had been implemented. With these innovations, the citizens of Reading have experienced a more responsive, effective police department, and support for police efforts is growing.

The prestigious J. Stannard Baker Award for Highway Safety is also sponsored by the IACP, along with the National Highway Traffic Safety Administration and the Traffic Institute, Northwestern University (see Box 14-7). This award recognizes law enforcement and civilian personnel who have shown unusual initiative and creativity in developing quality traffic safety programs.

Lt. Born pioneered the Ohio State Highway Patrol's Partners for Safety effort initiated in January 1998.[21] His vision for Partners for Safety as a sustained and concerted effort to mix law enforcement and public education in local communities is being realized. Patrol posts around the state have successfully

## BOX 14-7

### Who Was J. Stannard Baker?

The IACP's highway traffic safety award was named to honor J. Stannard Baker who made significant contributions to highway safety. Mr. Baker was a former physics professor at Northwestern University. A pioneer in accident reconstruction investigation, he developed this subject into a science by applying the laws of physics and developing mathematical equations to assist police in their investigations. The first books on accident reconstruction investigation were written by J. Stannard Baker and are still in use today.

*Source:* International Association of Chiefs of Police.

implemented meaningful Partners for Safety efforts to encourage motorist participation in highway safety efforts by developing a new telephone number to offer motorists highway assistance. Born worked with the Ohio Department of Transportation to erect 153 large highway signs on high traffic volume highways. The new number is also expected to reduce nonemergency calls to 911. As a result of an intensive publicity campaign and the distribution of promotional items, nonemergency telephone calls have been reduced.

The commitment to safety forged by Lt. Born among the Highway Patrol, private corporations, and the citizens of Ohio demonstrates that increased safety on the roads can be achieved through cooperative partnerships. These partnerships included the American Automobile Association; Ameritech Cellular; BP; Brickler & Eckler, LPA; Club (Winner International); Honda of America; Longaberger; McDonald's Championship racing; Ohio Automobile Dealer's Association (OADA); Ohio Hotel & Lodging Association (OH&LA); Ohio News Network; Ohio Trucking Association; State Farm Insurance; and Towing/Recovery Association of Ohio.

Lt. Born ensured that motorists in every Ohio county saw larger-than-life reminders from the Patrol to buckle their safety belts during the summer of 1998. By Memorial Day weekend, a project coordinated by Lt. Born resulted in over 300 billboards, financed with drunk driver fines, erected around the state urging motorists to become a "Partner for Safety" and "Join Us" in wearing their safety belts. These billboards were visible along U.S. and state routes with a high frequency of crashes.

The IACP also cosponsors the Community Policing Award with ITT Industries. One of the two winners from agencies serving populations of less than 20,000 was Beaufort, South Carolina.[22] The Beaufort Police Department (BPO) has 49 total employees and serves a daytime and nighttime population of 11,000.

The department started taking steps in 1994 to implement community policing. Since 1996, the department and the community have enjoyed many successful ventures and have formed partnerships to address community concerns. Within these partnerships a trusting bond has emerged between the department and the community. Teams have been formed to identify, analyze, and resolve crime, disorder, and community problems.

In 1994, an alarming increase in the number of crimes reported and an escalating level of violence prompted the implementation of community-oriented policing throughout the department. A twenty-block area was identified as the "Combat Zone," a place where drug dealers had taken over. The area had become run-down and had other crime-related problems.

It was clear that improving this situation would not be an easy task, as the twenty-block neighborhood was one of the poorest with many elderly residents. Lines of communication did not exist because trust did not exist between law enforcement and residents. The department committed itself to changing this condition and improving the relationship between the residents and the police.

In mid-1995, with the help of residents, officers identified the drug dealers and their methods. More than 130 arrest warrants were obtained for the sale and distribution of various drugs. When some of the toughest drug dealers were led away in handcuffs, residents realized that they could do something about controlling their neighborhood. The United Block Association (UBA) was formed to identify problem locations within the neighborhood in an effort to prevent problems before they got out of control. Due to this partnership, the twenty-block area has had a 58 percent reduction of Part 1 crimes.

Other programs grew out of this initiative, which allow the police and residents to interact. A Trespass Enforcement Program was established to relieve homeowners from the threat of drug dealers using their property to avoid the police. A partnership with local churches was formed to develop a volunteer program to work on community problems. A mentoring initiative selected department volunteers to work one-on-one with children to improve their learning skills. A School Resource Officer and a Student Police Academy at the high school were established. A citizen police academy was created to provide interaction between the citizens and officers.

For 25 years, the Beaufort Police Movie Club has been free to all children between the ages of five and twelve. The Movie Club attracts between 400 and 500 children each Saturday during the summer. The children see a movie and receive safety lectures from police officers and different public safety agencies within the community.

Members from the community were selected to participate in the Public Safety Advisory Council (PSAC). The PSAC identifies the problems and concerns of Beaufort Citizens and reviews current police resources as related to criminal activity. Community Mobilization Teams have been formed to eradicate problems and crime from individual neighborhoods. This initiative has been so successful that, in some areas of the city, crime has been cut in half. Substations within the city have further expanded the visibility of Beaufort's officers and allowed citizens to have easier accessibility to the officers that work in their neighborhoods.

The partners that assisted in these endeavors are as diverse as the community. Surveys indicate that residents are satisfied with the services and the performance of the department. There has been a dramatic decrease in the amount of crime and the overall fear of crime. The physical appearance of the community has improved, and residents are taking ownership and responsibility for their neighborhoods. Neighborhood organizations now are active and cooperating with law enforcement to make a difference.

## PROGRAM EVALUATION

As in the case of many other basic concepts, evaluation is one that everyone seems to understand and agree on until they begin to define it.[27] Then, a great deal of difference begins to emerge. Most definitions seem to look at evaluation from one or more of three perspectives:

1. As a process, which focuses on how evaluation is done, the steps and procedures involved in designing and conducting an evaluation.
2. As a product, meaning the findings or judgments that are made as a result of doing an evaluation.
3. In terms of its purpose, the end use of evaluation, such as for planning, policymaking, and decision making.[28]

These three perspectives can be grouped together logically to form a view of evaluation as a process, which results in a product, which has a purpose.[29] This section is not intended to provide information about how to do evaluation, on which there is ample literature, but rather about how to examine evaluation from an administrative point of view.

## Types of Program Evaluation

In its broadest context, *program* refers to an activity or group of related activities undertaken by a unit of government to provide a service to the public.[30] A program may be contained in a single agency, such as the police department, or spread among several agencies, such as emergency medical services. Again in the broadest context, *program evaluation* refers to the systematic assessment of an activity or group of related activities. Under the umbrella heading of program evaluation, three different types are recognizable.[31]

1. *Process evaluation.* This type of evaluation is not concerned with the ultimate usefulness or appropriateness of the program activities, but, rather, with only how well they are being performed. It looks at, for example, whether recruits are being hired and trained in sufficient time to meet the need for them. Process evaluation goes beyond program monitoring in that, in addition to describing what is happening, it determines "why or why not" these things are happening. Although often not recognized as such, process evaluation is an ongoing activity in police departments and is part of the way in which organizations are controlled. Illustrative are the periodic receipt and analysis of budget status reports and the system of administrative inspections that are conducted to determine if established policies and procedures are being followed, to identify deviations, and to recommend any needed corrective actions.

2. *Program evaluation.* This type of evaluation asks whether or not a program has met its ultimate objectives. It is concerned with the intended consequences of a police department's various programs. Police departments, although often not recognizing it, do more program evaluation than they realize. For example, the one-group pretest versus post-test design is represented in the following way:

$$O_1 \; X \; O_2$$

This design consists of a first observation ($O_1$), where a measurement is made; a treatment (X), such as a productivity improvement program, and a second observation ($O_2$). The difference between the two measurements is then considered to be a function of the treatment. However, this design is methodologically simple and subject to influences other than the treatment. To use an earlier example, a reduction in reported crime may not be due to anything that the police are doing but, instead, be a function of some event that occurred between $O_1$ and $O_2$, such as rumors sweeping the community that reduce confidence in the ability of the police to deal with crime, leading to a reduction in reported crime. The issue is not what the limitations of the one-group pretest versus post-test design are; rather, it is what forms of program evaluation the police should be, and are, engaged in.

3. *Impact evaluation.* Because this type of evaluation is the most difficult and costly to perform, it is the least used type of evaluation in police departments. Impact evaluation goes well beyond how well a program was operated and whether it met its objectives. Its heart is: "In both a positive and negative sense, what difference did this program actually make?"

   Assume that a local police department decides to fight drunk driving by using roadblocks at selected intersections on Thursday, Friday, and Saturday nights from 10:00 P.M. until 2:00 A.M. After 90 days, this effort has produced

111 driving under the influence and 17 no drivers license charges. Accidents attributable to drinking drivers have declined 82%. If only this information was considered, the program is a success.

But what if the roadblocks resulted in lengthy lines of cars waiting to pass through them and the opinion of motorists is running considerably against the police department? Factor in a case where an ambulance was involved in an accident trying to weave through traffic at the road block and the heart attack victim it was transporting nearly died due to the resulting delay in getting her to the hospital. To staff the roadblocks, officers were diverted from other assignments and as a result burglary rates have climbed 35 percent over the past 90 days. By doing an impact evaluation and looking at both the positive and negative consequences of the roadblock program you get a much clearer picture of what the program has meant.

There is an old saw that says, "Regardless what patients do regarding their appointment with a psychiatrist, some useful meaning can be gained by the psychiatrist." If patients are early, they are anxious; if they are on time, they are compulsive; if they are late, they are resistant. In a similar vein, historically police administrators have relied, to their own advantage, on reported crime as the evaluative measure of their department's performance. If crime was falling, cuts in personnel were resisted so that the "favorable position" could be maintained; if crime was increasing, additional officers were "required" to "turn the situation around." There is a sense in which program failure is essential for many organizations in that the effective solution of the problems they address would eliminate the purpose and, therefore, the very need for the organizations.[32] Recognizing this, the appropriators of funds and others began raising the question as to whether they should continue to support organizations that benefit from their own failures.[33]

Crime is a complex social issue on which the police have a negligible or marginal impact at best; the elimination of crime and consequently the need for the police are unlikely to happen. However, city managers, directors of departments of finance and management, and city councils are increasingly disinclined to accept the self-serving manipulations of some police chiefs to justify their budgets and characterize the performance of their departments. Consequently, there is an increasing use of some sort of benchmark, performance standard, or MBO system as a measure of program evaluation.

Despite these and related pressures, some chiefs resisted using—where they existed—their planning and research units for much more than tabulating statistics for the annual report and performing crime analysis for the line bureaus. Among the reasons for this posture were the following:

1. Police administrators did not understand, or would not acknowledge, the advantages to be gained from comprehensive program evaluation.
2. The policy preferences and positions of police administrators are translated into programs, and they were not very motivated to do anything that could discredit their stances.
3. The allocation of resources to the staff function of program evaluation was often viewed as a lower priority than the allocation of resources to line functions.
4. A distrust of evaluation existed that was coupled with a preference for relying on subjective judgments gained through years of experience.

**The Police Administrator and Evaluation**

5. Disfavorable evaluations were feared as a powerful tool for "outsiders" to criticize the administrator personally or the department, whereas favorable evaluations would not be accorded very much weight.

6. Initiating evaluation and then using the results involves a commitment to being change oriented, and sheer organizational inertia was a frequent barrier.

## Making Evaluation Work

The previously cited projects have yielded considerable debate similar to other controversial studies focusing on the impact of computerization on the police, the effectiveness of women officers, and the general role or function of uniformed police. It has become apparent that with respect to evaluations, there are two types of police administrators:

1. "Trapped" administrators believe in the efficiency, rightness, or perhaps the inevitability of their programs. If evaluations demonstrate a lack of effectiveness in the programs advocated by these administrators, they are likely to dismiss the evaluations as irrelevant, too academic, or invalid, or to simply shelve and ignore them. This posture creates problems for evaluation staffs and inhibits the intelligent development and execution of police programs.

2. "Experimental" administrators are not committed to a particular program, but to the concept of improving individual programs and the police department as a whole. If new or old programs are found as experimental administrators to be lacking, they are shelved or modified in attempts to find more successful ways. Experimental police administrators might be disappointed if evaluations show ineffectiveness, but unlike the trapped administrators they are not disorganized nor do they fail to act on the results. The experimental administrators are pragmatic and more interested in finding solutions than in justifying a particular course of action.[34]

By comparing the attributes of trapped and experimental police administrators, it is seen that the administrator is the key to whether evaluation will be a useful management tool. In order to make evaluation "pay off," police administrators must:

1. Adopt a genuinely supportive stance toward evaluation. Such a stance is reflected in the quality of staff selected for assignment to the evaluation function; in the resources made available to the evaluation effort; in according evaluation a place in the police organizational structure, which suggests its importance to the administrator; in the willingness to be involved in the evaluation process; and in ensuring a good relationship between the evaluation unit and the line bureaus.

2. Be willing to learn the key concepts in evaluation. There is a considerable amount of informative, but not overly technical, written material for police administrators, and they must avail themselves of it and other opportunities to learn, including attendance at workshops.[35]

3. Require informative evaluation. To "inform" means that the "information" being transmitted is understood. This requires not only that police administrators learn something of the key concepts and language of evaluation but also that they require evaluators to learn the key concepts and language of management.

4. Be assertive when dealing with researchers. Evaluators must know the specific expectations and informational needs of administrators. When evaluators

present concepts or procedures with which administrators are unfamiliar, administrators should require an explanation in terms they can understand. Nothing should be accepted "on faith."

5. Remember George Bernard Shaw's observation that every profession has its "conspiracy against the laity." Evaluation reports are often laced with dozens of complex statistical tables that are easily understood by evaluators but not necessarily by administrators. Evaluation, however, is a logical and not a statistical process. Complex statistical notations should be eliminated altogether, except perhaps as appendices, and the results stated in straightforward language. Reports that do not do so should be returned to the evaluators for redrafting.

6. Be able to describe the evaluation procedures and results to other nonresearchers, such as city managers, budget analysts, civic club members, and city councils or county commissions. Although administrators may have gained some sophistication in evaluation, they must guard against the use of "research jargon." Their purpose is not to display mastery but to win supporters for police programs.

7. Lose no chance internally or externally to praise the evaluation staff, their products, and their contributions.

8. Personally adopt and foster an environment supportive of experimentation.

9. Understand that much evaluative research is flawed, and can be criticized, but that the defects are seldom so great that all the information is useless. This means that police administrators must be willing to accept a certain element of risk in making policy and program decisions.[36]

## The Insider-Outsider Evaluator Question

Police administrators have several options with respect to who conducts the evaluation of experimental programs: (1) the police units conducting the activity may also perform the evaluation; (2) the evaluation may be done by the police department's planning and research unit; (3) another department of government, such as finance and management, may take responsibility; or (4) a contact may be executed with a research institute, a consultant, or some other related independent provider of services. These various possibilities raise certain questions, such as, "Is it appropriate for the police unit conducting an experimental program to evaluate itself?" Whereas the need to separate those who are carrying out an experimental program and those who evaluate it is apparent, the question of how much separation there should be gives rise to the "insider-outsider" evaluator question.

Several views should be considered when a police administrator is trying to decide whether to use the department's planning and research unit or an outsider to evaluate an experimental program:

1. The public and public officials may have more confidence in an autonomous outsider.
2. The outsider may have greater competence.
3. Outsiders may be perceived as being more objective.
4. An outsider may have a prestigious name that can be an asset in promoting the experimental program.
5. Outsiders may "sweeten" the results obtained by the program to gain favor and possible future business.
6. Insiders have greater knowledge of the operation of their particular department.

**FIGURE 14-5.** Santa Fe, New Mexico, policeman talks to senior citizens about "Neighborhood Watch" safety program. (Photo by Mimi Forsyth, Monkmeyer Press Photo Service.)

7. Insiders may see more practical ramifications to the results of the program than outsiders.

8. Insiders may suppress negative findings out of departmental loyalty or fear of personal and professional consequences to them.

9. Insiders may be more responsive to the legitimate directives of police administrators.

10. Insiders may have a "special axe to grind" and withhold or distort findings that reflect favorably on the program or on particular individuals.[37]

When such factors as cost, departmental staff capacity, and the availability of competent outsiders are added, the most advantageous way in which to proceed may still not be clear. In such matters, the identification of the issues is often a great deal easier to come by than is the answer. In other cases, there may be no decision to make other than who the external evaluator will be, because some grants are conditioned by the requirement of—and money is provided for—an independent evaluator who is external to the unit of government being used.

## SUMMARY

Productivity has two fundamental components: effectiveness and efficiency. Stated simply, effectiveness means that the police reached the objective they sought to achieve. In considering efficiency, the question is, "How much of our resources were required to achieve this objective?" Considerations of productivity also include the dimension of quality. In law enforcement circles, the Webber Seavey Award for Quality Policing—which was established in 1993 and is operated by the IACP and Motorola—is the equivalent of the Baldrige Award. Other key awards for achievement in law enforcement are the J. Stannard Baker Award for Highway Safety and the Community Policing Award.

Implementing a productivity management program involves seven sequential steps. Productivity programs may be—in terms of implementation—centralized, decentralized, or nondirective. Regardless of the implementation strategy, productivity programs require doing more with current resources, or maintaining or increasing output in the face of decreased resources. A natural adjunct to a productivity improvement program is an MBO (management by objectives) system. The measurement of productivity raises difficult challenges such as establishing some relationship between what the police do and the change in resulting conditions, and how to ensure that an increase in productivity does not have the unintended consequences of reducing the quality of service.

The evaluation of police programs is an absolute necessity. Three types of evaluation can be employed: (1) process, (2) program, and (3) impact. The police routinely, often without recognizing it, do process evaluation, and performance measures are often nothing more than a variant on some type of program evaluation design such as the one-group pretest versus post-test comparison. Police administrators can and must take certain steps to ensure useful evaluations. The issue of inside versus outside program evaluators raises a number of questions that must be considered in light of the specifics of the situation involved, as does the issue of "insiders versus outsiders" in organizational change, discussed in the next chapter.

## DISCUSSION QUESTIONS

1. What are twin pillars of productivity?
2. What is the classical definition of productivity?
3. Assume that the cost of responding to calls for police service in 2001 is $194 as compared to $168. Put this information into a measure of efficiency calculation and determine the percent change.
4. When implementing a productivity program, what is the first thing police leaders must be able to do?
5. Give at least three examples of how police departments can use volunteers to control policing costs.
6. What are the three characteristics of a well-stated objective?
7. Study the mission statements included in Box 14-5. How are those mission statements similar and different?
8. Explain the purposes of the IACP's Seavey, Stannard, and Community Policing awards.
9. Review Figure 14-3. At the bottom of the figure are illustrations of efficiency, quality, and effectiveness. Develop one performance measure for each of those measures. Specifically relate them to the PIE stated in Figure 14-3.
10. Distinguish between trapped and experimental administrators.
11. Identify and briefly discuss the three types of program evaluation.
12. What are the advantages and disadvantages of using an outside evaluator?

## NOTES

1. Frederick O'R. Hayes, "Leadership and Politics of the Productivity Process," in *Productivity Improvement Handbook for State and Local Governments,* ed. George J. Washnis (New York: John Wiley & Sons, 1980), pp. 19–23, with some changes and additions.

2. Edgar G. Crane, Jr., "Productivity in State Government," *Productivity Improvement Handbook,* p. 55.

3. Mark E. Keane, "Why Productivity Improvement?" *Productivity Improvement Handbook,* pp. 9–10.

4. The discussion of these three strategies is drawn from Frederick O'R. Hayes, "Implementation Strategies to Improve Productivity," in *Productivity Improvement Handbook,* pp. 26–27.

5. Hayes, "Implementation Strategies," p. 26.

6. Other terms that describe an MBO-type system include "cohesive management system" and "priority program planning system," both of which were used by the New York City Police Department in 1974 and 1975.

7. Peter Drucker, *Management: Tasks, Responsibilities, Practices* (New York: Harper & Row, 1973), p. 438. Also see George S. Odiorne, *Management by Objectives* (New York: Pittman, 1965), pp. 55–56. For an excellent synopsis on the empirical evidence on MBO, see Mark L. McConkie, "Classifying and Reviewing the Empirical Work on MBO: Some Implications," *Group Organization Studies,* 4:4 (1979), pp. 461–75.

8. Charles D. Hale, *Fundamentals of Police Administration* (Boston: Holbrook, 1977), p. 333.

9. Rodney H. Brady, "MBO Goes to Work in the Public Sector," *Harvard Business Review*, 51 (March–April 1973), 65–74.

10. Ronald G. Lynch, *The Police Manager*, 2nd ed. (Boston: Holbrook, 1978), p. 154.

11. C. D. Stein, "Objective Management Systems: Two to Five Years After Implementation," *Personnel Journal*, 54 (October 1975), 525.

12. Ibid.

13. McConkie, "Classifying and Reviewing," pp. 467–471.

14. Ibid., pp. 471–72.

15. Howard S. Gitlow and Shelly J. Gitlow, *The Deming Guide to Quality and Competitive Position* (Englewood Cliffs, N.J.: Prentice Hall, 1987), p. 7.

16. Ibid.

17. Ibid.

18. Ibid.

19. Ibid.

20. *http://www.TheIACP.org/awards/* (Available on-line February 6, 2000).

21. Ibid.

22. Ibid.

23. David A. Garvin, "How the Baldrige Award Really Works," *Harvard Business Review*, (November–December 1991), p. 81.

24. Ibid.

25. Ibid., pp. 82, 84.

26. Ibid., p. 84.

27. Jack Reynolds, *Management-Oriented Corrections Evaluation Guidelines* (Washington, D.C.: U.S. Government Printing Office, 1979), p. 3.

28. Ibid., p. 3.

29. Ibid., p. 3.

30. Harry P. Hatry, Richard E. Winnie, and Donald M. Fisk, *Practical Program Evaluation for State and Local Government Officials* (Washington, D.C.: Urban Institute, 1973), p. 8.

31. U.S. Department of Housing and Urban Development, *A Guide for Local Evaluation* (Washington, D.C.: U.S. Government Printing Office, 1976), pp. 1–2, with minor modification.

32. James F. Rooney, "Organizational Success Through Program Failure: Skid Row Rescue Missions," *Social Forces*, 58 (March 1980), p. 904.

33. Ibid.

34. For a description of the trapped and experimental administrators, see Donald T. Campbell, "Reforms as Experiments," in *Quasi-Experimental Approaches*, eds. James A. Caporaso and Leslie L. Rose, Jr. (Evanston, Ill.: Northwestern University Press, 1973), p. 224; Stuart Adams, *Evaluative Research in Corrections* (Washington, D.C.: U.S. Government Printing Office, 1975), pp. 19–20.

35. See, for example, Eleanor Chelmsky and William R. Shadish, editors, *Evaluation in the 21st Century* (Thousand Oaks, Calif.: Sage Publications, 1997); Joseph S. Wholey, Harry P. Hatry, and Kathryn E. Newcomer, editors. *Handbook of Practical Program Evaluation* (San Francisco: Jossey-Bass Publishers, 1994), and Carol H. Weiss, *Evaluation* (Englewood Cliffs, N.J.: Prentice Hall, 1997).

36. These points are restatements, with some additions, of material found in Michael P. Kirby, *The Role of the Administrator in Evaluation* (Washington, D.C.: Pretrial Services Resource Center, 1979), pp. 11–12.

37. On these points, see Carol H. Weiss, *Evaluation Research* (Englewood Cliffs, N.J.: Prentice Hall, 1972), pp. 20–21; Charles S. Bullock III and Harrell R. Rodgers, Jr., "Impediments to Policy Evaluation: Perceptual Distortion and Agency Loyalty," *Social Science Quarterly*, 57 (December 1976–1977), 506–519.

## INTRODUCTION

In the dynamic society surrounding law enforcement agencies today, the question of whether change will occur is not relevant. Instead, the issue is how police executives cope with the barrage of changes that confront daily those who attempt to keep their agencies viable, current, and responsive to community needs. Although change is a fact of life, police executives cannot be content to let change occur as it will. They must be able to develop strategies to plan, direct, and control change.[1]

To be effective in the change process, police executives must have more than good diagnostic skills. Once they have analyzed the demands of their environment, they must be able to adapt their leadership style to fit the demands and develop the means to change some or all of the other situational variables.[2]

This chapter has been organized to facilitate an examination of some of the critical dimensions of planned change. A police executive contemplating the implementation of change, especially on a large scale, will increase the likelihood of success if certain fundamental principles, discussed here, are followed.

# 15

# ORGANIZATIONAL CHANGE AND THE FUTURE

*There is nothing more difficult to take in hand, more perilous to conduct, or more uncertain of success, than to lead in the introduction of a new order of things.*

MACHIAVELLI, THE PRINCE

## WHY CHANGE OCCURS

The initiation of large-scale organizational change in American law enforcement tends to follow similar patterns. Often, a new police chief will be appointed either from within or from outside of the law enforcement agency as a prelude to a planned, large-scale reorganization desired by a city manager, mayor, or some other influential person or groups in the community. Before the appointment of the police chief, it is likely that one or more of the following events has transpired, giving impetus to the plan changes:

1. A new mayor is elected or a new city manager appointed who wants to replace the current chief with a new chief of his or her own choice.
2. The police department has been judged to be generally deficient in its crime-fighting capabilities by a study, the local media (see Box 15-1), by interest groups within the community, or by a commission of citizens created specifically to make a careful assessment of the capabilities of the department.
3. Police community relations are at a low, in part because of alleged acts of misconduct by the police (see Box 15-2).
4. The police department has a poor public image because of its low recruiting standards and failure to provide adequate training for its officers.
5. The previous police chief and/or other high-ranking police officials have been indicted for accepting payoffs relating to gambling, prostitution, liquor violations, or narcotics violations.

BOX 15-1

# The LAPD Is Treated to a Business Analysis, and It Comes Up Short

## Moving past issues like race, critics find inefficiency in a host of operations

## Entering a name 70 times

by Jeff Bailey

LOS ANGELES—Glorified in television dramas of years ago, the Los Angeles Police Department has more recently been reviled for the videotaped beating of Rodney King and ridiculed for its handling of evidence in the O.J. Simpson case.

Now, city leaders are looking at the LAPD in a new light: as if it were a business. A swarm of management consultants has been set loose on the $1 billion-a-year department in recent months, picking it apart the way they would a major service or manufacturing company. Their findings suggest the LAPD is far from a return to glory.

Officers who literally couldn't shoot straight, known internally as the "chronic 31," repeatedly failed firing-range tests yet were deployed as patrol officers. Some police-academy graduates aren't any good at using a radio because, the LAPD being short of radios, they were taught by pretending with wooden blocks. Some routine tasks—exchanging shotguns between shifts, scheduling the patrol force—are done in such outdated ways that, added together, they squander the services of hundreds of officers at a time when the crime-weary city is desperate to put more policing power on the streets.

### Call Waiting

"We were amazed at the lack of discipline and analysis," said Blue Marble Partners, one of the consulting firms called in to assess the LAPD, in its report.

Trying to figure out why the answering of 911 calls is so slow that nearly a quarter of callers hang up, LAPD officials couldn't even tell Blue Marble for sure how many people work in the operation. Says Gregory A. Zikos, a partner at the Torrance, Calif., consulting firm, "They have shortcomings in all of the areas of critical importance."

The LAPD says its training isn't deficient. It says the "chronic 31" have now all passed their shooting tests and that it is working on radio weaknesses.

The consultants' findings are adding to the turmoil at the nation's third-largest police force, after New York and Chicago. An unhappy Mayor Richard J. Riordan wants to get rid of Police Chief Willie Williams. The city council wants to slow down a four-year, 3,000-officer expansion program that is the centerpiece of the Republican mayor's 1997 re-election plan. And veteran police brass beneath Chief Williams, already shellshocked from five years of criticism following the King beating, the 1992 riots and the Simpson trial, seem at times frozen by all the conflicting advice and orders they are getting.

### 'Reluctant to Change'

"It's a lot of studies and a lot of process," Deputy Chief David J. Gascon says. "A lot of it is probably helpful, but at some point outsiders have to get out of the way and let us try to manage."

Can they? "As a group, they're the most reluctant to change I've ever seen," says Art Mattox, a Xerox Corp. executive who serves on the civilian Police Commission that oversees the department.

The police here long operated as a bureaucratic fortress under a series of chiefs who were all but immune to criticism because they couldn't be fired. A 1981 city audit found some of the same LAPD management weaknesses turning up today. Then-chief Daryl F. Gates responded by hurling a copy of the audit to the floor and stomping on it, calling it "harassment." It was the last city audit.

Then came the King videotape. A year later, a poor early response to the riots further undermined public confidence in the department. Mr. Gates quit under pressure. Sweeping examinations of police violence and racism began, and brutality complaints declined sharply.

### Calling the Consultants

But once the scrutiny got started, it spread to nearly every aspect of the LAPD. Eager to better understand and oversee their police, elected officials hired more than a dozen consulting firms. The result has been a rare top-to-bottom evaluation of a major law-enforcement agency's labor productivity and management methods.

As consultants' reports piled up, exposing many inefficiencies, the LAPD's own statistics began to suggest a state of disarray. For instance, Mayor Riordan's expansion—raising the number of police officers to about 11,000 by 1997 from about 8,000 in 1993—was meant to put more officers on the street; but by last October, only 24 more cops were on patrol, while the ranks of detectives—already flush, according to critics—had swelled by 152.

The mayor became incensed, and since then most of the new officers have gone to patrol. But in March,

LAPD figures showed that two key measures of effectiveness, the numbers of arrests and of traffic citations, had fallen. Arrests for the June 30, 1995, fiscal year were off 35% from a 1991 peak, and citations were down 38%.

With the police expansion forcing painful budget cuts elsewhere, the mayor was further angered. "We've given them the tools to succeed," he says. "The public has a right to an explanation."

Chief Williams's spokesman, Commander Tim McBride, says arrests fell because crime rates were lower and that ticket-writing fell because traffic cops were shifted to other duties. But he acknowledges a widespread belief within the department: The 1993 jailing of two officers involved in the King beating sapped some officers' enthusiasm for their job.

"There's not less crime," says Bill Hall, a lieutenant in robbery and homicide. "There's less *reported* crime." Patrol officers, he says, "are just driving around." Says Commander McBride: "There may be some of that occurring."

Assessing a police department isn't a straightforward matter. There isn't any widely agreed-upon management model to follow. Private-sector yardsticks can't be mechanically applied to a public-sector function such as policing.

But up close, when the work is broken down into discrete tasks, many LAPD functions don't seem so unique, and ways to improve performance become clearer.

## Presenting Arms
For instance, at every change of shift, LAPD patrol officers go through an elaborate sign-out procedure for shotguns, radios and other equipment. It eats up about 30 minutes per shift for each officer, Blue Marble consultants calculated, or the equivalent of 236 full-time cops. The time of 51 additional officers is required to manage the equipment exchange.

Blue Marble suggested this: Buy enough equipment so sharing isn't required. Cost: $5 million at most, producing more than $20 million a year in labor savings, equal to 287 cops.

While some consultants looked at long-term improvements that would cost hundreds of millions of dollars, Blue Marble looked for productivity gains in mundane LAPD tasks.

It found that scheduling and payroll timekeeping are handled in an exquisitely laborious process. Every four weeks, patrol cops spend about three hours each in the station—a combined loss equivalent to 51 full-time cops—deciding on and requesting in writing their desired days off.

The paperwork is gathered, and on the Thursday of the third week of each deployment period (every four weeks), typically a watch commander, captain, adjutant and timekeeper gather to draw up the deployment plan. It is reviewed and reworked, posted, manually transcribed into the brown time book, sent to division timekeeping and transcribed into the blue book, then onto the green sheets and finally into the city payroll system.

Underpayment and overpayment are common, Blue Marble found. And overtime payments run six weeks behind.

An automated timekeeping system could be had for $650,000 tops, Blue Marble says, producing labor savings among payroll workers of about $1.5 million a year.

Every arrest must be approved by the watch commander. So, two officers drive back to the station, locate the watch commander and get his approval. Often, they stop to shoot the breeze and have a cup of coffee, and then drive the suspect to jail. (Some stations have their own jail.) Since approval is rarely denied, the consultants recommend the policy be scrapped.

Arrest and booking forms require the entry of a juvenile drunken-driving suspect's name 70 separate times. And the forms, filled out manually, end up filed in half a dozen or more separate locations. Mayor Riordan brought a business friend in to see this, Kaufman & Broad Home Corp.'s chief executive officer, Bruce Karatz, and it reminded Mr. Karatz of something: selling a house.

"It's about as many forms as arresting someone," Mr. Karatz says, and that is why Kaufman's sales offices are highly computerized. He helped raise $15 million in private donations to buy personal computer networks for LAPD stations. And even though the department simply loaded 14 duplicative forms into the network—rather than consolidating them, as outsiders suggest—the time saved by reducing paperwork could raise patrol-officer and detective productivity by 10% to 15%, LAPD officials and others estimate.

Taken together, all of these proposed changes could free up the time of hundreds of officers and, by reducing their paperwork and other hassles, perhaps make their jobs a little less aggravating. That in turn could enable the city to improve the LAPD's training, buy some more real radios or perhaps slow the costly hiring program.

## Bar Codes
The LAPD is studying the equipment-exchange problem and now plans to buy a timekeeping system. It

*(continued)*

## BOX 15-1 (continued)

says watch-commander approval is an important quality-control step in arrests that perhaps could be made less time-consuming.

But unlike productivity-minded companies, the department and its overseers don't try to quantify labor savings from equipment or computer-system purchases in order to make informed choices between more bodies and more machines. "The city council thinks all we need to do is hire more cops and buy more cars. That's a Third World approach," says Joseph Bonino, a civilian LAPD manager who has long argued unsuccessfully for more investment in automation.

Bar-coding systems used in retailing, for instance, would let the department better track the thousands of guns, millions of dollars in cash and mounds of drugs it seizes as evidence each year.

And in detective work, the police could learn something from the financial community, which mines consumers' credit histories to develop lists of sales prospects for credit cards, insurance and the like. If the LAPD's many separate computer systems—which don't communicate with one another—could be connected, parolees' criminal histories and addresses for instance, could be matched against local crime patterns. The department is looking into both of these possibilities.

### Chief's Role

Reshaping the rigid LAPD bureaucracy, of course, would require tremendously strong leadership, and the department seems lacking in that. Chief Williams, though very popular with the public, has never gained the confidence of the troops since being hired from Philadelphia to replace Mr. Gates in 1992. Assistant Chief Bayan Lewis, head of operations, says "selling the chief to the troops" is one of his duties. "It's not an easy job," he says. "He's viewed as a carpetbagger without qualifications." Mr. Lewis doesn't share that view, he adds.

Chief Williams also isn't hands-on enough as a manager to suit the mayor—a former entrepreneur—Mr. Lewis notes. "Riordan wants a guy down there pressing buttons."

The city charter was amended after Mr. Gates left and gives the chief a maximum of two five-year terms. Chief Williams's first term ends next year, and he says he wants and expects a second one. He says the department was far worse off than anyone realized when he arrived and that his management and policies are turning it around. Police Commission members who will decide whether to keep him won't comment.

Whoever is in charge will face more tough choices. A culture that is transfer- and promotion-oriented has caused instability in some crucial areas.

The much-criticized crime lab, Blue Marble consultants note, has outdated equipment, too few clerks (so that professionals must do what they regard as scut work), and offices that are cramped and scattered over several buildings. Fingerprint examiners are short of cars, so they often keep patrol officers and detectives waiting at crime scenes. And because prints, photographs and other crime-scene materials are handled by three different staffs, detectives at times must make three separate calls for help.

The lab has had 13 commanders in 18 years. Blue Marble notes that "a commander who initiated a bad decision wasn't historically around to suffer the consequences."

### Directing Traffic

At the rank of commander, says Art Lopez, "I've averaged about one job a year." Currently he oversees traffic, including motorcycle-riding officers and collision investigators.

So how big is the traffic operation? "Somewhere between 350 and 400 collision investigators," he says, "and 250 to 300 motor officers." He pauses. "Make it 400 [collision investigators] and 260 motor officers." A subordinate says it is closer to 322 and 300.

How many accidents do they investigate? "I'm not quite certain where [that figure] is," Commander Lopez says.

It can be gleaned from the LAPD's statistical digest: They handled 55,114 accidents in 1994, the latest figures available or about 171 per investigator. That is fewer than one per work day.

Productivity isn't helped by deploying collision investigators two to a car. The larger Chicago police force gets by with just 40 crash investigators.

Productivity is tough to assess because the LAPD's statistics are often out-of-date or unreliable. George Callandrillo, a civilian in the traffic division, says he used to contact 22 separate sources to tally by hand how many citations each station issued. Information dribbled in. "It got too sketchy," he says. "I just said [forget] it."

More broadly, department employees don't trust the information, says Philip Friedman, an LAPD senior systems analyst, because "the people who put it in could care less."

*Source: The Wall Street Journal,* June 11, 1996, pp. A1 and A8. Reprinted by permission of *The Wall Street Journal,* © 1996 Dow Jones & Company, Inc. All rights reserved worldwide.

BOX 15-2

## Report Cites Many Problems With South Pasadena Police

**by Nicholas Riccardi and Richard Winton**

A city-ordered investigation of the scandal-racked South Pasadena Police Department released Wednesday night found so many basic flaws in the organization that the force is now "starting at square one," officials said.

An attitude promoted by retiring Chief Thomas Mahoney that off-duty conduct "is not a concern" was cited as a factor in officers allegedly covering up a hit-and-run crash and sexually exploiting an admitted manic-depressive volunteer, according to the report, compiled by Lewis Partners of Pasadena.

The report, presented to the City Council on Wednesday night, also alleges a new scandal: The department never investigated an officer who years ago shot a teenager while he was off-duty in another city. That youth won a five-figure settlement from South Pasadena, and officials Wednesday said the officer—whose identity they said they could not recall—was later arrested on suspicion of narcotics possession and fired.

The department also does not administer psychological testing to its officers and for years did not record civilian complaints, said Acting Chief John E. Anderson, who vowed to correct problems that he attributed to "lack of leadership."

"We're starting at square one," he said, adding that he was unsure of the qualifications of some of his men.

After being told he was about to be terminated last month, Mahoney—who has been on administrative leave since August—reached an agreement with the city to retire effective April 1.

In an interview Wednesday night, Mahoney said the investigators did not contact him.

"I, quite frankly, question its validity," Mahoney said of the report. He said the off-duty shooting was investigated and denied that he ignored off-duty conduct.

The first scandal the report addresses is a 1995 hit-and-run crash involving then-Officer Scott D. Ziegler, the son-in-law of a former mayor. Ziegler's name was apparently erased from a police report on the crash, the city-ordered investigation said.

After *The Times* reported on the crash in August, prosecutors charged Ziegler with misdemeanor hit-and-run. He pleaded no contest and was fired.

The district attorney's office and the FBI are probing the crash, and the woman whose car Ziegler damaged has filed a civil rights suit against the city. The second incident involves Theresa Goldston, who briefly volunteered with the department and said she had sexual relations with seven officers.

She later filed a claim against the city, which was settled for a reported $18,000.

*Source: Los Angeles Times,* February 6, 1997. Copyright 1997, *Los Angeles Times.* Reprinted by permission.

6. The former police chief, who had served for many years as the bulwark of traditionalism, recently retired.

7. The ranks of the police department and the community agree that morale among the police officers is dangerously low, as reflected in an abnormally high attrition rate, excessive use of sick time, incidences of injury to prisoners, high numbers of resisted arrests, increasing citizen complaints of officer misconduct, poor supervisory ratings, and generally poor performance of personnel throughout the organization.

8. The chief's personal style has become an issue in the community. In the extreme situation, part of the platform of a mayoral candidate is the pledge that if elected to office his or her first action will be to fire the chief of police. In one instance where this happened, the highly visible chief in a medium-size department went to the scene of an incident where an armed man had barricaded himself. When the man suddenly ran from the house firing at the officers, the chief and others shot the man dead. This incident raised questions as to how the chief could rule on the use of force if he had taken part in it and why he had taken part in it when there were so many well-armed officers

present. On the heels of other highly publicized incidents involving this chief, this spelled the end for him, and the mayor forced the chief out shortly after taking office.

9. The life cycle of the department may dictate the need for a change in leadership. The previous reform- or change-oriented chief may have pursued his or her programs so rapidly or insensitively that the department is in open revolt. In such instances the new chief is told to stabilize the situation and to "lay off" making substantial changes, unless they involve dismantling some of those instituted by the prior chief. Too, a lack of any change may cause a chief to be toppled. In one community there was widespread support for a bike patrol on the beach and in the downtown area. The chief opposed the idea and dragged his heels, creating barriers for implementation at every opportunity. This single issue led to his replacement, and ultimately a new chief activated the bike patrol very rapidly with great success.

The newly appointed police chief has likely been given a mandate to move forward with speed to rectify the difficulties in the department and is, more often than not, excited and enthusiastic about the prospect of implementing ideas formulated through years of professional growth and experience. It may appear that the chief is operating from a position of considerable strength and need not be too concerned with those who might try to thwart the change process. However, such an assumption could be very risky. Although there will be factions in the department and in the community that fully support the change effort, there will be powerful factions within the police department and within the community that will attempt to block any changes that appear to endanger their interests.

No chief can afford to overlook the impact that each type of group can have on the planned changes. In developing a strategy for change, certain elements must be built into the plan to identify and enhance the cooperation and support received by a group that desires change and to enhance the possibility of winning over the groups that may be neutral or only moderately opposed to the planned changes. Also, the plan must have a number of highly developed strategies to counteract or neutralize those individuals or groups that will make every possible effort to reduce the success of the planned changes.

The risks involved in implementing large-scale changes are considerable, but, surprisingly, many police executives either fail to take notice of these risks in their preplanning strategies or grossly underestimate them. This phenomenon has too often resulted in both goals and objectives falling far below expectations or failing to come to fruition at all. In other instances, the change effort encounters so many difficulties and obstacles, and so much opposition that the chief is eventually forced to resign or is fired.

## THE CHANGE AGENT

Throughout this chapter, the term *change agent* will be used to describe an individual or group from within or outside the police department whose role involves the stimulation, guidance, and stabilization of change. Within the context of planned organizational change, the role of the change agent is to assist in resolving organizational problems.[3] The specific person or group playing the role of change agent will vary. In some cases, the change agent will be the police chief or some person within the agency designated by the chief to assume responsibility for implementing change. In other cases, the change agent may be some individual or group of consultants hired from outside the organization to conduct a comprehensive study of all or certain segments of the organization and to produce a comprehensive report with specific recommendations for enhancing the operation of the police department. On occasion, outside consultants will also assist in implementing the recommended changes.

## ORGANIZATIONAL DEVELOPMENT (OD)

One general approach to planned change that has gained prominence over the last 30 years or so focuses primarily on people as the target of change. This approach—called *organization development*—is grounded largely in psychology and other behavioral sciences[4] (see Chapter 4, Organizational Theory).

Organizational development is formally defined as "a systemwide application of behavioral science knowledge to the planned development and reinforcement of organizational strategies, structures, and processes for improving an organization's effectiveness."[5] This definition reflects several important features of organizational development. First, OD deals with whole systems (departments, bureaus, and divisions) as opposed to a single individual or a single function within a system. Second, OD uses behavioral science knowledge, as in the areas of leadership, motivation, team functioning, rewards, conflict resolution, and change. This distinguishes it from such things as computer-systems or operations-research types of change approaches. Third, OD involves planned change, but not in the more rigid sense of organizational planning. Rather, it involves more of an adaptive, flexible, ongoing process of diagnosing and solving people-related problems. Fourth, it involves the creation and reinforcement of change with all the implications we have discussed thus far. Fifth, it can encompass strategy, structure, and process changes—although, traditionally, OD has focused on the people processes almost exclusively. Finally, OD focuses on improving organizational effectiveness, in terms of both productivity and quality of work life. An important aspect of the practice of OD is that effectiveness implies that organizations learn to solve their own problems and ultimately deal successfully with issues without the help of an outside consultant who specializes in OD.[6]

Organizational development is often carried out with the aid of a consultant, either from outside the agency or from within, who is separate from the team or group being assisted. An OD practitioner, often called a change agent, facilitates the change process by structuring learning experiences, diagnosing problems, helping to generate and implement solutions, and encouraging certain types of interaction processes. The actions of these agents of change are generally referred to as interventions because they attempt to hinder the erosion of the organization's effectiveness by modifying the ways its members function. Although OD practitioners usually have specialized training in the behavioral sciences, many have supplemented that expertise with training in other areas to give them the broader perspectives that are useful in facilitating change in today's complex organizations.

The focus of OD is often on the hidden or more subtle features of an organization. Although an OD intervention might change more visible features, such as structure, formal authority relationships, policies, and technology, OD tacitly recognizes the impact of the more hidden, informal organization and deals with many of these features to promote organizational effectiveness.[7]

# CHANGE AGENT ERRORS

Just as change agents can enhance the effectiveness of change programs by developing certain traits, they can limit the effectiveness of the program or team by committing certain errors. One serious error that a change agent can make is to become tied prematurely to a particular set of strategies and tactics. This problem is more severe when the commitment is made publicly and is compounded when individuals critical of the change process were not consulted before making the public statement about a change that will directly affect them or their areas of responsibility.

Planning for change should involve the identification of relevant groups affected by the change team's efforts, their interdependencies, and their need to feel involved in goal-setting and strategy design processes. Typically, the importance of cooperation is overlooked because a change agent may underestimate the value of the contribution that members of the organization can make in helping to structure and focus the change process. Sometimes the change agent is under the mistaken assumption that members of the police department do not want to participate actively in various aspects of change programs directed at them and/or they are unable to provide useful information through participation.[8]

Another error is inadequate planning for the initiation of the change process. The sudden creation of a formal commission, the quick institutionalization of a change team, the hasty hiring of a consultant, or some other rapid implementation of a formal change program may create immediate resistance. The change agent must not overlook the informal system, a problem likely to occur when the change agent is overly confident of his or her perception of the changes needed.

The change agent must also consider the roles played by individuals and groups outside the police department. This may include members of the local political community, citizen action groups, unions, and even spouses. The change agent must consider how the advocated change will affect these groups and what their perceived needs for change are, as well as what their expectations may be regarding the behavior of the change team and the consequences of the intervention.[9]

Change agents sometimes fail to identify or even recognize influential individuals or groups that may be willing to provide support for the change effort. Such persons or groups may be developed into strong advocates of the change if provided with adequate information in the appropriate manner. If an influential person or group is favorably disposed toward innovation, reinforcing information should be provided routinely, particularly if the advocated change is controversial and resisting groups are trying to alter the influential party's feelings and beliefs.[10]

# INTERNAL VERSUS EXTERNAL CHANGE AGENTS

When a decision has been made to reorganize a police department, one of the most important concerns is determining who will undertake the task. Should personnel from within the organization be selected? Should outside consultants be employed? Should a combination of sources from both groups be pooled in a cooperative effort? A number of useful guidelines can help to answer these questions.

Certain positive features associated with selecting a change agent from within an agency make this an attractive alternative. The internal change agent will have valuable insights into both the formal and the informal organization and will be aware of the potential sources of support for certain types of change as well as from which segments of the organization resistance is most likely to come. Such knowledge can prove quite useful in developing strategies for planned change. Because the change agent is a part of the organization, he or she will likely share certain values and attitudes with members of the organization with whom the agent will be working that will facilitate communications in all directions.[11] If the internal change agent has a reputation within the organization as a competent professional with unquestioned integrity, this, too, will enhance the change effort.

**Internal Change Agent: Pros and Cons**

One drawback to using an internal agent is the possible lack of acceptance of the person by the organization as an "expert." Colleagues who remember when the change agent was "just a wet-behind-the-ears rookie" or who have personal jealousies or animosities directed at the agent will make it difficult for the internal agent to establish credibility. Some important questions may be raised when internal change agents are used. For example, what possible personal or professional gain does the individual hope to acquire? Is the change agent overly concerned about the ways in which the changes will negatively impact on agency personnel that he or she knows personally? Does the internal change agent have some preconceived notions about the direction the change should take, thus limiting the range of viable alternatives that might be considered realistically?

Finally, individuals from within the agency acting as change agents will possibly have to be relieved of their present responsibilities, thus shifting the burden of their work to someone else. The extent to which this will impact on the organization depends on the amount of time involved in the change process, the amount of work to be shifted to subordinates, and the abilities of the subordinates.

The externally selected change agent has from the outset certain important advantages over the internal change agent. Individuals from outside the organization employed as change agents are selected because of their knowledge, experience, and professional reputation. Thus, when entering the police agency, they already enjoy considerable credibility as "experts" in their field. This legitimacy tends to bestow on the change agent a high degree of respect and deference. This, in turn, facilitates cooperation from key members of the organization, at least in the early stages of the change process. The external change agent has, more often than not, a broad range of experience with planned change and can complete the task both effectively and expeditiously.

**External Change Agent: Pros and Cons**

One of the important disadvantages faced by the external change agent is the absence of knowledge to identify with accuracy the major forces within the organization that can help or hinder the change process. For example, is a group of police officers within the agency fearful of certain changes and are these officers prepared to mobilize support in the community to resist such changes? Is the police union potentially supportive of some changes but opposed to others? Who are the informal leaders in the organization? Is the reorganization effort just a ploy by a city manager, mayor, or city council to embarrass the police chief into a forced resignation or dismissal?

Because external change agents rarely have to implement the changes they recommend, have no long-term commitment to any single agency, and may be unfamiliar with the factors outside their designated realm, they may make recommendations that are difficult or impossible for the agency to implement. It is not unheard of for a consulting firm to make some recommendations that cannot be implemented legally, especially if the consulting firm representatives are not familiar with the state laws, local ordinances, civil service regulations, or state-mandated police officers' standards. Other recommendations may be impossible to implement because of serious budgetary limitations related to a community's tax base or because agency personnel lack the experience or expertise to do so.

It could be argued that it is precisely because the external change agent does not have to be concerned about certain extraneous elements that he or she can make a fair and objective assessment. However, the external change agent, to be of maximum benefit to the police department, must be able to assist in improving the organization within the framework of its ability to change. There are those who would suggest that the closer someone comes to actually having to be responsible for implementing change, the less idealistic and more realistic that person becomes. Thus, some police departments actually require as a part of the contractual agreement with a consulting firm that the representatives of the firm remain with the agency for some reasonable period of time to implement the more difficult changes.

## LOCATING EXTERNAL CHANGE AGENTS

Once administrators decide on the type of evaluation needed, they can contact several police professional associations, such as the International Association of Chiefs of Police, the National Organization of Black Law Enforcement Executives, the Police Executive Research Forum, and the Police Foundation, to request a list of potential consultants.[12] Professional publications and journals and the National Criminal Justice Reference Service are also excellent sources for information on consultants. However, networking with other police executives may be the best way to find a consultant, because they most likely will refer one with whom they have worked and one familiar with the police subculture.

The next step is for administrators to contact prospective consultants to request a list of past clients. Administrators then should contact these clients for an assessment of the consultant's performance.

**Expertise of External Consultants**

Consultants who evaluate law enforcement agencies need to possess certain critical skills, including both substantive and methodology expertise. Methodology expertise includes knowledge of research design, data collection, and statistical analysis procedures. Substantive expertise includes knowledge of the problem and any law, rule, and regulation relating to it.

Consultants hired by law enforcement agencies also should have experience working with law enforcement professionals. A knowledge of current federal, state, and local laws; familiarity with standard, acceptable police procedures; and a thorough understanding of the police subculture are essential if evaluations and recommendations are to be accepted in the police environment. If consultants lack this knowledge and understanding, they may make impractical or unrealistic recommendations.

**Working with External Consultants**

Once a consultant is chosen, both the consultant and the police executive should work to establish mutual expectations and open communication. Clearly defined roles facilitate clear communication. Police executives must delineate both their perceptions of the problem and their expectations of the consultant. In turn, the consultants must detail their projected services to the department.

To delineate the department's problem effectively, police executives should avail themselves of critical resources. They can identify and contact knowledgeable community leaders and experts; listen to attendees at open forums held after the consultant's assignment; and check existing statistics, records, and data from surveys and censuses.

When executives clearly delineate problems, not simply the symptoms of an overall problem, the consultant can offer workable solutions. Unfortunately, many administrators focus on whatever flame is burning the brightest at the time. In six to eight months, however, when the consultant's study is completed, that flame may not be the brightest one, and the offered solutions may no longer be critical to the organization.[13]

With a clear understanding of both the problem and their expected role, consultants have the necessary foundation to evaluate and make a diagnosis, thereby avoiding helter-skelter research efforts. To facilitate this effort, administrators should assign a team or representative to act as liaison with the consultant. The liaison provides necessary information to the consultant and implements any new program after the consultant's assignment ends. Liaison is critical to a successful experience with consultants.

## Reviewing the Study

When a consultant's final report recommends changes in operational procedures, an overhaul of the organizational structure, or a reduction in the workforce, the police executives must carefully review the study and interpret its results before deciding what recommendations to implement. Organizational costs could be enormous if police executives implement inappropriate changes based on faulty research.

In order to determine whether any problem exists with the study, administrators first need to examine the specifics of how it was conducted. By doing this, they often can ferret out problem areas and adjust final recommendations accordingly.

To begin, administrators must attempt to separate good research from bad research. This means that today's police administrators must understand research methods. An understanding of these methods allows them to review the study to determine how the consultant reached certain conclusions and whether these conclusions are valid.

## RESEARCH TECHNIQUES

Applied research involves collecting and analyzing data regarding a specific problem to assist police managers in making decisions.[14] Police executives use applied research when they allocate personnel, decide what type of police equipment to purchase, study crime trends, and make other administrative decisions.

There are two types of applied research: descriptive and evaluative.[15] Descriptive research identifies the size of the problem, its causes, and people affected. For example, this type of research involves looking at calls-for-service data to determine the number of calls, the purpose of the calls, and the effect of the calls on officer work load.

Evaluative research, on the other hand, compares one program with an alternative program. Examples of this type of research include determining the effectiveness of having a traffic accident investigations unit or determining what model car would best suit the needs of the patrol unit. Evaluative research also ascertains whether a program, policy, procedure, or purchase is doing what it should do; how the program might be deficient; how the program can be improved; and whether the program should be eliminated.

## Problem Formation and Research Design

When reviewing a study, the administrator must determine whether the consultant had a clear problem formation and research design. It is the administrator's responsibility to delineate the purpose of the study—exploration, description, explanation, or a combination of these. For the most part, law enforcement agencies require a combination of descriptive and evaluative research.

## Variables

It is important for administrators to determine whether researchers clearly identified and defined the variables being studied and whether they operationalized these variables correctly. For example, if researchers report that crime in the city is up, administrators should determine how they arrived at this conclusion. Did the consultants rely on the agency's own figures for the most recently completed calendar year? Perhaps they used victimization rates as opposed to reported crime rates, or made a linear projection of reported crime for the next six months based on the preceding six months and by doing so ignored important seasonal fluctuations that would produce a lower estimate of crimes. The variables used in the study must not only be identified, but also be clearly defined.

In one case, a study asserted that the department had a slow response rate—an average of 15 minutes per call. However, individuals conducting the study arrived at this figure by averaging critical calls, such as those reporting shootings and felony crimes in progress, with complaints of loud music and barking dogs. Clearly, the consultants' approach to calculating response time skewed the findings. Administrators must always question whether the data obtained actually provide accurate information about what supposedly is being measured. Accurate results require the right data.

## Sampling Methods

Administrators then must look at the sampling methods employed by the consultant. Did the consultant select a sample of employees or were all employees contacted? When assessing a policy or a procedure in a large agency, sampling is probably appropriate. However, a modest sample from a small or medium-sized department may not reflect the true beliefs of the organization.

If a sample is used, it is crucial for the consultant to describe the type of sampling on which the information is based—convenience, simple random, systematic, or cluster sampling. How well a sample represents the entire agency depends on the sampling frame and the specific design of election procedures. Did the consultant select a sample out of convenience, or does the sample truly represent the organization? For example, did the study conveniently sample a particular segment of employees, such as detectives or day-shift officers, to the exclusion of others?

Statistically speaking, a sample can be representative of only the population included in the sampling frame. Each person in the organization must have a known chance of being selected by the sampling procedure used. Sampling and analyzing data from a sample can be fairly straightforward if an accurate employee list is used as a sampling frame, if a simple random or systematic sampling scheme is used, and if all respondents are selected at the same rate.

Also critical is whether the consultant selected an appropriate sample size and what percentage of the sample responded by completing the instrument (survey questionnaire). The sample should be representative of the organization and should reflect the gender, age, rank, ethnicity, and education level of the entire organization. The researcher must estimate the size of the sample in order to provide adequate representation of these organizational subgroups.

**Gathering Data**

Administrators must understand how the consultants gathered data. Did they use survey or field research, or did they analyze existing data or experimental research? Typically, consultants rely on several types of research methodology. However, several internal and external validity questions arise with each type of research method.

**Survey Instruments**

Research can be gathered using written or orally administered survey instruments. If researchers used a written survey, police administrators need to determine the validity of the questions. Additionally, if researchers administered an oral survey, police executives should ascertain whether interviewers asked the survey questions differently or perhaps even asked different questions.

Four types of questions can appear on surveys: demographic, behavior-oriented, knowledge, and attitude.[16] Researchers must construct the questions properly to obtain internal and external validity. They also must construct the questions in a manner that allows the respondents to give clear, unambiguous answers. Questions containing negative terms could cause respondents to misunderstand what is being asked.

There should be no compound questions, and the respondents should be capable of answering all questions. Survey questions should be applicable to all who are asked to answer them.

**Field Research**

Field research, sometimes called observation research, is appropriate to police research topics that defy simple quantification. This type of research may identify the nuances of specific attitudes or behaviors that might escape researchers using other methods. Researchers who employ this method go directly to the problem under study and observe it as completely as possible, which allows them to develop a deeper understanding of the problem.

However, field research has potential problems that can affect the validity of the study. For example, the researchers' own cultural identities or backgrounds could color their interpretations of what they observe. Not all researchers who observe the same events would classify things in the same manner.

## METHODS OF ORGANIZATIONAL CHANGE

Organizational change can be initiated in numerous ways, but approaches can be grouped into two broad categories: (1) those that focus on changing the individuals working in the organization and (2) those that focus on changing specific organizational structures. Effective programs of organizational change usually involve the simultaneous use of both approaches and a variety of intervention techniques.[17]

**Changing Individuals**

In general, future behavior is predicted by past behavior; that is, circumstances being equal, people will go on doing what they have always done. If an individual has been compliant, that person will continue to be compliant; if self-seeking, the individual will continue to be self-seeking. This picture is neither cynical nor pessimistic, it is simply realistic.[18]

Of course, individuals can change their attitudes and their behaviors. Certain conditions typically are associated with such change, and, by knowing what these conditions are, a person can increase the likelihood of affecting a desired change in behavior.[19] Lewin[20] suggests that change occurs in three phases: (1) the unfreezing of an old pattern of relationships, (2) the changing to a new pattern through change induced by a change agent, and (3) the refreezing of a new pattern of relationships (see Figure 15-1).

**Unfreezing**

A key motivator in the unfreezing phase of change is a feeling of discomfort with old behavior.[21] If a person feels no discomfort, no logic or force or threats will motivate the person to change. Certain techniques, however, can be employed to induce an individual to change.

The first step in a change program is to "unfreeze" or rearrange the environmental context that supports the individual's current behavior. Some of the mechanisms that might be used include removing reinforcement for the current behavior, inducing guilt or anxiety about the current behavior, making the individual feel more secure about change by reducing threats or barriers to change, removing the individual from the environment that supports current behavior, or physically changing the environment in which the person is behaving.

The following is an example provided by Reitz:

> a program designed to change a manager's leadership style could provide him with feedback that his current style is ineffective and inappropriate. It could involve changing his office location to make him more or less accessible to his employees. It could remove him from the situation and provide a "safe" climate in which he can experiment with alternative behaviors by sending him to a training program conducted away from the premises.[22]

**Changing to a New Behavior Pattern**

After the unfreezing of old behaviors, individuals seeking change must try an alternative behavior and determine its consequences.[23] Two important elements are necessary in this phase of the process. First, the change agent must be sensitive to the fact that experiences of success with a new behav-

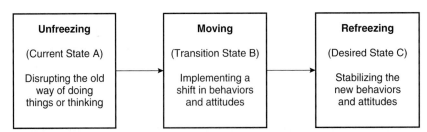

| **Unfreezing** | **Moving** | **Refreezing** |
|---|---|---|
| (Current State A) | (Transition State B) | (Desired State C) |
| Disrupting the old way of doing things or thinking | Implementing a shift in behaviors and attitudes | Stabilizing the new behaviors and attitudes |

**FIGURE 15-1.** Lewin's Model for Implementing Change (Reprinted by permission from page 52 of *Organization Development and Change*, 4th ed., by Thomas G. Cummings and Edgar F. Huse; Copyright © 1989 by West Publishing Company. All rights reserved.)

ior are so important that the behavior in the beginning should take place under controlled conditions. A change agent who wishes to establish problem-solving behavior, for example, should have individuals or groups participate in simulations or experiential learning situations that have predictable outcomes. By knowing that an exercise will demonstrate successful utilization of problem-solving skills, the change agent reinforces the knowledge, attitudes, and skills necessary to deal with more complicated, nonexperiential situations; success in an initially controlled training environment begets success in real-life situations.

Second, if an individual's regular environment is antithetical to the successful trial of a new behavior, the individual should, if it is practical, be removed from the existing environment until the new behavior is learned.[24]

## Refreezing

Refreezing is the stabilization and integration of the changed behavior. It is accomplished most effectively by providing the individual with a social and physical environment that will support the changed behavior.[25]

One authority has identified a number of subprocesses for the refreezing phase:

> If the new attitude has been internalized while being learned, this has automatically facilitated refreezing because it has been fitted naturally to the individual's personality. If it has been learned through identification, it will persist only so long as the target relationship with the original influence model persists unless new surrogated models are found or social support and reinforcement is obtained for expression of the new attitude.[26]

## CHANGING ORGANIZATIONAL STRUCTURES AND SYSTEMS

An alternative to attempting to change people who make up an organization is to change the structure of the organization itself or the systems and practices that guide its activities (see Box 15-3). Sometimes, the organizational change simply amounts to somebody pushing boxes around in an organizational chart, with nobody else knowing or caring much about it. In other instances, this approach to change can profoundly influence the patterns of activity that take place within organization boundaries, with important consequences for the long-term growth and health of the organization.[27]

In law enforcement agencies, changing organizational structures is not an unusual way in which to implement change. Naturally, the extent of any reorganization will be affected by a number of variables, including the availability of funds to create new positions; the support for change from the city manager, mayor, or other local officials; and the reasons for the reorganization in the first place.

A reorganization can be a very powerful tool for implementing change. It can be used to designate new priorities in the areas of enforcement, improve the quality and quantity of police service, or improve police minority relations.

BOX 15-3

## Plan Puts Deputy Chiefs on the Spot

### by Bill Bryan

The St. Louis Police Board is expected to vote today on a departmental reorganization in which deputy chiefs—not majors—would run the three area stations and report directly to Chief Ronald Henderson.

"I promised to deliver the highest level of police service available to the people in the neighborhoods, so what better way to do that than to put my most senior managers out there," Henderson said Tuesday.

"I'm giving three of my deputy chiefs each a third of the city and telling them, 'This is your real estate. I'm holding you responsible for its success or failure.' "

Henderson said that if the deputy chiefs report directly to him, "it will help me keep my fingers on the pulse of what's going on out there."

Henderson will make his pitch to the Police Board today for a one-year trial of the restructuring plan.

He said the plan has not created any controversy within the department, and he doesn't anticipate any problem with the board.

"When I told my deputy chiefs about it, they all were enthusiastically for it," the chief said.

Under Henderson's plan:

Lt. Col. Ray Lauer, who is now chief of the Bureau of Professional Standards, would replace Maj. Roy Joachmistaler as commander of Area I, which would be renamed the South Patrol Division.

Lt. Col. James J. Hackett, chief of the Bureau of Patrol Support, would replace Maj. Robert Zambo as commander of Area II, which would become the Central Patrol Division.

Lt. Col. Everett Page, chief of the Bureau of Auxiliary Services, would replace Maj. Gregory Hawkins as commander of Area III, which would be renamed the North Patrol Division.

Lt. Col. Joe Mokwa, the fourth deputy chief, would continue as chief of detectives, but the Bureau of Investigation would be renamed the Investigative Support Division.

The vacancy created by the recent retirement of Lt. Col. Charles McCrary, who had been in charge of community policing, would not be filled under Henderson's proposal.

Henderson would not comment Tuesday on the majors' new jobs.

*Source: The St. Louis Post-Dispatch, February 19, 1997. Reprinted with permission of The St. Louis Post-Dispatch, copyright 1997.*

## RADICAL VERSUS GRADUAL CHANGE

The objectives for any police chief contemplating change should be to do so in a manner that offers the greatest possibility of success, does not result in a reduction of the quality or quantity of service to the public, does not polarize the organization into warring factions, and does not result in the police chief being forced to resign or being fired. To achieve these goals, gradual changes are sometimes more effective than radical changes.

Conventional wisdom about change states that the way in which to change an organization is to bring in a new top executive, give the individual his or her head (and maybe a hatchet as well), and let the individual make the changes that he or she deems necessary. And, in fact, organizations (especially in times of crises) often use exactly that strategy to achieve change—sometimes unwittingly, sometimes not. What the conventional wisdom overlooks are the long-term consequences of unilateral, top-down change. It may often be the case, for example, that short-term problems are solved quickly, radically, and dramatically by executive action but that the "human problems" of the organization, which very well might have been causal in generating the short-term problem in the first place, are substantially worsened in the process.[28]

The problem with radical and unilateral change, then, is the possibility of creating a negative balance of the human resources of the organization, which can result in a severe backlash in the organization over the long term. The complementary problem for changes that are made very gradually and participatively is that, after years of meetings and planning sessions and endless questions, nothing very striking or interesting has actually happened in the organization, and in a spirit of resignation, organization members slowly abandoned their change activities and settled back into their old ways.[29]

Finding an appropriate pace for change to take place—neither too quickly and radically nor too slowly and gradually—is one of the most critical problems of planned organizational change. Trying to set the right pace often poses special problems for organizational consultants—especially those who are based outside the organization. On the one hand, if they suggest or induce change that moves too quickly or radically vis-à-vis a given organization, they risk losing their association with the organization and, therefore, any chance they might have to influence the effectiveness of the organization.[30] As one experienced observer notes in a list of "rules of thumb for consultants," the first task of the consultant is to "stay alive," one means of which is to take the level and pace of one's consulting activities in reasonable congruence with the current state of the organization.[31] Similarly, others counsel consultants explicitly about being careful not to introduce interventions that are too intense or deep for the change organization to handle.[32, 33]

The other side of the issue is, of course, that the consultant or change expert can be "seduced" by the existing values in the client system and ultimately find himself or herself co-opted by that system or even implicitly colluding with it in activities that restrict genuine change. For this reason, it is often useful for consultants to work in groups, so that they can maintain an independent point of reference that contrasts to that of the client organization. By this means, additional insurance is provided that the consultant will be more likely to adhere to professional values concerning change recommendations.

In summary, the tension between the readiness of (and capabilities of) the organization for change and the values and aspirations of the professional change consultant is a continuing problem for which no easy resolutions are available or appropriate. Somehow, the consultant must introduce material to the organization that is sufficiently discrepant from the status quo to provide impetus for change—but not so deviant as to be rejected out of hand by the organizational managers. That, as most practicing organizational interventionists know very well indeed, is a fine line to walk.[34]

As suggested earlier in this chapter, a police chief is sometimes appointed specifically to effect reform and thus may be under pressure to make changes (sometimes radical ones) quickly. Drastic changes, whether implemented or only planned, however, make the chief vulnerable to attack.

## RESISTANCE TO CHANGE

Over and above the general predisposition against change in the social climate of most organizations, specific proposals for change are almost certain to encounter rigorous obstacles in the form of organized resistance from individuals and groups both within and external to the organization.[35] Rather than being attributable to personality characteristics, the causes of resistance may be rooted in a past experience or past reinforcement history of those facing change. Lower level members of organizations in particular might have had direct experience that has led them to associate change with negative consequences.[36] If, for example, the last organizational change undertaken by a police department resulted in patrol officers having to work more evening hours to accommodate increased calls for service and increased crimes, and if this change disrupted the officers' off-duty personal lives and also failed to provide salary or other compensating differentials, then some officers will very likely be predisposed to believe that change, although perhaps beneficial to the organization, is not beneficial to them.

Most people who perceive, rightly or wrongly, that a proposed change will adversely affect them can usually be counted on to resist the change as mightily as they can.[37] In any case, most members of an organization have a vested interest in the status quo. They have adapted to the organization's environment and know how to cope with it; they have developed behavioral patterns that enable them to obtain satisfactory outcomes and to avoid unpleasant outcomes. Change means uncertainty; there is no assurance that a new scheme will be as satisfactory as the old one, even though the old one might have been flawed.[38] Thus, people sometimes resist innovations even when they cannot identify any results harmful to them simply because they grow anxious about consequences they cannot foresee that might injure their interests.

Occasionally, resistance to change is presented by individuals or groups even when it is known that their interests will not be compromised. These people may be obstructionists in the hope of exerting concessions or other advantages in return for their support or acquiescence.[39]

Some individuals may resist change because of the heavy psychic costs associated with change. According to Kaufman,

> The advocates of change naturally concentrate so heavily on the benefits to be derived from their recommendations that they sometimes lose sight of the personal effort and agony of people who have to accommodate the new patterns. Over and above advantages lost and penalties inflicted by opponents, beyond the humiliation of becoming a raw novice at a new trade after having been a master craftsman at an old one, and in addition to the expensive retraining and tooling, is the deep crisis caused by the need to suppress ancient prejudices, to put aside the comfort of the familiar, to relinquish the security of what one knows well. Put aside the social and financial incentives to stand fast; after those are excluded, it is still hard for most of us to alter our ways. The psychic costs of change can be very high, and therefore go into the balance sheet on the side of keeping things as they are. In addition, the psychic costs of pressing for an innovation are substantial. If the change is adopted and fails, the embarrassment and loss of stature and influence can be chilling to contemplate; the costs and benefits of the old ways are at least known. If battle is joined on behalf of change the proponents are likely to be opposed from all sides. Some critics will accuse the advocates of being too timid in the struggle, while others will portray the campaign as evidence of hunger for power; some will complain of the innovator's readiness to experiment wildly at the expense of those they serve, while others ridicule them for unwillingness to try something more daring than marginal adjustments. To win allies the proposed reforms must be amended and weakened and compromised until the expenditure of efforts seems hardly worthwhile. Meanwhile the drama of the struggle often arouses expectations among the beneficiaries out of all proportion to the realities of the improvement; instead of winning the applause and gratitude, the innovators often reap denunciation from those they thought they were helping as well as from their adversaries in the controversy. And anyone with experience in such a contest is aware that he or she may end up with obligations to supporters whose purposes he or she does not share and with fleeting credit but lasting enmities. On balance, then, the members or contributors to an organization are presented with

much stronger incentives to act warily than daringly. Precedent serves as a valuable guide because it clearly defines the safe path; in a mine field wise men step exactly in the footprints of predecessors who have successfully traversed the hazardous area.

The collective benefits of stability and the calculated opposition to change thus weigh heavily against innovation even when the dangers of inflexibility mount.[40]

Finally, it is often overlooked that police departments have a number of features that make them quite resistant to change. For example, the behavioral expectations for police officers, especially of those in medium-size and larger agencies, are usually specified in great detail and are divided very specifically. Every component must perform according to a set pattern, or there is a danger that the entire operation will be disrupted. Officers are therefore screened and groomed for the positions they will occupy; they are socialized and fitted into the ongoing system. Officers are chosen not only for skills and aptitudes but also for attitudes and personality traits. Their values and perceptions are then shaped by the organization. Officers learn their training manual, master the methods of their department, and forge understandings with their fellow officers until the whole system becomes second nature to them. Directives, orders, commands, instructions, inspections, reports, and all other means of organizational control, however irksome they might once have been, are gradually accepted as each officer's own premise of thought and action, until compliance with them is no longer reluctant or indifferent obedience, but an expression of personal preference and will.[41] Change after such indoctrination can be traumatic indeed.

## SUCCESS AND FAILURE PATTERNS IN A PLANNED CHANGE

A great deal can sometimes be learned by studying the success and failure patterns of organizations that have undertaken planned change. To discover whether there were certain dimensions of organizational change that might stand out against the background of characteristics unique to one organization, Greiner and others conducted a survey of eighteen studies of organizational change. Their findings were as follows:

Specifically, we were looking for the existence of dominant patterns of similarity and/or difference running across all of these studies. As we went along, relevant information was written down and compared with the other studies in regard to (a) the conditions leading up to an attempted change, (b) the manner in which the change was introduced, (c) the critical blocks and/or facilitators encountered during implementation, and (d) the more lasting results which appeared over a period of time.

The survey of findings shows some intriguing similarities and differences between those studies reporting "successful" change patterns and those disclosing "less successful" changes—i.e., failure to achieve the desired results. The successful changes generally appear as those which:

Spread throughout the organization to include and affect many people.

Produce positive changes in line and staff attitudes.

Prompt people to behave more effectively in solving problems and in relating to others.

Result in improved organization performance.

Significantly, the less successful changes fall short of all of these dimensions.

**Success Patterns**
Using the category breakdown just cited as the baseline for "success," the survey reveals some very distinct patterns in the evolution of change. In all, eight major patterns are identifiable in five studies reporting successful change, and six other success studies show quite similar characteristics, although the information contained in each is somewhat less complete. Consider

1. The organization, and especially top management, is under considerable external and internal pressure for improvement (see Box 15-4) long before an explicit organization change is contemplated. Performance and/or morale are low. Top management seems to be groping for a solution to its problems.

## BOX 15-4

### The Gang That Couldn't Examine Straight

by Elaine Shannon

The justice department report on the FBI lab delves deeply into fewer than two dozen cases and examines just three of the FBI's 35 specialized units, but its repercussions are enormous. By questioning the lab's credibility, the 500-page study has undermined thousands of cases that have coursed through the agency—the lab does as many as 600,000 examinations a year—especially those handled by the 10 lab workers faulted in the study. "We're going to get hundreds, if not thousands, of motions that are going to encompass every part of the lab, from latent-fingerprint comparisons to tire-tread analysis," says a ranking FBI agent.

A great deal of resources will have to be expended simply responding to defense motions, meritorious or not. Already next week there will be a motion to reopen the case of Jeffrey MacDonald, the Green Beret doctor now serving a life term in prison for killing his pregnant wife and two daughters in the infamous *Fatal Vision* murders in 1970. MacDonald's lawyer, Harvey Silvergate, says the motion will be based in part on affidavits of FBI agent Michael Malone, formerly a lab examiner, submitted during the lawyer's attempt to reopen the MacDonald case. According to last week's report, Malone exhibited "inexcusable" behavior in the corruption hearing filed against former judge Alcee Hastings when Malone testified to having performed a tensile-strength test that was not only beyond his expertise but was also carried out by another member of the lab. In the MacDonald case, Malone, who specialized in hair and fiber evidence, had asserted that filaments found in a hairbrush at the murder scene came not from a blond wig worn by an intruder, as MacDonald claimed, but more likely from a doll owned by one of the murdered little girls.

The Oklahoma City bombing case is the biggest of those cited by last week's report. It strongly criticizes explosives experts involved in the bombing investigation, particularly David Williams, who, according to the study, "reached conclusions that incriminated the defendants without a scientific basis," and Roger Martz, the chief of the chemistry-toxicology unit, who "improperly deviated from . . . protocol in his examination of some specimens." But Inspector General Michael Bromwich's study goes on to cite other cases that have the potential for coming undone in the legal system—or at least becoming embarrassing footnotes for the already red-faced bureau. Among them:

**The World Trade Center Bombing**
Five federal cases are being prosecuted in connection with the 1993 attack. While one is set for trial this summer, four have already resulted in convictions—which are being appealed. Of these, it is the case of Mohammad Salameh and three other defendants that has come in for scrutiny. The Bromwich report castigated Williams, then a top explosives examiner, who managed the on-site investigation, saying he "began with a presumption of guilt upon which to build inferences." It excoriated him for offering his opinion that the bomb had consisted of urea nitrate, when no intact urea-nitrate crystals were found at the scene. The report stated that Williams "tailored" his testimony to fit facts determined by the investigation.

**The Unabomber**
Terry Rudolph, an explosives examiner who worked at the lab from 1979 to 1988 and is retired, did some early work on the Unabom investigation. The Bromwich report opened with severe criticism of Rudolph for his work in the case against Steve Psinakis, an American accused of smuggling explosives out of the U.S. in 1982 in an alleged attempt to overthrow the regime of Philippine President Ferdinand Marcos. At trial in 1989, the judge was almost openly derisive about Rudolph's methods, commenting that "even with the FBI lab, completion of all necessary processes . . . is an awfully good idea, and leaving things undone because

2. A new administrator, known for the ability to introduce improvements, enters the organization, either as the official head of the organization, or as a consultant who deals directly with the head of the organization.

3. An initial act of the new person is to encourage a reexamination of past practices and current problems within the organization.

4. The head of the organization and all immediate subordinates assume a direct and highly involved role in conducting this reexamination.

5. The new person, with top management support, engages several levels of the organization in collaborative, fact-finding, problem-solving discussions to identify and diagnose current organization problems.

6. The new person provides others with new ideas and methods for developing solutions to problems, again at many levels of the organization.

7. The solutions and decisions are developed, tested, and found credible for solving problems on a small scale before an attempt is made to widen the scope of change to larger problems and the entire organization.

8. The change effort spreads with each success experience, and as management support grows, it is gradually absorbed permanently into the organization's way of life.

The likely significance of these similarities becomes more apparent when we consider the patterns found in the less successful organization changes. Let us briefly make this contrast before speculating further about why the successful changes seem to unfold as they do.

**Failure Forms**

Apart from their common "failure" to achieve the desired results, the most striking overall characteristic of seven less successful change studies is a singular lack of consistency—not just between studies, but within studies. Where each of the successful changes follows a similar and highly consistent route of one step building on another, the less successful changes are much less orderly.

**FIGURE 15-2.** Investigators examine the rubble in a parking garage below the World Trade Center in New York City where terrorists exploded a large bomb. The blast killed 5 people and injured 652. (Photo ©Reuters Newsmedia Inc./CORBIS.)

There are three interesting patterns of inconsistency:

1. The less successful changes begin from a variety of starting points. This is in contrast to the successful changes, which begin from a common point—i.e., strong pressure both externally and internally. Only one less successful change, for example, began with outside pressure on the organization; another originated with the hiring of a consultant; and a third started with the presence of internal pressure, but without outside pressure.

2. Another pattern of inconsistency is found in the sequence of change steps. In the successful change patterns, we observe some degree of logical consistency between steps, as each seems to make possible the next. But in the less successful changes, there are wide and seemingly illogical gaps in sequence. One study, for instance, described a big jump from the reaction to outside pressure to the installation of an unskilled newcomer who immediately attempted large-scale changes. In another case, the company lacked the presence of a newcomer to provide new methods and ideas to the organization. A third failed to achieve the cooperation and involvement of top management. And a fourth missed the step of obtaining early successes while experimenting with new change methods.

3. A final pattern of inconsistency is evident in the major approaches used to introduce change. In the successful cases, it seems fairly clear that *shared* approaches are used—i.e., authority figures seek the participation of subordinates in joint decision making. In the less successful attempts, however, the approaches used lie closer to the extreme ends of the power distribution continuum. Thus, in five less successful change studies, a *unilateral* approach (de-

cree, replacement, structural) was used, while in two other studies a *delegated* approach (data discussion, T-group) was applied. None of the less successful change studies reported the use of a *shared* approach.[42]

## POLICE FUTURES RESEARCH

Historically there has been great interest in forecasting the future, and there are a number of intriguing examples. Condorcet (1743–1794), a French philosopher, foresaw that all European colonies in the New World would become independent; social insurance would be provided for the aged, widowed, and orphans; education would become public and universal; women would receive equality with men; advances in medicine would eliminate infectious and hereditary diseases; and scientific knowledge would expand and improve technology.[43] Malthus (1766–1834) believed that unchecked human population growth would outstrip food supply, the result of which would be famine, disease, and poverty.[44] A Harvard sociologist, Sorokin (1889–1968), identified the basic characteristics and long-range trends of Western civilization, which he characterized as increasingly this-worldly, secular, materialistic, pragmatic, utilitarian, and hedonistic.[45] In 1967, Daniel Bell foretold of a "post-industrial society" to be created by a decline in "blue-collar" workers and a rise in "white-collar" employees.[46] What Condorcet, Malthus, Sorokin, and Bell share is having accurately forecast future events.

Despite the existence of a body of literature that one way or another reflects concern about social, technological, and economic change, the police have traditionally remained remarkably uninterested in futures research. There are a number of possible reasons for this disinterest: (1) a time horizon, for many law enforcement agencies, no longer than the next budget cycle; (2) a "hot stove" approach to managing, meaning that "we'll handle today's crisis now and worry about tomorrow when it gets here"; and (3) a lack of any perceived need to consider what conditions may be like in ten to twenty years.

In 1973, the California Commission on Peace Officer Standards and Training (POST) completed Project Star, a study of the impact of social trends on crime and criminal justice, the first major comprehensive futures study involving the police in this country.[47] After momentary excitement about Project Star, interest in law enforcement circles about futures research rapidly waned, although there was, in one form or another, intermittent interest among police scholars as evidenced by occasional publications.[48] Since roughly 1980, there has been growing interest among law enforcement executives in futures research. To no small degree this interest has been fueled by the growing imperative to make sense out of a turbulent and sometimes chaotic environment and the highly visible work of William Tafoya, who developed the nation's first graduate- and doctoral-level futures courses geared specifically to law enforcement. Echoing this development are several state agencies, such as California's POST, which now include a futures research component in their training curricula for law enforcement executives. In 1991, the Society of Police Futurists International (PFI) was organized, another indicator of the broadening prominence of police futures research.

**The Futures Research Unit**

Futures research is a discipline devoted to addressing potential changes in our society.[49] The use of the plural *futures* reflects a basic premise of this type of research: the future is not predetermined or predictable and can be influenced by individual and organizational choices.[50] Through the use of environmental scanning—analytically examining the right data with the appropriate forecasting methods—the futures research unit produces forecasts and policy options that allow law enforcement administrators to improve the odds of a preferable future from among the many existing alternatives.[51] One of the forecasting methods frequently used is the Delphi Technique. The Delphi was developed by the RAND Corporation in the mid-1950s and involves pooling the individual judgments of panel members selected on the basis of their expertise. Forecasts developed with a properly conducted Delphi Technique have had 85 percent or higher accuracy.[52] Unlike a prediction, which describes an event ahead of time and does not allow for error or probability, a forecast is a probabilistic statement of what may occur at some future time.

## Establishing a Futures Research Unit

A futures research unit (FRU) is not redundant if a law enforcement agency already has a planning unit because their missions are different and a great deal of planning, such as structuring a grievance procedure, is conducted without any real forecasting.[53] Moreover, futures research is also distinguishable from planning in that it assesses trends, countertrends, shifting values, and other indicators and attempts to provide an understanding of what they mean, where a department is going, and what should be done. In terms of organizational structure arrangements, the FRU can be placed within an existing planning component or made a separate unit altogether. The dynamics within individual agencies will dictate which approach to use.

To a substantial degree, any success the FRU has is indicative of access to and support from the agency's chief executive, reporting arrangements, and the quality of personnel selected for or by it. The FRU staff must be capable of using a variety of forecasting methodologies; be computer literate and statistically proficient due to the many types of data to be analyzed; and be self-starters who are imaginative, flexible, and inquisitive, relishing challenges.[54] To the greatest possible extent FRU personnel should come from the ranks of the police department, as opposed to being civilian experts, giving them one less issue with which to deal while on the road to gaining credibility.

As a minimum, all FRU members should have their own personal computers, have access to internal and external databases, and be provided with appropriate forecasting and database management software. Ideally, all computers would be networked to facilitate electronic mail (e-mail) and the sharing of information.[55] Selecting the right leader for a FRU is a crucial decision. Essentially the FRU is an organizationally sponsored center for creativity, and creative people can be difficult to manage. Tradition-bound leaders who require inflexible working hours, strict observance of rules and regulations, and reverence for their positions may find the situation unsatisfactory and possibly hamper performance. Moreover, creative individuals do not perform best in traditional, hierarchical organizational structures. Companies that manage creativity and innovation will work at fostering and nurturing these attributes.[56] The best choice for police departments may be to locate the FRU away from headquarters at sites where the FRU can develop its own work culture. In this way the culture of the larger organization remains intact while a separate environment is designed that maximizes productivity and impact.

Although FRUs are still evolving, often within the umbrella of a planning or planning and research unit, there are already a number of law enforcement agencies with futures capabilities, including the police departments in Madison, Wisconsin; Seattle, Washington; Portland, Oregon; Alexandria,

Virginia; Tulsa, Oklahoma; Santa Ana, California; and the San Diego County, California, Sheriff's Office. In such jurisdictions law enforcement executives know that futures research can help them understand how the conditions, events, and trends of today will impact on what may happen tomorrow. With such information, new programs can be initiated, personnel trained, equipment procured, the organizational structure modified, policies and procedures developed, and other measures instituted in thoughtful anticipation of, rather than in a crisis reaction to, the shifting environment.

# SUMMARY

The objectives of any police executive contemplating change should be to do so in a manner that offers the greatest possibility of success, does not result in a reduction of the quality and quantity of service to the public, and does not polarize the organization and the community into warring factions. In this chapter, we have examined some of the major components of the change process.

We started by examining some of the most common reasons for initiating change within a law enforcement agency. They tend to evolve from issues related to the crime-fighting capabilities of a police department, poor police–minority relations, poor public image, corruption, the retiring of a long-tenured police chief, and poor morale.

The person or persons who actually assumes the role of change agent will vary. In some cases it may be the police chief or some other person designated by the chief within the organization, or the change agent may be some individual or group of consultants hired from outside the organization.

A general approach to planned change, known as organizational development (OD), has gained prominence over the last thirty years. Its focus is primarily on people as the target of change. This approach is grounded largely in psychology and other behavioral sciences.

Change agents, extremely important components of the change process, must possess a number of basic qualifications: technical competence, the ability to develop realistic solutions, planning skills, and the ability to work well with members of the organization.

The most common change agent errors are: becoming tied prematurely to a particular set of strategies and tactics; failing to identify the groups affected by the change teams' effort; failing to recognize the relevant groups' need to be involved in goal setting and the strategy design process; planning inadequately for the initiation of the change process, and failing to consider the roles played by individuals and groups outside the police department.

Once the decision is made to implement change within the law enforcement agency, consideration must be given to using either internal change agents, external change agents, or a combination of both types. Internal change agents have the benefit of valuable insights into both the formal and informal organization as well as the potential sources of support or opposition. However, internal change agents sometimes experience difficulty in establishing credibility. Further, their motives may be questioned, and if the change process is a lengthy one, someone will have to assume their regular duties. External change agents frequently have the advantage of considerable knowledge and experience, which provides assurance that the planned change will be completed effectively and expeditiously. In addition, they also enjoy considerable credibility as experts in the field. One important disadvantage of external change agents is their unfamiliarity with the major forces within the organization that can help or hinder the change process.

Once the administrator decides to use an external change agent, he or she can contact several police associations in order to evaluate the suitability of this type of change agent, including the International Association of Chiefs of Police (IACP), the National Organization of Black Law Enforcement Executives (NOBLE), the Police Executive Research Forum (PERF), and the Police Foundation. Professional publications and journals in the National Criminal Justice Reference Service are also excellent sources for information on consultants. However, networking with other police executives may be the best way to find a consultant, because they most likely will refer one with whom they have worked and one familiar with the police subculture.

The actual methods by which organizational change can be initiated may vary, but generally they can be grouped into two broad categories: (1) those that focus on changing the individuals working within the organization and (2) those that focus on changing specific organizational structures.

One major problem faced in implementing change is determining a pace that is neither too quick or radical nor too slow and gradual. Setting the right pace often poses special problems, especially for outside consultants. On the one hand, if outside consultants suggest or introduce change too quickly or radically, they risk losing their association with the organization and therefore any chance they might have had to influence the effectiveness of the organization; on the other hand, the consultant or change agent may be "seduced" by existing values the client's system and ultimately find him- or herself co-opted by the system or even implicitly colluding with activities that restrict genuine change.

An understanding of why people resist change is absolutely essential to the successful accomplishment of a change process. Over and above the predisposition against change in the social climate of most organizations, specific proposals for change are almost certain to encounter rigorous obstacles in the form of organized resistance from individuals and groups both within and external to the organization. Resistance by individuals may be attributable to certain personality characteristics, but is more likely to be rooted in some unfavorable past experience with the change process. Most people who perceive that change will affect them adversely can be counted on to resist it. Also, police departments frequently have a number of features that make them quite resistant to change. These include highly defined behavioral expectations and a host of rules, regulations, policies, and procedures that are viewed as the organizational gospel. Thus, the officers' values and perceptions may be shaped by all these factors over the course of many years, and sudden change can be perceived as threatening.

Although there are no guarantees that any particular pattern of planned change will succeed or fail, a great deal can be learned from the experience of organizations that have undergone change. Greiner and others conducted a survey of eighteen organizations that had undertaken planned change and noted the following success and failure patterns. Success patterns were spread throughout the organization to include and affect many people; produced positive changes in line and staff attitudes; prompted people to behave more effectively in solving problems and relating to others; and resulted in improved organization change. The failure pattern included a lack of consistency in the planned change, wide and seemingly illogical gaps in the sequence of the change, a failure to achieve the cooperation and involvement of top management, and a failure to use a shared approach.

The likelihood of implementing successful organizational change will be enhanced considerably if certain aspects of the change process are handled appropriately. Failure to consider many of the factors discussed will likely result in both the goals and objectives of police executives falling far below their expectations or perhaps failing to come to fruition at all. In addition, a poorly planned and poorly timed change effort could result in certain powerful groups within the police agency and in the community joining together to force the police executive's resignation or dismissal.

There are numerous examples of the historical interest in forecasting the future, including the work of Condorcet, Malthus, Sorokin, and Bell. However, the police have traditionally been uninterested in futures research for a variety of reasons. The first major comprehensive futures study of U.S. police was Project Star, completed in 1974 by the California Commission on Peace Officer Standards and Training. Despite the ensuing publicity, there was little interest in police circles in futures research until the 1980s, in large measure due to the nationally visible work of Tafoya. One indication of the growing interest in futures is the creation in 1991 of the Society of Police Futures International. Futures research is a discipline devoted to addressing potential changes in our society and uses various forecasting tools, including the Delphi Technique. By knowing how the events and conditions of today may manifest themselves in the future, law enforcement administrators have greater lead time to make adaptive changes. Recognizing the contributions that can be made, some agencies such as those in Seattle, Washington; Tulsa, Oklahoma; Madison, Wisconsin; and Alexandria, Virginia, have created futures research capabilities in their police departments. When law enforcement executives contemplate creating a futures research unit, a number of factors must be considered, such as placement in the organizational structure, personnel, equipment, leadership, and physical location.

## DISCUSSION QUESTIONS

1. What types of events frequently give impetus to planned change within a police department?

2. How was the term *change agent* defined in this chapter?

3. How was the term *organizational development (OD)* defined in this chapter?

4. Name several important features of OD.

5. What are a police administrator's options when attempting to locate an external change agent?

6. What are the two types of applied research discussed in this chapter?

7. What is field research?

8. There are a number of patterns among those organizations experiencing less successful changes. What are they?

9. Define and discuss futures research.

10. What factors should be considered when a futures research unit is created?

# NOTES

1. P. Hersey and K. H. Blanchard, *Management of Organizational Behavior: Utilizing Human Resources,* 3rd ed. (Englewood Cliffs, N.J.: Prentice-Hall, 1977), p. 273.

2. Ibid.

3. G. N. Jones, *Planned Organizational Change* (New York: Praeger, 1969), p. 19.

4. R. D. Gatewood, R. R. Taylor, and O. C. Fovile, *Management—Comprehension, Analysis and Application* (Homewood, Ill.: Richard D. Irwin, 1995), p. 573.

5. T. G. Cummings and C. G. Worley, *Organization Development and Change,* 5th ed. (St. Paul, Minn.: West Publishing Company, 1993) p. 2.

6. Gatewood et al., *Management,* p. 573.

7. Ibid., p. 574.

8. G. Zaltman and R. Duncan, *Strategies for Planned Change* (New York: John Wiley & Sons, 1970), pp. 204–205.

9. Ibid., pp. 205–206.

10. Ibid., pp. 206–207.

11. E. M. Rogers and D. K. Bhowmik, "Homophily–Heterophily: Relational Concepts for Communications Research," *Public Opinion Quarterly,* 34:4 (Winter 1970–1971), 529.

12. J. M. Baird, "The Use of Consultants in Law Enforcement," *FBI Law Enforcement Bulletin* (October 1994), 9–14. This discussion was adapted from this article.

13. John H. Sheridan, "Where Bench-markers Go Wrong," *Industry Week* (March 1993), 28–31.

14. J. Eck, *Using Research: A Primer for Law Enforcement Managers* (Washington, D.C.: Police Executive Research Forum/National Institute of Justice, 1974), p. 3.

15. Ibid.

16. F. Leavitt, *Research Methods for Behavioral Scientists* (Dubuque, Iowa: William C. Brown, 1991).

17. L. W. Porter, E. L. Lawler III, and J. R. Hackman, *Behavior in Organizations* (New York: McGraw-Hill, 1975), p. 439.

18. A. C. Filley, *Interpersonal Conflict Resolution* (Glenview, Ill.: Scott, Foresman, 1975), p. 126.

19. Ibid.

20. K. Lewin, "Group Decision and Social Change," in *Readings in Social Psychology,* ed. E. E. Maccoby, T. M. Newcomb, and E. C. Hartley (New York: Holt, Rinehart and Winston, 1958), pp. 197–212.

21. H. J. Reitz, *Behavior in Organizations* (Homewood, Ill.: Richard Irwin, 1977), pp.546–547.

22. Ibid., p. 547.

23. Filley, *Interpersonal Conflict Resolution,* p. 133.

24. Ibid., pp.133–134.

25. W. G. Bennis et al., *Interpersonal Dynamics* (Homewood, Ill.: Dorsey Press, 1968), pp. 338–366.

26. E. H. Schein, "Management Development as a Process of Influence," *Industrial Management Review,* 2:11 (1961), 10.

27. Porter, Lawler, and Hackman, *Behavior in Organizations,* p. 446.

28. R. R. Blake and J. S. Mouton, *Building a Dynamic Corporation Through Grid Organization Development* (Reading, Mass.: Addison-Wesley, 1969), pp. 8–9.

29. Porter, Lawler, and Hackman, *Behavior in Organizations,* p. 479.

30. Ibid.

31. H. A. Sheppard, "Changing Relations in Organizations," in *Handbook of Organizations,* ed. J. G. March (Chicago: Rand-McNally, 1965), as cited in Porter, Lawler, and Hackman, *Behavior in Organizations,* p. 479.

32. R. Harrison, "Choosing the Depth of Organization Intervention," *Journal of Applied Behavioral Science,* 6 (November 1970), 118–202.

33. E. H. Shein, *Process Consultation: Its Role in Organizational Development* (Reading, Mass.: Addison-Wesley, 1969), as cited in Porter, Lawler, and Hackman, *Behavior in Organizations,* p. 479.

34. Porter, Lawler, and Hackman, *Behavior in Organizations,* p. 480.

35. H. Kaufman, *The Limits of Organizational Change* (Tuscaloosa: University of Alabama Press, 1971), p. 10.

36. Reitz, *Behavior in Organizations,* p. 545.

37. Kaufman, *Limits of Organizational Change,* p. 11.

38. Reitz, *Behavior in Organizations,* p. 545.

39. Kaufman, *Limits of Organizational Change,* p. 11.

40. Ibid., pp. 13–15.

41. Ibid., pp. 16–18.

42. L. E. Greiner, "Patterns of Organization Change," *Harvard Business Review,* 45:3 (1967), 124–25. This article is part of a larger study on organizational development involving Greiner and his colleagues, L. B. Barnes and D. P. Leitch, that was supported by the Division of Research, Harvard Business School.

43. California Commission on Peace Officer Standards and Training (POST), *The Impact of Social Trends on*

*Crime and Criminal Justice: Project Star* (Cincinnati, Ohio, and Santa Cruz, Calif.: Anderson and Davis, 1976), p. 12. For additional information on Condorcet's forecasts, see Burnham P. Beckwith, *The Next 500 Years* (New York: Exposition Press, 1967), pp. 6–7.

44. Ibid., p. 12.

45. Ibid., pp. 12–13. Also see Pitirim A. Sorokin, *Social and Cultural Dynamics* (Boston: Extending Horizon Books, 1957).

46. Ibid., p. 13. This idea is fully elaborated in his "Notes on the Post-Industrial Society," *The Public Interest,* 6 (Winter 1967), 25–35 (Part 1), and 7 (Spring 1967), 102–18 (Part 2).

47. POST, *Impact of Social Trends: Project Star.*

48. For example, see John E. Angell, "Organizing Police for the Future: An Update on the Democratic Model," *Criminal Justice Review* (Fall 1976), 35–51, and Gerald Caiden, *Police Revitalization* (Lexington, Mass.: Lexington Books, 1977).

49. John Henry Campbell, "Futures Research: Here and Abroad," *Police Chief,* 57:1 (1990), 30.

50. Ibid.

51. Ibid.

52. William Tafoya, "Rioting in the Streets: Deja Vu?," in *Bias Crimes: The Law Enforcement Response,* ed. Nancy Taylor (Chicago: Office of International Criminal Justice, University of Illinois at Chicago, 1991) p. 7.

53. Campbell, "Futures Research," 30.

54. Ibid., p. 31.

55. Ibid.

56. Ibid., p. 33.

Britz, M., 481
Broder, Michael S., 370
Broken windows theory, 18
Bromwich, Michael, 54, 646, 647
Brown, Gary, 289, 290
Brown, Lee, 93
Brown, Sam, 370
Brown, Walter, 105
Brown, Willie, 460
Bruère, Henry, 577
Brutality. *See* Police brutality
Bryan, Bill, 642
Bucqueroux, Bonnie, 55, 56–57
Budget
    definitions of, 563
    supplementation of, 591–596
Budget and Accounting Procedures Act,
    581
Budget cycle, 564
    approval, 568–571
    execution, 571, 573–575
    preparation, 565–568
Budget formats, 576–578
    hybrid budgets, 591
    line-item budgets, 578–581
    performance budgets, 581–582
    planning-programming budget system,
        582–584
    programmatic budgets, 584–585
    zero-based budgets, 585, 588–591
Budget unit analysis, 588
Buffalo County Sheriff's Department
    (Nebraska), 610
Buffett, Warren, 492
Buitrago, Adela, 129
Bulletin board systems (BBSs), 47–50, 77
Bureaucratic model, 127, 129–132, 165
Bureaucratic structures, leadership in,
    221–222
Bureau of Alcohol, Tobacco and Firearms
    (ATF), 529, 530, 536, 537
Bureau of Justice Assistance, 45
Burns, James, 226–232
Burns, Tom, 168–169, 170
Bush, George H. W., 70, 118
Butler, Marcus, 561
Butler, Richard, 115
Butler, Smedley, 6
Butterfly effect, 162

Caccese, Robert J., 304
Cahill, William, 460
Calderon, Milton, 378
Cali Cartel, 114
California Commission on Peace Officer
    Standards and Training, 649, 652
Callandrillo, George, 630
Campbell, Bill, 143
*Cannon v. Taylor,* 476
Cantamount, Kenneth, 460
Career development, 312, 327
Career status, 298–299
Carlyle, Thomas, 217
Carr, Keith, 23
Carraway, Melvin, 607, 608
*Carroll v. United States,* 70
Carter, D. L., 481
Carter, Jimmy, 585
Carter, William, 559

Case analysis and management system
    (CAMS), 35
*Case for Bureaucracy, The* (Goodsell),
    135–136
Cassidy, Terence J., 450
Castellini, Anthony, 359, 361
Center for Domestic Preparedness, 111
Central Intelligence Agency (CIA), 74
Centralization, 196–197
*Challenge of Crime in a Free Society, The*
    (President's Commission on Law
    Enforcement and Administration of
    Justice), 300
Chambers of commerce, 103–104
*Champ v. Baltimore County,* 286
Change. *See* Organizational change
Change agents, 632–633, 651
    errors, 634
    external, 634, 635–637
    internal, 634, 635
Change process. *See* Transitioning
*Changing Organizations* (Bennis), 153
Chaos theory, 159, 161–162
"Character flaw" theory of alcoholism,
    350
Character investigation, 296–297
Chemical tests, 331–332
Cherokee County Sheriff's Association, 96
Chicago Alternative Policing Strategy
    (CAPS), 26–29
CHIEFS, 43
Childbirth, 311
Christian, Jeffrey, 277
Christian fundamentalists, 114, 115
Christian Identity Church, 115, 539
Christian Patriots, 539
Churches, 104–105
Ciaccio, Peter, 378
Citizen involvement, 102–105
City councils, 85–87
City manager, 84–85
*Civil Action for Deprivation of Rights,* 75
Civilian Review Board, 395
Civilians, in police work, 321–324
Civil Rights Act (1871), 439–440
Civil Rights Act (1964), 291, 467, 484,
    487
Civil Rights Act (1991), 280, 294
Claiborne, James M., 228, 229
Clark, Jacob R., 55–58
Clark, John, 56
Clark, Steven, 101–102
Clayton, Lowell, 101–102
*Cleveland Board of Education v. Loudermill,*
    454
Cleveland, Frederick, 577
Click, Ben, 78
Clientele, grouping by, 183
Climate
    communication, 255–256
    organizational, 60
Climbers, 221
Clinton, William Jefferson, 39, 54, 55, 66,
    76, 228, 491–492
Closed shops, 400
Cluster chain, 254
Coalition of Hispanic American Police
    Associations (CHAPA), 405
Code of silence, 359–362

Cognitive nearsightedness, 549–550
Cognitive science applications, 42
Collection techniques, covert, 333
Collective bargaining, 398–400
College education, for police officers,
    300–305
Columbia University, 394
Columbine High School (Littleton,
    Colorado), 116–117
Colvin, Robert E., 468
Combined Law Enforcement Associations
    of Texas (CLEAT), 403
Combs, Terry, 96
Commission on Accreditation for Law
    Enforcement Agencies (CALEA),
    58, 79–81, 118, 161, 162
Common sense, 548–549
Communication, 245, 277–278
    barriers, 248–249, 271–273
    cross-cultural diversity in, 266–273
    cross-gender, 262–266
    electronic, 275–277
    interpersonal, 256–262
    oral, 275
    organizational, 249–256
    process, 245–248
    written, 273–275
Communication climate, 255–256
Communication network analysis,
    254–256
Communication officer documentation,
    381
Communications Workers of America
    (CWA), 401, 402–403, 405
Communicator, 247
Community policing, 18–21, 61–62
    artificial intelligence and expert
        systems, 42–47
    case examples, 21–22, 24–32
    crime analysis, 32–35, 37
    and Crime Bill of 1994, 32
    geographic information systems (GIS),
        37–42
    Internet, fax machines, and bulletin
        board systems, 47–50
    and organizational structure, 196–202
    problems with, 51–61
    technological impact on, 50–51
    transitioning, 23
Community-oriented policing (COP), 232,
    236
Community-Oriented Policing Services
    (COPS), 32, 54, 66, 403
Community Policing Award, 618
Competition, 238
Complaint procedures, 494
*Complex Organizations* (Perrow), 135
Computer-aided dispatch (CAD), 38, 39
Computers. *See* Information technology
Computer science applications, 42
Conceptual skills, 216–217
Condorcet, 649
Conduct unbecoming an officer, 464–465
Conflict
    and bargaining relationships, 408–410
    and leadership, 238–239
Conflicting interests, 545
Conflict resolution, 264–266
Conlin, Robert, 559